Access 2002:
The Complete Reference

Virginia Andersen

Osborne/**McGraw-Hill**

New York Chicago San Francisco
Lisbon London Madrid Mexico City
Milan New Delhi San Juan
Seoul Singapore Sydney Toronto

Osborne/**McGraw-Hill**
2600 Tenth Street
Berkeley, California 94710
U.S.A.

To arrange bulk purchase discounts for sales promotions, premiums, or fund-raisers, please contact Osborne/**McGraw-Hill** at the above address. For information on translations or book distributors outside the U.S.A., please see the International Contact Information page immediately following the index of this book.

Access 2002: The Complete Reference

34567890 DOC DOC 0198765432
Book p/n 0-07-213242-6 and CD p/n 0-07-213243-4 parts of
ISBN 0-07-213241-8

Publisher
  Brandon A. Nordin

Vice President & Associate Publisher
  Scott Rogers

Acquisitions Editor
  Megg Bonar

Project Editor
  Patty Mon

Acquisitions Coordinator
  Alissa Larson

Technical Editor
  Rima Regas

Copy Editor
  Marcia Baker

Proofreaders
  Marian Selig
  Paul Tyler
  Stefany Otis

Indexer
  Valerie Perry

Computer Designers
  Kelly Stanton-Scott
  Roberta Steele
  Carie Malnekoff

Illustrators
  Lyssa Sieben-Wald
  Beth E. Young

Series Design
  Peter F. Hancik

This book was composed with Corel VENTURA™ Publisher.

Contents

Part I

Getting Started

Part II

Retrieving and Presenting Information

Part III

Improving the Workplace

Part IV

Exchanging Data with Others

22 Exchanging Database Objects and Text 865

Part V

Application Development

About the Author

Virginia Andersen became a writer and consultant after retiring from her defense contracting career. Since then, she has written over 30 books about personal-computer–based applications, including database management, word processing, and spreadsheet analysis. Virginia spent nearly 15 years teaching computer science, mathematics, and systems analysis at the graduate and undergraduate levels at several southern California universities. During her years as a programmer/system analyst, Virginia used computers for many diverse projects, including lunar mapping, reliability engineering, undersea surveillance, weapon system simulation, and naval communications. Virginia is a certified MOUS Expert in Access 97 and 2000.

Acknowledgments

Although revising a book of this size and complexity isn't quite the monster challenge it was to write it in the first place, I owe a lot of gratitude to the talented and highly professional help of the Osborne editorial and production staff. Working with this team has been a most enjoyable experience. I would especially like to express my thanks to Megg Bonar, my acquisitions editor, for her friendly and most helpful guidance throughout. As acquisitions coordinator, Alissa Larson has earned an extra star for the highly professional and efficient escorting of the manuscript through the maze of publication. She and her staff have been a treat to work with.

I would also like to thank my project editor, Patty Mon, and her staff for the smooth and seemingly effortless passage of the pages through the system into the finished product. Rima Regas, my technical editor, and Marcia Baker, my copy editor, were very brave to take on such a huge job. Their talents are much appreciated. My sincere thanks also go to Marian, Paul, Stefany, Valerie, Melinda, and Lucie for their indispensable help with proofreading, indexing, and shipping this Complete Reference.

I also appreciate the contribution my friend, Brent Heslop, made with his help writing the chapter about data access pages and the Web for the previous edition. Thanks go, too, to the Coronado Police Department for sharing its Access database with me and my readers, as well as to my friends and neighbors who posed good-naturedly for the badge photos you can see in one of the databases. They tell me it's a good thing I'm a writer, not a photographer.

I also owe a big debt of gratitude to my alert literary agent, Matt Wagner of Waterside Productions, for opening this important opportunity.

Finally, my husband Jack and all the cats must get a lot of credit for being so patient with me throughout this long, involved process.

Introduction

This book is a total resource for anyone who wants to learn about Access, and how to create and maintain databases. The primary objective is to provide a solid base you can employ to become an accomplished information systems professional in the area of relational databases, specifically using Microsoft Access.

A successful database is efficient, quick, accurate, and easy to use. This book shows you how to create just such a database with Access 2002. The clearly written explanations of the database processes present exactly what you need to create an Access object or present information. The step-by-step exercises that follow the explanations further enhance your understanding by illustrating exactly how to complete the process successfully. The many tips, notes, and cautions help steer you to faster and better database management.

This book also meets the requirements for a certified study guide to use in preparing for the Microsoft Office User Specialist (MOUS) Certification examinations. After completing this book, readers should feel confident they have thoroughly reviewed all the skill objectives included in both the Core and Expert levels of the MOUS Access 2002 Certification examination.

Whom Is This Book For?

This book is the ideal resource for anyone currently using Access 2002 or who wants to learn how to use it. In planning this book, I envisioned it in the form of a large triangle— with the base scaled from the beginning user at the left end to advanced user at the right end. This book has enough material to get even the newest user of Access started with relational database management and enough is at the other end to help more advanced users wade into the depths of programming in Access.

The bulk of the material lies between the two extremes under the peak of the triangle and that is of the utmost interest to the readers who fall in between. This book is extremely rich in the art of designing and creating efficient relational databases with all the appropriate queries, forms, reports, and data access pages. Many different approaches are taken with respect to extracting and summarizing information in useful arrangements, including charts. After all, what good is data stored in a database if you can't get it out and turn it into useful and easy to interpret information?

This book is also intended for the users of the other Office applications, such as Word and Excel, who need to know how to interface with Access. With the boundaries between the programs rapidly vanishing, use of Access isn't limited to database managers. All the Office members can now interact with each other smoothly and with little translation.

The Complete Reference, the Ultimate Study Guide

If you aspire to become a Microsoft Office User Specialist in the field of Access 2002, *The Compete Reference* is the only book you need to prepare for the test. The book includes material that covers 100 percent of the skill set activities listed in the Microsoft Access 2002

Course Objectives. In addition, more than 80 percent of the skill set activities are addressed with step-by-step exercises. Because the actual test is a set of hands-on exercises, this material can be most important.

What's in This Book?

This book is organized so you can progress at your own pace beginning with basic database and Access principles, and followed by increasingly more advanced topics. The book is divided into five major parts, each focusing on a specific aspect of Access database management.

Part I: Getting Started

Part I takes a quick tour of Access 2002 and examines the concept of relational databases. Many tips are included to help you design an efficient database that is easy to maintain and can ensure data integrity. In Part I, the reader creates and relates tables, and then enters data into them. Several methods of validating new data are investigated and means of presenting data for editing are also addressed.

Part II: Retrieving and Presenting Information

Part II is concerned with retrieving information with filters and queries, as well as presenting that information in forms and reports. This important set of chapters includes how to create expressions to extract exactly the information you want. Five chapters are devoted to creating form and report designs, including synchronized data entry forms, creating reports that summarize grouped information, and even printing mailing labels in conjunction with Word 2002. The final chapter in this part describes how to create charts, pivot tables, and pivot charts to include in forms and reports.

Part III: Improving the Workplace

Part III is a little more advanced and discusses customizing the workplace with special toolbars, menus, and dialog boxes for the more interactive applications. Several important means of optimizing Access performance are included in this part. Part III also introduces programming techniques with chapters about using macros, as well as understanding events and when events occur.

Part IV: Exchanging Data with Others

Part IV discusses the important subject of exchanging information with other users of Access and with other applications, including via the Internet. Importing and exporting information in many forms, including text, is an integral part of developing a complete user application. In this part, you also learn how to create data access pages for displaying dynamic Access data on the Internet.

Part V: Application Development

Part V, the final part of the book, introduces Visual Basic and its uses in providing end-user applications. This part also covers using Access in a multiple-user environment and investigates measures to ensure information security. An example is presented that illustrates an end-user application complete with switchboards and dialog boxes tailored for user-interfaces. The final chapter in this part discusses converting databases created with previous versions of Access to Access 2000.

In Every Chapter

Every chapter is constructed to include some basic learning tools, such as the following:

- Complete explanations of all processes involved in the creation and management of effective relational databases.

- Numbered, step-by-step exercises with illustrations and explanations of each step.

- Many tips, notes, and cautions, which add shortcuts for many of the exam-related activities and pinpoint potential pitfalls that can occur.

- A summary at the end of each chapter that reviews the material covered and highlights the more important topics discussed in the chapter.

- A table following the summary that itemizes the specific MOUS skill set activities explored in the chapter. The table also directs you to the section in the chapter that discusses the topic.

Quick Reference

In addition to the chapter material, this book includes a Quick Reference section on the CD that accompanies it. The Quick Reference contains complete lists and descriptions of elements of Access 2002 database design and maintenance. This reference serves as an immediate resource for any details in question. It can save time when you need a specific piece of information by presenting concise lists and tables you can jump directly to without having to browse through the more descriptive chapter material.

What's on the Companion CD?

Appendix B presents a thorough explanation of the contents of the CD that accompanies this book. This appendix explains how to install the Access databases on your computer and how to look up specific information in the Quick Reference.

The CD includes the following:

- The Quick Reference lookup resource.

- The complete Home Tech Repair database.

- A set of tables to use as the basis for creating the Home Tech Repair database.

- The complete Police database.

- A set of tables to use as the basis for creating the Police database.

■ Miscellaneous files required by the two databases, such as scanned images and HTML files used by the data access pages.

Conventions Used in This Book

To help make this book more useful and interesting, we included a few conventions and margin art that can attract your attention to important pieces of information. Following are descriptions of these conventions:

This is a note. Notes further define terms used in the text or point you in the direction of more information about the subject under discussion.

This is a tip. Tips often provide shortcuts to the process under discussion or offer useful pieces of advice about how to make better use of Access 2000.

This is a caution. Cautions warn you to be careful when you're about to make crucial decisions or take risky steps. Access tries hard not to put you in harm's way, but this does happen now and then. I post a caution for you when this does happen.

This is an example of the margin icons that often accompany a step in the numbered exercises in this book. The margin icons illustrate the toolbar button to click to accomplish the activity under way.

Sidebars

This is a sidebar. Sidebars are set somewhat apart from the normal text and include information related to the current subject, but that doesn't necessarily fit in the flow of information. Rather than interrupt the flow, I set the sidebars aside where you can return later to read this tangential information in detail.

What's New?

This book attempts to show you the completely new look and feel that comes with Access 2002, including expanded Web-based connection to the rest of the world. Closer to home are the many time-saving and user-friendly features that make Access 2002 a total database management system.

New Features in the Office Arena

Many new features are shared by all users of Office XP programs. One of the most important advances toward seamless Web collaboration is the improvement in creating and publishing HTML and other Web documents. Office XP provides many new Web-oriented improvements that provide a pathway for users to cross between current, often obscure, Web technologies and the more user-friendly environment required by today's audience.

Some of the improvements that are more obvious to Access users involve the Office workspace and the Windows desktop. Here are some examples of these improvements:

- The New File side pane appears when you first start Access. This is where you can choose to open an existing file or create a new database.
- The new multiple clipboard side pane enables you to collect and paste up to 24 items. It also displays reviews of the items placed on it.
- The new Ask a Question box on the menu bar is a more convenient way to get help. The Help window is also faster and can be used alongside the Access window.
- A new Search task pane makes finding the elusive database you want to work with easier.

New Features in Access

Some of the new features in Access 2002 apply to database design, others apply to creating database objects or to customizing the workplace itself. Here are some of the more significant improvements covered in this book:

- You can now stack multiple undos and redos for more flexibility while in Design view.
- You can view any table, query, or form in PivotTable or PivotChart view and save a PivotTable or PivotChart as a data access page.
- You can now work on a subform or subreport design live in the main form or report Design view.
- Access 2002 provides many new events, properties, and shortcut keys.
- You can multiselect controls in data access pages design if you have Internet Explorer 5.5 installed.

Banded data access pages can now be made updateable by setting the group level properties.

Got Comments?

During my years spent teaching at the University of Southern California, I discovered, to my dismay, that I often learned as much from my students as I hoped they would learn from me. With this philosophy in mind, I invite you to share with me any new tricks or clever shortcuts you've devised. Please e-mail them to me at **vandersenz@aol.com**. In fact, I would enjoy hearing any other comments, good or bad, you might have about the book or the databases I have developed as examples. Only by tapping fresh minds can I hope to make these books better and better.

I've appreciated the many comments I received about the previous edition of the Complete Reference—some from as far away as South Africa and Japan. I have certainly benefited from the correspondence and I hope I could resolve some of the readers' problems as well.

The
Complete
Reference

Part I

Getting Started

The Complete Reference

Access 2002

Chapter 1

Quick Tour of Access 2002

In this, the Information Age, we're all surrounded by mountains of data. To use this data effectively, the information must be stored so it can be retrieved and interpreted with flexibility and efficiency. Microsoft Access 2002 is the ideal database management system that you can use for all your information management needs, from a simple address list to a complex inventory management system. It provides tools not only for storing and retrieving data but also for creating useful forms, reports, and interactive Web data pages. All you need is a basic acquaintance with Microsoft Windows and a sense of exploration to build the database you need.

This chapter shows you how to start Access 2002 and gives you a tour of the Access workplace. If you're already an experienced user, you may want to scan the material in this chapter quickly and move on to Chapter 2 for insight into the power of the tool called a relational database.

Starting Access and Opening a Database

You can start most software built for the Windows 95/98 environment in the same way: by clicking the Start button and pointing to Programs in the Start menu. Depending on how you installed Access 2002, the name may appear as a separate item in the Programs list or as one of the programs in the Microsoft Office XP menu. If you don't see Microsoft Access in the Programs list, choose Microsoft Office XP and then click Microsoft Access.

When first opened, the Access main window displays a floating New File side pane offering you a choice of creating a new database or opening one of the existing database files, as shown in Figure 1-1. The upper panel contains the names of databases that were recently opened (your list will be different). The Access opening window is where your session with Access begins.

The side pane in Figure 1-1 appears only when Access first starts or when you choose File | New. For now, click the Close button (the × in the upper-right corner) to close the side pane and leave the Access window empty for a tour of the window.

Launch Access and Start a Database at the Same Time

If you usually work with the same database in Access, you can quickly launch Access and open the database with one mouse click.

To start Access and open the database:

1. Click the Start button and point to Documents.

2. Choose your database file from the list (see Figure 1-2). The icon preceding the document name identifies the type of document. If your system displays file extensions, an Access database file shows the .mdb extension.

If your database doesn't appear in the list of recently opened documents, you must resort to the two-step method by first starting Access, and then opening the database.
NOTE: If you have more than one version of Access installed on your computer, the database will open in the latest version.

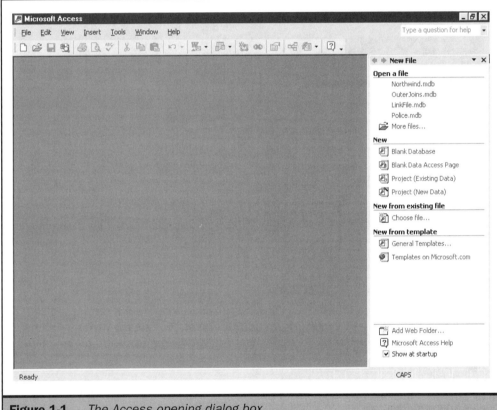

Figure 1-1.   *The Access opening dialog box*

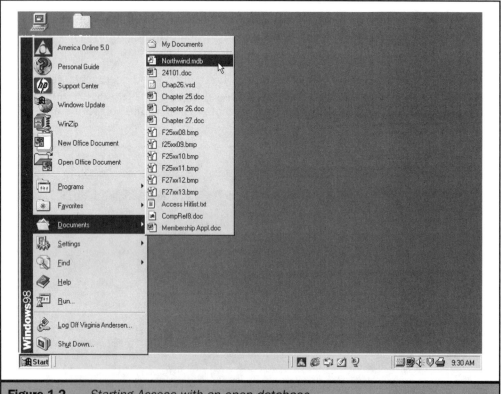

Figure 1-2.   *Starting Access with an open database*

Touring the Access Window

The Access window (see Figure 1-3) shows a title bar, a menu bar, and a toolbar common to Windows 95/98 programs. In addition to displaying the program name, Microsoft Access, the title bar contains buttons you can use to manipulate the window:

- The Close button closes the program.
- The Maximize button appears only when the window is less than maximum size and enlarges the window to fill the screen.

■ The Restore button replaces the Maximize button when the window is maximized and returns the window to its previous reduced size.

■ The Minimize button reduces the window to an icon on the Windows taskbar.

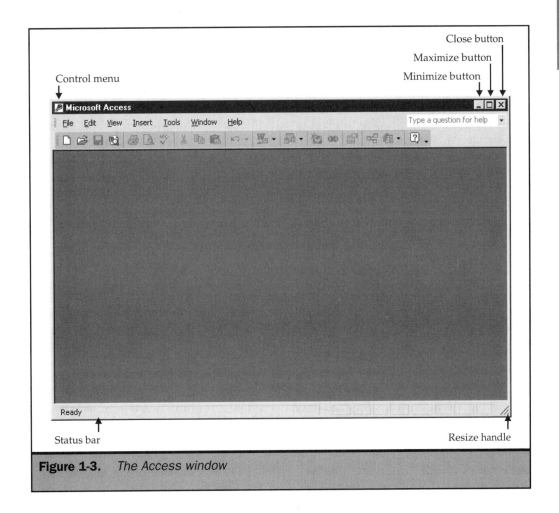

Figure 1-3.   *The Access window*

■ The Control Menu icon at the far-left end of the title bar opens a menu with the commands that accomplish the same things as the other buttons. Click the Control Menu icon to open the menu.

When the window is less than maximum size, you can move it to a new position on the desktop by dragging its title bar. You can also change its height and width by dragging its borders or the resize handle in the lower-right corner where you see the three diagonal lines.

Most of the menu commands are dimmed and unavailable in the empty Database window. The File menu offers options to create a new database or to open an existing one. Other options, such as the Toolbars option in the View menu, let you tailor the database workplace. All the Help menu options are available.

The buttons on the toolbar offer shortcuts to many of the commonly used menu commands. Most of the toolbar buttons are dimmed, which indicates they're also unavailable when no database is active. Even if a button is dimmed, you can still rest the mouse pointer on the button and see its name displayed below the button in a *ScreenTip* (called a *ToolTip* in earlier versions of Access). The toolbar, as well as the menu bar, presents different options, depending on the current activity.

The status bar, located at the bottom of the Access window, provides a running commentary about the ongoing task and the Access working environment. The right side of the status bar also shows boxes that indicate the presence of a filter and the status of various toggle keys such as INSERT, CAPS LOCK, SCROLL LOCK, and NUM LOCK.

If you're already familiar with Windows 95, you know the taskbar at the bottom of the screen shows a button for each program currently running. New with Windows 98, the taskbar shows a button for each open document, even if they are from the same program. These buttons make switching from one program or document to another quick and easy. Just click the name of the one you want to use and it becomes the active program or document. Notice the Microsoft Access button appears pressed in on the Windows taskbar, indicating it's the active application. If other programs are open, their buttons also appear in the taskbar, but only the currently active one appears pressed in.

Note   *As more and more programs are started, the Windows taskbar buttons are narrowed so all can be seen in the taskbar. With many programs running at once, only the programs' icons and the first few letters of their names may be visible on the taskbar buttons.*

Opening a Database

If the database you want to open is listed in the side pane that appears when Access starts, you can open it by simply double-clicking the filename or by selecting it and choosing OK. If the one you want isn't on the list, click More Files. The Open dialog box appears, as shown in Figure 1-4. (Your list of folders and files will be different.) The same dialog box appears if Access is already running when you choose File | Open or click the Open toolbar button.

The Groups bar at the left contains five buttons, which you can click to open other folders or to return to the Windows desktop.

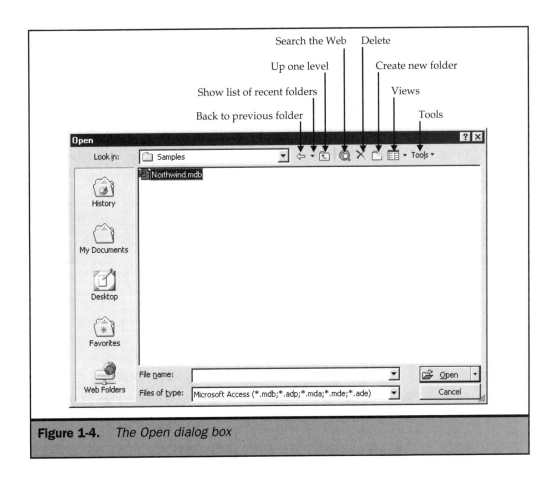

Figure 1-4.   *The Open dialog box*

- The top button, History, opens the new Recent folder that contains the name, size, type, and date of the last modification for each recently accessed database. When you click the History button, the Recent folder name appears in the Look in box.

- The second button, My Documents (or the name of your personal default folder) shows the contents of that folder. This is the default display in the Open dialog box.

- The Desktop button displays a list of the desktop components on your computer you can move to, including such items as My Computer, My Documents, Network Neighborhood, and Online Services.

- The Favorites button displays the names of any folders and objects you've added to the Favorites folder.

- The Web Folders button displays the folders and objects you saved in Web folders.

The trick is to know where you stored your database. If you used other applications, such as Word or Excel, you know how to find the file you want with the Open dialog box. You use the Look in box to zero in on the folder that contains the database, double-click the folder name or icon to open it, and then select the one you want from the list that appears in the dialog box.

The Open dialog box contains several buttons that help you find the file you want to open. You can see the name of each button by resting the mouse pointer on the button in the command bar. Table 1-1 describes the purpose of each of the buttons in the Open dialog box.

Button	Action
(left arrow)	Returns to the previous folder in the Look in box.
(down arrow)	Displays a list of recently accessed folders.
Up One Level	Retreats to the next higher level in the folder structure to look for an Access file.
Search the Web	Opens the Search page of your Internet browser.
Delete	Deletes the selected item. Access asks for confirmation before deleting the item.

Table 1-1.   *Open Dialog Box Buttons*

Button	Action
Create New Folder	Creates a new subfolder in the folder shown in the Look in box.
Views	Enables you to change the amount of information displayed for each item.
Tools	Displays a list of tools, such as Search, Delete, Rename, and Add to Favorites.

Table 1-1.   *Open Dialog Box Buttons* (continued)

The Views drop-down list includes the following options:

- **Large Icons**   Displays the names of the files and subfolders located in the folder specified by the Look in box in rows accompanied by large type icons.
- **Small Icons**   Displays the file and subfolder names in rows with small type icons.
- **List**   Displays the file and subfolder names in a columnar list.
- **Details**   Displays the size, type, and date last modified for each file in the list.
- **Properties**   Displays the properties of the currently selected file such as title, author and application.
- **Preview**   Shows a preview of the file, if one is available, without opening it.

■ **Thumbnails**   Creates thumbnail graphics of files in the selected folder if their file formats permit.

■ **WebView**   Shows the Web view of files in the selected folder, if available.

The Tools drop-down list includes the following options:

■ **Search**   Opens the Search dialog box you can use to locate a database by means other than its name.

■ **Delete**   Deletes the currently selected item. You are always asked to confirm the deletion before Access removes the file. Same as Delete command bar button.

■ **Rename**   Enables you to change the name of the item.

■ **Add to Favorites**   Adds a shortcut to the selected item to the Favorites folder. The item then appears in the dialog box list when you click the Favorites button in the left pane.

■ **Add to "My Places"**   Adds a shortcut to the Places bar. The item appears in the dialog box list when you click the My Network Places button (on Windows 2000) or the Web Folders button (on Windows 98/Windows NT 4).

■ **Map Network Drive**   Enables you to indicate the drive and path to a network connection.

■ **Properties**   Opens the Properties dialog box for the currently selected database.

To choose a different file type to open, click the down arrow next to the Files of type box and choose from the list of 17 types or All Files. The default file type for Access 2002 is Microsoft Access, which includes all Access databases and any other Office documents that have been linked to an Access database, such as an Excel spreadsheet or a Word document. Choose Access Databases to see only the database files in the current folder or Access Projects to see only the list of projects.

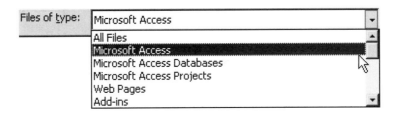

Once you locate the database you want to open, double-click the name or select it and click Open.

Note *The Open button offers other ways to open the database, such as read-only, exclusive, or both. More about these options in later chapters.*

To get started working with a database in Access 2002, let's open the Northwind sample database that comes with Microsoft Office XP. The *Northwind database* is an order-processing application that demonstrates the power and usefulness of a relational database. Even though the purpose of the database seems straight forward enough—taking and filling orders from customers for the company products—a lot of data still must be manipulated. The database is introduced in this chapter and discussed further in Chapter 2.

To open the Northwind sample database:

1. Start Access and double-click More Files in the opening New File side pane or select More Files and click OK. If Access is running and you canceled the opening side pane, click the Open button. The Open dialog box appears.

2. Click the Look in arrow at the top of the dialog box and click C: to revert to the root directory of your hard drive. (If Access is installed on another drive, choose that one instead.)

3. In the list of folders and files in the C: directory, double-click Program Files. Program Files now appears in the Look in text box and a list of the subfolders and files in that folder shows in the window.

4. Continue to open the folders for the Program Files\Microsoft Office\Office\ Samples path. If Office XP is installed in a different directory, use that designator.

5. Double-click Northwind. If the Northwind Traders welcoming screen appears, click OK to close the screen. The Northwind database opens as shown in Figure 1-5.

Tip *If you don't want to be greeted by the Northwind welcoming screen every time you open the database, check the "Don't show this screen again" check box.*

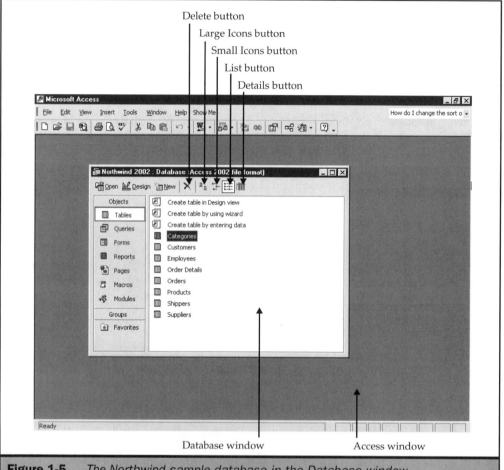

Figure 1-5.   *The Northwind sample database in the Database window*

Note   *In the next section, a distinction is made between the Access window with the menu bar and toolbars, and the Database window that contains lists of all the objects in the database and has a separate command bar.*

Installing Sample Databases

If you don't find the Northwind sample database, you may not have installed it when you installed Office XP. To install it now, do the following:

1. Close Access, if it's running and choose Start | Settings | Control Panel.

2. Double-click Add/Remove Programs.

3. Scroll down the list of programs in the Install/Uninstall tab of the Add/Remove Programs Properties dialog box until you find Microsoft Office XP.

4. Select Microsoft Office XP and click Add/Remove.

5. Click Add or Remove Features in the Microsoft Office XP: Maintenance Mode Options dialog box, and then click Next.

6. In the next dialog box, the Microsoft Office XP: Update Features, click the plus sign (+) next to Microsoft Access for Windows to expand the feature tree.

7. Expand the Sample Databases feature and click Northwind Database. Then choose Run from My Computer from the drop-down list.

8. Click Update and insert the Microsoft Office XP CD, when prompted. When the setup program is finished, allow Windows to restart your computer, if necessary.

You can choose to install the other sample programs as well, either as Run from My Computer or Installed on First Use, which waits to install the program until you call for it.

Touring the Database Window

The left pane of the Database window shows a set of buttons grouped under the Objects title button. The buttons are labeled with the names of the Access database objects: Tables, Queries, Forms, Reports, Pages, Macros, and Modules.

Another title button named Groups includes buttons that open other folders, such as the Favorites folder. In Access 2002, you can define and name your own custom groups similar to the Favorites group. A user-defined group can contain any type of Access objects, as well as objects from other Office applications, just like the Favorites group. When you click Groups, the Objects list collapses and the list of your custom groups appears in its place.

Before opening one of the tables in the Northwind database, let's examine the Database window more closely. More menu commands are now available, all of which are relevant to the open database. Many more toolbar buttons are also available now that a database is open.

The Database window is made up of several pages, each represented by a button in the left pane under Objects. Clicking an object button opens the page, which displays the names of any existing objects of that type. For example, if you want to see the names of all the forms you created for the database, click the Forms button in the left pane of Database window. Each object page also includes two or three "new object" shortcuts you can use to quick-start a new object design with or without the help of a wizard.

Note   *Not only can you resize the database window by dragging its borders, you can also change the width of the left pane by dragging the divider between it and the object pages.*

The command bar at the top of the Database window includes buttons to open an existing object for viewing or modification, to create a new object, or to delete an existing object. In addition, you can change how the objects are listed in the Database window.

You can list the objects using large or small icons in alphabetical order by name or another arrangement. In addition, you can show details with the object name. Each of these options is available by clicking a button on the Database window command bar or by selecting from the View menu.

Table 1-2 describes the object list viewing options.

Figure 1-6 shows the Northwind queries displayed with the Large Icons option. The object icons in the left pane also appear larger when you choose Large Icons.

Tip   *Notice the icon indicates the type of query. For example, the Customers and Suppliers by City query is a Union query, as specified by the joined rings icon, while the spreadsheet icon above the Quarterly Orders... query indicates a Crosstab query. See Chapters 8 and 9 for more information about creating and running queries.*

The list of tables shown in Figure 1-7 is displayed with the Details option. The details are actually the same object properties you can view when using the Windows Explorer. The columns can be widened to see more of the detail or narrowed to hide some of the information. To resize a column, move the mouse pointer to the column divider in the header and, when it changes to a plus sign with a double-pointed horizontal arrow, click-and-drag the boundary.

Option	Description
Large Icons	Displays a large icon above each object name, arranged alphabetically across rows.
Small Icons	Displays a small icon before each object name, arranged alphabetically across rows.
List	Displays a small icon before each object name, arranged alphabetically in one column. If the number of objects exceeds the table height, the list moves to a second column, and so on.
Details	Displays a small icon before each object name, arranged alphabetically in a list with a description, date last modified, date created, type, and, often, the owner.

Table 1-2.   *Access Object Viewing Options*

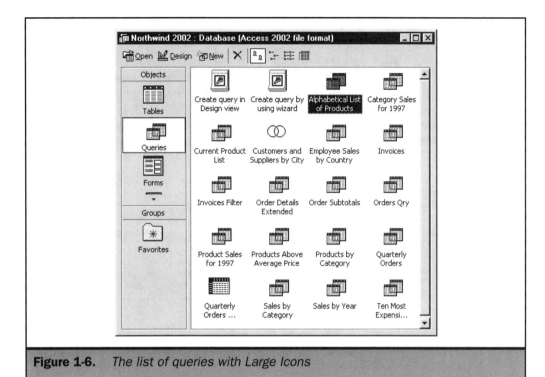

Figure 1-6.   *The list of queries with Large Icons*

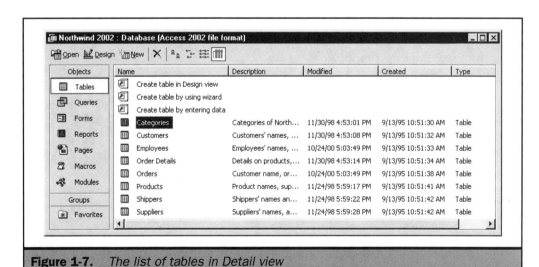

Figure 1-7.   *The list of tables in Detail view*

You can also rearrange the objects to list them in a different order, just as with the Windows Explorer. Choose Arrange Icons from the View menu and you have a choice of arranging in alphabetical order by name (the default), by type of object, by date of creation, or by the date the object was last modified (see Figure 1-8). All the arrangements are in ascending order, as you can tell from the arrows in the icons.

Note *The Arrange Icons command is also available on the Database window shortcut menu. To open the shortcut menu, click the right mouse button when the mouse pointer is on an empty area of the Database window. You learn more about shortcut menus in a later section in this chapter.*

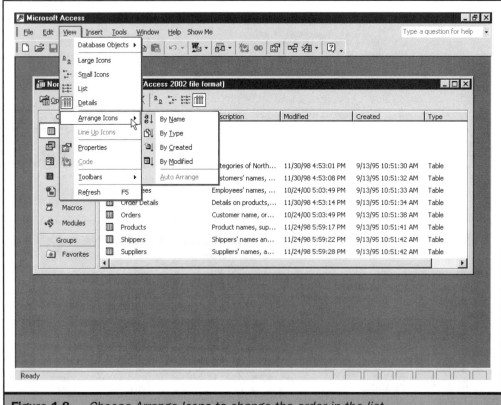

Figure 1-8. *Choose Arrange Icons to change the order in the list*

If you don't see the Arrange Icons command on the View menu right away, it's because Microsoft considers this a seldom used command. To save you the trouble of choosing from an unnecessarily long list of commands, the ones less commonly used are hidden when you first click the menu. To show these hidden commands, click the double pointers at the bottom of the menu or simply rest the mouse pointer on the menu for a moment. The newly revealed commands appear with a lighter shaded background.

If you choose one of these commands, it usually appears in the menu the next time you click the menu or the menu bar. See Chapter 20 for more information about Access menu bars and toolbars.

Each object page also has a command bar with a set of buttons appropriate to that object type. All the object pages include the Design and New buttons. The first button depends on the object:

- The Tables, Queries, Forms, and Pages pages show the Open button, which opens the selected object for data entering or editing.

- The Reports page shows the Preview button that displays the report as it will be printed.

- The Macros page shows the Run button that executes the selected macro.

- The first button is dimmed on the Modules page.

Note   *If you maximize the Database window, the command bar appears immediately below the Database toolbar in the Access window.*

In addition to the objects in the list, each object page—except the Macros and Modules pages—includes two or three shortcut items that start the process of creating a new object. For example, the Tables page, as shown earlier in Figure 1-5, has the following three items in the list:

- Create table in Design view
- Create table by using wizard
- Create table by entering data

More about using these features in later chapters.

Looking at Menu Options and Toolbar Buttons

The standard Database menu bar and toolbar appear in the Access window. Not all the options are available to all the database objects and, some, such as the Save button, aren't available until a table or other object is opened. The Paste button is dimmed until you copy something to the clipboard. Table 1-3 describes the Database toolbar buttons and their equivalent menu commands and keyboard shortcuts, if any.

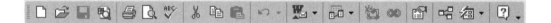

Tip *If you don't see the toolbar, right-click in the menu bar and check Database in the list of available toolbars.*

Button	Button Name	Menu Equivalent	Shortcut	Description
	New	File | New...	CTRL-N	Opens the New dialog box with options for creating databases using wizard templates or a blank database.
	Open	File | Open...	CTRL-O	Opens the Open dialog box where you can locate and open the desired database file.
	Save	File | Save	CTRL-S	Saves the current object. If not already named, prompts for a name.
	Search	File | Search	(none)	Opens the Search side pane, where you can specify search criteria.
	Print	File | Print	CTRL-P	Prints the current object. The button sends the document directly to the default printer. File | Print and CTRL-P Open the Print dialog box.
	Print Preview	File | Print Preview	(none)	Opens the current document in the Print Preview window.

Table 1-3. *Database Toolbar Buttons and Menu Options*

Button	Button Name	Menu Equivalent	Shortcut	Description
	Spelling	Tools | Spelling	F7	Checks the spelling of all text and memo fields in the current document. If no document is open, the currently selected object is opened and the spelling is checked.
	Cut	Edit | Cut	CTRL-X	Removes selected text or object and places it on the clipboard.
	Copy	Edit | Copy	CTRL-C	Copies selected text or object to the clipboard.
	Paste	Edit | Paste	CTRL-V	Copies contents of the clipboard to the active object or window.
	Undo/Can't Undo	Edit | Undo/Can't Undo	CTRL-Z	Reverses previous editing action. Not available if no reversible action has been taken.
	OfficeLinks	Tools | Office Links	(none)	Opens a submenu with options for linking with MS Word or MS Excel.
	Analyze	Tools | Analyze	(none)	Opens a submenu with choices of Analyzer tools.
	Visual Basic	View | Code or Tools | Macro | Visual Basic Editor	(none)	Opens the Visual Basic Editor window showing code for the selected object.

Table 1-3. *Database Toolbar Buttons and Menu Options* (continued)

Button	Button Name	Menu Equivalent	Shortcut	Description
	Microsoft Script Editor	Tools | Macro | Microsoft Script Editor	(none)	Opens the Microsoft Script Editor window where you can add or view data access page script.
	Properties	View | Properties	(none)	Opens the General property dialog box for selected object.
	Relationships	Tools | Relationships	(none)	Opens the Relationships window.
	New Object: AutoForm	Insert | AutoForm	(none)	Creates an AutoForm or other object based on selected table or query. Not available with other objects.
	Microsoft Access Help	Help | Microsoft Access Help	F1	Starts the MS Office Assistant.
	Add or Remove Buttons	(none)	(none)	Enables you to add buttons to or remove buttons from the toolbar.

Table 1-3.   *Database Toolbar Buttons and Menu Options* (continued)

Caution   *The Undo button works with a lot of actions, but not with all of them, so be careful. Some actions cannot be undone. When you're about to perform an action that's irreversible, Access displays a warning message. Take the time to read the message carefully and make sure you want to proceed.*

You can move the menu bar and toolbar to different locations in the window, docked at another edge or free-floating. To move either one, click the move handle located at the far-left edge of the bar (it looks like a stack of dash marks). Then drag the bar away from the top of the window to another edge or leave it in the center of the window. Dragging the bar borders resizes the floating bar. Figure 1-9 shows the toolbar floating over the Database window and the menu bar docked at the right edge of the window. To restore the menu bar to the top of the screen, click-and-drag the move handle at the left end of the bar. To restore the floating toolbar, drag it by its title bar to the top of the window.

Using Shortcut Menus

Shortcut menus are context-sensitive menus that appear when you click the right mouse button. The commands in the menu depend on where the mouse pointer is and what's happening when you click the button. The shortcut menu also appears when you press SHIFT-F10. Click anywhere outside the menu to close it. Pressing ENTER, ESC, or ALT also closes the shortcut menu.

Figure 1-10 shows the shortcut menu that appears when you right-click in a blank area of the Database window. Only the most commonly used commands are included in the shortcut menu, but they may also include commands from several different menus on the menu bar.

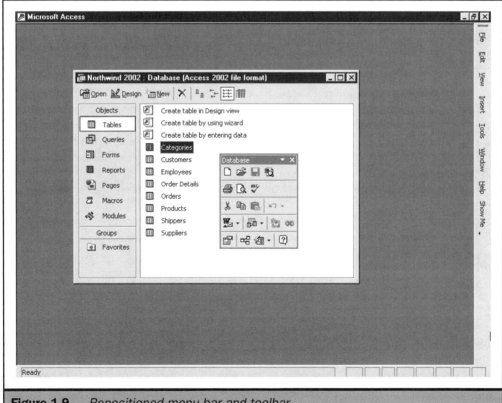

Figure 1-9.   *Repositioned menu bar and toolbar*

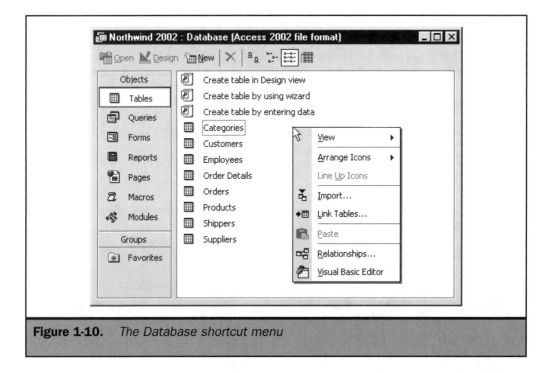

Figure 1-10. *The Database shortcut menu*

To choose a command from a shortcut menu, click the command or type the letter underlined in the name of the command. If the command shows a right arrow, such as View in Figure 1-10, it's a submenu. Rest the pointer on the item to open the list of commands, and then choose from the list. If the command shows an ellipsis (...) such as Import, a dialog box opens when you click it.

See Chapter 20 for information on how to customize menu bars, toolbars, and shortcut menus.

Opening a Table

To open one of the tables in the current database, double-click its name in the Tables page or select the name and click Open. The table appears with the data in rows and columns much like a spreadsheet. This view of table data is called *Datasheet view*. Figure 1-11 shows the open Northwind Orders table in Datasheet view. Each row contains a single record with all the information for one order. Each column contains values for one field. Each field has a unique name and contains a specific item of data, such as the customer or employee name. The column headings show the field names.

When you enter data in the table, you're putting actual values in the cells at the intersections of rows with columns.

You can also select an object by typing the first letter of the object name, which gives you a quick way to open the object. For example, to open the Order Details table, open the Tables page and type O, and then press ENTER, *which activates the default Open button. If more than one object on the page has the same first character, the first one in the list is selected. To open the next object, close the first one, type the character again, and then press* ENTER.

The Datasheet view window has scroll bars you can use to view different parts of the datasheet, as described in the next section.

Another way to open a table is to click the right mouse button on the table name in the Tables page, and then choose Open from the shortcut menu. Other commands on this menu will be useful later.

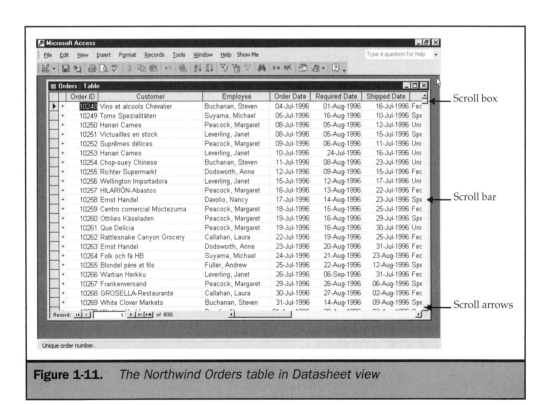

Figure 1-11.   *The Northwind Orders table in Datasheet view*

The status bar at the bottom of the Access window displays the description of the current field included in the table definition. For example, if the cursor is in the first field—Order ID—the status bar displays "Unique Order Number."

Touring the Datasheet View

You may have noticed some changes that occur in the window when you open a table. For example, the title bar of the Database window now shows the name of the open table.

 If the Database window is maximized, the name appears in the Access window title bar.

The menu bar includes two new options—Format and Records—that are relevant to the open table. More of the toolbar buttons are also available.

The datasheet window shows scroll bars at the right side and in the right side at the bottom. To the left of the bottom (horizontal) scroll bar is a set of navigation tools you can use to move through the records in the table. The following paragraphs give you more detail about the toolbar buttons and the scroll bars.

Looking at the Table Datasheet Toolbar

The Database toolbar has been replaced by the Table Datasheet toolbar, which has many new buttons.

 If you right-click anywhere on the toolbar, you can see the Table Datasheet option is checked in the shortcut menu. This is a sure way to tell which toolbar is visible on the screen. You can also choose additional toolbars from the list to show in addition to or instead of the default toolbar.

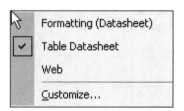

Table 1-4 describes the toolbar buttons on the Table Datasheet toolbar that didn't appear on the Database toolbar.

Button	Button Name	Menu Equivalent	Description
	View	View	The left side of the button switches to the view depicted on the button. The drop-down button opens a list of available table views. The View drop-down list always contains Datasheet View, Design View, PivotTable View, and PivotChart View. If you have created an AutoForm for the table, the Form View option also appears.
	Sort Ascending	Records | Sort | Sort Ascending	Sorts records in the active field in ascending order (lowest value to highest value).
	Sort Descending	Records | Sort | Sort Descending	Sorts records in the active field in descending order (highest value to lowest value).
	Filter By Selection	Records | Filter | Filter By Selection	Limits records in display to those with the same value as the selected data.
	Filter By Form	Records | Filter | Filter By Form	Opens blank datasheet form for entering filter criteria.
	Apply Filter	Records | Apply Filter/Sort	Applies the current filter.
	Remove Filter	Records | Remove Filter/Sort	Removes the filter, if already applied.

Table 1-4.   *Table Datasheet Toolbar Buttons*

Button	Button Name	Menu Equivalent	Description
	Find	Edit | Find	Opens the Find dialog box for locating specific records based on the value in one or all fields.
	New Record	Insert | New Record or Edit | GoTo | New Record	Adds a new record at the bottom of the datasheet.
	Delete Record	Edit | Delete Record	Deletes current record.
	Database Window	Window | *current database*:Database	Brings the Database window to the front.

Table 1-4.   *Table Datasheet Toolbar Buttons* (continued)

Among the buttons described in Table 1-4, the only buttons with keyboard shortcuts are Find (CTRL-F), New Record (CTRL-++), and Database Window (F11).

Using the Scroll Bars

When all your table data cannot fit into a single screen in Datasheet view, scroll bars appear down the right side and at the bottom of the datasheet window, as shown earlier in Figure 1-11.

A *scroll bar* has four important parts: the scroll bar itself, the scroll box, and the two small arrows at either end. The scroll bar represents the total area of the datasheet, both visible and hidden. The location of the scroll box in the bar indicates your approximate vertical or horizontal position in the datasheet. The size of the box indicates the relative amount or proportion of the total data visible currently. For example, if the scroll box is midway down the vertical scroll bar and occupies half the total length of the bar, you're viewing half the records that occur in the middle of your table.

You have four ways to move up and down among records in the datasheet with the vertical scroll bar:

- To move a few records up or down, click the up or down arrow.
- To scroll continuously through the records, point to one of the scroll arrows and hold down the mouse button until you reach the records you want.

- To move one window-length at a time, click in the scroll bar above or below the scroll box.

- To scroll to a particular record in the table, drag the scroll box to that record. As you drag the scroll box, a ScreenTip appears next to the pointer. The ScreenTip displays the number of the current record and the total number of records in the table.

+	10429	Hungry Owl All-Night Grocers	Leverling, Janet	29-Jan-1997	12-Mar-1997	07-Feb-1997	
+	10430	Ernst Handel	Peacock, Margaret	30-Jan-1997	13-Feb-1997	03-Feb-1997	
+	10431	Bottom-Dollar Markets	Peacock, Margaret	30-Jan-1997	13-Feb-1997	07-Feb-	Record: 178 of 830
+	10432	Split Rail Beer & Ale	Leverling, Janet	31-Jan-1997	14-Feb-1997	07-Feb-1997	

The horizontal scroll bar works just the same to move the datasheet sideways in the window through the columns.

Note
The scroll bars only move the data about on the screen, so you can see different areas of the datasheet. They don't move the cursor among records or fields.

Navigating Among Records and Fields

You can move the cursor around the records and fields in your table in several ways, including simply clicking the desired location if it's visible. You should try them all and settle on the one that suits you best. The other methods are

- Selecting from the Go To submenu on the Edit menu.
- Clicking the record navigation buttons at the bottom of the datasheet.
- Using keystrokes such as TAB and the arrow keys.

The Go To submenu on the Edit menu enables you to move to the first, last, next, previous, or to an empty new record.

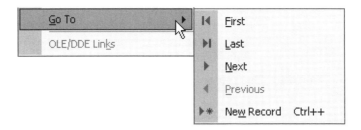

The record navigation buttons at the bottom of the datasheet window give you the same options as the Edit | Go To submenu. You can also enter a specific record number (if you know the number of the record you want to see) in the text box between the navigation buttons, and then press ENTER. This area also tells you what record the cursor is in and the total number of records in the table.

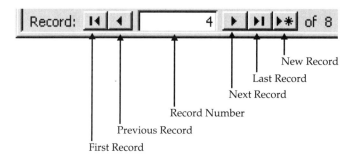

<table>
<tr><td colspan="2">New Record</td></tr>
<tr><td colspan="2">Last Record</td></tr>
<tr><td colspan="2">Next Record</td></tr>
<tr><td>Record Number</td></tr>
<tr><td>Previous Record</td></tr>
<tr><td>First Record</td></tr>
</table>

Note   *If this is a filtered subset of the table, then the word "(Filtered)" appears after the total number of records, which is the number of records remaining after the filter has been applied.*

Pressing a key or combination of keys can be a faster way to move around the datasheet once you get used to the correlation between the keys and the resulting cursor movement. Table 1-5 shows what happens when you press various keys and key combinations.

Keystroke	Resulting Cursor Movement
UP or DOWN ARROW	Up or down one record in the same field.
RIGHT ARROW or TAB	Right one field in the same record. If in the last field, to the first field in the next record. (If you're in Edit mode, RIGHT ARROW moves one character to the right.)
LEFT ARROW or SHIFT-TAB	Left one field in the same record. If in the first field, to the last field in the previous record. (If you're in Edit mode, LEFT ARROW moves one character to the left.)
PGUP or PGDN	Up or down one screen of records.

Table 1-5.   *Cursor Movement in Datasheet View*

Keystroke	Resulting Cursor Movement
HOME	To the first field in the same record. (If you're in Edit mode, HOME moves the cursor to the beginning of the active field.)
END	To the last field in the same record. (If you're in Edit mode, END moves the cursor to the end of the active field.)
CTRL-HOME	To the first field in the first record. (If you're in Edit mode, CTRL-HOME moves the cursor to the beginning of the active field.)
CTRL-END	To the last field in the last record. (If you're in Edit mode, CTRL-END moves the cursor to the end of the active field.)
TAB	Returns to the database window.

Table 1-5.   *Cursor Movement in Datasheet View* (continued)

    You can change the behavior of the ENTER *and arrow keys in the Keyboard Options dialog box. For example, you can prevent the cursor from moving to another record after you fill in the last field in one record. See Chapter 16 for information about customizing your workplace by setting options.*

Looking at a Subdatasheet

In a relational database, being able to view information related to the current data on the screen when you want to is important. This has always been possible with forms and subforms in which the main form contains data from one record in one table, while the subform contains data from one or more records in a related table.

Beginning in Access 2000, you have the same capability when viewing data in Datasheet view. The related data is displayed in a *subdatasheet,* which can be easily displayed. If the records shown in Datasheet view display a plus sign at the left end of the row, additional information in another table in the database is related to that record. To see this data, expand the subdatasheet by clicking the plus sign. The plus sign changes to a minus sign (-) when the subdatasheet expands. To collapse the subdatasheet, click the minus sign.

You can have as many subdatasheets expanded as you want in a single Datasheet view. Each subdatasheet corresponds to one record in the datasheet. You can expand them individually or set a table property that automatically expands all the subdatasheets when the table opens in Datasheet view. See Chapter 4 for information about setting table and other properties.

Figure 1-12 shows the Northwind Orders table with two subdatasheets expanded to show the products from the Order Details table, which were included in two of the orders in the Orders table. Notice the plus and minus signs indicating the current state of the subdatasheet.

Note   *If fields haven't been specified with which to link records in the subdatasheet with records in the datasheet, when you expand the subdatasheet, you'll see all the records in the related table. See Chapter 3 for more information about relating tables and what that can do.*

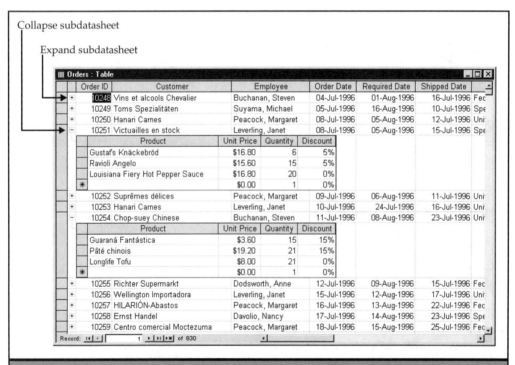

Figure 1-12. *Viewing subdatasheets in the Orders table in Datasheet view*

Looking at Data in a Form

So far, you've viewed the Northwind Products table data only in Datasheet view. This view is fine for reviewing the data in small tables, but the full datasheet is often too wide to fit all of the fields on a single screen. A much more convenient way to see the data is in a form with only one record on the screen at once. Then you can usually see all the fields and move freely among them without having to use the scroll bars. Forms are dual-purpose objects: You can use a form to look up data or to enter and edit data.

Creating the Form

To create an AutoForm for a table, you don't even have to open the table first. Simply select the table's name in the Database window and click the arrow next to the New Object button. Figure 1-13 shows the list of new objects you can create, including AutoForm and AutoReport. Notice you can use this button to begin creating any of the Access database objects.

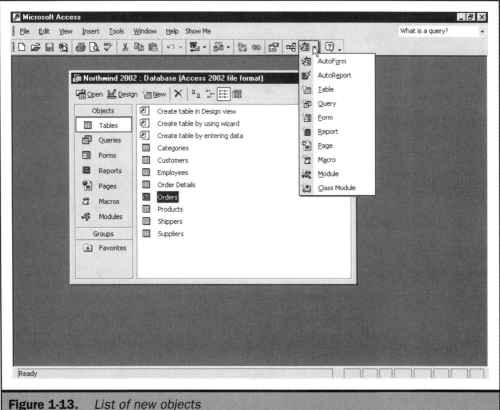

Figure 1-13.   *List of new objects*

If you simply click the New Object toolbar button without choosing from the list, you automatically create an AutoForm because it's first on the list and, therefore, the default option. To create one of the other objects, click the down arrow and choose from the list.

The AutoForm feature is a special Wizard that doesn't ask you for any input about how you want the form to look or what data you want it to show. It falls back on a default form layout and style. The form includes every field in the table, arranged in a single column with the field names to the left, so you can identify the fields. The name of the table appears in the title bar of the form window. Figure 1-14 shows the Northwind Orders table in Form view after creating the AutoForm.

The Orders table has a related table, Order Details, which was available as a subdatasheet (refer to Figure 1-12). When Access creates an AutoForm, it automatically creates a subform containing data from the related table, which corresponds to the current record in the main form.

If there are more fields than can fit on a single screen, you can use the vertical scroll bar to see the rest.

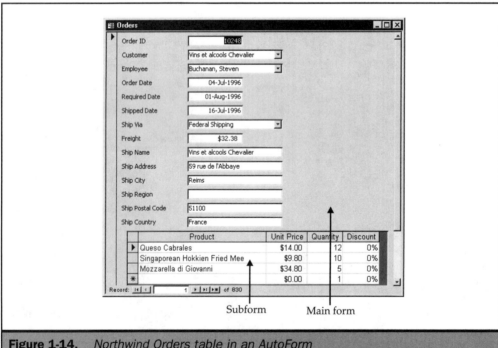

Figure 1-14. *Northwind Orders table in an AutoForm*

To use the form to add a new record to the Orders table, click the New Record navigation button to display an empty form. Use the TAB key to move from field to field as you enter data. To add a new record in the subform, enter the data in the blank row at the bottom of the subform datasheet.

When you finish with the form, you can give it a name and save it as a new database object or you can close the form without saving it. You can also choose to enter the form Design window and make changes to the AutoForm, and then save it as a custom form. You learn more about form design in Chapter 10.

Navigating in Form View

Moving about the table when it's in Form view isn't very different from moving around in Datasheet view. You still have the navigation buttons at the bottom of the window, which you can use to move to other records (and the Go To options in the Edit menu). The subform also has a navigation bar referring to the records in the subform. Moving from one field to another is a little different, however. Of course, you can simply click in the field you want to work with, but you may find using keystrokes easier. Table 1-6 shows how to move the cursor in a form with keystrokes.

Note *As with moving around in a datasheet, some of these keystrokes behave differently if you are in Edit mode. Refer to Table 1-5 for the details.*

Keystroke	Resulting Cursor Movement
TAB, ENTER, RIGHT or DOWN ARROW	To the next field. If in the last field of a record, to the first field of the next record.
SHIFT-TAB, LEFT or UP ARROW	To the previous field. If in the first field of a record, to the last field of the previous record.
PGDN, SHIFT-PGDN, or CTRL-PGDN	To the same field in the next record.
PGUP, SHIFT-PGUP, or CTRL-PGUP	To the same field in the previous record.
HOME	To the first field in the current record.
END	To the last field in the current record.
CTRL-HOME	To the first field in the first record.
CTRL-END	To the last field in the last record.

Table 1-6.   *Cursor Movement in Form View*

If the form contains a subform, pressing TAB cycles the cursor through all the fields of the main form, and then through the fields and records of the related subform. After leaving the last field of the last record in the subform, the cursor moves to the first field in the next record in the main form. The path is reversed when you press CTRL-TAB.

To switch back to Datasheet view, click the down arrow on the right side of the View button and choose Datasheet view from the list. You can also choose View | Datasheet view. The Form view option remains on the View drop-down list until you close the table without saving the new form.

Looking at the Wizards

If you used earlier versions of Access, you've already met some of the wizards, the experts that guide you through complicated processes in a few simple steps. Wizards can help create new databases, tables, and queries, as well as customize forms, reports, and data access pages with special features. A wizard presents each step as a dialog box in which you choose what you want to do and how you want the results to look. As you make choices, the wizard works in the background to create the Visual Basic code that can accomplish your goals.

Access 2002 has improved many of the old wizards and has added new ones, so you can get help with virtually anything you want to create. Table 1-7 describes the wizards installed when you choose Typical Wizards during Setup and where they are discussed in later chapters of this book. Additional wizards, such as the Security Wizard, Subform/Subreport Wizard, Input Mask Wizard, and many of the database utilities are installed when you select Additional Wizards from the feature tree during Setup. See the Quick Reference on the CD for a complete list of the wizards, builders, and add-ins, and how to reach them.

Wizard	Purpose	Refer to Chapter
AutoDialer	Adds a control to a form or datasheet or a button to a toolbar that dials a selected phone number.	12
AutoForm	Creates a basic data entry form based on the selected table or query.	11

Table 1-7.   *The Wizard Line Up*

Wizard	Purpose	Refer to Chapter
AutoFormat	Applies predefined styles to existing forms or reports. Also used to create custom styles.	13
AutoPage	Creates a basic data access page based on the selected table or query.	24
AutoReport	Creates a basic report containing all the fields in the selected table or query.	13
Combo Box	Creates a combo box control on a form.	12
Command Button	Creates a command button control on a form.	12
Crosstab Query	Creates a query that summarizes data in a compact, spreadsheet-like format.	8
Database	Creates a new database for a variety of uses based on prebuilt models.	3
Export	Exports data to the file format you specify.	23
Field Builder	Adds predefined fields to the current table.	4
Form	Creates a new form.	11
Import Exchange/ Outlook	Imports data and objects arriving via e-mail.	24

Table 1-7. *The Wizard Line Up* (continued)

Wizard	Purpose	Refer to Chapter
Import HTML	Imports HTML tables and lists from the Internet or an intranet into an Access table.	24
Import Spreadsheet	Imports an Excel or other spreadsheet into an Access table.	23
Import Text	Imports a text file into an Access table.	23
Label	Creates mailing labels in standard and custom sizes.	14
Link Exchange/Outlook	Links with data acquired by e-mail.	
Link HTML	Links an HTML table or list on the Internet or an intranet to an Access table.	24
Link Spreadsheet	Links spreadsheet data to an Access table.	23
Link Text	Links a text file to an Access table.	23
List Box	Creates a list box control on a form.	10
Lookup	Creates a lookup column in a table, which displays a list of values from which the user can choose.	6
Microsoft Word Mail Merge	Manages mail merge operations using letters stored in Word and addresses stored in Access.	23

Table 1-7. *The Wizard Line Up* (continued)

Wizard	Purpose	Refer to Chapter
Page	Creates a data access page based on a table or query.	24
Page Combo Box	Creates a drop-down list box control for a data access page.	24
Page Command Button	Creates a command button for a data access page.	24
Page List Box	Creates a list box control for a data access page.	24
PivotTable	Places an Excel PivotTable on an Access form.	15
Print Relationships	Prints the diagram displayed in the Relationships window.	5
Report	Creates a report based on a table or query.	13
Simple Query	Creates a select query from the fields you pick.	8
Switchboard Manager	Creates switchboards for custom user interfaces.	21
Table	Creates a new table.	4

Table 1-7.   *The Wizard Line Up* (continued)

Getting Help

No matter how easy Access makes database management, you can't possibly remember how to do every task. That's where the Access Help feature comes in. Three methods of getting help are available

- Ask a question and look in the Help file.
- Use the What's This? feature to see short explanations.
- Access the Microsoft Office Web site.

The Ask a Question box is always available in the upper-right corner of the menu bar, so you can always get help, no matter where you are or what you're doing in Access. The Help menu is always on the menu bar as well. The Help button is also available on all built-in toolbars.

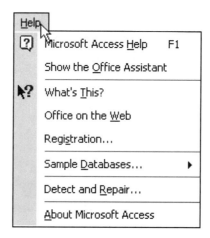

You have four ways to start the Microsoft Access Help feature:

- Type a question in plain English in the Ask a Question box.
- Choose Microsoft Access Help from the Help menu and ask the question of the Office Assistant.

- Press F1.
- Click the Microsoft Access Help toolbar button.

The first option displays a list of related topics from which you can choose. The other options can start the Office Assistant, an animated character that all the Office programs use interactively to offer help.

Asking a Question

The Ask a Question box on the menu bar is new to Access 2002. You can use it to get help quickly. Simply type a question in the box, press ENTER, and a list of related topics is displayed (see Figure 1-15). Click one of the topics or, if none seem to answer your question, click See More... to display additional topics. You may have to rephrase your question to zero in on the specific topic you need.

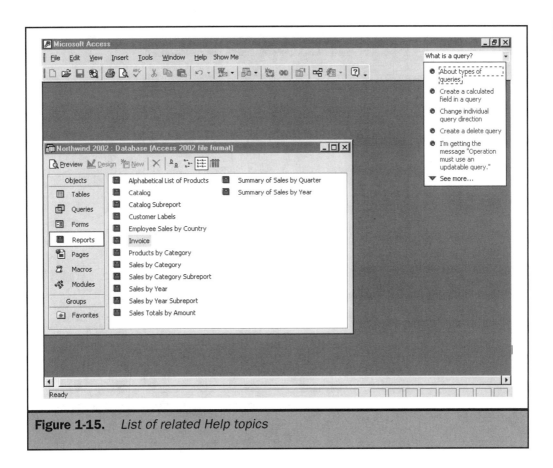

Figure 1-15. *List of related Help topics*

> **Tip**
> *The last item in the list displayed by the Ask a Question feature is None of the Above, Look for More Help on the Web, which takes you to a Help window from which you can start your Web browser and send the question to a site for further assistance.*

Click a topic and the Help window opens, displaying the topic you chose (see Figure 1-16). Only the right pane of the Help window containing the chosen topic may be visible at first. What's visible depends on which panes were visible when you last closed the Help window. The topic usually includes many expandable items, such as Select queries, Parameter queries, and the others in the list shown in the figure. To see the whole subtopic, click the expand arrow at the left of the selection.

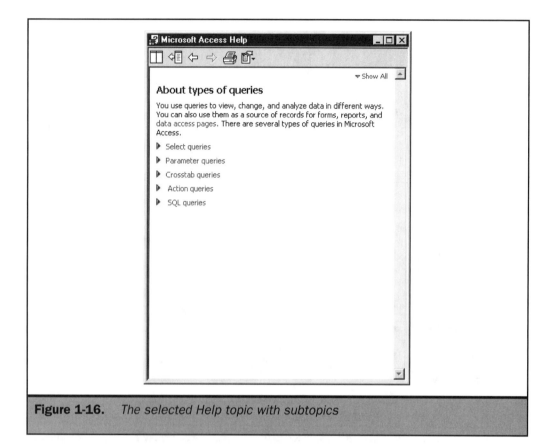

Figure 1-16. *The selected Help topic with subtopics*

If you want to see all the subtopics expanded, click the Show All button at the top right of the window (see Figure 1-17). In addition to the list of subtopics, you may see many terms showing in a different color, which indicates they're expandable to show definitions and other short explanations. These are also expanded when you click Show All. You can also expand them individually by clicking the colored term. To collapse a single item, click it again. To collapse all the items, click the Hide All button. All items automatically collapse when you move to another topic.

The left pane of the Help window contains additional means of getting assistance with Access. To open the other half, click the Show button. The left pane contains three tabs (see Figure 1-18), which give you different ways to look for help.

- The Contents page, which displays a complete list of major Help topics.

- The Answer Wizard, where you can type a specific question and the wizard responds with a list of Help topics that relate to the question.

- The Index page, where you can look for information by keyword, such as "queries" or "data access pages."

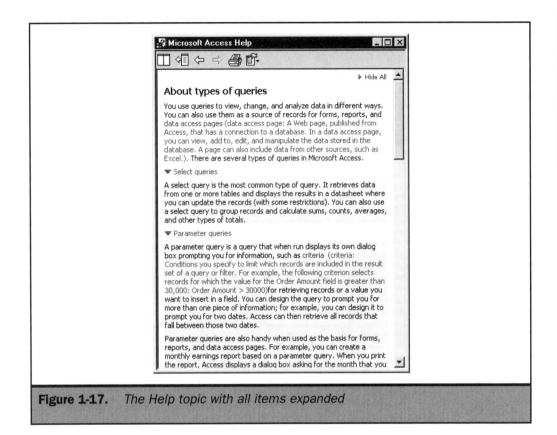

Figure 1-17.   *The Help topic with all items expanded*

Looking in the Contents

The Contents page shows a list of major topics, each represented by a closed book icon with an accompanying plus sign. Scroll down the list of major topics and, when you find the one you are interested in, click the plus sign to display the list of individual topics within that heading. Individual topics are indicated by a question mark. When you find the specific topic you want to read, click the title. Figure 1-18 shows the expanded Queries: Basics topic with one of the topics displaying in the right pane.

As you can see in Figure 1-18, when you rest the mouse pointer on a title that's too long for the width of the pane, a ScreenTip appears showing the complete title.

To collapse the list of individual topics in the Contents page, click the minus sign that replaced the plus sign when you expanded the topic.

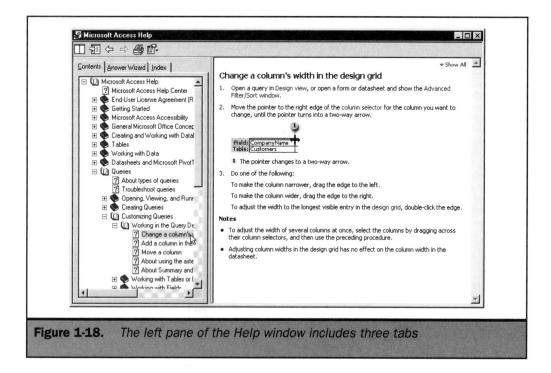

Figure 1-18. The left pane of the Help window includes three tabs

As you access different Help topics in your search for an answer, you can use the Help window buttons as follows:

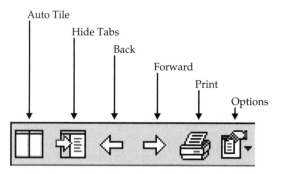

- The Auto Tile button opens the Help window tiled vertically with your current database, so you can get help on the fly.
- The Hide Tabs button removes the Help tabs pane.

- You can move back and forward among the recently accessed topics with the Back and Forward buttons.

- If you find a topic you want to print, click Print. If you've selected a topic heading, a dialog box appears offering to print the current page or all the topics under the current Contents heading. Otherwise, the Print dialog box appears.

- The Options button displays a list that includes the other button actions, plus Home, Stop, Refresh, and Internet Options all of which apply to seeking help on the Web.

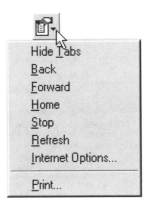

Asking the Answer Wizard

The Answer Wizard uses sophisticated keyword association techniques to locate relevant Help topics based on a question you ask. To use the Answer Wizard, type a question in the upper box of the Answer Wizard tab, and then click Search. Figure 1-19 shows the topics found in answer to the question, "How do I change the sort order of records?" As with the Index tab, the first topic is automatically displayed. Select another topic to display it. To look on the Web, click the Search On Web button.

Note   *If you type the same question in the Ask a Question box, only the first nine topics are offered plus the opportunity to seek help on the Web.*

Looking Up Help in the Index

Another way to find a Help topic is through the Index page shown in Figure 1-20. To use the Help Index, type a keyword in the upper box or select one from the alphabetical list in the center box. Then click Search. The search is not case-sensitive.

The topics Access finds relating to the keyword are listed in the lower box, along with the number of topics found. The first topic in the found list is automatically displayed in the right Help pane. If you want to see one of the others, select it.

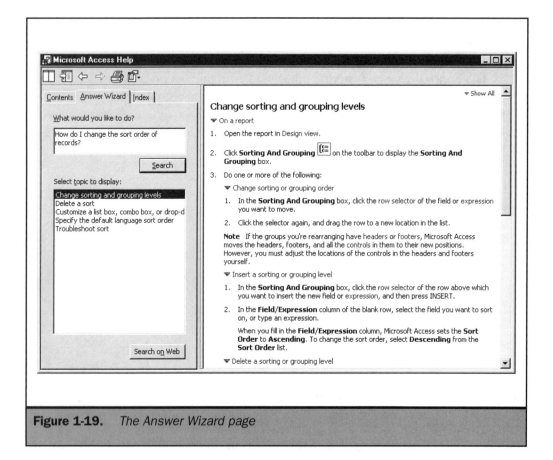

Figure 1-19. *The Answer Wizard page*

To look up topics for another keyword, click Clear and enter or choose a keyword as before. You can look up more than one key word at a time by typing them in the upper box, separated by semicolons.

Hiding the Help Window

To close the Help window, click the Close button in the title bar. If you want to keep it onscreen as you work, click the AutoTile button instead. You can also keep the Help window handy, but out of the way, by clicking the Minimize button. The Help window button then appears in the taskbar. To restore the Help window, click the taskbar button.

Asking the Office Assistant

Choosing Microsoft Access Help from the Help menu usually starts the animated paper clip known as *Clippit, the Office Assistant*. When you activate the Office Assistant,

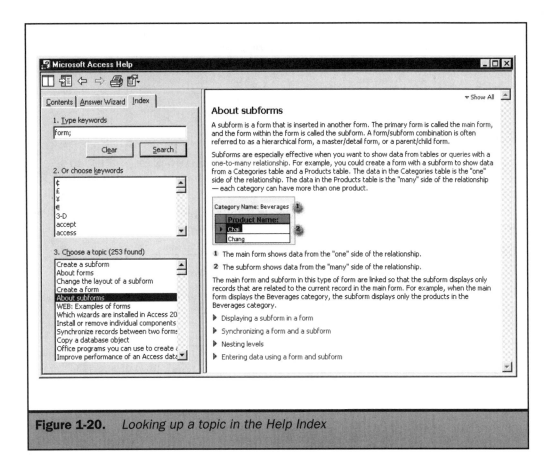

Figure 1-20.   *Looking up a topic in the Help Index*

a short list of Help topic descriptions with light bulb icons often appear in the window or Clippit may just ask what you want to do. Type your question in the text box and click Search. This functions much like typing your question in the Ask a Question box. You'll see a list of relevant topics and you can choose one to open the Help window.

To remove the Office Assistant from the screen, choose Help | Hide Office Assistant or right-click the character and choose Hide from the shortcut menu. If you want variety, you can choose from six other characters. See Chapter 16 for information about customizing the Office Assistant and other features of the Access workplace.

Asking What's This?

The *What's This?* help tool gives you short and quick information about a specific menu command, a toolbar button, or an element in a dialog box. Getting this type of help is a two-step process. First, activate the What's This? help feature. The mouse pointer changes to an arrow accompanied by a question mark. Then, click the command, button, or other object you want to find out about.

You have several ways to activate What's This? help:

- Choose Help | What's This?
- Click the ? button in a dialog box.
- Press SHIFT-F1.

For example, with a menu command highlighted, you can press SHIFT-F1 to see the What's This? explanation of the selection. In a dialog box, you can also right-click an object in question and choose What's This? from the shortcut menu to see a brief description. For example, click View on the menu bar and highlight—but don't click—List. Then press SHIFT-F1 to see an explanation of the command.

List (View menu)

Lists database objects by using small icons for the selected object type. Icons are alphabetized vertically within the Database window.

To return the mouse pointer to its normal state without opening What's This? help, repeat the button click or press ESC.

Note   *You can create your own custom help messages for ScreenTips and status bar messages. See Chapter 12 for information about adding such custom help to an Access form.*

Getting Help Off the Web

The fourth option in the Help menu is Office on the Web. When you choose this command, you can connect directly to the Microsoft Office Update and other Web sites via Microsoft Internet Explorer 5.0 or another browser. At these sites, you can have access to technical resources and also download your choice of product enhancements.

You can also reach the Web by choosing the None of the Above, Look for More Help on the Web from the Ask a Question or by clicking the Search On Web button on the Answer Wizard tab. This opens the Finding Help Topics window (see Figure 1-21) where you can click the *search tips* hyperlink to get information about using the window. You can also type more information about your dilemma. When you have added all the information you want, click the Send and go to the Web button to begin the search.

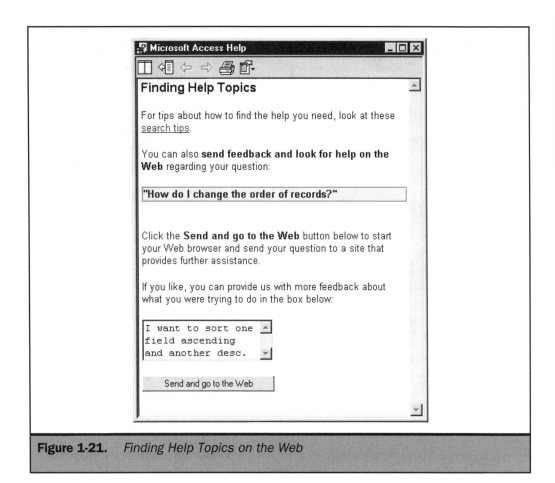

Figure 1-21. *Finding Help Topics on the Web*

Getting Help with What You're Doing

Without opening the Help window, Access gives you many hints and clues while you're working. The status bar offers information about the current activity or position of the cursor. Many design windows include hint boxes that tell you about aspects of the design. Other windows and dialog boxes include samples or previews of the selections made.

Figure 1-22 shows the table Design window with status bar information telling you how to move around the Design view and get help. The hint box on the right describes what should appear in the Field Name column.

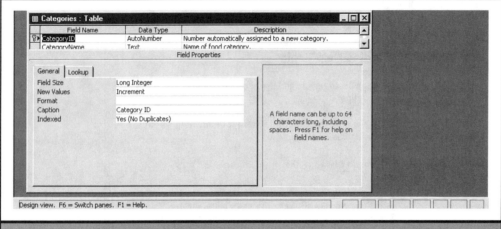

Figure 1-22. *Hints and status bar help*

Summary

This chapter has shown you ways to start Access 2002 and get around in the Access window. You had a chance to try out the viewing options, menu bar commands, and toolbar buttons. Using the Access 2002 Northwind sample database, you were given a tour of the Database window and a glimpse of the power behind the Access design capabilities, including the many available wizards.

The final section covered the ways to get help while you are working with Access: from the Help Contents and Index pages, by typing a question in the Ask a Question box, by asking the Answer Wizard, with guidance from the Office Assistant, or with the What's This? button.

Armed with this familiarity with the Access database management system, the next chapter introduces you to the concepts behind the relational database model and examines the types of relationships you can define between tables. That chapter also looks at the structure and components of a sample database and how the data is related for efficiency.

Subsequent chapters present details about designing and creating a database, as well as populating it with tables and other Access objects.

MOUS Exam Activities Explored in This Chapter

Level	Activity	Section Title
Core	Open database objects in multiple views	Opening a Table Touring the Datasheet View Looking at Data in a Form Looking at a Subdatasheet
Core	Navigate among records	Touring the Datasheet View Navigating Among Records and Fields Navigating in Form View

The
Complete
Reference

Chapter 2

The World of
Relational Databases

Every day, we're surrounded by databases ranging in complexity from the weekend gardening list to what resides in the archives at the Internal Revenue Service. Our ability to succeed in this information age is directly related to the ability to manage information. Managing information means storing it efficiently and retrieving it quickly—in such a form as can be instantly useful. The relational database model has been developed to meet those requirements.

What Is a Relational Database?

A *database* is an organized collection of related information used for a specific purpose, such as keeping track of ongoing work order activities or maintaining a library. If you gathered data about the climate in East Africa and about the mineral deposits in southern Utah, you wouldn't call this a database because the data wouldn't normally be used together for a specific purpose. If you collected information about your company's work orders, the customers who contracted for the work, and your employees who would carry out the work, however, this would constitute a database.

> **Note** *The terms "data" and "information" aren't interchangeable. Bits of data are combined in a logical way to impart specific information. For example, the numbers 999090009 constitute an item of data, but they don't constitute information until modified with special characters: 999-09-0009. Then the numbers become information in the form of a Social Security number.*

When you use a computerized database management system such as Access, the database is called *relational*. The principle behind a relational database is this: the information is divided into separate stacks of logically related data, each of which is stored in a separate table in the file. Tables are the fundamental objects at the heart of a relational database. They form the active basis for the information storage and retrieval system.

Once the information is arranged in separate tables, you can view, edit, add, and delete information with online forms; search for and retrieve some of or all the information with queries; and print information as customized reports.

In Access, the term *database* is more precisely used to define the collection of objects that store, manipulate, and retrieve data. These components include tables, queries, forms, reports, pages, macros, and modules.

Purpose of Relationships

Many advantages exist to distributing data among individual tables, rather than storing it all in one large two-dimensional table, called a *flat file*. Topping the list of advantages is the reduction of data redundancy, which not only reduces the required disk storage space, but also speeds processing. Other important advantages gained by implementing a relational database are the following:

- **Flexibility** If your data changes, you need to update the value in only one place. All the queries, forms, and reports look in that place for the current values.

- **Simplicity** The flat-file model used as the basis for a relational system dictates a simple, nonredundant method of data storage. Each table in the relational design is a single object containing data pertinent to a particular aspect of the database, such as an employee, a product, or an order.

- **Power** Storing the data in separate related tables allows grouping, searching, and retrieving the information in almost unlimited ways.

- **Ease of management** With smaller, less complicated tables, the information is much easier to locate and manage.

For example, if you're tracking customer work orders, you could put all the data in a single table, creating a flat-file database. A separate record would exist for every work order under contract. Storing all the customer data with the work order information would mean repeating the same information. In addition, if the customer's phone number changed, every record containing that customer's information would have to be updated. Employee information in the work order table would also be repeated.

How much more efficient to have one table for work order information and separate tables for the customer and employee information. A short field containing a customer identifier could be added to the customer and work order tables to form a connection between the tables, called a *relationship*. Similarly, an employee identifier can link the work orders to the employee who is acting as the job supervisor.

Figure 2-1 shows how to implement the work order database as a relational database. The information is split into an efficient three-table relational database with special fields added to provide the relationships.

The relationship line drawn between the CustomerID field in the Customers table and the CustomerID field in the Workorders table links the two tables. This relationship enables you to look up all the work order information for one customer, as well as the customer's name and phone number for a specific work order.

Similarly, the three relationship lines from the Employees table to the Supervisor, Principal Worker, and Helper fields in the Workorders table link the two tables in three ways. For example, you can ask Access for the name and pager number of the supervisor on a specific job.

Note   *Although the figure shows only one copy of the Employees table in the Relationships window, three copies of the table actually exist, one for each of the relationships. They have been moved so they're superimposed on one another for simplicity. If you do this yourself, you see two more copies of the Employees table in the window, named Employees_1 and Employees_2.*

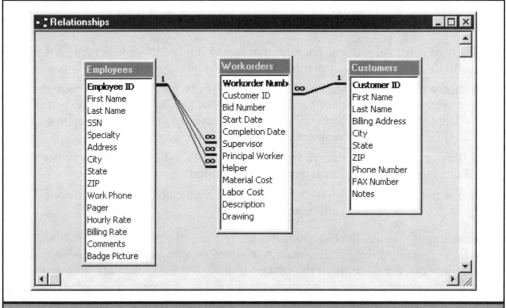

Figure 2-1. *An example of a relational database*

When you're building a database, one of the main tasks is to decide how to distribute the data. Three clues guide you while designing a relational database. First, the data can be divided by user, such as by the personnel office or the production manager.

The second clue is the data redundancy. For example, in a customer-related service company, one customer may contract for several services. Storing all the customer data with the work order information would mean repeating the customer information in every work order record. This would result in many copies of the same information (if your business were successful enough to have repeat business).

The third clue is the dimension of time. If you have information you seldom use, such as an archive of completed work orders, storing this separately—and out of the way—and bringing it out only as needed is better.

Types of Relationships

Tables can be related in three different ways: one-to-many, one-to-one, or many-to-many. The type you define depends on how many records in each table are likely to have the same value.

To relate tables, one of them must have a field that contains a unique value in every record. This can be a primary key field or a field with a unique index that allows no

What Is Normalization?

According to the *Academic Press Dictionary of Science and Technology*, the definition of *normalization* is the "process of restructuring data files." The ultimate goal of normalization is to reduce the data in a database to its simplest structure and minimize redundancy of data or, more specifically, to organize data fields to achieve the most efficient yet flexible way to store data.

Normalization has a complex mathematical origin that involves specific stages called *normal forms*. Each normal form represents a hurdle your database must overcome before it can progress to the next stage. The higher the normal form, the more restrictive the test. Achieving the third normal form is considered sufficient for a database.

The first normal form eliminates duplicate data. For example, the Workorders table included the names of the three employees who formed the team working on the job. If an employee was assigned to more than one job, the information would be repeated in other records.

The second normal form requires all data in the table to apply directly to the subject of the table, usually indicated by the primary key field. For example, customer names don't directly apply to the Workorder Number primary key field in the Workorders table, so the data should be removed and replaced by a short field that links the Workorders record with a Customers record.

The third normal form eliminates fields that can be derived from other fields. For example, if the Workorders table included a Total Cost field that showed the sum of the Labor Cost and the Material Cost fields, it would have to be removed to achieve the third normal form.

duplicate values. A primary key or unique index can also be a combination of two or more fields whose combined value is unique for all records.

The most commonly used type of relationship is the *one-to-many relationship*, in which one record in one table can have many matching records in another table. The table on "one" side is often called the *parent* table and the other is the *child* table. For example, the Customers table would have one record for each customer. The Workorders table may have more than one work order for the same customer. Both tables would include a field with a value representing that specific customer. In the parent table—Customers—the field must be the *primary key* or a field with an index that contains a unique value. In the child table, the field is called the *foreign key* and needn't be unique.

Tip   *You can speed processing, however, if the child table is indexed on the foreign key. See Chapter 4 for information on defining table structures including specifying indexes.*

In Figure 2-1, both relationships are one-to-many, as denoted by the symbols at the ends of the relationship lines. The 1 appears at the end of the line attached to the table on the "one" side and the infinity symbol appears at the table on the "many" side of the relationship. Primary key fields are indicated by the field name appearing in boldface in the field lists. As you can see in the figure, all three tables in the database have primary keys. The foreign keys are identified by the relationship line pointing to the field name in the child table field list.

The *one-to-one relationship* is a form of lookup, in which each record in one of the tables has a matching record in the other table. Neither table is designated as the parent. The key fields in both tables are the primary keys. One use for this type of relationship is to store additional, seldom-accessed information about an item in the first table, such as an abstract of a book or the details of a work order.

The *many-to-many relationship* isn't really permitted as such in a relational database. Many records in one table have the same values in the key field as many records in the second table. To implement this in Access, you must create a third table, called a *junction table,* to place between the first two, converting the many-to-many to two one-to-many relationships.

Figure 2-2 shows how the three types of relationships differ. Chapter 5 contains more information about defining and modifying relationships.

Referential Integrity

Referential integrity is an optional system of rules that guarantees the relationships are valid and the database will remain intact as data is entered, edited, or deleted.

The basic rule of referential integrity is this: for every record in a child table (the "many" side), one and only one matching record must be in the parent table (the "one" side). For example, in the relationship between the Customers table (parent) and the Workorders table (child), every current work order must have a reference to a customer. You cannot have a work order without a customer. The referential integrity rules also prevent you from deleting a customer record if work orders are still in progress.

To summarize the referential integrity rules that Access can enforce:

- You cannot enter a child record for which no parent exists (start a work order without a customer).

- You cannot delete a parent record if related child records still exist (remove a customer before the job is completed).

- You cannot change a child record so its foreign key doesn't have a match in the parent table (change the customer field in a work order record to a nonexisting customer).

- You cannot change the primary key value in a parent table as long as related records are in the child table (change a customer link before the work order is finished).

A one-to-one relationship links the Bid Data table to the Workorders table:

BID DATA TABLE

Bid Number	Bid Date	Award Date	Workorder Number
105	03/03/01	04/01/01	003
106	03/15/01		
107	03/20/01	04/10/01	004

WORKORDERS TABLE

Workorder Number	Start Date	Completion Date
003	04/20/01	04/25/01
004	04/15/01	04/20/01
005	05/10/01	05/15/01

A one-to-many relationship links the Employees table to the Workorders table:

EMPLOYEES TABLE

Employee ID	Last Name	Specialty
16	De Salle	Masonry
17	Howell	Labor
18	Gikos	Labor

WORKORDERS TABLE

Workorder Number	Employee ID
001	17
002	18
003	19
004	17

A many-to-many relationship links the Workorders table to the Suppliers table:

WORKORDERS TABLE

Workorder Number	Materials Code
004	L
005	E
006	E
007	E

SUPPLIERS TABLE

Materials	Supplier	Address	etc...
E	Smith Electric		
E	Johnson Supply		
E	Homestead Depot		

Figure 2-2.   *Three types of database relations*

These rules help to maintain an accurate and complete database with no loose ends. Before you can set referential integrity, you must make sure the following conditions are met:

- The matching field in the parent table is the primary key or at least has a unique value, such as an AutoNumber field.
- Relating fields are the same data type.
- Both tables are in the same Access database. You can set referential integrity between linked tables, providing they are both in Access format and you open the database that contains the linked tables.

The same rules can apply to a one-to-one relationship. Enforcing the referential integrity rules in such a relationship guarantees that every record in one table has one and only one matching record in the other table.

Defining Database Objects

Before going any further, let's take a closer look at the objects that make up a database. Access is an object-oriented *database management system* (*DBMS*), which means the entire database is composed of objects with certain characteristics or attributes called *properties* that determine their structure, appearance, and behavior. For example, table properties include a description of the table, the subject of the table, and the arrangement of records in the table, such as in alphabetic or chronological order, based on one or more fields.

In turn, each of the major Access objects is a container for other objects, which also have properties. For example, tables are made up of fields that are considered objects with properties of their own, such as name, size, format, data type, and so on. Reports and forms contain design objects, such as data fields, titles and labels, command buttons, page numbers, graphics, and so on. Each of these has a list of properties you can set to achieve the effect you want.

As you see in the Database window in the Access window, the major database objects are tables, queries, forms, reports, pages, macros, and modules. The *tables* are the containers for all the data in your database. In a relational database system, the data is distributed among several related tables, instead of placed in one large table.

A *query* is a question you ask of your database. You usually use a query to extract a specified set of records from one or more tables. For example, you may ask the database to show you a list of delicatessen customers who are vegetarians or who have a preference for exotic pasta products. Access answers your question by displaying the requested data. Because a query is a stored question instead of a stored answer, when you ask the question again, the results include the latest information. You not only can view the results, you can also use them in reports and forms.

Forms are often more convenient than a tabular datasheet for entering and editing table data, especially if a table includes more data than can fit across the screen and you have to scroll right to see the rest. A form can display a single record at a time, so all the data is visible at once and the fields can be arranged any way you want in a form design. You can also include data from more than one table or query as the basis for a single form. Forms are especially useful for creating a comfortable visual environment for data management. For example, you can create a form that resembles the paper form used to collect data in the workplace.

When you want print the data, you usually create a *report*. The report can be a quick and easy dump of the table data—useful for checking specific data items—or it can be a glossy presentation of the data in a custom format suitable for the stockholders or a business manager. The report can also include totals and other summaries of values in a particular field, such as gross sales and monthly profitability. Adding charts and graphs to a report makes the report even more visually informative.

Access provides a special type of report you can use for printing mailing labels or envelopes. If you keep a mailing list in a database table, this type of special report can come in handy. You can also create form letters and merge them with the address list to print a personalized copy for each recipient.

The *data access page* object, which was new to Access 2000, is a special document containing data from an Access database designed to be viewed on a Web site. The data access pages are designed specifically for Internet Explorer 5.0 and make use of dynamic *Hypertext Markup Language (HTML)*. More about data access pages in Chapter 24.

The final two types of objects are macros and modules. *Macros* contain a sequence of commands that perform a certain task and are useful for defining the actions that respond to button clicks or other events. *Modules* are programs written in Visual Basic, the programming language used by Access 2002. Procedures contained in the modules are the cornerstone of advanced Access applications.

Inspecting the Sample Database

The Northwind sample database introduced in Chapter 1 is an order-processing application. If it weren't for the use of the Access relational database management features, the process could be both cumbersome and time-consuming. The following sections examine the sample database in more detail.

Looking at the Data Distribution

As mentioned earlier, a relational database consists of several tables, each of which contains data focused on an aspect of the database. After distributing the data among the tables, the tables are related to one another by means of identifying the matching fields.

The Northwind data is distributed among eight tables as shown in Figure 2-3. The principal tables are Products, Orders, and Customers. The other tables support the

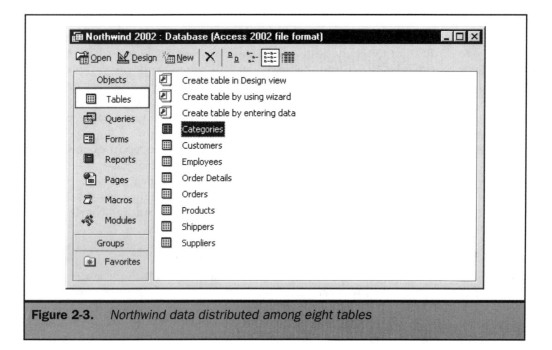

Figure 2-3.   *Northwind data distributed among eight tables*

order-processing by providing additional data, such as the name of the employee who took the order, the category of product, product suppliers, and shipping methods. Each of these tables is a good example of grouping data items used for the same purpose.

The Orders table contains all the order information, such as order number; customer identifier; employee identifier; order date, date required, and date shipped; shipping method; and the complete name and address of destination.

The Customers table contains the customer identifier and the complete address and phone number. If this weren't in a separate table, the information would be repeated in every order placed by the customer.

The Products table contains the current state of the inventory of each product. The fields include the product identifier, name, supplier identifier, category, quantity per unit, unit price, units in stock and on order, the reorder level, and a field that indicates whether the product has been discontinued.

The other tables contain peripheral information for the purpose of reducing data redundancy. The Employees table contains the employee identifier, birth date and hire date, name and address, telephone, a photo, the name of the employee's supervisor, and a memo field for notes. The Suppliers table includes the supplier identifier, name and address, and a point of contact. The Shippers table contains the company name and phone number, as well as the shipper identifier. The Categories table lists the categories of products with an identifier for each.

The last table—Order Details—is a junction table that links Products and Orders. This table is required to establish the many-to-many relationship between the Products and Orders tables. (An order may contain several products and a product may appear in several orders.)

Viewing Table Relationships

Most of the tables in the Northwind database are related in some way. To see the relationship scheme, click the Relationships button in the Database toolbar or choose Tools | Relationships. The Relationships window (see Figure 2-4) shows the eight tables with their relationship lines.

Each of the eight tables is related to at least one other table, thereby creating a relational database. All the relationships are one-to-many and specify the following:

- The *Suppliers table* is related to the Products table using the SupplierID as the linking field. The linking fields needn't have the same name, but it should be the same data type. More about creating relationships in Chapter 5.

- The *Categories table* is related to the Products table by the CategoryID field in both tables.

- The *Products table* is related to the Order Details table by the ProductID field in both tables.

- The *Orders table* is related to the Order Details table by the OrderID field in both tables.

- The *Employees table* is related to the Orders table by the EmployeeID field in both tables.

- The *Customers table* is related to the Orders table by the CustomerID field in both tables.

- The *Shippers table* is related to the Orders table by the ShipperID field in the Shippers table and the ShipVia field in the Orders table.

Identifying Primary Keys and Linking Fields

As you can tell from the symbols at the end of the relationship lines, all these relationships are one-to-many, the most common type. The parent table must be linked to the child table by its primary key. The primary key field appears in bold in the table field list. Notice all the primary keys are short identifiers for the subject of the table: customer, employee, order, category, supplier, and shipper. The primary key field in the Order Details junction table consists of two fields: OrderID and ProductID. This combination guarantees the primary key will have a unique value.

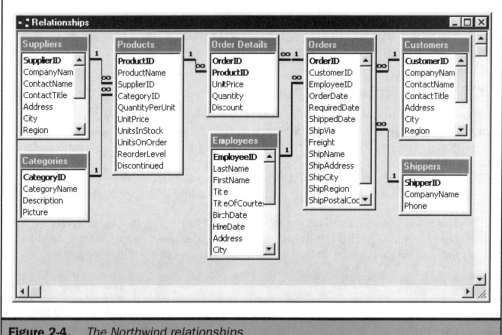

Figure 2-4. *The Northwind relationships*

Looking at Relationship Properties

In addition to the relationship type, you can find out more about a relationship, such as whether referential integrity is enforced, the specific names of the linking fields, and the type of join implemented. Figure 2-5 shows the Relationships dialog box that opens when you right-click the middle of a relationship line and choose Edit Relationship from the shortcut menu, or when you choose Relationships | Edit Relationship. This dialog box specifies which are the linking fields in each table, the enforcement of referential integrity, and the type of relationship.

If you click the Join Type button, a second dialog box opens in which you can choose the join property you want to use for the relationship. See Chapter 5 for more information on join types and how they affect the data displayed.

The Payoff

In addition to the efficiency of data storage, a relational database system offers large benefits when it comes to data retrieval. Forms can be designed for entry or display of

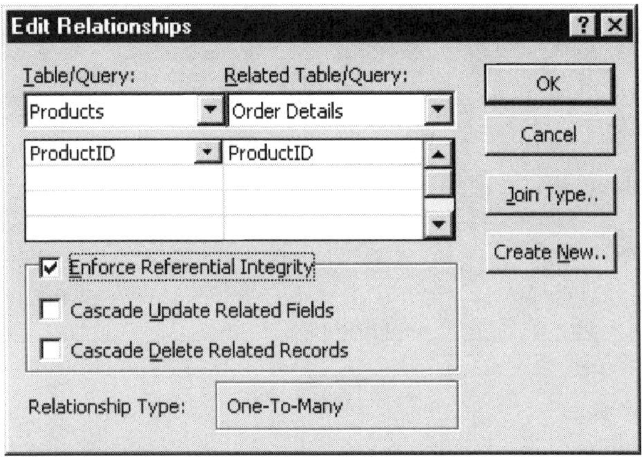

Figure 2-5. *Choose Edit Relationships to open the Relationships dialog box*

data from related tables. As you enter data in the form, it's dispersed to and updates the proper table. As you view data in a multiple-table form, the data is synchronized automatically.

A Custom Form

The Northwind sample database includes several custom forms. To view the Orders form (shown in Figure 2-6), do the following:

1. In the Access window, choose File | Open and locate the Northwind database in the Open dialog box. Select the database name and click Open.

2. Click the Forms object button in the database window to show the Forms page.

3. Then double-click the Orders form name or select it and click Open.

The form is used to enter new orders or to view existing orders. Each order includes data from the related Customers, Employees, Products, and Shippers tables. While this form looks complicated, you'll see in Chapter 12 that such forms are easy to construct with Access 2002.

The Bill To: field has a down arrow button that controls the display of a list of customers derived from the Customers table. The user selects from the list or enters a new customer name. If the name is selected from the list, the address is automatically filled out in both the billing and shipping areas of the form. The user can enter a different shipping address, if necessary, as you can see from the white background

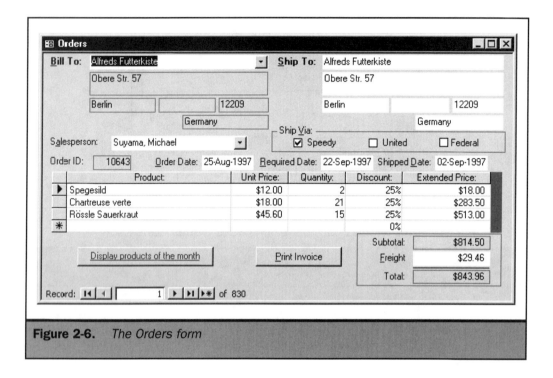

Figure 2-6. *The Orders form*

in that area. The billing information is not editable from within the form, as indicated by the background shading in that area.

The Salesperson is also filled in from a list of employees. When the user checks the shipping method in the Ship Via group, the shipper information is automatically copied to the invoice, which is then printed by clicking the Print Invoice button.

The Order ID is a special type of field that's automatically incremented by Access, thereby guaranteeing a unique value for each record. The Order Date has a default value set to the current date, while the other dates must be entered.

The Product information is contained in a subform and the name is selected from a drop-down list. The Unit Price is copied from the Products table, while the quantity and discount fields are entered by the user. The Extended Price, Subtotal, Freight, and Total fields are calculated based on the entered information.

The Display products of the month button is a hyperlink to a list of products currently being offered at a discount price. The Products list is a Word 2002 document.

The Orders form has several class modules, such as the OnClick event procedure that executes when the Print Invoice button is clicked. Figure 2-7 shows the printed invoice for the order in Figure 2-6.

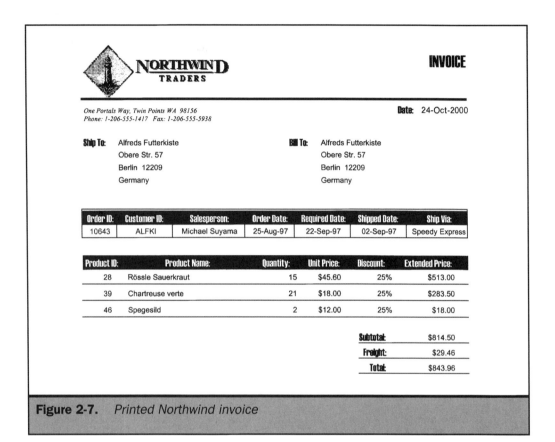

Figure 2-7.   *Printed Northwind invoice*

A Custom Report

To preview the Products by Category report in the Northwind database, click the
Reports button in the Database window. Then double-click the report name or select
it and click Preview. Figure 2-8 shows a preview of the Products by Category report.

The Products by Category report is an example of a report containing information
from more than one table. The report is based on a select query that gathers
information from the Products and Categories tables. The query also excludes
discontinued products.

The products are grouped in this report by category with a count of the number
of products in each category.

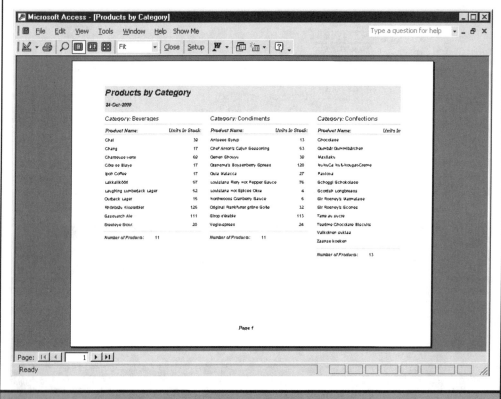

Figure 2-8. *The Products by Category report*

Summary

This chapter contains some insight into the theory of relational database systems and how they can be used for efficient information storage and retrieval. The major building blocks of an Access database—tables, queries, forms, reports, pages, macros, and modules—were briefly discussed and samples shown. The relationships among the tables in the Northwind sample database were examined.

The next chapter discusses in-depth the process of designing a relational database and how to distribute data among tables. You see how to create a new database with the Database Wizard and how to create a blank database without the help of the Database Wizard.

MOUS Exam Activities Explored in This Chapter

Level	Activity	Section Title
Beg/Intermed	Enforce referential integrity	Referential Integrity
Expert	Establish one-to-one relationships	Types of Relationships
Expert	Set Cascade Update and Cascade Delete options	Referential Integrity

The
Complete
Reference

Chapter 3

Creating a Database

The information in a relational database system is distributed among related tables to optimize information storage and retrieval. Common fields relate the tables so information can be extracted and presented in useful ways. A *database* can be an essential tool in managing personal or business information if it's properly designed and constructed. A poorly designed database is of less than no value. The more time spent on task and data analysis, the better the results. Once the design is completed and reviewed, building the database with Access is easy, with or without the Database Wizard.

Designing the Database

The design process begins with an analysis of the tasks to be required of the database. First, you find out what the system is intended to do for the prospective users. Interview all the users and get thorough descriptions of their expectations. What's essential to remember is the design process is also an iterative one: As the users get used to a new system, they can think of more features they can use, such as an additional data entry form, a special query, or a calculated field.

On the other hand, freezing the design at some point is critical, so you can proceed with the development. Then you can accumulate the user's later requirements and desires for the upgraded version.

Also important is to acquaint the user with the comprehensive form and report capability of Access 2002 by demonstrating some data entry forms and showing examples of printed reports.

The database design process can be broken down into eight steps, each with specific goals and products:

1. Determine what the users want from the database and what data is needed to provide the output.

2. Plan the data distribution.

3. Identify the fields for each table.

4. Assign a unique field for each table that ensures no two records are the same.

5. Determine how the tables are related to one another.

6. Review design and step through procedures with users.

7. Create tables and enter data.

8. Analyze and optimize database performance.

While numbering steps in a process implies one step is completed before the next begins, in reality, the design process is more fluid—each step overflowing into the next. You can return to a previous step anywhere along the line.

This chapter covers only the design and creation of the database itself. Chapter 4 discusses creating tables with and without the Table Wizard, while Chapter 6 contains more information on entering and editing data in the database.

Introducing Home Tech Repair

The example used in the first chapters of this book is the Home Tech Repair database. *Home Tech Repair* is a small company specializing in maintenance and improvement of home structures. Its specialties are electrical, plumbing, structural, painting, and heating and air conditioning systems in the home. It doesn't undertake large construction or remodeling jobs.

The main purpose of the database is to keep track of work orders and to print invoices. Figure 3-1 shows an example of the manual record-keeping system in use before the development of the Access database.

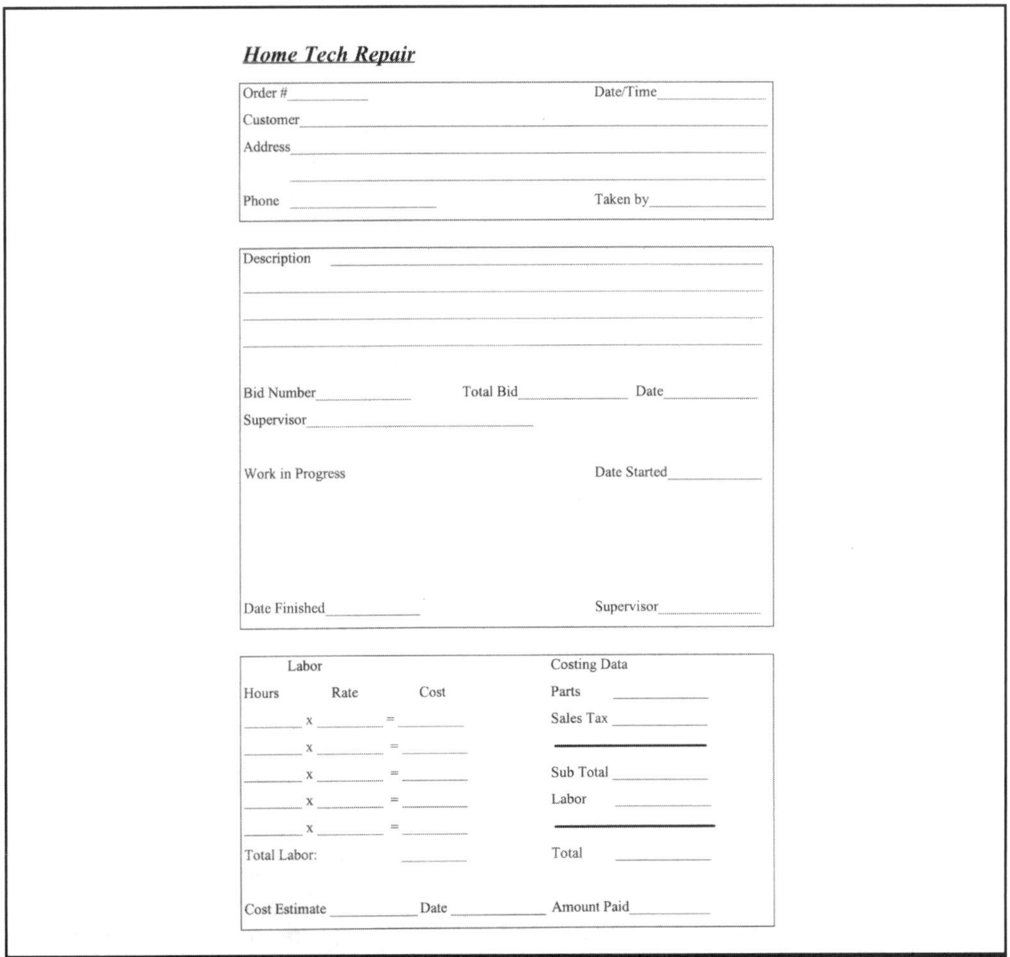

Home Tech Repair

Order # ____ Date/Time ____
Customer ____
Address ____
Phone ____ Taken by ____

Description ____

Bid Number ____ Total Bid ____ Date ____
Supervisor ____
Work in Progress Date Started ____
Date Finished ____ Supervisor ____

Labor

Hours		Rate		Cost
____	x	____	=	____
____	x	____	=	____
____	x	____	=	____
____	x	____	=	____
____	x	____	=	____
Total Labor:				____

Costing Data
Parts ____
Sales Tax ____
Sub Total ____
Labor ____
Total ____

Cost Estimate ____ Date ____ Amount Paid ____

Figure 3-1. *The Home Tech Repair manual work order record*

Determining Goals of the Database

Step 1. Determine What the Purpose Is of the Database. What do the users want to get from the database? What kind of reports do they want, and how do they want the information arranged and summarized? If adequate data collection forms already exist, use them as patterns for the Access forms. Look at other databases that address similar information management situations. Once the tasks are defined, a list of the required data items can be developed.

The main purpose of the Home Tech Repair database is to maintain up-to-date information about current work orders. To do this, the information must include forms for data entry and viewing of all table data, and it must relate the individual work orders to specific customers or employees.

In addition to the work-order tracking, the owner wants to conduct financial analyses, for example, to determine how much revenue has been generated by each employee or to review the total sales on a monthly basis. These analyses can include summary reports with charts and graphs depicting trends, as well as proportional distributions of types of jobs over a period of time. Such studies are helpful when planning for future work.

Distributing the Data

Step 2. Determine How the Information Should Be Divided Among the Tables. This isn't as easy as it sounds, but here are some guidelines to follow:

- A table shouldn't contain duplicate information among its records. With only one copy of each data item, you need to update it in only one place.

- The information in a table should be limited to a single subject. This enables you to maintain data about each subject independently of the others.

In the Home Tech Repair case, employee and customer information is repeated on several work order sheets. To reduce the redundancy, pull out both sets of information and put them in separate tables. Keeping payments in a separate table would add flexibility, especially if the work is paid for in installments, such as a deposit at the start of the contract and the remainder during the work.

If specific parts are routinely used, such as plumbing fixtures or electrical devices, the list should be kept in a separate table. The data in the parts table can be accessed by the form or report that brings the work order expenses together.

Other peripheral data can be included in separate small tables, such as shipping or payment methods. The Home Tech Repair company information can also be kept separate in one place, accessible to the report that prints the invoice. This table can include the company address, phone and FAX numbers, Internet address, and any short, standard message to include in correspondence.

Step 3. Determine the Fields to Contain the Individual Facts About Each
Subject.   All the fields should relate directly to the subject and not include any information that can be derived from other fields. Include all the information you need, but nothing extra. Break up the information into small logical parts, such as First Name and Last Name fields, rather than a single field. Name the fields so you can locate specific records and sort by individual field values. You can always combine the fields later for finding and searching, if necessary.

 The word "Name" is also a reserved word in Access. Name *is one of the properties of Access objects and controls, as discussed in later chapters. Using a word that has a special meaning to Access as a field name isn't a good idea because this can cause unpredictable problems.*

Table 3-1 lists the fields in each of the Home Tech Repair tables and shows the data type and size, as well as a brief description of the data to be stored in the field.

Field	Data Type	Field Size	Description
Workorders Table			
Workorder Number	Number	Integer	Uniquely identifies work order
Customer ID	Text	50	Customer name
Bid Number	Text	5	Original bid number
Start Date	Date	N/A	Scheduled start date
Completion Date	Date	N/A	Expected completion date
Supervisor	Text	20	Name of employee in charge
Principal Worker	Text	20	Name of employee who is second in charge
Helper	Text	20	Name of helper
Material Cost	Currency	2 decimals	Cost of materials
Labor Cost	Currency	2 decimals	Cost of labor
Description	Memo	N/A	Description of work order

Table 3-1.   *Distributing Data Among Home Tech Repair Tables*

Field	Data Type	Field Size	Description
Drawing	Hyperlink	N/A	File of drawing, as required
Employees Table			
Employee ID	Number	Integer	Uniquely identifies employee
First Name	Text	20	Employee's first name
Last Name	Text	25	Employee's last name
SSN	Text	10	Social Security number
Specialty	Text	25	Special labor skills
Address	Text	50	Employee's home address
City	Text	50	City
State	Text	2	State
ZIP	Text	9	ZIP code
Work Phone	Text	12	Office phone or pager
Pager	Text	12	Home phone
Hourly Rate	Currency	2 decimals	Salary hourly rate
Billing Rate	Currency	2 decimals	Customer's billing rate
Comments	Memo	N/A	Additional information
Badge Picture	OLE Object	N/A	Employee picture
Customers Table			
Customer ID	Number	Integer	Uniquely identifies customer
First Name	Text	20	Customer's first name
Last Name	Text	25	Customer's last name
Billing Address	Text	50	Address to send bill to
City	Text	50	City

Table 3-1. *Distributing Data Among Home Tech Repair Tables* (continued)

Field	Data Type	Field Size	Description
State	Text	2	State
ZIP	Text	9	ZIP code
Phone Number	Text	12	Customer's phone
FAX Number	Text	12	Customer's FAX number
Notes	Memo	N/A	Additional customer information

Table 3-1. *Distributing Data Among Home Tech Repair Tables* (continued)

The AutoNumber data type would be better for the fields you intend to use as the primary key fields, such as Employee ID, Customer ID, Bid Number, and so on. Access creates the AutoNumber values to ensure they're unique within a table. The Home Tech Repair business already had a system of identifying the employees, work orders, and so on and, sometimes, it's easier to accommodate the users with codes they're familiar with. You can set those field properties so the value is always unique.

After arranging the data in the tables, review the distribution carefully for further normalization. Remove any redundancies and make sure all fields in each table apply directly to that subject. For example, the overhead and the total work order costs are calculated fields, and so aren't included in the Workorders Table.

Specifying Key Fields and Relationships

Step 4. Be Sure Each Table Has a Field That Will Contain a Unique Value.   If no field exists, plan on asking Access to assign a special field to act as the primary key, so you can be sure each record in the table is unique.

Each of the three main tables of the Home Tech Repair database has a field that uniquely identifies a record: Workorder Number, Employee ID, and Customer ID. The values in these fields can be entered by the user or assigned by Access in the form of an incremental AutoNumber. If the number has no other significance, such as identifying the general location of the job, let Access enter the number, and then you can be sure no duplicates occur.

Step 5. Determine How the Tables Will Relate to One Another.   Identify the common fields and the type of relationship.

The Workorders table has a field named Customer ID. Instead of using the name, use the Customer ID, which is the primary key in the Customers table and can be used as the linking field between the two tables. Similarly, use the Employee ID in the Supervisor, Principal Worker, and Helper fields in the Workorders table, instead of the employee names. The Employee ID is the primary key field in the Employees table, which links it to three foreign keys in the Workorders table.

The relationship between the Customers and Workorders table is one-to-many because a customer may contract for more than one job. The relationship between the Employees table and the Workorders table is also one-to-many because an employee can work on more than one job at a time and in one of three slots in a single job.

Figure 3-2 shows the Home Tech Repair tables in the Access Relationships window. The field lists have been lengthened to display all the fields.

Three instances of the Employees table are in the Relationships window because it's linked to three separate fields in the Workorders table. Chapter 5 contains information about working in the Relationships window and defining relationships.

Completing the Database

Step 6. Thoroughly Review the Design, Complete with Sketches of Planned Reports and Prototype User Interfaces.   Now it's time to consult with the users for additional comments and suggestions. Step through the operations you plan to carry out with the information.

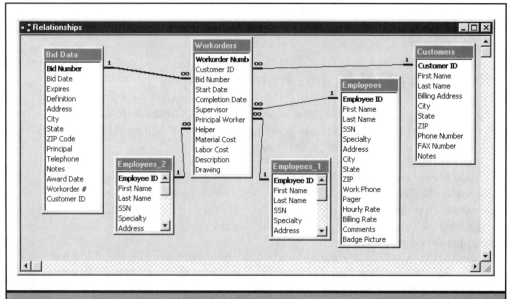

Figure 3-2.   *The Home Tech Repair tables*

Step 7. Create the Table Structures in Accordance with the Design and Enter Data. You may want to limit the data to only enough to test the application and complete the tables later. Create the forms, reports, and queries. If the database is for inexperienced users, you can add a switchboard and other custom tools to make their jobs easier. A *switchboard* is the user's main interface with the database and displays a list of actions the user may take. Clicking an item in the list opens a data entry form, previews a report, or offers the chance to change items on the switchboard. Carefully test the entire system. Time spent refining and verifying the design can save time later revising the database after it's been populated with data.

Step 8. Optionally, Run the Access Performance Analysis Tools to Be Sure the Design Is as Efficient as Possible. Run the Table Analyzer to inspect the distribution of information among the tables. Run the Performance Analyzer to go over the entire database and make recommendations for improvement.

Using Access 2002

Access 2002 provides three important analysis tools that can help you construct an efficient database:

- The Table Analyzer Wizard
- The Performance Analyzer Wizard
- The Database Documenter

The *Table Analyzer Wizard* helps you normalize your data structure. It moves sequentially through the three normal forms. Refer to Chapter 2 for a discussion of database normalization.

First, the Table Analyzer looks for repeated data and offers suggestions for improvement. If you agree to the changes, Access creates the new tables and relationships, copies the data to the new tables, and renames all the tables. In the last step, the Analyzer creates a query that puts it all back together, so the view looks like the original table.

The *Performance Analyzer* examines any or all of the objects in the database, not only the tables that contain the data. You tell it which objects you want analyzed. It can check the relationships you defined and review the program modules you wrote. The Performance Analyzer makes suggestions for improving the database performance, such as creating an index on the foreign key field of a child table, which would speed processing. You may choose to implement or decline any or all of the suggestions.

When the database is complete, you can run the third analysis tool, the *Database Documenter* to document the completed database fully. This can provide a valuable service later when you need to upgrade the database.

See Chapter 17 for more information about using the Table Analyzer and other performance-enhancing tools.

After the design is established, Access gives you three ways to create a new database:

- Starting with the Database Wizard
- Starting from scratch with a blank database

If you start a new database with help from the wizard, you have a choice of ten different types of commonly used database templates, such as Contact Management or Order Entry. When you choose one, the wizard creates a complete version of the database, with all the relevant tables, forms, reports, and queries. You can even ask for sample data in the new database to try out the database and see how it looks with your own data.

When you build a new database from scratch, the Database window opens as before, but all the pages are blank because the database contains no objects as yet.

> **Note** *A third method is via the Windows Start menu where you again have a choice between a blank document and one of the wizard's templates. When you make your selection, Access launches and you proceed as usual.*

Using the Database Wizard

If you need a database for a common personal or business purpose, the Database Wizard can get you started. Once you build the database with the help of the wizard, you can add your own data and make modifications to the forms and reports that came with the turnkey application.

To start the Database Wizard, do either of the following:

- If you're just launching Access, choose General Templates from the side pane.
- If you're already running Access, whether or not you have another database active, choose File | New, or click the New toolbar button, and then select General Templates.

The Templates dialog box has two tabs: General and Databases. The General tab originally contains the Blank Database option, a Blank Data Access Page template, and two blank project templates: one for an existing database and one for a new database. The Databases tab (see Figure 3-3) contains ten database templates for prefabricated applications, ranging from a list of categorized expenses to a complex event-management system.

You can scroll through the sample templates on the Databases tab to find one close to the system you want. Looking through the icons, the Service Call Management database seems to match the Home Tech Repair requirements most closely.

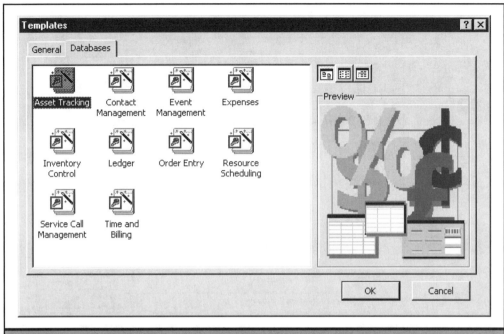

Figure 3-3.   *The Databases tab shows predefined database templates*

Previewing the Database Templates

The Service Call Management database used as an example in this chapter uses nine related tables to contain all the relevant data. As you highlight each icon, the Preview pane shows an image reflecting the template style.

To get an idea of what information each database contains, you can start the Database Wizard. After defining the location where you want to store the database, the next window describes the information the database tables will contain. After reviewing the contents of the database template, you can proceed with the wizard or click Cancel and start over.

To start the Database Wizard, double-click the icon in the Templates dialog box, or select it and choose OK. The File New Database dialog box opens (see Figure 3-4), where you specify the location for the database file and give it a name or accept the suggested name. Then click Create to continue with the wizard.

A blank Database window appears briefly while the wizard is looking for the database elements in the template, and then a window appears listing the contents of the tables to be in the design. Figure 3-5 shows the opening Database Wizard screen for the Service Call Management database.

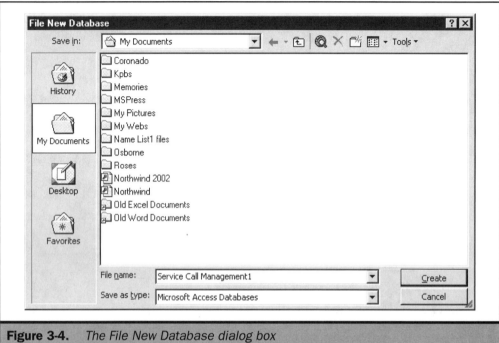

Figure 3-4. *The File New Database dialog box*

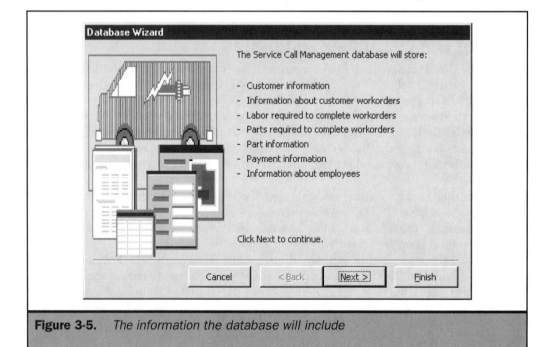

Figure 3-5. *The information the database will include*

Table 3-2 briefly describes the information contained in the templates offered by the Database Wizard.tW

Database	Contents
Asset Tracking	Asset information with depreciation and maintenance history. Employee, department, and vendor information.
Contact Management	Contact and call information, including contact type and date.
Event Management	Event type, attendee, and registration information. Employee and pricing information.
Expenses	Employee expense reports containing expense details and categories with the employee information.
Inventory Control	Product information including product categories, buying and selling data, and employee and customer records.
Ledger	Complete accounting of transactions, accounts, and classification of account numbers.
Order Entry	Customer and order information with order details. Payment, product, and company information.
Resource Scheduling	Information about the scheduling of company resources, including details of the specific resources and customer activities.
Service Call Management	Information about customers and their work orders. Details of work orders include time and material costs, as well as payment information. Also includes employee and part information.
Time and Billing	Time card information for billing clients for time spent on projects. Also includes employee, client, payment, and project information.

Table 3-2. *Prefabricated Database Templates*

Stepping Through the Wizard

Once you select the basis for your database—asset management, membership maintenance, order control, or whatever—the wizard leads you through a series of design steps. The steps include

- Adding optional fields from a list of suggested fields for each table.
- Selecting your preferred screen display appearance.
- Selecting a report style for printed output.
- Entering a title for the new database.
- Including a picture to appear in forms and reports, such as a company logo.

You have a chance to customize your database to a limited degree during the process. After the wizard is through, you have much more flexibility with the design.

To continue creating the Home Tech Repair database with the Service Management template as the basis, choose Next to accept the template.

Selecting Tables and Fields

The second wizard dialog box displays the list of tables to appear in the Home Tech Repair database. You have no choice about the table list, but you can add more fields than the wizard has planned. As you highlight each table name, a list of fields appears in the right box. The field names that appear in regular font are required fields and are already checked. Optional fields appear in italic and aren't checked. Checking an optional field adds it to the table. Figure 3-6 shows the CCAuthoriz. # field as an optional field that can be added to the Payment information table. Click Next to move to the third dialog box.

 Remember, if you change your mind or forget to select a particular option, you can always return to previous dialog boxes by clicking Back.

Choosing Form and Report Styles

The next two dialog boxes give you a choice of ten different screen displays and six report styles. As you select an option, a sample appears in the preview pane on the left. Figure 3-7 shows the screen display style list and Figure 3-8 shows the report styles.

Tip *The screen display and report style formats are also available when you click the AutoFormat button on the Form or Report Design toolbar. When you open the AutoFormat dialog box, you also have a chance to customize the format and put it back on the list either as an updated format or as a new format. The customized formats are then available to the Database Wizard. More about custom formatting in Chapter 10.*

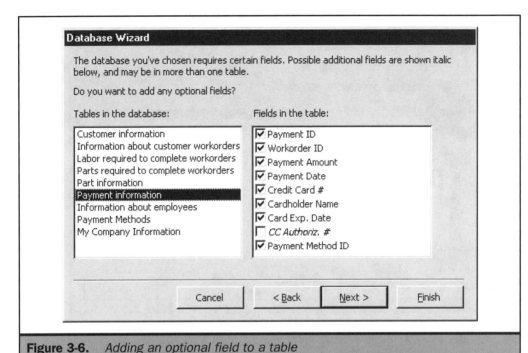

Figure 3-6. *Adding an optional field to a table*

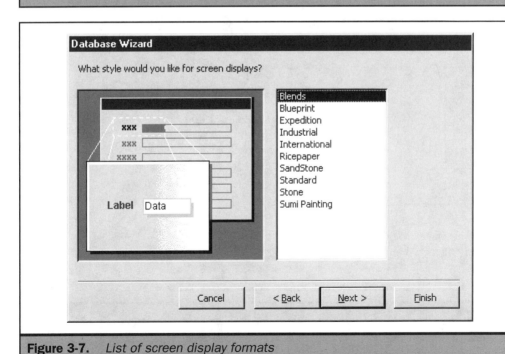

Figure 3-7. *List of screen display formats*

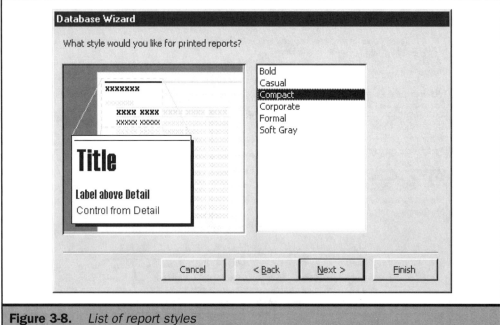

Figure 3-8. *List of report styles*

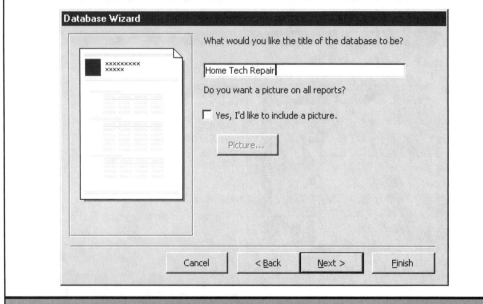

Figure 3-9. *Enter a name for the database*

After viewing the screen display and report style options, choose Next to continue with the wizard.

Naming the Database

In the last wizard dialog box (see Figure 3-9), you can give the database a special name to appear in the switchboards and the title bar. You can also include a picture. The picture you specify in this dialog box automatically appears in the header of all the reports generated by the wizard. If you don't select the picture in this dialog box, you have to add it individually to each report later.

To add a picture, check the "Yes, I'd like to include a picture" option and click the Picture button. The Insert Picture dialog box opens, in which you can browse for the folder that contains the picture you want. As you select images from the list, a preview appears in the right pane. Click OK to add the selected image and return to the previous dialog box. Choose Next, and then accept the option in the last dialog box to start the database and click Finish.

As the wizard is constructing the database, you can see the process in the background behind the odometers. After a while, a message appears asking for your company name, address, and related information. Click OK and fill in the dialog box. When you close the form, the main switchboard for the new database appears on the screen (see Figure 3-10). This is the main user interface for working with the database.

Note *The minimized Service Call Management Database window appears in the lower-left corner of the screen. Click the Database toolbar button or press F11 to restore the Database window at any time. You can also click the Control button in the minimized title bar and choose Restore.*

When the wizard is finished, you have a complete database application, with all the relevant reports, forms, and queries. All you need to do is input your data.

Figure 3-11 shows the structure of the application the Database Wizard created with the Service Call Management template. The Main Switchboard leads to several forms for entering and viewing table data, many of which include data from more than one table. The application also includes five reports that present and summarize current information.

Running the New Application

The Home Tech Repair application automatically displays the main switchboard at startup. The first option opens the main form for the application, Workorders by Customer, where you can enter new work orders or edit existing records (see Figure 3-12).

To see individual work order information, select the work order in the subform and click the Workorders command button. The Workorders form (see Figure 3-13) contains specifics about a single work order, including the employees who work on the

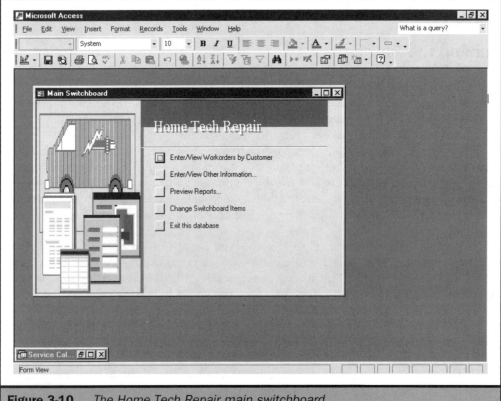

Figure 3-10. *The Home Tech Repair main switchboard*

job, their billing rate, and the hours spent. The costs are calculated and displayed with payments credited to the work order and the remaining balance computed. To return to the previous form, close this form.

To see the payment history of a specific work order, select the work order and click the Payments command button. To preview an invoice for the work order, click the Preview Invoice command button. When you display the Print Invoice dialog box (see Figure 3-14), you have the opportunity of rewording the default message that accompanies the invoice. The message is part of the company information table.

The third option in the main switchboard opens another switchboard listing the other data entry forms you can use. Figure 3-15 shows the list of reports designed and included in the Home Tech Repair application. Most of them require some user entry, such as a time interval, to create the report.

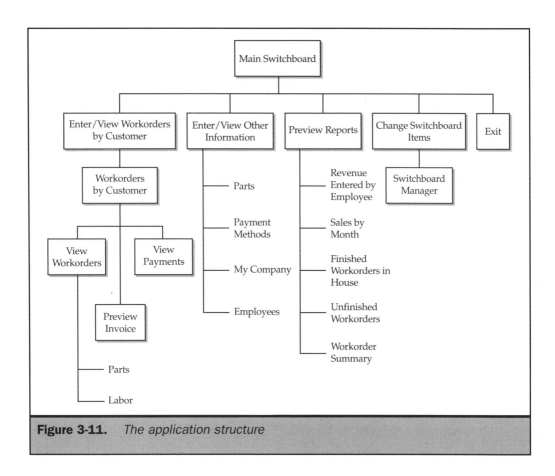

Figure 3-11.   *The application structure*

Caution   *When you let the wizard create your database, many of the components are linked together by common fields. If you try to change field names in a table, you must also change them in any query, form, or report that refers to that field name. The wizard doesn't let you customize the field names during the building process.*

Many changes are required to have the wizard's database conform to the needs of the Home Tech Repair Company. Some fields are unnecessary and should be removed; others should be renamed. Additional forms and reports that depend on different queries, filters, or sort orders may be necessary. All these changes can be made to the Home Tech Repair database built from the Service Call Maintenance template.

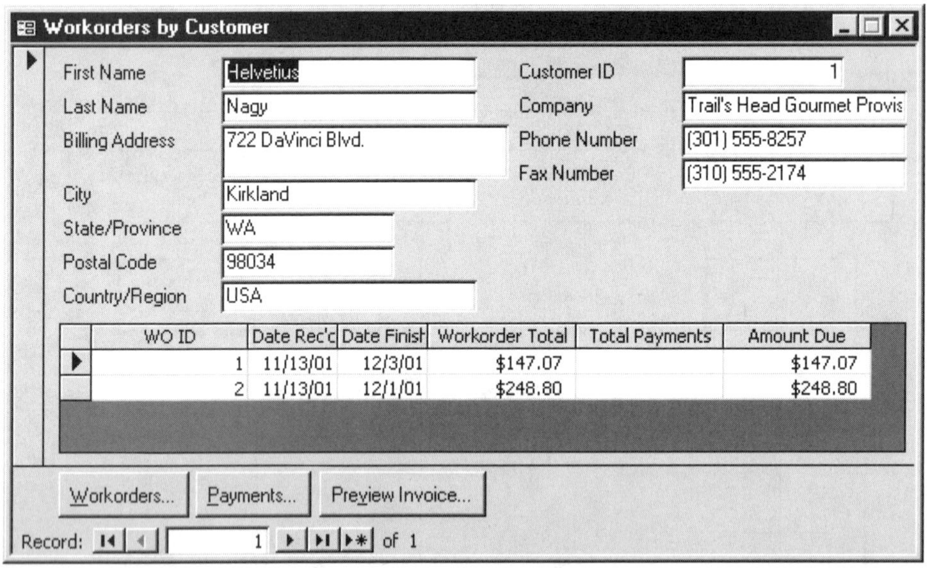

Figure 3-12. *The main form in the Home Tech Repair application*

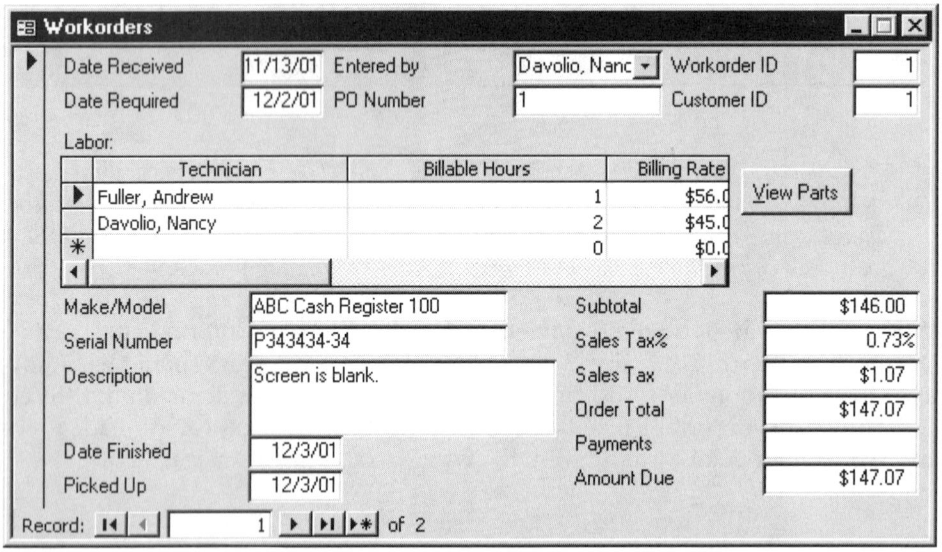

Figure 3-13. *Individual work order information*

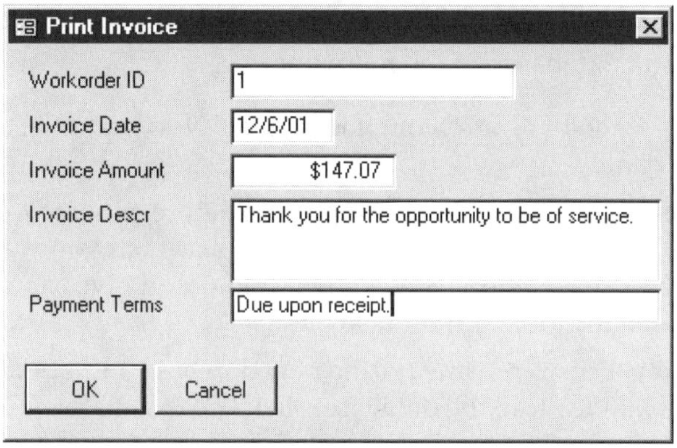

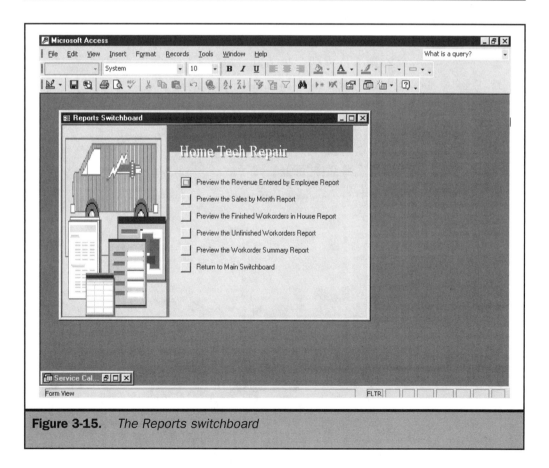

Figure 3-14. *Previewing a work order invoice*

Figure 3-15. *The Reports switchboard*

Starting with a Blank Database

To create a new blank database, do the following:

1. Click the New toolbar button or choose File | New and select Blank Database on the side pane.

2. The File New Database dialog box opens as before, where you can enter a name for the new database and specify the folder in which you want to store it. By default, Access opens the My Document folder and gives a unique name to the new database: db1, db2, db3, and so on.

3. After entering a custom name for the new database and opening the folder where you want to store the database, click Create.

An empty Database window opens (see Figure 3-16) showing the Tables page. The first thing to do when starting a new blank database is to create one or more tables. To start a new table, do one of the following:

■ Click New.

■ Double-click "Create a new table in Design view."

■ Double-click "Create a new table by using wizard."

■ Double-click "Create a new table by entering data."

Figure 3-16. *The new Database window*

More information about creating and modifying tables is available in Chapter 4.

 If you're just starting Access and you want to create a new blank database, click "Blank Database" in the side pane.

Starting a New Database from Windows

Although you may not think of a database as a document, Office considers all the products of Office applications as documents. Excel spreadsheets, PowerPoint presentations, and Access database are all documents, just as Word documents are documents to Office. You can start a new database from Office without even launching Access first.

Choose New Office Document from the Windows Start menu to open the New Office Document dialog box. The General tab has icons for blank documents from all the Office applications that are installed (see Figure 3-17—your icons may be different). To see the other types of templates, choose another tab. The Databases tab contains icons for all the Database Wizard templates you saw earlier.

When you select a template and choose OK, the appropriate application launches and the process begins, either with a blank document or with the help of one of the wizards.

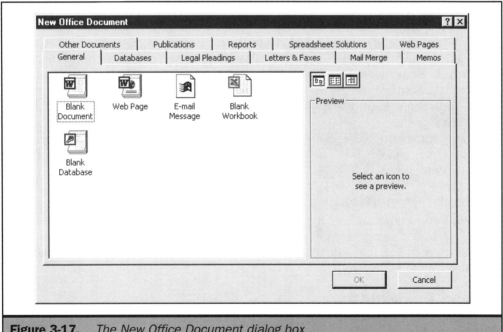

Figure 3-17. *The New Office Document dialog box*

Looking at Database Properties

Databases are Access objects and, as such, possess properties that range from the filename and size to the location, to the date it was last modified and by whom. The many database properties are grouped in five categories: General, Summary, Statistics, Contents, and Custom. Choose File | Database Properties, or right-click the Database window title bar and choose Database Properties from the shortcut menu.

The General and Statistics properties are set by Access, but you can specify your own properties in the other categories.

General and Statistics Properties

The General properties include the filename (both Windows 98 and MS-DOS), type, location, size, and the dates the database was created, modified, and accessed. These properties are the same as the Windows Explorer displays when you right-click a file and choose Properties from the shortcut menu. Four attributes set by Access also appear in the General tab: Read Only, Hidden, Archive, and System.

The Statistics properties include the same dates as in the General group, plus the date of last printing, editing information such as the revision number, total editing time, and the name of the person who last saved the file, if appropriate.

Summary Properties

Summary properties include descriptive information about the database. These properties are useful in trying to find an elusive file because Access searches for a file by subject, author, keywords, or category. For example, you could ask Access to find the database using the keyword "repair" as the search criterion. The more information you enter in these properties, the easier it will be to locate the database when you forget its filename. Figure 3-18 shows the Summary properties for the Home Tech Repair database.

Access automatically sets the Author and Company properties from the User Info tab of the Options dialog box, but you can change them in this dialog box. All the others you must enter yourself.

Contents Properties

The *Contents properties* tab lists the names of all the objects in the database grouped by category: tables, queries, forms, reports, data access pages, macros, and modules. As you add more objects to the database, such as queries, forms, and reports, you see the Contents properties change.

Custom Properties

The database *Custom properties* can also help you to locate a database file without knowing the filename. As with some of the Summary properties, you can set Custom properties and use them as advanced search criteria to open a database from Access, Word, or Excel. The Access advanced search can look for values in over 80 different properties of a database, such as Category, Company, Keyword, or Last Saved By.

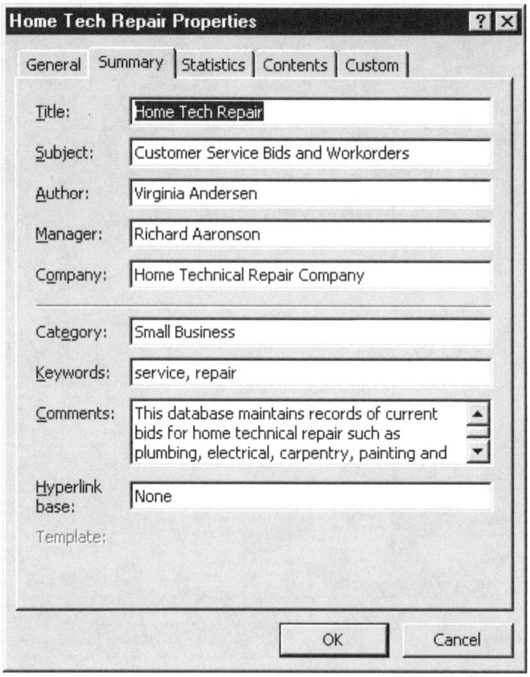

Figure 3-18.   *The Summary properties of the Home Tech Repair database*

To set the Custom properties, select the Name of the property you want to specify in the top box. In the Type box, select the type of entry you want to make: Text, Date, Number, or Yes/No. Then move to the third box, enter the value of the property, and click Add. The property is placed on the list in the Properties pane. You can add as many properties as you like, and then click OK to store the values and close the Properties dialog box. Figure 3-19 shows some Custom properties for the Home Tech Repair database.

Summary

In this chapter, the eight-step database design process was described and put into practice in the design of the Home Tech Repair database. You saw how to distribute the data among the tables, and then how to determine the key fields and specify the relationships between the tables. After completing the design, the wizard was invoked to create a database similar to the one the Home Tech Repair Company requires.

This chapter also addressed starting a new application from a blank database, rather than a prefabricated template. Finally, the database properties were examined.

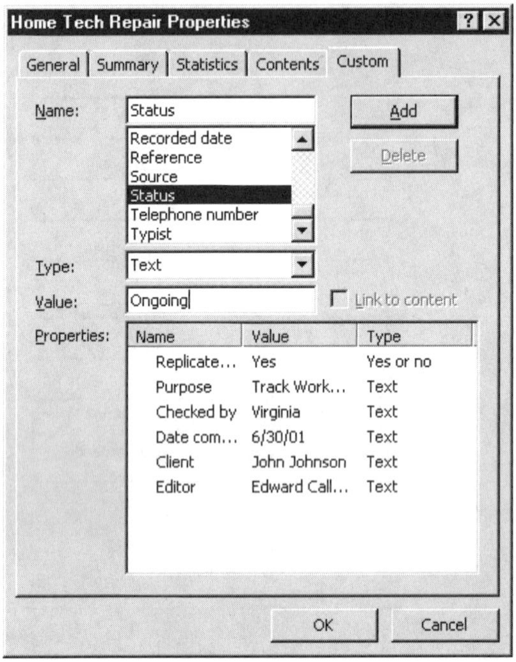

Figure 3-19. *Entering Custom database properties*

In the next chapter, you learn how to create and modify new table structures. The many field properties that determine the appearance and behavior of the data are also discussed. You also learn how to improve the value of the information in a database by adding validation rules, default field values, and other features.

MOUS Exam Activities Explored in This Chapter

Level	Activity	Section Title
Core	Create Access databases	Designing the Database
		Determining the Goals of the Database
		Distributing the Data
		Stepping Through the Wizard
		Starting with a Blank Database
		Starting a New Database from Windows

Chapter 4

Creating and Modifying Tables

Tables form the essential foundation of a relational database and the development of a database begins with building the tables to store the distributed data. Carefully designed table structures can make the difference between a smooth-running, error-free information system and a total disaster.

Access provides many useful tools for creating and customizing tables that help ensure accurate data entry and facilitate information selection and retrieval. This chapter covers not only how to create a new table structure, but also how to customize the design for your specific data requirements.

Creating a New Table Structure with the Table Wizard

In Access, a wizard is only a click away, no matter where you want help. Creating a new table is no different. The quickest way to start the Table Wizard is to double-click the Create Table by Using Wizard item in the Tables page of the Database window.

You can also begin a new table structure with the Table Wizard by choosing from the New Table dialog box (see Figure 4-1). To start the Table Wizard, do the following:

1. Open the New Table dialog box with one of the following actions:

   - Click the New button in the Tables page of the Database window.
   - Click the arrow on the New Object button and choose Table from the list.
   - Choose Insert | Table.

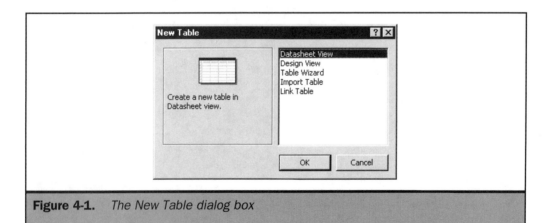

Figure 4-1.   *The New Table dialog box*

> **Note** *In the New Table dialog box, the Table Wizard is only one option. You can also start from Design view or Datasheet view, import a table from an external source, or link with an external table. This chapter first discusses starting with the Table Wizard, and then looks at using Design view and Datasheet view. Tapping external sources is covered in Chapters 22 and 23.*

1. Double-click Table Wizard in the New Table dialog box or select the option and click OK.

2. The first Table Wizard dialog box (see Figure 4-2) contains two lists of sample tables: one with the names of 25 common business tables and the other with 20 tables for storing data with more personal applications. Each sample table in the list contains a list of appropriate sample fields. You use this dialog box to build the basis for your new table by selecting the fields you want in the table.

3. Choose the category of table and the fields you want. Click the Business or Personal radio button, and then scroll down the list of sample tables until you see the one that most closely matches your requirements. When you select a table in the list, the sample fields available for that table appear in the middle box.

The next step is to select the fields you want in the new table from the list of sample fields in the sample table.

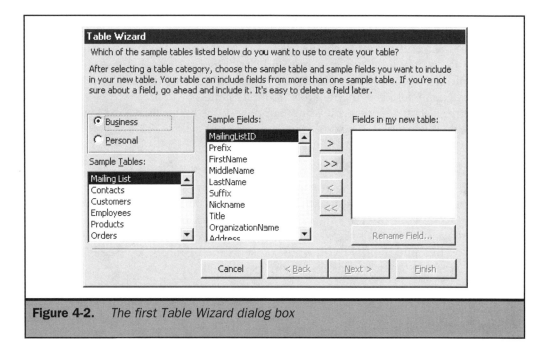

Figure 4-2. *The first Table Wizard dialog box*

Adding Fields

You can add all the fields from the sample table or only selected ones using the following methods:

- To include all the fields, click the double right arrow button.
- To remove all the fields from the new table list and start over, click the double left arrow button.
- To add one field at a time, select the field name and click the single right arrow button.
- To remove a field from the new table list, select the field name and click the single left arrow button.

> **Tip** *You aren't limited to the fields in the sample table you chose. Fields from other tables can be added to the new table list. Simply select another sample table and choose fields from that. If you discover you've added unnecessary fields later, they're easy to remove from the table structure.*

The fields appear in the table design in the order in which you select them from the list, so planning ahead pays. If you placed them in the wrong order, you can remove one or more and reinsert them, or you can rearrange them later in Design view. A field is inserted above the currently selected field in the new field list.

You also have the opportunity to rename the fields while you are creating the table design. Select the field in the Fields in My New Table list and choose Rename Field. Edit the name or enter a new one and click OK. Figure 4-3 shows the Table Wizard dialog box where a new Customer table is under construction and the default ContactFirstName field is being renamed to First Name.

After you select the names you want to appear in the table, click Next to move to the next Table Wizard dialog box.

Setting the Primary Key

The second Table Wizard dialog box lets you name the new table and offers to set a primary key for you. You can accept the default sample table name or enter your own. If you want to set your own primary key, choose the second option, No, I'll Set The Primary Key, and then choose Next. If you chose to set your own key, the next dialog box asks you to name the field you want to use as the primary key (see Figure 4-4). If you let Access set the primary key, this box is skipped.

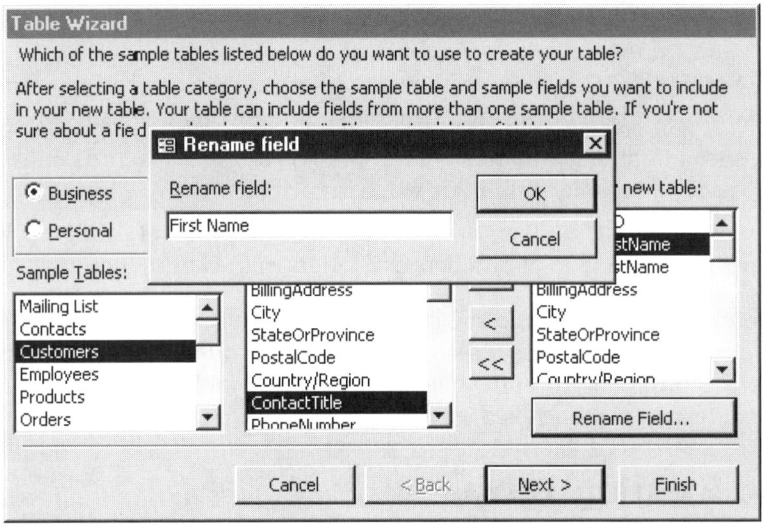

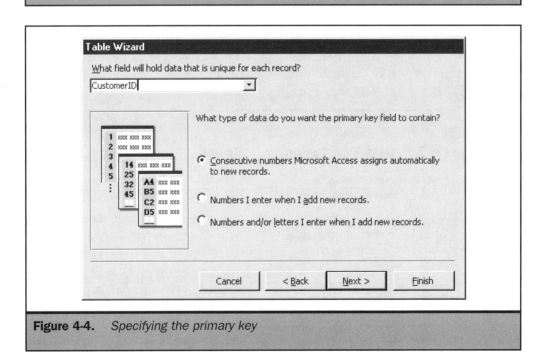

Figure 4-3.   *Renaming a field for the new Customers table*

Figure 4-4.   *Specifying the primary key*

In the dialog box shown in Figure 4-4, you also specify what type of data the primary field will contain:

■ The first option, Consecutive Numbers Microsoft Access Assigns Automatically to New Records, requires Access to make sure the field contains unique values.

■ The second option, Numbers I Enter When I Add New Records, relies on the user to assign a unique numeric value in each record.

■ The third option, Numbers and/or Letters I Enter When I Add New Records, allows a combination of numbers and letters in the key value.

The choices made in this and the previous dialog box dictate the primary key definition in the new table. Table 4-1 describes the results of the choices made, assuming the table is based on the Customers sample table. The choice in the first dialog box determines who sets the primary key.

Relating to Existing Tables

In the next dialog box (see Figure 4-5), the wizard inquires about the relationship of the new table to the other tables in your database. To define a new relationship, select the appropriate Not Related To statement and click the Relationships button.

The Relationships dialog box opens (see Figure 4-6), where you can choose the type of relationship to exist. Notice Access is quite specific about the one-to-many relationship because it knows the Customers table has the Customer ID field as the primary key, so it must be the parent table. The Bid Data table also has a field named Customer ID, but it isn't the primary key, so this table must be the child table.

Who Sets Primary Key?	Data Type Option	Result
Access	Access assigns consecutive numbers.	Customer ID is the primary key, defined as AutoNumber data type.
You	Access assigns consecutive numbers (option 1).	Your choice for primary key is defined as AutoNumber data type.
You	You enter numbers (option 2).	Your choice for primary key is defined as Number data type.
You	You enter numbers and/or letters (option 3).	Your choice for primary key is defined as Text data type.

Table 4-1. *Results of Setting Primary Key Definition*

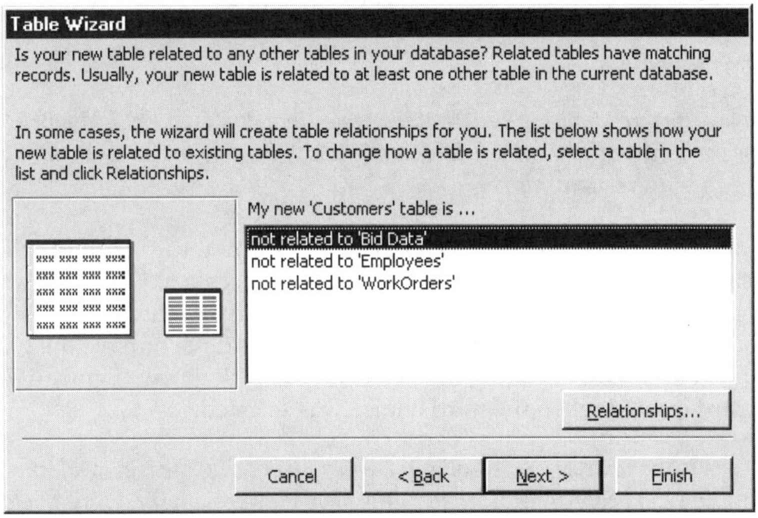

Table Wizard

Is your new table related to any other tables in your database? Related tables have matching records. Usually, your new table is related to at least one other table in the current database.

In some cases, the wizard will create table relationships for you. The list below shows how your new table is related to existing tables. To change how a table is related, select a table in the list and click Relationships.

My new 'Customers' table is ...

not related to 'Bid Data'
not related to 'Employees'
not related to 'WorkOrders'

Relationships...

Cancel   < Back   Next >   Finish

Figure 4-5.   *Examining existing relationships*

If there's an obvious similarity between fields in the new table and those in an existing table, Access may assume a relationship exists and the previous dialog box says Related To instead of Not Related To. If this happens, you can accept the link or delete the relationship by selecting the statement and clicking Relationships. In the Relationships dialog box, choose The Tables Aren't Related and click OK. Access

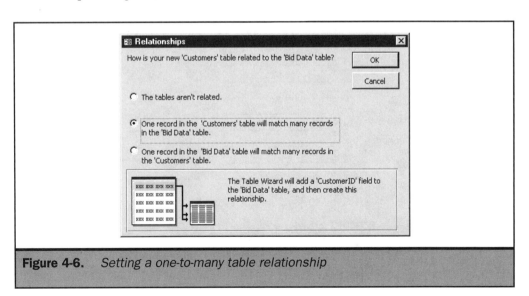

Relationships   ✕

How is your new 'Customers' table related to the 'Bid Data' table?   OK

                                                              Cancel

⚬ The tables aren't related.

⦿ One record in the 'Customers' table will match many records in the 'Bid Data' table.

⚬ One record in the 'Bid Data' table will match many records in the 'Customers' table.

The Table Wizard will add a 'CustomerID' field to the 'Bid Data' table, and then create this relationship.

Figure 4-6.   *Setting a one-to-many table relationship*

removes the relationship and the Table Wizard dialog box now shows the tables aren't related. You can also reverse the roles of the tables by choosing the third option in the Relationships dialog box.

If you specify a relationship between two tables that don't have a field name in common, Access copies the primary key field name to the child table to use as the foreign key, and then creates the relationship.

After clicking OK in the Relationships dialog box, you return to the Table Wizard where you can relate the new table to other tables, as necessary.

In the final dialog box, you can choose to go directly to the table Design view to make changes, open the table in Datasheet view to enter data, or have the wizard create a form for data entry. After making the final choice, click Finish. Figure 4-7 shows the form the wizard created when the third choice was selected.

This form is the same as the AutoForm created by clicking the New Object:AutoForm button. You can begin entering data in the form now or name and save the form design for later data entry.

Creating a New Table from Scratch

The easiest way to start a new table from a blank table design is to double-click the Create Table from Design View item in the Tables page of the Database window. You can also open the New Table dialog box as before and double-click Design view, or select Design view and click OK. An empty table appears in the table Design window, ready to add fields as shown in Figure 4-8.

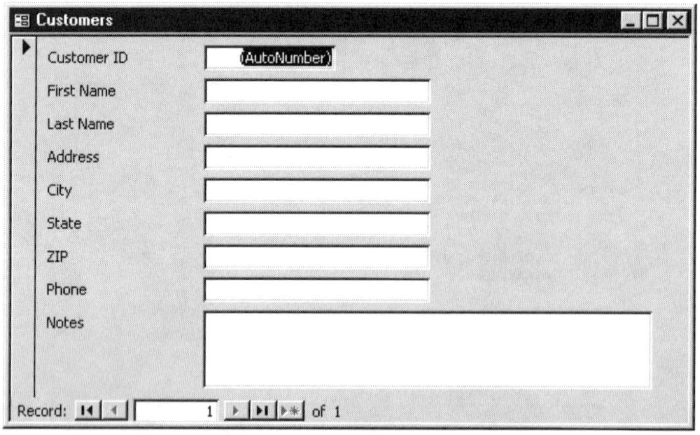

Figure 4-7.   *The data entry form for the new Customers table*

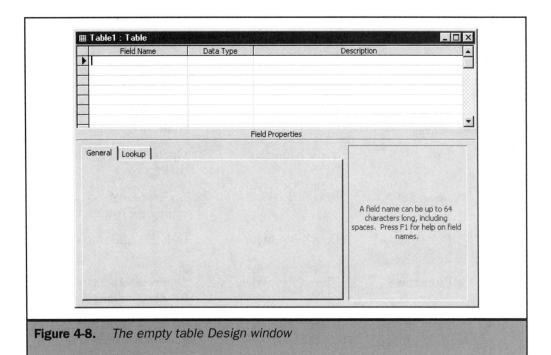

Figure 4-8.   *The empty table Design window*

Touring the Table Design View

The table Design window is divided horizontally into two panes. The upper pane is the field entry area where you enter the field name, data type, and an optional description. You also specify the field to serve as the primary key for the table in the upper pane. The lower pane is devoted to specifying the individual field properties such as size, display appearance, validity rules, and many more. The list of properties depends on the type of field you're entering. To the right of the Field Properties pane is a description of the currently active area of the screen. Once you start adding fields to the design, you can jump from one pane to the other, simply clicking where you want to be or pressing F6 with the cursor in an active row.

Some new buttons on the Table Design toolbar relate to the task of creating and modifying a table definition.

Table 4-2 describes the Table Design toolbar buttons.

	Button	Menu Equivalent	Description
▦	Datasheet View	View ∣ Datasheet View	Switches to Datasheet view.
⚷	Primary Key	Edit ∣ Primary Key	Sets selected row or rows as the primary key.
▤	Indexes	View ∣ Indexes	Opens the Indexes dialog box.
⮡	Insert Rows	Insert ∣ Rows	Inserts one or more new rows.
⮡	Delete Rows	Edit ∣ Delete Rows	Deletes selected rows.
▣	Properties	View ∣ Properties	Opens the Table Properties dialog box.
◈	Build	(none)	Starts the Field Builder.

Table 4-2.   *Table Design Window Toolbar Buttons*

Note   *No preset keyboard combinations exist that you can use as a substitute for these buttons.*

Adding Fields

To begin adding fields to the table structure, do the following:

1. Click the first row of the field entry area and type the first field name. Field names can have up to 64 characters, including letters, numbers, and spaces. Don't begin a field name with a space, however. You also cannot use any of the characters Access attaches special meanings to, such as a period, exclamation mark, and brackets. Using a mixture of uppercase and lowercase letters can help explain the field to the user, but Access doesn't differentiate between cases in field names.

2. Choose an appropriate data type from the Data Type drop-down list.

3. Enter an optional description that can provide additional information about the field. The description appears in the status bar when the field is selected in a datasheet or form.

4. Move to the Field Properties panel and set any desired properties for each new field, such as a default value, a custom format, or a validation rule.

Although including spaces in field names makes them easier to read, if there's a possibility you might want to export the table or the complete database to another database program, use a mixture of uppercase and lowercase instead. Access accepts spaces, but other applications may not.

Because the most commonly used field type is Text, Access automatically specifies a new field as a Text field by default. To change it to another type, select from the drop-down list in the Data Type box.

Once you get used to the names of the available data types, you can simply type the first letter of the type name and Access then fills in the name.

Figure 4-9 shows the data types in the drop-down list.

Field descriptions are helpful. For example, if the field name itself isn't informative enough or you want to remind yourself the field is a link to another table, add a description. The text you enter in the Description column appears in the status bar when the field is highlighted in Datasheet view or in a form.

Specifying Field Data Types

Several factors come into play as you decide what data types to use, including the following:

- The kind of values you plan to allow in the field and how you plan to use them.

- The availability of storage space. With some data types, the field size can be reduced for efficiency.

- The types of operations you can execute with the data. You can count the number of records containing a specific value of most data types in a field, but you can add up values only from Number and Currency fields.

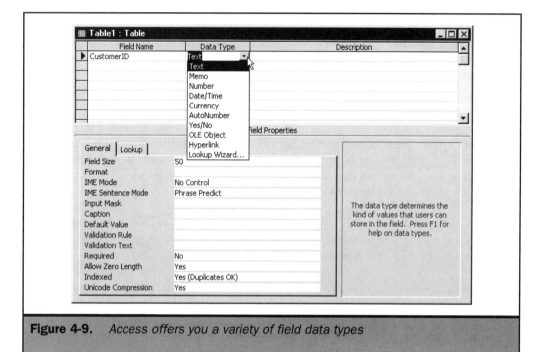

Figure 4-9. *Access offers you a variety of field data types*

- The way you want to sort or index records. You normally cannot sort on a Memo, Hyperlink, or OLE Object field. You can index on any field type except OLE Objects.

- The way you want to group records for a report or query. You can group on any field type except (again) Memo, Hyperlink, and OLE Object fields.

You can use the Access Field Builder to help add new fields to your table. Simply click an empty row in the table design and click the Build toolbar button (the one that looks like a magic wand). The Field Builder contains the same sample table and field lists as the Table Wizard. The predefined fields are complete with names, data types, and other common properties (see Figure 4-10).

The following paragraphs briefly describe each of the ten data types and how they're used. If you're interested in the amount of disk space each type of field requires, refer to the Quick Reference on the CD that accompanies this book.

Text The Text data type is the most common data type and can contain any combination of up to 255 characters and/or numbers. You would use the Text type for storing values that contain combinations of numbers and letters, such as addresses and

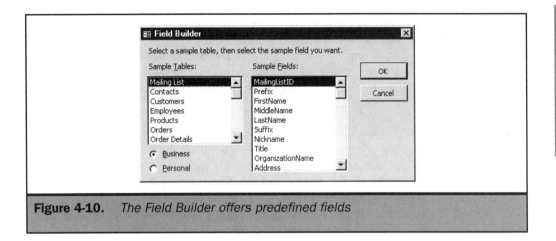

Figure 4-10.   *The Field Builder offers predefined fields*

job descriptions. Even when you think the field will contain only numbers, but you aren't expecting to perform any calculations with the values in the field, it's better to use the Text type. For example, ZIP codes may seem like numbers, but they often contain a dash, which isn't considered a number. In addition, you won't be computing the sum or average of all ZIP codes, so using a Text type is more efficient.

Tip   *If you're planning to sort records on a field that will contain only numbers, but won't perform any calculations, you're better off using the Number type rather than Text. When Access sorts numbers in a Text field, it reads the numbers from left to right, instead of right to left. For example, the numbers 9, 46, and 175 in a Text field would be sorted (ascending) in the reverse of their numerical order: 175, 46, and 9 because Access reads the first digits and sorts accordingly. If the first digits are the same, it reads the second, and so on.*

Access gives Text fields a default size of 50 characters, but you can reduce the size to 1 or increase it up to a maximum of 255 characters. If you expect the field to contain more characters than 255, you should consider using the Memo field type instead, which can contain much more data.

Memo   Use a Memo field to store long, but variable-length, text possibly relating to the other field data. For example, you could add comments to your employee records about their efficiency on the job or their skills when dealing with customers. You don't expect every record to include memo data, but when one does, the text can vary in size from a few words to up to 65,535 characters.

Note   *The handy Spelling Checker can be used to catch misspelled words in Text and Memo fields. See Chapter 6 for more information about this useful tool.*

Number   Select the Number data type when you plan to sort on the values or use them in calculations, such as adding up the labor hours for a plumbing job or the hours worked by a certain employee during the fall season. If you're working with dollar sales figures, it's better to use a Currency type because you can choose from several monetary display formats. Currency values also maintain higher precision during calculations.

Currency   Use the Currency type when you want to store monetary values, such as the cost and bid price of contracted jobs. Currency fields can be used in arithmetic calculations, just like the Number fields. You have many more ways to specify the display appearance of Currency fields than Number fields, including how to indicate negative values. Currency values are accurate to 15 digits to the left of the decimal point and four digits to the right. Using Currency instead of the Number data type prevents inaccuracies caused by rounding off the results of calculations to two decimal points.

Caution   *Number and Currency fields are automatically assigned 0 as the default value. This can cause a problem if you plan to use the field to store lookup values. This also becomes a problem if you want to count records that contain a value in the field. Zero is considered a value and the record is then falsely included in the count. To prevent this complication, remove the setting in the Default Value property. See Chapter 6 for more information about lookup lists.*

AutoNumber   When you specify an AutoNumber field, Access guarantees each record in the table has a unique value in the field, thereby creating a field you can use as a primary key. Access generates a unique value for the field as you enter each new record. You have a choice of two types of AutoNumbers: Long Integers and Replication ID numbers. If you choose Long Integer, you have a choice of how Access generates new values: Increment or Random. Incremental numbers, which simply count the records as you add them, are the most commonly used.

Date/Time   The Date/Time type is most useful when you want to sort records chronologically by the value in the field. You can also use a Date/Time field in calculations to determine elapsed time. With the Date/Time data type, you have a variety of ways to display the data as well. Formatting Date/Time and other data types is discussed in a later section in this chapter.

Yes/No   The Yes/No field is useful when you want the equivalent of a check mark in your records. For example, suppose you want to know if a transaction has been posted or a job has been completed. By default, a Yes/No field appears as a check box control in a datasheet, as well as in forms and reports. You can choose to display Yes or No, On or Off, or True or False. You can also create your own display for Yes/No fields.

The Yes/No data type is also called "Boolean" because of its binary logic.

OLE Object   When you want to embed or link an object from another source in your table, you use an OLE Object type field. With this type of field, you can acquire data from such objects as an Excel spreadsheet, a Word document, graphics, sound, or other binary data.

Hyperlink   When you want the field to jump to another location, or to connect to the Internet or an intranet, store the hyperlink address in a hyperlink field. A *hyperlink field* can contain up to four parts, separated by the pound sign (#):

- **DisplayText**   Optional text that's displayed instead of the full hyperlink address (commonly referred to as a "friendly" link).
- **Address**   A *Universal Resource Locator* (*URL*) or a *Universal Naming Convention* (*UNC*) path.
- **SubAddress**   A page within the Web address or a location within the file.
- **ScreenTip**   Text that displays when the mouse pointer rests on the hyperlink.

Only the address is required unless the subaddress points to an object in the current Access database. The other parts are optional.

Lookup Wizard   The *Lookup Wizard* creates a field limited to a list of valid values. When you select this data type, a wizard helps you create the list and actually attaches it to your table. You can type in the values you want to use or have the Lookup Wizard consult another table for the set of valid values. Then, as you enter table data, you can choose the value you want from a drop-down list. The field inherits the same data type as the primary key field in the lookup list, which is the value stored in the lookup field.

Setting Field Properties

Field properties determine how the values in the field are stored and displayed. Each type of field has a particular set of properties. For example, you may want certain currency values displayed with two decimal places, a dollar sign, and a comma as the thousands separator. Or, you could specify the currency values be rounded off to the nearest whole dollar.

Another field property is the Caption, which is the text that appears in the column header in Datasheet view and as the label attached to a field in a form or report. The Caption property can display a more descriptive name for the values than the field name itself.

Table 4-3 lists the field properties and indicates the data types to which each applies.

Property	Text	Memo	Number	Date/Time	Currency	Auto Number	Yes/No	OLE Object	Hyper-link
Field Size	X		X			X			
New Values						X			
Format	X	X	X	X	X	X	X		X
IME Mode	X	X		X					X
IME Sentence Mode	X	X		X					X
Precision			X						
Scale			X						
Decimal Places			X		X				
Input Mask	X		X	X	X				
Caption	X	X	X	X	X	X	X	X	X
Default Value	X	X	X	X	X		X		X
Validation Rule	X	X	X	X	X		X		X
Validation Text	X	X	X	X	X		X		X
Required	X	X	X	X	X		X	X	X
Allow Zero Length	X	X							X
Indexed	X	X	X	X	X	X	X		X
Unicode Compression	X	X							X

Table 4-3.　*Field Properties and Data Types*

Access attaches default properties to every field. You can accept or change the settings to customize your fields. Because Text fields are the most common and most of the field properties apply to the Text data type, let's look at their properties first. Table 4-4 describes the properties of a Text field, most of which are also available to other types of fields, although they have different default settings for different data types.

Property	Effect
Field Size	Specifies the maximum number of characters allowed in the field. Default is 50.
Format	Determines the display appearance, such as forcing uppercase or lowercase characters. In a text field, a default format isn't specified.
IME Mode	Sets the IME mode for a field when focus is moved to it. IME is a program that enters East Asian text into programs by converting keystrokes into complex East Asian characters. Default is No Control.
IME Sentence Mode	Sets the type of IME sentence. Default is Phrase Predict.
Input Mask	Provides a template for data conforming to a pattern, such as telephone numbers or Social Security numbers, and adds literal characters to the field, if desired. Default is none.
Caption	Displays a name other than the field name in datasheets, forms, and reports. Default is none.
Default Value	Automatically enters the specified value in the field. Default is none.
Validation Rule	Specifies an expression that checks for invalid data. Default is none. (Unless the validation rule specifies that the field may be left blank, it can also have the same effect as setting the Required property to yes.)
Validation Text	Displays this message if the entered data fails the validity rule. Default is none.
Required	Indicates this field may not be left blank. Default is No.

Table 4-4. *Text Field Properties*

Property	Effect
Allow Zero Length	Differentiates between a blank field and a field containing an empty string of text (""). Helpful when a value is known not to exist (such as a FAX number). Default is No.
Indexed	Indicates the table is indexed on this field. Default is No.
Unicode Compression	Allows string data that's now stored in Unicode format to be compressed to save storage space. Default is Yes.

Table 4-4. *Text Field Properties* (continued)

The Text, Number, and AutoNumber field types are the only ones for which you can specify a field size. Access automatically sets fixed field sizes for the other types. Number and Currency fields also have a property that lets you specify the number of decimal places to display. The AutoNumber data type also has the New Values property, which determines the method of assigning a unique number to the new record.

To specify a property setting, first select the field in the field entry pane (the upper portion of the window) in Design view, and then click the desired property in the Field Properties pane. Many of the properties show a down arrow when they're selected. Clicking the arrow displays a list of property options from which to choose. In most cases, you can also type in the setting you want.

Other properties, such as Input Mask and Validation Rule, include a Build button that shows as a button displaying three dots (...) to the right of the property text box, which you can click to get help with the property. For example, if you click the button next to the Validation Rule property, the Expression Builder dialog box opens where you can get help with creating a valid expression. If you don't need help building an expression, you can simply type it in the property box. If the expression is invalid, Access lets you know. You learn more about validation rules later in this chapter.

Choosing a Field Size

A text field such as a postal code or job number that contains only a few characters doesn't need to take up the default 50 characters of disk space. You can change the size of the field by entering a different number. Another reason to specify the field size is to prevent data entry errors by limiting the number of characters that can be entered.

Number fields are sized a little differently, specifying the name of the number layout, rather than the number of characters. The options are

- **Byte**, which is used to store positive integers (whole numbers) between 1 and 255.

Save space with Number field sizing. If you know the field will contain only small integers, choose the Byte field size property to save disk space. This may not sound like much of a savings, but with extremely large tables the results are significant.

- **Integer**, which is used to store larger integers and negative integers, between –32,768 and +32,768.
- **Long Integer**, the default Number field size, which is used to store even larger integers between roughly –2 billion and +2 billion.
- **Single**, which stores single-precision floating-point numbers in IEEE format.
- **Double**, which stores double-precision floating-point numbers in IEEE format.
- **Replication ID**, which is used to store a *globally unique identifier* (*GUID*).
- **Decimal**, which makes the Precision and Scale properties available to control number entries.

AutoNumber fields are limited to Long Integer and Replication ID field sizes.

Changing the size of a Number field only changes the way it's stored, not the appearance of the numbers. To change their appearance, you need to change the Format property.

Formatting Field Data

The Format property is used to specify the appearance of the value when displayed; it has no effect on the way the value is stored and it doesn't check for invalid entries. A format makes sure all the field values look alike, no matter how you entered the data. For example, you can force all names to be displayed in uppercase characters or all dates to include four-digit year values. Access provides predefined formats for most data types, but you can also create custom formats for all data types except OLE Object.

You can change the Country setting on the Regional Settings tab of the Windows Control Panel to apply to foreign currency and other formats to field values. For example, changing English (United States) to English (United Kingdom) in Windows 98 changes the currency symbol from dollars ($) to pounds (£).

When you set a field's Format property in Design view, Access applies that format to the values in Datasheet view. Any new controls on forms and reports also inherit the new formatting. Controls added to the form or report design prior to setting the custom formats are unaffected.

Table 4-5 describes the custom formatting symbols that can be used with any data types.

Symbol	Effect
!	Enters characters from left-to-right instead of right-to-left, forcing left alignment.
(Space)	Enters a space as a literal character when the SPACEBAR is pressed.
"xyz"	Displays the characters or symbols within the quotation marks.
*	Fills available space with the character that follows.
\	Indicates the character that follows is to be treated as a literal character. Often used with reserved symbols and characters.
[color]	Displays the field data in the color contained within the brackets. You can use black, blue, green, cyan, red, magenta, yellow, or white.

Table 4-5. *Custom Formatting Symbols*

Other custom formatting symbols are valid only for specific data types, as described in the following paragraphs.

Text and Memo Fields   Text and Memo fields use the same format settings, some of which are character placeholders that apply to individual characters and other settings affecting the entire entry. Table 4-6 describes the settings you can use with Text and Memo field data.

Custom Text and Memo format settings can have two sections, separated by a semicolon. The first section applies to fields containing text and the second applies to fields containing zero-length strings or Null values.

Symbol	Effect
@	Indicates a character or a space is required.
&	Indicates a character or a space is optional.
<	Converts all characters to lowercase.
>	Converts all characters to uppercase.

Table 4-6. *Text and Memo Format Settings*

The following are some examples of using the Text and Memo Format settings:

Format Setting	Entered As	Displays
@@@-@@-@@@@	123456789	123-45-6789
>	Jimmy	JIMMY
<	JIMMY	jimmy
@\!	Hello	Hello!
@;"No Data"	horse	horse
@;"No Data"	(blank)	No Data

Number and Currency Fields   You can format your Number and Currency data with one of Access's predefined formats or create your own using the special formatting symbols. The Format property of a Currency field is automatically set to Currency, but you can change it to any of the other settings. The Format property of a Number or Currency field displays a list of the predefined formats, as described in Table 4-7.

Setting	Effect
General Number	Displays number as entered. Default for Number fields.
Currency	Displays number with currency symbol and thousands separator. Negative values appear in parentheses. Default is two decimal places. Default for Currency fields.
Euro	Displays number with Euro currency symbol and thousands separator. Negative values appear in parentheses. Default is two decimal places.
Fixed	Displays at least one digit. Default is two decimal places.
Standard	Displays thousands separator. Default is two decimal places.
Percent	Displays value multiplied by 100 with added percent sign (%). Default is two decimal places.
Scientific	Uses standard scientific notation with exponents. For example, 243 displays as 2.43E+02.

Table 4-7.   _Number, AutoNumber, and Currency Predefined Format Settings_

Tip   *When you specify the Percent format for a number field, you must change the Field Size property from the default Long Integer to Single. Otherwise, the field displays only the integer portion of the number you enter and leaves off the fraction. For example, if you enter **1**, the field displays 100.00%, but if you enter **1.25**, the field still displays 100.00%.*

The custom Number and Currency formats also use special characters to indicate how you want the values to appear. Some of the characters are used as digit placeholders similar to the character placeholders in Text and Memo formats, while others affect the whole value. Table 4-8 describes these symbols and their effects.

In addition, you can use the space, quotation marks, exclamation mark, and color settings with Number and Currency fields as with Text and Memo fields.

The following are examples of using a format string with number fields:

Format String	Entered	Displays
$#,##0.00	1234.56	$1,234.56
$#,##0.00	0	$0.00
##.00%	1.235	123.50%
##.00%	0	.00%

Symbol	Effect
. (period)	Indicates the decimal point that separates the parts of a number.
, (comma)	Used as the thousands separator.
0	A digit placeholder that displays a digit if one is there or, if none are there, displays zero.
#	A digit placeholder that displays a digit if one is there or, if none are there, closes up the adjoining digits.
$	Displays a dollar sign.
%	Value is multiplied by 100 and a percent sign is added.

Table 4-8.   *Number and Currency Custom Formatting Symbols*

Symbol	Effect
E– or e–	Used to display numbers in scientific notation. Includes a minus sign (-) before negative exponents, but no plus sign (+) before positive exponents.
E+ or e+	Same as the previous, except displays plus and minus signs before the exponent.

Table 4-8. *Number and Currency Custom Formatting Symbols* (continued)

Custom Number and Currency formats can have up to four sections, separated by semicolons. Each section applies to a different type of number:

- The first section specifies the format for positive numbers.
- The second section specifies the format for negative numbers.
- The third section specifies the format for zero values.
- The fourth section specifies the format for Null values.

For example, the custom currency format

$#,##0.00[Yellow];($#,##0.00)[Blue];"Zero";"Don't know"

displays positive values in yellow, negative values in blue, and, enclosed in parentheses, the word "Zero" for zero values and "Don't know" for Null values.

Null vs. Zero-Length Strings in Text and Memo Fields

As you saw, you can use sections 3 and 4 of the custom format for Number and Currency fields to specify what value to display when the value is Null and another value when it's a zero-length string.

Text and Memo field custom formats can display a specific value when the field is blank for either reason, but can't differentiate between the two types of blanks. To do that, you must use the IIf() function to test for the Null value and assign the format text according to the outcome of the test. For example, you could assign the text "Don't know" to the second section of the custom format if the IIf() function returns Yes (Null value) and "None" if it returns No (anything but a Null value). You learn more about using functions and procedures in Chapter 25.

Date/Time Fields Date/Time fields include seven predefined format settings, in addition to some symbols you can use to create your own custom formats. Table 4-9 describes the formats Access provides. Date and Time format settings are specified according to the setting in the Regional Setting Properties dialog box in the Windows Control Panel.

Note *In Access 2002, Date/Time field data is always stored with four digits. However, the user may have entered only two digits to represent the year. The Short Date setting assumes any dates between 1/1/00 and 12/31/29 are in the twenty-first century, that is, between January 1, 2000 and December 31, 2029. Dates between 1/1/30 and 12/31/99 are assumed to be in the twentieth century, between January 1, 1930 and December 31, 1999.*

Using special characters to represent the hour, minute, and second in a time format and the day, week, month, and year in a date format, you can create almost any display format you choose. The letter *d*, for example, can display the day of the month as one or two digits or as the full name, depending on how many times you use the letter *d* in the string. The letter *m* can also be used to represent the month from one or two digits to the full name. Table 4-10 describes the custom formatting available for Date/Time values.

Setting	Description
General Date	(Default) Combination of Short Date and Long Time settings. If no time, only date is displayed; if no date, only time. Examples: 5/21/01 3:30:00 PM (US) 21/5/01 15:30:00 (UK)
Long Date	Uses Long Date Regional setting. Examples: Monday, May 21, 2001 (US) Monday, 21 May 2001 (UK)
Medium Date	21-May-01
Short Date	Uses Short Date Regional setting. Examples: 5/21/01 (US) 21/5/01 (UK)
Long Time	3:30:00 PM
Medium Time	3:30 PM
Short Time	15:30

Table 4-9. *Date/Time Predefined Format Settings*

Symbol	Description
: (colon)	Time separator as set in the Regional Settings Properties dialog box.
/	Date separator.
C	Applies General Date predefined format as set in the Regional Settings Properties dialog box.
d	Day of the month in one or two digits, as required (1 to 31).
dd	Day of the month in two digits (01 to 31).
ddd	First three letters of the day of the week (Sun to Sat).
dddd	Full weekday name (Sunday through Saturday).
ddddd	Same as Short Date format.
dddddd	Same as Long Date format.
w	Day of the week by number (1 to 7).
ww	Week of the year by number (1 to 52).
m	Month in one or two digits, as needed (1 to 12).
mm	Month in two digits (01 to 12).
mmm	First three letters of month name (Jan to Dec).
mmmm	Full name of the month (January to December).
q	Quarter of the year (1 to 4).
y	Number of the day in the year (1 to 366).
yy	Last two digits of the year (01 to 99).
yyyy	Full year (0100 to 9999).
h, n, s	Hour, minute, or second in one or two digits, as needed (0 to 23, 1 to 59).
hh, nn, ss	Hour, minute, or second in two digits (01 to 23, 01 to 59).
tttt	Same as Long Time.
AM/PM, am/pm	12-hour clock with two-character uppercase or lowercase designators.
A/P, a/p	12-hour clock with one-character uppercase or lowercase designators.
AM/PM	12-hour clock with morning/afternoon designators, as specified in Regional Settings Properties dialog box.

Table 4-10.   *Date/Time Formatting Symbols*

The character n is used as the minute format symbol to avoid confusion with the month symbol, m.

To include literal characters other than the date and time separators with the Date/Time values, enclose them in quotation marks. Some examples of using these special formatting symbols are

Setting	Displays
ddd", "mmm d", "yy	Tue, Jan 15, 02
dddd", "mmmm d", "yyyy	Tuesday, January 15, 2002
h:n:s AM/PM	9:15:35 AM

In addition, you can add other characters to the display format by enclosing them in quotation marks. For example, entering the value 5/21/01 in a field with the format setting

"Today is " dddd " in week number " ww "."

displays

Today is Monday in week number 22.

Notice the spaces within the quotation marks that separate the characters in the string from the date values and the period added to the end of the expression.

 If you specify a custom Date/Time format that's inconsistent with the settings in the Regional Settings Properties dialog box, the custom format is ignored.

Yes/No Fields   Access automatically displays a default check box control when you specify a Yes/No data type. Any format settings you make are ignored with this choice. To display values in any other format, first change the Display Control setting on the Lookup tab to a text box or a combo box, and then you can have some fun formatting Yes/No field values. Access provides three predefined formats for displaying Yes/No, On/Off, or True/False, but you can also create a custom format that displays other text for the two values.

To change a Yes/No field Display Control property, open the table in Design view and do the following:

1. Select the Yes/No field.

2. Click the Lookup tab in the Field Properties pane.

3. Select Text Box from the Display Control list.

4. Return to the General tab to choose the desired display format.

The Yes/No custom format contains up to three sections, separated by semicolons. The first section isn't used, but you still need to enter the semicolon before entering another section. The second and third sections specify what to display when the value is Yes and No, respectively. For example, the following format:

;"Yes, indeed!"[Green];"No, never!"[Red]

displays

Yes, indeed!

in green when the value is Yes, and

No, never!

in red if the value is No.

 If you choose Combo Box as the Display Control property instead of Text Box, more properties appear on the Lookup page where you can set the appearance and values of the list the combo box will display. More about using combo boxes and lookup lists in Chapter 6.

Setting the Number of Decimal Places

The Field Size, Precision, Scale, Format, and Decimal Places properties of Number and Currency fields are all related. The Field Size property determines whether the number is stored as an integer or with fractional values, and also specifies the degree of mathematical precision.

The Precision property applies only to Number fields with the Field Size set to Decimal. This property is used to limit the total number of significant digits that can be entered on both sides of the decimal point in a Number field. Leading and trailing zeros aren't counted, they're truncated. Enter a positive integer between 0 and 28 in the Precision property of the Number field. The default setting is 18.

The Scale property also applies only to Number fields with Decimal Field Size property. Scale limits the number of significant digits that can be entered to the right of the decimal point, not counting any trailing zeros. Enter a positive integer between 0 and 28 in the Scale property. The default setting is 0.

The Format property adds display features, such as dollar or percent signs, and commas as thousands separators.

The Decimal Places property determines how many digits to display to the right of the decimal point in a Number or Currency field. The Decimal Places setting has no effect on the precision of the stored number; that's specified by the Field Size or the Precision property. If the value is stored as an integer (Byte, Integer, or Long Integer data type), a number of zeros appear to the right of the decimal point equal to the setting in the Decimal Places property.

The default Decimal Places setting for Number and Currency fields is Auto, which displays two decimal places for fields with Format property settings of Currency, Fixed, Standard, Percent, and Scientific. You can choose any number from 0 to 15.

However, the Decimal Places property has no effect unless you already specified the appropriate Format property for the field.

To change the number of Decimal Places in the display, click the arrow in the Decimal Places property box and choose a number from the list or simply enter the desired number.

If the field retains the default Long Integer property, the values are then rounded to the nearest integer no matter how many decimal places you specify for the display.

 You can also set the Decimal Places property in a query, report, or form design and override the setting you specified in the table design.

To change the number of decimal places stored in the field, change the Field Size property to one of the settings for real numbers, such as Single, Double, or Decimal, which aren't limited to integers.

Including a Caption

If someone else is going to use the database and you think the field names aren't descriptive enough, you can use the Caption property to change the column heading in the Datasheet view. A caption can contain up to 255 characters, in any combination of letters, numbers, special characters, and spaces.

The new caption also appears in queries and replaces the text in the field labels attached to controls in report and form designs. The field names remain the same; only the labels show the new caption text.

 If you rename the field later in Datasheet view, the Caption property is deleted. To prevent this, rename fields only in Design view.

Choosing a Primary Key

In a relational database system, being able to gather and retrieve related information from separate tables in the database is important. To do so, each record in one table must be unique in some way. The field or fields that contain the unique value is the *primary key*. Access neither permits duplicate values in the primary key nor does it permit Null values. A valid unique value must be in the primary key field or field combination throughout the table.

Setting a Single-Field Key

If your table has a field you're sure won't contain any duplicate values, you can use that field as the primary key. In the table Design view, click the field row you want to use as the primary key, and then you have three ways to designate the field as the primary key:

- Click the Primary Key toolbar button.
- Choose Edit | Primary Key.
- Right-click the field row in the upper pane and choose Primary Key from the shortcut menu.

To remove the primary key designation, repeat any one of the previous steps.

Note *If you choose the field as the primary key after you enter data and there are duplicate values or one of the records has a blank value in that field, Access won't set the key. However, you can run a Find Duplicates query to locate and correct any duplicate entries. More about queries in Chapters 8 and 9. You can also solve the problem by choosing a different field as the primary key, adding another field to the key, or adding an AutoNumber field to use as the key.*

Setting a Multiple-Field Primary Key

If you can't guarantee the values in a single field will be unique throughout the table, you can combine two or more fields as the primary key. For example, in a list of customers, you may have several with the same last name, so that field couldn't be used as a primary key. However, you could combine first and last names to create unique values or, if that still doesn't work, combine first, last, and middle initial or ZIP code.

Tip *The multiple-field primary key field is left over from the days before Microsoft invented the AutoNumber data type. Rather than create a multiple-field primary key, adding an AutoNumber field to do the job is much simpler and safer. Access makes sure every record is unique. The main use for a multiple-field primary key is in a junction table, which is used to bridge two tables that are related with a many-to-many relationship, as described in Chapter 5.*

To set a primary key that combines two or more fields, hold down CTRL while you select each field. If the fields are contiguous in the list, select the top field row and hold down SHIFT while you select the last row you want to include. After you select all the fields you want in the key, use the Primary Key button or a menu option as before. Key icons appear in each row included in the multiple-field primary key. The following table has a three-field primary key that includes the first and last names with the ZIP code.

Field Name	Data Type	Description
CustomerID	AutoNumber	Unique customer number
Last Name	Text	Customer last name
First Name	Text	Customer first name
Address	Text	Billing address
City	Text	
State	Text	
ZIP	Text	

Customers : Table

The multiple-field primary key is constructed in the same order as the fields in the table structure. If a different field order is important, you can rearrange the fields in the Indexes window. More about the Indexes window in a later section.

Letting Access Set the Key

The AutoNumber field type is an Access tool that can guarantee unique records in a table. Designating an AutoNumber field as the primary key for a table is probably the simplest way to set the key. You needn't worry about inadvertently entering duplicate values because Access uses unique numbers to identify each record. Once the number is generated, it can't be changed or deleted.

You can choose to have incremental numbers, random numbers, or Replication ID numbers, also called GUIDs. With incremental values, Access adds 1 to the value for each record you add. When you choose random numbers for the AutoNumber field format, Access uses a random number generator to create the value. Replication ID numbers are used to identify and synchronize database replicas uniquely.

When you finish a table design using the Table Wizard without having designated a primary key, Access asks if you want it to create one for you. If you answer Yes, Access either applies the primary key to an AutoNumber field—if one exists—or creates an AutoNumber field, which it then designates as the primary key. You can respond No and leave the table without a key for the time being.

The only problem with using an AutoNumber field as the primary key can occur when you use an append query to add records from one table to another. Access won't append records that have duplicate values in the primary key field. If you need to append records that contain AutoNumber primary keys, don't include the AutoNumber field in the query. Access numbers the added records with unique values. Access gives the first appended record a value that's one higher than the highest number assigned in the original table. More about append queries in Chapter 9.

Creating Other Indexes

Indexes help Access find and sort records faster, just as an index helps you find topics in a reference book: An *index* contains a pointer to the location of the data, rather than the data itself. The primary key in a table is automatically indexed, so I'm talking about secondary indexes created with other fields. An index can include a single field or multiple fields.

When deciding which fields to use as indexes, look at the fields you expect to search frequently for particular values or those by which you want to sort. Also, if you expect to use a field to create a relationship with another table, you might want to create an index on the field to improve performance. A field that may have many records containing the same value isn't a good candidate for an index because an index on such a field won't speed things up much.

Adding a Single-Field Index

To set a single-field index, simply change its Indexed property to Yes and decide whether to permit duplicate values.

To view the indexes specified for a table, click the Indexes toolbar button or choose View | Indexes. Figure 4-11 shows the Customers table with two currently defined indexes. The primary key, Customer ID, is listed with the key icon as the first index and a single-field index based on the customer's last name as the second. Notice the primary key properties, shown in the Index Properties pane, specify the index as Primary with Unique values and not to ignore Null values in the field.

Creating a Multiple-Field Index

In many cases, you may want to search or sort records based on more than one field at once. Creating a multiple-field index enables you to do just that. When you sort records using a multiple-field index, the records are sorted initially by the first field in the index. If Access finds duplicate values in the first field, it sorts by the next field and so on. For example, you want to see records for customers in particular areas of the city. To do this, you can create an index using both the City and ZIP code fields.

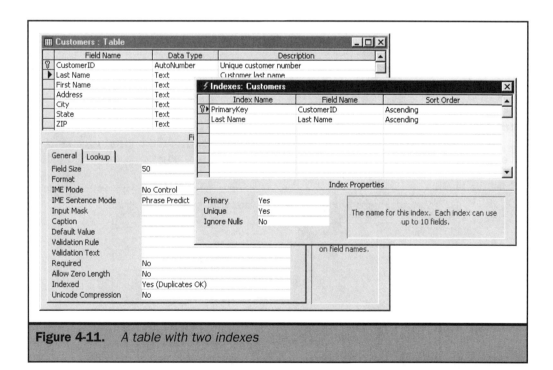

Figure 4-11. *A table with two indexes*

To create a multiple-field index follow these steps:

1. With the Customers table open in Design view, click the Indexes toolbar button.
2. Click in the first empty row in the Indexes window.
3. Enter a name for the new index, such as **City Region**, and then press TAB to move to the Field Name column.
4. Click the down arrow and select City from the list of available fields.
5. Accept Ascending as the sort order for the City field and click in the Field Name in the next row (leaving the Index Name blank because both fields are used in the same index).
6. Choose ZIP from the field list and change the sort order, if necessary.
7. If the index is intended to be the primary key, set the Primary property to Yes. (You must click the first row of the index, which contains the index name, to display the Index Properties pane.) If you want the index to contain unique values for each record, change the Unique property to Yes. If you want the index to ignore Null values, change the Ignore Null property to Yes. Figure 4-12 shows the completed two-field City Region index.
8. Close the Indexes dialog box, and then save the changes to the table.

You can specify up to ten fields in one index with a mixture of ascending and descending orders for the fields. If you want to insist on having unique values in the composite index, you can set its Unique property to Yes.

Saving the Table Design

The table design needn't be complete before you save it. In fact, a good idea is to save the design now, and then save it again during the design process to guard

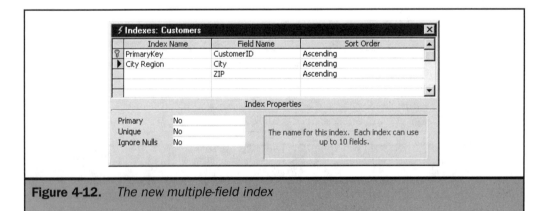

Figure 4-12.   *The new multiple-field index*

against catastrophes. Access requires you to save the design before you can switch to Datasheet view to enter data. To save the table design, click the Save button or choose File | Save. The first time you save a new table, Access prompts you for a name.

The table name can have up to 64 characters in any combination of letters, numbers, and spaces, but it cannot begin with a space. You can also include special characters except for those that have a special meaning to Access, such as a period (.), an exclamation point (!), a back quotation mark (`` ` ``), or brackets ([]). You also cannot use any control character with an ASCII value between 0 and 31.

 If you want to undo the changes you just made to the table design, close the table design and respond No when Access asks if you want to save the changes.

Modifying the Table Design

Even though you tried to include all the necessary features and properties in your table design, you'll undoubtedly find things that need changing. You may want to change the order of the fields in the table, so the ones you want to see most often always appear on the screen without scrolling to the right in the Datasheet view. Or, you may want to add a new field or delete one that isn't needed, after all. Maybe some of the field properties aren't quite what were expected or you want to change the field size or type.

You can make any of these changes to an empty table with no problems, but after you enter data, you risk losing data with some of the changes. Adding fields, increasing a field size, and rearranging the field order won't cause any data loss. But, if you decide to delete a field or reduce a field size in a table that already contains data, Access displays a warning if data loss may occur. Problems can also occur when changing a field type. Making a backup of the data before you make any changes to the table design is always a good idea.

Copying Tables and Other Objects

Before making changes in a table or any other Access object, make a backup copy in case something goes wrong. This is especially true with tables because, if you make the wrong change, you can lose a lot of data in the blink of an eye. Luckily, Access warns you of impending data loss, but it's still better to be careful.

With many other operations, Access gives you several ways to copy tables from the Tables page of the Database window to the clipboard:

- Select the table name and choose Edit | Copy.
- Select the table name and click Copy.
- Right-click the table name and choose Copy from the shortcut menu.

Once the table is on the clipboard, click an empty area in the Tables page and do one of the following:

- Choose Edit | Paste.
- Click Paste.
- Right-click and choose Paste from the shortcut menu.

All three of the Paste choices open the Paste Table As dialog box where you name the copy and choose to paste both the structure and the data, copy only the structure, or append the data to another table. Enter a name for the copy or accept the default Copy of... name and choose Structure and Data. Click OK to complete the copy procedure.

This method also works for queries, forms, reports, and data access pages, and it can be a time-saving tool for creating new objects that resemble existing ones.

The following paragraphs discuss how to make changes to an existing table and the implications the changes may have.

Switching Table Views

If you enter data in Datasheet view and you decide some changes need to be made in the table structure, you can quickly return to the Design view in one of the following ways:

- Click the View (Design) button.
- Choose View | Design View.
- If the window isn't maximized, right-click the Table window title bar and choose Table Design from the shortcut menu.
- If the window is maximized, right-click any empty area in the Table window outside the datasheet and choose Table Design from the shortcut menu.

Use the same methods to switch back to Datasheet view.

If you're viewing data in the AutoForm, switching to Design view takes you to the form Design view, not the table Design view. To switch to table Design view, you must first switch to Datasheet view, and then click the Design button.

Adding/Deleting Fields

A new field can be added to the bottom of the list of fields or inserted anywhere among the existing fields. To add one to the bottom, click the first blank field and enter the field definition. To insert a field among existing fields, click the row below where the new one is to appear, and then do one of the following:

- Click the Insert Rows toolbar button.
- Choose Insert | Rows.
- Right-click the row and choose Insert Rows from the shortcut menu.

Whichever method you choose, the new blank field row is inserted above the row that contains the cursor and all the fields below are moved down one row. The insertion point is in the new row ready to enter the field definition.

 If you select the existing row instead of clicking it, the new row is selected on insertion. You must click in the row to deselect it before you can begin entering the new field definition.

For example, add a new field to the Workorders table that will contain a hyperlink to a drawing used for that job, such as a schematic for installing a bay window. To add the new field, do the following:

1. Right-click the Workorders table on the Tables page of the Database window, and then choose Design from the shortcut menu.
2. Click in the first empty row in the Field Name column and enter **Drawing**.
3. Click the Data Type arrow and choose Hyperlink from the list.
4. Add a description, such as Layouts of project, and then click Save.

 Another way to add a new field, one that inherits the same properties as one already in your table, is to copy the existing field to the clipboard, and then paste it in an empty row. Of course, you must change the new field's name before you can save the table because no two fields can have the same name. Only the field definition is copied; no previously entered data is copied.

If you want to add several new rows at once, select the number of contiguous rows in the table design equal to the number of new fields you want to insert, and then use one of the previous methods. The same number of new blank rows appears above the top row in the selected group. Then click one of the new rows and begin entering the field definitions.

When you delete a field from the table design, you aren't only deleting the field name, but any data entered in the field. Before deleting a field that contains data, Access warns you'll permanently lose the data and asks if you really want to delete the field.

To delete a field, in Design view, click the row selector for the field (the gray button to the left of the field name) and do one of the following:

- Press the DEL key.
- Choose Edit | Delete Rows.
- Click the Delete Rows toolbar button.

■ Right-click in the row and choose Delete Rows from the shortcut menu.

To delete several rows at once, select them all and delete them as a group.

Using the DEL *key works only if the row is selected. The other three methods delete the row that contains the insertion point, even if it isn't selected.*

You can cause a problem by deleting a field you've used in a query, form, or report. Be sure you remove any references to the field you're about to delete from the other objects before you try to delete it. Access won't let you delete a field that's a link in a relationship to another table without deleting the relationship first.

Changing the Field Order

To change the order of fields in both the stored table and in the Datasheet view, rearrange them in Design view. To move a field to a new position in the table design, click the row selector to select the row, and then drag the row selector to move the field to its new position.

You can move several contiguous fields at once by selecting them all, and then dragging them as a group. To select more than one, use one of the following methods:

■ Click the top field row selector and drag through the row selectors until all are selected.

■ Click the top field row selector and hold down SHIFT while you click the field row at the end of the group.

While you can select noncontiguous field rows by holding down CTRL *as you select the rows, you cannot drag the group to a new position.*

If you want to keep the field order in the stored table, but would like to view them in a different order in the datasheet, you can rearrange the datasheet columns. See Chapter 6 for information about changing the appearance of a datasheet.

Changing a Field Name or Type

You saw earlier how to change the name that appears in the column heading in Datasheet view by changing the field Caption property. You can also change the actual field name in the design. Changing the field name has no effect on the data already entered into the field. However, any references to the field in other objects, such as queries, forms, and reports or in an expression, must be changed as well, unless you have checked the Name AutoCorrect option.

To change a field name in Design view, simply type the new name. After changing the name, you must save the table again.

Using Name AutoCorrect

Since the arrival of Access 2000, you no longer need to be so careful about changing the names of fields used in forms and other database objects. The Name AutoCorrect feature automatically corrects most side effects that occur when you rename fields, tables, queries, forms, reports, and controls included in form and report designs. When you open a form or other object, Access searches for and fixes any differences between the form and the fields and the controls on which it depends. By checking the date/time stamp for the last revision of the table and the form, Access can tell if any names have changed since the last time the form was saved. If the stamps are different, Access automatically performs Name AutoCorrect.

Name AutoCorrect is automatically set on by default in any database you create in version 2000 or 2002. If you convert a database from an earlier version of Access, you must turn it on in the Options dialog box. Read more about Name AutoCorrect and other options you can set to customize the workplace in Chapter 16.

Changing a field type is a little more complicated if the table already includes data. If no data is in the table, you can safely change any field data type. Some types convert easily to another type, but other conversions may result in loss of data. If data is going to be lost, Access displays a message showing the number of values to be affected before it makes any changes. If you used the field in an expression, you may also need to change the expression.

To change a field type, do the following:

1. Click the Data Type column.

2. Click the arrow and select the new data type.

3. Save the table design. If Access displays a warning message, respond No to cancel the changes or Yes to go ahead and make the changes. If no data is in the table, Access doesn't display any warnings.

You won't encounter any difficulties converting other data types to Text. Number fields convert to text with a General Number format, while Date/Time fields convert to text with the General Date format. Currency fields convert accurately to Text, but without the currency symbols.

Table 4-11 describes the relevant considerations when converting between data types.

Caution   *If the field you're converting is a primary key field or a unique index and the conversion would result in duplicate values, Access deletes the entire record. Access warns you first, so you can prevent the deletion.*

Tip   *Once a table contains data, you cannot change any type of field to AutoNumber, even if you know the field contains unique values. If you need an AutoNumber field, add a new field and select the AutoNumber data type. Access assigns each existing record a sequential number.*

From	To	Results	Comments
Text	Number, Currency, Date/Time	Converts to appropriate values.	Values must fit new data type. Others are deleted. Date/Time and Currency formats follow Regional Settings.
Text	Yes/No	Converts to appropriate values.	Yes, True, or On convert to Yes. No, False, or Off convert to No.
Number	Yes/No	Converts to appropriate values.	Zero or Null values convert to No and non-zero values to Yes.
Memo	Text	Direct conversion.	Memo data longer than field size is truncated.
Number	Text	Converts values to text.	Numbers appear in General Number format.
Currency	Text	Converts values to text.	No currency symbols are included.
Date/Time	Text	Direct conversion.	Values appear in General Date format.
Yes/No	Text	Direct conversion.	None.
AutoNumber	Text	Direct conversion.	Values may be truncated, depending on field size.
Currency	Number	Direct conversion.	Values may be truncated, depending on field size.
AutoNumber	Number	Direct conversion.	Values may be truncated, depending on field size.

Table 4-11. *Converting Between Data Types*

Changing a Field Size

Changing the Field Size property has no effect on the data if you're increasing the size. Obviously, if you want to reduce the field size, especially for a Number field, you should make sure no values are larger than permitted by the new field size. If the values are too large to fit the new field size, they're replaced with Null values. If the new field size doesn't permit the number of decimal places currently specified, the values are rounded off.

Modifying or Deleting the Primary Key

You might find the primary key doesn't always have a unique value after all and decide to use a different field or create a primary key with two or more fields.

To change the primary key, select the row you want as the primary key and click the Primary Key button. The key icon is removed from the old key field and appears in the new one.

To add another field to the existing primary key, select both the old and new key fields, and then click the Primary Key button. The key icon appears in the row selector of both rows.

At times, you might want to disable the primary key temporarily—for example, if you're importing records from another table, some of which may contain values that duplicate your original table. You must remove any duplicates in the new data before restoring the primary key. This has no effect on the data stored in the field designated as the key, it removes the key field feature temporarily.

To remove the primary key designation, select the primary key field and click the Primary Key button. If the key is used in a relationship, you must delete the relationship before you can remove the key.

Modifying or Deleting an Index

To delete a single-field index, change the field's Indexed property to No. This removes only the index; it has no effect on the field itself or the underlying data.

In the Indexes dialog box, you can add or delete fields from a multiple-field index, change the sort order for any field in the index, or change the index properties. You can also change the field order in the index.

- To remove a field from a multiple-field index, display the Indexes dialog box, select the field row, and then press the DEL key.

- To remove the entire index, display the Indexes dialog box, select all the rows in the index, and then press the DEL key.

- To insert an additional field into the index, display the Indexes dialog box, select the field below where you want the new field to appear, press INSERT, and then enter the new field name.

- To change the field order in a multiple-field index, select and drag the field selector to the desired position in the index definition.

- To change the sort order for any of the fields in the index, choose from the Sort Order list.

After making changes to the table's indexes, be sure to save the table. Access reminds you to do so if you try to close the table or if you return to Datasheet view without saving.

Ensuring Data Validity

You've seen a few of the ways Access helps you ensure the values entered in your database are valid. The data type you choose for the field can limit the values to, for example, date and time values. You can also limit the number of characters in a Text field and prevent duplicate values. A direct way to ensure valid data is to set some rules the values must obey.

You can specify two kinds of data validation rules: field validation and record validation. A *field validation* rule can limit the value to a few specific values or to a range of values. The rule is checked when you try to move to another field in the same or another record. For example, a rule could limit a numeric value to a range between 1 and 100 or insist a date value fall in 2001.

A *record validation* rule is handy for comparing the values in two fields in the same record. The rule is checked when you move out of a record and Access attempts to save the record. Access won't save a record with a conflict between fields. For example, a record validation rule could prevent saving a record in which the Job Cost is greater than the Bid Price. Another record validation rule could ensure the elapsed time between dates in two separate fields doesn't exceed a specific value.

When either type of rule is broken, Access displays a message in a warning box that explains the violation and doesn't leave the field or record. The message you want to display is the Validation Text property in the table or field property. If you don't enter message text, Access creates a standard default message, such as the one shown here.

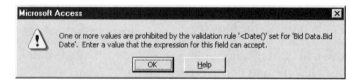

Defining Field Validation Rules

To define a field validation rule, follow these steps:

1. Select the field name in the upper pane of the Design window, and then click Validation Rule in the Field Properties pane.

2. Type the expression you want in the property box. For example, if the value must not exceed 100, enter **<=100** (less than or equal to 100).

3. Then move to the Validation Text property box and enter the message you want to display when the rule is broken.

GETTING STARTED

 The Validation Rule property has a Build button you can use to open the Expression Builder if you need help with the expression. See Chapter 8 for information about using the Expression Builder.

You can also type wildcards in the expression. These are the same placeholders used in search strings: ? stands for a single character and * stands for any number of characters. When you enter an expression with a wildcard, Access converts it to an expression using the Like operator and adds quotation marks. For example, if you type **C*** in the property text box, it turns into Like "C*" when you move out of the property box. This expression means all values entered in the field must begin with the letter *C* or *c*. The expression is not case-sensitive.

A validation rule defined for a Date/Time field also includes special symbols when translated by Access. To enter a rule that says the date entered must be earlier than January 1, 2002, you type **<01/01/02** and Access converts it to <#01/01/02# to make sure it isn't confused with a Number value.

Validation rules can include more than one criterion for the same field by combining them using the AND or OR operators. Table 4-12 describes some examples of validation rules, the corresponding Access expression, and an appropriate Validation Text message.

Figure 4-13 shows the Bid Data table structure with a validation rule added to the State field. The rule specifies the State value must be either CA, AZ, or NV and, if the rule is violated, the message Bid contracts only in California, Arizona or Nevada displays in an information box.

Rule	Access Version	Typical Message
<>0	<>0	Value must not be 0, but it may be negative.
100 Or 200	100 Or 200	Value must be either 100 or 200.
C*	Like "C*"	Value must begin with C.
C* Or D*	Like "C*" Or Like "D*"	Value must begin with C or D.
C??t	Like "C??t"	Value must be four characters long, begin with C, and end with t.
>=01/01/01 And <01/01/02	>=#1/1/01# And <#1/1/02#	Value must be in 2001.
Not CA	Not "CA"	Field may contain any value but CA.

Table 4-12. *Examples of Validation Rules and Text*

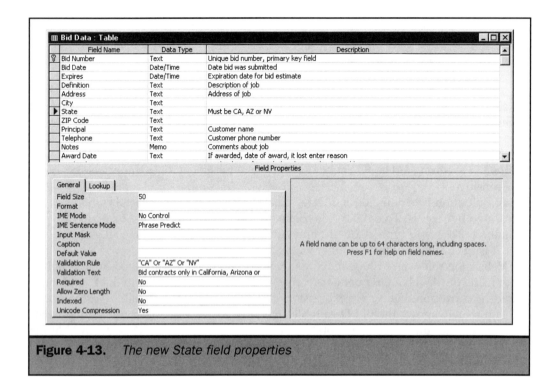

Figure 4-13. *The new State field properties*

Figure 4-14 shows the error message displayed when UT was entered in the State field and an attempt was made to move to another record.

Note *The previous State validation rule causes a violation if the field is left blank because it insists on one of three values. If you want to leave the field blank, add Null to the list of valid values. You can also create a more complex record validation rule that insists on a value only if a no value is in the corresponding City field to allow for customers who deal solely over the Internet instead of by mail.*

As you add validation rules to a table, you can test them against existing data to see if any of the field values violate the new rule. To do this, choose Edit | Test Validation Rules or, if the Design window isn't maximized, right-click the Design window title bar and choose Test Validation Rules from the shortcut menu.

Access warns you the process also checks the Required and Allow Zero Length properties, may take a long time, and asks if you want to do it anyway. If you respond Yes, you're told you must save the design before testing the rules. Choose Yes to save the design and continue testing. If Access finds no violations, it displays a message saying all the data was valid for all the rules you defined. If a violation is found, Access

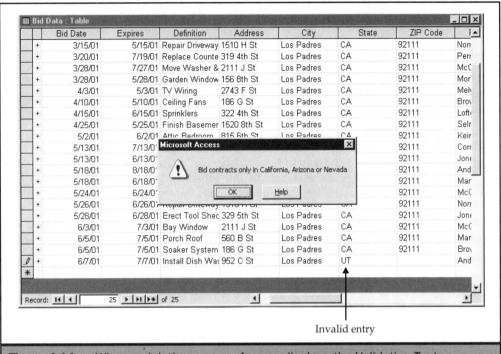

Invalid entry

Figure 4-14.   *When a violation occurs, Access displays the Validation Text*

stops checking and displays a message indicating which rule was violated and asks if you want to continue with the rule testing.

Field validation rules are enforced whenever you enter or edit data whether it's in the datasheet, in a form, or by means of an append or update query. These rules are also enforced on data entered by *Visual Basic for Applications* (*VBA*) code or imported from another table.

Defining a Record Validation Rule

A record validation rule is a table property rather than a field property. You can define only one record validation rule for a table, but if you want to apply more than one criterion, you can combine them in an expression using the AND or OR operators.

The record validation rule is applied whenever you enter or edit table data. When you leave a record, Access checks the new record against the rule you defined. As with field validation rules, if you define a record validation rule for a table that contains data, Access asks if you want the rule applied to the existing data when you save the table.

To add a record validation rule to a table, open the Table Properties dialog box by one of the following methods:

- Click the Properties toolbar button.

- Choose View | Properties.

- Right-click the field entry area or the table Design window title bar (if the window isn't maximized) and choose Properties from the shortcut menu.

- Press F4

Enter a description of the table in the Description property for later reference, the validation rule expression, and the text to display when the rule is violated. For example, the Expires date for a bid in the Bid Data table must be later than the Bid Date.

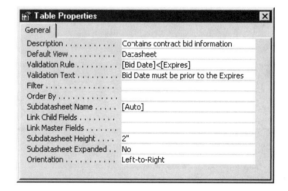

Using Field Names in Expressions

When you use a field in an expression, such as in a validation rule or to create a calculated field, the field name is called an *identifier* and must conform to certain rules. For Access to recognize the identifier as a field value, it must be enclosed in square brackets ([]).

If the field comes from a different table open in the current database, you must also add a *qualifier*. For example, to refer to the Last Name value in the Employees table, use the identifier: Employees![Last Name]. The bang (!) operator tells Access that what follows is a name created by the user.

When you use an object name in an expression, such as the Employees table name, you needn't enclose it in square brackets unless it contains a space or a special character, such as an underscore.

Requiring an Entry and Preventing Duplicates

One of the field properties is Required, which is set to Yes or No. The default value is No, but you can change it to Yes if the field should never be left blank. For example, every employee record must have a Social Security number, so you would change the field's Required property to Yes.

  All field and index properties that have only Yes and No settings can be toggled back and forth by double-clicking the property box.

The Indexed property helps prevent duplicate values. A single-field primary key field always requires unique values, but you can have only one such field in a table. You might want to prevent duplication in other fields without assigning them as the primary key. To add this restriction, change the field's Indexed property to Yes (No Duplicates). If you open the Indexes window, you see the new single-field index with its Unique property set to Yes.

You can prevent duplicate values in a group of fields by creating a multiple-field index on the combination of fields. Once the index is created, change the Unique property in the lower pane of the Indexes window to Yes. Then no two combinations of the values in these fields may be the same.

Handling Blank Fields

You might leave a field blank because you don't know the value or because no value exists for that field in that record. Access distinguishes between those two kinds of blank values with Null values and zero-length strings.

A *Null value* indicates a missing or unknown value for the field. You would leave a field blank if you don't know the value or it isn't relevant to the current record. Access recognizes this and stores the value as a Null value. Pressing ENTER without entering anything stores a Null value.

A *zero-length string* is a string that contains no characters. If you know no value exists for this field (not that you simply don't know what the value is), you enter a zero-length string by pressing SPACEBAR or by typing a pair of double quotation marks ("") with no space between. The marks disappear when you move to the next field, but Access stores a zero-length string.

A good demonstration of the difference between Null values and a zero-length string is the Pager field in the Customers table. If you don't know if the customer has a pager or, if she does, but you don't know the number, leave it blank. If you know the customer doesn't have a pager, enter a zero-length string.

Two special field properties control how blank fields are handled. The Required property determines whether a blank field is acceptable or the field must contain a value. The Allow Zero Length property, when set to Yes, permits zero-length strings. This property is available only to Text, Memo, and Hyperlink fields.

These two properties work together as follows:

- If you want to leave the field blank and don't care why it is blank, set both the Required and Allow Zero Length properties to No. This is the default combination setting for new Text, Memo, or Hyperlink fields.

- If you never want to leave a field blank, set Required to Yes and Allow Zero Length to No. You cannot leave the field without entering a value, even if it's only "Don't know" or "None."

- If you want to tell why the field is blank, set Required to No and Allow Zero Length to Yes. Then you would leave the field blank if the information isn't known or enter quotation marks ("") to indicate the field doesn't apply to the current record (no pager exists).

- If you want to leave the field blank only if you know the field isn't relevant to a record, set both properties to Yes. Then the only way for you to leave the field blank is to enter a zero-length string either by typing "" or pressing the SPACEBAR.

Table 4-13 shows the results of three methods of leaving blank values with the two properties set in all possible combinations. To leave a field blank, you can press ENTER, press the SPACEBAR, or type "".

Required	Allow Zero Length	Action	Resulting Value
No	No	Press ENTER.	<Null>
		Press SPACEBAR.	<Null>
		Type "".	Not allowed
Yes	No	Press ENTER.	Not allowed
		Press SPACEBAR.	Not allowed
		Type "".	Not allowed
No	Yes	Press ENTER.	<Null>
		Press SPACEBAR.	<Zero-length string>
		Type "".	<Zero-length string>
Yes	Yes	Press ENTER.	<Null>
		Press SPACEBAR.	<Zero-length string>
		Type "".	<Zero-length string>

Table 4-13. *The Results of Entering Blank Values*

GETTING STARTED

Note *When you allow blank fields, you can still use the Find and Replace options from the Edit menu to locate fields with Null values or zero-length strings. To find records with blank values, place the insertion point in the field and choose Edit | Find or click the Find toolbar button. Type* **Null** *in the Find What box to find the Null values or type "" to find fields with zero-length strings. In the Match box, be sure to ask Access to match the whole field or you'll find a lot of fields with blanks between words. Also be sure to clear the Search Fields As Formatted check box. See Chapter 6 for more information about locating specific records.*

Assigning a Default Value

If one of your fields usually has the same value—for example, the State field in a list of local customers—use the Default Value property to have that value automatically entered when you add a new record. You can still change it to a different value when you enter data, but a default value can save time during data entry, especially if it's a long value like California or Pennsylvania. A newly assigned default value doesn't affect values already entered in the table; only new entries are affected.

A default value can be assigned to any type of field except an AutoNumber or OLE Object. To assign one, enter the value in the Default Value property for the field. The type of value you enter depends on the data type. The value must also conform to the property settings and data type requirements. Some examples of default values are

Field	Data Type	Value
State	Text	CA
City	Text	"Los Padres" (If the value contains punctuation or spaces, it must be enclosed in quotation marks.)
Hours	Number	8
Deposit	Currency	500
Entry Date	Date/Time	Date() (Automatically enters current system date.)

 If you assign or change a default field value after entering record data, you can change the existing values to the new value by pressing CTRL-ALT-SPACEBAR *with the insertion point in the field.*

 If you want to assign a Yes/No field default value for use in a foreign country, enter an equal sign before the choice (=Yes) and the equivalent word from the local language will be displayed. For example, a Yes value would be displayed as Oui *in France.*

Inherited Properties

Other database objects, such as queries, forms, and reports inherit most of the properties you specify for the underlying table. For consistency, a good practice is to set the properties in table Design view so all objects based on the table inherit the same properties. If you need to modify a property setting later for a specific form or report, the change doesn't affect the underlying table.

A query inherits all the properties of the underlying table by default. If you change a property in table Design view after creating the query, the change is automatically inherited by the query, unless you already customized the query properties and overridden the inherited properties. When you change a property in the query design, the change blocks more property changes from the table design, but has no effect on the table.

Fields used in form and report designs also inherit table properties. Which properties they inherit depends on the type of field. Properties such as Format, Decimal Places, Input Mask, and Status Bar Text (from the Description in the field row) are inherited properties. The Default Value, Validation Rule, and Validation Text aren't inherited, but they are enforced. In other words, the setting for these properties don't appear in the control's property sheet, but Access enforces them. If you change the Default Value property in the form design, it overrides the field property previously set in table Design view.

See Chapter 10 for more information about form and report controls, and their properties.

Creating a New Table in Datasheet View

You needn't be in Design view to create a new table; you can do it right in Datasheet view by entering data directly into a blank datasheet. Access automatically analyzes the data you enter and assigns the appropriate Data Type and Format to the field. If any ambiguity occurs, the field is considered to be a Text field.

To begin a new table in Datasheet view, do the following:

1. Start a new datasheet by one of the following methods:

   ■ Double-click the Create Table by Entering Data item in the Database window.

   ■ Open the New Table dialog box, choose Datasheet view, and then click OK.

2. A blank datasheet opens displaying ten columns and twenty-one rows. The columns are named Field1, Field2, and so on.

3. Enter the field names in each column by double-clicking the column header and replacing the default Field*n* caption. If you enter the fields in the wrong order, you can always change the order later in Design view.

4. Enter the field data for each record, and then click Design view.

To copy the field value from the previous record, use the ditto key combination, CTRL-' (apostrophe).

5. Switch to Design view and save the table with the desired name. Access offers to assign a primary key when it saves the new table or you can designate one in Design view.

Figure 4-15 shows the design of a table created in Datasheet view.

Access has automatically assigned data types to the fields depending on the data you entered. The unused fields are also eliminated from the design.

Copying an Existing Table Structure

If you already have a table with a structure similar to what you need now, you can save time by copying the structure to a new table without the data. Then change the

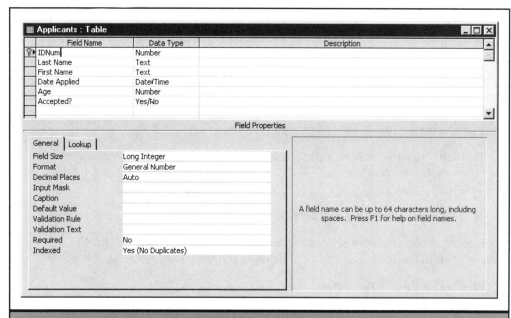

Figure 4-15. *The design of table created in Datasheet view*

field names and properties as necessary. To copy the table structure, follow these steps:
Select the existing table name in the Database window.

1. Click Copy on the toolbar or choose Edit | Copy.

2. If you want to copy the structure to a different database, close the current one and open the target database; otherwise, keep the Database window open.

3. Click Paste or choose Edit | Paste to open the Paste Table As dialog box.

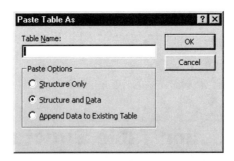

4. Enter a name for the new table, choose Structure Only, and then click OK.

The new table inherits the field properties from the original table.

Setting Table Properties

Two types of table properties are available in an Access database: table object properties and table definition properties. *Table object properties* include name, owner, dates of creation and last revision, and attributes, such as Hidden or Replicable. You can view these properties by one of the following methods:

- Right-click the table name in the Database window and choose Properties from the shortcut menu.

- Select the table name and choose View | Properties.

- Select the table name and click the Properties button.

Table definition properties related to the table structure itself are available when the table is open in Design view. To open the table property sheet, do one of the following:

- Choose View | Properties.

- Click the Properties toolbar button.

- Right-click the field entry area and choose Properties from the shortcut menu.

This is the same properties sheet shown earlier when entering a record validation rule. Table 4-14 describes these table properties.

Property	Description
Description	The text that appears in the Description column in the Database window when you select Details view for the tables list.
Default View	Sets the default display arrangement for the table data: Datasheet, PivotTable or PivotChart.
Validation Rule	Defines a rule that applies to complete records in the table.
Validation Text	Message displayed in the status bar when the validation rule is violated.
Filter	Sets a selection criterion and the Order By property establishes the sort order.
Order By	The sort order saved with the table. Can be applied when table data is used as the basis for a form or report.
Subdatasheet Name	The name of the related table, if any, or [Auto].
Link Child Fields	The field or fields in the child table that link it to the master table.
Link Master Fields	The field or fields in the master table that link it to the child table.
Subdatasheet Height	The default height measure for displaying the subdatasheet with the master datasheet. Default is 2".
Subdatasheet Expanded	When set to Yes, automatically displays the subdatasheet without clicking the expansion sign (+).
Orientation	Sets the reading order, alignment, and visual appearance of bidirectional text and documents. Default is left-to-right.

Table 4-14.   *Table Properties*

How to Change the Default Table Design Properties

You learned earlier that the default field size for a Text field is 50 characters. This is one of the default table design properties you can change. To modify this and other default properties, choose Tools | Options, and then click the Tables/Queries tab (see Figure 4-16). The options include

- **Text Field Size (default 50)** To change the default Text field size, enter the desired number.
- **Number Field Size (default Long Integer)** To change the Number field, choose from the drop-down list of Number field sizes.
- **Default Field Type (default Text)** To change the default field type, choose from the drop-down list of field types. Notice the list doesn't include Lookup Wizard as a field type.
- **AutoIndex on Import/Create** This option gives you the opportunity to specify text often used at the beginning or ending of a field name as the basis for indexes when importing or creating tables. For example, typing **"ID";"num";"code"** automatically creates indexes for all fields containing those characters either at the start or the end of the field name. For example, with this setting, an imported table would be indexed on fields named Customer ID, JobNum, and ZIP code.

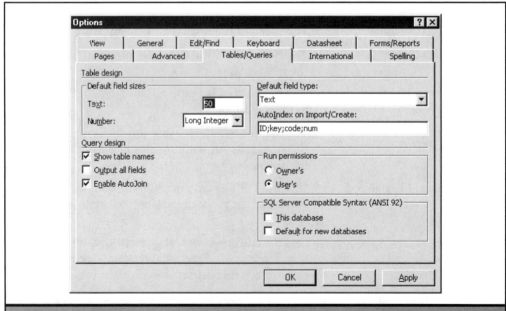

Figure 4-16. Setting the table design default properties

Summary

This chapter contained a great deal of information about constructing and modifying new Access tables, beginning with the Table Wizard. A table was also created by entering field specifications directly into a blank table design. It included choosing the best data type depending on what value you intend to store in the field and the operations with which you intend to use it. Other field properties were discussed as were primary key fields and creating indexes on one or more fields.

Modifying a table structure can be troublesome in some cases, such as changing the data type or shortening the field size. Ensuring data validity is one of the most important features Access offers. Several means were discussed, including requiring specific fields, adding validity rules, and assigning default values.

In the next chapter, you learn how to relate tables by linking the common field. The chapter also covers specifying the type of relationship and modifying an existing relationship. It also discusses the types of joins that control the way data is retrieved by queries.

MOUS Exam Activities Explored in This Chapter

Level	Activity	Section Title
Core	Open database objects in multiple views	Switching Table Views
Core	Create and modify tables	Creating a New Table Structure with the Table Wizard Creating a New Table from Scratch Creating a New Table in Datasheet View
Core	Modify field properties	Changing the Field Order Changing a Field Name or Type Changing a Field Size Modifying or Deleting the Primary Key Assigning a Default Value
Expert	Use data validation	Defining Field Validation Rules Defining Record Validation Rules Ensuring Data Validity Requiring an Entry and Preventing Duplicates

Chapter 5

Relating Tables

The advantages of relating tables in a database are many. For example, information retrieval routines operate much faster with matched fields and errors are less likely to get into the database during data entry. Tables related at the table level are ready for use in queries, forms reports, and data access pages. When tables are related, you can add a subform or subreport that includes corresponding information from the related table.

You can define relationships between tables at any time, but the best time is when the tables are new and contain little or no data. When you design the database, one of the important steps is to decide on the relationships between the tables and which fields they have in common. As you create new tables, the Table Wizard can help you define relationships or you can wait until you have all the table structures built, and then define all the relationships at once.

Defining a Relationship

To define a relationship between two tables, all you need to do is specify which fields the tables have in common. In a one-to-many relationship, the field in the parent table is called the *primary key* and must be either the table's primary key or a unique index. The field in the child table is called the *foreign key* and it needn't have a unique value. Data retrieval is faster, however, if the child table is indexed on the foreign key.

In a one-to-one relationship, both fields are primary keys or unique indexes in their tables. A many-to-many relationship is really two one-to-many relationships in which a third table is created whose primary key is a combination of the common fields from the other two tables. The junction table becomes the "one" side for relationships to both the original tables.

Defining table relationships at the table level keeps the relationships active and makes the database easier to use. You can link two tables temporarily in a query when you want to draw information from more than one table, but the permanent relationship is preferred. You can always break it later if necessary.

Ready-Made Relationships

If you used the Table Wizard to create a new table, you may already have some defined relationships with the other tables in your database. As you saw in Chapter 4, when you add a new table to your database with the help of the Table Wizard, one of the dialog boxes asks you to specify how the new table is to relate to the existing tables in the database, if at all.

The first database illustrated in this chapter was created by adding tables to a blank database with the Table Wizard. Figure 5-1 shows the relationships created by the Table Wizard that link the existing Employees and Customers tables to the newly created Time Billed table. The Employees and Customers tables weren't linked until the Time Billed table was added to the database.

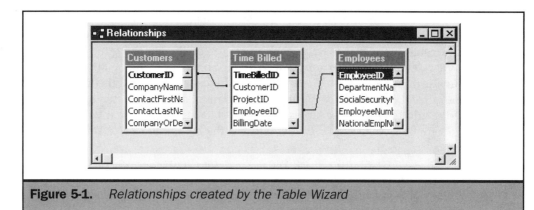

Figure 5-1. *Relationships created by the Table Wizard*

The sequence in which you add tables to the database determines which relationships the wizard automatically builds. If you added the Time Billed table before the Employees table, Access wouldn't relate the Employees table to the Time Billed table.

The lack of symbols at the ends of the relationship lines indicates that referential integrity rules aren't enforced. When the Table Wizard creates a relationship, it doesn't automatically set referential integrity. To add this, you must modify the relationship in the Relationships window. You can still tell which is the "one" side of a one-to-many relationship by the primary key, which appears in bold. Because it must have a unique value, only one record in that table can match the field in the other table.

Using the Relationships Window

Access provides a powerful, graphical tool to help you define and modify relationships. The Relationships window has all the tools you need to add a table

Creating a Relationship with the Lookup Wizard

The Lookup Wizard field data type was introduced in Chapter 4. When you define a field by choosing the Lookup Wizard data type in the table design, you have a choice of entering a list of values or retrieving the values from another table or query. If you choose to enter a list of values, the list is stored with the table. If you choose to get values from another table, such as the Categories table in the Northwind database, you must tell Access where to find the values and a relationship is defined between the tables.

The Lookup table field is the primary key and the Lookup column in the base table is the foreign key. See Chapter 6 for more information about using the Lookup Wizard to define a field.

to the relationship, relate the tables, specify the type of relationship, set up the referential integrity rules, and choose the join type. To open the Relationships window, choose Tools | Relationships, or click the Relationships button on the Database toolbar. If no relationships are defined in the current database, the Show Table dialog box appears in a blank Relationships window. The dialog box displays a list of all the tables and queries in the current database (see Figure 5-2). This database was created by using the Table Wizard to add the first three tables to a blank database. Then the Invoices table was created from the table Design window without the help of the Table Wizard.

If any relationships already exist between tables in the database, Access goes directly to the Relationships window without displaying the Show Table dialog box. To add a table to the Relationships window, click the Show Table button or choose Relationships | Show Table to open the Show Table dialog box.

To add the tables you want to relate from the list, do one of the following:

- Double-click the table's name or select the table and click the Add button.
- To select multiple adjacent tables, select the first table to be included, hold down SHIFT as you select the last table in the list to be included, and then click the Add button. If the table names aren't adjacent in the list, hold down CTRL while you select the names.
- Click the Queries tab to add a query to the Relationships window.
- Click the Both tab to have access to a combined list of tables and queries.

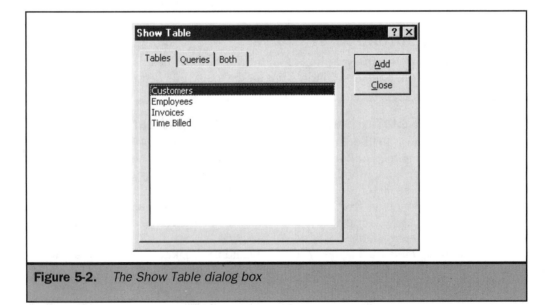

Figure 5-2. *The Show Table dialog box*

After you add all the tables and queries you want to work with in the Relationships window, click Close.

Touring the Relationships Window

The Relationships window shows the field lists of the tables you chose. The lists display the primary key field, if any, in boldface. Use the scroll bars to see all the fields, or resize a field list box by dragging the bottom border to see more names or the right border to see complete field names. You can also drag the field list boxes around in the window for better viewing. Figure 5-3 shows the Relationships window with all four tables, three created by the Table Wizard, and the Invoices table created from scratch. Relationships exist only among the first three.

 Note *If you use the Table Wizard to create all four of the tables, they would all show relationships.*

Before going on to join the tables, look at the new toolbar buttons on the Relationships toolbar and menu options in the Relationships window. Table 5-1 describes the buttons and their menu bar equivalents.

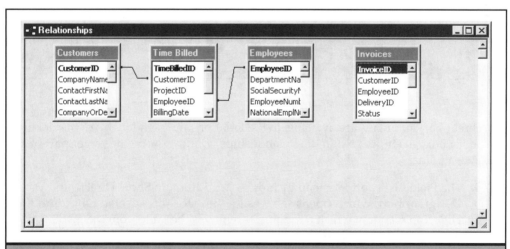

Figure 5-3. *The Relationships window shows the selected tables*

Button	Name	Menu Equivalent	Description
	Show Table	Relationships | Show Table. Also available in Relationships window shortcut menu.	Opens the Show Table dialog box with lists of all tables and queries in the current database.
	Show Direct Relationships	Relationships | Show Direct. Also available in Field List shortcut menu.	Displays the relationships for the selected table. If all related tables are already displayed, this has no effect on the display in the Relationships window.
	Show All Relationships	Relationships | Show All. Also available in Relationships window shortcut menu.	Displays all relationships in the current database. If all tables are already displayed, this has no effect on the display in the Relationships window.
	Clear Layout	Edit | Clear Layout.	Removes the display of all tables and relationships from the Relationships window. This doesn't alter the relationships themselves.

Table 5-1. *The Relationships Window Toolbar Buttons*

Three shortcut menus are available in the Relationships window by right-clicking a field list box, an empty area in the Relationships window, or on the center part of a relationship line:

■ The Field List shortcut menu includes—in addition to Show Direct—the Table Design option, which opens the Design view for the selected table, and the Hide Table option, which temporarily removes the table from the display, not the layout. Hide Table is also available from the Relationships menu.

■ The Relationships window shortcut menu includes—in addition to Show Table and Show All—the Save Layout option, which saves the current arrangement of field list boxes in the Relationships window.

■ The Relationship line shortcut menu includes Edit Relationship, which opens the Edit Relationships dialog box, and Delete, which removes relationships between the tables. Edit Relationship is also available from the Relationships menu.

Drawing the Relationship Line

It couldn't be easier to relate two tables. You simply drag a field (usually the primary key) from one table and drop it on the corresponding field (the foreign key) in the other table. The field names needn't be the same, but they usually need to be the same data type and contain the same kind of information. If you intend to enforce referential integrity, the fields must be the same data type. If the fields are Number fields, they must also have the same Field Size property.

Two exceptions occur to the requirement to match data types in the related fields.

■ An AutoNumber field with the New Values property set to Increment can be linked to a Long Integer Number field. AutoNumber values are stored as four-byte numbers. For the foreign key to have a matching value, it must contain a number of the same size: a Long Integer.

■ An AutoNumber can be linked to a Number field if both fields have the Field Size property set to Replication ID.

Tip *Dragging the foreign key field from the related table to the primary key field in the primary table creates the same relationship.*

To relate the Customer table to the Invoices table by CustomerID, do the following:

1. Click the CustomerID field in the Customers field list and drag it to the CustomerID field in the Invoices field list.

2. Drop the linking field into the child table. The Edit Relationships dialog box opens (see Figure 5-4).

Tip *Notice that Access recognizes this relationship as a one-to-many because one of the fields is a primary key and the other is not. If both fields were primary keys, Access would recognize the relationship as one-to-one. If neither field is a primary key nor has a unique value, Access calls the relationship Indeterminate.*

3. Verify the field names that relate the tables, and then do one of the following.

■ If you want to change the field at either side of the relationship, you can select a different field from the drop-down field list under the table name.

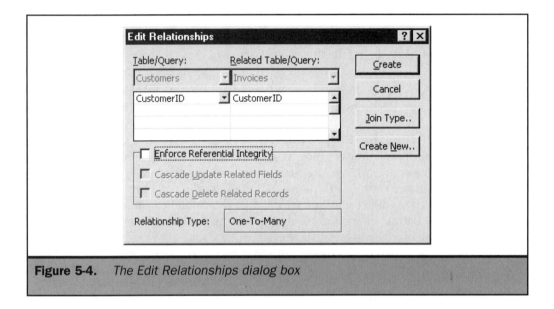

Figure 5-4. The Edit Relationships dialog box

- If you want to add another relationship between the same tables that relates two different fields, move to an empty row in the grid, click the down button, and choose from the list for each table.

- If you chose the wrong foreign key, choose Cancel in the Edit Relationships dialog box and start over in the Relationships window.

Tip *If you type the first few letters of the field name in the Edit Relationships dialog box grid, Access will fill in the rest for you.*

1. To complete the relationship, choose Create and you return to the Relationships window. Figure 5-5 shows the Relationships window with the new link drawn between the tables.

2. Repeat the procedure above to draw the relationship line from the EmployeeID field in the Employees field list to the EmployeeID field in the Invoices field list.

Note *When an Access wizard creates a relationship, it doesn't automatically check referential integrity. You can tell by the relationship lines that referential integrity hasn't been set. When it is set, symbols representing the relationship type appear at each end of the line.*

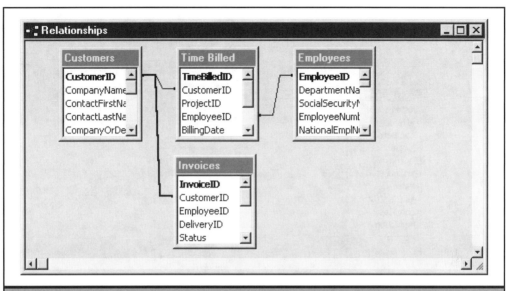

Figure 5-5. *A relationship line is drawn between two tables*

Relating to Two or More Foreign Keys

If you need to create relationships from a primary table to two or more foreign keys in the same table, Access creates additional instances of the table in the Relationships window. You don't have two copies of the table in the database, only in the Relationships layout. Figure 5-6 shows a Relationships window with three copies of the Employees table with the EmployeeID primary key field relating to the Supervisor, Principal Worker, and Helper foreign keys in the Workorders table.

Note, the relationships all have referential integrity enforced, as you can tell by the symbols at the ends of the relationship lines. Referential integrity is discussed in the next section.

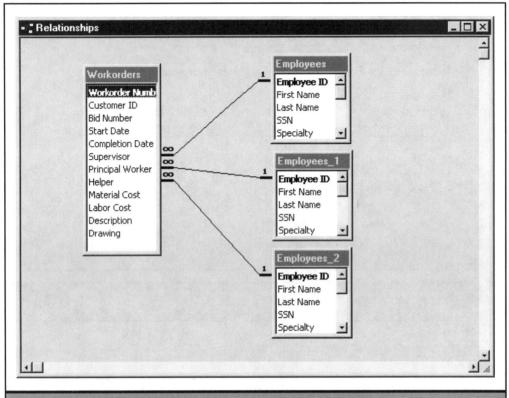

Figure 5-6. *Relating one table to three fields in another table*

Enforcing Referential Integrity

As discussed in Chapter 2, referential integrity is a set of rules that attempts to keep a database complete and without loose ends. No related records can exist without a parent. When you want Access to enforce the referential integrity rules on the relationship you are defining, check Enforce Referential Integrity in the Edit Relationships dialog box. If, for some reason, the tables already violate one of the rules, such as the related fields not being of the same data type, Access displays a message explaining the violation and doesn't apply the enforcement.

Referential integrity isn't enforced on queries included in a relationship.

When you check the Enforce Referential Integrity option, two options become available that let you override some restrictions. When you set these options, you're permitted to perform delete and update operations that normally wouldn't be allowed.

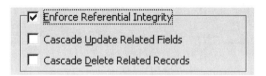

With these options checked, if you delete a record from the parent table or change one of the primary key values, Access automatically makes changes to the child table to preserve referential integrity. Without checking one of these options, Access displays a warning message if you try to delete a parent record that still has child records.

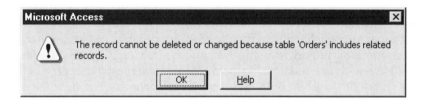

The Cascade Update Related Fields option lets you change the value in the primary key field in the parent table and Access automatically changes the foreign key value in the child table to match. For example, if you change the CustomerID value in the Customers table, all records for that customer in any related table are automatically updated to the new value. This option preserves the relationship. Access doesn't display a message that the update operation is taking place. If the primary key in a table serves as a link to more than one table, you must set the Cascade Update Related Fields property for each of the relationships. If not, Access displays a message that referential integrity rules would be violated by the cascading operation and refuses to delete or update the record.

Note *Setting the Cascade Update option has no effect if the primary key is an AutoNumber field because you can't change the value of an AutoNumber field.*

The Cascade Delete Related Records option enables you to delete a parent record, and then Access automatically deletes all the related child records. When you try to delete a record from the parent table of a relationship with this option selected, Access warns you that this record and the ones in related tables will be deleted. For example, if you delete an Employee record, Access automatically deletes all the records for that employee in the related tables.

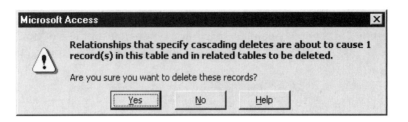

 Caution *Setting the Cascade Delete Related Fields property can be dangerous. If you delete records using a Delete query, Access automatically deletes the related records without issuing a warning.*

Creating a One-to-One Relationship

At times, you might want to store information about a particular subject—such as an item of merchandise or an employee—separate from the main pieces of information. For example, you may have data about an employee, such as name, address, and Social Security number in one table where they're readily available, but keep other data, such as the resume and employment history, in another table. These two tables are then related using a one-to-one relationship because only one record in each table matches one record in the other table. Both tables include a primary key field such as the employee identification number.

To relate two tables with a one-to-one relationship, do the following:

1. Choose Tools | Relationships or click the Relationships toolbar button in the Database window.

2. If the tables you want to relate don't appear in the Relationships window, click the Show Table button.

3. Select the tables in the Show Table dialog box, and then click Close.

4. Drag the primary key field from one table and drop it on the key field on the other table. The direction you go doesn't matter; the same one-to-one relationship is created.

Specifying the Join Type

One of the most powerful Access tools is the query that extracts and brings together data from more than one source. Many queries also carry out an action with the data. For example, you may want to see how much time each employee spent working on service for each current customer. To do so, you need information from the Time Billed, Employees, and Customers tables. Once the data is extracted, the query adds up the hours for records with matching employees and customers.

For a query to know how to associate records from the three tables, the tables must be related. When you define the relationship, you can also specify the type of join you want for the tables. The join type specifies which records to display in a query based on

How to Create a Many-to-Many Relationship

In a many-to-many relationship, a record in one table (call it Table A) can have several matching records in another table (Table B) and vice versa. Neither table is considered the parent table because the linking field isn't the primary key in either table. The only way you can create such a relationship is by creating a third table, called a *junction* table. This new table has a primary key that's actually a combination of at least the primary keys from tables A and B. The junction table acts as a bridge between the two tables when you build two one-to-many relationships between them. You can add other fields to the junction table like any other table.

Figure 5-7 shows a junction table linking the Orders and Products tables. Because several products could be included in a single order and several orders could include the same product, this represents a many-to-many relationship. To define the relationship in Access, the junction table Order Details was created with a primary key that combines the foreign keys from the Products table (ProductID) and from the Orders table (OrderID). Both field names appear in boldface in the Order Details table, indicating that, together, they constitute the primary key. Two one-to-many relationships then link the Products and Orders tables to the Order Details table.

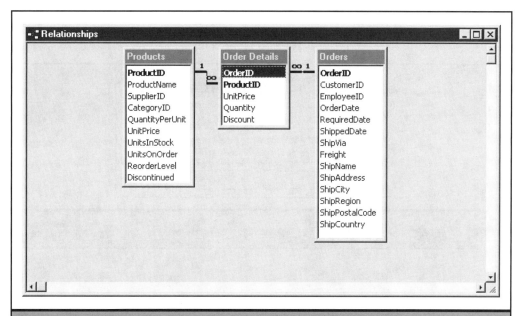

Figure 5-7.   *Creating a junction table for a many-to-many relationship*

related tables when they don't correspond exactly. For example, do you want the parent record to appear only if corresponding child records exist or do you want to see all parent records even if there are no related child records?

The join type doesn't affect the relationship, it just tells Access which records to include in a query.

To modify the relationship between the Employees and Invoices tables, and set the join type, do the following.

1. In the Relationships window, right-click in the middle of the relationships line joining the Employees table with the Invoices table and choose Edit Relationship from the shortcut menu. The Edit Relationships dialog box opens.

2. Click the Join Type button. Figure 5-8 shows the Join Properties dialog box.

3. Select option 2 as the type of join for this relationship because you want to see all the Employee records even if they have no related records in the Invoices table. Notice the explanatory text is specific with respect to the tables you related.

4. Click OK in the Join Properties dialog box.

5. Click OK in the Edit Relationships dialog box.

Figure 5-9 shows the completed layout for four tables in a database that tracks customer billing and prepares invoices. The relationships that include referential integrity show a 1 on the "one" side and an infinity sign (∞) on the "many" side.

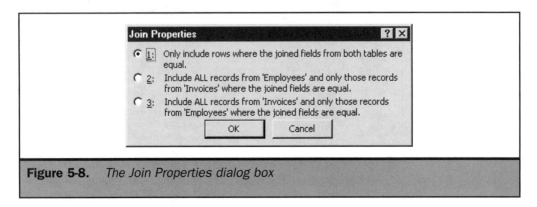

Figure 5-8.   *The Join Properties dialog box*

Understanding Joins

You can specify three types of joins through the Join Properties dialog box:

- Option 1 includes only records where both parent and child have the same values in the linking fields (no orphans and no childless parents). This is called an *inner join* or an *equijoin* and it's the default join type.

- Option 2 includes all the records from the table on the left, even if no corresponding values are in the other and only the matching records from the table on the right. This is called *a left outer join* (all parents, including the childless, but no orphans).

- Option 3 is the opposite of option 2 and includes all the records from the table on the right and only matching records from the left table. Called a *right outer join* (all children but no childless parents). If Referential Integrity is enforced, there will be no children without a parent.

If you have trouble deciding which table is the "left" in the relationship, look at how we read a sentence: from left to right. Read a relationship from primary table (left) to related table (right). Physical positioning in the layout doesn't matter.

If you select an outer join, an arrow at one end of the relation line points to the table whose value must match to be included in the query results. In a one-to-many relationship, the one side is considered the left table and the many side is the right table.

Note, you can also create a fourth type of join: a *self join*, which includes records from two instances of the same table. For example, you can add a self join to a query design to display the Supervisor's name instead of the Supervisor ID when extracting records from the Employees table. The Supervisor's name is in the Name field in the Employee record with the Supervisor ID value in the EmployeeID field. See Chapter 8 for more information about queries.

Relationships with no referential integrity enforced appear as lines with small dots at each end. Relationship lines with no arrows represent inner joins. An arrow on a relationship line means the join is an outer join and the arrow points to the table whose values must match to be included in the query results. The relationship between Employees and Time Billed tables is a left outer join with referential integrity enforced.

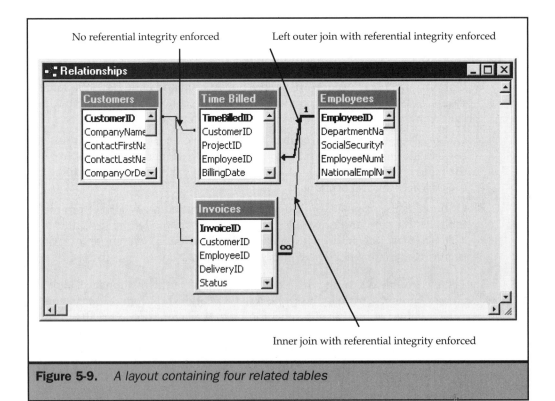

Figure 5-9. *A layout containing four related tables*

Saving the Relationships Layout

All relationships are saved when you create them. You can also save the *layout*, the arrangement of the field lists in the Relationships window. Saving the layout has no effect on the tables in the database.

To save the layout, do one of the following:

■ Right-click anywhere in the Relationships window (except on a field list) and choose Save Layout from the Relationships shortcut menu.

■ Choose File | Save.

■ Press CTRL-S.

If you made changes in the layout and try to close the Relationships window without saving the layout, Access prompts you to save it. If you want to discard the changes, choose No. When you open the Relationships window again, the previously saved layout is displayed.

Another Way to Tell the Kind of Join

You can read the symbols in the Relationships window and see what kind of joins you specified for the tables in the database. Another way to tell the join types explicitly is by reading the *structured query language (SQL)* statements in a query design. When you create a query, Access builds the SQL statements in the background. To see them, change the query view to SQL view. A simple select query that extracts data from the Employees and Invoices tables results in the following SQL statement.

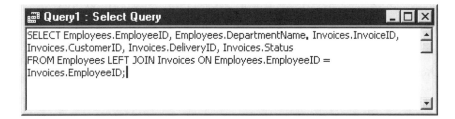

The SQL statement

FROM Employees LEFT JOIN Invoices ON Employees.EmployeeID = Invoices.EmployeeID;

specifies the join as left outer with the EmployeeID fields in both tables as the matching fields. The SELECT statement specifies the fields to include in the query results. See Chapter 9 for more information on creating advanced queries and using SQL.

 While you're defining relationships, you can always call for help. You can type a specific question in the Ask a Question box and press ENTER.

Viewing and Editing Relationships

To look at the relationships you defined for a database, open the Relationships window. If you plan on making any changes, be sure to close all open tables first.

Viewing Existing Relationships

 You have a choice of viewing all the relationships you set in your database or only those involving a specific table. In the database window, click the Relationships toolbar button or choose Tools | Relationships.

You can quickly switch to the database window by pressing F11.

In the Relationships window, do one of the following:

■ To view all the relationships in the current database, click the Show All Relationships toolbar button.

■ To see only the relationships for the table selected in the database window, click the Show Direct Relationships.

If all the relationships already appear in the Relationships window, perform the following steps to see only one table's relationships:

1. Clear the layout by clicking the Clear Layout toolbar button.

2. Click the Show Table button, double-click the table name in the Show Table dialog box, and then choose Close. This adds the table back to the Relationships window.

3. In the Relationships window, click the Show Direct Relationships button. All the tables related to the first are added to the layout and the relationship lines are drawn.

Hiding or Deleting a Table

If the Relationships window becomes too crowded, you can hide a table or delete it from the layout. To delete the table from the layout, select the table and press DEL, or choose Delete from the Edit menu. This affects only the display of the layout and doesn't remove the relationship or the table from the database.

If you want to remove the table temporarily to make room for manipulating the relationships, hide the table instead. To hide the table, choose Relationships | Hide Table, or right-click the table and choose Hide Table from the shortcut menu. The next time you view the Relationships window, all the tables will reappear, unless you save the layout with the changes.

Restoring All Relationships

To restore the relationships layout to its previous arrangement, close the window without saving the changes. When you reopen the window, the old layout returns. If you want to keep the window open, right-click in the Relationships window and choose Show All from the shortcut menu, click the Show All Relationships toolbar button or choose Relationships | Show All Relationships.

Modifying or Deleting a Relationship

Relationships aren't cast in concrete. You use the same Relationships window to edit a relationship that you used to create one.

You can even open a Table Design window from the Relationships window and modify the table structure. This comes in handy if you need to make sure the related fields are the same data type or if you want to create an index to speed processing.

 You can view the relationships while tables are open, but be sure to close all open tables before trying to modify a relationship.

Editing a Relationship

To edit an existing relationship, do the following:

1. Open the Relationships window as before.

2. If you don't see the relationship you want to change, choose Show Table from the Relationships menu, double-click the missing table, and choose Close.

3. When you see the join line that represents the relationship you want to change, do one of the following to open the Edit Relationships dialog box:

   ■ Double-click the line.

   ■ Right-click the line and choose Edit Relationship from the shortcut menu.

4. Make the changes you want, and then click OK.

 If you want to find out about a specific item in the Relationships dialog box, click the What's This button (the question mark), and then click the item. A message appears that explains what the item is for and how to use it.

Deleting a Relationship

To delete a relationship, click the join line to select it and do one of the following:

■ Press DEL.

■ Choose Delete from the Edit menu.

■ Right-click the line and choose Delete from the shortcut menu.

Access asks for confirmation before permanently deleting the relationship, no matter which method you use. Be careful not to delete a relationship used by a query.

 Pressing DEL with a table selected only removes the table from the layout, while pressing DEL with a relationship line selected permanently removes the relationship between the tables.

Changing a Table Design from the Relationships Window

You may need to make a change in a table design to create the relationship you want. For example, the primary key might be a Text field, while the foreign key is a Number field. This is all right unless you want to enforce referential integrity, which requires the same data type in both fields. You can open the child table design and change the field type to Text. If you already set a relationship between the tables, you must delete the relationship before you can change the table design. You may also want to add a secondary index on the foreign key in the child table to speed processing.

To switch to the Table Design view from the Relationships window, right-click anywhere in the table's field list box and choose Table Design from the shortcut menu. When you finish changing the table design, save the changes and close the window. You then return automatically to the Relationships window.

Printing the Relationships

Documentation is always helpful, especially if you work with several databases or develop applications for others. Once you define all the relationships for the database, graphically documenting the structure is easy.

To print the table relationships diagram, do the following:

1. In the Relationships window, right-click in an empty area and choose Show All.

2. When all tables appear in the layout, choose File | Print Relationships. Figure 5-10 shows the printed layout of the Home Tech Repair database relationships.

Although the primary key fields don't appear in bold in the printed diagram, you can use the join line symbols as a guide to the linking fields.

You may need to run Page Setup and reduce the left and right margins or change to Landscape orientation to print the entire diagram on one page.

If you want more precise information about the relationships you established in the database—including the attributes such as referential integrity and the relationship type—you can use the Documenter, one of the Access analytical tools.

1. Choose Tools | Analyze | Documenter. The Documenter dialog box opens showing eight tabs applying to the database objects and the database itself. If you see a message that the Documenter isn't installed, you can have it installed now.

2. When the Documenter dialog box opens, click the Current Database tab and select Relationships (see Figure 5-11).

3. Click OK to print the relationships in table form. A preview of the Relationships document appears after a few moments. Figure 5-12 shows the printed first page of the documented relationships that exist in the sample Northwind database that comes with Access 2002.

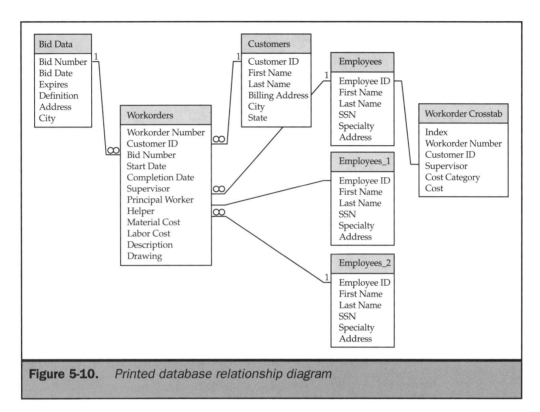

Figure 5-10. *Printed database relationship diagram*

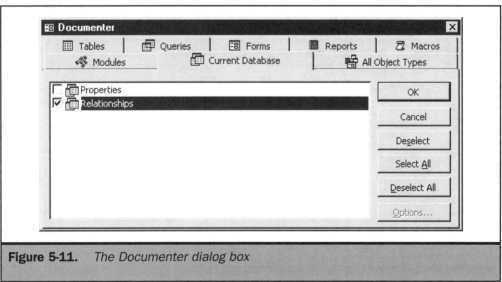

Figure 5-11. *The Documenter dialog box*

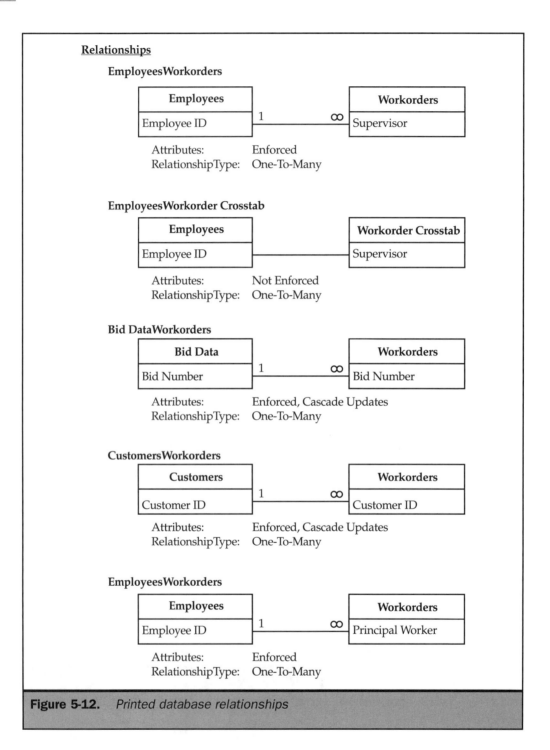

Figure 5-12. *Printed database relationships*

See Chapter 26 for more information about database administration and maintenance using the Access Analyze tools.

Summary

In these first chapters, you have learned the importance of creating relationships among tables in a database. The tables and their relationships form the structure on which the other database objects are based. Queries can extract related information from multiple sources. Forms and reports can include data from many tables.

You have seen how to create and modify tables and, in this chapter, you saw how to create and modify relationships between the tables and set other properties, such as referential integrity and join type. Referential integrity matches data from different tables and helps to ensure data validity. The join type determines which records are to be extracted by a query.

Now you are ready to move on to entering and editing the table data you'll use in later chapters. The next chapter goes into detail about entering and editing data in tables, including creating lookup lists and customizing data entry. You also see how to use the versatile Spelling tool and the AutoCorrect feature that corrects your spelling as you type.

After the information is stored in your database, the world is yours. You can retrieve some or all of the information, display it in forms, and print it in reports. You can even export it to other applications or publish it on the Internet.

MOUS Exam Activities Explored in This Chapter

Level	Activity	Section Title
Core	Create one-to-many relationships	Creating a Relationship with the Lookup Wizard Using the Relationships Window
Core	Enforce referential integrity	Modifying or Deleting a Relationship Using the Relationships Window Enforcing Referential Integrity
Expert	Establish one-to-may relationships	Using the Relationships Window—Specifying the Join Type
Expert	Establish many-to-many relationships	How to Create a Many-to-Many Relationship

The
Complete
Reference

Access
2002

Chapter 6

Entering and
Editing Data

Data errors have a way of burrowing deep into the database where they're difficult to detect and remove. Trying to prevent errors from getting into the database in the first place makes a lot of sense. Access provides many helpful tools to ensure data validity, including specifying the data type, format, field size, and validation rules discussed in Chapter 4.

This chapter discusses more tools that improve the chances for achieving data validity, as well as speeding the data entry process. Techniques such as copying quantities of data from other sources, selecting values from lookup lists, and using shortcut keys all help ease the chore of data entry. Other tools, such as the spelling checker and AutoCorrect features, also help to keep the database accurate and complete.

Entering New Data

When you open a new table, it appears in Datasheet view, ready for data entry. To add a new record, do one of the following:

- Click the New Record toolbar button.
- Click the New Record navigation button.
- Choose Edit | Go To | New Record.
- Choose Insert | New Record.

To navigate among records, use the vertical scroll bar, the navigation buttons at the bottom of the Datasheet view window, keyboard shortcuts, or the Go To command in the Edit menu. To move among fields or columns, use the horizontal scroll bar, the TAB or ENTER keys, or keyboard shortcuts. See Chapter 1 for details about moving about in Datasheet view.

When the insertion point moves to an empty field, type in the data. If you specified a custom format, the entered value adapts to that format when you move to the next column. If you created an input mask for that field, the mask appears when you enter the field and before you begin to type the data. See a later section in this chapter for details about input masks and how they compare with display format settings.

Date/time data can be entered in any valid format and Access converts it to the format you specified in the field property. Don't try to enter decimal fractions in number fields that are defined as integers.

Choosing Records | Data Entry opens a blank datasheet for the current table where you can enter new records without having to view the existing records. This is called the data entry or add mode and can be applied to forms, as well as to datasheets. After entering the new data and closing the additive datasheet, the new records are added to the underlying table.

When the table contains many fields, some of them may not always be visible. Instead of scrolling right and left to enter data in long records, you can use the Go To Field box on the Formatting (Datasheet) toolbar.

The Formatting (Datasheet) toolbar may already be showing when you're in Datasheet view, but if you don't see it, you can display it easily. Right-click the menu bar or another toolbar and click Formatting (Datasheet) in the list. You can also choose View | Toolbars and select Formatting (Datasheet) from the list.

The Go To Field box is leftmost on the toolbar and contains a list of all the fields in the current datasheet. Click the arrow next to the box to display the list of fields in the current table (see Figure 6-1). When you click a field name in the list, the insertion point moves to that field in the current record.

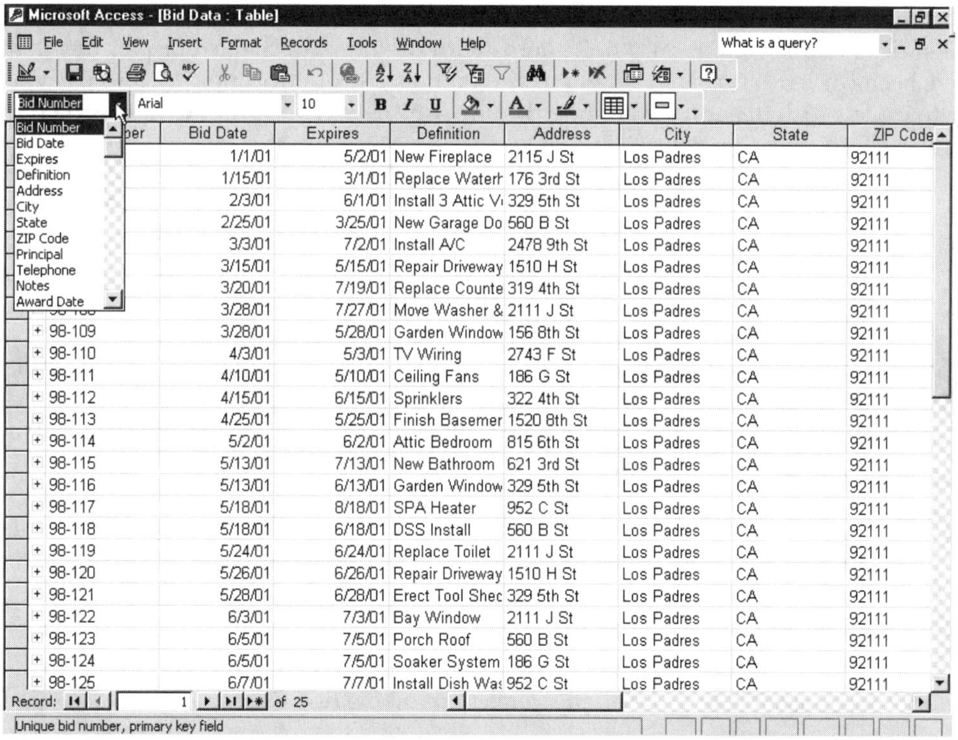

Figure 6-1. *The Go To Field box shows a list of all fields in the datasheet*

Entering a large amount of text in a Memo field can be difficult in Datasheet view. One way to see all the text in the field is to use the Zoom box while you're entering the data. Press SHIFT-F2 to open the Zoom box and press ENTER to close it after entering the text. If you want to start a new paragraph or enter a blank line in the memo text in the Zoom box, press CTRL-ENTER. The Zoom box isn't limited to Memo fields. It can be used anywhere text is entered to give you a larger entry area.

Copying and Moving Data

Access provides some shortcuts for entering repetitive data by copying or moving existing data. You can copy or move all the data or only individual field values from one record to another. Copying creates exact duplicates of the data in the new location. Moving cuts the data from one location and places it in another, leaving only one copy of the data.

When you collect items by copying or cutting them from their source, they're placed on the Office clipboard, which is shared by all Office programs. In Office 2000, the clipboard was a toolbar that could hold up to 12 items. In Office XP, the clipboard is a side pane that can hold up to 24 items with previews of the text or pictures that have been copied. You can paste them singly or as a group to a new location. If you try to place a 25th item on the clipboard, a message asks if you want to delete the first item or not to copy the 25th.

To paste an item from the clipboard, place the insertion point where you want to paste it and click the item in the clipboard. To delete an item from the clipboard, click the down arrow to the right of the item and choose Delete from the menu. To close the clipboard side pane, click the Close button in the upper-right corner. To display it later, choose Edit | Office Clipboard or click the icon on the Windows taskbar.

You can modify the behavior of the clipboard by clicking the Options button at the bottom of the pane. The options include Automatically Show Office Clipboard, Always Copy to Office Clipboard, Show Office Clipboard Icon on Taskbar, and Show Tips When Copying. All but the second option are selected by default.

You can cut or copy items using the Edit menu or the toolbar buttons. You can also display the Clipboard side pane and use it to copy-and-paste items.

- Click Copy to add the selected item to the clipboard.
- Select one item in the clipboard and click Paste.
- Click Paste All to paste all the items to the same document.

The items you've collected on the clipboard remain there until you close all the Office programs you have running on your computer. If a number of items are still on the clipboard when you close Access, Access asks if you want to keep them there for use by another Office program.

GETTING STARTED

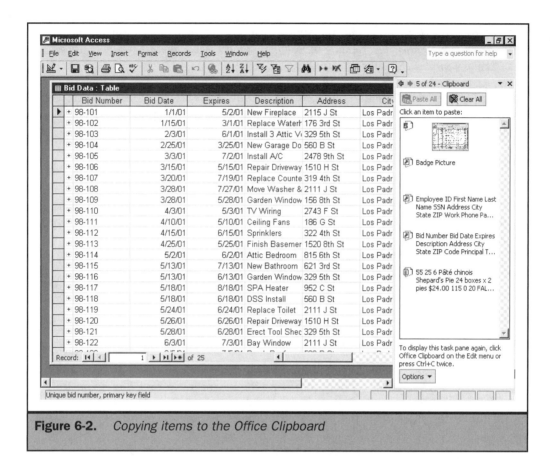

Figure 6-2.   *Copying items to the Office Clipboard*

Copying and Moving Within the Same Table

To copy a record within the same table, first select the record you want to copy by clicking the record selector—the small gray button to the left of the record. Then click the Copy toolbar button or choose Edit | Copy. This copies the data to the clipboard. Click the record selector in the record you want to replace and click Paste. The new record contains an exact copy of the original record. If you want to add the copy as a new record rather than replace an existing one, select the empty record at the bottom of the datasheet, and then click Paste Append. To remove the data, once the record is selected, use the Cut option instead of Copy.

Access tries to save the copied record when you move out of it. If the table has a primary key or a unique index, Access won't let you leave the new record until you replace the duplicate value with a unique one.

If the primary key field is an AutoNumber data type, Access automatically increments the number rather than copying the original number—just another reason to use an AutoNumber field as the primary key.

To copy or move more than one record, select all the records before choosing Copy or Cut. When replacing records, select the same number of existing records as you placed on the clipboard, and then click Paste. If you want to append the new records to the table instead of replacing existing ones, do one of the following:

- Select the new empty row at the bottom of the datasheet and click Paste.
- Choose Edit | Paste Append.

In either case, Access asks for confirmation when you try to paste multiple records.

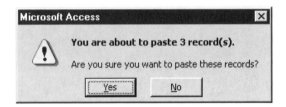

If the table has a primary key or a unique index that isn't an AutoNumber, you can't paste multiple records without removing the key or index first. Unlike pasting a single record, Access would have to save all but one of the records and this would create duplicate values in the field. If you try, Access displays an information message.

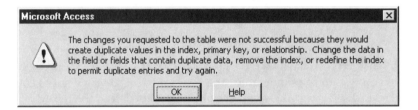

If you need to paste the value in a single field to the next record while you're entering data, you can quickly copy the value from the corresponding field in the previous record to the new record by pressing CTRL-' (apostrophe).

Copying and Moving from Another Table

To copy or move records from another table, select the records in the source table and choose Copy or Cut. If you choose Cut, you are asked to confirm that you want to delete the record(s) from the source table. Then switch to the destination datasheet and select the blank row at the bottom of the datasheet. When you click Paste, the new records are added to the destination datasheet.

The fields in the copied records are pasted in the same order as they appeared in the original datasheet, regardless of the field names. You may need to rearrange the columns in the destination datasheet before pasting so they correspond with the incoming fields. Inconsistent data types or sizes between the incoming records and the destination can result in problems.

If you want to replace certain records in the destination datasheet with records from another table, select the records you want to replace before clicking Paste.

To append records from another table to the existing datasheet, choose Edit | Paste Append. If the source table has more fields than the destination table, the excess fields aren't pasted.

If you're pasting records from another application, be sure to check the arrangement of the data before attempting to copy or move it into an Access datasheet. It should be arranged in a spreadsheet, a word-processor table, or as text separated by tab characters before you select it. See Chapter 23 for more information on exchanging data with other applications.

Fixing Paste Problems

You've heard this warning before, but here it is again—always save a backup copy of your data before attempting anything new. This applies to many of the copying and moving operations, which aren't vulnerable to Undo. If Access asks for confirmation before executing the operation, it most likely can't be undone once you say Yes.

When errors occur during a paste operation, Access creates a Paste Errors table and displays a message advising you of the errors as each is added to the table. To view the Paste Errors table, double-click the table name in the Tables page of the Database window.

Some of the problems you may encounter when trying to paste data into a datasheet include the following:

- You may try to paste values of incompatible data types, such as pasting a value that contains letters and numbers into a Currency field.

- The value you try to paste may be too long for the destination field. Compare the Field Size properties of both fields.

■ You may have tried to paste a value into a hidden field. Return to the datasheet and choose Unhide from the Format menu to reveal the hidden columns.

■ A value you are trying to paste may violate one of the property settings, such as the Input Mask, Validation Rule, Required, or Allow Zero Length setting.

When you open the Paste Errors table, you may be able to paste the data in the destination table field by field.

Inserting Pictures

The Home Tech Repair Employees table has a field reserved for the employee's badge picture. The Badge Picture field is an OLE Object data type and stores a file containing the digitized photograph.

An *Object Linking and Embedding* (OLE) object is created by an application outside Access and can be inserted into an Access table. Objects can be images, sounds, charts, video clips, or nearly any product of another application. Source applications can include Word, Excel, sound or video recorders, or an image scanner.

The object can either be linked to the Access table or embedded in it. *Linking* is the process by which the object remains in its source application and Access reaches it by means of a link or pointer to the object's location. If the linked object changes in the source application, the Access version also changes. *Embedding* an object actually stores a static copy of the object in the Access table, form, or report. Changes in the original don't reach the Access copy automatically.

Two other definitions are called for here: bound and unbound objects. A *bound object* is one stored directly in an Access table as part of the stored data. An *unbound object* is one added as an element to a form or report design, and isn't directly related to the table data.

The Badge Picture photos are OLE objects created by a scanner and are contained in image files such as .tif, .gif, or .pcx. Because the photos aren't expected to change, they are embedded in the table. In addition, they represent the value stored in the Badge Picture field, which means they're bound objects.

To insert an image in the Badge Picture field:

1. Place the insertion point in the Badge Picture field and choose Insert | Object, or right-click the field and choose Insert Object from the shortcut menu.

2. In the Insert Object dialog box, choose Create from File (see Figure 6-3).

3. Type the path and filename of the image file in the File box, or click Browse and look for the object.

4. After entering the filename, choose OK to embed the picture in the field.

When you return to Datasheet view, the field now contains the name of the source of the OLE object. In this case, the Microsoft Photo Editor was used, so the field shows Microsoft Photo Editor 3.0 Picture. Other entries indicate other types of objects. To see the image, create a form by clicking New Object: AutoForm. Figure 6-4 shows the first Employee record with the Badge Picture embedded.

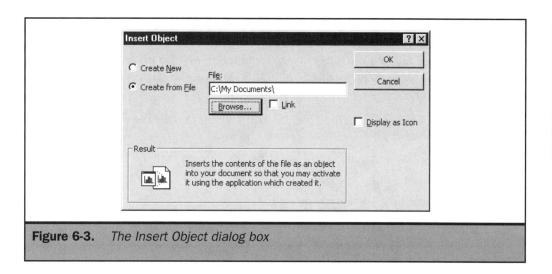

Figure 6-3. *The Insert Object dialog box*

Note   *You may need to double-click the added object to activate the OLE source program before you can see the image.*

Figure 6-4. *A Badge Picture inserted*

Another Way to Insert a Photo

You can also use the familiar cut-and-paste routine to insert a photo. For example, when you view the photo in an image application, such as the Microsoft Photo Editor, do the following:

1. While viewing the picture, choose Edit | Copy to copy the picture to the clipboard.

2. Switch to the Access table and place the insertion point in the OLE object field.

3. Then do one of the following:

   ■ Choose Edit | Paste to embed the image.

   ■ Choose Edit | Paste Special to link the image.

Other options in the Insert Object dialog box include

■ Link, which creates a link to the OLE Object, rather than embedding it.

■ Display As Icon, which displays only an icon representing the source object, instead of the object itself.

Note *Chapter 10 contains more information about using OLE and other objects when creating form and report designs.*

Inserting Hyperlinks

A *hyperlink* is a connection to an object in the same or another Access database, to a document created in another Office program, or to a document on the Internet or your local intranet. You can link to any OLE or ActiveX application on your computer or local area network. The *hyperlink field* contains the address of the target object and, when you click the hyperlink, you jump to it. If the object is the product of another application, that application is automatically started.

In the Home Tech Repair database, the Workorders table contains a hyperlink field that contains the engineering drawings for that work order. The scanned drawings are saved as .gif files in the same folder as the database itself.

Defining the Hyperlink Address

A hyperlink address can contain up to four parts, separated by the pound sign (#)

> *displaytext#address#subaddress#screentip*

of which only the address or, in some cases, the subaddress is required.

■ The *displaytext* is optional text to display in the field in place of the actual address. If you don't include display text, the hyperlink address or subaddress appears instead.

- The *address* is an absolute or relative path to the target. An absolute path is a *Uniform Resource Locator* (URL) or *Universal Naming Convention* (UNC) path to the document. A *relative path* is related to the current path or the base path specified in the database properties. An address is required unless you added a subaddress that points to an object in the current database.

- The *subaddress* contains a named location within the target object, such as a bookmark in a Word document, a particular slide in a PowerPoint presentation, or a cell range in an Excel spreadsheet.

- The *screentip* is the text that appears when you rest the mouse pointer on the hyperlink. If you don't specify a ScreenTip, the address is displayed.

Table 6-1 describes some examples of valid hyperlink addresses.

Note *Notice the UNC addresses that point to files in folders on your disk use backward slashes, while the URL addresses that point to Web pages use forward slashes.*

Address	Description
Form Workorders	Jumps to the Workorders form in the current database.
Presentation#c:\Demos\ HomeTech.ppt#1#Click to preview Home Tech slide	Jumps to the first slide in the PowerPoint presentation named HomeTech. Displays Presentation in place of the address and shows a ScreenTip.
#c:\MSOffice\Access\Samples\ Northwind.mdb#Form Products	Jumps to the Products form in the Northwind database.
Rhythm&Blues#c:\Favorites\Old Tunes.doc#RandB#Click to see a list of old tunes	Jumps to the RandB Bookmark in the Word document named Old Tunes in the Favorites folder. Displays Rhythm&Blues in place of the address and shows a ScreenTip.
Labor Rates#c:\My Documents\ Labor.xls#By Category!C12	Opens the Excel Labor workbook in the My Documents folder and goes to cell C12 in the By Category worksheet. Displays Labor Rates.
Microsoft Corporation#http:// www.microsoft.com#	Jumps to the Microsoft page on the Web. Displays Microsoft Corporation.

Table 6-1. *Examples of Hyperlink Addresses*

Entering the Hyperlink Address

You have several ways to enter a hyperlink address that's unique for each record in a form or datasheet, depending on the intended target of the hyperlink:

- Type the hyperlink address directly in the field.
- Use the Insert Hyperlink tool.
- Copy-and-paste a hyperlink or hyperlink address from another source.
- Copy-and-paste text from another Office document.
- Drag-and-drop an Internet shortcut.

 If you type the address, you must include the pound signs (#). If you use the Insert Hyperlink feature, Access adds them to the address for you when it assembles the address parts.

The scanned drawings for the Workorders Drawing field are stored in the folder with the database. To use Insert Hyperlink to enter the hyperlink address, do the following:

1. Place the insertion point in the Drawing field in the Workorders datasheet.
2. Click Insert Hyperlink or choose Insert | Hyperlink. The Insert Hyperlink dialog box opens (see Figure 6-5).
3. Click the Existing File or Web Page button under Link to, if not already chosen. Then do one of the following:
   - Type the path to the drawing file in the Address box. For example, **c:\My Documents\Osborne\fireplace.gif**.
   - If you've accessed the target of this hyperlink before, you can select it from the list of Recent Files or Browsed Pages.
   - Click the Browse For File button (the open folder) and locate the file in the Link to File dialog box (see Figure 6-6). Then click OK.
4. Back in the Insert Hyperlink dialog box, enter the text you want to show in the field in place of the address in the Text To Display box. For example, you could enter **Fireplace**.
5. If you want to show a ScreenTip, click the ScreenTip button and enter the text in the Set Hyperlink ScreenTip dialog box. Then click OK.

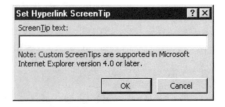

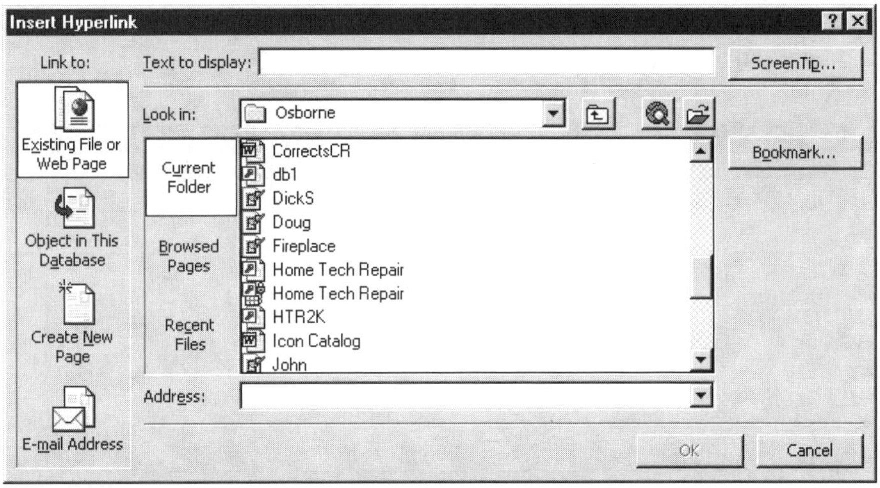

Figure 6-5. *The Insert Hyperlink dialog box*

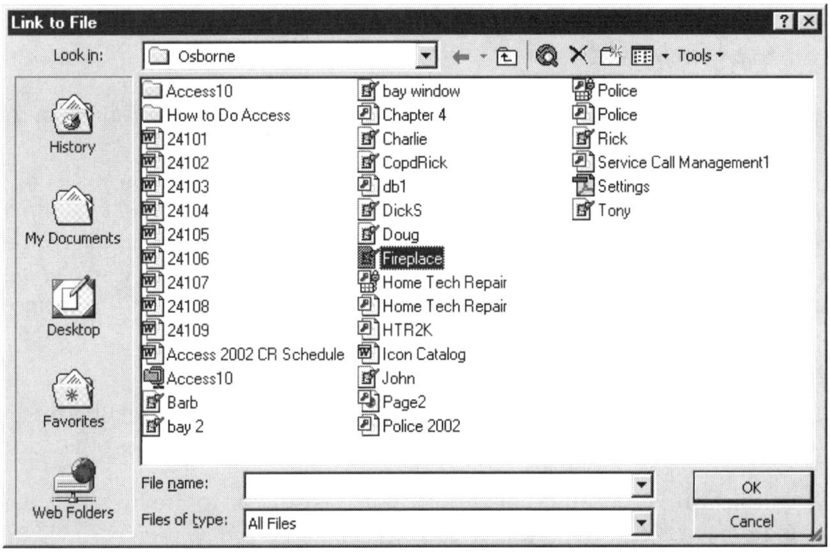

Figure 6-6. *The Link to File dialog box*

6. Click OK to finish inserting the hyperlink and return to the Workorders datasheet where the hyperlink appears in the Drawing field. When you rest the mouse pointer on the hyperlink, you see the ScreenTip.

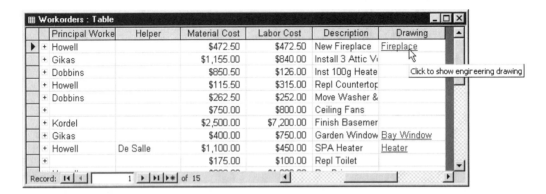

7. Click the hyperlink to test it and Microsoft Internet Explorer opens, displaying the scanned fireplace drawing, as shown in Figure 6-7.

The other Link to buttons in the Insert Hyperlink dialog box help you:

- Link to objects in the current database.
- Create and link to a new document.
- Link to an e-mail address.

You can also click the Bookmark button and indicate a specific location in the target document. More about hyperlinks in Chapter 12.

   By default, a hyperlink you haven't clicked appears underlined and in blue. After it has been followed the first time, the text changes to purple. This and other hyperlink options can be set in the General tab of the Options dialog box by clicking the Web Options button. See Chapter 16 for more information about personalizing your Access workplace.

Editing and Deleting Hyperlinks

Editing a hyperlink address is a little different than editing normal text because if you click on the address, you jump to the target. You have two ways to edit the address:

- Open the Edit Hyperlink dialog box, which is similar to the Insert Hyperlink dialog box, and edit the address directly.
- Move to the field and switch to Edit mode.

To open the Edit Hyperlink dialog box, right-click the hyperlink, point to Hyperlink in the shortcut menu, and click Edit Hyperlink in the submenu.

GETTING STARTED

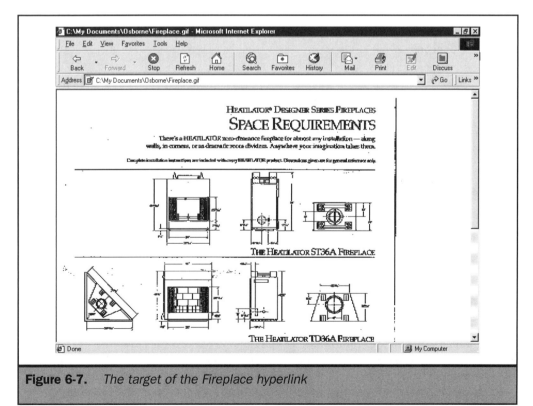

Figure 6-7. *The target of the Fireplace hyperlink*

Make the changes to the address in the Address box. You can also edit the display text and ScreenTip in the Edit Hyperlink dialog box the same way you specified them.

To Edit the complete address in the datasheet, use the keyboard to move to the field. (Don't click in the field or you'll jump to the target.) Then press F2 to enter Edit mode and make changes in the address. You can change all parts of the address this way. The two consecutive pound signs between the address and the ScreenTip indicate no subaddress exists, but its relative position is preserved.

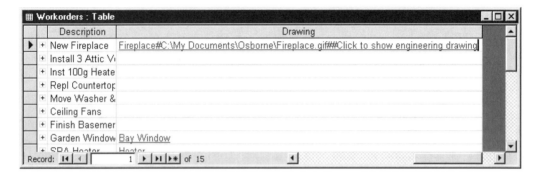

To delete a hyperlink address from a field, right-click the hyperlink and choose Cut from the shortcut menu. You can also point to Hyperlink in the shortcut menu and click Remove Hyperlink.

Although Access removes the hyperlink address without asking for confirmation, you can easily restore it by clicking Undo or choosing Edit | Undo Delete.

If you want to delete all the hyperlink addresses you inserted in a field, delete the field from the table design.

Customizing Data Entry

Data entry is, by nature, a time-consuming task. Access offers many tools to help improve its efficiency, some of which minimize the data entry process, while others assist in navigation in a datasheet or give you access to special symbols. The basic rule is "The more help you can provide the better."

Adding Custom Input Masks

An *input mask* is a field property similar to the Format property, but with different purpose. An input mask displays a fill-in blank for data entry, while a format is used to display field data with a consistent appearance. Setting the Format property affects how data is displayed after it's entered and offers no control over or guidance for the data being entered. Input masks can be used with Text, Number, Date/Time, and Currency fields.

GETTING STARTED

To decide between a Format property and an Input Mask property, use the following guidelines:

- If you want to make sure the field values look the same when displayed, use the Format property to specify the desired appearance.

- If you want to have some control over data entry, use an input mask to guide data entry and make sure it's entered properly.

An input mask appears when the insertion point reaches the field, before any data is entered. The mask displays fill-in blanks with literal characters separating them. When you use an input mask, you can be sure the data fits the specifications you set by limiting the number of fill-in spaces. Depending on the characters you use in the mask, you can leave some fill-in spaces blank, but you cannot add more characters than spaces.

An input mask also can specify what kind of values you can enter in each space. Telephone numbers offer a good example to show the difference between Format and Input Mask properties.

- The format (@@@) @@@-@@@@ displays nothing on the screen before data is entered and displays (619) 555-8867 after you enter the phone number.

- The input mask (000) 000-0000 displays (___) ___-____ before data is entered and displays the same (619) 555-8867 after the number is entered.

The format above displays the literal characters and the characters you enter or leaves the spaces blank if no character is entered, but only after the record has been saved. The previous input mask contains zeros, which require all entries contain the right number of digits (and only digits) to represent a U.S. telephone number.

Input masks also speed data entry by automatically entering the literal characters. The user need enter only the values that belong in the fill-in spaces between the literal characters.

If you set both a display format and an input mask, Access uses the input mask for entering and editing data and the format setting for displaying entered data. If your results don't look quite right, you may have specified conflicting settings.

You can create an input mask for Text and Date/Time fields with the Input Mask Wizard. If you want an input mask for a Number or Currency field, you must create it manually.

To create an input mask with the Input Mask Wizard, move the insertion point to the field in table Design view. Then do the following:

1. Click the Build button (...) at the right of the field's Input Mask property. The first Input Mask Wizard dialog box opens (see Figure 6-8) where you can select from a list of ten predesigned input masks appropriate for commonly used fields. The Try-It box shows how the mask works when displayed in Datasheet or Form view. Access may prompt you to save the table design before opening the first dialog box.

Input Mask Wizard

Which input mask matches how you want data to look?

To see how a selected mask works, use the Try It box.

To change the Input Mask list, click the Edit List button.

Input Mask:	Data Look:
Phone Number	(206) 555-1212
Social Security Number	531-86-7180
Zip Code	98052-6399
Extension	63215
Password	*******
Long Time	1:12:00 PM

Try It: |

Edit List   Cancel   < Back   Next >   Finish

Figure 6-8. *Predesigned input masks*

2. After selecting the mask, click Next to move to the second dialog box. In this dialog box, you can make any necessary changes to the mask, such as changing the placeholder that displays as the fill-in blanks (the default is an underline character), and then click Next.

3. Choose to store the literal characters with the data, if desired. This uses more disk space, but the symbols are available when you want to use the value in a form or report, rather than having to specify them in the field format in the form or report design.

4. Click Finish to close the wizard.

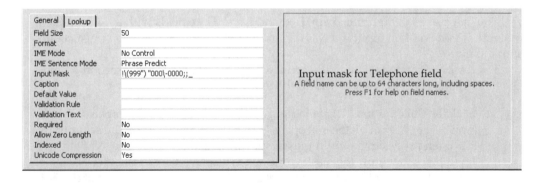

General	Lookup
Field Size	50
Format	
IME Mode	No Control
IME Sentence Mode	Phrase Predict
Input Mask	!\(999") "000\-0000;;_
Caption	
Default Value	
Validation Rule	
Validation Text	
Required	No
Allow Zero Length	No
Indexed	No
Unicode Compression	Yes

Input mask for Telephone field
A field name can be up to 64 characters long, including spaces.
Press F1 for help on field names.

The new Telephone Input Mask property contains some special features discussed in a later section in this chapter.

If you have a customized field that isn't part of the Input Mask Wizard's repertoire, you can easily create your own mask manually with special symbols. The special symbols are placeholders that specify which entries are required and define what type of characters can be entered at each position in the mask. You can even add a custom mask to the wizard's list of predefined input masks. You cannot create an input mask for a Memo, AutoNumber, Yes/No, OLE Object, or Hyperlink field.

To build an input mask manually, enter the desired characters directly in the Input Mask property in Design view. Table 6-2 describes the symbols you can use in an input mask and whether they require an entry in that position.

In addition to the symbols in the previous table, you can add any of the characters that represent date and time separators, a decimal point, or a thousands separator.

Symbol	Entry	Entry Required?
0	Digit (0 through 9) with no + or – sign. Blanks display as zeros.	Yes
9	Digit with no + or – sign. Blanks display as spaces.	No
#	Same as 9, but allows +/– signs.	No
L	Letter (*A* through *Z*).	Yes
?	Letter.	No
A	Letter or digit.	Yes
a	Letter or digit.	No
&	Any character or space.	Yes
C	Any character or space.	No
<	Converts letters to lowercase.	N/A
>	Converts letters to uppercase.	N/A
!	Characters typed into the mask fill it from left to right. Can appear anywhere in the mask.	N/A
\	Next character is treated as a literal.	N/A

Table 6-2. *Input Mask Symbols* (continued)

When you add these characters to the input mask, they appear in the fill-in field for data entry. Here are some examples of the effects of using input masks:

Input Mask	Description	Sample Valid Value
00000-9999	Zeros represent required entries, the 9s are optional.	92118-2450 or 92118-
(999) AAA-AAAA	Allows letters or digits. Area code is optional.	(301) 555-CALL
!>L0L 0L0	Converts all letters to uppercase. Fills left to right.	N0C 1H0
>L<??????????	Converts required initial letter to uppercase. Other characters are optional and converted to lowercase.	Henrietta
>LL0000-000	Two required letters converted to uppercase and seven required digits.	BT5430-115

To make a change in one of the wizard's masks, select the mask first in the Input Mask Wizard dialog box, and then click Edit List and proceed as in the previous to make the desired changes.

Three sections separated by semicolons are available in an input mask definition, as you saw in the Phone input mask created earlier by the wizard:

!\(999") "000\-0000;;_

- ■ The first section contains the mask itself, which has some interesting features. The exclamation mark tells Access to enter the characters from left to right. The opening parenthesis is preceded by a backslash telling Access the character that follows is a literal character. The closing parenthesis and space that follows it are enclosed in quotation marks to indicate they are also literals. The dash separating parts of the phone number is also preceded by a backslash indicating a literal.

- ■ The second section determines whether to store the literal characters with the data. Enter **0** in this section to store the characters; enter **1** or leave blank to store only the characters entered in the fill-in blanks in the mask. In this example, the second section is blank.

- ■ The third section specifies the character to use as the blank fill-in spaces in the displayed mask. For example, type **a plus sign** to use + in place of the default underline character. If you want to leave the fill-in spaces blank, type " " (space between the double quotation marks).

Note *Input masks defined in table Design view are automatically applied to the queries based on the table. They're also inherited by bound controls in forms and reports based on the table, if the form or report was designed after the mask was defined. Input masks for unbound controls must be manually set in form or report Design view. If you want to override the table-defined mask for a query or form (or report) design, change the Input Mask property for the control in the design. Clicking the Build button in the control's property sheet opens the Input Mask Wizard dialog box where you can make the changes. See Chapter 10 for more information on setting control properties in form and report designs.*

Caution *Once you add a new input mask to the wizard's list, there's no way to remove it. But you can change it to create a different mask.*

Creating Lookup Fields

A *lookup field* is an Access tool that makes entering data quicker and more accurate. A lookup field displays a list of values from which to choose. The most common type of lookup field, called a *lookup list*, gets its values from an existing table or query. The advantage of this type of lookup field is that the tables are actually related and, as the source list changes, the current values are available to the lookup field. The lookup table becomes the parent table and its primary key links it to the lookup field, which is actually the foreign key in the main data table.

Creating a Custom Input Mask

If you have a field that commonly appears in your tables or forms, such as the Canadian postal code, you can create a new input mask and save it in the Input Mask Wizard's list of predefined masks.

In table Design view, click the Input Mask property for the field, and then click the Build button to open the Input Mask Wizard dialog box.

1. Click Edit List. Figure 6-9 shows the Customize Input Mask Wizard dialog box with the Phone Number input mask.

2. Click the New Record navigation button at the bottom of the dialog box to show a blank form.

3. Enter a description of the new mask, the mask itself, the symbol you want to use as the placeholder, and a sample of the data you intend to enter into the field.

4. Then select the Mask Type: Text/Unbound or Date-Time. Figure 6-10 shows the completed definition for the Canadian postal code input mask.

5. Click Close. The new definition appears in the list of predefined masks.

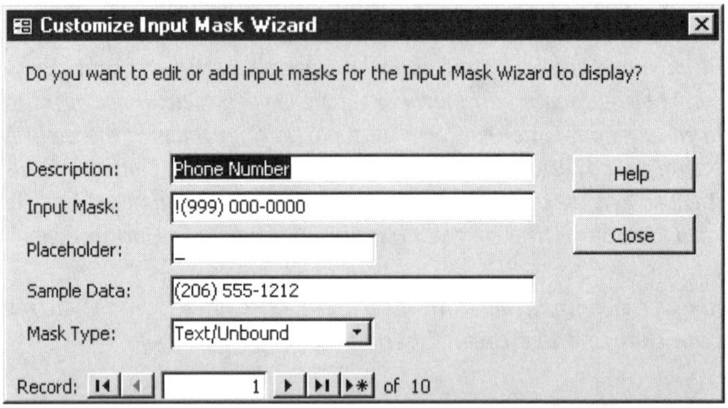

Figure 6-9. *The Customize Input Mask Wizard dialog box*

The second type of lookup field gets its values from a list you type in when you create the field. This type is called a *value list* and is best used when the list is limited to a few values that don't change often, such as a short list of product categories or preferred suppliers. Once you add the list to a field, the list stays with it when you add the field to a data entry form.

You can add either type of lookup field in either Design or Datasheet view. If the field already exists in the table design and you want to change it to a lookup field, you must change the data type in Design view. To add a new lookup field to a table, do one of the following:

■ In Design view, add a new field row and select Lookup Wizard from the Data Type list.

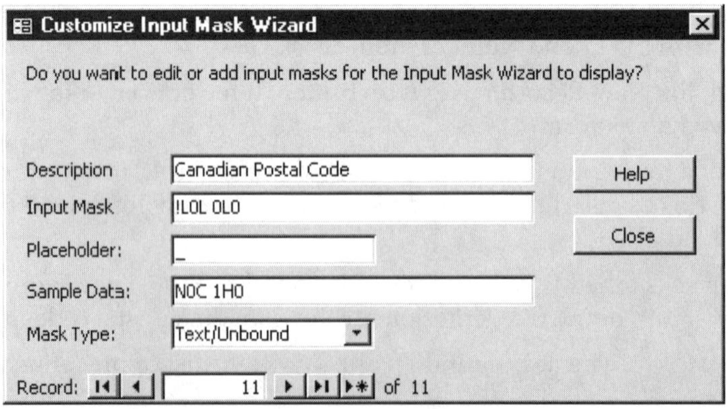

Figure 6-10. *An input mask for a Canadian postal code field*

■ In Datasheet view, click in the column to the right of where you want the new lookup field, and then choose Insert | Lookup Column. You may have to expand the menu list to see Lookup Column.

Either method starts the Lookup Wizard that displays a series of dialog boxes in which you specify the details of the lookup field. In the first dialog box (see Figure 6-11), you decide which type of lookup field to create: a lookup list that relates to a table or query, or a value list you type in.

If you choose to type in your list of values, the wizard displays a dialog box where you specify the number of columns you want in the list and enter the values. If you choose to get the values from another table, the wizard displays several more dialog boxes in which you do the following:

■ Select the source table or query from the current database.

■ Select the fields from the table you want to include.

■ Specify how you want the columns to look and whether to hide the primary key in the lookup table.

■ Specify which field in the table is the key field.

■ Enter a name for the lookup field.

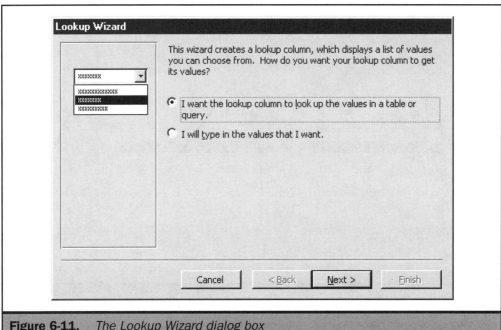

Figure 6-11. *The Lookup Wizard dialog box*

Specifying a Lookup Column

As an example of defining a lookup field that gets its values from another table, insert a new field in the Workorders table of the Home Tech Repair database. The Workorders information can be easier to enter and read if a lookup field is used for the Supervisor, Principal Worker, and Helper fields. The list can display the last name of all the employees at Home Tech Repair. Then, rather than requiring the users to remember each employee's ID code, they can select the last name from a lookup column and have Access store the corresponding Employee ID value in the field. The Last Name is displayed, but the Employee ID will be stored.

To add a lookup field to the Workorders table, follow these steps:

1. Open the Workorders table in Design view and insert a field named Supervisor between Completion Date and Principal Worker, choosing the Lookup Wizard data type.

2. In the first Lookup Wizard dialog box, choose the first option, I Want The Lookup Column To Look Up The Values In A Table Or Query. Then click Next.

3. Select Employees from the list of tables and click Next.

4. In the next dialog box, double-click the Employee ID and Last Name fields in the list of available fields in the Employees table (see Figure 6-12). Then click Next.

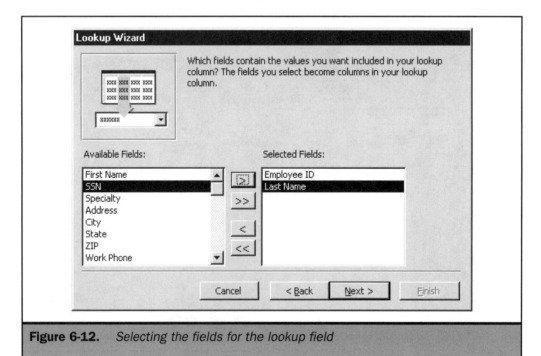

Figure 6-12.   *Selecting the fields for the lookup field*

5. The next dialog box (see Figure 6-13) shows you how the field values will look in the lookup column. If the column width is insufficient or unnecessarily wide, drag the right edge of the column header to change the width. In addition, check the Hide Key Column (Recommended) option, so you needn't view the Employee ID key value, only the last name. Click Next.

6. Accept the name Supervisor for the lookup column and click Finish. Access prompts you to save the table so the relationships may be completed. Choose Yes and you return to the table Design view.

The Lookup Wizard has set the properties for the new field based on your selections in the dialog boxes, which you can view on the Lookup tab of the Field Properties pane.

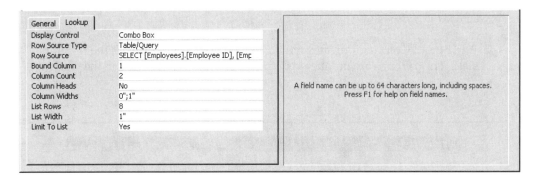

The Lookup properties specify the appearance and behavior of the lookup field when it appears in a datasheet or a form.

- The Display Control property determines the type of control implemented. The wizard chose a Combo Box. Other options are Text Box and List Box.

- The Row Source Type indicates where the values come from that are displayed in the lookup column. Here the source is Table/Query. Other Row Source Types are Value List and Field List.

- The Row Source property specifies exactly the table and fields that comprise the list. To see the entire entry, right-click in the property text and choose Zoom from the shortcut menu. You can edit the statement in the Zoom box, if necessary, or change the font properties.

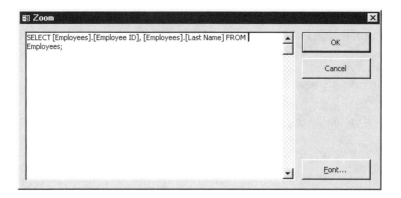

Note   *The SELECT statement in the Row Source property is a SQL statement created by the Lookup Wizard. See Chapter 9 for more information about creating and using SQL statements.*

■   The Bound Column indicates which column in the list contains the linking field. The columns are numbered in the order they were selected in the wizard's

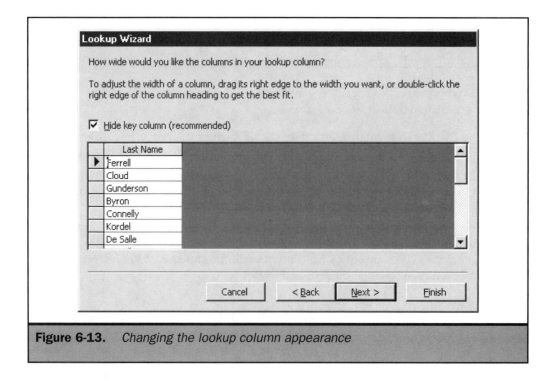

Figure 6-13.   *Changing the lookup column appearance*

dialog box. The Employee ID field—selected first—is the primary key in the Employees table, and so is assigned as the bound column for the lookup column.

■ The Column Count specifies two columns from the related table are involved. One, the Employee ID, is stored in the Workorders table and the other, Last Name, is displayed in the lookup column.

■ The No setting for Column Heads prevents the captions from the Employees table from displaying in the lookup list.

■ The first Column Width setting is 0, which keeps the first column, the Employee ID field, from being displayed. This selection was made when you checked the Hide key column option. The Last Name column is set to the width adjusted in the Lookup Wizard dialog box.

■ List Rows tells Access how many rows to display at once, which indicates the height of the drop-down list.

■ List Width specifies the overall width of the displayed list. If the text to be displayed in the list exceeds the column width in the datasheet or form, you can increase this value.

■ The Limit to List property prevents the user from entering a value that isn't on the list. This is required in this case because the displayed value must be in the source table for the primary key value (Employee ID) to be retrieved and stored in the foreign key field in the Workorders table.

Tip *With Limit To List set to Yes, you may still be permitted to leave the field blank. The combo box accepts Null values unless the Required property of the Supervisor field is set to Yes.*

Figure 6-14 shows the Workorders table with a new lookup field used to locate employee names in the Employee table. The lookup field links the Employee table to the Workorders table by the Employee ID field. Although the employee's last name is displayed, the foreign key, Employee ID, is stored in the field, but isn't displayed.

Specifying a Lookup List

A static value list can be helpful when entering data in the Employees table. Because only a few valid values are in the Type field, this is a good candidate for streamlining. In the first Lookup Wizard dialog box, choose the second option, I Will Type In The Values I Want, and move to the next dialog box where you enter the values for the list. Figure 6-15 shows the list of employment types for the Employees table.

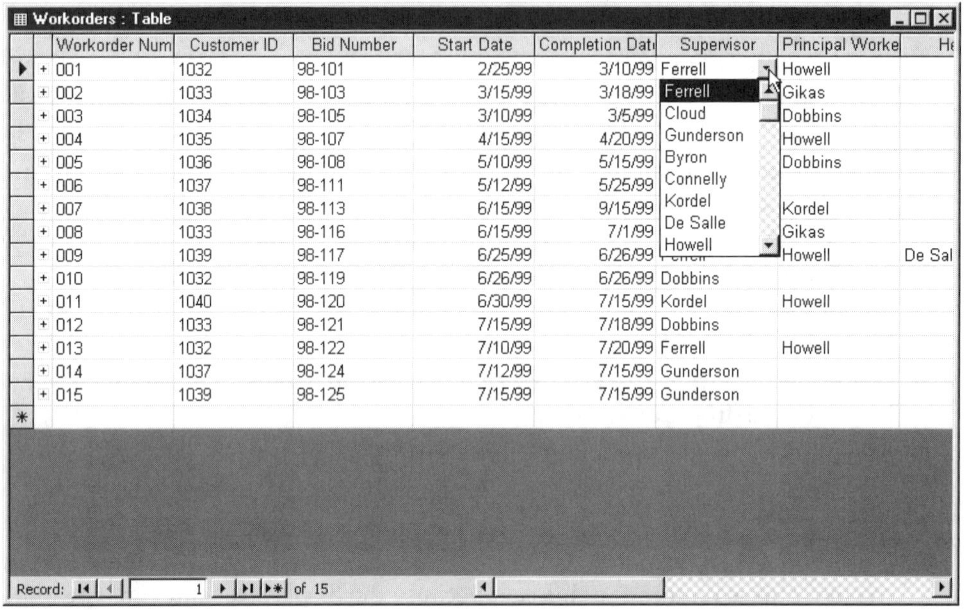

		Workorder Num	Customer ID	Bid Number	Start Date	Completion Date	Supervisor	Principal Worke	He
▶	+	001	1032	98-101	2/25/99	3/10/99	Ferrell	Howell	
	+	002	1033	98-103	3/15/99	3/18/99	Ferrell	Gikas	
	+	003	1034	98-105	3/10/99	3/5/99	Cloud	Dobbins	
	+	004	1035	98-107	4/15/99	4/20/99	Gunderson	Howell	
	+	005	1036	98-108	5/10/99	5/15/99	Byron	Dobbins	
	+	006	1037	98-111	5/12/99	5/25/99	Connelly		
	+	007	1038	98-113	6/15/99	9/15/99	Kordel	Kordel	
	+	008	1033	98-116	6/15/99	7/1/99	De Salle	Gikas	
	+	009	1039	98-117	6/25/99	6/26/99	Howell	Howell	De Sal
	+	010	1032	98-119	6/26/99	6/26/99	Dobbins		
	+	011	1040	98-120	6/30/99	7/15/99	Kordel	Howell	
	+	012	1033	98-121	7/15/99	7/18/99	Dobbins		
	+	013	1032	98-122	7/10/99	7/20/99	Ferrell	Howell	
	+	014	1037	98-124	7/12/99	7/15/99	Gunderson		
	+	015	1039	98-125	7/15/99	7/15/99	Gunderson		

Record: I◀ ◀ 1 ▶ ▶I ▶* of 15

Figure 6-14. *Using the new lookup field in the Workorders table*

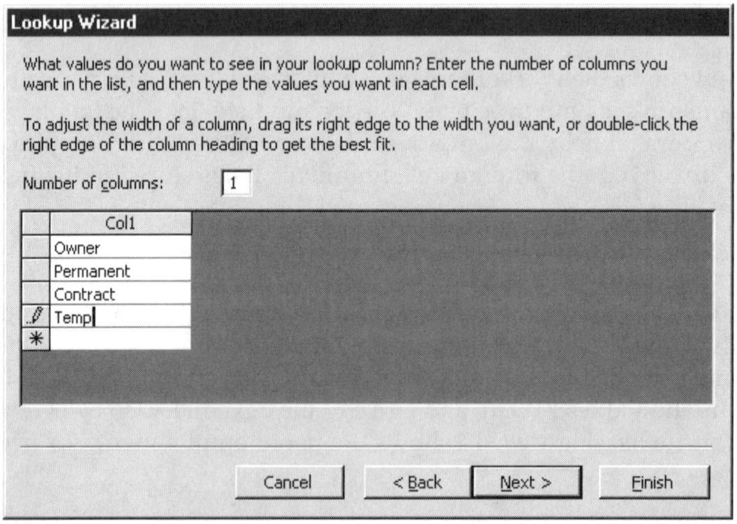

Lookup Wizard

What values do you want to see in your lookup column? Enter the number of columns you want in the list, and then type the values you want in each cell.

To adjust the width of a column, drag its right edge to the width you want, or double-click the right edge of the column heading to get the best fit.

Number of columns: 1

Col1
Owner
Permanent
Contract
Temp

Cancel | < Back | Next > | Finish

Figure 6-15. *Completing a lookup list for the Type field*

Field properties are inherited by forms and reports, including the lookup fields created in the table design. Figure 6-16 shows the new Type value list in the Employees AutoForm.

 When you use the value list in a form, you can set the control properties to allow the user to add values to the list during data entry. Be aware, though, if you change a value list definition after adding it to a form design, you must modify the control's Row Source property in the form's Design view to include the correct list. See Chapter 12 for more information about customizing form controls.

Changing the Datasheet Appearance

Datasheet properties include the layout of the fields and records—the order in which the fields appear, the dimension of the rows and columns, and the column headings. Other properties are the font size and style, the colors of the text and the background, and special cell effects, such as raised or sunken.

You also have the option of hiding some fields from view if the data needn't be visible to all users of the database. Finally, if you have too many fields to view on the

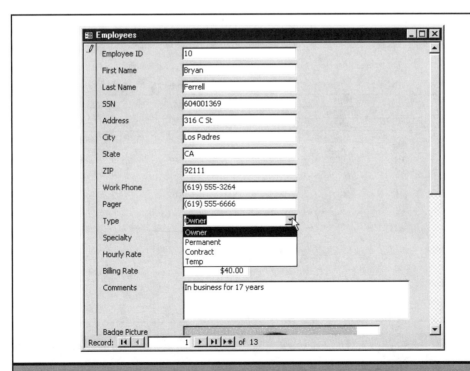

Figure 6-16.   *The lookup field property is inherited by the AutoForm*

screen at once, you can keep one or more of the key fields on the left of the screen as you scroll right, so you can identify the current record.

Saving the modified datasheet appearance with the table preserves the appearance, so the next time you open the table in Datasheet view, it will look the same.

Some datasheet properties, such as column width, can be changed directly in the Datasheet view. Others are accomplished with menu commands or dialog box options. Most of the formatting can be done easily by clicking buttons on the Formatting (Datasheet) toolbar.

Displaying Subdatasheets

After you open a table or query in Datasheet view, you can display a subdatasheet related to a row by clicking the expand indicator (+) to the left of the row. The indicator turns into a minus sign (–). To remove the subdatasheet from view, click the collapse indicator.

If the subdatasheet has a subdatasheet of its own, expand and collapse it using the same method. You can nest up to eight levels of subdatasheets. Each datasheet or subdatasheet can have only one nested subdatasheet. Figure 6-17 shows the Bid Data datasheet with three nested subdatasheets expanded: linked to the workorder, the supervisor, and other workorders supervised by the same employee.

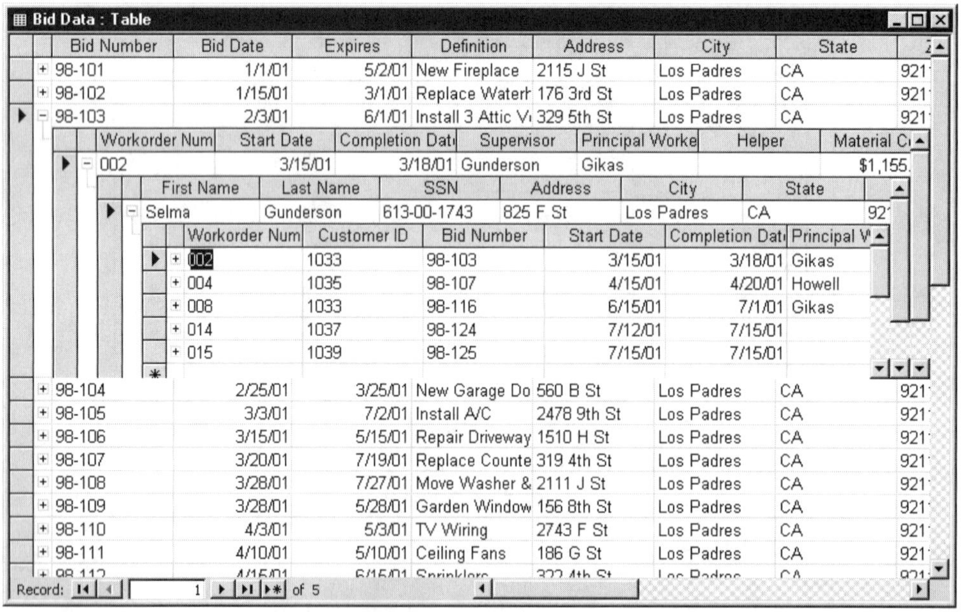

Figure 6-17. *Expanding subdatasheets*

Notice that the navigation buttons at the bottom of the Datasheet window refer to the active subdatasheet.

You can expand the subdatasheets for as many rows as you want. To display all the subdatasheets in the datasheet, choose Format | Subdatasheet | Expand All. To collapse them, choose Format | Subdatasheet | Collapse All.

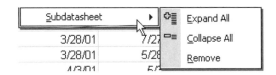

By default, Access doesn't display the foreign key or matching field in the subdatasheet. The column is hidden from view. If you want to display the field, choose Format | Unhide Column. Displaying the column is only temporary. The next time you open the datasheet containing the subdatasheet, the column is hidden again.

 Hiding and showing the columns in a datasheet or subdatasheet changes only the display and has no effect on the source object of the relationship.

Moving and Resizing Columns and Rows

Access displays the data fields in columns in the same order as the fields appear in the table design, unless you change the column order. The columns, by default, are all the same width, so you may be unable to see the whole field value or the entire text of some of the field names. Other columns may be wider than necessary and waste screen space. The rows are also a standard height. You can change any of these datasheet properties. Figure 6-18 shows the datasheet elements you can use to change the column and row properties.

Rearranging the Columns

You may always want some fields in your table to be visible in Datasheet view. If they are far down in the list of fields in the table design, they may be off the screen to the right. One solution is to change the order of the fields in the design, but it's easier to change the column order on the screen. You can move them to the left, so you won't have to scroll to see them.

To move a column, click the field selector and release the button. Then move the mouse pointer to the field selector. When the mouse pointer changes shape to an arrow with a small rectangle, click-and-drag the column to the desired position. When you begin to move the column, a dark vertical line moves with it, showing you where the left boundary of the moving column is at that moment. The column itself doesn't move until you release the mouse button.

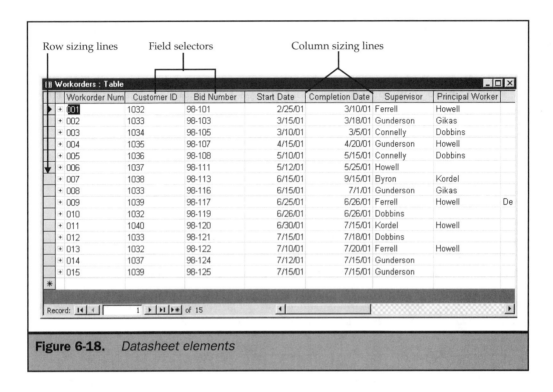

Figure 6-18.   *Datasheet elements*

Changing the relative position of a column in the datasheet has no effect on the way the fields appear in the design or the way they're stored on the disk.

Changing the Column Width

Obviously, if all the columns are the same width, but your data and field names are all different widths, some adjustments may make the datasheet look better and make more efficient use of the screen area.

You can change a column width in three ways:

- By dragging the sizing line at the right border of the field selector button.
- By double-clicking the column sizing line.
- By setting the width in a dialog box.

Dragging to a new width with the mouse is the easiest way to change a column width, but it isn't precise. To change the width with the mouse, move the mouse pointer to the column's right boundary line in the field selector. When the pointer reaches the right place, it changes shape to a plus (+) sign with right- and left-pointing arrows. Then click-and-drag the boundary to the right to increase or to the left to decrease its width.

If you drag the boundary all the way to the left until it reaches the left boundary, the column disappears. This is one way to hide a column. More about hiding columns a little later.

If you want the column just wide enough to fit the contents, double-click the right edge of the column heading.

If you need to be more precise about a column width, you can set the exact width in a dialog box. You can reach the Column Width dialog box in two ways after selecting one or more columns:

■ By choosing Format | Column Width.

■ By right-clicking the field selector and choosing Column Width from the shortcut menu.

The Column Width dialog box shown here displays the current column width, measured in characters, in the text box.

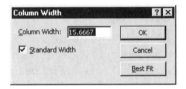

To change the width, type a new value in the Column Width text box, click to place a check mark in the Standard Width box to return to the default column width, or click Best Fit. The Best Fit option resizes the selected column or columns to fit the longest data in the field or the text in the column heading, whichever is longer.

The only disadvantage to setting the column width to Best Fit is you might later enter some new data that's longer than anything before and, unless you return to the Column Width dialog box and recheck Best Fit, it won't be fully displayed in the new column width.

If you want to change several or all column widths at once, so they fit the data and captions, you can select the columns before choosing Best Fit in the Column Width dialog box. Selecting Best Fit adjusts all the selected columns according to their contents.

You cannot undo the changes you made in the column width by choosing Edit | Undo or by clicking the Undo toolbar button. If you want the columns restored to their original width, close the datasheet without saving the changes to the layout.

Changing the Row Height

You can change column widths individually, but rows are different: they're all the same height and when you change the height of one, you change them all. For example, suppose you have a Memo field that usually contains two or three lines of text and you want to read them in Datasheet view. If you increase the row height to double or triple, you can fit the text in the space allowed. You may be able to combine adjusting the column width with increasing the row height to achieve the proper balance of dimensions.

The row height is modified the same way as the column width: by dragging a sizing line with the mouse or by entering the new height in a dialog box. To change the row height with the mouse, move the mouse pointer to any one of the row sizing lines in the record selector area. The mouse pointer changes shape to a plus sign again but, this time, with the arrows pointing up and down. Click-and-drag the line until the rows reach the desired height, and then release the button. All rows will be the same height.

To set a more exact row height, choose Format | Row Height to open the Row Height dialog box. The insertion point can be anywhere in the datasheet when you choose Format | Row Height. To use the shortcut menu, you must right-click in a selected row or any row selector, and then choose Row Height. The Row Height dialog box is similar to the Column Width dialog box, except there's no Best Fit option. The height is measured in points and the default height depends on the default font size.

Freezing and Hiding Columns

Two other properties of a datasheet deal with the display of the data. *Freezing* a column causes the data in it to remain on the screen as you scroll right to see fields in a long record. *Hiding* a column prevents the data from displaying in the datasheet. Neither of these properties change the way the data is stored, only the way it's displayed.

Freezing and Unfreezing Columns

If your datasheet has more columns than can fit across the screen, some of the information moves off the screen as you scroll right to see the rest of the data. One or two of these fields may contain information, such as the product number or a customer name that identifies the record. When you're editing the table data, it's helpful to keep this data on the screen, so you can be sure you're editing the right records. When you freeze a column on the screen, the column and its contents are automatically moved to the left of the datasheet and kept on the screen, even when you scroll right.

To freeze a column, place the insertion point anywhere in the column you want to freeze, and then choose Format | Freeze Columns, or right-click in the column header and choose Freeze Columns from the shortcut menu. To freeze several adjacent columns, select them all before choosing Freeze Columns. If you want to freeze nonadjacent columns, freeze them one at a time in the order you want them to appear at the left of the screen. Access then moves them, one by one, to the left side of the datasheet.

To unfreeze the columns, choose Unfreeze All Columns from the Format menu.

Unfortunately, Access doesn't return the thawed column to the position it was in before freezing and moving it to the left. You have to move the thawed column back yourself or close the table without saving the changes in the layout to restore the original arrangement.

Hiding and Unhiding a Column

If your table contains irrelevant information to the current activity, you may not want it to take up space on the screen. In this case, you can hide one or more columns from view. Again, this changes only the appearance of the datasheet, not the data stored in the table.

You saw earlier that you can hide a column by reducing its width to nothing. Another way to hide a column is to place the insertion point anywhere in the column and choose Format | Hide Columns. You can also right-click in a selected column or in the field selector and choose Hide Columns from the shortcut menu. The column immediately disappears from the screen. If you want to hide several adjacent columns, select them all first. If you want to hide nonadjacent columns, reposition them so they are adjacent, and then hide them as a group or hide them one at a time.

Note *If you try to copy or move records to a datasheet that currently has hidden columns, the data won't be entered and you'll get paste errors. Be sure to unhide all the hidden columns before attempting to copy or move records.*

To return the hidden columns to the datasheet display, choose Format | Unhide Columns. The Unhide Columns dialog box appears with a list of all the fields in the datasheet. Check marks next to the field names indicate the fields currently in view. If a field doesn't show a check mark, it's currently hidden. To return a field to the datasheet display, check the box next to its name. You can see the data being restored to the screen behind the dialog box when you click the check boxes. Choose Close when you've returned all the desired fields to the display.

You can also use the Unhide Columns dialog box to hide columns at the same time by removing the check marks.

Changing the Font

Access uses 10-point Arial as the default font for datasheets. The font setting applies to all the characters in the datasheet—data and captions alike. You might want to reduce the font size to get more data on the screen. Or, you might want to enlarge the font size to make it more visible if a group is going to view the screen from a short distance. You can also change to any font your computer system supports. The row height and column widths are automatically adjusted to accommodate the font changes.

To change the datasheet font, choose Font from the Format or the shortcut menu to open the Font dialog box (see Figure 6-19). Select the font, size, and effects you want, and then click OK.

You can also use the Formatting (Datasheet) toolbar buttons to change the font properties. Any changes you make affect the entire datasheet.

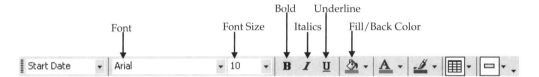

Changing Grid Lines and Cell Appearance

Now comes the fun part—making some dramatic changes to the appearance of the datasheet with colors and special effects. The *grid lines*—the horizontal and vertical lines that separate the datasheet into rows and columns—are displayed by default, but you can remove either the horizontal or vertical lines, or both. The *cells* are the boxes at the intersection of the rows and columns. In addition to changing the appearance of the grid lines, you can apply special effects to the cells to make them appear raised or sunken.

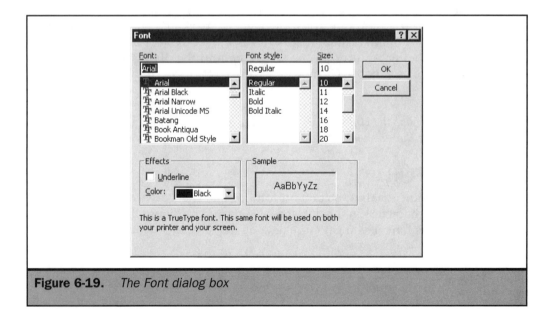

Figure 6-19.   *The Font dialog box*

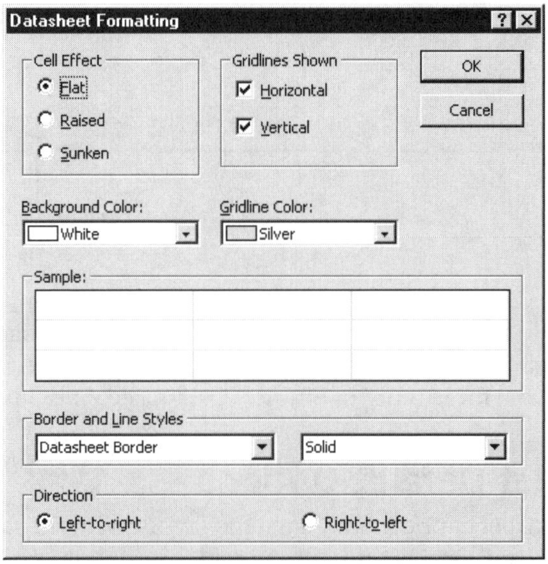

Figure 6-20.   *The Datasheet Formatting dialog box*

To change the datasheet properties, choose Format | Datasheet. The Datasheet Formatting dialog box opens, as shown in Figure 6-20.

In the Datasheet Formatting dialog box, you can make the following changes:

- Set a special cell effect, such as Raised or Sunken.
- Show or hide either or both the horizontal and vertical gridlines.
- Change the color of the gridlines and the cell background.
- Change the style of the borders and gridlines to weights ranging from transparent to double-solid.
- Change the column display direction from left-to-right (the first field appears in the first column, the second in the column to the right, and so on) to right-to-left (the first field appears in the right-most column, the second in the column to the left, and so on).

As you make changes in the dialog box, the combined effects are shown in the Sample panel.

You can also use buttons on the Formatting toolbar to change the appearance of the datasheet gridlines and cells.

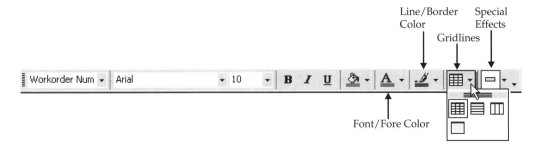

Clicking either color button displays a palette of colors from which to choose. Clicking the Gridlines button opens a palette with options for displaying both the horizontal and vertical gridlines, either, or none. Clicking the Special Effects button shows a palette with the three types of effects: Flat, Raised, and Sunken.

Setting Datasheet Default Options

To save the new datasheet appearance, save the layout with the table. To create a custom datasheet layout for use with all the tables in the database, change some of the default datasheet options. Choose Tools | Options to open the Options dialog box and click the Datasheet tab, as shown in Figure 6-21.

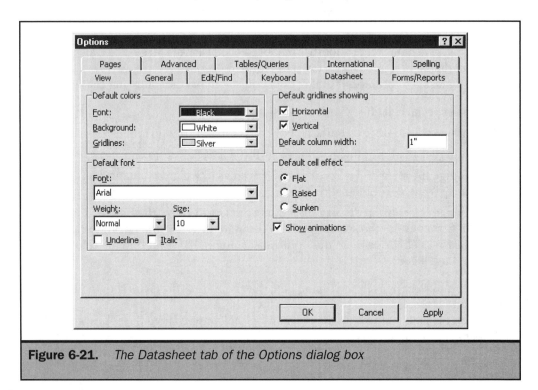

Figure 6-21.   *The Datasheet tab of the Options dialog box*

The available options are

- *Default colors*, which lists 16 colors you can use for the font, background, and gridlines.

- *Default font*, which specifies the font, weight, size, and style. The text appears in the color set in the Default Colors box.

- *Default gridlines showing*, which displays or hides horizontal and vertical gridlines. Gridlines displayed appear in the color set in the Default Colors box.

- *Default column width*, which sets the standard width for all the columns in the datasheet.

- *Default cell effect*, which specifies one of three cell effects: Flat, Raised, or Sunken.

- *Show animations*, which, when checked, turns on the animations features, such as showing the columns sliding over to make room when you insert a new column.

Changing Table Definition in Datasheet View

Although the best place to modify the table definition is in Design view, you can make some limited changes in Datasheet view.

Inserting a Subdatasheet

If the Subdatasheet Name property for the table on the "one" side of a one-to-many relationship is set to Auto, Access automatically creates a subdatasheet with records from the table on the "many" side. The datasheet and subdatasheet are related by matching the primary key and foreign key fields.

You can add a subdatasheet to any table or query by specifying the source name in the Subdatasheet Name property and setting the linking fields. You can also use the Insert menu to add a subdatasheet to a table. Open the table or query in Datasheet view, and then do the following:

1. Choose Insert | Subdatasheet. The Insert Subdatasheet dialog box opens showing three tabs: Tables, Queries, and Both.

2. Click the tab that contains the datasheet you want to use for the subdatasheet.

3. Select the table or query name in the list.

4. Choose the foreign key field for the subdatasheet table or query in the Link Child Fields box.

5. Choose the primary key or matching field for the open datasheet in the Link Master Fields box (see Figure 6-22).

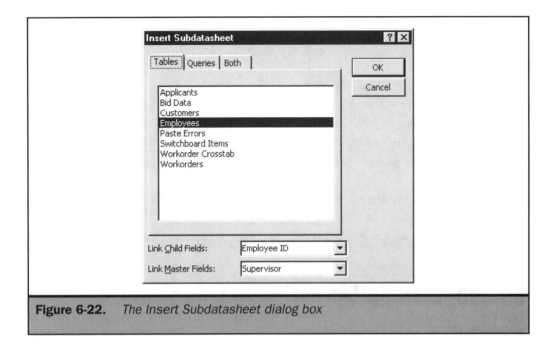

Figure 6-22. *The Insert Subdatasheet dialog box*

6. You can add other subdatasheets to the active table datasheet using the Insert Subdatasheet dialog box and, when you finish, click OK.

If you want to link by more than one field, separate the field names with semicolons. Both field lists must contain the same number of field names and be in the same order.

To remove a subdatasheet from a table or query, open the table or query in Datasheet view and choose Format | Subdatasheets | Remove. The subdatasheet is only removed from the display. The data isn't affected and the relationship remains intact.

If your subdatasheet shows the same data for all the rows in the datasheet, you might not have specified the linking fields.

Inserting/Deleting a Column

As you saw in Chapter 4, you can create a new table in Datasheet view by entering data directly in a blank datasheet. Access defines the data type to agree with the values you enter. The same principle applies to adding a new field in a table in Datasheet view. Insert a new column, change the caption to the name you want for the field, and then type in the data.

To insert a column, place the insertion point in the column to the right of where you want the new one and choose Insert | Column. A new blank column appears and the columns to the right move over. Double-click the field selector—usually labeled Field1—and rename the column with the appropriate field name.

> **Note** *If you want to change the data type Access assumes for the field, define a validation rule, or change other properties, you must switch to Design view.*

As discussed earlier in this chapter, the Insert menu offers two special columns: Lookup and Hyperlink. If you choose Lookup Column, the Lookup Wizard starts. Choosing Hyperlink Column inserts a new blank column, but the field is automatically specified as the Hyperlink data type.

To delete a column in Datasheet view, click anywhere in the field, and then choose Edit | Delete Column. Access warns you the deletion will be permanent. This is one of those cases where Undo doesn't work. Choose Yes to go ahead with the deletion or No to cancel.

> **Note** *You cannot delete a field that's part of a relationship without first deleting the relationship. Either open the Relationships window to delete the relationship if you want to or accept Access' offer to delete it for you.*

Changing Field Names

You already learned how to create a name for a field in Design view. You also saw how to give a field a new name when you created a table from a blank datasheet. In Datasheet View, you have three ways to rename an existing column:

- Double-click the text in the field selector and type the new name.
- Select the column and choose Format | Rename Column.
- Right-click the field selector and choose Rename Column from the shortcut menu.

All three methods place the insertion point in the field name text where you can replace or edit the existing name. In addition, any existing field Caption properties are deleted.

Editing Record Data

The standard methods of moving around a datasheet or form to edit record data haven't changed with Access 2002. You use the Edit | Go To menu or the navigation buttons at the bottom of the datasheet or form to move to another record: Next, Previous, First, Last, or New. The TAB key and the RIGHT ARROW and LEFT ARROW keys move to another field.

To change the entire value in a field, select the field and enter the new value. To edit only part of the value, change to Edit mode by clicking in the field or pressing F2.

Once in Edit mode, the RIGHT ARROW and LEFT ARROW keys move the insertion point through the characters instead of among the fields.

The icons that appear in the record selector at the far left of the datasheet row are the record indicators that show the status of the current record. Table 6-3 describes the indicators and their meanings.

 A fourth record indicator, a circle with a diagonal line through it—the international symbol meaning Don't—shows the record is undergoing changes and is locked by another user. If this appears, you must wait to make your changes to the record.

The behavior of the ENTER, TAB, and the arrow keys can be customized as described fully in Chapter 16. For example, by default, when you press ENTER to move to the next field, the field is selected. You can change this so the insertion point arrives at the first or last character in the value instead of selecting the field.

Selecting Records and Fields

The mouse is a convenient tool for selecting characters, fields, and records in Datasheet view. Table 6-4 describes the mouse techniques for selecting data.

You can also use many keyboard shortcuts to select data. The results of pressing certain keys and key combinations depend on the current mode in Datasheet view. When viewing a table in Datasheet view, you have a choice between Navigation or Edit mode. In *Navigation mode,* the insertion point isn't visible and you can move between fields and records using the arrow keys. If you're in *Edit mode,* the insertion point appears in a field and the arrow keys move it among the characters in the field.

To switch between Edit and Navigation modes, press F2 or click in the current field. While in Navigation mode, you can switch between selecting the first field of the current record or the entire record by pressing SHIFT-SPACEBAR.

Icon	Meaning
▶	Current record, not in the process of editing.
..✎	Changes are underway in the current record. Access saves the record when you move to another record.
✳	Blank row for entering a new record.

Table 6-3.   *Record Indicators*

To Select	Mouse Action
Characters in a field	Click at the start and drag across the data.
Entire field	Click the left edge of the field when the mouse pointer changes to a hollow plus sign.
Adjacent fields	Click the left edge of the first field and drag to extend the selection.
Column	Click the field selector.
Adjacent columns	Select the first column and, without releasing the mouse button, drag over the adjacent columns.
Record	Click the record selector.
Adjacent records	Select the first record and drag over the adjacent records.
All records	Choose Edit	Select All Records.

Table 6-4.   *Using the Mouse to Select Fields and Records*

Table 6-5 describes the shortcut keys you can use to select table data, records, and columns.

If you often need to extend a selection, you can switch to Extend mode by pressing F8 one or more times. Each time you press F8, the extension applies progressively to the word, to the field, to the record, and, finally, to all the records. While in Extend mode, the right and left arrow keys extend the selection across the characters in the current field. If the entire column is selected, the arrow keys extend the selection to the adjacent columns in the datasheet. The UP ARROW and DOWN ARROW keys extend the selection to adjacent rows. If you change your mind, cancel the extension by pressing SHIFT-F8. To cancel Extend mode, press ESC.

 You can tell you're in Extend mode by the letters EXT appearing in the Datasheet view status bar.

Locating Records

If a table doesn't contain a lot of records, you can probably find the record you want by scrolling down through the records in the datasheet or form, especially if the records are sorted by the field you are searching. If your table contains hundreds of records, however, that method is rather time-consuming. In the unlikely event that you know the number of the record you want to locate, you can find it using Edit | Go To or the navigation button.

To Select	Press
Text in a field (in Edit mode)	
Extend one character to the right	SHIFT-RIGHT ARROW
Extend one character to the left	SHIFT-LEFT ARROW
Extend one word to the right	CTRL-SHIFT-RIGHT ARROW
Extend one word to the left	CTRL-SHIFT-LEFT ARROW
Fields or records	
Next field	TAB (depends on keyboard option setting)
Current record	SHIFT-SPACEBAR
Extend to previous record (with current record selected)	SHIFT-UP ARROW
Extend to next record (with current record selected)	SHIFT-DOWN ARROW
All records	CTRL-A or CTRL-SHIFT-SPACEBAR
Columns	
Current column	CTRL-SPACEBAR (also cancels column selection)
Extend to column on the right (with current column selected)	SHIFT-RIGHT ARROW
Extend to column on the left (with current column selected)	SHIFT-LEFT ARROW

Table 6-5.   *Shortcut Keys for Selecting Table Data*

Another way to locate a specific record is by the value in a specific field. Access has provided you with the Find feature, available as a toolbar button, as well as a menu option. Just tell Access what you want to find and where and how to search for the value. The search can apply to the complete value in the field or only to certain characters within the field.

Note   *If you're looking for values in a datasheet with a subdatasheet or a form with a subform, Access searches only the object that contains the insertion point.*

Finding an Exact Match

To find a record with a specific value in one of the fields, place the insertion point anywhere in the column and click the Find toolbar button, or choose Edit | Find. The Find and Replace dialog box opens, and you specify the search you want to conduct.

For example, place the insertion point in the Specialty field in the Employees table of the Home Tech Repair database and click Find. In the Find and Replace dialog box (see Figure 6-23), enter **Labor** as the value to look for in the Find What box, and then click Find Next. The insertion point moves to the next record with that value.

Clicking Find Next again finds subsequent records with the same value in the field. After Access has found the last record that matches the value, choosing Find Next displays an information dialog box indicating no more records exist with that value. The Find in Field dialog box remains on the screen until you click the Close command button.

If you placed the insertion point in the middle of the table, Access searches to the last record, and then begins at the first record until all records have been examined.

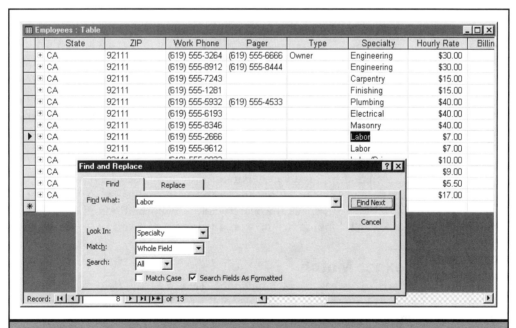

Figure 6-23. *The Find and Replace dialog box*

Limiting or Expanding the Search

By default, Access searches only the specified field in all the records. In the Look In box, you have a choice between the field that contains the insertion point or the entire table. You can expand the search by choosing the whole table—for example, Employees:Table—in the Search box. Access searches for the value in all the Text and Memo fields in the table. This is slower than limiting the search to a single field, but it comes in handy for finding specific values in all fields, especially when you want to replace one value with another globally.

 One way to speed up the search process is to index a field if you expect to search it often with Find and Replace.

Two of the options can be used to limit or expand the search. If you're interested in finding only one occurrence of the value rather than all of them, you can limit the search to a subset of the records. The Search option drop-down list includes

- *All* (the default setting), which begins at the current record, searches to the end of the table, and begins again at the first record.
- *Up*, which searches from the current record toward the first record.
- *Down*, which searches from the current record through the remaining records.

 You can close the Find and Replace dialog box anytime—you needn't find all the occurrences of the value before you can go on to something else.

The Match Case option, when checked, treats uppercase and lowercase letters as different characters. For example, if you enter the value "labor" in the Find What box and check Match Case, Access won't find "Labor." If you check Match Case, Search Fields As Formatted isn't available.

The Search Fields As Formatted option lets you look for the field based on the display format, rather than the stored value. For example, suppose you have a date field displayed in the format 15-May-01, but it's stored as the value 05/15/01. If you want to look for it as 15-May-01, check the Search Fields As Formatted option. This type of search is slower than looking for the stored value.

Finding an Inexact Match

Access offers two ways to find an inexact match in a Text or Memo field: by setting the Match option to limit the search to only part of the field or by using wildcards in the search string.

The Match options specify whether to require a complete and exact match or to accept a match with only part of the field. The Match options include:

■ *Whole Field* (default), which finds only records containing values that exactly match the search string.

■ *Any Part of Field*, which finds records whose field contains the search string anywhere in the field. For example, if you want to find all work orders with the word "heater" somewhere in the description, you would ask Access to find a match anywhere in the field.

■ *Start of Field*, which specifies the first one or more characters to match with the field values. For example, if you want to locate records for all customers whose last name begins with *A*, you would use the Start of Field Match option.

Several wildcard characters can be used in the search string to represent one or more characters. For example, if you know only part of the value you want to find or if you want to find records that match a specific pattern, wildcards can be used in the search string.

Wildcards can be mixed and matched to create the string combination you need. Most of them can also be used in queries and expressions, as you see in Chapters 8 and 9. Table 6-6 describes the wildcard characters and gives examples of how each can be used.

Wildcard	Matches	Example
*	Any number of characters.	**b*** finds "bird," "belt," and "blueberry"
?	Any single character.	**b??l** finds "ball," "beal," "bell," "bowl," and so on
[]	Any character within the brackets.	**b[aeo]ll** finds "ball," "bell," and "boll" but not "bill" or "bull"
!	Any character not in the brackets.	**b[!ae]ll** finds "bill," "boll," and "bull" but not "ball" or "bell"
- (hyphen)	Any character in the specified range of characters. The range must be in ascending order.	**B[a-d]t** finds "bat," "bbt," "bct," and "bdt"
#	Any single numeric character.	**10#** finds "100," "101," "102," and so on but not "10A"

Table 6-6. *Wildcard Characters*

Looking for Wildcard Characters

The field value you're looking for may include one of the characters Access recognizes as a wildcard, such as an asterisk(*), a question mark (?), a number sign (#), an opening bracket ([), or a hyphen (-). If you use the character directly in a search string, Access treats it like a wildcard.

When you use wildcards in a string to look for one of these characters, you must enclose the item you're looking for in brackets. For example, to find a value that begins with ?B, you would use the string **[?]B***.

But, if you are looking for a hyphen along with another wildcard character, you need to treat it a little differently. Access interprets a hyphen (-) or a tilde (~) as an indication of a sequence of acceptable characters. You must put it before or after all the other characters inside the brackets, not between them. If you placed an exclamation point (!) inside the brackets to indicate a match excluding the characters within the brackets, place the hyphen right after the exclamation point.

If you're searching for an exclamation point or a closing bracket, you needn't use the brackets at all. Just place the characters in the string with the rest.

While wildcards are intended for use in search strings that locate values in Text and Memo fields, they can sometimes be used with dates and other data types. If you changed the Regional Settings properties for the other data types, the wildcards probably won't work.

Wildcards can appear anywhere in the search string in the Find What box. For example, you can enter the string **12##*[BC]*** to find all addresses in the 1200 block of any street that begins with *B* or *C*.

If you included A inside the square brackets, Access would also find addresses on streets with Avenue as part of the street name.

Finding Zero-Length Strings and Null Values

As mentioned in Chapter 4 in the discussion of zero-length strings and Null values, you can use Find to locate records with blank fields. This is useful when you enter incomplete record data because all the information wasn't yet available. Then, when more data arrives, you can quickly look for the records that need to be filled in. If the field contains a zero-length string, you know no relevant value exists for that field in that record. But, if the field contains a Null value, this means the value was unknown at the time.

To find fields with Null values, enter **Null** or **Is Null** in the Find What text box. To find fields with zero-length strings, type a pair of quotation marks ("") with no space between them. When Access finds a record with a blank in the field, the record selector moves to the record, but the field isn't highlighted. When you close the Find and Replace dialog box, the insertion point appears in the blank field, ready for you to enter data.

If you created a custom format for a Text or Memo field, which specifies a certain display if the field contains a Null value, and a different display if it contains a zero-length string, you need to watch how you apply the Search Fields As Formatted option.

- If the field is unformatted, you can find a blank field by entering **Null** or **Is Null** in the Find What box and making sure the Search Fields As Formatted option isn't checked.

- If the field is formatted so a Null value displays text such as "Not known," enter that string and make sure the Search Fields As Formatted option is checked.

- If you're looking for zero-length strings, make sure the Search Fields As Formatted option isn't checked.

In addition, be sure to select Whole Field in the Match box when you're looking for either a Null value or a zero-length string.

Finding and Replacing Data

A variation of the Find feature is the Replace tool that lets you specify a value you want in the field in place of the one already there. The search options are the same. The only difference between the Find tab and the Replace tab is the addition of the Replace With box in which you type the replacement value.

To replace a certain value in a field with another value, click the Find button and open the Replace tab or choose Edit | Replace. (The Replace command may be in the expanded Edit menu.)

For example, suppose you want to replace all occurrences of the word "Lost" in the Award Date field of the Bid Data with the words "Not awarded." Follow these steps:

1. Place the insertion point in the Award Date column.

2. Choose Edit | Replace to open the Replace tab of the Find and Replace dialog box.

3. Enter **Lost** in the Find What box and **Not Awarded** in the Replace With box (see Figure 6-24). Notice you have the same search options as with finding records.

4. Click Find Next, and then do one of the following:

   - Choose Replace to replace this instance of Lost. Access moves automatically to the next occurrence.

   - Choose Find Next to skip replacing this occurrence and move to the next.

   - Choose Replace All to replace all the values without reviewing them.

5. Access displays a message when it finishes searching the records. Click Cancel to close the dialog box.

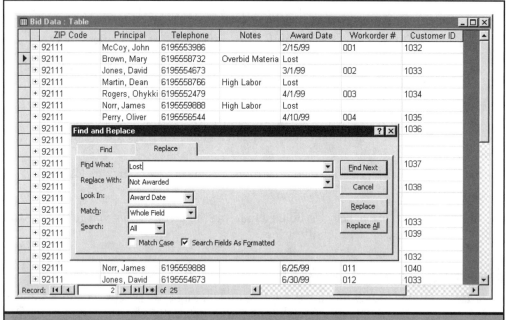

Figure 6-24. *Replacing Lost with Not Awarded*

> **Note**
> *You cannot replace Null values and zero-length strings with Find and Replace. You can use Find to locate them one at a time and replace them manually or run an update query to replace them all at once.*

If you have a large amount of data to replace, you can do that faster by using an update query. The only disadvantage is the update query replaces all the values without your confirmation of individual replacements. If you want to find and replace values in more than one field, the update query isn't as convenient as Find and Replace.

> **Note**
> *As with searching for a value, if the datasheet contains a subdatasheet or the form contains a subform, the replacement occurs only in the object containing the insertion point.*

Setting Edit/Find Options

Many of the Edit and Find options you choose in the Find and Replace dialog boxes have default settings that can be changed in the Edit/Find tab of the Options dialog box (see Figure 6-25). The Default Find/Replace Behavior options present combinations of the Search and Match settings in the Find and Replace dialog boxes as follows:

- *Fast search* searches the current field and matches the whole field.

GETTING STARTED

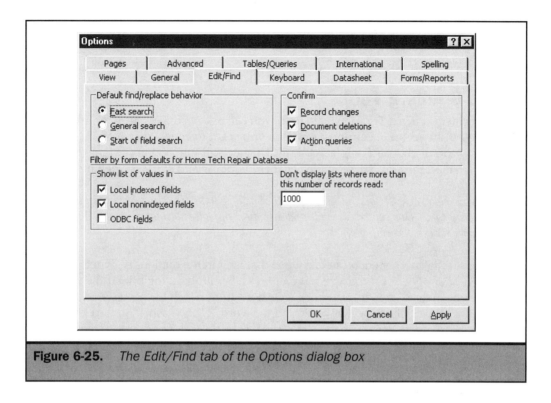

Figure 6-25.   *The Edit/Find tab of the Options dialog box*

- *General search* searches all fields and matches any part of the field.
- *Start of field search* searches the current field and matches the beginning characters in the field.

 The Confirm options specify when Access is to display a confirmation message: before changing records, deleting a document, or running action queries. A good idea is to leave these options all enabled because these actions cannot be reversed by Undo.

The Filter By Form default settings are discussed in Chapter 7.

Deleting Data

To delete individual characters, place the insertion point in the field and press DEL to remove the next character or press BACKSPACE to remove the previous character. To delete all the data in the field, select the field and press DEL or BACKSPACE. Characters deleted from a field can be restored by choosing Edit | Undo Delete.

To delete an entire record, select the record and press DEL or choose Edit | Delete. Deleting a record cannot be reversed, so Access warns you before deleting the record.

To delete several records, select them all, then proceed as previously described. To delete a record without selecting it, place the insertion point anywhere in the record and click Delete Record.

Using the Spelling Tool

After you enter data in a Text or Memo field, you can ask Access to check for misspelled words. Select the records, columns, or fields you want to check, and then click the Spelling button or choose Tools | Spelling. To check all the Text and Memo fields in the table, select the table name in the Database window and start the spelling checker.

If you make no selection, Access checks the spelling in all Text and Memo fields in the current table. This can take a while and display many false alarms with fields that contain proper names, for example.

If the spelling checker encounters a word that isn't in the dictionary, whether it's misspelled or simply not recognized, it displays a Spelling dialog box. If the word resembles one in the dictionary, a list of suggestions from which to choose is presented. In Figure 6-26, the spelling checker has found the word "Dishwassher" in the Description field of the Workorders table. You can choose one of the three suggestions as a replacement, change the word yourself, or ignore the word and go on with the checking.

To change the spelling, do one of the following:

■ Click Change to accept the selected suggestion in the Suggestions box.

■ Select one of the other suggestions in the list, and then click Change.

■ Double-click the desired suggestion.

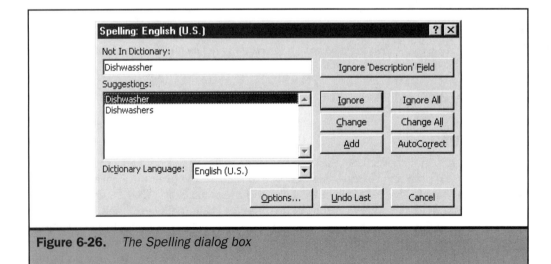

Figure 6-26. *The Spelling dialog box*

- If none of the suggestions is what you want, but you still want to change the word, type the new word in the Not In Dictionary and click Change.
- To change all subsequent occurrences of the same word to the word in the Not In Dictionary, choose Change All.

The other options in the Spelling dialog box are as follows.

- *Suggestions* displays a list of possible replacements for the word in the Not In box. If the Always Suggest option in the Spell Options dialog box isn't selected, no suggestions are displayed.
- *Ignore 'Description' Field* instructs the spelling checker to ignore the current field.
- *Ignore* skips the current instance of the word, while *Ignore All* skips this and all subsequent instances of it.
- *Add* adds the word in the Not In Dictionary box to the Custom dictionary shown in the Add Words To box.
- *Dictionary Language* specifies the dictionary to which the flagged word should be added.
- *AutoCorrect* adds the word to the list of words to correct automatically the next time it occurs. The advantage to this approach is, if you misspell the word later, Access is equipped to correct it for you.
- *Options* opens the Spell Options dialog box described next.
- *Undo Last* reverses the previous change. You can use this more than once to reverse several previously changed values.

Note *If the currently selected records, columns, or fields don't contain any fields that can be checked for spelling, Access displays a message box with that information. Only Text and Memo fields are spell-checked.*

Setting Spelling Options

You can specify some of the spelling options, such as what suggestions to make, what types of errors to ignore, and which language dictionary to use as a reference. To change these spelling options, click the Options button in the Spelling dialog box. Figure 6-27 shows the Spelling Options dialog box. By default, all four options are checked and the English (U.S.) dictionary is used.

The Suggest options, when checked, always try to suggest a correction from the main dictionary. Deselect the Suggest From Main Dictionary Only option to have the spelling checker also consult a custom dictionary.

Tip *You can choose to use the English (United Kingdom) dictionary instead of the English (U.S.) one, so the spelling checker doesn't flag words like theatre or labour.*

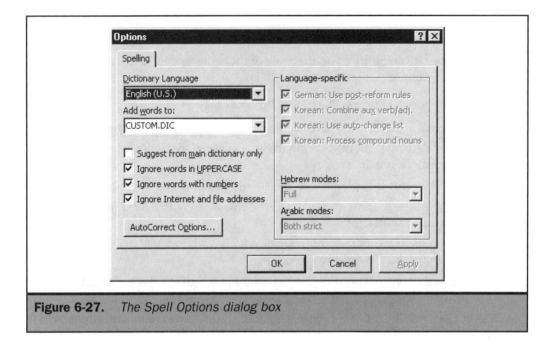

Figure 6-27. *The Spell Options dialog box*

The Ignore options speed up the spell checking by telling Access not to bother with words in uppercase, such as acronyms, or words with numbers, or internet or file addresses.

Using AutoCorrect

If you want Access to correct misspelled words and ones you habitually mistype as you enter text, activate the AutoCorrect feature. This feature can also be used to replace abbreviations with longer words. For example, you could speed up data entry by having Access convert "Jr" to "Junior." When you type **Jr** and press SPACEBAR, TAB, ENTER, or a punctuation mark, Access automatically replaces it with "Junior."

To start automatic correction, choose Tools | AutoCorrect. The AutoCorrect dialog box opens (see Figure 6-28) with five options, plus a list of corrections and other replacements it's prepared to make.

The first four options are self-explanatory and correct some of the commonly occurring spelling oversights, such as two initial capital letters or accidentally leaving the CAPS LOCK key set.

Caution *The AutoCorrect feature is used by all the Microsoft Office programs. Any entries you make in other programs are applicable to misspellings in Access.*

Adding to the Replacement List

The fifth option contains a list of replacements for many typical spelling errors. You can add more replacements to the list. For example, if you commonly misspell the word "there" as "theer," you can add it to the AutoCorrect list, as follows.

1. Choose Tools | AutoCorrect.

2. Type **theer** in the Replace box. As you type the Replace entry, the list scrolls down accordingly. This enables you to see if the entry is already there.

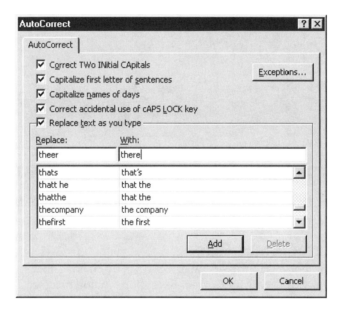

3. Type **there** in the With box.

4. Click Add.

5. Click OK to close the AutoCorrect dialog box.

To delete an entry from the AutoCorrect list, select the line in the list below the Replace and With boxes, and then click Delete.

AutoCorrect doesn't correct any text typed prior to checking the Replace Text As You Type option. Also, additions to the AutoCorrect list don't act on entries made before the addition was made.

GETTING STARTED

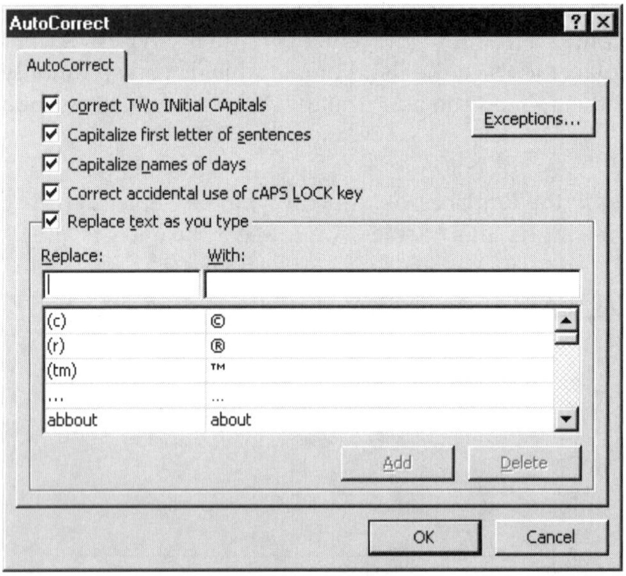

Figure 6-28. *The AutoCorrect dialog box*

Excluding AutoCorrect Rules

You can specify exceptions to the AutoCorrect rules by clicking Exceptions in the AutoCorrect dialog box. The AutoCorrect Exceptions dialog box (see Figure 6-29) has two tabs: First Letter and INitial CAps.

The First Letter tab contains a list of common abbreviations, all ending with a period. Normally, Access assumes a period signals the end of a sentence and capitalizes the first letter of the next word. To add this to the list of exceptions, type the entry (with the period) in the Don't Capitalize After box and click Add. To remove one from the list, select the entry and click Delete.

The INitial CAps tab is empty until you type text in the Don't Change box and click Add.

Printing Table Data

The quickest way to print table data is to click the Print button with the table open or with the table name selected in the Database window. This sends the data directly to the default printer. You can also right-click the table name in the Database window and choose Print from the shortcut menu. This also sends the data directly to the printer.

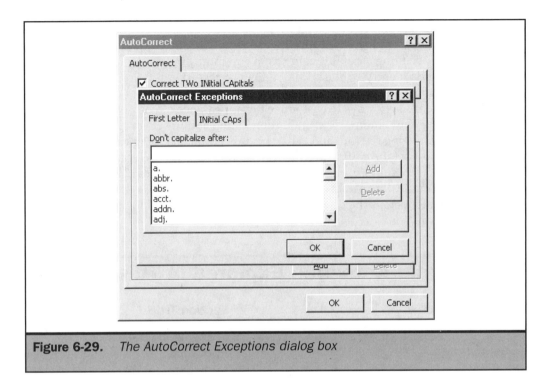

Figure 6-29. *The AutoCorrect Exceptions dialog box*

Note *If you want to print the subdatasheet data, expand the subdatasheet before printing.*

If you want to choose other print options, such as printing multiple copies or printing only the selected records, you need to open the Print dialog box. To see how the printed data looks before you print it, open the Print Preview window. This is useful when you think the data might not fit across the page with the current page layout. If you want to adjust the page margins, paper size, or the page layout, open the Page Setup dialog box.

See Chapter 14 for complete information about previewing and printing reports, including changing print options and running Page Setup.

Summary

Access 2002 has included several new tools to make your data entry and editing quicker and easier. Many of the table field properties can be set to ensure valid and complete data in all the tables in your database.

One of the most versatile of the Access data entry tools is the Lookup Wizard, which helps you create a list from which to choose the proper value for a field. The list can retrieve values from another table or merely specify a set of fixed values.

Access treats blank values in different ways, depending on why they are blank. The Required and Allow Zero Length properties can together control the entry and display of blank fields. Specifying a default value for a commonly occurring field value can save time during data entry, while adding a field or record validation rule can guard against incorrect data entry.

Access provides many ways to customize the appearance of your Datasheet view, including changing the column width and order, hiding and freezing columns, adjusting the row height, changing the font and cell appearance, and changing the field names.

Among the most helpful editing tools is the spelling checker, which can check spelling as you type and offer suggestions for replacing misspelled words. The AutoCorrect feature can automatically correct commonly misspelled words.

The next chapter begins the discussion of manipulating table data by sorting and filtering the information.

MOUS Exam Activities Explored in This Chapter

Level	Activity	Section Title
Core	Format datasheets	Changing the Datasheet Appearance
Core	Add a pre-defined input mask to a field	Customizing Data Entry
Core	Create Lookup fields	Creating Lookup Fields
Core	Modify field properties	Adding Custom Input Masks Changing Field Names
Core	Enter, edit, and delete records	Entering New Data Locating Records Finding and Replacing Data Deleting Data Using the Spelling Tool Using AutoCorrect
Expert	Create and modify Lookup field properties	Creating Lookup Fields
Expert	Create and modify input masks	Adding Custom Input Masks Creating a Custom Input Mask

The Complete Reference

Access 2002

Part II

Retrieving and Presenting Information

Chapter 7

Sorting, Filtering, and Printing Records

Once you've stored all the information in the related tables of your database, you need to retrieve specific data and arrange it in meaningful ways. The Access Sort and Filter features help you do just that. *Sorting* arranges the records in a specified order, while *filtering* hides records you don't want to see. Combining these two tools gives you the power to display only the records you want in the order you want.

Sorting Records

Access automatically sorts records by the value in the primary key field. During data retrieval and presentation, times will occur when you'll want the records arranged in a different order. For example, you may want to look up all the work orders sorted by the employee who's acting as the supervisor, so you can keep tabs on the workload.

To see records with this information grouped together in Datasheet or Form view, you can sort the records based on the value in a specific field. In Datasheet view, you can sort up to 255 characters in one or more fields to achieve a sort within a sort. The ascending sort order arranges text values in alphabetical order (*A* to *Z*), date/time values from earliest to latest, and number/currency values from lowest to highest. Use descending to reverse the order. You cannot sort on Memo, Hyperlink, or OLE Object fields.

Sorting on a Single Field

To sort by a single field in a datasheet or form, click within the field you want to sort by, and then do one of the following:

- Click Sort Ascending.
- Click Sort Descending.
- Choose Records | Sort | Sort Ascending.
- Choose Records | Sort | Sort Descending.
- Right-click in the field and choose Sort Ascending from the shortcut menu.
- Right-click in the field and choose Sort Descending from the shortcut menu.

Figure 7-1 shows the Home Tech Repair Employees records sorted in ascending order by Last Name.

To restore the records to their original order, choose Records | Remove Filter/Sort or right-click in the datasheet and choose Remove Filter/Sort from the shortcut menu.

To sort records in a subdatasheet, display the subdatasheet by clicking the expand indicator (the plus sign (+) in the left margin), and then proceed as with a datasheet. When you specify a sort order for one subdatasheet in Datasheet view, all the subdatasheets of that level are also sorted accordingly.

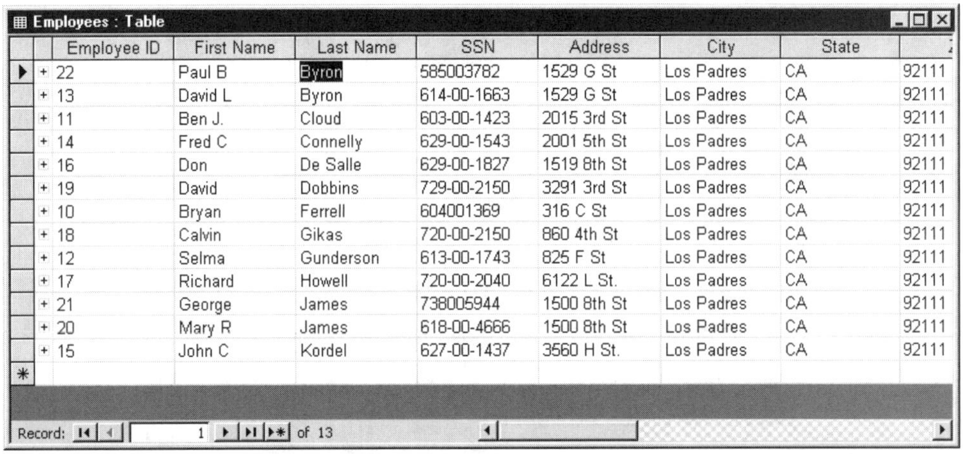

Employee ID	First Name	Last Name	SSN	Address	City	State	
+ 22	Paul B	Byron	585003782	1529 G St	Los Padres	CA	92111
+ 13	David L	Byron	614-00-1663	1529 G St	Los Padres	CA	92111
+ 11	Ben J.	Cloud	603-00-1423	2015 3rd St	Los Padres	CA	92111
+ 14	Fred C	Connelly	629-00-1543	2001 5th St	Los Padres	CA	92111
+ 16	Don	De Salle	629-00-1827	1519 8th St	Los Padres	CA	92111
+ 19	David	Dobbins	729-00-2150	3291 3rd St	Los Padres	CA	92111
+ 10	Bryan	Ferrell	604001369	316 C St	Los Padres	CA	92111
+ 18	Calvin	Gikas	720-00-2150	860 4th St	Los Padres	CA	92111
+ 12	Selma	Gunderson	613-00-1743	825 F St	Los Padres	CA	92111
+ 17	Richard	Howell	720-00-2040	6122 L St.	Los Padres	CA	92111
+ 21	George	James	738005944	1500 8th St	Los Padres	CA	92111
+ 20	Mary R	James	618-00-4666	1500 8th St	Los Padres	CA	92111
+ 15	John C	Kordel	627-00-1437	3560 H St.	Los Padres	CA	92111

Record: 1 of 13

Figure 7-1. *Employee records sorted by Last Name*

When several records have the same value in one of the fields you want to sort by, you can sort on two or more fields at the same time in Datasheet view. In Form view, records can be sorted by only one field with the Sort feature.

Note   *If you're building a database for a different language, you can set the sort order accordingly. Choose Tools | Options and click the General tab. The New database sort order list (see Figure 7-2) offers a variety of language settings. Before you change the sort order to another language, be sure your operating system supports that language. Just to be safe, always back up your database before making such drastic changes.*

Sorting by Two or More Fields

To sort by more than one field, the fields must be adjacent in the datasheet. In addition, Access uses a sort precedence from left to right, so the records are sorted first by the values in the left column. If duplicate values appear in that column, a secondary sort is performed on those records by the values in the next column to the right. If the columns involved in the sort aren't adjacent or are in the wrong relative position in the datasheet or subdatasheet, move the columns before sorting the records. When all are in position, select the columns you want to sort on and click one of the Sort buttons as before, or choose from the Records or the shortcut menu.

Figure 7-3 shows the Employees Last Name and First Name columns repositioned and selected, ready to sort by values in those fields.

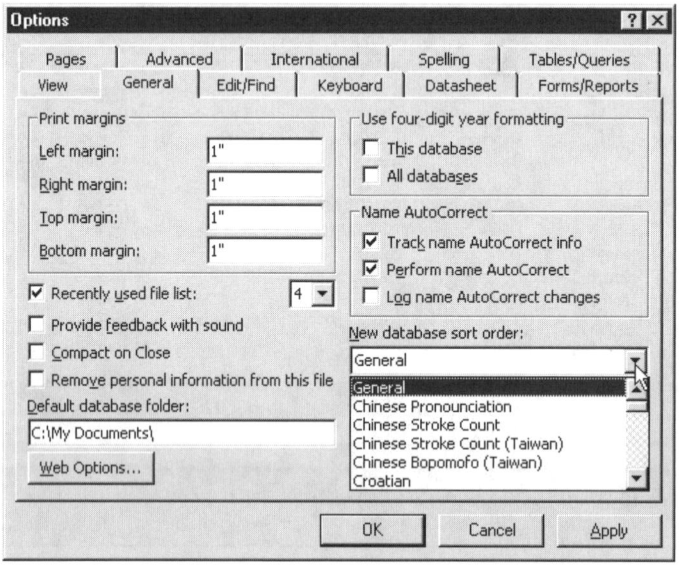

Figure 7-2. *Changing the sort order list to a different language*

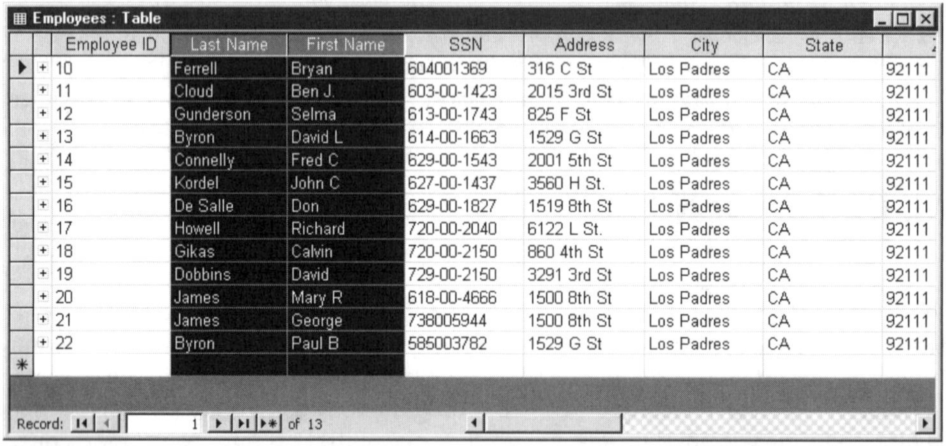

Figure 7-3. *Sorting Employees by Last and First Names*

Sort Tips

- If you stored numbers in a Text field, they are sorted as a character string instead of by numeric value. However, you can get around this by filling out the values with leading zeros, so the strings are all the same length. For example, the result of sorting the values 5, 15, 33, 242 in a Text field would be 15, 242, 33, 5. But, if you store them as 015, 005, 033 and 242, they are sorted properly in numeric order. Better yet, convert the field to Number if you're sure it won't ever contain letters or other characters.

- If your table includes records with zero-length strings or Null values, those records appear first in the ascending sort order: Null values first, followed by zero-length strings.

Note   *When you sort records by two or more fields, Access performs a "simple" sort, in which the values in the fields are all sorted in the same order, ascending or descending. It won't mix ascending and descending orders. To mix sort orders, you must use the Advanced Filter/Sort operation described later in this chapter.*

Saving the Sort Order

If you close the table after sorting the records, Access asks if you want to save the changes to the design (which includes the sort order). Responding Yes saves the sort order with the table and, the next time you open the table, the records appear in that order. Responding No saves the table in the original, primary key order. In addition, any new forms or reports you create based on the table inherit the sort order and apply it to the new object.

Filtering Records

When you want to see only certain records in your datasheet, subdatasheet, or form, you can filter out the ones you don't want to see. The *filter* process screens the records and lets through only those that meet your criteria. The *criteria* is a set of conditions you specify to limit the display to a certain subset of records.

This can save time by focusing your attention on only the records that are important at the moment. Filtering doesn't remove the records from the table, it only removes them from your view of the table. A filter consists of conditions you specify that can be as simple as "all the records for work orders in March 2001" or as complex as "all bids submitted during February or March that exceeded $500 and were awarded within 30 days of the bid offer."

The difference between finding records and filtering records is when Access finds a record, the cursor moves to the record and leaves all the rest on the screen. With a filter, the nonqualifying records are removed from the screen, leaving only the records you want to see.

In Access, you have five ways to filter records, depending on the conditions you want to set and whether you want the records sorted in a particular order.

- *Filter By Form* screens records with the criteria you enter into a table skeleton.

- *Filter By Selection* leaves only the records with the same value as the one you select in one of the records.

- *Filter Excluding Selection* leaves only the records that don't include the same value as the one you select in one of the records.

- *Advanced Filter/Sort* gives you, in addition to filtering, the capability to specify a complex sort. With a *complex sort* you can sort the records by two or more fields using different orders, ascending or descending.

- *Filter For Input* displays a box in the shortcut menu where you enter the filter criteria directly.

When the records you see on the screen are the result of a filter, Access reminds you in three ways that you aren't viewing the entire table. The status bar shows FLTR, indicating a filter is in effect, and the navigation bar gives you the number of records qualified by the word (Filtered). In addition, the Apply Filter toolbar button appears pressed and the ScreenTip has changed to Remove Filter. Figure 7-4 shows the Workorders records filtered, so only records of jobs supervised by Ferrell are visible.

Picking a Filter Type

To decide what type of filter you should use, look at what you want it to do.

- If you want to search for records that meet more than one criteria at once (combined with AND), you can use any of the five types of filters. Using Filter By Selection, you must specify and apply the criteria one at a time.

- If you want to combine criteria with the OR operator or enter expressions as criteria, you must use either Filter By Form, Filter For Input, or Advanced Filter/Sort.

- If you also want the records sorted as part of the filter process, you must use the Advanced Filter/Sort. You can, however, sort the results of the other types of filters after applying the filter by clicking one of the Sort buttons on the toolbar.

Microsoft Access - [Workorders : Table]

File   Edit   View   Insert   Format   Records   Tools   Window   Help   Type a question for help

		Workorder Num	Customer ID	Bid Number	Start Date	Completion Date	Supervisor	Principal Worker	Helper
▶	+	001	1032	98-101	2/25/01	3/16/01	Ferrell	Howell	
	+	009	1039	98-117	6/25/01	6/26/01	Ferrell	Howell	De Salle
	+	013	1032	98-122	7/10/01	7/20/01	Ferrell	Howell	
*									

Figure 7-4.   *Workorders filtered by Ferrell as supervisor*

When you apply a filter to a datasheet, the same filter is applied to any subdatasheets within it. When you create a filter on a subdatasheet, the filter is also available when you open the table in Datasheet view.

Filtering By Selection

Filtering By Selection is the most commonly used and the easiest filtering method. Simply select the value you want to use as the match for the records and click a button. When you apply the Filter By Selection, the records that remain on the screen are only those that contain the selected value. You can Filter By Selection on a value in any type of field, even hyperlink fields, except OLE Object fields.

Specifying the Filter Value

To set the filter value, find one occurrence of the value in the datasheet or subdatasheet and select all or only part of it. You can also place the insertion point in the field that contains the value for which you want to filter. Once you've defined the value, apply the filter in one of the following ways:

■ Choose Records | Filter | Filter By Selection.

■ Click Filter By Selection on the toolbar.

■ Right-click the desired value and choose Filter By Selection from the shortcut menu.

The way you select the value determines what records pass the filter. Table 7-1 describes the various ways of selecting values for filtering and equates them to match settings in the Find dialog box, as discussed in Chapter 6.

Selection	Returns Records Where	Find Match Equivalent
Entire value or place insertion point in the field without selecting any characters	Whole field matches selected value	Whole Field Match option
Part of value, including first character	Field starts with selected characters	Start of Field Match option
Part of value, not including first character	Field with matching value anywhere in field	Any part of Field Match option

Table 7-1. *Value Selections for Filtering*

Let's try out a few filters on the Home Tech Repair tables. First, filter the Employees table to show records for electrical specialists only.

1. With the Employees table open in Datasheet view, place the insertion point in a Specialty field with the value Electrical.

2. Click Filter By Selection. Only two records remain on the screen, both with Electrical in the Specialty field.

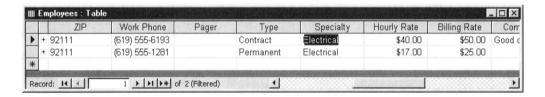

3. Click Remove Filter. All the records return to the datasheet or subdatasheet.

> **Tip** *After you remove the filter and restore all the records to the display, you can reapply the most recently used filter by clicking the Apply Filter toolbar button or choosing Records | Apply Filter/Sort.*

As an example of filtering to a partial value, filter the Bid Data table so you see only records that contain the word "heater" in the Description field.

1. In the Bid Data datasheet, select the "heater" part of Replace Waterheater in the Description field of the Bid Number 98-102 record.

2. Choose Records | Filter | Filter By Selection. Two records remain, both with the word "heater" at the end of the Description field.

Bid Data : Table						
	Bid Number	Bid Date	Expires	Description	Address	City	Stat
▶ +	98-102	1/15/01	3/1/01	Replace Waterheater	176 3rd St	Los Padres	CA
+	98-117	5/18/01	8/18/01	SPA Heater	952 C St	Los Padres	CA
*						

Record: ◄◄ ◄ 1 ► ►◄ ►* of 2 (Filtered)

3. Click Remove Filter. All records return to the datasheet.

Filter By Selection applies only one filter condition at a time. If you need to filter based on a combination of two or more values, you can apply the second Filter By Selection criterion to the records that remain after the first filter is applied. This is equivalent to combining the filter criteria with an AND operator. For example, you may want to see records for work orders for heater jobs supervised by Ferrell. Apply a filter that limits the records to heater jobs, and then apply a second filter to the results of the first. The second filter further limits the result to records with both values. The order of applying the filters doesn't make any difference; the result is the same either way.

If you press TAB to reach the Drawing field (don't click it or you'll jump to the hyperlink target), and then click Filter By Selection, you can see all the records that refer to the same drawing. For example, the Bay Window drawing is used for two work orders.

Using an Exclusion Filter

Instead of telling Access which records you want to see, sometimes it's easier to specify which ones you don't want to see. In this case, you can use the Filter Excluding Selection option, which screens out the records with the value you select, instead of including them. Filter Excluding Selection works much like Filter By Selection because you select the value or partial value in the datasheet or form.

For example, suppose you want to see the records for all work orders except those supervised by Ferrell. You select the value as before, and then choose Records | Filter |

Filter Excluding Selection, or right-click the selection and choose Filter Excluding Selection from the shortcut menu. Filter Excluding Selection is also available from the Records | Filter menu.

Filtering By Form

Filter By Form isn't much different from Filter By Selection. Instead of selecting a value from the datasheet or subdatasheet as a filter criterion, you enter the value in a filter grid. The grid is a table skeleton that resembles a blank record showing all the filterable fields in the table with space to enter filter values. One advantage of using Filter By Form is you can combine filter criteria. You can specify two or more conditions, so a record must meet any one or all of them to survive the filter. The multiple criteria can apply to a single field or to more than one field.

If you want to filter the records in a subdatasheet, click the expand indicator to display the subdatasheet records, and then proceed as with a datasheet filter.

Entering Filter Criteria

When you choose Filter By Form, the table grid appears on the screen as shown in the following illustration. The most recent filter saved with the table shows in the filter grid. Notice Access has created an expression from your Filter By Selection criterion. The expression *Like "*heater"* means to show all records that have a value in the Description field ending with heater.

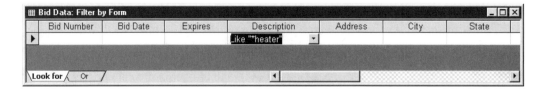

 *The asterisk in front of "heater" in the filter indicates the characters you selected appeared at the end of the value. The filter shows all other records that end with "heater." If you want records with the value anywhere in the field, add another asterisk, so the filter becomes Like "*heater*".*

 The Filter By Form toolbar has three handy buttons. The Clear Grid button removes the filter that appears in the skeleton; so you needn't delete every entry individually. The other button is the familiar Apply Filter button. The Close button lets you return to the datasheet without applying any filter.

To create a new filter, clear the grid of any existing filter and move to the field where you want to specify a value. When you move the insertion point to a field in the grid, an arrow appears in the field. Clicking this arrow displays a list of unique values that currently exist in the field, sorted in ascending order. Figure 7-5 shows the list of values in the Completion Date field of the Workorders table. To filter on one of these values, select the value, and then click Apply Filter. This is equivalent to using Filter By Selection.

If you display a value list in one of the employee-related fields (Supervisor, Principal Worker, or Helper), you see the values in the lookup table you created in the last chapter. The values in the list are only for display. Access stores the value from the primary key field of the lookup list in the Workorders table. This creates a bit of a problem, as you can see in the section that discusses Advanced Filter/Sort, later in this chapter.

RETRIEVING AND PRESENTING INFORMATION

Filtering Memo, OLE Object, and Hyperlink Fields

Although you cannot sort by Memo, OLE Object, or Hyperlink fields, you can filter by such fields. When you apply Filter By Selection, you can see all the records with the same values in the field. But with the other three filter operations, you can only filter based on whether the field has a value or is empty. When you click the drop-down list in one of these fields, the only available values are Is Null and Is Not Null. This filter option is also available for calculated fields in queries.

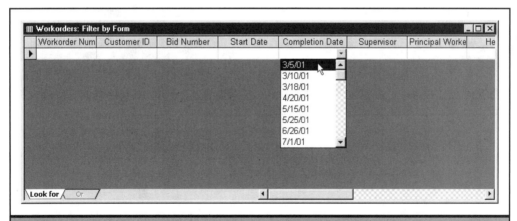

Figure 7-5. *List of Completion Date values*

If you don't see the value list in the table skeleton, the option may be turned off. To restore the option, choose Options from the Tools menu, and then click the Edit/Find tab. One group of the options on this page is Show list of values in, which offers the choices of Local indexed fields, Local non-indexed fields, and ODBC fields. Check the first two options to display the value list for all fields in the skeleton. More about customizing the workplace in Chapter 16.

To filter Workorders records to show only those whose scheduled completion date is before July 1, 2001, follow these steps:

1. In the Workorders datasheet, click Filter By Form on the toolbar. The filter grid appears.

2. If entries are in the grid, click Clear Grid to remove them.

3. Place the insertion point in the Completion Date field and select 7/1/01 from the value list. Access automatically adds the date/time delimiter symbols (#) to the date you select from the list.

4. Place the insertion point at the beginning of the date and enter < (less than). You can also press F2 to switch to edit mode, press HOME, and then enter the less than symbol (<).

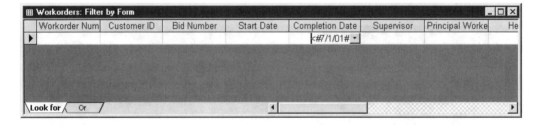

5. Click Apply Filter. Only the eight records of Workorders scheduled to be completed before July 1, 2001 remain on the screen.

Workorder Num	Customer ID	Bid Number	Start Date	Completion Date	Supervisor	Principal Worke
+ 001	1032	98-101	2/25/01	3/10/01	Ferrell	Howell
+ 002	1033	98-103	3/15/01	3/18/01	Gunderson	Gikas
+ 003	1034	98-105	3/10/01	3/5/01	Connelly	Dobbins
+ 004	1035	98-107	4/15/01	4/20/01	Gunderson	Howell
+ 005	1036	98-108	5/10/01	5/15/01	Connelly	Dobbins
+ 006	1037	98-111	5/12/01	5/25/01	Howell	
+ 009	1039	98-117	6/25/01	6/26/01	Ferrell	Howell	De S
+ 010	1032	98-119	6/26/01	6/26/01	Dobbins	

Record: 1 of 8 (Filtered)

6. Click Remove Filter or choose Records | Remove Filter/Sort to restore all the records. Remove Filter/Sort is also available from the Datasheet shortcut menu, which displays when you right-click anywhere in the datasheet.

Using Wildcards and Expressions in a Filter

You can use wildcards in filter criteria for Text and Memo fields the same way as in the Find criteria. They apply only to character strings. Refer to Chapter 6 for examples of using wildcards.

You can also enter an expression as the filter criterion, such as the earlier example of <7/1/01 entered in the Completion Date field in the Filter By Form grid. To use an expression as a criterion, enter it directly in the filter grid. Table 7-2 shows some examples of expressions you can use as filter criteria.

Field	Expression	Result
Address	Like "*3rd*"	Displays records with addresses on 3rd street.
Completion Date	Between #5/1/01# And #7/31/01#	Displays Workorders records for all jobs scheduled to be completed during May, June, and July 2001.
Last Name	>="P"	Displays records for Customers whose last name starts with letters *P* through *Z*.

Table 7-2. *Examples of Filter Expressions*

Field	Expression	Result
Completion Date	Between Date() And Date()+30	Uses the Date() function to display Workorders records for jobs scheduled to be completed within 30 days from today.
Bid Date	Year([Bid Date])=2001	Uses the Year() function to display Bid Data records with Bid Dates in 2001.
Workorder #	Is Null	Displays Bid Data records with empty Workorder # fields.

Table 7-1. *Examples of Filter Expressions* (continued)

You need to obey a few rules when entering expressions in a filter condition, whether you're using the Filter By Form, Filter For Input, or Advanced Filter/Sort method.

- If a Text field value contains a space, any punctuation, or an operator character, the value must be enclosed in quotation marks. For example, "George" is OK, but "George Bart" must be entered as "George Bart". If the entry is one of the values in the list, Access adds the quotation marks for you after you leave the criteria grid.

- To filter a Memo field, use the asterisk (*) wildcards to filter on embedded text.

- For Number, Currency, and AutoNumber fields, don't include characters, such as the currency symbol or the thousands separator. If you do, you'll see a data type mismatch error message. Decimal points and minus signs are okay.

- For Date/Time field values, abide by the options set on the Date tab of the Regional Settings Properties dialog box of the Windows Control Panel. These settings control the sequence of the month, day, and year values within the field. Access encloses the date or time value in pound signs (#).

- For Yes/No fields, you can enter Yes, -1, On, or True to filter for Yes values; No, 0, Off, or False for No values.

Combining Filter Criteria with AND

You can use complex criteria that combine two or more filter conditions in the Filter By Form window. If you combine two conditions with the AND operator, you are limiting the records to those that meet both conditions. For example, you could ask Access to limit the Workorders records to only those with a Material Cost less than $1,000 and a Labor Cost greater than $500. This would give you a list of labor-intensive contracts.

To combine two filter conditions with AND:

1. In the Workorders datasheet, click Filter By Form on the toolbar.

2. Click Clear Grid to remove the previous filter conditions and click in the Material Cost field. Figure 7-6 shows the stored values in the Material Cost fields without the dollar signs, which are part of the display format, not stored with the values.

3. Type **<=1000** and press TAB to move to the Labor Cost field, and type **>=500**, and then press ENTER.

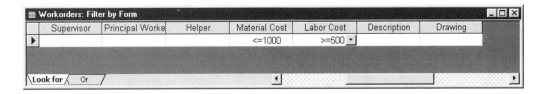

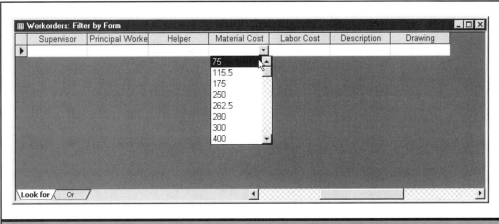

Figure 7-6.   *List of Material Cost stored values*

4. Click Apply Filter. Four records meet the combined filter conditions that show the labor-intensive contracts.

5. Click Remove Filter to restore all the records in the datasheet.

The previous example combined filter conditions in different fields with the implied AND operator. You can also combine filter conditions in the same field with AND by typing AND between the expressions. For example, if you enter the filter condition >=500 AND <=1000 in the Material Cost field, you would see only the records for work orders requiring between $500 and $1,000 worth of materials, inclusive. Another way to express the same criterion is to use the Between…And…operator: Between 500 And 1000.

Combining Filter Conditions with OR

Using the AND operator to combine filter conditions reduces the resulting record set by demanding both criteria be met in each record. The OR operator, on the other hand, expands the resulting record set by including records that meet either of the conditions, but not necessarily both.

When you use Filter By Selection, you can combine conditions only with the implied AND operator by imposing a second filter on the set of records already filtered by the first criteria. With Filter By Form, you can apply as many filters as you want in one operation, using both AND and OR operators.

The Filter By Form window contains two tabs at the bottom of the window: Look for and Or. You enter the first filter condition, and any others you want to combine with it, using AND on the Look for page. If you want to add an OR filter condition, click the Or tab and enter the condition on the second page. If you change your mind and want to delete the Or tab, select it and choose Edit | Delete Tab.

Another Or tab appears when you begin to add a filter to the first Or page.

The OR combination comes in handy when you want to find records with any one of several values in a field. For example, suppose you want to see all the Workorders records for jobs on B or H Streets. You would enter * **B*** in the Address field in the filter grid on the Look for page, and then enter * **H*** in the Address field on the Or page.

If you don't include a space before the H in the filter criterion, you'll see all records with the letter H anywhere in the Address field. For example, addresses on any street with "th," such as 5th or 6th.

To combine two filter conditions with OR:

1. In the Bid Data datasheet, choose Records | Filter | Filter By Form. The Filter window opens with the last filter condition in the grid.

2. Click Clear Grid, enter * **B*** (with a space before the *B*) in the Address field on the Look for page, and then press ENTER. Access translates the expression to *Like "* B*"*.

3. Click the Or tab at the bottom of the window. The Or page opens with the same empty grid as the Look for page. Notice a third tab now shows at the bottom of the window.

4. Place the insertion point in the Address field, enter * **H***, and then press ENTER. The expression is changed to *Like "* H*"*.

5. Click Apply Filter on the toolbar. The datasheet now shows the five jobs with addresses on B or H Streets.

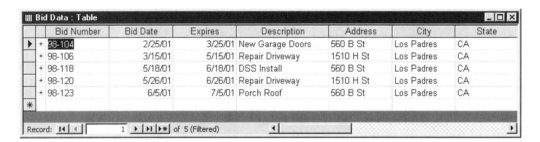

	Bid Number	Bid Date	Expires	Description	Address	City	State
+	98-104	2/25/01	3/25/01	New Garage Doors	560 B St	Los Padres	CA
+	98-106	3/15/01	5/15/01	Repair Driveway	1510 H St	Los Padres	CA
+	98-118	5/18/01	6/18/01	DSS Install	560 B St	Los Padres	CA
+	98-120	5/26/01	6/26/01	Repair Driveway	1510 H St	Los Padres	CA
+	98-123	6/5/01	7/5/01	Porch Roof	560 B St	Los Padres	CA

Record: 1 of 5 (Filtered)

6. Click Remove Filter to restore all the records.

AND and OR Can Get Confusing

The logic can get a little confusing when you begin combining filter conditions with both AND and OR. For example, you might want to see all Bid Data records for jobs on B and H Streets that were lost. If the job was lost, Lost appears in the Award Date field. Obviously, B and H Streets are combined with the OR operator, but where does the Award Date (Lost) condition go? The answer is to combine the Award Date filter with both the B and H Street filters using the AND operator in each case. On the Look for page, enter **"Lost"** in the Award Date field in the grid with * B* in the Address field. On the Or page, again enter **"Lost"** in the Award Date field with * H* in the Address field. If you didn't repeat the Lost value in both conditions, you would see all the bids for jobs on B Street that were lost, together with all the jobs bid on H Street, regardless of the outcome.

If your filter doesn't return any records, you might have set conflicting criteria that were impossible to meet. For example, you might have asked for bids that were for jobs on both B and H Streets, when clearly a job cannot be in two places at once.

Optimizing Filter By Form

In the Filter By Form grid, when you move to a field, you can display the list of unique values stored in that field by clicking the down arrow. To display the list, Access reads all the records and picks out the unique values.

In a very large table, the value lists can be quite lengthy and take a long time to display. To improve performance, you can display lists only for indexed fields in the current table and let the user enter the values to look for in the nonindexed fields, instead of choosing from a value list.

To make changes in the Filter By Form default settings, choose Tools | Options and click the Edit/Find tab (see Figure 7-7). The *Show lists of values in* group of options includes the following:

- *Local indexed fields* displays value lists for all the indexed fields in the current table.

- *Local nonindexed fields* displays value lists for other fields in the current table.

- *ODBC fields* displays value lists for linked tables in an external file.

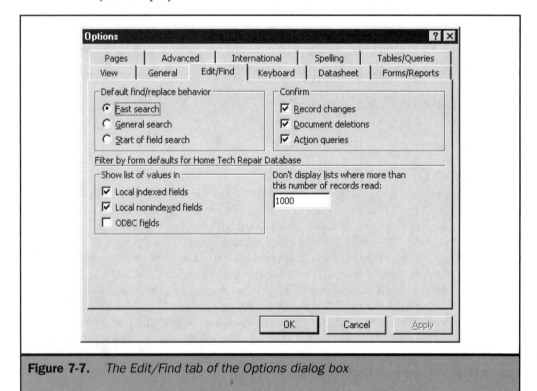

Figure 7-7.   *The Edit/Find tab of the Options dialog box*

Check only the Local indexed fields box to speed up the value list display. If this still takes too long, also clear that option.

The other option that affects Filter By Form is the *Don't display lists where more than this number of records read:* option. This represents the maximum number of records Access has to read to come up with the list of unique values. If the number of records exceeds the number in this box, Access stops reading the records and no value list is displayed.

If you checked one or more of the *Show lists of values in* options and still don't see a value list for one or more fields, you may need to increase the number in the Don't display lists… box.

If you use the same nonindexed field in several filters, you might save time and improve performance by indexing it.

Note *Be aware these option settings apply to the entire database, not only to the current table.*

Filtering For Input

The new Filter For Input option lets you filter records by entering the condition right in the open Datasheet or Form view. You use the same conditions and expressions you would use in the Filter By Form grid. To apply the filter, right-click in the field whose values you want to filter and type the value or expression in the Filter For box. For example, you may want to see only records in the Bid Data table with expiration dates before July 1, 2001 (see Figure 7-8).

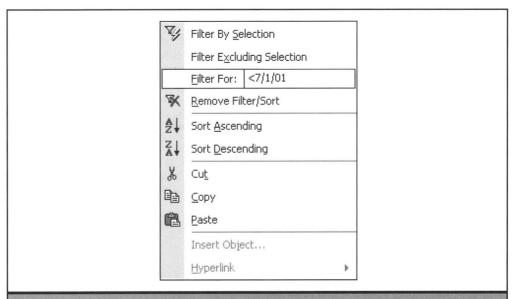

Figure 7-8.   *Entering a criterion in the Filter For box*

After entering the value or expression, press ENTER to close the shortcut menu and apply the filter. If you want to apply the filter and keep the shortcut menu open to specify additional criteria, press TAB instead. You can add as many criteria as you need to refine the filter to only the records you want to see. This is equivalent to applying successive filters with Filter By Selection or combining conditions with AND in Filter By Form. The conditions are cumulative.

To filter more than one value in the same field, enter an expression that combines the criteria with an OR operator. You cannot combine criteria in different fields with an OR operator using Filter For Input.

 To remove the filter, click the Remove Filter button, or choose Remove Filter/Sort from the Records menu or the shortcut menu.

Like the other filters, when you save the table, the filter is saved with it if you respond Yes to saving the table design. You can reactivate the filter when you reopen the table, if desired, by clicking Apply Filter.

Filtering with Advanced Filter/Sort

The Advanced Filter/Sort feature is the most flexible and comprehensive of the Access filtering tools. Not only does this feature include all the features of Filter By Form, it also enables you to specify mixed sort orders for different fields in the table. You enter all the filtering and sorting specifications in a single window.

The Advanced Filter/Sort window is divided horizontally into two parts, as shown in Figure 7-9. The upper part contains a box with a list of the fields in the table. The lower part is the design grid where you specify which fields you want to filter, the values to use as filters, and how you want the records sorted in the resulting record set. You can drag the dividing line between the two window panes to resize them if necessary. If you applied a filter recently, the criteria appears in the Criteria row of the grid. Click Clear Grid to remove it.

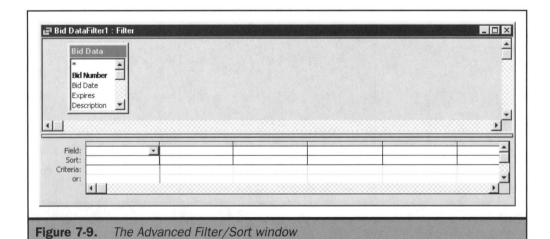

Figure 7-9.   *The Advanced Filter/Sort window*

The design grid contains several blank columns, each with four named lines. The first line, Field, is for the field names and contains a drop-down list box from which you can select the field you want. The second line, Sort, specifies the sort order, if any. You enter the filter criteria in the third and remaining lines. You can have up to nine criteria rows.

Selecting Fields to Filter or Sort

When creating an advanced filter, you need to add the fields to the design grid you want to use for sorting and specifying the filter criteria. Even though you place only a few fields in the design, all the fields are displayed in the resulting record set.

To add a field to the grid, do one of the following:

- Drag-and-drop the field name from the field list box in the upper pane of the window down to the design grid in the lower pane.

- Double-click a field name in the field list box to add it to the first empty column in the design grid.

- Select from the field list in the Field row of a grid column.

If you want to filter on more than one field, select them all in the field list and drag the whole group to the design grid. Depending on their position in the field list, you have different ways of selecting the fields:

- To select a block of contiguous fields, hold down SHIFT, and then select the first and last fields in the block.

- To select noncontiguous fields, hold down CTRL as you select the fields one by one.

Once you select the group you want to use in the filter, drag them together to the design grid. If you added more than one field, Access places them in separate columns in the order they appeared in the field list.

 If you're using most of the fields in the filter design, it may be easier to add them all, and then delete the few you don't need.

If you add a field to the design, and then change your mind, you can remove it. Select the column by clicking the gray field selector button at the top of the column, and then press DEL or choose Edit | Delete Columns.

Recall that Access sorts records first by the field in the leftmost column, and then works to the right. If you want to change the order of the fields in the design, so the records are sorted the way you intend, select the column and drag it to the desired position, just as with columns in a datasheet.

Let's try designing an advanced filter that limits the Bid Data records to bids submitted in February or March 2001, which were either lost or awarded within 45 days of bid submission. In addition, sort the resulting records first by Award Date in ascending order, and then by Bid Date in descending order.

First, select fields for the Advanced Filter/Sort.

1. With the Bid Data table open in Datasheet view, choose Records | Filter | Advanced Filter/Sort.

2. If any filter criteria appear in the grid, click Clear Grid on the toolbar to remove them.

3. Double-click Award Date in the field list. The Award Date field appears in the first column of the design grid.

4. Click-and-drag the Bid Date field to the second column in the grid.

5. Select the Expires field from the field list in the next empty column.

6. The Expires field is unnecessary in this filter, so remove it by selecting the field name in the grid and pressing DEL. You can also choose Edit | Delete Columns to remove a field from the grid.

Tip   *While you're designing an advanced filter, you may want to refer to the table data in the datasheet. The Datasheet window is still open, but not active, so it's easy to switch between windows by selecting from the Window menu.*

Next, set the sort orders and enter the filter criteria.

Setting Sort Orders and Filter Criteria

The Sort row in the design grid contains a list box in which you have three choices: Ascending, Descending, and [not sorted]. The fields in the advanced filter that aren't used for sorting can be left blank or set with the [not sorted] option. If you want to sort records on more than one field, you must arrange the fields in the order you want the sorts performed. Access starts with the leftmost Sort field, and then sorts on the next Sort field to the right, and so on. You can sort on as many as ten fields in an Advanced Filter/Sort.

To add the sort order specifications to the advanced filter that sorts first by Award Date in ascending order, and then by Bid Date in Descending order, follow these steps:

1. Click the Sort cell list box in the Award Date column and choose Ascending from the list.

2. Click the Sort cell list box in the Bid Date column and choose Descending. Keep the advanced filter design open for the next steps.

You enter the filter conditions for a field in the Advanced Filter/Sort grid much the same as in the Filter By Form grid. The only difference is you don't have a value list from which to choose. You can enter specific values and expressions, and use wildcards. The Criteria row holds the same conditions you would put on the Look for page in Filter By Form and the Or row works like the Or page. When you enter a condition on the Or line, an additional Or line becomes available below it just as a new Or tab appears in a Filter By Form design.

Multiple Values in the Same Field

If you want to filter records that have any one of several values using Advanced Filter/Sort, you have three ways to enter the criteria. For example, if you want to see all records with *x*, *y*, or *z* in the Alpha field:

- Enter the expression **x OR y OR z** in the Criteria row of the Alpha column.

- Enter **x** in the Criteria row, **y** in the first Or row, and **z** in the second Or row.

- Use the In() function: Enter **In(x,y,z)** in the criteria row.

To add the filter criteria to the Bid Data advanced filter that includes the bids submitted during February and March 2001, which have either been lost or awarded within 45 days, follow the next procedure.

1. Place the insertion point in the Criteria cell of the Award Date column and type **Lost**, and then press the DOWN ARROW key. Access adds the quotation marks when you move to the next row.

2. In the Or cell of the Award Date column, type **<[Bid Date]+45**, and then press ENTER.

3. Click the Criteria cell of the Bid Date column and type **Between 2/1/01 AND 3/31/01.** Note, the insertion point is still in the Criteria cell.

4. Press SHIFT-HOME to select the expression you entered in step 3 and click Copy.

5. Press the DOWN ARROW key to move to the Or cell of the Bid Date column and click Paste. The same criterion now appears in both cells of the Bid Date column. Figure 7-10 shows the completed advanced filter design.

*Access has converted the Or criterion for the Award Date field to a string expression because the field is a Text data type. If it were a Date/Time data type like the Bid Date field, you wouldn't be able to enter text such as **Lost**. Access also added the date delimiters (#) to the date values in the Bid Date criteria.*

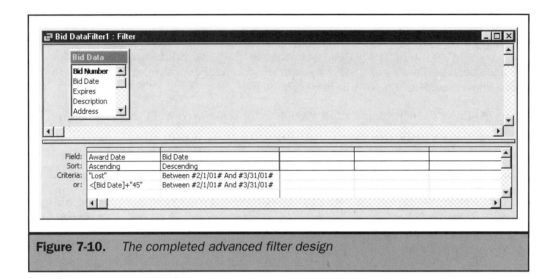

Figure 7-10. *The completed advanced filter design*

Applying the Advanced Filter

Anytime during the design of an advanced filter, you can apply it to see if you're getting the data you want. Access gives you three ways to apply the filter:

- Click Apply Filter on the toolbar.
- Choose Filter | Apply Filter/Sort.
- Right-click anywhere in the upper section of the Design window and choose Apply Filter/Sort from the shortcut menu.

Figure 7-11 shows the resulting record set. Notice the toolbar and the navigation key area both warn you this is a filtered record set. If you want to abandon the filter design without applying it, click Close on the toolbar.

To remove the filter, do one of the following:

- Click the Remove Filter button.
- Choose Records | Remove Filter/Sort.
- Right-click and choose Remove Filter/Sort from the shortcut menu.

You can base a new form or report on a filtered set of records if you create it while the filtered record set is displayed in Datasheet view or if you saved the filter with the table. While the filter and sort properties are inherited by the form or report, you can still override the settings in the form or report property sheets. See Chapter 10 for more information about creating forms and reports, and changing their properties.

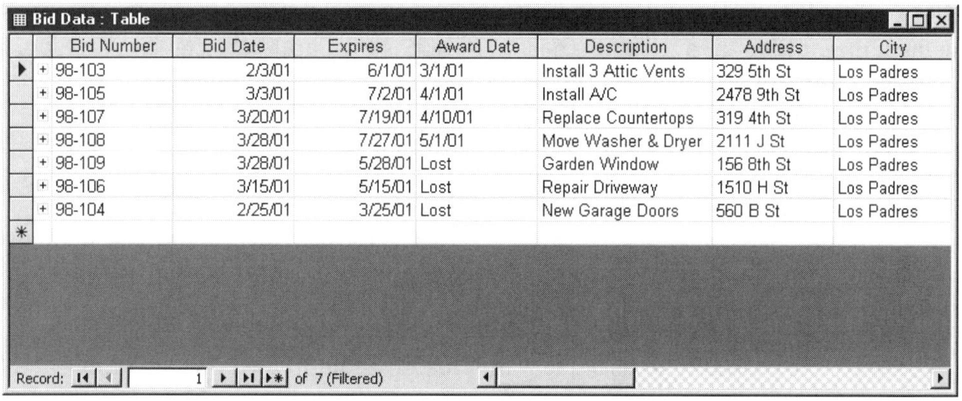
Bid Data : Table

Bid Number	Bid Date	Expires	Award Date	Description	Address	City
98-103	2/3/01	6/1/01	3/1/01	Install 3 Attic Vents	329 5th St	Los Padres
98-105	3/3/01	7/2/01	4/1/01	Install A/C	2478 9th St	Los Padres
98-107	3/20/01	7/19/01	4/10/01	Replace Countertops	319 4th St	Los Padres
98-108	3/28/01	7/27/01	5/1/01	Move Washer & Dryer	2111 J St	Los Padres
98-109	3/28/01	5/28/01	Lost	Garden Window	156 8th St	Los Padres
98-106	3/15/01	5/15/01	Lost	Repair Driveway	1510 H St	Los Padres
98-104	2/25/01	3/25/01	Lost	New Garage Doors	560 B St	Los Padres

Record: 1 of 7 (Filtered)

Figure 7-11. *The filtered record set*

Filtering by Lookup Fields with Advanced Filter/Sort

Filtering on a field that gets its value from a lookup list with Advanced Filter/Sort can present a slight problem. When you choose to filter records by values in a Lookup field in Filter By Form, you pick from the value list that contains all the values in the lookup list created by the Lookup Wizard. What you don't see in the list are the values actually stored in the field. The value in the primary key field of the lookup list is stored instead of the more informative displayed value.

When you use Advanced Filter/Sort, you don't choose from the lookup list because only one table is in the Filter window. This means you must enter the stored value in the Criteria row to filter on a Lookup field. For example, to filter on Ferrell in the Supervisor field of the Workorders table with Filter By Form, you can select Ferrell from the list or type **Ferrell** in the grid. To do the same in Advanced Filter/Sort, you must enter **10**, Ferrell's Employee ID number, in the Criteria row.

Modifying a Filter

You use the same techniques to modify a filter that you used to create it. You can add more criteria or change existing ones in any type of filter. You can even switch between Filter windows to see how the filter is progressing or apply the filter during the process to see how the records are selected.

Note *When you filter a table, the records you see are limited to those that pass the criteria you set. You still see all the fields in every record. To limit the fields, as well as the records in the resulting set, you need to use a query. Chapter 8 discusses the difference between filters and queries, and tells how to decide which to use.*

Saving a Filter

The most recent filter is saved with the table—not as a separate object—if you respond Yes to save the table changes. When you reopen the table, the filter is no longer in effect, but you can reapply it by any of the methods discussed earlier. If you create a new filter, but want to keep the previous one available with the table, respond No when asked if you want to save the changes. Of course, if you've made other changes you do want to keep, you'll save the filter with them.

If you want to have more than one filter available to a table or want to save a filter permanently, you must save it as a query. Queries are stored as separate Access database objects. When you want to use the filter again, you can bring it back from the query to the Filter window or simply run it as a query.

To save an advanced filter as a query and load it again in the Filter window:

1. With the Filter window displayed, click the Save As Query button. You can also choose Save As Query from the shortcut menu or the File menu. Access asks for a name for the new query in the Save As Query dialog box.

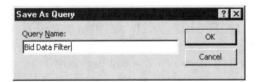

2. Name the query and choose OK.

3. To restore the specifications to the Filter window, open a blank Advanced Filter/Sort window and click the Load From Query button. You could also choose Load from Query from the shortcut menu or the File menu. Load from Query may still be in the File expanded menu, if you haven't used the command before.

4. The Applicable Filter dialog box shows a list of queries based on the Bid Data table.

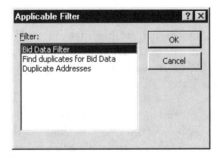

5. Choose the query you want and click OK. All the filter parameters are returned to the grid, where you can choose to apply the filter or make changes.

If all you want to do is filter the records, simply run the query you saved from the filter. If you want to use the query as the basis for a new filter, load the filter from the query and make the changes.

Removing and Deleting Filters

A difference exists between removing and deleting a filter. Removing a filter simply returns all the records to the datasheet or form. You can reapply the filter later. Deleting the filter erases the filter criteria and the filter cannot be reapplied without reconstructing it.

To remove a filter from a datasheet or form, do one of the following:

- Click Remove Filter.
- Choose Records | Remove Filter/Sort.
- Right-click anywhere in the datasheet and choose Remove Filter/Sort from the shortcut menu.

When you remove a filter from a datasheet, any filter you applied to a subdatasheet within it is also removed.

To delete a filter entirely, you need to clear the filter grid and apply the empty filter to the datasheet by the following method:

1. Switch to the Advanced Filter/Sort window. It doesn't matter how you created the filter; you can still see it in the filter grid.

2. Click Clear Grid or choose Clear Grid from the Edit or the shortcut menu.

3. Click Apply Filter.

4. Click Close to close the datasheet and respond Yes to save the changes.

When you open the table again, the Apply Filter button is dimmed indicating the filter has been removed. If you want to use the filter again, you have to reconstruct it.

Printing Table Data

You needn't create a fancy report to print your table data. You can print the datasheet as it appears in the Datasheet view or print in the default report format, called the AutoReport. To print a single copy of the datasheet, click the Print button. If you want to adjust the margin settings, the paper size, or the page layout, use the Page Setup dialog box. If you want to choose other print options, such as multiple copies or selected pages, you need to open the Print dialog box.

To see how the printed report looks before you print it, you can click the Preview toolbar button. This is useful when you think the datasheet may not fit across the page with the current page layout, in which case you can change the page setup before printing the data.

Previewing the Printout

The Print Preview window shows you how the printed datasheet or report looks on the page. You have many options in the window for displaying pages and zooming in on specific areas of a page.

To open the Print Preview window, do one of the following:

- Right-click the table name in the Database window and choose Print Preview from the shortcut menu.

- Select the table name in the Database window or open the table in Datasheet view and choose File | Print Preview. Print Preview may be in the expanded menu list if you haven't used it before.

- Select the table name in the Database window or open the table in Datasheet view and click Print Preview.

The Preview window toolbar includes some new buttons that offer options for viewing the printout as described in Table 7-3.

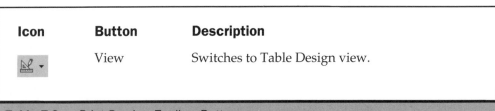

Icon	Button	Description
	View	Switches to Table Design view.

Table 7-3. *Print Preview Toolbar Buttons*

Icon	Button	Description
🖨	Print	Prints the datasheet.
🔍	Zoom	Zooms in on a specific area of the preview.
⊟	One Page	Displays one page.
⊟⊟	Two Pages	Displays two pages.
⊞	Multiple Pages	Displays multiple pages, selected by dragging over a layout palette. Maximum four rows and five columns of pages.
100% ▾	Zoom	Zooms in or out with a specific percentage of magnification.

Table 7-3.   *Print Preview Toolbar Buttons* (continued)

Figure 7-12 shows the Bid Data datasheet previewed in three pages.

> *The Bid Data datasheet requires three page widths to print all the fields. If the page orientation were changed to landscape in the Page Setup dialog box, the data would fit on two pages.*

The Preview window shortcut menu contains many of the same options. It also includes the Page Setup option you can use to open the Page Setup dialog box and make changes, such as to the margin settings and the page orientation.

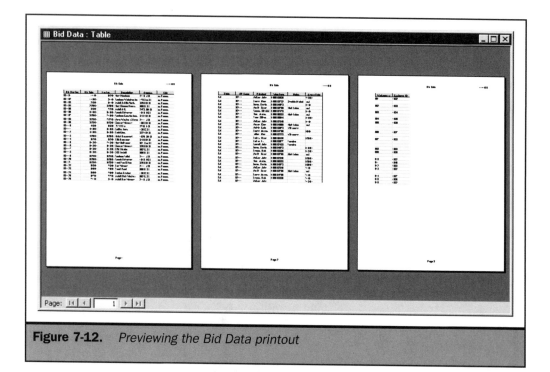

Figure 7-12. *Previewing the Bid Data printout*

Choose Close to close the Preview window and return to Datasheet view.

Running Page Setup

The Page Setup options determine what printer to use and how your data is to be printed on the page. The table or report must be open before you can use Page Setup. To run Page Setup, choose Page Setup from the File menu or from the Preview window shortcut menu. The Page Setup dialog box has two tabs, as shown in Figure 7-13. The Margins page contains options that let you set the width (in inches) of all four page margins and choose whether to print the field names in the column headings.

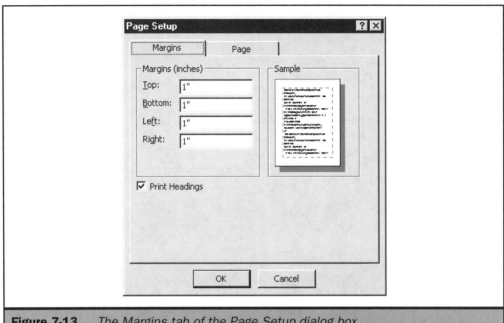

Figure 7-13.   *The Margins tab of the Page Setup dialog box*

When you finish setting the margin options, click the Page tab to choose the orientation, paper size, and source options, and to select a printer. Figure 7-14 shows the Page tab of the Page Setup dialog box. Many of these options depend on the printer you're using. If you have more than one printer available to your system, you can select Use Specific Printer, and then click the Printer button to see a list of installed printers.

One of the most useful options on this tab is Orientation, which lets you decide whether the document should be printed down (Portrait) or across (Landscape) the page. When your datasheet is too wide to fit in the default portrait orientation, you can choose to print it in landscape orientation.

When you finish modifying the Page Setup options, click OK to implement the changes or Cancel to abandon the changes.

Changing the Print Options

You can specify exactly what you want printed by choosing from the Print dialog box shown in Figure 7-15. Among the options are changing printers and even printing to a disk file for printing later or for transporting to a printer at a different location. The default settings include printing a single copy of all the pages in the report.

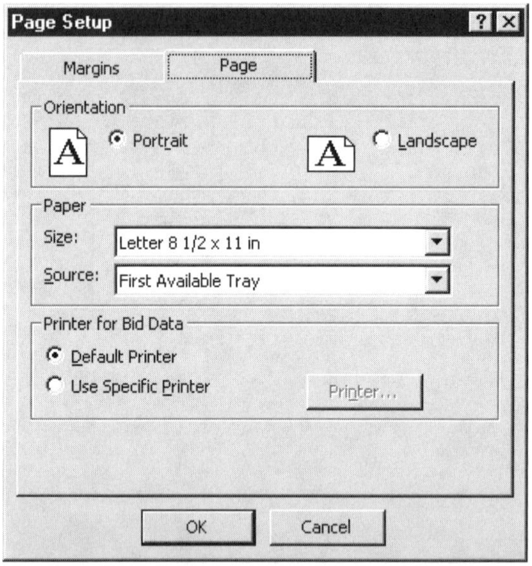

Figure 7-14. *The Page tab shows printer and paper options*

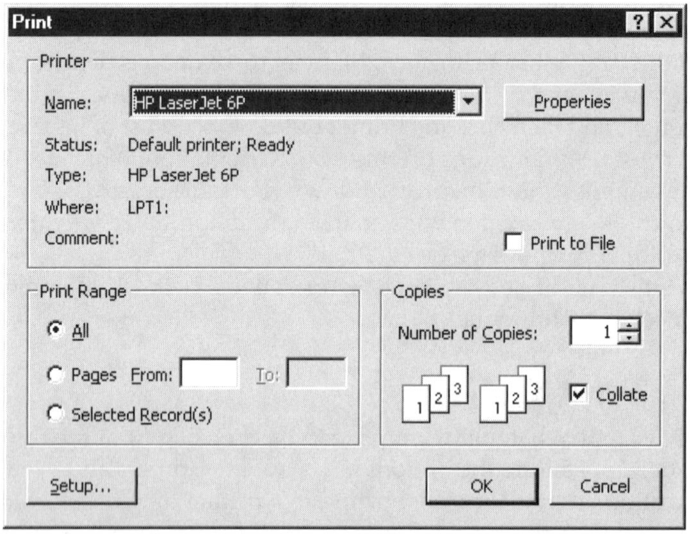

Figure 7-15. *The Print dialog box*

If you don't want to print the entire datasheet, you can select the range of pages to print by specifying the beginning and ending page numbers. If you want to print only a few of the records, select them before opening the Print dialog box. Then choose Selected Records in the Print Range options.

To print more than one copy of the report, click the up arrow on the Number of Copies spin box or enter the number of copies you want printed in its text box. You also have a choice of collating the multiple copies (putting them in sequence) or printing all the copies of one page before printing the next page.

Clicking the Setup button in the Print dialog box opens the Margins page of the Page Setup dialog box.

Any customizing you have done in Datasheet view, such as changing row height or column widths, rearranging columns, or changing the font or cell effects, is carried over to the printout.

Printing from a Shortcut

Access gives you a shortcut to printing the table data without even having to open the table first. When you right-click the table name in the Tables page of the Database window, a shortcut menu opens with Print as one of the options available in the shortcut menu.

Selecting Print from the shortcut menu sends the report directly to the printer, just as clicking the Print button does. If you want to preview the report before printing, you still have to open it first.

Chapter 13 describes in more detail the process of previewing and printing reports. Chapter 14 discusses special printing tasks such as envelopes and mailing labels.

Summary

You've now seen how to store information in related database tables and how to retrieve data using different type of filters. Filtering records has some limitations:

- You can limit only the records, not the fields. You can see all the fields of the resulting recordset.
- You can save only one filter or sort order with a table.
- Filtering is limited to records in a single table.

Queries provide an alternative to filters with distinct advantages, such as choosing specific fields from related tables and being stored as separate database objects. The next chapter introduces you to the subject of queries and their applications.

MOUS Exam Activities Explored in This Chapter

Level	Activity	Section Title
Core	Sort records	Sorting Records Filtering with Advanced Filter/Sort
Core	Filter records	Filtering By Selection Filtering By Form Filtering For Input
Expert	Create and apply advanced filters	Filtering with Advanced Filter/Sort

Chapter 8

Extracting Information with Queries

W hen you work with information in an Access datasheet, you can filter and sort the records in many ways, but you can have even more flexibility with queries. You can not only limit the records to a specific subset, but you can also specify which fields you want to see in the result.

Query is a general term synonymous with question, inquiry, or quiz. In Access, to query a database is to ask a question about the information in the database. A query can be about the data in a single table or multiple related tables.

Access provides several types of queries, ranging from the popular select query that extracts specific data to the more exotic action queries that can actually insert, update, and delete records. This chapter discusses select queries and a few special purpose queries, while the next chapter covers the more advanced types.

How Do Queries Work?

Several types of queries do quite different things but, in general, an access query is a set of explicit specifications that tell Access exactly what information you want to see and how you want it arranged or manipulated in the results. In the query, you specify the fields you want to include, add selection criteria that limit the records in the resulting record set, select the desired order for them to appear, and define any summary fields.

With Access queries you can

- View data from multiple tables sorted in a specific order.
- Perform many types of calculations on selected groups of records.
- Find and display duplicate or unmatched records.
- Update data, delete records, or append new records to a table.
- Create a new table with records from one or more tables.

Note *The result of running a query is called a dynaset, which is short for dynamic subset. This is called "dynamic" because if you make a change to the data in the dynaset, Access makes the same change in the data in the tables that provided the basic information. This can be useful when updating data, but it's not always what you want to do. Later, you see how to change the query properties to create a "static" result, so you can change the data in the resulting recordset without affecting the underlying table information.*

Access Query Categories

Access queries fall into four general categories: select, special purpose, action, and SQL-specific. A select query is the most common category and is used for extracting specific information from one or more tables in a database. The results of a select query are displayed in a datasheet for viewing or editing, or used as the basis for a form or report. With a select query, you can also group records and perform calculations on field values in the groups, such as sum, count, average, minimum and maximum, and other totals.

An example of a *special purpose query* is the *crosstab* (meaning *cross-tabulation*) query that displays summarized values from one field in the table, grouped in two ways. Other special purpose queries locate duplicate records in a table or unmatched records in a relationship.

Action queries are used to perform global data management operations on tables, such as updating or deleting groups of records, making a new table from an existing one, and appending new records to an existing table.

SQL-specific queries are accessible only through structured query language (SQL) statements. All queries have SQL statements in the background, but SQL-specific queries are constructed with the programming language, instead of a design grid like other types of queries.

Access has some new Query Wizards to help create many of these queries. You learn about the select and the special purpose queries you can create with a wizard for now, but you learn about the more advanced queries in Chapter 9.

RETRIEVING AND PRESENTING INFORMATION

Specific Types of Access Queries

The Access select queries include the following:

- *Simple Select queries* display data from one or more tables sorted in a specific order. You can also perform many types of predefined or custom calculations on values in all records or within groups of records.

- *Find Duplicate queries* display all records with duplicate values in one or more specified fields. For example, you can query to find customers who have more than one work order. You can include any other fields you want.

- *Find Unmatched queries* display records in one table that have no related records in another table. For example, you can query to find customers who have no current work orders.

Special purpose queries include the following:

- *Parameter queries,* when run, display a dialog box where you enter the criteria for retrieving data or a value to insert into a field.

- *AutoLookup queries* automatically fill in certain field values in a new record in one or more tables.

- *Crosstab queries* calculate a sum or count and group the results in a spreadsheet format that correlates the data with two types of information. For example, total sales by product and quarter or district.

Action queries include the following:

- *Update queries* make global changes to a group of records in one or more tables. For example, raise all labor rates by 15 percent.
- *Append queries* add a group of records from one or more tables to the end of one or more other tables.
- *Delete queries* remove a specific group of records from one or more tables. For example, remove all records from the Bid Data table with "Lost" in the Award Date field.
- *Make-table queries* create a new table out of data from one or more tables.

SQL-specific queries include the following:

- *Union queries* combine fields from one or more tables into one field in the result.
- *Pass-Through queries* send instructions directly to ODBC databases using commands specific to the server.
- *Data-Definition queries* create or change database objects in an Access, SQL server, or other server database.
- *Subqueries* are SQL SELECT or other server statements that form a SELECT query within another query.

When to Use a Filter and When to Use a Query

It may seem like filters and queries do the same thing, but some differences occur in the results. Filters and select queries both retrieve a subset of records from a table or another query. As a rule of thumb, use a *filter* to view or edit some records temporarily in a datasheet or form. If you want to return to the subset of records at a later time, you should use a query. Queries are separate database objects that appear in the Database window, while a single filter is saved with a table.

If you use a query, you needn't open the table first because a query is an object in its own right. With a filter, you must open the table first before you can view the results of the filter or design a new filter.

Use a query if you want to extract data from multiple tables, control which fields to display, or perform calculations on field values. None of these operations are permitted with filters.

The results of both filters and queries can be used as the source of data for forms and reports. You can also sort the results of both and save the sort order for use in a later work session. Both methods let you edit the data displayed in the results, if editing is otherwise permitted.

Even if you decide you need to have a query, you can use the easy Filter By Form or Filter By Selection tools to create a filter, and then save it as a query. Access translates your filter design into a proper query.

Table 8-1 summarizes the difference in capabilities between filters and queries.

Creating Select Queries

As usual, Access gives you a choice of ways to begin a new query design:

- Click the New command button on the Queries page in the Database window.
- Click New Object and select New Query.
- Choose Insert | Query.

All three approaches open the New Query dialog box, as shown in Figure 8-1. As you can see, you can call on wizards for help with several types of queries.

If you want to create a select query, you can either start from scratch by selecting Design View in the New Query dialog box or choose one of the wizards to help you.

Capability	Queries	Filters
Use as basis for a form or report	Yes	Yes
Sort records in the result	Yes	Yes
Edit data in the result, if editing is allowed	Yes, depending on type of query	Yes
Add another table and include those records in the result	Yes	No
Select only specific fields to include in the result	Yes	No
Store as a separate Access object in the database	Yes	No
See results without opening the underlying table, query, or form	Yes	No
Include calculated and aggregate values in result	Yes	No

Table 8-1.   *Differences Between Filters and Queries*

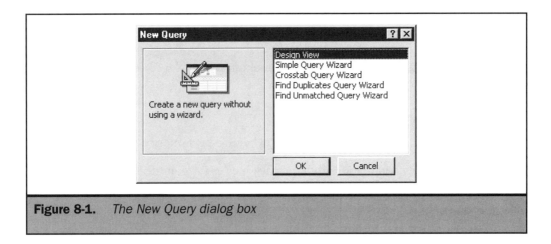

Figure 8-1. *The New Query dialog box*

Choosing Design View takes you directly to the Query Design window, which looks a lot like the Advanced Filter/Sort Design window. To create a select query with the wizard, choose Simple Query Wizard, which guides you through choices about the basic design of the select query. You can then go to the Design window to customize the query design, if necessary.

Using the Simple Query Wizard

To start the wizard, double-click Simple Query Wizard or select it and click OK. The Simple Query Wizard displays a series of dialog boxes in which you specify the fields and records you want to include in the query and enter a name for the saved query. You can include fields from any of the tables or other queries in your database. Figure 8-2 shows the first Simple Query Wizard dialog box.

To add all the fields from a table, click the double right arrow (>>). To add a field to the Selected Fields list, double-click the field name or select the field in the Available Fields list and click the right arrow (>). If you change your mind about including a field, double-click it in the Selected Fields list or select it and click the left arrow (<). To add fields from another table, select the table (or query) from the Tables/Queries list box, and then select fields from the new list.

Double-clicking the field name switches it from one list to the other. The fields appear in the query result in the order you selected them in the first dialog box. You can change the order later in Query Design view.

To select more than one field at once, do one of the following:

■ If the field names are contiguous, hold down SHIFT while you click the first and last names in the group.

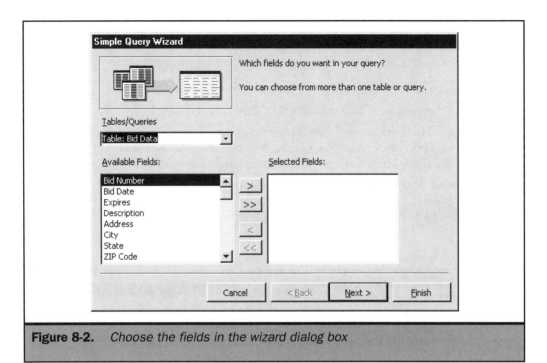

Figure 8-2. *Choose the fields in the wizard dialog box*

■ If the field names aren't contiguous, hold down CTRL while you click each name, one by one.

After selecting the fields, click the single right arrow. After you add all the fields you want in the query, click the Next button. The second Simple Query Wizard dialog box gives you two options:

■ Create a detail query with all the record data.

■ Create a summary query that calculates totals based on the field values. When you choose to summarize field values, you need to specify the summary options in another dialog box, which is discussed in a later section in this chapter.

  If you haven't selected any Number or Currency type fields, no fields appear to summarize. The wizard then skips this dialog box and takes you directly to the third and last dialog box.

In the final wizard dialog box, you enter a name for the query. You also choose whether to view the information immediately or go to the Query Design window to make modifications to the query.

Let's try out the Simple Query Wizard by building a list of current work orders and include information from both the Workorders and Bid Data tables.

To create a Current Workorders query:

1. In the Database window, click Queries, and then click New.

2. Select Simple Query Wizard from the New Query dialog box.

3. Select Table:Workorders from the Tables/Queries list box and use one of the methods previously discussed to move the Workorder Number, Supervisor, Material Cost, Labor Cost, and Description fields to the Selected Fields list.

4. Select Table:Bid Data from the Tables/Queries list box and add the Address, Bid Number, and Principal fields to the Selected Fields list. Figure 8-3 shows the complete list of fields to include in the new query.

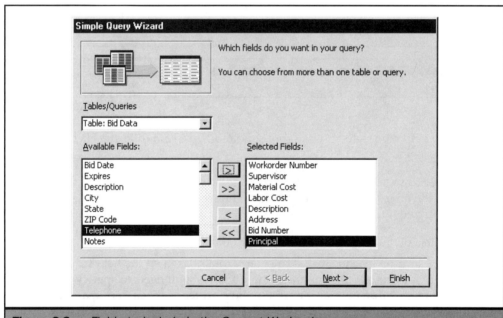

Figure 8-3. *Fields to include in the Current Workorders query*

5. Click Next and accept the Detail option, which shows every field of every record, and then click Next.

6. Enter Current Workorders as the name for the new query (see Figure 8-4) and accept the default option to open the query to view information.

7. Click Finish. The query results appear in a datasheet showing only the eight fields you selected, but all the records (see Figure 8-5). The column widths and record height are adjusted in the figure to show all the information.

The wizard has helped you with the basic query definition; now it's up to you to add the final touches, such as adding selection criteria to limit the records, changing the query and field properties, adding another table, specifying a sort order, or adding calculated fields.

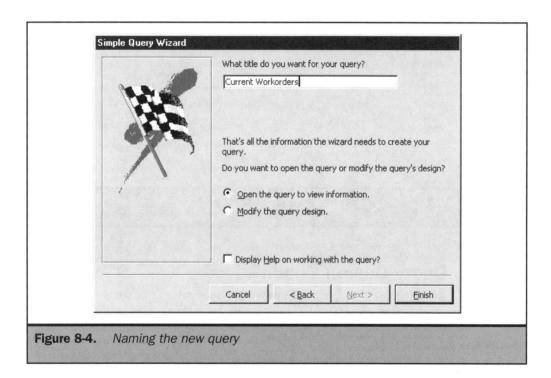

Figure 8-4. *Naming the new query*

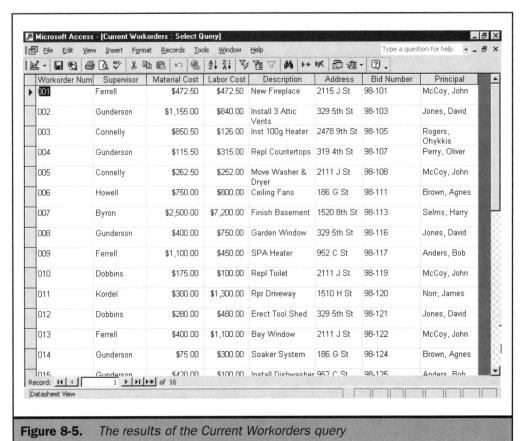

Figure 8-5. The results of the Current Workorders query

Touring the Query Design Window

Like all Access objects, a query can be displayed in more than one view. Tables, for example, can be viewed as a datasheet in which you are looking at the data in the table. You can also look at the table in Design view to see the table structure and all the information about the fields, indexes, formats, and so on.

A query, like a table, can be viewed as a datasheet or a design. The Datasheet view shows you the data that results when you run the query (refer to Figure 8-5). The Design view is where you can look at the query structure and make changes to the query design or even create a new one. The third query view is the SQL view, which shows the SQL statements Access creates behind the scenes to implement the query. The SQL view has no counterpart with table objects.

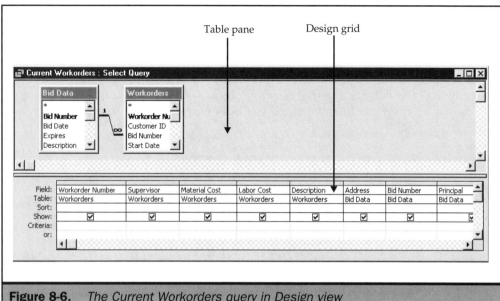

Figure 8-6. *The Current Workorders query in Design view*

 To switch to Design view, click View and choose Design View, or choose View |
Design View.

The Query Design window (see Figure 8-6) looks a lot like the Advanced
Filter/Sort window with two sections:

- The upper pane is the table pane, which displays the field lists for all the tables
  in the query.

- The lower pane is the *Query By Example* (*QBE*) design grid, which shows the
  elements of the query design.

The table pane for the Current Workorders query shows the two tables from which
you selected fields: Bid Data and Workorders. Access has accepted the one-to-many
relationship between the tables joining the Bid Number fields.

The design grid shows the field names you selected in the wizard dialog box,
including the name of the table (or query) from which they came. The Sort, Criteria,
and Or rows are the same as in a filter grid. The check marks in the Show row indicate
all the fields are to appear in the dynaset. Clearing the check mark hides the field from
the query result. This is helpful when you want to filter or sort the results based on a
field that you don't want to appear in the query results.

Drag the dividing line between the two panes up or down to change their relative heights. You can also drag the field list boxes in the table pane to see more of the field names and the grid column dividers to change the column width.

The Query Design toolbar has some new buttons and the menu bar also includes new options. Table 8-2 describes the new buttons and shows their menu equivalents. The shortcut menu is specified by where you right-click to display it: in the table pane or the design grid.

Icon	Button	Description	Menu Equivalent	Shortcut Menu
	Query Type	Choose from six query types	Query | (query type list)	Table pane: Query Type
	Run	Displays query results	Query | Run	
	Show Table	Opens the Show Table dialog box	Query | Show Table	Table pane: Show Table
Σ	Totals	Adds the Total row to the design grid	View | Totals (expanded menu)	Design grid: Totals
All	Top Values	Shows a list of numbers and percentages for limiting the records to high or low values		
	Properties	Opens the query property sheet	View | Properties	Design grid: Properties
	Build	Starts the Expression Builder		Criteria row of the design grid: Build

Table 8-2. *Query Design Toolbar and Menu Options*

The menu bar and shortcut menu have a few additional choices as follows:

■ View | Table Names shows or hides the Table row in the design grid.
The design grid shortcut menu also shows the Table Names option.

■ With the insertion point in the Criteria row or an Or row, the design grid
shortcut menu has the Zoom option that opens a window where you can enter
and view long expressions.

■ When a relationship line is selected in the Table pane, View | Join Properties
opens the Join Properties dialog box (see Figure 8-7). Right-clicking the join line
and choosing Properties from the shortcut menu also opens the dialog box.
Double-clicking the join line opens the Join Properties dialog box without using
a shortcut menu. You can change the join properties to get different results with
the query. Refer to Chapter 5 for a description of the types of joins.

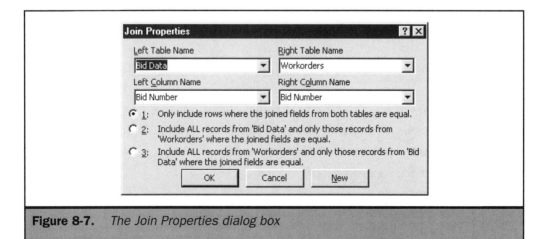

Figure 8-7.   *The Join Properties dialog box*

■ Edit | Clear Grid (in the expanded Edit menu) removes all entries in the design grid. The field lists remain in the table pane.

Clear Grid is one of those actions that cannot be reversed by choosing Undo.

■ Query | Parameters opens the Query Parameters dialog box where you define the parameters to prompt for when running a parameter query. The table pane shortcut menu also includes the Parameters option. More later about creating a parameter query.

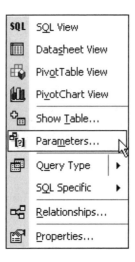

Without the Wizard

Six basic steps create a query without the help of a wizard:

1. Select one or more tables and queries that contain the information you want to retrieve.

2. Choose the fields from the field lists in the table pane and add them to the design grid.

3. Specify the sort orders for the field values, if any.

4. Add selection criteria that limits the records in the query results.

5. Add calculated fields that display the results of functions or expressions, if any.

6. Add summarizing expressions, if any.

When you finish with these steps, run the query.

You can actually run the query to test the results while you're creating it by switching to Datasheet view or clicking Run. The query isn't saved until you close it.

Each of these steps has many features, as you can see in this and subsequent sections.

To bypass the wizard and create your query from scratch, select Design view from the New Query dialog box. The Show Table dialog box opens, in which you select the tables or queries you want to query.

As an example of creating a new query without the wizard, Home Tech Repair needs a list of work orders showing the following fields from the Bid Data and Workorders tables arranged in the following order:

Bid Number (Bid Data)
Supervisor (Workorders)
Job Address (Bid Data)
Description (Workorders)
Award Date (Bid Data)
Start Date and Completion Date (Workorders)

Later, you add the customer's Last Name and Phone Number from the Customers table. In addition, you add the cost data and compute the total cost. Then add criteria based on start date, total cost, and other factors to limit the records in the result.

To create the new query, do the following:

1. Choose New in the Queries tab of the Database window.

2. Select Design View and click OK. The Show Table dialog box opens with three tabs that display a list of Tables, Queries, or Both in the current database. Figure 8-8 shows the Tables tab of the Show Table dialog box in front of an empty Query Design window. (Your lists of tables and queries will be different.)

3. Select Bid Data (if not already selected) and choose Add. You can see the field list added to the query table pane behind the dialog box.

4. Double-click Workorders in the Show Table list, and then choose Close. Figure 8-9 shows the query design with the two tables. (Field lists have been resized in the figure, so you can see the linking fields.)

5. Keep the Query window open for adding fields to the design grid.

The next task is to choose the fields you want to appear in the query result and arrange them in the desired order. But, first, look at the relationships Access shows for the two Home Tech Repair tables, and then add a third table to the design.

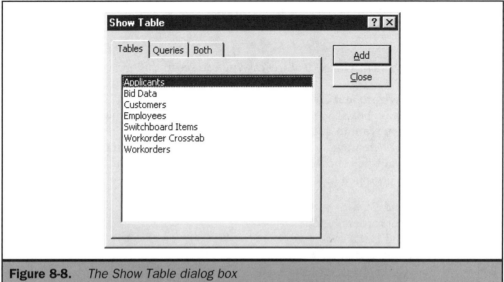

Figure 8-8. *The Show Table dialog box*

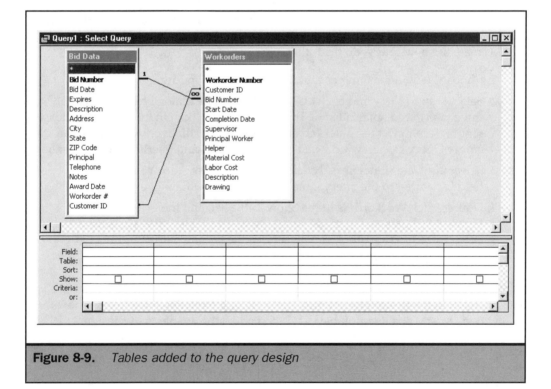

Figure 8-9. *Tables added to the query design*

Relating Multiple Tables in a Query

You begin to see the power of a relational database system when you build a query using more than one table. As you add tables, the query has access to more and more information.

To add a table to an existing query, click Show Table or choose Query | Show Table. If the tables are already related at the table level, Access automatically displays the join lines when you add the table to the query design. You can tell by the appearance of the line if referential integrity is enforced and which table is the "one" side and which is the "many."

If the tables aren't related before adding them to the query, Access often assumes a relationship between them based on fields with the same name and data type, especially if one of them is a primary key. When Access joins the tables, referential integrity is not enforced.

If the tables aren't related at the table level and Access cannot join them, you must join them in the query or you'll get what is called a Cartesian product: *each of the* n *rows in one table is matched with every one of the* m *rows in the second table, resulting in a recordset with n×m records.*

In the Home Tech Repair database, the relationship between the Bid Data and the Workorders table was defined as one-to-many, linked by Bid Number and with referential integrity enforced. The Workorders table is related to the Bid Data table, but referential integrity isn't enforced. You can see these relationships in the query table pane.

Add the Customers table to the new query and include the Last Name and Phone Number in the results, so you won't have to look them up to reach the customer.

To add the Customers table, do the following:

1. Click Show Table to open the Show Table dialog box.

2. Double-click the Customers table and click Close. The Customers table is added to the query design and the join lines show the relationships with the Bid Data and Workorders tables (see Figure 8-10). Referential integrity is enforced on the relationship with the Workorders table, but not on the relation with the Bid Data table. The tables have been rearranged slightly in the figure to show the relationships more clearly.

Another way to add a table to a query design is to drag it from the Tables tab of the Database window. To do this, press F11 *to switch to the Database window, and then choose Window | Tile Vertically to split the screen. Click the Tables tab in the Database window and drag the table name from the Database window to the table pane in the query design.*

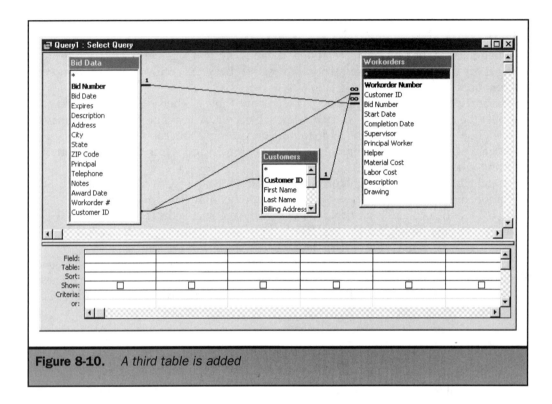

Figure 8-10. *A third table is added*

If you added a table and decide you don't need it after all, click the field list in the table pane and press DEL, or right-click the field list and choose Remove Table from the shortcut menu. The table is removed from the query design, but it remains untouched in the database. Any fields you already placed in the design grid are also removed.

 You can also add a second copy of the same table and create a self-join.

Adding/Removing Fields

Adding fields to a query grid is much the same as adding them to an Advanced Filter/Sort grid. You can add all the fields at once, a selected group of fields, or one field at a time.

To add all the fields in a table to the grid at once, do one of the following:

- Double-click the asterisk (*) at the top of the field list. This method places the table or query name in the Field row of the column followed by a period and an asterisk—for example, Customers.*.

- Drag the asterisk from the field list to an empty column in the grid. This method does the same as the previous one.

■ Double-click the field list title bar to select all the fields, and then drag the group to the grid. Access places each field in a separate column across the grid in the order in which they appeared in the field list.

> **Tip**
>
> *Using the asterisk method of adding all the fields to query is both an advantage and a disadvantage. The advantage is if fields are added or deleted from the underlying table or query, this query automatically makes corresponding changes to the design. The only disadvantage is if you want to sort or filter using one of the fields, it must be added separately to the grid.*

To add a group of fields to the grid at once, select them and drag them as a group. The standard use of SHIFT and CTRL to select adjacent and nonadjacent field names works here the same as with filters. When you drag the block of selected field names to the grid, Access spreads them to empty columns, beginning where you drop the group. If fields are already in the grid, the ones to the right of where you drop the group move over to make room.

To add fields to the grid one at a time, do any of the following:

■ Double-click the field name to place it in the first empty column.

■ Drag the field to an empty column or insert it between filled columns.

■ Select the field name from the Field row drop-down list. The list in a blank column contains all the fields in all the tables in the table pane, as well as the table names with a period and asterisk.

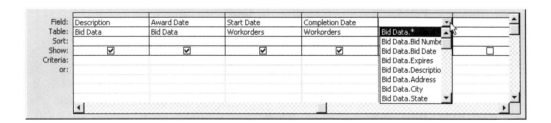

> **Note**
>
> *Fields added to a query inherit the properties from the underlying table or query. You can override some of these field properties in the new query design. More about changing field properties later in this chapter.*

To delete a field from the grid, click the column selector and press DEL, or choose Edit Delete Column. If you remove the check mark from the Show cell in a column with no Sort or Criteria entries, the field will be removed from the grid the next time you open the query.

A quick way to delete a column from the design grid is to shrink the column width down to nothing.

You can adjust the column widths and drag a column to a new position, just as in a datasheet or advanced filter. Changing the column width has no effect on the query results datasheet unless you reduce it to zero and the adjustments aren't saved with the query.

Note

You can ask Access to adjust a column width to fit its longest visible entry in the design grid, which may be the field name or one of the selection criteria. Move the mouse pointer to the right edge of the column selector and double-click when the pointer changes to a two-way arrow. This sets a fixed column width and, if you enter a longer value in the column later, you'll need to readjust the width to see it all.

Figure 8-11 shows the new query, still unnamed, with all the required fields in place. The columns have been resized to fit their contents and some are off the screen out of sight.

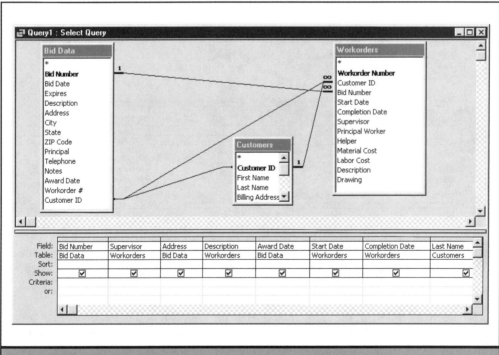

Figure 8-11. *Fields added to the new query*

Running and Saving the Query

As you progress with the query design, a good idea is to run the query to see if you are getting the information the way you want it. You have three ways to run the query:

- Click Datasheet view.
- Click Run.
- Choose Query | Run.

You needn't save the query design before looking at the results. Figure 8-12 shows the unfinished query in Datasheet view. The column widths and row heights have been adjusted, so all data appears onscreen.

With Access 2002, you can now view your query results in two other arrangements: PivotTable and PivotChart. These provide a shortcut to analyzing the data produced by the query. See Chapter 15 for details of creating PivotCharts and PivotTables.

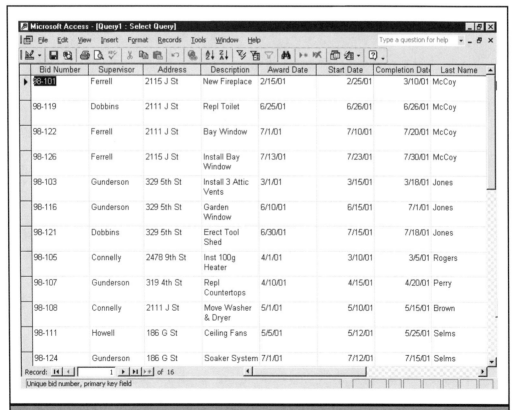

Bid Number	Supervisor	Address	Description	Award Date	Start Date	Completion Date	Last Name
98-101	Ferrell	2115 J St	New Fireplace	2/15/01	2/25/01	3/10/01	McCoy
98-119	Dobbins	2111 J St	Repl Toilet	6/25/01	6/26/01	6/26/01	McCoy
98-122	Ferrell	2111 J St	Bay Window	7/1/01	7/10/01	7/20/01	McCoy
98-126	Ferrell	2115 J St	Install Bay Window	7/13/01	7/23/01	7/30/01	McCoy
98-103	Gunderson	329 5th St	Install 3 Attic Vents	3/1/01	3/15/01	3/18/01	Jones
98-116	Gunderson	329 5th St	Garden Window	6/10/01	6/15/01	7/1/01	Jones
98-121	Dobbins	329 5th St	Erect Tool Shed	6/30/01	7/15/01	7/18/01	Jones
98-105	Connelly	2478 9th St	Inst 100g Heater	4/1/01	3/10/01	3/5/01	Rogers
98-107	Gunderson	319 4th St	Repl Countertops	4/10/01	4/15/01	4/20/01	Perry
98-108	Connelly	2111 J St	Move Washer & Dryer	5/1/01	5/10/01	5/15/01	Brown
98-111	Howell	186 G St	Ceiling Fans	5/5/01	5/12/01	5/25/01	Selms
98-124	Gunderson	186 G St	Soaker System	7/1/01	7/12/01	7/15/01	Selms

Record: I◄ ◄ 1 ► ►I ►* of 16

Unique bid number, primary key field

Figure 8-12. *The query in Datasheet view*

When you try to close the query either from the Design view or from one of the query result views, Access prompts you to save the design.

Save the new query design before adding the sort order and filter criteria.

1. Return to the Query Design view and click Save.

2. Enter **Workorder Cost Sheet** in the Save As dialog box, and then choose OK.

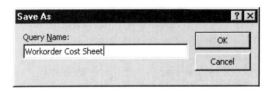

   You can usually cancel a query when it's running by pressing CTRL-BREAK. *Very long queries may not comply, however.*

Analyzing and Optimizing Query Performance

If you created an important query, but it seems to take a long time to run, ways to streamline it may exist. The Performance Analyzer is an Access tool that can look over any or all of the objects in your database and come up with recommendations, suggestions, and ideas for improvement. To start the Performance Analyzer, choose Tools | Analyze | Performance. Click the Query tab in the Performance Analyzer dialog box, check the query you want to examine, and then choose OK.

The Performance Wizard isn't installed with the Typical installation, so you may need to install it before you can analyze the query.

When the Performance Analyzer finishes, it displays a list of results. You can have Access implement any of the recommendations or suggestions.

You can also do the following to optimize a query:

■ Make sure all the foreign keys in the related tables are indexed.
   If a field cannot be indexed, try not to sort on it.

■ Include in the design grid only those fields necessary in the results.
   Extra fields take more time to display.

■ Make sure you aren't using exorbitantly large data sizes.
   Unnecessarily large fields waste disk space and slow processing.

Hiding/Showing Fields

You might want to use one or more fields in filtering or sorting the query results, but you don't want the information to appear in the results. The check box in the Show cell of the design grid determines whether the field values will be displayed. Clear the check mark to hide the field; check it to show the field.

When you reopen the design of a query in which you hid some of the fields, you may think they were removed. Actually, Access moved the hidden fields to the rightmost columns in the design grid when you saved the query and they may be off the screen. However, if no Criteria or Show entries existed, the field is, indeed, removed from the design.

Specifying the Record Order

One of the features of Access is you can sort the results of a query in the Datasheet view by clicking one of the Sort buttons without having to set the sort order in the design. This gives you flexibility, but if you want to specify a sort order saved with the query, you should set it in the query design.

Setting a sort order in a query design is the same as setting it in an advanced filter. You choose from the Sort cell list box in the column containing the field you want to sort by. If you want to sort on more than one field, make sure you have the fields arranged in the proper order from left to right. They needn't be adjacent.

A sort order is saved with the query if you specify it in the design. Any new form or report based on the query then inherits the sort order. It needn't be applied, but it is an inherited property of the form or report.

Sorting on a lookup field can have confusing results. For example, Figure 8-13 shows the results of sorting the Workorder Cost Sheet records first by Supervisor, and then by Completion date. The lower window shows the underlying query grid with both fields sorted in ascending order.

The Completion Dates are in the correct order within the set of records for a given Supervisor. The Supervisor fields, however, don't appear to be in alphabetic order, either ascending or descending. When you specify a sort in the query grid, Access sorts on the stored value, which in this case is the Employee ID number, not the employee name. If you want the records sorted by the displayed value, you need to sort in the Datasheet view which has access to the related lookup list values.

The same is true when you try to filter records based on a value in a lookup field. You must enter the stored value in the Criteria cell in the query grid only with filtering on a lookup field with Advanced Filter/Sort, as discussed in the last chapter.

Like a sort order, you can apply a filter to the query results, instead of making it part of the query design. This has the same effect as adding the criteria to the design, but the filter won't be saved with the query.

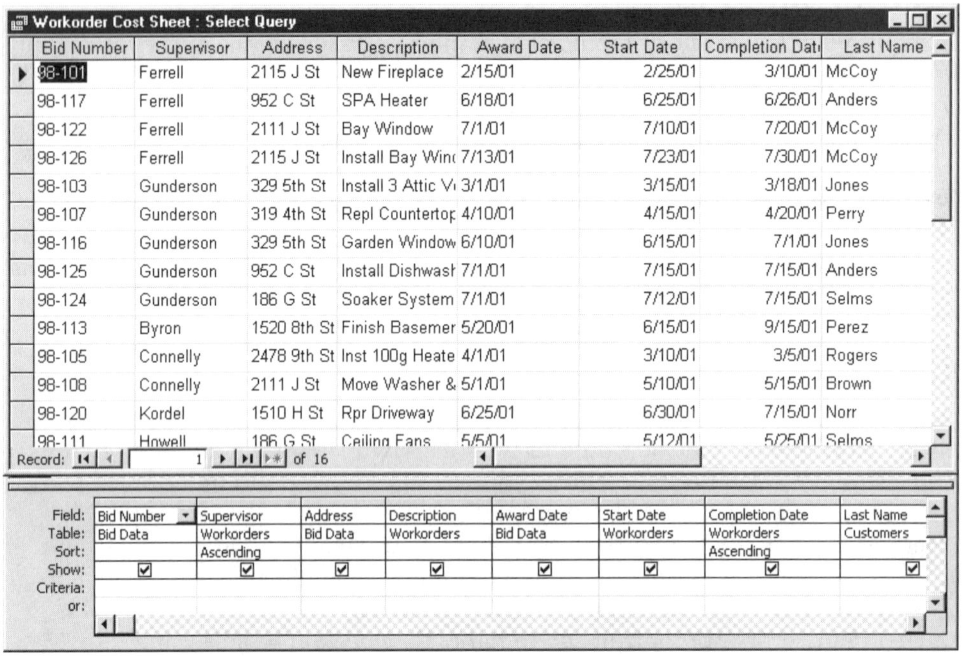

Workorder Cost Sheet : Select Query

Bid Number	Supervisor	Address	Description	Award Date	Start Date	Completion Dat	Last Name
98-101	Ferrell	2115 J St	New Fireplace	2/15/01	2/25/01	3/10/01	McCoy
98-117	Ferrell	952 C St	SPA Heater	6/18/01	6/25/01	6/26/01	Anders
98-122	Ferrell	2111 J St	Bay Window	7/1/01	7/10/01	7/20/01	McCoy
98-126	Ferrell	2115 J St	Install Bay Win	7/13/01	7/23/01	7/30/01	McCoy
98-103	Gunderson	329 5th St	Install 3 Attic V	3/1/01	3/15/01	3/18/01	Jones
98-107	Gunderson	319 4th St	Repl Countertop	4/10/01	4/15/01	4/20/01	Perry
98-116	Gunderson	329 5th St	Garden Window	6/10/01	6/15/01	7/1/01	Jones
98-125	Gunderson	952 C St	Install Dishwash	7/1/01	7/15/01	7/15/01	Anders
98-124	Gunderson	186 G St	Soaker System	7/1/01	7/12/01	7/15/01	Selms
98-113	Byron	1520 8th St	Finish Basemer	5/20/01	6/15/01	9/15/01	Perez
98-105	Connelly	2478 9th St	Inst 100g Heate	4/1/01	3/10/01	3/5/01	Rogers
98-108	Connelly	2111 J St	Move Washer &	5/1/01	5/10/01	5/15/01	Brown
98-120	Kordel	1510 H St	Rpr Driveway	6/25/01	6/30/01	7/15/01	Norr
98-111	Howell	186 G St	Ceiling Fans	5/5/01	5/12/01	5/25/01	Selms

Record: 1 of 16

Field:	Bid Number	Supervisor	Address	Description	Award Date	Start Date	Completion Date	Last Name
Table:	Bid Data	Workorders	Bid Data	Workorders	Bid Data	Workorders	Workorders	Customers
Sort:		Ascending					Ascending	
Show:	☑	☑	☑	☑	☑	☑	☑	☑
Criteria:								
or:								

Figure 8-13. *Sorting on a lookup field*

Showing Highest or Lowest Values

Limiting the results to the few highest or lowest values in a field can be handy for isolating the more labor-intensive jobs or finding the employees who could use a raise. For example, you can ask Access to display only the records with the 15 highest or lowest values in a field or the records with the highest or lowest 15 percent of values.

You use the Top Values box on the toolbar to specify how many or what percentage of the records to include in the results. The Top Values list includes 5, 25, and 100 records, and 5 percent and 25 percent of the values to choose from, as well as All. You can also type any percentage or number of values you want directly in the box.

Access selects the records starting from the top of the list, so before you select the Top Values setting, you must sort (descending) on the field you want to display the highest values. If you want the lowest values, sort in ascending order. If you specified a sort on any other field in the query, make sure the sorted field is to the right of the top values field, so the values will be subordinate to the Top Value list.

If you specify the number of top values you want to see, all values that match the last value in the list are also included, so you may see more than you expected. If you don't want to see the duplicate records, change the UniqueValues query property to Yes. You can also use the TopValues query property to limit the records to the top or bottom values. More about query properties in a later section in this chapter.

Adding Selection Criteria

The last chapter introduced you to the concept of adding selection criteria when filtering records with Advanced Filter/Sort. The selection criteria in queries are also expressions defining a condition that must be met for the record to be included in the subset. An *expression* is a combination of symbols, values, identifiers, and operators used for many purposes, many of which you have already seen, and others you learn about in later chapters, including:

- Establishing field and record validation rules.
- Setting default field values.
- Defining filter criteria.
- Computing calculated field values.
- Specifying conditions under which a macro runs.
- Using as arguments in Visual Basic functions and procedures.

Symbols used in expressions include quotation marks, colons, asterisks, and other special characters. *Values* can be expressed as literal values, constants, the result of a function, or an identifier. *Identifiers* refer to the value of a field, a control in a form or report, or a property. An *operator* is a symbol or word that indicates an operation to be performed on one or more elements in the expression.

 Another feature of Access 2002 is you can apply a filter to the query results datasheet, instead of making it a part of the query design. This has the same effect as adding the criteria to the design grid, but the filter won't be saved with the query.

Using Wildcards and Operators

If you want to set a criterion for a text field and you want to match only part of the field, you can use the same wildcards you used in filters: ? to represent a single character and * to represent any number of characters. For example, to find all Bid Data records for jobs on J Street, enter the expression

J St

in the Criteria cell in the Address column and press ENTER. Access examines the expression and completes the syntax by adding special characters:

Like "*J St*".

Operators are the key to more flexible expressions. Access has several classes of operators: arithmetic, comparison, concatenation, and logical. Table 8-3 lists the operators you can use in query criteria expressions and gives examples of each.

Operator	Description	Example	Limits Records to
Arithmetic Operators			
+	Addition	=Cost+50	Values equal to 50 more than the value in the Cost field
–	Subtraction	=Cost-50	Values equal to 50 less than the value in the Cost field
*	Multiplication	=Cost*2	Values twice the amount in the Cost field
/	Division	=Cost/2	Values half the amount in the Cost field
\	Integer division	=Cost\2	The integer portion of values that results from dividing the Cost field value by 2
Mod	Modulo division	=Cost Mod 2	The remainder of dividing the Cost value by 2
Comparison Operators			
=	Equals	=Books *or* ="Books"	Text value Books
>	Greater than	>7/15/01 *or* >#7/15/01#	Dates later than July 15, 2001

Table 8-3. *Operators Used in Expressions*

Operator	Description	Example	Limits Records to
<	Less than	<1500	Values less than 1500
>=	Greater than or equal to	>=15	Values greater than or equal to 15
<=	Less than or equal to	<=1/1/02 *or* <=#1/1/02#	Dates on or before January 1, 2002
<>	Not equal to	<>NY *or* <>"NY"	Values other than NY
Between…And	Between two values, inclusive	Between 100 And 500	Numbers from 100 to 500, inclusive
In	Included in a set of values	In("Germany", "France")	Either Germany or France
Is Null	Field is empty	Is Null	Records with no value in the field
Is Not Null	Field is not empty	Is Not Null	Records with a value in the field
""	Field contains zero-length string	=""	Records with zero-length string in the field
Like	With wildcards, matches a pattern	Like C* *or* Like "C*"	Any text values that begin with C
Logical Operators			
And	Both conditions are True	>=10 And <=100	Values between 10 and 100, inclusive
Or	Either condition is True	Books Or Videos *or* "Books" Or "Videos"	Either Books or Videos
Not	Not True	Not Like AB* *or* Not Like "AB*"	All values except those beginning with AB

Table 8-3.   *Operators Used in Expressions* (continued)

When filtering on a Date field, you can use one of the date functions in the criteria expression. Table 8-4 shows examples of the date functions included in expressions used as criteria to limit the records in the Workorders table by values in the Completion Date field.

Note *If the field name contains a space, a colon (:), or any Access special character, the name must be enclosed in brackets ([]) when used in an expression.*

Function	Expression	Result
Date()	<Date()+45	Displays work orders with Completion Date less than 45 days from today.
DateAdd()	>DateAdd("m",6,Date())	Displays work orders with Completion Date more than six months from today. The *m* isolates the month value.
Year()	Year([Completion Date])=2001	Displays work orders whose Completion Date falls in 2001.
DatePart()	DatePart("q",[Completion Date])=2	Displays work orders whose Completion Date is in the second calendar quarter. The *q* isolates the calendar quarter.
Month()	Year([Completion Date])=Year(Now) And Month([Completion Date])=Month(Now)	Displays work orders with Completion Dates in the current year and month.

Table 8-4. *Using Date Functions in Expressions*

Using a Single Criterion

You add a single selection criterion to a Criteria cell in the query design grid, exactly the same as in an advanced filter. For example, if you want to see information from the Workorder Cost Sheet for only those jobs supervised by Gunderson, do the following:

1. Open the Workorder Cost Sheet query in Design view and enter **12** (the Employee ID number for Gunderson) in the Criteria cell of the Supervisor column, and then press ENTER. Access adds quotation marks around 12 because the field is a text data type.

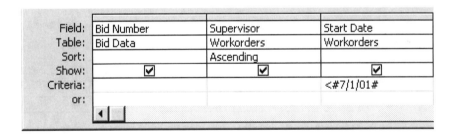

Field:	Bid Number	Supervisor	Address	Description	Award Date	Start Date
Table:	Bid Data	Workorders	Bid Data	Workorders	Bid Data	Workorders
Sort:						
Show:	☑	☑	☑	☑	☑	☑
Criteria:		"12"				
or:						

2. Switch to Datasheet view to display the five records for Gunderson's jobs.

3. Now you want to see the records for all jobs started before July 1, 2001, without regard to the supervisor. Return to Design view and delete the Supervisor criteria by selecting the expression and pressing DEL.

4. Enter **<7/1/01** in the Start Date Criteria cell and press ENTER. Access adds the date delimiters.

Field:	Bid Number	Supervisor	Start Date
Table:	Bid Data	Workorders	Workorders
Sort:		Ascending	
Show:	☑	☑	☑
Criteria:			<#7/1/01#
or:			

5. Run the query to see the eleven records for jobs started before July 1, 2001.

When you move out of the Criteria cell after entering the expression, Access automatically parses the expression and inserts characters to complete the syntax:

- Brackets ([]) around field names
- Number signs (#) around dates
- Double quotation marks ("") around text
- Equal sign (=) before a calculated field expression

Using Multiple Criteria

To apply more than one selection criterion, you combine them with the And or Or operators, using the same logic as with filters:

- Use And to require both criteria be met to include the record in the query result.
- Use Or to extract records that satisfy either expression.

Table 8-5 displays two truth tables that show the result of combining criteria with And and Or.

Note *If you want to select records based on field values, the field must be in the design grid, even if you don't show it in the results.*

Where you enter the expressions in the design grid depends on how you want them applied:

- In one field using Or, enter one expression in the Criteria row and the second in the Or row.

Field:	Bid Number	Supervisor	Start Date
Table:	Bid Data	Workorders	Workorders
Sort:		Ascending	
Show:	☑	☑	☑
Criteria:		"12"	
or:		"10"	

■ In one field using And, enter both expressions in the Criteria row combined with the And operator. This combination is seldom used because a field can't have two different values at once, but it can be used to find a combination of text strings in a memo field.

Tip   *If the expression is wider than the input area, press* SHIFT-F2 *with the insertion point in the cell where you enter the expression. This opens the Zoom box where you can enter and edit the expression. Even though the text wraps to multiple lines in the Zoom box, the expression is only one line.*

■ In two fields using Or, enter one expression in the Criteria row of one column and the other expression in the Or row of the other column. It doesn't matter which is which.

Field:	Bid Number	Supervisor	Start Date
Table:	Bid Data	Workorders	Workorders
Sort:		Ascending	
Show:	☑	☑	☑
Criteria:		"12"	
or:			<#7/1/01#

■ In two fields using And, enter both expressions in the Criteria row.

Field:	Bid Number	Supervisor	Start Date
Table:	Bid Data	Workorders	Workorders
Sort:		Ascending	
Show:	☑	☑	☑
Criteria:		"12"	<#7/1/01#
or:			

■ In three fields using both And and Or, enter one pair of And expressions in the Criteria row and the other pair in the Or row. Figure 8-14 shows the results of this query sorted by Supervisor (actually by Supervisor ID).

Field:	Bid Number	Supervisor	Start Date	Address
Table:	Bid Data	Workorders	Workorders	Bid Data
Sort:		Ascending		
Show:	✔	✔	✔	✔
Criteria:		"12"	<#7/1/01#	
or:			>#6/1/01#	Like "*J St*"

The Advanced Filter/Sort saved as a query in the last chapter provides an example of a slightly different arrangement of multiple selection criteria in the design grid.

Field:	Award Date	Bid Date
Table:	Bid Data	Bid Data
Sort:		
Show:	✔	✔
Criteria:	"Lost"	Between #2/1/01# And #3/31/01#
or:	<[Bid Date]+"45"	Between #2/1/01# And #3/31/01#

The criteria specified in the Look for tab appear in the Criteria row of the design grid and the expressions entered in the Or tab appear in the Or row. The Bid Date

		Expression 1			**Expression 1**	
	AND	*True*	*False*	*OR*	*True*	*False*
Exp 2	*True*	Select	Reject	Exp 2	*True*	Select	Select
	False	Reject	Reject		*False*	Select	Reject

Table 8-5. *Results of Combining Two Expressions*

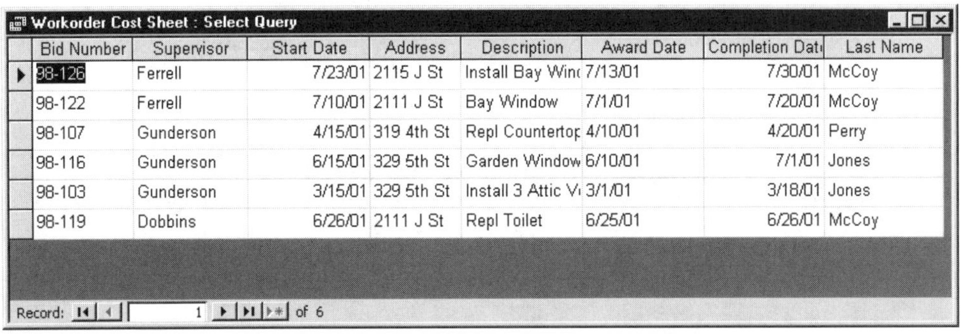

Bid Number	Supervisor	Start Date	Address	Description	Award Date	Completion Dat	Last Name
98-126	Ferrell	7/23/01	2115 J St	Install Bay Win	7/13/01	7/30/01	McCoy
98-122	Ferrell	7/10/01	2111 J St	Bay Window	7/1/01	7/20/01	McCoy
98-107	Gunderson	4/15/01	319 4th St	Repl Countertop	4/10/01	4/20/01	Perry
98-116	Gunderson	6/15/01	329 5th St	Garden Window	6/10/01	7/1/01	Jones
98-103	Gunderson	3/15/01	329 5th St	Install 3 Attic V	3/1/01	3/18/01	Jones
98-119	Dobbins	6/26/01	2111 J St	Repl Toilet	6/25/01	6/26/01	McCoy

Figure 8-14. *The results of the query*

column has been widened to show the entire expression. Another way to view the complete expression is to right-click the cell and choose Zoom from the shortcut menu to open the Zoom box.

Tip *When working with expressions, you can use the Cut, Copy, and Paste buttons as shortcuts to enter criteria.*

Getting Help from the Expression Builder

When you need to enter a complicated expression in a query design as a selection criterion or you want to construct a calculated field, you can call on the Expression Builder for help. To open the Expression Builder, click Build in the Query Design view. You can also right-click in the cell where the expression will go and choose Build from the shortcut menu. If the cell already contains an expression, this is copied to the Expression Builder. Figure 8-15 shows the Builder with an Award Date criterion left over from an earlier query.

Notice the Workorder Cost Sheet folder is open and a list of fields is displayed in the center of the lower section.

The upper pane of the Expression Builder is where you enter the expression. The lower pane consists of expression elements divided into three levels. The leftmost panel contains all the groupings in the current session. When you open a folder in this panel, the contents of the selected item are listed in the middle panel. Selecting an item in the center panel opens a list of individual elements in the right panel. You can add one of these to the expression by double-clicking the name, or by selecting it and clicking Paste.

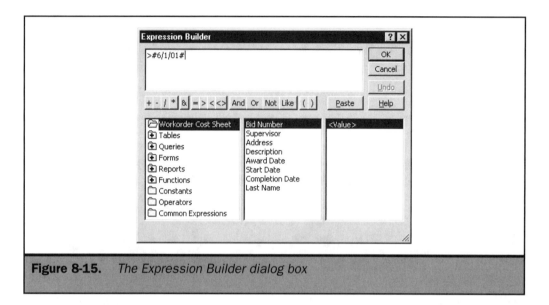

Figure 8-15. *The Expression Builder dialog box*

For example, suppose you want to use the Month() function to define a selection criterion on the Start Date field in the Workorder Cost Sheet query to display only records for jobs started in June. To accomplish this, do the following:

1. In the Query Design view, right-click in the Criteria cell of the Start Date column and choose Expression Builder from the shortcut menu.

2. Double-click the Functions folder to open two subfolders: Built-In Functions and Home Tech Repair.

3. Open the Built-In Functions folder. A list of function categories appears in the center panel.

4. Choose Date/Time. The right panel shows a list of all the date- or time-related built-in functions.

5. Scroll down the list and select Month, and then choose Paste. The Month() function is copied to the upper pane with the correct syntax (see Figure 8-16).

6. The Month() function requires an argument—a number—to tell Access which month you want to specify in the expression. Click to highlight <<number>> in the parentheses and enter **6** (for June).

7. Click OK. You return to the Query Design window where Month(6) now shows in the Criteria cell of the Start Date column.

The row of buttons between the upper and lower panes gives you a quick way of adding many of the commonly used operators and symbols.

You see more of the Expression Builder in Chapter 19 when you add condition expressions to macros.

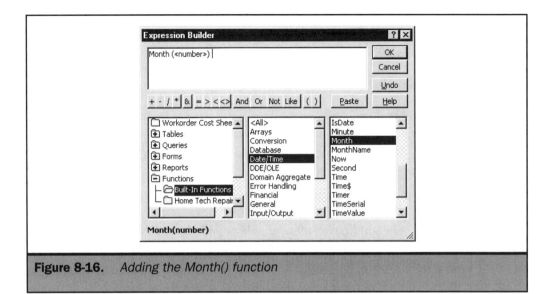

Figure 8-16. *Adding the Month() function*

Handling Blank Fields

Fields containing Null values and zero-length strings can affect the query results. Consider these aspects when you work with potentially empty fields:

- If the field has been left empty because of incomplete data, it's easy to display those records in a datasheet where you can add the missing data. Use Is Null as the criteria to find Null values and "" to find zero-length strings.

- Query results that include data from related tables display only those records in which neither matching field has a Null value.

- When you use a field in an aggregate calculation, such as sum or count, Access doesn't include records with Null values in that field. If you want to include records with a Null value when you count the number of records, use Count with the * wildcard.

- If one of the fields in an expression that uses an arithmetic operator (+, –, *, /, \, ^) has a Null value, the entire expression returns a Null value.

- You can convert Null values to zero-length strings with the Nz() function. More about functions in Chapter 25.

- If you want to display records with zero-length string values but no Null values, use Like "*" as the selection criterion.

Setting Query Properties

Like all other database objects, a query has a set of properties that controls its appearance and behavior. To open the Query Properties dialog box (see Figure 8-17), place the insertion point in the table pane, and then do one of the following:

- Click Properties.
- Choose View | Properties.
- Right-click anywhere in the design window outside the field lists and choose Properties from the shortcut menu.

Table 8-6 describes the query properties and lists the available property settings for each.

If the subdatasheet height doesn't allow display of all records in the subdatasheet, Access adds a vertical scroll bar. If you're permitted to add records to the subdatasheet, a New Record row is also included.

Note   *The field lists in the query design have two properties: Alias and Source. The Alias property usually is the underlying table or query name, but if you have more than one copy of a table in the query design, you can use the Alias property to rename one of them. Right-click the field list and choose Properties from the shortcut menu. The Source property specifies the name of an outside source for the field list.*

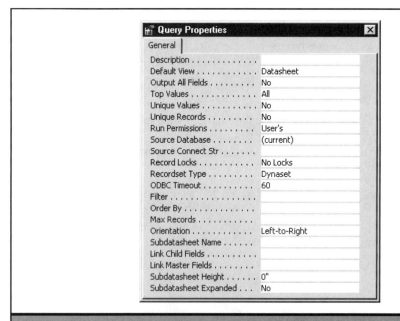

Figure 8-17.   *The Query Properties dialog box*

Property	Description	Settings
Description	Optional description of the query.	Enter up to 255 characters.
Default View	Sets the default view for the query result.	Datasheet (default), PivotTable, or PivotChart.
Output All Fields	Same as checking Show for all fields.	Yes or No (default).
Top Values	Limits the records to some quantity or proportion of the top values, measured by the number of records or percent of total based on the leftmost sorted field.	5, 25, 100, 5%, 25% or All (default), or enter a value.
Unique Values	Returns only those records with unique values. Often used when only one field is used in the design grid.	Yes or No (default).
Unique Records	Similar to Unique Values, except displays records that are unique, based on all the fields in the data source, not only the one in the design grid.	Yes or No (default).
Run Permissions	Gives an end user permission to take an action otherwise not permitted.	User's (default) or Owner's.
Source Database	Specifies the underlying data source.	Default (current), but can indicate an external database.
Source Connect Str	Works with Source Database and indicates where the tables and queries are stored.	Name of the external database. Default is none.

Table 8-6. *Query Properties*

Property	Description	Settings
Record Locks	Determines how records are locked in multiuser systems.	No Locks (default), All Records, or Edited Record.
Recordset Type	Specifies the behavior of the result.	Dynaset (default), Dynaset(Inconsistent Updates), or Snapshot.
ODBC Timeout	Length of time to check network connection for a response before giving up.	Sets a value in seconds. Default is 60 seconds. Setting to 0 turns the feature off.
Filter	Indicates any filter applied after the query was run. Usually filtering the datasheet with Filter By Form or Filter By Selection.	Expression created by the filter tool. No default.
Order By	Sorts order specified by Sort Ascending or Sort Descending applied to query result.	Lists fields in sort order. No default.
Max Records	Determines maximum number of records to return from an ODBC database.	Default is 0, which returns all records. Enter a number to have query stop after returning that number of records.
Orientation	Sets the reading direction.	Left-to-right (default) or right-to-left.
Subdatasheet Name	Specifies the subdatasheet.	Name of related table or query.

Table 8-6.   *Query Properties* (continued)

Property	Description	Settings
Link Child Fields	Specifies linking field name(s) in the subform or subreport.	One or more field names.
Link Master Fields	Specifies linking field name(s) in the main form or report.	One or more field names.
Subdatasheet Height	Specifies the maximum height for an expanded subdatasheet.	Default 0″.
Subdatasheet Expanded	Saves all subdatasheets automatically expanded with main datasheet.	Yes or No (default).

Table 8-6. *Query Properties* (continued)

Modifying a Query

To open a query for modifying the design, select the query in the Queries page of the Database window and click Design. If you want to view the results of the query first, click Open, and then switch to Design view. You can also right-click the query name and choose Open or Design from the shortcut menu.

You use the Query Design window to make changes to the query, just the same as if you were creating it. You can add or delete a field, rearrange the columns, show or hide any of the fields, change the resulting records sort order, and add one or more selection criteria.

Inserting a Field and Changing the Field Order

If you want to add another field to the grid, drag the field name to the Field row of the column where you want the field. The field is inserted and the other columns move to make room.

Tip *If you double-click the field name, Access puts it at the end of the line in the first empty column.*

Moving a field in the design grid works the same as in a datasheet. Select the field by clicking the column selector (the mouse pointer changes to a down arrow). Release the mouse button and click again when it changes to a left upward arrow. Then drag the column to a new position. When you see the dark vertical line where you want the column's left margin to appear, release the mouse button. The column moves and the other columns slide over to oblige.

Changing Field Properties

The fields that appear in the query results inherit the properties from the table design. You may want the field to look different or show a different name in the query results, however, especially if you're going to use them as the basis for a custom form or report. You cannot change all a field's properties, only those that appear in the field's property sheet in the query.

When you make changes to field properties in the table design, any new or existing queries usually inherit those changes. The exception to this rule is this: if you already changed field properties in the query design, any changes in the table design aren't carried over to override the query customization.

You may want a field to show a more descriptive name. For example, Access assigns default names to calculated fields, such as Expr1 or CountOfAddress, which aren't very informative. When you change the name in the query design, the new name appears in the datasheet and in any new forms or reports based on the query. The new name doesn't affect the underlying table or any existing forms or reports.

To rename a field in the query design, do the following:

1. Place the insertion point to the left of the first letter of the name in the grid.

2. Type the new name followed by a colon (:). If you're replacing Expr1 or another Access-assigned name, replace only the name, not the expression following the colon.

3. Press ENTER.

If you want to keep the name in the grid, but show a different name in the datasheet, change the field's Caption property in the property sheet.

To change other field properties, click in the field on the grid and click Properties. You can also choose View | Properties or right-click the field and choose Properties from the shortcut menu. Entries in the field property sheets are blank; they don't contain the settings defined in the table design. Any entries you make in the Query Design window override the preset properties. Figure 8-18 shows the property sheet for the Completion Date field with a list of Date/Time formats.

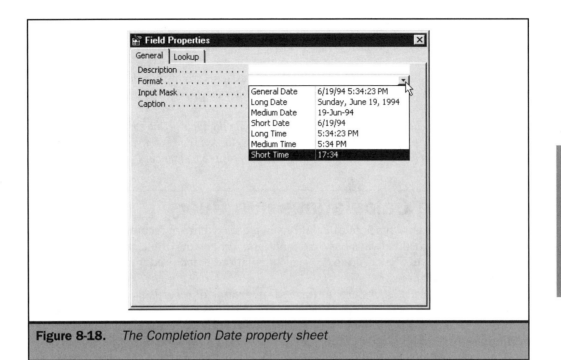

Figure 8-18.   *The Completion Date property sheet*

The field property sheet has two tabs: General and Lookup. The General tab shows four properties you can change in the query design, as follows:

- The *Description* is the text displayed in the status bar when you click the field in the Datasheet view. Any text entered here replaces the Description entered in the table definition. You can enter up to 255 characters.

- *Format* shows a list of applicable formats for the field. A Text field has no list, but you can enter a custom format.

- An *Input Mask* creates a data entry skeleton. You can either type the mask in the box or click Build to start the Input Mask Wizard.

- The *Caption* property specifies the column header for a datasheet, form, or report in place of the field name.

- If the field is a Number field, the *Decimal Places* property also appears in the property sheet.

If the field is a lookup field, the Lookup tab has one option where you can change the Display Control to a Text Box, List Box, or Combo Box. The other properties on the Lookup tab are the same as those in the table design. If the field isn't a lookup field, this tab is blank.

If you want to change several field properties or even a query property, keep the property sheet open and the options will change when you click another object in the query design.

When you finish with the property sheet, click Close. Changing field properties in a query design has no effect on the underlying table design.

 Calculated fields don't inherit any properties from the table because they didn't exist in the table. The properties must be set in the query design. For example, if the calculated field contains currency data, set the Format property to Currency.

Performing Calculations in a Query

You can perform many types of calculations in a query that are recomputed each time the query is run, so you always have current data. The results of the calculations aren't stored in the table. In a query, two types of calculations exist: predefined calculations and custom calculations.

The *predefined calculations* are performed on groups of records and provide totals, counts, averages, and other information about field values in all records or in groups of records. Think of these aggregate calculations as vertical computations. For example, add up the number of jobs on J Street or calculate the average labor cost for all jobs.

The *custom calculations* actually create new fields in a record by combining the values in other fields in the record, producing a horizontal computation. You can create new numeric, date, or text fields for each record using custom calculations. For example, use the expression

[Completion Date]-[Start Date]

to create a new field named Job Time. After creating a calculated field, you can use the predefined calculations to analyze the data further. For example, after finding the Job Time for each job, you can compute the average time. Or, you can even add a selection criterion to limit the records to jobs in a specific area or supervised by a specific employee.

Adding a Calculated Field

To add a new field that displays the results of a calculation based on other fields in the grid, click the Field row of an empty column and enter an expression. The field names must be enclosed in brackets so Access recognizes them as fields.

For example, add a calculated field to a query of the Home Tech Repair Workorders table that shows the total cost of each current job:

1. In the Query Design view, drag the fields you want to see in the result to the grid, including Material Cost and Labor Cost.

2. Click in the Field cell on the first empty column and enter the expression: **[Material Cost]+[Labor Cost]**, and then press ENTER. Access adds a default field name to the new field, Expr1. You can change the default field name to one that's more descriptive.

3. Move the insertion point to the left in the Field cell and replace Expr1 with **Total Cost**, keeping the colon.

4. Click Datasheet view. Figure 8-19 shows the results of the new calculated field.

If you want to see the total cost of each job, including a 15 percent markup for overhead expenses, add another calculated field using the expression:

[Total Cost]*1.15.

Tip   *When you run the query, if you misspell a field name in an expression, Access assumes it's a parameter needed by the query and asks you to enter the value. Click Cancel to close the Enter Parameter Value dialog box and to return to the grid to correct the field name.*

RETRIEVING AND PRESENTING INFORMATION

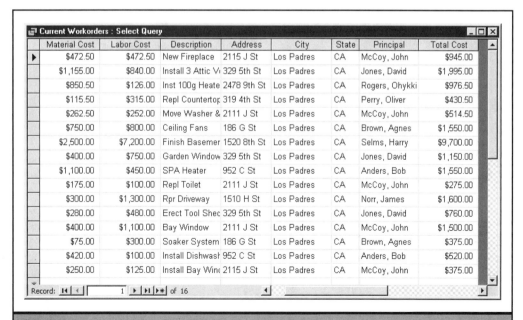

Figure 8-19.   *Displaying the new Total Cost field*

You aren't limited to Number and Currency fields in calculated fields. Text fields are easily combined with the concatenation operator (&). For example, if you want to create a new field showing employees' complete names in one field, use the following expression:

[First Name]&" "&[Last Name]

The quotation marks between the field names add a space.

If you want to include only the employees' initials and add some text to the display, use an expression such as the following:

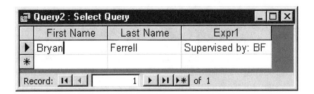

Field:	First Name	Last Name	Expr1: "Supervised by: " & Left([First Name],1) & Left([Last Name],1)	
Table:	Employees	Employees		
Sort:				
Show:	☑	☑	☑	
Criteria:				
or:				

The Left function extracts characters from the left of the field value and the integer argument in the function indicates how many of these characters you want to see, only one in this case. The result of this calculated field looks like this:

Query2 : Select Query

	First Name	Last Name	Expr1
▶	Bryan	Ferrell	Supervised by: BF
*			

Record: 14 4 | 1 | ▶ ▶I ▶* of 1

If you need help with a more complex expression, click Build to open the Expression Builder as described earlier.

Note   *If two tables in the query have a field with the same name, you must use the table name, as well as the field name in the expression, separated by an exclamation mark (!)—for example, [Bid Date]![Start Date] or [Employees]![Employee ID].*

Once you add the calculated field to the design grid, you can change its properties like any other field in the query. You can also summarize on a calculated field, as well as on a basic table field as described in the next section. By using more complex functions in expressions, you can create a wide variety of calculated fields using many data types, as discussed in a later section.

You cannot edit a calculated field in the dynaset. If you want a different value, change one of the fields in the expression.

Summarizing with the Wizard

As mentioned earlier in this chapter, if the query you're creating with the Simple Query Wizard contains any number, currency, or date/time fields, you're given the opportunity to create summary fields.

The second wizard dialog box offers two choices: Detail, in which all records are shown, or Summary. If you choose Summary and click the Summary Options button, the Summary Options dialog box opens where you can specify the types of summarization you want. Figure 8-20 shows the Summary Options dialog box for a query containing three fields from the Workorders table: Supervisor, Material Cost, and Labor Cost.

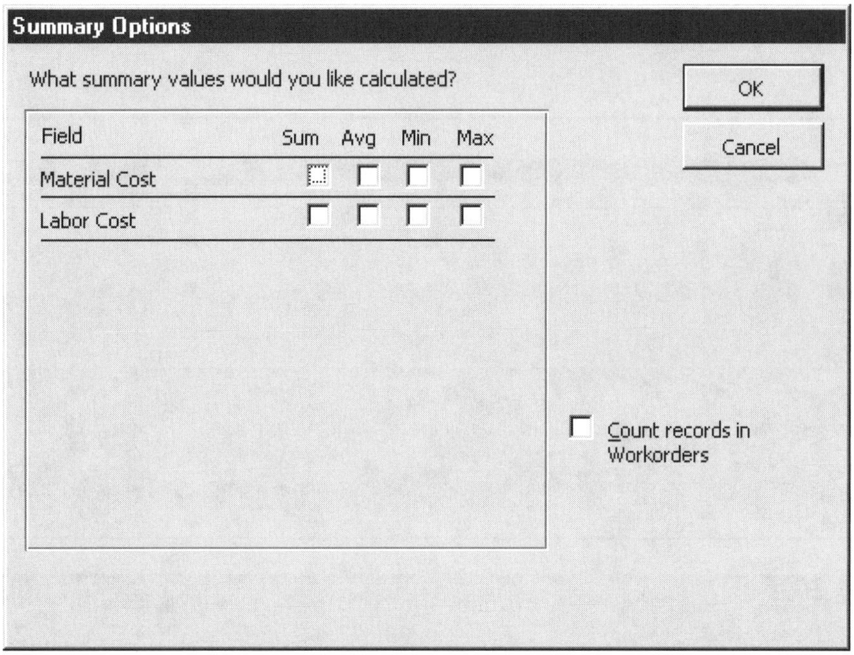

Summary Options

What summary values would you like calculated?

Field	Sum	Avg	Min	Max
Material Cost				
Labor Cost				

OK

Cancel

☐ Count records in Workorders

Figure 8-20.   *The Summary Options dialog box*

The two currency fields are listed with check boxes where you can choose the type of summary for each field. In addition, you have the option of counting the number of records in each group. After making your choices in this dialog box, click OK and return to the wizard. If any date/time fields are in the query, you have an opportunity to group on those values as well, by month, quarter, year, and so on.

Figure 8-21 shows the results of choosing to calculate the total and average of both cost fields, as well as to count the number of work orders for each supervisor. When you add summaries to the query design, you can be much more creative.

Summarizing with Aggregate Functions

If you want to know the material cost of all the current jobs or the average billing rate for all employees, you can add a summary calculation. The summaries work with values in a field from multiple records. You can summarize all the records in the result or group the records based on a specific field value—such as Supervisor—and calculate the summary value for each group separately.

Note *A summarizing query produces a snapshot instead of a dynaset and none of the fields in the result can be edited.*

Supervisor	Sum Of Material Cost	Avg Of Material Cost	Sum Of Labor Cost	Avg Of Labor Cost	Count Of Workorders
Ferrell	$2,222.50	$555.63	$2,147.50	$536.88	4
Gunderson	$2,165.50	$433.10	$2,305.00	$461.00	5
Byron	$2,500.00	$2,500.00	$7,200.00	$7,200.00	1
Connelly	$1,113.00	$556.50	$378.00	$189.00	2
Kordel	$300.00	$300.00	$1,300.00	$1,300.00	1
Howell	$750.00	$750.00	$800.00	$800.00	1
Dobbins	$455.00	$227.50	$580.00	$290.00	2

Figure 8-21. *A summary query created by the Simple Query Wizard*

Summarizing All Records

To summarize field values in a query, start with a select query, add the field you want to summarize, and then specify the way you want the fields summarized. For example, to find the total and average Material Cost for current work orders, do the following:

Σ

1. Start a new select query of the Workorders table and drag the Material Cost field to the grid.

2. Click Totals to add the Total row to the grid. You can also choose View | Totals or right-click in the grid and choose Totals from the shortcut menu.

3. Click the Total cell in the Material Cost column and choose Sum from the drop-down option list.

4. To summarize on the same field in two ways, you need another copy of the field in the grid. Drag another copy of the Material Cost field to the next empty column and choose Avg from the Total list.

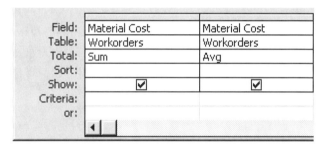

5. Switch to Datasheet view to see the results.

SumOfMaterial	AvgOfMaterial Cost
$9,506.00	$594.13

Query2 : Select Query

This example is summarized over all the records in the table. You can also base a summary on a subset of records by using the Group By option in the Total cell for the fields that make up the group. For example, you could count the number of jobs assigned to each supervisor.

You have a choice of 12 options in the Total drop-down list, seven of which perform mathematical calculations, two return specific records, and the other three indicate other uses for the field. Table 8-7 describes the Total list options and with which data types they can be used.

Option	Result	Use with Data Types
Sum	Total of values in the field	Number, Date/Time, Currency, AutoNumber
Avg	Average of values in the field	Number, Date/Time, Currency, AutoNumber
Min	Lowest value in the field	Text, Number, Date/Time, Currency, AutoNumber
Max	Highest value in the field	Text, Number, Date/Time, Currency, AutoNumber
Count	Number of values in the field, not counting blanks	All
StDev	Standard deviation of values in the field	Number, Date/Time, Currency, AutoNumber
Var	Variance on values in the field	Number, Date/Time, Currency, AutoNumber
First	Field value from first record in result set	All
Last	Field value from last record in result set	All

Table 8-7. *Options in Total List*

The other three options are

- *Group By,* which defines the groups you want the calculations to apply to—for example, show the average material costs for work orders grouped by supervisor.
- *Expression,* which creates a calculated field with an aggregate function in the expression.
- *Where,* which specifies selection criteria in a field not used in grouping. This field is hidden by default.

Note *Summaries usually don't include blanks, except in the case of Count. If you want to count records with Null values, use Count with the asterisk (*) wildcard character: Count*.*

Summarizing by Group

When you add fields to the grid with the Total row visible, the default entry is Group By. To group records with the same value in that field, leave the Group By option in the Total cell. For example, to count the number of work orders under control of each supervisor, do the following:

1. Start a new select query with the Workorders table and drag the Supervisor, Workorder Number, and Labor Cost fields to the grid.

2. Enter the expression **Avg([Labor Cost]+[Material Cost])** and press ENTER.

3. The Total cell still holds the Group By option. Change this to Expression and press ENTER.

4. Change the default Expr1 name to **Average Total**.

Field:	Supervisor	Workorder Number	Labor Cost	Average Total: Avg([Labor Cost]+[Material Cost])
Table:	Workorders	Workorders	Workorders	
Total:	Group By	Count	Avg	Expression
Sort:				
Show:	☑	☑	☑	☑
Criteria:				
or:				

The results of this query are shown in Figure 8-22.

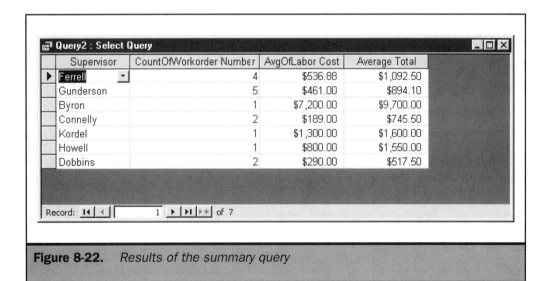

Supervisor	CountOfWorkorder Number	AvgOfLabor Cost	Average Total
Ferrell	4	$536.88	$1,092.50
Gunderson	5	$461.00	$894.10
Byron	1	$7,200.00	$9,700.00
Connelly	2	$189.00	$745.50
Kordel	1	$1,300.00	$1,600.00
Howell	1	$800.00	$1,550.00
Dobbins	2	$290.00	$517.50

Record: 1 of 7

Figure 8-22. *Results of the summary query*

You can also sort the groups by the values computed in the summaries. For example, you could reorder the previous records in descending order of the average total cost of the work orders assigned to each supervisor.

Adding Criteria

You can add selection criteria to summary queries to limit the result in three ways:

- To limit the records before they're included in the group and before the group calculations are performed, add the field whose records you want to limit, and then enter the criterion. For example, in the Supervisor's group, you could include only those work orders whose labor costs exceed $500. If you're calculating any totals in the same query, change the Total cell to Where.

- To limit the groupings after the records are included in the group, but before the group calculations are performed, enter the criterion in the Group By field. For example, you could include a summary for specific Supervisors.

- To limit the results of the group summaries, enter the criterion in the field that contains the calculation. For example, you could display results only for Supervisor groups whose average total cost exceeds $1,000.

Adding Customized Expressions

To create your own customized expressions in a summary query, you can use any of the built-in Access functions in the query grid. The most useful functions for summarizing data in a query come in three basic groups:

- *Aggregate Functions*, such as you already saw that calculate statistical values from field data—for example, Avg, Sum, Count, and so on.

- *Domain Aggregate Functions* that compute the same statistical values, but use all the values in the table or query. Domain Aggregate Functions override any grouping restrictions. Examples are DAvg, DSum, DCount, and so on.

- *Formatting Functions* that extract and display parts of the data and combine or format the results in many ways. Examples are Format, Left, Mid, and Right.

 If you use an Aggregate or Domain Aggregate Function that computes the standard deviation or variance with a group containing only two records, the result is a Null value.

Creating Special Queries with the Query Wizard

As you saw in the New Query dialog box, more Query Wizards exist than the Simple Select Wizard. The list includes wizards that create crosstabs, queries that find duplicate records, and queries that find unmatched records in related tables.

Creating a Find Duplicates Query

A Find Duplicates query locates and displays records in which the specified field has the same values. For example, you could use a Find Duplicates query to display all the work orders supervised by a specific employee or all the bids made on jobs at a particular address. The Find Duplicates Wizard can create the query for you using the following steps:

1. Click New in the Queries page of the Database window and double-click Find Duplicates Query Wizard in the New Query dialog box. The first dialog box asks you to select the table or query you want to search.

2. Choose Bid Data and click Next.

3. In the next dialog box (see Figure 8-23), double-click Address in the Available Fields list to add it to the Duplicate-value fields list, and then click Next.

4. Next, select all the fields you want to display in addition to the field in which duplicates may occur—for example, Bid Number, Bid Date, Description, and Principal. Then click Next.

5. In the last dialog box, enter Duplicate Addresses as the name for the query and click Finish. Figure 8-24 shows the results of the new Find Duplicates query.

RETRIEVING AND PRESENTING INFORMATION

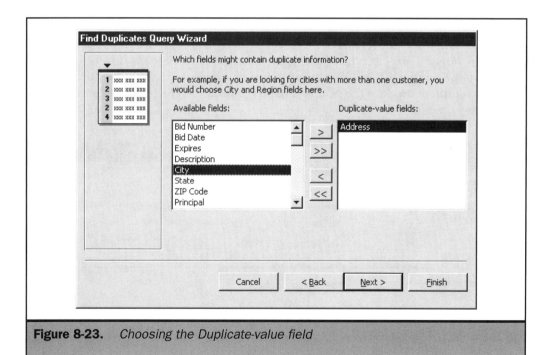

Figure 8-23. *Choosing the Duplicate-value field*

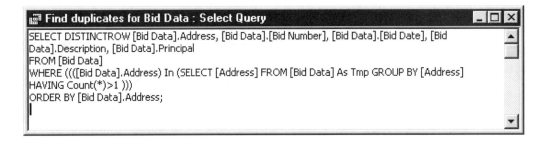

Figure 8-24. *Showing work orders with duplicate addresses*

If you want to sort the results or modify the query in another way, choose to modify the query in the last wizard dialog box, instead of to view the results.

The following shows the SQL statement the wizard created as the criteria in the Address column to produce the results. Chapter 9 discusses creating and using SQL statements in more detail.

```
Find duplicates for Bid Data : Select Query

SELECT DISTINCTROW [Bid Data].Address, [Bid Data].[Bid Number], [Bid Data].[Bid Date], [Bid
Data].Description, [Bid Data].Principal
FROM [Bid Data]
WHERE ((([Bid Data].Address) In (SELECT [Address] FROM [Bid Data] As Tmp GROUP BY [Address]
HAVING Count(*)>1 )))
ORDER BY [Bid Data].Address;
```

Creating a Find Unmatched Query

With the Find Unmatched Query Wizard, you can locate and display records in one table that have no match in a related table. For example, you can find customers who have no work orders, so you can send a letter to remind them of your services.

To create a Find Unmatched query, do the following:

1. Start a new query with the Find Unmatched Query Wizard.

2. In the first dialog box, choose Customers as the table whose records you want to display and click Next.

3. In the next dialog box, choose Workorders as the table you want to match with the Customers table. If there are any customers with no corresponding work orders, the Customer record is included in the result. Click Next.

4. In the next dialog box, specify the joining field. If the fields have the same name, Access predetermines the relationship (see Figure 8-25). Click Next.

5. Then select the fields you want to see in the result, such as name, address, and phone number.

6. Accept the query name as Customers Without Matching Workorders and click Finish.

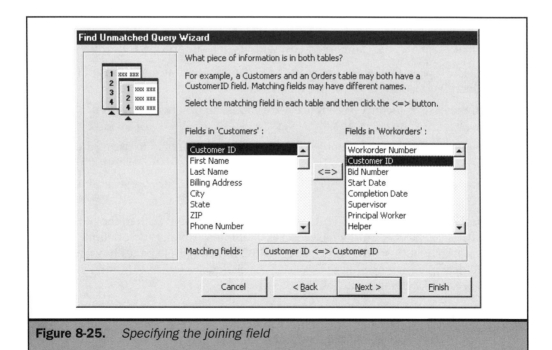

Figure 8-25. *Specifying the joining field*

	First Name	Last Name	Billing Address	City	State	ZIP	Phone Number
▶	Patricia	Gonzales	2595 9th St	Los Padres	CA	92111	(619) 555-1543
	Phillip	Armstrong	3401 F St	Los Padres	CA	92111	(619) 555-7843
	Thomas	Barrett	871 G St	Los Padres	CA	92111	(619) 555-2103
*							

Record: ◀◀ ◀ 1 ▶ ▶◀ ▶◀* of 3

Creating a Crosstab Query

A *crosstab query* is a special type of summary query that correlates summary values between two or more sets of field values, such as sales of types of products within certain sales regions or categories of workorder costs correlated with the active supervisor. One set of facts is listed as row headings at the left of the crosstab and the other is listed as column headings across the top. The summarized values, sums, averages, or counts are contained in the body of the crosstab.

To create a crosstab, you need at least three output fields: row headings, column headings, and values. You can create a crosstab query from scratch or with the help of the Crosstab Query Wizard. The result of running a crosstab query is a snapshot and none of the data in the results is editable.

As an example of creating a crosstab query, use the table named Workorder Crosstab, which has all the costs in one field, with an additional field that indicates the category of the cost: labor or material. To use the Crosstab Query Wizard to create a crosstab that correlates the category of cost with the job supervisor, follow these steps:

1. Click New on the Queries page of the Database window and choose Crosstab Query Wizard from the New Query dialog box.

2. In the first dialog box (see Figure 8-26) choose the Workorder Crosstab table as the basis for the query and click Next.

3. In the next dialog box, double-click Supervisor as the field to use as the row heading and click Next.

4. In the next dialog box (see Figure 8-27), choose Cost Category as the column heading and click Next.

5. In the next dialog box, select Cost as the value field and Sum in the Function list. Clear the check mark next to "Yes, include row sums" if you don't want to see a Total of Costs column (see Figure 8-28). The sample pane shows how the fields will be arranged in the crosstab. Click Back to return to a previous dialog box to make changes or click Next to finish the query.

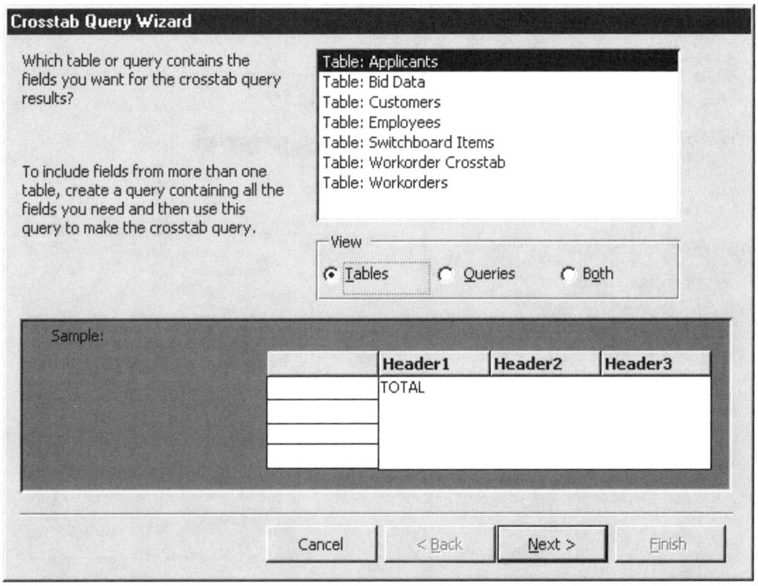

Figure 8-26. *The first Crosstab Query Wizard dialog box*

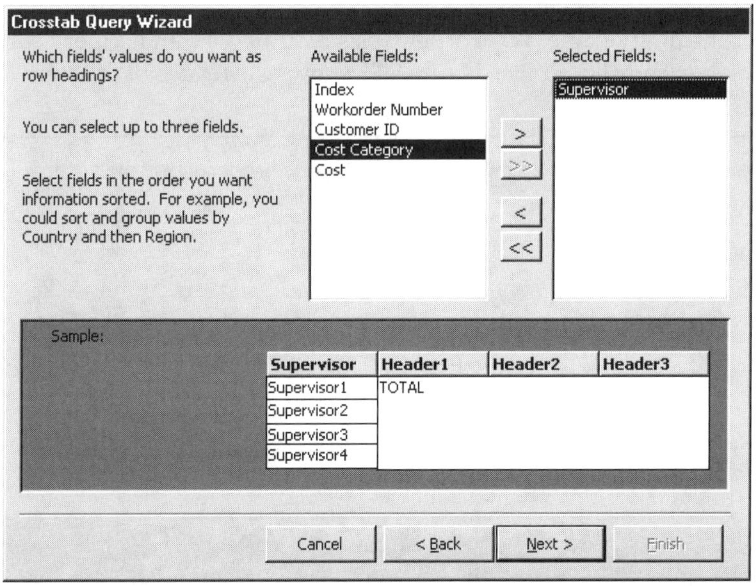

Figure 8-27. *Choosing the row heading*

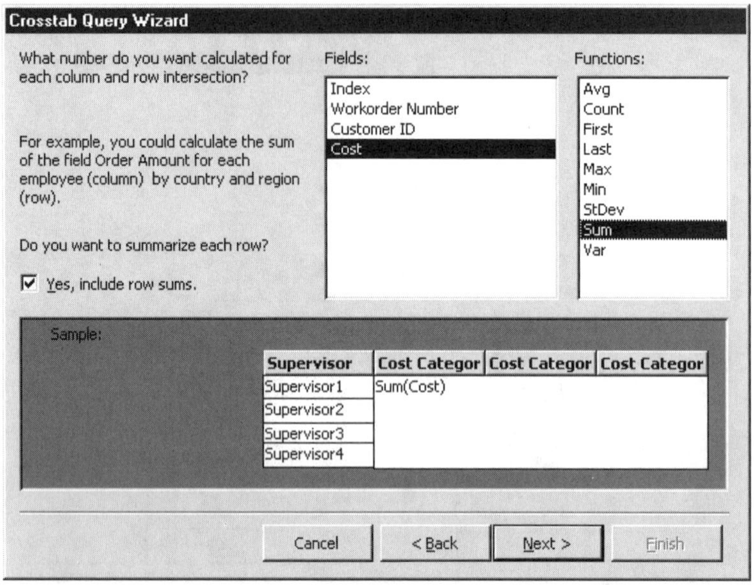

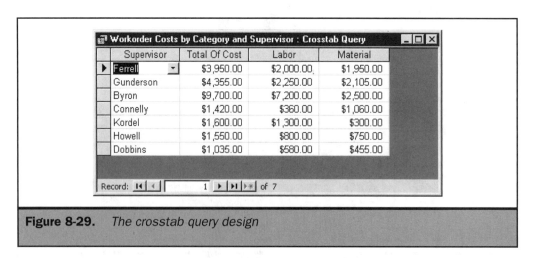

Figure 8-28. *Choosing the values for the crosstab*

6. Enter the query name, Workorder Costs by Category and Supervisor in the final dialog box and click Finish. Figure 8-29 shows the results of the completed query.

Workorder Costs by Category and Supervisor : Crosstab Query

Supervisor	Total Of Cost	Labor	Material
Ferrell	$3,950.00	$2,000.00	$1,950.00
Gunderson	$4,355.00	$2,250.00	$2,105.00
Byron	$9,700.00	$7,200.00	$2,500.00
Connelly	$1,420.00	$360.00	$1,060.00
Kordel	$1,600.00	$1,300.00	$300.00
Howell	$1,550.00	$800.00	$750.00
Dobbins	$1,035.00	$580.00	$455.00

Record: 1 of 7

Figure 8-29. *The crosstab query design*

Note   *The icon that accompanies the query name in the Database window indicates it's a crosstab query.*

      You can also create a crosstab query from the Design view by starting a new query based on the same table. Then click Query Type and choose Crosstab Query. The crosstab row is added to the design grid. Figure 8-30 shows the design of the query created by the Crosstab Query Wizard.

You can make changes to the query design after the wizard is finished with it. For example, you can limit the records included in the crosstab by adding the field you want to set the limit on and setting the Total cell to Where. Then leave the Crosstab cell blank and enter the expression in the Criteria cell.

If you want to change the column headings in the crosstab, return to the query design and open the query property sheet. Enter the titles you want for the columns in the Column Headings property, in the order they are to appear in the result. Separate the headings with semicolons (;) or new line breaks (CTRL-ENTER). You can also type the list of column headings enclosed in double quotation marks separated with commas.

You can have up to three row heading fields. The additional row headings effectively become subgroupings of the data. Each additional row heading multiplies the number of records in the result: two row headings doubles the records in the result; three headings triple the result.

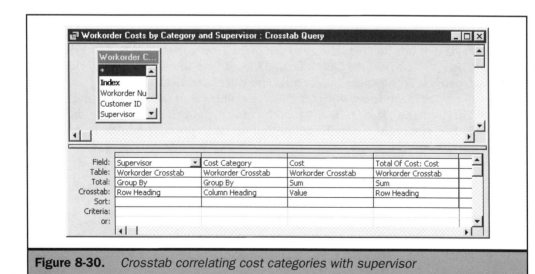

Figure 8-30.   *Crosstab correlating cost categories with supervisor*

Printing the Query Results

After you finish the query design and run the query, you can print the results in the datasheet the same way you print a table datasheet. To send the datasheet directly to the printer, click Print. If you want to select some of the printer options, such as multiple copies or specific pages, choose Print from the File menu, and then select options from the Print dialog box.

To preview the datasheet before printing, click Print Preview. You can use all the viewing and zoom capabilities you used with datasheets.

Deleting a Query

To delete a query, select the query in the Database window and choose Edit | Delete. You can also right-click the query name and choose Delete from the shortcut menu. Access then asks for confirmation before actually deleting the query. Remember, the query will be deleted permanently and you won't be able to get it back once you delete it.

Summary

The subject of queries is a difficult and complex one, not easily covered in one chapter. You have almost limitless options when you want to extract and arrange data from one or more tables. This chapter attempted to introduce you to the basics of query design and construction with select queries and some special purpose queries.

Query Wizards can create queries that can at least get you started with the design you need. Then you can use the Query Design view to modify the query to include additional features, such as selection criteria and calculated fields.

The next chapter continues with query development and delves into some of the more advanced queries, such as the Parameter query that prompts for criteria from the user, and several types of action queries that update, append, or delete records in one or more tables.

MOUS Exam Activities Explored in This Chapter

Level	Activity	Section Title
Core	Create and modify Select queries	Creating Select Queries Adding Selection Criteria Setting Query Properties Modifying a Query
Core	Add calculated fields to Select queries	Adding a Calculated Field Summarizing with the Wizard
Core	Create queries	Using the Simple Query Wizard Summarizing with the Wizard Creating Special Queries with the Wizard—Find Duplicates, Find Unmatched, Crosstab Queries
Expert	Specifying multiple query criteria	Using Multiple Criteria
Expert	Use aggregate functions in queries	Summarizing with Aggregate Functions

RETRIEVING AND
PRESENTING INFORMATION

Chapter 9

Creating Advanced Queries

Queries are the primary means of retrieving information stored in an Access database. In addition to the popular select query discussed in the previous chapter, Access offers more flexible ways to retrieve data. Queries also can perform data management operations, such as adding, updating, or deleting data. You can even use an Access query to run a procedure stored in an external database.

In this chapter, you see how versatile Access queries can be. After examining two special purpose queries, the chapter discusses action queries and SQL-specific queries.

Creating Special Purpose Queries

Data retrieval queries needn't be static, always extracting the same information. They can be tailored at run time by the user entering the search criteria in a special dialog box. When you want to specify which group of data you want, use a parameter query. A parameter query is much the same as a common select query except Access prompts for one or more of the selection criteria before running the query.

Another special purpose query is the *AutoLookup query* that automatically fills in certain field values in related tables. The *AutoLookup field* can save data entry time by looking up the value you enter in the matching field and entering corresponding information into fields in the related tables.

Parameter Queries

Parameter queries are especially useful for looking up such information as activities during a specific time period, for example, sales during the holiday season or work orders started during the month of June. When you enter the starting and ending dates, Access retrieves all records whose values in that field fall between the two dates. You can have as many parameters in the query as you need. Access prompts separately for each one.

Parameters can be set in almost all types of queries, including select and action queries. You can use a parameter in any field in which you can type text in the Criteria row.

Note *You can create parameter queries from the design grid, with SQL statements, or in the Record Source property of a form or report.*

To create a parameter query, start with a normal select query and, instead of entering the criteria in the Criteria cell, enter the text for the prompt enclosed in brackets ([ ]). The text you enter becomes the prompt in the dialog box, so be sure it's informative enough for the user to know how to respond. You cannot use the field name itself as the prompt, but you can include it in the prompt text.

For example, Home Tech Repair would like a list of a specific customer's current work orders. To allow the user to specify which customer, create a parameter query as follows:

1. Click New in the query page of the Database window, choose Design view in the New Query dialog box, and then click OK.

2. Choose the Workorders, Bid Data, and Customers tables from the Show Tables dialog box, clicking Add with each one. Then click Close.

3. Drag the Supervisor, Description, Start Date, and Address fields from the field lists to the grid. Then add the customer's Last Name field, which is the parameter the user enters.

4. Type **[Enter customer's last name]** in the Criteria row of the Last Name column (see Figure 9-1). This displays as the prompt in the Enter Parameter Value dialog box when you run the query.

5. Click Run and the Enter Parameter Value dialog box appears. Enter the desired Last Name (**McCoy**, in this example) and click OK.

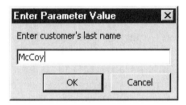

6. When this query is run, the result shows four current work orders for McCoy (see Figure 9-2).

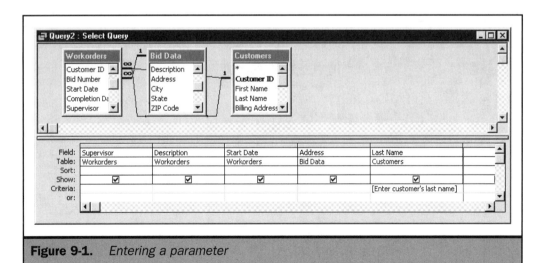

Figure 9-1. *Entering a parameter*

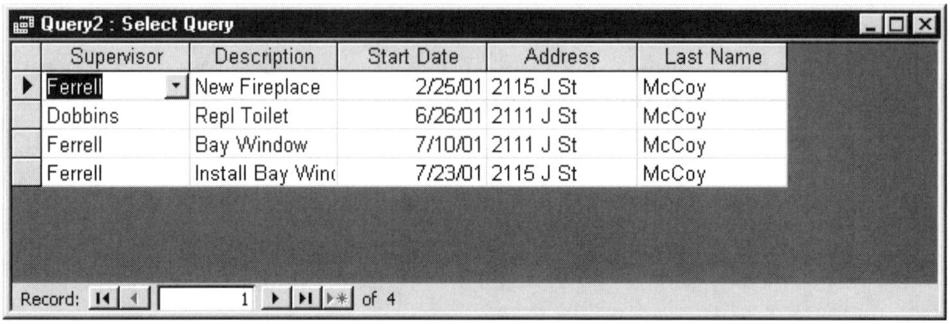

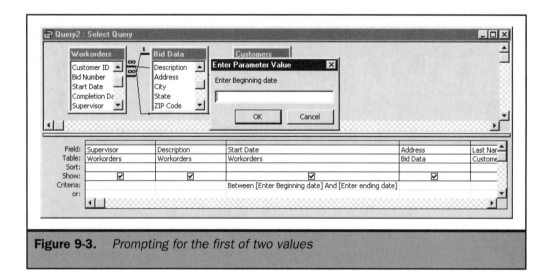

Figure 9-2. Four work orders for customer McCoy

You can also use a parameter query to find records that have a range of values, such as a time period. For example, you can show all the work orders started in the month of June. To do this, include parameters in the Between...And expression in the Criteria row. Access prompts for each parameter in a separate dialog box. Figure 9-3 shows the query grid and the first Enter Parameter Value dialog box.

After entering 6/1/01 in the first prompt box and 7/1/01 in the second, Access runs the query and displays records for the five work orders begun during June.

Figure 9-3. Prompting for the first of two values

Query2 : Select Query					_ □ ×
Supervisor	Description	Start Date	Address	Last Name	
► Byron ▼	Finish Basement	6/15/01	1520 8th St	Perez	
Gunderson	Garden Window	6/15/01	329 5th St	Jones	
Ferrell	SPA Heater	6/25/01	952 C St	Anders	
Dobbins	Repl Toilet	6/26/01	2111 J St	McCoy	
Kordel	Rpr Driveway	6/30/01	1510 H St	Norr	

Record: I◄ ◄ [1   ] ► ►I ►* of 5

By default, the data type of a parameter is Text. You can specify a different data type, however, by opening the Query Parameters dialog box while in the Query Design view using one of the following methods:

■ Choose Query | Parameters.

■ Right-click in the table pane and choose Parameters from the shortcut menu.

In the Query Parameters dialog box, enter the parameter exactly as it appears in the Criteria row (without the brackets), and then choose the data type from the Data Type drop-down list. Repeat this for each parameter for which you want to specify a data type, and then click OK.

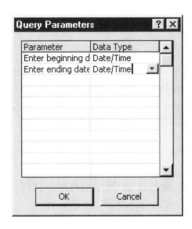

Note   *In most cases, Access can tell the data type of the parameter, but you must specifically define the data type for parameters if the field is a Yes/No data type or if it's used in a crosstab query. You must also set the Column Headings property for a crosstab query that prompts for a parameter.*

If you want to display the entered parameter value itself in the query result, add a calculated field with the parameter's name. For example, if you want to see the beginning date in the result of the previous query, enter the following expression in the Field row of an empty column: **Job Start:[Enter beginning date]**. The value will be the same in all the records in the result.

 *You can use the Format function to customize the parameter display. For example, use the expression **Job Start:Format([Enter beginning date],"d mmm yyyy")** to display the date as 1 Jun 2001 in the query result, such as a query, form, or report.*

Parameter queries are an excellent basis for reports. For example, you can print monthly reports simply by entering the month of interest and let Access do the rest.

 Sometimes Access prompts for a parameter in a field you haven't designated as a parameter. This can be caused by misspelling the field name or changing the name in the table, but not changing it in other database objects. If you checked the Name AutoCorrect option, filed name changes are projected to all objects that include that field.

In Chapter 12, you see how to create custom dialog boxes that prompt the user for input used in the form.

Place the parameter prompt in the Criteria cell for the field used as the parameter.

AutoLookup Queries

The AutoLookup query was invented to save time during data entry. The query does so by being used as the basis for a data entry form that contains data from more than one table. When you enter a valid Customer ID, for example, the query fills in all the rest of the information in the datasheet or form. An AutoLookup query uses two tables with a one-to-many relationship in which the matching field on the "one" side is either the primary key or a unique index. Referential integrity needn't be enforced.

Return All Records with a Parameter Query

Suppose you created a parameter query that extracts special fields from a specific set of records, but you also want to use the same query design to return all the records. You can add a criterion to the query that returns all the records if you don't enter a parameter value.

Place the parameter prompt in the Criteria cell for the field used as the parameter. Then move to the Or cell and enter the same parameter prompt followed by Is Null.

When you run the query, if you click OK or press ENTER without entering a value, you get all records in the result because the parameter is a Null value, one of the acceptable criteria.

Note   *An AutoLookup query is different from a lookup field because the query automatically fills in the data for you, while the lookup field merely displays a list from which to choose.*

To create an AutoLookup query, add the two related tables to the query design, and then drag the join field from the table on the "many" side to the grid. This type of query looks for the related record in the parent table—the "one" side—and retrieves values from other fields in the matching record. The field on the "one" side must be the primary key or have a unique index. But the field on the "many" side can neither be the primary key nor can it be a unique index.

Figure 9-4 shows an AutoLookup query that fills in the customer's name and address when you enter the Customer ID value. Notice the Customer ID field in the design grid is from the Workorders table, the "many" side of the relationship.

In the query result datasheet, when you add a new record or change the value of the join field on the "many" side, Access automatically looks up and displays the associated values from the table on the "one" side. Figure 9-5 shows a new record being entered in which the Customer ID value—1033—was entered and the TAB key was pressed. The remaining three fields were filled in by Access.

Caution   *Be sure the value entered in the join field on the "many" side exists in the table on the "one" side. If not, Access displays an error message when you try to leave the record. In addition, be sure to include all the required fields and those with validation rules in the query design grid and make sure their Show boxes are checked.*

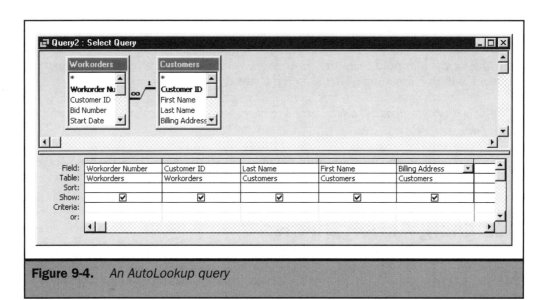

Figure 9-4.   *An AutoLookup query*

Workorder Num	Customer ID	Last Name	First Name	Billing Address
001	1032	McCoy	John, C	2115 J St
002	1033	Jones	David	329 Fifth
003	1034	Rogers	Phyllis	2478 9th St
004	1035	Perry	Oliver	2001 J St
005	1036	Brown	Agnes	186 G St
006	1037	Selms	Harry	1520 8th St
007	1038	Perez	Antonio	1656 F St
008	1033	Jones	David	329 Fifth
009	1039	Anders	Bob	952 C St
010	1032	McCoy	John, C	2115 J St
011	1040	Norr	James	1510 H St
012	1033	Jones	David	329 Fifth
013	1032	McCoy	John, C	2115 J St
014	1037	Selms	Harry	1520 8th St
015	1039	Anders	Bob	952 C St
016	1032	McCoy	John, C	2115 J St
017	1033	Jones	David	329 Fifth

AutoLook : Select Query

Record: 17 of 17

Figure 9-5. *Using the AutoLookup query*

You can always update the value of the join field from the "many" side and Access looks up and displays the associated values from the "one" side. If you want to update the value of the join field from the "one" side, you must have referential integrity enforced with the cascading updates option enabled for the relationship.

Note   *Whenever you update the data, Access recalculates any summary totals and expressions using that data.*

Once you design and save an AutoLookup query, it can be used as the basis for a data entry form, a report, or a data access page.

Designing Action Queries

Action queries are used to perform global data management operations on one or more tables at once. The four types of action queries reflect the most common database activities: updating field values, adding new records, deleting records, and creating new tables.

Types of Action Queries

- An *update query* makes global changes to fields in a group of records. For example, you can run an update query to raise all the labor costs for jobs in a certain area of the city.

- An *append query* adds a group of records from one or more tables to the end of other tables. For example, when you consolidate another contractor's business with your own, add his customer list to your own.

- A *delete query* deletes a group of records from one or more tables. For example, you can use a delete query to delete records for completed work orders. This type of action query is less popular than the others, so the option appears in the expanded Query and Query Type menus. Click or rest the mouse pointer on the arrows at the bottom of the menu to see the expanded menu.

- A *make-table query* creates a new table from data in one or more existing tables. For example, you can archive outdated information into a new table or make a backup copy of an important table.

Note   *The results of action queries aren't valid dynasets and cannot be used as a record source for forms or reports. And you can't create an AutoForm or AutoReport from the result of an action query. However, if you save the result as a table first, you can use the table as a record source.*

Before undertaking any kind of action query, make a backup copy of the tables that will be involved. If several tables are to be changed, back up the entire database. To create a copy of a table, right-click the table name in the Tables tab and choose Copy. Then right-click in an empty area and choose Paste. Enter a name for the copy in the Paste Table As dialog box and choose OK. Adding Copy to the original table name helps keep track of the tables as your database grows.

Tip   *An additional safety precaution you can practice while designing an action query is to switch to Datasheet view to check your progress, instead of running the query. Showing the results in Datasheet view doesn't actually run the query and carry out the intended action, so no data is changed.*

The Edit/Find tab of the Options dialog box contains three Confirm options, one of which is Action Query. By default, this option is checked so Access always asks for confirmation before carrying out an action query. You can clear this option to prevent the display of the confirmation box, but this is risky. Double-clicking a query name in the database window and running a query, even an action query, is so easy. If you cleared the Confirm option, you won't even be warned an action query is about to run.

Update Query

Update queries are used to change one or more field values in many records at once. You can add criteria that screen the records to be changed, as well as update records in more than one table. Update queries can use most types of expressions to specify the update. Table 9-1 shows some examples.

For example, in the Home Tech Repair database, several bids have expired, but can be renewed. To renew the bids, the costs must be increased slightly to reflect inflation and a new expiration date set. This involves finding records in the Bid Data table whose Expires date is before June 15, 2001, for example, and then making changes to the related Workorders table to increase the Material Cost and Labor Cost values. If no corresponding Workorder record exists, the Update query doesn't change the Expires value because the relationship is defined as an inner join.

Field Type	Expression	Result
Currency	[Material Cost]*1.05	Increases Material Cost value by 5%
Currency	[Workorders].[Material Cost]+[Workorders].[Labor Cost]	Updates the field with the sum of the costs from the Workorders table
Date	#8/25/01#	Changes the value to August 25, 2001
Text	"Completed"	Changes the value to Completed
Text	"WO"&[Design]	Adds characters WO to the beginning of the value in the Design field
Yes/No	Yes	Used with criteria, changes specific No values to Yes

Table 9-1. *Sample Update Expressions*

To create this update query, start with a new query design with the Bid Data and Workorders tables, and then do the following:

1. Click Query Type and choose Update Query from the list. You can also choose Query | Update Query or right-click the table area and choose Query Type | Update Query from the shortcut menu. A new row, Update To, appears in the grid.

2. Drag the Expires, Material Cost, and Labor Cost fields to the grid.

3. Enter the expression **<6/15/01** in the Criteria cell in the Expires column to limit the records. Access adds the pound sign (#) date delimiters.

4. Enter the following update expressions:

   ■ **[Material Cost]*1.05** in the Update To cell in the Material Cost column.

   ■ **[Labor Cost]*1.05** in the Labor Cost column.

   ■ **[Expires]+90** in the Expires column.

Figure 9-6 shows the completed query design.

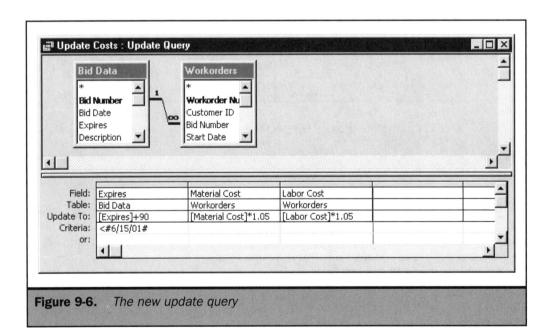

Figure 9-6. *The new update query*

5. Click Datasheet view to see which records will be affected by the update query. If the selection isn't correct, return to the Design view and make changes.

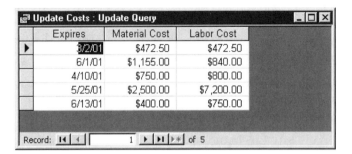

6. Click Design view to return to the Query Design window and save the query as Update Costs, if you haven't already, and then click Run or choose Query | Run. Access displays a message warning that the update is irreversible.

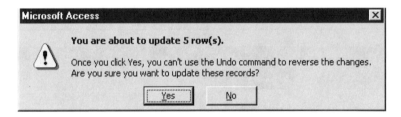

7. Choose Yes to update the records or No to abandon the process.

To stop the query after it's started, quickly press CTRL-BREAK.

To see if the changes were correctly made, open both the copy of the original tables and the updated version, and then compare the results. Figure 9-7 shows a comparison of the updated Bid Data records with the backup copy. The five records that appeared in the datasheet of the update query are now updated.

As you can see in Figure 9-7, two records in the Bid Data table (numbers 98-102 and 98-104) still have an Expires date prior to June 15, 2001. This may seem confusing or an error but, as mentioned earlier, they aren't updated because no matching record is in the Workorders record. The join is an inner join, which includes in the result only those records with matching values in the join field.

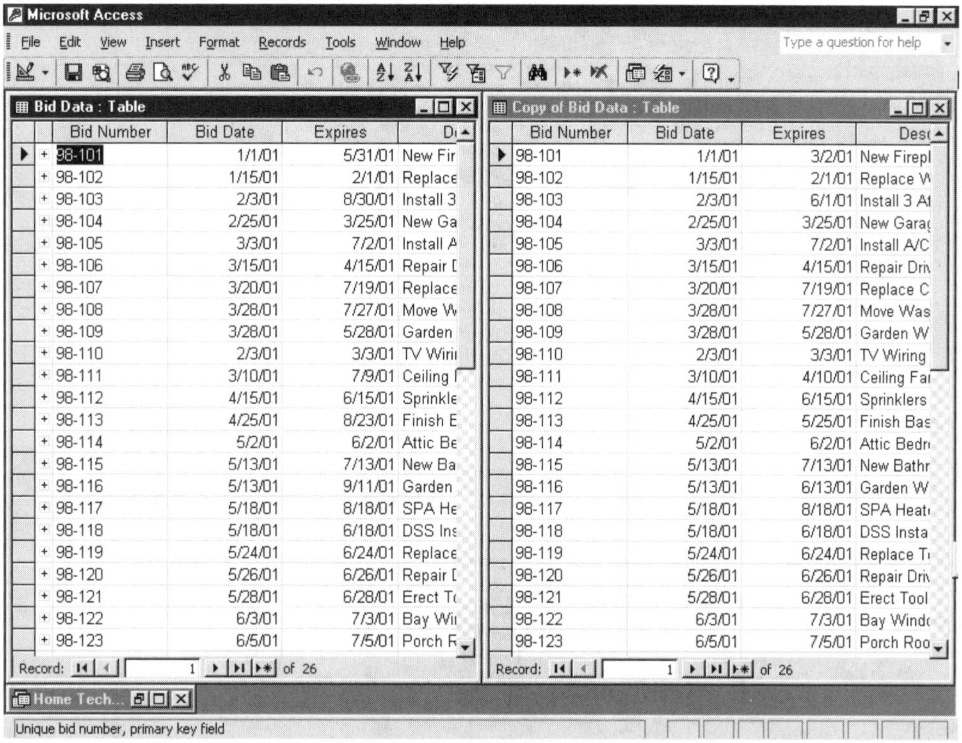

Figure 9-7. *Comparing updated and backup tables*

Note *If you enforced referential integrity between related tables in the database and checked the Cascade Update Related Records option on the "one" side, Access applies the updates to the matching fields on the "many" side, even if they aren't included in the query.*

When you name and save the query, it appears in the Queries tab with a warning icon. All the action queries appear with an exclamation point attached to the icon, which warns you that double-clicking this query runs some sort of action. Access displays a confirmation message, however, before running the query, unless you have turned off that option.

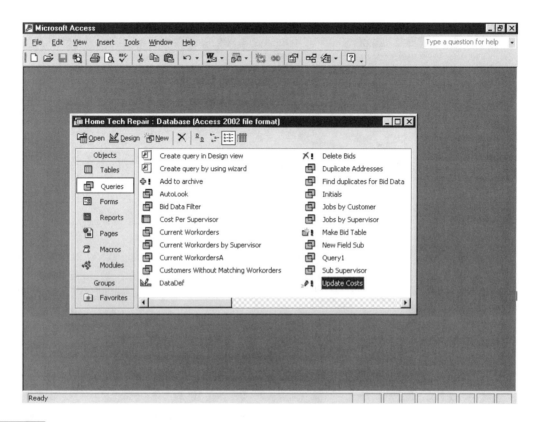

Tip

If you start a new query and you decide you want to create a different type, you needn't scrap the one you're working on. You can change the query type and proceed. To change the query type while in Design view, choose the type you want from the Query menu or right-click in the table area of the Query window, point to Query Type, and choose the type from the shortcut menu.

Append Query

When you want to add records from one or more source tables to other tables, you first decide which fields you want to append, and then locate the target table and determine which fields in the target table correspond to the fields from the source. The field values are only copied—they aren't moved—to the target table.

Note

To be matched, fields needn't have the same names, but they do need to be of the same data type. The target table also needn't have exactly the same structure as the source table.

You can append records to a table in the current database or another Access database; establish a path to a FoxPro, Paradox, or dBASE database, or you can even enter a connection string to a SQL database.

For example, the Home Tech Repair Bid Data table gets infinitely large if none of the records are removed. The bids that have been lost are no longer needed in the current table, but they may be useful in an archive history of past bidding. Before you can archive the records, you need to create a new table structure to hold the records with the following steps:

1. Right-click the Bid Data table name in the database window and choose Copy.

2. Right-click in the Tables page and choose Paste.

3. In the Paste Table As dialog box, name the new table Lost Bid Archive, choose Structure Only, and then click OK.

The new table name appears in the Tables page of the database window. Now you're ready to create the append query that will copy the records with Lost in the Award Date field to the Lost Bid Archive table. If the target table has the same field names as in this case, Access automatically fills in the field names in the query grid. If they aren't the same, you must enter the target field names.

To create the append query, do the following:

1. Start a new query, adding only the Bid Data table from the Show Tables dialog box, and then click Query Type, and choose Append Query. The Append dialog box appears.

2. Enter the table name, **Lost Bid Archive**, in the Table Name box, choose Current Database, and then click OK.

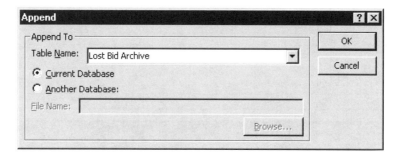

3. Because you want all the field data in the selected records to be archived, drag the asterisk (*) from the Bid Data field list to the grid. If you don't want all the fields appended, drag the fields individually to the grid.

4. To add the Lost criteria, drag the Award Date field to the grid and enter **"Lost"** in the Criteria cell.

5. Remove the field name from the Append To cell, so you won't append two copies of the Award Date field. Figure 9-8 shows the completed append query design.

6. Switch to Datasheet view to make sure the right records will be appended, and then switch back to Design view and save the query as Add to Archive.

7. Click Run. Access displays a message asking for confirmation to append six records.

8. Choose Yes to complete the addition or choose No to cancel the operation.

Delete Query

The *delete query* may be the most dangerous action query of all. No action queries can be reversed, but deletion seems the most drastic. All the more reason to make a backup copy of all the tables before you begin a delete query.

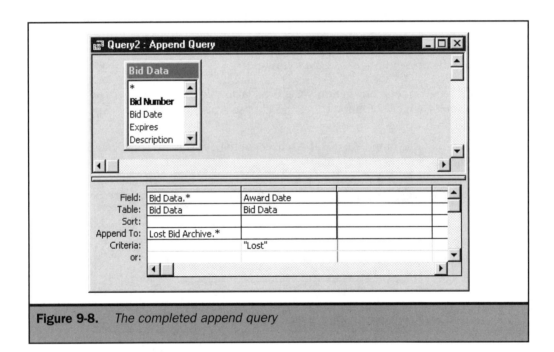

Figure 9-8. *The completed append query*

Tips for Creating and Using Append Queries

■ If the source and target tables have identical structures, drag the asterisk (*) to the grid. If you add any criteria, delete the field name from the Append To cell or you'll have two copies of the field.

■ If you're appending fields to which Access automatically assigns AutoNumber values, don't add the AutoNumber field from the source table to the grid. If Access doesn't automatically assign AutoNumbers and you're sure the AutoNumber fields won't experience any duplicate values with the existing records in the target table, add the AutoNumber field to the grid. Records with duplicate AutoNumber values aren't appended.

■ If you have only a handful of records to append, select the records and use the Copy and Paste Append commands instead.

■ If you're appending more fields than the target table contains, the excess fields are ignored. If the target table has more fields than the source table, Access appends the fields with matching names and leaves the rest blank in the target table.

■ If you get an error message when trying to append records, click the Help button in the message box to see a related Help topic.

A delete query removes entire records from the table, not only the specified fields. You can remove records from a single table, multiple tables related one-to-one, or multiple tables related one-to-many.

Deleting from a Single Table

Deleting records from a single table or several one-to-one tables is straightforward: Add the tables to the query design and specify the criteria for deleting the record, for example, the account is paid in full, the work order is completed, or the house has been sold.

To delete records from a single table:

1. Start a new query with the table from which you want to delete records, such as a copy of the Bid Data table.

2. Click Query Type and choose Delete Query or choose Query | Delete Query. The Delete Query command is on the expanded menu in both cases. The Delete row is added to the grid. The only choices in the Delete row are Where and From.

3. Drag the asterisk from the field list to the grid. The Delete row now shows From.

4. Drag the field containing the value that indicates the record is to be deleted (for example, the value Lost in the Award Date field) and enter the criteria expression in the Criteria row.

Field:	Copy of Bid Data.*	Award Date	
Table:	Copy of Bid Data	Copy of Bid Data	
Delete:	From	Where	
Criteria:		"Lost"	
or:			

5. Switch to Datasheet view to preview the records to be deleted and make any necessary changes in the query design.

6. Return to Design view and run the query. Respond Yes to proceed or No to cancel the operation.

As with the other action queries, to stop the query after you respond Yes, quickly press CTRL-BREAK.

Deleting from Related Tables

Deleting records from a table or multiple tables that are related with a one-to-many relationship can get complicated, especially if you're enforcing referential integrity and have selected Cascade Delete Related Records for the relationship.

About Cascade Delete

Checking the Cascade Delete Related Records option when enforcing referential integrity can be even more disastrous than the Cascade Update option. With Cascade Delete checked, Access automatically deletes all matching records whether or not the table is included in the query. For example, if you deleted a customer, records for all the bids and work orders for that customer would also be deleted.

Before you use a delete query, examine the relationships you've established between the table and others in the database. Of course, if referential integrity is enforced on a relationship without the cascade options, you may not be permitted to delete the records on the "one" side if this would leave orphans on the "many" side.

If you have Cascade Delete Related Records enabled for the relationship, all matching records on the "many" side are deleted with the records on the "one" side. If the option isn't selected, you must run two delete queries to accomplish the job. First, delete the records from the tables on the "many" side, and then go after the records on the "one" side.

To delete records from multiple related tables, start a new query with all the involved tables, and then do the following:

1. Click Query Type and choose Delete Query.
2. Drag the field to use for criteria to the grid.
3. Drag the asterisk (*) from all the field lists of the tables on the "many" side of the relationships to the grid. Don't drag the "one" table to the grid yet.
4. Click Datasheet view to preview the records that will be deleted.
5. Return to Design view and click Run.
6. Remove the "many" side tables from the Query window.
7. Drag the asterisk (*) from the "one" table to the grid and run the query again to delete the records from that table.

You can combine an append query with a delete query using the same query design to create the two-step archive operation that adds the selected records to the history table and deletes the same records from the source table. After making sure you selected the right records to archive, run the append query to add the records to the target table. Then, in the Query Design view, click Query Type and change the query to a delete query. When you run the query again, it deletes the same records from the source table.

Make-Table Query

The *make-table query* does exactly what it advertises: it makes a new table out of records from one or more tables or queries. Make-table queries are useful in many circumstances. Here are a few:

- To export records to another database, for example, to create a table of completed work orders to send to the billing department, which uses another system.

- To export consolidated information from related tables to a nonrelational application, such as Excel or Word.

- To control the information that's exported, such as screening out confidential or irrelevant data.

■ To use as a record source for a report of events that occurred during a specific period of time. For example, a report of bids offered during June and July, and the results, including work order information.

■ To start the archive file by adding the first set of records, and then using an append query to add more later.

■ To replace records in an existing table with a new set.

Make-table queries copy the data to the target table. The source tables and queries are unaffected.

To build a make-table query, start a new query with the tables and queries you want records from, and then do the following:

1. Click Query Type and choose Make-Table Query. Access displays the Make Table dialog box requesting a name for the table, either a new table or an existing one.

2. Do one of the following:

■ If the target table is in the same database, enter the table name and click OK.

■ If the target table is an existing table, choose the table name from the drop-down list.

■ If you want the new table in a different database, select Another Database, type in the full path and filename of the database, enter the table name, and click OK. If the target isn't an Access database, follow the database name with the name of the application, such as "Paradox."

3. Drag the fields from the field lists to the design grid and include record selection criteria, the same as you do with a select query.

4. Click Datasheet view to preview the records to be included in the new table.

5. Return to the Design window and click Run.

6. If you're replacing records in an existing table, Access asks for confirmation before proceeding:

   ■ Respond Yes to continue.

   ■ Respond No to abandon the operation.

   ■ Click No and change the name of the target table by clicking Query Type and choosing Make-Table Query again. Then choose another table or enter a new table name.

7. Respond Yes or No to the final confirmation box that completes the make-table query.

Although you cannot undo an action query, including the make-table query, if the table isn't what you want, you can delete it and start over.

The only field properties inherited by the table created with a make-table query are the field size and data type. All other properties—including the primary key, format, default values, and input masks—aren't inherited and must be reset in the new table or in the form or report that uses the new table as a record source.

Make-table queries create snapshots of the data as it was at the time it was run and, as such, aren't updateable manually. If the data in the source tables changes, run the query again to update the values.

If you don't get the results you want with an action query, Access may be able to point you to a solution. The Help topic, Troubleshoot Queries, contains solutions to many of the problems you may encounter, such as appending the wrong records or dealing with key violations.

Introducing Structured Query Language

Structured query language (SQL) is the language Access uses behind the scenes to program query operations. SQL is comprised of statements, each complying with specific language syntax and conventions. To view or edit SQL statements while working on a query, switch from Design view to SQL view.

Some types of queries can only be created with SQL statements. You learn about these SQL queries in the next section in this chapter.

You can enter a SQL statement in most places where you would enter a table, query, or field name, such as the record source for a form or report. If you use a Wizard to create a form or report, the record source is a SQL statement created by Access.

Using SQL statements instead of saved queries as record sources simplifies the database by having fewer objects to store and maintain.

Looking at SQL Statements

Before going too far into the details of the language, look at some simple examples of SQL statements. The SELECT statement is the most common—and the most important—statement in SQL. Nearly all queries start with the SELECT statement. For example, if you create a query that retrieves all the fields in records from the Bid Data table with "Lost" in the Award Date field, the SQL version would look like this:

```
SELECT *
FROM [Bid Data]
WHERE [Award Date]="Lost";
```

- The SELECT* command means to include all the fields, as does SELECT ALL.
- The FROM clause names the table that contains the records to retrieve.
- The WHERE [Award Date]="Lost" clause specifies the selection criteria. This is the same value you entered in the Criteria row of the Award Date column. SQL statements always end with a semicolon (;).

 If you create the query in the design grid, and then switch to SQL view, you see a lot of extra parentheses Access adds to keep things straight. You can enter the SQL statement as it's shown here and it'll work fine.

If you don't want to retrieve all the fields, use the SELECT command with a list of field names. The following query displays the Bid Number and Expires fields for Bid Data records in which the Award Date field contains "Lost" or the Expires value is prior to June 1, 1999:

```
SELECT [Bid Number], Expires
FROM [Bid Data]
WHERE [Award Date]="Lost" OR Expires<#6/1/99#;
```

 A field name that contains a space, such as Bid Number, must be enclosed in brackets. If no space is in the field name, you needn't add brackets, but Access usually does to be safe.

All the queries created in this and the previous chapter resulted in SQL statements that can be viewed by switching to SQL view. Choose SQL view from either the View button or the View menu.

Figure 9-9 shows the SQL views of a few queries in the Home Tech Repair database, including the action queries from the previous section.

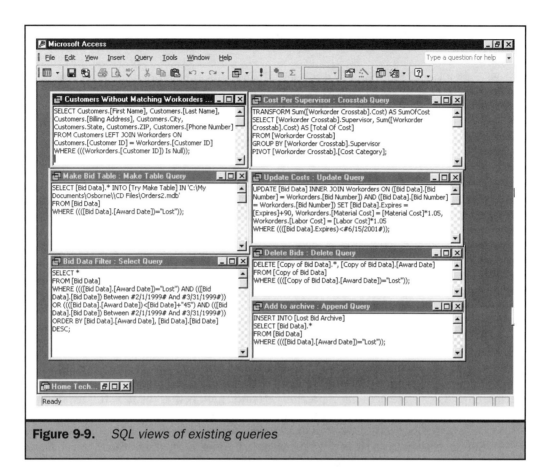

Figure 9-9.   *SQL views of existing queries*

Before going into the conventions and syntax of the SQL language, look at the Customers Without Matching Workorders (shown in the upper-left corner in Figure 9-9). This query was created to locate records in the Customers table that had no matching records in the Workorders table. The entire SQL statement is shown here:

```
SELECT DISTINCTROW Customers.[First Name], Customers.[Last Name],
Customers.[Billing Address], Customers.City, Customers.State,
Customers.ZIP, Customers.[Phone Number]
FROM Customers LEFT JOIN Workorders ON Customers.[Customer ID] =
Workorders.[Customer ID]
WHERE (((Workorders.[Customer ID]) Is Null));
```

This statement has two clauses in addition to the SELECT command: FROM and WHERE.

- The SELECT command determines which fields are included in the query result. Because two tables are involved in the query, field names must be qualified with the table name separated by a period (.).

- The FROM clause shows the table name and also specifies the join type that relates the Customers table with the Workorders table as a left outer join, using the Customer ID as the matching field.

- The WHERE clause limits the result to Customer records with no matching records in the Workorders table. That is, the Customer ID field has a Null value because no matching record exists.

Each clause begins on a separate line for readability; the entire statement is treated as a single line by Access.

SQL Conventions and Syntax

Like all programming languages, SQL has strict conventions and grammatical syntax. The more sophisticated the language, the more complex the rules and procedures. See the Quick Reference for information about SQL syntax. For the complete details of the SQL language, refer to the many Help topics Access provides.

The most significant elements in SQL are the statements, clauses, predicates, and declarations. Each statement has a precisely defined syntax that must be followed. The syntax is expressed using typical programming language conventions.

SQL statements can be used in more places than just a query design. For example, they can be used in other expressions, as arguments in procedures, and as property settings for forms and reports. An easy to way to get a correct SQL statement is to create the query in Design view, and then switch to SQL view and copy the statement. To copy the statement to the Clipboard, select all or part of it and press CTRL-C, or right-click and choose Copy from the shortcut menu. Then place the insertion point where you want the statement and press CTRL-V, or right-click and choose Paste.

Reading SQL Conventions

When you look up a SQL command or other element in the Help file, the syntax is expressed using certain conventions:

- All SQL keywords are in uppercase—for example, SELECT, WHERE, and FROM.

- Optional items are in italics and enclosed in brackets ([])—for example, SELECT [*predicate*].

- Choices are enclosed in curly braces ({}) and separated by vertical bars (|)—for example, {* | *table*.* | [*table*.]*field1*[,[*table*.]*field2*[,…]]}, which gives you the choice among including all records in a single table query (*), including all records in a named table (*table*.*), or specifying the fields one at a time, separated by commas.

- The ellipses in the previous example indicate a repeating sequence.

Understanding SQL Syntax

The main elements in SQL are the statements and clauses that accompany the statements. You've already seen examples of the SQL statements (refer to Figure 9-9):

- SELECT retrieves all or specific records from one or more tables or queries.

- SELECT…INTO creates a new table from fields in existing tables (the make-table query).

- INSERT…INTO adds one or more records to a table (the append query).

- UPDATE changes specific values based on specified criteria (the update query).

- DELETE removes records from one or more tables (the delete query).

- TRANSFORM calculates values for a crosstab query.

The following shows the syntax of the SELECT statement. The other statements are similar in structure, using many of the same clauses and options.

```
SELECT [predicate]{*|[table.*|[table.]field1
[AS alias1][,table.]field2[AS alias2][,…]]}
FROM tableexpression [,…][IN externaldatabase]
[WHERE…]
[GROUP BY…]
[HAVING…]
[ORDER BY…]
[WITH OWNERACCESS OPTION]
```

Table 9-2 explains the parts of the SELECT statement.

Part	Explanation
predicate	One of the four standard optional predicates: ALL to include all records, DISTINCT to omit records with duplicate data in selected fields, DISTINCTROW to omit data based on entire duplicate records, or TOP*n* [PERCENT] to limit the records to a certain number or percentage of records.
*	Includes all fields from the specified table or tables.
table	Names the table containing the fields that determine which records to select.
field1, field2	Names the fields containing the data to retrieve.
alias1, alias2	Specifies text to use as column headers instead of the field names.
tableexpression	Names the table or tables containing the data to retrieve.
externaldatabase	Name of database containing the tables, if not in the current database.

Table 9-2.   *Parts of the SELECT Statement*

Note   *Using the DISTINCT or DISTINCTROW predicate in the SELECT statement is equivalent to setting the query's Unique Values or Unique Records property to Yes.*

The SELECT statement has several clauses, most of which are optional. The only required one is the FROM clause, which specifies one or more tables or queries containing the fields listed in the SELECT statement. The FROM clause can include the IN clause to retrieve data from an external database.

The other clauses in the SELECT statements are

- WHERE, contains a criteria expression that specifies which records to retrieve from the tables in the FROM clause.

- GROUP BY, combines records with identical values in the specified field. You can specify up to ten groupings. The order of the field names in the list determines the grouping levels from the highest to the lowest.

- HAVING, specifies which grouped records to display. After the records are grouped in accordance with the GROUP BY clause, HAVING applies a criteria expression to the group.

■ ORDER BY, sorts the resulting records in ascending or descending order based on the value in one or more specified fields. ORDER BY is usually the last clause in a SELECT statement.

■ WITH OWNERACCESS OPTION, gives the user running the query the same permissions as the query's owner in a declaration.

You can use any valid expression in a SQL SELECT statement or in WHERE, ORDER BY, GROUP BY, or HAVING clauses. The same rules apply to expressions used in query statements as apply elsewhere.

When included, the INNER JOIN, LEFT JOIN, and RIGHT JOIN commands follow the FROM clause and specify the type of join to be used in the query. The update query created earlier resulted in the SQL statement shown in Figure 9-9 (second window on the right side). This query includes the command:

```
UPDATE [Bid Data] INNER JOIN Workorders ON ([Bid Data].[Bid Number]
= Workorders.[Bid Number]) AND ([Bid Data].[Bid Number] =
Workorders.[Bid Number]) SET [Bid Data].Expires = [Expires]+90,
Workorders.[Material Cost] = [Material Cost]*1.05,
Workorders.[Labor Cost] = [Labor Cost]*1.05
WHERE ((([Bid Data].Expires)<#6/15/2001#));
```

The INNER JOIN operation establishes the Bid Number as the joining fields in the two tables. The SET operation contains the expressions entered in the Update To rows used to update the three fields.

Note *The Expires field name is enclosed in brackets in the expression [Expires]+90, even though it doesn't include an embedded space. The brackets tell Access this is a field name.*

The WHERE clause contains the criteria expression that specified which records to update.

Refer to Chapter 5 for a review of the join types and how they can affect query results.

Caution *If you query two or more tables, you must include a WHERE or JOIN clause or you get the Cartesian product of the number of records in the tables. For example, if one table has 50 records and the other 100, the query result will contain 5,000 records.*

Updating Query Results

Many queries are run for the purpose of isolating records that need to be updated. Some query results allow updating, while others do not. Running the right query is important if you plan to update the results.

- Queries based on a single table or on tables related with a one-to-one relationship produce results that are always updateable.
- Queries extracting data from tables with a one-to-many relationship are usually updateable, but some restrictions might occur, such as updating one of the join fields.
- The results of the following queries are never updateable:
    - Queries based on two one-to-many relationships including a junction table.
    - Crosstab, SQL pass-through, and union queries.
    - Any query whose Unique Values property is set to Yes.
    - A query with more than one table or query that isn't joined by a join line in Design view.
    - A query with a linked ODBC table with no unique index or a Paradox table with no primary key.
    - A query that performs a calculation on values in a field.
    - An update query that references a field from a crosstab query, select query, or subquery that contains totals or aggregate functions.

Certain fields in query results may not be updateable as well.

- Memo, Hyperlink, and OLE Object fields in query results are always updateable.
- Calculated fields, read-only fields, and fields in a record that has been locked by another user aren't updateable.

Alternatives to getting around the ban on updating query results may exist. The Access Help topics can be a source of such solutions.

Creating SQL-Specific Queries

SQL-specific queries are queries that can be built only using SQL statements. SQL queries include

- *Union queries* that combine corresponding fields from two or more tables or queries into one field in the query results.
- *Pass-through queries* that send commands directly to ODBC databases.
- *Data-definition queries* that create or edit Access or SQL Server tables.

All SQL queries are created directly in the SQL view window. To reach the SQL window to start a SQL query without first specifying any tables in the Design view, do the following:

1. Click New in the Queries page of the Database window, select Design view in the New Query dialog box, and then click OK.

2. Close the Show Table dialog box without adding any tables to the design.

3. Point to SQL Specific in the Query menu and select the type of query you want to create.

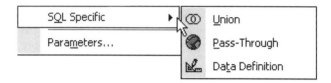

  If you convert a SQL-specific query to another type, such as a select query, the SQL statement will be deleted.

Creating a Union Query

Union queries are useful when you want to combine two or more separate lists containing similar information into a single list. For example, you can combine the Home Tech Repair address and description data with the same information from a newly acquired business database.

A union query consists of a SQL SELECT statement for each table involved in the compilation. The following example produces a new list that combines data from the Workorders table and the new business.

```
SELECT [Address],[Description]
FROM [Workorders]

UNION SELECT [Address],[Description]
FROM [New Business]
```

Each SELECT statement must return the same number of fields and the fields must appear in the same order. The corresponding fields must also have compatible data types. The exception to this rule is you can have number and text fields as corresponding fields in the two lists.

You can add WHERE clauses to both SELECT statements to limit the result of the union query. You can also use a GROUP BY or HAVING clause in each of the SELECT statements to group returned data. Adding an ORDER BY clause as the last entry sorts the combined list.

Normally, the union query returns only unique values, but you can have duplicates included in the result by using the ALL predicate: UNION ALL SELECT.

The columns are named using the column names from the table in the first SELECT statement. If you want to see other names, rename the field with the AS [*alias*] clause.

Creating a Pass-Through Query

A *pass-through query* works directly with an ODBC database server, such as Microsoft FoxPro. You don't link to the table. You send commands directly to the table on the server to retrieve data. Pass-through queries are often used to run procedures stored on an ODBC server.

To create a pass-through query, start a new query as before and select Pass-Through from the SQL-Specific list in the Query menu. Then, in the SQL window, do the following:

1. Click Properties or choose View | Properties. If the window isn't maximized, you can also right-click the title bar and choose Properties from the shortcut menu.
2. Type the connection information in the ODBC ConnectStr property or click Build and enter the server information in the Select Data Source dialog box.
3. If your query won't return records, set the Returns Records property to No.
4. If the query can return messages as well as data, change the Log Messages property to Yes. Access creates a table to contain any returned messages.

5. Type the query SQL statement in the Query window and click Run. If the query will return records, you can switch to Datasheet view instead.

If you don't specify a connection string in the ODBC ConnectStr property, Access uses the default ODBC string. This can be a nuisance because Access asks for the connection information every time you run the pass-through query.

Creating a Data-Definition Query

A data-definition query creates, deletes, or alters tables in the current database. It can also be used to create an index in an existing table. The four data-definition statements are

- CREATE TABLE creates a new table.
- ALTER TABLE adds or drops a field or constraint, such as an index or a primary key.
- DROP deletes a table or removes an index.
- CREATE INDEX builds an index for a field or group of fields.

To create a data-definition query, start a new query as before and choose Data Definition from the SQL-Specific list. Then type the SQL statement in the window.

For example, suppose you want to create a new table named Members in the current database that stores names, addresses, and other information about the club members. After you decide how to structure the table, you can use the following statement to define the table design with field names, data types, indexes, and a primary key.

```
CREATE TABLE Members
([Member ID] integer,
[Last Name] text,
[First Name] text,
[Title] text,
[Member Since] date,
[Dues Paid] yes/no,
[Notes] memo,
CONSTRAINT [Index1] PRIMARY KEY ([Member ID]));
```

PRIMARY KEY is only one of the constraints you can impose on the new table. The others are

■ UNIQUE, which specifies a field as a unique index.

■ FOREIGN KEY, which designates the field as the match for a primary key in a related table.

You can use the ALTER TABLE statement to add or drop a column or constraint. For example, the statement

```
ALTER TABLE Members ADD COLUMN Office TEXT(25)
```

adds a new field named Office that is a 25-character text field.

To create a new index named FullName for the Members table based on the members' names, use the following statement:

```
CREATE INDEX FullName ON Members ([Last Name],[First Name])
```

 The CREATE INDEX statement has other keywords that set the index properties, such as UNIQUE, PRIMARY, ASC, DESC, DISALLOW NULL, and IGNORE NULL. See the Access Help topics for more details about data-definition queries.

When you run a data-definition query, Access displays a warning message that you're about to modify data in your table. Choose Yes to continue creating the table or No to abandon the query.

Creating a Subquery

Subqueries are select queries within other select or action queries. You can use a subquery to specify a criterion for selecting records from the main query or to define a new field to include in the main query.

Defining a Criterion

To define a criterion, enter the SELECT statement directly in the Criteria cell in the query design grid or in a SQL statement in place of an expression in a WHERE or HAVING clause.

For example, suppose you want to see fields from the Workorders table for all the jobs run by supervisors who have at least one job incurring more than $1,000 in material costs. Start a new query and add the Workorders table, and then place the Workorder Number, the Bid Number, Supervisor, and Material Cost fields in the grid.

To place this subquery in the query grid, type **IN (SELECT Supervisor FROM Workorders WHERE [Material Cost]>1000)** into the Supervisor field Criteria cell. Be sure to enclose the SQL statement in parentheses. If you switch to SQL view, you can see both the main query and the subquery created from the criteria:

```
SELECT Workorders.[Workorder Number], Workorders.[Bid Number],
Workorders.Supervisor, Workorders.[Material Cost]
FROM Workorders
WHERE (((Workorders.Supervisor) In (SELECT Supervisor FROM
Workorders WHERE [Material Cost]>1000)));
```

Figure 9-10 shows the results of this query. Supervisor Ferrell has four jobs listed, one of which has Material Cost over $1,000. Gunderson has five jobs, only one of which has Material Cost over $1,000, and Byron only has one job listed. You can compare the results of this query/subquery to the full Workorders table to see how it works.

Other predicates you can use with subqueries include

- ANY or SOME, which are synonymous and retrieve records in the main query that satisfy the comparison with any of the records retrieved by the subquery.

- ALL is more restrictive and retrieves only those records in the main query that satisfy the comparison with all the records retrieved by the subquery. For example, all the supervisor's jobs would have to have over $1,000 in material costs for the records to be retrieved by the main query.

- IN retrieves records in the main query for which some record in the subquery meets the comparison.

- NOT IN is the opposite of IN and retrieves records in the main query for which no record in the subquery meets the comparison.

- EXISTS is used in true/false comparisons to determine whether the subquery returns any records at all.

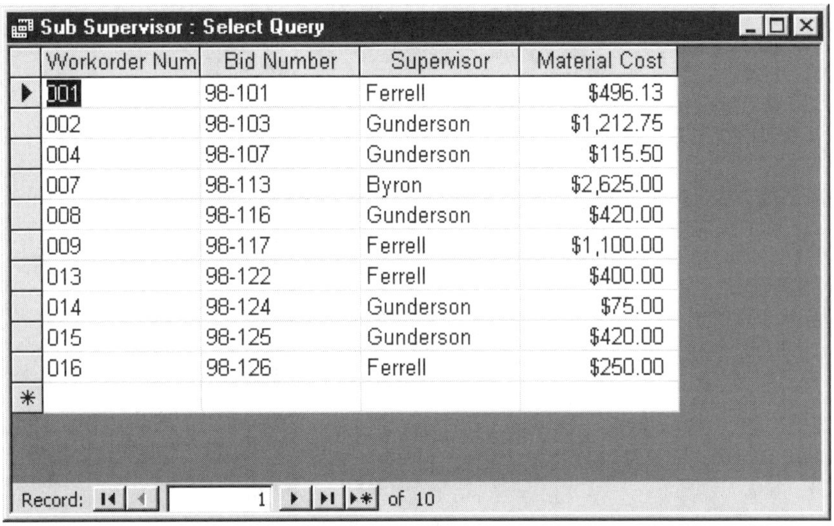

Sub Supervisor : Select Query

Workorder Num	Bid Number	Supervisor	Material Cost
001	98-101	Ferrell	$496.13
002	98-103	Gunderson	$1,212.75
004	98-107	Gunderson	$115.50
007	98-113	Byron	$2,625.00
008	98-116	Gunderson	$420.00
009	98-117	Ferrell	$1,100.00
013	98-122	Ferrell	$400.00
014	98-124	Gunderson	$75.00
015	98-125	Gunderson	$420.00
016	98-126	Ferrell	$250.00

Record: 1 of 10

Figure 9-10. *The results of using a subquery as a criterion*

Defining a New Field

To use a subquery to define a new field, type the statement in the Field cell of an empty column. For example, the following subquery adds the field Address from the Bid Data table to the grid.

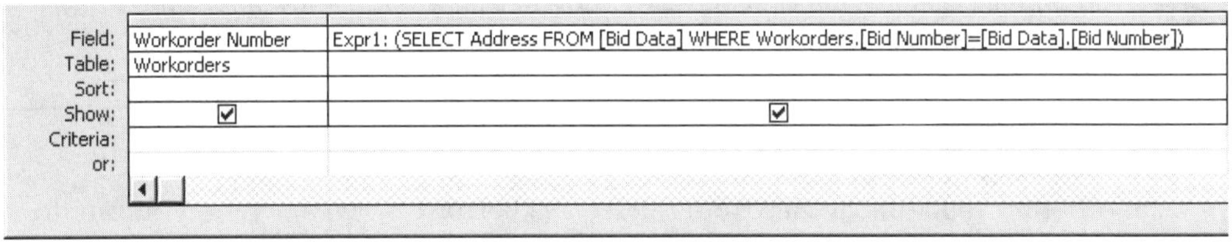

Field:	Workorder Number	Expr1: (SELECT Address FROM [Bid Data] WHERE Workorders.[Bid Number]=[Bid Data].[Bid Number])
Table:	Workorders	
Sort:		
Show:	☑	☑
Criteria:		
or:		

You can return to the Field cell and change the Expr1: default field name to a more informative one. Be sure to keep the colon (:), however. Figure 9-11 shows the results of this subquery.

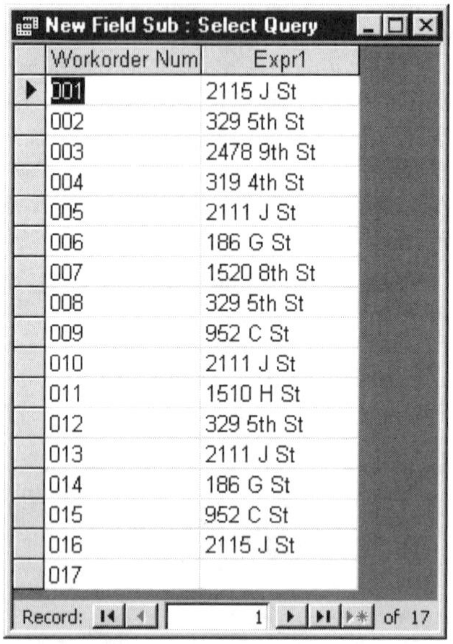

Workorder Num	Expr1
001	2115 J St
002	329 5th St
003	2478 9th St
004	319 4th St
005	2111 J St
006	186 G St
007	1520 8th St
008	329 5th St
009	952 C St
010	2111 J St
011	1510 H St
012	329 5th St
013	2111 J St
014	186 G St
015	952 C St
016	2115 J St
017	

Figure 9-11. *Using a subquery to create a new field*

Although this is a simple example, you can see that using subqueries to define fields based on values found in other tables can reduce the number of tables you need in a query. In this case, you didn't have to add the related Bid Data table to the query design to include the job address.

Note *You cannot calculate totals with, or group records by, fields defined with subqueries.*

Optimizing Query Performance

In addition to soliciting advice from the Access Performance Analyzer, you can do several things to speed up your queries.

- Index any field you use as a selection criteria and index fields on both sides of a join. If you set a relationship between the tables, Access automatically indexes the foreign key, if it isn't already indexed.
- Keep the field sizes down to the smallest data type that can be used with the data and give join fields the same or compatible data types.

- Compact the database regularly. Compacting reorganizes the table records so they're ordered by primary key value in adjacent database pages, which improves the sequential scan of the data pages.

- Add only the fields you need to the grid. Clear the Show box in fields used as criteria if you don't need to display them in the results.

- Avoid calculated fields in subqueries that slow down the running of the main query.

- When you group records by a joined field, use the field that's in the same table as the field on which you're totaling. Use Group By as little as possible.

- Avoid setting restrictive criteria on calculated fields and nonindexed fields.

- When using restrictive criteria on the join field in a one-to-many relationship, placing the criteria on the field on the "one" side may run faster than placing it on the "many" side.

- Index all fields used to specify sort orders.

- If you aren't working with volatile data, use the make-table query to create and save a table that can be used later as the basis for a form or report without having to run the query every time.

As you work with Access queries, you'll probably come across other techniques for improving performance.

Summary

In the first chapters of this book, you learned how to construct tables and databases, store information efficiently, and now you've seen how to create a wide variety of queries that help you retrieve the information. Many queries selectively retrieve information based on carefully specified criteria, while others perform data management operations on records in one or more tables.

Queries have been the mainstays of data retrieval in the past and continue to provide valuable service. One of the principal uses for queries has been as the basis for form and report designs. With the development of the new form and report design capabilities, you may find you don't need to create a query first, that you can do it right in the object design. The Form and Report Wizards also help select the proper data by filtering records and adding calculated controls.

The next five chapters discuss designing standard and custom forms and reports, including user-interactive data entry forms, special reports used for printing envelopes and mailing labels, and charts and graphs that visually represent trends and other data.

MOUS Exam Activities Explored in This Chapter

Number	Activity	Section Title
Expert	Create and run parameter queries	Creating Special Purpose Queries – Parameter Queries
Expert	Create and run action queries	Designing Action Queries – Update, Append, Delete, Make-Table

The Complete
Reference

Chapter 10

Creating Form and Report Designs

Now that you've seen how to store data efficiently in a related database and how to retrieve the information you want in exactly the arrangement that will be most helpful, it's time to look at how you can present the information to the world. Information can be displayed on the screen in forms suitable for viewing or editing. These forms can contain data from more than one table, and they have a custom appearance that enhances the understanding of the information and improves the chances for accurate data entry.

If you need to print the information, such as for an annual report or form letter, or simply to transport the information to the outside world, Access offers you a variety of reporting features. You can even create a report that prints on preprinted forms, such as those required by the Internal Revenue Service.

This chapter begins the series that covers form and report development. With Access 2002, designs of the two objects contain mostly the same ingredients, so these common features are discussed in this chapter. Subsequent chapters delve more into features and capabilities that are limited to one object or another.

Deciding Which Database Object

Access 2002 offers four ways to arrange information for display or distribution. The choice of database object type depends on the specific purpose of the object and how you plan to distribute the information.

- Forms are commonly used for data entry and editing, as well as viewing. You can also print data from a form or save the form as a report for more customizing and printing.

- Reports are used primarily for distributing printed information to recipients within the organization.

- Report snapshots are high-fidelity versions of a report that preserve the two-dimensional layout, graphics, and other embedded objects of the report. A snapshot is stored in a separate file that can be distributed via e-mail.

- Data access pages are used for data entry and editing within an Access project or via the Internet or an intranet outside a database. They are also used to distribute live data via e-mail.

This chapter focuses on the design elements common to forms and reports. See Chapter 13 for a discussion on report snapshots, including how they are distributed and viewed. Chapter 24 discusses data access pages and other aspects of using Access on the Internet.

Describing the Common Design Elements

Forms are used mostly for data entry and viewing. They can include user-interactive elements for acquiring additional information and executing user choices. Reports are mainly for presenting information in a static format, often printing the report for distribution to other members of the organization. Data access pages are bound to data in the database and are used like forms, but they're designed to be run in the Internet Explorer Web browser.

The design elements common to forms, reports, and data access pages include the record source that contains the data and the graphic objects added to the design. Many of the properties set to control the appearance and behavior of the form or report are also common to both. Page properties are related to the appearance and behavior of the dynamic Web page when it's accessed on the Internet. These unique properties are discussed in Chapter 24.

Choosing a Record Source

The source of the data you want in the form or report can be one or more tables or queries, or a SQL statement. For example, if you want to display a list of the Home Tech Repair customers, you would choose the Customers table as the record source for the form. If you want to print cost information for the current work orders, you would base the report on the Workorder Cost Sheet query that relates three tables and retrieves data from all three. A SQL statement can also be used in place of a query.

When you create a new form or report with the Form or Report Wizard, the first question asks what the record source is. Similarly, when you create a new object from scratch in the Design window, the first thing you do is choose the record source from the tables or queries in the current database. The individual fields in the underlying tables and queries become controls in the design.

Any sort orders and filters you saved with the table or query are inherited by the form or report. They aren't applied by default, but they are inherited, so you can easily apply them to sort or filter the information in the form or report.

The record source is one of the properties of every form and report. The only exceptions are special-purpose forms used for user input, such as pop-up forms, or switchboard forms that present alternative courses of action and don't involve data fields.

Using a Query Instead of a SQL Statement as the Record Source

When you get help from a wizard to create a form or report, the record source becomes a SQL statement created by the wizard. There may be times when you are better off converting the wizard's SQL statement to a saved query and using that as the record source. In the following cases, you should base the form or report on a query instead of a SQL statement:

- If speed is important, use the query. A form or report based on a query opens faster than one based on a SQL statement.

- If you want to use the expression in the SQL statement in more than one form or report, save the SQL statement as an independent query that can be used in more than one form or report.

■ If you need to restrict the records that will appear in the form or report, you must modify the SQL statement to add the criteria because the wizard cannot set criteria in the SQL statement. You can add the criteria to the SQL statement, and then save the query, or you can save it first, and then add the criteria to the query.

You learn how to convert the SQL statement to a query in the form or report design by working on the Record Source property later in this chapter.

Understanding Controls

The form or report design is made up of elements called controls. All the information shown on a form or report is represented by controls. A *control* is a graphical object you place on a form or report to display data, perform an action, or enhance the appearance of the form or report. Examples of controls are boxes that show field values, field labels, lines and rectangles, and command buttons. Many of these controls are also available to pages.

Controls come in three basic types, depending on their relationship to values in the tables:

■ A *bound control* gets its value from a field in the table and, as the data changes, the value of the bound control changes with it. The data fields you add to a form design are examples of bound controls.

■ An *unbound control* has no tie to the underlying table data and retains the value you enter. Examples of unbound controls are lines, rectangles, labels, and images.

■ A *calculated control* gets its value from values in the table and is actually an expression containing functions and operators, in addition to fields, that produces a result. The value shown in a calculated control changes as the values in the underlying fields change, but you cannot directly edit a calculated control.

Table 10-1 shows a list of the most common controls used in form, report, and data access pages designs. Most of them can be used in all, but a few are unique to one or another type of design. Although the user-interactive controls such as command buttons and combo boxes appear on the report toolbox, they aren't usually used in report designs.

Note   *The page objects referred to in Table 10-1 are data access pages, in contrast with page controls, which are pages within a tab control. Tab controls and their pages are discussed in Chapter 12.*

Control	Description
Bound object frame	A container that displays an OLE object stored in the record source.
Check box	A control that displays a Yes/No value from the record source. Can be used to represent one of a set of mutually exclusive options in an Option Group control.
Combo box	A control that combines a drop-down list of values with a text box for data entry. In page design, this control is called a *drop-down list control*.
Command button	A button that initiates an action, such as opening a linked form, running a macro, or calling a VBA procedure. Often shown with an image instead of text.
Image	An unbound picture, such as a company logo.
Label	Descriptive text, such as titles, captions, or instructions.
Line	A straight line used to divide parts of the design.
List box	A control that displays a list of choices, such as values for a field or search criteria.
Option button	A standalone control that displays a Yes/No value. Can be used to represent one of a set of mutually exclusive options in an Option Group control.
Option group	A frame with a limited set of alternatives in the form of check boxes, option buttons, or toggle buttons that relate to the same action or type of field value.
Page break	A control that creates a form with more than one page or causes a report to move to the next printed page.
Rectangle	A box that can be drawn for visually grouping fields or other text.
Subform/Subreport	A form or report contained within another form or report that shows data from related tables.

Table 10-1.   *Access Design Controls*

Control	Description
Tab	A control that shows a multiple-page form with tabs at the top of each page.
Text box	A control that displays field data from tables, queries, or calculated fields.
Toggle button	A button that represents an on or off setting.
Unbound object frame	A container for displaying an object not tied to an underlying table.

Table 10-1. *Access Design Controls* (continued)

Figure 10-1 shows a form with many of the typical controls you can add to your form and report designs. The option group contains a set of option buttons but, in this case, they could also be check boxes or toggle buttons. The combo box is shown expanded to display the value list. Controls are all accessible from the toolbox, which you can display in the Design window.

 Note *In Chapter 12, you learn about more special controls you can add to forms, including hyperlinks.*

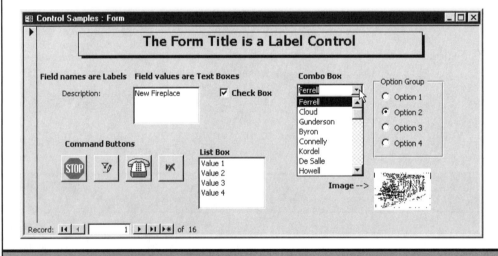

Figure 10-1. *Common controls used in form and report design*

Form and Report Design Properties

You saw in earlier chapters that databases, tables, queries, and fields have properties you can set to customize their appearance and behavior. Forms and reports, as well as all their controls, also have properties. This chapter discusses properties that apply primarily to forms and reports, as well as the controls they contain. Data access page properties are discussed in Chapter 24.

Forms and reports have some of the same properties, such as record source, caption, width, and filter, but each has a few unique properties which you learn about in a later chapter. For example, forms have properties that apply to user interfaces and events that occur when a user edits data, clicks a button, or presses TAB. Reports, on the other hand, have properties such as page header/footer text and record grouping for summary reports.

Each type of control also has an appropriate set of properties, such as name, caption, source, format, decimal places, color, filter, position, and size. All the properties relevant to the currently selected control are displayed in a window called a *property sheet*. You see how to examine and set these properties later in this chapter.

Working in the Design Window

Similarities also exist in the form and report Design windows. The toolbars and menus are nearly identical and the design surface looks the same. The only difference between them shows up at the beginning of a new design. The report Design window shows the page header and footer sections by default, but in the new form Design window, the form header and footer sections are optional and only the detail section is shown at the outset. You can add the headers and footers to the form design, if needed.

Because the two Design windows are so similar, the following paragraphs focus on the form Design window, while pointing out any significant differences in the report Design window.

Touring the Form Design Window

To start a new form, choose Objects | Forms in the Database window, and then do one of the following:

- Double-click the Create Form In Design View shortcut item on the Forms page. This opens a blank form design that isn't based on any existing table or query.
- Double-click the Create Form By Using Wizard shortcut item on the Forms page. This starts the Form Wizard.
- Click New on the Forms page.
- Choose Insert | Form.

Starting a New Report or Page

The Reports page and the Pages page of the Database window have similar options for starting new object designs. Shortcut items on both pages enable you to start a new design from Design view or with a wizard. In addition, the Pages page includes a shortcut item that enables you to edit an existing data access page.

The New Report dialog box has some of the same options, but has only two AutoReport options—Columnar and Tabular—and the Label Wizard has replaced the PivotTable Wizard. The New Data Access Page dialog box has four choices: Design View, Existing Web Page, Page Wizard, and AutoPage:Columnar.

The last two methods both open the New Form dialog box (see Figure 10-2) where you can choose to use one of the Form Wizards, create one of five different AutoForm designs, or create the design directly in the Design view.

In addition to choosing the method of creating the new form, you have the option of selecting a table or query as the basis for the form. This isn't required for either a form or a report unless you plan to add fields to the design. A switchboard is an example of a form without any data and a cover sheet for a report needn't contain any field data.

After choosing Design view and selecting a table as the basis, choose OK to open the empty form design. Access arms you with tools to help with creating the form, including a design toolbar and a formatting toolbar, some new menu items, a control toolbox, a field list, and a group of property sheets. The design surface also has a grid and rulers that help you align and space the controls in the design. Figure 10-3 shows the form Design window with all the tools visible, including the field list from the Workorders table. All these dialog boxes can be displayed by clicking a toolbar button

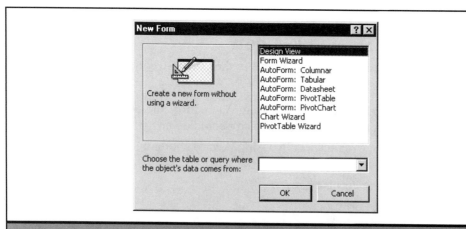

Figure 10-2. *The New Form dialog box*

or by choosing from the menu bar. The next section explains what these tools are used for and how to reach them.

To show either of the toolbars or the toolbox, right-click in the menu bar or in a toolbar, and then choose from the displayed list. To hide the toolbar or the toolbox, clear the check mark from the list.

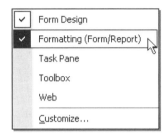

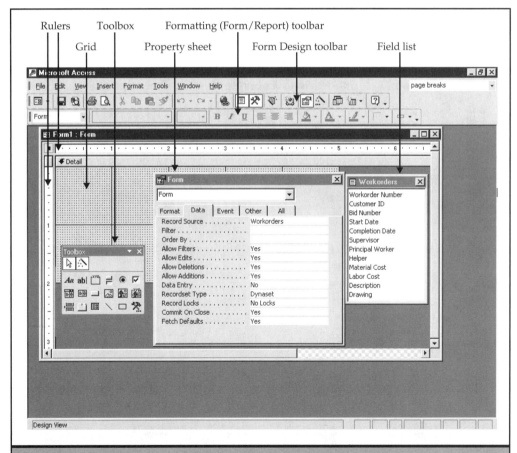

Figure 10-3.   *The Design window and its tools*

You can also choose from the View menu to show or hide them. Use the Toolbox button on the Form Design toolbar to display or hide the toolbox.

Toolbars are usually "docked" at the top of the window. You can quickly convert the toolbars into floating windows by dragging the move handle (the double vertical lines at the left end of the bar when it's docked) away from the docked position. You can also click a line between two buttons and drag the bar away from the dock, but it's easier to use the move handle. That way, you won't accidentally start something by clicking a button. To return a toolbar to the top of the window, drag it by the title bar until the frame stretches out to the width of the window and loses its title bar, and then release the mouse button.

The Form Design Toolbar

The Design window also displays the special Form Design toolbar and, optionally, the Formatting (Form/Report Design) toolbar. Table 10-2 describes the new buttons on the Form Design toolbar.

	Button	Menu Equivalent	Description
	View	View | Form View	Switches to Form view. Other options are Datasheet view and Design view.
	Format Painter	(none)	Copies formatting properties from one control to another.
	Insert Hyperlink	Insert | Hyperlink	Inserts a hyperlink address that's attached to the form or report, not to a table field.
	Toolbox	View | Toolbox	Displays the control toolbox.
	AutoFormat	Format | AutoFormat	Opens the AutoFormat dialog box to change the design style.

Table 10-2. *Form Design Toolbar Buttons*

	Button	Menu Equivalent	Description
	Visual Basic	View | Code	Opens the VB Editor window to display object module used in the design.

Table 10-2. *Form Design Toolbar Buttons* (continued)

The Report Design toolbar has most of the same buttons with only two exceptions:

- The Print Preview button shows instead of the Form View button.

- An additional button, Sorting and Grouping, appears between the Toolbox and AutoFormat buttons.

The Formatting Toolbar

Forms and reports use the same toolbar for customizing the appearance of the elements in the design. The buttons on the Formatting toolbar become available when one or more controls are selected in Design view. More about selecting form sections and controls later in this chapter. Table 10-3 describes the buttons found on the Formatting (Form/Report Design) toolbar. There are no menu equivalents to these toolbar buttons.

	Button	Description
CustomerID ▾	Object	Displays a list of all the sections and controls in the design. Click the name to select it.
Arial ▾	Font	Changes the font of the selected controls.
10 ▾	Font Size	Changes the font size of selected controls.
B	Bold	Changes selected text to bold.

Table 10-3. *Formatting (Form/Report Design) Toolbar Buttons*

	Button	Description
I	Italic	Changes selected text to italic.
U	Underline	Underlines selected text.
≡	Align Left	Aligns text in selected controls to the left margin.
≡	Center	Centers text in selected controls.
≡	Align Right	Aligns text in selected controls to the right margin.
	Fill/Back Color	Displays a color palette to use for fill and background colors.
A	Font/Fore Color	Displays a color palette to use for font and foreground colors.
	Line/Border Color	Displays a color palette to use for line and border colors.
	Line/Border Width	Displays a palette of line widths.
▭	Special Effect	Displays a palette of special effects, such as raised, sunken, etched, shadowed, and chiseled.

Table 10-3. *Formatting (Form/Report Design) Toolbar Buttons* (continued)

The Toolbox

Most of the buttons on the toolbox represent the controls you can add to the design. To add a control, click the desired button and click the design where you want the control. For some controls, you can draw an outline to specify the size of the control.

The first two buttons are special, however. When the first button, Select Objects, is pressed in, you can click one of the control object buttons to add a control to the design.

Note *You can't actually turn off the Select Objects button, but when you want to add several controls of the same type, you can lock down that control button by double-clicking it. This deactivates the Select Objects button until you click it again or press ESC to unlock the control button.*

The second button is the Control Wizards button, which automatically invokes one of the Control Wizards when you add its control to the design. Wizards are available for adding list boxes, combo boxes, option groups, command buttons, subforms, and subreports. If the button is deactivated, a wizard won't be forthcoming when you add one of those controls.

Note *The Option Group Wizard and the Subform/Subreport Wizards are part of the Additional Wizards group. If they don't start when you add one of these controls, you need to run the Access Setup program again and check Additional Wizards.*

Table 10-4 describes each of the buttons in the toolbox.

RETRIEVING AND
PRESENTING INFORMATION

	Button	**Description**
▷	Select Objects	When on, selects one control to add to the design.
✶	Control Wizards	When on, starts a wizard when certain controls are added to the design.
Aa	Label	Adds a space for entering text.
ab|	Text Box	Adds an unbound text box with attached label.
[xyz]	Option Group	Starts the Option Group Wizard or adds an empty option group if Control Wizards is off.
⊐	Toggle Button	Adds a toggle button.
◉	Option Button	Adds an option button.

Table 10-4.   *Toolbox Buttons*

	Button	Description
☑	Check Box	Adds a check box.
	Combo Box	Starts the Combo Box Wizard or adds an empty combo box if Control Wizards is off.
	List Box	Starts the List Box Wizard or adds an empty list box if Control Wizards is off.
	Command Button	Starts the Command Button Wizard or adds an empty command button if Control Wizards is off.
	Image	Opens the Insert Picture dialog box where you can locate and select an image.
	Unbound Object Frame	Opens the Insert Object dialog box where you can locate and select an object.
	Bound Object Frame	Creates a frame for displaying the contents of an OLE Object field from the record source.
	Page Break	Places six small dots at the left margin of the form design, indicating the beginning of a new page.
	Tab Control	Adds a tab control with two pages.
	Subform/Subreport	Starts the Subform or Subreport Wizard, or adds an unbound subform or subreport.

Table 10-4.   *Toolbox Buttons* (continued)

	Button	Description
	Line	Changes mouse pointer to a pencil for drawing a line.
	Rectangle	Draws a box.
	More Controls	Opens a window showing a list of additional controls that have been installed.

Table 10-4.   *Toolbox Buttons* (continued)

The toolbox is usually a floating window, which means you can drag it by the title bar to any location on the screen to get it out of the way. You can also dock the toolbox on one side, the top, or the bottom of the Design window. To dock it, drag the toolbox all the way to the side of the window. When docked, the title bar disappears so when you want to drag it back into the window, drag it away from the edge by the move handle. You can also drag the toolbox borders to change the dimensions of the floating window. To remove the toolbox from the screen, click the Close button.

The Property Sheets

Property sheets list all the properties that pertain to the form or the selected form section or control. The properties are grouped by category into four tabs, with a fifth tab showing the entire list. The categories are Format, Data, Event, and Other.

You use the property sheets to view the properties set for the controls and make any necessary changes. Some properties have drop-down lists of valid settings, others include the Build option.

If you have selected more than one control, the property sheet shows only those properties the group has in common. If the selected controls have no properties in common, the sheet is blank.

The Field List

The field list resembles the lists you saw in the Relationships window and in a query design, but without the asterisk. You use the field list to add fields to a design by dragging the name to the design grid. A text box control in the design displays the field value and an attached label shows the field caption, which may be different than the field name.

The Alignment Tools

The horizontal and vertical *rulers* help you place controls accurately in the design. The rulers are optional; you can show or hide them by selecting View | Ruler while you're in Design view. The single command, Ruler, applies to both the vertical and horizontal rulers. You can also right-click an empty area of the form design and choose Ruler from the shortcut menu.

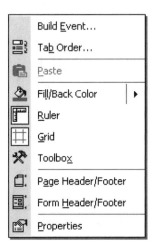

 You can also use the rulers when you want to select more than one control in the design, as you see in a later section that discusses selecting controls.

The *grid* shows as faint dots and lines in the design background. To show or hide the grid, choose View | Grid. One of the settings you can choose from the Format menu is Snap To Grid. With this setting selected, Access automatically aligns the controls to the nearest grid mark.

 You can also change the grid granularity to increase or decrease the precision of the control placements. The grid fineness is actually a property of the form or report design itself, and is set in the Format tab or the property sheet. The grid is preset to 10 increments per inch horizontally and 12 per inch vertically. You can change either of these settings to any value from 1 to 64 by entering the value in the GridX (horizontal) or GridY (vertical) form property. A setting finer than 20 dots per inch is a little difficult to see.

Starting a New Design

To illustrate creating a new form design, let's build a data entry form for Home Tech Repair to enter new work order data. To start the new form, click Forms in the Objects bar in the Database window, and then do the following:

1. Click New or click the arrow next to New Objects on the toolbar, and then choose Form from the list. The New Form dialog box opens as shown earlier in Figure 10-2.

2. Choose Design view.

3. Click the drop-down arrow in the lower box and choose Workorders from the list of existing tables and queries, and then click OK. The blank form shows in Design view.

4. Click the Field List and Toolbox buttons or choose both from the View menu. You can also right-click the empty design and choose Toolbox from the shortcut menu.

5. Keep the form design open for adding fields and titles.

By default, the form design doesn't fill the window, but you can resize the design grid by dragging the form borders.

A new form consists only of the detail section where most of the information is to be displayed. If you want some text or other information displayed in a form header or footer, add the section by choosing View | Form Header/Footer. You can also right-click the form design and choose Form Header/Footer from the shortcut menu. Both sections are added to the design. If you want one and not the other, you can shrink the unwanted section to nothing. Report designs automatically include page headers and footers in addition to the detail section. You can add report headers and footers by choosing View | Report Header/Footer.

You can also add page headers and footers to forms. In a form, the information placed in the page header and footer appears only when the form is previewed or printed, not when it's open in Form view. Choose Page Header/Footer from the View menu or the shortcut menu to add a form page header and footer.

Adding Controls

You can add all types of controls to the design with the toolbox, but it's easier to use the field list to add text box controls for the table fields. In the following paragraphs, you see how to add fields from the Workorders table, a form title and subtitle, and some calculated fields.

From the Field List

The Field List contains the names of all the fields in the record source. When you drag a field from the list to the design, Access creates a new text box control that shows field values in the Form view. You can add fields from the list to the design in three ways:

- Drag a field name from the list to the design. Dragging the field name to the design looks much like dragging a field name to the query grid. When you drop the button, the control appears showing the text box and the attached label.

- To add all the fields to the design at once, double-click the field list title bar to select all the names, and then drag the group to the design. The text boxes and attached labels appear in a tight column in the form design.

- Use the standard SHIFT-click or CTRL-click to select contiguous or dispersed field names, and then drag the group to the design.

The field list remains open until you click the Close button, or click the Field List button again, or choose View | Field List.

To get back to the Home Tech Repair data entry form and add fields from the Workorders table, do the following:

1. Click the Workorder Number field in the field list and drag the button to the design at about the 1-inch mark on the horizontal ruler, as shown in Figure 10-4.

2. Drag the other fields from the field list to positions in the design resembling Figure 10-5. You need to expand the form both horizontally and vertically to place the fields as shown.

Once you have all the fields you want in the design, you can close the field list to make more room on the screen. Next, add a form header and use the toolbox to add a title and subtitle to the header.

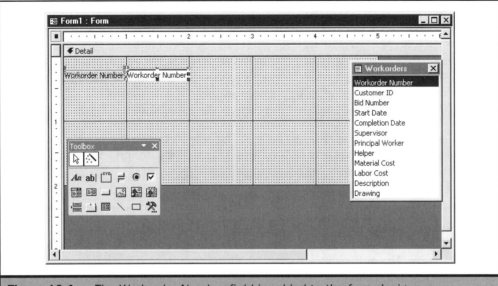

Figure 10-4. *The Workorder Number field is added to the form design.*

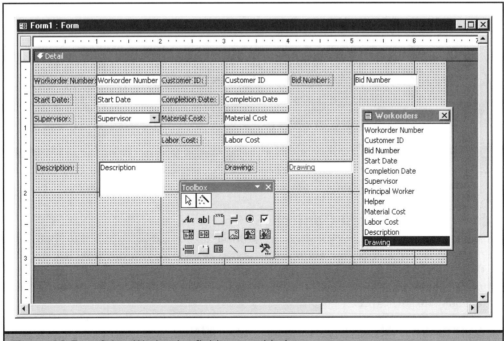

Figure 10-5. *Other Workorder fields are added.*

From the Control Toolbox

To add a control, click the appropriate button and draw the control outline in the design. What happens next depends on the type of control you're adding. If it's a Label control, the insertion point appears inside the outline ready to enter the label text. If you want to add several controls of the same type, you can double-click the button to lock it down and not have to click it for every control.

To add a title in the Workorders form header, do the following:

1. Choose View | Form Header/Footer. The new sections are added to the form design. You can also right-click an empty area of the design and choose Form Header/Footer from the shortcut menu.

2. Move the mouse pointer to the dividing line between the Form Header and Detail sections and, when it changes shape to a double vertical arrow, click-and-drag the line down ½ inch on the vertical ruler.

3. Click the Label toolbox button and draw an outline in the Form Header across the form. The outline appears with the insertion point at the left, ready to type text.

4. Type **Home Tech Repair** and click outside the label box, and then click it again to select the label control.

5. Use the Formatting toolbar to change the font size to 18, italic, and centered. Figure 10-6 shows the form design with the new header.

6. Widen the form header section some more to add a subtitle.

7. Click the Label toolbox button and draw a box beneath the title, and then type **Data Entry Form — Workorders** in the label control.

8. Use the Formatting toolbar to customize this text, so it's bold and font size 10.

9. Switch to Form view to see how the design looks now (see Figure 10-7).

Tip *You can draw a straight line anywhere in your design from one point to another. If you want to make sure the line is exactly horizontal or vertical, hold down SHIFT while you draw the line. Access automatically aligns the new line with the grid marks.*

Adding a Calculated Control

A calculated control contains values from multiple text, number, currency, or date fields in the record source. For example, in an earlier chapter you saw how to combine text values from first and last name fields into a single whole name field. Another example is to create a single field address from separate address, city, state, and ZIP code fields with the expression:

[Address]&", "&[City]&" "&[State]&" "[ZIPcode]

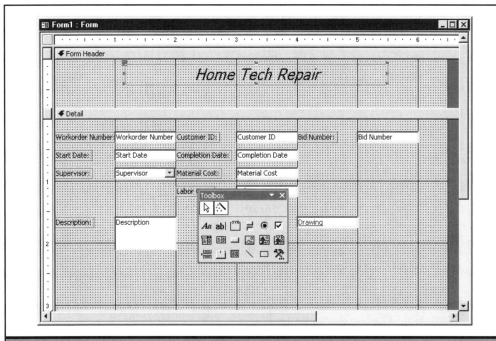

Figure 10-6.   *Adding a title in the form header*

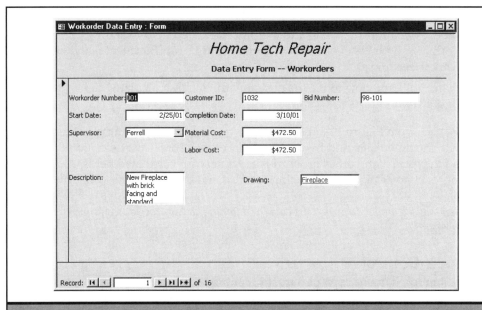

Figure 10-7.   *The Workorder Data Entry Form in Form view*

The quotation marks enclose embedded spaces and a comma that separate the values. You can also combine currency or date fields, for example:

- **[Birthday]-Date()** displays the number of days until your next birthday.
- **[Price]*1.07+[Shipping&Handling]** computes and displays the sales price, plus 7 percent tax, and adds the shipping and handling charges.

 You can often save processing time by performing the calculations at the query level instead of in the form or report design. Then use the query as the basis for the form or report.

Now add two calculated fields to the Workorders data entry form that will display the total cost of the job and the number of days estimated to complete the work by doing the following:

1. Click the Text Box control button in the toolbox and click the area to the right of the Material Cost field.

2. Double-click a control or click the Properties button to open the property sheet for the new unbound text box. You can also right-click a control and choose Properties from the shortcut menu.

3. Click the Data tab and enter the following expression in the Control Source property box: **=[Material Cost]+[Labor Cost]**. Notice you must start the expression with an equal sign (=) or Access assumes the expression is a field name.

4. Double-click the attached label that shows Text*n* and type **Total Cost**.

5. Repeat steps 1 through 4 to add another calculated field to show estimated work time with the expression **=[Completion Date]-[Start Date]** and label it **Work Time (days)**.

6. Switch to Form view to see the design with the new calculated fields (see Figure 10-8).

You can see from Figure 10-8 that while the two cost fields retain the currency format with the dollar sign and two decimal places, the Total Cost field did not. You have to set the format and other properties separately for calculated fields. A later section in this chapter discusses selecting controls and changing their properties.

 A simple calculated control is the current date. In the Control Source property, type the expression: =Date().

Copying a Control

If you want more than one copy of the same control, you have two ways to do that: copy-and-paste or duplicate. You can make as many duplicates as you want.

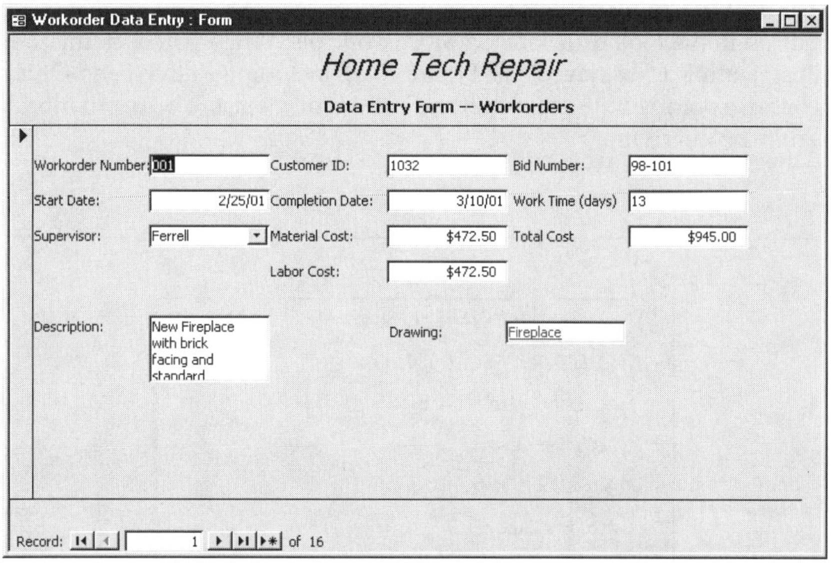

Figure 10-8. *Form with calculated fields*

To duplicate a control, click the control to select it, and then choose Edit | Duplicate. A copy of the control appears just below the first. You can repeat this technique to build a column of evenly spaced duplicate controls, which you can move around the design after duplicating them.

Tip *If the control has a label, click the control, not the label.*

If you don't care if the copies are evenly spaced, use the standard copy-and-paste routine. Select the control and click Copy, or right-click and choose Copy from the shortcut menu. If no other control is selected when you click Paste, the copy appears in the upper-left corner of the design. Then you can drag it to the desired location in the design. If you select a control near where you want the copy, the copy is pasted just below the selected control.

When you copy a control, Access includes any associated properties. A copy of a text box control includes a copy of the attached label.

Note *If you only want to copy the format of a control to other controls, rather than add more controls, use the Format Painter.*

Looking at More Controls

The last button in the toolbox is labeled More Controls. When you click this, a long list of additional controls is displayed (see Figure 10-9), including ActiveX and OLE controls. Move the mouse pointer to the arrow at the bottom of the list to see even more controls (your list may be different).

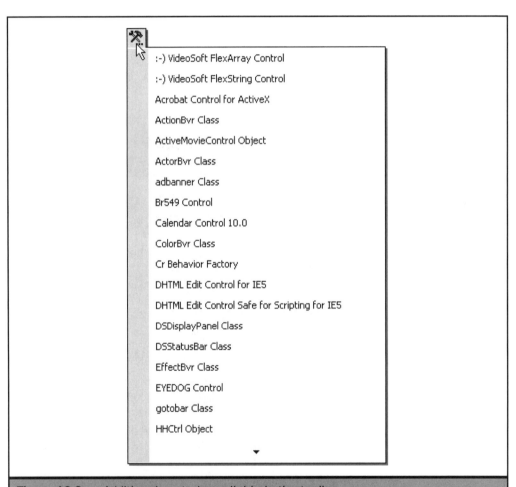

Figure 10-9.   *Additional controls available in the toolbox*

To add one of these to the form design, click the control name and draw the outline in the design where you want to see the control. If you select an OLE control, you must have the OLE server registered. The Calendar Control that you add later in this chapter, for example, is one of the options when installing Microsoft Office XP.

Note *You can also add these ActiveX controls to a form design by choosing Insert | ActiveX Control and selecting the control you want from the Insert ActiveX Control dialog box.*

Dressing Up with Lines and Rectangles

While they aren't essential, lines are useful in forms and reports to create a visual separation between parts of the design. A heavy line can help focus attention on a specific area. You can draw a line anywhere in a form or report section.

To draw a line, click the Line toolbox button and click where you want the line or drag the pointer to draw the line. If you only click within the design, Access draws a solid horizontal line, 1 inch long and 1 point thick. When you drag to draw the line, you can drag it in any direction and any length. To make sure the line is horizontal or vertical when you draw it, hold down SHIFT while you draw.

Rectangles come in handy as boxes that group related data or as a means to emphasize another control. For example, in a form, you can draw a box around a set of command buttons to set them off from the rest of the design.

To draw a rectangle, click the Rectangle toolbox button and draw the box in the design. After drawing the line or rectangle, you can use the Formatting toolbar buttons to change the line or border thickness, choose colors, and add a special effect. You can also use the property sheet to change the line or rectangle border style to a dashed or dotted line, for example.

TIP: If you draw a rectangle around other controls and add a background color, you may obscure the other controls. To cure this, select the rectangle and choose Format | Send To Back to place it behind the others.

Modifying Controls

You can customize the controls you add to a form or report design to present information in just the right way. Controls can be moved about in the design, resized, and any of their properties can be changed to create the appropriate effect. To change any control, you must first select the control to focus Access on the object you want to work with.

Selecting Controls and Other Objects

You have many ways of selecting the form or report design, one of the design sections, or one or more controls. The Object button on the Formatting toolbar displays a complete list of every element of the design from the form (or report) itself to each of its sections and all the controls in the design, including any added lines and text. The list is in alphabetical order. To select one of these, choose from the list. You may need to scroll down the list to find the element you want to select.

Selecting the Form or a Form Section

You can select the form itself in the following ways:

- If the rulers are displayed, click the form selector, the small square in the upper-left corner where the horizontal and vertical rulers meet.

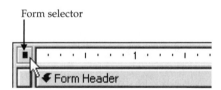

Form selector

- Choose Edit | Select Form (or Report).
- Click anywhere in the plain gray background outside the form design.

When the form is selected, the form selector shows a small black square. After selecting the form, you can view and change any of its properties, including the record source, in the form property sheet.

In addition to choosing from the Object list, you can do one of the following to select a form or report section:

- Click the section selector, the small box in the vertical ruler opposite the section bar.

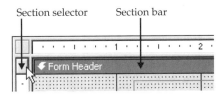

Section selector   Section bar

- Click the section bar.
- Click anywhere in the gray background of the section.

When a section is selected, the section bar, the horizontal divider that contains the section title, appears shaded.

Selecting Controls

That leaves the controls themselves. To select one control, you can simply click the control or choose the control name from the Object list on the Formatting toolbar. When you select a control, a set of small dark squares called *handles* appear around the control. You use these handles to move and resize the controls. The larger squares are the *move handles* and the smaller ones are the *sizing handles*. More about moving and resizing later in this chapter.

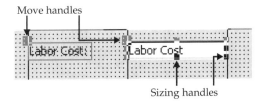

Move handles

Sizing handles

If you want to make the same change to several controls at once, you can select more than one of them in one of the following ways:

- Hold down SHIFT as you click each control.
- To select a column of controls, click the selection arrow in the horizontal ruler above the controls.
- To select a row of controls, click the selection arrow in the vertical ruler to the left of the controls.
- To select a block of controls, click the selection arrow in one of the rulers and drag to draw a rectangle around the controls. This selects all the controls inside or partially within the rectangle.

- To select a block of controls within the design, but not a complete column or row, click the design outside of any control and draw a rectangle around the controls.

- To select all the controls in the design, choose Edit | Select All.

 When you click one of the rulers and draw a rectangle to select a row or column of controls, you can choose to include controls completely or only partially enclosed within the rectangle. Choose Tools | Options and click the Form/Report tab. The Selection Behavior options include Partially Enclose (the default) and Fully Enclosed.

To remove the selection, click anywhere outside the selected objects. To remove only a few controls from a group of selected controls, hold down SHIFT and click each of the controls you want to exclude.

A text box control is a special case because it contains two parts that can be treated together or separately. The attached label is usually the field name and the edit region displays the field value. If you click the edit region to select a text box control, both parts are selected and any changes you make apply to both. If you click the attached label, only the label is selected and you can change its properties or move it separately.

You can tell by the size and number of handles that appear around the control, whether you have selected them both or only the label. The following shows two text box controls: both the label and the edit region of the Labor Cost control are selected, while only the label of the Material Cost control is selected.

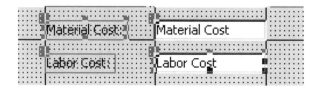

Once you select the controls you want to work with, you can move, resize, align, or space them equally or change any of their properties.

Grouping Controls

If you have several controls you want to look and behave alike, you can define them as a single group and format them all at the same time. To create the control group, select all the controls you want to include and choose Format | Group. A frame appears around the set of controls, which doesn't show up in Form view. The new form, shown next, contains the cost fields in a single group. The text box controls were aligned right and displayed underlined and in italic.

Material Cost	Material Cost	Total Cost	=[Material Cost]+[
Labor Cost	Labor Cost		

To remove the group designation, choose Format | Ungroup. The Group and Ungroup commands may appear on the expanded Format menu.

Moving and Resizing Controls

One reason to select a control is to change its size or move it to a different position in the design. As mentioned earlier, when you select a control, handles appear around the control. These handles are used to move and resize a control or a selected group of controls.

Moving Controls

To move a control in the design, move the mouse pointer to the move handle—the larger square in the upper-left corner of a selected control. When the pointer changes shape to an open hand, click-and-drag the control to the desired position. You can drag it over other controls to place it where you want it.

Again the text box control is a special case because it has two move handles. The move handle in the upper left of the edit region moves the whole control together if the pointer shows as an open hand. If the mouse pointer changes to a pointing hand, instead of an open hand, you can move the edit region by itself. When you move the mouse pointer to the move handle of the attached label, it always changes to a pointing hand, so you can move the label by itself. You can't move both parts with the move handle in the label.

Dragging a control by its move handle can be inaccurate, so if you want to move a control a smaller or more precise distance, hold down CTRL *and press the appropriate arrow key. Each key press moves the control one fourth of a grid unit in the direction of the arrow. Holding down* CTRL *while you drag a control temporarily turns off the Snap To Grid feature.*

If you selected more than one control, you can drag any one of them and they'll all move together.

Resizing Controls

A selected control has seven sizing handles, one on each side and one at each corner. Dragging one of the side handles changes the width or height, while dragging a corner handle can change both height and width at once.

If you selected several controls, they all change to the same size when you drag the sizing handle of one of them.

If you need to make more precise adjustments in the size of the selected control, hold down SHIFT while you click the appropriate arrow key. Each keypress increases or decreases the size of the control by one fourth of a grid unit.

The Format menu and the shortcut menu also have options that help you size one control or a group of controls, so they match in length or width. First select the controls you want to resize, and then choose Format | Size, or right-click and point to Size in the shortcut menu. The Size command may be in the expanded Format menu. Figure 10-10 shows the commands available from the Size menu.

The first command, To Fit, resizes a control to fit its contents. For example, if you've drawn a long label control and entered short text, choose the To Fit command to reduce the size of the control to fit the entered text. The second command, To Grid, automatically adjusts the size of the control, so all four corners fall on the nearest grid points.

Double-clicking one of the sizing handles automatically resizes the control to fit the contents.

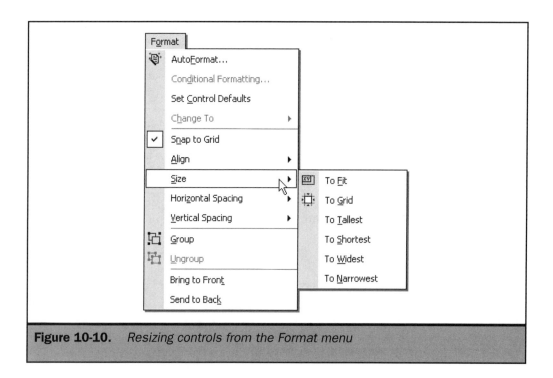

Figure 10-10.   *Resizing controls from the Format menu*

The remaining four commands adjust the size of each control in a group of controls relative to the tallest, the shortest, the widest, or the narrowest of the group.

 The Snap To Grid command, when checked, automatically adjusts the control size when you drag the size handles, so their boundaries are on gridlines.

Aligning and Spacing Controls

Having the controls in a form evenly lined up helps give the form a professional look. To align a group of controls, select them first, and then choose Format | Align, or right-click and point to Align in the shortcut menu. Figure 10-11 shows the choices you have for alignment relative to the members of the group.

The last command in the Align menu, To Grid, places the upper-left corner of all the selected controls on a grid mark. If you have Snap To Grid checked, this is automatically done.

 When aligning controls, be sure to select only those in the same row or same column. If you have controls in the group from a different area of the form, they will be aligned with the rest, creating a confused appearance.

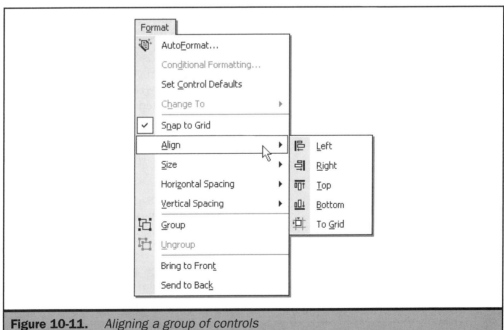

Figure 10-11. *Aligning a group of controls*

RETRIEVING AND PRESENTING INFORMATION

When you have a row or column of controls that you want uniformly spaced across or down the form or report, you can use the Horizontal Spacing or Vertical Spacing commands in the Format menu. These commands are also used to increase or decrease the spaces evenly between the controls.

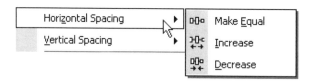

Table 10-5 describes the choices in the Horizontal and Vertical Spacing options.

Spacing	Command	Result
Horizontal	Make Equal	Controls at the left and right of the group remain fixed and the controls between are moved to equalize the intervening spaces.
Vertical	Make Equal	Controls at the top and bottom of the group remain fixed and the controls between are moved to equalize the intervening spaces.
Horizontal	Increase	The leftmost control remains fixed and the space between the remaining controls is increased by one grid interval.
Vertical	Increase	The top control remains fixed and the space between the remaining controls is increased by one grid interval.
Horizontal	Decrease	The leftmost control remains fixed and the space between the remaining controls is decreased by one grid interval.
Vertical	Decrease	The top control remains fixed and the space between the remaining controls is decreased by one grid interval.

Table 10-5.   *Spacing Commands*

Using Property Sheets

Properties establish the characteristics of form and report design elements. Everything in a form or report design has properties: controls, sections, and even the form or report itself. Control properties set the structure, appearance, and behavior of the controls. Properties can also determine the characteristics of the text and data contained in a control.

Property sheets contain lists of all the properties that pertain to the selected control or group of controls. To open a property sheet for a control, do one of the following:

- Double-click the control.
- Select the control and choose View | Properties.
- Select the control and click Properties on the toolbar.
- Right-click the control and choose Properties from the shortcut menu.

The list of properties depends on the current selection. Figure 10-12 shows the property sheet for the Workorder Number text box control. As you can tell by the scroll bar, more properties are in the list.

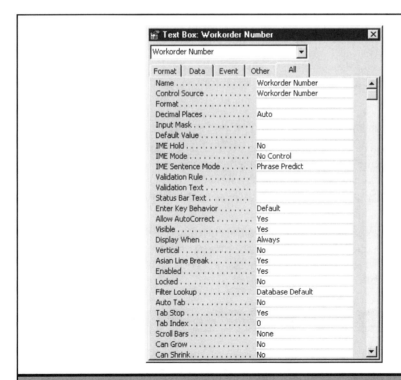

Figure 10-12.   *The Workorder Number property sheet*

The properties are grouped in the sheet by type: Format, Data, Event, Other, and All. Click the tab that will show the properties you want to change or stay with All to see the entire list.

To change a property, click the property in the list, and then do one of the following:

- Type the desired setting in the property box.
- If an arrow appears in the property box, select the desired setting from the list.
- If a Build button (…) appears, click it to display a builder or a dialog box with a choice of builders, depending on the type of control.

When you click a property in the property sheet, you can see a description of the property in the status bar. If you need more information about the property or how to use it, press F1.

The calculated field, Total Cost, which we added to the Workorders data entry form earlier, needs to show currency symbols. To set the format property, do the following:

1. In the form Design window, double-click the edit region of the Total Cost text box control. The property sheet opens.

2. Click the arrow in the Format property box and choose Currency from the list (see Figure 10-13).

Other items of interest are in the property sheet for the Total Cost text box. For example:

- Look in the status bar for a description of the Format property.
- The Name property isn't Total Cost, but Text12. Recall that Total Cost isn't a real field name, but is only the label attached to the unbound text box control. Access automatically assigns a name to a new control when it's added to the design. This name is an identifier that Access uses in expressions, macros, and procedures.
- You can see the expression that defines the calculated field. If it is a long expression, right-click the Control Source property line and choose Zoom from the shortcut menu to see the entire expression. You can also click the property box and press SHIFT-F2 to open the Zoom box.

To apply the same property settings to a group of controls of the same type, first select them all, and then open the property sheet. Only those properties common to all members of the group are visible in the sheet.

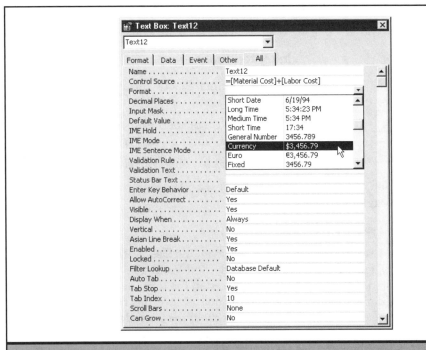

Figure 10-13. *Setting the Total Cost Format property to Currency*

Once you open a property sheet, it remains on the screen until you close it. To set properties of a different object in the design, either select the object from the drop-down list at the top of the property sheet or select the control in the design.

Inherited Properties

Access copies many of the properties from a field in the underlying table or query to the form or report design when you drag a field from the field list to create a bound control. For example, when the Material Cost field was dragged to the Workorders form, the currency format and number of decimal places were applied to the bound control in the form.

Changing a control's property setting in the form or report doesn't affect the field in the table or query. If you change the field property in the table structure after you add the field to the design, the changes aren't carried over to the form or report. Some properties, such as Format, Decimal Places, Input Mask, Validation Rule, Validation Text, and Default Value are best set in the underlying field rather than in the form or report design, so they're consistent throughout the application.

The following table lists the properties inherited by each type of bound control.

Bound Control	Inherited Properties
Text box	Format, Decimal Places, Input Mask, Caption, Status Bar Text
List box	All the Lookup properties set in the table Design view, Caption, and Status Bar Text
Combo box	Same as List box, plus Format and Input Mask
Check box, option button, option group, toggle button, bound object frame	Status Bar Text and Caption

The Status Bar Text property gets its value from the Description column in the table design. The Default Value, Validation Rule, and Validation Text properties aren't really inherited, although they are enforced in the form or report. If they were truly inherited, they would appear in the bound control's property sheet in Design view. If you set a Validation Rule property in the form design, both that and the one set in the table design will be enforced. On the other hand, a Default Value property set in the form design overrides the value set in the table design.

Assigning a Default Value

When you assign a default value to a bound control in a form or report design, the value you enter overrides any default value set in the underlying table design. Unless you enter a different default value, the one you assign is stored in the field when a new record is entered in the form. For example, if you're entering new bid data and one of the fields in the form is the date, you can assign the current date as the default value. This automatically stores the current system date in the new record.

To assign the current date as the default value, type **=Date()** in the control's Default Value property box.

Note *Another way to include the current date in a form or report is to choose Insert | Date and Time to open the Date and Time dialog box. Then click Include Date and choose a date format. To include the time, check Include Time and choose a time format. If a header section is in the form or report, Access places the Date/Time text box there; otherwise, it goes in the Detail section. Date and time values added this way are part of the design and aren't stored in the underlying table.*

Specifying a Validation Rule

To apply a validation rule to a control in the form or report, enter the expression in the Validation Rule property box. You can also click the Build button to use the Expression

Builder to construct the rule. The validation rule you enter as a control property is enforced, in addition to any that were set in the table design.

If your expression is long, you can press SHIFT-F2 to open the Zoom box, where you can see the whole thing.

Type the message you want displayed when a violation occurs into the Validation Text property box.

Changing Default Control Properties

Access has provided a default set of properties for each type of control. The set specifies the general appearance and behavior of that type of control. For example, the default properties for a text box control determines the font size and alignment of text within the attached label. Another default text box property automatically includes the field name as an attached label. This set of properties is called the *default control style* for that control type.

If you find you're making the same changes to most of the controls of a certain type, you can change the default property setting. For example, if you usually want a larger font size in your text boxes, change the Font Size from the default size of 8 to a larger size. Or, if you don't want the attached labels for every text box, change the Auto Label property on the Format tab to No.

When you change a default setting to the one you use most, it saves space. Access doesn't have to store both the default and custom settings.

To change a default property setting, do the following:

1. Click the tool in the toolbox for the desired control type.

2. Click Properties on the toolbar. The property sheet for that control type opens, but the title bar indicates these are the default settings, instead of the settings for a particular control in the design.

3. Change the setting in the default property sheet.

Figure 10-14 shows the Default Text Box property sheet. As with other property sheets, the status bar displays an explanation of the currently selected property. In this case, the Enter Key Behavior property determines what happens when you press ENTER while the insertion point is in a text box control: either start a new line to enter more text or move in accordance with the setting in the Move After Enter option in the Keyboard tab of the Options dialog box.

To change the default properties of other controls, keep the Default Properties box open. Then select the name of the control from the drop-down list at the top of the box.

The changes you make affect only the new controls you add to the design; the existing controls aren't changed. The changes remain in effect for the current design until you change them again.

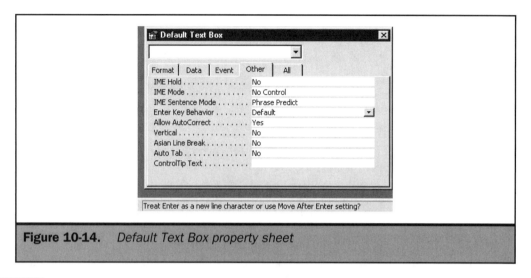

Figure 10-14. *Default Text Box property sheet*

Some of the text box control properties can be set only in the Default Text Box property sheet. For example, Auto Label and Auto Colon (on the Format tab) work together. When both are set to Yes, Access automatically adds the field name as an attached label followed by a colon. Label X, Label Y, and Label Align, which position the attached label with respect to the text box, also appear only in the default property sheet. See the Quick Reference on the CD for a complete description of text box and other control default properties.

If you already made changes to a control and you like what you see, you can copy the changes quickly to the control type's default style. Any new controls then would use the properties from the existing control as a default control style. Select the control with the characteristics you want as defaults for subsequent controls, and then choose Format | Set Control Defaults.

Using the Formatting Toolbar

The Formatting toolbar is a quick way to change the appearance of the text in selected controls. The toolbar is optional when you're designing a form or report. To see the Formatting toolbar, choose View | Toolbars and check Formatting (Form/Report). You can also right-click any menu bar or toolbar and choose Formatting (Form/Report) from the shortcut menu.

The Formatting toolbar has, in addition to the Object button already discussed, eight buttons for formatting text in the design. These eight buttons change the font name, size, and style, and align the text within the control boundaries. The last five buttons give you a quick way to change the color and style of many elements in the design.

The three color buttons display a color palette you can use to change the color of the background, the font, or the border of a control. The fourth button changes the thickness of the selected control's border and the last button adds special effects to a control or an entire section, such as raised, sunken, shadowed, etched, chiseled, and flat effects. If you want to keep one or more palettes on the screen to make several changes at once, drag the palette away from its toolbar button. Click the Close button on the palette to close it. Figure 10-15 shows all the palettes open in a form Design window.

 If you want to apply the same formatting property changes to a group of similar controls, select them all, and then change the common property.

Formatting Conditionally

Conditional formatting was introduced in Access 2000. You can use it with text boxes and combo boxes. With conditional formatting, you can specify a default format for the control and up to three additional formats that are applied under special conditions: the current value of the field, when the field gets focus, or when an expression evaluates to True. The expression can refer to the values in other fields in the same record. For example, if the date in a field is more than 30 days ago, display the value in this field underlined and in red on a light green background.

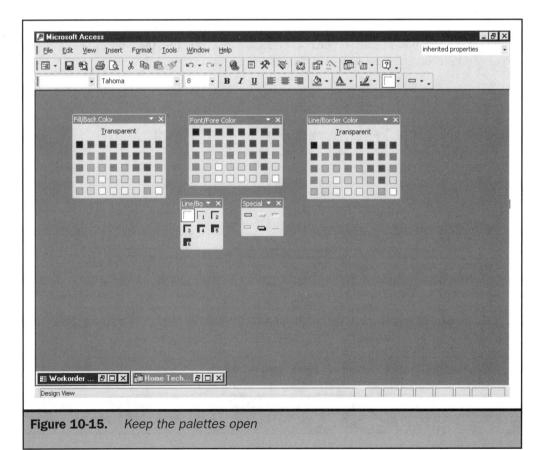

Figure 10-15.   *Keep the palettes open*

To activate conditional formatting, select the control you want to apply it to and choose Format | Conditional Formatting. The Conditional Formatting dialog box (see Figure 10-16) shows two areas: one for setting the default format and one for specifying a conditional format to be applied under specific conditions.

The formatting choices include bold, italic, and underline, as well as text and background colors. The button on the right end of the condition box enables or disables the control. When a control is enabled, you can reach it by pressing TAB. If a control is disabled, it's skipped in the tab order. The box in the middle displays an example of how the chosen formatting will look.

To set conditional formatting, first set the default format, and then move to Condition 1. In the first box, you have a choice of conditions:

■ *Field Value Is*   Defines the value or range of values for which to apply the format settings.

■ *Expression Is*   Applies the formatting if the expression you enter evaluates to True.

■ *Field Has Focus*   Applies the formatting to the field as soon as it gets focus.

Depending on which selection you make in the first condition box, other specifications can be made in the other boxes. If you choose Field Value Is in the first box, you have a choice of several comparison operators.

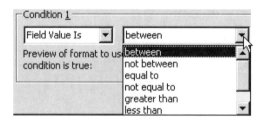

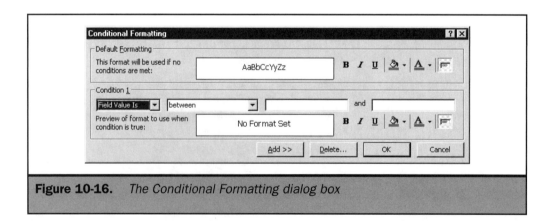

Figure 10-16.   *The Conditional Formatting dialog box*

If you choose Expression Is, you have only one box in which to enter the expression. Field Has Focus requires no additional criteria.

Choose Add to add another condition. You can specify up to three conditional formatting scenarios for each text box or combo box control. The conditions are ranked with the first one taking precedence. If the first condition isn't met, the second is evaluated, and so on. Figure 10-17 shows the Conditional Formatting dialog box with settings for the Total Cost text box control. The three conditions are the following:

- If the Total Cost exceeds $5,000

- If the Total Cost is less than $1,000

- If the Labor Cost is greater than the Material Cost

If you want to remove a condition, choose Format | Conditional Formatting again and click Delete in the dialog box. The Delete Conditional Format dialog box opens, where you can check the conditions you want to delete, and then click OK.

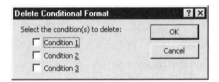

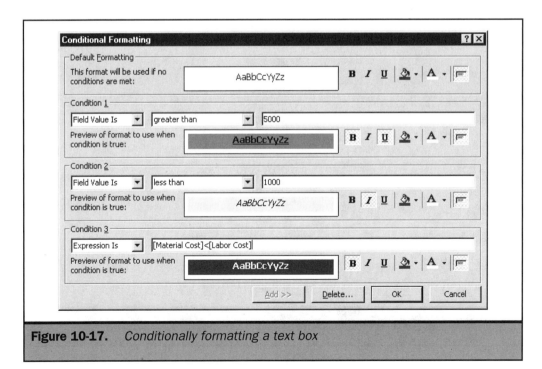

Figure 10-17.   *Conditionally formatting a text box*

Changing a Control Type

When you change your mind about what type of control you want in the form or report, Access lets you change the control type dynamically. Not all types can be converted and you're limited to the types you can convert to, depending on the original control type.

To change a control type, click the control you want to change and choose Format | Change To. You can also right-click the control and point to Change To in the shortcut menu. A list appears displaying the list of controls to which the selected control can be changed. Click the new type of control. If a control type is dimmed in the list, you cannot change the selected control to that type. Table 10-6 describes the types of conversions permitted by Access.

When you change to another type of control, the applicable properties are copied from the original control to the new control. If the original control has property settings that don't exist for the new control, they're ignored. If the new control has properties that weren't used in the original control, Access assigns the default settings for the new control.

Deleting Controls

 To delete a control, select the control and press DEL or choose Delete from the Edit menu. If you change your mind, you can restore the control by clicking Undo on the toolbar (or choosing Edit | Undo). With the new Office XP stacked Undo/Redo, you needn't act immediately. You can select the action to undo from the Undo drop-down list. You can delete more than one control by selecting them all, and then pressing DEL.

Original Control	Permitted Conversions
Label	Text box
Text box	Label, list box, combo box
List box	Text box, combo box
Combo box	Text box, list box
Check box	Toggle button, option button
Toggle button	Check box, option button
Option button	Check box, toggle button

Table 10-6. *Permitted Control Conversions*

Adding Other Objects and Special Effects

One of the important aspects of Access is you can add objects created by other applications to a form or report. For example, you can add a chart you created in Excel, a picture from Paint, an image from Photo Editor, or a document from Word, to name just a few.

You can add a picture, a sound clip, or another object either as a bound or unbound object, depending on the purpose of the object. A *bound object* is stored in the underlying record source and changes as you move from record to record. For example, a picture of an employee is stored in each record in the Employees table.

An *unbound object* is part of the design instead of the record source and is stored with the design. It remains the same when you move to a new record in the table. A picture of a company logo in a form header or a letterhead is an example of an unbound object.

Linking vs. Inserting Objects

You have two ways to add an object to your design: inserting or linking. When you *insert* a picture or other object in your form or report design, Access stores a copy of the object in your database where it's always available. You can make changes to an inserted object from Access.

When you *link* to a picture or other object, it remains in its original file and isn't stored in your database. You can make changes to the object file separately and the changes will show in your form or report.

One advantage to linking over inserting is you don't increase the size of your database with large picture files. If the linked object file is moved or renamed, however, you lose the link and must restore it.

Table 10-7 shows examples of uses for bound objects, unbound objects, and images, as well as whether they should be linked or inserted.

Example	Type of Control	How Added
An image that needn't be modified, such as a company logo	Image control	Insert if you have sufficient disk space, otherwise link
A chart from Excel that will change often	Unbound object frame	Link

Table 10-7.   *Examples of Inserted and Linked Controls*

RETRIEVING AND PRESENTING INFORMATION

Example	Type of Control	How Added
A complete description of a construction job	Bound object frame	Link and display as an icon
A Word document that needs to be referenced, but changes little	Unbound object frame	Insert
An employee badge picture	Bound object frame	Insert

Table 10-7.   *Examples of Inserted and Linked Controls* (continued)

The advantage of linking objects is they're updated automatically. Linked objects in reports are updated when the report is previewed or printed. Linked bound objects in forms are updated when the object gets focus in Form view. Linked unbound objects in forms are updated when the form is opened.

When you link an object to a form or report, Access creates an automatic link by default. You can change the links to bound and unbound object frames to manual updating. Remember, if the control is a bound object, you must change the link for every record. Background pictures and pictures in image controls are always updated automatically.

Adding Bound Objects

When you have an OLE Object field in your table, you can add it as a bound object to your form or report. To add the object to the design, drag the field name from the field list to the design. Access creates a bound object frame to contain the field. The frame is part of the design, while the bound object is still part of the underlying record source.

You can add a bound object frame control to the design first using the toolbar, and then bind it to the field by setting the frame's Control Source property to the name of the OLE Object field.

To edit a bound object in a specific record, open the form in Form view and locate the record you want to change. Then go to the Edit menu, point to the corresponding Object command, and click Edit.

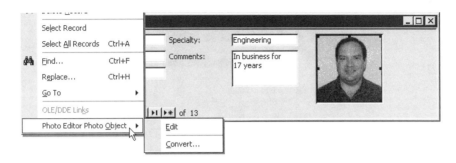

The source application launches where you can make the desired changes to the object.

 If you want to save disk space, choose Convert from the Edit | Object menu instead and check Display As Icon in the Convert dialog box.

Adding an Unbound Object

You can add an existing object to a form or report design, or you can create a new one using the source program from within the Access Design window. To add an unbound object to the design, begin by doing the following:

1. Click the Unbound Object Frame toolbox button and draw an outline of the object in the design. You can also choose Insert | Object after clicking the design. The Insert Object dialog box opens (see Figure 10-18). (Your list may be different.)

2. Choose Create New to build a new object or choose Create From File to choose an existing object.

3. If you chose to create a new object, select the type of object and click OK. The source program in which you can create the object launches. When you finish creating the new object, close the program and you return to Access.

4. If you chose to get the object from a file, a dialog box opens where you can enter the filename including the complete path or click the Browse button to look for the file. Other options in the box include Link, which you check if you want to link to the file instead of embedding a copy. After entering the filename, click OK.

 Another option available to both new and existing objects is Display as Icon, which shows the object as an icon in the form or report, instead of displaying the whole object.

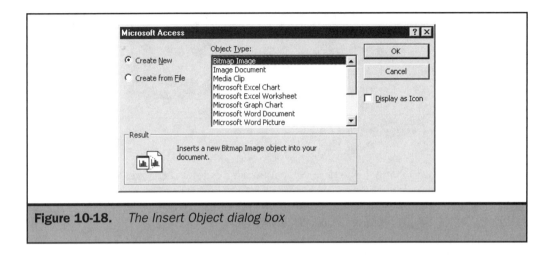

Figure 10-18. *The Insert Object dialog box*

When you finish in the Insert Object dialog box, the object appears in the form or report design. If you want to modify the object later or play the sound in Form view, open the property sheet for the new object and change its Enable property to Yes.

To edit an object in Design view, double-click the object, or right-click and choose *name of source program* Object | Edit from the shortcut menu. You can also select the object and choose Edit | *name of source program* Object | Edit. All these methods launch the source program where you can edit the object.

You can still use the clip art, sounds, and short videos from Microsoft Media Gallery (formerly called Clip Gallery) but there's no longer a jump directly to the Media Gallery from within Access. Notice Microsoft Media Gallery doesn't appear in the Insert Object dialog box list of Object Types. If you want to use clip art in an Access form or report, you need to drag/drop or copy/paste it from the Media Gallery to your destination.

If you're working in the source program, you can use the standard copy-and-paste procedure to insert the object into the Access form or report. Select the object you want to add and copy it to the clipboard. Then switch to Access, click the design where you want the object, and choose Edit | Paste or click Paste.

Adding a Picture

Image controls are used to display pictures or other images. To add a picture to the form or report design, click the Image toolbox button and draw the outline of the picture in the design. You can also choose Insert | Picture. The Insert Picture dialog box opens where you can locate and select the picture you want. If you click the arrow next to the View button in the Insert Picture dialog box and choose Preview, you can see a display of the picture (see Figure 10-19). Once you select the picture, click OK to insert it in the design.

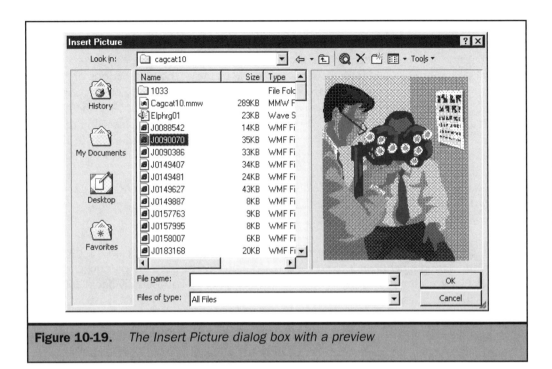

Figure 10-19.   *The Insert Picture dialog box with a preview*

Tip   *If you add an image control by clicking in the design instead of drawing an outline, Access automatically creates a 1-inch square frame. When you add the picture, the frame automatically resizes to fit the picture.*

If you use the Insert menu to add the picture, the form or report design expands to fit the picture. If you created an image control, the picture is limited to the outline you drew and you probably need to enlarge the frame or change the object's Size Mode property.

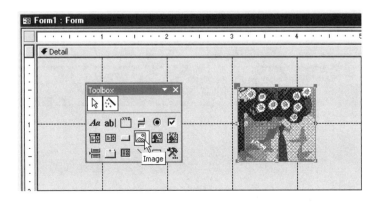

The Size Mode property sets the size of the image with respect to the frame that contains it. The options are Clip, Stretch, and Zoom. The Clip option crops the image to fit the frame, leaving the center portion of the picture in the frame. The Stretch setting sizes the image to fit both dimensions of the frame. If the proportions of the image aren't the same as the frame, the image appears distorted. The Zoom setting sizes the image to fit either the width or the height of the frame, whichever is the more restrictive, and keeps the original relative height and width. The Zoom setting can leave spaces either on both sides, or on the top and bottom of the frame. Figure 10-20 shows examples of each of the Size Mode property settings.

Image controls can also be used to display unbound objects. Image controls load much faster than unbound object frames, so unless you want to update the object, insert it as an image control.

You can also change the background color of an inserted picture from the default transparent setting by choosing from the color palette. To display the palette, click Fill/Back Color on the toolbar or right-click the control and choose Fill/Back Color from the shortcut menu.

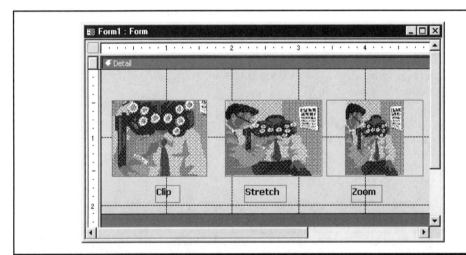

Figure 10-20.   *Size Mode property settings*

When you add a picture to a form or report, the image file is automatically inserted into the database file. If you plan to use the picture in several forms and reports, you can save disk space by linking the picture and storing only one copy of the file. To link a picture you already inserted, change the Picture Type property to Linked.

Changing Pictures

If you change your mind about the picture and want to see a different one, you can delete the control and add another one, or you can simply change the Picture property on the control's property sheet. The Picture property shows the complete path and filename of the picture in the image control. Click the Picture property box, and then click the Build button to open the Insert Picture dialog box. Then choose another picture to replace the first one and click OK.

Bitmap vs. Metafile

You can use either bitmap files (with .bmp or .dib file extensions) or metafiles (with .wmf or .emf file extensions) to add background pictures, pictures in image controls, or bound or unbound frames.

Bitmap files are better if:

- Scaling and disk space aren't a concern.
- You don't have the capability of creating a metafile.
- You want to tile a background picture that doesn't need to be scaled.
- You need to make pixel-level changes to the picture.

Metafiles are better if:

- You need to change the size of the picture. Metafiles scale better because they're composed of lines rather than a pattern of dots.
- Disk space is a concern. A metafile requires less disk space than an equivalent bitmap.

Some graphics programs let you save a file as a metafile. Check the program documentation. You must create the picture in a graphics program. If you paste a bitmap into a graphics program and save it as a metafile, you get a bitmap embedded in a metafile, not a real metafile.

Changing Form and Report Properties

Forms and reports have many properties in common, such as Record Source, Filter, Order By, Width, and several event properties. Each of these can be changed in the object's property sheet and some can also be changed in Design view.

Changing the Record Source

To change a form or report record source, do the following:

1. Click the form or report selector, and then click Properties.
2. Click the Data tab and click the down arrow in the Record Source property box.
3. Choose the new record source from the drop-down list of all tables and queries in the current database.

You can also click the Build button to the right of the Record Source property box to start the Query Builder where you can create a new query to use as the record source.

 When you change the record source, some of the text boxes no longer represent fields in the underlying record source. When you switch to Form or Report view, those text boxes show #Name? because no field exists in the new record source with that name.

Applying Filters and Sort Orders

When you create a form or report based on a table or query with a filter or a specified sort order, both are included in the object's properties. The sort order is automatically applied, but the filter may or may not be, depending on how you created the form or report:

- If you created the form or report from a closed table or query, the filter and sort order are inherited, but not applied. You must apply them when you need them.
- If you created the form or report from an open table or query containing filtered data, the filter is applied every time you open the report, but only the first time you open the form. The next time you open the form, you must apply the filter yourself by clicking Apply Filter.

 If you change the filter in the underlying table or query after the form or report was created, it has no effect on the records in the form or report.

Resizing a Form or Report

You have two ways to change the width of a form or report design: Drag the right border or, for a more precise setting, change the Width property in the Format tab of the property sheet. The height of a report is usually determined by the page setup and the height of a form is usually limited by the screen size.

To change the height of a section in a form or report, drag the section bar below the section you want to change up or down. You can also open the section's property sheet and set the Height property to a more precise measure.

Note *If you created a form that doesn't fill the window, you can resize the Form view window to fit the form. With the form window less than maximized, choose Windows | Size to Fit Form, and then save the form. If the Default View property is set to Single form, the window is cropped to fit one record in the form. If the property is set to Continuous Forms, the form is cropped to remove a partial record at the bottom of the form. If only one record is displayed partially, the window is expanded to show as much of the record as possible. See Chapters 11 and 12 for more information about customizing form properties.*

Using AutoFormat

Access has provided several attractive formats for forms and reports that add style to the design. To apply the style to a form or report under construction or already completed, do the following:

1. Open the object in Design view and click the form or report selector.
2. Click the AutoFormat button or choose Format | AutoFormat.

Figure 10-21 shows the AutoFormat dialog box for forms. The report AutoFormat list of styles is different. The Options button has been clicked in the figure to show you can apply the font, color, and border attributes selectively.

If you click Customize, you open another dialog box where you can do the following: create a new AutoFormat based on the form design you're working on, modify the selected AutoFormat in the AutoFormat dialog box with attributes in the current form design, or delete the selected AutoFormat completely. This last option is handy if you create a custom AutoFormat, and then decide it's no longer useful.

Note *If you want to apply AutoFormat to only one section in the form or report design, click the section selector before you open the AutoFormat dialog box. You can also use AutoFormat for a single control.*

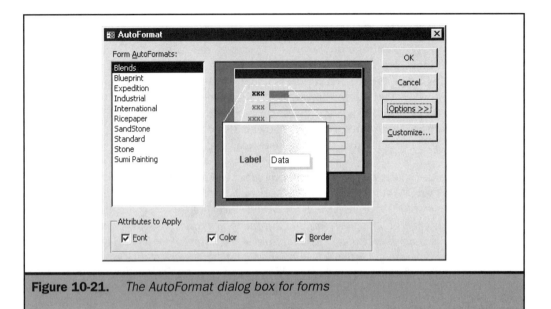

Figure 10-21.   *The AutoFormat dialog box for forms*

Adding a Background Picture

Adding a picture in the background of a form or report is a little different than adding one as a control. A background picture is a property of the form or report, and is found on the Format tab of the form or report property sheet. To add a background picture, do the following:

1. Select the form or report with one of the following methods:

   ■ Click the form selector.

   ■ Choose Edit | Select Form (or Report).

   ■ Choose Form or Report from the Object list on the Formatting toolbar.

2. Then open the property sheet and click in the Picture property box on the Format tab.

3. Click the Build button, select the picture you want from the Insert Picture dialog box, and then click OK.

Figure 10-22 shows the title page of a report with a sketch of a Home Tech Repair worker in the background.

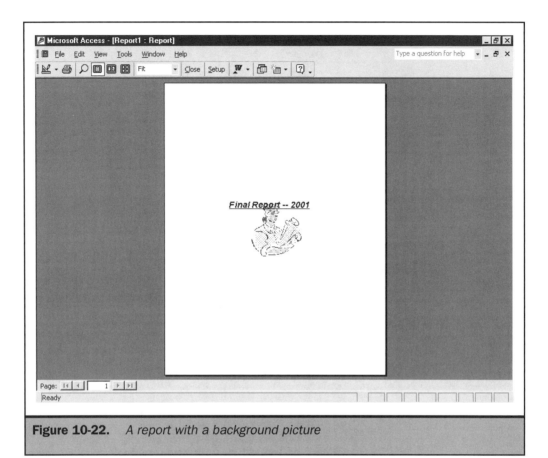

Figure 10-22.   *A report with a background picture*

Changing Front-to-Back Order

In some designs, you may want to overlap controls with one in the foreground and the other behind. The Bring To Front and Send To Back commands on the Format menu determine which of the controls is in the foreground. Figure 10-23 shows a form with an image and some text. In the left example, the text has been placed in back of the image, while in the right example, the text is in front.

To accomplish this, select the control you want in the background and choose Format | Send To Back.

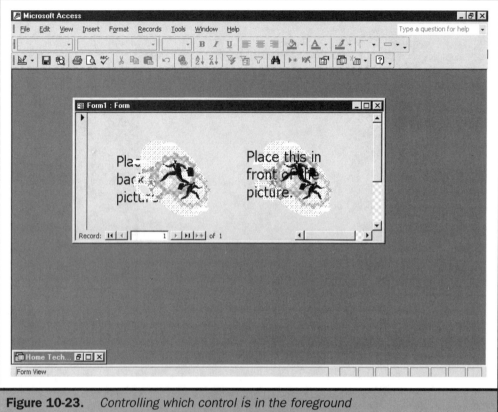

Figure 10-23. *Controlling which control is in the foreground*

Adding a New Object to a Group

If your database is accessed by several people who have different uses for the information, you can group the database objects based on their area of interest. You can use the standard Favorites group that Access provides or create a new group. For example, one group may apply to Workorders and another to Employees.

To add an object to a group, right-click an object name in the Database window and choose Add to Group from the shortcut menu. Choose the group from the list of existing groups.

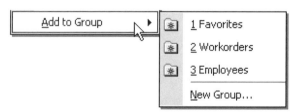

If you want to create a new group, choose New Group instead of the name of an existing group, enter the group name in the New Group dialog box, and then click OK. The object is added to the new group. As you add groups, their names appear under Groups in the Database window.

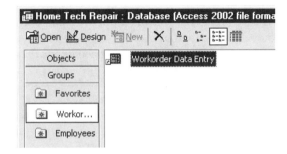

Using AutoForm and AutoReport

When you click the New Object button to use AutoForm and AutoReport, you have no choice of format or style. Both prepare a columnar arrangement of data from a single table. When you click New on the Form page of the Database window, the New Form dialog box gives you five choices of AutoForm style: Columnar, Tabular, Datasheet, PivotTable, and PivotChart.

The New Report dialog box is similar to the New Form dialog box, but has only two options for an AutoReport: Columnar and Tabular. After you create an AutoForm or AutoReport, you can change the appearance by switching to the Design window.

Using a Design as a Template

When you create a form or report without the help of a wizard, Access applies the Normal template to define the characteristics of the design. The template determines all the default property settings for the form or report, including all the sections and controls. For example, by default, a new form doesn't include form or page header and footer sections. You need to add these if you want them.

You can use any existing form or report as the template for a new design. In fact, you can create a form or report for the express purpose of using it as a template. To specify the new template, choose Tools | Options, and then click the Forms/ Reports tab in the Options dialog box. Type the name in the Form template or Report template box.

Changing the template in the Options dialog box doesn't affect any of the existing forms or reports, it affects only the ones you create after changing the template. When you use the template for a new form or report, it only sets the characteristics of the design and doesn't create any controls.

The template options are saved in the workgroup information file, which is where the Options dialog box gets its information. A change in the option setting is applied to any database you open or create.

To use the template you created for one database in another, you need to copy or export the template to the other database.

Summary

With the information in this chapter, you're equipped with all the building blocks you need to create substantial forms and reports. This chapter included instructions for applying the tools Access provides to help with the efforts.

The next chapter discusses the Form Wizard and the way to use it to create impressive forms. This wizard lets you choose the form layout and style. After the wizard is finished, you can make changes in the design to get exactly the effect you want. The following chapter continues with form customization.

MOUS Exam Activities Explored in This Chapter

Level	Activity	Section Title
Core	Create and display forms	Working in the Design Window Using AutoForm and AutoReport
Core	Modify form properties	Modifying Controls Deleting Controls Changing Form and Report Properties

The Complete Reference

Access 2002

Chapter 11

Using the Form Wizard

Armed with the basic information about creating Access forms and reports, now it's time to put the Form Wizard to work. With this wizard, you can create many types of forms for data entry and viewing. Special forms you can build with the wizard include hierarchical forms showing data from two or more related tables, PivotTables and PivotCharts for summarizing data, and a wide variety of other charts that graphically represent table data.

In this chapter, you can see how to use the Form Wizard to create a data entry form based on an existing query. Then the Form Wizard's finished product is modified in a number of ways.

Creating a New Form Design

Access forms are used for viewing and entering data. Designing a form that presents the data so the information is easily understood and data entry is as foolproof as possible is important. While the Access Form Wizard can do all—or most—of the work for you, this wizard only does what you ask. So, it pays to plan ahead and design the form on paper before invoking the wizard.

 If you have data collection forms already in use, you may want to create a replica of the form on the screen to make computerized data entry look familiar to the user.

Designing the Form

The Home Tech Repair production manager wants a form that shows the current work orders with the following information: work order and bid numbers, address, customer's name, supervisor's name, job description, plus all the cost information, including the extended cost that adds the overhead expenses. Although she hasn't specified the arrangement of the data in the form, you should sketch it out and show it to her for approval before starting to create the form. Figure 11-1 shows a rough sketch of the new Current Workorders form.

After reviewing and incorporating the comments returned by the prospective users of the form, you must search for the data you need in the form design.

In Chapter 8, you designed a query that linked the Bid Data and Workorders tables. The query has most of the fields needed in the Current Workorders form and also has two calculated fields: Total Cost and an additional expression that adds 15 percent overhead expenses to the Total Cost value. This query would be a good basis for the new form. If you need to add more fields to the form, you can add them to the query first or add them to the form design after the wizard is finished. If the query is used for

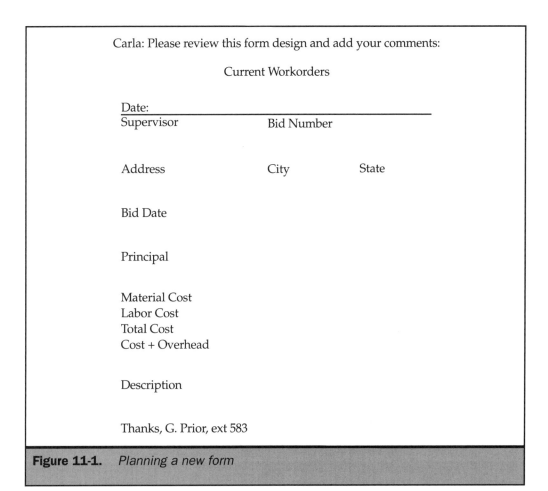

Carla: Please review this form design and add your comments:

Current Workorders

Date:

Supervisor   Bid Number

Address   City   State

Bid Date

Principal

Material Cost
Labor Cost
Total Cost
Cost + Overhead

Description

Thanks, G. Prior, ext 583

Figure 11-1.   *Planning a new form*

other purposes, modifying the form, rather than changing the query design, is better. Figure 11-2 shows the Current Workorders query in Design view.

When you use the Form Wizard, you choose one or more tables or queries as the basis, and then select the fields in the order they are to appear in the form.

Starting a New Form

As discussed in Chapter 10, you can start a new form from a number of places and in a number of ways, many of which lead to the New Form dialog box (see Figure 11-3)

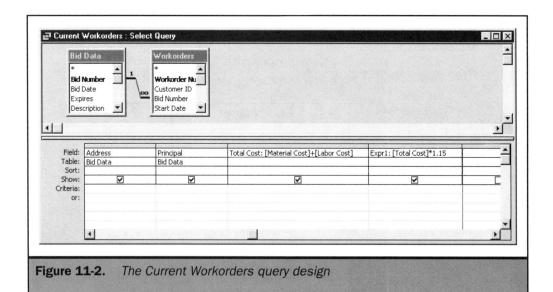

Figure 11-2. *The Current Workorders query design*

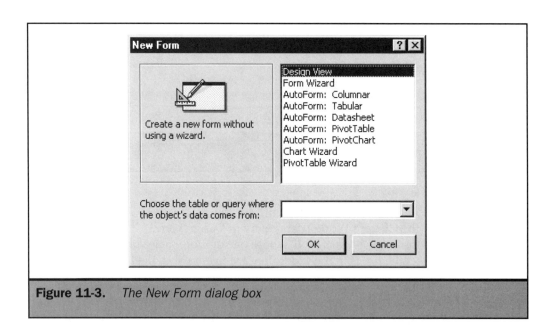

Figure 11-3. *The New Form dialog box*

where you choose the type of form you want to create. To open the New Form dialog box, do one of the following:

■ If you want to base the form on a single table, select the table or query name in the Tables or Queries page of the Database window, click the New Object toolbar button, and then choose Form from the list.

■ To start a new form with a table or query open in Datasheet or Design view, click New Object and choose Form.

If you create a new form while the table or query is open in Design view, you won't be able to see the form in Form view until you close the underlying table or query.

■ Click the Forms button in the Objects bar and choose New.
■ Click anywhere in the Database window and choose Insert | Form.

If you selected a table or query name before opening the dialog box, that name is displayed in the box. If not, you can choose one from the drop-down list or wait and choose one in the wizard's first dialog box. Choose the type of form you want to create or choose one of the wizards to help you out and click OK.

If you choose one of the AutoForm designs or the Chart Wizard, you must choose a table or query to use as the basis before proceeding.

You can also start a new form by double-clicking one of the shortcut items in the Forms page:

■ Create form in Design view
■ Create form by using wizard

The Form Wizard creates forms using one or more tables or queries and displays data from the record source. The Chart Wizard, the PivotTable Wizard, and the PivotChart Wizard build special purpose forms. These are discussed briefly in a later section in this chapter.

Choosing an AutoForm

In the New Form dialog box, you have a choice of AutoForm styles or wizards, in addition to starting with a blank form design. The *AutoForm* choices include the Columnar style, which is the same as the form you see when you click the New Object: AutoForm button. Other AutoForm options in the New Form dialog box include Tabular and Datasheet. Figure 11-4 shows examples of the three most commonly used styles. PivotTable and PivotChart styles are discussed in more detail in Chapter 15.

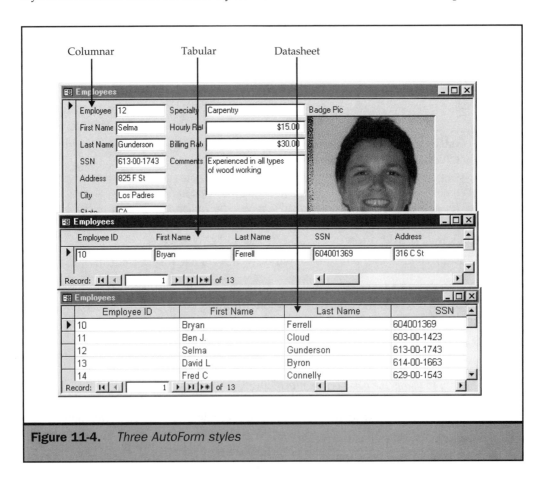

Figure 11-4.   *Three AutoForm styles*

■ The *Columnar* style arranges all the fields on the screen in one or more columns, depending on the number and size of the fields.

■ The *Tabular* style places all the data for one record in a line across the form. If the record has many fields, you must scroll to the right to see them all.

■ The *Datasheet* style is similar to the table Datasheet view. This style is often used for subforms that show data from multiple records related to the record displayed in the main form—for example, details of the work orders (subform) run by a specific supervisor (main form).

■ The *PivotTable* style summarizes and analyzes data in a table, query, or form. You can apply different levels of detail and organize data dynamically by dragging fields and items in the PivotTable.

■ The *PivotChart* style is similar to the PivotTable, except it shows a graphical analysis of the data in a table, query, or form. You use the same means of dragging fields and items in the design.

Choose the AutoForm style you want and click OK, or simply double-click the choice. All the AutoForms arrange the fields in the same order as in the table structure or the query grid. The table or query name appears in the form title bar and the form adopts the most recently used style.

 Note *The new form isn't automatically saved. If you try to close a new form without saving it, Access displays a message prompting you to save the form. If you don't enter a name, Access gives it a default name—Form—followed by a sequential number.*

Selecting the Form Data

When you choose Form Wizard from the New Form dialog box or double-click the shortcut item, the first wizard dialog box opens where you choose the table or query to use as the basis for the new form.

To start a new form design based on the Current Workorders query, do the following:

1. Select the Current Workorders query in the Queries page of the Database window, click the New Object button, and then choose Form.

2. Double-click Form Wizard in the New Form dialog box or select Form Wizard and click OK. The first Form Wizard dialog box opens (see Figure 11-5).

Note *If you haven't selected a table or query either before opening the New Form dialog box or from the list in it, the Form Wizard automatically selects the first table in the alphabetic list of tables and queries. You can change the record source in the first dialog box, if necessary.*

RETRIEVING AND PRESENTING INFORMATION

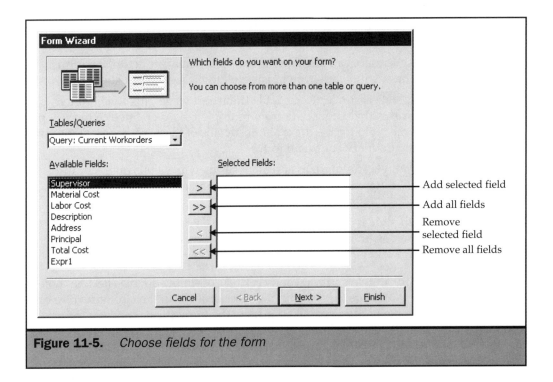

Figure 11-5. *Choose fields for the form*

The Current Workorders query name shows in the Tables/Queries box and the Available Fields list shows all the fields in the query, including the calculated fields. The fields appear in the same order as in the query design grid. To place the desired fields in the Selected Fields list, do any of the following:

- To add all the fields in the Available Fields list, click the double right chevrons.
- To add a single field, double-click the field name or select the field name and click the single right chevron.
- To remove a field, double-click the field in the Selected Fields list or select the field and click the single left chevron.
- To remove them all, click the double left chevrons.

To continue with the Current Workorders form, do the following:

1. Click the double right chevrons to add all the fields from the Current Workorders query to the Selected Fields list.
2. Click Next. The Form Wizard's second dialog box opens.

> **Tip**   *If the fields in the Available Fields list aren't in the order you want to see in the form, choose the fields, one at a time, in the order you want them to appear. You can also insert a field name in the Selected Fields list by selecting the field name above where you want the new one, and then selecting the field from the Available Fields list and clicking the right chevron. Selecting them in the right order in the Form Wizard dialog box saves having to move the controls around in the form design.*

If you select fields from more than one table, the Form Wizard creates a main form with one or more subforms. Creating hierarchical forms is discussed in a later section in this chapter.

Choosing the Form Layout and Style

The second Form Wizard dialog box offers a choice of six form layouts: Columnar, Tabular, Datasheet, Justified, PivotTable, and PivotChart (see Figure 11-6). When you select a layout, a sample appears in the left pane. The first three are the same as the AutoForm layouts shown earlier. The Justified layout resembles the Tabular layout, except all the fields appear on the screen without having to scroll. The row of fields is

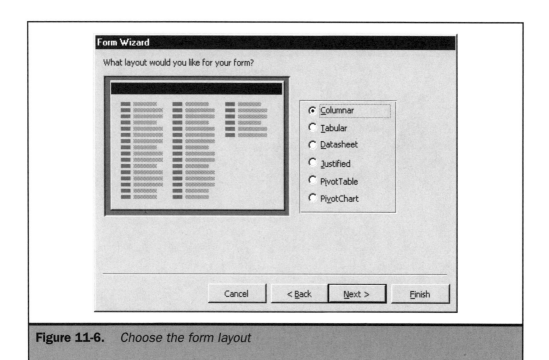

Figure 11-6.   *Choose the form layout*

wrapped to multiple lines, as necessary. The last two arrange the fields as a PivotTable or PivotChart. Select each layout option and look at the preview pane.

For the Current Workorders form, select the Columnar layout and click Next.

When working with any of the Access wizards, you can always click Back and return to the previous dialog box to change a setting. After you click Finish, you cannot return to the wizard to change that design; you must work in the Design window.

After selecting the desired layout, click Next to choose the style. The next dialog box shows a list of ten styles from which to choose. These are the same styles you see when you click the AutoFormat toolbar button, as shown in the previous chapter. Choose a style and click Next to reach the final Form Wizard dialog box (see Figure 11-7).

In this dialog box, you name the form and decide whether to view the data in the new form or to go directly to the Design view to modify the design. After entering the form name, click Finish to save and open the form. Figure 11-8 shows the new form in Form view. Once the wizard is finished, you can go about customizing the form for your special needs. For example, you will want to edit the Expr1 label and rename the control itself.

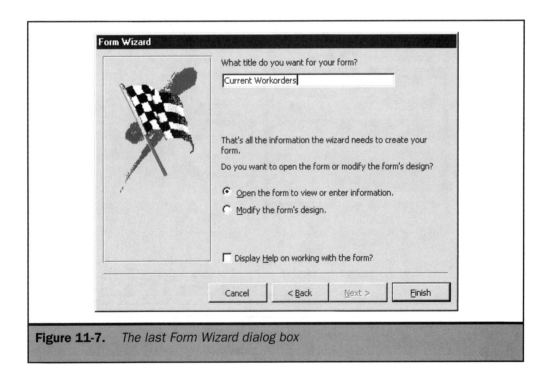

Figure 11-7. *The last Form Wizard dialog box*

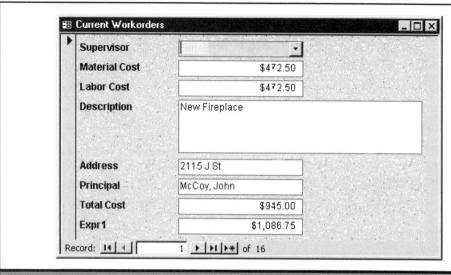

Figure 11-8. *The Current Workorders form*

Tip   *A calculated field created in the query design inherits the format from the fields used in the calculation. So, the Expr1 field automatically includes the currency symbol and two decimal places. If you create the calculated field in the form design using =[Total Cost]*1.15 as the Control Source, the result doesn't inherit the format and is simply a number without the currency symbol.*

What If the Form Is Blank?

When you finish with the Form Wizard, the form opens in Form view unless you have checked Modify the form's design in the final dialog box. If all you see is the style background with no data or field names, one of the following may be to blame:

■ You might have based the form on a table that doesn't contain any data. Open the table and see if it has records.

■ You might have based the form on a query that doesn't return any data. For example, the criteria may be so strict, they exclude all the records. To see if the query returns data, do the following:

1. Switch to Design view and click the form selector.

2. Click the Build button to the right of the Record Source property to open the Query Builder.

3. Click View to run the query.

Other reasons for an empty form aren't likely to occur when you use the Form Wizard, but they may occur when you create a form in Design view. For example:

■ The form might not be bound to any record source. Check the Record Source property in the form property sheet.

■ The form might be in Data Entry mode, in which case a blank record is displayed when you open the form.

■ If you have added a form header or footer section, they may be so big, the detail section doesn't appear on the screen.

More about how to resolve these problems in later sections in this chapter.

Modifying the Form Design

While the Form Wizard does a good job of creating a form, you can do a lot to improve the result. For example, you can

■ Add a form header with a title.

■ Resize the form to fit the window.

■ Resize the window to fit the form.

■ Add special controls, such as the current date.

■ Move, resize, and reformat the controls.

■ Change the text of attached labels.

■ Add lines and rectangles for emphasis.

■ Change the progression of the cursor through the controls when the TAB key is pressed (the tab order).

Before starting to modify the new Current Workorders form, look at the form properties to see how they influence the appearance and behavior of the form.

Looking at the Form Properties

To examine the form properties, double-click the form selector to open the property sheet.

The Format properties control all aspects of the form appearance from the caption in the title bar to the palette source that controls the colors.

The Data properties determine what data is displayed and affect how the form handles the data, including the filter and sort order, and whether to use the form only for data entry.

The Event properties are used to specify what is to happen when the form opens or closes, or when the user does something such as update a record, press a key, or click a command button. Forms have over 30 event properties to which you can attach actions when creating an application. Chapter 18 discusses events and event procedures.

The Other tab includes miscellaneous properties such as Pop Up and Modal, which determine the form's behavior with respect to the rest of the work space. Other properties also specify custom menus and toolbars and add links to custom help topics.

The All tab of the property sheet contains the complete list of form properties.

Table 11-1 describes the form Format properties and shows valid settings where used. Default settings appear in **bold** type.

Property	Description	Settings
Caption	Text to be displayed in the form title bar.	Name entered in the final wizard dialog box or other text entered in the property box.
Default View	Layout of form in Form view.	**Single Form**, Continuous Forms, Datasheet
Allow Form View	Includes Form View in the View menu and View button list.	**Yes,** No
Allow Datasheet View	Includes Datasheet View in the View menu and View button list.	**Yes,** No
Allow PivotTable View	Includes PivotTable View in the View menu and View button list.	**Yes,** No
Allow PivotChart View	Includes PivotChart View in the View menu and View button list.	**Yes,** No
Scroll Bars	Displays scroll bars when not all data fits on the screen.	Horizontal Only, Vertical Only, **Both**
Record Selectors	Displays record selector at the left of the form.	**Yes**/No

Table 11-1.   *Form Format Properties*

Property	Description	Settings
Navigation Buttons	Displays navigation buttons at the bottom of the form.	**Yes**/No
Dividing Lines	Displays lines between records in a continuous form.	**Yes**/No
Auto Resize	Automatically sizes the form to display complete records.	**Yes**/No
Auto Center	Automatically centers the form in the window when the form is opened.	Yes/**No**
Border Style	Sets the type of border and border elements to display.	None, Thin, **Sizable**, Dialog
Control Box	Displays the control box at left end of title bar (if form window isn't maximized) or the menu bar (if maximized).	**Yes**/No
Min Max Buttons	Enables minimize and maximize buttons at the right end of title bar (if not maximized) or in the menu bar (if maximized).	None, Min Enabled, Max Enabled, **Both Enabled**
Close Button	Displays Close button (*X*) in title bar (if not maximized) or the menu bar (if maximized).	**Yes**/No
What's This Button	Adds the What's This button to a form's title bar or menu bar. The Min Max buttons property must be set to None to display the What's This button.	Yes/**No**
Width	Specifies the width of the form.	Derived from the form design or enter a value.
Picture	Specifies a background picture for the form.	Path to file containing picture.
Picture Type	Specifies how the picture is attached.	**Embedded**, Linked

Table 11-1. *Form Format Properties* (continued)

Property	Description	Settings
Picture Size Mode	Determines how the picture appears in the frame.	**Clip**, Stretch, or Zoom
Picture Alignment	Specifies where the background picture is to appear on the form.	Top Left, Top Right, Center, Bottom Left, Bottom Right, **Form Center**
Picture Tiling	Specifies whether multiple copies of a background picture are tiled across the entire form.	Yes/**No**
Grid X	Specifies number of grid dots per inch horizontally in form design.	**24** or enter value
Grid Y	Specifies number of grid dots per inch vertically in form design.	**24** or enter value
Layout for Print	Specifies whether the form uses printer or screen fonts.	Yes (printer fonts)/**No** (screen fonts)
Subdatasheet Height	Sets the default height for expanded subdatasheets.	**1 inch** enter any number of inches.
Subdatasheet Expanded	Automatically expands all subdatasheets.	Yes/**No**
Palette Source	Specifies the color palette for the form.	Enter the path to the palette file. **(Default)**
Orientation	Specifies the visual layout of the form and its controls.	**Left-to-right**, Right-to-left
Movable	Specifies whether the form can be moved.	**Yes**/No

Table 11-1. *Form Format Properties* (continued)

The second tab in the form property sheet contains Data properties that dictate the way data is used in the form. Table 11-2 describes the Data properties. The default settings, if any, appear in bold.

Property	Description	Settings
Record Source	Specifies name of table or query used as basis for form or contains a SQL statement.	Drop-down list shows names of all tables and queries in current database.
Filter	A string expression that defines a subset of records to display when a filter is applied.	Often inherited from the table or query.
Order By	Names of the fields to be used for sorting.	Often inherited from the table or query.
Allow Filter	Specifies whether records can be filtered.	**Yes**/No
Allow Edits	Permits changing existing records.	**Yes**/No
Allow Deletions	Permits removing existing records.	**Yes**/No
Allow Additions	Permits entering new records.	**Yes**/No
Data Entry	Opens the form with a blank record only for data entry. No existing records are displayed.	Yes/**No**
Recordset Type	Determines which type of recordset to use for bound controls and how the user can edit and view data.	**Dynaset**/Dynaset (Inconsistent Updates)/Snapshot
Record Locks	Determines how records are locked when data in a multiuser environment is updated.	**No Locks**/All Records/Edited Record
Commit On Close	Specifies whether edits are saved when the form closes.	**Yes**/No
Fetch Defaults	Specifies whether to retrieve default values.	**Yes**/No

Table 11-2. *Form Data Properties*

Note
To make a form read-only, set the Allow Edits, Allow Deletions, Allow Additions, and Data Entry properties all to No.

Dynasets vs. Snapshots

Dynasets and snapshots are both results of running a query. A *dynaset* is a dynamic subset of records that can be edited, while a *snapshot* is a static subset of records that cannot be edited. Although both of the query result sets contain the same data, they are built differently when you run the query.

Cache memory is a block of high-speed memory in your *random access memory* (*RAM*) that acts as a staging area for data or program statements. Access assumes you will scroll down the screen and want to have data ready to display, so it places the next group of records in cache when you first run the query. This process is called *caching* (pronounced *cashing*).

Both dynasets and snapshots populate the recordset with enough records for the first screen or two, after which, the snapshot continues to populate the recordset by copying and caching the remaining records from the query. A dynaset, however, populates the rest of the result set by retrieving and caching only the primary key values. When the user moves to other records, the dynaset has to perform another query using the cached primary keys to obtain the values in the remaining columns.

Snapshots are better for small queries whose results don't require editing. You can scroll through and retrieve the results from a small snapshot recordset faster than from a dynaset because you have to run the query only once. Dynasets are faster and more efficient for larger result sets because they deal with primary keys, instead of whole records.

The form Recordset property has three settings:

- *Dynaset,* which enables you to edit bound controls based on a single table or one-to-one related tables. You cannot edit controls bound to the join field on the "one" side of a one-to-many relationship unless you have enabled the Cascade Update option in the relationship.

- *Dynaset (Inconsistent Updates),* which enables you to edit all tables and controls bound to their fields.

- *Snapshot,* which prohibits any editing of tables or controls bound to their fields.

Each control in the form also has a Locked property, which you can set selectively to prevent editing of data, rather than globally preventing edits.

The Other tab contains form properties that don't fall into one of the first three categories but, nevertheless, are important in setting the form behavior. Table 11-3 describes the properties on the Other tab. Again, default settings are shown in bold.

Property	Description	Settings
Pop Up	Allows form to remain on top of other forms on the screen. Often used to define floating toolbars and menu bars.	Yes/**No**
Modal	Keeps form on the screen until user closes it. Often used to create custom dialog boxes.	Yes/**No**
Cycle	Specifies what happens when user presses TAB with the cursor in the last control in the tab order of the form: to the first field in the next record, back to the first field in the current record, or back to the first field on the current page.	**All Records**/ Current Record/ Current Page
Menu Bar	Specifies a custom menu bar to display with the form. If left blank, Access displays the built-in menu bar or the application's global menu bar	Name of custom menu bar.
Toolbar	Specifies a custom toolbar to display with the form. If left blank, Access displays the built-in toolbar.	Name of custom toolbar.
Shortcut Menu	Specifies whether to display a shortcut menu when you right-click an object on a form.	**Yes**/No
Shortcut Menu Bar	Specifies a custom shortcut menu that appears when you right-click on the form or on a control on the form. If blank, Access displays the built-in shortcut menu appropriate to the object you right-clicked.	Name of the shortcut menu.
Fast Laser Printing	Specifies whether lines and rectangles are replaced by text character lines similar to the underscore (_) and vertical bar (	) characters to speed up printing a form using most laser printers.	**Yes**/No

Table 11-3. *Form Other Properties*

Property	Description	Settings
Help File	Specifies the name of a custom Help file for the current form.	String expression that contains the path and file name of the help file.
Help Context ID	Specifies the context ID of a topic in the custom Help file specified by the Help File property setting.	Long integer/0
Tag	Stores extra information about a form, such as an identification string.	A string expression up to 2,048 characters long/**zero-length string (" ")**.
Has Module	Specifies whether the form has a class module associated with it. Setting this to No speeds up loading the form and reduces storage requirements.	Yes/**No**
Allow Design Changes	Specifies whether design changes can be made only from Design view or from any view. If set to All Views, a property sheet remains on the screen when you switch to Form or Datasheet view.	Design View Only, **All Views**

Table 11-3.   *Form Other Properties* (continued)

RETRIEVING AND PRESENTING INFORMATION

Changing Form Sections

Access forms can contain several sections:

- The *detail section* contains the record data. You can show data from one record in the detail section or as many records as can fit on the screen.

- The *form header section* contains information to show at the top of the screen for every record—for example, a title, instructions, or command buttons that open another form or print the current form. The information is printed at the top of the first page.

- The *form footer section* contains information to show at the bottom of the screen for every record and at the bottom of the last page of the printed form.

- The *page header section* contains information such as a title, graphics, or column headings that appear at the top of each page when the form is printed or previewed. This section isn't visible in Form view.

- The *page footer section* contains information that appears at the bottom of each page when the form is printed or previewed. This section isn't visible in Form view.

Adding Form Header and Footer Sections

By default, a form created by the wizard from a single table or query has only one section: the detail section. You can also add form header and footer sections to contain information that appears at the top and bottom of the form. This information remains on the screen as you scroll through records in the detail section.

To add a header section to the Current Workorders form, open the form in Design view and choose View | Form Header/Footer. A thin form header section appears above the detail section. If you scroll down the form design, you also see the footer section. To increase the size of the form header section, move the mouse pointer to the detail section bar. When the pointer changes to a black plus sign (+) with up and down arrows, click-and-drag the bar down.

To add a title to the form, do the following:

1. Open the toolbox, click the Label control button, and then draw a frame in the form header section.

2. Type **Current Workorders** in the new label.

3. Click outside the label control, and then click it again to select it.

4. Using the Formatting toolbar, change the font size to 18, and make it bold and centered.

5. Right-click the label and choose Size | To Fit from the shortcut menu, or choose Format | Size | To Fit. The label box frame shrinks to the size of the text in it.

Figure 11-9 shows the Current Workorders form design with a title in the new header section.

When you check Form Header/Footer in the View menu, both sections are added to the form design. If you don't have information to put in the footer and you don't want the section to take up room in the form, you can drag the bottom form border up to reduce the footer section space to zero.

Changing Section Properties

All the sections in a form have the same properties. Double-click one of the section selectors to open the property sheet for the section. The sheet shows fewer properties than the form itself. Most of the section properties apply to formatting. There are no

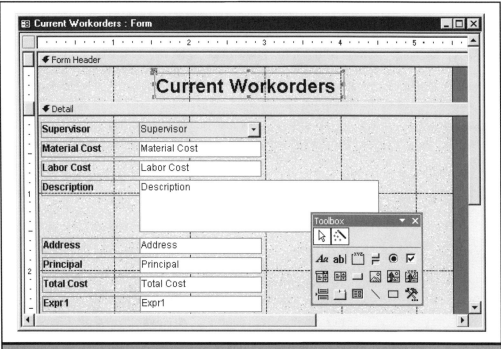

Figure 11-9.   *Adding a title to the form header section*

Data properties and only five Event properties for form sections. Table 11-4 describes the section Format and Other properties. The default settings appear in bold.

Page header and footer sections have fewer properties because the information in them doesn't appear in Form view; it only appears when the form is printed. You can set the height, color, and any special effect for the page sections.

Note   *The header and footer sections needn't have the same properties.*

Moving and Adding Controls

The wizard places controls in the form in a straightforward way according to the layout you choose in the dialog box, not always in the most logical arrangement. When the wizard is through, you almost always need to move some controls around and resize some that display short values to reduce empty space and add more controls. If the query didn't have all the fields you want in the form, now is the time to add them to the record source.

Property	Description	Settings
Force New Page	Starts printing on a new page, rather than on the current page before and/or after printing this section.	**None**/Before Section/After Section/Before & After
New Row Or Col	Starts printing in a new row or column within a multiple-column form before and/or after printing this section.	**None**/Before Section/After Section/Before & After
Keep Together	Applies only to group sections in reports; not used with forms.	Yes/**No**
Visible	Shows or hides a form section or control. Useful when you want to keep information confidential.	**Yes**/No
Display When	Specifies whether the section is to be displayed on screen and/or in print. Applies only to the detail, form header, and form footer sections.	**Always**/Print Only/Screen Only
Can Grow	Allows a section automatically to expand vertically to print or preview all the data in the section. Doesn't apply to page header or footer sections.	Yes/**No**
Can Shrink	Allows a section automatically to reduce vertically to print or preview the data in the section with no empty space. Doesn't apply to page header and footer sections.	Yes/**No**
Height	Specifies the height of the section.	Number in inches

Table 11-4. *Form Section Properties*

Property	Description	Settings
Back Color	The color used to fill a control or section's interior.	A numeric expression that corresponds to the background color.
Special Effect	Specifies a special effect for the section.	**Flat**/Raised/Sunken
Name	An identifier for the section: either default or custom.	Name of section (FormHeader, and so forth)
Tag	Stores extra information about a form, such as an identification string.	A string expression up to 2,048 characters long/ **zero-length string (" ")**

Table 11-4. *Form Section Properties* (continued)

In the next paragraphs, you see how to modify the form by changing and adding controls, including the current date. Refer to Chapter 10 if you need to review how to select controls, and how to use the moving and sizing handles.

Moving and Resizing Controls

With the Current Workorders form in Design view, rearrange the text boxes so the Address and Principal fields are below the Supervisor field, leaving some space below the Principal text box. Then drag the Description text box to the right side of the form next to Labor Cost. Resize the Description text box, so it's more square and fits in the space.

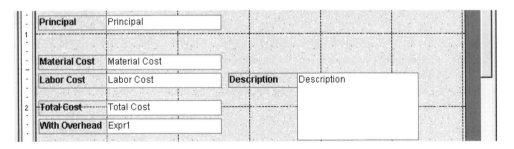

Note *When you are moving a control past other controls, you can drag it right over the other controls without interfering with them.*

Modifying a Label

The calculated field that added 15 percent overhead to the total cost amount needs a little work. If you didn't rename the field in the query design grid, the label would still say Expr1, the name given the field in the query. Use one of the following ways to change the text in the label to **With Overhead**:

- Double-click the label and edit the text.
- Select the label and enter the new text in the Caption property in the Format tab.

Adding New Controls

The Current Workorders query doesn't have all the fields you want to see in the Current Workorders form. To add more bound text box controls, change the form's Record Source property and include the additional fields.

 If you're planning to use a form for data entry, be sure the design includes all the required fields and that you set the same validation rules in the form as in the tables.

To add more fields from the related tables used in the query, open the form in Design view and do the following:

1. If the property sheet is already visible, click the form selector or select Form from the drop-down list. If not, double-click the form selector to open it.

2. Click in the Record Source property box on the Data tab, and then click the Build button. This starts the Query Builder, which looks much like the query design grid (see Figure 11-10) except for the words "Query Builder" in the title bar.

3. Hold down CTRL while you select the Bid Number, City, and State fields in the Bid Data field list, and then drag the group to the grid. The position in the grid is unimportant right now.

4. Click Save, and then click the Close button to return to the form design.

 If you try to close the Query Builder without saving the changes, Access prompts you to save.

The additional fields are now available to the form and the field list is displayed. You can add fields to the form in two ways:

- The quickest way is to drag the fields from the field list to the form design.
- You can also add a new bound text box control for each of the fields and set the control source to the field you want to add.

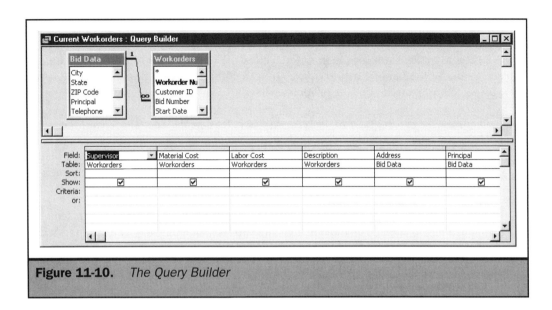

Figure 11-10.   *The Query Builder*

Follow the next steps to complete the addition of the Bid Number, City, and State fields:

1. Select Bid Number in the field list and drag it to the four-inch mark on the horizontal ruler in line with the Supervisor field.

2. Select the City field and drag it to a position in the design below the Bid Number field, and then drag the State field next to the City field.

3. Resize the City and State labels to fit the text, and then resize the State text box because it will contain only two characters. Move the State text box next to its attached label.

4. To make the three address fields all the same height, click the vertical ruler level with the row of text boxes to select all three and choose Format | Size | To Tallest.

5. Now align them by choosing Format | Align | Top while they're still selected.

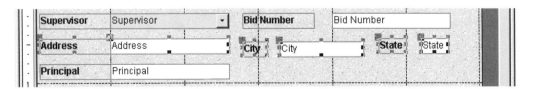

You can also add a line to separate the material and labor cost from the calculated fields that show the total and extended costs. First, move the two calculated fields down a little to make room for the line. Then click the Line control button and draw a line across under the Labor Cost text box. You can change the line thickness, style, and color by selecting from the Border properties lists.

Don't use the vertical ruler to select the two calculated fields. You'll also select the Description text box.

The last control to add to the Current Workorders form is the current date, which appears in the form header section. To add the date, do the following:

1. Choose Insert | Date and Time. The Date and Time dialog box appears (see Figure 11-11). The Date and Time command may be included in the expanded Insert menu.

2. Check Include Date (if not already checked) and select the middle date format (Medium Date), which displays dates as dd-mmm-yy.

3. Clear the Include Time check box and click OK. The expression = *Date()* appears in the upper-left corner of the form header section.

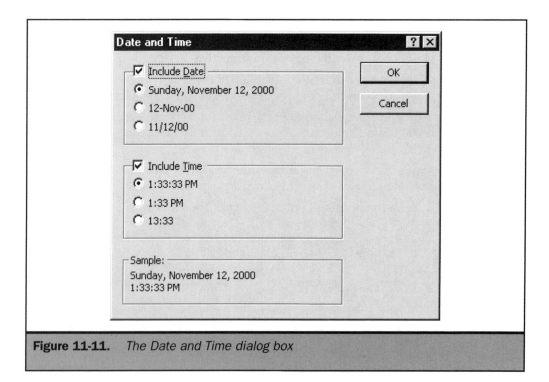

Figure 11-11.   *The Date and Time dialog box*

4. Drag the date control down to just above the detail section bar.

Figure 11-12 shows the completed Current Workorders form design and Figure 11-13 shows the form in Form view.

When you switch to Form view, choose Window | Size to Fit Form to resize the window. This works only if the form Design view wasn't maximized.

Sorting and Filtering Data in a Form

Once you're viewing data in the form, you can filter the records just as in a datasheet: use Filter By Selection, Filter By Form, Filter For Input, or Advanced Filter/Sort to limit the records. To sort records in the form, place the cursor in the field you want to sort on and click one of the Sort buttons. You can also enter filter and sort expressions in the form's property sheet.

If the form is based on a table or query that already has a sort order or filter saved with it, the form inherits both properties. A sort order is automatically applied to the

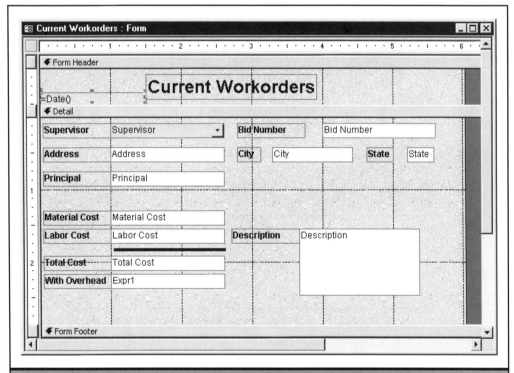

Figure 11-12.   *The completed Current Workorders form design*

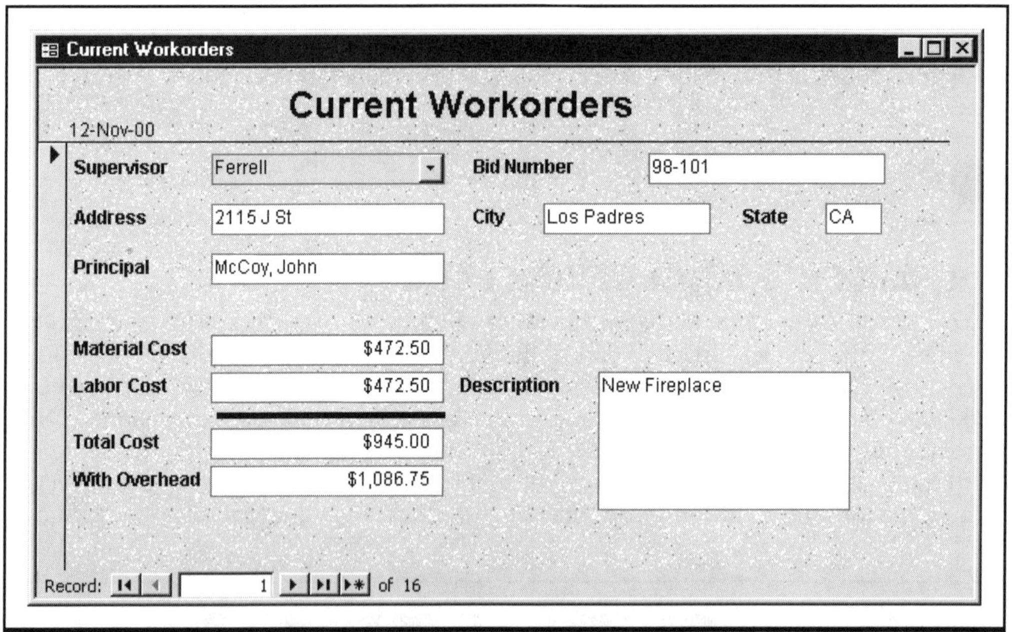

Current Workorders

Current Workorders

12-Nov-00

Supervisor	Ferrell
Address	2115 J St
Principal	McCoy, John

Bid Number 98-101

City Los Padres   **State** CA

Material Cost $472.50

Labor Cost $472.50   **Description** New Fireplace

Total Cost $945.00

With Overhead $1,086.75

Record: 1 of 16

Figure 11-13. *The Current Workorders form in Form view*

records in the form. Whether the filter is automatically applied to the records in the form depends on the status of the table or query when you created the form.

- If the table or query was open and the filter applied when you created the form, the filter is automatically applied to the records in the form. The word "(Filtered)" appears to the right of the navigation buttons at the bottom of the form and "FLTR" appears in the status bar to remind you of the filter. To remove the filter, click the Remove Filter button, which appears pressed in when a filter is applied, or choose Records | Remove Filter/Sort.

Record: 1 of 4 (Filtered)

- If the table or query was closed and saved with the filter, the filter is inherited by the form, but isn't automatically applied. Click the Apply Filter button or choose Records | Apply Filter/Sort.

If you construct and apply a different filter or sort order, the new property replaces the one inherited from the underlying table or query.

To disable all filtering of records in the form, set the Allow Filters property to No. This disables the Filter By Selection, Filter By Form, Filter For Input, and Advanced Filter/Sort.

Using the Form

Forms are the principal user interface with the database information. You can view all the data, search for specific records, enter new records, and edit existing records. To accomplish these tasks efficiently, you must know how to get around in the form and how to move through the records in Form view.

To open a form in Form view where you can view and edit data, double-click the form name in the Forms page of the Database window or select the form name and click Open. In Form view, you can add a new record by clicking the New Record button to show a blank form. You can also edit existing records using the navigation tools or the Edit menu.

To open a form in Design view where you can modify the design, select the form name and click Design.

You can also right-click the form name in the Database window and choose Open (to open in Form view) or Design view from the shortcut menu.

The Form view toolbar buttons are the same as in Datasheet view. The View button has five options: Design view, Form view, Datasheet view, PivotTable view, and PivotChart view. When you view the form that includes a subform in Datasheet view, you can see the related records from the subform by clicking the expansion symbol (+) next to the record row. The View menu has the same five commands.

Sizing the Form

If you created a form that doesn't fill the screen, you can adjust the form window to fit the form. In Design view, drag the form boundaries in to fit the contents of the form, and then switch to Form view and do the following:

1. If the form window is maximized, click the Resize button in the title bar to reduce it.
2. Choose Window | Size To Fit Form. Access adjusts the window around the form boundaries.
3. Click Save to save the new form size.

If the form's Default View property is set to Single Form, the window is cropped or expanded to fit the displayed record. If a single record is too large for the screen, Access expands the window to display as much of the record as possible.

If the Default View is set to Continuous Forms, Access crops any partial record showing at the bottom of the screen. If only one record fits in the window, Access expands the form window to display as much of the record as possible.

In the following discussion, the terms cursor *and* insertion point *are used interchangeably. Both indicate a control has focus. Insertion point is often used to refer to the blinking vertical bar that appears in text during edit mode. Cursor and focus are more general terms, but they basically mean the same thing.*

Navigating in the Form

As with datasheets, you can operate in two different modes in a form: navigation and editing. In Navigation mode, the cursor moves to other fields; in Editing mode, it moves among characters in a field. The keypresses have different consequences, depending on the current mode. For example, in Editing mode, pressing RIGHT ARROW moves the insertion point one character to the right. In Navigation mode, it moves the cursor to the next field and usually selects the value.

To change modes, do the following:

■ To switch from Editing mode to Navigation mode, press F2 or click in a field label. You can also press TAB or SHIFT-TAB to leave Editing mode and move to another field.

■ To switch from Navigation mode to Editing mode, press F2 or click the text box.

Clicking the navigation buttons at the bottom of the form moves the cursor to the first, previous, next, or last record in the recordset. You can enter a specific record number to move to that record. Choosing from the Edit | Go To menu also moves the cursor to other records. These methods move the cursor to the same field in another record.

Table 11-5 describes the keystrokes you can use to navigate through records and fields in a form.

Destination	Keystrokes
First field of first record	CTRL-HOME
First field of current record	HOME
Last field of current record or the first record in the current record's subform	END
Last field of last record or the first record of the last record's subform	CTRL-END
Current field in next record	CTRL-PGDN
Current field in previous record	CTRL-PGUP
Next field	TAB or RIGHT ARROW

Table 11-5. *Navigating with Keystrokes*

Destination	Keystrokes
Previous field	SHIFT-TAB or LEFT ARROW
Specific record	F5, enter record number, and press ENTER
Previous record or page	PGUP
Next record or page	PGDN

Table 11-5. *Navigating with Keystrokes* (continued)

Note *You recall the options set in the Keyboard tab of the Options dialog box affect the behavior of the* TAB, ENTER, *and* ARROW KEYS. *If you change their default settings, some of the keystrokes in these tables may behave differently.*

When you're in editing mode, you need to move around in the field data and insert or delete characters. Many of the same keys are used, but with different results. Table 11-6 describes the effects of the navigating and editing keystrokes while in editing mode.

To Do This	Press This
Move to start of field	HOME or CTRL-HOME if in a multiple-line field
Move to the end of the field	END or CTRL-END if in a multiple-line field
Move one word left or right	CTRL-LEFT ARROW or RIGHT ARROW
Move one character left or right	LEFT ARROW or RIGHT ARROW
Delete one character left of insertion point	BACKSPACE
Delete one character right of insertion point	DEL
Delete several characters	Select characters and press DEL
Delete to the end of the word	CTRL-DEL

Table 11-6. *Editing Field Data with Keystrokes*

To Do This	Press This
Delete to the beginning of the word	CTRL-BACKSPACE
Replace value with default value for field	CTRL-ALT-SPACEBAR
Insert new line	CTRL-ENTER
Insert current system date	CTRL-; (semicolon)
Insert current system time	CTRL-: (colon)
Copy value from same field in previous record	CTRL-' or CTRL-"

Table 11-6. *Editing Field Data with Keystrokes* (continued)

Changing the Tab Order

Each time you press TAB in Form view, the cursor moves to another field. The progression of the cursor through the fields in the form is called the *tab order*. Each text box control is assigned a tab index number indicating its position in the sequence. The first control in the order has 0 as the tab index number, the second has 1, and so on. Access sets the tab order to match the order in which the fields were added to the design.

If you open the Current Workorders form in Form view and press TAB a number of times, you see the order isn't logical. The tab order reflects the way the fields were originally positioned in the query grid. Some of the fields have been moved in the design and the tab order doesn't automatically change to match. The three fields added later are at the end of the tab order.

To change the tab order so the cursor moves more logically through the records, do the following:

1. Open the form in Design view and click the detail section.

2. Choose View | Tab Order. The Tab Order dialog box (see Figure 11-14) opens showing a list of all the text box controls in the detail section.

3. To reposition a control, click the row selector, move the mouse pointer to the row selector, and then drag the row to a new position. You can also select a group of rows and reposition them as a group.

4. Repeat step 3 until you have the order the way you want it, and then click OK.

 Clicking the Auto Order button in the Tab Order dialog box rearranges the controls in order from left-to-right and top-to-bottom. If this is the way you want the cursor to move through the fields, click Auto Order instead of moving the controls by hand.

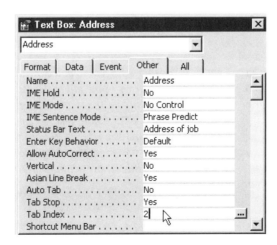

Figure 11-14.   *The Tab Order dialog box*

When you change the tab order in the form design, Access rearranges the fields in the form's Datasheet view to match.

Text box controls have three properties that involve the tab order:

■ Tab Stop, which you can set to No to keep the cursor from reaching the field by means of pressing TAB. You can still select the field for editing; it just isn't part of the tab order.

■ AutoTab, which when set to Yes, automatically moves the cursor to the next field in the tab order when the last character permitted by an input mask is entered.

■ Tab Index, which indicates the control's position in the order, beginning with 0. For example, if you choose Auto Order in the Tab Order dialog box, the third control in the order, Address, has a tab index of 2.

Locating Records

Searching for specific records by examining the value in one or more fields is the same in a form as in a datasheet. You use the same Find and Replace dialog box to specify the search string and the scope of the match, part or all of the field.

To display a specific record in the form, place the insertion point in the field you want to look for and click Find, or choose Edit | Find. If you want to replace the current field value with another, choose Edit | Replace, or click the Replace tab in the Find and Replace dialog box. Refer to Chapter 6 for more information about using Find and Replace.

Viewing Multiple Records

If you want to see more than one record on the screen, you can switch to the form's Datasheet view or change the form's Default View property from Single Form to Continuous Forms. When you choose Form view from the View button or from the View menu, the form appears with as many records as can fit on the screen.

Home Tech Repair uses a form named Roster as a quick way to look up employees. When the Roster form is set to Single Form, only one record appears on the screen, as the following shows. The Form view window has been resized to fit the form by choosing Window | Size to Fit Form.

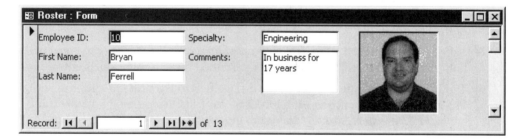

Figure 11-15 shows the same Roster form with the Default view set to Continuous Forms.

When you use the scroll bar to move through records in a continuous form view, Access always makes sure a complete record appears at the top of the screen, while only a partial record may appear at the bottom, depending on the size of a single record. Using PGUP and PGDN causes the previous or next set of whole records to appear onscreen. For example, in the Roster form, only four complete records are visible at once with a partial record at the bottom of the screen. When you press PGDN, the partial record moves to the top where it appears in its entirety with three more complete records below it and another partial record at the bottom.

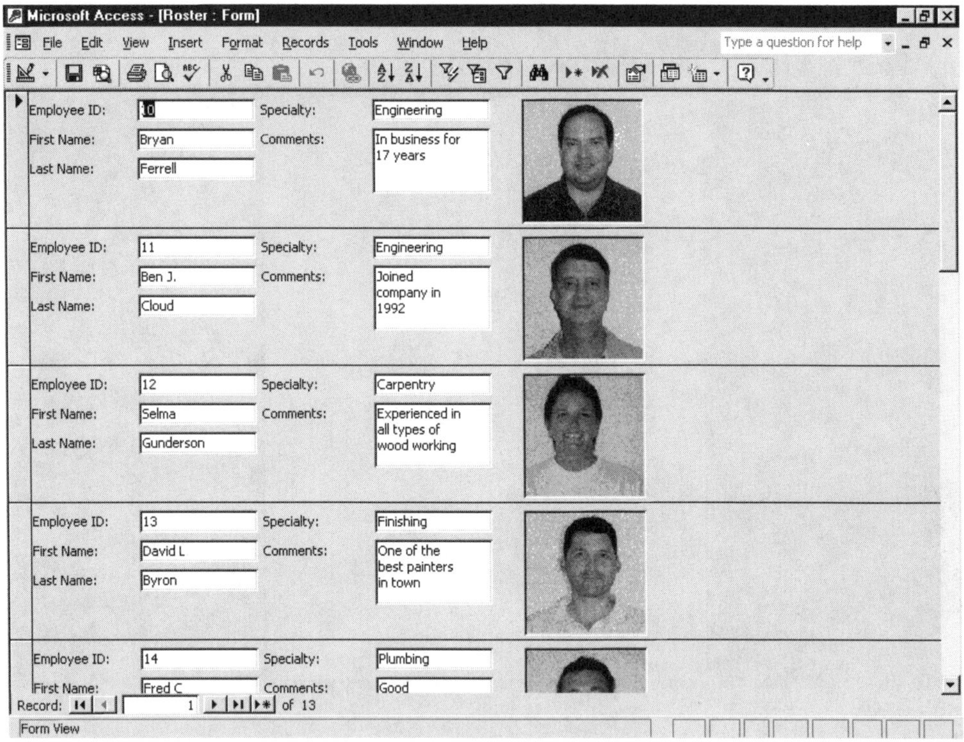

Figure 11-15.   *The Roster continuous form*

Printing the Form

Although forms are used mostly for data viewing, entering, and editing, you can also preview and print the form. Click the Print Preview button to see how the form will look when printed. Figure 11-16 shows a preview of the Roster form. See Chapter 13 for information about setting printing options and running the page setup for special print jobs.

Looking at the Other Wizards

Two other wizards are available from the New Form dialog box: the Chart Wizard and the PivotTable Wizard. The Chart Wizard converts data in your tables into a variety of

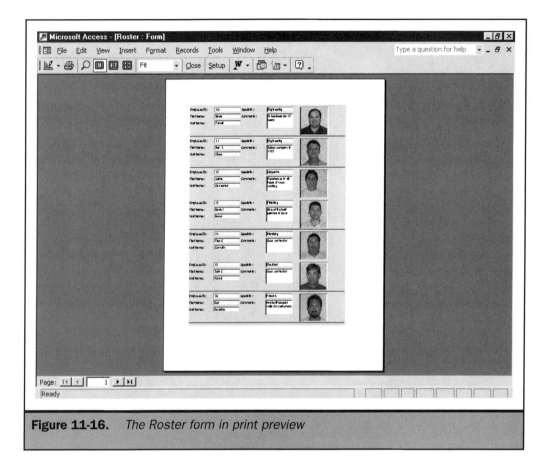

Figure 11-16. *The Roster form in print preview*

charts, including bar charts, pie charts, and line graphs. If you want to illustrate trends over a period of time, you use a bar chart or a line graph. If you want to show relative frequencies or other proportions, use a pie chart. Figure 11-17 shows a pie chart based on the Home Tech Repair Workorders table that illustrates the percent of jobs started in each month.

Note *You must have Microsoft Graph installed to use the Chart Wizard.*

The chart has been added to a blank form as an OLE Unbound object frame by the Chart Wizard. To make changes to the chart, such as exploding the pie, as shown in Figure 11-17, or adding captions to the pie wedges, use the Microsoft Graph applet. To launch it, switch the form to Design view and double-click the chart.

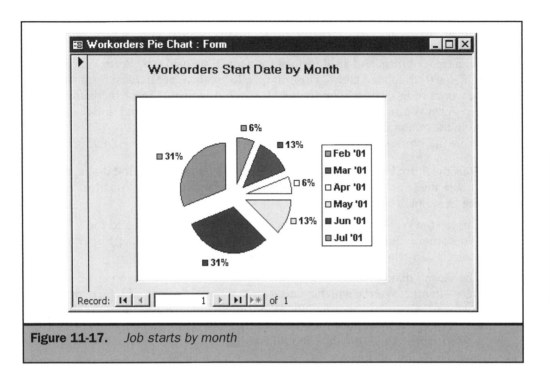

Figure 11-17.   *Job starts by month*

Note   *The colors in the pie chart don't show up in the figure, but the legend refers to the wedges starting at 12 o'clock and moving clockwise: 6 percent started in Feb '01, 13 percent in March '01, 6 percent in April, 13 percent in May, and so on.*

The PivotTable Wizard takes large amounts of data from your tables and summarizes it in rows and columns in a similar, but more flexible, way to crosstab queries. You need to have Excel installed to modify PivotTables created by the wizard.

Chapter 15 contains more information about creating visual form and report elements containing charts, graphs, PivotTables, and PivotCharts.

Creating a Hierarchical Form from Related Tables

A *hierarchical form* usually consists of a main form and one or more subforms. The main form shows data from records on the "one" side of a one-to-many relationship and the subforms show data from records on the "many" side.

If your main form has many controls and no room exists for a subform, you can link the forms instead. When you click a command button in one form, it opens the other form showing data that's synchronized with the record in the first, much like clicking the subdatasheet expansion button in Datasheet view.

You can create a form and a subform at the same time using the Form Wizard by choosing fields from related tables. For example, to create a hierarchical form showing the list of work orders currently under way for each customer, choose fields from both tables. The Form Wizard can determine how the tables are related and decide which data goes in the main form and which goes in the subform.

To create the Workorders By Customer hierarchical form, do the following:

1. Start the Form Wizard with the Customers table and, in the first dialog box, choose the Customer ID, First Name, Last Name, and Billing Address from the Customers table.

2. Choose the Workorders Table in the Tables/Queries list and add the Workorder Number, Bid Number, Start Date, Completion Date, Supervisor, Material Cost, and Labor Cost fields. Then click Next.

The second dialog box (see Figure 11-18) asks how you want to view the data—in other words, which records go in the main form and which in the subform? Access has assumed the Workorders data (on the "many" side of the relationship) goes in the subform. The other two options in the dialog box let you specify whether the data should be arranged as a form with a subform or as separate, linked forms.

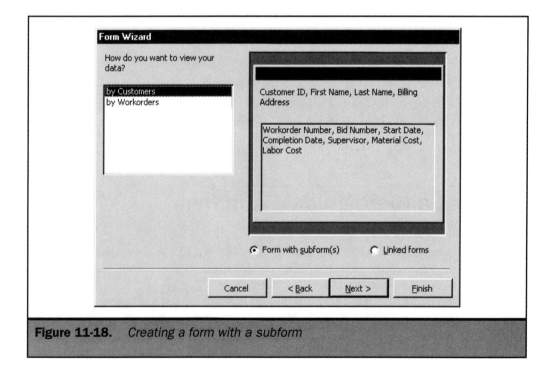

Figure 11-18. *Creating a form with a subform*

3. Accept the default options and click Next. The next dialog box offers four layouts for the subform: Tabular, Datasheet, PivotTable, or PivotChart. Choose Datasheet and click Next.

4. Choose the style for the form in the next dialog box and go on to the final box, in which you name the form and the subform, and then choose to view the form or open the form in Design view.

5. Enter the name Workorders by Customer Form for the main form and leave the default name for the subform. Then click Finish.

Figure 11-19 shows the completed hierarchical form with a few modifications, such as a title in the form header. The columns in the subform have also been resized to fit the screen. You can modify the subform in place. To modify the subform design, open the main form in Design view and click the subform selector or any of the controls in the subform. Modify the subform and its controls the same as in the main form.

You can also add a new or an existing form as a subform within another form by using the Subform/Subreport Control Wizard.

See the next chapter for more information about creating subforms and linking forms to see related information.

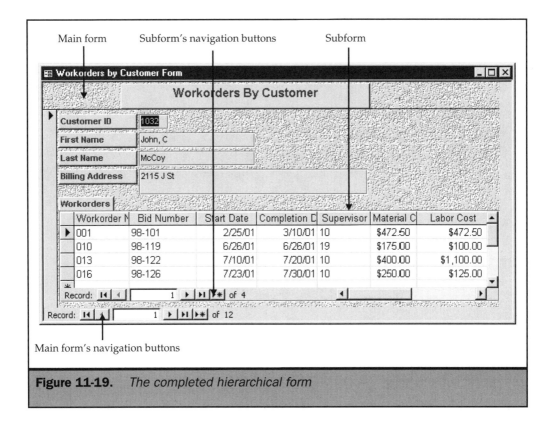

Figure 11-19.   *The completed hierarchical form*

Summary

You have seen in this chapter how helpful the Form Wizard can be when you want to create a form. More wizards can help construct the perfect form. Control Wizards can help when you want to add combo boxes, list boxes, option groups, and command buttons. In the next chapter, you see how to use these tools in new forms.

When you use Access, you see pop-up forms that prompt for user action, such as dialog boxes where you make choices about what to do next. In the next chapter, you see how to create your own custom dialog boxes and other special types of forms, such as switchboards, for user interaction.

MOUS Exam Activities Explored in This Chapter

Level	Activity	Section Title
Core	Navigate among records	Navigating in the Form
Core	Modify form properties	Modifying the Form Design
Core	Enter, edit, delete records	Using the Form
Expert	Add subform controls to Access forms	Creating a Hierarchical Form from Related Tables

The
Complete
Reference

Access
2002

Chapter 12

Customizing Forms

With all the building blocks at your disposal, including the help of the Form Wizard, you're ready to explore some of the ways you can make forms more flexible and practical. This chapter offers constructive ideas for creating custom forms. You can add special controls to a form that help with data entry, print records, or open another related form to see additional information. Access provides tools that help you add command buttons to perform specific actions, as well as improve data entry accuracy and validity.

This chapter continues with examples from the Home Tech Repair database and also introduces you to a real-life, operational database-management system in use by local law enforcement personnel. The Police database referred to later in the chapter is primarily user interactive and demonstrates some of the special applications of Access forms.

The forms created in this chapter are based on tables or queries. In Chapter 21, you complete the form scenario by learning how to create forms with no underlying data—forms that open automatically and offer a list of actions you can take. In Chapter 24, you see how to create data access pages, which are dynamic forms for displaying Access information as a Web page.

Starting a New Custom Form

When you start a new custom form without the help of the Form Wizard or one of the AutoForm templates, you begin with an empty Design view window. If you chose a table or query in the New Form dialog box to use as the basis for the form, you can display the field list and drag the fields into the form design. If you haven't already chosen the basis for the form, you can define it in Design view by selecting the table or query from the form's Record Source property list.

No law says you have to base a form on data. You can create a form that displays courses of action from which to choose or one that simply displays a welcoming screen, which times out after a few seconds. The first sections of this chapter dwell on forms that contain data, while later sections discuss special-purpose forms.

Placing and Customizing Data-Related Controls

In the last chapter, you saw how to add bound text box controls to a form design by dragging the field names from the field list. In addition to the text box controls in which you enter and edit data, list and combo boxes enable you to choose from a list of values. List boxes limit your choice to values in the list, but combo boxes usually let you type entries, as well as choose from the list. Either of these can be bound or unbound. If *bound*, the selected or entered value is stored in the field to which it's bound. If *unbound*, the value isn't stored in a table, but can be used by another control or as a search criterion.

Creating List and Combo Boxes

Selecting a value from a list is often quicker and safer than trying to remember the correct value to type. Because list and combo boxes are similar, how do you decide which type of control to use in the form?

- The values in a list box are always visible and you're limited to the values in the list. To choose from the list, click the entry and press ENTER or TAB. You can also choose one of the values by typing the first letter of the value and pressing ENTER or TAB. (If you have more than one value starting with the same letter, the first one is selected.) You cannot enter a value that isn't on the list. List boxes are best when you're limited to only a few values because, otherwise, the list box takes up valuable viewing space.

- The values in a combo box aren't displayed until you click the arrow to open it, so these values take up less room on the screen than a list box. Like the list box, you can select one of the values by clicking it or by typing the first few characters of the value into the text box area of the combo box. If the Auto Expand property is set to Yes, the default setting, Access automatically fills in the rest of the value. In addition, you can type in values that aren't in the list unless you set the combo box Limit To List property to Yes.

Note
When the characters you type match the first few characters in one of the values, the combo box Auto Expand property specifies whether Access automatically fills in the text box portion of the combo box with a value from the underlying list. As you type, Access displays the first value in the list that matches the characters. If you set the Limit to List property to Yes and the combo box list is dropped down, Access automatically fills in the matching value as you type in the text box, even if the Auto Expand property is set to No.

List boxes and combo boxes consist of rows of data with one or more columns, which can appear with or without headings. One of the columns contains the values you want to store in the field (bound control) or use for other purposes (unbound control); the other columns contain explanatory information.

Figure 12-1 compares examples of list and combo boxes that contain lists of the employee last names from the Home Tech Repair database. The figure also shows a text box for comparison. The list box is always open, but is limited to the size you draw in the form design. If the list is wider or longer than the space allowed, Access adds scroll bars. The combo box list is, by default, the same width as the control in the design, but you can change the width to fit the list. Scroll bars are also added to combo boxes, when necessary.

To add a list box or combo box to a form design based on the Employees table, open a blank form in Design view and do the following:

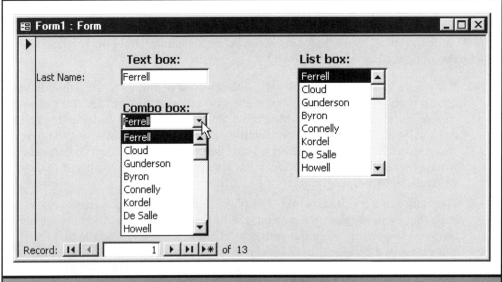

Figure 12-1. Last names in a list box and combo box

1. Make sure the Control Wizard button is pressed, and then click the List Box or Combo Box tool in the toolbox.

2. Click the form design or draw an outline where you want the control to appear. The wizard's first dialog box opens (see Figure 12-2). For both the List Box Wizard and the Combo Box Wizard, the first dialog boxes are nearly identical.

3. Choose one of the options (both wizards offer the same options):

   ■ **I want the box to look up the values in a table or query.** If you choose this option, the box displays field values from the table or query you choose.

   ■ **I will type in the values that I want.** If you choose this option, the list contains values you type into the next dialog box.

   ■ **Find a record on my form based on the value I selected in my combo box.** This option is used to create a combo box that acts as a search string to find a specific record and display it in the form. This option creates an unbound control.

4. After making a choice in the first dialog box, click Next. Depending on your choice in step 3, do one of the following:

   ■ If you chose the first option, select the table or query that contains the values the box will display. Then click Next, select the fields you want to see in the list, and click Next again.

   ■ If you chose to type in the values, enter the number of columns you want to see and the values to display. Choosing this option skips the next dialog box.

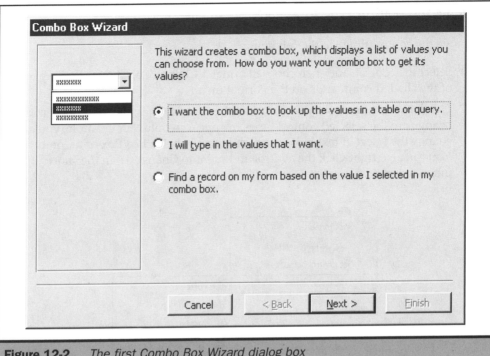

Figure 12-2. *The first Combo Box Wizard dialog box*

Tip *Press* TAB *to move to the next row in the list of values. If you press* ENTER, *you advance to the next wizard dialog box. In that case, click Back to return to the value list dialog box.*

- ■ If you chose the third option, choose the field whose values you want to see. The value you choose in Form view acts as a search value. Then click Next.

5. In the next dialog box, adjust the column widths to show the values and decide to show or hide the primary key field. Then click Next.

6. The next dialog box asks what you want Access to do with the value you select in the list box or combo box:

- ■ **Remember the value for later use.** Saves the value for use by a macro or procedure. When you close the form, the value is erased.

- ■ **Store that value in this field.** With this option, you select the field in which you want to store the selected value.

7. If you want a label attached to the box, type it in the last dialog box and click Finish.

Changing the Control Type to Combo Box or List Box   If you want a list or combo box in place of a text box already in a form, changing the control type is easy. To change the control type, do the following:

1. Select the control, and then choose Format | Change To. Change To may be one of the shaded commands on the Format menu.

2. The list that appears shows a list of all the control types; the only types you can change are the selected control types to appear in bold. For example, you can change the selected text box control only to a Label, a List Box or a Combo Box. You can also right-click the control and point to Change To in the shortcut menu to see the same list.

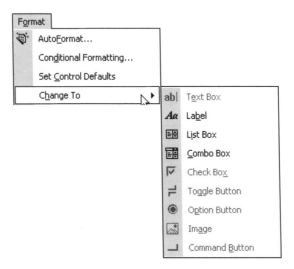

3. Choose the kind of control you want. The control is changed in the design.

4. Open the combo box or list box control's property sheet and click the Build (...) button next to the Row Source property to start the Query Builder.

5. Select the Employees table in the Show Table dialog box, click Add, and then click Close.

6. Drag the Last Name field to the query grid and close the query window. The Query Builder places the following SQL query statement in the Row Source property box:

```
SELECT Employees.[Employee ID], Employees.[Last Name] FROM Employees;
```

7. Change other properties as necessary.

Note   *Refer to Chapter 10 for a list of which controls can be changed to which other types.*

Creating Unbound List and Combo Boxes

An *unbound list* or *combo box* can display either a set of fixed values you enter when you create the box or specific values from a table or query. The value chosen from the control list isn't stored in a field in the underlying table. You can use the value for other purposes, such as looking up a record with that value in a field.

To add a combo box to an Employee form that displays the record for a selected employee, do the following:

1. Start a new form based on the Employee table and add the desired fields to the form.

2. Start the Combo Box (or List Box) Wizard as before and, in the first dialog box, choose the third option: Find a record in my form based on the value I selected in my combo box. Then click Next.

3. Choose Last Name as the field value to show in the list, and then click Next.

4. Choose Hide key column (recommended) and click Next.

5. In the final dialog box, enter **Show record for:** as the control label and click Finish.

Figure 12-3 shows a form with an unbound combo box control that displays the record for the selected employee. When you use the combo box in Form view, you select a value from the list and Access moves to the first record with that value in the corresponding field. This option gives you a quick way to move to a specific record in Form view.

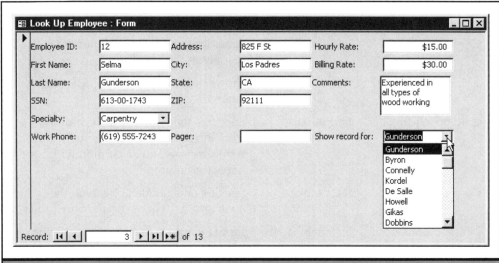

Figure 12-3.   *Using a combo box to find a record*

If you click Back to return to the dialog box where you selected Last Name, you see Access added the primary key field, Employee ID, to the list when you weren't looking. You chose to hide it in the next box, so it won't appear in the list.

Setting List and Combo Box Properties

If your form contains a bound list box or combo box, the control inherits most of its properties from the field properties you set in the table design. When you use a wizard to create one, Access sets certain other properties for you. You can modify these properties by changing the settings in the property sheet to make them work the way you want. Table 12-1 shows some of the properties you can change to customize the control.

Property	Location	Description
Auto Expand	Data tab	Automatically fills in the remaining characters with a value in a combo box when you type the first few characters of the value. Default is Yes.
Bound Column	Data tab	Specifies the number of the column in the list to use as the value for the control. If bound to a field, the value in that column is stored in the field named in the Control Source property. If set to 0, Access stores the list index instead of the value in the list.
Column Count	Format tab	Specifies the number of columns to display in the list.
Column Heads	Format tab	Shows or hides field names as column heads.
Column Widths	Format tab	Specifies the width of each column, from left to right, separated by semicolons. Setting a column width to 0 hides the column.
Control Source	Data tab	Specifies what data appears in the control: a field name or an expression.
Limit To List	Data tab	Limits values accepted in a combo box to those on the list. Default is No.

Table 12-1. *Combo Box and List Box Properties*

Property	Location	Description
List Rows	Format tab	Specifies the maximum number of rows to display in the list box portion of a combo box.
List Width	Format tab	Specifies the width of the list box portion of a combo box when the box is open (may be wider than the control in the form).
On Not in List	Event tab	Names a procedure to execute when the entered value isn't in the combo box list. You can use this to add new values to the list.
Row Source	Data tab	If the Row Source Type is set to Table/Query or Field List, specifies the name of the table or query or a SQL statement. If the Row Source Type is set to Value List, displays a list of items separated by semicolons. If the Row Source Type is a user-defined function, this property is blank.
Row Source Type	Data tab	Specifies Table/Query, Value List, Field List, or a user-defined function.

Table 12-1. *Combo Box and List Box Properties* (continued)

Adding Yes/No Controls

Three different types of controls can be used to view or enter a Yes/No value in the underlying table or query: check boxes, option buttons, and toggle buttons. When you have a limited number of alternative choices in one field, you can also group the controls together in an option group. The grouped options work as a single control and only one of them can be selected. The *option group* can display the list of choices as any of the three types of Yes/No controls.

When you select or clear a check box, option button, or toggle button, Access displays the value in the table or query according to the format property set in the table design (Yes/No, True/False, or On/Off). Figure 12-4 shows how the various Yes/No controls appear when the values are Yes and No.

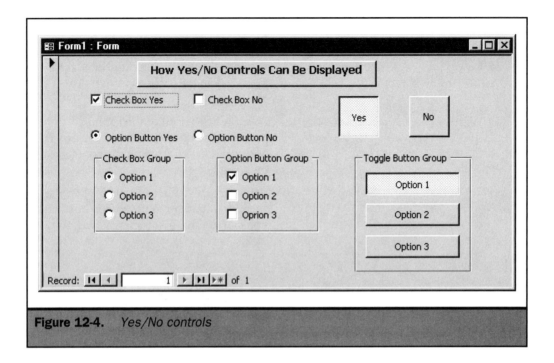

Figure 12-4. *Yes/No controls*

You can also use these as unbound controls in custom dialog boxes to accept user input instead of field values. See Chapter 21 for information about creating custom dialog boxes.

Check Boxes and Option Buttons

A check box displays a check mark in a small box if the value in the underlying field is Yes. The box is empty if the value is No. An option button displays a black dot in a circle if the value in the underlying field is Yes. The circle is empty if the value is No.

Toggle Buttons

When the toggle button appears pressed in, the value in the underlying field is Yes. If the button appears raised, the value is No. You can enter a caption for the button by entering text in the control's Caption property box.

One attractive thing about toggle buttons is you can use a picture on the button instead of text, creating a more interesting appearance.

Option Groups

An option group offers a limited set of mutually exclusive alternatives, usually four or less. The *option group control* consists of a frame around a set of check boxes, option buttons, or toggle buttons. If the option group is bound to a field, the frame itself is the bound object, not the individual controls in the group. When you create an option group, you specify the values of the options in terms of meaningful numbers to the underlying field. When you select an option in the group, that value is stored in the field.

If Access isn't bound to a field, it uses the value of the option you choose to carry out one of a list of actions, such as print the report you chose or open another form.

Although you can create an option group without the help of the wizard, taking advantage of the wizard is much easier. To create an option group, make sure the Control Wizard button in pressed in on the toolbox, and then do the following:

1. Click the Option Group tool and click the form design where you want the upper-left corner of the group to appear. The wizard draws a one-inch square box. Then click Next.

2. In the first wizard dialog box (see Figure 12-5), enter the text you want to see as choices in the group.

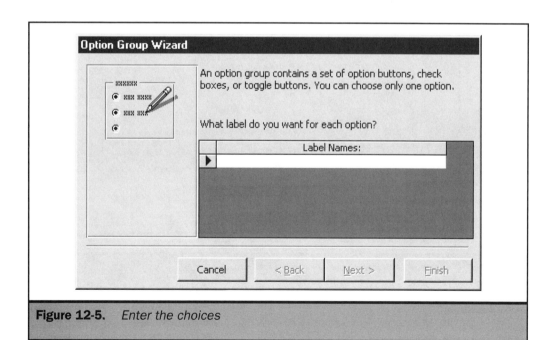

Figure 12-5. *Enter the choices*

After entering an option label, press TAB or the DOWN ARROW or click the record selector to move to the next row. If you press ENTER, you move to the next dialog box.

3. In the second dialog box, set the default option, if desired, and then click Next.

4. Specify the Option Value property for each of the options in the group. This property must always be a number. This is the value passed to the field when the option is selected. By default, the values are consecutive integers: option 1 has the value 1, option 2 has the value 2, and so on. Then click Next.

5. The next dialog box asks you which field you want to store the value in (bound) or if you want Access to save the value for later (unbound). If the form doesn't have a record source, the wizard skips this dialog box.

6. Next, choose the type of control and the style you want to see in the option group (see Figure 12-6), and then click Next.

7. In the final wizard dialog box, enter the name you want as the label for the group. This text then appears in the group frame. Then click Finish.

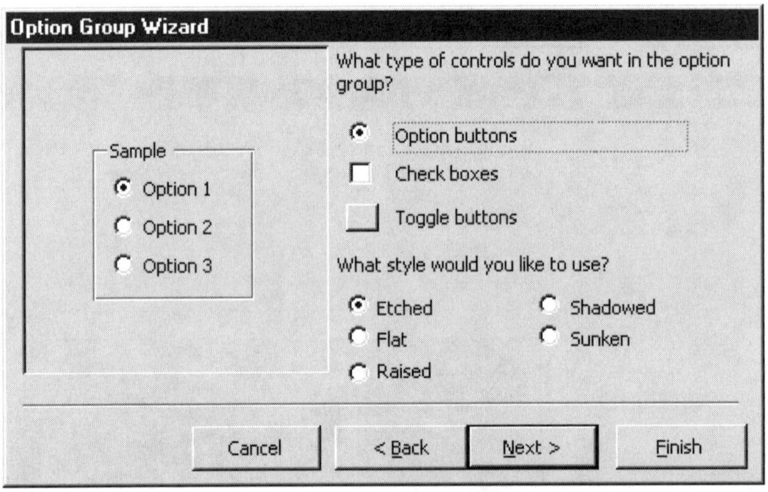

Figure 12-6.   *Choose the control type and style*

If you want to use an option group to store text values in the underlying field instead of numbers, you can create an intermediate lookup table that translates the number values returned by the options to the corresponding text values.

If you have a set of options that relate to the same type of information, but apply to different fields, you can still keep them together in the form. Arrange the independent options in a group and draw a rectangle around them to resemble an option group. The options won't be automatically set to be mutually exclusive, however.

Adding User-Interactive Controls

Because a form is often used to enter data, the user is constantly interacting with the form and the controls it contains. Some of the controls are directly associated with table data, such as text boxes, list boxes, combo boxes, and the option type with which you can set a Yes/No value. The most common control unrelated to data is the command button, used in Form view to perform an action. When the user clicks a command button, Access recognizes this event, and then carries out the response you specified for the event.

Introducing Events and Event Properties

Access is an object-oriented, event-driven application. Nothing happens until the user tells it what to do by pressing a key or clicking the mouse button. An *event* is an occurrence recognized by an Access object. You can define a response to events by setting the event property of the object or the control.

Examples of events include

- Pressing or releasing a key.
- Opening or closing a form.
- Moving the cursor to or away from a control.
- Applying a filter to records in a form.
- Changing or deleting the value in a control.

Every time you press a key or click a button, you're initiating an event to which Access will respond. The action Access takes depends on the event property specified. For example, clicking the Open command button (the event) in the Database window opens the selected object (the response). When you move to another record after entering or editing data, the event causes Access to check any validation rules automatically and, if no violation exists, to save the record. These actions are triggered by the system, based on the built-in event properties.

You can set event properties for any of the controls in your form or report design to carry out the appropriate action. When you set an event property, you attach a set of commands to the event. These commands can be in the form of a macro or an event procedure containing Visual Basic statements. Then, when you click that command button or press that key, Access knows what to do.

The Access wizards also provide a number of predefined methods you can attach to standard events, such as clicking a command button. The Click event occurs when you quickly press and release the left mouse button on a control. The On Click event property specifies what is to happen when you click the left mouse button on that control.

Note   *You can also set an On Dbl Click event property to a different action that takes place when you double-click the mouse button. Forms don't, however, have an On Right Click property for responding to clicking the right mouse button.*

Another important term when discussing events is *focus*; a control is said to get focus when it becomes active and able to receive user input via the keyboard or the mouse. For example, when you press TAB to move through the controls on a form, focus is shifted from one control to another according to the tab order.

Adding Command Buttons

The Command Button Wizard is on hand to help create over 30 different types of command buttons, ranging from moving to the next record to closing the form. The wizard guides you through the selection of the category of action you want and the specific procedure to execute. It also lets you identify the button with text or a picture.

To add a command button to a form, do the following:

1. Make sure the Control Wizard button is pressed in, click the Command Button tool, and then click in the form design. The first Command Button Wizard dialog box appears (see Figure 12-7). The list at the left shows the available action categories. The list at the right shows specific actions that fall into the selected category. Each category has a different set of actions. As you highlight an action in the list, a sample appears in the left pane.

2. Select the category you want, select the specific action, and click Next. Depending on your choice of action, the wizard displays additional dialog boxes requesting information, such as the name of the form to open or the report to preview.

3. After choosing the options required by the action you selected, the next wizard dialog box lets you choose between text and a picture for the button. You can accept the default text or enter your own. If you don't like the default picture, click Show All Pictures and choose another one, or click Browse and look in another folder. After making your choice, click Next. As you select a picture from the Show All Pictures list, you can see how it looks in the left Sample panel.

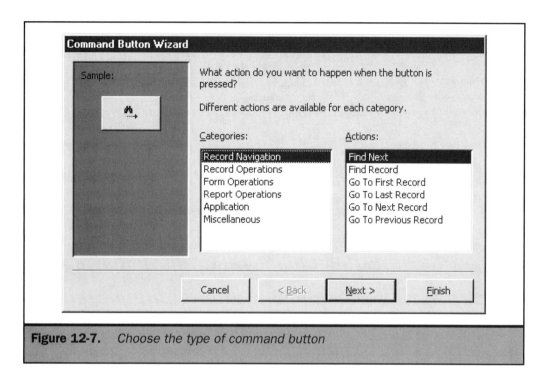

Figure 12-7. *Choose the type of command button*

4. Enter a name for the button or accept the default name. Then click Finish.

5. You can modify the properties of the command button later to change between a picture and text. Of course, you can always move and resize a command button just like any other control in the form design. Command buttons are included in the tab order of the form design. That is, as you press TAB to move around in Form view, a command button gets focus when its turn comes. Then pressing ENTER is the same as clicking the command button.

Tip *If you use a picture on a button, creating a control tip, which explains what happens when the button is clicked, is a good idea. A control tip automatically displays below the button when you move the mouse pointer over the command button. You can customize the tip the wizard provides. If you created a status bar message, it appears in the status bar when you select the control to which it applies. You can create your own custom help, as you see later in this chapter.*

When the Command Button Wizard builds the button for you, it writes an event procedure containing Visual Basic code to place in the form's class module. For example, you can use the wizard to add a command button to print the current record in the Current Workorders form (see Figure 12-8). To add this button, start the wizard, choose the Record Operations category and the Print Record action in the first dialog box, and then click Finish to accept the remaining default options.

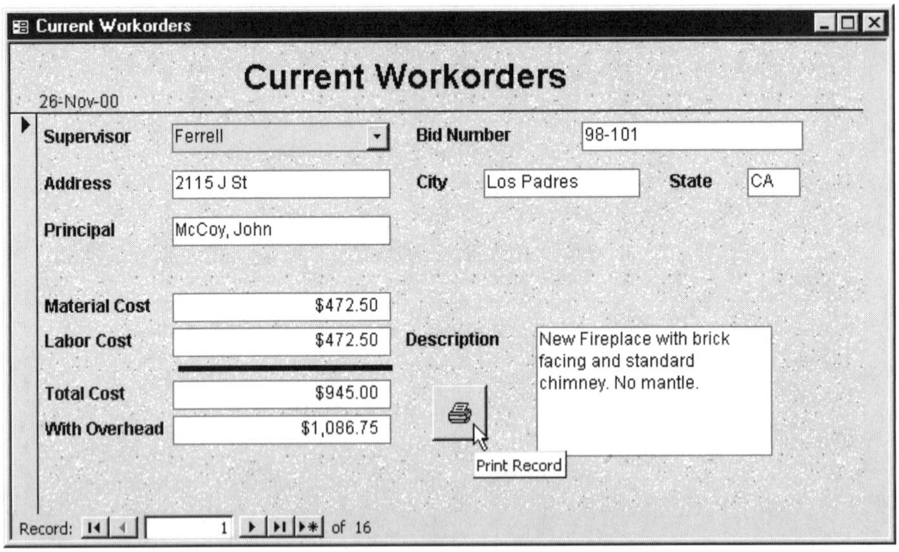

Figure 12-8. *A Print command button added to a form*

Looking Behind the Scenes

The wizard writes an event procedure that contains the necessary instructions and stores it in the form's class module. To see the code, click Code while in Design view. The default name for the button control is Command39. Access always makes provisions for an error occurring with the On Error statement, which branches to the statement that displays the error message.

```
Private Sub Print_Record_Click()
On Error GoTo Err_Print_Record_Click
    DoCmd.DoMenuItem acFormBar, acEditMenu, 8, , acMenuVer70
    DoCmd.PrintOut acSelection
Exit_Print_Record_Click:
    Exit Sub
Err_Print_Record_Click:
    MsgBox Err.Description
    Resume Exit_Print_Record_Click
End Sub
```

> The DoCmd.DoMenuItem statement specifies which menu command to obey: the eighth available option in the Edit menu on the Form menu bar, which is Select Record. The statement also specifies the Access 7.0 version of the menu bar. The next statement, DoCmd.PrintOut acSelection, tells Access to print the selected record. In Chapter 25, you learn more about creating and using Visual Basic procedures.

Note *If you choose Form Operations and Print Form as the action to take, Access prints all the records as one continuous form.*

Adding Hyperlinks

In Chapter 6, you saw how to add a hyperlink field to a table and how to insert a hyperlink address in the field. A hyperlink in a table can jump to a different address for each record. For example, the hyperlink field Drawing in the Home Tech Repair Workorders table contained addresses of files containing scanned engineering drawings.

The hyperlink address you enter in the field in a record appears in Form view, like other fields. To add the field to the form design, drag the hyperlink field name from the field list to the form design.

If you don't need to tie the hyperlink address to a record, you can add it to the form in Design view as an unbound control. You can add a hyperlink to a form design either as a label or an image. Both jump to the target address when you click the control in Form view.

To add a hyperlink as a label to the Home Tech Repair Roster form that will jump to the Employees table, do the following:

1. With the form open in Design view, click the Insert Hyperlink toolbar button or choose Insert | Hyperlink. The Insert Hyperlink dialog box opens (see Figure 12-9).

2. Enter the filename for the hyperlink in the Address text box, as follows:

   ■ Select the file from the list.

   ■ If the file you want to jump to is in the folder, type the filename preceded by two periods and a backslash, for example: **..\HomeTech Repair.mdb**.

   ■ If the file isn't in the current path, type the entire path and filename.

   ■ Click the Browse for File button (the open folder icon).

3. Next, click Bookmark to open the Select Place in Document dialog box where you can specify the object to jump to.

4. Click the plus sign (+) next to Tables and select Employees from the list of tables in the database (see Figure 12-10). Then click OK.

5. Enter **Lookup Employees** in the Text to display box to see it in the hyperlink instead of the address.

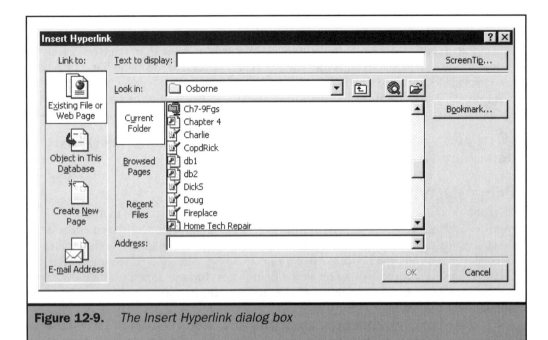

Figure 12-9. The Insert Hyperlink dialog box

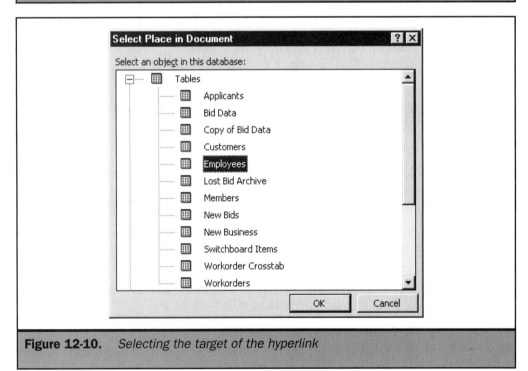

Figure 12-10. Selecting the target of the hyperlink

6. Click ScreenTip and enter **Display Employees table** in the Set Hyperlink ScreenTip dialog box, and then click OK. The default is the complete hyperlink address.

7. Click OK to close the Insert Hyperlink dialog box.

8. Drag the hyperlink control to the position you want in the form design.

You can test the new hyperlink in the form design by right-clicking and choosing Hyperlink | Open Hyperlink from the shortcut menu.

When you switch to Form view, the hyperlink appears as an underlined label. Rest the mouse pointer on the hyperlink to see the ScreenTip. Click it to open the Employees table in Datasheet view.

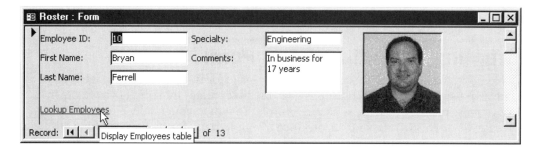

Note   *If you select a control in the form before inserting the hyperlink, the new hyperlink appears just below the label of the selected control. If no control is selected, the hyperlink appears in the upper-left corner of the form. From there, you can drag the hyperlink to any position in the form design.*

To add a picture that follows a hyperlink, add an image control to the design and change its Hyperlink Address and Hyperlink Subaddress properties to specify the target file.

Tip   *To add a hyperlink in the form of a command button or an image, turn off the Control Wizard before adding the button or image control to the form design. After placing it in the design, select the button and enter the Hyperlink Address and Hyperlink Subaddress properties. Also, set the Caption property to the text you want to display on the button.*

RETRIEVING AND
PRESENTING INFORMATION

Copying a Hyperlink

If another Microsoft Office document, an Excel spreadsheet, or a Word document has a hyperlink already defined that you can use, you can easily copy it to your form or report.

1. Open the document that contains the hyperlink.

2. Right-click the hyperlink and choose Hyperlink | Copy Hyperlink in the shortcut menu.

3. Switch to the Access form or report Design view and choose Edit | Paste As Hyperlink.

Access adds a label control to the design that represents the copied hyperlink. Change the control's Caption property to change the displayed hyperlink address to more meaningful text.

 Tip *Be sure to select only the hyperlink and not to include any nearby text. If you copy any characters that aren't part of the hyperlink, you'll jump to the text instead of the hyperlink address.*

 # Creating a Multiple-Page Form

Access gives you two ways to create a multiple-page form: by inserting a page break control or using the new tab control. A page break separates the form horizontally into two or more pages, which are separate controls. To move sequentially among the pages, press PGUP or PGDN. Tab controls produce multiple-page forms that combine all the pages into a single control. To move between pages in a tab control, click the desired tab.

Using the Page Break Control

To insert a page break, click the Page Break Control tool in the toolbox, and then click in the form where you want the split. Access shows a short dotted line at the left border where the break occurs.

Page break

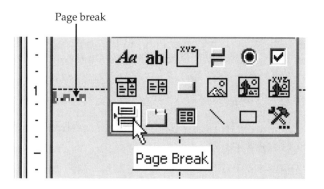

 Be sure you place a page break between controls. If the page break lines up horizontally within part of a control, the data in the control is then split between the pages.

Pages aren't necessarily full-screen height. If you want every page the same size and show only one page at a time, design the form with evenly spaced page breaks. Use the vertical ruler to help place the page breaks.

After placing the page break, change some of the form properties as follows:

- Change the Cycle property on the Other tab from the current default All Records to Current Page, which keeps you from moving to the next page when you press TAB at the last control in the tab order on one page.

- Change the Scroll Bars property on the Format tab from Both to Horizontal Only to remove the vertical scroll bar. This prevents scrolling to a different page. If the form isn't wider than the screen, you can set the property to Neither and remove both scroll bars.

Switch to Form view and press PGDN and PGUP to see if the page breaks are properly placed.

 Each page is a separate section. If you plan to print the form and want each form page printed on a separate page, change the section's Force New Page property to Yes.

Adding a Tab Control

Tab controls, which were new to Access 97, are easier and more efficient than page breaks because all the pages in the form belong to a single control. They are useful for presenting groups of information that can be assembled by category. Tab controls are also widely used as dialog boxes. For example, the Options dialog box (Tools | Options) has a tab for each of 11 categories of options, such as Keyboard and Tables/Queries.

RETRIEVING AND
PRESENTING INFORMATION

To create a tab control, do the following:

1. In Design view, click the Tab Control tool in the toolbox, and then click in the design where you want the tab. Access places a tab control with two pages (see Figure 12-11).

2. Add controls to each page, just as with a single-page form, clicking the tab to change pages. The only exception when adding controls is, while you can copy-and-paste controls from one page to another or from another part of the form, you can't drag them.

3. Next, do any of the following:

   ■ Change the default tab name by double-clicking the page and entering the new name in the Caption property.

   ■ Add another tab or delete a tab by right-clicking the tab control border and choosing Insert Page or Delete Page from the shortcut menu. When you delete a page, the last page to be inserted is removed.

   ■ Change the order of the tabs by right-clicking the tab border and choosing Page Order from the shortcut menu. Select the page and click Move Up or Move Down to reorder the pages by selecting and dragging the control names in the list. Choose Auto Order to set the tab order relative to the control locations in the design.

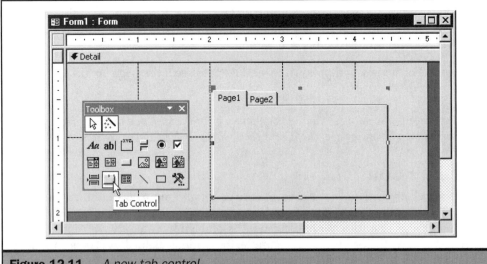

Figure 12-11. *A new tab control*

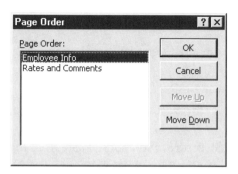

- Change the tab order of controls on a page by right-clicking in the page and choosing Tab Order. Rearrange the list of controls in the Tab Order dialog box.

4. After placing the controls on the pages, check each one to make sure it fits. You can resize the tab by dragging the borders. All pages of the tab control will be the same size.

5. Switch to Form view and test the new tab control.

Tip   *If you try unsuccessfully to make the tab control smaller, the controls on one of the pages may prevent the reduction. Access doesn't crop any controls to fit the tab control. You may need to move or reduce a control on one of the pages first.*

Figure 12-12 shows the Roster form as a two-page tab control.

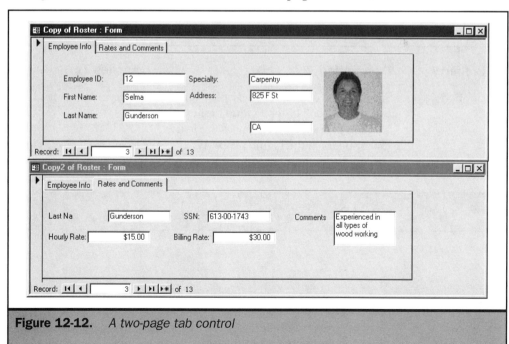

Figure 12-12.   *A two-page tab control*

To create this form, do the following:

1. Open the Roster form in Design view and maximize the window.

2. Click the Tab Control tool in the toolbox and draw a tab control frame in the lower half of the form design across the width.

3. Use the vertical ruler to select all the controls in the upper half and click Copy on the toolbar.

4. Right-click in the tab control and choose Paste from the shortcut menu. The controls from the Roster form appear in the first page of the tab control.

5. Click the second page tab and drag the other fields from the field list.

6. Double-click in a page to open the property sheet and change the Caption property. Then click in the other page and also change its caption.

7. Delete the controls from the upper half of the form and reduce the form height to show only the tab control, and then switch to Form view.

Customizing a Tab Control

Two property sheets are used to customize a tab control: the tab control property sheet and the page property sheet. To customize the tab control, double-click the control border outside of a page to open the property sheet. To set individual page properties, double-click in the page area.

Table 12-2 describes some of the properties you can use to create the custom tab control.

Property	Description	Applies To
Caption	Specifies the characters to display on a tab. If you don't enter a value in the Caption property, Access uses the text that appears in the Name property, usually Page*n* numbered in sequence.	Page in tab control

Table 12-2. *Tab Control and Page Properties*

Property	Description	Applies To
MultiRow	Allows the tab control to show more than one row of tabs. If set to the default No, the tabs are truncated if, together, they exceed the total width of the tab control and a horizontal scroll bar is added at the top of the tab control. The individual tabs aren't shrunk, but not all of them are displayed.	Tab control
Style	Specifies what to display at the top of the tab control. Choices are Tabs (the default), Buttons, or None. If set to Tabs or Buttons, you can set the Tab Fixed Height, Tab Fixed Width, and MultiRow properties to change their appearance.	Tab control
Tab Fixed Height	Sets the height of tabs. If set to the default 0, each tab is tall enough to fit its contents. Uses unit of measure set in Windows Control Panel.	Tab control
Tab Fixed Width	Sets the width of tabs. If set to the default 0, each tab is wide enough to fit its contents. Uses unit of measure set in Windows Control Panel.	Tab control
Picture	Adds a bitmap graphic to a tab, which appears to the left of the tab name specified in the Caption property. If you want only the graphic and not the text, press SPACEBAR in the Caption property. Metafiles cannot be used on page tabs.	Page in tab control

Table 12-2. *Tab Control and Page Properties* (continued)

Note *A tab control makes an excellent custom dialog box, which requires you also change other tab control properties. See Chapter 21 for information on how to create custom dialog boxes and other special-purpose forms.*

Creating a Shortcut to a Form

Your Windows desktop probably contains many shortcuts, such as My Computer, In Box, and Recycle Bin, which you can click to start working with the object. You can create a desktop shortcut that launches Access and opens your custom form at startup. To create a shortcut to a form, do the following:

1. Open the Database window and click Forms under Objects in the Database window.

2. Right-click the form name and choose Create Shortcut from the shortcut menu. The Create Shortcut dialog box opens showing the path and filename of the selected form.

3. Click OK, and then minimize the Access window to see the new shortcut.

 Double-clicking the shortcut launches Access and opens the form for browsing, entering, and editing data. If you right-click the shortcut, the shortcut menu has many more options, such as opening the form in Datasheet or Design view, previewing the form as it would be printed, or sending the form directly to the printer. You can also use the Send To command to copy the shortcut to a floppy disk or to send it to a recipient via e-mail or fax. To delete the shortcut from the Windows desktop, right-click the icon, choose Delete from the shortcut menu, and respond Yes when asked to confirm the deletion.

Adding Special Controls

In addition to images, unbound option groups, lines, and rectangles, you can add other special controls to a form design to enhance its appearance or provide additional information. Calculated controls can combine data from more than one field into processed or summary information. Remember, one of the rules of relational databases is you don't include a field in a table that could be derived from fields already in the table.

Other special controls fall into the category of *ActiveX controls*, which were called *OLE Custom Controls* in earlier versions of Access. The More Controls toolbox button mentioned in Chapter 10 opens the list of all the custom controls available in your system, including the ActiveX controls.

Adding Calculated Controls

Including a calculated field in a form or report is often helpful. For example, in the last chapter, a query was used to add two calculated fields to the Current Workorders form. One field totaled the labor and material costs, and the other added a 15 percent overhead cost. You can also add a calculated field to a form directly without using a query. An unbound text box control is usually used for a calculated field, but you can use any control that has a Control Source property, which tells Access where to get the information to display. Combo boxes, list boxes, bound and unbound object frames, toggle buttons, option buttons, and check boxes all have a Control Source property.

The calculation is based on an expression you enter in the Control Source property box. An *expression* always begins with an equal sign (=). The expression contains operators and functions in addition to the names of the fields or controls involved in the calculation.

Three types of operators are available for use in expressions:

■ *Arithmetic operators,* such as +, -, *, ^, /, \, and Mod, which are used to compute results.

■ *Comparison operators,* such as = <, >, <=, >=, <>, and Between, which are used to create criteria expressions.

■ *Logical operators,* such as And, Eqv, Imp, Not, Or, and Xor, which produce a Yes or No value.

Note *See the Quick Reference on the CD for a compete list of operators used in Access expressions.*

Access provides nearly 200 built-in functions to help create the expression you want for the calculated control. All functions are followed by parentheses, which enclose the arguments of the function. *Arguments* identify the values the function uses to come up with a value.

Brackets around an identifier in an expression indicate the name of an Access object, such as a table, query, field, form, report, or control. If you type in the expression, you must include the brackets if the name includes a space or special character, such as an underscore. Otherwise, Access automatically adds the brackets.

Note *When you create a calculated field, Access gives it a default name, such as Textnn, where nn is a sequential number created as Access adds the controls. If you change the Name property to another name, be sure you don't use the name of any of the controls in the expression.*

Table 12-3 shows examples of expressions you can use as the Control Source property for a calculated field.

Expression	Result
=[Labor Cost]+[Material Cost]	The sum of the values in the Labor Cost and Material Cost text box controls.
=[Completion Date]-[Start Date]	The number of days between the dates in the Completion Date and the Start Date text box controls.
=[Cost]*.075	The product of the value in the Cost text box control and .075. (Computes 7.5 percent sales tax.)
=[Labor Cost]/[Total Hours]	The quotient of the values in the Labor Cost and Total Hours text box controls. Computes the average hourly labor cost.
=Date()	Current date in the mm-dd-yy format.
=Format(Now(),"ww")	Number of the week of the current year.
="Home Tech Repair"	Displays Home Tech Repair.
=[First Name]&" "&[Last Name]	Displays first name, a space, and last name.
=Left([Last Name],2)	Displays first two characters of the value in the Last Name field.
=Trim([City])	Uses the Trim function to remove leading or trailing spaces around the value in the City field.
=IIf([Award Date]="Lost","Review bid","Create workorder")	Uses the IIf (immediate if) function to test the value in the Award Date field. If the field contains the word "Lost," the value of the calculated field is "Review bid"; otherwise, it displays "Create workorder."
=Avg([Material Cost])	Displays the average of all the values in the Material Cost field.
=Count([Bid Number])	Displays the number of records with a value in the field.
=Sum([Qty]*[Price])	Displays the total of the values obtained by multiplying values in the Qty and Price fields in each record.

Table 12-3.   *Examples of Calculated Field Expressions*

You can use the name of a calculated control in another expression if the expression doesn't use an aggregate function, such as Avg or Sum. You can use only field names from a table, query, or SQL statement in aggregate functions.

To add a calculated field to a form design, do the following:

1. In Design view, click the Text Box control tool, and then click in the form design to place the control.

2. Enter the expression using one of the following methods:

   ■ Type the expression directly into the calculated control box. Be sure to precede the expression with an equal sign (=).

   ■ Type the expression, again preceded by an equal sign, in the Control Source property box in the property sheet.

   ■ For more complex expressions, click Build next to the Control Source property to open the Expression Builder.

3. Switch to Form view to test the new calculated field.

 If you created an expression in a query that you can use in a calculated field in a form, copy and paste it in the Control Source property of the calculated control. Then place an equal sign in front of the expression.

Using the Expression Builder

The *Expression Builder* is a modal form, which means you can't do anything else until you close the form by clicking either OK or Cancel. The dialog box (see Figure 12-13) is divided into two parts: the upper part contains the expression under construction; the lower part contains all the elements you can add to the expression. Between the two is a row of buttons you can use to add operators to the expression.

The lower half of the form contains three columns, the leftmost of which lists all the different groupings of elements, such as database objects, functions, constants, operators, and common expressions. The figure shows the Expression Builder as it appears when you click Build (...) in the Control Source property of a new calculated field in the Current Workorders form. Notice the Current Workorders folder appears open in the left column and the center column displays all the elements of the form design. The objects and functions available in the Expression Builder depend on where you were when you launched it.

Double-click any item in the list that shows a plus sign to expand it to show all the elements in the group. When you select an item in the left column, the elements in the item are listed in the center column. The right column lists elements from the selected item in the center column. If you select a field or control name in the center column, the right column shows <Value>, plus an alphabetical list of related properties. To add the item to the expression, double-click it in the right column or select it and click Paste.

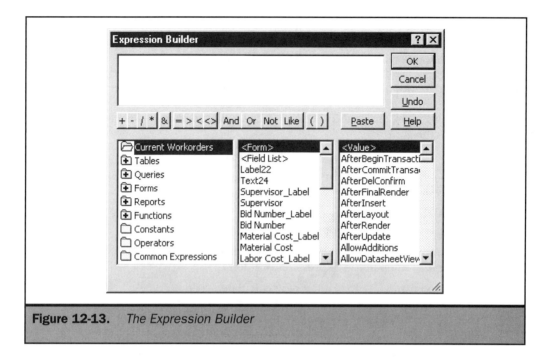

Figure 12-13. *The Expression Builder*

> **Tip** *A shortcut to adding a field or control value to the expression is to double-click it in the center column.*

To add the expression [Total Cost]*1.15 in the Expression Builder, do the following:

1. With the Current Workorders folder open in the left column, scroll down the center column and double-click the Total Cost control name. Notice Access automatically encloses the control name in brackets.

2. Click the asterisk (*) operator button to add it to the expression.

3. Type **1.15** to finish the expression and click OK. The Expression Builder dialog box closes and you return to the form design.

> **Note** *If you look at the Control Source property for the calculated control, you see Access has added the equal sign at the beginning of the expression.*

If you want to add a function to an expression, double-click Function to open the folder, and then choose the function category from the center column and the function itself from the right column. Each function has a set of arguments of various data types—some required and others optional. The message at the bottom of the Expression

Builder dialog box shows the function syntax. See the Access Help topic for an individual function for information about the proper use and the exact requirements.

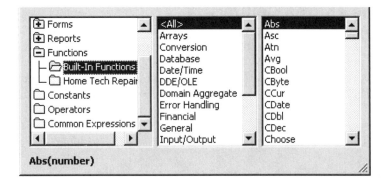

Adding Common Expressions

One of the folders in the left column of the Expression Builder dialog box is labeled Common Expressions. When you click the folder to open it, you see a list of six common expressions dealing with page numbers, date/time values, and current user.

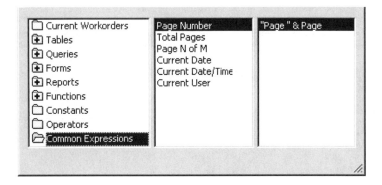

ActiveX Controls

ActiveX controls extend your reach to products supplied by third-party developers. Each one is a separate file with the .ocx file extension. The file contains all the code, methods, events, and properties necessary to function in an Access environment.

Some ActiveX controls come with Access 2002 and others can be installed later. After you install the control according to its installation program, all you must do is register it, so Access knows the program exists in your system and where to find it. Some ActiveX controls are automatically registered during installation, while others must be registered manually.

After adding an ActiveX control to a form design, you can open the property sheet for the control and change its properties as necessary.

Registering ActiveX Controls

To see which ActiveX controls are already registered in Access, choose Tools | ActiveX Controls. The ActiveX Controls dialog box (see Figure 12-14) lists all the controls currently registered. Your list may be different. If you don't see the control you want, click Register to open the Add ActiveX Control dialog box. Locate the folder and file where the control was installed, select it, and click Open. The control is added to the list.

 If you're sure you won't be using the ActiveX control any more, you can take it out of the registry by selecting it in the ActiveX Controls dialog box and clicking Unregister.

Adding a Calendar Control

The *Calendar control,* one of the most popular ActiveX controls, displays dates graphically on a calendar. The custom control has properties that enable you to set and retrieve dates in a table. For example, Figure 12-15 shows the Workorders Form with a Calendar control that displays the Start Dates of the work orders in Workorders table.

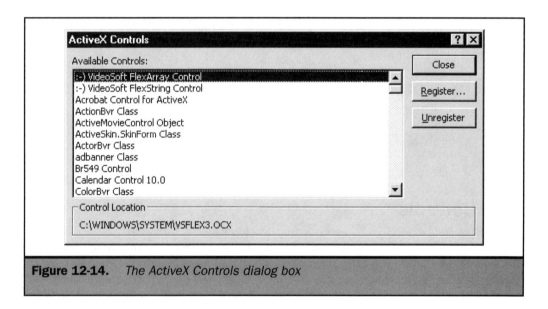

Figure 12-14.   *The ActiveX Controls dialog box*

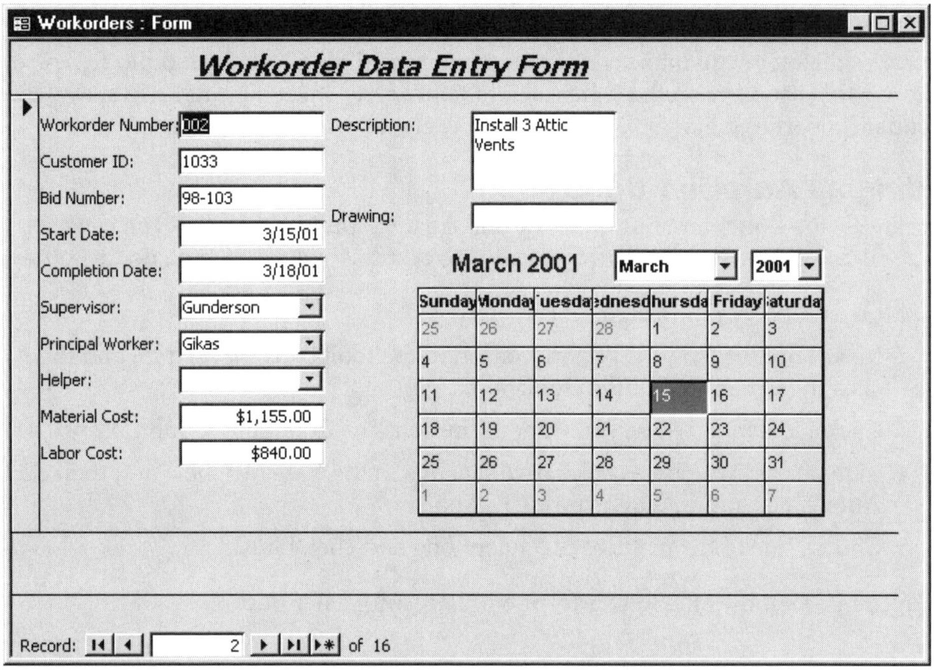

Workorders : Form

Workorder Data Entry Form

Workorder Number:	002
Customer ID:	1033
Bid Number:	98-103
Start Date:	3/15/01
Completion Date:	3/18/01
Supervisor:	Gunderson
Principal Worker:	Gikas
Helper:	
Material Cost:	$1,155.00
Labor Cost:	$840.00

Description: Install 3 Attic Vents

Drawing:

March 2001   March   2001

Sunday	Monday	Tuesday	Wednesday	Thursday	Friday	Saturday
25	26	27	28	1	2	3
4	5	6	7	8	9	10
11	12	13	14	15	16	17
18	19	20	21	22	23	24
25	26	27	28	29	30	31
1	2	3	4	5	6	7

Record: 2 of 16

Figure 12-15.   *Adding a Calendar control*

As you navigate among the records, the month changes to show the value in the Start Date as a pressed-in date in the calendar.

To add a Calendar control to a form, do the following:

1. Start a new form based on the Workorders table and add the fields to the design.

2. With the form open in Design view, do one of the following:

   ■ Click the More Controls tool in the toolbox, and then select Calendar Control 10.0 from the displayed list. Now draw a frame in the form design where and in the size you want the calendar to appear.

   ■ Choose Insert | ActiveX Control and select Calendar Control 10.0 in the Insert ActiveX Control dialog box, and then click OK. The calendar is automatically placed in the form design in the upper-left corner and showing the default size.

3. Open the property sheet for the Calendar control, click the arrow next to the Control Source property, and choose Start Date from the list.

The Calendar control has many properties you can set to create a custom appearance. In addition to the individual properties in the property sheet, you can open the Calendar Properties dialog box to make changes. To open the dialog box, click Build (...) next to the Custom property on the Other tab of the property sheet. Figure 12-16 shows the Calendar Properties dialog box with three tabs: General, Font, and Color.

Adding an AutoDial Control

You can use the Command Button Wizard to create a command button you can click to dial a selected phone number automatically. To add this special control, do the following:

1. Open the form in Design view.

2. Make sure the Control Wizard button in the toolbox is pressed in, and then click the Command Button tool.

3. Click in the form where you want the button. The Command Button Wizard starts.

4. In the first dialog box, click Miscellaneous in the Category box, and then click AutoDialer in the Actions box. Click Next.

5. Choose one of the pictures of a telephone and click Finish.

Figure 12-17 shows the Roster form with an AutoDialer button.

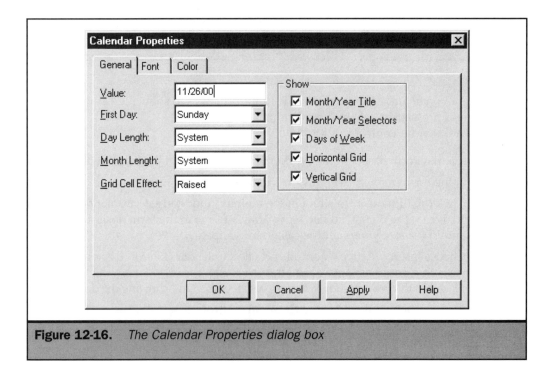

Figure 12-16. *The Calendar Properties dialog box*

Figure 12-17. *The AutoDialer command button*

When you click the button in Form view, the AutoDialer dialog box opens. If you moved the cursor to a telephone number field before clicking the button, the number appears in the box. If not, you can enter a number in the empty Number box. Choose OK to dial the number.

The Setup button in the AutoDialer dialog box opens a dialog box where you can set the modem properties.

If you want to see the code the wizard wrote to make the button work, click Build (…) in the On Click event property box of the new AutoDialer button.

Adding a Web Browser Control

If you want to view a Web page on a form, you can add the Microsoft Web Browser control. You must have Microsoft Internet Explorer installed to add this ActiveX control. With the form open in Design view, do the following:

1. Click More Controls on the Toolbox.

2. Scroll down the menu list of registered ActiveX controls and select Microsoft Web Browser.

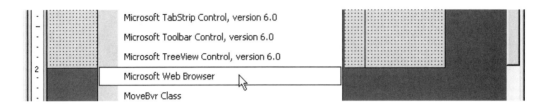

Microsoft TabStrip Control, version 6.0

Microsoft Toolbar Control, version 6.0

Microsoft TreeView Control, version 6.0

Microsoft Web Browser

MoveBvr Class

3. Click in the form where you want the Web page to appear. You can resize and move it if necessary.

Introducing the Police Department Database

The Police database is used 24 hours a day by a local police department in support of law enforcement and on behalf of citizens. This is a mostly user-interactive data management system that tracks incidents and maintains records of all people who report, or who are involved in, activities that require police attention—for example, crimes such as burglaries, auto theft, vandalism, and spousal abuse; traffic collisions, with or without injuries; and even people who come in to be fingerprinted as a requirement for employment.

The people who use the database include

- Police officers in the field who call the station to find out if the person they have stopped for speeding has a previous violation. The dispatcher at the station looks in the database for prior contacts.

- Victims of traffic accidents who need case information to send to their insurance companies.

- Parents of missing children who want to know if the child has been located.

The database consists of four tables: two main tables and two collateral tables used mainly for lookup.

The *Alpha Card table* lists all people who have filed a report or called in an incident, or who may be a suspect in some sort of incident, for example:

- A rental car agency reports a stolen vehicle.

- A home owner reports a burglary.

- A police officer responds to a two-car injury accident and identifies both drivers and one passenger. This report results in three separate records in the Alpha Card table.

The *Alpha Entry table* contains details of the report and is related to the Alpha Card table with a one-to-many relationship. The Index primary key field in the Alpha Card table links to the Index field, the foreign key, in the Alpha Entry table. Figure 12-18 shows the relationships between the four tables in the Police database.

The third table, *Entry Explanation,* contains more understandable explanation of the police shorthand descriptions in the Entry field on the Alpha Entry table. This table is related one-to-one with the Alpha Entry table with a left outer join. Referential Integrity has also been enforced so Cascade Delete could be enabled. This has been found to be convenient because when the Alpha Entry record is deleted the corresponding Explanation record is also deleted and the user doesn't have to look for the Explanation record to delete it.

The last table, Penal Codes, is a list of penal code numbers and their descriptions used as a lookup list.

The principal user interface is the Alpha Card form (see Figure 12-19), which shows all the entries linked to that individual. The main form in the upper half shows the data from the Alpha Card table. The lower half is a subform that shows all the related entries from the Alpha Entry table. Both the main form and the subform have record navigation buttons. The printer command button prints the current record and the Explanation button opens a pop-up form displaying an explanation of the entry. These special controls are discussed in subsequent sections in this chapter.

Another major form in the Police database is the Alpha Entry form, which is a tabular form showing all the records in the table. The Alpha Entry form also includes a command button that opens the Alpha Card form with the same index number, so the officer can see the identity of the person involved, as well as any prior entries for that person.

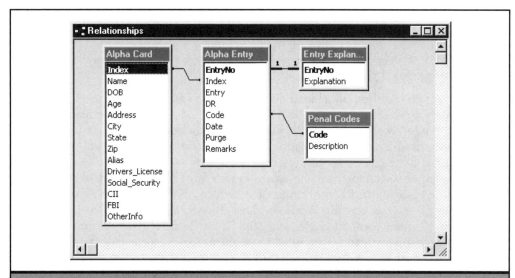

Figure 12-18.   *The relationships in the Police database*

RETRIEVING AND PRESENTING INFORMATION

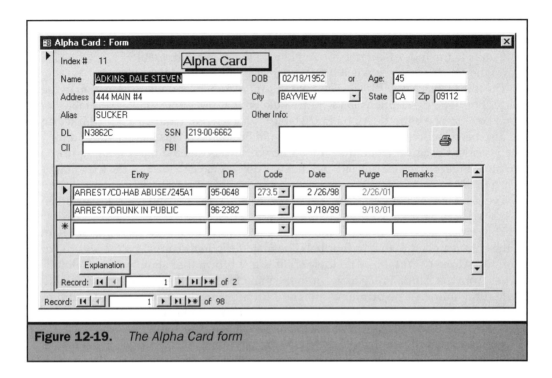

Figure 12-19. *The Alpha Card form*

Note
If you're unable to open the Alpha Card form, you may not have imported the custom menus and toolbars with the database. See Appendix B for instructions about importing the database from the CD.

Adding a Subform

The main form and subform in a hierarchical form are synchronized so the subform displays only the records related to the record currently displayed in the main form. You can enter new records in either the main form or the subform. A main form can have as many subforms as you need and you can even nest subforms up to two levels, which means you can have a subform within a subform.

You saw in the last chapter how to create a main form and a subform at the same time using the Form Wizard. Simply create a new form with fields from two or more related tables. If the relationship is one-to-many, the wizard shows fields from the "one" side in the main form and fields from the "many" side in the subform. If you already have a main form and want to add a subform to it, you can use the Subform/Subreport Wizard available in the control toolbox.

With the Subform Wizard

You can use the Subform Wizard to create and insert a new subform or to insert an existing subform into a main form. To use the wizard to add the Alpha Entry Subform to a copy of the Alpha Card form, do the following:

1. Open the Copy of Alpha Card form in Design view.

2. Make sure the Control Wizard button is pressed in and click the Subform/Subreport tool in the toolbox.

3. Click in the form design and draw an outline where you want the subform. You usually want the subform to span the width of the detail section in the form below the information in the main form. After the wizard starts, do one of the following:

   ■ If creating a new subform, click Using existing tables and queries, and then click Next. Now choose from the Tables/Queries list and fields lists, just as when you create a regular form with the Form Wizard. Then click Next.

   ■ If you already created and saved the form you want to insert, click the Forms tab and select Alpha Entry Subform from the drop-down list (see Figure 12-20), and then click Next.

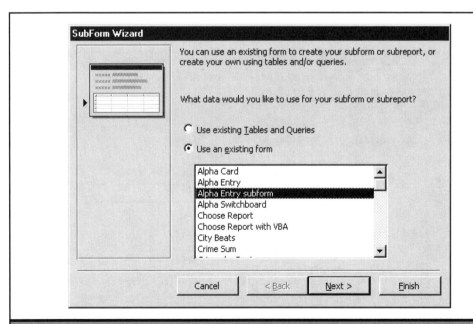

Figure 12-20. *Choosing an existing form as the subform*

4. In the next dialog box, you can choose from a list of links assumed by Access or choose to define your own. If you choose to define you own, the dialog box includes boxes where you can choose the fields that link the main form to the subform (see Figure 12-21). Choose the Index field in both forms, and then click Next.

5. Enter a name for the subform or accept Alpha Entry Subform, and then click Finish.

6. Open the property sheet and click the subform border (not the label).

7. Click the Data tab and make sure the Link Child Fields property refers to the foreign key in the subform and the Link Master Fields property refers to the linking field in the main form.

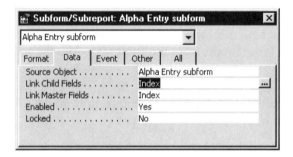

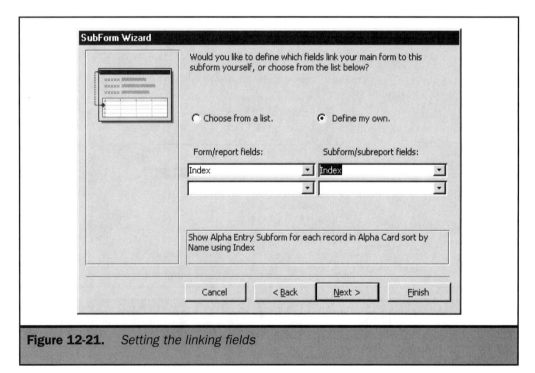

Figure 12-21. *Setting the linking fields*

Without the Subform Wizard

If you already created and saved the form you want to insert into the main form as a subform, the easiest way is to drag it to the form design from the Database window. To accomplish this, do the following:

1. Open the main form in Design view, and then press F11 or click Database Window.
2. Choose Window | Tile Vertically, so you can see both windows at once.
3. Click the Forms tab in the Database window and drag the Subform icon from the Database window to the form design, usually into the Detail section (see Figure 12-22).
4. Open the property sheet and click the Data tab.
5. Click the subform border, and then check the Source Object and linking properties as before.

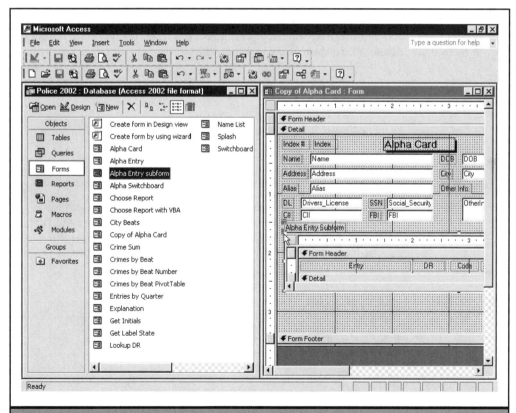

Figure 12-22.   *Dragging the subform to the form design*

Using the Hierarchical Form

To move from the main form to the subform, click in the subform, usually in a record selector or an editable area. To return to the main form, click an editable control or its label. When you work in Navigation mode, some special key combinations move the cursor from the subform back to the main form, for example:

- Pressing CTRL-TAB moves the cursor through the sequence of editable controls in the main form, and then moves to the first record in the subform. Pressing the combination again moves to the first control of the next record in the main form.

- Pressing CTRL-SHIFT-TAB moves the cursor to the previous control in the main form or, if the cursor is anywhere in the subform, it moves the cursor to the last control in the tab order of the main form.

- Pressing CTRL-SHIFT-HOME moves the cursor to the first editable field in the main form, even if it was pressed while the cursor was in the subform.

Each form has its own set of navigation buttons that you can use to move among the records. The subform also has a vertical scroll bar to move other records into view. You can add new records, or edit or delete existing records in either the main form or the subform using the standard data entry techniques.

 Make sure the cursor is in the right place—in the main form or the subform—before you try to add or delete records.

You can also sort records and set filters to limit records in either the main form or the subform using standard sorting and filtering methods.

Modifying a Subform

The complete subform design is included with the main form design. You can make changes to it in place. Select the control in the subform you want to change, and then change it as usual. If you want to work on the subform in its own window, right-click the subform and choose Subform in New Window from the shortcut menu. You can also choose View | Subform in New Window.

 The subform control in the main form is a separate control and has different properties than the subform object. To select the subform control, click one of the subform boundaries. To select the subform for making changes in the subform itself, click the form selector for the subform.

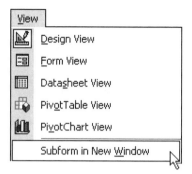

Linking and Synchronizing Forms

Each month, the Los Padres Police Department purges entries that were kept the required period of time. To do this, the user opens the Alpha Entry form. This is a tabular form showing all the entries in DR number order. One of the fields is Purge, which contains the date when the record should be removed from the file. If this entry is the last one connected to the individual, the Alpha Card should also be removed. To view the related record in the Alpha Card file, use the Command Button Wizard to add a command button at the right end of the Alpha Entry record that opens the Alpha Card form for the same Index number.

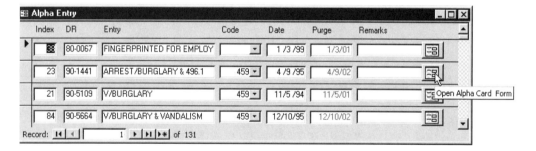

When you click the command button in Form view, the Alpha Card form opens showing only that single record. The word "(Filtered)" in the navigation button area indicates that only the one record has been extracted. Figure 12-23 shows the Alpha Entry form and the resulting Alpha Card record with the windows tiled vertically. The record for Index 4 is the current record in the Alpha Entry form and the Alpha Card form shows the related record.

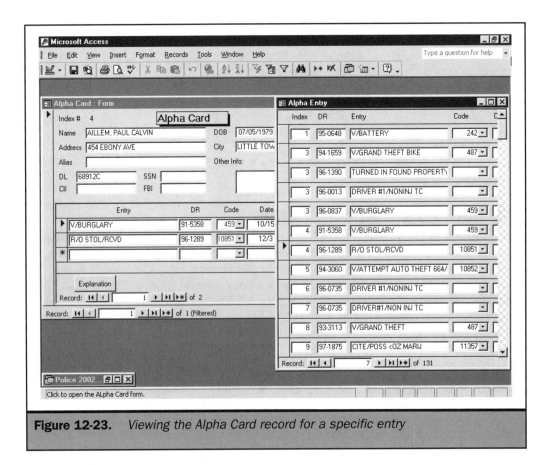

Figure 12-23. *Viewing the Alpha Card record for a specific entry*

The Police database includes one other form that's linked to the Alpha Entry subform. The Explanation form is a pop-up form displaying an explanation of the entry that appears in the Alpha Entry subform. To add this feature, first create the pop-up form. A *pop-up form* is a special-purpose form, like the toolbox or property sheet, which can be kept on the screen while you're doing other things. The pop-up form remains on the screen until you close it.

In contrast, a dialog box doesn't let you do anything else until you respond to the options presented in the box and click OK, Close, Cancel, or another button in the box. In Chapter 21, you see how to create custom forms that can be used as dialog boxes.

To create a pop-up form that displays an explanation of the entry selected in the Alpha Entry subform, start a new form based on the Entry Explanation table. Add both fields to the design and resize the form to the smallest possible height and width.

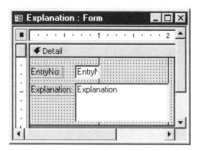

Then open the property sheet for the form and change the following properties:

■ Set Scroll Bars to Neither.

■ Set Record Selectors, Navigation Buttons, Dividing Lines, Auto Resize, and Auto Center all to No.

■ Set Border Style to Thin.

■ Set Min Max Buttons to None.

■ On the Other tab, set Pop Up to Yes.

Now add a command button to the form footer of the Alpha Entry subform that opens the Explanation form for the selected entry by doing the following:

1. Open the Alpha Entry subform in Design view by one of these methods:

   ■ In Alpha Card form Design view, click the subform form selector.

   ■ Choose Alpha Entry subform in the Forms tab of the Database window, and then choose Design.

2. The form already has a header and footer section. Drag the lower border of the form down to make room for a command button, if necessary.

3. Make sure the Control Wizard button is pressed and click the Command Button tool. Then click in the left end of the form footer section.

4. Choose Form from the Categories list, Open Form from the Actions list, and click Next.

5. Choose Explanation as the form to open, and then click Next.

6. In the next dialog box, choose Open the Form and Find Specific Data to Display, and then click Next.

7. Select EntryNo and the linking fields in both tables. Then click Next.

8. Choose Text instead of Picture for the button, enter Explanation in the box, and click Next.

9. Enter Explanation as the name for the command button and click Finish.

Figure 12-24 shows the explanation of the entry selected in the Alpha Entry subform. The pop-up form remains onscreen until you close it.

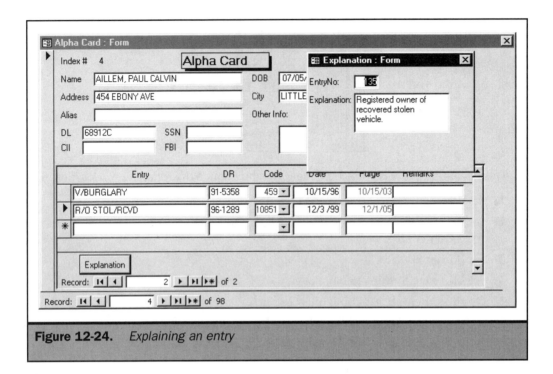

Figure 12-24. *Explaining an entry*

Note *The way the form is designed, when you move to another entry, you must click the Explanation button again to see the explanation for that entry. If you want to synchronize the two forms so the Explanation form follows the subform selection, you need to add a macro or an event procedure to one of the event properties. Chapter 19 discusses creating and using macros.*

Adding Custom Help

You've already seen some of the ways you can get help from Access. When you move the mouse pointer over a toolbar button, a tool tip pops up, displaying the name of the button. The status bar displays messages related to the current activity or object, including the description you entered for the fields in your table design.

Then, in nearly every window, you can click the Help button to get an explanation of virtually any object on the screen. Pressing F1 also brings you context-sensitive Help messages. If all else fails, type a question in the Ask a Question box and press ENTER to look for help on a certain subject.

When you design your own application, times may occur when a quick reminder can help with entering data, creating a filter, or printing a report. Access lets you create your own custom tips and status bar messages as properties of a form or report. You can also create custom tips that pop up when you click a What's This button (the one with a question mark) on your form, and then click one of the controls.

RETRIEVING AND
PRESENTING INFORMATION

Custom Control Tips

The *Control Tip Text property* specifies the message that appears when you move the mouse pointer over a control in the form. Short tips are best, but you can enter up to 255 characters, if you want. To create a Control Tip, select the control and type the message in the Control Tip Text property box on the Other tab.

Status Bar Messages

A *status bar message* is a good way to display instructions for entering data in a control or explaining the options in an option group. *Status Bar Text* is a control property available for any control on a form you can select. The message displays when the control gets focus.

To specify a message to display in the status bar, type the text in the Status Bar Text property box on the Other tab. You can enter up to 255 characters, but the amount of text displayed is limited by the physical space across the status bar. This depends on the size of the window and the font you use for the message.

 Try to keep the status bar messages brief. A lengthy message can be truncated and cause some confusion on the part of the user.

Validating or Restricting Data in Forms

Access gives you several ways to validate or restrict data entered in forms. You can create controls such as check boxes that limit the data to Yes/No values or a list box that requires a value be picked from the list. You can also set certain form and control properties that limit or restrict data entry.

Validating with Properties

When you designed your tables, you added field properties to help ensure valid data. You created input masks, entered validation rules, and specified default values for some of the fields. This is the preferred way to validate data because you only have to do it once. Any bound control you add to a form inherits the properties you set in the table design. If you wait and add the validations and restrictions to a form, you need to do it for every form that refers to that data.

Times may occur, however, when you want to superimpose more validation in the form. For example, you may want to display different error messages when the data is invalid or prevent entering data in a field altogether. If you want to validate unbound controls, you must do it in the form design. The validation rules for controls in a form are created the same as for a field in table design. You can ask for help from the Expression Builder if you need it.

Table 12-4 describes the control and form properties you can use to validate or restrict data in a form.

Property	Description
Default Value	Enters default value for new records. Set in table design or control property sheet.
Validation Rule	Specifies validation rule. If data entered in the control violates the rule, Access displays an error message. Set in table design or control property sheet.
Validation Text	Specifies the error message to display when the data is invalid. Set in table design or control property sheet.
Input Mask	Specifies format for entered data. Set in table design or control property sheet.
Enabled	Determines whether a control can have focus. If set to No, the control appears dimmed and cannot receive focus in Form view. Yes is default for all controls except unbound object frames. Set in control property sheet.
Locked	Determines whether data can be changed in Form view. If set to Yes, control becomes read-only. No is default for all controls except unbound object frames. Set in control property sheet.
Allow Edits	Determines whether user can edit existing records in the form. Set in form property sheet.
Allow Additions	Determines whether user can add new records in the form. Set in form property sheet.
Allow Deletions	Determines whether user can delete a record in the form. Set in form property sheet.
Data Entry	Determines whether form opens with a blank record for data entry or with all records appearing. Set in form property sheet.

Table 12-4. *Data Validation and Restriction Properties*

If you set one of these properties in the table design and set the same property to a different value in the form design, the bound control property overrides the field property. For example, if you want to set the default value for a date field to today's date in the form instead of the value set as the field property in the table design, type **=Date()** in the control's Default Value property box. This takes precedence over the setting in the field property.

The order in which validation rules are applied is as follows:

1. Rule specified by a macro or event procedure that responds to the Before Update event.
2. Rule specified as control Validation Rule property.
3. Rule specified as the field Validation Rule property.
4. Rule specified as the table Record Validation Rule.

If you change any of the validation rules in table Design view, these changes are enforced on controls based on those fields, even if you added the controls to the form before making the changes.

You can combine property settings to accomplish specific purposes. For example, if you want the form to be read-only, set Allow Edits, Allow Additions, and Allow Deletions all to No.

Combining the Enabled and Locked property settings for a control can create custom results as shown in Table 12-5.

RETRIEVING AND PRESENTING INFORMATION

Enabled Setting	Locked Setting	Results
Yes	Yes	Control can receive focus. The data is displayed normally and can be copied but can't be edited.
Yes	No	Control can receive focus. Use this combination to allow editing of objects in unbound object frames. The data is displayed normally and can be copied or edited.
No	Yes	Control cannot receive focus. Data is displayed normally, but can't be copied or edited.
No	No	Control cannot receive focus. Control and data both appear dimmed and are disabled.

Table 12-5. *Combining Enabled and Locked Properties*

You can also combine the Enabled and Tab Stop properties. If you set Enabled to Yes and Tab Stop to No, the control can't be selected by pressing TAB, but it can still be selected by clicking the control or its label.

By combining the Enabled property with the After Update event property, you can disable a control until the user has entered text in another control. For example, disable a command button that prints an envelope until the user has entered the ZIP code for the address.

Validating with Events

Attaching macros or event procedures to form and control event properties can give you additional flexibility and power over data entry. For example, you can require that at least two of three fields must be filled in before you can save the record. You would also use an event procedure if the validation refers to controls on other forms or if the control contains a function.

If you want to validate the data before the whole record is updated, add the procedure to a form event. To validate the data before moving to the next control, add the procedure to a control event. Table 12-6 shows a few of the form and control events that can be used for data validation.

See Chapter 18 for more information about events and their sequence of occurrence.

Event	Description
Before Update (form)	Rule enforced before saving new or changed data in a record.
On Delete (form)	Rule enforced before deleting a record.
Before Update (control)	Rule enforced before saving new or changed data in a control.
On Exit (control)	Rule enforced before leaving control.

Table 12-6. *Data Validation Events*

Optimizing Form and Subform Performance

Performance is a function of both speed and efficiency of memory use. If your form runs slowly or takes up too much memory, it won't perform up to its potential. You can do several things to optimize form and subform performance:

- Don't load up the form or subform with bitmaps and graphics. They take a lot of space and time to load. When you do use them, try to use black-and-white bitmaps rather than the larger color versions.

- Change unbound object frames used to display graphics to image controls, which are more conservative of disk space.

- Try to avoid overlapping controls in a form.

- Keep open only the forms you're using. Close all others.

- If the record source has a lot of records and you use the form mostly for entering new data, set the form's Data Entry property to Yes. Otherwise, Access has to scan all the existing records before it reaches the blank one at the end of the recordset.

- Sorting takes time, especially in a multiple-table query. Don't sort records in an underlying query unless it's necessary.

- If a subform doesn't need all the fields in a table, create a query with only the essential fields and use that as the basis for the subform.

- Index all the fields in a subform used to link with the main form. Also index all subform fields used in criteria.

- If the form or subform has no code behind it, change the Has Module property to No, so Access won't reserve space for the class module or waste time looking for it.

After you do everything you can think of to improve form and subform performance, you can use the Performance Analyzer to see if you can do anything else.

Summary

You may never want to add hyperlinks or a calendar to a form but, if you do, this chapter contains all the information you need to add these and other special controls. The most important aspect of form design isn't "What new and exotic things can I add to it?" but, rather, "What does the user need to see and know to do his or her job?"

One of the most flexible features of form design is the capability to link subforms g to a main form to show related data from more than one table. You saw examples of using subforms in this and the preceding chapter where records from a table on the "many" side of a one-to-many relationship were displayed in a subform with the data from the "one" side in the main form.

Starting with the next chapter, you learn how to create reports for distributing information to outside users. You also make further use of the Police database introduced in this chapter, as well as continue to see examples using the Home Tech Repair database. You create reports first with the help of the Report Wizard, and then from scratch in report Design view. Chapter 14 also discusses special reports that group and summarize data, or print envelopes and mailing labels.

MOUS Exam Activities Explored in This Chapter

Level	Activity	Section Title
Expert	Use data validation	Validating with Properties Validating with Events
Expert	Create and modify Lookup field properties	Placing and Customizing Date-Related Controls
Expert	Create forms in Design View	Starting a New Custom Form
Expert	Add subform controls to Access forms	Adding a Subform
Expert	Add a Web browser control to Access forms	ActiveX Controls—Adding a Web Browser Control

The Complete Reference

Access 2002

Chapter 13

Using the Report Wizard

The Access Report Wizards help you prepare many types of reports—from simple ones that contain complete information from one or more tables to reports that calculate and summarize information and present it in a variety of visual representations. You can also create multiple column reports to be used for printing mailing labels of all kinds and use Access tables for mail merge applications.

In this chapter, you see examples of reports using different databases: the Access Northwind sample database, as well as the Home Tech Repair and Police databases introduced in earlier chapters. No single database has all the elements necessary to display the versatility of Access report writing.

The Report Wizard, described in this chapter, guides you through creating a simple report based on one table, a more complex report based on two tables, and, finally, a summary report that groups records and calculates summary values. After using the Report Wizard, you can then modify the design to add special features and set report properties. Chapter 14 continues the discussion of reports by addressing customization, subreports, and mailing labels.

Creating a New Report Design

Although you create Access reports using the same techniques as for creating forms, major differences exist between forms and reports with respect to the design concepts. Forms deal with data and the processes of data management, such as data entry, validation, and retrieval. Reports, on the other hand, deal with information derived from the data. For example, the numbers 999900000 are simply data and mean nothing to you until you turn the sequence into information: 999-90-0000.

Forms are used primarily by people who are acquainted with computers and database management systems, so forms can be somewhat abbreviated, assuming the user understands the process at hand. *Reports* are much more widely distributed, sometimes to people who may never have seen a computer, so they must be self-explanatory and focus on the purpose of the report in plain language.

What Is the Purpose of the Report?

The differences between forms and reports necessitate a much wider range of report design features, which, in turn, creates a more complex design problem. As with form design, you start the process by defining what you want out of the report. Concentrate first on the intended recipients and the level of detail they want to see. Management wants to see information to help it make strategic decisions, such as trends in sales and summary economic data. Operational personnel wants more detailed information relating to ongoing business, such as stock levels and employee performance.

Figure 13-1 shows examples of three types of reports. You can see all these reports in the Northwind database in the Program Files\Microsoft Office\Office\Samples folder.

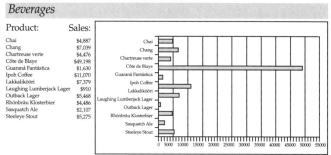

Sales by Category

Wednesday, February 28, 2001

Beverages

Product: Sales:

Chai	$4,887
Chang	$7,039
Chartreuse verte	$4,476
Côte de Blaye	$49,198
Guaraná Fantástica	$1,630
Ipoh Coffee	$11,070
Lakkalikööri	$7,379
Laughing Lumberjack Lager	$910
Outback Lager	$5,468
Rhönbräu Klosterbier	$4,486
Sasquatch Ale	$2,107
Steeleye Stout	$5,275

Alphabetical List of Products

A

Product Name:	Category Name:	Quantity Per Unit:	Units In Stock:
Aniseed Syrup	Condiments	12 - 550 ml bottles	13

B

Product Name:	Category Name:	Quantity Per Unit:	Units In Stock:
Boston Crab Meat	Seafood	24 - 4 oz tins	123

C

Product Name:	Category Name:	Quantity Per Unit:	Units In Stock:
Camembert Pierrot	Dairy Products	15 - 300 g rounds	19
Carnarvon Tigers	Seafood	16 kg pkg.	42
Chai	Beverages	10 boxes x 20 bags	39
Chang	Beverages	24 - 12 oz bottles	17
Chartreuse verte	Beverages	750 cc per bottle	69
Chef Anton's Cajun Seasoning	Condiments	48 - 6 oz jars	53
Chocolade	Confections	10 pkgs.	15
Côte de Blaye	Beverages	12 - 75 cl bottles	17

E

Product Name:	Category Name:	Quantity Per Unit:	Units In Stock:
Escargots de Bourgogne	Seafood	24 pieces	62

F

Product Name:	Category Name:	Quantity Per Unit:	Units In Stock:
Filo Mix	Grains/Cereals	16 - 2 kg boxes	38
Fløtemysost	Dairy Products	10 - 500 g pkgs.	26

INVOICE

One Portals Way, Twin Points WA 98156
Phone: 1-206-555-1417 Fax: 1-206-555-5938

Date: 28-Feb-2001

Ship To: Ernst Handel
Kirchgasse 6
Graz 8010
Austria

Bill To: Ernst Handel
Kirchgasse 6
Graz 8010
Austria

Order ID:	Customer ID:	Salesperson:	Order Date:	Required Date:	Shipped Date:	Ship Via:
11072	ERNSH	Margaret Peacock	05-May-1998	02-Jun-1998		United Package.

Product ID:	Product Name:	Quantity:	Unit Price:	Discount:	Extended Price:
2	Chang	8	$19.00	0%	$152.00
41	Jack's New England Clam	40	$9.65	0%	$386.00
50	Valkoinen suklaa	22	$16.25	0%	$357.50
64	Wimmers gute Semmelknödel	130	$33.25	0%	$4,322.50

Subtotal:	$5,218.00
Freight:	$258.64
Total:	$5,476.64

Figure 13-1.   *Sample reports*

If you installed Office XP in a folder other than the default, the path to Northwind will be different.

The top report shows a summary of sales by product category, complete with a chart illustrating the information. This type of report is suitable for a manager who makes decisions based on product popularity. The second report shows a detailed list of all products in the store in alphabetic order. This kind of report is used by operational personnel to look up an item when a customer calls to ask if the product is in stock. If you want to carry this kind of report into the stock room to check current inventory levels, you might want to add the storage location field, and then sort or group the records by that value.

The lower report is an example of a special purpose report used for printing invoices. The report is based on a query that extracts information from several related tables containing shipper, customer, order, product, and salesperson data.

 A report can be designed to print on a preprinted form, which can be scanned and saved as a report template. See Chapter 14 for information on printing reports on preprinted forms.

Consulting the future users of the report is essential to the design process and drawing a sketch of the proposed report for review by the intended users is helpful. Unfortunately, even experienced business people don't always predict everything they want in a report until they see the finished product; then they identify other things they need in the report. For this reason, you should plan on the design process being an iterative one that continuously improves the product.

Selecting, Sorting, and Grouping the Data

Once you collect the requirements for the report content and appearance, you can begin to locate the required data in the database. It may be stored in a single table or distributed among several related tables. If the data is stored in several tables in the database, make sure the tables can be linked, if they aren't already related.

Sorting Records

Next define the sort order for the records in the report. For example, do you want the records in chronological order or by some identifier, such as the primary key? If a sort order is saved with the table, you can apply it automatically in the report. For example, if you have a mailing list for sending promotional material to your customers, you may want to sort the outgoing mail by ZIP code to save on postal costs.

Filtering Records

At times, you might want to limit the records in a report based on a certain filter criterion. For example, you might want to prepare a report for the ordering clerk to use in placing orders. The report would include only those products that have fewer items in stock than the minimum number recommended. You can base the report on a query that extracts only the data you want or apply a filter to the report later. To complete the report, you could also include the name and telephone number of the supplier of each product.

Grouping Records

Records are often grouped in a report. This is a good way to relate data from several records and convert it into meaningful information. For example, you could group sales by quarter in an attempt to predict future inventory requirements. You can even include charts and graphs in your report that illustrate the information even more clearly.

Specifying Summary and Calculated Fields

Once the records are grouped, summaries and calculated fields can add an important element to reports. They can save the readers time by doing much of the data evaluation work for them. For example, the report shown in Figure 13-1a is intended to compare the sales of various beverage products. The manager is considering eliminating some of these product lines and needs information to decide which ones are no longer popular. If the report summarizes sales data over a period of time and presents it in a report, the manager then has all the required numeric information already summarized.

Starting a Report

You have three basic ways to create a report:

- Use the Access AutoReport feature.
- Use one of the Report Wizards.
- Create your own design in the report Design view.

Like most Access activities, you have several ways to start a new report design. Once you try them, you can decide which is your favorite method. You can begin from anywhere in the Database window. Use one of the following methods to open the New Report dialog box (see Figure 13-2):

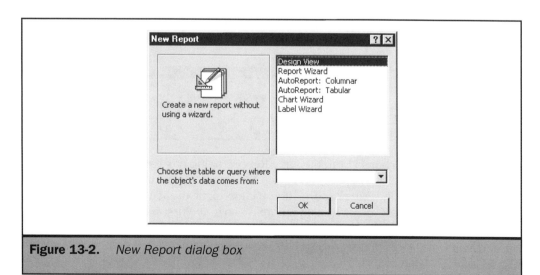

Figure 13-2.   *New Report dialog box*

■ Click Reports under Objects in the Database window, and then click New.

■ Choose Insert | Report from any object page.

■ Click the New Object button and choose Report from the list.

■ Click Tables or Queries under Objects and select a table or query name. Then choose Insert | Report, or click the New Object button and choose Report from the list.

■ From an open Datasheet (table or query) view, choose Insert | Report, or click the New Object button and choose Report.

The New Report dialog box offers six ways to create a report, including three wizards and two AutoReport layouts. If you select or open a table or query before starting the new report, the name also appears in the dialog box.

While you're working on a table in Design view, you can start a new report by choosing Report from the New Object button list. You can create and save the report design, but you cannot preview the report while the table is open in Design view. You must close the table Design window before you can switch to the report Print or Layout Preview.

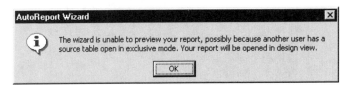

The next step is to choose from the New Report dialog box list and select a table or query as the basis for the report, if desired. You must select a table or query if you want to choose one of the AutoReports. If you choose one of the wizards without first selecting a table or query as the basis, you can do so in the first wizard dialog box. If you choose Design view without naming a table or query, you don't have access to any field names unless you enter a table or query in the Record Source property, but you can add other controls to the design.

Click OK after making the selections in the New Report dialog box to move on to the report building process.

Choosing an AutoReport

AutoReport creates a quick report of all the data in a table or query. The report isn't fancy, but it's useful for checking and verifying the data in your table. When you print the records from Datasheet view, the data appears in a tabular layout resembling the datasheet itself. The default AutoReport created by choosing Insert | AutoReport or by choosing AutoReport from the New Object button list is columnar with the field names down the left column and the field values in the right column. Figure 13-3 shows a preview of the Home Tech Repair Customer default AutoReport. No style is applied and no report title, page numbers, or dates are included.

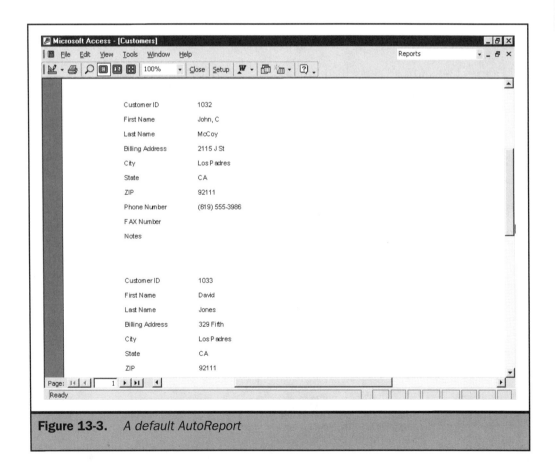

Figure 13-3.   *A default AutoReport*

AutoReport places all fields in the same order as they appear in the table or query, and uses the table or query name as the report title. The name also appears in the Report window title bar even though the report isn't yet saved. When you try to close the report preview, the report Design view appears. If you try to close the Design view, Access asks if you want to save the report.

You have more flexibility when you create an AutoReport by selecting from the New Report dialog box. You have a choice of Columnar or Tabular styles. Again, you must select a table or query as the basis before Access creates an AutoReport.

AutoReports created by choosing from the New Report dialog box use one of the predefined report styles, including a title, formatted field names, page numbers, and the current date. To create an AutoReport, do the following:

1. Use one of the previously described methods to open the New Report dialog box.

2. Choose AutoReport: Columnar or AutoReport: Tabular.

3. Click the drop-down arrow and select the table or query name to use as the basis for the report.

4. Click OK. Access creates the report design and displays the report in Print Preview.

Figures 13-4 and 13-5 show the printed first pages of columnar and tabular AutoReports created for the Home Tech Repair Customers table.

Customers

Customer ID	1032
First Name	John, C
Last Name	McCoy
Billing	2115 J St
City	Los Padres
State	CA
ZIP	92111
Phone Number	(619) 555-3986
FAX Number	
Notes	

Customer ID	1033
First Name	David
Last Name	Jones
Billing	329 Fifth
City	Los Padres
State	CA
ZIP	92111
Phone Number	(619) 555-4673
FAX Number	
Notes	Repeat customer

Figure 13-4.   *The Customers columnar AutoReport*

Cust	First Name	Last Name	Billing Address	City	State	ZIP	Phone Num	FAX Numb	Notes
1032	John, C	McCoy	2115 J St	Los Padres	CA	92111	(619) 555-3986		
1033	David	Jones	329 Fifth	Los Padres	CA	92111	(619) 555-4673		Repeat customer
1034	Phyllis	Rogers	2478 9th St	Los Padres	CA	92111	(619) 555-2979		
1035	Oliver	Perry	2001 J St	Los Padres	CA	92111	(619) 555-2345		
1036	Agnes	Brown	186 G St	Los Padres	CA	92111	(619) 555-4766		Guard dog on site.
1037	Harry	Selms	1520 8th St	Los Padres	CA	92111	(619) 555-6489		
1038	Antonio	Perez	1656 F St	Los Padres	CA	92111	(619) 555-6489		Call in evening.
1039	Bob	Anders	952 C St	Los Padres	CA	92111	(619) 555-3335		
1040	James	Norr	1510 H St	Los Padres	CA	92111	(619) 555-9888		
1041	Patricia	Gonzales	2595 9th St	Los Padres	CA	92111	(619) 555-1543		
1042	Phillip	Armstrong	3401 F St	Los Padres	CA	92111	(619) 555-7843		
1043	Thomas	Barrett	871 G St	Los Padres	CA	92111	(619) 555-2103		

Wednesday, February 28, 2001   Page 1 of 1

Figure 13-5. *The Customers tabular AutoReport*

The style of the AutoReport created this way is the one chosen for the most recently created report. To change to another style, choose Format | AutoFormat or click the AutoFormat toolbar button, and then choose a different style from the AutoFormat dialog box. More about changing report properties and appearance later in this chapter.

After creating the AutoReport, you can print it as it appears or switch to Design view and make changes. An AutoReport is so quick and easy, unless you plan to use it quite often, don't bother to name and save it. To close the report without saving the design, choose Close from the File menu and respond No when asked if you want to save the changes.

Using the Report Wizard

The *Report Wizard* is quite similar to the Form Wizard, and it presents a series of dialog boxes that guide you through the design process. Most of the dialog boxes present the same kinds of options, but the Report Wizard includes a couple of new ones that let you choose the sorting, grouping, and summarizing specifications. The examples in the remainder of this chapter use the Home Tech Repair database, as well as the Police database introduced in the previous chapter. The Police database is used on a 24-hour basis and maintains a log of incidents reported to the department. It provides a central source of information in support of the officers in the field, as well as the citizens in the community.

Creating a Single-Table Report with the Report Wizard

In the first example, the Report Wizard creates a report based on the Alpha Entry by Code Query that limits the data in the Alpha Entry table of the Police database to only those with a numeric incident code. This screens out the employment fingerprint and traffic collision reports that don't involve a crime.

Field:	EntryNo	Index	Entry	DR	Code	Date
Table:	Alpha Entry	Alpha Entry	Alpha Entry	Alpha Entry	Alpha Entry	Alpha Entry
Sort:						
Show:	☑	☑	☑	☑	☑	☑
Criteria:					Not =0	
or:						

To create this new report with the help of the Report Wizard, do the following:

1. With the Police database open, click Reports under Objects and double-click the Create Report by Using Wizard option. You can also open the New Report dialog box and choose Report Wizard.

2. The first dialog box is the same as in the Form Wizard in which you choose the fields you want to include in the report from the tables and queries in the database. Select all the fields in the Alpha Entry by Code Query and click Next.

3. In the second dialog box, the wizard asks if you want to group the records by any of the field values. Select Code as the name of the field you want to group by and click the right arrow (>), as shown in Figure 13-6.

   ■ If you change your mind, select the field name and click the left arrow (<) to remove the group designation. The up and down arrows near Priority change the grouping order level.

   ■ If you're grouping on a field with numeric values, you can group by an interval such as 50 or 100. Click Grouping Options and choose from the drop-down list in the Grouping Intervals dialog box.

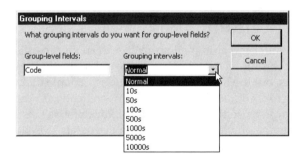

- If one of the fields you're grouping on is a number or currency field, the Summary Options button becomes available. More about adding summaries in a later section.

4. The next dialog box, which is another one unique to the Report Wizard, asks if you want to sort your records within the groups in other than primary key order. The groups are automatically sorted in ascending order by the group field value. Figure 13-7 shows a sort specified by Date in ascending order. You can sort on up to four fields by clicking the arrow next to the sort box and choosing the field from the list. If you want the sort in descending order, click the Ascending button to the right of the sort box.

Tip *The fields needn't all be sorted in the same order. You can sort by one field in ascending order and the next in descending order.*

5. In the next dialog box (see Figure 13-8), you select the layout you want for the report and the print orientation. If you select a lot of fields, you might want to change the orientation to landscape. Select Align Left 1 and click Next.

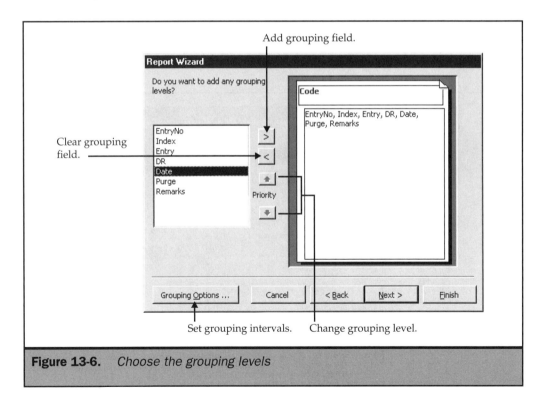

Figure 13-6. *Choose the grouping levels*

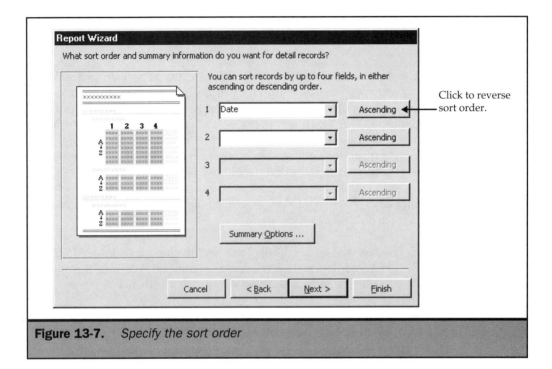

Figure 13-7. *Specify the sort order*

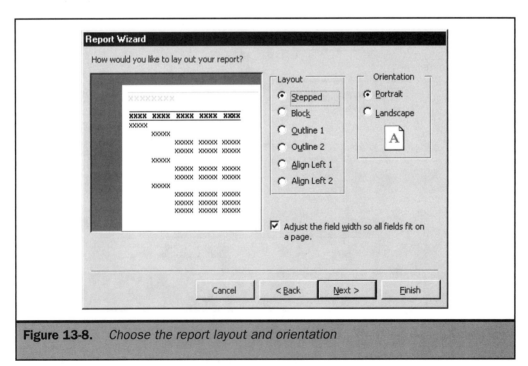

Figure 13-8. *Choose the report layout and orientation*

Tip
An option also asks the wizard to adjust the width of the fields so they can all fit on the page. This may result in losing characters in the column headings or currency symbols in the field data, but you can adjust the column widths later in Design view.

6. The next wizard dialog box offers six different styles from which to choose. The styles apply to the font size and style, the line spacing, and color, much like with the Form Wizard, but are more suited to printed output. As you select each style, an example is displayed in the sample pane on the left. Select the desired style and click Next.

7. The final dialog box is the same as with the Form Wizard: You give the report a name and choose whether to view the report or go directly to Design view. Enter **Alpha Entry by Code Report** as the report name and click Finish.

Figure 13-9 shows a Print Preview of the Alpha Entry by Code Report generated by the Report Wizard. If you also want an interpretation of the code to appear with the code number in the group header, add the Description field from the Penal Codes table to the query.

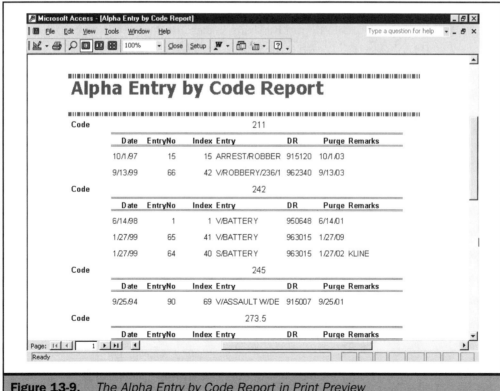

Figure 13-9. *The Alpha Entry by Code Report in Print Preview*

You can see the title text box isn't wide enough to contain the whole report name. Switch to Design view and widen the control. At the same time, you can also make the separation between groups clearer by adding a group footer and drawing a line across the section as a visual group divider.

Creating a Three-Table Report with the Report Wizard

When you use the Report Wizard to create a report based on two or more tables or queries, you can specify which table contains the main data and which contains the subordinate data. In the example in this section, the Alpha Card table is specified as the parent table and the Alpha Entry table as the related child table. The Entry Explanation table, which is related one-to-one to the Alpha Entry table, is also included. The resulting report shows multiple Alpha Entry records for a single Alpha Card record.

   When you choose fields from one or more tables, the Report Wizard automatically creates a query, which is run every time to open the report. The query is a SELECT statement that appears as the report Control Source property. If the query is complex, you can save processing time by creating the query yourself and using it as the basis for the report.

To create the three-table report, do the following:

1. Double-click the Create Report by Using Wizard item on the Reports page, or open the New Report dialog box, choose Report Wizard, and then click OK.

2. In the first dialog box, choose the Index and Name fields from the Alpha Card table; the EntryNo, Entry, Code, and Date fields from the Alpha Entry table; and the Explanation field from the Entry Explanation table. Then click Next.

If you select fields from two or more tables that aren't related, Access displays a message box asking if you want to quit the Report Wizard and edit the relationships. Click OK to open the Relationships window and the Show Table dialog box. After relating the tables, you must restart the Report Wizard. If you don't want to relate the tables, click Cancel and you return to the first dialog box where you can remove the unrelated fields.

3. In the second dialog box (see Figure 13-10), the wizard asks how you want to view the data. This dialog box appears only if you chose fields from more than one table or query. Access assumes the parent table of the relationship is to appear as the main data. Accept the choice and click Next.

The Show me more information button opens the Report Wizard Tips window where you can ask to see several examples of how the wizard can group your data in the report. Click Close to return to the Report Wizard.

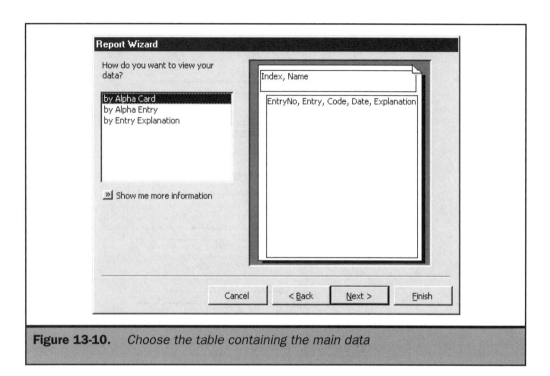

Figure 13-10.   *Choose the table containing the main data*

4. The next dialog box, similar to the one shown earlier in Figure 13-6, shows the Alpha Card fields in the upper box and the Alpha Entry and Entry Explanation fields in a list below. Select any grouping levels you want in this dialog box. Click Next twice to skip this and the Sort Options dialog box to reach the Layout dialog box in which you select a layout.

5. Choose Outline 1 and click Next twice.

6. In the last dialog box, name the report **Alpha Card with Entries** and click Finish.

Don't use any special characters, such as an ampersand (&), in the title you give the wizard. Although the file is named using the character, when the title appears on the first page of the report, the character is converted to an underline.

Figure 13-11 shows the printed first page of the new Alpha Card with Entries report. As you navigate through the pages, you see several improvements should be made. For example, the column headers may appear on one page and the corresponding Alpha Entry data carried over to the next. To correct this, you can group on the Index field and specify the group not be broken between pages. The next chapter discusses this and other modifications you can make to improve the report design. You may also like to see a group divider between the index lists. The report title text is again incomplete.

Alpha Card with Entries

	Index		1		
	Name		ALLEN, FRANK ROGER		

EntryNo	Date	Entry	Explanation	Code
1	6 /14/95	V/BATTERY	Victim of battery	242

	Index		3		
	Name		AIYER, ROBERT L		

EntryNo	Date	Entry	Explanation	Code
134	7 /11/96	V/BURGLARY	Victim of house burglary	459
133	1 /8 /96	DRIVER #1/NONINJ TC	Driver #1 in a non-injury traffic collision.	
132	10/21/96	TURNED IN FOUND	Turned in jewelry found in store parking lot.	
2	4 /25/94	V/GRAND THEFT BIKE	Victim of grand theft. Bicycle was stolen.	487

	Index		4		
	Name		AILLEM, PAUL CALVIN		

EntryNo	Date	Entry	Explanation	Code
3	10/15/93	V/BURGLARY	Victim of burglary	459
135	12/3 /96	R/O STOL/RCVD	Registered owner of recovered stolen vehicle.	10851

	Index		5		
	Name		AIZENBAUM, ESTELA		

EntryNo	Date	Entry	Explanation	Code
4	8 /6 /94	V/ATTEMPT AUTO THEFT	Victim of an attempted auto theft.	10852

	Index		6		
	Name		AKEN, HAILESILASSIE B		

EntryNo	Date	Entry	Explanation	Code
5	3 /31/96	DRIVER #1/NONINJ TC	Driver #1 in non-injury traffic collision	

Wednesday, February 28, 2001

Figure 13-11.   *Printed Alpha Card with Entries report*

Troubleshooting the Report

If the relationships between the three tables used in this report aren't set properly, the report may not contain complete information. For example, the default relationship uses an inner join. An *inner join* includes only records where both parent and child have the same value in the linking field. So, if an Alpha Entry is related to the Entry Explanation table with an inner join, you won't see any Alpha Entry records that have no corresponding Entry Explanation record.

To solve this problem, edit the relationship and change it to the second option in the Edit Relationship dialog box, a left outer join. This will include all the records from the Alpha Entry table and only those from the Entry Explanation table that match.

Another useful feature of this relationship is to enforce referential integrity and choose Cascade Delete. This automatically cleans up the database by deleting the explanation records when the entry record itself is deleted.

Creating a Summary Report with the Report Wizard

The Report Wizard's summarizing capabilities are useful when creating reports involving numeric or monetary information. When you choose to group records, the wizard makes summarizing options available with which you can compute the total value; determine the average, minimum, and maximum of the group of values; compute a grand total; and calculate the percent of the grand total represented by each of the groups. The wizard may not create exactly the report you want to see, but it can save you a lot of time with the arithmetic. You can always modify the report appearance later.

For this example, turn back to the Home Tech Repair database. This database has some currency fields that can demonstrate the summary options by creating a report that summarizes the work orders grouped by supervisor. When you choose to group the records by Supervisor, the next dialog box in which you set the sort order now has the Summary Options button available. Clicking this button opens the Summary Options dialog box (see Figure 13-12), which shows the names of all the fields in the report that contain number or currency data.

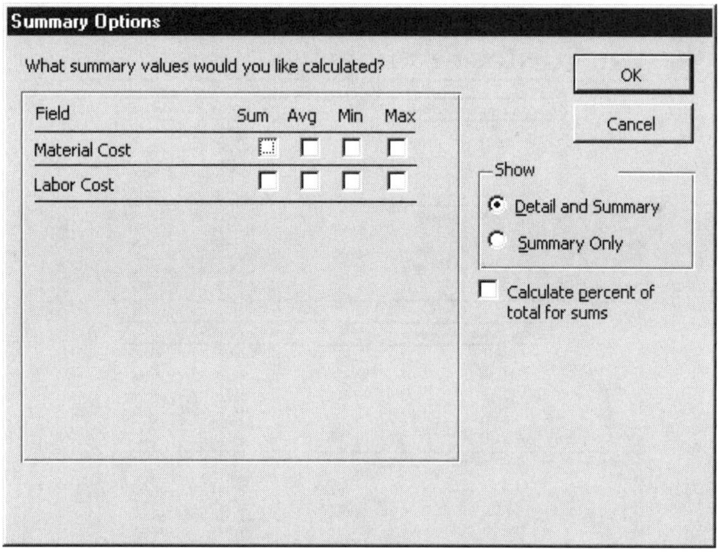

Figure 13-12.   *The Summary Options dialog box*

Click the check boxes for all the summary values you want the wizard to calculate for you. In the Show option group, you can choose to include the detail records with the summaries or show only the summary values. The other option, Calculate percent of total for sums, includes the relative size of each group sum compared to the grand total, which is calculated and printed at the end of the report.

Figure 13-13 shows the printed first page of a report that groups the Home Tech Repair work orders by supervisor and computes the sum, average, minimum, and maximum of the Material Costs and Labor Costs for each group of work orders. The Report Wizard has also automatically counted the number of detail records in each group and displays it at the top of the summary section. A two-point dash-dot line has been added to the group footer as a visual way to separate one supervisor's work orders from the next.

Tip   *The group containing work orders headed by Supervisor 13 is split between pages 1 and 2 in the report. One of the group section properties is Keep Together, which can be set to No, Whole Group, or With First Detail. Set this property to Whole Group if you want to keep the group header, detail section, and the group footer together on the page. Chapter 14 contains more information on grouping records in a custom report and setting group properties.*

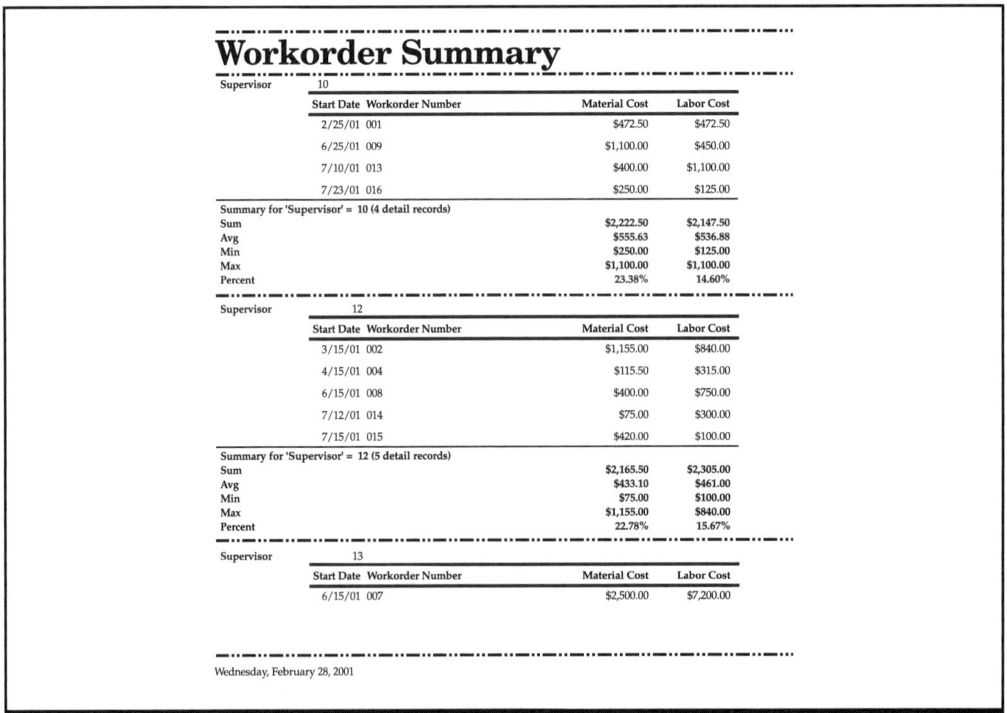

Workorder Summary

Supervisor	10		
Start Date Workorder Number		**Material Cost**	**Labor Cost**
2/25/01 001		$472.50	$472.50
6/25/01 009		$1,100.00	$450.00
7/10/01 013		$400.00	$1,100.00
7/23/01 016		$250.00	$125.00

Summary for 'Supervisor' = 10 (4 detail records)
Sum		$2,222.50	$2,147.50
Avg		$555.63	$536.88
Min		$250.00	$125.00
Max		$1,100.00	$1,100.00
Percent		23.38%	14.60%

Supervisor	12		
Start Date Workorder Number		**Material Cost**	**Labor Cost**
3/15/01 002		$1,155.00	$840.00
4/15/01 004		$115.50	$315.00
6/15/01 008		$400.00	$750.00
7/12/01 014		$75.00	$300.00
7/15/01 015		$420.00	$100.00

Summary for 'Supervisor' = 12 (5 detail records)
Sum		$2,165.50	$2,305.00
Avg		$433.10	$461.00
Min		$75.00	$100.00
Max		$1,155.00	$840.00
Percent		22.78%	15.67%

Supervisor	13		
Start Date Workorder Number		**Material Cost**	**Labor Cost**
6/15/01 007		$2,500.00	$7,200.00

Wednesday, February 28, 2001

Figure 13-13.   *Summarizing work order costs by supervisor*

Looking at the Other Report Wizards

Two additional wizards are available from the New Report dialog box: the Chart Wizard and the Label Wizard. You can use the *Chart Wizard* to create a chart from data in one or more tables or queries. You have a choice of 20 different types of charts, depending on the analysis you want to present graphically. The chart can be free-standing or you can embed it in a form or report. To use the Chart Wizard, you must have the Microsoft Graph applet installed. Graph isn't a feature of the Typical setup, so you might need to run Setup again and add it. See Chapter 15 for more information about creating and editing charts.

The *Label Wizard* helps you create multicolumn reports for predesigned or custom labels. See Chapter 14 for details on creating and printing mailing and other labels.

Previewing the Report

When the Report Wizard has finished creating the report design, you have a choice of going directly to the report Design view or previewing the report as it will be printed. If you haven't used the Report Wizard or you want to preview an existing report, select the desired report name in the Reports page of the Database window, and then do one of the following:

- Click the Preview button in the Database window.
- Click the Print Preview toolbar button.
- Right-click the report name in the Reports tab and choose Print Preview from the shortcut menu.

The Layout Preview is another way you can check the report design. The window looks like the Print Preview window, but it doesn't include all the records in the report. The layout shows all the design elements and just enough records to verify the design is correct. Layout Preview is available from the View button only when the report is open in Design view.

Working in the Print Preview Window

The Access Print Preview window gives you many ways to view the report, including moving around a single page and among pages, looking at several pages at once, and changing the magnification so you can see the details more clearly. Returning to the Police database, Figure 13-14 shows the Alpha Card with Entries report in Print Preview.

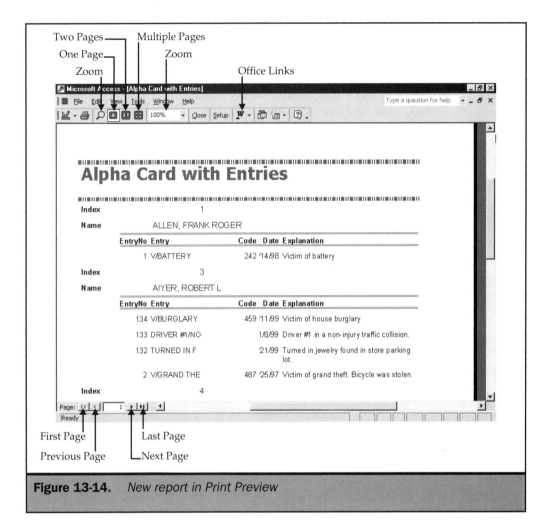

Figure 13-14. *New report in Print Preview*

To close the Print Preview window, do one of the following:

■ Click the Close toolbar button.

■ Press C or ESC.

■ Choose File | Close.

When the Preview window closes, you return to the Database window or the report Design view, depending on where you were when you opened the Print Preview.

Navigating in the Preview

The horizontal and vertical scroll bars enable you to move about on the current page. The navigation buttons at the bottom of the Print Preview window let you move among pages in the report. Click one of the buttons to move to the first, previous, next, or last page of the report. You can also enter the page number in the page number box and press ENTER to move to a specific page.

You can use shortcut keys to navigate in a report preview, as well. Table 13-1 describes the key combinations you can use in the Print Preview window.

Shortcut Keys	Result
F5	Move to page number box to enter target page number.
PAGE DOWN	View next page (when Fit is selected in the magnification box). Scroll down one full screen (when Fit isn't selected).
PAGE UP	View previous page (when Fit is selected in the magnification box). Scroll up one full screen (when Fit isn't selected).
DOWN ARROW	View next page (when Fit is selected in the magnification box). Scroll down by small increments (when Fit isn't selected).
UP ARROW	View previous page (when Fit is selected in the magnification box). Scroll up by small increments (when Fit isn't selected).
CTRL-DOWN ARROW	Move to the bottom of the current page.
CTRL-UP ARROW	Move to the top of the current page.
RIGHT ARROW	Scroll right in small increments.
END or CTRL-RIGHT ARROW	Move to the right edge of the current page.
CTRL-END	Move to the lower-right corner of the current page.
LEFT ARROW	Move left in small increments.
HOME or CTRL-LEFT ARROW	Move to the left edge of the current page.
CTRL-HOME	Move to the upper-left corner of the current page.

Table 13-1. *Shortcut Keys for Navigating in Print Preview*

RETRIEVING AND PRESENTING INFORMATION

If you have a Microsoft IntelliMouse installed, rolling the wheel button also moves you around the current page in the Print Preview window.

Viewing Multiple Pages

Using the Print Preview toolbar buttons, you can view one or two pages adjusted to fit the screen or up to 20 pages arranged in four rows of five pages each.

To view one complete page at a time, do one of the following:

- Click the One Page toolbar button.
- Right-click and choose One Page from the shortcut menu.
- Choose View | Pages and choose One Page from the list.

To view two or more complete pages adjusted to fit the screen, choose Fit in the Zoom box, and then use one of the following methods:

- Click the Two Pages toolbar button.
- Click the Multiple Pages toolbar button and drag the mouse pointer over the grid to select the number of pages and the arrangement you want. Figure 13-15 shows three pages of the Alpha Card with Entries report in Print Preview.

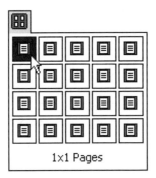

- Choose View | Pages and choose the number of pages from the list. You have a choice of 1, 2, 4, 8, or 12 pages.

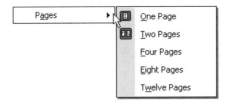

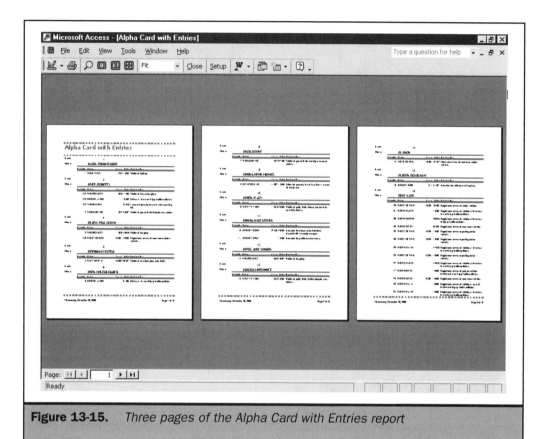

Figure 13-15. *Three pages of the Alpha Card with Entries report*

■ Right-click and choose Multiple Pages from the shortcut menu. Then drag the mouse pointer over the grid to select the number of pages and the arrangement you want to see.

Note *If you used the Pages toolbar button to view multiple pages, the shortcut menu shows the same palette of page arrangements. If you were viewing one page of the report, the shortcut menu option is limited to two-by-three pages.*

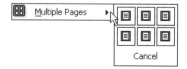

To return to previewing a single page, click the One Page toolbar button.

Changing the Magnification

When you first open the Print Preview window, the report is automatically displayed at 100 percent magnification. You can increase or decrease this degree of magnification to almost any value or ask Access to adjust the report to fit on the screen.

To change the magnification, click the arrow next to the Zoom button on the toolbar and choose a percentage between 10 percent and 200 percent from the list, or enter a value, and then press ENTER. You can also choose Fit from the Zoom button list, which adjusts the magnification to fit the screen. The number of pages you chose to preview at once determines the degree of magnification when you choose Fit.

You can also right-click anywhere in the report preview and click Zoom in the shortcut menu, where you have the same choices as with the toolbar Zoom button.

When the mouse pointer passes over the report preview, it changes to a magnifying glass, which you can click to zoom in and out in the report. This alternates the preview between Fit and the percentage you chose. When the glass shows a minus sign (-), clicking zooms out making the preview less magnified; clicking the magnifying glass with a plus sign (+) zooms in on the area where the pointer was when you clicked it. This provides a quick way to zoom in on a specific part of the report, for example, a group summary field.

Using the Layout Preview

You have another way to preview a report, called Layout Preview, which shows just enough data to demonstrate every section of the report. If your report contains many detail records, it's helpful to see several components on the screen at once, instead of having to navigate through it page by page. You must be in Design view to switch to the Layout Preview.

To see the Alpha Card with Entries report in Layout view, do the following:

1. Click View and choose Design view, or choose View | Design view. If you opened the Print Preview window from the Design view, click Close to return to the Design view.

2. Click View and choose Layout Preview, or choose View | Layout Preview.

The Layout Preview of the report shows an abbreviated version of the Print Preview. For example, the Layout Preview of the Alpha Card with Entries report is reduced from 15 pages in Print Preview to 2 pages. To return to Print Preview, close the Layout Preview, and then switch from Design view to Print Preview.

Printing the Report

You can print the report from either preview window, the Design view, or from the Database window without opening the report. Printing from the Layout Preview only prints the layout pages, not the complete report. Some print commands send the report directly to the printer without opening the Print dialog box; others open the dialog box where you can select other print options.

To print the report from the Layout or Print Preview window, do one of the following:

- Click the Print toolbar button. This sends the report directly to the printer.

- Right-click the report and choose Print from the shortcut menu. This also sends the report directly to the printer.

- Choose File | Print. This opens the Print dialog box.

 If you're viewing the report in Layout Preview, only the elements that appear in the layout are printed, not the entire report.

To print a report from the Database window, select the report name, and then do one of the following:

- Click the Print toolbar button. This sends the report directly to the printer.

- Choose File | Print. This opens the Print dialog box.

- Right-click the report name and choose Print from the shortcut menu. This sends the report directly to the printer instead of opening the Print dialog box as when you select with the report open.

You can also print the report from Design view by clicking the Print toolbar button and sending the report directly to the printer, or by choosing File | Print, which opens the Print dialog box. This prints the report itself, not the report design.

If you want to change any of the page options, such as the margins, the page layout, the printer selection, the number of columns on the page, or the page size, you need to run Page Setup. After setting the page specifications, you can choose the print options, such as number of copies and the range of pages to print.

Running Page Setup

You can open the Page Setup dialog box from any view of a report or from the Database window without opening the report by starting File | Page Setup. If you're in the Database window, select the report name before choosing Page Setup. If you're previewing the report in either the Layout or Print Preview, you can also right-click the report and choose Page Setup from the shortcut menu.

The page settings are stored with the report, so you need to set them only once and they'll be in effect every time you print the report. The Page Setup dialog box has three tabs: Margins, Page, and Columns.

■ Click the Margins tab to set the width of each of the four page margins and also choose whether to print the data only, without any of the labels or other unbound objects. Figure 13-16 shows the Margins tab of the Page Setup dialog box.

If you want to change the default page margins so you don't have to change them for each report separately, choose Tools | Options and click the General tab. Specify the margins in the Print margins group and click Apply or OK. This affects only new forms and reports, not existing ones. See Chapter 16 for more information about customizing the Access workplace.

Click the Page tab to set the orientation of the print on the page, the paper size and source, as well as to select a different printer if you have more than one in your system. Figure 13-17 shows the Page tab of the Page Setup dialog box. The choice of paper sources depends on the printer you're using.

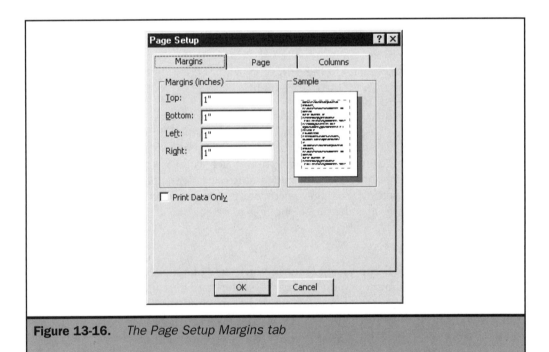

Figure 13-16. *The Page Setup Margins tab*

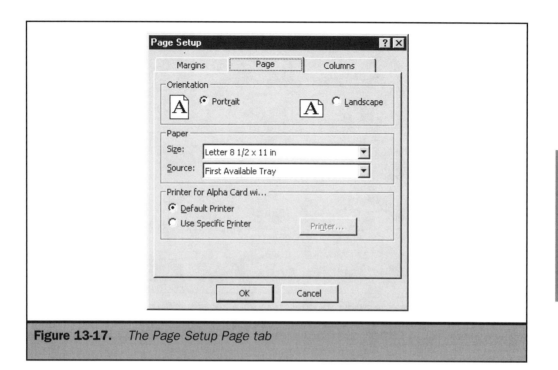

Figure 13-17. *The Page Setup Page tab*

If you want to print using a printer other than the default printer, click Use Specific Printer, and then click the Printer button. This opens a dialog box that displays a list of the printers currently installed in the system. Select a different printer and click OK to return to the Page Setup dialog box.

Note *Use the Column tab to choose the number of items across the page, their row and column spacing, their size, and the layout on the page. This is used mostly for printing mailing labels that come in predesigned sheets. Access offers ready-made layouts for most of the commercially available label sheets. Chapter 14 describes using the Columns tab when printing mailing labels.*

After you make all the desired changes to the page setup, click OK to return to the previous view of the report or the Database window.

Choosing Print Options

When you choose File | Print, the standard Windows Print dialog box opens (see Figure 13-18) and gives you several choices regarding printing. If you have more than one printer in your system, you can select one other than the default printer by clicking the arrow next to the Name box and selecting from the list of installed printers.

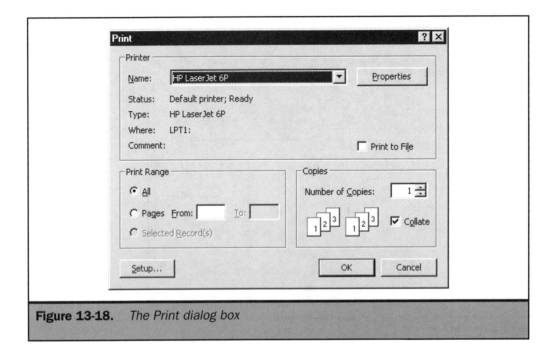

Figure 13-18. *The Print dialog box*

Table 13-2 describes the other options available in the Print dialog box.

Option	Description
Properties	Opens the Setup dialog box for the selected printer. The options depend on the printer model.
Print to File	Writes the report to a disk file for printing later. When you click OK, the Print to File dialog box opens where you name the file and choose the folder in which to store it.
All	Prints all the pages in the report.

Table 13-2. *Print Dialog Box Options*

Option	Description
Pages From:	Specifies the page numbers of the first and last pages of the range you want to print.
Selected Record(s)	If you selected records in a form or datasheet, this option is available. Prints only the selection.
Number of Copies	Specifies the number of copies to print.
Collate	When checked, collates the pages in numeric order. When cleared, Access prints all copies of one page, then prints all copies of the next page, and so on.
Setup	Opens the Page Setup dialog box with only the Margins and Columns tabs.

Table 13-2.   *Print Dialog Box Options* (continued)

After you set all the options you want, click OK to print the report.

Printing from a Shortcut

To create a shortcut on the desktop for a report, select the report name in the Database window and choose Edit | Create Shortcut, or right-click the report name in the Database window and choose Create Shortcut from the shortcut menu. With either method, the Create Shortcut dialog box opens showing the Object Type and Name, the host database name and path, and the location of the shortcut file. Click OK to complete the shortcut.

Minimize any open windows and look at the shortcut on the Windows desktop. Now you have two ways of printing the report using the shortcut icon, both of which send the report directly to the printer without opening the Print dialog box:

- Right-click the shortcut and choose Print from the shortcut menu.
- Click Start, choose Settings, and then choose Printers to open the Printers dialog box. Drag the shortcut icon and drop it on the icon of the printer you want to use in the Printers dialog box.

Modifying the Report Design

The method you use to open a report in Design view depends on where you start:

- From the Database window, select the report name and click Design, or right-click the report name and choose Design from the shortcut menu.

- From the Print Preview or Layout Preview window, click Close if you previewed the report from Design view, or click the View button and choose Design view if you previewed from the Database window.

- From a shortcut on the Windows desktop, right-click the shortcut and choose Design from the menu.

Working in the report Design view is almost identical to working in the form Design view. The controls are the same, although you include fewer user-interactive controls in reports. The ways you select sections and controls and change their properties are the same as with form designs. Placing, positioning, and sizing controls in the report design also use the same techniques.

Touring the Report Design Window

The report Design window is similar to the form Design window. The menu bar is the same, and the only new toolbar button is the Grouping and Sorting button, which you use a little later. The View button shows Print Preview in the report Design window instead of the Form View icon shown in the form Design view. The Formatting toolbar is exactly the same and the report control toolbox is identical to the one you saw when working with forms. To switch between views of the report, click the View button. When working in report Design view, the View button list includes Design view, Print Preview, and Layout Preview.

Examining Report Sections

If the report design looks more cluttered than the form designs you worked with in the last chapter, it's probably because of the extra sections—the Page Header and Footer sections. The wizard automatically adds these sections when it creates a report. The *Page Header section* contains information to be printed at the top of each page, such as the field names used as column headings. The *Page Footer section* contains information to be printed at the bottom of each page, such as the current date and the page number.

The *Report Header and Footer sections* contain information to be printed only once, at the beginning or the end of the report. The *Detail section* contains the bulk of the data in the report.

Two optional sections, the *Group Header and Footer sections*, contain information to be printed at the top and bottom of each group of records. These sections are used when you group the records by the values in a specific field, such as by Code as in the Alpha Entry by Code Report shown earlier.

You select a section in a report design the same way as in a form design by using one of the following methods:

- Click the Object toolbar button and choose the desired section from the list.
- Click the section selector at the left of the section label line.
- Click anywhere in the section label line.
- Click anywhere in the section, outside of any control.

To change the size of a report section, select the section and drag the lower boundary up or down. The report and page sections come in pairs, so if you want to remove one, reduce its height to zero. The section must be empty before you can do that. When you add a group, you needn't use both the header and footer. You can choose whether you want a group header or footer, or both, by setting the group properties.

Setting Report and Section Properties

You open and use the property sheets in a report design the same as in a form design, and many of the properties are the same. Table 13-3 describes properties unique to reports. The default settings appear in bold.

Tab	Property	Description	Settings
Format	Page Header	Specifies whether to print the page header information on all pages of the report or to suppress printing on the same page as the report header and/or footer.	**All Pages**, Not With Rpt Hdr, Not With Rpt Ftr, Not With Rpt Hdr/Ftr
Format	Page Footer	Same as Page Header, except refers to printing the page footer information.	Same as Page Header

Table 13-3. *Properties Unique to Reports*

RETRIEVING AND
PRESENTING INFORMATION

Tab	Property	Description	Settings
Format	Grp Keep Together	Works with the group Keep Together property to specify whether to keep the group together in the same column or same page.	**Per Column**, Per Page
Data	Filter On	Applies filter saved with underlying table or query.	Yes, **No**
Data	Order By On	Applies sort order saved with underlying table or query.	Yes, **No**
Other	Record Locks	Specifies whether records are locked while the report is being previewed or printed.	**No Locks**, All Records
Other	Date Grouping	Specifies how you want to group dates in a report. U.S. Defaults setting causes the week to begin on Sunday. So if you group a Date/Time field by week, the report groups dates from Sunday to Saturday.	**Use System Settings**, U.S. Defaults

Table 13-3.   *Properties Unique to Reports* (continued)

Tip   *When you create a report with a special title page and you don't want to print the page header or footer information on the same page, set the Page Header and Page Footer report properties to Not With Rpt Hdr. Then set the report header Force New Page property to After Section to continue printing on a new page.*

If you want the report footer information also printed on a separate page at the end of the report, set both the Page Header and Page Footer properties to Not With Rpt Hdr/Ftr, and then set the report footer Force New Page property to Before Section.

When you create a report based on a table or query saved with a sort order or a filter, the report inherits both properties, but doesn't apply them until you say so. If you look at the report properties, you can see the Filter and Order By expressions saved with the table. To apply the filter, set the Filter On property to Yes. To use the inherited sort order, set the Order By On property to Yes. To remove them, change the settings to No. If you want to change the filter or sort order, type a new expression in the Filter or Order By property box.

Note	*Reports also have two unique event properties: On No Data and On Page. The No Data event occurs if no data is in the report to print. You can attach a procedure or macro to this event property to suppress printing an empty report and to display an explanation message. The Page event occurs after a page is formatted for printing, but before it's printed. This event is also useful for controlling report printing. See Chapter 18 for more discussion of events and how you can harness them for useful purposes.*

Each of the report sections also has a list of properties you can set to get exactly the appearance and behavior you want. Table 13-4 describes the properties common to all sections in a report design with the default settings appearing in bold. Other section-unique properties are discussed subsequently.

Property	Description	Settings
Name	Specifies the string expression that identifies the name of a section.	**Section name** or a string expression up to 64 characters long
Visible	Shows or hides the section in previewing and printing.	**Yes**, No
Height	Specifies the height of the section.	Height, in inches
Back Color	Specifies the background color of the section.	Number corresponding to the selected color
Special Effect	Adds a special effect to the section.	**Flat**, Raised, Sunken
Tag	Stores extra information about the section.	**Zero-length string (" ")** or a string expression of up to 2,048 characters

Table 13-4.   *Common Report Section Properties*

Note   *All report sections also possess two event properties: On Format and On Print. The* Format *event occurs when Access determines which data belongs in a section, but before the section is formatted for previewing or printing. The* Print *event occurs after data in a report section is formatted for printing, but before the section is printed. See Chapter 18 for more information on events and when they occur.*

Page headers and footers have no additional properties, but the remaining sections—report header and footer, group header and footer, and detail sections—share several other properties, as described in Table 13-5. The default settings appear in bold.

Property	Description	Settings
Force New Page	Specifies whether report sections (header, detail, footer) are printed on a separate page, rather than on the current page.	**None**, Before Section, After Section, Before & After
New Row Or Col	Specifies whether a section is printed in a new row or column within a multiple-column report.	**None**, Before Section, After Section, Before & After
Keep Together	Specifies whether to print a section all on one page or to print across two pages.	**Yes**, No
Can Grow	Allows the section to grow vertically, so all data it contains can be printed or previewed.	Yes, **No**
Can Shrink	Allows the section to shrink vertically, so the data it contains can be printed or previewed without leaving blank lines.	Yes, **No**

Table 13-5.   *Other Common Section Properties*

Note *These sections also have the On Retreat event property in common. The* Retreat *event occurs when Microsoft Access returns to a previous Report section during report formatting, for example, to determine where certain controls and sections are located on a report and whether they fit in a given space.*

The Group Header section has one more property unique to that section: *Repeat Section,* which is used to specify whether a group header is repeated on the next page or column when a group spans more than one page or column. The default setting is No. If the group header contains column headings and other relevant information, you might want to print it at the top of each page or column.

Placing and Adjusting Controls

You place controls in a report design using the control tools in the toolbox. To select a control, click the control. To select more than one control, do one of the following:

- Click the horizontal or vertical ruler and drag to draw a box around the controls you want to select.

- Click the report design outside of any control and draw a box around the controls you want selected.

- Hold down SHIFT as you click each control in the group you want to select.

To resize and move controls, you can drag the handles and use the options in the Format menu. All the methods are the same as with form design.

Changing the Report Style

One of the Report Wizard dialog boxes showed you a list of styles from which to choose. If you don't like the style you selected there, you can change to one of the other styles in the list by clicking the AutoFormat toolbar button in Design view. You can also choose Format | AutoFormat to open the same dialog box. Figure 13-19 shows the AutoFormat dialog box after clicking the Options button.

You can use the options to apply the font, color, and border formatting selectively. By default, all three options are checked. If you clear them one at a time, you can see the difference in the displayed sample.

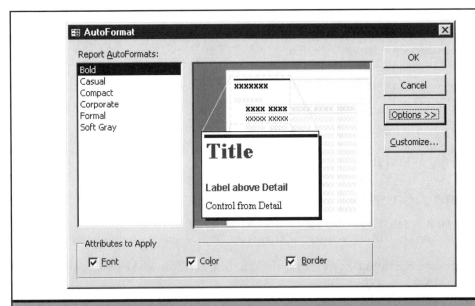

Figure 13-19. *The AutoFormat dialog box*

Customizing a Report AutoFormat

Using the Customize button in the AutoFormat dialog box, you can create a custom format and add it to the list of AutoFormats available to your reports. You have three options:

- Create a new AutoFormat based on the one used in an open report.
- Modify an existing AutoFormat with the changes you made to the format of the open report.
- Delete an AutoFormat from the list.

Before starting to customize a format, click the Options button, check the attributes you want modified, and then click Customize.

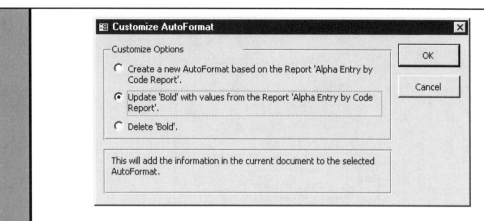

As you select an option, an explanation is displayed in the lower panel. Select one of the three Customize Options, and then click OK or click Cancel to return to the AutoFormat dialog box. If you choose to create a new AutoFormat, Access asks you to enter a name for it. Once you save the new AutoFormat, it's available to any new reports.

Adding Page Numbers and Date/Times

The Report Wizard automatically added page numbers and the current date/time to the Page Footer section of the Alpha Card with Entries report. A *page number* is an unbound text box control that you can add to a report design and format in several ways. A date/time field is also an unbound control and is based on your current system date/time settings.

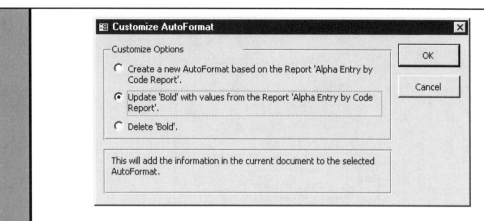

Adding a Page Number

If you haven't used the Report Wizard and you want to add a page number to your report, choose Insert | Page Numbers to open the Page Numbers dialog box (see Figure 13-20). You have several options in the Page Numbers dialog box regarding the page number format, position, and alignment. You can also suppress printing the page number on the first page of the report.

The dialog box offers two page number formats: Page *N* and Page *N* of *M*, where *N* is the page number and *M* is the total number of pages.

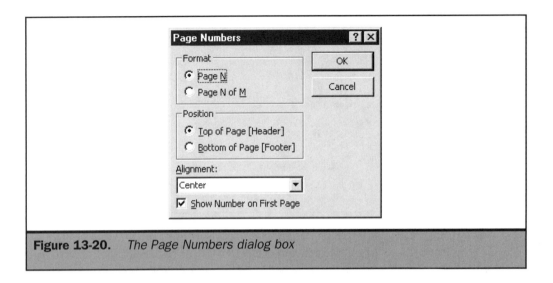

Figure 13-20. *The Page Numbers dialog box*

You can see the Report Wizard used the Page N *of* M *option in specifying the page numbers in the Alpha Entry by Code Report. The expression that appears in the page number text box control is =*"Page "&[Page]&" of "&[Pages]. *This expression concatenates alphabetic characters with the Page (current page number) and Pages (total number of pages) field values. The characters enclosed in quotation marks appear in the page number field. Notice spaces follow the word "Page" and are on both sides of the word "of" to separate the words from the numbers. The ampersand signs (&) are the concatenation operators. The result is, for example, Page 12 of 25 pages.*

You can position the page number either in the page header or footer by selecting from the Position options.

The page number alignment options include

- *Left,* which places the text box at the left margin.
- *Center,* which places the text box centered between the right and left margins.
- *Right,* which places the text box at the right margin.
- *Inside,* which places the text box at the left margin on odd pages and at the right margin on even pages.
- *Outside,* which places the text box at the right margin on odd pages and at the left margin on even pages.

If you don't want to print the page number on the first page of the report, clear the check in the Show Number on First Page box.

Changing the Page Numbers Format

The Page Numbers dialog box gave you a choice of two formats for the page number text box. You can also enter a custom expression in the Control Source property of the page number text box, which includes characters with the values. Some other expressions you might want to use for page numbers are

Expression	Displays
=[Page]	1, 2, 3
="Entry Report: Page "&[Page]	Entry Report: Page 1, Entry Report: Page 2, Entry Report: Page 3
=[Page]&"/"&[Pages]&"Pages"	1/3 Pages, 2/3 Pages, 3/3 Pages

Adding a Date/Time Control

To add the current date and time to the report, choose Insert | Date and Time. The Date/Time dialog box shown in Figure 13-21 lets you include the date and/or the time and gives you a choice of formats for each.

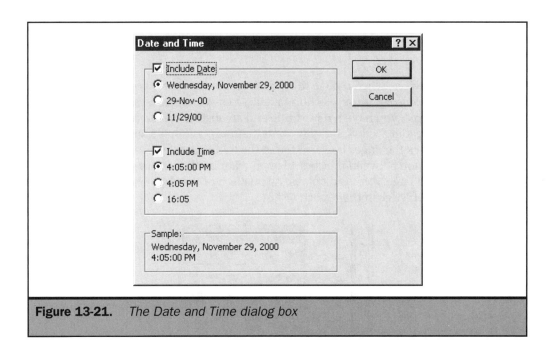

Figure 13-21.   *The Date and Time dialog box*

If the report design has a Report Header section, the date/time control is automatically placed there. If not, it goes in the Detail section. You can drag it to any place you want in the design.

The Report Wizard added the expression =Now( ) to the Page Footer section of the Alpha Card with Entries report. This prints the current system date at the bottom of each page. You could also use the expression =Date( ) to insert the current system date. Many other built-in Date/Time functions are available from the Expression Builder, which return the date and time components (day, month, year, hour, week, and so on) in a variety of ways.

If you look at the properties of the date/time control in the report, you can see the Control Source property is the expression =*Now()* and the Format is Long Date. This displays the date with the day of the week, as well as the date, for example, Monday, January 14, 2002. You can change the Format property in the property sheet to one of the other Date/Time formats.

If you're grouping records by date interval, such as week or month, the values are grouped according to the country or locale selected in the Regional Settings section of the Windows Control Panel. If you're set up to run in Finland, for example, and you want to use the US-type date display, you can change the date/time group property to US Default. The US Default setting uses Sunday as First Day and the week beginning January 1 as First Week.

Adding Page Breaks

If left to its own devices, when a page fills up, Access starts a new page. You can add a page break control within a section to tell Access where you want a new page to begin. For example, you have a report title and an abstract of the report's contents all in the Report Header section, but you want them printed on separate pages. To accomplish this, click the Page Break button in the toolbox and place the control in the Report Header section between the controls you want on the first page and those you want on the second page. Access displays the position of the page break as a short dotted line at the left edge in the report design.

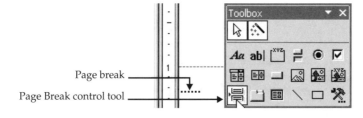

Page break
Page Break control tool

Saving the Report Design

When you create a report with the help of the Report Wizard, it's saved for you using the name you entered in the final wizard dialog box. If you don't use the wizard, save the report design frequently as you refine it. This guards against catastrophe and gives you a recent starting point if something goes wrong. Choose File | Save or click the Save toolbar button to save the report without closing the Design window. To close the report, choose File | Close.

You have two other options when saving a report design:

■ Save As, which opens the Save As dialog box where you can choose to save the report design to the current database with the same or a new name.

■ Export, which opens the Export Report To dialog box (see Figure 13-22), where you locate the folder in which you want to save the report and enter a report name. See Chapter 22 for more information about exporting Access reports and other objects.

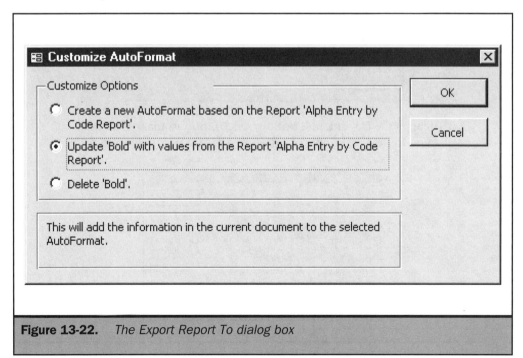

Figure 13-22.   *The Export Report To dialog box*

Documenting the Report Design

In Chapter 5, you saw how to use the Documenter analysis tool to examine and document table relationships. You can also use it to save and print a complete definition of form and report designs. The definition includes the properties, code, and permissions for the report. It also includes the names and properties of all the sections and controls in the report. You can even choose which property categories to include (referring to the tabs in the property sheet). Excluding some of the properties you haven't used can speed up the process.

Note: If you made changes since you last saved the report, the Documenter asks you to save the file before proceeding with the analysis.

The report may be open in any view or you can start the Documenter from the Database window. To start the Documenter, do the following:

1. Point to Analyze in the Tools menu, and then select Documenter.

2. In the Documenter dialog box, click the Reports tab and select the name of the report. The default options print all the names and properties of all the sections and controls, as well as the report properties and any code that may be included.

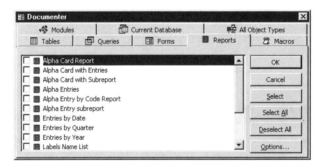

3. To change the Documenter options, click Options, make the desired changes in the Print Report Definition dialog box, and then click OK.

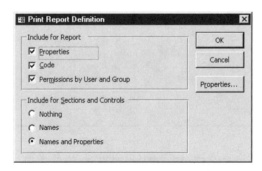

4. If you want to limit the properties to print, click Properties in the Print Definition dialog box and deselect the ones you don't need to print in the Properties Categories dialog box. You have a choice of not printing Data, Event, Layout, and Other properties. If Properties isn't checked in the Print Definition dialog box, the Properties button isn't available. Then click OK twice to return to the Documenter dialog box.

5. To print the report definition, click OK. Be prepared to get a cup of coffee or pick up the cleaning while the Documenter Wizard does its stuff because it's a time-consuming process.

The complete printed definition for the Alpha Card with Entries Report runs nine pages.

Tip   *If you want to save the definition, choose File | Save As Table. Access saves it as a table in the current database with the default name, Object Definition. You aren't prompted for a name for the table. If you want to save more than one object definition, you can rename the first definition with a custom name or let Access save the second as Object Definition1, and so on.*

Using Report Snapshots

Access 2002 offers a new type of report called a *report snapshot,* which is a separate file with the .snp extension that contains a copy of every page of an Access report. The copy includes high-fidelity graphics, charts, and pictures, and it preserves the colors and the two-dimensional layout of the report.

The advantage of a report snapshot is you can save time and money by distributing the report electronically, rather than photocopying and mailing the printed version. The recipients can then preview online and print only the pages they want.

To view, print, or mail a report snapshot, you need the Snapshot Viewer program installed. The *Snapshot Viewer* is a standalone executable program that comes with its own control, help file, and related files. By default, the Snapshot Viewer is installed by Access 2002 the first time you create a report snapshot. You can use the Snapshot Viewer to view a snapshot from the Internet Explorer version 3.0 and later or from any application that supports ActiveX controls.

Note   *While you need Access 2002 to create a report snapshot, the recipients don't need Access to view the snapshot. They need only a combination of the Snapshot Viewer and another program, such as Windows Explorer, a Web browser, or an e-mail program, such as Microsoft Exchange or Microsoft Outlook.*

Creating a Report Snapshot

To create a report snapshot from an existing report, do the following:

1. Select the name of the report in the database window and choose File | Export.

2. The Export Report As dialog box opens (see Figure 13-23) where you choose Snapshot Format in the Save as type box.

3. If you don't want to use the same name as the Access report, choose the drive and folder to export to in the Save in box and enter the filename in the File name box.

4. Click Save.

The Snapshot Viewer automatically starts and displays a preview of the report snapshot. The new report snapshot inherits any current sort order and filter settings in the underlying recordset.

Note *You can also use the OutputTo macro action to create a report snapshot. The OutputTo action has six arguments: Object Type (Report), Object Name, Output Format (Snapshot Format), Output File (filename), AutoStart, and Template File.*

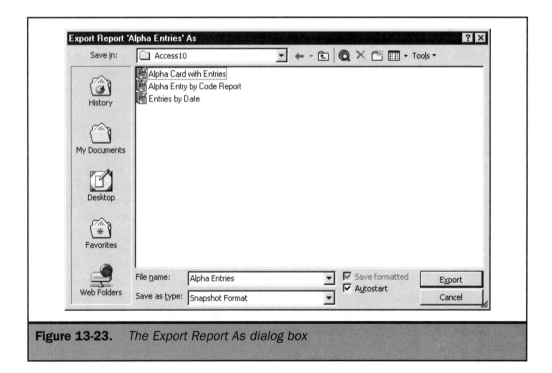

Figure 13-23. *The Export Report As dialog box*

Viewing the Report Snapshot

The Snapshot Viewer window (see Figure 13-24) has a standard menu bar with commonly used File, View, Window, and Help menus. It also shows a navigation bar at the bottom of the window you can use to move among the pages in the report snapshot. The Print button opens the Print dialog box.

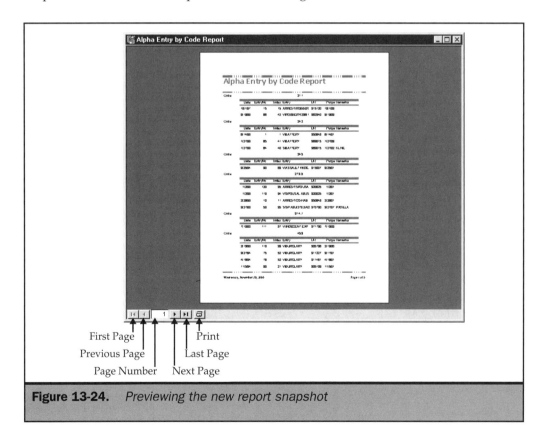

Figure 13-24.   *Previewing the new report snapshot*

The Snapshot Viewer works much like the Print Preview window in Access. You can change the magnification by clicking in the page. If the whole page shows on the screen, clicking it increases the magnification. If already magnified, clicking reduces the preview to its former magnification. The Fit command shows one complete page in the window. The Fill command widens the page to fill the width of the window.

If you saved the report snapshot and want to view it again, you can open the Snapshot Viewer from the Windows Explorer. Start the Window Explorer and locate the .snp file. Double-click the filename and the Snapshot Viewer launches and displays the report snapshot.

Sending the Report Snapshot

You can send the report snapshot to others in electronic mail by using the Send command in the Snapshot Viewer. With the report snapshot open in the Snapshot Viewer, choose File | Send. Your electronic mail program starts and displays an empty message.

Summary

This chapter has only begun the discussion of the variety of printed material Access and the Report Wizards can produce. So far, you learned the fundamentals of report construction and how to use the Report Wizard for creating standard detail and summary reports. You also had a glimpse of the advantages of using report snapshots for electronic distribution of Access reports.

The Report Wizard can create reports from several related tables and arrange the information in almost any way you choose. You have the opportunity to summarize any numeric or currency field values in several ways to include more useful, analytic information.

The next chapter delves deeper into customizing reports and creating special purpose reports, such as a report based on a parameter query that requests information from the user. You see how to create a report from scratch and add special types of controls, including a subreport that contains the detail data related to the data in the main report. The chapter also describes how to create columnar reports for such purposes as printing mailing labels.

Chapter 15, the final chapter in this trio of chapters dealing with printed Access products, looks at the analytical tools provided by the Chart, PivotTable, and Pivot Chart Wizards.

MOUS Exam Activities Explored in This Chapter

Level	Activity	Section Title
Core	Create and format reports	Starting a Report Choosing an AutoReport Using the Report Wizard Setting Report and Section Properties Changing the Report Style
Core	Add calculated controls to reports	Selecting, Sorting, and Grouping the Data—Specifying Summary and Calculated Fields Placing and Adjusting Controls
Core	Preview and print reports	Working in the Print Preview Window Using the Layout Preview Printing the Report
Expert	Create and modify reports	Placing and Adjusting Controls Adding Page Numbers and Date/Times Adding Page Breaks
Expert	Sort and group data in reports	Selecting, Sorting, and Grouping the Data—Sorting Records Selecting, Sorting, and Grouping the Data—Grouping Records Using the Report Wizard—Creating a Summary Report with the Report Wizard

RETRIEVING AND PRESENTING INFORMATION

The
Complete
Reference

Access
2002

Chapter 14

Customizing Reports

When you create reports with Access, you're limited only by your imagination. Access offers so many tools and features for creating custom reports, you can design and print information any way you like.

In addition to printing table or query data grouped and arranged in special orders, you can create reports that print data in columns on the page. A special type of columnar report can be used to print mailing labels or labels for other purposes, such as book plates or floppy disk labels.

This chapter discusses creating custom reports from the Design view, as well as printing labels with the help of the Label Wizard. Most of the examples deal with data in the Police database introduced in an earlier chapter. You may want to keep the Police database open as you work through this chapter.

Creating a New Report Design

Creating a new report with the help of the Report Wizard is by far the easiest way to start a custom report, but you can also start from an empty report design. All you need to do is double-click the Create report in Design view shortcut on the Reports page of the Database window. Then specify the underlying table or query in the Record Source property.

You can also open the New Report dialog box, choose Design View, and then click OK. If you want to base the report on a table or query, do one of the following:

- Select the table or query name in the Database window before opening the New Report dialog box.
- Select the table or query name in the New Report dialog box before clicking OK.

If the report isn't based on table or query data, you can insert only unbound controls such as labels, lines and rectangles, and unbound objects. You can also include hyperlinks to other objects.

Figure 14-1 shows the new Design view for a report based on the Alpha Card table in the Police database. All three report design tools appear in Figure 14-1: the toolbox, the property sheet, and the field list. Notice the page header and footer sections are automatically added to the design with the detail section. A new form design contains only the detail section by default.

After opening the report Design view, use the field list to drag the fields to the design. Use the toolbox to place other controls and the property sheet to create the appearance you want.

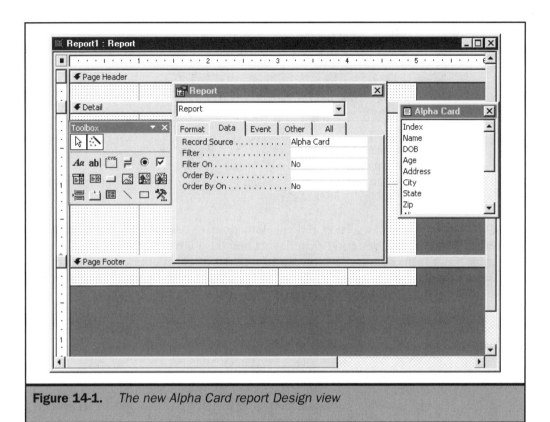

Figure 14-1.   *The new Alpha Card report Design view*

Controlling Headers and Footers

A report design can include a pair of header and footer sections: one for printing information at the beginning and end of the report, and one for printing information at the top and bottom of each page. To add a header/footer pair, choose View | Page Header/Footer or View | Report Header/Footer.

To delete the header/footer pair, choose View and remove the check mark before the Page Header/Footer or Report Header/Footer option. If there are any controls in the section you try to delete, Access displays a message asking if you want to delete all the controls in the sections. Click Yes to delete them or No to abandon the deletion.

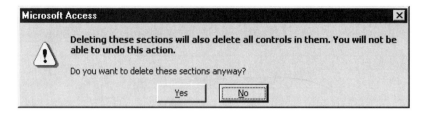

 All deletions are permanent. Always save the report design before you delete controls or sections so you have a copy to fall back on. Then, if you change your mind, you don't have to start over. You can close the design without saving the changes and open it later in its original condition, before the deletions.

To change the height of a section, drag the lower section boundary up or down. If the section contains controls, you can't shrink it beyond the control borders. To keep from having too much blank space when you print a report with no information in the header or footer, do this: shrink the height by dragging the lower boundary up or by setting the Height property to 0. You needn't select the section first to drag the boundary.

 If you selected the section and the property sheet is open when you resize the section, you can see the Height property value change as you drag the boundary.

To suppress the printing of a section that contains information, set the section's Visible property to No. The section still appears in Design view; it just doesn't print.

The Page Header and Page Footer properties on the Format tab of the report property sheet control whether to print the information on the first page with the report header or on the last page with the report footer. The settings for both properties are

- *All Pages* prints the information on every page.
- *Not with Rpt Hdr* prints on all but the first page.
- *Not with Rpt Ftr* prints on all but the last page.
- *Not with Rpt Hdr/Ftr* prints on all pages except the first and last.

Figure 14-2 shows the Alpha Card Report in Design view. The report header section contains a title and the current date. The page header has been reduced to a zero height and the page number has been added in the center of the page footer. If you need to review how to insert dates and page numbers, refer to Chapter 13. A line control was added to the bottom of the detail section to separate the detail information of each record. Finally, the Soft Gray style was chosen from the AutoFormat dialog box. Figure 14-3 shows the report in Print Preview.

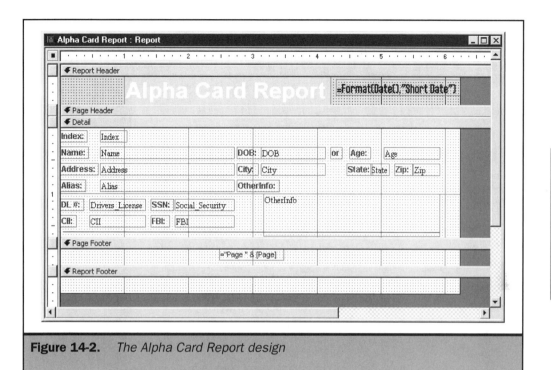

Figure 14-2.   *The Alpha Card Report design*

Customizing with Special Controls

Reports are not user interactive, so they can contain fewer types of special controls. Command buttons and option groups, for example, have no place in reports. You can add calculated fields, graphics, and images to a custom report, either bound or unbound. You can also add hyperlinks, although they are not "live" within the report.

Adding Calculated Fields

Reports often include calculated fields contained in an underlying query. You can also add calculated controls as described in Chapter 10. A *calculated control* is an unbound text box whose Control Source property is set to an expression that produces the desired value. The expression can contain combinations of text, number, currency, or date/time fields from the record source.

Calculated controls are often used to show summary information in reports with grouped records. A later section in this chapter discusses grouping records and summarizing data with expressions and aggregate functions.

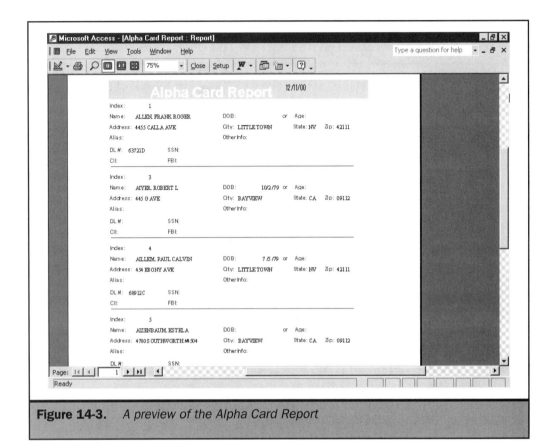

Figure 14-3. *A preview of the Alpha Card Report*

Adding Graphics and Images

As discussed in Chapter 10, you have two ways to insert a graphic or image in a report: as an image control or as an OLE object in an unbound object frame. The advantage of using an image control is it loads quicker than the OLE object in a frame. If you think you might need to edit the OLE object, embed it in an unbound object frame where you can double-click to open the application that created the object.

To add an image control to a report, do the following:

1. Click the Image control tool and click in the report design where you want to place the upper-left corner of the image. Access draws a square frame for the image and opens the Insert Picture dialog box.

2. Locate and select the image you want and click OK. The frame expands to accommodate the full size of the image.

3. Resize the image frame by dragging the sizing handles.

4. Change the image control Size Mode property to Stretch or Zoom.

To insert the image in an unbound object frame, click the Unbound Object Frame tool and draw the frame in the report design. The Insert Object dialog box opens where you can locate and select the image you want in the report.

If the object you want to insert in the frame is an existing Office document or other file originated by an application that supports OLE, check Create from File and type in the path of the file you want to insert.

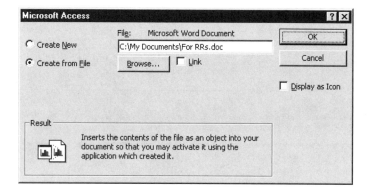

Figure 14-4 shows a report design with a photograph of two roses embedded as an image and a Word document embedded as an OLE Object in an unbound object frame. If you want to edit the Word document, double-click the object in Design view and edit it in place. The photograph in the image control is not editable.

Note *You can also link an OLE Object to a report design, instead of embedding it by choosing Link in the Insert Object dialog box. Linking leaves the object in the host application and provides a path to the object in the report. This saves disk space and ensures the latest version of the object, but it can cause problems if the path to the linked object is changed.*

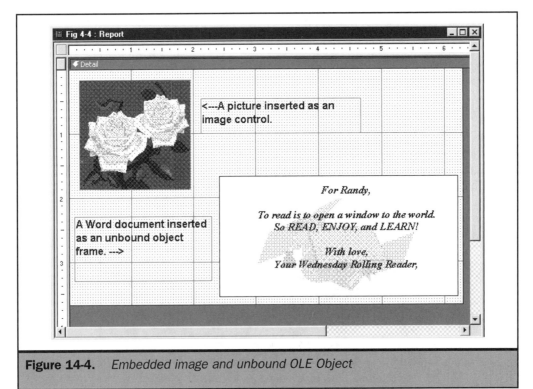

Figure 14-4. *Embedded image and unbound OLE Object*

Adding a Bound OLE Object

Bound OLE Objects are actually OLE Object data type fields from the underlying table or query. To add a bound object to the report design, simply drag the field name from the field list to the design. Access automatically draws the bound object frame for the object.

 An OLE Object data type is actually only a pointer to the object. Such a field cannot be used to sort or index records.

You can also draw the bound object frame first using the control tool, and then bind it to the field in the underlying record source by setting its Control Source property to the name of the field.

Adding a Hyperlink

 You can add a hyperlink to a report design the same way as to a form design by clicking the Insert Hyperlink button or choosing Insert | Hyperlink. After you specify the target of the hyperlink, you can test it in the report Design view by right-clicking the hyperlink and choosing Hyperlink | Open Hyperlink from the shortcut menu.

The hyperlink isn't live in the report in Access Print Preview, but it does become active when you export the report to another Office application, such as Word or Excel.

From the receiving application, you can open the document and click the hyperlink to jump to the address.

When you add a hyperlink to a report design, Access places it in the upper-left corner of the detail section. From there, you can move it to any position in the report design.

> **Note** *When you enter a value in the report Caption property, the text is displayed in the report title bar and it can also be used·as a hyperlink that jumps to this report from another object.*

Adding a Background Picture

Pictures can serve a special purpose in a report other than as an illustration—for example, as a watermark that shows behind the printing. When you add a background picture to a report, it applies to the whole page and is a report property. To add a watermark to the Alpha Card Report design, do the following:

1. Open the report in Design view and double-click the report selector. The property sheet opens showing the report properties.

2. Enter the path and filename of the picture in the Picture property. If you don't know the name or path, click the Build button (...) and locate the file you want in the Insert Picture dialog box and click OK.

3. Set the five other report properties that relate to pictures as follows:

    ■ The Picture Type property specifies whether the picture is embedded or linked.

    ■ The Picture Size Mode property can be set to one of the three size modes: Clip, Stretch, or Zoom. Refer to Chapter 10 for a description of the effects of setting size modes.

    ■ The Picture Alignment property determines the position of the picture in the report. The available settings are Top Left, Top Right, Center, Bottom Left, and Bottom Right.

    ■ When the Picture Tiling property is set to Yes, the picture is repeated across and down the page, beginning at the position specified by the Picture Alignment property and it spreads in four directions. For example, if you set the alignment to Center, a complete picture appears in the center of the page with perhaps incomplete versions fanning out from it. If you choose to tile the picture, use the Clip size mode setting.

    ■ The Picture Pages property specifies on which pages to print the background picture: All Pages, First Page, or No Pages.

4. Switch to Print Preview to see how the report looks with the new background picture. Figure 14-5 shows a preview of the Alpha Card Report with an information icon as a background picture. The picture is aligned in the center of the page and tiled both horizontally and vertically from the center.

RETRIEVING AND PRESENTING INFORMATION

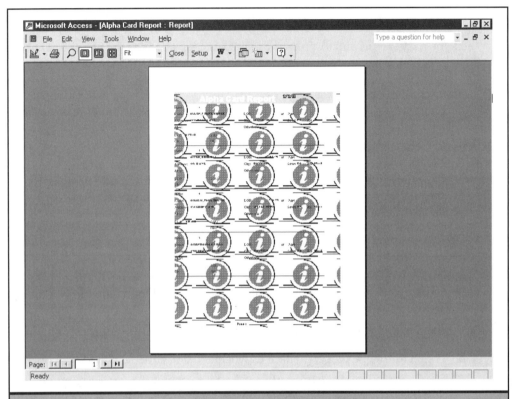

Figure 14-5. *The Alpha Card Report with a background picture*

Bitmap Files vs. Metafiles

Pictures used in bound or unbound object frames, image controls, or as background pictures can be either bitmap files or metafiles. Bitmap files have .bmp or .dib file extensions, while metafiles have .wmf or .emf file extensions.

If you think you might need to adjust the size of the picture, metafiles are easier to scale than bitmaps. This is because metafiles consist of arrangements of lines, rather than a collection of dots. In addition, if disk space is a concern, metafiles are often much smaller than the equivalent bitmaps.

Some graphics programs let you save a picture file as a metafile. Check the program documentation. Pasting a bitmap into a graphics program and saving it as a metafile doesn't convert it to a metafile; it's still a bitmap.

Bitmaps are satisfactory if you don't have a program that generates metafiles and if disk space and scaling aren't a concern. If you need to make small changes in the picture, bitmaps are also more convenient because you can edit individual pixels.

Basing a Report on a Parameter Query

Basing a report on a parameter query enables the user to set the criteria for the report at the time it's run. For example, the police department would like to see a list of incidents reported during a specific time period. When you try to run the report based on the parameter query, you're prompted to enter the parameters, the same as when you try to run the query itself.

Access also gives you the tools to print the entered parameters in the report, usually in the report header section.

Creating the Parameter Query

To create a parameter query that extracts Alpha Entry records having a date within an arbitrary time period, do the following:

1. Select the Alpha Entry table in the Database window and choose Insert | Query, or click the New Object button and choose Query.

2. Choose Design view in the New Query dialog box and click OK.

3. Double-click the asterisk in the Alpha Entry field list to add all the fields to the query.

4. Double-click the Date field to add it to an empty column in the grid and clear the check mark in the Show row, so the value won't appear twice in the report.

5. Type the following in the Criteria row of the Date field:

Between [Type beginning date] And [Type ending date]

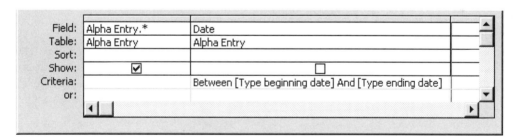

6. Save the query as Entries by Date.

If you run the query, Access displays two parameter prompts: one requesting Type beginning date and the other, Type ending date. Enter the desired dates and click OK to see the list of Alpha Entries reported within that time period.

Creating the Report

A report based on the parameter query also prompts for the parameter values when you open the report in Print Preview. To create a simple report based on the parameter query, do the following:

1. Select the Entries by Date query in the Database window and choose Insert | Report, or click the New Object button and select Report.

2. Choose AutoReport: Tabular in the New Report dialog box and click OK.

3. Because Access immediately opens the new report for preview, it prompts for the parameters.

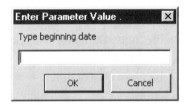

4. Enter the desired beginning date in any valid date format and press ENTER or click OK.

5. Repeat step 4 to enter the ending date. When you click OK, the report opens in Print Preview.

6. Click Close to switch to Design view where you can modify the report design as required.

Printing the Parameters in the Report Header

Access treats the prompt expression as a valid control source for an unbound text box. The selection parameters can be printed with the report by adding unbound text box controls to the design. You can add two text boxes: one for each parameter or combine the parameters in an expression in a single text box. To print the parameters in the report header as one text box, do the following:

1. Click the Text Box control tool and place the control in the report header section.

2. Click outside the new control, and then select the attached label and press DEL to remove the attached label.

3. Double-click the new text box control to open the property sheet and enter the following expression in the Control Source property box:

="Between "&[Type beginning date]&" and "&[Type ending date]

RETRIEVING AND
PRESENTING INFORMATION

(More about combining text and field values in report designs in a later section in this chapter.)

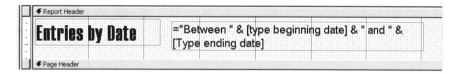

4. Resize the control to fit the expression.

5. After making the final touch-ups, save the report and switch to Print Preview. Figure 14-6 shows a preview of the report displaying Alpha Entries reported between January 15, 1999 and January 15, 2000.

If you choose to add the parameters as two text box controls, you can edit the attached labels to read "Between" and "and." This method requires more alignment and size adjustments than putting both parameters in one text box.

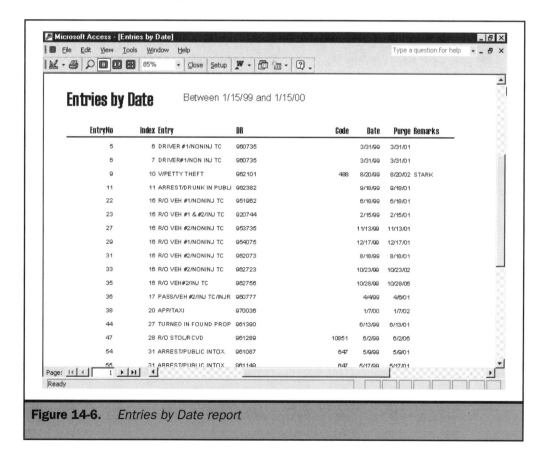

Figure 14-6.   *Entries by Date report*

If you're unexpectedly prompted for parameters when you try to print or preview a report, you may have misspelled a field name in the report design. The name in the design doesn't match any in the underlying table or query. If you created an expression using field names, one of them may also be misspelled. Another possibility is you used a control name, instead of a field name in an aggregate function, such as Sum or Count. Aggregate functions must use field names, not control names.

Troubleshooting Custom Reports

When you design a report, several problems can occur. For example, when you print the report, you see too much white space. To solve this problem, reduce the size of the controls to fit the values they contain and move them closer together.

If every other page is blank when you preview or print the report, the width of the report exceeds the available width of the paper and spill-over pages result. The total of the width of the report and the right and left margin settings must not exceed the width of the paper. To correct this problem, either reduce the width of the report or change the margin settings with Page Setup.

If the report prints a blank page at the end, you may need to reduce the size of the report footer. If no controls are in the report footer, reduce its height to zero by dragging the lower boundary or by setting the Height property to 0.

If data spills over to the next page, reduce the overall height of the report or decrease the top and bottom margins.

If you see *#Name?, #Num? or #Error* instead of a field value in the report preview, other errors may have occurred. For example, if you change the Record Source for the report, some controls may no longer be valid and you'll see *#Name?* in their place. Either delete the offending controls or change their Control Source property to a valid field or expression that relates to the current Record Source.

#Num? occurs when the control is based on an expression and the expression attempts to divide by zero. The divisor may be a field name or an expression that has evaluated to 0. One solution to this problem is to use the IIf (Immediate If) function to test for a zero divisor and, if it evaluates to 0, display 0 instead of the quotient.

The IIf function has three arguments: a statement that evaluates to True or False, the value to return if the statement is True, and the value to return if the statement is False. The expression *IIf([Divisor]=0,0,[Dividend]/[Divisor])* returns 0 if the Divisor evaluates to 0 and the result of the division if not.

#Error can occur if you enter an incorrect expression in a calculated field. It also occurs if you created a circular reference in an expression in which the expression uses the control name in the expression. For example, you added a control named Gate and entered the expression *=[Total Sale]*[Mark Up]+[Gate]*. Return to Design view and correct the expression.

Sorting and Grouping Records in a Report

As you saw in the previous chapter, one of the most useful features of Access reports is the capability to sort and group records based on the value in one or more of the fields. After doing so, you can summarize the information in many ways to illustrate trends and draw conclusions. Such summaries are critical to the decision-making process and Access can do most of the arithmetic for you.

You can change the sort order the report has inherited from the underlying record source. Records can be grouped on Text, Number, Date/Time, Currency, or AutoNumber field types or expressions containing those field values. Access nests up to ten group levels, each group subordinate to the previous group.

Depending on the data type of the group-on field, you have different options about how to group the records. For example, if the field is a Text field, you can group on the entire value or the first few characters of the value. Date/Time values can be grouped by each value or any time increment of the value—year, day, hour, minute, and so on.

Changing the Sort Order

You can remove or reapply the sort order inherited from the record source by setting the report's Order By On property. Choose No to remove the sort order or Yes to reapply it.

To sort the records in the report in a different order than the underlying table or query, set the report's Order By property as follows:

- To sort the records by values in one field in ascending order, type the field name enclosed in brackets followed by ASC—for example, **[Code] ASC**.

- To sort the records by values in one field in descending order, type the field name enclosed in brackets followed by DESC—for example, **[Last Name] DESC**.

- To sort the records by values in more than one field in ascending or descending order, type each field name enclosed in brackets followed by ASC or DESC and separated by commas. For example, the setting **[Code] ASC, [Last Name] DESC** sorts first by the Code field in ascending order, and then by the Last Name field in descending order.

If you don't specify ASC or DESC, Access automatically sorts in ascending order. The new setting overrides the inherited sort order without affecting the data source. Be sure to set the Order By On property to Yes to effect the new sort order.

Note   *If you create the report with the Report Wizard and specify a sort order, it overrides the inherited sort order. You can still change the order in the Design view if you change your mind.*

RETRIEVING AND PRESENTING INFORMATION

Adding Group Sections

To illustrate grouping records in a report, create a new report based on a query that extracts only those records with a value in the Code field. This eliminates Alpha Entry records not related to a potentially criminal offense. The Alpha Entry by Code query contains the expression <>0 in the Criteria row of the Code column in the grid. After dragging the field names from the list to the detail section of the new Entries by Year Report, you can proceed to group the records by the year the incident was reported.

To add a group section to an existing report, switch to Design view and click the Sorting and Grouping toolbar button or choose View | Sorting and Grouping. This opens the Sorting and Grouping dialog box in which you set the sort order and choose the field or expression on which you want to group. To group the records, do the following:

1. Select the field to group on from the drop-down Field/Expression list or enter an expression.

2. Select the order in which you want the groups arranged. (The detail records within each group appear ordered by the value in the primary key field of the parent table or query unless you change the report Order By property.)

3. Set the group properties in the lower pane of the Sorting and Grouping dialog box.

4. Set one or both group sections' properties to Yes to add a group header or footer.

Figure 14-7 shows the Sorting and Grouping dialog box with settings that group the records by the year value in the Date field. The Date groups appear in ascending order from the earliest year to the latest, and the report has both a group header and a group footer section. You can see the new Date group header and footer sections in the design behind the dialog box.

The properties in the lower pane of the Sorting and Grouping dialog box apply to the way the groups are formed and displayed. The Group Header and Group Footer properties add the group sections when set to Yes.

Note *You must choose a group header or footer for Access to group the records. If you don't select Yes in either the Group Header or Footer property, the records aren't grouped. Instead, the records are only sorted by the field or expression.*

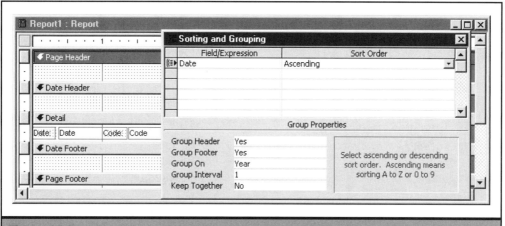

Figure 14-7.   *Sorting and Grouping dialog box*

The options available in the Group On property list vary with the data type of the field or expression entered in the Field/Expression column. Table 14–1 describes the options. Each Value is the default setting for all data types.

Data Type	Group On Property	Groups Records With
Text	Each Value	The same value in the field or expression.
	Prefix Characters	The same beginning characters. Enter the number of characters in the Group Interval property.
Date	Each Value	The same date value in the field or expression.
	Year	Dates in the same year.
	Qtr	Dates in the same quarter.
	Month	Dates in the same month.

Table 14-1.   *Group On Options by Data Type*

Data Type	Group On Property	Groups Records With
	Week	Dates in the same week.
	Day	Dates on the same day.
	Hour	Times in the same hour.
	Minute	Times in the same minute.
AutoNumber, Currency, or Number	Each Value	Groups contain records with the same value in the field or expression.
	Interval	Values that fall within the interval specified in the Group Interval property.

Table 14-1. *Group On Options by Data Type* (continued)

The Group Interval property specifies the interval or the number of characters on which to group. For example, you may want to group records by values in a currency field in $50 increments. Set the Group Interval property to 50 and the first group then includes values from $0 to $49, the second from $50 to $99, and so on.

The Keep Together property can prevent a group that occupies less than a page from being split over two pages. If the group is larger than one page, this property is ignored. The options are

- *No* (the default), which allows the group to be split.
- *Whole Group*, which keeps the entire group together on one page.
- *With First Detail*, which keeps the group header and the first record in the detail section together on the same page.

The group sections also have a Keep Together property, which is a little different from the group property set in the Sorting and Grouping dialog box. The group property refers to the entire group, while the section properties refer only to that section. However, if you want the group Keep Together property to take effect, the group section Keep Together properties must be set to Yes.

Customizing Group Headers and Footers

You must include one of the group sections to group records in a report, but you needn't print the information in it. Changing the section Visible property to No suppresses previewing and printing the section. If no information is in the group section, you can reduce its height to 0, exactly as any other section in the report.

To remove a group header or footer, open the Sorting and Grouping dialog box, and then change the corresponding property to No. If you placed information in the section you try to delete, Access warns you will delete the information with the section.

> **Tip** *You can set the Repeat Section property of the group header section to Yes to have the information printed on the next page when the group spans more than one page or column.*

If you switch the Entries by Year Report to Print Preview, you can see the Alpha Entry records are, indeed, grouped by year, but it's not obvious. The grouping would stand out more if the year value appeared in the group header section. Moving the field labels to the group header would also allow more room for the field data in the detail section. Unfortunately, attached labels can't be dragged to a different section, so delete them and place unattached label controls in the group header above the text box controls.

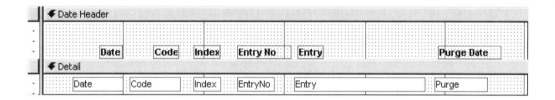

Next, to add a new unbound text box control to the group header that shows the year value for the group, do the following:

> **ab**

1. Click the Text Box control tool in the toolbox and place the control in the group header section.

2. Open the property sheet and enter the expression **=Year([Date])** in the Control Source property box. The Year() function extracts the year value from the Date field. You can also click the Build button (...) and use the Expression Builder to create the expression.

3. Select the attached label, click in it, and then replace Text*n* with **Year Reported:** as the label for the year control.

> **Note** *If you look at the label's property sheet, you can see the control's name is still Labeln. Understanding the difference between the control's name and the caption it displays is important. When you start programming with macros and Visual Basic, you'll use the control's name, not its label.*

4. Switch to Print Preview to see the year value in the group header.

Alpha Entries Grouped by Date Reported

Year Reported:	1993					

Date	Code	Index	Entry No	Entry	Purge Date
12/19/93	459	93	118	V/BURGLARY	12/19/00

Adding Summaries and Running Totals

In Chapter 10, you saw how to add calculated controls to form and report designs by using expressions. You can also use calculated controls to summarize data in a report. In the last chapter, you saw how the Report Wizard offered to add summaries to a report that contained groupings. You were limited to arithmetic summaries involving number, currency, or AutoNumber fields. When you design your own report with groupings, you can use many more types of group summaries, including running totals that accumulate the value throughout the report.

Calculated text boxes are unbound controls that rely on values in table or query fields for their values. You can use any expression with operators and functions to compute the summary value by setting the Control Source property of the control. You saw an example earlier when the year value was added to the Date group header in the Entries by Year Report.

Adding a Count Summary

Now let's add a summary to the group footer to the Entries by Year Report that counts the number of Alpha Entry records in each group, and then adds another summary to the report footer that shows the total number of records in the report.

1. In the report Design view, click the Text Box control tool in the toolbox and click in the group footer at the left end of the section.

2. Open the property sheet and type **=Count([Entry])** in the Control Source property box.

3. Change the Align property to Left, so the number appears closer to the label.

4. Change the label to **Total This Year:**. Then move and resize the text box and label controls to fit.

5. Increase the height of the report footer section to make room for the grand total summary field.

6. Select the calculated control in the group footer and click Copy. Next, click in the report footer near the left end, and then click Paste. A copy of the group summary control appears in the report footer.

7. Click in the label and change the caption to **Grand Total:**.

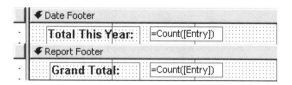

Tip *The expression you used in the group footer works just as well in the report footer. Access expects you to summarize over all the records in the report when you place the control in the report footer.*

Adding a Running Total

When you deal with financial data, being able to show running totals, within groups and overall is often important. You can add a calculated control that sums up the values in a group, accumulates the values from group to group, and, finally, prints the overall total for the whole report.

When you create a calculated control using one of the aggregate functions, such as Sum, Avg, Count, and so on you can set the Running Sum property to Over Group or Over All. The Over Group setting accumulates the values in the group, and then resets the value to 0 at the beginning of the next group. The Over All setting accumulates the values to the end of the report, printing subtotals at intermediate points, as required.

Tip *If you're only interested in the summary data in a report, you can suppress printing the details by changing the detail section Visible property to No.*

Numbering Items in a Report

Sometimes having each of the items in a report numbered is handy, so you can reference it uniquely by number—for example, if you are taking part in a teleconference and need to be sure you all are talking about the same item. To number the items, do the following:

1. Add a calculated text box control to the detail section in a prominent position at the left of the record data.

2. Remove the new text box label.

3. Double-click the new control to open its property sheet and change the Control Source property to the expression **=1**.

4. Set the Running Sum property to Over All, which increments the calculated text box value by 1 for each record in the detail section.

This works for grouped records as well. To number the records in each group separately, add the calculated control to the detail section, as shown previously, but set the Running Sum property to Over Group instead of Over All.

RETRIEVING AND
PRESENTING INFORMATION

Applying the Finishing Touches

To finish the Entries by Year Report, add a title in the report header. Because the information in the report header prints only on the first page of the report, you can add a continuation title and the page number to the page header, which prints on every page except the first. To do this, choose View | Page Header/Footer and shrink the page footer section because nothing will be placed in it. Then change the report Page Header property to Not with Rpt Hdr.

Finally, draw some lines under the titles to separate the report header and page header from the rest of the report, and then draw another line at the bottom of the group footer to separate the groups.

Figure 14-8 shows the completed report in Design view and Figure 14-9 shows the printed first page of the report.

 Reduce the width of the Year and Count controls to move the values closer to the attached labels.

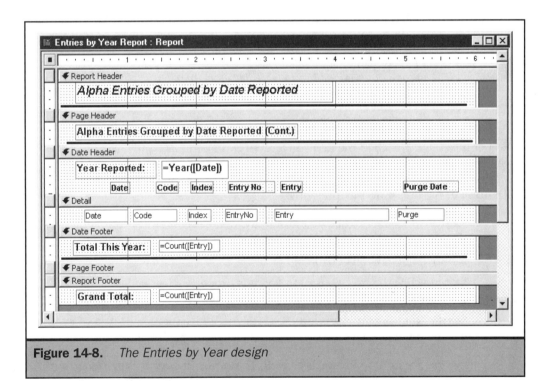

Figure 14-8. *The Entries by Year design*

Alpha Entries Grouped by Date Reported

Year Reported: 1990

Date	Entry No.	Cod	Inde	Entry	Purge Date
6 /24/90	73	488	50	V/PETTY THEFT	6 /24/02

Total This Year: 1

Year Reported: 1993

Date	Entry No.	Cod	Inde	Entry	Purge Date
12/19/93	118	459	93	V/BURGLARY	12/19/00

Total This Year: 1

Year Reported: 1994

Date	Entry No.	Cod	Inde	Entry	Purge Date
10/26/94	19	20001	16	R/O VEH #1/H&R FELONY	10/26/01
11/5 /94	39	459	21	V/BURGLARY	11/5 /01
4 /16/94	76	459	52	V/BURGLARY	4 /16/01
3 /27/94	75	459	52	V/BURGLARY	3 /17/01
9 /25/94	90	245	69	V/ASSAULT W/DEADLY	9 /25/01
12/18/94	92	459	71	V/BURGLARY	12/18/04

Total This Year: 6

Year Reported: 1995

Date	Entry No.	Cod	Inde	Entry	Purge Date
4 /9 /95	41	459	23	ARREST/BURGLARY & 496.1	4 /9 /02
12/10/95	107	459	84	V/BURGLARY &	12/10/02

Total This Year: 2

Year Reported: 1996

Date	Entry No.	Cod	Inde	Entry	Purge Date
10/15/96	3	459	4	V/BURGLARY	10/15/03
8 /7 /96	7	487	8	V/GRAND THEFT	8 /7 /03
7 /5 /96	26	10851	16	R/O STOL VEH	7 /5 /03
7 /16/96	28	10851	16	R/O/STOL VEH	7 /16/03
7 /18/96	30	10851	16	R/O/STOL VEH	7 /18/03
12/20/96	48	10851	29	R/O STOL TRLR	12/20/03
1 /29/96	51	10851	30	R/O/RCVD VEH	1 /29/03
1 /27/96	50	10851	30	R/O/STOL VEH	1 /27/03
8 /6 /96	61	10851	37	R/O/STOL VEH	8 /6 /03

Figure 14-9.   *Printed first page of the Entries by Year Report*

Modifying and Adding Groups

To change the sort order of the records in an ungrouped report or of the groups in a grouped report, open the Sorting and Grouping dialog box and choose from the Sort Order drop-down list.

If you want to change the grouping levels of existing groups, click the row selector of the group you want to move. Then click it again and drag the row to the desired position in the list of groupings. If the groups you move have headers or footers, Access moves them and all the controls they contain to the new positions in the report design. The controls may need some adjustment after repositioning.

To change the group-on field or expression, select it and choose another field from the drop-down list or enter a different expression. If you want to add an additional grouping level, click the next empty Field/Expression row and choose the field from the drop-down list or enter an expression. You can also insert a grouping level above an existing one by clicking the row selector where you want the new level and pressing INSERT.

To remove a grouping, click the row selector and press DEL.

Adding a Second Level Grouping

As an example of adding a second grouping level, group the Entries by Year Report by quarter within the year group by doing the following:

1. Open the Entries by Year Report in Design view, and then click the Sorting and Grouping button.

2. Click the Field/Expression column of the empty second row and choose Date from the drop-down list.

3. In the lower pane, leave the Group Header and Footer properties as No.

4. Change the Group On property to Qtr and leave the Group Interval at 1.

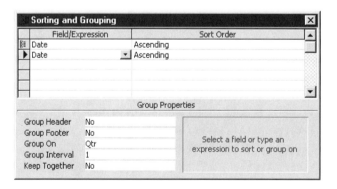

5. Close the Sorting and Grouping dialog box.

6. Add an unbound text box to the left end of the detail section and enter the expression **=DatePart("q",[Date])** in its Control Source property box.

7. Change the Hide Duplicate property to Yes.

8. Delete the new control's attached label and place a label in the top Date Header section reading **Qtr**.

9. Save the report as Entries by Quarter and switch to Print Preview to view the changed report.

Figure 14-10 shows a preview of the report that now groups the Alpha Entry records by the year the entry was reported, and then by quarter. You could also edit the report title accordingly.

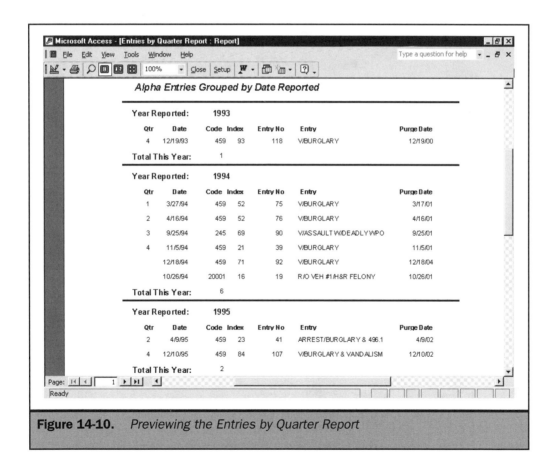

Figure 14-10.   *Previewing the Entries by Quarter Report*

The DatePart function extracts a specific part of an existing date value. The syntax contains two arguments: datepart and date. Datepart is an abbreviation of the part of the date you want to extract, which also specifies the format in which to display the date. For example, "yy" extracts a two-digit year value, while "m" extracts a one-digit month value. The datepart values are the same as the Date/Time formatting expressions and must be enclosed in quotation marks. The second argument, date, is a literal date value, such as "Dec 15, 2001" or the name of a Date/Time field.

Printing an Alphabetic Index

By combining the Group On and Group Interval settings, you can create an alphabetic list of items grouped by the leading character. For example, to create a list such as the one shown in Figure 14-11, do the following:

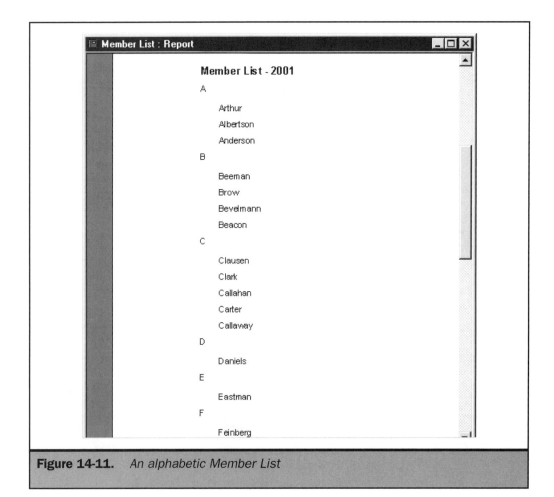

Figure 14-11. *An alphabetic Member List*

1. Select the Member List table in the Database window and choose Insert | Report.

2. Select Design view in the New Report dialog box and click OK.

3. Place the LastName field in the detail section and delete the attached label.

4. Click the Sorting and Grouping button, choose LastName as the field to group on, and set the following group properties:

   ■ Set Group Header to Yes.

   ■ Set Group Footer to No.

   ■ Set Group On to Prefix Characters.

   ■ Set Group Interval to 1.

5. To place the initial character in the group header, add a text box control to the group header and delete the attached label.

6. Set the new text box control Control Source property to **=Left([LastName],1)**. Figure 14-12 shows the completed report design and the Sorting and Grouping dialog box.

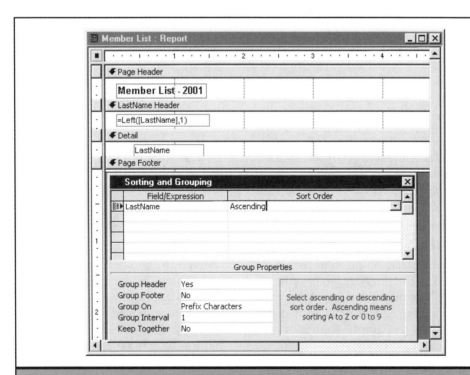

Figure 14-12. *The Member List report design*

Hiding Duplicates and Other Tips

Duplicate values appearing in the detail section can clutter a report. For example, a report grouping the Alpha Entry records by code would show multiple records with the same code value. You have two ways to alleviate the problem: Move the Code field to the group header section where it will be printed only once or leave it in the detail section and change a control property.

- To move the control, drag it from the detail section to the desired position in the group header.
- To leave the control in the detail section and suppress printing duplicate values, open the control property sheet and set the Hide Duplicates format property to Yes.

Two other properties are useful when printing reports containing memo fields that may contain a varying amount of data or, possibly, none at all. Changing the Can Shrink property to Yes prevents blank lines when no value is in the field. Changing Can Grow to Yes lets the field value expand, if necessary.

If you have lengthy groups that span several pages in a report, you may want to set the groups apart as separate sections when you print the report. You can have each group start on a new page and reset the page number to 1. This involves setting the Force New Page property to Yes and creating a macro that resets the page number when the new group section is formatted. See Chapter 19 for more information on creating macros and attaching them to event properties.

Be careful not to use the word "Name" as a field name. Access reserves that word as the name of the current object. If you use the expression =Left([Name],1) in the group header, you will see "M" (the first letter of the report name) in every group header. Many more reserved words are in the Access language.

Adding a Subreport

A *subreport,* a complete report in its own right, is inserted into another report, called the *main report.* A main report can be either bound or unbound. A *bound main report* is based on a table or query and its subreports contain related information. For example, the main report could contain details about the year's business, while the subreport could show charts and graphs summarizing and illustrating the numbers in the main report. A bound main report may also have two or more subreports that provide parallel information, but only relate to the main report and not to each other.

An *unbound main report* isn't based on a table or query, but can serve as a container for one or more subreports—for example, an annual report in which the main report is a title page with some introductory information, and the subreports contain parallel information unrelated to each other about the business during the previous year.

A main report can include as many subreports and subforms as necessary. You can also add up to two levels of subreports. A first-level subreport can contain another subreport or a subform. If the first level is a subform, it can contain only another subform, not a subreport, as the second level.

Creating a Subreport

You use the Subform/Subreport control tool in the toolbox to create a new subreport in the current report design. The Subform/Subreport Wizard creates the subreport based on your selections in the series of dialog boxes. It also saves the finished subreport as a separate report whose name appears in the Reports tab of the Database window.

As an example of creating a new subreport, let's add the Alpha Entry information to the Alpha Card Report, relating the two reports by the Index field. To be safe, save the Alpha Card Report with a different name before adding the subreport as follows:

1. Right-click the Alpha Card Report name in the Database window and choose Save As from the shortcut menu.

2. Enter the new name, **Alpha Card with Subreport**, in the Save As dialog box and click OK.

To create the subreport containing related Alpha Entry information, do the following:

1. Open the Alpha Card with Subreport report in Design view and open the toolbox. Make sure you press in the wizard button.

2. Increase the height of the detail section and move the line to the bottom to make room for the subreport in between.

3. Click the Subform/Subreport tool and click in the report design between the last row of controls and the line at the bottom of the detail section. Access draws a square frame in the report design and opens the first dialog box, where you can select an existing report or form as the subreport or create a new one, as shown in Figure 14-13.

Note   *You can also draw a custom subreport frame to the desired size before releasing the mouse button and starting the wizard.*

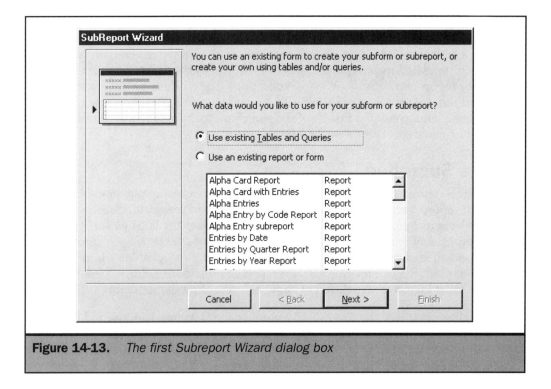

Figure 14-13. *The first Subreport Wizard dialog box*

4. Choose Use existing Tables and Queries to create the new subreport, and then click Next.

5. In the next dialog box, select Alpha Entry from the Tables and Queries drop-down list, click >> to select all the fields, and then click Next.

6. Accept the link the wizard suggests, which links the report and subreport by the Index field, as shown in Figure 14-14, and click Next.

7. Accept Alpha Entry subreport1 as the report name or enter a different name, such as **Alpha Entries**, and then click Finish to return to the main report Design view.

8. Delete the subreport label, if necessary, and then move and resize the subreport control as appropriate.

Figure 14-15 shows a preview of the report with the new subreport. The style adopted for the subreport depends on the style most recently accessed. Your subreport's style may be different. As you can see in the preview, you can make several refinements in the subreport to improve its appearance. For example, you could hide the Index field and spread out the remaining controls to make room for the Entry information. In addition, the

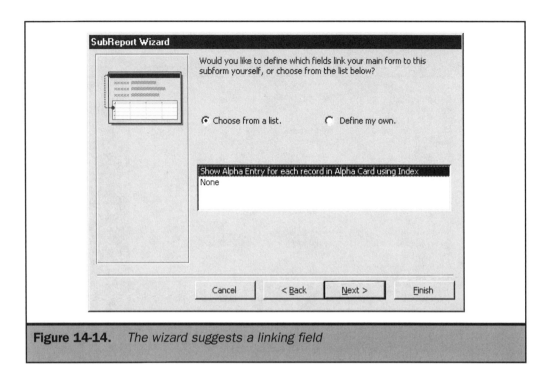

Figure 14-14. *The wizard suggests a linking field*

Code field doesn't need so much room. These and other modifications to a subreport are discussed later in this chapter.

Access doesn't print the page header and footer sections in a subreport. If you put the column labels for your subreport in the page header, they won't appear when you print the report. If the subreport doesn't exceed the page length, you can place the column headings in the subreport report header section, which is printed. The wizard placed the column headings in the report header section in the previous Alpha Entry subreport. If the subreport is likely to span two or more pages, place the column headings in the subreport group header and set the Repeat Section property to Yes.

Inserting an Existing Subreport

To use an existing report as a subreport, make sure the underlying tables or queries are properly related to the main report, and then open the Subform/Subreport Wizard as previously shown. Instead of choosing Table/Query in the first wizard dialog box, choose Reports or Forms, and then select the desired report or form from the drop-down list of all the reports and forms in the current database. Follow the instructions in the remaining wizard dialog boxes.

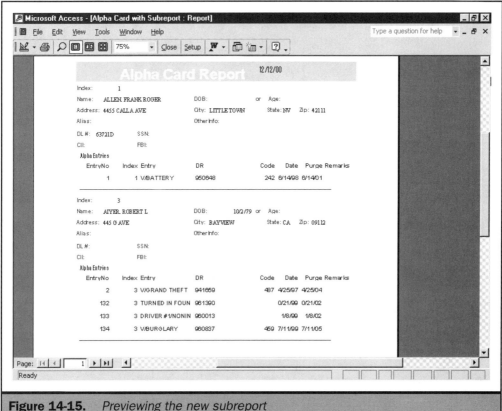

Figure 14-15. *Previewing the new subreport*

Tip   *A quick way to insert an existing report into another report as a subreport is to drag it from the Database window. Open the main report in Design view, and then press F11 to switch to the Database window. Drag the name of the report you want as the subreport to the section where you want the subreport to appear in the main report. Access adds the subreport control to the design.*

You can also drag a datasheet from the Tables page of the Database window to the report, in which case the Subreport Wizard starts with the dialog box suggesting the linking field. You must have the Control Wizard button on the toolbox pressed in for this to work.

Linking the Report and Subreport

If you insert the subreport in a bound report, the underlying tables must be linked so both reports contain corresponding data. You need to set the links in the Relationships window before trying to insert the subreport.

When you use the wizard to create a subreport or drag an existing report or datasheet from the Database window, Access automatically links the main report and subreport if one of the following conditions is met:

- The reports are based on related tables.
- The main report has a primary key and the table in the subreport contains a field with the same name and the same or compatible data type.
- Both reports are based on queries whose underlying tables meet either of those same conditions.

The linking fields must be included in the underlying record source, but you don't have to show them in either report. The wizard automatically includes linking fields even if you don't select them with the field picker.

If, for some reason, the wizard hasn't linked the tables properly, you can set the properties yourself by doing the following:

1. Open the main report in Design view.
2. Select the subreport control and open the property sheet.
3. Enter the name of the linking field in the subreport in the Link Child Fields property box.
4. Enter the name of the linking field in the main report in the Link Master Fields property box.

Tip *You must use the field name, not the name of the control. If you aren't sure of the field names, click the build button (...) next to one of the linking properties to open the Subform/Subreport Field Linker dialog box. Click Suggest to see the same link suggestions presented by the SubReport Wizard.*

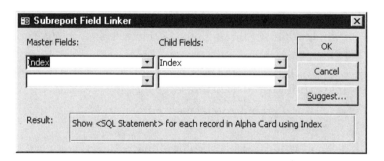

You can link on more than one field by entering the field names in the property sheet, separated by semicolons.

Modifying a Subreport

The first thing you may want to do with a new subreport is to edit or delete the attached control label. Do this in the main report Design view. Then make changes in the subreport design to match the style and arrangement of the controls in the main report.

You make modifications to a subreport design just like any other report—in the main report design window.

Subreport controls share many of the properties with other types of controls, for example, the position and size properties, as well as the Special Effect and border properties. By default, the Can Grow property is set to Yes and the Can Shrink property to No. In addition to the link field properties, the subreport has a Name property, set to the name you saved the file with, or the name you entered in the Subform/Subreport Wizard dialog box.

The Source Object property is unique to subforms and subreports, and contains the type and name of the object, for example, the Source Object property of the subreport in the Alpha Card with Subreport is Report.Alpha Entries subreport.

Note *The period separating the object type, Report, from the report name is called the dot operator, which indicates what follows is an item defined by Access. In this case, the name of the report is a property of the report as defined by Access. When you want to refer to a property you defined, you use the ! operator instead. More information about operators and how they're used in SQL statements and Visual Basic is in later chapters.*

Optimizing Report and Subreport Performance

Reports can get quite involved when you start adding subreports and graphics, and they can take quite a while to print, especially if your tables are large. Do as much as possible to create efficient reports and minimize the printing time. Here are some tactics you can use

- Don't overlap controls, although they can create an attractive appearance in a report.

- Don't overdo with graphic objects. They use more disk space and take more time to print because they're large files.

- Convert unbound graphics to image controls, unless you think you might need to update them.

- Use black-and-white instead of color bitmaps, unless you need to print in color.

- Don't sort or group on expressions that must be evaluated each time they're encountered.

- If you have a lot of calculated fields in the report, create a query that performs the calculations, and then base the report on the query.

- Use indexes as much as possible for fields that link to the main report, fields used in criteria, and fields on which you sort or group.

- If you don't need all the fields from the table, base the report or subreport on a query that includes only the required fields.

If you are bent on efficiency, you can ask the Performance Analyzer to look at the report or subreport. If the Analyzer finds any way to improve the design, it will tell you so. To start the Analyzer, you must close the report or subreport you want analyzed, and then do the following:

1. Select the report name in the Database window, choose Tools | Analyze, and then click Performance. The Performance Analyzer opens with the Reports tab in view.

2. Check all the reports and subreports you want analyzed and click OK.

The Performance Analyzer examines all the parts of the report, the subreport, and the underlying tables, and then displays any recommendations that may improve the efficiency of the design. For example, if you run the Performance Analyzer and choose the Alpha Entry report, it comes up with the "idea" to improve performance by converting the DR field data type from Text to Long Integer. Although all DR values currently in the Alpha Card table are integers, however, you know DR values aren't always integers, so you can ignore the idea.

Designing a Multiple-Column Report

Another way to arrange information in a report is in columns. When information is arranged in a tabular layout, it's easy to scan down a column of data and compare values in different records. Arranging the information in columns makes focusing on individual records easy because all the data for one record is grouped together.

The Report Wizard gives you a choice of tabular or columnar layout in one of the dialog boxes. Choosing Columnar creates a report with the fields arranged in a single column on the page. Using Page Setup, you can change the layout to include as many columns as can fit across the page. For example, if you rearrange and resize the controls in the report design, you can reduce the width of a column to two inches, and then specify three columns on the page. Figure 14-16 compares the columnar report created by the Report Wizard with the same data in a three-column report.

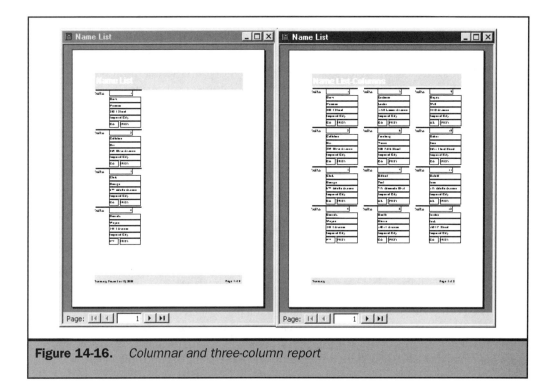

Figure 14-16. *Columnar and three-column report*

You can place controls anywhere in the page or in the report header and footer sections because they span the entire width of the page when you print the report. If you grouped the records, the group header and footer, as well as the detail section, span only the width of the column. So, place the controls you want in the group sections within the width you allow for the column.

When designing a multiple-column report, use the following formula as a guide to the page layout:

Column width * Number of columns + Column spacing * (Number of columns -1) + Right margin + Left margin >= Paper width

To create this three-column report, do the following:

1. Select the Name List table in the Database window and choose Insert | Report.

2. Choose AutoReport: Columnar from the New Report dialog box.

3. In Design view or Print Preview, choose Page Setup from the File menu. The three-tab Page Setup dialog box opens.

4. Click the Columns tab and change the Number of Columns to **3**.

5. Leave the Column Spacing at the default **.25"**. If you left some space between the bottom control in the detail section and the lower boundary of the section, you can also leave the Row Spacing at **0**.

6. In the Column Size group, set the Width to **2"**. You can also set the Height here or use the height drawn in Design view.

7. Choose OK. If you were in Print Preview, the report shows the new layout. If not, switch to Print Preview to see how the report looks.

If the report design exceeds the page width, Access displays a warning when you try to switch to Print Preview. Then you can either enter a smaller column width, reduce the column spacing, or reduce the size of the side margins. If you reduce the column width, be sure to change the controls in the group and detail sections to fit.

Another setting in the Columns dialog box is the Column Layout option group. This option determines the order in which the records are laid out on the page. The default is Down, then Across, which places records down the page in the first column to the bottom of the page, and then moves to the second column, and so on. The alternative choice is Across, then Down, which places the records across the first row to the right margin of the page, and then moves to the second row, and so on.

Grouping Records in a Multiple-Column Report

When you create a multiple-column report with grouping levels, you can specify to keep the groups together in a row or column, depending on the Column Layout setting, when printing the report. You can also have a group start in a new row or column by setting combinations of group and report properties.

Starting a Group in a New Row or Column

If you grouped the records in the report and want to set each group apart, you can ask Access to start a new column or row with each new group by setting the group section (header or footer) New Row Or Col property. Your choices are

- *None*, which lets the setting in the Page Setup dialog box and the available space on the page determine the row or column breaks.

- *Before Section*, which starts printing the group section (usually the header) in a new row or column, and then prints the next section (usually the detail) in the same row or column.

- *After Section*, which starts printing the group section in the current row or column, and then prints the next section in a new row or column. This option can be used to print the group headers alone in the first row or column, and then the detail section in the second row or column.

■ *Before & After*, which starts printing the group section in a new row or column, and then prints the next section in a new row or column. This option can be used to cause the information in the group header section to stand apart from the information in the detail section.

You may have to play around with combinations of the Column Layout options in the Columns dialog box and the New Row Or Col group section property settings to get the effect you want in the report.

Keeping Groups Together in Rows or Columns

Earlier in this chapter, you saw how to keep data together on a page by setting group properties in the Sorting and Grouping dialog box, and by setting report properties in the property sheet. If you arranged the records in columns and you want to keep the group together, do the following:

1. In Design view, click the Sorting and Grouping button to open the dialog box.

2. Click the group level you want to keep together and set the Keep Together property in the lower pane to Whole Group or With First Detail.

3. Display the report property sheet and change the Grp Keep Together property to Per Column.

 If you set the Column Layout in the Columns dialog box to Across, then Down, the group is kept together in a row. The Down, then Across setting keeps the group together in a column.

Printing Mailing Labels and Envelopes

Labels are used for many purposes: mailing addresses, name tags, disk labels, and book-plates (From the library of.......). Because labels are usually smaller than a sheet of paper, you can print many of them on one page. This leads to a multiple column per page report layout like the one in the previous section. Label printing is so common, Access has provided a special Label Wizard to help with the layout.

After you create the label design, you can use it to print addresses on envelopes as well, with a few changes to the page layout. Through the Label Wizard, you can create your own custom label size and layout, and then save it to use again.

Using the Label Wizard

In one of the Label Wizard's series of dialog boxes, you can select from a long list of predefined label layouts that match commercially available label stock. You can prepare labels for printing on continuous-feed or sheet-feed printers. The Label Wizard helps with every stage of the label design, including choosing the layout, changing the text appearance, adding field data to a prototype label, and even offering to sort the labels for you before printing.

As an example of printing mailing labels, the local police department keeps the names and addresses of the *Retired Senior Volunteer Program* (*RSVP*) members in the Name List table in their Access database, so monthly notices can be mailed to the members.

To create mailing labels for the volunteers, do the following:

1. Open the New Report dialog box and choose Label Wizard. If you haven't already selected the table or query that contains the label data, select Name List from the drop-down list and click OK.

2. In the first dialog box (see Figure 14-17), you can set the following options:

   ■ Choose the desired label size from the list. The dimensions are specified as height × width.

   ■ Select the desired Unit of Measure: English or Metric.

   ■ Select the Label Type: Sheet feed or Continuous.

   ■ Choose the brand of label from the Filter by manufacturer drop-down list.

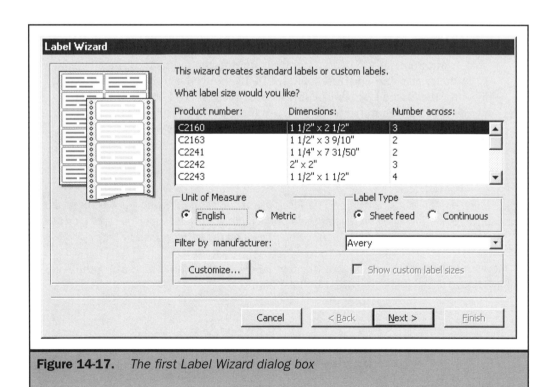

Figure 14-17. *The first Label Wizard dialog box*

- If you want to create a custom label size, click the Customize button. More later about creating and printing custom labels.

- If you already created some custom label sizes, you can choose Show custom label sizes to see that list.

3. Click Next to open the second dialog box where you can select the font name, size, and weight, and text colors. Italics and underlining are also options here.

Note   *These settings apply to all the text in the label. You can change individual lines of text later in the Design view. For example, you may want the addressee's name to be in bold text, but not the address.*

4. Click Next to continue. The next Label Wizard dialog box displays a blank label prototype where you arrange the data.

- To move a field to the prototype label, double-click the field name in the Available Fields list or select it and click >.

- To remove a field from the prototype label, select the field and press DEL.

- To move to the next line, press ENTER.

- Enter spaces, punctuation, and other characters as necessary as you place the fields.

Access automatically concatenates the values in the fields and trims the spaces from the names and addresses. Figure 14-18 shows the completed prototype label for the Name List labels. Notice the spaces entered between the field names and the comma entered between the City and State fields.

5. Click Next to move to the next dialog box where you can choose to sort the records before printing the labels. Then click Next to move to the last Label Wizard dialog box where you enter a name for the label design.

Note   *If you don't specify a sort order, the labels are arranged in the same order as the source table, ascending based on the first field in the table. If the label report is based on a query, the labels are arranged in ascending order based on the leftmost field in the grid.*

Figure 14-19 shows a preview of the new labels for the Name List, using the Avery 5160 label size. The labels are sorted by Last Name.

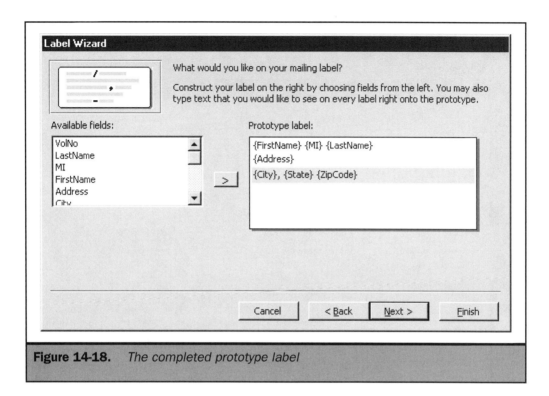

Figure 14-18.   *The completed prototype label*

Tip   *A good idea is to print one page of the new labels on plain paper and compare it with your label stock before committing to print many pages of labels on expensive label sheets.*

Note   *You can create a new label report without the Label Wizard by designing a report with only a detail section, sized to match the label stock. Then add text boxes or calculated controls with expressions, including the Trim function and & operator, to the detail section, making sure they don't overlap. Then run Page Setup and set the Printer, Page, and Margins options. If more than one label is across the page, treat it as a multiple-column report and enter the number of labels across in the Number of Columns box in the Grid Settings group, and then set the Column Spacing and Row Spacing measurements.*

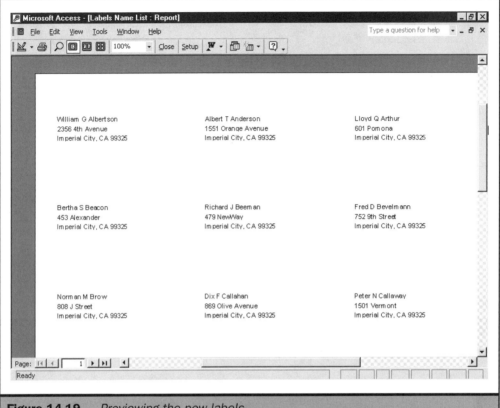

Figure 14-19. *Previewing the new labels*

Printing Labels with a Dot Matrix Printer

If you want to print the labels on a dot matrix or tractor-feed printer, you'll probably have to make some changes to the page size definition. Before creating the label report, use the Windows Control Panel to set the default printer and the paper size as follows:

1. In the Windows desktop, click Start, point to Settings, and click Printers.

2. Click the icon for the dot matrix printer and choose File | Set As Default.

3. Choose File | Properties and click the Paper tab.

4. Scroll right and click the Custom icon to open the User-Defined Size dialog box.

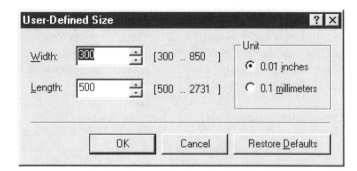

5. Select the unit of measure, and then enter the width and length. The width is measured from the left edge of the leftmost label to the right edge of the rightmost label. The length, however, is measured from the top of the first label to the top of the second, which includes one label height, plus the space between the labels.

6. Click OK twice to save the settings and return to the desktop.

Now you can create the labels for the dot matrix printer with or without the Label Wizard.

Manipulating Text Data

If you close the label Print Preview window, the new Name List label appears in Design view. Now you can see how the Label Wizard created the calculated text box controls. The Label Wizard combined the text values in special expressions using the concatenation operator (&) and the Trim function. The *concatenation operator* serves to combine the values in the field with any other characters you want, enclosed in quotation marks. The *Trim function* displays the field value without leading or trailing spaces.

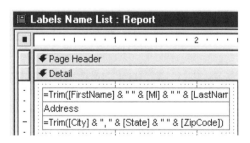

Other text functions are also useful when combining text values. In addition to the Trim function, the *Ltrim function* removes only the leading spaces, while the *Rtrim function* removes only the trailing spaces. Be sure to add a space between the field names and literal characters in the same line in the prototype label or all the characters will run together.

The Left function used earlier when creating the alphabetic list report lets you display only the first few characters of the text value. The number of characters to display is specified as the second argument in the function statement. The Right function displays the last few characters.

Tip   *Some names or addresses might be longer than can fit across the label. You can set the Can Grow property of the fields to Yes and the control adjusts vertically to accommodate all the data. Conversely, if the field contains no data, setting the Can Shrink property to Yes can avoid blank lines. If you look at the property sheets for the controls in the label design created by the Label Wizard, you can see both those properties are set to Yes for all three controls.*

You can create your own calculated control expressions to combine text values by using these tools and functions. Type the expression in the Control Source property box of the calculated text box or directly into the control in the design. Always begin the expression with the equals sign (=). Table 14-2 shows other examples of expressions you can use in calculated controls placed in forms and reports.

Expression	Result
="None"	Displays None.
="Mr/Ms"&" "&[First Name]&" "&[Last Name]	Displays first and last names preceded by Mr/Ms and separated by a space.
=Trim([City])	Displays the City field value with no leading or trailing spaces.
=Left([LastName],3)	Displays the first three characters in the LastName field.
=Right([Code],2)	Displays the last two characters in the Code field.

Table 14-2.   *Examples of Combining Text Values*

Expression	Result
=IIf(IsNull([MI]),[FirstName]&" "&[LastName],[FirstName]&" "&[MI]&" "&[LastName])	Uses the IIf function to test the MI field for a Null value. If the field is Null, only the first and last name values are displayed. If the field is not Null, all three field values are displayed.

Table 14-2.   *Examples of Combining Text Values* (continued)

  If you need help constructing a valid expression, click the Build button next to the Control Source property box and use the Expression Builder.

Customizing a Label Layout

After the Label Wizard has finished the label design, you can make changes to the appearance of the text. For example, you can change the font name, size, and style by selecting the control and clicking the appropriate Formatting toolbar button. To change the size of a control, drag the sizing handles.

You can also change the page layout by running Page Setup. If you want to make significant changes, you're probably better off starting over with the Label Wizard.

If you have some preprinted labels that aren't the same size as any of the ones provided in the wizard's list, you can create your own label size and add it to the list. To do this, do the following:

1. Start the Label Wizard as before and click Customize in the first dialog box. The New Label Size dialog box opens, displaying any previously designed custom labels. If any are there, you can modify them by clicking Edit.

2. Click New to open the New Label dialog box (see Figure 14-20) where you enter the label specifications.

3. After selecting the Unit of Measure, Label Type, and Orientation, enter the Number Across. Then type the label dimensions directly into the boxes in the sketch of the label sheet.

4. Type a name for the new label and click OK. You return to the New Label Size dialog box, now showing the name of the new label size and with the dimensions and number of labels across.

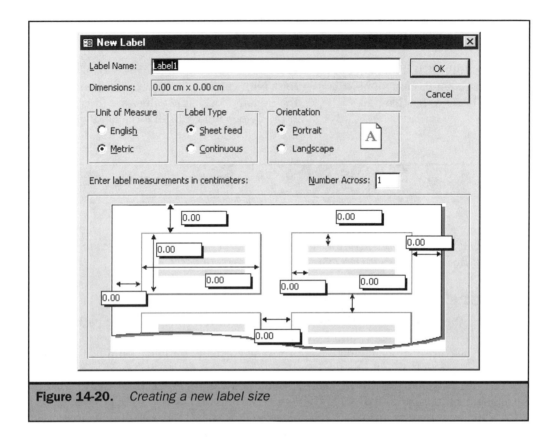

Figure 14-20. *Creating a new label size*

5. Click Close to return to the Label Wizard, which now shows the list of custom label sizes instead of the predefined labels.

When you start the Label Wizard to create a new label report, click the Show custom label sizes option to display the list of the custom layouts you designed. Choose the desired label from the list and proceed as with a standard label.

Printing Addresses on Envelopes

You can use the same report design you created for printing the labels to print the addresses on envelopes. All you need to do is change the Page Setup options to reflect the different size and arrangement of the controls. First, save the report you created for printing labels with a different name, and then open the report in Design view and make any changes to the text in the report.

To print the name and address on a standard #10 envelope, do the following:

1. First, increase the size of the text in all the controls. You can also change the name control to bold to make it stand out better on the envelope. This may necessitate moving and enlarging the controls themselves.

2. Choose File | Page Setup and make the following changes:

   ■ On the Page tab, change the orientation to Landscape, the Paper Size to Envelope #10 4 $\frac{1}{8}$ × 9 $\frac{1}{2}$ in, and the Paper Source as necessary for your printer.

   ■ On the Margins tab, change the Top margin to **2"** and the Left margin to **4.5"**.

   ■ On the Columns tab, change the Number of Columns to **1**.

3. Click OK to return to the report Design view, and then click Print Preview.

Publishing a Report

Printing a report isn't the only method Access provides for publishing a report. Microsoft Office XP specializes in creating a seamless work environment in which documents can be passed from one user or application to another with little effort. Another new feature is the ease with which Office documents can be shared with the outside world by transferring them to the Internet.

You have five major ways to share Access reports and other objects with external databases or other applications:

■ Exporting Access documents to external formats for use by other applications by choosing Export from the File menu or from a shortcut menu.

■ Using Office Links to publish the report in Word or Excel by choosing Tools | Office Links or clicking the OfficeLinks toolbar button.

■ Attaching the report to an electronic mail message as another format by choosing Send from the File menu or a shortcut menu. You have a choice of four file formats from which to choose.

■ Creating a Report Snapshot you can print or distribute to others via e-mail or on the Web.

■ Publishing to the Web using a wizard.

Chapters 22 through 24 discuss in detail the sharing of Access objects with other databases, other applications, and the Internet.

Printing a Report on a Preprinted Form

Many of the reports you file in the world today must be printed on preprinted forms. The Internal Revenue Service isn't the only one: your company's invoices, an insurance claim, or a mail order might also have to be formatted to fit into the spaces on a form. People pay good money for the software to do just that, but there's no reason you can't create your own report to print information on these forms.

If you have a scanner in your system, you can scan the form and save it as a bitmap file. Be sure to crop the image and size it to fit your screen. If you don't have a scanner, the neighborhood office supply store can probably scan the form and create the file for you.

The table that will contain the data to be printed on the form must have a field for every blank in the form, even if you don't plan to enter data in every field. Next, create and save an AutoForm based on the table, and then insert the scanned image in the form by entering the image file name in the Picture property box. Then set the other picture properties as follows:

- Set Picture Type to Embedded.
- Set Picture Size Mode to Clip.
- Set Picture Alignment to Center.
- Set Picture Tiling to No.

Finally, move and resize the controls to their correct locations in the form and delete the attached labels.

TIP: When you design such a form, setting a finer grid in the Design window is helpful, so you can make more precise adjustments in the positioning of the controls in the design.

You can save the form as a report, or you can save it as a form and print the filled-in report from the form. If you're printing on preprinted forms, you can choose to print data only by choosing Setup in the Print dialog box and choosing Print Data Only.

Summary

This chapter covered designing custom reports for many purposes, but an almost unlimited number of features and tools are still in the Access repertoire. As you work with report designs and begin to realize how versatile Access can be in presenting information in a variety of ways, you'll gain even greater understanding.

The last remaining piece of information retrieval and presentation involves graphically presenting information in such a way that the viewer can perform analyses and detect trends in the underlying data. The next chapter discusses three tools for doing this: the Chart Wizard, the PivotTable Wizard and the PivotChart Wizard. The

Chart Wizard helps create charts and graphs from Access table data, which you can edit using the Microsoft Graph applet. The PivotTable Wizard helps create spreadsheet-like tables from Access table data that you can edit using Excel. The PivotChart Wizard presents a graphical analysis of data in a table, query, or form.

MOUS Exam Activities Explored in This Chapter

Level	Activity	Section Title
Core	Preview and print reports	Printing Mailing Labels and Envelopes Publishing a Report
Expert	Create and run parameter queries	Creating the Parameter Query
Expert	Create and modify reports	Creating a New Report Design Sorting and Grouping Records in a Report
Expert	Add Subreport controls to Access reports	Creating a Subreport Inserting an Existing Subreport Linking the Report and Subreport

Chapter 15

Creating Charts, PivotTables, and PivotCharts

611

Charts and graphs enhance data presented in forms and reports by summarizing the information and illustrating it in easily understood ways. With these tools, the reader can analyze trends and make comparisons. Access offers a wide variety of chart types including column, bar, line, pie, XY scatter, area, and many others. Many of the types can also be shown in three dimensions. You can create standalone charts or embed them in forms and reports. If you want the chart to reflect the values in the currently displayed record, you can also link the chart to a field in the underlying table or query.

PivotTables and PivotCharts are additional tools provided by Access that help you summarize data in a tabular or chart layout. The flexible PivotTable and PivotChart features enable you to switch rows and columns as well as filter values to display summaries in many dramatic ways.

Creating a New Chart

When you decide to add a chart to a form or report, you must understand the purpose of the chart. Do you want to point out trends over a period of time or compare the relative values summarized by groups? The local police department, for example, is interested in the increase or decrease of violent crimes over the last four years. This type of chart would involve tabulating the number of crimes reported during each year and displaying the results as a column chart or a line chart.

The police are also concerned with the crime rates in different areas of the city. Such a comparison can be illustrated with a bar or column chart, as well as a pie chart in which each area is represented by a slice of the pie.

Other decisions that must be made during the planning stage are whether to embed the chart in the form or report, or to create a free-standing chart that can be available to more than one form or report. If you embed the chart in the form or report, you can link the chart to data in the underlying table or query and the chart then changes for each record. If you want the chart to remain the same as you move through records, leave the embedded chart unlinked.

If you create a chart in another application, such as Excel, you can import the chart to your form or report.

The fundamental rule when you design a chart or any other user-oriented object is to keep it simple. Just because Access and the other Office applications offer all kinds of bells and whistles, this doesn't mean you need to clutter your products with a lot of touches that may obscure the point you're trying to make. Keep the purpose of the chart in mind as you look at the tools Access and Graph offer.

The Anatomy of a Chart

A chart is composed of *elements*, some of which relate to the data, while others relate to the structure of the chart itself. Figure 15-1 shows a typical chart based on data taken

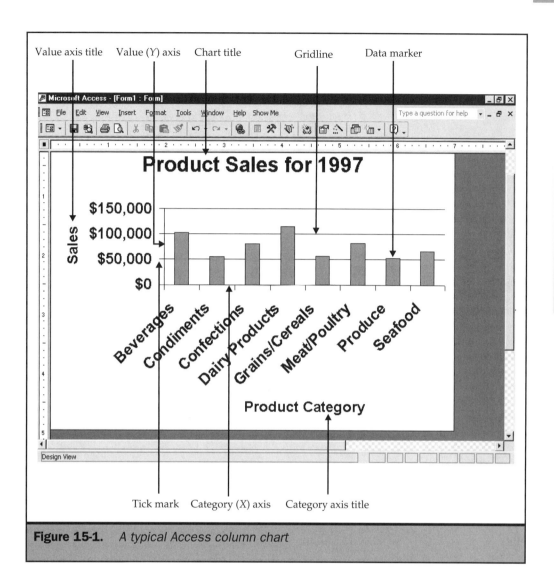

Figure 15-1. *A typical Access column chart*

from the Northwind sample database that came with Access. This chart compares the sales of eight categories of products during the year 1997.

Many other types of charts can show comparisons among data groups. For example, Figure 15-2 shows the same data displayed in an exploding pie chart. Many of the same elements appear in this chart, in addition to a few new ones: a legend, a slice, and data labels. Data labels can be displayed with the data name, the percentage of the whole the group represents, or both, as the figure shows.

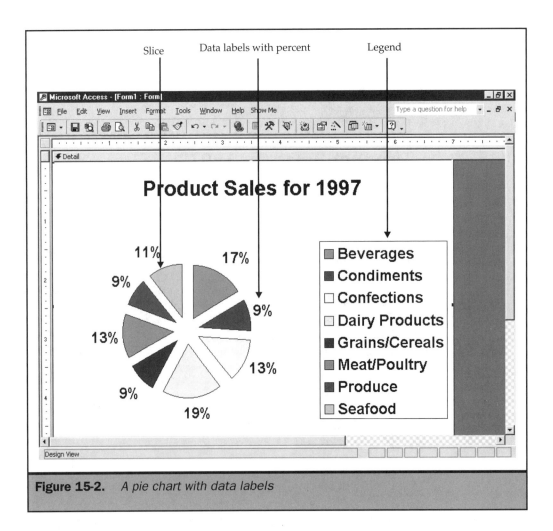

Figure 15-2.   *A pie chart with data labels*

Another reason to include charts in a form or report is to show trends over a period of time. Figure 15-3, which uses data from the Police database, shows a line chart that tracks the number of crimes reported over a four-year period. The crimes are grouped as violent or nonviolent and a legend is included that identifies the lines. This chart includes the data labels, which show the number of crimes at each data point on the lines. The legend that appears at the right of the chart identifies the individual categories of information.

Note   *The lines appear in different colors when displayed on the screen, but when they're printed in black and white, you must rely on the shape of the data points to identify the data series.*

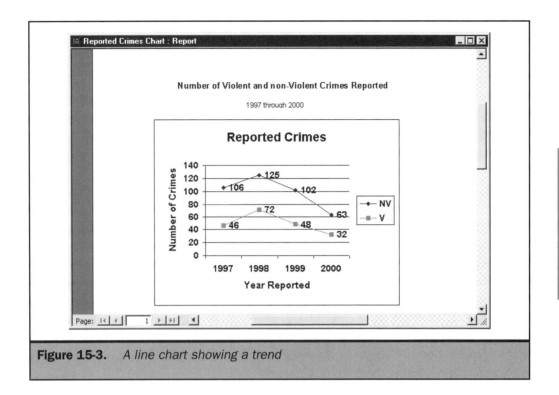

Figure 15-3. *A line chart showing a trend*

The line chart has been embedded in a simple report with a title and subtitle added to the page header. The report could be much more comprehensive in real life.

Before I move on, understanding each of the main elements in a standard chart is important.

- The *Category (X) axis* is the horizontal line at the bottom of the chart that usually identifies the data in the chart. For example, when you plot sales by product, the product name appears on the Category axis.

- The *Value (Y) axis* is the vertical line that measures the values in the chart data—for example, the sales in dollars or other currency.

- The optional *Z axis* appears in 3-D charts and also measures values. The Z axis projects outward from the chart.

- A *series* is a group of related data values from one field in the underlying record source. For example, in a sales by product chart, each year's sales total would represent one of a series of values. The values are grouped together in one category: the product type. A series is a further partitioning of grouped field data, which adds more detail to the chart.

- *Titles* help explain the purpose and scope of the chart. Titles are optional and can appear at the top of the chart and by each axis.

- *Gridlines* are horizontal or vertical lines that appear across the chart at the tick marks.

- *Tick marks* are short lines that appear on the axes to mark evenly spaced segments. They help to read the values and determine the scale of the chart.

- *Scale* defines the range of values in the chart and the increments marked by tick marks on the axes. This is usually determined by the Chart Wizard, but you can change the scale and spacing of the tick marks.

- A *slice* is a wedge of a single-field pie chart, which represents the relative value of one data point with respect to the whole.

- *Data markers* are the elements that show the value of the data—for example, bars, columns, slices of a pie chart, small icons on a line chart, and so on.

- *Data labels* are the actual values that can be displayed above or near the data markers. Figure 15-2 shows data labels with each slice of the pie.

- The *legend* is the list that identifies the members of a series of data values. For example, in Figure 15-3, the legend next to the chart indicates which line represents which type of crime.

Selecting the Data for the Chart

Once you decide on what you want the chart to accomplish, you can begin locating the data the chart will require. If the data is all contained in one table, you can use the table as the basis for the chart. If not, you can create a select or crosstab query that groups and summarizes the data for the chart. With a select query, you can combine data and add calculated fields such as an extended price, as well as add totals that summarize field values.

You can use up to six fields of any data type, except OLE and Memo. Only two requirements exist:

- You must include at least one field for categorizing data, such as the year the crime was reported or the area of the city where it occurred.

- You must also include a field or a calculated field that you can add up, average, or count, such as the number of violent crimes or the sales during the third quarter of 1998.

 If you include a date/time field in the chart, you can group the values with the wizard instead of creating a query to do the job.

A simple chart might contain only two fields—one as the category and the other as the data or value that corresponds to the category. For example, in Figure 15-1, only two fields exist: Product Category used as the category and Sales, which was summed to form the value.

If you include sales figures for 1998 through 2000, you would create a series within the chart: the sales of beverage products shown separately for each year. The chart would now show four contiguous vertical data marker columns for each of the products. These four columns represent sales figures for each of the four years. The legend would then identify the year that corresponds to the color and position of the data marker column. You can see examples of this type of chart in later sections.

If you want to create a chart with fixed data that won't change with the underlying record source, create a Make Table query that extracts and summarizes the data, and then base the chart on the resulting table.

Using the Access Chart Wizard

The way you begin to create a new chart depends on the type of chart you want. Do you want a standalone chart in its own form or report design, or a chart embedded in an existing form or report? In either case, you eventually use the Chart Wizard to create the chart.

To create a new chart, start the Chart Wizard by doing one of the following:

- If you're creating a free-standing chart, start a new form or report, and then choose Chart Wizard in the New Form (or Report) dialog box. Then select the table or query you want to use as the basis for the chart and click OK.

You can also use one of the other methods you learned in the previous chapters to open the New Form or New Report dialog box.

- If you want to insert a new chart in an existing form or report, open the form or report in Design view and choose Insert | Chart. Then click in the design where you want to place the chart. The Chart Wizard opens and, in the first dialog box, asks you to select the table or query to use as the basis for the chart.

You must have Microsoft Graph installed to use the Chart Wizard. If you used the Typical setup when you installed Office XP, you need to run Setup again to install Microsoft Graph. Choose Settings | Control Panel from the Start menu, click Add/Remove Programs in the Control Panel window, and then follow the instructions onscreen. If you need more help, see the Office XP installation instructions.

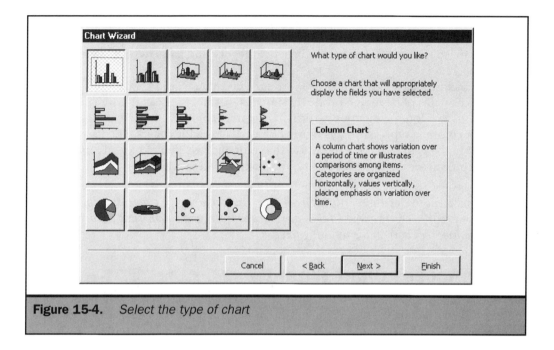

Figure 15-4. *Select the type of chart*

Once you specify the underlying record source, follow the instructions in the wizard dialog boxes as follows (this example uses the Crimes by Beat Number table in the Police database):

1. Choose the fields you want to use in the chart—for example, Year, Crime Type, and Number of Crimes. You need at least one field as the category and one as the data. You can choose up to six fields. Then click Next.

2. In the next dialog box, select the type of chart you want to create (see Figure 15-4), and then click Next. You can click each type of chart and read a description in the right pane. A 3-D column chart has been selected in this example.

3. The next dialog box (see Figure 15-5) shows you Access's interpretation of the arrangement of the fields in the layout of the sample chart.

   This isn't always what you had in mind. Click the Preview Chart to see how this arrangement would look.

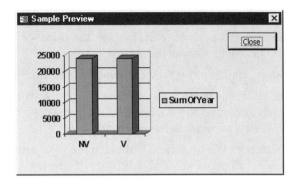

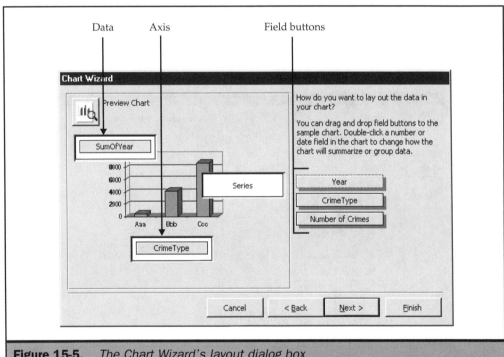

Figure 15-5.   *The Chart Wizard's layout dialog box*

The preview doesn't show what the chart is meant to present—the number of crimes by type reported in each year. It shows the number of years in which violent and nonviolent crimes were reported.

4. To change this layout, close the Preview window and do the following:

   a. Drag the SumOfYear label to the area below the chart to replace Crime Type. The label changes to Year because it represents a category on the *X* axis, rather than a numeric value on the *Y* axis.

   b. Drag the Number of Crimes field button to the Data area below the Preview Chart. The label changes to SumOfNumber of Crimes.

   c. Drag the Crime Type field button to the Series area.

   d. To remove a field from the Preview Chart, drag it off the chart. The field name is replaced by Series, Data, or Axis, depending on the chart area. Figure 15-6 shows the new layout.

5. Click the Preview Chart button again to see the effects of the changes.

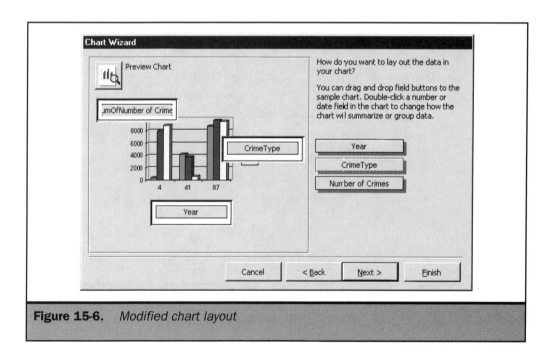

Figure 15-6. *Modified chart layout*

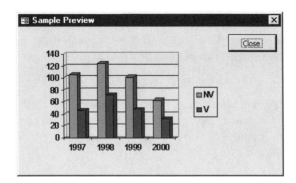

6. Close the Preview window and click Next.

7. In the final Chart Wizard dialog box, you can enter a name for the chart, such as "Crimes by Year Chart," or accept the name of the table or query you used as the basis. You also have the option of displaying a legend explaining the series data. When you close the dialog box, you can open the form or report and display the chart, or you can go directly to Design view to edit the form or report.

8. Click Finish and see the chart in the new form (see Figure 15-7). You may have to resize the form or the chart to get the appearance you want.

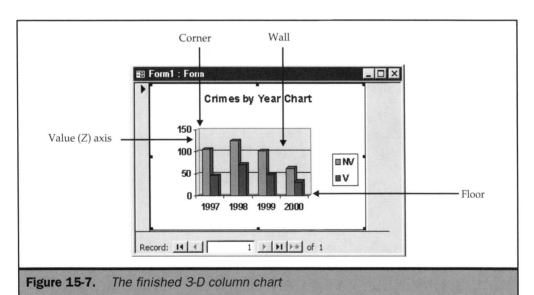

Figure 15-7.   *The finished 3-D column chart*

A *3-D chart* has a third dimension, depth that creates a back wall, an end wall on the left, side walls, and a floor. The back wall and end wall meet at the corner. You can set the pattern and color properties of each of these features to get the appearance you want in the chart.

 When you drag a field to the Value area in the sample chart, the Chart Wizard assumes you want to use the Sum aggregate function to create the value, but you can change to another function by double-clicking a number field, choosing from the Summarize dialog box, and then clicking OK.

A 3-D column chart has some additional elements, as you can see in the figure. The depth of the chart is the Z axis and can represent a third dimension of data. In this example, only two dimensions exist: the year the crime was reported and the type of crime. If you added the Beat Number to the chart, you could use the 3-D version to illustrate this. A 3-D chart can get confusing if it isn't laid out carefully.

 When the Chart Wizard creates a chart, it builds the Row Source property as a structured query language (SQL) statement. To view the SQL statement, switch to Design view and open the property sheet for the chart control. Right-click the Row Source property and choose Zoom from the shortcut menu. The chart created in the previous exercise has the following Row Source SQL statement:

TRANSFORM Sum([Number of Crimes]) AS [SumOfNumber of Crimes] SELECT [Year] FROM [Crimes by Beat Number] GROUP BY [Year] PIVOT [CrimeType];

You see more about PivotTables and PivotCharts later in this chapter.

Creating a New Chart Without the Chart Wizard

If you want to add a chart to a form or report based on data outside the current database, you can create a new chart without using the Chart Wizard. To create the chart, open the form or report in Design view, and then do the following:

1. Click the Unbound Object Frame toolbox button and click the design where you want the chart.

2. In the Insert Object dialog box, choose Create New.

3. Scroll down the list of OLE programs on your computer, choose Microsoft Graph Chart, and click OK.

Microsoft Graph places a datasheet and chart showing unrelated sample data in the Access window (see Figure 15-8). To add the data you want in the chart, you can either type it into the datasheet or import it from the outside source. To clear the datasheet of the sample data, click the Select All button (the rectangle at the upper-left corner of the datasheet where the row and column headers meet) and press DELETE. Then enter data by selecting each cell and typing the value. If you don't clear the datasheet, whatever you type will replace the contents of the cell. Use the arrow and TAB keys to move around the datasheet.

To import a text or spreadsheet file, click the datasheet where you want the first cell to appear, and then choose Edit | Import File. Select the type of file you want to import in the Files Of Type box, and then double-click the filename. Depending on the type of file you're importing, you must respond to some additional prompts. If you're importing a

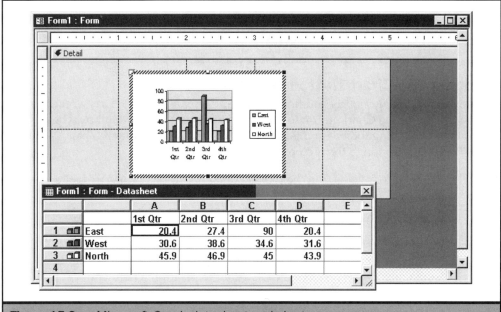

Figure 15-8.   *Microsoft Graph datasheet and chart*

text file, the Text Import Wizard opens with a series of dialog boxes requesting information with respect to delimiters, field widths, and other specifications. See Chapter 22 for more information about using the Import Text Wizard.

If a chart is created in Excel and you want to import its data to use in an Access chart, choose Microsoft Excel Files as the file type, double-click the chart you want to import, and follow the instructions.

 You see more later in this chapter about working with Microsoft Graph from within Access to edit a chart.

Printing and Saving the Chart

In the final Chart Wizard dialog box, you assigned a title to the new chart, but you haven't yet named the host form or report, as you can see from the Form1: Form name in the title bar. To name and save the form or report containing the chart, choose File | Save and enter the desired filename. The new name is added to the Database window.

When you reopen the form or report containing the chart, it contains the current data from the underlying record source.

 If you want a "snapshot" chart that contains fixed data, rather than the current values, you can convert the chart to an image while it shows the data you want to keep.

When you preview the chart in Form view or Print Preview, you can print it or switch to Design view to make changes.

Adding the Chart Button to the Toolbox

If you're producing reports and find you need to create a lot of charts, you can save time by adding the Chart button to the form and report control toolbox. The *toolbox* is actually a floating toolbar and is customized just like any other toolbar.

To add the button to the toolbox, do the following:

1. Right-click anywhere in the toolbox and choose Customize from the shortcut menu.

2. Click the Commands tab and, in the Categories box, click Toolbox.

3. Move the Customize dialog box out of the way, so you can see the toolbox.

4. Scroll down the list of commands and drag the Chart button from the Customize dialog box to the toolbox at the position where you want it to appear.

5. Close the Customize dialog box.

If you want to remove the Chart button, open the Customize dialog box again and drag the button off the toolbox. Then click Close.

See Chapter 20 for more information about customizing menus and toolbars.

Linking to Record Data

When you start a new chart from within a form or report design, Access assumes you want to link the chart to one of the fields in the underlying record source, so a different chart displays with each record. To do this, you first create the host form or report, and then insert the new or existing chart.

For example, create a columnar form based on the City Beats table, which contains only two fields: the beat number and a brief description of the territory. Then create a new chart by doing the following:

1. Choose Insert | Chart and click in the design just below the text box controls in the form. (Or, use the Chart button in the toolbox if you added it.) Be sure you have made room in the section for the embedded chart.

2. In the first Chart Wizard dialog box, choose the Crimes by Beat Number table as the basis for the chart and click Next.

3. In the second dialog box, select the fields you want in the chart. For this chart, choose Year, BeatNo, Crime Type, and Number of Crimes from the field list, and then click Next.

4. In the next dialog box, choose a simple column chart and click Next.

5. In the layout dialog box, drag the Year field to the Axis area, the Number of Crimes to the Data area, and the Crime Type to the Series area. Then click Next.

6. In the next dialog box (see Figure 15-9) the wizard suggests BeatNo as the linking fields in both the form and chart because they have the same name. If no matching names are between the tables, the wizard makes no suggestion. You can change the linking field names or choose not to link the chart to the form at all by choosing <No Field>. Click Next to move to the final dialog box, which is the same as before, and name the form "City Beats."

> **Note** *The linking fields needn't have the same names, but they must have the same kind of data and be of the same or compatible data types.*

Figure 15-10 shows the finished form with the linked chart. As you move through the records, the heights of the data column markers change to reflect the number of crimes reported in that beat area.

> **Tip** *Reconstructing the chart when you move to the next record may take a few seconds, so be patient.*

If you open the form in Design view and look at the properties of the chart control, you will see that the Link Child Fields and Link Master Fields are both set to the BeatNo field.

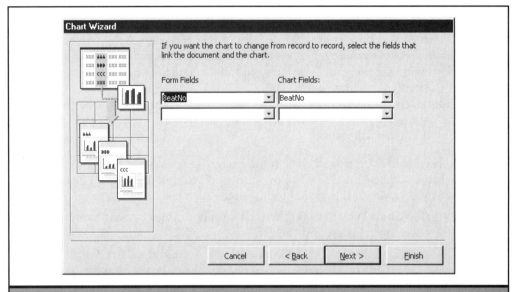

Figure 15-9. *The Chart Wizard offers to link the chart to records in the form*

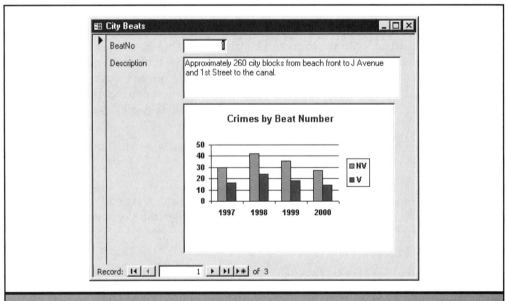

Figure 15-10. *The new form with a linked chart*

Note *If you already created the chart and want to embed and link it in a form, you can set the Link Child Fields and Link Master Fields properties yourself in the chart control property sheet.*

Adding an Existing Chart

You can insert an existing chart created within the current database or in another Access database into a form or report. To add a chart created in the same or another Access database, you can use the cut/copy/paste method or drag-and-drop to move or copy the chart from one form or report to the other. To use drag-and-drop to insert the chart from another database, you must have two instances of Access running.

To insert a new chart created with another program, open the form or report in Design view and do the following:

1. Click the Unbound Object Frame toolbox button and click where you want the chart. You can also draw the frame in the design.

2. In the Insert Object dialog box, click Create From File and enter the path to the file, or click Browse to locate the file if you don't know the path.

3. If you want to link the chart to the form or report, select Link. If you want the chart to appear as an icon instead of the full chart, select Display As Icon. Then click OK.

Note *You won't be able to change the data in an imported chart by changing the data in your database.*

Modifying the Chart

The tools you use to modify a chart depend on what kind of changes you want to make. If you want to change any of the properties or the position of the control, do so in Access. If you want to change the underlying data, you can create a new query and change the Row Source property of the chart within Access. You can also edit the SQL statement in the Row Source property rather than create a new query.

However, if you want to change any of the chart's elements, such as the axis titles or the chart type, or change the appearance of the chart, you must activate Microsoft Graph for in-place editing.

Note *You can also modify the appearance of a chart by creating Visual Basic procedures and attaching them to the chart control. See Chapter 25 for information about writing Visual Basic procedures.*

Modifying with Access

To modify the chart with Access, open the host form or report in Design view and select the chart control frame. With the frame selected, you can do the following:

- Drag the frame to a different position in the form or report.
- Drag the sizing handles to change the frame size. This resizes only the frame. Double-click the chart object to activate Graph and change the size of the chart itself.
- Use the Formatting (Form/Report) toolbar to change the frame's fill color, border color and width, and special effect.
- Open the property sheet and change any of the control properties including the Row Source, Link Master Fields, and Link Child Fields.

For example, to unlink the Crimes by Beat Number chart from the form, do the following:

1. Open the City Beats form in Design view.
2. Select the chart control and open the property sheet.
3. Delete the BeatNo field names from the Link Master Fields and Link Child Fields properties.

When you return to Form view and move through the records, you can see the chart no longer changes with each record. Instead, it shows the total crimes for all beats with each record.

> **Tip**   *If disk space is a concern, you can save space by converting the unbound object control to an image control. Select the chart in form or report Design view and choose Format | Change To. Then select Image, the only option available to an unbound OLE object control. The data shown in the chart won't be updated with changes in the underlying record source. Use caution with the transformation because it can't be undone.*

Editing the Row Source Property

The Chart Wizard creates a query whose SQL statement becomes the row source for the chart. You can modify the row source using the query grid or by editing the SQL statement itself.

To change the row source, do the following:

1. Open the form or report in Design view and open the property sheet for the chart.
2. Click the Build button (…) next to the Row Source property to open the SQL Statement: Query Builder dialog box (see Figure 15-11), which shows the Sum

Crimes Chart created from the Sum Crimes query, together with the Query
Builder dialog box.

3. To limit the chart to crimes occurring in specific years, enter **Between 1998
And 2000** in the Criteria row of the Year column.

4. Close the Query Builder dialog box and respond Yes to save the changes.
Then switch to Print Preview.

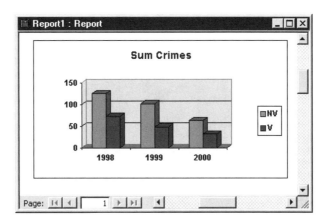

Note   *If you plan to limit the time interval before finishing with the wizard, you could also
set the chart interval in the Chart Wizard dialog box.*

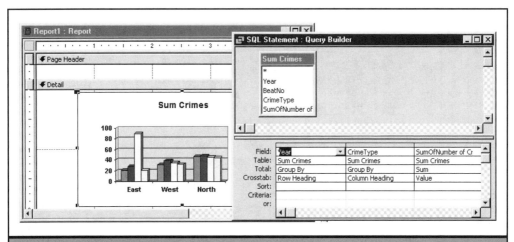

Figure 15-11.   *The Query Builder dialog box*

Editing the Chart Legend

When you add a series to the chart layout that summarizes data within the category, as shown in Figure 15-12, the legend isn't always as informative as possible. The charts illustrate the same data and are based on tables that contain the same data, but use different table structures.

The chart on the left is based on the Crimes by Beat Number table:

SumLine	Year	BeatNo	CrimeType	Number of Crim
1	1997	1	V	16
2	1997	1	NV	30
3	1997	2	V	12
4	1997	2	NV	35
5	1997	3	V	18
6	1997	3	NV	41
7	1998	1	V	24
8	1998	1	NV	42

The Chart Wizard created a crosstab query that totals the number of both types of crimes reported for each beat.

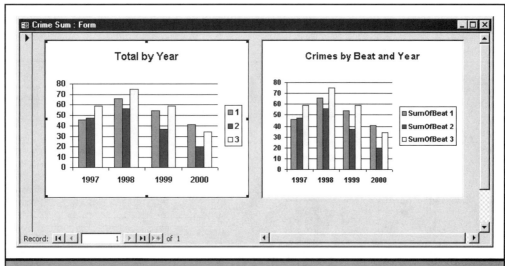

Figure 15-12. *Two charts illustrating the same data*

Field:	Year	BeatNo	Number of Crimes
Table:	Crimes by Beat Number	Crimes by Beat Number	Crimes by Beat Number
Total:	Group By	Group By	Sum
Crosstab:	Row Heading	Column Heading	Value
Sort:			
Criteria:			
or:			

The chart legend in the chart on the left takes its values from the value of the field whose Crosstab row shows Column Heading, which is BeatNo (1, 2, and 3). The legend would be more informative if you edited it to read Beat 1, Beat 2, and Beat 3. You have two ways to do this after opening the Query Builder for the Row Source property:

- Change the BeatNo field in the query grid to the expression **"Beat "&[BeatNo]**. Be sure to include a space after **Beat** within the quotation marks to separate it from the number.

Field:	Year	Expr1: "Beat " & BeatNo	Number of Crimes
Table:	Crimes by Beat Number	Crimes by Beat Number	Crimes by Beat Number
Total:	Group By	Group By	Sum
Crosstab:	Row Heading	Column Heading	Value
Sort:			
Criteria:			
or:			

- Choose View | SQL View (or click the View button and choose SQL View) and change the PIVOT clause from:

```
PIVOT [BeatNo];
```

to:

```
PIVOT "Beat "&[BeatNo];
```

 **Tip** *If you make the change in the grid, the SQL statement changes to match and vice versa.*

When you save the design, close the Query Builder dialog box, and switch to Form, you can see the change in the legend.

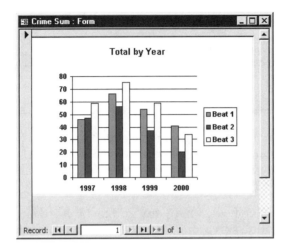

The chart on the right in Figure 15-11 is based on the more compact Crimes by Beat and Year table.

LineNo	Year	Type	Beat 1	Beat 2	Beat 3
1	1997	V	16	12	18
2	1997	NV	30	35	41
3	1998	V	24	18	30
4	1998	NV	42	38	45
5	1999	V	18	10	20
6	1999	NV	36	27	39
7	2000	V	14	8	10
8	2000	NV	27	12	24

For this chart, the Chart Wizard created a select query that sums the value in each of the Beat*n* fields by year. The legend shows SumOfBeat 1, SumOfBeat2, and SumOfBeat3. You can use the same two methods to change the legend text: add expressions to the Field row of the query grid or edit the SQL statement.

Open the form in Design view and start the Query Builder as before. Then do one of the following:

Field:	Year	Beat 1	Beat 2	Beat 3	
Table:	Crimes by Beat and	Crimes by Beat and	Crimes by Beat and	Crimes by Beat and	
Total:	Group By	Sum	Sum	Sum	
Sort:					
Show:	☑	☑	☑	☑	
Criteria:					
or:					

- Type **Beat 1:** before the Beat 1 field name. Repeat for Beat 2 and Beat 3 field names.
- Switch to SQL view and edit the AS clauses by deleting "SumOf" from each clause.

Be sure to leave the brackets around the field names because they contain spaces.

SQL Statement : Query Builder

```
SELECT [Crimes by Beat and Year].Year, Sum([Crimes by Beat and Year].[Beat 1]) AS
[SumOfBeat 1], Sum([Crimes by Beat and Year].[Beat 2]) AS [SumOfBeat 2], Sum([Crimes by
Beat and Year].[Beat 3]) AS [SumOfBeat 3]
FROM [Crimes by Beat and Year]
GROUP BY [Crimes by Beat and Year].Year;
```

Save the changes and switch to Form view. Figure 15-13 shows the two charts with their new legends.

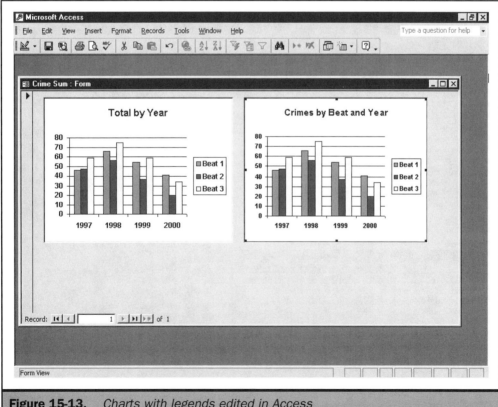

Figure 15-13. *Charts with legends edited in Access*

Editing with Microsoft Graph

Microsoft Graph is an applet you can use from within Access to edit the charts you created with the Chart Wizard. When you activate Graph, special toolbars appear in the Access window you use to edit the chart in place.

Graph serves many programs and not all its features apply to Access charts. In this chapter, I cover the main features that help you modify charts you included in Access forms and reports, and leave you to experiment with others.

To activate Microsoft Graph, double-click the chart control in the form or report Design view. Figure 15-14 shows the Entries by Quarter form in the Access window when Graph is active. In addition to the form window containing the chart, a Datasheet window appears containing sample data. Notice the cross-hatched border around the chart that indicates Microsoft Graph is currently running.

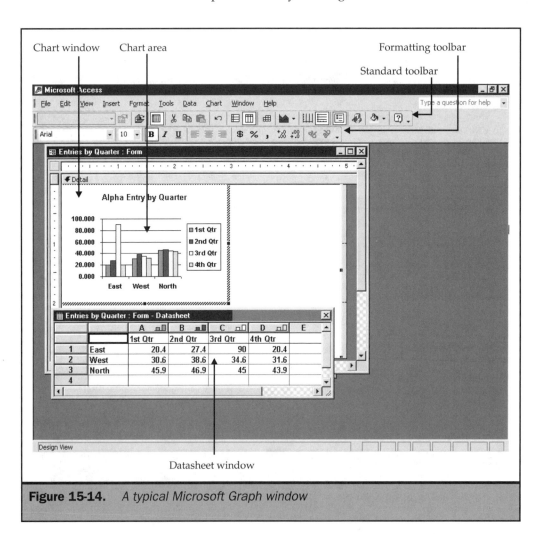

Figure 15-14. *A typical Microsoft Graph window*

The title you entered in the Chart Wizard dialog box appears as the chart title in Graph, but the data shown in the datasheet is all sample data used for illustration only.

> **Note**   *If you want to bother entering the actual data into the Graph datasheet, the chart would use it instead of the sample data.*

To show or hide the datasheet, do one of the following:

- Choose View | Datasheet, which toggles the Datasheet window in focus and out.
- Right-click the Chart window and choose Datasheet from the shortcut menu.

To leave the Microsoft Graph window and return to the Access form or report Design view, click anywhere outside the chart object. The changes you made to the chart in Graph are shown in the Access chart. You must save the form or report design to save the changes.

Looking at the Graph Toolbars

The Graph window normally has two toolbars: Standard and Formatting. Three other toolbars are available on demand: Drawing, Picture, and WordArt, which you can use to add special objects to the chart. To add a toolbar, right-click in any toolbar and select the one you want to add. You can also choose from the View | Toolbars menu.

Table 15-1 describes the buttons unique to the Graph Standard toolbar and their menu equivalents. The first combo box on the Standard toolbar is used to select a chart object.

Button	Name	Description	Menu Equivalent
	Chart Objects	Opens Format dialog box for selected object.	Format	Selected *chart element*
	Import File	Imports Excel, Lotus 1-2-3, or text file.	Edit	Import File
	View Datasheet	Shows/hides the datasheet.	View	Datasheet
	By Row	Displays data series in rows.	Data	Series in Rows
	By Column	Displays data series in columns.	Data	Series in Columns

Table 15-1.   *Graph Standard Toolbar Buttons*

Button	Name	Description	Menu Equivalent
	DataTable	Adds data in grid to bottom of chart.	Chart | Chart Options
	Chart Type	Displays palette of chart types.	Chart | Chart Type
	Category Axis gridlines	Displays gridlines upward from Category (*X*) axis.	Chart | Chart Options
	Value Axis Gridlines	Displays gridlines across from Value (*Y*) axis.	Chart | Chart Options
	Legend	Displays legend with chart.	Chart | Chart Options
	Drawing	Shows/hides the Drawing toolbar.	View | Toolbars
	Fill Color	Displays palette of colors for chart background.	Format | Selected *chart element*

Table 15-1.   *Graph Standard Toolbar Buttons* (continued)

The *Graph Formatting* toolbar has many of the common font name, size, weight, and alignment buttons, in addition to a few unique to Graph, which are described in Table 15-2. All these formatting activities are available by selecting the chart element and choosing Format \| Selected chart element.

Changing the Chart Appearance

To change the size of the chart, select the chart area and drag the sizing handles until it reaches the proper size.

If you have both the Access and Graph windows visible at once, you can see the change at once. When you widen the chart in Graph's Chart window, the chart in the Access frame widens, but the frame doesn't, which causes some of the chart to move out of the frame. Click in the Access window and widen the frame to match.

Button	Name	Description
$	Currency Style	Adds currency symbol to selected axis numeric values.
%	Percent Style	Adds percent sign to selected axis numeric values.
,	Comma Style	Uses comma as thousands separator.
+.0 .00	Increase Decimal	Adds one decimal place to the right of the decimal point.
.00 +.0	Decrease Decimal	Removes right-most decimal place.
⍺	Angle Clockwise	Tilts selected text downward 45 degrees. Click again to undo.
⍺	Angle Counterclockwise	Tilts selected text upward 45 degrees. Click again to undo.

Table 15-2. *Graph Formatting Toolbar Buttons*

Formatting Text Elements   You have the same options when formatting most of the text elements in the chart. Select the element and choose Format | Selected object to open the Format dialog box. The dialog box has three tabs: Patterns, Font, and Alignment (see Figure 15-15).

Note   *Select Fill Effects in the Format dialog box to open another dialog box where you can choose gradients, fill textures, or patterns, and even select a picture to use as a background.*

The Font tab contains the standard font name, size, weight, colors, and effects, such as underline, strikethrough, superscript, and subscript. When you select the chart title or one of the axis titles and choose Format | Selected, the Alignment tab appears in which you can choose the text alignment, plus the orientation. You can have the text displayed vertically or at a specific angle by clicking the arc in the Orientation area.

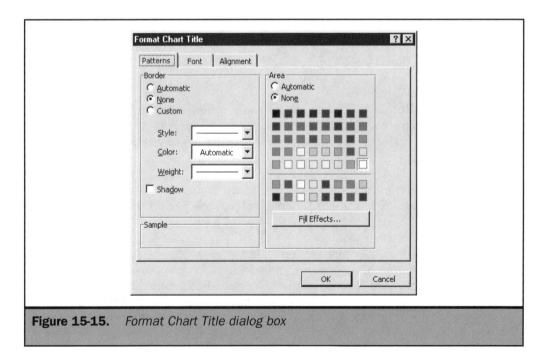

If you select the legend and choose Format | Selected Legend, the Alignment tab is replaced by the Placement tab, in which you can choose to display the legend at the bottom, corner, top, right, or left of the plot area.

Figure 15-15. *Format Chart Title dialog box*

Formatting Other Chart Elements When you select one of the axes and choose Format | Selected, the Format Axis dialog box shows five tabs: Patterns, Scale, Font, Number, and Alignment. The Patterns, Font, and Alignment tabs are the same as for text elements. The other tabs offer the following options:

- The options in the Scale tab depend on which axis you select. If you select the Value (*Y*) axis, you can choose to set the minimum and maximum values manually for the axis, as well as the major and minor units for the gridlines and tick marks. The alternative is to let Graph set these values automatically. You can also specify where the Category (*X*) axis is to cross the Value axis and whether to arrange the values in reverse order (see Figure 15-16).

- The Number tab gives you a selection of number categories and specific formats for the values on the Value (*Y*) axis. Also, a check box links the values to the source data. Clear this to create a snapshot chart that doesn't update with changes in the underlying data.

- When you select the Category (*X*) axis, the formatting options are slightly different. The Scale tab contains options that relate to data categories instead of values.

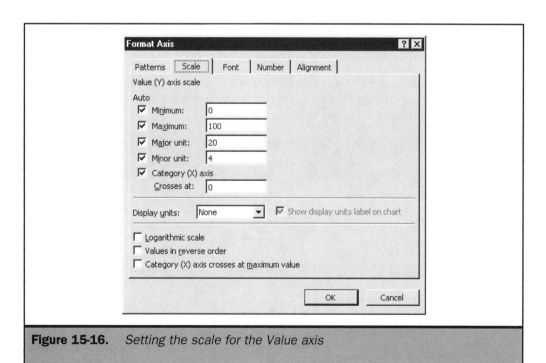

Figure 15-16. *Setting the scale for the Value axis*

When you format the data series by clicking one of the columns, bars, or other representation of the data, the Format dialog box contains five tabs: Patterns, Axis, Y Error Bars, Data Labels, and Options. The Patterns tab offers the same color, border, and fill options as before. The other tabs offer the following options:

■ The Axis tab specifies whether to plot the series on the primary or secondary axis. The secondary series is plotted against values placed in a Value axis on the right side of the plot area. A sample chart illustrates the choice.

■ The Y Error Bars tab gives you the option of displaying the statistical error estimation or the standard deviation in the values either as values or percentages. You can choose to display plus errors, minus errors, or both. This option is handy for presenting the results of statistical survey for which you need to express the validity.

■ In the Data Labels tab, you can choose to display the data values and labels with the data series. You can display the values as percentages or in the unit of the value itself.

■ In the Options tab, you can choose to have the series overlap and set the amount of overlap, as well as specify the amount of space between the sets of data series.

 You can add graphics, such as lines, arrows, and shapes, to the chart in Graph by displaying the Drawing toolbar and clicking the appropriate button. You may need to use the Format | Placement menu to move the shape in front or in back of the chart elements.

When you choose to format the data table you added below the chart, you see only two tabs in the Format dialog box: Patterns and Font. To format the plot area or the walls of a chart, you have only the Patterns options.

Changing Chart Type   You have two means of changing the chart type:

■ Click the Chart Type toolbar button and choose from the palette containing 18 chart types.

■ Choose Chart | Chart Type and choose from the Chart Type dialog box (see Figure 15-17). The Standard Types include 14 types with many sub-types for each. In the Standard Types tab, press and hold the button below the Chart subtype pane to see a sample of the selected chart. The Custom Types tab shows an additional 20 chart types from the built-in list of charts and, if you created any custom chart types, they're displayed when you choose Select from User-Defined.

After making your selection, click OK to apply it to the current chart. You can also specify a chart type as the default chart.

Setting Chart Options   When you choose Chart | Chart Options, the Chart Options dialog box opens with six tabs: Titles, Axes, Gridlines, Legend, Data Labels, and Data Table as shown in Figure 15-18.
The tabs offer the following options:

■ In the Titles tab, you enter the text you want to display as the chart title and the axes titles. You can specify a primary and secondary title for each axis, but only one for the chart itself.

■ In the Axes tab, you specify whether to display the axes and choose the method by which to display the Category (X) axis.

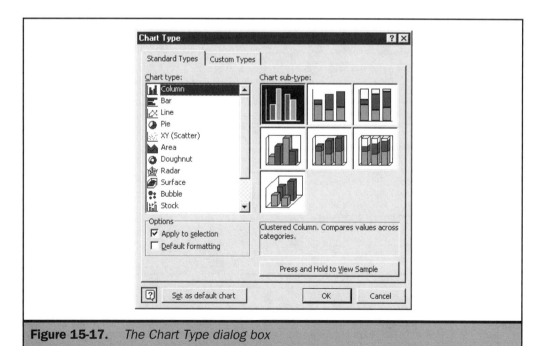

Figure 15-17.   *The Chart Type dialog box*

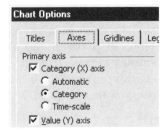

- In the Gridlines tab, you specify whether to display the gridlines on one or both of the axes. You can choose to display both major and minor gridlines on each axis.

- In the Legend tab, you choose whether to display the legend with the chart. The Legend tab also gives you the same options as the Placement tab of the Format dialog box for placing the legend: Bottom, Corner, Top, Right, or Left.

- The Data Labels tab includes the same options as the Data Labels tab in the Format Data Series dialog box.

- In the Data Table tab, you can choose to display the data in the underlying data source in a grid attached to the bottom of the chart. When you choose to display the data table, you can also display the legend keys with it. Figure 15-19 shows the Total by Year chart with the corresponding data table. If you choose not to

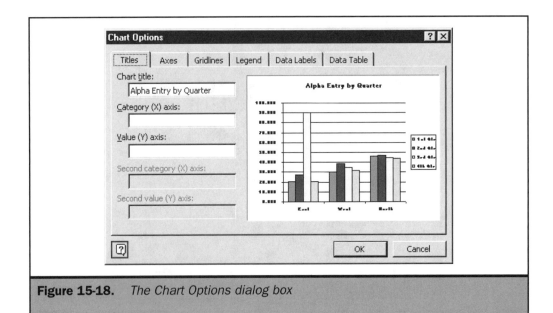

Figure 15-18. *The Chart Options dialog box*

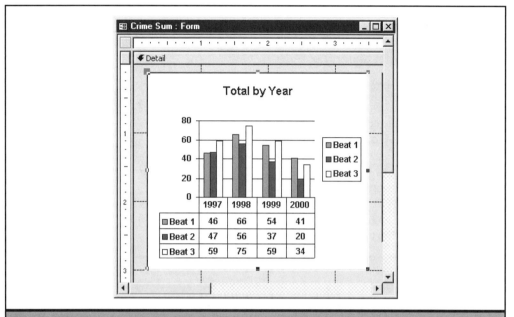

Figure 15-19.   *The Data Table added to the chart*

display the legend keys, then the colored squares at the left of the data table row headings don't appear. The Data Table option isn't available for several of the chart types, such as pie, XY scatter, and surface.

Note   *If you need a statistical analysis of the data, you can add a trendline. The Add Trendline option in the Chart menu draws a line in the chart, which can be used in regression analysis of a large sample of recorded data. Once a trend is established, the line can be extended to predict future performance. Trendlines are also used to create a moving average, which smoothes out fluctuations in data and shows the pattern or trend more clearly.*

Troubleshooting Charts

Sometimes the changes you make in Graph fail to show up in the chart when you switch to Form view or Print Preview in Access, even though they appeared in Design view. For example, you can change the column headings in the Graph datasheet to display the text you want in the legend. When you return to Access, the new labels appear in the design, but not in Form view or Print Preview.

The reason for this seeming inconsistency is you have several places in which to specify the chart information and Access must set an order of precedence to decide which values to use. The order is

■ First, the data in the underlying table or query—for example, the field names or the expressions in the Field row of the query grid.

■ Second, the contents of the Row Source property.

■ Last, the data entered in Graph.

So, if you set the legend text in Graph, but the underlying query column headings are different, they override the Graph settings.

If the columns don't appear in the order you want in the chart, open the Query Builder and rearrange the fields, left to right, in the order you want them sorted. Then choose the Sort order for each.

Creating PivotTables and PivotCharts

PivotTables and their alter egos, the PivotCharts, are actually Excel objects, but Office XP also makes them available from Access. A *PivotTable* is a spreadsheet-like table you can use to analyze data dynamically in different ways. A PivotTable is similar to a crosstab in appearance, but it's far more powerful. When you make a change in the PivotTable, the summary values are recalculated immediately. The calculations performed in a PivotTable include the individual amounts that appear in each cell, totals of each row, and totals of each column.

A *PivotChart* is a similar flexible tool that presents the data in chart form instead of in a spreadsheet. As with PivotTables, you can dynamically switch row and column data, and add filters to analyze the underlying data on the fly.

Figure 15-20 shows a PivotTable containing data from the Police database. The PivotTable has two row fields: BeatNo, which is the primary row designator, and CrimeType, which is secondary. Year is the column field and the calculated field, Number of Crimes, appears in the detail area.

Figure 15-21 shows the same data in a PivotChart form. If you want to reverse the rows and columns, choose View | PivotChart View, and then click the By Row/By Column toolbar button.

To create a PivotTable, first create and save a query that contains the data you want to analyze, and then start the PivotTable Wizard. You can also start a PivotTable or PivotChart from scratch by choosing AutoForm: PivotTable or AutoForm: PivotChart in the New Form dialog box. The next section describes how to create a PivotTable with the PivotTable Wizard using information in the Police database.

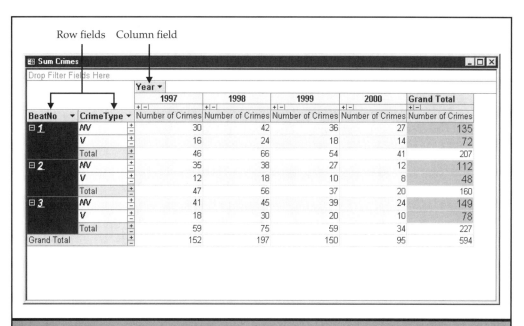

Figure 15-20. *A sample PivotTable*

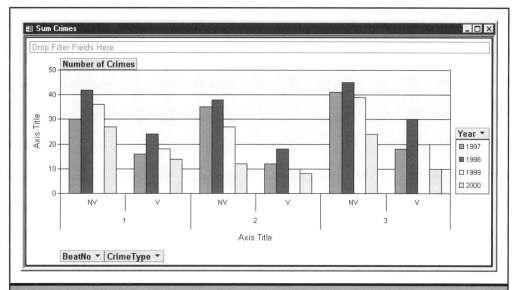

Figure 15-21. *A sample PivotChart*

Using the PivotTable Wizard

The Access PivotTable Wizard creates a PivotTable and embeds it in an Access form. This example uses the Crimes by Beat Number table as the basis for the PivotTable. To create a new PivotTable in the Police database, do the following:

1. In the Database window, select Crimes by Beat Number on the Tables page and choose Insert | Form to open the New Form dialog box.

2. Choose PivotTable Wizard and click OK.

3. The first wizard dialog box describes PivotTables and explains the process of creating the table. After reading the information, click Next.

4. The second wizard dialog box (see Figure 15-22) asks you which of the fields to include in the PivotTable. If you're basing the PivotTable on a query you created just for this purpose, you probably want all the fields, so click the double right chevrons. Otherwise, select each field and click the single right chevron. For this exercise, choose all fields except SumLine from the list of fields, and then click Finish.

An empty PivotTable layout design appears where you arrange the field data in the areas you want them (see Figure 15-23). The field list contains all the fields you included in the design.

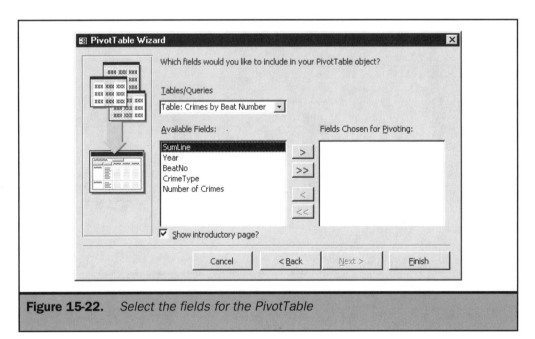

Figure 15-22. *Select the fields for the PivotTable*

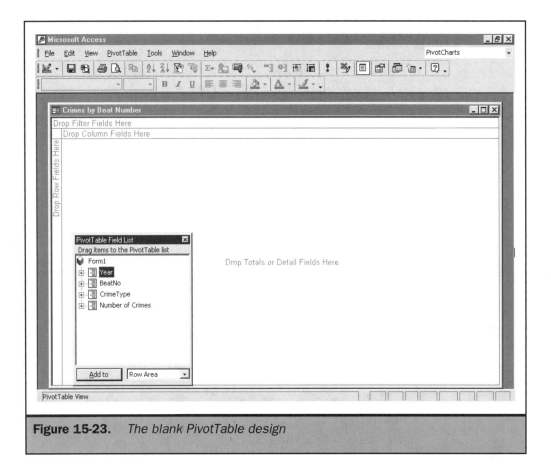

Figure 15-23.   *The blank PivotTable design*

To place the fields in the PivotTable layout, drag-and-drop the field names from the Field List to the specific areas as follows (blue lines appear to indicate in which area you are dropping the field):

■ The Year field to the Column Fields area.

■ The BeatNo field to the Row Fields area.

■ The Crime Type field to the Row Fields area to the right of the BeatNo field.

■ The Number of Crimes field to the Detail Fields area.

Note   *You can also select the field in the Field List, select the destination area from the drop-down list, and then choose Add To.*

Figure 15-24 shows the PivotTable under construction. Now, you need to add totals and grand totals as follows:

1. Select one of the detail field values and click the AutoCalc toolbar button. You can also right-click the detail field and point to AutoCalc in the shortcut menu.

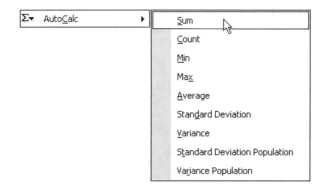

2. Choose the type of calculation you want from the list, Sum, in this case.

3. Select the whole table and choose PivotTable | Hide Details to collapse the detail sums for every row. You can also click the Hide Details button.

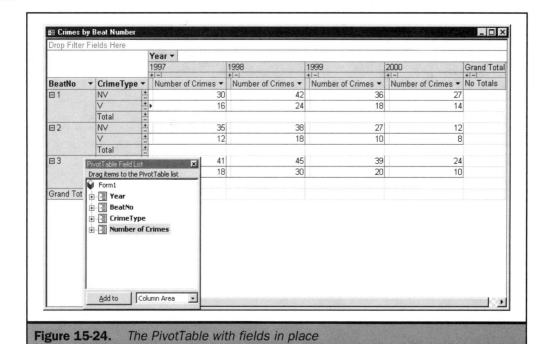

Figure 15-24. *The PivotTable with fields in place*

4. Click in a column header and choose View | Properties or click the Properties toolbar button.

5. Click the Captions tab in the Commands and Options dialog box (see Figure 15-25) and select Total in the Select Caption box. You can also set the format for the captions using the Format tab.

6. Delete the Sum Of part of the caption to reduce the table column width.

7. Close the Commands and Options dialog box. When you rest the mouse pointer on a cell in the PivotTable, a ScreenTip displays the information about that cell.

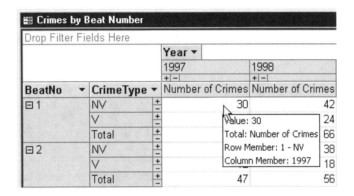

8. Save and name the form containing the PivotTable.

You can change many more properties in a PivotTable. See the Access or Excel Help topics for more ways you can customize your PivotTables.

Filtering the PivotTable Data

You needn't view all the data in a PivotTable. In fact, one of the most important aspects of PivotTables and PivotCharts is the capability to analyze the data dynamically. You can choose to have only specific categories displayed. For example, to see crimes only for the years 1999 and 2000, do the following:

1. Click the down arrow next to Year in the Column header area.

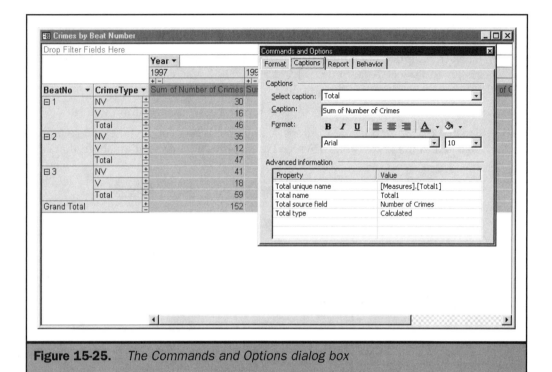

Figure 15-25. *The Commands and Options dialog box*

2. Clear the check boxes next to 1997 and 1998, and then click OK.

3. To restore them, repeat step 1, choose All, and then click OK.

Creating a PivotChart

Once you build the PivotTable, you can instantly convert it to a chart, as follows:

1. Open the PivotTable in PivotTable View.

2. Choose View | PivotChart View or click the View button and choose PivotChart View from the list.

The resulting PivotChart presents the same data as the PivotTable (refer to Figures 15-20 and 15-21). When you close the PivotChart, it isn't saved as a separate object, but reverts to the PivotTable form saved following the PivotTable design.

Modifying the PivotChart

When you first convert the PivotTable to a chart, no legend describes the categories of data. To add a legend to the PivotChart, choose PivotChart | Show Legend or click the Show Legend toolbar button.

Notice the *X* and *Y* axes have only generic titles. To add titles to the axes, do the following:

1. Select the Category Axis Title and click Properties.
2. Click the Format tab and enter the title text you want in the Caption box (see Figure 15-26). You can change the font, size, and appearance at the same time.
3. Keep the Commands and Options dialog box open and select the *Y*-axis title.
4. Enter an appropriate title in the Caption box and click the dialog box.

You can filter the data displayed in PivotCharts, the same as with PivotTables. Click the down arrow next to the item you want to filter on and check only those values you want to see in the chart. For example, if you want to focus on violent crimes, click the arrow next to CrimeType and clear the check mark from NV. Then click OK.

RETRIEVING AND PRESENTING INFORMATION

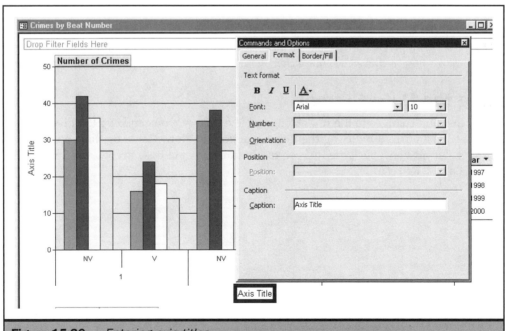

Figure 15-26.   *Entering axis titles*

Earlier in this chapter, you saw how to change a regular chart to a different type, for example, from a column chart to a line chart. You can do the same with PivotCharts. To do this, click anywhere outside the plot area and click the Chart Type button. You can also choose PivotChart | Chart Type. Then choose the type of chart you want from the Type tab of the Commands and Options dialog box. Most of the choices are the same as with Microsoft Graph.

Creating PivotTables and PivotCharts Without the Wizard

You don't have to use a wizard to create PivotTables and PivotCharts, but you do need to specify the table or query that contains the data you want to analyze.

1. Open the New Form dialog box as usual and choose AutoForm: PivotTable.

2. Select the table or query that will provide the data, and then click OK. The blank PivotTable layout appears just the same as after you choose the fields with the PivotTable Wizard, except the Field List includes all the fields in the table or query.

3. Drag the fields to the desired areas as before and set other properties as necessary.

When you choose AutoForm: PivotChart, the layout shows a blank chart grid with the Category, Series, Data, and Filter drop areas (see Figure 15-27). Drag the fields from the field list to the appropriate areas and set the properties as necessary.

 You can also create PivotTables and PivotCharts in reports using the same techniques. The only difference between a PivotChart in a form and one in a report is the default chart type is a clustered column chart for a form and a stacked column chart for a report.

Keeping the Data Current

When the data changes in the underlying table or query, you can keep the PivotTable or PivotChart current by using the Refresh action. With the table or chart open in Form or Report view, click the Refresh toolbar button or choose PivotTable (or PivotChart) | Refresh.

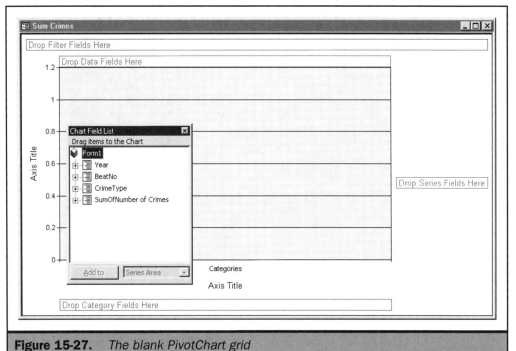

Figure 15-27.   *The blank PivotChart grid*

Summary

This chapter concludes the discussion of customized output from Access and brings to a close the part of the book devoted to retrieving and presenting information. Trying to anticipate what every reader needs in the area of information storage and retrieval is impossible, but I did attempt to give you a wide view of the capabilities within Access. The many Help topics can expand on the information presented in these nine chapters.

The next chapter begins the discussion of improving the Access workplace. The topics covered include changing the workplace options, setting startup options, and adding commands to the startup sequence. Later, in the next part of the book, you learn about creating and using macros to further automate the database application further.

MOUS Exam Activities Explored in This Chapter

This chapter contains no information directly related to the MOUS Certification Exam activities, although the information is important to understand how to use Access for effective database management.

The Complete Reference

Part III

Improving the Workplace

Chapter 16

Customizing the Workplace

657

M any of the features discussed in this chapter have been briefly mentioned in previous chapters and some are covered later. The purpose of this chapter is to capture all the workplace options in one place for easy reference. Using the many Access and Windows options, you can change the default appearance and behavior of a database application, keyboard actions, hyperlinks, search and filter routines, and form and report design windows, among many other aspects of your workplace.

In addition to the changes you can make that affect the current Access database, you can change many startup options, such as displaying a startup form, opening a specific database, and displaying custom menus and toolbars.

This chapter also discusses changes you can make to set the appearance and behavior of the helpful Office Assistant.

Personalizing the Workplace

You needn't accommodate yourself to the layout and behavior of the Access environment the way it is when first installed. The Access developers attempted to design a workplace that would be appropriate for most users, but if you want to change some aspects, this is easy. For example, if you have a large screen, you may want to see a larger font size. You can, of course, change each of these factors every time you work with Access, but changing the default settings saves time.

Rearranging Icons

In the Database window, each page displays icons representing objects of that type in the current database. You can change the icon size and amount of detail shown with the icons, as well as arrange them in a specific order.

The buttons at the top of the Database window and the commands in the View menu contain the means for displaying the object icons as follows:

- *Large Icons* shows expanded object icons in rows with the name below each one.

- *Small Icons* shows smaller object icons in rows, but with the name beside each one.

- *List* shows the object icons in columns with the name beside each one.

- *Details* shows each object icon in a single row with its name and four additional columns containing other information about the object: the description you entered in the object property dialog box, the time/date the object was last modified, the time/date the object was created, and the type of object.

The last two settings are the same as settings you can choose from the View drop-down list in the Open dialog box.

To add a description to an object, right-click the object icon in the Database window and choose Properties from the shortcut menu. Enter the description in the Description box in the General tab and click OK.

When you show the object icons with the details, you can make other adjustments to the display:

- Resize the column width by dragging the vertical column separator in the column heading.

- Resize the column width to fit the widest information in it by double-clicking the column separator.

- Sort the icons by one of the detail categories by clicking once in the column heading to sort in ascending order. Click the column heading again to change the order to descending.

The View | Arrange Icons commands sort the icons in ascending order by name, type, date/time created, or date/time modified. These commands accomplish the same arrangements as clicking once in the column headings of the details. The Auto Arrange command, which is available only if you selected Large Icons or Small Icons, moves the icons back into the specified arrangement.

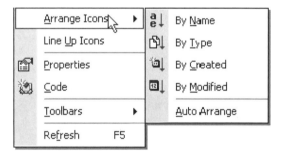

You can drag the icons to another position in the Database window, and then use the View | Lineup Icons command to straighten up the rows and columns. The Lineup Icons command moves the icons slightly to the nearest row/column intersection. Lineup Icons is only available if you're showing large or small icons.

Hiding the Taskbar

It isn't necessary to show the Windows taskbar at the bottom of the screen. You can remove it temporarily to allow more screen space for your database activities. Auto hide is one of the Taskbar Options in the Taskbar Properties dialog box. When Auto hide is checked, the taskbar remains off the screen until you move the mouse pointer to the edge of the screen where it appeared before it was hidden.

To hide the taskbar, do the following:

1. Right-click in an empty space on the taskbar and choose Properties from the shortcut menu. You can also click the Start button and choose Settings | Taskbar & Start Menu to open the Taskbar Properties dialog box (see Figure 16-1).

2. Make sure Always on top is checked, and then check Auto hide and click OK. The taskbar disappears from the screen.

3. Move the mouse pointer all the way to the edge of the screen—below the application status bar—to return the taskbar to the screen temporarily.

4. To return the taskbar to the screen permanently, open the Taskbar Properties dialog box again and clear the Auto hide option.

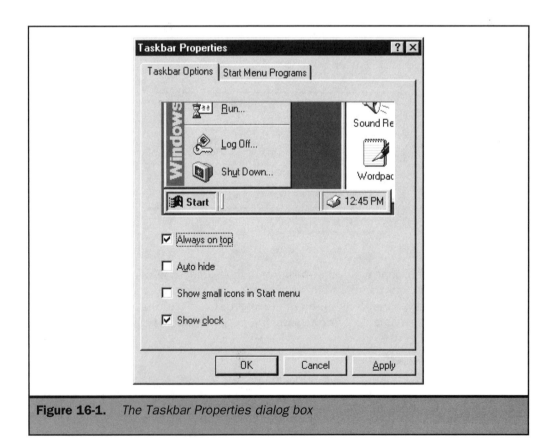

Figure 16-1. *The Taskbar Properties dialog box*

If you can't remember where the taskbar was before you hid it, move the mouse pointer to each side of the screen until it reappears.

Creating a Shortcut

If you use an Access object regularly, you can create a shortcut that launches Access and opens the database object directly from the Windows desktop. The easiest way is to drag the object from the Access Database window to the Windows desktop. You must first resize the Access window so you can see the area where you want to place the shortcut icon. When you double-click the shortcut, Access opens the database that stores the object and displays the object.

Note *To delete a shortcut, click it and press* DEL. *This doesn't delete the object itself, only the shortcut.*

Another way to create a shortcut is to use the Create Shortcut command on the object shortcut menu. With this method, you can create a shortcut in a location other than the desktop by entering a path in the Create Shortcut dialog box (see Figure 16-2). Type a new path in the Location box or click Browse to search for the desired location and have Access fill in the path for you. If the database is on a network, Access automatically selects This Database is on the Network and fills in the path in the Full Network Path box.

Figure 16-2. *The Create Shortcut dialog box*

If you moved the database that's the destination of a shortcut, remove the shortcut and create a new one with the new path.

Setting Workplace Options

Access is installed with certain characteristics set as defaults. For example, the width of the print margins, the default database folder, the color of hyperlinks, the gridlines and font styles in a datasheet are all set by default. If you find yourself changing specific default values when you work with a database, you can reset the default value to the one you use the most. All default values can be overridden later, if necessary.

 Access stores most option settings in the workgroup information file, instead of in your database file. Changes you make to those settings in the Options dialog box apply to any database opened or created by anyone who uses the same workgroup information file.

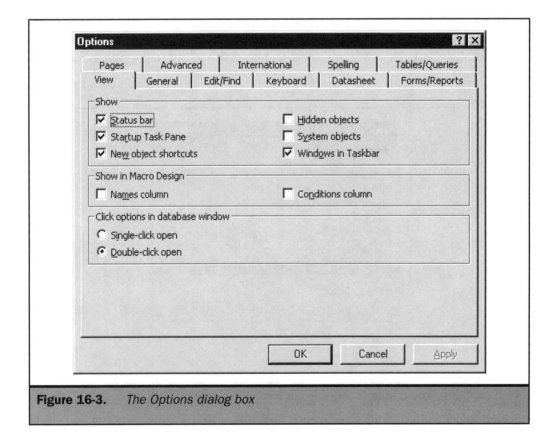

Figure 16-3. *The Options dialog box*

To change default values, choose Tools | Options and click the tab that contains the values you want to change. To change values on more than one tab, choose Apply to keep the Options dialog box open, and then click another tab. When you finish setting the default values, click OK to close the dialog box.

If you want to know more about any of the settings in the Options dialog box, click the question mark (?) at the upper-right corner of the dialog box, and then click the item. Sometimes you must click in the option box rather than on the option name.

The Options dialog box has 11 tabs, as shown in Figure 16-3. The following sections describe the options on each of the tabs.

When you open the Options dialog box, the visible tab is the one you last accessed.

View Options

The options on the View tab (refer to Figure 16-3) all relate to what you see at startup, while working in the Database window, or when creating a macro.

In the *Show* group, you can choose to show or hide the following items:

- *Status bar* displays the status bar at the bottom of the screen.
- *Startup Task Pane* displays the opening Access side pane that enables you to select an existing database or to create a new one.
- *New object shortcuts* displays the two or three items in the Database window you can double-click to start a new database object. For example, "Create form by using wizard."
- *Hidden objects* displays any object in the Database window that's been specified as hidden by setting the Hidden property to Yes. The object appears as a dimmed icon.
- *System objects* displays system tables created by Access or the user as dimmed icons. The names of system objects created by Access all begin with MSys and aren't normally displayed. A user can also create a system object by giving it a name with USys as the first four characters.
- *Windows in Taskbar* places a button on the Windows taskbar for every open database object or window. Must have Internet Explorer Active Desktop installed to use this feature.

In the *Show in Macro Design* group, you have only two options, both of which relate to creating and editing macros.

- The *Names column* setting displays the Macro Name column by default in the macro design grid where you enter an optional macro name.

■ The *Conditions column* setting displays the Condition column by default in the macro design grid where you enter the conditions under which the macro action is to take place.

See Chapter 19 for more information about creating macros.

The *Click options in database window* setting offers you the choice between clicking once or double-clicking to open an object in the Database window. The default is Double-click open but if you want to click only once to open an object, change to Single-click open.

 If you change to single-click in the Control Panel, you also have to change it in Access. Choose Tools | Options and click the View tab. Then check the Single-click open option.

General Options

The General tab (see Figure 16-4) shows options that don't fit into one of the other categories of settings.

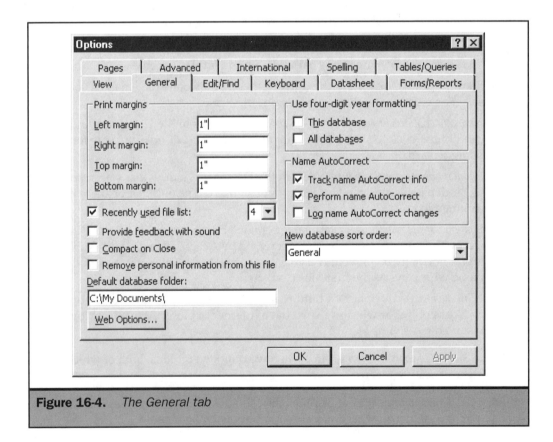

Figure 16-4. *The General tab*

■ You can enter any number in the *Print margins* group that's compatible with your printer and paper size, ranging from 0 to the height or width of the printed page. Override the default settings established here by running Page Setup before printing a form or report.

■ The *Recently used file list* setting determines the number of filenames to display when you choose File in the menu bar or when the opening task pane appears. Enter the desired number or choose from the drop-down list.

■ If you select the *Provide feedback with sound* option, you activate sounds to accompany such tasks as a print job completion or an alert notification. You can customize sounds for this option through the Sounds dialog box in the Windows Control Panel. If you installed a sound card after you installed Office XP, you must reinstall the .wav files from Office Setup.

Caution   *The sound option affects all Office programs.*

■ Checking *Compact on Close* automatically compacts and repairs the database when you close it, if the size will be reduced by at least 256K.

■ Checking *Remove personal information from this file* automatically deletes your name, the name of your company and any other personal information you have entered.

■ The *Default database folder* specifies the default folder in which you want to save new databases. Enter the complete path to the folder.

■ The *Web Options* button opens a dialog box (see Figure 16-5) in which you can specify the default appearance of new hyperlinks. You can choose colors for hyperlinks before and after click it to jump to the target, and include underlining.

■ The *Use four-digit year formatting* applies the default format to the current database or to all databases.

■ In the *New database sort order* setting, you can choose from a list of 15 languages that change the default alphabetic sort order for new databases. The General setting applies to English, French, German, Italian, Portuguese, and modern Spanish. To change the sort order for an existing database, select the language, and then compact the database.

The *Name AutoCorrect* group offers three options that help fix common side-effects that occur when you make changes in an object via a user interface. Access stores an identifier for each object and tracks naming information. When Access notices an object has been changed since the last Name AutoCorrect, it runs it again for all items in that object. For example, if you added a text box to a form that's bound to the Alpha Card table and you change the Alpha Card table name to Alpha Card Plus, Access can track down all the items from the original Alpha Card and change their names to match the new table name.

IMPROVING THE
WORKPLACE

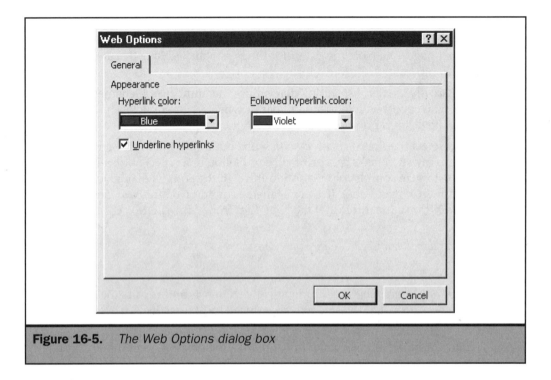

Figure 16-5. *The Web Options dialog box*

The three options you can check for Name AutoCorrect are

- *Track name AutoCorrect info* stores information it needs to correct naming errors, but doesn't immediately correct them.
- *Perform name AutoCorrect* repairs naming errors as they occur.
- *Log name AutoCorrect changes* creates a log named AutoCorrect Log that contains the changes it makes to the database each time it runs Name AutoCorrect.

Edit/Find Options

The Edit/Find tab (see Figure 16-6) shows settings that all relate to finding, replacing, and filtering records in the current database.

The *Default find/replace behavior* setting determines the extent of the search. These options are also available on an immediate basis in the Find/Replace dialog box.

- *Fast search* searches the current field only and matches the entire field.
- *General search* searches all the fields and matches any part of the field.
- *Start of field search* searches the current field and matches only the beginning characters in the field.

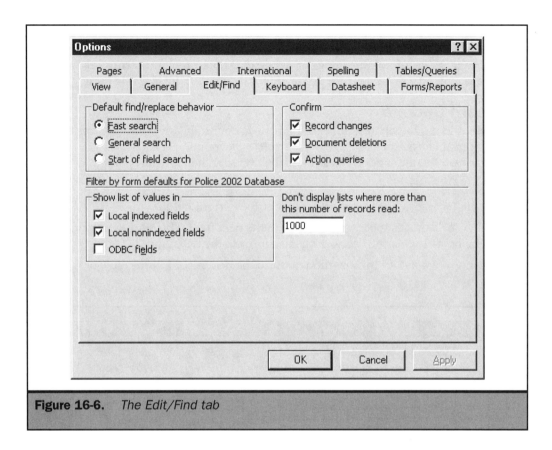

Figure 16-6.   *The Edit/Find tab*

The *Confirm* group requires Access to display a message requiring a confirmation of the current operation under specific conditions, such as when a record changes (*Record changes*), when you delete a database object (*Document deletions*), or when you run an action query (*Action queries*).

The *Filter by form defaults for...* group contains options that limit or extend the size of the value list displayed in the Filter By Form window and sets the maximum number of records to read to build a value list for a given field. The more fields you include in the filter operation, the longer it takes. These settings apply only to the current database.

- *Local indexed fields* limits the value list to the indexed fields in the current database.

- *Local nonindexed fields* includes the fields in the current database that aren't indexed.

- *ODBC fields* includes fields in a linked table in an external source.

■ Enter a number in the Don't Display Lists Where More Than This Number of Records Read box to set the maximum number of records you want to read to build the list of unique values or the field. If the number of records exceeds this amount, no values at all are displayed for the field in the Filter By Form window.

Keyboard Options

The settings in the Keyboard tab (see Figure 16-7) determine the consequences of pressing certain keys, such as ENTER, TAB, RIGHT ARROW, and LEFT ARROW.

The *Move after enter* option refers to the behavior of the insertion point after pressing ENTER.

■ *Don't move* keeps the insertion point in the current field.

■ *Next field* moves the insertion point to the next field. This setting works with the *Behavior entering field* settings to complete the behavior.

■ *Next record* moves the insertion point to the next record in the table or form.

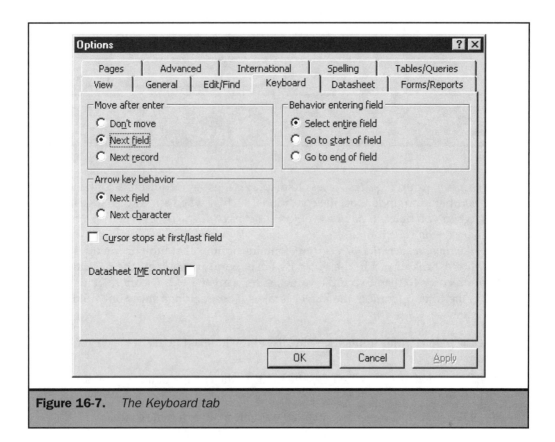

Figure 16-7. *The Keyboard tab*

The *Arrow key behavior* settings specify what occurs when you press RIGHT ARROW and LEFT ARROW.

■ *Next field* moves the insertion point to the next or previous field when you press RIGHT ARROW or LEFT ARROW. To move the insertion point within the field, press F2.

■ *Next character* moves the insertion point to the next or previous character in the current field when you press RIGHT ARROW or LEFT ARROW.

The *Behavior entering field* group determines what happens when the insertion point enters a field.

■ *Select entire field* selects all the characters in the field.

■ *Go to start of field* places the insertion point in front of the first character in the field without selecting any characters.

■ *Go to end of field* places the insertion point at the end of the field after the last character without selecting any characters.

The *Cursor stops at first/last field* setting locks the insertion point within the current record and prevents the RIGHT ARROW and LEFT ARROW keys from moving the insertion point to the next or previous record.

Checking the *Datasheet IME control* specifies the *Input Method Editor* (*IME*) Mode property is set to No Control when entering data in a datasheet. If you clear this option, the IME behavior is determined by the IME Mode property of the individual fields.

Datasheet Options

The Datasheet tab (see Figure 16-8) includes the following default value settings:

■ *Default colors* enables you to specify the default font, background, and gridline colors for the datasheet. When you click the drop-down arrow, a list of 16 colors with samples appears. Click the desired color.

■ *Default font* enables you to select the font name from the list of fonts installed on your system. You can also choose from nine font weights ranging from Thin to Heavy; the default setting is Normal. Choose the font size from the drop-down list that contains font sizes ranging from 8 to 72 points or enter a number in the box. Check Italic and/or Underline to set that style as default.

■ *Default gridlines showing* determines whether to show or hide the horizontal and vertical gridlines in the datasheet.

■ *Default column width* specifies the width of the columns in a new datasheet. You can change the width easily in the datasheet by dragging the column dividers. Type a new default width in the box. The default width uses the system unit of measure.

IMPROVING THE WORKPLACE

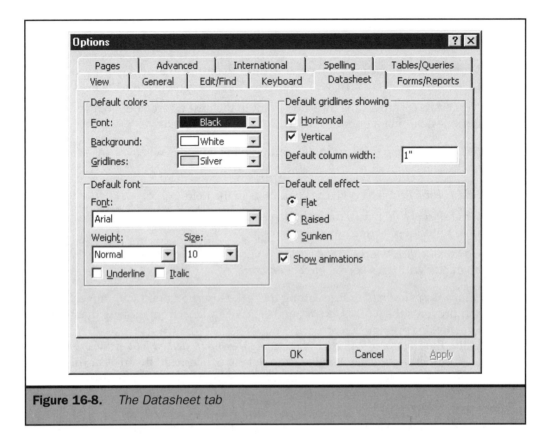

Figure 16-8. *The Datasheet tab*

■ *Default cell effect* is normally set to Flat, but you can change this to Raised or Sunken to create a special effect in the datasheet.

■ *Show animations*, when checked, shows movement in the datasheet. For example, when you insert or delete a column, the other columns can be seen to slide over.

Form and Report Options

The settings in the Forms/Reports tab of the Options dialog box (see Figure 16-9) all relate to designing a form or report.

■ The *Selection behavior* group relates to the results of dragging a rectangle in the design to select controls. *Partially enclosed* selects all controls with any part within the drawn rectangle, while *Fully enclosed* selects only those controls totally within the drawn rectangle.

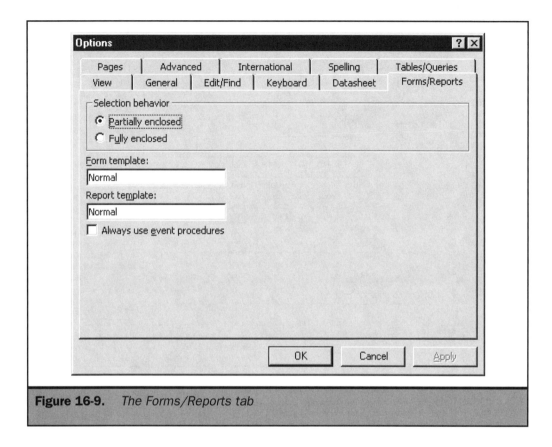

Figure 16-9.   *The Forms/Reports tab*

■ The *Form template* and *Report template* settings enable you to specify an existing form or report as the template for new designs. Type the name of the form or report you want to use as the default template.

■ The *Always use event procedures* setting, when selected, takes you directly to the VB Editor window when you click the Build button in a property sheet, bypassing the Choose Builder dialog box. With the setting cleared, the Choose Builder dialog box appears, offering the choice of Expression Builder, Macro Builder, or Code Builder.

Page Options

The Pages tab (see Figure 16-10) contains two groups of options: Default Designer Properties and Default Database/Project Properties.

The Default Designer Properties include

■ Section Indent, which specifies the default indent for each section.

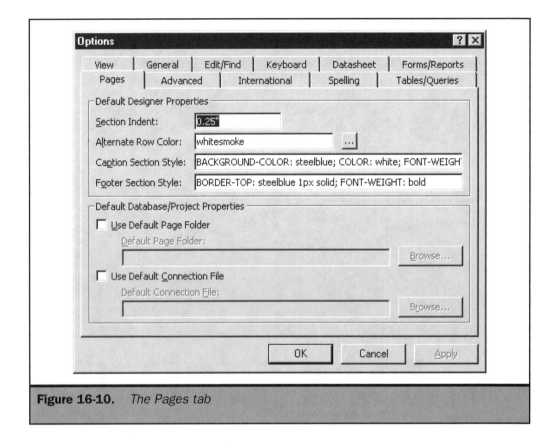

Figure 16-10. *The Pages tab*

- Alternate Row Color, which defines the color to display in alternate rows of the group header and footer sections.

- The Caption Section Style box names the default style for the caption section.

- The Footer Section Style names the default footer section style.

In the Default Database/Project Properties group, you can select Use Default Page Folder and enter the folder to use as the default page folder. Select the second option, Use Default Connection File, to enter an ODC or Microsoft Data link to use as the default connection file.

Advanced Options

The Advanced tab (see Figure 16-11) contains five groups of options and a list of timing settings. Many of the settings in this tab relate to a multiple-user environment and interfacing with external applications.

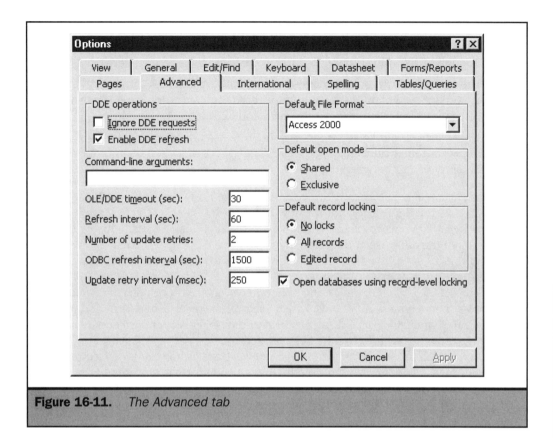

Figure 16-11. *The Advanced tab*

■ Use the *DDE operations* options to set the behavior of the database when dealing with other applications. *Ignore DDE requests* does just that—it ignores *Dynamic Data Exchange* (*DDE*) requests from external sources. *Enable DDE refresh* allows updating DDE links at an interval specified in the Refresh Interval setting. See Chapter 23 for more information about interacting with external applications.

■ Enter the name of the one or more values you want the Command function to return in the *Command-line arguments* text box.

The next group of selections in the Advanced tab deals with shared databases and interactions with external sources.

■ *OLE/DDE timeout (sec)* sets the period of time after which Access reattempts to perform an OLE or DDE operation that failed. Enter a number between 0 and 300 seconds.

■ The *Number of update retries* refers to the number of times Access tries to save a changed record locked by another user. Enter a number between 0 and 10.

■ Set the *ODBC refresh interval (sec)* to a number between 1 and 32,766 to specify the interval after which Access automatically refreshes records you are accessing through ODBC. This is only used if the database is shared on a network.

■ The *Refresh interval* option relates to the *Enable DDE refresh* option and specifies the time after which Access automatically updates records in a Datasheet or Form view. Enter a number between 1 and 32,766.

■ The *Update retry interval* option sets the time (in milliseconds) after which Access automatically tries to save a changed record locked by another user. Enter a number between 0 and 1000.

In the *Default File Format* option, you can choose between Access 2000 and Access 2002 as the default format for new databases.

In the *Default open mode* group, you have a choice between *Shared*, which allows others to open the database at the same time you have it open, and *Exclusive*, which gives you sole access to the database. See Chapter 28 for more information about running Access in a shared environment.

You can set the *Default record locking* option to *No locks*, which doesn't lock records while they're being edited; *All records*, which locks all the records in a form or datasheet (and the underlying tables) as long as the form or datasheet is open; or *Edited record*, which locks only the record currently being edited.

The last option in the Advanced tab is *Open databases using record-level locking*, which minimizes the page size required by the Unicode format representation. When you check this option, instead of locking an entire page that may include several records, only one row or record is locked at a time.

International Options

The International tab (see Figure 16-12) contains options that deal with the direction and alignment of text and the movement of the cursor through data. These have been added to accommodate the Middle Eastern language users.

The *Default Direction* group offers the choice between Left-to-right and Right-to-left.

■ The *Left-to-right* selection starts entering data in the left-most column and places the next data in the column to the right, and so on.

■ *Right-to-left* places the first field in the right-most column and places the next in the column to the left, and so on.

In the *General Alignment*, you have a choice between Interface mode and Text mode.

■ The *Interface mode* sets General alignment consistent with the user interface language. For example, if the direction is left-to-right, the text is aligned left.

■ The *Text mode* sets General alignment according to the direction of the first language-specific characters it encounters.

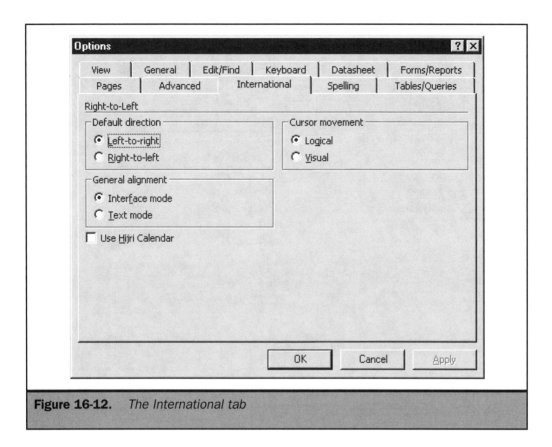

Figure 16-12.   *The International tab*

Check *Use Hijri Calendar* to change to the Middle Eastern calendar.
In the *Cursor Movement* group, you have a choice between Logical and Visual.

- If you choose *Logical*, the cursor moves within bidirectional text according to the direction of the language it's encountering. For example, if you have English and Arabic words in the same sentence, the insertion point moves left-to-right in the English text, and then starts at the rightmost character of the Arabic word and continues to move in a right-to-left direction.

- If you choose *Visual*, the cursor moves within bidirectional text by moving to the next adjacent character. For example, if you have English and Arabic text in the same sentence, the insertion point moves left-to-right through the English text and continues at the leftmost character of the Arabic word and continues in the left-to-right direction.

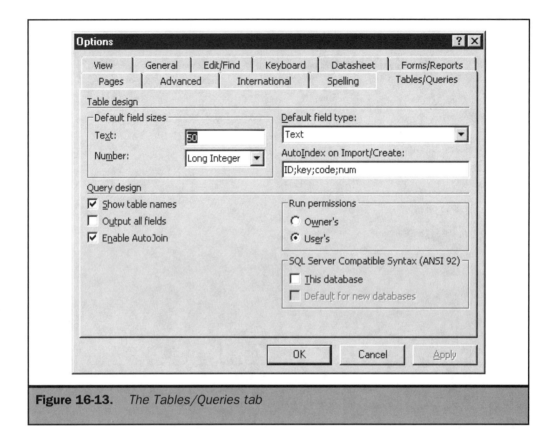

Figure 16-13. *The Tables/Queries tab*

Spelling Options

The Spelling options tab is the same as the Spelling dialog box described in Chapter 6.

Table and Query Options

The Tables/Queries tab of the Options dialog box is divided into two sections: one for table design and the other for query design (see Figure 16-13).

The Table Design group includes field size and type choices as well as specifying prefixes to use for automatically indexing fields. The Table design default settings include the following:

- The *Default field sizes* group includes the default size for text and number data type fields. You can enter any number in the Text box and choose from the drop-down list in the Number box. The number choices are Byte, Integer, Long Integer, Single, Double, and Replication ID.

- *Default field type* setting is usually Text, but you can select any of the nine field types as the default, including OLE Object, Hyperlink, or Memo.

- The *AutoIndex on Import/Create* setting is used when you import a table from an external source or create a new table in Design view. This setting tells Access to index on all fields automatically that begin or end with the characters you type in the box. Multiple entries are separated by semicolons. For example, the entries in the AutoIndex box instruct Access to create an index on all fields whose names begin or end with the characters ID, key, code, or num.

The Query Design default settings include the following:

- Checking *Show table names* displays the table names in the Table row of the query grid. This helps to keep track of the field source when multiple tables are used in a query.

- Checking *Output all fields* displays all the fields in a query's underlying tables and queries when you run the query. The fields aren't added to the query grid. When you select this option, only the new queries are affected.

- The *Enable AutoJoin* option automatically creates an inner join between two tables in the query grid. If you want to define the relationships yourself, clear the option. For two tables to be autojoined, they must have fields with the same name and of the same data type, and one of the fields must be the primary key field for that table.

- The *Run permissions* setting determines whether others are permitted to view data retrieved by queries or to run action queries. The User's setting applies the permissions defined for that classification of user. If you change it to Owner's, all users have the owner's permission to view or run the query, but only the owner can save changes to the query or change the ownership of the query. Changing the default setting affects only new queries.

- Choose the SQL Server Compatible Syntax (ANSI 92) option if you want Access to format queries for the current or all new databases exclusively in ANSI 92 standard syntax. This setting ensures SQL server compatibility.

IMPROVING THE
WORKPLACE

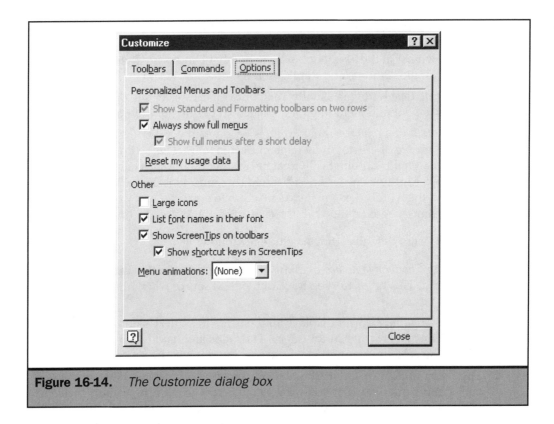

Figure 16-14. *The Customize dialog box*

Setting Some Command Bar Default Options

Access provides the opportunity to change some of the command bar default options, such as whether to show ScreenTips and, if you do, also to show the shortcut key combinations that accomplish the same thing. You can change the size of the buttons on the default toolbars and add animation to the menu bar as well.

To change default command bar settings, choose View | Toolbars | Customize or right-click anywhere in a toolbar or the menu bar and choose Customize from the shortcut menu. In the Customize dialog box, click the Options tab (see Figure 16-14).

In the Other group of options in the Options tab, check Large Icons to enlarge the toolbar buttons. To return the buttons to their original size, check the option again.

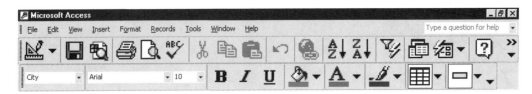

When you click the drop-down arrow next to Font in one of the Formatting toolbars, you see the names of the available fonts, each displayed in its respective font. If you want to view the font names in the default font (usually Arial), clear the List font names in their font option.

Although the ScreenTips that pop up when you rest the mouse pointer on a toolbar button can be helpful, you can suppress them by clearing the Show ScreenTips setting. To restore the ScreenTips, repeat the process and check the option. If you check Show ScreenTips, the Show shortcut keys in ScreenTips option becomes available, displaying the corresponding shortcut key combination—for example, Cut (CTRL-X).

  These settings affect all the Office programs, so make sure you want these settings in effect when you're working in Word or Excel.

Choose from the *Menu animations* drop-down list to change the way menus display when you choose a command. You have the choice of (None), Random, Unfold, and Slide.

See Chapter 20 for more information about customizing menus and toolbars, and how to make use of the other two tabs in the Customize dialog box.

Creating Custom Groups

If you want to begin grouping objects from your Access database in a group other than the default Favorites, you can create a new custom group. You can also add objects from other applications to the group. To create a new group, right-click one of the objects you want to add to the group and choose Add to Group | New Group from the shortcut menu. A New Group dialog box opens where you enter the name for the new group. Then click OK.

You can also create a new group without adding an object to it immediately by right-clicking an existing group button, such as Favorites, and choosing New Group from the shortcut menu. Then name the group and click OK.

The new group name is added to the Groups list in the left pane of the Database window.

To add another object to the group, right-click the object in the Database window, and then point to Add to Group in the shortcut menu and select the name of the group where you want to place the object.

You can also drag the object icon to the group name in the left pane of the Database window and drop it there.

The object always remains in its original location. Only a shortcut is added to the group.

To rename or delete a group, right-click the group button and choose Rename Group or Delete Group from the shortcut menu. If you choose to delete a group that contains shortcuts, Access warns you all the shortcuts will also be permanently deleted. The original object is unaffected by deleting the shortcut from the group.

If you choose to rename the group, a Rename Group dialog box opens where you can type a new name, and then click OK.

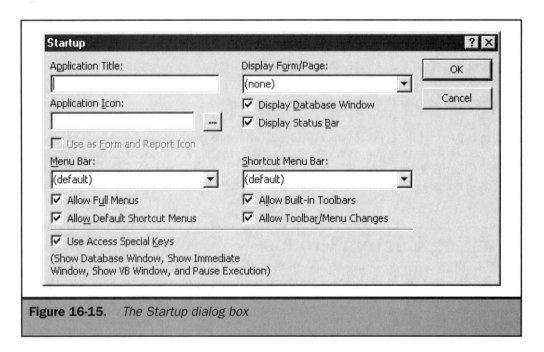

Figure 16-15.   *The Startup dialog box*

Changing the Way Access Starts

Access receives information from several sources that tell it how to start and what to show when it does start. Some startup settings affect only the current Access database, while others affect the way Access itself appears and behaves.

You have two major ways to control Access at startup: by setting options in the Startup dialog box and by opening Access with command-line options.

 You can also modify the database startup properties and options with Visual Basic. See Chapter 25 for information about writing Visual Basic procedures.

Setting Startup Options

The startup options you set in the Startup dialog box apply only to the current database, so you can choose different options for each of your databases or applications. When you set a startup option, such as a title bar with a custom name and icon, Access automatically sets the corresponding database property for you. To set startup options, choose Tools | Startup to open the Startup dialog box (see Figure 16-15).

Most of the changes in the startup options take effect the next time you open the database. Only the Application Title and Application Icon options take effect as soon as you close the dialog box.

 After you set startup options, you can bypass them by pressing SHIFT when you open the database.

- *Application Title*   To display a custom title in the Database window title bar, enter the text you want to display in the Application Title box.

- *Application Icon*   To add a custom icon to the title bar in place of the default Access icon in the Windows title bar, type the name of the bitmap (.bmp) or icon (.ico) file in the Application Icon box. If you don't know the name of the file you want to use, click the Build button next to the box and use the Icon Browser to locate the file.

 If you're creating an application to be distributed to multiple users, you should place the icon file in the same folder as the host application.

- *Menu Bar*   When you create your own custom global menu bar that offers limited commands, you can control what your users can do with the database. Use this option to replace the default menu bar with your custom menu bar by choosing the name of the menu from the drop-down list. This choice has no effect on the custom menu bars you created for a form or report. See Chapter 20 for information about creating custom startup menu bars.

Note   *The user may still be able to have access to the built-in global menu if the Allow Full Menus option is checked.*

- *Allow Full Menus*   When this option is checked, the user can have access to all the built-in menus. If you clear this option, Access hides certain menus, such as View and Insert, which give the user the power to open an object in Design view and make changes.

- *Allow Default Shortcut Menu*   Leave this option checked to allow access to the built-in shortcut menus that appear when right-clicking an object, a toolbar, or a menu bar. Clear the option to disable all shortcut menus. If you want the user to use the shortcut menus, but not to customize toolbars and menu bars, leave the option checked, but clear the Allow Toolbar/Menu Changes check box.

- *Display Form/Page*   Many applications display a special form or data access page when opening—either as a welcoming screen or as a switchboard with a list of choices of actions to take next, such as enter/edit data or preview a report. After you create the special form and save it in the current database, you can use it as the startup form. To choose a form for display at startup, click the drop-down arrow in the Display Form box and choose the form from the list of forms in the current database.

- *Display Database Window*   If you don't want the user to see the Database window behind the opening form, clear the Display Database Window check mark. The Database window may still be accessible by pressing F11. If you hide the Database window, the startup form must be a switchboard with navigation tools for using the database. See Chapter 21 for more information about creating and using switchboard forms.

- *Display Status Bar*   Clear this option to prevent displaying the status bar at the bottom of the window.

Tip   *This option applies only to the current database, but you can keep from displaying the status bar in all databases by clearing the Status Bar option in the View tab of the Options dialog box.*

- *Shortcut Menu Bar*   Select the name of a custom shortcut menu to replace the built-in shortcut menus for forms and reports in the current database. Choose Default to use the built-in shortcut menus.

- *Allow Built-in Toolbars*   Check this option to give the user access to all the built-in toolbars in the current database or to clear the option to prevent user access. If you want the user to use, but not to modify, the built-in toolbars, select this option and clear the Allow Toolbar/Menu Changes option. If you want the user to use and modify the toolbars, select both options.

- *Allow Toolbar/Menu Changes*   Check this option to permit the user to modify any of the built-in or custom toolbars and menu bars in the database. Clear the option to lock the toolbars, which disables the right mouse button click on a toolbar and the Tools | Customize command.

Tip   *If this option is cleared, the user can still move, size, and lock toolbars and menu bars, unless specifically denied in the Customize dialog box for the toolbar or menu bar.*

- *Use Access Special Keys*   When selected, you can use the special key combinations that display the database or debug window, menu bars, or modules in the Module window. If you cleared this option and specified a custom menu bar, the built-in menu bar isn't accessible. The special keys are

  - F11, which brings the Database window to the front

  - CTRL-G, which displays the Immediate window

  - CTRL-BREAK, which, in a project, stops retrieving records from the server

  - ALT-F11, which starts the Visual Basic Editor

Caution   *You can use the selections in the Startup dialog box instead of, or in conjunction with, the actions contained in the AutoExec macro. An* AutoExec macro *is a series of actions that take place when you open the database, but after the Startup options have taken effect. In view of the sequence of events, avoiding conflicts between the two is important. For example, the AutoExec macro could undo the options you set in the Startup dialog box. See Chapter 19 for more information about AutoExec macros and how they are used.*

Adding Startup Command-Line Options

All programs including Access are started by executing a command, such as msaccess.exe. You can add options to the command that starts Access to customize the way it starts, for example:

- Open a specific database automatically
- Run a macro
- Supply a user account name or password
- Open a database for exclusive access or as read-only

Access can be launched from two places: the Windows Start menu or a shortcut on the Windows desktop. You can add startup options to the command lines in either location.

Specifying command-line options with the Start menu applies those options when you open Access through the Start menu. Command-line options added to a shortcut apply the options when you launch Access by double-clicking the shortcut icon.

Adding to the Start Menu

To add options to the command line in the Start menu, do the following:

1. In the Windows desktop, click the Start button, point to Settings, and click Taskbar & Menu Programs.

2. Click the Start Menu Programs tab, and then click Add.

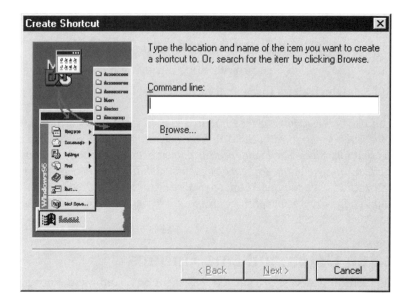

3. In the Create Shortcut dialog box, enter the path to Access or click Browse.

 By default, Access is installed in the C:\Program Files\Microsoft Office\Office folder. If you have installed it in another folder, enter that path.

4. If you click Browse, locate the Access program file and click Open.

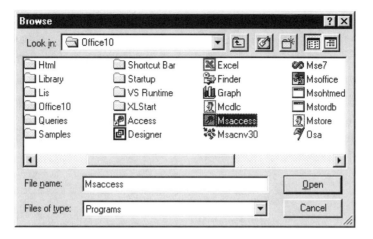

5. Place the insertion point at the right end of the Access startup command in the Command Line box and type the desired option. For example, enter **"C:\MY Documents\Osborne\Police.mdb"** to open the Police database when Access starts (see Figure 16-16). Be sure to enclose the path in quotation marks.

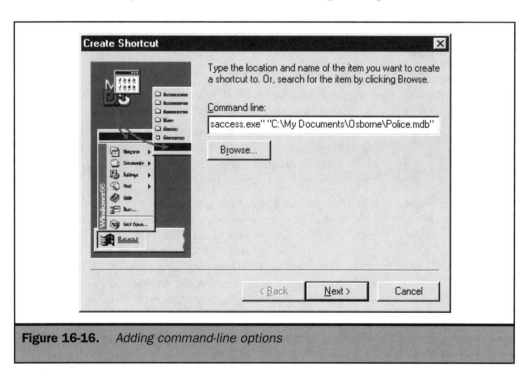

Figure 16-16. *Adding command-line options*

6. Click Next and select the folder where you want the new shortcut to appear in the Start Menu Programs list.

7. Click Next and enter a name for the new shortcut. For example, Police DB, then click Finish.

You can also add switches to the command line to customize the way the database opens. For example, the /ro switch tells Access to open the database for read-only. See Table 16-1 in the next section which describes the switches that are available for Access command-lines.

Option	Description
database or *project*	Opens the specified database or project. The default path is My Documents, but you can include the path with the database name.
/excl	Opens the database for exclusive access. Not available for projects.
/ro	Opens the database or project for read-only access.
/user *user name*	Starts Access with the specified user name. Not available for projects.
/pwd *password*	Starts Access with the specified password. Not available for projects.
/profile *user profile*	Starts Access with the options in the specified user profile instead of the standard Windows Registry settings created when Access was installed. Replaces /ini setting used in earlier versions.
/compact *target database* or *target project*	Compacts and repairs the database or project named before the /compact switch to the specified target database and closes Access. If no target is specified, the database or project is compacted to the original name and folder. If no path is included with the target database or project name, the compacted database or project is saved in the My Documents folder. Doesn't compact SQL Server databases.

Table 16-1. *Startup Command-Line Options*

Option	Description
/repair	Repairs the database named before the /repair switch and closes Access. In Access 2000 and later, compact and repair are combined in the /compact switch. /repair is retained for backward compatibility.
/convert *target database*	Converts the database named before the /convert switch from an earlier version of Access to an Access 2002 database, saves the new version with the specified name, and then closes Access. Not available for projects.
/x *macro*	Starts Access and runs the specified macro. This is an alternative to using an AutoExec macro when you open a database.
/cmd	Indicates what follows is the value to be returned by the Command function. This option must appear last in the command line. A semicolon (;) can be used as a substitute for /cmd.
/nostartup	Starts Access without displaying the Startup task pane in which you can choose an existing database or create a new one.
/wrkgrp *workgroup information file*	Starts Access using the specified workgroup information file. Not available for projects.

Table 16-1.   *Startup Command-Line Options* (continued)

Note   *Be sure to enclose the path and filename in quotation marks, but keep the switches outside.*

Adding to a Shortcut

You can also add different options to the shortcut command line to give you an alternative way to start Access. In fact, you can create multiple shortcuts, each offering a different set of command-line options—for example, opening a different database or supplying a different user account name.

In an earlier section in this chapter, you saw how to create a shortcut that launches Access and opens a database object in a specific database. You can accomplish the same thing by adding command-line startup options to a shortcut that launches Access with or without opening a database.

To create a shortcut that launches Access, do the following:

1. On the Windows desktop, double-click the My Computer icon and locate the folder where Access is installed. By default, it is installed in the C:\Progam Files\Microsoft Office\Office folder.

2. Right-click the Access icon and choose Create Shortcut in the shortcut menu.

3. Drag the new shortcut from the My Compter dialog box to the desktop.

4. Right-click the shortcut, choose Properties on the shortcut menu (see Figure 16-17).

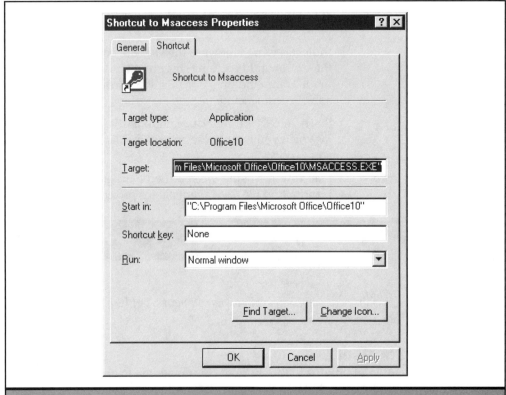

Figure 16-17. *The Shortcut tab of the Shortcut to Msaccess Properties*

5. Click at the right end of the Target box and add the command-line options to the path. Again enclose the path to the database in quotation marks but keep any switches out.

6. If you want to see a different picture on the new shortcut, click Change Icon (see Figure 16-18).

7. Select a new icon and click OK twice. The new shortcut appears on the desktop.

You can add the startup options and switches to either the Start menu command line or the shortcut icon command line.

Note   *Both the forward slash (/) and the semicolon (;) are special characters in command-line options. If you need to use one of them in the option—in a password, for example—type the character twice.*

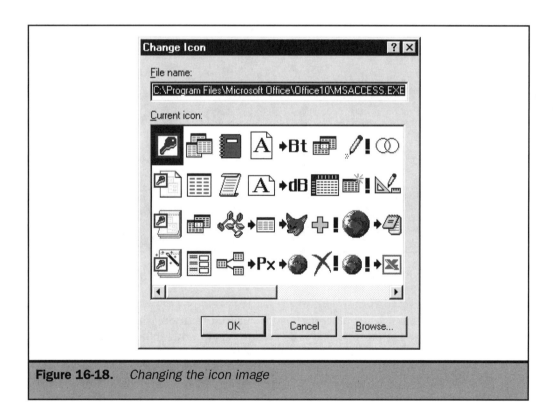

Figure 16-18.   *Changing the icon image*

Customizing with Windows 98 Control Panel

If you've worked with Windows 98 a lot, you know you can set many of the hardware and program options with the Control Panel. Access uses the settings you set in the Control Panel, many of which affect the appearance of the screen and the behavior of the mouse and the keyboard. To use the Windows 98 Control Panel, click the Start button, and then click Control Panel. The Control Panel window contains 24 icons relating to different categories of settings. The icons in your window may be different, depending on your system configuration.

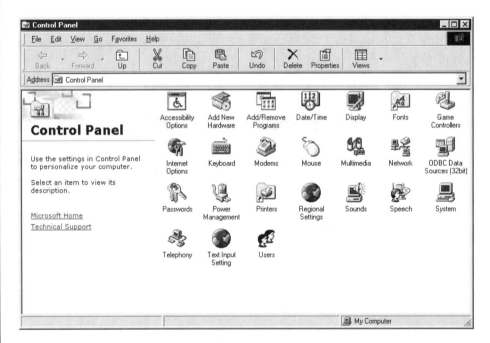

Look at some of the settings that can affect the way Access looks and works for you:

- The Accessibility group contains options for modifying the keyboard to slow down the multiple keypresses, such as ALT-TAB, to permit one-handed use. Tones can be added to alert the user of visual warnings, and captions can substitute for speech and sound messages. You can change a setting to control the mouse pointer with the number pad keys.

- The Display settings control the background pattern and wallpaper, the style of screensaver, the colors of all parts of the active and inactive windows, and adjust the resolution, font size, and color palette.

- The Keyboard settings control the character repeat and delay speeds, the cursor blink rate, and the language represented by the keyboard.

- The Mouse settings depend on the type of mouse you have, but may include the mouse pointer icons, the button click assignments, and the cursor speed and acceleration.

- ODBC Data Sources (32bit) lets you add, remove, or reconfigure the ODBC drivers on your system and shows you how to connect to data providers. *Open Database Connectivity (ODBC)* is a programmed interface that gives a program access to data in a database management system that uses the SQL language as a data access standard. The Regional Settings options let you specify the language to use and change how the number, currency, and time/date values are displayed.

- With the Sounds settings, you can change the system and program sounds. You can preview each one in the Sounds dialog box.

When you make changes in the workplace with the Control Panel, remember, most of the changes will affect all the Windows programs in the system. If you have other users on the same machine, you might want to consult them before making too many changes.

Modifying the Office Assistant

If you decide you want to use the *Office Assistant*, it can offer help and tips, as well as answer questions relating to the Office program you're currently using. Just like the list you see when you type a question in the question box, the Assistant can display the list, plus specific tips about using the features or keyboard shortcuts more effectively and a variety of messages.

The Assistant is an animated character with sound, which you can change to any one of the six characters that come with Office. You can drag the Assistant anywhere on the screen to be less obtrusive. You can also set many options to customize the Assistant to match your needs.

Showing, Hiding, and Resizing

To open the Office Assistant, choose Help | Show the Office Assistant. To show the Assistant after opening a Help topic, either close the Help topic or click anywhere in the Access window.

To hide the Assistant, right-click the character and choose Hide from the shortcut menu. You can also choose Help | Hide Office Assistant to close the assistant. To close the Office Assistant balloon, click the character.

Setting Office Assistant Options

To customize the help offered by the Assistant, you can change some of the options. If the Assistant balloon is visible, click Options to display the Options dialog box (see Figure 16-19). If the balloon isn't visible, right-click the character and choose Options from the shortcut menu.

To prevent the Office Assistant from appearing at all, clear the Use the Office Assistant option. The other options, except for the Reset my tips button, become unavailable.

The remaining options in the upper group specify the Assistant's behavior.

- When checked, the *Respond to F1 key* option displays the Assistant instead of the Help window when you press F1.

- *Help with wizards* makes the Assistant available to help when you're running an Access wizard. An option at the bottom of the final wizard dialog box offers this choice.

- *Display alerts* displays messages from Access in the Assistant window instead of a message box, if the Assistant is open.

- Select the *Search for both product and programming help when programming* option if you want both Access and programming help when generating VBA code.

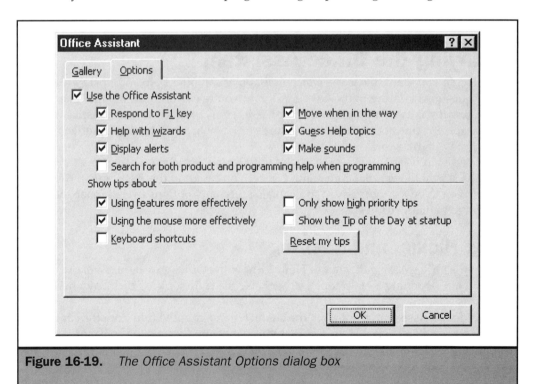

Figure 16-19. *The Office Assistant Options dialog box*

- *Move when in the way* moves the Assistant out of the way of other screen elements, such as dialog boxes. This option also shrinks the Assistant to the smaller size, if it isn't accessed for five minutes.

- *Guess Help topics* displays a list of Help topics related to the actions you've been performing in Access before asking for help.

- If you have a sound card and speakers installed, *Make sounds* turns on the sound effects for the Assistant. The sounds vary with the character.

The selections in the *Show tips about* group tells the Assistant what types of tips to display.

- *Using features more effectively* displays tips about getting the most from Access features.

- *Using the mouse more effectively* displays tips about speeding up your work with the mouse.

- *Keyboard shortcuts* shows you shortcut keys that can also speed up your work.

- Selecting *Only show high priority tips* displays only important tips, such as those that save time.

- *Show the Tip of the Day at startup* displays a randomly selected tip each time you start an Office program.

- Click the *Reset my tips* button to allow the Assistant to repeat tips already shown.

Choosing a Different Assistant

To change the character used by the Office Assistant, click Options in the Assistant balloon, and then click the Gallery tab (see Figure 16-20). Use the Next and Back buttons to preview each of the alternative characters, watch their actions, and hear the accompanying sounds.

When you find the one you want, click OK. You're prompted to insert the Office CD to install the new Assistant.

After the change of character, the Office Assistant dialog box closes.

If you have access to the Internet, you can download other Assistants from the Microsoft Office Web site. To reach the Web site, choose Help | Microsoft On The Web and click Microsoft Home Page.

Summary

This chapter has given you an overall view of the changes you can make to your Access environment using several different tools. Most of the customization deals with the appearance and behavior of Access and its objects, such as rearranging the desktop and creating shortcuts to commonly used objects.

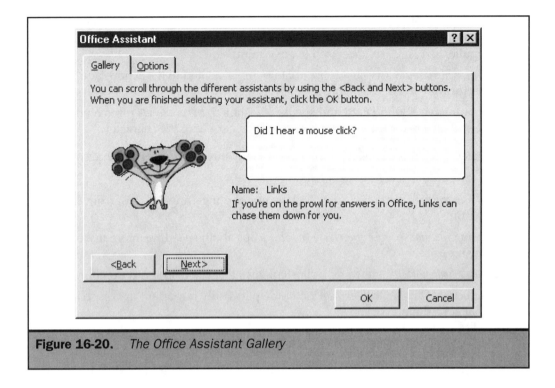

Figure 16-20. *The Office Assistant Gallery*

The many options available in the Options dialog box are discussed and the valid settings are listed. You can also change the way Access starts by specifying a startup form and a custom title bar and icon. Adding options to the command line that launches Access can alter the way it starts, as well.

The Office Assistant is a helpful tool when first learning how to use Access. You can even customize the Assistant by changing the options or installing a new animated character. Once you become familiar with the basics, you can eliminate the busy Office Assistant.

The next chapter concentrates on improving Access performance, especially with large databases. It discusses using the Access Analyzer Wizards and the Database Utilities to streamline your database and ensure reliability.

MOUS Exam Activities Explored in This Chapter

Level	Activity	Section Title
Expert	Create a switchboard and set startup options	Setting Startup Options Adding Startup Command-Line Options

The
Complete
Reference

Chapter 17

Improving Database Performance

n this hectic information age, we're always looking for ways to speed operations and improve the accuracy and consistency of the results. Optimization is the ultimate goal and stacking up performance improvements is a way to get close. Access includes many ways you can help yourself create an efficient database, including the Analyzer tools, which can examine the organization of your database and suggest ways you can improve the distribution of information among the tables and speed overall database performance.

For the purpose of security and reliability, you also have tools to back up and restore databases in case of emergency. Other tools compact the database to take less disk space and repair damaged databases.

When you want to optimize your database performance, look at not only the database, but also the conditions under which it operates. You can take a top-down approach and start with the Windows settings, and then work down through the Access program settings to the database and each of its elements. This chapter steps you through such a process.

Improving System Performance

Overloaded memory and crowded hard disks can slow performance to unacceptable levels. Although Windows 98 tries to optimize the system as much as possible, you can still watch for and correct some things.

Optimizing Memory Use

Access 2002 requires a minimum of 32MB of memory to run in Windows 98 or later and 64MB if you're using Windows NT. Increasing your memory beyond the minimum requirement significantly speeds processing. Another way to speed processing is to release unnecessarily occupied memory by closing all the programs you aren't currently using.

Other general memory conservation tips are

- If you're using a fancy wallpaper full-screen background in Windows, you're using more memory than you must. Delete the wallpaper or change to a solid color background or a pattern bitmap.

- Screensavers can also occupy valuable memory. If you need to have a screensaver, use a blank one.

Optimizing in Windows

Windows is the operating system that connects you and your application programs with the computer. You have some control over how Windows handles the system and the software in it. Although the operating system attempts to create the most efficient environment, you might be able to improve on the default settings.

One of the aspects of optimization that's entirely up to you is the allocation of space on the hard disk. As you save more and more files to the hard disk, it becomes overloaded and can noticeably slow processing. When this becomes a problem, you must take measures to clean out unneeded files from the disk.

Setting System Performance Properties

Through the Windows 98 Control Panel, you can discover any system performance problems and set the performance properties to suit your requirements. To reach the System Properties dialog box, do the following:

1. Click Start, point to Settings, and then click Control Panel on the submenu.

2. Double-click the System icon to open the System Properties dialog box, and then click the Performance tab (see Figure 17-1). If Windows hasn't detected any difficulties, the message "Your system is configured for optimal performance" is displayed. If any system optimization problems exist, such as too many programs open at once, Windows displays a comment documenting the problem in the lower pane. Select the comment and click Details to see an explanation and recommendations for correcting the problem.

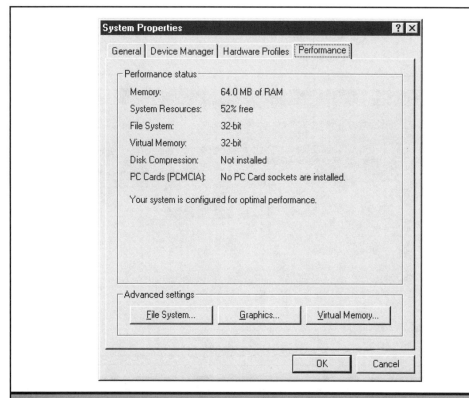

Figure 17-1.   *The Performance tab of the Systems Properties dialog box*

3. Click File System to open the File System Properties dialog box (see Figure 17-2) where you can use the Hard Disk tab to choose the principal use for your system: Desktop computer, Mobile or docking system, or Network server.

4. Drag the Read-ahead optimization slider button to the Full setting to maximize the size of the increment reads to 64K. Click OK.

5. Click Virtual Memory in the System Properties dialog box to change the virtual memory settings, which determine how much of your hard disk space is to be used as additional memory (see Figure 17-3). Windows 98 recommends you let Virtual Memory take care of the allocation, unless you really know what you're doing. Click the first option, and then click OK to return to the Performance tab of the System Properties dialog box.

6. Click Close. If you made any changes, you must restart your computer before the changes take effect.

Cleaning Up the Hard Disk

While you're working with applications in the Window environment, a lot of unnecessary files build up on your hard disk, which can slow processing. When Access needs to place bits and pieces of a database in various places on the disk—because no large contiguous storage is available—storing and retrieving the data takes time. If you periodically clean up the hard disk and empty the Recycle Bin, your database will run much faster.

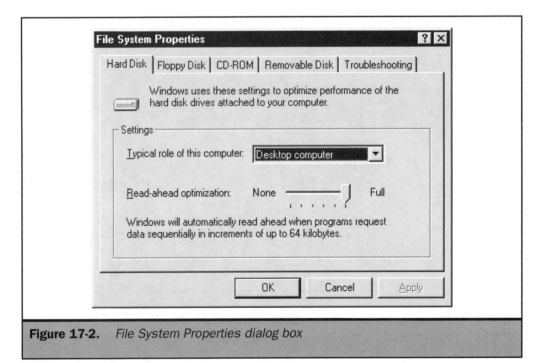

Figure 17-2. *File System Properties dialog box*

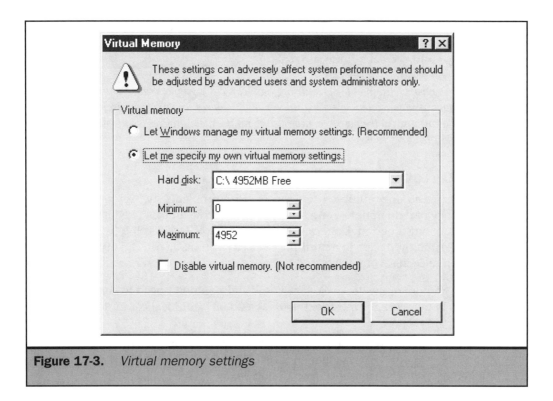

Figure 17-3.   *Virtual memory settings*

Note   *As a disk begins to fill, files are broken into segments and stored in scattered areas on the disk. This is called* fragmenting. *The process of defragmentation reorganizes the files on the disk, so the segments are reunited and the whole file is placed in a larger, contiguous area on the disk.*

The disk clean-up process has four steps:

1. Delete all the files you no longer need. Look in other programs, in addition to Access.

2. Right-click the Recycle Bin shortcut, choose Empty Recycle Bin, and respond Yes when asked to confirm the deletion. If you aren't sure what's in the Recycle Bin, choose Open first and look over the list. You can delete the items one at a time by right-clicking the item and choosing Delete from the shortcut menu.

3. Compact the Access databases. A later section in this chapter discusses the Compact and other Access database utilities.

4. Run the Disk Defragmenter. The Disk Defragmenter is one of the system tools found in the Accessories menu. Click Start, point to Programs | Accessories |

IMPROVING THE
WORKPLACE

System Tools, and then click Disk Defragmenter. Select the drive from the list in the Select Drive dialog box and click OK. The process may take a while, but you are kept informed about the progress.

While the Disk Defragmenter is running, you can click Stop or Pause anytime. If you click Show Details, you see a screen full of small squares in a grid representing the disk storage locations. As the defragmenter cleans up the disk, progress is displayed by color changes in the grid cells.

Speeding Up Access 2002

Sharing databases among multiple users causes extra problems such as availability of data, consistency of data updates, and security. Productive time can be lost if the data is locked for too long a period. Data can become corrupt if access is too freely offered. When you are running Access in a multiple-user environment, you can optimize Access performance in several ways.

- If one or more of the databases are yours and you don't need to share with others in the workgroup, store the databases on your local computer, rather than on the server.

- If you're the only one who uses a database, open it in exclusive mode, so no one can lock you out. When you open the database, choose Open Exclusive from the Open drop-down list in the Open dialog box.

- Store the tables from a database shared by the workgroup on the server, but store all the other objects on the local computers.

See Chapter 26 for more information about using and optimizing Access in a multiple-user environment.

Optimizing a Database

Access provides two analytical tools that can save you a lot of time and help you optimize a new database. You can also help to optimize the performance of a database without using the Analyzers by focusing on each of the elements that comprise the database—for example, the user's access to the database, the features of the database, including the filters and indexes, as well as the objects themselves.

Using the Analyzer Wizards

The Table Analyzer examines the distribution of data among the tables and presents suggestions and ideas for further improvements. Another tool, the Performance Analyzer, looks at any or all of the objects in the database and also makes suggestions for improving their performance. The Performance Analyzer can also examine the relationships you've established in the database and the set of all Visual Basic code modules in the database, including class and standard modules.

Both of these tools are available by choosing Tools | Analyze and selecting from the submenu.

Table Analyzer

When you design a new database, you do the best you can to reduce the redundancy of data by creating a set of related tables. The Access Table Analyzer can look at the data distribution and, perhaps, make suggestions for additional optimization, including adding more indexes and further normalization.

To start the Table Analyzer, choose Tools | Analyze | Table. The first two dialog boxes give you a good description of the process of table optimization by first describing the problem, and then showing possible solutions to the problem. Each dialog box also offers a look at examples of the problems and the solutions. Figure 17-4 shows the first of the two introductory dialog boxes.

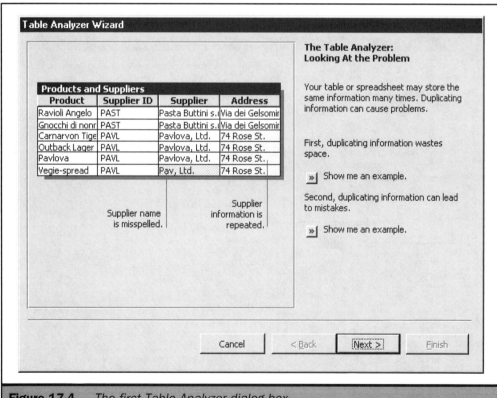

Figure 17-4. *The first Table Analyzer dialog box*

The second Table Analyzer dialog box shows how it plans to solve the problem by splitting tables so that each piece of data is stored only once.

The third Table Analyzer dialog box shows a list of tables in the current database (see Figure 17-5). Select the table that contains repeated data and click Next. In the next dialog box, you can choose to let the wizard decide how to split up the data or do it yourself. If you let the wizard decide, the next dialog box presents a diagram of the suggested redistribution of information.

If you expect to use the Table Analyzer often and don't want to see the two introductory dialog boxes each time, clear the check mark next to Show introductory pages? in the dialog box showing the list of tables.

In Figure 17-6, the Table Analyzer found that the values in the ZIP code and City fields are repeated many times in the Police Name List table. It suggests you create a lookup table for each field with a link from the new Table2 to the original Name List table and an additional link from the new Table3 back to Table2. Notice the wizard hasn't changed any table names; this is only a suggestion that you change the table names.

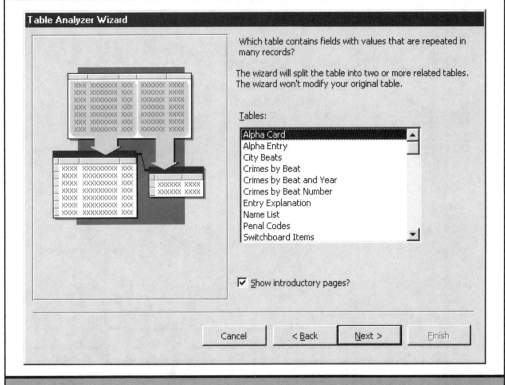

Figure 17-5.   *Select a table to analyze*

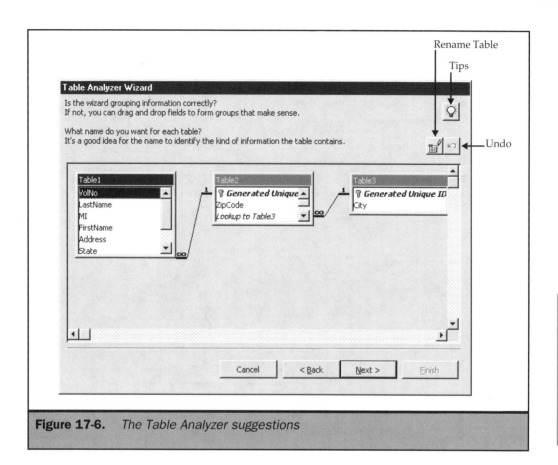

Figure 17-6. *The Table Analyzer suggestions*

Tip *Click the Tips button (the light bulb icon) to get instructions about how to handle the wizard's suggestions.*

To change a table name, select the table, click the Rename Table button in the upper-right corner of the dialog box, and enter a new name. When you change the name of the related table, the wizard changes the table name in the linked field in the primary table to match. If you change your mind about the new name you entered for a table, click the Undo button next to the Rename Table button.

If the way the fields are grouped doesn't make sense to you, drag the field names from one table to the other to change them. Click Next to move to the dialog box in which you verify the primary key fields are correct (see Figure 17-7). The wizard has, by default, added a unique field to each new table and corresponding linking fields.

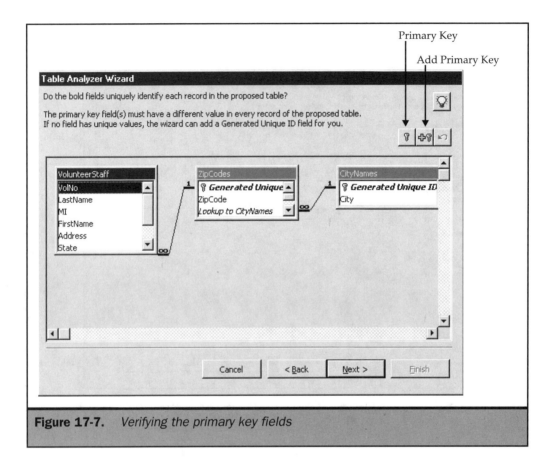

Figure 17-7.   *Verifying the primary key fields*

Each of the new tables has a designated primary key field, but Table1 (VolunteerStaff) has no primary key field. You can specify a primary key for Table1 in two ways:

■ Select an existing field that you know has unique values and click the Primary Key button. The key symbol appears next to the field name.

■ Select the table and click the Add Primary Key button. A new Generated Unique ID field is added to Table1.

After adding key fields click Next. In the final dialog box (see Figure 17-8), the wizard offers to create a query for you that uses the same name as the original table and looks like the original table. Allowing the wizard to do this lets you work with the data all in one place and guarantees all the forms and reports you created using the original table as a basis will continue to work properly. You can also choose to create this query yourself, if you prefer.

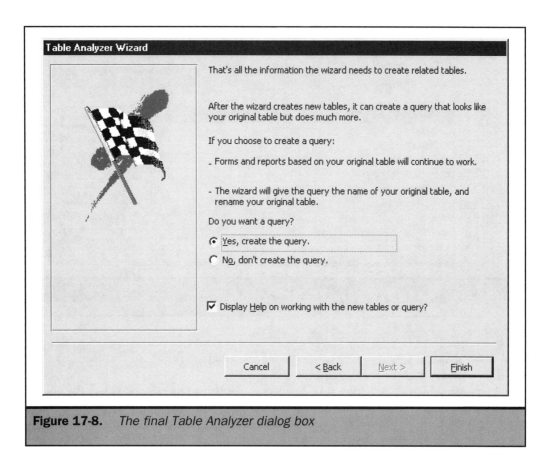

Figure 17-8. *The final Table Analyzer dialog box*

If you chose to decide which fields to place in which tables, the next dialog box shows only the original table without the new Table2. You can create the new table by dragging a field name from the list in Table1. You can also rename the tables and define the primary key field for the new table using buttons in the dialog box. After you click Next, the wizard offers to create a query for you as before.

Performance Analyzer

The *Performance Analyzer* looks at any or all of the objects in the database and suggests ways you can improve the application's performance. When you finish with the Performance Analyzer, many of the suggestions can be implemented automatically. To start the Performance Analyzer, choose Tools | Analyze | Performance. The first dialog box (see Figure 17-9) includes a tab for each type of database object. Each tab contains the names of all those objects in the current database. The Current Database tab contains the Relationships and VBA Project options. The All Object Types tab contains all the names in one place.

IMPROVING THE WORKPLACE

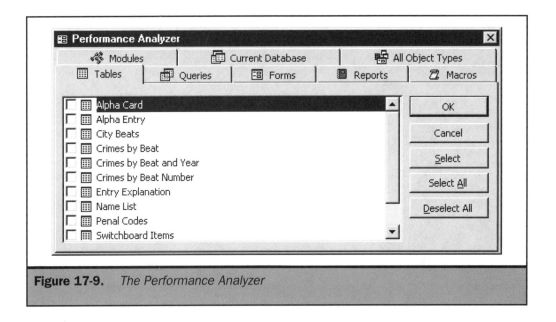

Figure 17-9. *The Performance Analyzer*

Tip *The accompanying object icons identify the object type.*

To choose which objects to examine, select the appropriate tab and select the object names. Click Select All on a tab to choose all the objects. To analyze the entire database, click the All Object Types tab, choose Select All, and then click OK. A message box keeps you informed about the progress of the analysis and, when all the objects have been inspected, the wizard displays a dialog box with a list of recommendations, suggestions, and ideas (see Figure 17-10). Any problems that have been fixed are also denoted. The Analysis Notes pane describes the general overall findings. When you select one of the items in the list, additional explanations are displayed in the Analysis Notes pane.

Tip *If you include queries in the objects to analyze, be sure to have enough data in the tables to give the query a good workout.*

The Analyzer has recommended you add an index to the DR and the Date fields of the Alpha Entry table. When you select one of these recommendations, the Analysis Notes shows that, if you index on this field, it benefits the Alpha Entry table and your queries run faster. To implement a recommendation, select it and click Optimize. After considering all the items in the list, click Close to close the Performance Analyzer.

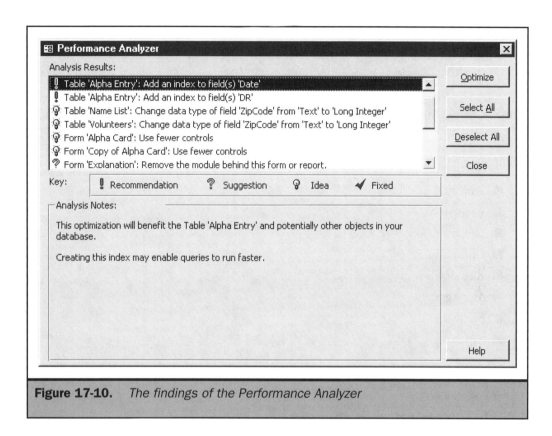

Figure 17-10. *The findings of the Performance Analyzer*

Caution *The Performance Analyzer doesn't always have the whole picture. Accept its recommendations and suggestions carefully. For example, adding indexes may improve query performance, but they also increase the disk space needed for the database and may slow entering and editing data.*

Using Database Properties

In a single-user environment, locating a particular database may be no problem, but when multiple users are accessing multiple databases, locating the database you want to work with may be more difficult. Adding custom database properties can be to your advantage when you're looking for the database. Some of the database properties are automatically set by Access and aren't available to you, but other properties can be set so they assist in locating the file when you use the Advanced Search feature.

Databases have three types of properties:

- *Built-in summary properties,* such as author, title, and subject in which you can enter values.

- *Custom file properties* to which you can assign any value you want.

- *Automatically updated properties,* such as file size, and the dates of creation and modification, over which you have no control.

You can always search for a file based on the date it was last modified or by the author's name, but what if you want to find the database containing information about cat pedigrees or the latest tastes in taco mixes? Of the over 30 properties listed in the Advanced Search dialog box, you can specify values for eight of them in the Summary tab of the database Properties dialog box:

- Author
- Category
- Comments
- Company
- Keywords
- Manager
- Subject
- Title

Values you specify for these properties can be combined with other search criteria to locate the file you need.

Optimizing Tables and Queries

After you've done all you can to normalize the database and distribute data efficiently among the tables, you can do a few other things to speed data processing. Some examples are

- Choose the appropriate data type for each field to save space and improve join operations. In addition, if you know the range of values to be stored in the field, choose the smallest field size the data type will accept. You have no choice with Date/Time fields, but you can reduce the default 50-character field size for Text fields if the data is, for example, a ZIP code.

- Make sure the fields on either side of a relationship are of the same or a compatible data type.

Optimizing with Indexes

In addition to the primary key, which is automatically indexed, you can create indexes on one or more fields to find and sort records faster. Indexes can speed queries if the fields on both sides of the join are indexed. In a one-to-many relationship, the primary table is already indexed on the primary key field, but creating an index for the field in the related table helps when the query is run. In addition, indexing any field used in a criteria rule in the query reduces processing time for the query.

Multiple-field indexes help distinguish between records that may have more than one record with the same value in the first field. If you're creating a multiple-field index, use only as many fields as necessary.

Note	*While indexes can speed searches, sorts, and queries of related tables, they can also add to the database size. Each index represents a condensed lookup table. Additional problems can occur in a multiple-user environment because indexes can reduce the concurrency of the database, thereby limiting the ability of more than one user to modify data at the same time.*

Optimizing Queries

Among the guidelines for optimizing queries are the following:

- Include only the fields you need in the query. If a field isn't needed in the result set, but you're using it as a criteria, clear the Show check box in the query grid.

- Avoid calculated fields in a query as much as possible. If you nest the query in another query as a subquery, you slow the operation considerably. If you need an expression in the result of the query, instead, add a control to the form or report and use the expression as the control source. If necessary, prompt the user to enter a value required by the expression in a parameter query.

- Use Between…And… in a criteria expression rather than the > and < operators.

- If you want to count all the records in the recordset, use Count(*) instead of Count([*fieldname*]).

- Don't use domain aggregate functions, such as DSum, in a query. Access must retrieve all the data in the linked table before running the query, even if the data isn't included in the query.

- When grouping records by values in one of the joined fields, be sure to place the Group By aggregate function in the field that's on the side of the join that contains the values you want to summarize. If you place Group By in the joined field, Access must join all the records, and then calculate the aggregate using only the necessary fields.

- Use as few Group By aggregates as possible. You may, instead, be able to use the First function in some cases.

- Try not to use restrictive criteria on nonindexed or calculated fields.

- If you need to place criteria on one of the fields used to join two tables in a one-to-many relationship, you can place it on either field in the grid. Run some tests to see which placement results in a faster query.

IMPROVING THE
WORKPLACE

■ If you're working with fairly static data, consider running a make-table query and using the resulting table instead of the query as the basis for forms and reports. You can always run the make-table query again if the data changes. Be sure to add indexes to the resulting table.

■ When you create a Crosstab query, try to use fixed column headings to avoid the time it takes to update them.

To save even more time running queries, always save the query in a compiled state. When you simply save the query after making modifications in Design view, you are saving the query file. A query isn't compiled until it is run. To save the compiled query, run it by opening it in Datasheet view, and then save it. The query is optimized if it's compiled with the same amount of data as your application will have.

Working with Linked Tables

Although linked tables look just like your own tables when you use them in forms and reports, they're actually stored in another database file. Every time you access the linked table, Access must retrieve the records from that file, which takes time. If the linked table is on a network or in a SQL database, this may take even more time because of the network traffic.

You can reduce the time it takes to retrieve the records from a network or a SQL database in these ways:

■ If you don't need to see all the records from the linked table, use filters or queries to limit the number of records and reduce transfer time.

■ Paging up and down among records causes Access to load the records into memory, which takes time. If you want to add new records to the linked table, choose Records | Data Entry. This avoids loading all the records into memory, and then having to page through them to the end of the recordset to add new records when the table first opens in Datasheet or Form view.

■ If you usually add new records to the linked table, create a data entry form and set the form's Data Entry property to Yes. This also avoids loading and displaying all the records from the linked table.

■ When you need to query a linked table, don't use functions in the criteria. And, especially, don't use domain functions, which require Access to load all the data in the linked table before executing the query.

■ You can also create problems for the other users on the network who want to use the same data. Lock the records no longer than necessary.

You can improve performance with linked tables using Visual Basic code in other ways. See Chapter 25 for examples.

Optimizing Filter By Form

The Filter By Form defaults for database name settings in the Edit/Find tab of the Options dialog box can improve the performance of all tables and queries, as well as all text box controls that use the Database Default setting in the Filter Lookup property. As discussed in Chapter 16, the Filter By Form Defaults group of options can limit the displayed list of values to indexed fields only or include local indexed and nonindexed fields. You can also set a limit on the number of values to display in the list in the displayed filter form.

If the list of field values takes too long to display, you can optimize the Filter By Form for a single text box control on a form by setting the control's Filter Lookup property (on the Data tab) to Never. This suppresses displaying the field values on the drop-down list in the Filter By Form window.

Optimizing Forms and Reports

Most of the optimization strategies can be used on both forms and reports as well as subforms and subreports. You can also apply techniques to individual text box and combo box controls to improve their performance in forms and reports.

The following tips apply to both forms and reports:

- Base the subform or subreport on a saved query that includes only the required fields and with a filter that results in only the required set of records.

- If the record order isn't important, you can save time by not sorting records in an underlying query, especially if the query uses fields from multiple tables.

- Try not to sort or group on expressions.

- Make sure the underlying query is itself optimized before loading the form or report.

- Index on the fields you use for sorting or grouping.

- Don't overdo the design with bitmaps and graphic objects. But, when you need to add graphics, convert the unbound object frame controls to image controls, which take less time to load.

- You can save a lot of disk space by using black and white bitmaps rather than color.

- Don't overlap controls unless absolutely necessary. Access must go over the screen twice to place overlapping controls.

- Use subforms and subreports sparingly; they occupy as much space as the main form or report. Base all subforms and subreports on queries instead of tables. Include only the necessary fields because more fields decrease performance.

- Index all fields in a subform or subreport linked to the main form or report. In addition, index all fields used in criteria.

■ When you need to include data from an external table, you can save time by importing the table, rather than linking. This does take more space, however.

■ If the form or report has no event procedures associated with it, make sure the form or report Has Module property is set to No. The form or report can load faster and take less disk space without the reserved class module space.

Specially for Reports

When you're opening a report from a procedure, you can test the Has Data property to see if the underlying recordset is empty. If it has no records, you save time by branching to the next operation and avoiding opening the useless report.

Before printing a report, set the Fast Laser Printing property (on the Other tab) to Yes if you're using a laser printer. If you're using a nonlaser printer, printing in landscape orientation can take more time because of the mechanical motion across the page.

Specially for Forms

A few more strategies apply only to forms:

■ Don't leave a form open if you aren't using it. Access still must refresh the window whether or not you're working in it.

■ Design a form with as few controls as possible. More controls reduce the efficiency of the form. If you need a lot of controls, consider adding a tab control to create a multiple-page form with controls grouped logically on the pages.

■ If the underlying record source contains a lot of records and you're planning to use the form primarily for data entry, change the form's Data Entry property to Yes. When the form opens, it automatically moves to the end of the recordset and displays a blank record in the form. If you open the form with records showing, Access must read every record before it can display a blank new record.

■ If you don't expect to edit the records in a subform, you can save time by setting the subform's Allow Edits, Allow Additions, and Allow Deletions properties all to No. An alternative is to set the Recordset Type to Snapshot, instead of the default Dynaset.

■ Use a hyperlink instead of a command button to open a form. Command buttons added with the help of the Command Button Wizard result in an event procedure written in VB code. Without VB code, you can eliminate the class module and save space and time.

Optimizing Data Access Pages

When data access pages take too long to load, you can do some things to speed it up in Page view or Internet Explorer. Some of the same recommendations for forms and reports apply to pages: avoid overlapping controls, use bitmaps sparingly, and stick to black-and-white, index on fields used for sorting, grouping, or filtering, and, if the page is to be used for data entry, set the DataEntry property to True.

Other strategies apply only to data access pages, for example:

- Set the ExpandedByDefault property in the Group Level property sheet to False for the highest group level. Using the same setting for lower group levels also speeds interactions once the page is opened.

- Set the DataPageSize property in the Group Level property sheet to a lower number, so fewer records are displayed on a page. Displaying many records on a single page takes longer.

- With grouped pages, if they contain records with a one-to-many relationship, group the records by table, rather than by a field or expression. Also bind each section to a table rather than a query. If you bind the section to a query, all the records are retrieved before displaying any records, which takes longer. Use a query only to limit the records to display on a page.

- If the data on the page isn't updatable, use bound span controls instead of text boxes. Also use bound span controls on grouped pages.

- Save time by closing all database objects that aren't being used when you view a page in Access. If you are viewing the page in Internet Explorer, close all windows you don't need.

Optimizing Controls

List box, combo box, and drop-down list box controls all show field values from which you can choose. They are bound to a field in the underlying record source. When you use a wizard to create the list box or combo box control, it automatically constructs a SQL statement and assigns it to the control's Record Source property. You can save time by basing the control on a saved query instead of the SQL statement, which must be evaluated each time you activate the control.

To convert the wizard's SQL statement to a saved query, do the following:

1. Open the control's property sheet and click the Build button next to the Row Source property. The SQL statement appears in the Query Builder window.

2. Choose File | Save and enter a name for the query.

3. When you close the Query Builder window, Access asks if you want to save the query with that name and update the property with the query name. Respond Yes.

Base the drop-down list box—the data access page version of a combo box—on a saved query, instead of a table. The Wizard that creates the drop-down list automatically uses the table name as the List Row Source. Change this property to the query name instead.

You can optimize the behavior of these controls in several more ways:

- Include only the necessary fields in the query that you specify as the Row Source or List Row Source property for the control. Adding extra fields slows the display of the list.

- If they are different fields, be sure to index on both the first field displayed in the combo box, the list box, or the drop-down list box, as well as in the bound field in the underlying table.

- Set the AutoExpand property of the combo box control to No if you don't require the fill-in-as-you-type feature.

- If you do use the fill-in-as-you-type feature by setting the AutoExpand property to Yes, be sure the first field in the displayed list is a Text data type, rather than a Number data type. Access converts the numeric value to text to find a match for completing the entry. Using text in the first field eliminates the need for this conversion.

- You usually include the bound field in a lookup combo box list but, if you don't, don't use expressions for the bound field or the displayed field. Also, use single-table (or query) row sources and don't add restrictions to the row source.

- If you don't expect the data to change, base the control on imported, rather than linked, data.

- Use the default format and property settings for the controls. Access saves only the exceptions to the default settings with the form. If you find you are changing the same property frequently, you can change the default setting for the control.

Backing Up and Restoring a Database

To reduce the risk of losing data, a good idea is to have a backup copy of your database. The database must be closed before you can back it up. If you're working in a multiple-user environment, make sure all the users have closed the database before you start the backup process. You can make a backup copy in several ways:

- Drag the file name in the Windows Explorer list from the hard disk to another disk drive.

- Double-click the My Computer shortcut and open successive folders until you locate the folder that contains your database. Right-click the database shortcut and point to Send To in the shortcut menu, and then click the drive to which you want to copy.

- Use Microsoft Windows 2000 Backup and Recovery Tools, the MS-DOS Copy command, or other third-party backup software. Some programs also offer the options of compressing the files.

If your database file is too large to copy to one floppy disk, you can't use Windows Explorer or My Computer to back up the file. Microsoft Backup and other backup software enable you to copy the file over more than one disk.

If you're working in a multiple-user environment, also be sure to make a backup copy of the workgroup information file. You won't be able to start Access if the file is damaged or missing. See Chapter 26 for more information about workgroups and shared databases.

You can also back up individual objects of your database without copying the entire file. To do this, create a new, blank database and import the objects into it from the original database.

To restore the database from a copy, use the recover feature of the same method you used to make the backup copy. If you used Windows Explorer, drag the file name from the floppy disk list to the database folder on the hard drive.

Caution *If the backup copy and the existing database in the database folder have the same name, you can replace the existing database when you restore the backup copy. If you want to save the original database, rename it before restoring from the backup copy.*

Compacting and Repairing a Database

Access provides some useful tools for managing databases. One of these tools converts databases to or from previous versions of Access. Another creates an MDE file from the current database. An MDE file contains compiled versions of all the code in the database with none of the source code. MDE databases run faster, but the user cannot access the source code for viewing or editing.

 See Chapter 29 for information about converting databases to and from Access 2002.

Another utility repairs and compacts a database to use disk space more efficiently. As you delete tables and queries, your database can become scattered about on the disk with useless small blocks of space between. Compacting the database makes a copy of the database and rearranges the file to make better use of the disk space.

If a database becomes damaged in some way, Access usually detects this when you try to open the database or if you try to compact, encrypt, or decrypt it. When damage is found, Access offers the option to repair the database at once. If, however, your database begins to act strangely, but Access hasn't noticed any damage, you can use the Compact and Repair Database utility manually.

IMPROVING THE WORKPLACE

You can compact an open database in place by choosing Tools | Database Utilities | Compact and Repair Database. Access takes only a few moments to compact the database, showing progress in the status bar.

If the database isn't open, you can compact it to the same file name or to a different name, drive, or folder. To compact and repair a closed database, do the following:

1. Close all databases and, from the empty Access window, choose Tools | Database Utilities | Compact and Repair Database.

2. In the Database to Compact From dialog box (see Figure 17-11), select the name of the database you want to compact and click Compact.

3. In the Compact Database Into dialog box, specify the drive and folder for the compacted database and enter a name for the copy or choose a name from the list.

4. Click Save. If you choose the same name as the original database, Access asks for confirmation before replacing the file.

Tip   *You can stop the process at any time by pressing* ESC *or* CTRL-BREAK.

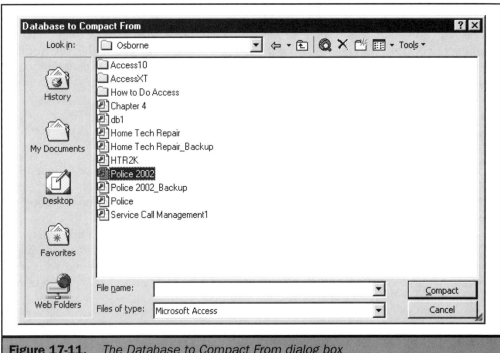

Figure 17-11.   *The Database to Compact From dialog box*

If the compaction has been successful, and you've chosen to use the same name and path for the compacted file, Access replaces the original database file with the compacted version. If Access isn't successful with compacting a database, one of the following reasons may be to blame:

- Another user may have the database open.

- Your disk didn't have enough free space for both the original copy and the compacted copy of the database. To remedy this, delete as many unnecessary files and try compacting the database again.

- You might not have permission to copy all the tables in the database. You need both Open/Run and Open Exclusive permissions to make copies of the data. If you aren't the owner of this database, find the owner and try to obtain permission. If you are the owner, update the permissions for all the tables.

- Some earlier versions of Access allowed the back quote character in a database object name. This is no longer permitted. Open the database in the previous version and change the object name and all references to the object in queries, forms, reports, macros, and code.

- The database may be on a read-only network or the file attribute may be set to Read Only.

Note   *If the file size would be reduced by more than 256K, you can save time by specifying the database is automatically compacted when you close it. Check the Compact on Close option on the General tab of the Options dialog box. If another user has the database open, Access won't compact it until the last user closes it.*

Repairing with the Help Menu

The Access Help menu has a Detect and Repair command you can use to find and fix errors automatically in an application. When you choose Help | Detect and Repair, Access displays an explanation of the process and offers to restore shortcuts while repairing the database. Another option is to discard many of your custom settings and revert to the defaults. This option is useful if you need to eliminate potentially corrupt personalized settings, such as user name or the list of recently used files.

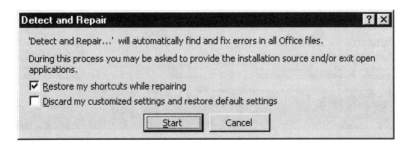

IMPROVING THE WORKPLACE

Click Start to begin the rather lengthy process. Access runs the Office 2002 Installer and will probably ask you to insert the installation disk. It may also ask you to close certain open applications. Be aware, reparation can take a long time and you can click Cancel at any time to abort the process.

Documenting a Database

One of the most important tasks in a database management system is documentation, especially if many people are involved with its development and use. One of the Access analysis tools is the *Documenter*, which analyzes the current database and prints a report of the details of the entire database or only specified parts.

To run the Documenter, do the following:

1. Choose Tools | Analyze | Documenter. The Documenter dialog box opens, showing nearly the same eight tabs as the Performance Analyzer. Each tab displays a list of objects in the database.

2. Select the items on each tab you want documented or choose Select All on the All Object Types tab to select everything in the database, including the relationships and the database properties (see Figure 17-12).

3. If you want to limit the amount of information to print in the table definitions, click Options and check the desired options in the Print Table Definition dialog box (see Figure 17-13).

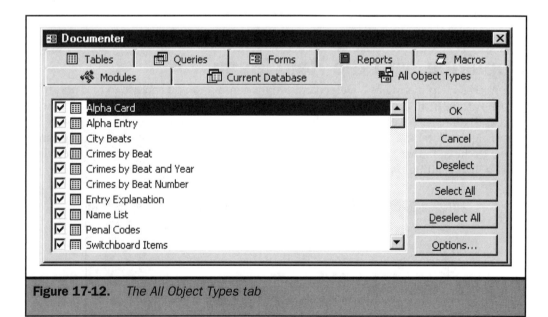

Figure 17-12. *The All Object Types tab*

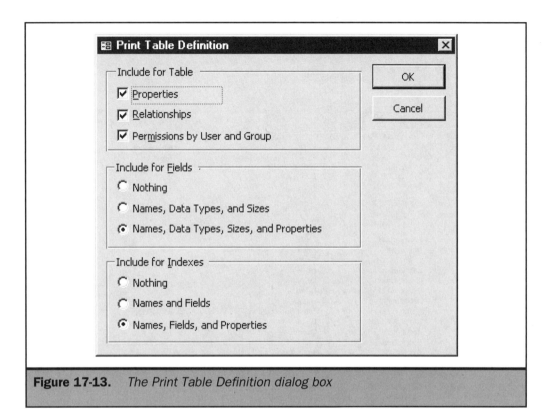

Figure 17-13. *The Print Table Definition dialog box*

4. To limit the information in another object type, select one of them and click
   Options. Each object has a list of details from which to select.

5. After making all your selections, click OK twice to start the Documenter.

Tip   *You can stop the Documenter any time by pressing* CTRL-BREAK.

The status bar shows the progress of the analysis with messages and odometers.
When the Documenter is finished, the report is opened in Print Preview. Figure 17-14
shows the first printed page of the Documenter's analysis of the Products table in the
Northwind database.

C:\My Documents\Osborne\To CD\Police 2002.mdb
Table: Alpha Card

Tuesday, February 13, 2001
Page: 1

Properties

DateCreated:	9/16/00 4:53:13 PM	GUID:	{guid {05ED137C-652B-46B7-825A-9C1E29FE15C9}}
LastUpdated:	11/26/00 4:21:06 PM	NameMap:	Long binary data
OrderByOn:	False	Orientation:	Left-to-Right
RecordCount:	98	Updatable:	True

Columns

Name		Type	Size
Index		Long Integer	4

AllowZeroLength:	False
Attributes:	Fixed Size, Auto-Increment
CollatingOrder:	General
ColumnHidden:	False
ColumnOrder:	Default
ColumnWidth:	Default
DataUpdatable:	False
GUID:	{guid {C8766057-35FE-4893-8601-5280ADD1B045}}
OrdinalPosition:	0
Required:	False
SourceField:	Index
SourceTable:	Alpha Card

Name		Type	Size
Name		Text	27

AllowZeroLength:	False
Attributes:	Variable Length
CollatingOrder:	General
ColumnHidden:	False
ColumnOrder:	Default
ColumnWidth:	Default
DataUpdatable:	False
DisplayControl:	Text Box
GUID:	{guid {3682F7A8-8DDD-490A-BC49-C0C964CABAF4}}
OrdinalPosition:	1
Required:	False
SourceField:	Name
SourceTable:	Alpha Card
UnicodeCompression:	True

Name		Type	Size
DOB		Date/Time	8

AllowZeroLength:	False
Attributes:	Fixed Size
CollatingOrder:	General
ColumnHidden:	False
ColumnOrder:	Default
ColumnWidth:	Default
DataUpdatable:	False
GUID:	{guid {9E580737-CE40-4C5F-99FD-26FB4F863C42}}
OrdinalPosition:	2
Required:	False
SourceField:	DOB
SourceTable:	Alpha Card

Figure 17-14.   *First page of the Northwind Products table definition*

You may want to look at how many pages the definition report contains before you start to print it. Some definitions, even with small databases, are quite lengthy.

If you want to save the report, you can output the definitions to one of several file formats: HTML format, an Excel worksheet, a Rich Text Format file, a DOS text file, or as a file in report snapshot format. Choose File | Export to open the Export Report To dialog box and select the desired file format from the Save as type box, enter a name for the report, and then click Export.

Summary

While this chapter might seem to contain a lot of unrelated and detailed information, all the suggestions are relevant to producing an efficient database. Both time and space have visible effects on efficiency and whatever you can do to optimize both factors can help.

Some of the suggestions relate to the computer system itself, others relate to the Windows workplace. Access provides many tools for optimization in its own workplace. Each of the Access database objects can be optimized by following the rules and guidelines presented in this chapter.

The next chapter begins to explore the world of creating an application that can be controlled by the user. In an event-driven program—such as Access—understanding the concept of events and learning when and in what sequence events occur is important. After you become familiar with events, you can proceed to create macros and event procedures that carry out specified actions when events occur.

MOUS Exam Activities Explored in This Chapter

Level	Activity	Section Title
Core	Use Access tools to maintain and repair databases	Backing Up and Restoring a Database Compacting and Repairing a Database Repairing with the Help Menu
Expert	Compact and repair databases	Compacting and Repairing a Database Repairing with the Help Menu

IMPROVING THE WORKPLACE

Chapter 18

Understanding Events and the Event Model

A lthough you can manage a database adequately using the Access wizards and other tools without knowing anything about events, when you begin to build a customized application that the user can control, you need to understand events and know when they occur. Then you can create macros and Visual Basic event procedures to carry out appropriate responses to all the user's actions.

This chapter contains most of the details about events necessary to create a basis for subsequent chapters that discuss writing macros and event procedures to automate an Access application. Skim through this chapter to get enough of an understanding of events, and then refer to it from later chapters to find specific information.

What Are Events?

Access is an *event-driven program,* which means it responds to a variety of events as they occur. In fact, if no event occurs, nothing happens at all. An *event* is something that happens to a certain object, a recognized action that occurs and triggers some type of response. For example, when you click a command button, the click event occurs and the command button's event property specifies a response.

Events are usually caused by the user, but Access also responds to events resulting from system changes or external influences. For example, a specified timer interval expires, data in the table changes, linked data is updated, or a filter finds no records that match the criteria. When an event occurs, you can have Access respond with a specific action by running a macro or executing an event procedure.

The macro or event procedure is attached to an *event property* of the object to which the event occurs. For example, when the user clicks a command button, you want the Alpha Entry form to open. You would create a macro or event procedure that opens the form and specifies it as the On Click event property for the command button.

Actually, when you create a command button using the Command Button Wizard, the wizard automatically creates an event procedure and adds it to the button's On Click property.

The next chapter discusses creating macros that respond to events. First, let's take a close look at events, what they are, and when they occur.

None of the events discussed in this chapter apply to data access pages. Pages have no event properties.

Types of Events

Events are grouped into eight categories, depending on the effects of the event. For example, some events relate to the data, others to filters, and still others to keyboard actions. The following sections describe each type of event and show tables listing the events that fall into each classification.

Each event corresponds to a property of the object to which it applies. For example, the Change event corresponds to the On Change property of several controls. You can set the property to respond to the event in a specified way.

Data Events

A data event occurs when data is entered, edited, or deleted in a datasheet or a form. For example, when the user enters data into a text box control in a form or selects a value from a combo box, a data event occurs. In addition, when the entry focus moves from one record to another, it is classified as a data event. Table 18-1 describes the data events and the Access objects to which each applies.

Event	Applies To	When It Occurs
AfterDelConfirm	Forms	After you respond Yes or No to the confirmation message Access displays when you choose to delete records and after the records are actually deleted or the deletion is canceled. The event won't occur if you set Confirm Record Changes to Off on the Edit/Find tab of the Options dialog box.
AfterFinalRender	Forms (PivotChart view)	After the find generation of the graphical representation of the date.
AfterInsert	Forms	After a new record has been added to the database.
AfterLayout	Forms (PivotChart view)	After the PivotChart elements have been assigned to the chart.
AfterRender	Forms (PivotChart view)	After a change in the graphical representation of the date has been made.
AfterUpdate	Forms, controls	After a control or record is updated with modified data. Also occurs when the control or record loses focus or you choose Records	Save Record to update the current record without moving to another. Occurs for both new and existing records.

Table 18-1.   *Data Events*

Event	Applies To	When It Occurs
BeforeDelConfirm	Forms	After one or more records are deleted, but before Access displays the confirmation message box. Occurs after the Delete event in the sequence of events.
BeforeInsert	Forms	When you begin to type the new data in a new record, but before you add the record to the database.
BeforeQuery	Forms (PivotTable view)	Before running the query that extracts the date for the PivotTable.
BeforeRender	Forms (PivotChart view)	Before generating the graphical representation of the date.
BeforeUpdate	Forms, controls	Before a control or record is updated with modified data. Occurs when the control or record loses focus or you choose Records | Save Record. Occurs for both new and existing records.
Change	Controls	When the contents of a text box control or the text box portion of a combo box control changes. When you type a character in the control or change its Text property with a macro or a procedure.
Current	Forms	When focus moves to a record and it becomes the current record. Occurs when the form is first opened and when focus moves from one record to another in the form. Also occurs when you requery the form's record source by choosing Records | Remove Filter/Sort or with a macro action.

Table 18-1. *Data Events* (continued)

Event	Applies To	When It Occurs
DataChange	Forms (PivotTable view)	When tha data in the PivotTable is updated or edited.
DataSetChange	Forms (PivotChart view)	When the data set in the PivotChart is updated or edited.
Delete	Forms	When a record is deleted, but before you confirm the deletion and it's actually carried out.
Dirty	Controls	When the current record has been changed since it was last saved. Also applies to data in Datasheet view.
NotInList	Controls	When you enter a value in a combo box that isn't in the combo box list.
PivotTableChange	Forms (PivotTable view)	When a change occurs in the PivotTable.
Query	Forms (PivotTable view)	After running the query that extracts data for the PivotTable.
Undo	Forms, controls	After Undo is requested, but before changes to a record are undone.
Updated	Controls	When an OLE object's data has been modified by the source application.

Table 18-1.   *Data Events* (continued)

IMPROVING THE
WORKPLACE

Note

Don't confuse the BeforeUpdate and AfterUpdate events with the Updated event. BeforeUpdate and AfterUpdate apply to record data. The Updated event applies only to OLE objects updated by their source program. All three events may occur when an OLE object data changes, but not always. If all three occur, the Updated event usually occurs before the other two.

Here's some additional information about the data events and what they can be used for:

- The BeforeUpdate and AfterUpdate don't occur when the value in a calculated field changes.

- You can use the BeforeUpdate record event to validate data, especially with complex validation rules that involve more than one value. You can display different error messages for different data, giving the user the opportunity to override the rule violation, if desired. Use the Validation Rule property for controls in a form, as well as the Validation Rule and Required properties specified in the table design for fields and records in forms.

- The BeforeUpdate event can also be used to cancel updating the record before moving to another record in case of an error. It can also check to see if a value was already entered in the control.

- You can use the AfterInsert event to requery the underlying recordset to incorporate new data when a record is added to the form.

- The Change event can be used to coordinate data among several controls in the form.

- The Delete event transfers the records to a temporary buffer instead of actually deleting them. You can restore them to the recordset if you cancel the BeforeDelConfirm event. Use the Delete event to display a dialog box before deleting each record, asking if the user really wants to delete it, thereby offering a selective deletion process.

- A problem can occur when you use the NotInList event to enable the user to add a value to the combo box list. If you set the AutoExpand property for the combo box control to Yes, Access selects matching values from the list as you enter characters in the text box part of the control. So, if you want to add the name John to the list, but Johnston is already on the list, the AutoExpand property fills out the complete Johnston value and the NotInList event doesn't occur. The cure for this is to enter a space after you enter the new value, so it no longer matches a value in the list. Then the NotInList event occurs when you move to the next control.

The Change event can result in cascading events—a never-ending loop. If the Change event procedure alters the contents of the control, the Change event occurs again, which triggers the Change event procedure again, and so on. If you plan to use the Change event, don't create two or more controls that affect the contents of each other.

Error Events

One error event, *Error,* is important in an application for handling errors during operation. The other error event, *Timer,* is used for synchronizing data on forms and reports by refreshing the data at regular intervals. Table 18-2 describes the Error events.

The Error event is often used to intercept Access error messages and replace them with more helpful messages that relate to the application.

Filter Events

Filter events (see Table 18-3) apply only to forms and occur when you apply an existing filter or create a new filter for the form.

Event	Applies To	When It Occurs
Error	Forms, reports	When a Microsoft Jet Database Engine error occurs while in a form or report. A Visual Basic run-time error doesn't trigger an Error event.
Timer	Forms	When the time interval specified in the form's Time Interval property has elapsed. The Timer event is used to keep data synchronized in a multiple-user environment by requerying and refreshing the data in the form at regular intervals.

Table 18-2. *Error Events*

IMPROVING THE WORKPLACE

Event	When It Occurs
ApplyFilter	When you choose Records | Apply Filter/Sort, choose Filter | Apply Filter/Sort in the Filter window, or click the Apply Filter toolbar button. Applies the most recently created filter, using Filter By Form or the Advanced Filter/Sort window.
	When you choose Records | Filter and click Filter By Selection, or click the Filter By Selection toolbar button. Applies a filter based on the selection in the form.
	When you choose Records | Filter and click Filter Excluding Selection. Applies a filter that excludes the current selection in the form.
	When you choose Filter | Advanced Filter/Sort or Filter | Filter By Form in the Advanced Filter/Sort window.
	When you choose one of the filter options in the shortcut menu when a bound control has focus.
	When you choose Records | Remove Filter/Sort or click the Remove Filter toolbar button.
	When you close the Advanced Filter/Sort or the Filter By Form window.
Filter	When you choose Records | Filter and click Filter By Form, or click the Filter By Form toolbar button, which opens the Filter By Form window.
	When you choose Records | Filter and click Advanced Filter/Sort, which opens the Advanced Filter/Sort window.
	When you choose Filter | Advanced Filter/Sort in the Filter By Form window or choose Filter | Filter By Form in the Advanced Filter/Sort window.

Table 18-3.   *Filter Events*

The *ApplyFilter event* can be used to change a form display so it hides or disables controls, depending on the filter criteria.

You can use the Filter event to remove an earlier filter so extraneous criteria aren't carried over to the next filter. To do this, set the form's Filter property to a zero-length string using a macro or event procedure that completely clears the filter criteria.

Focus Events

Focus events (see Table 18-4) occur when a form or control gets or loses focus. Two focus events apply to both forms and reports, and they occur when the object becomes active or inactive. The remaining focus events apply to forms or controls in forms.

Event	Applies To	When It Occurs
Activate	Forms, reports	When a form or report becomes the active window by opening it, by clicking it, or by clicking a control on a form.
Deactivate	Forms, reports	When a different Access window replaces the form or report as the active window, but before it actually becomes the active window. Doesn't occur when focus moves to a window in another application, a dialog box, or a pop-up form.
Enter	Controls	Before a control receives focus from another control or as the first control in a newly opened form. Occurs before the GotFocus event.
Exit	Controls	Just before a control loses focus to another control on the same form. Occurs before the LostFocus event.
GotFocus	Forms, controls	When a control receives focus or a form with no active or enabled controls receives focus. The form receives focus only if no controls are on the form or if all visible controls are disabled.
LostFocus	Forms, controls	When a form or control loses focus.
RecordExit	Forms	After the record has lost focus, but before focus leaves a record and moves to the form.
SelectionChange	Forms (PivotTable, PivotChart views)	When the field selected in a filter field area changes.

Table 18-4. *Focus Events*

The *Enter event* occurs before focus moves to a control, so you can use the event to display instructions for entering data in the control or other information.

You can use the *GotFocus* and *LostFocus events* to set the control's Visible and Enabled properties. These events are also used to display a message in the status bar when a control, such as an option button, has focus. The message clears when the control loses focus.

Keyboard Events

All *keyboard events* (see Table 18-5) apply to forms and controls that have focus. A control has focus when it can receive user input by means of the mouse or keyboard action. A form can receive focus only if it contains no controls or if all visible controls are disabled and cannot get focus. The object with focus receives all the keystrokes. When the Key Preview form event property is set to Yes, the keyboard events are invoked for the form before they're invoked for the controls on the form. The default setting is No.

Event	When It Occurs
KeyDown	When you press any key on the keyboard while the form or control has focus.
	When you send a keystroke to a form or control using a macro with the SendKey action or a Visual Basic procedure SendKey statement.
	A form receives all KeyDown events before the controls do if you set the form's Key Preview property to Yes.
	Holding the key down causes repeated KeyDown events.
KeyPress	When you press and release a key or any key combination that produces a standard ANSI character while the form or control has focus.
	When you send a keystroke to a form or control using a macro with the SendKey action or a Visual Basic procedure SendKey statement.
	A form receives all KeyPress events before the controls do if you set the form's Key Preview property to Yes.
	Holding the key down causes repeated KeyPress events.

Table 18-5. *Keyboard Events*

Event	When It Occurs
KeyUp	When you release a pressed key while a form or control has focus. The object that has focus receives the keystrokes.
	When you send a keystroke to a form or control using a macro with the SendKey action or a Visual Basic procedure SendKey statement.
	A form receives all KeyUp events before the controls do if you set the form's Key Preview property to Yes.
	Holding the key down causes the KeyUp event to occur after all the KeyDown and KeyPress events have occurred.

Table 18-5.   *Keyboard Events* (continued)

KeyUp and KeyDown are often used to recognize function keys, navigation keys, key combinations that use CTRL, SHIFT, or ALT with another key, and number keys from the keyboard or the number key pad. KeyUp and KeyDown don't occur when you press ENTER if the form has a command button whose Default property is Yes. Pressing ENTER is the same as clicking the command button. They also don't occur when you press ESC if the Cancel property is set to Yes.

The KeyPress event doesn't indicate the physical state of the keyboard, it only indicates the character pressed. The event accepts any printable character, CTRL combined with a character, ENTER, or BACKSPACE.

 Pressing BACKSPACE *results in an ANSI character and triggers the KeyPress event, but pressing* DEL *does not.*

Mouse Events

All the mouse events (see Table 18-6) apply to both forms and controls. A form can receive focus only if it contains no controls or if all visible controls have been disabled and cannot get focus.

The *Click event*, one of the most common events, occurs when you press the left mouse button. Click and DblClick only apply to the left mouse button. The other mouse buttons don't trigger the Click or DblClick event. You can use the MouseUp or MouseDown event to differentiate between the mouse buttons.

IMPROVING THE
WORKPLACE

Event	When It Occurs
Click	When you press and release the left mouse button on a control or its label.
	When you click a record selector or an area outside a section or control in a form.
	When you select a combo box or list box by pressing TAB or an arrow key, and then press ENTER.
	When you press SPACEBAR while a command button, check box, option button, or toggle button has focus.
	When you pass the mouse pointer over a hyperlink and click the left mouse button when the pointer changes to a pointer hand.
DblClick	When you press and release the left mouse button twice on a control or its label.
	When you double-click a record selector or a blank area in a form.
MouseDown	When you press the left mouse button while the mouse pointer is on a form or control.
	If you cancel the MouseDown event with the CancelEvent macro action for a form or control, the shortcut menu for the form or control is disabled. You cannot display the shortcut menu by right-clicking the form or control.
MouseMove	When you move the mouse pointer over a form, form section, or control.
MouseUp	When you release the mouse button while the pointer is on a form or control.
MouseWheel	When you use the mouse wheel to adjust the focus on the screen.

Table 18-6.   *Mouse Events*

The mouse events don't apply to attached labels, they apply only to free-standing labels. Clicking or double-clicking an attached label triggers the event for the associated control.

The result of the DblClick event depends on the type of control you clicked:

- If the control is a text box, double-clicking selects the entire word.
- If the control is an OLE object, the source application starts where you can edit the object.

If you don't double-click quickly enough, the action is treated as repeated Click events.

 The MouseMove event can occur when a form moves under the mouse pointer, even if the pointer doesn't move. If you run a macro or event procedure that moves the form, you can generate unexpected MouseMove events.

Print Events

Print events (see Table 18-7) apply only to reports and they occur for each section of the report when the report is either being printed or formatted for printing.

Event	When It Occurs
Format	When Access determines what data goes in each report section, but before the section is formatted for previewing or printing. You can use the data in the current record to change the page layout by creating a macro or event procedure for this event.
NoData	After Access formats a report for printing and discovers the report is based on an empty recordset, but before the report is printed. You can use this event to cancel printing a blank report.
Page	After the page is formatted, but before it's printed.
Print	After the data is formatted for a section, but before the section is printed.
Retreat	When Access has to back up one or more report sections to perform multiple formatting passes. Occurs after the section's Format event, but before the Print event. You can use this event to undo changes you made during the Format event for a section. Applies to all report sections except page headers and footers.

Table 18-7.   *Print Events*

Depending on the section of the report, the *Format event* applies to a different set of data:

- In the detail section, Format occurs for every record.
- In the group header, Format applies to all the data in the header section, plus the first record in the detail section.
- In the group footer, Format applies to all the data in the footer section, plus the last record in the detail section.

The *NoData event* occurs when a report has an empty recordset. If the report isn't bound to a table or query, it doesn't occur and it doesn't occur for empty subreports either. If you want to hide an empty subreport, you can attach a macro or event procedure that suppresses previewing or printing to the subreport's Has Data property.

The *Page event* can be used to draw a border around a page or add a graphic to the report. This can save disk space that would otherwise be used for storing the graphic with the report design.

The *Print event* occurs after formatting, but before actually printing the report. A macro or event procedure attached to it can be used to perform calculations, such as running page totals after the data is prepared for printing on a page.

Window Events

Window events (see Table 18-8) occur when you open, close, or resize a form or report window.

Event	Applies To	When It Occurs
Close	Forms, reports	When a form or report is closed and is no longer on the screen.
Load	Forms	When a form is opened and records appear on the screen. Occurs after the Open event and before the Current event.
Open	Forms, reports	When a form opens, but before the first record is displayed. When a report opens, but before it begins printing.

Table 18-8. *Window Events*

Event	Applies To	When It Occurs
Resize	Forms	When you change the size of a form or when the form is first displayed and expanded to its previously saved size.
Unload	Forms	When a form is closed and the records are unloaded, but before it leaves the screen. Occurs before the Close event.
ViewChange	Forms (PivotTable view)	When you change the PivotTable series to categories or the categories to series.

Table 18-8.   *Window Events* (continued)

You can use the *Load event* to specify default control settings or display calculated data in the form.

When you open a form, you can use the Open event to display a message asking if the user wants to add new records. If the response is Yes, the form can go quickly to a blank record at the end of the recordset. If not, it continues to display the first record.

Forms and reports behave differently when based on an underlying query. When you open a form, the query runs before the form is displayed. When you open a report, the Open event occurs before the query is run, giving you the opportunity to enter query parameters or other criteria.

You can use the Resize event to cause certain controls on the form to be repositioned or resized to accommodate the change in the form size.

Understanding the Sequence of Events

Many types of events can happen to an object in a short period of time. When you begin to create macros and procedures that will govern how an application operates, understanding not only when events occur, but also the sequence in which they occur is important. This is especially important if you intend to have two or more procedures executing in response to events and want them executed in a specific order. You must know to which events to attach the actions.

IMPROVING THE WORKPLACE

Form Control Events

Two types of events occur when you're moving about the controls in a form. When focus moves from one control to another, *focus events* occur. When you add or change data in a control, *data events* occur.

Moving Among Controls

When you move to another control on the same form, the Enter and GotFocus events occur in that order.

An exception to this rule is this: the Enter event doesn't occur for the items grouped in an option group, only to the option group control. The Exit event also applies only to the option group control. The toggle buttons, check boxes, or option buttons in the option group experience only the GotFocus and LostFocus events.

If you're opening a form that has one or more active controls, certain other events occur before those two:

Open(form)→Activate(form)→Current(form)→Enter(control)→GotFocus(control)

Conversely, when you move to another control, the control loses focus and the Exit and LostFocus events occur in that order.

If you're closing a form that has one or more active controls, other form events occur as well:

Exit(control)→LostFocus(control)→Unload(form)→Deactivate(form)→Close(form)

Working with Data in a Form

When you enter new data or change existing data, and then move focus to a different control, the BeforeUpdate and AfterUpdate events occur in that order. Then the Exit and LostFocus events for the changed control follow immediately after.

Whenever the contents of a text box or combo box control changes, the Change event occurs before either the BeforeUpdate and AferUpdate events occur. In fact, the Change event occurs in conjunction with keyboard events every time you press a key to enter or edit data. The sequence for each time you press a key while in the text box or the text box portion of a combo box is

KeyDown→KeyPress→Dirty→Change→KeyUp

In the special case, when you enter a value in the text box portion of a combo box control that isn't in the displayed list of values, the NotInList event occurs after the Change event, but before any other control or form events. If the Limit To List property for the combo box control is set to Yes, this also triggers an Error event. The sequence is as follows:

KeyDown→KeyPress→Dirty→Change→KeyUp→NotInList→Error

This sequence of events is often used to display a message box asking if you want to add the value to the list, even though the property specifies limiting the values to those in the list.

Form Record Events

Events occur for records in forms on several occasions:

- When the record gets focus
- When you update the data in a record by moving to the next or previous record
- When you delete one or more records
- When you add a new record

When you move from one record to another in a form or save the current record by choosing Records | Save Record, the update events apply to the current record in the form. By contrast, when you move from one control to another within the same record in a form, the update events apply to the individual controls in the form. Only when you move to another record do the form update events occur.

Moving Focus and Updating Data

At the top level are the form events that occur when you move focus to a record on the form, enter or edit the data in the record, and, finally, move to another record. The form events that occur are

Current(form)→BeforeUpdate(form)→AfterUpdate(form)→Current(form)

If you changed the data in a record and leave the record, the Exit and LostFocus events occur for the last control that got focus in that record, before you enter the next record. The form itself becomes current when you are moving to the next record. The events occur after the AfterUpdate event for the form and before the Current event for the form as follows:

AfterUpdate(form)→Exit(control)→LostFocus(control)→RecordExit(form)
→Current(form)

As you move among the controls within the same record on a form, several events occur for each control that gets focus. When you open a form and change the data in a control, the following events occur

Current(form)→Enter(control)→GotFocus(control)→BeforeUpdate(control)
→AfterUpdate(control) →Exit(control)

Then, if you move focus to another control, the events reflect the shift in focus:

Exit(control1)→LostFocus(control1)→Enter(control2)→GotFocus(control2)

When you finish working in one record and move to the next, the following events occur in which the record is updated and the form itself becomes current until another control gets focus with the Enter event:

BeforeUpdate(form) →AfterUpdate(form) →Exit(control2) →LostFocus(control2) →RecordExit(form) →Current(form)

 When moving between records, the BeforeUpdate and AfterUpdate events apply to the form. When moving between controls in the same record in the form, they apply to the controls.

Creating New Records

To add a new record, you move to the blank record on the form and type data in a control. Creating a new record triggers the following sequence of events:

Current(form) →Enter(control) →GotFocus(control) →BeforeInsert(form) → *(control update events)* →AfterInsert(form)

The BeforeUpdate and AfterUpdate events for the controls and for the new record occur between the BeforeInsert and AfterInsert form events.

Deleting Existing Records

When you delete a record from the form, Access displays a dialog box asking for confirmation of the deletion and the following events occur:

Delete→BeforeDelConfirm→AfterDelConfirm

The confirmation dialog box is displayed after the BeforeDelConfirm event. If you cancel the deletion with a macro or event procedure with the Delete event, the dialog box isn't displayed at all, and the BeforeDelConfirm and AfterDelConfirm don't occur.

Form and Subform Events

Events occur when you work with forms whenever you open or close a form, move between two forms, move between a main form and a subform, or work with the data displayed in the form.

Opening or Closing a Form

When you open a form, the sequence of events depends on whether the form has any enabled controls. If it does, the sequence of form events is

Open→Load→Resize→Activate→Current

These events are followed by the control events. If no active controls are on the form you open, the GotFocus event occurs for the form between Activate and Current.

When you close a form, the following events occur for the form:

Unload→Deactivate→Close

If no active controls are on the form, the LostFocus event occurs for the form between Unload and Deactivate.

 Open occurs before Load so you can cancel Open, but you can't cancel Load. Conversely, Close occurs after Unload, so Unload can be canceled, but Close cannot.

Moving to Another Form

More than one form can be open at a time, but only one form can be the active form. When you switch between two open forms, the Open, Load, and Resize events occur for the second form while the first is still active. Then the Deactivate event occurs for the form you're leaving and the Activate event occurs for the form you're switching to and it becomes current.

Deactivate also occurs for the form when you switch to another open window unless the window is one of the following:

- A dialog box
- A form whose Popup property is set to Yes
- A window in another application

When you move to a form that's already open, the Open event doesn't reoccur for the form.

Changing Data in a Form

When you work with data in a form, the form and control events occur in a sequence as you move between records and edit the data in them. The form events occur first as you open the form and move to the first control, and then the control events take over. When you first open the form the following events occur:

Open(form)→Load(form)→Resize(form)→Activate(form)→Current(form)
→Enter(control)→GotFocus(control)

When you finish entering data in the last control in the form and close the form, the following sequence of events occurs

Exit(control)→LostFocus(control)→Unload(form)→Deactivate(form)→Close(form)

If any of the data in a control in the form is changed, the BeforeUpdate and AfterUpdate events for both the form and the control occur before the Exit event for the control takes place and starts the form closing sequence.

Using Subforms

All the events that occur for a form also occur for a subform. The subform and its data are loaded before the main form, using the same sequence of events. The exception is the *Activate event,* which occurs only for the main form.

When you close a form that contains a subform, a similar sequence of events occurs, but in reverse order: the form and its records are unloaded before the subform and its records. Also, the *Deactivate event* occurs only for the main form. To summarize, the closing events for the main form, the subform, and the controls occur in the following order:

1. The events for the controls on the subform, including Exit and LostFocus

2. The events for the controls on the main form, including the subform control

3. The events for the form, including Deactivate and Close

4. The events for the subform

Keystrokes and Mouse Click Events

Keyboard and mouse events are initiated by the user while working in a form or with controls in the form. Keyboard events occur when you press a key or key combination while the form or control has focus. A keyboard event also occurs if you use a SendKey macro action or a procedure to send the ANSI character keystroke equivalent to the control.

Mouse events occur for forms, form sections, and controls on the form when you manipulate the mouse or press one of its buttons. Releasing a mouse button also triggers an event.

Using the Keyboard

When you press a key on the keyboard while a control has focus, the following events occur

KeyDown→KeyPress→KeyUp

If you press the key and hold it down, the KeyDown and KeyPress events alternate repeatedly until you release the key. Then the KeyUp event occurs.

If the key you press isn't an ANSI character, the KeyDown and KeyUp events occur, but not the KeyPress event. Pressing and holding down a non-ANSI key causes the KeyDown and KeyUp events to alternate repeatedly.

If the key you press changes the data in a text box control, the Change event occurs between the KeyPress and KeyUp events.

If the keystroke moves focus from one control to another, the KeyDown event occurs for the first control, while the KeyPress and KeyUp events occur for the second control. For example, if you edit the data in a text box control, and then press TAB to move to the next control, the following sequence of events occurs

KeyDown(control1)→BeforeUpdate(control1)→AfterUpdate(control1)
→Exit(control1)→LostFocus(control1)→Enter(control2)→GotFocus(control2)
→KeyPress(control2)→KeyUp(control2)

Using the Mouse

When you place the mouse pointer on a control in a form and click the mouse button, the following events occur

MouseDown→MouseUp→Click

Notice the Click event doesn't occur until after the MouseUp event.

The mouse events occur when you press any of the mouse buttons—the left, right, or center, if you have one. When you write an event procedure for the MouseUp and MouseDown events, you can distinguish between the mouse buttons. You can also use code to interpret mouse-keyboard combinations that use the SHIFT, CTRL, and ALT keys with a mouse click.

If you use the mouse to move focus from one control to another, the sequence of events is as follows:

Exit(control1)→LostFocus(control1)→Enter(control2→GotFocus(control2)
→MouseDown(control2)→MouseUp(control2)→Click

If you move to another control by other means, such as pressing TAB, and then clicking the mouse button, the Current event for the form occurs between the LostFocus event for the first control and the Enter event for the second.

When you double-click a mouse button on a control other than a command button, both the *Click* and *DblClick events* occur, each with a corresponding MouseUp event, as follows:

MouseDown→MouseUp→Click→DblClick→MouseUp

If the control is a command button, a second Click event follows the second MouseUp event.

The *MouseMove event* is independent of the other mouse events and occurs when you pass the mouse pointer over the form, a form section, or control. The MouseMove event is often used to display ScreenTips and other comments explaining parts of a form. *The Mouse Wheel event* is also independent of the other mouse events and occurs whenever you use the mouse wheel to move the pointer.

Report and Report Section Events

Report and *report section events* occur when you open or close a report. Opening a report for previewing and printing both trigger the same sequence of events. Some of the report section events occur during or after section formatting and before printing the section.

Working with Reports

If you open a report for previewing or printing, and then close the report or switch to a different Access window, the following events occur

Open→Activate→Close→Deactivate

If you have two reports open and you switch between them, the Deactivate event occurs for the first report, followed by the Activate event for the second. The Deactivate event doesn't occur for the report if you switch to a dialog box, a pop-up form, or a window in a different application.

When the report you open is based on a query, the Open event occurs before the query is run. This is useful for entering the criteria for the query in a procedure that responds to the Open report event. The procedure could open a dialog box in which the user is prompted to enter a value to be used in the parameter query.

Working with Subreports

When you preview or print the report, each section is formatted individually and prepared for printing after the Activate report event and before the Close report event. When all the sections are formatted for printing, the report is closed and deactivated. The sequence is as follows:

Open(report)→Activate(report)→Format(section)→Print(section)→Close(report)
→Deactivate(report)

Some special events can occur while a section is being formatted or after formatting is complete, but before printing. These events are

- *Retreat*, which occurs when Access returns to a previous section to make changes during formatting. For example, if you set a group's Keep Together property to Whole Group or With First Detail, Access must return to the previous report section to determine if the controls can all fit on the page. The Retreat event is also useful for maintaining the positioning of report items on a page.

- *NoData*, which occurs if no records are in the report.

- *Page*, which occurs after formatting, but before printing. If you want to add special formatting to customize the report's appearance, you can attach a procedure to this event.

Setting Event Properties

Event properties are used to run a macro or an event procedure each time the associated event occurs. The tables in an earlier section of this chapter describe the events and indicate to which objects each applies. When an event applies to a form, control, or report, that object has an event property that corresponds to the event. This is this property you set to create the appropriate response to the event.

For example, enter the name of a macro in the On Click property of a command button and it will run when you click the button.

To set an event property, open the property sheet for the object, and then click the Event tab. Figure 18-1 shows the Event property sheet for a form.

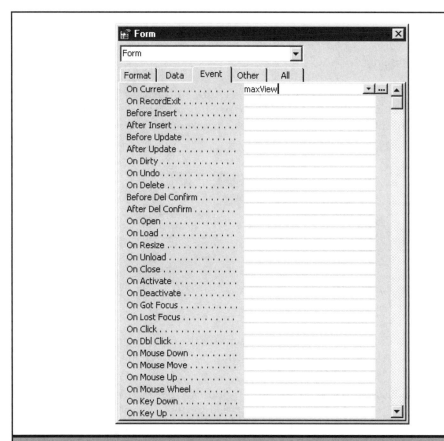

Figure 18-1. *A form Event property sheet*

Depending on how you intend to create a response to the event, do one of the following:

- To set the property to an existing macro, choose the macro name from the drop-down list in the event property.

- To set the property to a macro in a macro group, choose the name from the drop-down list. The name then appears in the list as *macrogroupname.macroname*.

- To set the property to an existing event procedure, choose [Event Procedure] from the drop-down list. Only one event procedure can exist for each event property, named with the name of the property.

- To set the property to an existing user-defined function, enter an equal sign (=) followed by the function name, and then empty parentheses: *=functionname()*.

Note *The status bar displays a brief description of the event property when the insertion pointer is in the property box.*

If you want to create a new macro, event procedure, or function for the event property, click Build (...) to the right of the property box or right-click the property and choose Build from the shortcut menu. In the Choose Builder dialog box, do one of the following:

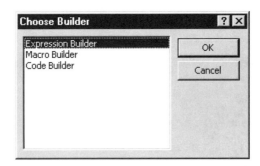

- Select Macro Builder to create a new macro for the property or edit the already specified macro. See Chapter 19 for information about creating and editing macros and macro groups.

- Select Code Builder to open the Module window where you can create a new event procedure or edit one already specified for this property. See Chapter 25 to learn how to write event procedures.

- Select Expression Builder to choose or create a user-defined function for this property.

See the Quick Reference on the CD for a complete list of event properties and the objects to which they apply.

Summary

This chapter presented an overview of events and how they can be harnessed to customize an application. In addition, it listed many of the common types of events and the objects to which they apply, as well as the sequence in which they occur. Once you have an understanding of events, you're ready to proceed to creating your own macros and event procedures, so the application responds properly to each user action and system event.

As you're building macros in the next chapter, you can refer to the event details in this chapter. Attaching the macro action to the proper event for it to execute at the intended time and operate on the intended object is important.

The next chapter launches into automation with macros and gives many useful examples of macros that display message boxes, filter records, and even change the flow of operations.

MOUS Exam Activities Explored in This Chapter

This chapter contains no information directly related to the MOUS Certification Exam activities, although the information is important for you to understand how to use Access for effective database management.

IMPROVING THE
WORKPLACE

Chapter 19

Automating
with Macros

Macros provide a quick and easy way to program your Access application to do just what you want. With macros, you can specify customized responses to user actions, such as clicking a button, opening a form, or selecting an option in an options group. Macros can also respond to system conditions, such as an empty recordset.

Although the Access Control Wizards offer an easy way to add user interaction to a form or report, they don't always have exactly the right response. Creating a macro as a response to an event is an alternative to using a Control Wizard. Writing event procedures in Visual Basic is another alternative, but it requires some skill in programming with precisely constructed commands written in established syntax. Macros are easier because you select the actions and their arguments from predefined lists, which virtually precludes any errors in construction.

This chapter discusses macros, how to create them, and how to attach them to events to get the desired response. In subsequent chapters, you see how to use macros to customize menus and toolbars, as well as how to create opening switchboards for an application. The Police database introduced earlier is used as the sample database in this chapter.

How Do Macros Work?

A *macro* is a list of one or more actions that work together to carry out a particular task in response to an event. Each action carries out one particular operation. You create the list of actions in the order in which you want them to execute. In addition to selecting the action to be taken, you specify other details of the action called *arguments,* which provide additional information, such as which form to open or how to filter the records to be displayed.

You can also set conditions under which the macro action is to be performed, such as to display a message box if a field contains a certain value or is blank. The macro runs only if the condition evaluates to True. If the condition is False, the action is skipped. Then, if another action is in the macro, it's executed. If not, the macro stops.

Once an event occurs, the macro assigned to it automatically executes, beginning with the first action in the list. For example, a macro that opens a form and moves to a blank record for data entry can be assigned to the On Click event property of a command button on a switchboard or other form. When you click the button, the macro executes.

The process of using macros to automate an application is a simple one, composed of these steps:

1. Create and save the macro.

2. Open the form or report to which the macro applies and select the specific control.

3. Open the property sheet for the control and click the Event tab.

4. Click the desired event property and choose the macro name from the drop-down list.

5. Close and save the form or report.

Macros are individual Access objects listed in the Macros tab in the Database window. Once you create and save a macro, it's available for attaching to an event property of any object in your database. Not all macro actions are appropriate for all objects, however, just as not all events occur to all objects. For example, if you create a macro that opens a form, you would probably attach it to the On Click event property of a command button or an option group, but not to a control in a report.

A later section in this chapter describes categories of macro actions and how they're used.

Note *Access macros are quite different from the recorded macros you may have used in other programs. Access doesn't record keystrokes in a macro. You select specific actions from a list of more than 50 predefined actions and add the action arguments.*

Creating a Macro

The first step in creating a macro is to design the macro carefully by listing the actions you want performed when the event occurs. Each action may require specific arguments or need to be performed only under certain conditions.

Next, verify you're choosing the right event for the macro to respond to. Refer to Chapter 18 for information about events and when they occur.

When you complete the planning and design of the macro action list, you're ready to open the Macro design window.

Touring the Macro Design Window

To start a new macro, click New in the Macros tab of the Database window. The Macro window opens showing a blank macro sheet (see Figure 19-1).

The drop-down list in the Action column contains a list of actions from which to choose. Entries in the Comment column are optional, but highly recommended as a reminder of what the macro is meant to accomplish.

Tip *Comments are especially useful because macros are stored as separate objects, not linked with a particular form or report. The comments can explain how the macro is used and to which events it's attached. This can be important if you rename the macro. You need to find all the references to the macro and change the name there, as well.*

Once you select an action from the list, the lower pane displays the associated arguments. Some are required, while others are optional, depending on the action.

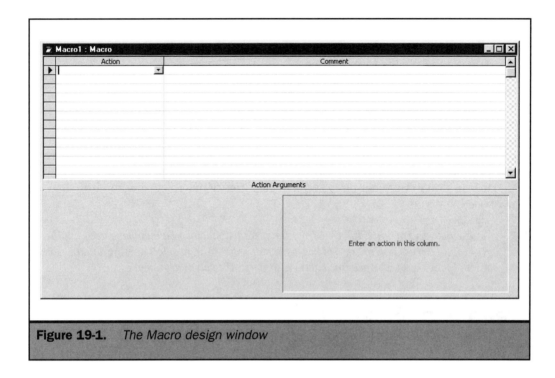

Figure 19-1. *The Macro design window*

The Macro window toolbar has some new buttons and new menu commands:

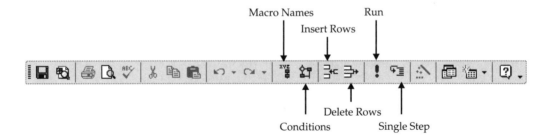

- The Macro Names button adds the Macro Name column to the macro sheet. Also use View | Macro Names.

- The Conditions button adds the Condition column to the macro sheet. Also use View | Conditions.

- The Insert Rows button inserts one or more blank rows in the grid above the selected row. If you select more than one row, that number of rows is inserted. Also use Insert | Rows.

- The Delete Rows button deletes the selected row or rows. Also use Edit | Delete Rows.

- The Run button runs the macro. Also use Run | Run.

- The Single Step button runs the macro one action at a time and displays intermediate information. Also use Run | Single Step.

The lower-right pane in the Macro window displays information about the currently active part of the macro sheet. For example, in Figure 19-1, the first row is selected and the message Enter an Action in This Column is displayed in the information pane. As you work in the macro sheet, the pane shows other information and comments.

The Macro Name and Condition columns are, by default, not displayed when you start a new macro. If you want them to appear when you first open the Macro window, choose Tools | Options and click the View tab. Then, in the Show In Macro Design group, check Names Column and Conditions Column. You can remove them later from the macro sheet by clearing the menu command or clicking the toolbar button.

Creating a Simple Macro

As an example, create a macro in the Police database that opens the Alpha Card form in read-only mode by doing the following:

1. Click New in the Macros tab of the Database window to open the blank macro sheet.

2. Click the Action drop-down arrow and choose OpenForm from the list.

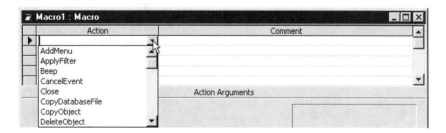

The Action Arguments pane now contains the arguments for the OpenForm action and the information pane describes the selected OpenForm action (see Figure 19-2). The Form Name argument is required. Other required arguments show selections. The optional arguments are blank in the pane.

3. Click the Form Name box in the Action Arguments pane and select a form from the drop-down list of all the forms in the current database.

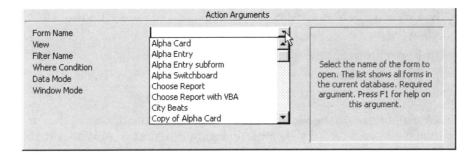

4. Set the other arguments as follows:

- View (required): Choose from the list of options including Form (default), Design, Print Preview, Datasheet, PivotTable, or PivotChart. Leave the default Form view.

- Filter Name (optional): Enter the name of the filter to limit or sort the records in the form. This can be a query or a filter saved as a query. Leave this blank because you want all the records.

- Where Condition (optional): Enter a SQL WHERE clause that limits the records in the form. You can click the Build button next to the argument box to start the Expression Builder if you need help. Again, you want all the records, so don't add a Where Condition.

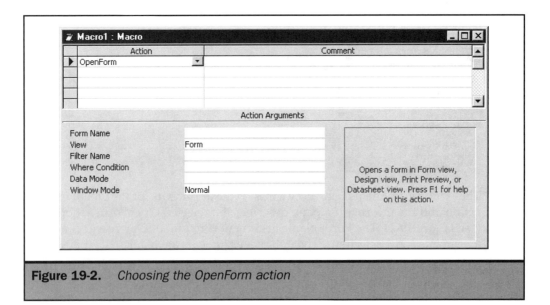

Figure 19-2.   *Choosing the OpenForm action*

■ Data Mode (optional): Choose from the list of data entry modes: Add, to allow adding new records; Edit, to allow editing of existing records; or Read Only, to prevent any additions or editing. Choose Read Only from the list.

■ Window Mode (required): Choose from the list of window modes, including Normal (default); Hidden, which hides the form; Icon, which displays the form minimized; or Dialog, which sets the form Popup and Modal properties both to Yes. Leave the Window Mode with the default Normal setting.

5. Close the Macro window, enter a name for the macro in the Save As dialog box, and then click OK. If you return to the Macros tab of the Database window, you can see the name of the new macro.

Choosing Actions

Access offers actions that cover data management activities, such as opening forms and reports, printing reports, filtering data, validating data, moving among records in a form, playing sounds, displaying message boxes, and even exchanging data with other programs.

To add an action to a macro, you can either choose from the drop-down list or type the name yourself. As with many lists offered by Access for choosing an item, if you begin to type the name of the action, Access automatically fills in the remaining characters for you.

Table 19-1 describes the categories of database activities and lists the macro actions you can use for those purposes.

Category	Activity	Macro Actions
Work with data in forms and reports	Limit data.	ApplyFilter
	Navigate among controls, records, and pages.	FindNext, FindRecord, GoToControl, GoToPage, GoToRecord
Execute a command or run an operation	Carry out a command.	RunCommand
	Leave Access.	Quit

Table 19-1. *Categories of Macro Actions*

Category	Activity	Macro Actions
	Run a query, another macro, a procedure, or another application.	OpenQuery, RunSQL, RunMacro, RunCode, RunApp
	Stop execution.	CancelEvent, Quit, StopAllMacros, StopMacro
Import, export, or link objects with other applications	Export Access objects to other applications.	OutputTo, SendObject
	Transfer data to other formats.	TransferDatabase, TransferSpreadsheet, TransferSQLDatabase, TransferText
Manipulate Access objects	Copy, delete, rename, or save the object.	CopyDatabase, CopyObject, DeleteObject, Rename, Save
	Modify a window.	Maximize, Minimize, MoveSize, Restore
	Open, close, or select an object.	Close, OpenDataAccessPage, OpenDiagram, OpenForm, OpenFunction, OpenModule, OpenQuery, OpenReport, OpenStoredProcedure, OpenTable, OpenView, SelectObject
	Print an object.	OpenForm, OpenQuery, OpenReport, OpenStoredProcedure, OpenTable, OpenView (set the View argument to Print Preview), PrintOut

Table 19-1. *Categories of Macro Actions* (continued)

Category	Activity	Macro Actions
	Set the value of a field, a control, or a property of a form, control, or report.	SetValue
	Update an object with the latest data or update the screen display.	RepaintObject, Requery, ShowAllRecords
Other actions	Create custom command bars and shortcut menus, including global menu bars and global shortcut menus.	AddMenu
	Set the state of a menu item on a custom menu bar or shortcut menu— for example, dimmed or selected.	SetMenuItem
	Display a message to the user or other information.	Echo, Hourglass, MsgBox, SetWarnings
	Generate keystrokes.	SendKeys
	Show or hide custom or built-in command bar.	ShowToolbar
	Play a beep sound.	Beep

Table 19-1. *Categories of Macro Actions* (continued)

 See the Quick Reference on the CD for a complete description of all the macro actions and their arguments.

Setting Action Arguments

Most macro actions have a list of associated arguments that give Access more information about how you want to carry out the action. Some arguments are required and others are optional. When you add an action to a macro, the argument list appears in the lower pane.

Drag an Action

A quick way to add an action to a macro that carries out a specific action on an Access object, such as opening a form, report, or query, is to drag the object from the Database window to the Action row in a macro sheet. You need to have both the Database window and the Macro window open at the same time, tiled vertically.

Click the tab that contains the object you want to drag to the macro, select the object name, and then drag the object to the first empty row in the macro sheet.

Dragging any object except a macro to the macro sheet adds an action, which opens that object. If you drag a macro from the Database window to the macro sheet, the added action runs that macro.

When you add an action by dragging an object, Access automatically sets all the required arguments to their default values.

You can usually type the value you want in the argument box, but many offer drop-down lists. If you enter a value, some require it to be included in the list. A description of the current argument is displayed in a pane to the right of the argument list. If you need more help, press F1 with the insertion point in the argument box.

In some cases, choices for one argument can determine which choices are available for an argument further down in the list. For this reason, setting the arguments in the order they are listed in the Action Arguments pane is best.

If the argument requires an object name, you can enter the name or drag the object from the Database window to the argument box. When you drag an object from the Database window, Access automatically sets the appropriate arguments for that action.

Instead of selecting from a list or entering a value, you can enter an expression that evaluates to the argument value you want to use. Always precede the expression with an equal sign so Access recognizes it as an expression instead of an identifier. For example, the expression =*[EntryNo]* sets the argument to the value in the EntryNo control.

The equal sign rule has two exceptions: The Expression argument of the SetValue action and the RepeatExpression argument of the RunMacro action give unexpected results if you use an equal sign. They evaluate the expression twice.

If you want help from the Expression Builder, click the Build button, which appears at the right of the argument box when you click an argument that accepts an expression.

Not all arguments accept expressions. For example, you must select from the list for the ObjectType argument. If you use an expression where one isn't permitted, you get an error message.

If you want to refer to a control on another form, you must use the full object identifier syntax: [Forms]![formname]![controlname]. The ! symbol indicates what follows is an object named by the user. If the object was named by Access, you would use a period (.) to separate the object names. In addition, both forms must be open.

Testing and Debugging a Macro

After you complete the macro, you can run it to see if it behaves as planned. You have a choice of running the complete macro at once or stepping through each action one at a time. If an error occurs in the macro or you don't get the results you expect, use the stepthrough method of running the macro.

Starting the Macro

After you finish adding the actions and setting the arguments, you can run a macro in several ways. While still in the Macro window, click the Run button or choose Run | Run.

After you name and save the macro, you can run it from the Database window by one of the following methods:

- Select the macro name and click Run.
- Double-click the macro name.
- Right-click the macro name and choose Run from the shortcut menu.

If your macro depends on a particular form or report being open before it can run, open the form or report first, choose Tools | Macro | Run Macro and then enter the macro name in the Run Macro dialog box.

If an error occurs during the operation, Access displays an error message. Read the message, and then click OK to open the Action Failed dialog box (see Figure 19-3), which tells you which action in the macro failed and the arguments being used at the time. The Arguments box in Figure 19-3 shows the second argument is missing from the GoToRecord action. It also shows any conditions that were in effect. Your only option in this dialog box is to click Halt to stop the macro. Before closing the dialog box, note the action name and other data about where the fault occurred. Then, it's up to you to switch to the Macro window to correct the problem.

 While you're debugging a macro, you can enter False as a condition in an action row to disable the action temporarily.

Stepping Through a Macro

 If you create a macro with many actions and it contains an error, you can use the Single Step method to move through the macro, one action at a time. You must be in the Macro window to step through the macro actions. To start stepping through the macro, click Single Step or choose Run | Single Step, and then click Run or choose Run | Run to carry out the first action. A Macro Single Step dialog box opens showing the details of the first step in your macro (see Figure 19-4).

 The Single Step mode remains in effect until you turn it off. Click the Single Step button again, or choose Run and clear the Single Step command.

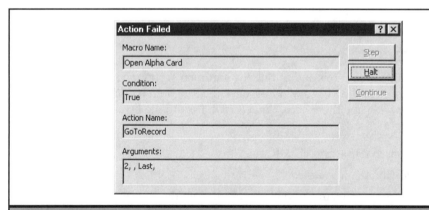

Figure 19-3. *The Action Failed dialog box*

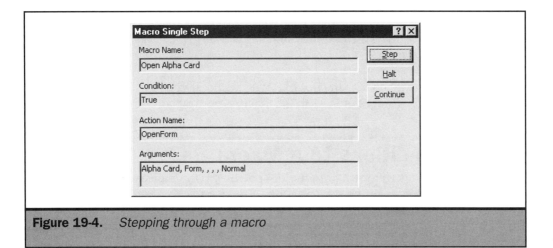

Figure 19-4.   *Stepping through a macro*

Your options in this dialog box are

- Step (default), which moves to the next action.
- Halt, which stops macro execution.
- Continue, which stops Single Step mode and runs the rest of the macro without stopping. If another error occurs, the macro stops and an Action Failed dialog box appears.

  Your macro may cause other macros to run. For example, an OpenForm action in a macro may open a form that has other macros assigned to the OnOpen, OnLoad, or other event properties. If other macros run as a result of the macro you're testing, their steps are also displayed in the Macro Single Step dialog box. You can tell it's a different macro by the name in the Macro Name box.

Modifying a Macro

After you see how a macro runs, you may decide to make some changes to it, such as adding an action, changing the order of the actions, adding a condition to the action, adding a Where Condition argument to limit the records, or creating additional macros to include in a macro group.

To open a macro for modification, select the macro name in the Database window and click Design. Use the Insert Rows and Delete Rows toolbar buttons or the Insert and Edit menu commands to add or delete actions. You can also use the standard Cut, Copy, and Paste operations to edit a macro. The Undo button is available to reverse the recent changes, as well.

Tip *If the macro operates on important data, make a temporary copy of the data to use during the modification process. This way, if anything goes wrong, you haven't destroyed valuable information.*

After making the changes to the macro, save it again. If you save it with a different name, be sure to change all references to the macro accordingly.

Adding Conditions to a Macro

When you want a macro to run only under specific circumstances, you can add a condition to one or more of the macro actions. The macro condition effectively states: If this condition is true, run this action. If it is not true, go to the next action, if any. This is a highly useful tool when programming an application. You can use conditions to set values of controls or control properties and even run additional macros. Such test comparisons aren't case-sensitive.

Some examples of using conditions are

- If the balance of an account is negative, change the color of the number to red.
- If a student's grades are exemplary, print a congratulatory message.
- If the inventory level of an item is low, display a message to remind the user to reorder.
- If the order exceeds a specific total, calculate the amount due with a volume discount.

Note *Don't confuse the macro condition that determines whether the action takes place with the Where Condition that limits the records in the form or report. The macro condition is entered in the Condition column of the macro sheet and the Where Condition is an argument of many macro actions.*

Normally, a condition applies only to the action on the same row in the macro sheet. If the condition isn't met, the next action is executed. To continue the condition to the next action, enter an ellipsis (...) in the Condition column of the next row. You can apply the condition to several sequential actions.

Tip *When you're debugging a macro, you can temporarily disable an action by entering False in the Condition column. This can help to isolate the problem.*

You can also use conditions to create an If...Then...Else structure in a macro. This conditional logic runs one or more actions if the condition is met and a different set if the condition evaluates to False.

To add the Condition column to the macro sheet, click the Conditions button or choose View | Conditions. Type the logical expression for the condition in the row with the action you want to carry out if the condition is True. If you want to use the Expression Builder to help with the expression, right-click in the Condition column and choose Build from the shortcut menu.

You cannot use a SQL expression as a condition in macro. SQL expressions are used only in Where Condition arguments.

Running a Macro with a Condition

When you run the macro, Access evaluates the condition and does the following:

- If the condition is True, Access runs the action on that row, and all actions directly following it, that have an ellipsis (…) in the Condition column. Then Access runs any additional actions that have blank conditions until it encounters another condition, a macro name in the Macro Name column, or the end of the macro.

- If the condition is False, the action is ignored as are any additional actions with an ellipsis (…) in the Condition column. Then Access moves to the next action, if any.

Table 19-2 shows some examples of expressions you can use as conditions with macro actions. All the fields in the expressions are in the form from which the macro originates, unless otherwise specified.

Expression	Evaluates to True if:
[State]="CA"	CA is the value in the control.
IsNull[Purge]	The Purge field on the form contains a Null value. Uses the IsNull function.
Forms![Alpha Entry]![Purge]<Date()	The Purge field on the Alpha Entry form is earlier than the current date.
[State] In ("CA","AZ","NV","NM") And Len([ZipCode])<5	The State value is one of those in the list and the value in the ZipCode field contains less than five characters. Combines two conditions into a single expression.

Table 19-2.   *Examples of Conditional Expressions*

IMPROVING THE
WORKPLACE

Expression	Evaluates to True if:
DCount("*","Alpha Entry", "[Index]=Forms![Alpha Card]![Index]")>5	There are more than five records in the Alpha Entry table whose Index value matches an Index value in the Alpha Card table. Uses the DCount aggregate function.
MsgBox("Do you really want to delete this Entry?", 1) = 1	The user responds to the message box by clicking OK. If the user clicked Cancel, the returned value is 0 and the condition is False and Access ignores the corresponding action.

Table 19-2. *Examples of Conditional Expressions* (continued)

Note *Notice the use of identifiers to specify a control in a form other than the one from which the macro was launched. The referenced form must be open at the time the macro runs.*

Assigning a Macro to an Event Property

Once you create the macro to carry out the action you want, you need to decide when you want it to happen. Access responds to all kinds of events that occur when you are working with a form or report, including mouse clicks, changes in data, changes in focus, and opening or closing a form or report.

Chapter 18 contains a complete description of events, including when they happen and in what sequence. Assigning the macro to the right event in a sequence is important.

After you decide when you want the macro to run, you set the corresponding event property of the form, report, or control to the name of the macro. For example, if you want to run a macro that sounds a beep when a form opens, assign the macro to the On Open property of the form.

To attach a macro to an event property, do the following:

1. Open the form or report in Design view, and then:

   ■ To attach the macro to a form or report event, click the form or report selector or choose Edit | Select Form or Edit | Select Report.

   ■ To attach the macro to a section of the form or report, click the section selector.

   ■ To attach the macro to a control in a form, select the control.

2. Open the property sheet and click the Event tab to see a list of events that can occur for the selected object.

3. Click the property whose event you want to run the macro and choose the macro name from the drop-down list.

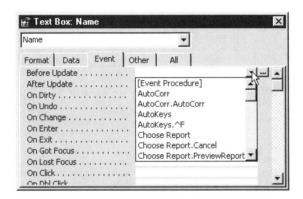

4. Save and close the form or report design.

If you select a macro name, and then click Build (…) next to the property box, you open the macro Design window where you can view and edit the selected macro.

When the event occurs, the built-in response, if any, occurs first, and then the macro runs. For example, when you click a button, the built-in response occurs and the button appears pressed. If you attach a macro to the On Click event property, the macro runs next.

If you want the macro to occur when you click either the control or its label, select them both before opening the property sheet. Then choose the macro name in the On Click event property for the multiple selection.

Deciding Which Event

Although the property sheet shows quite a long list of event properties for forms and controls, you'll use a few of them more often. Table 19-3 lists some of the commonly used form and control event properties.

Reports have fewer event properties because little user interaction occurs with a report. Some of the more common event properties used to attach macros and event procedures to reports are

■ On No Data, which runs a macro when the report has an empty underlying recordset. Use to cancel the print event.

■ On Open, which runs a macro when the report opens, but before printing begins. Use to prompt for a filter for the records to be included in the report.

■ On Page, which runs a macro after the page is formatted, but before printing begins. Use to add a graphic or border design to the report.

Report sections also have a few event properties to which you can attach a macro or event procedure.

Property	Occurs	Use To
On Open	When the form opens, but before the first record is displayed.	Open, close, or minimize other forms or maximize this form.
On Current	When the form is opened and focus moves to a record or the form is refreshed or requeried.	Synchronize data among forms or move focus to a specific control.
Before Update	After focus leaves a record, but before the data is saved in the database. After a control loses focus, but before the control is changed.	Display a message to confirm the change. Validate data for a control.
After Update	After the record changes are saved in the database. After a control loses focus and after the control is changed.	Update the data in other controls, forms, or reports. Move focus to a different page, control, or record in the form. Also transmit new data to other applications.
Before Insert	Upon entering data in a new record and again before adding the new record to the database.	Verify the data is valid and display information about adding new data.
On Click	When you press and release a mouse button over a control.	Carry out commands and command-like actions.
On Enter	When you move to a control, but before it gets focus.	Display information about data to enter in the control or a request for user password.

Table 19-3.   *Commonly Used Form and Control Event Properties*

Default Events

Most of the macros used in an application are attached to the default events for the object. A *default event* is the event most often associated with a particular object, not one that occurs automatically. For example, the Click event is the most common event associated with command buttons and check boxes, while Open is the most common event for forms.

When you use the Macro Builder to create a macro for an object, the macro is automatically attached to the default event. To create a macro with the Macro Builder, do the following:

1. Open the form or report in Design view.

2. Right-click a control, such as a text box on a form, and choose Build Event from the shortcut menu.

3. In the Choose Builder dialog box, select Macro Builder and click OK.

4. A blank macro sheet opens with a Save As dialog box in front. Enter a name for the macro and click OK.

5. Create the macro as before, and then close it.

When you open the form or report in Design view and look at the property sheet for the text box control, you see the name of the macro in the Before Update event property.

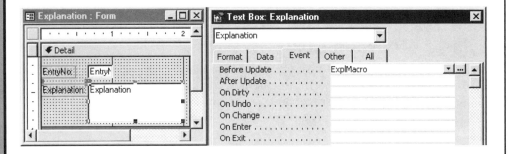

Table 19-4 lists the default events and the Access objects to which they apply. Not all objects and controls have default events.

When you use the Code Builder to create an event procedure for an object or control, the code is also attached to the object's default event.

Default Event	Objects
Click	Detail section of a form and the following controls: check box, command button, image, label, option button, rectangle, and toggle button
BeforeUpdate	Combo box, list box, option group, and text box
Updated	Bound and unbound object frame and chart
Enter	Subform
Load	Form
Open	Report
Format	Report section

Table 19-4. *Default Events for Access Objects*

Some Common Uses for Macros

When you work with a database, Access causes many things to happen in response to your actions. You may not be aware that you can customize the database with macros to accomplish many similar operations according to your designs. Here are some of the more common applications for macros.

Displaying a Message Box

The *MsgBox action* is one of the most useful macro actions when interacting with the user. You can use it to display warnings, alerts, and other information. The MsgBox action has four arguments: Message, Beep, Type, and Title. Table 19-5 describes the values you enter in each of the arguments.

 Don't enclose the message in quotation marks unless you also want the marks displayed.

If you like the format of the built-in Access error messages, you can create the same effect with your own messages. The Message action argument can contain three sections separated by the @ character. The first section is text displayed as a bold heading and can be used as an alert. The second section appears in plain text below the heading and is used for an explanation of the error. The third section appears below the text of the second section, also in plain text, with a blank line between.

Argument	Description
Message	Enter the text of the message you want displayed when the macro runs. You can enter up to 255 characters; the box expands accordingly. You can also enter an expression preceded by an equal sign (=) that evaluates to a text message.
Beep	Specifies whether to sound a beep signal when the message box opens. Set to Yes (default) or No.
Type	Sets the type of message box, each of which displays a different icon. Choices are None (default), Critical (a red circle with an *X*), Warning? (a bubble with a question mark), Warning! (a yellow triangle with an exclamation mark), or Information (a bubble with a lowercase *I*).
Title	Text that displays in the message box title bar. If left blank, the box is titled Microsoft Access.

Table 19-5. *MsgBox Action Arguments*

Validating Data

Usually, you ensure valid data is entered in a form by specifying a validation rule for the control in the form or by setting record and field validation rules in the underlying table design. For more complex data validation, use a macro or an event procedure to specify the rule.

The recommendation is that you use a macro or an event procedure if any of the following situations are present:

- You want to display different error messages for differing errors in the same field. For example, if the value is above the valid range, display one message; if the value is below the valid range, display another.

- You want the user to be able to override the rule. In this case, you can display a warning message and accept the user's confirmation or cancellation.

- The validation refers to controls in other forms.

- The validation contains a function.

- The validation rule involves conditions based on more than one value. For example, if the user checks Credit Card as the method of payment, be sure the number and expiration date are also entered in the form.

- You have a generic validation rule that can be used for more than one form. When you want to apply it to a control on a form, run the SetValue macro action that sets the Validation Rule property for the control.

One example of using a macro to validate data is checking to make sure certain reports of serious criminal activity in the Police Alpha Entry table are never purged from the database. The macro is based on a condition that compares the Code value, which identifies the crime, with the value in the Purge field. The Purge field contains the date when the record may be erased from the file. The report of certain crimes is never to be erased. If the Code is in a certain range, no date should be entered in the Purge field. Figure 19-5 shows a macro that would accomplish this data validation. Attach the macro to the Before Update event property of the text box control that contains the data in question.

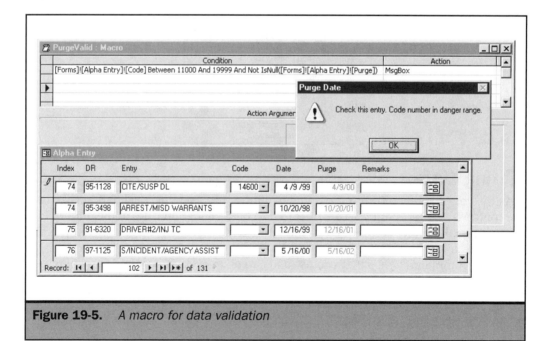

Figure 19-5. *A macro for data validation*

Filtering Records

The Northwind sample database that comes with Access contains a clever example of using a macro to filter records. The macro is associated with the Customer Phone List form (see Figure 19-6), which contains an alphabetic list of all the current customers. When you click one of the buttons at the bottom of the form, the list is filtered to show only those customers whose company name begins with the selected letter. The All button at the right of the row of buttons shows as pressed in, indicating all the names appear in the list.

The Northwind database is located in the Program Files\Microsoft Office\Office\ Samples folder. If you don't see the Samples folder, it may not be installed with Access. Run Setup again and change the Access options to include the Sample Databases.

The Alpha Buttons macro applies a filter to the list, depending on which button is pressed. The row of buttons is actually an option group control, which returns a value representing the option selected. By default, the first item returns 1, the second returns 2, and so on. The macro (see Figure 19-7) uses the returned value in a condition for the ApplyFilter action. The Where Condition argument for each ApplyFilter action specifies the appropriate filter.

Company Name:	Contact:	Phone:	Fax:
Alfreds Futterkiste	Maria Anders	030-0074321	030-0076545
Ana Trujillo Emparedados y helados	Ana Trujillo	(5) 555-4729	(5) 555-3745
Antonio Moreno Taquería	Antonio Moreno	(5) 555-3932	
Around the Horn	Thomas Hardy	(171) 555-7788	(171) 555-6750
Berglunds snabbköp	Christina Berglund	0921-12 34 65	0921-12 34 67
Blauer See Delikatessen	Hanna Moos	0621-08460	0621-08924
Blondel père et fils	Frédérique Citeaux	88.60.15.31	88.60.15.32
Bólido Comidas preparadas	Martín Sommer	(91) 555 22 82	(91) 555 91 99
Bon app'	Laurence Lebihan	91.24.45.40	91.24.45.41
Bottom-Dollar Markets	Elizabeth Lincoln	(604) 555-4729	(604) 555-3745

A B C D E F G H I J K L M N O P Q R S T U V W X Y Z All

Record: 1 of 91

Figure 19-6.   *The Northwind Customer Phone List form*

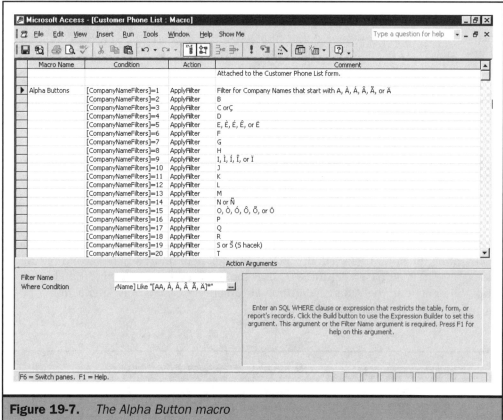

Figure 19-7. *The Alpha Button macro*

> **Note** *Because Northwind Traders deal with customers worldwide, the filter must accommodate alphabet symbols from other languages, as well as English.*

The resulting recordset includes all records whose CompanyName field begins with any of the letters enclosed in brackets in the Where Condition argument.

When no records match the filter, you see an empty datasheet if no provisions are made for that case. If you scroll down the macro actions to the final rows (see Figure 19-8), you can see that if the record count is greater than 0, the records are displayed and the macro stops. The ellipsis (…) in the StopMacro row carries over the condition from the previous row.

If no records are returned by the filter, a message is displayed. When the user clicks OK to clear the message, all the records return to the screen because the SetValue action changes the value of the option group to 27, the number of the All button. The

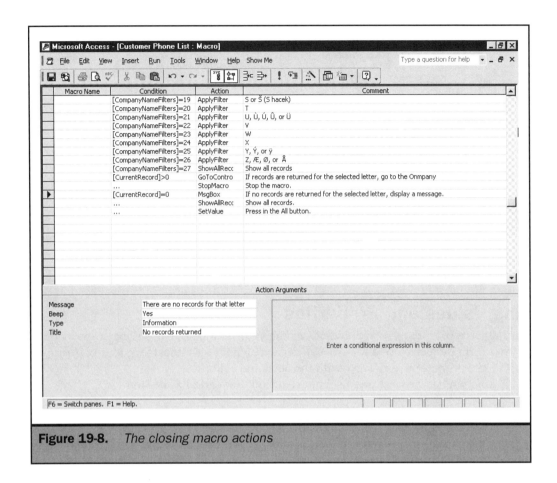

Figure 19-8.   *The closing macro actions*

All button also appears pressed. The condition is carried over three actions in this sequence.

Note *In the last rows of the macro,* [RecordsetClone].[RecordCount] *is used in the condition to represent the number of records returned by the filter. This is a bit of Visual Basic code, where RecordsetClone is a copy of the form's underlying record source, either a table or a query. RecordCount is a property that counts the number of records in the recordset object. So, using the two together returns the number of records in the result of the query that is the basis for the form.*

To see how the macro is attached to the form, switch to Form view and look at the event property sheet for the option group. The After Update event property is set to the Customer Phone List.Alpha Buttons macro, which causes the macro to run when the user clicks one of the buttons in the option group.

IMPROVING THE WORKPLACE

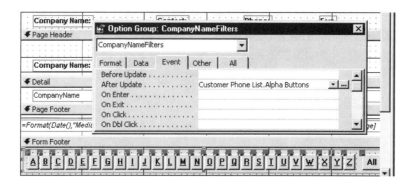

Note *The Alpha Buttons macro is part of a macro group named Customer Phone List. When referring to a macro that's one of a group of macros, you must use the full name:* macrogroupname.macroname. *The names needn't be enclosed in brackets or quotation marks, even if they include spaces. More about macro groups later in this chapter.*

Setting Values and Properties

SetValue is a useful macro action that sets the value of a field, control, or property of a form, a form datasheet, or a report. You can set a value for almost any control, form, and report property in any view with the SetValue action.

The action has two arguments, both required: Item and Expression.

- The *Item argument* contains the name of the field, control, or property whose value you want to set. When you enter the name in the Item argument box, you use the control name if the control is on the form or report from which the macro is called. If the control is on another form or report, you must use the full identifier including the form or report name: Forms!*formname*!*controlname*. If you're setting the value of a property, add the property name to the identifier preceded by a period: Forms!*formname*!*controlname.property*. If it's a form or report property, omit the control name.

Tip *Many of the errors that occur in macro design are the result of incorrect identifiers.*

- The *Expression argument* contains the value you want to set for the item. Again, use full syntax when referring to any Access objects in the expression. Use the Expression Builder if you need help. Don't precede the expression with an equal sign.

Setting Control Values

In addition to entering the value itself, you can set the value of a control based on the value of another control in the same or a different form or report. You can also use the result of a calculation or the value returned by an option group to set the value of a control.

For example, when you're adding new records to the Alpha Entry recordset in the subform of the Alpha Card form, you can compute the value of the Purge field. Depending on the Code value, the entry may be purged from the person's file after a certain length of time, usually three or seven years. To save data entry time, you can write a macro that examines the Code value and uses the DateAdd function to set the Purge date by adding a specified number of years to the Date field value.

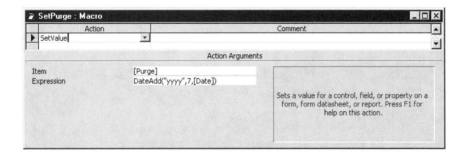

The first argument in the DateAdd function, yyyy, indicates that the interval you want to increment is the year part of the date value. The second argument is the number to add and the third names the control that contains the original date.

When you are setting a control value in a different form from the one that launched the macro, you need to use the complete identifier syntax. For example, to copy the Name field from the Alpha Card form to a new form when certain conditions are met, use the macro shown in Figure 19-9.

Because the macro is called from the Alpha Card form, you normally wouldn't need to use the full syntax for the field whose value you are copying. However, Access recognizes "Name" as a reserved word, representing the name of the current object. So, you must include the complete identifier; otherwise, the value "Alpha Card" appears in the New Form. You can save time and prevent errors if you get in the habit of using the full identifier. You won't have to remember which form called the macro.

The SetValue action triggers table-level validation rules if the control is bound to an underlying field, but it doesn't trigger form-level validation rules. The SetValue action pays little attention to any input mask you defined for the control or its underlying field.

Setting Control Properties

Many of the properties of forms, reports, and controls can be set by running a macro. For example, you can hide a control from view on the form or disable it so the user can't enter data in it. You can also change colors, fonts, and other appearance properties.

As an example of setting a property with a macro, disable the Drivers License control if the subject of the Alpha Card report is younger than 16. To do this, set the Enabled property to No. When a control is disabled, it still appears on the screen, but it's dimmed and you can't reach it by pressing TAB.

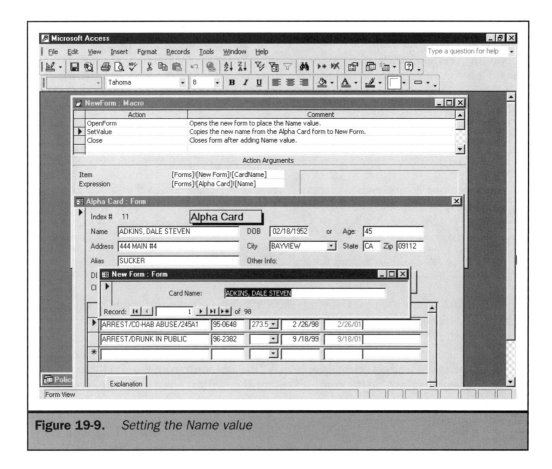

Figure 19-9. *Setting the Name value*

To make sure you enter the correct identifier, you can use the Expression Builder. After adding the SetValue action to the macro, click Build (…) next to the Item argument to open the Expression Builder, and then do the following:

1. Double-click the Forms folder, and then double-click the All Forms folder in the left panel to open the list of forms in the current database.

2. Choose the Alpha Card form. A list of all controls and labels in the form appears in the center panel.

3. Choose Drivers_License. A list of all the properties that apply to the Drivers License text box control appears in the right panel.

4. Choose Enabled and click Paste. Figure 19-10 shows the resulting expression. When you click OK, the expression is placed in the Item argument box.

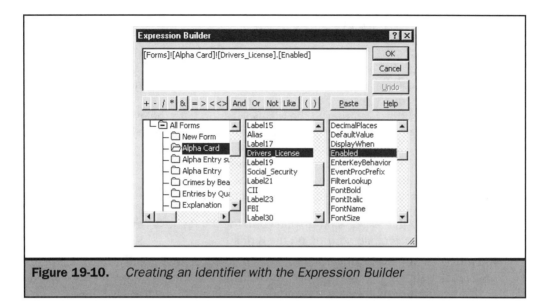

Figure 19-10. *Creating an identifier with the Expression Builder*

To complete the macro, enter No in the Expression argument and add a condition to the action row that runs the macro only if the Age value is less than 16. Then attach the macro to the Age control's After Update event property. You probably want to add another macro to reenable Drivers_License when you move to the next record.

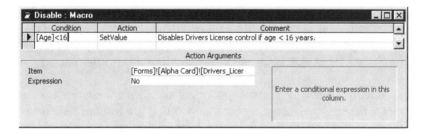

If you want to hide a control, set its Visible property to No.

If the property value is a string expression, enclose it in quotation marks in the Expression argument box.

Note   *Not all properties can be set with macros. Some can only be set in Design view.*

To set section properties, refer to the section by its number.

Changing the Flow of Operations

Adding conditions that determine whether a macro action is carried out is one way to control the flow of operations. If the condition evaluates to True, the corresponding action takes place. You can add the MsgBox function to a macro condition to let the user decide which action to carry out.

The MsgBox function is similar to the MsgBox action with the exception that the function returns one of seven different values, depending on which button the user clicks in the message box. The MsgBox function displays a dialog box containing the message and waits for the user to click a button indicating the user's choice. Several arrangements of buttons are available in the dialog box.

The MsgBox function has three main arguments; only the first is required:

- *Prompt* is a string expression displayed in the dialog box. You can display up to 1,024 characters, depending on the font size.

- *Button* is a number equal to the sum of three values that specify the visual characteristics of the message box, such as the number and type of buttons, the default button, the icon style, and the modality of the message box.

- *Title* is a string expression displayed in the dialog box title bar.

Two additional optional arguments can specify a Help file and context number in the file where you can find context-sensitive help.

You can display seven different buttons in various arrangements, as well as a choice of four icons. You can also specify which of the buttons is the default. Table 19-6 lists the button arrangements and dialog box features with their numeric values. The buttons are placed in the message box in the order—from left to right—they're listed in the table.

For example, if you want the message box to display the Yes, No, and Cancel set of buttons (3) with the Warning Query icon (32) and set the Yes button as the default (0), enter the sum 3+32+0 = **35** as the second argument in the MsgBox function.

> **Note** *The message box normally opens as application modal, which requires the user to respond to the message box before continuing. But, if you want to make it system modal, which suspends all applications in the system until the user responds, add 4096 to the other values in the second argument.*

When the user clicks a button in the message box, the corresponding value is returned, which the macro condition can use to determine the next action to take. Table 19-7 lists the values returned by each type of button.

> **Note** *Each of the values in Tables 19-6 and 19-7 corresponds to a Visual Basic constant, which you can use in a procedure to solicit user response. For example, the value 0, meaning Display only the OK button, corresponds to the constant vbOKOnly.*

Value	Description
	Buttons to display:
0	Display only the OK button.
1	Display the OK and Cancel buttons.
2	Display the Abort, Retry, and Ignore buttons.
3	Display the Yes, No, and Cancel buttons.
4	Display the Yes and No buttons.
5	Display the Retry and Cancel buttons.
	Icons to display:
0	Display no icon.
16	Display the Critical Message icon.
32	Display the Warning Query icon.
48	Display the Warning Message icon.
64	Display the Information Message icon.
	Specify the default button:
0	Set the first button as default.
256	Set the second button as default.
512	Set the third button as default.
768	Set the fourth button as default.
	Specify modality:
0	User must respond before continuing work in current application.
4096	All applications are suspended until user responds to message box.
16384	Adds Help button.
65536	Places message box window in the foreground.
524288	Right-aligns message text.
1048576	Text reads right-to-left on Hebrew and Arabic systems.

Table 19-6. *MsgBox Function Button Argument Settings*

Button	Returned Value
OK	1
Cancel	2
Abort	3
Retry	4
Ignore	5
Yes	6
No	7

Table 19-7.   *Values Returned by MsgBox Function*

When you use the MsgBox function in a macro condition, you can compare the returned value to a specific number and carry out the action if the comparison is True. For example, you can use the MsgBox function to display a confirmation message before deleting a record. The box contains three buttons: Yes, No, and Cancel. If the user clicks the Yes button, the function returns 6, so if any other value is returned, the user didn't click Yes. Figure 19-11 shows a macro using the MsgBox function in a condition that evaluates to True if the function returned any value except 6 (Yes). If the value isn't 6, the deletion event is canceled. You could add other conditions that carry out actions as a result of the other button selections.

Note   *The Button argument in the MsgBox function is 291, the sum of the Yes, No, Cancel button arrangement (3), the Warning Query icon (32), and setting the second button (No) as the default (256).*

After you save the Verify Deletion macro, it's attached to the form's Before Del Confirm event property. The message box displays when you select a record and press DEL. In Figure 19-11, the Alpha Entry record for Index 23 was selected before pressing DEL. You can see it has been deleted from the Form view, but isn't confirmed yet. If you respond by clicking Yes, Access displays another confirmation message if the deletion can result in cascade deletions of other records or interfere in some other way with the relationships in the database.

Synchronizing Data

In Chapter 12, you saw how to add a command button to a form that displays related data in another form. When you click the Explanation button in the Alpha Card form,

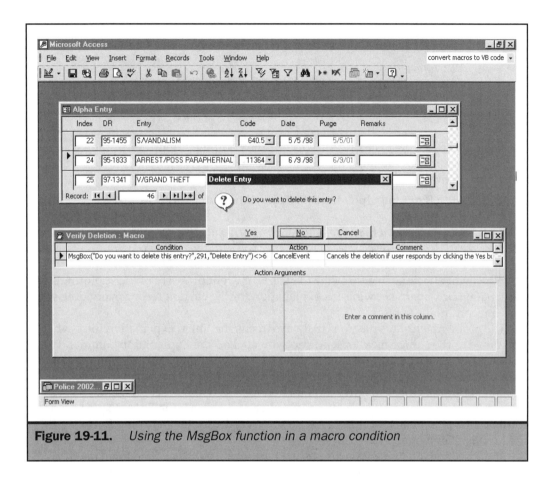

Figure 19-11. *Using the MsgBox function in a macro condition*

the Explanation form opens, showing a more understandable description of the abbreviated Entry field in the Alpha Entry subform.

The only shortcoming of this technique is you must click the button again after you move to another Alpha Entry record if you want to see its explanation. Having the Explanation box synchronize the explanation with the current entry without having to click the command button again would be more convenient.

A simple macro can be used to synchronize the records in the Alpha Entry subform with the records in the Explanation form. The ExplainIt macro contains a single action, OpenForm. The action arguments specify the Explanation form with a Where Condition that shows the Explanation record whose EntryNo matches the EntryNo in the Alpha Entry subform.

Form Name	Explanation
View	Form
Filter Name	
Where Condition	[EntryNo]=[Forms]![Alpha Card]![A
Data Mode	Read Only
Window Mode	Normal

The only tricky part is being sure to use the complete identifier in the Where Condition argument. You must include all parts of the identifier, including the names of both the main form and the subform:

[EntryNo] = [Forms]![Alpha Card]![Alpha Entry subform]![EntryNo]

Note *Be sure you included EntryNo in the Alpha Entry subform, even though you don't want to see it. Set the Visible property to No after you add it to the form design.*

When you attach the macro to the On Current event property of the subform, the Explanation box opens showing the explanation for the current record every time you click a record in the subform.

The problem with this macro is it always opens the Entry Explanation form when you move to the subform, whether or not you clicked the Explanation command button. This can become a nuisance and get in the way of data entry. You need to add a condition if you want to open only the Entry Explanation form when you click the command button. Once the Entry Explanation form is open, synchronize the records with the Alpha Entry subform. The condition checks to see if the Entry Explanation form is already open and, if it is, moves to the record with the matching EntryNo. If the form isn't open, the macro doesn't run.

The Northwind sample database uses a custom Visual Basic function named IsLoaded, which returns Yes if the form is open or No if it isn't open. The only argument for the function is the name of the form. Use this function in a macro condition and execute the macro action only if the form is already open.

Tip *You can copy the module that contains this function from the Northwind Modules window and save it in your database Modules window using the Export command. Right-click the Utility Functions module in the Northwind Database window and choose Export from the shortcut menu. Then locate your database in the Export Module...To dialog box and choose Save. You can accept the same name or enter a new name for the module in the Export dialog box. Then click OK.*

To see the code in the function, select the module in the Database window and choose Design. Don't worry about the statements in the function now. You will learn about statements in Chapter 25.

Figure 19-12 shows the completed macro with the new IsLoaded function added as a condition.

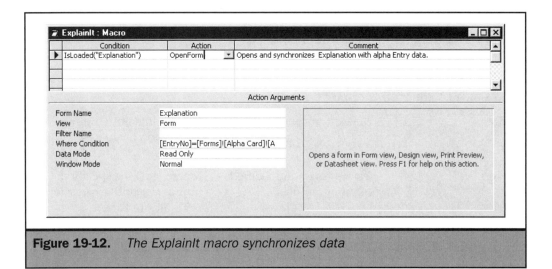

Figure 19-12. *The ExplainIt macro synchronizes data*

Nesting Macros

If you want to run one macro from another, use the RunMacro action and set the Macro Name argument to the name of the macro you want to run. The RunMacro action is similar to choosing Tools | Macro | Run Macro, and then selecting the macro name. The only difference is the Tools command runs the macro only once. With the RunMacro action, you can repeat the macro many times.

The RunMacro action has two arguments in addition to the Macro Name:

- Repeat Count, which specifies the maximum number of times the macro is to run.

- Repeat Expression, which contains an expression that evaluates to True (-1) or False (0). The expression is evaluated each time the RunMacro action occurs. When it evaluates to False, the called macro stops.

The Repeat Count and Repeat Expression arguments work together to specify how many times the macro runs. Table 19-8 describes the number of times the RunMacro action occurs and the called macro runs when both arguments are used.

When the called macro is finished, Access returns to the calling macro and runs the next action after RunMacro.

You can call a macro in the same macro group, as well as a macro in another group. If you enter a macro group name as the Macro Name argument, the first macro in the group runs.

Repeat Count Argument Value	Repeat Expression Argument Value	
	Blank	Expression
Blank	Macro runs once.	Macro runs until the expression evaluates to False.
Number	Macro runs the specified number of times.	Macro runs the specified number or until expression evaluates to False, whichever occurs first.

Table 19-8.   *Running the Macro More Than Once*

You can nest macros to more than one level. The called macro can, in turn, call another macro, and so on. As each macro finishes, it returns control to the macro that called it.

Macros vs. VB Event Procedures

You can accomplish a lot with macros but, at times, you need to use a Visual Basic procedure instead. Macros are easy to create and relatively error-free, while procedures require programming and are more difficult, especially for the beginner. When you need to automate a process in your database, deciding whether to use a macro or Visual Basic depends on what you want to do.

When to Use Macros

Macros are best for accomplishing simple tasks such as opening and closing forms, running reports, and displaying custom toolbars. Access provides a list of actions to choose from and helps with the setting of action arguments. You must use a macro in two cases:

- When you want to assign specific actions to a key combination for global use in the entire database.
- When you want a series of actions to take place when the database starts up. The Startup options can also execute some actions, such as opening a switchboard form at startup. Macro actions occur after those set for startup.

When to Use Visual Basic

Using Visual Basic procedures instead of macros creates a more easily maintained database because the procedures are stored with the form or report definition and are always available. Macros are treated as separate Access objects and are stored individually. You can also create custom functions with Visual Basic to perform special calculations or logical operations.

If you want to trap and respond to run-time errors, you must use an event procedure assigned to an On Error event property.

If you want to process a set of records—one record at a time—you need to create a procedure to handle the transactions.

Many more reasons exist to use Visual Basic when you are creating automated database management applications. See Chapter 25 for an introduction to the art of designing and writing Visual Basic code.

Creating a Macro Group

If you create several macros that apply to controls on the same form or report, you can group them together as one file. Using macro groups offers two advantages:

- It reduces the number of macro names in the Database window.

- You can find all the macros for a single form or report in one place where they're easy to edit, if necessary.

To create a macro group, open the macro sheet as usual and display the Macro Name column by clicking the Macro Names button or choosing View | Macro Names. Add a macro to the sheet and enter a name for it in the Macro Name column of the first row of the macro. Add the rest of the actions to the macro.

To add another macro, enter the name in the Macro Name column and add the actions you want to occur.

When Access runs a macro in a group, it begins with the action in the row that contains the macro name and continues until it finds no more actions or encounters another macro name. After adding all the macros to the group, close and save it as usual with the group name.

Tip *The macros in a group are much easier to read if you leave at least one blank row between the macros.*

When you assign macros from a group to an event property, you need to use the group name, as well as the macro name. In the property sheet for a control, the drop-down list in an event property shows compound names for all the macros in a group, as well as the names of all the single macros. The group name and the macro name both appear separated by a period: *macrogroupname.macroname*.

Assigning AutoKeys

Access offers a special macro group named *AutoKeys,* in which you can assign an action or set of actions to a specific key or key combination. Pressing the key or combination of keys carries out the action you specify. You can add as many individual macros to the group as you need, each one named with the key or key combination that runs it.

For example, the following macro opens the Alpha Card form when the user presses CTRL-F.

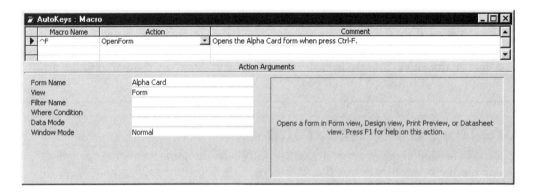

If you use a key combination Access already uses, such as CTRL-C *for Copy, your actions replace the Access key assignment.*

Table 19-9 shows a list of valid AutoKeys key combinations. These combinations are part of the set that can be used by the Visual Basic SendKeys statement. The SendKey syntax form is used as the macro name. The carat symbol (^) represents CTRL and the plus sign (+) represents SHIFT. Function keys and other key names are enclosed in curly brackets.

Key Combination	SendKey Syntax for Macro Name
CTRL+Any letter or number key	^A, ^4
Any function key	{F1}
CTRL+Any function key	^{F1}
SHIFT+Any function key	+{F1}
INS	{INSERT}

Table 19-9. *AutoKeys Key Combinations*

Key Combination	SendKey Syntax for Macro Name
CTRL+INS	^{INSERT}
SHIFT+INS	+{INSERT}
DEL	{DELETE} or {DEL}
CTRL+DEL	^{DELETE} or ^{DEL}
SHIFT+DEL	+{DELETE} or +{DEL}

Table 19-9.   *AutoKeys Key Combinations* (continued)

Documenting Macros

Because macros are database objects, they're listed in the database Properties dialog box on the Contents tab. To view the list, choose File | Properties and click the Contents tab. Then scroll down the list until your reach the macro section.

If you want to keep documentation for the macros and macro groups in your database, you can print the macro description. With the macro name selected in the Database window, choose File | Print or click Print. In the Print Macro Definition dialog box, check the categories of information you want to print:

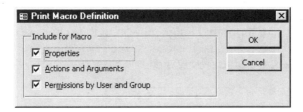

- ■ *Properties* includes the container, date created, date of last update, owner, and user.

- ■ *Actions and Arguments* lists all the actions with their conditions, if any, and the values of all the arguments.

- ■ *Permissions by User and Group* lists user permissions, such as admin, and group permissions, such as Admins and Users.

Note   *If you only want to view the definition on the screen, choose File | Print Preview instead of File | Print and make the same selections in the Print Macro Definition dialog box.*

Creating an AutoExec Macro

You can create a special macro that runs when you first open a database. The AutoExec macro can carry out such actions as open a form for data entry, display a message box prompting the user to enter his or her name, or play a sound greeting.

All you must do is create the macro with the actions you want carried out at startup and save it with the name, AutoExec. A database can have only one macro named AutoExec.

When you open a database, all the startup options you set in the Startup dialog box take place first. Then Access looks for a macro named AutoExec, if one exists, and executes the actions in it.

You can bypass both the startup options and the AutoExec macro by pressing SHIFT when you open the database.

Caution   *Many of the same options can be set in the AutoExec macro as in the Startup dialog box. Be careful not to include conflicting settings in the macro. See Chapter 18 for information about the startup settings.*

Converting Macros to Visual Basic Code

Working with macros gives you a good introduction to writing Visual Basic code because many similarities exist. All the macro actions have equivalent Visual Basic methods with the same name.

You can convert all the macros you created for a form or report to Visual Basic procedures that are saved with the form or report object. Then you can remove the macro object from the Database window. To convert the macros associated with a form, open the form or report in Design view, and then choose Tools | Macro | Convert Form's Macros to Visual Basic. If you're converting a report's macros, choose Convert Report's Macros to Visual Basic.

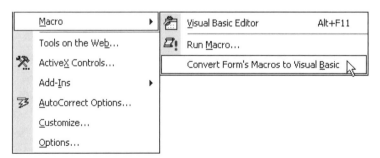

If you created a special macro that isn't associated with a specific form or report, such as the AutoKeys or AutoExec macro, you can still convert it to code using a different method. Open the macro in Design view and choose File | Save As. Then choose Module from the As list in the Save As dialog box and click OK.

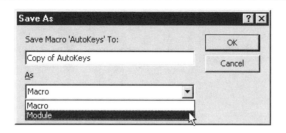

The next dialog box gives you the option of including error-handling code with the generated functions and the macro comments in the module. Make your selections, and then click Convert. After the conversion is complete, you'll find a module with the same name as the macro in the Modules tab of the Database window.

Summary

Properly constructed macros carry out actions when you want them to and in the way you want. They're useful for responding to user input and manipulating data. As you work with macros, you can begin to see their potential. An additional advantage to working with macros is the experience actually prepares you for the step into Visual Basic coding.

In the next two chapters, macros are used to customize command bars and to create switchboard forms that open when you start an application. The switchboards give the user a list of activities from which to choose, such as enter or edit data, preview a report, or go to another list of activities.

MOUS Exam Activities Explored in This Chapter

This chapter contains no information directly related to the MOUS Certification Exam activities, although the information is important to understanding how to use Access for effective database management.

Chapter 20

Customizing Menus and Toolbars

In Access 97, Microsoft began blending the three types of user interaction tools into a single global concept: the command bar. While the terms *toolbars, menu bars,* and *shortcut menus* are still valid in Access 2002 and do describe differing implementations, the methods used to create and modify custom command bars are the same for all types. The purpose is to make them more consistent, as well as easier to use and customize.

Many of the command bar elements are interchangeable among the three types. For example, you can add toolbar button images to menu bars and shortcut menus or add menus and menu commands to toolbars.

You've worked with all these interaction tools extensively during the previous chapters in this book and when running other Office programs. In this chapter, you see how to work with and customize built-in command bars, as well as create custom command bars for an application.

Using Access Command Bars

The basic element of toolbars, menu bars, and shortcut menus is the command the user chooses to cause an action to take place, such as to print a report or run a query. You reach a command by the single act of clicking a toolbar button or by making choices from a hierarchy of menus and submenus.

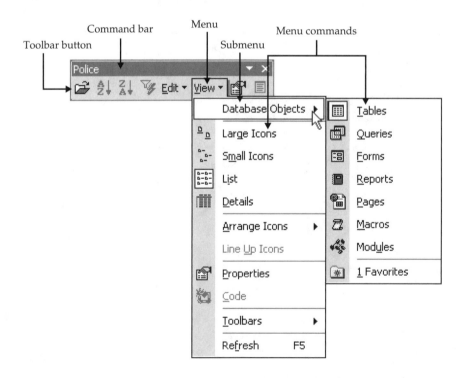

The command can appear as a button with an image or a menu command showing text. Menu commands with equivalent toolbar buttons often also display the icon that appears on the button. You can set options, so both menu commands and buttons can show text and images.

The commands can be grouped as a set of items in several ways:

- In a menu such as the New, Open, Get External Data, and Close commands on the File menu.

- On a toolbar such as the Save, Print, and Spelling buttons on the Form View toolbar.

- In a shortcut menu such as Cut, Copy, and Paste commands.

- In a submenu such as the Import and Link Tables commands on the File | Get External Data submenu.

In any of these groupings, the individual commands can be represented by images, text, or both.

Some command bars are classified as *global* and are available to any database or application. *Built-in* command bars are predefined and are automatically displayed in specific views in any database. *Custom* command bars are user-defined and are limited to the database in which they were created. Custom command bars can also be attached to specific forms or reports.

IMPROVING THE WORKPLACE

Access 2002 Personalizes Your Command Bars

Access 2002 automatically personalizes your menus and toolbars to fit your needs. When you first start Access, only the most basic commands appear in the menu bar. These appear in the short version of the menu. The other commands are relegated to the expanded menu, which you can see by double-clicking the menu or clicking the arrows at the bottom of the list of commands.

When you expand the menu, the additional commands appear dimmed—not because they are unavailable, but because they haven't been used lately. If you expand one menu, all the other menus appear expanded until you choose a command or close the menu.

When you choose a command that was on the expanded list, it's added to the short version. If you don't use it for a while, it reverts to the expanded list.

To save room on the screen, you can place toolbars next to each other on the same row across the screen. If there isn't enough space to show all the buttons, only the most commonly used buttons appear at first. If you want to see a list of all the buttons on the toolbars, click Toolbar Options at the end of the toolbar and choose Add or Remove Buttons. To add a button to the visible toolbar, check the button's name in the drop-down list. Buttons that weren't used recently, like menu commands, are dropped to the Toolbar Options list.

Showing/Hiding Built-in Toolbars

The built-in Access toolbars appear automatically in certain contexts. For example, when you're in Form Design view, the default toolbars are Form Design and Formatting (Form/Report). If you right-click one of the toolbars, you see that you can also display several other toolbars.

To add toolbars not in the list to the window, open the Customize dialog box (see Figure 20-1) using one of the following methods:

■ Choose Customize at the bottom of the shortcut menu.

■ Choose View | Toolbars | Customize.

■ Choose Tools | Customize.

The Toolbars tab of the Customize dialog box contains a list of all the available toolbars, both built-in and custom. Click the check box of any toolbar you want to add to the display, and then click Close.

As you can see in the figure, the two default toolbars for the Form Design view are already checked, as well as Menu Bar, the global menu. To remove them from the display, clear the check mark and click Close. Toolbars are immediately added to or removed from the screen behind the dialog box when you click a check box in the Customize dialog box. You cannot remove the global Menu Bar this way.

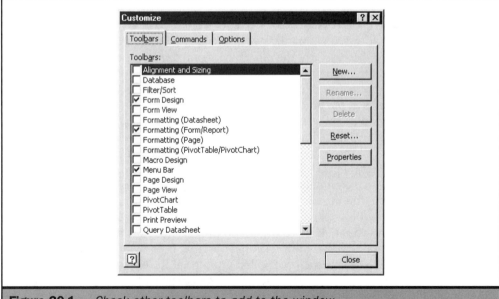

Figure 20-1. *Check other toolbars to add to the window*

You can also remove a toolbar from the display by right-clicking any toolbar and removing the check mark from the name in the drop-down list. If the toolbar isn't the default for this view, the name will also be removed from the drop-down list. Default toolbar names remain on that list even though they aren't showing.

Note   *If you open a toolbar in a view it doesn't normally appear in, it stays on the screen until you close it, even if you close and open the database. Similarly, if you close a toolbar in a context where it normally appears, the toolbar remains closed until you reopen it. To reopen the toolbar, check it in the Customize dialog box's list of toolbars or right-click in a toolbar and check the toolbar in the drop-down list.*

The drop-down list of available toolbars includes Web in any Access view. Other toolbars are optionally available in many views. Table 20-1 lists the Access view windows and indicates which built-in toolbars are displayed by default or are available from the drop-down list besides the Task Pane, Web, and any custom toolbars you created.

View	Default and Optional Toolbars
Database window	Database
Filter By Form or Advanced Filter/Sort	Filter/Sort
Form Design view	Form Design, Formatting (Form/Report), Toolbox
Form view	Form View, Formatting (Form/Report)*
Macro Design view	Macro Design
Page Design view	Data Outline, Field List, Formatting (Page), Page Design, Toolbox
Page view	Page View, Formatting (Page)*
Print Preview	Print Preview
Query Datasheet view	Query Datasheet, Formatting (Datasheet)
Query Design view	Query Design

* The formatting toolbars are available in Form or Page view only if their Allow Design Changes property is set to All Views.

Table 20-1.   *Access Views and Their Available Toolbars*

View	Default and Optional Toolbars
Relationships window	Relationship
Report Design view	Report Design, Formatting (Form/Report), Toolbox
Table Datasheet view	Table Datasheet, Formatting (Datasheet)
Table Design view	Table Design
Visual Basic Editor view	Standard (Visual Basic), Debug, Edit, UserForm (Visual Basic)

Table 20-1. *Access Views and Their Available Toolbars* (continued)

The names of three additional toolbars that aren't defaults for any view appear in the Toolbars list in the Customize dialog box:

- The Source Code Control toolbar displays buttons you can use to control changes while creating Visual Basic code in a multiple-developer environment.

- The Utility 1 and Utility 2 toolbars are empty, built-in toolbars you can use to create custom global toolbars, as described in a later section in this chapter.

Two other items on the Toolbars list that aren't really toolbars are Menu Bar and Shortcut Menus. Menu Bar displays the default menu bar for the current view. The names of any new custom menus you create appear at the end of the list.

Note *The default property settings of the Menu Bar command bar don't let you remove it from the display. If you try to clear Menu Bar, a beep sounds. To remove the menu bar from the screen, you need to check the Allow Showing/Hiding property. More about changing command bar properties in the "Modifying Command Bars" section.*

When you check Shortcut Menus in the Toolbars list, a menu bar is displayed containing all the built-in shortcut menus. As shown in Figure 20-2, clicking Table on the Shortcut Menus menu bar displays a list of shortcut menus associated with various elements of a table object, such as Datasheet View Title Bar or Design View Upper Pane. When you click one of the elements in the list, you see the shortcut menu that displays when you right-click that part of the table.

If you create custom shortcut menus, the names aren't displayed separately in the Toolbars list. Instead, they're listed as menu items in the Custom category on the Shortcut Menus menu bar.

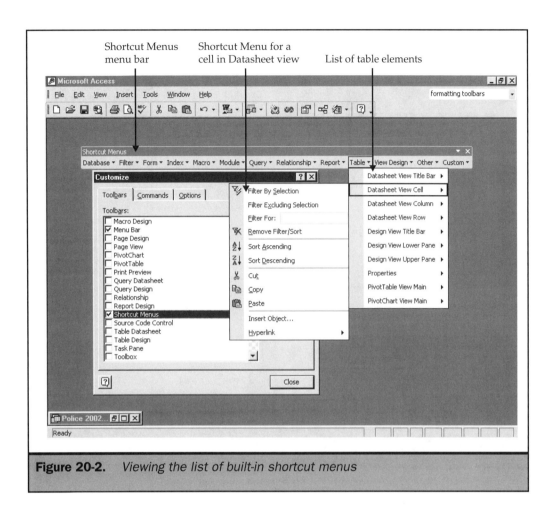

Figure 20-2. *Viewing the list of built-in shortcut menus*

Showing/Hiding Toolbar Buttons

You needn't display all the default toolbar buttons on a toolbar. Using the Toolbar Options button, you have a choice of which buttons to display. Click the Toolbar Options button on the right end of the toolbar (or at the right end of the title bar next to the Close button if the toolbar is floating) to display the list of buttons available to that toolbar. Then click the Add or Remove Buttons drop-down arrow and point to the toolbar name in the list of toolbar buttons currently showing. Figure 20-3 shows the list of buttons normally displayed on the Table Datasheet toolbar. The arrow at the end of the list indicates additional buttons aren't in view.

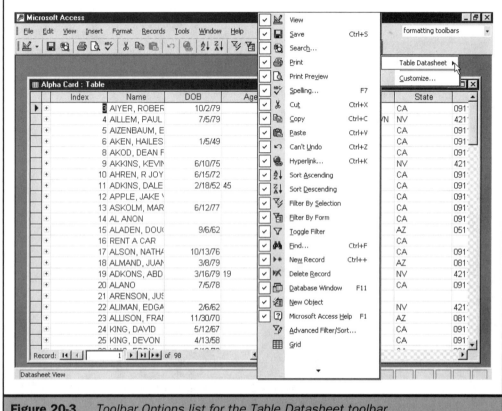

Figure 20-3.   *Toolbar Options list for the Table Datasheet toolbar*

To remove a button, clear the check mark next to the button name. To restore the button to the toolbar, check it in the list again.

Note   *When you remove a button from the toolbar, the equivalent menu command isn't removed from the menu.*

You also have a choice of resetting the toolbar to its original default button set or opening the Customize dialog box to make more complex changes.

Moving/Resizing Command Bars

A command bar is *docked* if it's fixed to one side of the window. Menu bars and toolbars normally appear docked at the top of the window. You can drag them away from the edge and turn them into *floating* command bars, which can be moved about on the screen. A docked command bar has no title bar, while a floating command bar has an identifying title bar. The Form and Report Design Toolbox is an example of a toolbar that is, by default, a floating toolbar, which can be docked if you want.

 When a toolbar is floating, the Toolbar Options button is at the right end of the title bar next to the Close button. When a menu bar is floating, the Toolbar Options button is also at the right end of the title bar.

To move a toolbar or menu bar from its docked position, click-and-drag its moving handle (the stack of small dash lines at the left end of the bar). You can also click an empty space or any separator bar in the menu bar or a toolbar to drag it away from the dock.

To dock the command bar to an edge of the window, drag it to the side until it spreads to the full height or width of the window.

 You can dock a command bar at any edge of the window unless you set the bar's Docking property to restrict its placement. More about setting command bar properties later in the "Modifying Command Bars" section.

After moving the command bar away from the edge of the window, you can drag the toolbar borders to change the height and width of the bar. To close a floating toolbar, click the Close button in the title bar. You cannot close a floating menu bar because it doesn't include a Close button.

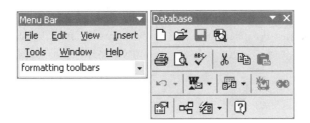

You can also change the arrangement of the menu bar and the toolbars when they're docked. For example, if you want the toolbar to appear above the menu bar, click the toolbar's moving handle and drag it over the menu bar.

Changing Menu and Toolbar Options

In addition to repositioning and resizing a built-in menu or toolbar, you can use the Options tab of the Customize dialog box (see Figure 20-4) to set other features. The upper pane sets options for the menus and toolbars as personalized by Access. The lower pane contains options that change the way command bars look and behave. Table 20-2 describes the effects of each option.

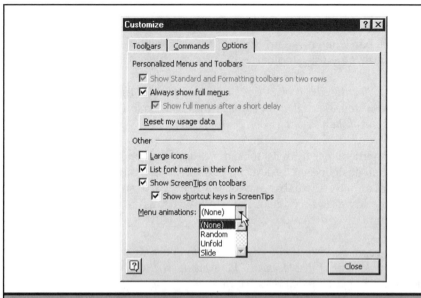

Figure 20-4. *The Options tab of the Customize dialog box*

Option	Description
Show Standard and Formatting toolbars on two rows	Displays the two default toolbars that appear when you're editing a chart in Access in separate rows.
Always show full menus	Shows all commands on menus. Clear the check mark for this option to show only the basic or frequently used commands on personalized versions of the menus. Affects all Office programs.
Show full menus after a short delay	Expands the menu when you open the menu and rest the mouse pointer on it. Always checked unless previous option is cleared; then it may also be cleared.

Table 20-2. *Menu and Toolbar Options*

Option	Description
Reset my usage data	Clears the menu and toolbar settings that were automatically saved as you chose menu commands and toolbar buttons.
Large icons	Displays larger button images. Affects all Office programs.
List font names in their font	Displays the drop-down list of fonts in the Formatting toolbars as a sample of the font.
Show ScreenTips on toolbars	Displays the name of the button when the mouse pointer rests on it. Affects all Office programs.
Show shortcut keys in ScreenTips	Includes the shortcut key combination to the button name in the ScreenTip. Affects all Office programs except Excel.
Menu animations	Determines the way menus react when displayed. Choices are Random, Unfold, Slide, and (None), the default.

Table 20-2.   *Menu and Toolbar Options* (continued)

The following toolbar has large icons and displays both ScreenTips and shortcut keys. Notice the double arrows at the right end of the toolbar, indicating additional buttons are out of view off screen.

These option settings all remain in effect until you change them.

Hiding the Windows Taskbar

If you want to have more free space in your Access window, you can hide the Windows taskbar that normally appears at the bottom of the screen. You have two ways of hiding the taskbar:

- The easiest way is to move the mouse pointer to the top edge of the taskbar and, when it changes to a double-pointed vertical arrow, drag the taskbar down off the screen. To restore the taskbar to the screen, move the pointer to the bottom and drag the visible edge back up to the screen.

- The second method is to use the Auto Hide property. Auto Hide moves the taskbar off the screen when you aren't accessing it. To set this property, right-click an empty area of the taskbar and choose Properties from the shortcut menu. In the Taskbar Options tab of the Taskbar Properties dialog box, click Auto Hide, and then click OK. The taskbar disappears from the screen. To restore it temporarily, move the pointer to the area where the taskbar last appeared, such as the bottom of the screen, and it'll pop into view. To restore it permanently, clear the Auto Hide property.

In Windows 98, after you close the Taskbar Properties dialog box, click anywhere in the desktop to hide the taskbar.

You can also move the taskbar to a different position on the screen by clicking an empty area between two buttons and dragging it to another side of the window. The taskbar won't float on the desktop; it must be docked at one side of the window.

Customizing Command Bars

Access provides so many useful menu bars and toolbars, why would anyone want to create custom command bars? One reason could be you don't want the user to be able to make changes in a form or report design. You can remove the View button from the toolbar to keep the user from switching to Design view.

Other possible customizations are

- Adding a Save Record button to the toolbar, so the user can quickly test the validity of the data just entered without leaving the record.

- Removing the New Object button from the toolbar to keep the user from designing new forms, reports, or other Access objects.

- Tailoring the commands and button options to match the terminology and practice of a specific application.

The same dialog box is used to create and customize all three types of command bars. As discussed earlier, the Customize dialog box is reached by one of three methods:

- Choosing View | Toolbars | Customize.

- Choosing Tools | Customize.
- Right-clicking anywhere on a toolbar or menu bar, and then choosing Customize from the shortcut menu.

Modifying built-in command bars and creating new custom command bars use the same techniques and tools. The difference between a modified built-in command bar and a new customized command bar is that the modified command bar is available to all databases, while the custom bar is available only to the database where it was created.

In the Customize dialog box, you can do any of the following:

- Choose any of the built-in toolbars or menu bars to make changes.
- Create new global or custom command bars.
- Select a command to place on a command bar and specify how it will appear: as an icon, text, or both.
- Choose options, such as displaying ScreenTips and increasing the size of the icons for individual command bars.

After adding menu commands and buttons to a new or modified command bar, you can set many of its properties to achieve the appearance and behavior you want. For example, you can control whether the command bar can be docked, moved, or resized, and even specify the type of animation to show when commands are selected. You can change button icons and also create your own images.

The Customize dialog box also contains the option to restore a modified built-in command bar to its original state.

Note *When designing a new custom toolbar or menu bar, give some thought to the arrangement of buttons and menus on the bar. If you're using buttons and menus the user may already be accustomed to using, try to keep them in the same relative arrangement in the custom toolbar or menu bar. Also try to keep the menu commands in the same menus as with the Access default menus, rather than adding them to other menus where they may be difficult to find.*

Creating a Global Toolbar

You have two ways to create a custom toolbar that's available to all your databases: modify a built-in toolbar or create a new global toolbar. The list of available toolbars in the Customize dialog box includes the blank Utility 1 and Utility 2 built-in toolbars. When you add buttons and menu commands to them, they become custom global toolbars and are available to all the databases and Access client projects. They actually are treated as modified built-in toolbars, not custom toolbars.

Note *You cannot rename the global toolbars created in Utility 1 and Utility 2. You can modify them later if you need to place different buttons and menu commands on them or you can modify a different built-in toolbar to use as a global toolbar.*

Creating Custom Toolbars and Menu Bars

Whether you're creating a new custom toolbar, a menu bar, or a shortcut menu, it all begins the same way:

1. Open the Customize dialog box using one of the methods described earlier.

2. Click the Toolbars tab, click New, and then type a name for the new toolbar in the New Toolbar dialog box.

3. Click OK. A tiny, empty toolbar appears in front of the Customize dialog box and the toolbar name, Alpha Card, appears in the Toolbars box.

4. On the Toolbars tab, click Properties. The Toolbar Properties dialog box opens (see Figure 20-5).

5. Here's where the processes diverge. Do one of the following:

   ■ To continue with a custom toolbar, set the toolbar properties, as described next.

   ■ If you want to create a new menu bar, choose Menu Bar from the Type list and then set the properties.

   ■ If you want to create a new shortcut menu, choose Popup from the Type list and set the properties.

6. Choose Close when you finish setting the properties.

The Selected Toolbar box in the Toolbar Properties dialog box shows the name of the toolbar. Click the down arrow to see the list of all toolbars, menu bars, and shortcut menus in the current database. Table 20-3 describes each of the properties you can set for custom toolbars and menu bars. Although the properties are called Toolbar Properties, they apply equally to menu bars. Shortcut menus have fewer properties available.

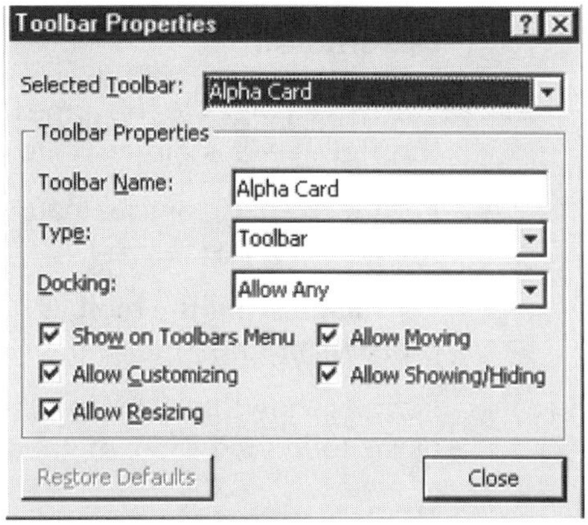

Figure 20-5.   *The Toolbar Properties dialog box*

Property	Description
Toolbar Name	Shows the name entered in the New Toolbar dialog box or the name of the selected built-in toolbar. Edit the name here, if desired.
Type	Shows the type of the selected toolbar. Toolbar is the default setting. Click the arrow to see a list of command bar types: Menu Bar, Toolbar, and Popup (shortcut menu). To change the type of a selected command bar, choose a different type.
Docking	Specifies the type of docking you want to permit for this toolbar: Allow Any (default), Can't Change, No Vertical (limits docking to the top and bottom of the screen), or No Horizontal (limits docking to the sides of the screen). If you choose any setting but Can't Change, be sure to select Allow Moving, too.
Show on Toolbars Menu	Displays the toolbar name in the list when you right-click a toolbar or choose View | Toolbars.

Table 20-3.   *Toolbar Properties*

Property	Description
Allow Customizing	Permits changes to the appearance and behavior through the Customize dialog box.
Allow Resizing	Permits resizing of the floating toolbar. Docked toolbars can't be resized.
Allow Moving	Permits moving the toolbar between the docked position and floating.
Allow Showing/Hiding	Permits showing or hiding the toolbar with any of the following three methods:
	■ Right-click a toolbar and check or clear the toolbar in the shortcut menu.
	■ Choose View	Toolbars and check or clear the toolbar name in the list.
	■ Check or clear the toolbar name in the Customize dialog box.

Table 20-3. *Toolbar Properties* (continued)

Note *If you change the toolbar type to Popup to create a shortcut menu, the only property available is Allow Customizing. All others are dimmed. Access displays a warning if you try to change a toolbar or menu to a popup.*

After setting the desired properties for the new toolbar, menu bar, or shortcut menu, you can proceed to add buttons and menus.

If you're modifying a built-in toolbar, some of the properties aren't available. For example, the Toolbar Name and Type properties are dimmed because you can't rename a built-in toolbar or change its type. Also, the Show on Toolbars Menu option is dimmed because the built-in toolbars in context with the current view are always shown on the list when you right-click the toolbar or choose View | Toolbars. The Restore Defaults button, which you can click to restore a built-in toolbar to its original condition, does become available, however.

Adding/Deleting Toolbar Buttons

Once you begin creating a new toolbar, you can add buttons to it in two ways:

- Copy or move a built-in or a previously created custom button from another toolbar.

- Select the button from the list of commands in the Commands tab of the Customize dialog box.

Figure 20-6 shows the commands in the Query Design toolbar. The commands in the list that show an ellipsis (...) after the text, such as Parameters, open a dialog box. Ones with a vertical bar and a black triangle, such as Query Type, open a submenu.

Many types of commands are available in the Commands box, including the built-in buttons that appear in built-in toolbars. The commands are grouped into categories. Click the desired category to see the commands available in that category. You may have to examine more than one category to find the button you want—some are stored in unusual categories.

Table 20-4 lists some other types of buttons you can add from the Command box. Many of them apply to objects in the current database.

Note *You can also add buttons that run Visual Basic code.*

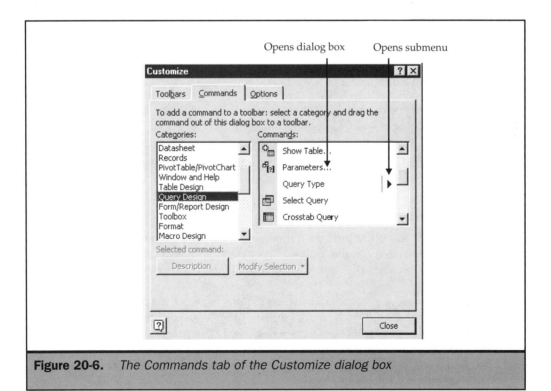

Figure 20-6. *The Commands tab of the Customize dialog box*

Category	Includes Buttons That
ActiveX Controls	Create custom controls
All Forms	Display a form in Form view
All Macros	Run a macro
All Queries	Display a query in Datasheet view
All Reports	Display a report in Print Preview
All Tables	Display a table in Datasheet view
All Web Pages	Display a data access page in Page view
Source Code Control	Help protect and manage source code in a multiple-developer environment
Tools	Start Office Links and analyzers, run a macro, back up and restore files, and start other tools and managers

Table 20-4.   *Categories of Commands*

To add a button from the Customize dialog box:

1. Choose the type of command you want in the Categories list. The Commands list shows images and text of commands in that category.

2. To see more information about a command, select the command and click Description. The description shows the button ScreenTip and tells you what the command does.

3. When you find the button you want, drag it to the toolbar. When you see a dark I-beam, drop the button on the toolbar.

4. Continue to add other buttons to the toolbar. You can drop a button between two buttons already in the toolbar. The bar expands as you add buttons. To move a button already in place, drag it to the desired position.

Tip   *If you want to use the button to open a specific form or report, or you want to run a query, choose All Forms, All Reports, or All Queries in the Categories list. The Commands box then shows the names of all the objects of that type in the current database. Drag the name of the object from the Commands box to the toolbar. The default button for that type of object appears on the toolbar—for example, the Form View button for a form or the Print Preview button for a report.*

If another toolbar has a button you can use, you can move or copy it to the new toolbar. Using an existing button is easier than starting from scratch. An additional advantage is, when you copy or move a command from a built-in toolbar, the command keeps all the pointers to Access Help topics.

Caution   *Moving a button from one toolbar to another removes it from the source toolbar.*

You must have both toolbars showing to do this. The Customize dialog box may be open or closed. To copy a button from another toolbar:

- If the Customize dialog box is open, hold down CTRL while you drag the button.
- If the Customize dialog box isn't open, hold down CTRL-ALT while you drag the button.

Caution   *If you copy a built-in button, the copy isn't independent of the original button. If you make changes to the copy of the button, the same changes also affect the built-in button. If you intend to make changes to the button, creating a new custom toolbar and dragging the buttons from the Commands box is better.*

To move a button from another toolbar:

- If the Customize dialog box is open, drag the button to the new toolbar.
- If the Customize dialog box isn't open, hold down ALT while you drag the button.

Tip   *If you want to add a button that opens a database object in its default view, you can simply drag the object from the Database window to the toolbar. The Customize dialog box must be closed to do this. The button ScreenTip displays the name of the object it opens.*

To remove a button with the Customize dialog box open, drag it off the toolbar or right-click the button and choose Delete from the shortcut menu. When you delete a built-in button, it's still available from the Commands box, but deleting a custom button removes it permanently. If the Customize dialog box isn't open, hold down ALT while you drag the button off the toolbar.

Tip   *If you want to keep custom buttons for later use instead of deleting them completely, create a new toolbar for storing them until you need them. Move the buttons from one toolbar to the other, and then hide the new toolbar by clearing the check mark in the Toolbars box of the Customize dialog box.*

You can customize toolbar buttons in many ways, including adding text and shortcut keys. Buttons on a toolbar may be grouped by category or special purpose with vertical separator bars. See the section, "Modifying Command Bars," for information about customizing toolbar buttons and menu commands.

Adding Built-in Menus

You can add built-in menus to a toolbar or a menu bar by the same two methods: drag from the Commands box of the Customize dialog box, or move or copy from an existing toolbar or menu bar. The only difference between adding toolbar buttons and menus is that the menus, by default, show only text, while the buttons show only an image. These properties can be changed and customized.

With the new menu bar or toolbar showing, open the Customize dialog box and click the Commands tab. Scroll down the Categories list and select Built-in Menus. Figure 20-7 shows some of the available built-in menus.

Drag the menu you want to add from the Commands box to the menu bar or toolbar, and then drop the menu when you see the dark I-beam.

Moving and copying menus is the same as moving and copying buttons. Deleting built-in menus is also the same as deleting buttons.

Most of the commands in the built-in menu are carried over, depending on the context of the new menu bar or toolbar.

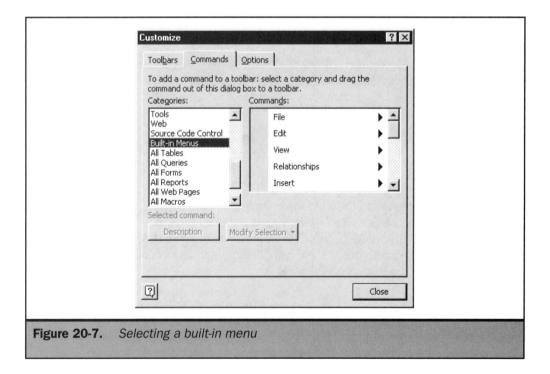

Figure 20-7.   *Selecting a built-in menu*

Adding Custom Menus

If you want to add a custom menu to a toolbar or menu bar, you create it in place on the bar. To add a new custom menu, do the following:

1. With the toolbar or menu bar showing, open the Customize dialog box and click the Commands tab.

2. Click New Menu in the Categories dialog box.

3. Drag New Menu from the Commands box to the menu bar or toolbar.

4. Right-click the new menu and enter a name in the Name box of the shortcut menu and press ENTER.

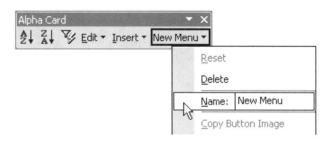

5. Add commands to the new menu by choosing from the Commands dialog box or moving or copying from other menus.

Adding Menu Commands to a Toolbar or Menu Bar

Menu commands can be added to both toolbars and menu bars using the same procedure. The menu commands are placed in a column under the menu in the menu bar or toolbar.

IMPROVING THE WORKPLACE

To add a menu command, do the following:

1. With the menu bar, toolbar, or shortcut menu showing, open the Customize dialog box and click the Commands tab.

2. Click the appropriate menu or view category in the Categories box.

3. Drag the command from the Commands box over the menu in the menu bar or toolbar. When you see the list of commands already in the menu (or, if the menu is new, an empty box) and drag the command to the position where you want it to appear, a horizontal bar appears in the drop-down menu just above the position where the command is to be inserted. When the bar is in the right place, release the mouse. If the menu is new, release the mouse button over the empty box.

In the following example, the Print Preview command is added as the first command in the new custom menu, Forms/Reports.

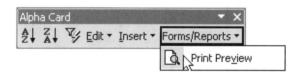

| Note | *If you add a menu command to a built-in menu, such as the File menu that appears in more than one view, that command appears in all views of the menu.* |

You can also move or copy a menu command from another menu bar, toolbar, or shortcut menu. If you're moving or copying a menu command to a menu in a different menu bar or toolbar, both the source and destination bars must be showing. The Customize dialog box must also be open to move or copy a menu command.

■ To move the command, drag it over the menu where you want it to appear and, when you see the list of the commands in the menu, release the mouse at the desired position.

■ To copy the command, press CTRL while you drag the command to the new menu or toolbar.

| Note | *You can always drag the command to a new position on the command bar later, if necessary.* |

To delete a menu command from a menu or toolbar, do the following:

1. Open the Customize dialog box and show the menu bar or toolbar that contains the command you want to delete.

2. Click the menu on the menu bar or toolbar that contains the command you want to remove.

3. Drag the command off the menu and away from the other menu bars or toolbars.

If you remove a command from a built-in menu, the command is removed from the menu in every menu bar in which it appeared.

Adding a Submenu

A *submenu* is a menu within a menu and it's created the same way as a menu. To add a custom submenu to an existing menu, do the following:

1. Drag the New Menu command from the Commands box to the menu you want to contain the submenu. When you see the horizontal line, release the mouse and the New Menu control is placed with the other menu commands. The only difference is it shows a pointer indicating it opens another list of menu commands.

 You can also add one of the built-in menus or toolbar buttons that opens a submenu and customize its commands.

2. Right-click New Menu and type a name for the submenu, such as **Run Queries**, and then press ENTER.

3. Slowly click the new submenu to display a small empty box to the right of the submenu where the menu commands are to be placed. If you click too fast, the box doesn't appear.

4. Select and drag a command, such as a query name from the All Queries category, to the empty box and, when the I-beam appears, release the mouse. Figure 20-8 shows the Forms/Reports menu with two submenus: the built-in View menu and a custom submenu for running queries.

5. Drag the names of the other queries you want in the submenu from the All Queries list to the submenu.

Adding Commands to a Shortcut Menu

When you close the Toolbar Properties dialog box after choosing Popup as the toolbar type, the new shortcut menu is added to the Custom category on the Shortcut Menus toolbar. The *Shortcut Menus toolbar* is the group designation for all shortcut menus in the application. When you're ready to complete the shortcut menu, do the following:

1. Open the Customize dialog box and click Shortcut Menus in the Toolbars box on the Toolbars tab. The Shortcut Menu toolbar appears at the top of the screen.

2. Click the Custom category on the Shortcut Menus toolbar.

3. Add menu commands from the Customize dialog box the same way as for menu bars and toolbars. You can also move or copy commands from other menus.

 A shortcut menu can be global or context-sensitive. To specify a shortcut menu as global, set the option in the Startup dialog box as described later in this chapter. A context-sensitive shortcut menu contains commands that relate to the object to which it's attached.

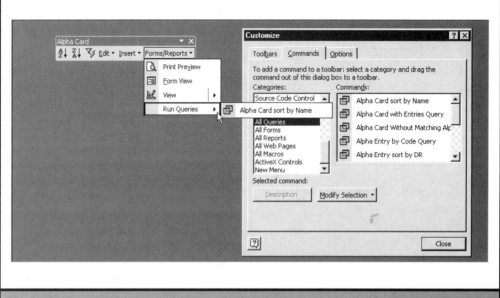

Figure 20-8. *Adding commands to a submenu*

Importing Custom Command Bars

If you created custom toolbars, menu bars, and shortcut menus for one database, you can import them to another database. This can save time and improve consistency among databases. To import custom command bars, do the following:

1. Open the receiving database and choose File | Get External Data, and then click Import.

2. In the Import dialog box, select Microsoft Access in the Files of type box.

3. Use the Look in box to choose the drive and folder where the source database is stored, and then double-click the database name.

4. In the Import Objects dialog box, click Options to expand the dialog box with the advanced import options.

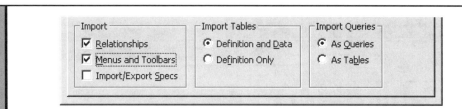

5. Click Menus and Toolbars in the Import group and click OK.

Access imports all the custom menus and toolbars from the source database, except those with the same names as ones in the receiving database.

Attaching a Custom Command Bar to an Object

Reports, forms, and controls have properties that specify which, if any, command bar is to be displayed when the object is in view.

- The *Menu Bar property* specifies the menu bar to display when a database, form, or report has focus. If the property is left blank, Access displays the built-in menu bar for the report or the global menu bar as defined in the Startup dialog box.

- The *Toolbar property* specifies the toolbar to use with a form or report when it's opened. If the property is left blank, Access displays the default toolbar for the form or report.

- The *Shortcut Menu Bar property* specifies the shortcut menu to display when you right-click a form, report, or a control on a form (but not a control on a report). If the property is left blank, Access displays the default shortcut menu or the global shortcut menu as defined in the Startup dialog box.

To set one of these properties, open the object's property sheet and click the Other tab. Select the name of the command bar from the drop-down list next to the appropriate property box. Repeat the process for each form, report, or control to which you want to attach a command.

Figure 20-9 shows the property sheet for the Alpha Card form in the Police database.

Note   *Forms and controls have an additional command bar property, the Shortcut Menu property, which is set to Yes or No, depending on whether you want the user to be able to open the shortcut menu. You can set this property to No in the property sheet or with a macro to protect the form from unauthorized changes, which could be made with commands that appear in the default shortcut menu.*

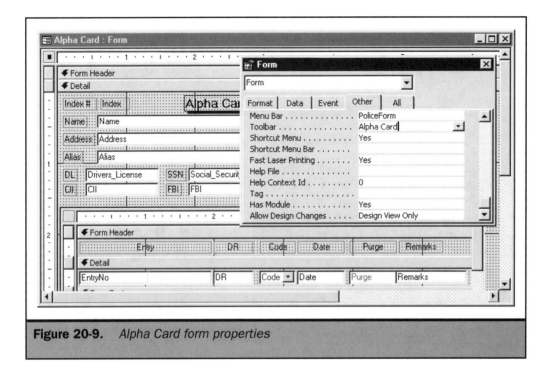

Figure 20-9. *Alpha Card form properties*

When you attach a custom command bar to a form, the bar appears only when the form is in Form view. Similarly, a custom command bar attached to a report appears only in Print Preview.

Specifying Global Command Bars

A global menu bar replaces the built-in menu bar in all the windows in an application, except where you specify a custom menu bar for a form or report. A global shortcut menu replaces the shortcut menus for datasheets, forms, form controls, and reports.

To specify a custom menu bar or a custom shortcut menu as the default for the entire database or application, you need to change the settings in the Startup dialog box. To set global command bars to replace the defaults, do the following:

1. Choose Tools | Startup to open the Startup dialog box.

2. Click the arrow next to the Menu Bar box and select the name of the menu bar to use instead of the default (see Figure 20-10).

3. Click the arrow next to the Shortcut Menu Bar box and select the shortcut menu to use instead of the default.

4. Click OK to close the dialog box.

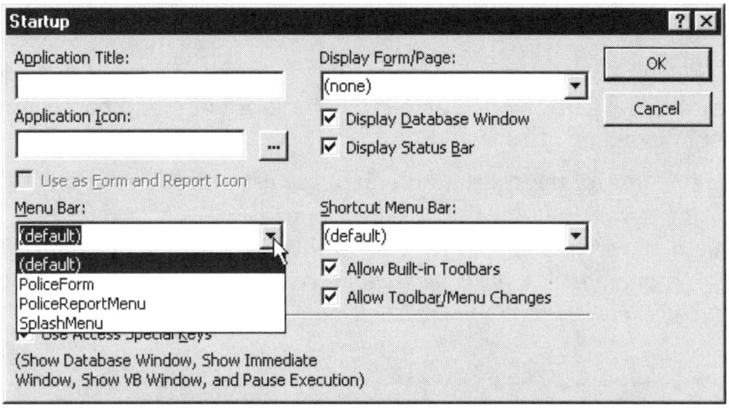

Figure 20-10.   *Setting startup options*

Other settings can restrict the user's access to full menus, default shortcut menus, and built-in toolbars. See Chapter 16 for more information about setting startup options.

The changes take effect the next time you open the database. To bypass the startup options, press SHIFT while the database is opening.

> **Tip**   *If all the built-in toolbars or some of the built-in menus no longer appear on the screen when they're supposed to, you may have changed some settings in the Startup dialog box. Be sure to check Allow Built-in Toolbars and Allow Full Menus to bring them back to their default views. If you still don't see all the menus, they may have been removed from the menu bar. The menus are still available from the Customize dialog box, so you can easily return them to the built-in menu bar.*

Deleting a Custom Command Bar

To delete a custom toolbar, menu bar, or shortcut menu, open the Customize dialog box as usual and click the Toolbars tab. Select the item you want to delete and click Delete. If the toolbar or menu bar is a built-in one you modified, the Delete button isn't available. Instead, click Reset to remove the custom features and restore the built-in command bar to its original default state.

Deleting a shortcut menu is a little different. You must convert it to a toolbar before you can delete it. Perform the following steps to delete a custom shortcut menu:

1. Open the Customize dialog box and click the Toolbars tab, and then select the toolbar you want to delete.

2. Click Properties to open the Toolbar Properties dialog box (shown earlier in Figure 20-5).

3. In the Selected Toolbar box, choose the name of the shortcut menu you want to delete.

4. Choose Toolbar in the Type list to change it to a toolbar, and then click Close to return to the Customize dialog box. The shortcut menu name is added to the list of toolbars.

5. Select the name of the shortcut menu in the list of toolbars and click Delete.

If you delete a custom command bar you specified as a property for a form, form control, or report, be sure to delete the name from the corresponding property or you'll get an error message the next time you try to open the form or to preview the report.

Modifying Command Bars

All changes to command bars are made with the Customize dialog box open. You can add more buttons, menus, and menu commands, and rearrange them on the bar. To move a command, drag it to the desired position. When you're moving a control on a menu bar or toolbar, the vertical I-beam appears to the left of the current position. A horizontal bar appears above the current position when you're moving a menu command or a submenu. Drop the control when the line appears in the desired position.

To rename the command bar, select the custom command bar in the Toolbars tab of the Customize dialog box and click Properties. Type a new name for the command bar in the Toolbar Name box. You can change other properties at the same time, and then click Close.

Note *You cannot rename a built-in command bar.*

Grouping Controls

When you have a set of buttons, commands, or menus that relate to similar operations, you can group them in a command bar by adding separator bars between controls. For example, the Print, Print Preview, and Spelling buttons appear in a group on the Database toolbar with a bar before Print and another after Spelling.

To add a bar at the left of a button or menu, or above a menu command, right-click the control and choose Begin a Group from the shortcut menu. The Begin a Group option isn't available for a leftmost or top control in the command bar.

To remove the separator bar, repeat the process and clear the Begin a Group check mark.

Note *If you drag the control you have set as the beginning of a group to a new position, the dividing line may move with the control or be deleted. The results appear inconsistent.*

Editing Buttons and Menu Commands

Many customizing options are available on the individual control shortcut menu. Buttons and menu commands have more options than menus. With the command bar showing and the Customize dialog box open, right-click a built-in or custom toolbar button to open the shortcut menu (see Figure 20-11). To edit a menu command, click the menu on the menu bar or toolbar, or the shortcut menu that contains the command, and then right-click the command.

Table 20-5 describes the commands contained on the shortcut menu. The commands are available to all built-in and custom buttons, as well as menu commands. Some of the commands are also available to menus. Five image-related commands are also on the shortcut menu, which are described separately in later paragraphs.

Note *When you rename a toolbar button that doesn't display text, you can see the new name in the ScreenTip.*

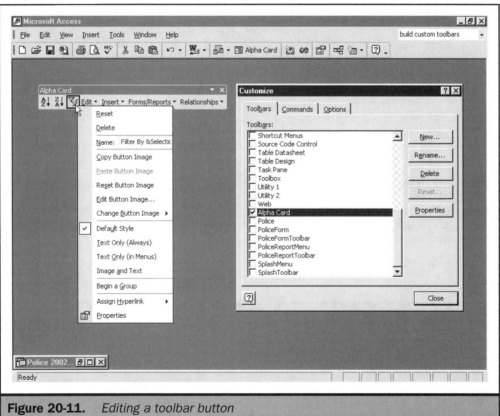

Figure 20-11. *Editing a toolbar button*

Shortcut Menu Command	Description
Reset	Restores the default properties of a built-in button, menu, or menu command. Not available for custom buttons, menus, or menu commands.
Delete	Removes the button, menu, or menu command from the toolbar. Built-in objects are still available in the Commands box, but custom objects are deleted permanently.
Name	Enter a new name in the Name box and press ENTER. You can rename both built-in and custom buttons, menus, and menu commands. Choosing Reset restores the default name of a built-in control.
Default Style	Displays a button with only an image and a menu command with text and an image, if one exists.
Text Only (Always)	Displays text only with no image on both buttons and menu commands.
Text Only (in Menus)	Displays text only with no image on menu commands and only an image with no text on buttons.
Image and Text	Displays both an image, if one exists, and text on buttons and menu commands.
Begin a Group	Adds a dividing line before or above the button, menu, or menu command.
Assign Hyperlink	Assigns a hyperlink to the command or removes an existing link.
Properties	Opens the Control Properties dialog box for the selected toolbar, menu bar, or shortcut menu.

Table 20-5.   *Editing Buttons and Menu Commands*

Tip   *Once you select a menu, button, or menu command on a toolbar or menu bar, you can also open the shortcut menu previously described by clicking Modify Selection on the Commands tab of the Customize dialog box.*

Adding an Access Key

Characters that appear underlined in the text of a menu or menu command represent *access keys*, or *hot keys*, as they're sometimes called. Pressing ALT plus the access key character selects that menu or menu command. When you customize toolbars and menu bars, you can specify access keys.

To designate a character in the name as the access key, precede the character by an ampersand (&). When the command is displayed, the character appears underlined.

 When you specify access keys for menu commands in a single menu, be sure to assign a different character to each command. If two commands have the same access key, only the first in the list is activated when you press ALT plus the key character.

Changing the Width of a Combo Box Button

Some of the buttons on built-in toolbars are actually combo boxes that display a list of options when you click the drop-down arrow next to the button—for example, the Object button on the Formatting (Form/Report) toolbar, which displays a list of the sections and controls in the current form or report. If the items in the list are longer than the box is wide, you may want to widen it. If the button takes up more room on the toolbar than is necessary, you can decrease the width.

To change the width of a combo box button, do the following:

1. Open the Customize dialog box and click the combo button. A blank rectangle appears within the combo box button.

2. Move the mouse pointer to the right or left edge and, when it changes to a double-pointed arrow, drag the edge of the box. You get the same result by dragging either edge.

Adding and Editing Images

Built-in toolbar buttons and many of the built-in menu commands show icon images, which you can customize for your application. You can copy images from one button or command to another, copy a graphics image from another program, choose from a palette of existing images, or even design your own image with the Image Editor.

To copy from one toolbar or menu bar to another, you must have the Customize dialog box open, as well as both bars showing. Then do the following:

1. Right-click the button or command that contains the image you want to copy and choose Copy Button Image from the shortcut menu.

2. Then right-click the button or command you want to show the image and choose Paste Button Image from the shortcut menu.

Note *If you change the image for a command on a built-in menu, all views showing that menu reflect the changed image.*

To copy an image from a graphics program, copy the image to the clipboard, right-click the button or command you want the image to appear on, and then choose Paste Button Image from the shortcut menu.

 You get the best results if you choose a graphics image the same size as the built-in image, which is 16 × 16 pixels. Resizing the imported image can blur the resolution.

To change a button icon to one of the predefined images, right-click the image you want to change and choose Change Button Image from the shortcut menu. Click an image in the palette that appears to copy it to the button or command.

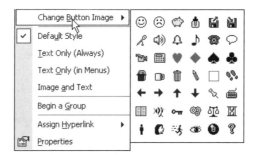

If you really want to use your imagination, open the Button Editor and create your own image. To start the Button Editor, right-click the button or command and choose Edit Button Image from the shortcut menu. The Button Editor dialog box (see Figure 20-12) opens showing the selected image on a 16 × 16 cell grid.

 When you edit an instance of an existing button image, the original icon is still in the Commands box on the Commands tab of the Customize dialog box.

■ To add to the image, click one of the color buttons, and then draw in the image grid. You can drag the pointer over the cells to create a line or block of color or click in individual cells. You can also right-click a cell in the picture to repeat a special color.

■ To erase parts of the image, click the Erase button, and then drag the pointer over the cells you want cleared. When you erase a color, the cell assumes the color of the background of the button.

■ To move the image about on the grid, click the Move buttons. Each click moves the image one row or one column. If the image is against one side of the frame, the Move button pointing that way isn't available.

■ To erase the entire image and start over, click Clear.

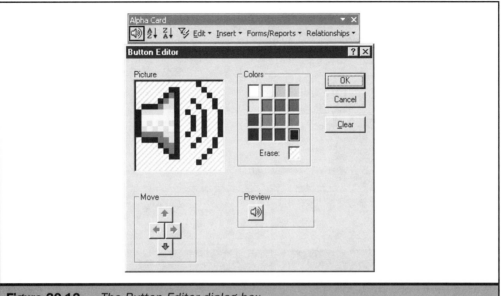

Figure 20-12. *The Button Editor dialog box*

Tip *If the button or command doesn't show the new icon image after you click OK, the command's style may be set to Text Only. To correct this, open the Customize dialog box and right-click the control. Then change the Style property in the shortcut menu to Default Style or Image and Text.*

Assigning a Hyperlink

You can add a custom button or menu command to a command bar that jumps to a specified hyperlink in the current database, to another location on your hard drive or local network, or to a Web page. To add a hyperlink command, open the Customize dialog box and do the following:

1. Drag the Custom command from the Commands list to the command bar. Custom is the first command in the File category.

2. Right-click the new Custom button and change its properties, as desired. For example, rename the command and add an image.

3. Right-click the button again and choose Assign Hyperlink | Open.

4. In the Assign Hyperlink dialog box scroll down the list of files in the Current Folder (see Figure 20-13) and select the hyperlink address to which you want to jump. See Chapter 12 for information about browsing for hyperlink addresses.

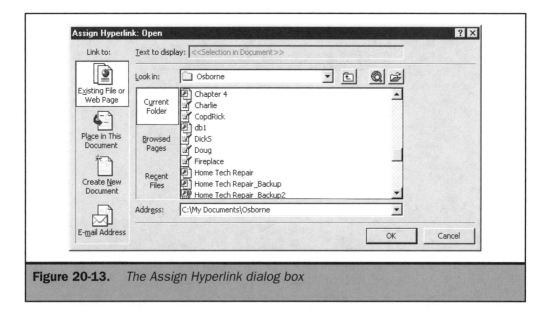

Figure 20-13. *The Assign Hyperlink dialog box*

Changing Control Properties

The last command on the shortcut menu opens the Control Properties dialog box, where you can make further modifications to the buttons, menus, and menu commands on a menu bar or toolbar. Figure 20-14 shows the Control Properties dialog box for the Filter By Selection button.

All the properties can be set for buttons and menu commands. Some are also available for menus. The control properties you can set are

- **Caption**   Enter or edit the name of the control. The ampersand (&) before *S* indicates it as the access key for this button. Available for menus.

- **Shortcut Text**   Enter the text you want displayed next to the menu command to indicate the shortcut key or key combination, such as CTRL-C. The shortcut key is defined in the AutoKeys macro. With a menu command, the shortcut key text appears to the right of the command. With a toolbar button, the shortcut key text is displayed in the ScreenTip (if you checked the Show Shortcut Keys in ScreenTips box for the button on the Options tab of the Customize dialog box).

- **ScreenTip**   Enter the text to be displayed in the ScreenTip when the mouse pointer rests on the control. If you leave this blank, the control name is displayed as a ScreenTip. Available for menus.

- **On Action**   Enter the name of the macro or the Visual Basic function procedure you want to run when the control is selected. Select from the list, which displays the names of all the macros in the current database, or type a function name. A function name must be preceded by an equal sign (=). The On Action property works like an event property for other objects. Available for menus.

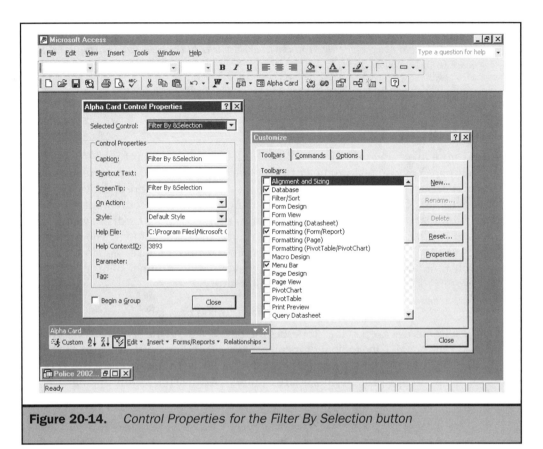

Figure 20-14.   *Control Properties for the Filter By Selection button*

- ■ **Style**   Choose from the same four style options that appeared in the shortcut menu: Default Style, Text Only (Always), Text Only (in Menus), or Image and Text.

- ■ **Help File**   Enter the path and filename of the compiled Help file that contains the What's This? tip text. Built-in commands have Help files in the Office folder. Available for menus.

- ■ **Help ContextID**   Enter the context ID number of the What's This? tip text in the Help file indicated in the Help File box. The Filter By Selection tip text is number 3893 in the file. Available for menus.

- ■ **Parameter**   Enter the name of any parameter to be passed to the event procedure specified in the On Action property.

- ■ **Tag**   A string that can be used to refer to the control in an event procedure. You can use a tag to assign an identification string to an object without affecting any of its other property settings or causing other side effects.

To change the properties of other controls on the current toolbar or menu bar without closing the dialog box, click the drop-down arrow next to the Selected Control box and choose from the list of controls.

Click Close when you finish making all the desired changes.

Restoring Built-in Command Bars

You can restore all or any part of a modified built-in command bar to the original default settings. You can restore the entire toolbar or menu bar to show the original buttons and menus with or without restoring the original default properties. Or, you can choose to restore only certain individual menus, buttons, or commands.

When you restore an entire built-in toolbar or menu bar, Access displays all the buttons and commands in their original appearance and arrangement. The property settings for the toolbar or menu bar are also restored, including the screen location and size, as well as showing or hiding the bar, whichever was its original state.

To restore a toolbar or menu bar, do the following:

1. Open the Customize dialog box and click the Toolbars tab.

2. Click Properties to open the Properties dialog box and, in the Selected Toolbar box, select the name of the toolbar or menu bar you want to restore. Figure 20-15 shows the Toolbar Properties dialog box for the Database toolbar. Notice the Toolbar Name and Type property boxes are dimmed because it's a built-in toolbar.

3. Click Restore Defaults and click Close.

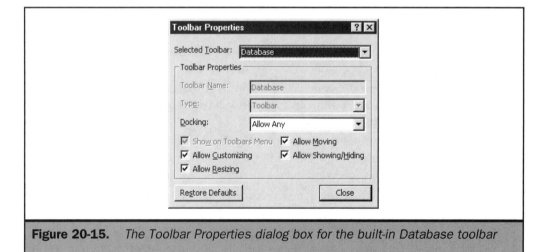

Figure 20-15. *The Toolbar Properties dialog box for the built-in Database toolbar*

If you want to reset only the buttons and menus on a built-in toolbar, menu bar, or shortcut menu, you can do so from the Customize dialog box. On the Toolbars tab, choose the name of the toolbar or menu bar you want to restore, and then click Reset. If you want to reset a shortcut menu, select Shortcut Menus in the list of toolbars and click Reset. This resets all the shortcut menus you modified.

Note *The Reset button isn't available for custom toolbars or menu bars. And the Reset button also isn't available unless you've made changes to the selected toolbar, menu bar, or one of the built-in shortcut menus.*

You can restore the original settings of a single toolbar button or menu command in a toolbar, menu bar, or shortcut menu. To restore the settings, open the Customize dialog box and click the menu bar or toolbar that contains the settings you want to restore. The menu bar or toolbar appears on the screen behind the dialog box. Then do one of the following:

- To restore a menu, right-click the menu in the menu bar or toolbar and choose Reset in the shortcut menu.

- To restore a toolbar button, right-click the button and choose Reset in the shortcut menu.

- To restore a menu command, click the menu in the menu bar or toolbar, or click the shortcut menu that contains the command. Then right-click the command and choose Reset from the shortcut menu.

Note *If you restore a menu that appears in more than one menu bar, such as File or Edit, you also restore the menu in the menu bars for all other views that use this menu.*

If the button you want to restore opens a list of options, you cannot use the Reset command to change back to the default image. Instead, if you changed the image on the built-in button or menu command and you want to restore it to the original image, right-click and choose Reset Button Image in the shortcut menu.

Converting Macros to Command Bars

If you used macros in earlier versions of Access to create custom menus and menu commands, you can easily convert them to the new style command bars. The process doesn't delete the macro but, instead, builds a new command bar from the macro actions. You can still maintain the macro if necessary.

To convert the macro to a command bar, do the following:

1. Click Macros under Objects in the Database window.

2. Select the name of the macro for which you want to create a toolbar.

3. Choose Tools and point to Macros, and then do one of the following:

- To create a menu, click Create Menu from Macro.
- To create a toolbar, click Create Toolbar from Macro.
- To create a shortcut menu, click Create Shortcut Menu from Macro.

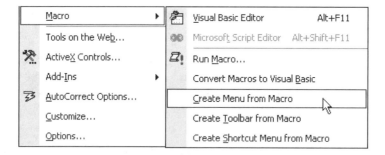

4. Customize the new command bar as necessary, including changing the name.

You can attach macro-conversions to forms and reports or designate them as global command bars, the same as command bars created with the Customize dialog box.

Summary

Creating and using customized command bars gives you many opportunities to build exactly the application you want. You can include only those menus and commands that apply to the job. You can exclude irrelevant menus and commands, as well as those that may even jeopardize the integrity of the database as a whole.

The next step in creating a unique operating environment for your application is to add dialog boxes that serve as decision points for the user. In these switchboards, the user can choose the next action to take and can even make further choices from pop-up dialog boxes that offer alternatives. Creating switchboards and other user-interactive tools is covered in the next chapter.

MOUS Exam Activities Explored in This Chapter

This chapter contains no information directly related to the MOUS Certification Exam activities, although the information is important to understanding how to use Access for effective database management.

Chapter 21

Creating Custom Switchboards and Dialog Boxes

When creating an application for a user who wants to concentrate on its purpose and the special tasks it requires, you can add custom user interfaces. Two special-purpose forms can be added to an application that can be used as switchboards for choosing activities and as dialog boxes for acquiring user input.

A switchboard can offer the user a single point of entry into the application with a list of custom activities. With a mere click on a switchboard item, the user branches to the operation.

Working with Windows applications, you're no doubt familiar with dialog boxes and their many uses. A dialog box offers a set of options from which to choose, such as which form or report to open, which filter to apply, or what action to take next. Custom dialog boxes can also prompt the user for data. You can create custom dialog boxes that contain options relevant to the application in easily understood text.

Creating Switchboards

Switchboard is a term borrowed from the telephone industry that's used to indicate a single point of entry into an application with a list of connections to activate next. When the Access Database Wizard creates a new database, it always adds at least one switchboard as the user interface. Figure 21-1 shows the main switchboard for the Asset Tracking database.

In addition to the main switchboard, two other switchboard pages are included in the user interface in the Asset Tracking database:

- The Forms Switchboard, reached by clicking Enter/View Other Information item.
- The Reports Switchboard, reached by clicking Preview Reports.

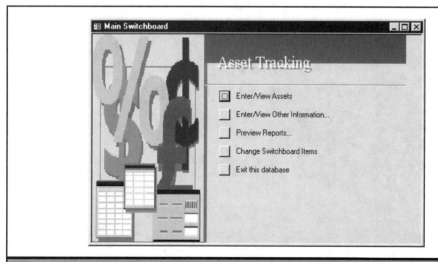

Figure 21-1. *The Asset Tracking database main switchboard*

The ellipsis (…) following each of those items tells users they open secondary switchboard pages.

You can make changes to any of the switchboards the wizard creates for you. For example, you can add an item to the Main Switchboard to access the Internet or add other reports to the list in the Reports Switchboard. Access includes the Switchboard Manager to help make changes to wizard-built switchboards, as well as create your own from scratch. Notice that one of the items on the Main Switchboard in Figure 21-1 is Change Switchboard Items, which launches the Switchboard Manager. Editing a switchboard created by the Database Wizard is the same as editing one you created with the Manager. A later section in this chapter discusses modifying switchboards.

Using the Switchboard Manager

The switchboard system is the last piece of an application that's designed and created after all the forms, reports, and queries are completed. The switchboard system for a database consists of a hierarchical arrangement of switchboard *pages,* beginning with the main switchboard, usually branching out to two or more subordinate pages. Each page contains a set of *items* with commands that carry out a specified activity. Most items also include an *argument* that specifies which form to open, which report to preview, which macro or procedure to run, and so on.

To start the Switchboard Manager, choose Tools | Database Utilities | Switchboard Manager. If your database doesn't already have a valid switchboard, the Manager displays a message asking if you want to create a new one. Click Yes.

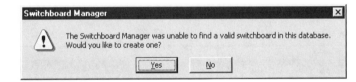

The first Switchboard Manager dialog box (see Figure 21-2) starts with the mandatory default main switchboard page.

In addition to Close, the options in the dialog box are

- *New,* which opens a dialog box where you can build a new page.
- *Edit,* which enables you to edit the selected page in this dialog box.
- *Delete,* which removes the selected page from the switchboard system.
- *Make Default,* which assigns the selected switchboard page as the default that can be set to display at startup.

Adding Items to the Page

The first step is to add items to the main switchboard by selecting the page in the Switchboard Manager dialog box and clicking Edit. This opens the Edit Switchboard Page dialog box (see Figure 21-3) which has only one available option at this time: New.

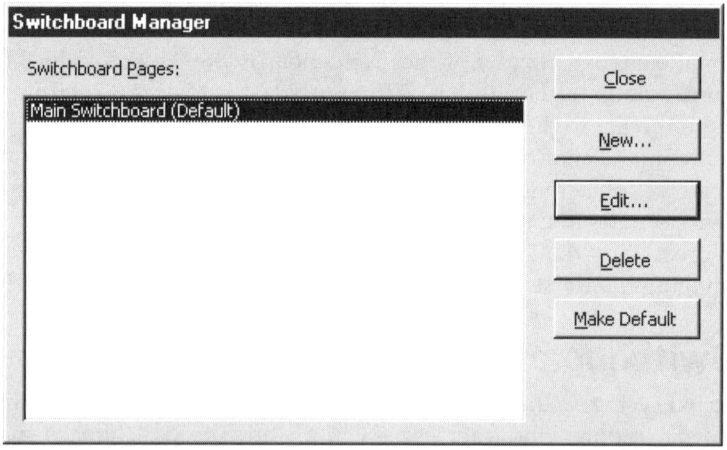

Figure 21-2. *Starting a new main switchboard*

No items are in the main switchboard for the Police database yet. Before adding them to the switchboard, enter Bayview City Police as the switchboard name in place of Main Switchboard. Then begin adding the list of items you decided should appear when the database starts up. To start placing the choices on the switchboard, click New to open the Edit Switchboard Item dialog box.

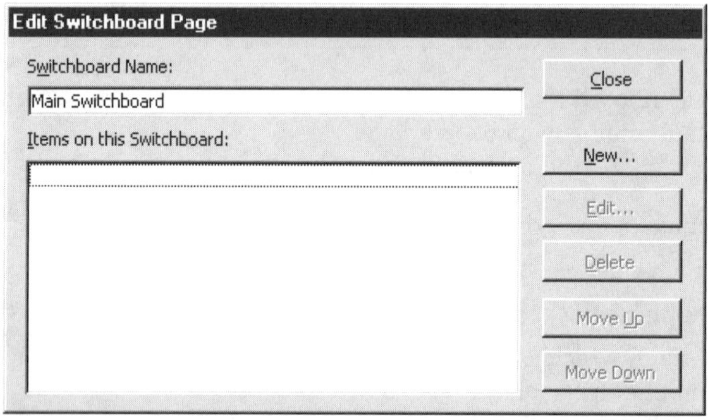

Figure 21-3. *The Edit Switchboard Page dialog box*

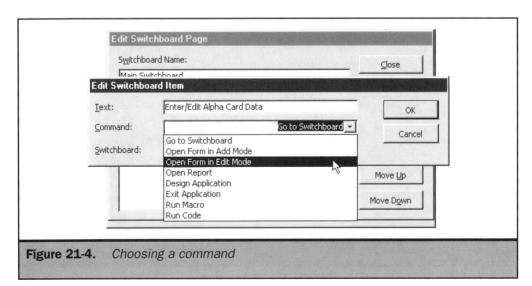

 Tip   *To return to the main switchboard, always add an item at the end of the list on all switchboard pages, except the opening switchboard. The item moves control back up the switchboard tree to the main switchboard. The opening switchboard should have an item that closes the database.*

Three entries define a switchboard item:

- Enter the text you want to appear in the list of items in the Text box.
- Choose the command you want from the drop-down list next to the Command box.
- Depending on which command you choose, enter the command argument in the third box. The title of the box varies with the command chosen.

The activity most often carried out in the Police application is to look up or enter Alpha Card information in the Alpha Card form. This form also displays the Alpha Entry information in a subform. To begin the Police switchboard system, do the following:

1. Type **Enter/Edit Alpha Card Data** in the Text box in the Edit Switchboard Item dialog box.

2. Click the drop-down arrow next to Command and choose Open Form in Edit mode (see Figure 21-4).

Figure 21-4.   *Choosing a command*

You can use the ampersand (&) character in the item's Text box to specify access keys for the items in the switchboard. Then the user has a choice of clicking the item or pressing ALT *with the access key.*

The Switchboard Manager offers eight different commands, which cover most of the actions you would want to initiate from a switchboard. Table 21-1 describes the commands and the arguments they require, if any.

After you choose the command, the third line changes to the appropriate argument name, in this case, Form.

When you click the drop-down arrow next to the Form box, the Manager displays a list of all the forms in the Police database (see Figure 21-5). Choose Alpha Card and click OK. You return to the Edit Switchboard Page dialog box where you now see the new item in the Items on this Switchboard list.

Repeat the same steps to add the following two items to the main switchboard:

■ Enter/Edit Alpha Entry Data, which opens the Alpha Entry form in Edit mode.

■ Preview Alpha Card with Entries, which opens the Alpha Card with Entries report.

Command	Description	Argument
Go To Switchboard	Opens another switchboard and closes this one.	Name of destination switchboard
Open Form in Add Mode	Opens a form for data entry with a blank record showing.	Form name
Open Form in Edit Mode	Opens a form for viewing and editing data.	Form name
Open Report	Opens a report in Print Preview.	Report Name
Design Application	Opens Switchboard Manager to make changes to current switchboard.	None
Exit Application	Closes active database.	None
Run Macro	Runs a macro.	Macro name
Run Code	Runs a Visual Basic procedure.	Procedure name

Table 21-1. *Commands Offered by the Switchboard Manager*

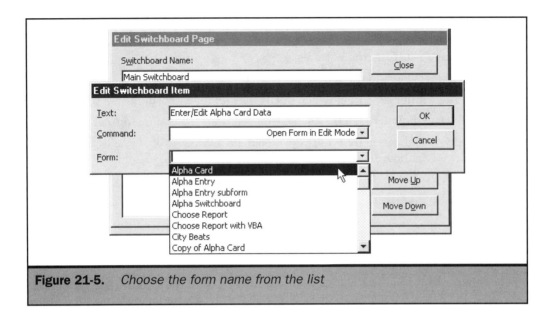

Figure 21-5. *Choose the form name from the list*

Adding a New Switchboard Page

The Police database user may want to open several more forms and reports, but not as often as the ones already added as items to the main switchboard. The less frequently used forms and reports can be grouped on secondary switchboard pages. To add a new page to the switchboard system, do the following:

1. Click Close to close the Edit Switchboard Page and return to the Switchboard Manager dialog box.

2. Click New to start a new page.

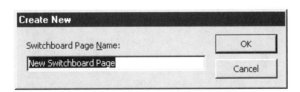

3. Type **Enter/Edit Other Data** in the Switchboard Page Name box and click OK. Include an ampersand if you want to specify an access key for this item.

4. The new page name is added to the list in the Switchboard Manager dialog box. Select the Enter/Edit Other Data switchboard page and click Edit to open the Edit Switchboard Page dialog box as before.

5. Click New to open the Edit Switchboard Item dialog box and type **Enter/Edit City Beats**. Then choose Open Form in Edit mode from the Command list and City Beats from the Form list.

6. Repeat step 5 to add the following items to the list:

   ■ Enter/Edit Name List, which opens the Name List form in Edit mode.

   ■ Enter/Edit Entry Description, which opens the Explanation form in Edit mode.

7. Finally, add the item that returns to the main switchboard: Type **Return to Main Switchboard**, choose Go To Switchboard from the Command list, and choose Bayview City Police from the Switchboard list.

Figure 21-6 shows the completed Edit/Enter Other Data page.

 As you add pages to the switchboard tree, remember to add items to the main switchboard to branch to the page, as well as adding the item to the page that moves back up the tree.

The items are added to the page in the order you define them. If you need to rearrange them, select an item in the Edit Switchboard Page dialog box and click Move Up or Move Down to change its position in the list. Each click moves the item up or down one position.

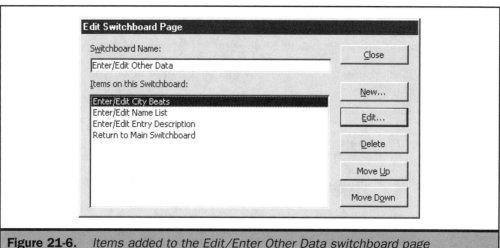

Figure 21-6. *Items added to the Edit/Enter Other Data switchboard page*

To complete the Police switchboard system, create another page titled Preview Other Reports, and add the items to it that will open other reports as specified in the item text:

- Alpha Entry
- Entries by Code
- Entries by Qtr
- Entries by Year
- Print Labels
- Return to Main Switchboard

 When you create a subordinate switchboard page, you needn't add items to it right away. You do need to create the page, however, before you can place an item on the main switchboard that will open it. One development strategy is to create all the pages first, and then add the items.

When all the pages are completed for the switchboard system, close the Switchboard Manager. The Switchboard form now appears in the Forms page of the Database window. Double-click the form name to open the form in Form view. Figure 21-7 shows the completed Main Switchboard for the Police database.

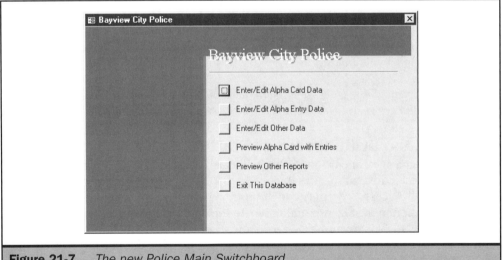

Figure 21-7.   *The new Police Main Switchboard*

A new table has also been added to the Tables page named Switchboard Items, which you examine later.

The Switchboard Manager has used the same colors and arrangement for your switchboard as the Database Wizard used for the Asset Tracking database. All it lacks is a picture to make it complete.

Adding a Picture

The blank area at the left of the switchboard items in the Access template is intended for a company logo or other image. You can add a picture to the switchboard form just as with any other form. When you add a picture to one switchboard page, the same picture appears on all the pages.

To add a picture to the switchboard, open the form in Design view and do the following:

1. Choose Insert | Picture.

2. In the Insert Picture dialog box, locate the picture you want to use and click OK. Access places the picture in the upper-left corner of the form. It most likely covers up some of the switchboard.

3. Resize the picture to fit within the solid background.

4. Click the Properties toolbar button to open the property sheet for the picture and change the Size Mode property to Stretch. If the image is distorted, change the property to Zoom and resize the frame to fit the picture dimensions

5. Switch to Form view. Figure 21-8 shows the Preview Other Reports page of the completed switchboard.

The picture used here is the contacts.gif file found in the Dbwiz subfolder in the Office\Bitmaps folder. This is one of the pictures used by the Database Wizard.

Displaying the Switchboard at Startup

When you select a switchboard in the Switchboard Manager dialog box and click Make Default, you designate that form as the one to display when the database opens. You still have to tell Access to display the default switchboard by setting the Display Form/Page option in the Startup dialog box to the name of the default switchboard.

Choose Tools | Startup and click the arrow next to the Display Form/Page box and choose Switchboard or another form name from the list. The change takes effect the next time you start the database. To bypass the switchboard display after setting it as the default startup form, hold down SHIFT while the database opens.

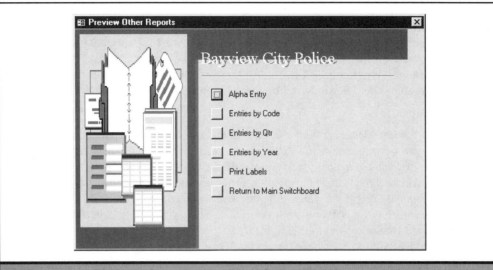

Figure 21-8.   *The completed Preview Other Reports page*

   Even though you designate the switchboard as the startup form, the Database window appears on the screen behind a switchboard that isn't maximized. To prevent the user from having access to the Database window, clear the Display Database Window option in the Startup dialog box. After the database is opened, you can still bring the Database window to the front by pressing F11.

Modifying the Switchboard

To edit any item on a switchboard page, open the Switchboard Manager and use the Edit buttons. If the Database Wizard created the switchboard, open the Switchboard Manager by clicking Change Switchboard Items in the opening switchboard. If you used the Switchboard Manager directly to create the switchboards, start the Manager by choosing Tools | Database Utilities | Switchboard Manager. Then do the following:

1. Choose the switchboard you want to change and click Edit.

2. To add an item, click New and enter the text. Then choose a command and an argument.

3. To change an item, select it and do one of the following:

   ■ To change the displayed text, the command, or the argument, click Edit.

   ■ To delete the item, click Delete.

   ■ To move the item in the list, click Move Up or Move Down.

4. Close the Switchboard Manager.

You can also delete an entire switchboard by selecting it in the Switchboard Pages dialog box and clicking Delete. The page and all its items are deleted.

To change the switchboard that displays when you start the database, select the switchboard you want to display instead and click Make Default. The startup option is still set to display the Switchboard form, but the Switchboard Manager has designated a different screen as the default switchboard. This takes effect the next time you open the database.

Note   *The Switchboard Manager allows a maximum of eight items on a page. You can add more if you want to change the Visual Basic coding for the form. To exceed this default setting, first add the items, just as you would the first eight, and then add the records to the Switchboard Items table to match. In the OnOpen event procedure for the form, a loop is limited to eight iterations. All you need to do is increase the value of the constant, conNumButtons, that controls the loop to the total number of items on the switchboard. Then add Case statements for the added items. See Chapter 25 for more information about editing Visual Basic code created by Access Wizards.*

Changing the Picture

Whether the Database Wizard added a picture to the switchboard or you inserted it in the one you created with the Switchboard Manager, you can swap it for another picture. The pictures the wizard uses are specially designed and sized for use in switchboards.

To change the picture to another special switchboard bitmap, do the following:

1. Open the switchboard form in Design view.

2. Double-click the picture control to open its property sheet.

3. Click the Format tab, and then click the Build (...) button next to the Picture property.

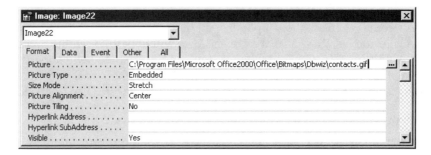

4. The Insert Picture dialog box opens where you can locate the image you want. The special images used by the Database Wizard are located in the Bitmaps\Dbwiz folder where you installed Office. The picture shown in the Asset Tracking switchboard is the assets.gif file in that folder.

If you selected a different type of image, you can replace it this way or delete the picture control and insert another as before by choosing Insert | Picture (see Figure 21-9).

Figure 21-9.   *Inserting a different switchboard picture*

Viewing the Switchboard Items Table

When you use the Switchboard Manager to create a switchboard, Access creates a new table named Switchboard Items. Each record in the table represents an item in one of the switchboard pages and each field in the record describes what command the button carries out and the argument it uses. Figure 21-10 shows the table created for the Police database switchboards.

Table 21-2 describes the contents of the Switchboard Items table.

 The first row of each switchboard contains 0 in both the ItemNumber and the Command field, indicating the ItemText is the switchboard caption and is to be displayed in the title bar.

The Argument field needs a little explanation. The first row contains Default in the Argument field, indicating the Main Switchboard has been specified as the default switchboard to be displayed at startup if the Display Form/Page option is set to Switchboard. A number in the Argument field represents the ID number of the switchboard as the goal of the command, Go To Switchboard. For example, the fourth row shows 2 in the Argument field, indicating the command is to display switchboard number 2, Enter/Edit Other Data.

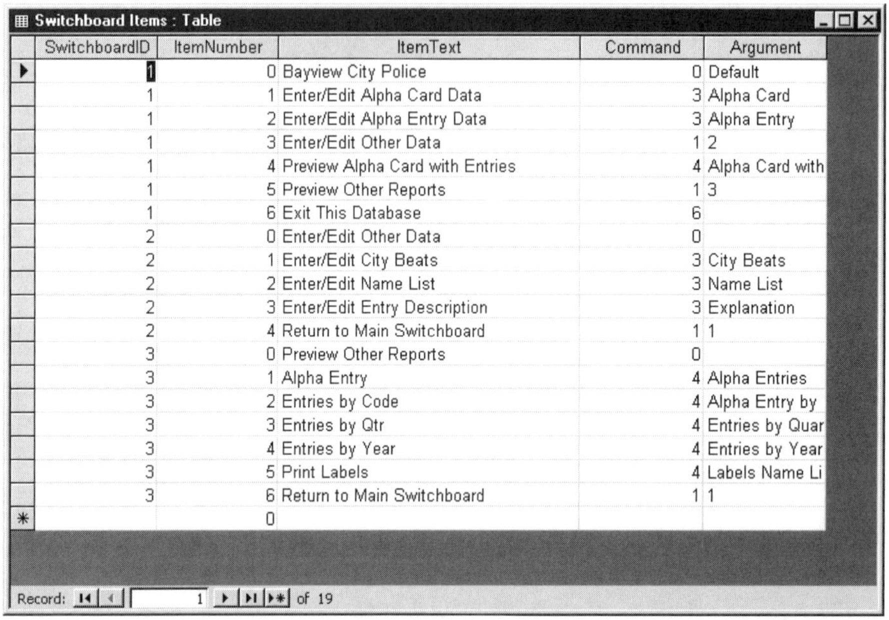

Switchboard Items : Table

SwitchboardID	ItemNumber	ItemText	Command	Argument
1	0	Bayview City Police	0	Default
1	1	Enter/Edit Alpha Card Data	3	Alpha Card
1	2	Enter/Edit Alpha Entry Data	3	Alpha Entry
1	3	Enter/Edit Other Data	1	2
1	4	Preview Alpha Card with Entries	4	Alpha Card with
1	5	Preview Other Reports	1	3
1	6	Exit This Database	6	
2	0	Enter/Edit Other Data	0	
2	1	Enter/Edit City Beats	3	City Beats
2	2	Enter/Edit Name List	3	Name List
2	3	Enter/Edit Entry Description	3	Explanation
2	4	Return to Main Switchboard	1	1
3	0	Preview Other Reports	0	
3	1	Alpha Entry	4	Alpha Entries
3	2	Entries by Code	4	Alpha Entry by
3	3	Entries by Qtr	4	Entries by Quar
3	4	Entries by Year	4	Entries by Year
3	5	Print Labels	4	Labels Name Li
3	6	Return to Main Switchboard	1	1
*	0			

Record: 1 of 19

Figure 21-10. *The Switchboard Items table*

Field	**Contents**
SwitchboardID	A sequential number assigned to the switchboard page.
ItemNumber	A sequential number assigned to each item on a page, beginning with 1. Together with the SwitchboardID, forms the primary key that uniquely identifies the item and switchboard page.
ItemText	Text entered in the Text box of the Edit Switchboard Item dialog box.
Command	Number representing the command selected from the Commands list in the Edit Switchboard Item dialog box. Commands are numbered sequentially in the order they appear in the list.

Table 21-2. *The Switchboard Items Table*

Field	Contents
Argument	Number of the switchboard, the name of form, report, macro, or procedure to be used by the command in the Commands list in the Edit Switchboard Item dialog box.

Table 21-2. *The Switchboard Items Table* (continued)

You can make changes in the switchboards by editing the information in the table, but it's easier and safer to use the Switchboard Manager. When you make changes with the Switchboard Manager, the changes are also made to the items table. If you make changes to the form in Design view, they aren't necessarily translated to the table and, if you do a lot of customizing to the form, it may not work the way you want. You might be better off creating a form from scratch with all the customization, and then designating it as the startup form.

Creating a Switchboard from Scratch

The purpose behind creating a switchboard from scratch is so you can build a customized form without being subjected to the limitations imposed by the Switchboard Manager. The form should be designed to help the user run all the tasks required of the application, such as entering data and printing reports. The switchboard form is usually the last piece of the application to be created, after all the tables, queries, forms, and reports are designed and saved in the database.

To create a switchboard from scratch, start with a blank form that isn't bound to an underlying table or query, and then add command buttons that trigger macros or event procedures to carry out the actions you want. The properties of a switchboard form are quite different from the normal data entry form that shows record navigation buttons and scroll bars.

To begin a new switchboard form, do the following:

1. Open the Forms page in the Database window and click New.

2. In the New Form dialog box, choose Design view, leave the lower box blank, and click OK. A new blank form appears in the window.

Before you begin placing command buttons on the form, change some of the form properties, so it appears more like a switchboard.

Setting the Form Properties

Open the form property sheet by double-clicking the form selector or choosing Edit |
Select Form, and then clicking the Properties toolbar button. You can also choose Form
in the Object toolbar button and click Properties. On the property sheet, set the form
properties as follows:

- Enter the text you want to see in the switchboard title bar in the Caption
  property box.
- Make sure the Default view is Single Form.
- Leave the Allow Form View property as Yes and change the other three
  Allow... properties to No.
- Change Scroll Bars to Neither to remove both the horizontal and vertical
  scroll bars.
- Change Record Selectors to No because there won't be any data on the form.
- Change Navigation Buttons to No because the user won't be moving
  among records.
- Change Dividing Lines to No.
- Set Auto Resize to Yes so the form always appears the same size in Form view.
- Set Auto Center to Yes to ensure the form opens in the middle of the window
  where it's easier to view and use.

If you want the switchboard form to display a different color, click the detail section
selector to change to the section property sheet. Then click the Build button next to the
Back Color property box and choose from the color palette. You can also click the
Fill/Back Color button on the Formatting (Form/Report) toolbar and choose a color
from the drop-down palette.

After setting all the desired properties, save and name the form. When you open
the form in Form view, it appears totally blank, but colorful.

Adding Command Buttons with the Wizard

The next step is to begin adding controls to the form that will carry out the desired
actions. You can add command buttons to carry out specific actions or hyperlinks
to jump to a different form or other location. The type of control you use for a
switchboard depends on what it's intended to do.

- If the switchboard item is designed to carry out a single action, such as open
  a form in Form view, you can use the Command Button Wizard to add a
  command button.

- If the item must carry out two or more actions, you need to add the button without the Command Button Wizard and create a macro or Visual Basic event procedure to attach to the button's OnClick event property.

- Hyperlinks can also be used to open another form or preview a special part of a report.

See Chapter 10 for more information about Control Wizards and how to use them.

Before you begin to add command buttons and labels to the switchboard, you may want to draw a rectangle in which to place them. This helps to group the items and give your switchboard a special flavor. You can also add pictures and titles outside the rectangle.

If you place buttons on the form, and then draw the rectangle, the box will be in front of the buttons and their labels. To fix this, select the rectangle and choose Format | Send to Back.

Add the first item, Enter/Edit Alpha Card Data, to the main switchboard with the Command Button Wizard as follows:

1. Open the blank form in Design view and click the Toolbox button.

2. Click the Control Wizards button, and then click the Command Button control tool.

3. Choose Form Operations in the Categories list and Open Form in the Action list, and then click Next.

4. Choose Alpha Card from the list in the next dialog box and click Next.

5. Choose the option Open the form and show all the records, which opens the form in Edit mode, and then click Next.

6. Choose Text and delete the caption so the button is blank, and then click Next.

7. Enter **Alpha Card Data** as the name for the button and click Finish.

8. In the Design window, resize the button to a small square, then add a Label control next to the button and enter the text **Enter/Edit &Alpha Card Data**.

9. Select the button and look at the OnClick event property in the property sheet. The [Event Procedure] entry refers to the code the wizard created to carry out the choices you made in the dialog boxes.

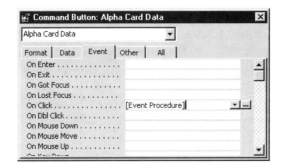

 The ampersand (&) creates an access key for the label that carries out the action attached to it. So far, no action is associated with the label—only the button—but you can attach the same event procedure the wizard created for the button with a few slight changes.

Copying the Button Event Procedure

 You are about to be introduced to some Visual Basic code and given a chance to modify it for your button label. To see the procedure, click the On Click event property box and click Build (…) next to [Event Procedure], or click the Code button on the Form Design toolbar. The Visual Basic Editor window opens, showing the following procedure. Alpha_Card_Data is the name of the button and Click is the event. (Text following the apostrophes are newly added comments and would be ignored by the program.)

```
Private Sub Alpha_Card_Data_Click()
On Error GoTo Err_Alpha_Card_Data_Click

    Dim stDocName As String          'These two statements declare
    Dim stLinkCriteria As String     'variables as strings.

    stDocName = "Alpha Card"         'This statement names the form
                                     'to open. The next statement opens
                                     'the form and sets the filter.
    DoCmd.OpenForm stDocName, , , stLinkCriteria
Exit_Alpha_Card_Data_Click:         'Quits the procedure.
    Exit Sub

Err_Alpha_Card_Data_Click:          'Traps any run time errors.
    MsgBox Err.Description             'Displays an error message.
    Resume Exit_Alpha_Card_Data_Click  'Goes to the Exit above.
End Sub
```

To add this procedure to the label's On Click property, do the following:

1. In the Visual Basic Editor window, select all the statements of the procedure except the first (Private Sub...) and the last (End Sub), and then click Copy to place it on the clipboard.

2. Click the View Microsoft Access button to return to the form Design view.

3. Select the button label and open the Event property sheet.

4. Click Build next to the On Click property and select Code Builder to open the Visual Basic Editor window for this event property.

5. Place the insertion point in the line below the Private Sub line and click Paste.

Because you want the label to carry out the same action as the button when you click it, all you need to do is change the button name to the label name wherever it appears. The easiest way to do this is to copy the label's name from the Sub statement—**Label2** in this case—to the clipboard and paste it in place of the button name (Alpha_Card_Data) in four places. After copying the label name to the clipboard, select the complete button name, Alpha_Card_Data, and click Paste. Be careful to retain the underline characters that replace spaces in the names in their proper places.

Adding Command Buttons and Attaching Macros

When you add command buttons or other controls to the form without the help of the Control Wizard, you must create your own macros or Visual Basic code to carry out the desired action. To avoid cluttering up the Database window with a lot of little macros, build all the macros for the switchboard in one group, and then specify the individual macros in the On Click event properties for the buttons and their labels.

If the switchboard opens other switchboard pages, create the blank forms for the secondary pages, and then save and name them, so you have all the form names and can create all the macros at once. The macro group for the Alpha Card main switchboard may look like the following. (The first item in the Police main switchboard was added earlier by the Command Button Wizard and doesn't require a macro.)

EXCHANGING DATA WITH OTHERS

Macro Name	Action	Comment
Alpha Entry	OpenForm	Switchboard item to open Alpha Entry form.
Other Data	OpenForm	Switchboard item to open Other Data page.
Card Report	OpenReport	Switchboard item to preview Alpha Card report.
Other Reports	OpenForm	Switchboard item to open Other Reports page.
Exit	Close	Closes the main switchboard.

SwitchMacro : Macro

By attaching a macro or procedure to the label, as well as to the button, and including access keys in the switchboard item labels, you have four ways to trigger the action: Click the button, click the label, press ALT with the access key, or press TAB to move focus to the button, and then press ENTER.

To add a command button without the wizard, do the following:

1. Be sure the Control Wizard button isn't pressed in, click the Command Button tool, and then click the form design where you want the button.

2. Select the button name, Command*n*, in the command button and press DELETE. You can also open the property sheet and delete the Caption property.

3. Resize the button to a small square that matches the first button.

4. Click the Label tool and draw a label next to the new button, and then type **Enter/Edit Alpha &Entry Data** in the new label. The label identifies *E* as the access key for the control.

5. Use the Format | Align and Format | Size commands to make the buttons the same size and line up the new controls.

6. Click outside the label control and hold down SHIFT while you select the command button and its label. By selecting both controls, you can attach a macro to them both at once.

7. Open the property sheet for the multiple selection and click the Event tab.

8. Click the arrow next to the On Click property and select SwitchMacro.Alpha Entry from the drop-down list of macros (see Figure 21-11).

9. Switch to Form view and test the new buttons.

Continue to add the rest of the items to the main switchboard, and then proceed to the other secondary switchboard pages using the same methods.

Another way to create a command button that runs a macro is to create the macro, and then drag it from the Database window to the form design. The following DBWindow runs the DBWindow macro, which contains only two actions: SendKeys, which sends the F11 keystroke to the application to open the Database window, followed by Close, which closes the switchboard form.

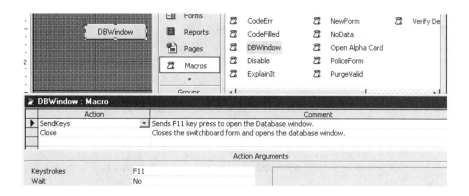

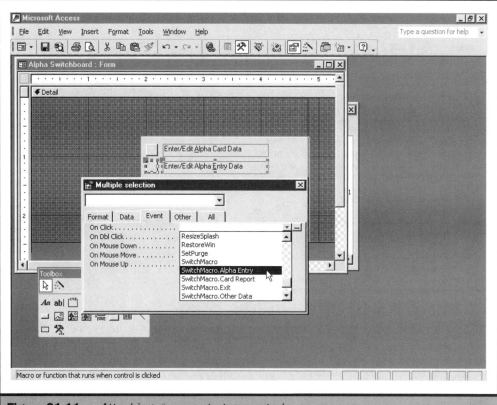

Figure 21-11. *Attaching a macro to two controls*

Adding a Hyperlink Command Button

You may want to jump to your Web site or another location on the hard drive. For this, you can add a command button that follows a hyperlink. To add a hyperlink command button, do the following:

1. Turn off the Control Wizard and click the Command Button tool. Then click the switchboard form where you want the button.

2. Resize as necessary and open the new button's property sheet.

3. Enter the text you want to see on the button in the Caption property box.

4. Click the Hyperlink Address property and enter the path to a file on the hard drive, a UNC path, or a URL. If you need help, click Build next to the Hyperlink Address property and use the Edit Hyperlink dialog box to help compose the correct address.

In the following illustration, the command button opens the Alpha Card Report in Print Preview. The caption is underlined because it's a hyperlink. The Hyperlink Address property is blank because the report is an object in the active database. The Hyperlink SubAddress shows the object type, Report, followed by the report name.

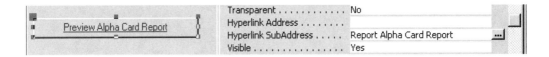

When you switch to Form view and click the hyperlink command button, the report opens for preview.

See Chapter 12 for details about adding hyperlinks to form designs.

Creating a Custom Dialog Box

A *dialog box* is a special type of window that pops up and stays on the screen until you make a selection, even if this selection is only to cancel the box. Creating custom dialog boxes for an application is much like creating switchboards. You start with a blank, unbound form and add controls that you can select to carry out specific actions. After completing the form, you create macros or event procedures, and then attach them to the corresponding controls on the form.

In this section, you create a dialog box that offers a choice of Police reports when the user clicks the Print button on the Alpha Card form. You create this custom dialog box in four major steps:

■ Create the form and add an option group control with a list of available reports from which to choose and three command buttons. One button to show the selected report in Print Preview, the second to print the report and the third to close the dialog box.

■ Create a macro group with a macro for each of the options in the group.

■ Attach the macros to the event property of the option group.

■ Set the form properties to look and act like a dialog box.

Designing the Form

To create the Choose Report dialog box for the Police database, do the following:

1. Start a new form without choosing a table or query as a basis.

2. In form Design view, click the Toolbox button if the toolbox isn't showing and make sure the Controls Wizard button is pressed.

3. Click the Option Group control tool and draw a frame in the empty form design to start the Option Group Wizard.

4. In the first wizard dialog box (see Figure 21-12), enter the label names for the options in the group. After entering a name, press DOWN ARROW or TAB to move to the next line. If you press ENTER, you move to the next dialog box. After entering all the option labels, click Next.

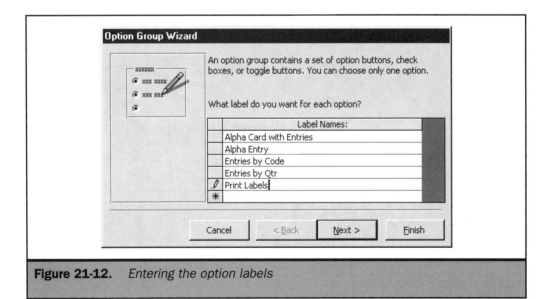

Figure 21-12. *Entering the option labels*

5. In the next wizard dialog box, you can choose one of the options you just entered as the default or choose not to have a default option. Accept the first option as the default and click Next.

6. When the user selects an option from the group, a value is returned. In this dialog box (see Figure 21-13), you can change the default sequential integer values. Unless you have a special reason to change the returned values, accept the default and click Next.

7. The next wizard dialog box (see Figure 21-14) shows a variety of styles for the option group and the options in it. Choose Option buttons as the type of control and Raised as the style, and then click Next.

8. In the final wizard dialog box, enter **Choose Report** as the caption for the group to be displayed at the top of the group frame, and then click Finish.

9. Select the option group frame and open the property sheet. Choose the Name property on the Other tab and enter **Choose Report** as the name for the option group.

10. Save and name the new form.

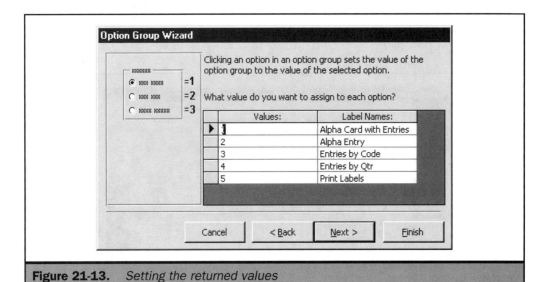

Figure 21-13.   *Setting the returned values*

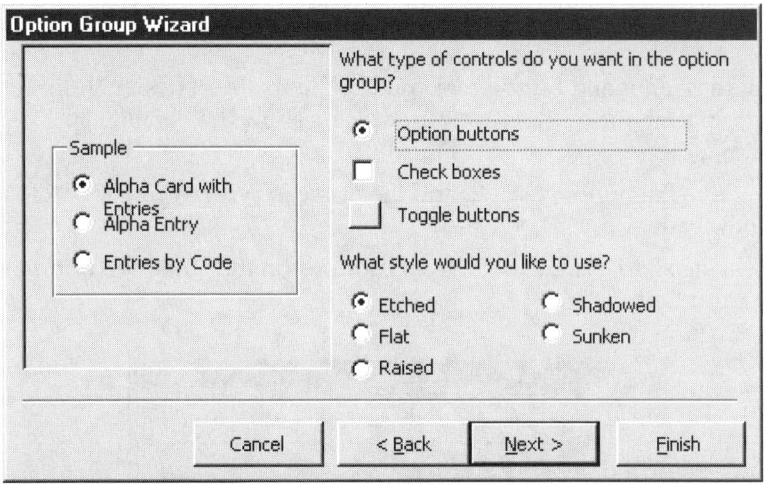

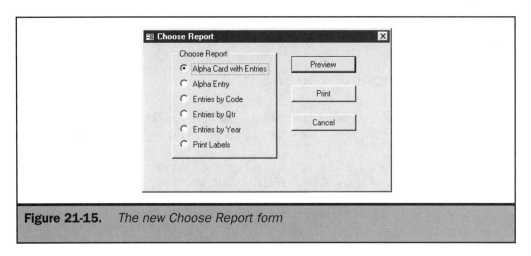

Figure 21-14. *Setting the option group style*

Figure 21-15 shows the new form in Form view. The next step is to add the command buttons. Do this without the help of the Command Button Wizard because you want to attach macros to the buttons instead of using the default operations offered by the wizard.

Figure 21-15. *The new Choose Report form*

To add the three command buttons, make sure the Controls Wizard button on the toolbox is *not* pressed, and then do the following:

1. Click the Command Button tool and click in the form design. Repeat twice more, spacing the buttons as desired. They show the default captions: Command*n*.

2. Select the first button, click it, and then type **Preview**. Press ENTER to save the new caption.

3. Repeat step 2 to change the default captions on the other two buttons to **Print** and **Cancel**.

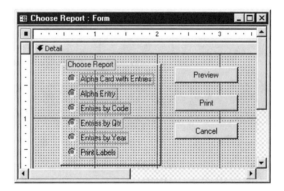

4. If the buttons aren't evenly spaced or accurately aligned, select all three and use the Format I Align or Format I Vertical Spacing command to adjust the buttons.

So far, the controls on the Choose Report form don't carry out an action. You need to create the macros that run when the control is clicked and do what is intended.

Creating and Attaching the Macros

You need a macro for each of the command buttons in the form. In addition, you must convey to the Print and Preview macros which report to open. The macros you attach to the Preview and Print buttons must distinguish among the reports and open the one chosen in the option group.

The option group returns a value depending on which item in the group was selected. As you saw, the Option Group Wizard set default return values so that if you click the first item, the group value is 1, if you click the second item, the value is 2, and so on. You can use this value in the macro condition to choose the specific report to preview or print.

Creating the Macro Group

To build a macro for the Preview button, do the following:

1. Click New in the Macros tab of the Database window, and then click the Macro Names and Conditions toolbar buttons to show the two optional columns.

2. Type **PreviewReports** as the name of the first macro and choose OpenReport as the Action.

3. In the Action Arguments pane, choose Alpha Card with Entries from the drop-down list of Report Names and choose Print Preview as the View argument.

4. Next enter the condition under which to preview the report: **[ChooseReport]=1**. ChooseReport is the name of the option group and 1 is the value of the group when you select the first item in the group.

If you're in doubt about the name of the control, look at the Name property on the Other tab of the control's property sheet.

5. Move to the next row and repeat steps 3 and 4 to open the Alpha Entry report in print preview with the condition that the ChooseReport group value is 2.

6. Continue to define macro actions to open the remaining reports in print preview. You should have six actions in the PreviewReports macro, each opening a different report in print preview.

7. The last action in the macro closes the Choose Report form so you can see the Print Preview window. Set the following arguments for the Close action:

   ■ Object Type — Form

   ■ Object Name — Choose Report

   ■ Save — No

8. Leave an empty row and create a new macro named PrintReports to print each of the reports using the same conditions. Don't include the Close action with the second macro, so the pop-up dialog box remains on the screen for further selections.

An easy way to add the conditions to the PrintReports macro is to copy the [ChooseReport]= part of the condition and paste it in subsequent lines, and then add the values.

The macro command for the Cancel button can be simply Close with the Choose Report form name as the argument. Figure 21-16 shows the completed macro group from the Choose Report form.

EXCHANGING DATA WITH OTHERS

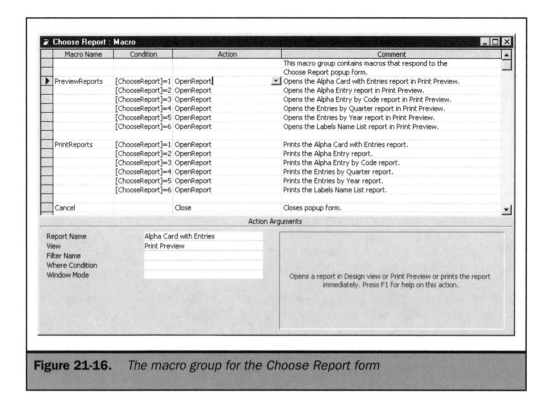

Figure 21-16.   *The macro group for the Choose Report form*

Attaching the Macros to Form Controls

To attach the macros to the command buttons, do the following:

1. Double-click the Preview command button to open the property sheet.

2. Click the Events tab and choose the macro name from the drop-down list next to the On Click event property. Figure 21-17 shows attaching the PreviewReports macro in the Choose Report macro group as the action to carry out when the button is clicked.

3. Repeat steps 1 and 2 to attach the PrintReports macro to the Print button and the Cancel macro to the Cancel button.

Setting Form Properties and Style

The last phase of creating a custom dialog box is to change some of the form properties to make it look and act more like a dialog box than a data entry form. A dialog box is a pop-up modal form. *Pop-up* means it opens and stays on top of other windows, even

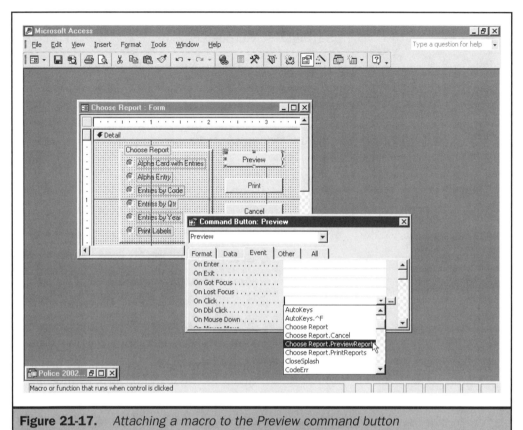

Figure 21-17. *Attaching a macro to the Preview command button*

when it no longer is the active window. *Modal* means you must hide or close the form before you can work in any other object or menu command.

To set these and some other properties, open the form in Design view and double-click the form selector to open the form property sheet. Then set the form properties as described in Table 21-3. All the properties are on the Format tab, except PopUp and Modal, which are on the Other tab.

Always leave a way for the user to close the form, such as the control menu box, the Close button, or a button that runs a Close macro action. If you accidentally create and display a modal form without a means to close it, you can use the CTRL-F4 *key combination to close the form. Then return to the Design view and add a visible means to close it.*

Property	Setting	Purpose
PopUp	Yes	Form remains on top of other windows.
Modal	Yes	Form retains focus until it's closed.
Caption	Choose Report	Displays text in title bar in Form view instead of form name.
Allow Form View	Yes	Permits the form in Form view.
Allow Datasheet View	No	Prevents switching to Datasheet view.
Allow PivotTable View	No	Prevents switching to PivotTable view.
Allow PivotChart View	No	Prevents switching to PivotChart view.
Scroll Bars	Neither	Removes scroll bars from the form.
Record Selectors	No	Removes record selectors from the form.
Navigation Buttons	No	Removes navigation buttons from the form.
Dividing Lines	No	Removes horizontal lines from the form.
Auto Center	Yes	Centers the form automatically when it opens. If you want the form to appear in a special place, set to No.
Border Style	Dialog	Form has a thick border and includes only a title bar with a control menu box.
Control Box	Yes	Displays the control menu box in the title bar in Form view so the user can close the form.
MinMax Buttons	None	Prevents the user from resizing the form in Form view.

Table 21-3. *Property Settings for a Custom Dialog Box*

Two additional features that help turn a form into a dialog box are the default button for the form and the Cancel button:

■ The command button specified as the default button is pushed automatically when the user presses ENTER. The default button shows with a darker border than the rest of the buttons on the form.

■ The command button specified as the Cancel button is pushed automatically when the user presses ESC.

You can assign any one button in the form as the default button and another button as the Cancel button by setting the Default or Cancel control property to Yes.

While you're working with the command button properties, you can add ScreenTips that appear when you rest the mouse pointer over the button. To add ScreenTips, type the text in the button's Control Tip property box on the Other tab of the property sheet.

If the form shows too much blank space in Form view, return to Design view and drag the right border in until it nearly touches the controls.

 You can't use the Window | Size to Fit Form command with this form because it is modal. This means you can't do anything outside the form while it is open, even clicking a toolbar button.

Figure 21-18 shows the finished Choose Report dialog box.

Creating a Dialog Box for User Input

In Chapter 9, you saw how to create a parameter query that prompts the user to enter the criteria for the query. You can use a custom dialog box to accomplish the same thing. For

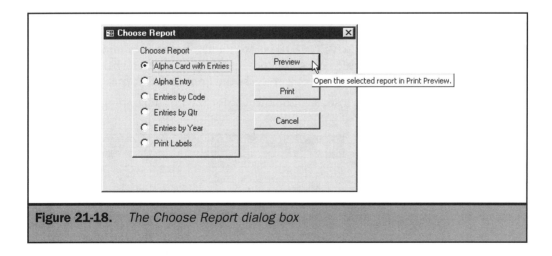

Figure 21-18.   *The Choose Report dialog box*

example, the following dialog box prompts the user to enter the DR value of the Alpha Entry records he wants to see. It includes instructions to ensure a valid input value.

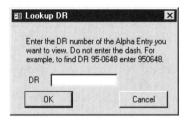

After entering the DR value and clicking OK, a query runs using the value as the criteria for the DR field. For this example, make a copy of the Alpha DR Query and name it Lookup DR. Then you can change the criteria of the DR column to get the value from the dialog box instead of a parameter prompt.

Setting the Input Form Properties

The Lookup DR form has several special features, in addition to the properties that make it a dialog box, as described in the previous section. These include

- The DR box is an unbound text box named FindDR.
- The FindDR text box is first in the tab order with a Tab Index property of 0.
- The OK command button Default property is set to Yes, so the user can simply press ENTER after typing the DR value to run the query.
- The Cancel command button Cancel property is set to Yes.

Creating the Macros

The LookUpDR macro group contains two macros, one for each command button:

- The Run Query macro, which is attached to the OK button, contains two actions: OpenQuery, which runs the Lookup DR query in Datasheet view in read-only mode, and Close, which closes the Lookup DR form.
- The CloseForm macro closes the Lookup DR form without running the query.

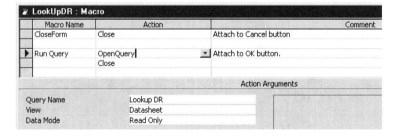

Modifying the Query

To pass the DR value from the form to the query, the Criteria must be set to the unbound text box control in the form. To do this, type **[Forms]![Lookup DR]![FindDR]** in the Criteria row of the DR column in the query grid.

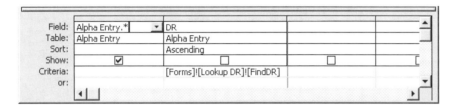

You see more of this type of naming convention when you start working with Visual Basic. Each of the three parts of the statement is enclosed in square brackets to indicate each is an identifier that refers to objects and controls. The first element defines the object type, Forms. The exclamation point (!) indicates the element that follows was named by the user. The second element identifies the specific form, Lookup DR, and the third identifies the unbound text box control, FindDR, in the form.

Be sure to clear the check box in the Show row of the DR column or you'll have two copies of the DR values in the query results.

Summary

The switchboards and custom dialog boxes discussed in this chapter can add significantly to the efficiency of an end-user application by presenting interfaces tuned to the goal of the application and to the level of the intended user. A switchboard system can help the user perform the tasks required of the application by offering a list of activities from which to choose. A main entry point into the application can be set to appear when the database first starts.

Custom dialog boxes can be used for many purposes, each of which can get information from the user before continuing to carry out an action. Such dialog boxes can be designed to look and perform like the built-in Access dialog boxes.

Both switchboards and custom dialog boxes require a means to carry out an action, either a macro or an event procedure attached to the controls. Macros were used in this chapter and, in Chapter 25, you see how Visual Basic event procedures can be created to carry out more complex actions.

EXCHANGING DATA WITH OTHERS

MOUS Exam Activities Explored in This Chapter

Level	Activity	Section Title
Expert	Create a Switchboard and set startup options	Using the Switchboard Manager Creating a Switchboard from Scratch

The Complete Reference

Part IV

Exchanging Data with Others

The
Complete
Reference

Access
2002

Chapter 22

Exchanging Database
Objects and Text

Your application developments can proceed more rapidly when database objects are reused or modified rather than being developed from scratch. Access provides a number of useful functions and tools to enable you to exchange database objects between Access databases. Functions also exist that support the exchange of Access objects with other types of databases, such as dBase or Paradox. You can also exchange Access data in the form of text files.

This chapter, together with the next two, covers the exchange of information between Access and the outside world. The next chapter expands the discussion of data exchange by including other programs, such as word processors and spreadsheets, as well as covering mailing the data to another destination. Chapter 24 discusses submitting Access data to a Web site in the form of static or dynamic pages. The Access data access page is an important object that creates and displays data dynamically in a Web page. The page can also include data from other sources, such as Excel.

Access database objects include tables, queries, reports, forms, pages, macros, and modules. This chapter describes techniques for exchanging many of these database objects by:

- Copying objects among Access databases
- Importing or linking Access data
- Importing or linking other database formats
- Using linked or imported tables
- Exporting to Access databases
- Exporting objects to other database formats
- Importing and exporting text files

Copying Objects Among Access Databases

Modifying existing objects is generally easier than developing tables, forms, and reports from scratch. A first step in the modification of existing Access database objects is to copy the objects you want to edit or modify.

Efficient and simple techniques exist for copying objects among Access databases. Standard copy-and-paste operations, as well as drag-and-drop techniques, can be used to copy objects from one Access database to another.

Copy and Paste

To copy and, subsequently, to paste an Access database object, you must select the object to be copied from the Database window. Objects in this window are selected by first clicking the appropriate button under Objects, and then selecting an object on that page.

To copy the Alpha Card table from the Police database:

1. Click Tables under Objects in the Database window.
2. Select the Alpha Card table from the list of tables.
3. Use one of the following to copy the table to the clipboard:

   ■ Click the Copy toolbar button.
   ■ Choose File | Copy.
   ■ Right-click the table name and choose Copy from the shortcut menu.

If your objective at this point is to copy the table to the same database, you have three ways to paste the table:

   ■ Click the Paste toolbar button.
   ■ Select Edit | Paste.
   ■ Right-click the Tables page outside any table name and choose Paste from the shortcut menu.

When tables are copied, options are presented in a Paste Table As dialog box (see Figure 22-1), which asks for a name for the table, as well as presents the following options:

   ■ Pasting the structure of the table (without its data)
   ■ Pasting the structure of the table and its data
   ■ Appending the data to an existing table

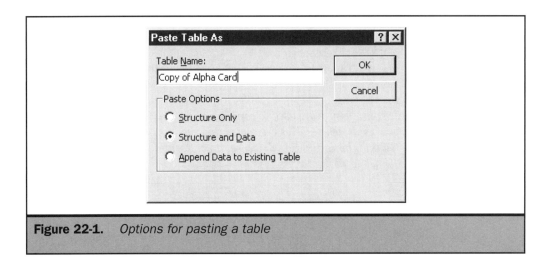

Figure 22-1. *Options for pasting a table*

If you choose to append the data to an existing table, you might have problems with duplicate primary key fields or unique index values. You also need to consider differing table structures. See Chapter 9 for information dealing with append queries and how to solve those problems.

If you're copying an object to another database (rather than within its own database with a different name), you can start a second instance of Access and open the destination database. Then tile the two Access windows in a split-screen format. Next, copy the object from the source database, select the object category in the destination Database window, and paste into the destination database. If you don't want to use two instances of Access, close the source database after you copy the object, open the corresponding page in the destination database, and then click Paste.

 Copying an object generates a copy of all the properties of that object. For example, when a form is copied, the format, source data, event specifications, filters, and all other properties are copied with the form.

Drag-and-Drop

A drag-and-drop technique can also be used to copy objects between databases. To use drag-and-drop, two instances of Access must be active at the same time. The source database must be open in one Access window and the destination database must be open in another Access window.

To drag an object from one window to another:

1. Make sure both Database windows are open to the same object page, and then select the object to be copied in the first database.

2. While holding the left mouse button down, drag the item to the destination database.

3. Release the mouse button and the new object appears in the destination database.

 When drag-and-drop techniques are used to copy tables, the Paste Table As window doesn't appear. As a result, when tables are copied this way the table structure and its data are both pasted into the destination database. If you want only the structure, open the copied table and delete all the records.

Importing or Linking Access Data

Two other important techniques for adding Access data to an Access database or project are importing and linking. *Importing* is used to copy Access data or other objects into an Access database from other Access databases. Importing is also used to bring data into an Access database from dissimilar sources, such as a dBASE or Paradox application; this is discussed later in this chapter (see "Importing or Linking to Other Databases"). *Linking* is a way of connecting to and using data in an Access database without actually copying the data from the other database.

You can import or link data from Access versions 2.0, 7.0/95, 8.0/97, and 9.0/2000 to Access 2002 databases or projects.

 Note   *If you're importing or linking a database that requires a password, you must enter the password before you can proceed.*

Importing Objects

The first case to look at is the importing of all objects from one Access database to another. To start importing an object, do the following:

1. Choose File | Get External Data. You have a choice of Import or Link Tables.

2. Choose Import. The Import dialog box opens (see Figure 22-2) where you locate and select the database file that contains the objects you want to import. You can also right-click in the Database window and choose Import from the shortcut menu.

Import vs. Link

You should choose to import data into an Access database if you expect to use the data only in Access and not depend on another program to maintain the data. Access is more efficient when working with its own tables and you can modify the data just the same as native-grown data.

You should choose to link with data in another program if you rely on the source program to update the information. Linking is also useful in a multiuser environment where you split an existing database and place the data on a network server. Users can then share the database and create their own forms, reports, and other objects.

EXCHANGING DATA
WITH OTHERS

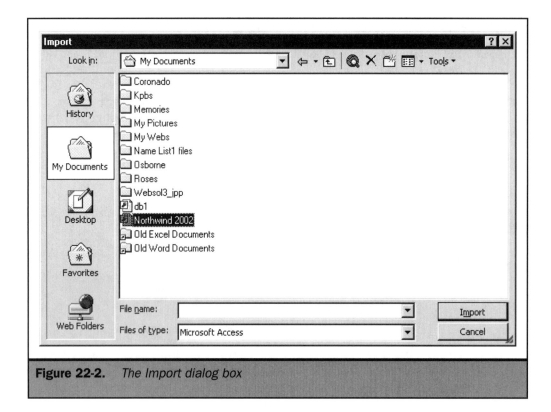

Figure 22-2. *The Import dialog box*

3. When you locate the database file from which you want to import objects, select it and click Import. The Import Objects dialog box opens (see Figure 22-3) where you can choose just which objects to import. In this example, the Northwind database is selected from sample Access applications, and the Products and Categories tables are imported.

4. To choose which objects to import, click the desired object tab and do one of the following:

■ Select each object name individually.

■ Click Select All.

■ To remove an object from the import list, select it again, or click Deselect All to remove all selected objects.

5. Repeat step 4 for all the desired object types.

6. After selecting all the objects you want to import, click OK to close the Import Objects dialog box and return to the Database window where you can see the imported objects.

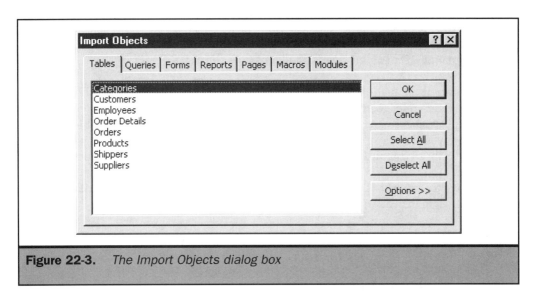

Figure 22-3.   The Import Objects dialog box

Note   *When you import a data access page, you import only the link to the underlying HTML file. The HTML file location is unchanged unless you specify a new location for it.*

Figure 22-4 shows the Police Database window with the newly imported Catefories and Products tables. The imported tables are now part of the Police database and don't appear different from the native tables.

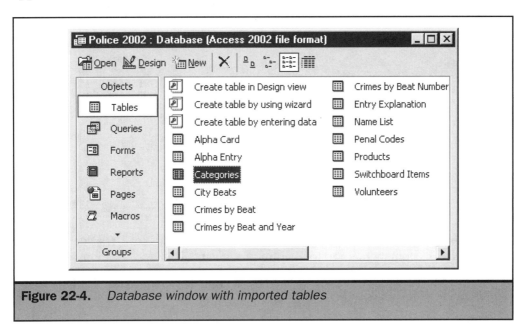

Figure 22-4.   Database window with imported tables

You can't append imported data to existing tables directly. You must import the table first, and then run an append query to add the data to the other table. See Chapter 9 for information about append queries and how to use them.

If you import a table that includes Lookup fields, remember to import the tables or queries the fields refer to and get their values from. Otherwise, every time you open the table in Datasheet view, you'll get an error message for each missing table or query. If you don't want to or can't import the supporting value tables or queries, you can change the imported table design by changing the field Display Control property on the Lookup tab to Text Box for each Lookup field.

If you try to import a table that's already linked to another table, you link to the source table data instead of importing it.

 Importing objects from an earlier version of Access is an easy way to convert the object to Access 2002.

Setting Import Options

When you click Options in the Import Objects dialog box, the box expands to show a lower pane with three sets of import options.

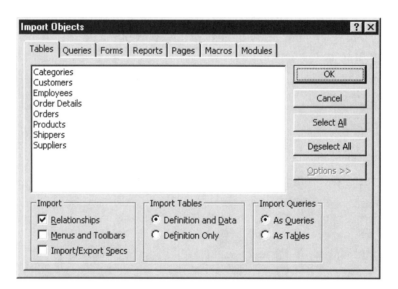

The first set of options supports the importing of other table features, such as the relationships, custom menus and toolbars, and some database specifications.

■ The Relationships option is selected by default and includes the relationships you defined for the tables and queries you import.

■ The Menus and Toolbars option includes all the custom menus and toolbars in the database from which you're importing. However, Access won't import any menu or toolbar that has the same name as one in the destination database.

■ The Import/Export Specs option includes all the import and export specifications set for the source database.

The second set of options, Import Tables, applies to the imported tables and determines whether to import both the table definition and the data (default) or only the definition. This is useful for creating a copy of the table structures for a new database without including any existing data.

The third set of options, Import Queries, applies to any queries you selected to import and specifies whether to import queries as queries (default) or run the query and import the resulting recordset as a table. Importing queries as tables can create a read-only database.

Once opened, as you click other object tabs, the Options pane remains open.

Caution *Reasons for importing some objects or combinations of objects must be examined carefully. For example, importing a form without importing its underlying tables or queries can result in problems that may be difficult to resolve. An attempt to invoke the form generates an error message indicating the underlying record source is missing. Logical, useful groupings of objects should be imported and, in most cases, this means tables should be imported to provide the field definitions and data for all the forms, queries, reports, pages, macros, and modules you choose to import. Relationships should also be included whenever importing more than one table.*

Linking Access Tables

Linking to tables in another Access database makes them available without copying them into the active database. Linking saves space and reduces the need to maintain redundant data. Linking also ensures you always have access to current information. However, linking also means you're dependent on an object that actually resides in another environment where it may be renamed, moved, or deleted. Objects that are linked may be moved from one folder or from one disk to another, which could break the link.

Caution *If you're linking to a table in a database that's password-protected, you must enter the correct password to continue. When you enter the password, it's stored in an unencrypted form with the link information and any user who can open your database can also open the linked, password-protected database. See Chapters 26 and 27 for more information about multiple users and security.*

To link to a table in another Access database, do the following:

1. Open the destination database, in this example, Police.

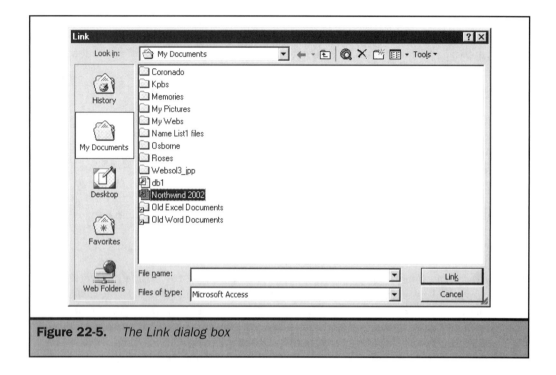

Figure 22-5. The Link dialog box

2. Start the linking process by choosing File | Get External Data from any page in the Database window and click Link Tables. You can also right-click in the Database window and choose Link Tables from the shortcut menu. The Link dialog box appears, which is similar in appearance to the Import dialog box (see Figure 22-5).

3. In the Link dialog box, select the Microsoft Access file type, and then select the database you want to link to your active database. Then click Link. In this example, the sample Northwind database is selected as the source of the linked table. The Link Tables dialog box opens (see Figure 22-6), showing only a Tables tab because tables are the only Access objects to which you can link.

4. Select one or more of the available tables and click the OK button. In this example, the Suppliers table is linked to the Police database. The table is marked in the list of tables with an arrow indicating the table is a linked table (Figure 22-7).

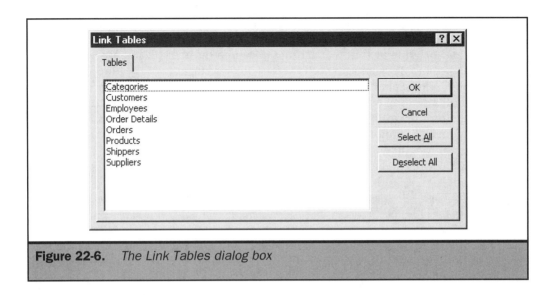

Figure 22-6.   *The Link Tables dialog box*

Note   *If you link two related tables from the same database, the relationship is retained.*

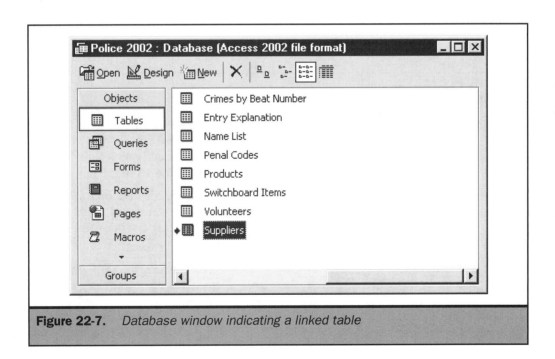

Figure 22-7.   *Database window indicating a linked table*

Importing or Linking to Other Databases

Access can import data or link to existing tables in a number of the most prevalent database management systems, as well as from other sources, such as word processors or HTML files. Access provides specific recognition of some database table formats. The process of importing or linking to foreign databases that aren't Access databases is similar to the import or link functions for Access databases. This section discusses importing from or linking to dBase and Paradox databases, as well as techniques for importing data from other sources supported by Access.

Table 22-1 lists the database formats Access can successfully import from or link to.

Tip   *If data is in the database or a data format that isn't supported by Access 2002, the source program may be able to convert or save the data in a format that is supported, such as dBASE or Paradox. For example, you can't directly import or link to a Microsoft Works database, but Works can save the file as a dBASE IV file, which is supported by Access. Most unsupported programs, including some working with different operating systems, are also able to export data to a delimited or fixed-width text file, which you can then import or link to Access.*

Data types are generally compatible among these database management systems, although they aren't labeled consistently. Table 22-2 shows the data types in other database applications and what data type is designated in Access.

Format	Import/Link
dBASE III, III+, IV, 5, 7	Both import and link. However, for version 7, linking (read/write) requires updated ISAM drivers available from Microsoft Technical Support or the Borland Database Engine 4.*x* or later.
Paradox 3.*x*, 4.*x*, 5.0, 8.0	Both import and link. Again, for version 8.0, linking (read/write) requires updated ISAM drivers available from Microsoft Technical Support or the Borland Database Engine 4.*x* or later.

Table 22-1.   *Database Formats Usable in Access*

dBASE	Paradox	Access
Character	Alphanumeric	Text
Numeric	Number	Number with Field Size property set to Double
	Short Number	Number with Field Size property set to Integer
Float	Currency	Number with Field Size property set to Double
		Number with Field Size property set to Double
Logical		Yes/No
Date	Date	Date/Time
Memo	Memo	Memo
	OLE	OLE Object
	Graphic, Binary, Formatted Memo	Not supported

Table 22-2.   *Data Type Conversions*

Using Data from dBASE or Paradox

Importing a dBASE table or a Paradox file into an Access database is similar to importing a table from an Access database. The example shown here imports a dBASE table into the Access database. To import the foreign table, do the following:

1. Choose File | Get External Data, and then select Import or right-click in the Database window and choose Import from the shortcut menu. This brings up the Import dialog box as before.

2. In the Files of type area, select the database file types. Then locate and select the file you want to import.

3. In the case illustrated here, select the Employee.dbf file and click Import.

4. After a few seconds, you should see a message indicating EMPLOYEE has been successfully imported into the open Access database (see Figure 22-8). Click OK.

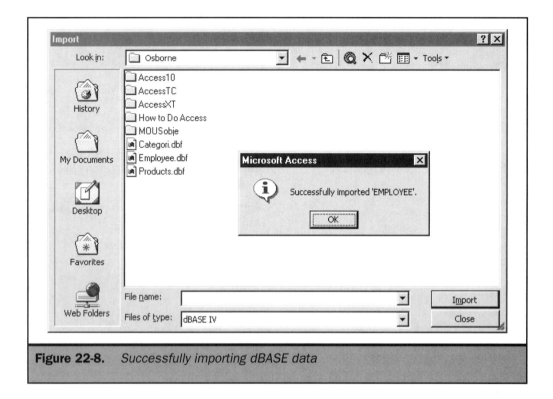

Figure 22-8. *Successfully importing dBASE data*

5. Locate and import other files as necessary or click Close to close the dialog box
and return to the Police database window.

Once the table is imported, it looks and behaves just like an Access table. Importing
Paradox files uses the same procedures.

Another approach to making use of data from a dBASE or Paradox database is to
use the Link Tables operation by choosing File | Get External Data and selecting the
Link Tables option. You can also right-click the Database window and choose Link
Tables from the shortcut menu. The Link dialog box appears (refer to Figure 22-5), in
which you select the appropriate file type and the specific file to be linked.

When you import a dBASE file, Access creates a table with the same name as the
.dbf file and imports the data. When you link to a dBASE file, Access also requires the
associated dBASE index files be linked. If you choose to link to a dBASE file, the Select
Index Files dialog box appears where you can choose the indexes (.ndx and .mdx files)
associated with the .dbf file.

■ If there are none, click Cancel and proceed with the link operation.

■ If you select one or more index files, the Select Unique Record Identifier dialog box prompts you to select the corresponding index field. Your index must have a unique value for each record or difficulties may occur when you try to update records.

After importing or linking a dBASE file, you can set field properties for the table. If you import a file with no primary index, you can set one in Access. When you update the file with Access, the index is automatically updated as well. If you use dBASE to update the file, you must also update the corresponding index in dBASE before trying to open the file in Access.

Figure 22-9 shows a linked dBASE file in the Database window by displaying the arrow (indicating a linked file) and a dB icon indicating NewCats is a linked dBASE file.

If you select a Paradox table to link to, you need the index (.px) file and the memo (.mb) file, if the table has any. Without these files, you won't be able to open the linked table in Access. If the Paradox table doesn't have a primary index, you must create one in Paradox to update the table in Access.

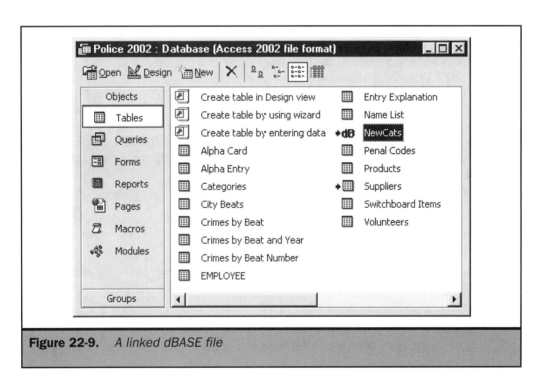

Figure 22-9.   *A linked dBASE file*

EXCHANGING DATA
WITH OTHERS

Using Data from Later Versions of dBASE and Paradox

Linking a dBASE 7 or Paradox 8.0 table can require additional resources, depending on whether you want both to read and write data in the tables you select. To alter the contents of a table, you need to have the *Borland Database Engine* (*BDE*) 4.0 or ISAM drivers installed. BDE version 4.0 is obtained by installing dBASE 7, Paradox 8.0, or Delphi, or by upgrading older versions of BDE from Borland's Web site. You can get the ISAM drivers from Microsoft Technical Support.

Importing and Linking SQL Data

Importing or linking SQL database tables or data requires SQL server drivers to be installed for each type of SQL database you want to use. Even in the case of the Microsoft SQL Server, the appropriate driver won't be installed with the typical Access installation. Prior to importing or linking Microsoft SQL Server database tables, you must run Setup to install the correct *Open Database Connectivity* (*ODBC*). If you're linking to or importing data from some other SQL server (such as Oracle or Sybase), the correct driver files and documentation must be acquired from the vendor.

In defining the connection to a SQL table, you must specify the source of the data as either a machine data source or a file data source. *Machine data sources* store the connection information in the Windows Registry with a user-defined name and are limited to use on the computer on which they're defined.

File data sources store the connection information in a text file, called the *Data Source Name* (*DSN*) file, rather than in the Windows Registry and, consequently, are more flexible because they can be copied to another computer. You can also place a file data source on a server and make it available to other computers on the network. File data sources can also be made unshareable, so they reside on a single computer and point to a machine data source.

To import or link with SQL tables, do the following:

1. Choose File | Get External Data, and then choose Import or Link Tables as before. You can also right-click the Database window and choose either command from the shortcut menu.

2. In the subsequent dialog box (Import or Link), select the ODBC Databases from the list of possible file types in the Files of type box.

3. A Select Data Source dialog box (see Figure 22-10) appears, listing the defined data sources for all the ODBC drivers you have installed. Do one of the following:

   ■ Click the File Data Source tab and enter the desired DSN.

   ■ Click the Machine Data Source tab and double-click the machine data source.

   ■ The New button enables you to define a new file or machine data source in accordance with the requirements of each ODBC driver.

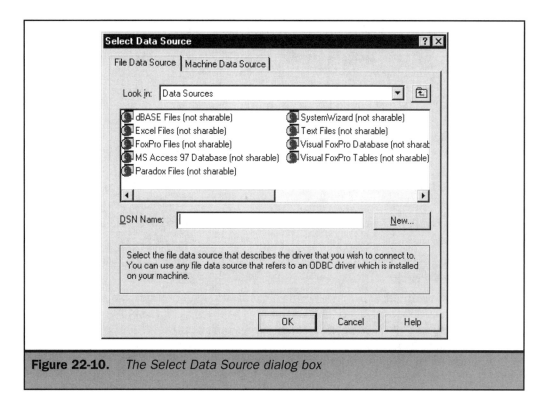

Figure 22-10. *The Select Data Source dialog box*

4. If the ODBC data source requires you to log on, enter your logon ID and password, and then click OK.

5. After you select the data source, Access connects to it and displays the tables available for importing/linking. You may be required to log on when you select a data source.

   ■ If you're linking to the table, choose the Save the Login ID and Password check box to save the information.

   ■ If you leave it cleared, you must enter the logon ID and password each time you open the table with Access.

6. Once a table is selected for importing or linking, click OK.

Note *If you're linking to a table that doesn't have a unique index, Access displays the field list. Select a field or a combination of fields to identify each record uniquely and click OK. If the field you select contains duplicate values in some of the records, you won't be able to update those records.*

For more information about using SQL tables, see the Access 2002 Help topics.

EXCHANGING DATA
WITH OTHERS

Using SQL Server Database Utilities

When you link an Access database to a SQL Server database, the Microsoft SQL Server database utilities become available. With these, you can back up your database or add security. To use these database utilities, you must have *Microsoft Data Engine* (*MSDE*) or Microsoft SQL 2000 installed on your computer. Once these database administrator components are available, you can do the following with your SQL Server database.

- Choose Tools | Database Utilities | Backup to create a backup copy of the database.

- Choose Tools | Database Utilities | Restore to restore the database from a previous backup.

- Choose Tools | Database Utilities | Drop SQL Database to delete the link to the SQL database.

- Choose Tools | Security | Database Security to add or modify security for the database.

- Choose a command from the Tools | Replication submenu to manage the SQL server database replicas. The commands are Synchronize Now, Create Publication, Pull Subscription, Push Subscription, Subscription Properties, Publisher Properties, and Conflict resolution. See Windows Help topics for more information about using SQL Server databases.

See Chapter 26 for information about creating and maintaining replica databases, and see Chapter 27 for information about adding security to your Access databases.

Importing and Linking Text Files

Text files are useful when importing or linking the data to Access tables. Most relational, hierarchical, or network-oriented database management systems can generate a text version of the data using some kind of record selection function. Once text files have been generated they are either *fixed-width* text files (files consisting of rows of data of the same length) or *delimited* text files (files containing records that use special characters—typically commas—to indicate the separation between data fields). Fixed-width or delimited text files can be imported or linked to an Access database using the same external data importing and linking functions used for data from any source.

Using Delimited Text Files

Importing or linking a delimited text file begins with the same sequence as other importing and linking operations. Prior to starting the importing/linking process, however, you must specify a table ready to receive the data—either a new table definition with the appropriate field definitions or an existing table to which this new data can be appended.

Note *Creating a table definition to receive the data from delimited text files can be accomplished using basic table definition techniques (see Chapter 4) or by copying the table definition from an existing table. Care must be taken to account for the proper number of fields, field length, and data type selection to import text data correctly.*

To import a text file, open the Import dialog box as before, and then do the following:

1. In the Import window, select Text Files in the Files of type box.

2. Locate the text file you want to import and double-click its name, or select it and click Import.

3. The Import Text Wizard dialog box appears, displaying sample data from the selected text file. The Import Text Wizard actually analyzes the selected file and determines whether it's a fixed-width text file or a delimited file. Figure 22-11 shows the text file we're importing, SENIORS.TXT, has been determined to be a delimited text file.

4. Click Next to see how the file is formatted. In the case illustrated here (see Figure 22-12), the wizard determined the fields in this file are delimited by commas, text fields are bound by quotation marks, and the first row doesn't contain field names.

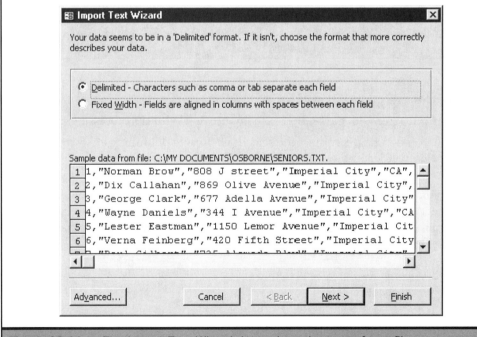

Figure 22-11. *The Import Text Wizard determines the type of text file*

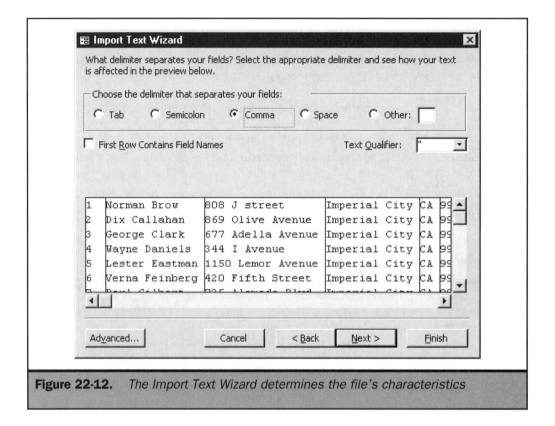

Figure 22-12. *The Import Text Wizard determines the file's characteristics*

5. Next, do one of the following:

■ If you agree with the results of the Import Text Wizard's processing, click Next.

■ If you don't agree, adjust the selections (for the delimiting character, the text qualifier, and whether the first row contains field names) until you're satisfied they're accurate, and then click Next.

6. At this point, you must decide whether to import the data to a new table or append to an existing table. If you select In an Existing Table, select a table name from the drop-down list and click Finish. Figure 22-13 illustrates an example of selecting an existing table to receive the data.

Note   *You can append text files to an existing table if the first row of the text file matches the table's field names.*

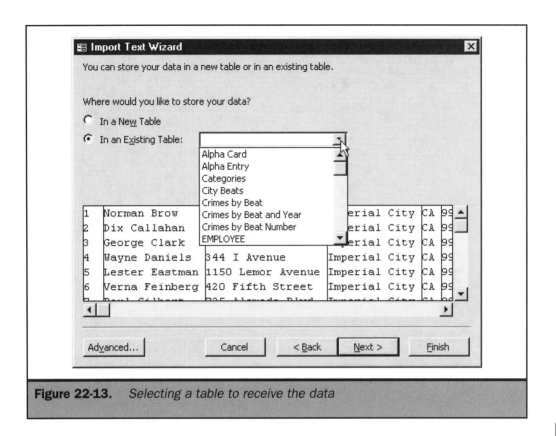

Figure 22-13. *Selecting a table to receive the data*

7. Because the field names aren't in the first row of the text table, choose to import the data to a new table and click Next. The Import Text Wizard asks you to specify information about each field in the file (see Figure 22-14). Enter or verify the field name, data type, if the field is indexed, and whether you want to import or skip that field.

8. After completing the field information, click Next and the wizard suggests specifying a primary key field, either by letting the wizard add one, specifying an existing field, or choosing not to have a primary key (Figure 22-15). Click Next.

9. The final step in importing the data is to enter a name for the new table and click Finish.

If the import process seems to take a long time, errors may be occurring. Press CTRL-BREAK to cancel any time during the process.

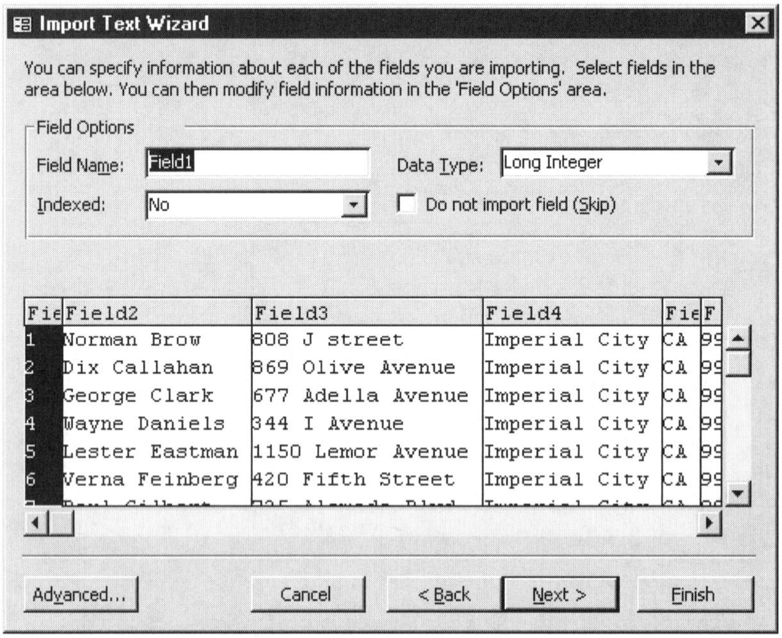

Figure 22-14. *Setting imported field information*

Import Errors

Improperly defined data or data of an improper length could cause errors that are recorded in an import processing error table. If this occurs, Access creates an Import Errors table containing descriptions of the errors that occurred when importing the text file or spreadsheet to an Access database. The table shows the field names and row numbers of the data that caused the error. An Import Errors table isn't created when you import a text file to an Access project.

Some of the possible import errors are

- **Field Truncation**, which occurs when the text value is longer than the Field Size property setting for the destination field.

- **Type Conversion Failure**, which occurs when a value is the wrong data type for the destination field.

- **Key Violation**, which occurs when a duplicate primary key value appears.

■ **Validation Rule Failure**, which occurs when a field value breaks the rule defined in the Validation Rule property for the destination field.

■ **Null in Required Field**, which occurs when the Required property of the destination field is set to Yes and a Null value occurs.

■ **Unparsable Record**, which occurs when a text value contains a character specified as the text delimiter character.

If the problem is with the data, edit the file. If you're trying to append data to an existing table, you may need to change the table definition. After correcting the problems, import the file again. When a value contains the delimiter character, edit each field to repeat the character twice.

Linking delimited text files with the Link Text Wizard involves the same process as importing with two exceptions: you aren't asked if you want to link to an existing table or create a new one, and you're also not prompted for a primary index because you're not creating a new table.

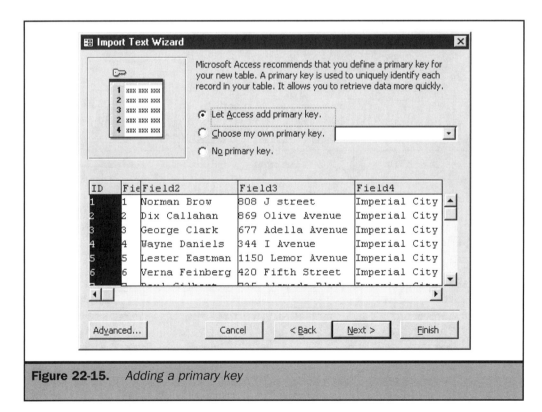

Figure 22-15. *Adding a primary key*

Using Fixed-Width Text Files

The Import Text Wizard reacts a little differently once fixed-width text files are detected. The second Wizard dialog box (see Figure 22-16) shows the fixed-length data with vertical lines between fields and a ruler at the top. The wizard asks you to confirm whether the lines seem to indicate the proper separation point between fields and provides guidance as to how to move or reposition the lines:

- To create a line, click the position where a field separation is desired.
- To delete a line, double-click the line to remove the field separation.
- To move a line, click-and-drag the line to the proper position.

Once adjustments are completed, the process of identifying the destination table and completing the import or link is the same as with delimited files.

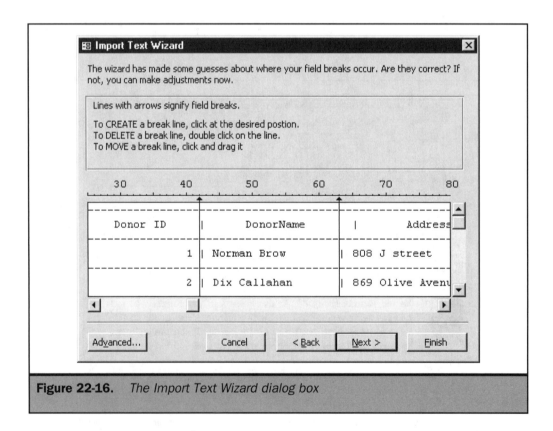

Figure 22-16.   *The Import Text Wizard dialog box*

Changing Import Specifications

The import specifications for a text file can be changed using the Advanced features of the Import Text Wizard. When the Advanced button is clicked, an Import Specification dialog box appears (Figure 22-17), which enables you to specify a number of table characteristics including:

- The file format (delimited or fixed-width)

- If delimited, the field delimiter and text qualifier characters

- The language and code page in which you can choose a different language and set the logical text layout to one of the right-to-left reading codes. As a step toward compatibility with Asian markets, you can set the code for importing or exporting text files in a right-to-left reading direction. Click the Code Page drop-down arrow in the Import Specification box to see the list of code page conversion options.

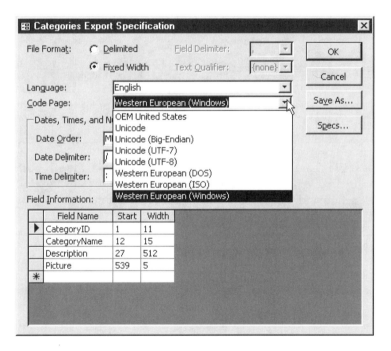

- The specifications for dates, times, and numbers

- Information for each incoming field, such as name, starting and ending position in the record, data type, whether the field is to be indexed, and whether to omit the field from the import

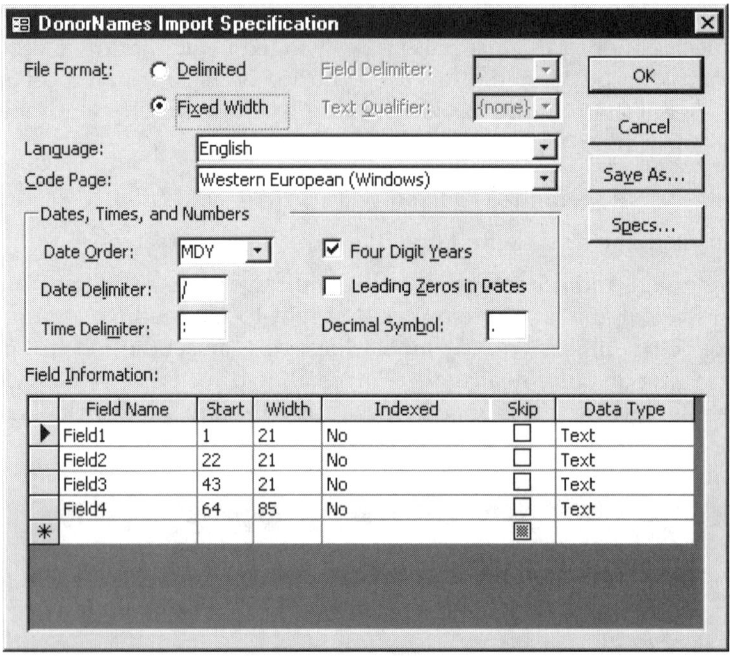

Figure 22-17. *The Import Specification dialog box*

Once the text file characteristics are satisfactorily specified, the OK button returns you to the Import Text Wizard dialog box, where clicking the Finish button completes the text import action and places the table in your Access database.

Using Linked or Imported Tables

Linked or imported tables are used just as any other Access table with some precautions. Imported tables have essentially become new tables within your Access database. Linked tables, however, still reside within the environments in which they were created. Thus, issues such as renaming the table or changing its characteristics have implications for relating the linked table to its original source environment.

Renaming a Table in Access

The linked table may have a name that isn't meaningful in our Access database. You can give it a more relevant name without disturbing the link. Renaming a linked table is the same as renaming a native table.

1. Select the table in the Database window.

2. Select Edit | Rename or right-click and choose Rename from the shortcut menu, and then edit the old name or enter a new name.

Note

When a linked table is renamed in Access, the name of the linked table isn't changed in its original environment. Renaming the linked table in an Access database simply changes the name used within that particular database. The longer table names in Access (up to 64 characters) can support more descriptive naming conventions than other applications offer, some of which still limit table names to eight characters and don't allow spaces.

Changing Table Properties

Table properties of linked tables are usually set by the database that owns the table. The field properties and the validation rules are also set by the source database. Data entered in Access must conform to most of the properties set for the originating database fields, such as default values, minimum or maximum values, field format, text options, and any other validation requirements.

Field properties you can change in a linked table include Format, Decimal Places, Input Mask, and Caption. If you want to change other field properties in a form, set them for the controls bound to the fields.

Changing the basic properties or validation rules of a linked table requires access to the table through its original database application. If the table is in a database environment other than Access, that database management system must be available to support efforts to change table properties.

Updating Links with the Linked Table Manager

When the location of a linked table is changed, using the Linked Table Manager database utility within Access is a recommended method of reestablishing the proper path or linkage to the table. The Linked Table Manager doesn't physically move files, it only updates the path leading to the file location. The Linked Table Manager may be consulted in two cases:

■ To examine or refresh links

■ To change the path or location of linked tables

Note

The Linked Table Manager doesn't move database or table files; it only updates the path to the object. If you want to move the file to a new location, use the Windows Explorer, My Computer, or the MS-DOS Move or Copy commands. After you move the file, you can use the Linked Table Manager to refresh the link.

EXCHANGING DATA
WITH OTHERS

To refresh links, do the following:

1. To start the Linked Table Manager, select Tools | Database Utilities | Linked Table Manager. The Linked Table Manager dialog box displays a list of all tables linked to the current database with the table name and the current path (see Figure 22-18).

2. Click Select All or check only the table links you want to refresh and click OK.

3. If the Manager is successful in locating the file, it displays a message to that effect. If not, it prompts for the location of the table by displaying a Select New Location Of Tablename dialog box where you can locate the file and change the path.

 The Linked Table Manager has no way of refreshing links to tables whose names were changed in the source database after linking. Delete the current link and start over.

To change the path to a linked table, open the Linked Table Manager, as previously discussed, and do the following:

1. Select the Always prompt for new location option in the Linked Table Manager dialog box.

2. Check the tables whose paths you want to change and click OK.

3. Designate their new location in the Select New Location of Tablename dialog box and click Open. If you need to, you can use the Search feature (choose Tools | Search) in the Select New Location dialog box to locate elusive files.

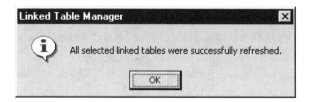

4. Click OK to close the message box, then click Close.

 If more than one of the tables you selected were moved to the new location, all the links are updated at once.

Unlinking Tables

Unlinking a table actually removes the linkage to a table in another (source) database. The procedure for unlinking a table is identical to that for deleting a table, however, the Delete function doesn't actually delete the linked table. It only deletes the link to the database.

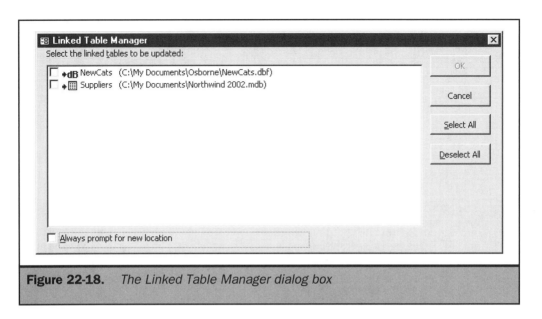

Figure 22-18. *The Linked Table Manager dialog box*

Caution *If your intention is to delete a link to a table in another database and not to delete a complete table and its data, be sure to select a table name with the arrow indicating it's a linked table. If you inadvertently select a regular table, as opposed to a linked table, and perform a Delete, the table and its data will be lost.*

To unlink a table, do one of the following:

■ Select the linked table to be unlinked and press DELETE or choose Edit | Delete.

■ Right-click the table name and choose Delete from the shortcut menu.

Respond Yes when Access asks for confirmation of the deletion.

Exporting to an Existing Access Database

Exporting data or database objects to another Access database is a straightforward process. Exporting has the same functionality as copying and pasting. The same data formats are supported as with importing.

1. To export a table, select the table name in the Database window and choose File | Export, or right-click the table name and choose Export from the shortcut menu.

2. An Export Table To dialog box appears in which to locate and select the destination database and select the export file type in the Save as Type box (Figure 22-19).

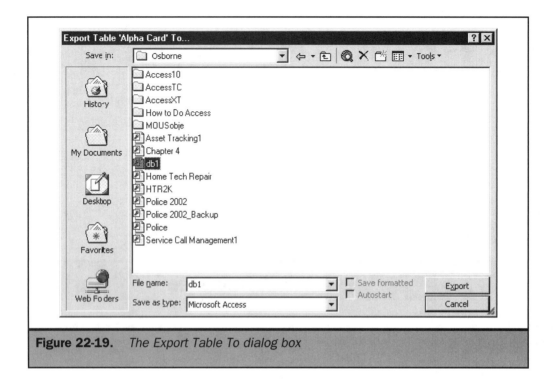

Figure 22-19. *The Export Table To dialog box*

3. Click Export.

4. Accept the existing name or enter a new name for the destination table in the Export dialog box.

5. Select to export both the table definition and data, or only the definition.

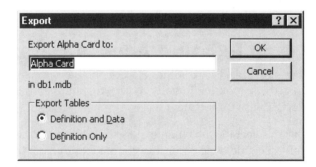

6. Click OK.

When you're exporting database objects other than tables, the basic steps are the same. The exception is the final step isn't required because you're exporting only an object design without any data.

Most objects other than tables cannot be exported directly to Access databases created and maintained in versions of Access prior to 2000. Access databases created in earlier versions of Access must be converted to the current version of Access before exporting objects other than tables.

Exporting database objects operates as a one-at-a-time function. When multiple objects are to be exported to an Access database, it may be more expedient to open the destination database and use the Get External Data/Import functions, which can be used to import multiple objects at once.

Exporting to Another Database Format

Access supports exporting data to the same database and text formats as are acceptable for importing and linking. Access can also export data in the proper formats for other applications, such as spreadsheets (Excel and Lotus 1-2-3), text files, HTML, or XML files, as discussed in the next chapter.

When you export data to dBASE or Paradox, which limit table names to eight characters, not including the file extension, the longer table names are truncated to comply with the limitation. This can result in duplicate names. To prevent this, make a copy of your table with a shorter name before exporting the copy.

To export data to these formats, follow these steps:

1. Select the table in your active database and select File | Export, or right-click the table name and choose Export from the shortcut menu.

2. In the Export Table To dialog box, choose the dBASE or Paradox file format in the Save as Type box (refer to Figure 22-19).

3. Click the arrow next to Save in and select the drive and folder to export to.

4. Enter the destination filename in the File name box and click Save.

Exporting to Text Files

When you want to export data from an Access database to a text file, you call on the Export Text Wizard, which works much like the Import Text Wizard described earlier. The wizard helps you specify the format of the exported Access file and determine where the output is to be stored. The following steps describe how to export data to a text file using the Export Text Wizard.

1. In the Tables page of the Database window, select the table containing the data you want to export to a text file.

2. Choose File | Export or right-click and choose Export from the shortcut menu.

3. In the Export Table ... To dialog box, select Text Files in the Save As Type box.

4. In the Save in box, select the folder to receive the exported text data.

5. In the File name box, enter the name of the text file you want to assign to the exported data or select an existing file to receive the data. Click Export.

6. The Export Text Wizard dialog box (see Figure 22-20) appears displaying data from the selected table. You have the choice between saving a fixed-width text file or a delimited file.

7. Click Next.

8. If you chose Delimited, the next dialog box (see Figure 22-21) contains the specifics of the delimiters, text qualifiers, and other features of each field.

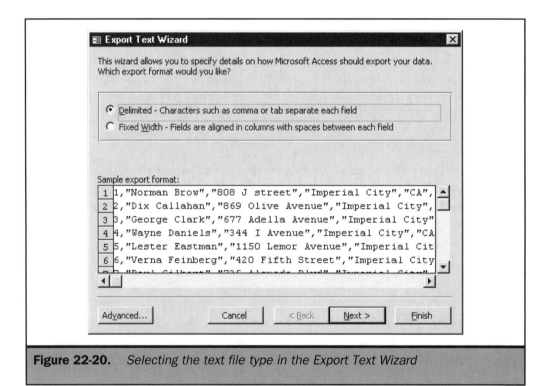

Figure 22-20. *Selecting the text file type in the Export Text Wizard*

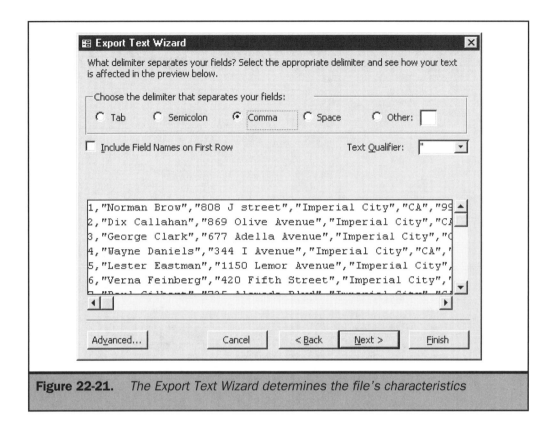

Figure 22-21.   *The Export Text Wizard determines the file's characteristics*

- If you agree with the results of the Export Text Wizard's processing, click Next.
- If you don't agree, adjust the selections (for the delimiting character, the text indicator, and whether the first row contains field names) until you're satisfied they're accurate. Then click Next.

9. If you chose Fixed Width, the next dialog box asks for verification of the field breaks. Figure 22-22 shows the same table being exported as fixed width.

10. Click Finish to complete the export.

You can also use the Export Text Wizard to customize the export specifications for a text file the same way you set the import specifications with the Import Text Wizard. When you click the Advanced button in the Export Text Wizard, an Export Specification dialog box appears, enabling you to specify the file format (fixed-width or delimited), the language and code page settings, the specifications for dates, times, and numbers, and field information. The options are the same as for importing, including encoding for a right-to-left language.

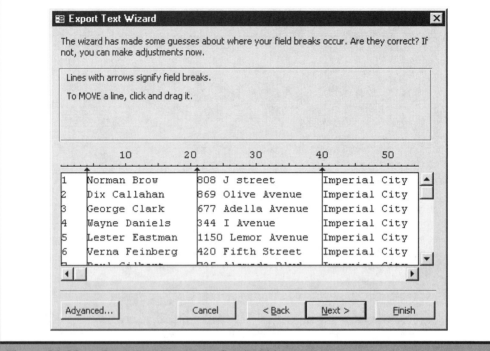

Figure 22-22. *Exporting the text as fixed width*

Automating Data Transfer

When you want to speed up a routine data transfer activity—importing, exporting or linking—you can create a macro or Visual Basic procedure to do it for you. Then you can attach the macro or procedure to a command button or an event property of a form, such as On Close or On Update.

Five types of transfer actions and Visual Basic methods are available

■ **TransferDatabase** action, which imports or exports data between the current Access database or project and another database. This is also used to link a table from another database to the current Access database. The TransferDatabase method carries out the macro action in a procedure.

■ **TransferCompleteSQLDatabase** action, which imports or exports a complete SQL Server database to another SQL database. The TransferSQLDatabase method carries out the macro in a procedure.

- **TransferSpreadsheet** action, which imports or exports data between the current Access database and a spreadsheet file. This is also used to link Excel spreadsheet data to the current Access database. The TransferSpreadsheet method carries out the macro action in a procedure.

- **TransferText** action, which imports or exports text between the current Access database and a text file. This is also used to link data in a text file to the current Access database. If you link to data in a text file or HTML file, the data is read-only in Access. The TransferText method carries out the macro action in a procedure.

- **ImportXML** and **ExportXML** actions, which import and export between the current database and a XML file. The ImportXML and ExportXML methods carry out the same actions in a procedure.

Each of the macro actions has a set of arguments that represent the same choices you make in the series of wizard dialog boxes. Open an Access Help topic to read more information about these actions and methods and their syntax.

Refer to Chapter 19 for information about creating, attaching, and running macros. See Chapter 25 for information about writing and applying VBA procedures.

Summary

Importing, linking, and exporting data are important ways of sharing data between Access databases, and also with other applications. These data exchange functions are essential tools in exchanging data with other Microsoft Office XP applications, as well as Paradox, dBASE, and other database management systems. These functions are also important in sharing data across networks and, as I explain in Chapter 24, can play a pivotal role in exchanging data with potential users on the World Wide Web. The functions that support these data exchange operations, such as Get External Data, Export, and the Import and Export Text Wizards, have a number of options and should be the subject of considerable experimentation to ensure the results are useful and reliable. In the next two chapters, you learn about the issues of exchanging data with outside sources and various techniques to access the Internet and to make Access data available on the Web.

▚ MOUS Exam Activities Explored in This Chapter

Level	Activity	Section Title
Core	Import data to Access	Importing or Linking Access Data Importing or Linking to Other Databases Importing and Linking Text Files Using Linked or Imported Tables
Core	Export data from Access	Exporting to an Existing Access Database Exporting to Another Database Format Exporting to Text Files
Expert	Link tables	Linking Access Tables Updating Links with the Linked Table Manager
Expert	Link tables to Structured Query Language (SQL) Server database	Importing and Linking SQL Data
Expert	Using SQL Server 2000 functions	Using SQL Server Database Utilities

The Complete Reference

Access 2002

Chapter 23

Exchanging Data with Outside Sources

The last chapter focused on exchanging data within the Access management realm, with other database management systems, and with text files. In this chapter, you learn how to exchange information between an Access database and an outside source—data from a word processor, a spreadsheet or an HTML or XML document. A successful exchange of data with these outside sources involves a sequence of steps, which are intended to ensure the end result is useful. For example, records moved into Access from a word processor or spreadsheet need to be evaluated and, in some cases, edited to be compatible with the table's data structure.

This chapter describes the procedures you can use for data exchange operations with outside data sources. Procedures are described for:

- Copying or moving records from word processors and spreadsheets
- Saving Access objects as external files
- Working with Microsoft Word
- Working with Microsoft Excel
- Working with HTML and XML
- Mailing Access database objects

Copying or Moving Records

To copy or move records from other applications to Access, make sure the data is arranged in an appropriate format, and then use the selection, copy, and paste functions in Access to move the records you want. The following sections describe specific approaches for moving data among word processors and spreadsheets.

Copying or Moving Data from a Word Processor

You can use two approaches to copy or move records from a table created with a word processor. The first approach is to save the desired records to a text file with fixed length or delimited records, and then import them into the target table. Procedures for importing these text files to an Access table are described in the previous chapter.

The second approach to moving records from a word processor to Access is to perform a copy-and-paste operation. For this copy/paste approach to work properly, be aware of these two major points:

- The records in the word processing file must already be in a table or properly separated by tab characters.
- The columns in the word processor table should be in the same order as the fields in the Access table you're targeting.

When you copy data, you place a copy of that data in the destination file and leave the original data alone in the source file. When you move data, you actually delete it from the source and place it in the target file.

When performing copy or moving operations, the Access database must be open to receive the new data. You can add new records to either a datasheet or a form. If you're adding records to a datasheet, the columns aren't required to have the same names as the fields, but the data being copied or moved should be the same data type.

If you're adding records to a form, the data is copied or moved to text box controls, which have the same names as the incoming data columns. If the column names don't match the control names or the columns have no names, the data is moved or copied to the form in the tab order.

On the receiving end, you can replace existing records or add to the records already in the datasheet or form. When you replace records in a datasheet, you select the same number of records to eliminate as you selected to bring in from the word processor. In a form, you can replace only the current record.

To move or copy word processing data, do the following:

1. In the word processor application, select the records you want to move or copy using the selection method provided by the application. In Microsoft Word, this can be as simple as clicking the left mouse button on the first record you want, and then holding the left mouse button down as you drag the cursor down the file until the last desired record is highlighted (see Figure 23-1).

2. Then, do one of the following, both of which place the selected records on the clipboard:

   ■ If you actually want to move the records from the word processing file to the Access database, choose Edit | Cut or click the Cut toolbar button.

   ■ If you want to copy the records, as opposed to moving them, choose Edit | Copy or click the Copy toolbar button.

 In Word, you can also right-click the selection and choose Cut or Copy from the shortcut menu. Other word processing programs have other methods for placing text on the clipboard. If the application you're getting the records from doesn't have the Cut and Copy commands, use the comparable commands to place the data on the Windows clipboard.

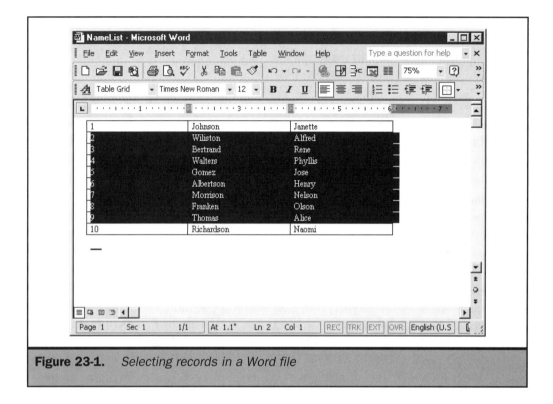

Figure 23-1.   *Selecting records in a Word file*

3. Open the datasheet or form you want to paste the records into, and then do one of the following (whichever method you choose, you will be asked to confirm the paste action, as shown in Figure 23-2):

- If you're replacing records in Datasheet view, select the records you want to replace, and then choose Edit | Paste or click the Paste toolbar button. If you select fewer records in the target than in the source table, the selected records are replaced and the excess records from the source table are ignored. If you select more records in the target table, they're replaced with the records selected in the source table beginning at the top of the table. The excess selection in the target table is untouched.

- If you're replacing a record in a form, move to the record you want to replace and click the record selector or choose Edit | Select Record, and then choose Edit | Paste or click the Paste toolbar button.

- If you're adding the data to the target datasheet, choose Edit | Paste Append.

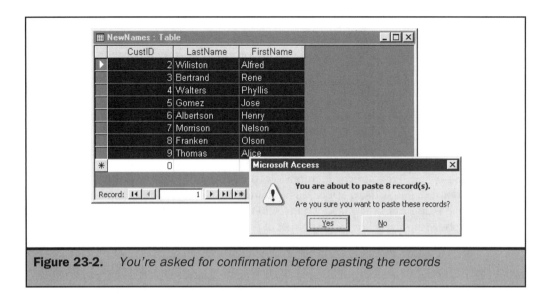

Figure 23-2.   *You're asked for confirmation before pasting the records*

Copying or Moving Data from a Spreadsheet

Copying or moving records from a spreadsheet is similar to the process for copying or moving records from a word processor. The advantage in the case of the spreadsheet is this: the data needn't be arranged in or converted to table form because it's already in tabular form on the spreadsheet. The same cautions apply as in the case of the word processor:

- The columns in the spreadsheet must be in the same order as the data elements in the table for the data copy/move to be useful.

- If the records are to be added to a form (as opposed to being added to a datasheet), the column names in the spreadsheet should be the same as the names of the corresponding text box controls on the database form.

Copying or Moving Records from Access to Another Application

Copying or moving records from a datasheet or a form to another application is much the same as bringing new records into Access from a source application. When you paste Access records to a different application, the field names appear in the first row of the table in a word processor or worksheet in a spreadsheet.

If you're copying from a datasheet that has subdatasheets, only one level is copied at a time. To copy the subdatasheet, open it, and then perform the same copy or move operation.

Use the same four basic steps:

1. Select the Access data you want to copy or move, and then copy or cut it to the clipboard.

2. Open the other application.

3. If you're replacing existing data, select that data. If adding to existing data, place the insertion point where you want to begin pasting the data.

4. Use the other application's command to paste or append the Access data.

If you're pasting Access records into a Word document, place the insertion point where you want the records to appear. The data is pasted in the document as a table.

If you're pasting to Excel, place the insertion point in the cell where you want the first column heading to be located. The rest of the Access data fills out columns and rows to the right and down in the Excel worksheet.

Tip   *You can also use the drag-and-drop method to move database objects among applications. You must have both applications running, and then click an Access table or query in the Database window and drag it to a Word document or Excel worksheet. Going in the other direction, you can create an Access table by dragging-and-dropping a range of cells from an Excel worksheet to the Database window.*

Saving Access Output as an External File

The previous chapter discusses saving Access data and objects in other database management systems or in text format. You can also export the data from Access tables, queries, forms, and reports to a number of other file formats both within and external to Microsoft Office. Table 23-1 lists the export file formats available in the Access Save as Type list in the Export dialog box.

Application	Versions or Formats
Excel	3, 4, 5-7, 97–2002
Lotus 1-2-3 (tables and queries)	.WK1, .WK3, and .WJ2
HTML Documents	N/A
Microsoft Active Server Pages	N/A
Microsoft IIS	1-2

Table 23-1.   *Access Export File/Data Formats*

Application	Versions or Formats
Rich Text Format	N/A
Snapshot Format (reports only)	N/A
XML Documents	N/A
Microsoft Word Merge (tables and queries only)	N/A
ODBC Databases (tables and queries only)	Depending on ODBC drivers installed

Table 23-2. *Access Export File/Data Formats* (continued)

To save the data from an Access table in one of these file formats, do the following:

1. In the Database window, select the table containing the data you want to export.

2. Choose File | Export or right-click and choose Export from the shortcut menu.

3. When the Export Table To dialog box appears, select a file type in the Save as Type box and click OK. Depending on your choice of file type, the dialog box title bar may show Export Table As.

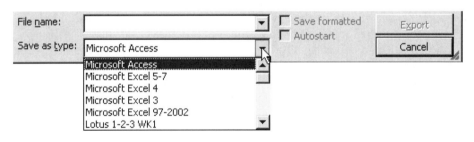

4. Use the Save In box to locate the destination folder.

5. Then enter a name for the output file and click Export.

If you export the Access object to Excel 5–7 or 97–2002, HTML Documents, or Text Files you can also check two other options:

- *Save Formatted*, which preserves as much of the formatting as possible.

- *AutoStart*, which becomes available when you choose Save Formatted. This option launches the destination application and opens the exported file for viewing or editing when you click Export.

If you choose Rich Text Format, XML Documents, Microsoft IIS 1-2, or Active Server Pages, the Save Formatted option is checked by default. AutoStart is available with Rich Text Format and XML Documents file type, but not with IIS or ASP.

Working with Word

You have four ways to use Access data in Word:

- Save the Access data as Rich Text Format, and then open with Word.
- Send the Access data to Word as a mail merge source file.
- Load Access data into Word with the Publish It With Microsoft Word Office Link.
- Use the Merge It With Microsoft Word Office Link to include Access data in a mail merge operation.

Note   *Office Links is a tool that provides smooth interaction with the other Office programs, such as Word and Excel. You can reach the Office Links commands from the Tools menu or by clicking the Office Links toolbar button.*

Saving in Rich Text Format

Rich Text Format (RTF) is a standard format used by Word and other word processing and desktop publishing programs for Windows. Settings, such as fonts and styles, are kept intact when files are saved as RTF files.

To save the output of an Access datasheet, query, form, or report as an RTF file, choose Rich Text Format from the Save as Type box in the Export...As dialog box. When you choose the Rich Text Format file type, the Save Formatted option is automatically selected and cannot be cleared. The AutoStart option becomes available, which, if checked, launches Word for editing the file when you click Export to close the Export dialog box.

Figure 23-3 shows the Alpha Card table as an RTF file in the Word 2002 window.

Saving an Access Table or Query as a Mail Merge Data Source

An easy way to make Access mailing data available to the Word mail merge process is to save the table or query as a mail merge data source document. In the Export...To dialog box, choose Microsoft Word Merge as the file type. When you click Export, Access creates and saves the data source with the Access field names and record data. You can export Access data to any version of Word for use with the Word mail merge feature.

When you start the mail merge process in Word and choose the exported file as the data source, the first record, called the *header row*, contains the field names and the rest

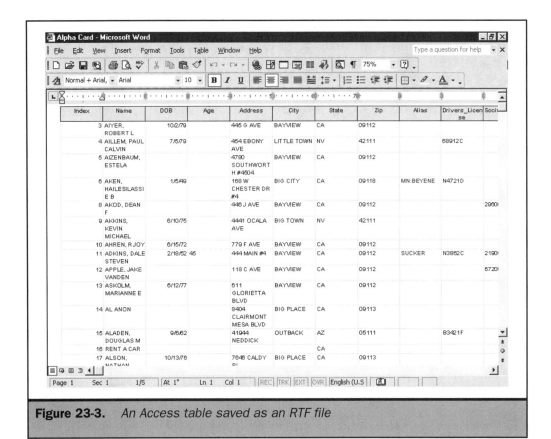

Figure 23-3. *An Access table saved as an RTF file*

of the records comprise the *data rows*. The field names in the header row must match the field names placed in the Word mail merge main document. If they don't match, you must edit either the Access data source or the Word main document.

Be sure the Access table or query has no field names longer than 20 characters. Word's mail merge feature truncates excess characters, which can result in duplicate field names. In addition, spaces and special characters in field names are converted to underscores.

Publishing with Word

You can use an Office Link to save the output of a datasheet, form, or report automatically as an RTF file and load the file into Word. For example, suppose you created a custom form or report that you want to include in your company's annual report being created in Word. After creating the form or report design, simply load the output into the Word document.

The file is saved in the folder where Access is installed. When you launch Word, you can open the Access file from Word. Access refers to this as "publishing" the data in Word.

One of the differences between this process and the process of saving a datasheet as a mail merge data source is that forms and reports can be published, as well as tables and queries. For mail merge, tables and queries are the only accepted Access objects.

To publish an Access object into Word, do the following:

1. Select the name of the table, query, form, or report you want to save and load into Word. If you want to load only part of a datasheet, open the datasheet first and select the records you want to load.

2. Choose Tools | Office Links or click the Office Links toolbar button, and then click Publish It with Microsoft Word.

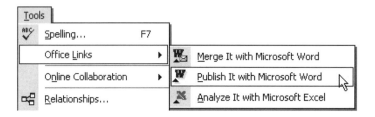

The list of Office Links commands depends on the applications you have installed.

This saves the selected object or data in a file in the Access folder, opens Word automatically, and opens the file for review and editing. The file is saved in a table in Rich Text Format. Figure 23-4 shows the result of publishing the Alpha Entry by Code query table in Word.

Using Merge It with Word

An Access database is often an ideal place to store addresses and names of customers, business associates, or friends. Being able to use these names and addresses in correspondence is a valuable capability. Once the link between Access and Word is established, you can open Word at any time to print form letters, envelopes, or labels using the current data from Access.

A query may be the ideal way to simplify Access data structures for this mail merge function. Your table for customer names and addresses may have a number of other fields, such as a telephone number or date of last order, which you needn't pass on. A query that selects only those fields relevant to addressing correspondence can be designed to support mail merge actions (that is, Name, Title, Company, Street Address, City,

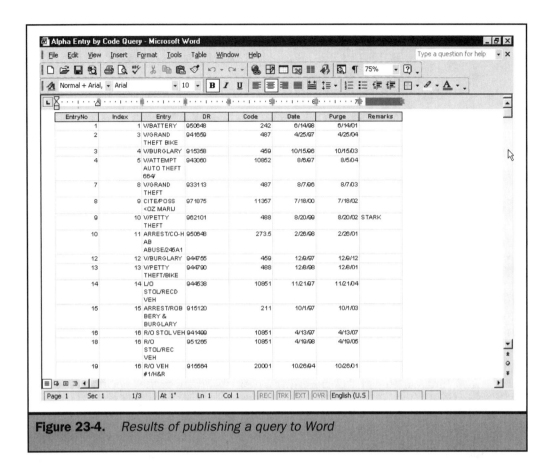

Figure 23-4. *Results of publishing a query to Word*

State, ZIP code). The Word mail merge feature can do this after receiving the table data as well, but you might as well not clutter the exchange of data with unnecessary fields.

To merge data from an Access table or query using the Microsoft Word mail merge functions, follow these steps:

1. In the Database window, select the table or query containing the data.

2. Choose Tools | Office Links or click the Office Links toolbar button, and then select Merge It with MS Word.

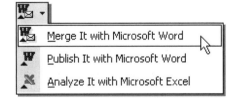

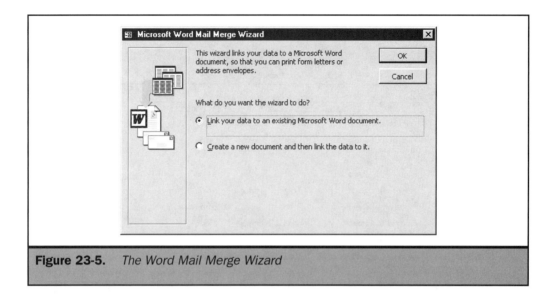

Figure 23-5.   *The Word Mail Merge Wizard*

3. The Microsoft Word Mail Merge Wizard dialog box appears (see Figure 23-5), giving you a choice of linking your data to an existing Microsoft Word document or creating a new one. Once you select one of these options and click OK, Word starts up and opens either a new document or the specific document you selected.

4. In Word, a toolbar appears with a button called Insert Merge Field. When you click this button, the list of fields from the Access table is displayed. Select the specific fields you want to insert in your document and place them in the document. Figure 23-6 shows a new Word document with the NameList Access table as the data source. For further information about how mail merge works, consult your Microsoft Word documentation.

Working with Excel

The association between Excel and Access can be a two-way street. You can make use of Excel data in Access by importing or linking. You have three ways to make use of Access data in Excel or another spreadsheet program:

- Export the Access datasheet as unformatted data.
- Save the output of a datasheet, form, or report as an Excel file or worksheet.
- Load the output of a datasheet, form, or report directly into Excel.

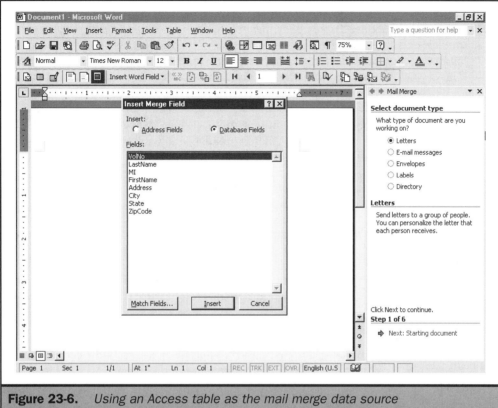

Figure 23-6. *Using an Access table as the mail merge data source*

When you use one of the last two methods, most of the formatting is preserved. A form is saved as a table of data. If you are saving a report that includes grouped data, the group levels are saved as outline levels in Excel.

Importing from and Linking to Excel Spreadsheets

Before you try to import or link to data from an Excel or other spreadsheet, make sure the data is arranged in a tabular format. The spreadsheet must also have the same type of data in each column as the target Access datasheet and the rows must contain the same field in each position.

You can choose to import or link an entire spreadsheet, or only the data from a named range of cells within the spreadsheet. Usually, you create a new table from the imported or linked spreadsheet data, but you can also append the data to an existing datasheet if the spreadsheet column headings are the same as the table field names.

Access tries to assign appropriate data types to the imported data fields, but it doesn't always make the correct assumption. Before you do any work on the new table, be sure the field data types are what you want. You should also check the assumed field properties and set additional properties, such as formatting, to fit the intended table use in Access. Number field formatting may differ between Excel and Access.

If you're importing from Excel version 5.0 or later, you can select one or more of the worksheets in the workbook. You can't import multiple spreadsheet files from Excel 4.0 or from Lotus 1-2-3. If you want one of these spreadsheets, you must open the program and save each spreadsheet as a separate file before importing.

Note *You can import from other spreadsheet programs as well if they have the capability of saving the files in Excel or Lotus 1-2-3 format.*

To import or link an Excel spreadsheet, invoke the Import Spreadsheet Wizard by doing the following:

1. Choose File | Get External Data and click Import or Link Tables. You can also right-click the Database window and choose Import or Link Tables from the shortcut menu.

2. In the Import (or Link) dialog box, select Microsoft Excel in the Files of Type box.

3. In the Look In box, select the drive and folder where the spreadsheet file you want is located, and then select the filename and click Import.

4. In the first Import Spreadsheet Wizard dialog box (see Figure 23-7), you can choose to import a specific worksheet or a named range of cells, and then click Next.

5. In the next wizard dialog box, check First Row Contains Column Headings (see Figure 23-8), and then click Next. Clear the check box if the first row contains field data instead of column headings.

Note *If you indicate the first row contains the column headings and some headings contain data that can't be used for valid Access field names (if, for instance, the heading is blank), Access displays a message to that effect and automatically assigns valid field names.*

6. In the third wizard dialog box, choose to store the data in a new table or in an existing one. If you want to store the data in an existing table, select the table name from the list of tables in the current database. Click Next.

7. In the next wizard dialog box (see Figure 23-9), you can set the field options for each field in the worksheet:

   ■ Enter a new name for the field in the Field Name box. For example, change 13500 (the amount of the loan) to Pmt No.

   ■ Choose Yes in the Indexed box to create an index on that field.

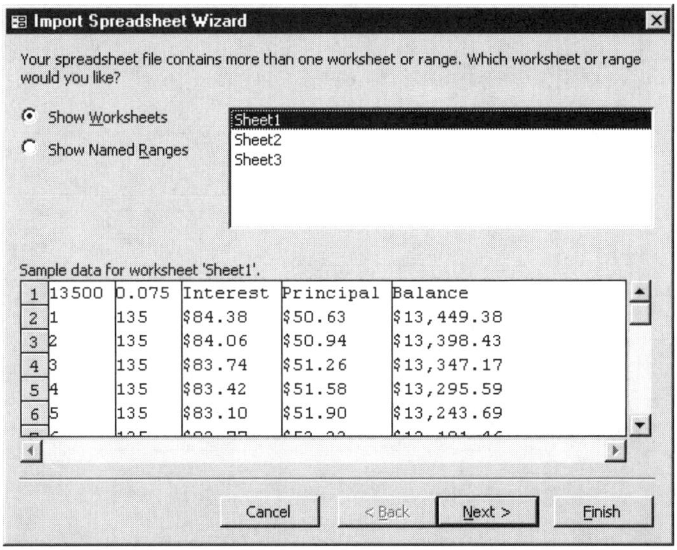

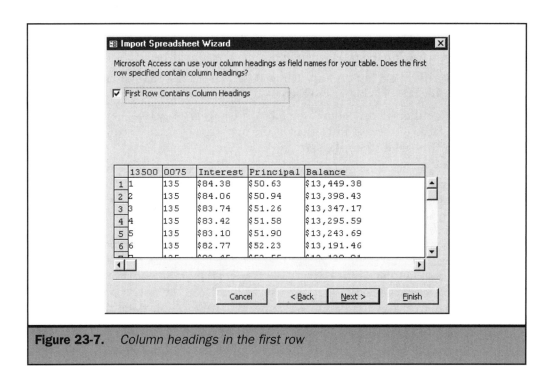

Figure 23-8.   *The first Import Spreadsheet Wizard dialog box*

Figure 23-7.   *Column headings in the first row*

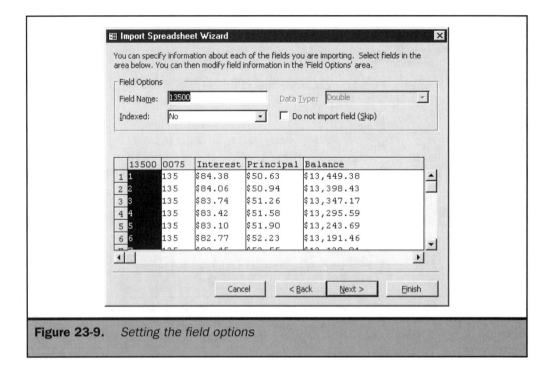

Figure 23-9. *Setting the field options*

■ Change the data type, if applicable, in the Data Type box.

■ Choose to skip the field when importing the spreadsheet.

8. Click the next field header and change 0075 (the interest rate) to Pmt Amt. After making the desired changes to each field, click Next.

9. In the next dialog box, choose Pmt No as the primary key (see Figure 23-10). You can also let Access add a field as the primary key or choose not to have a primary key at all. Then click Next.

10. In the final wizard dialog box, you can accept the same name as the Excel range or enter a new name for the Access table, and then click Finish. An option in this dialog box lets you run the Table Analyzer with the new table to see if it can be made more efficient.

The new Payment Table in Access contains the data that was in the Excel range of cells (see Figure 23-11).

Figure 23-12 shows the table design created by the Import Spreadsheet Wizard. Notice the Pmt No is specified as the primary key field. You can now change the Pmt Amt data type to Currency to improve the appearance of the table data.

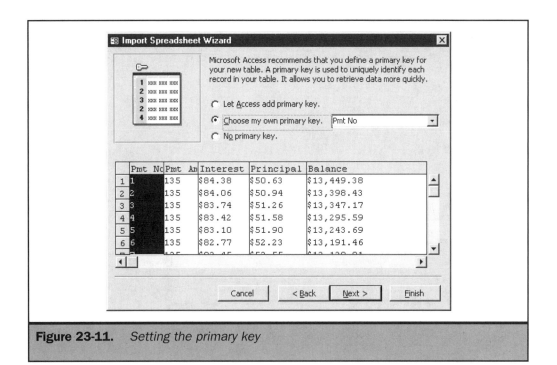

Figure 23-11. *Setting the primary key*

Payment Table : Table

Pmt No	Pmt Amt	Interest	Principal	Balance
1	135	$84.38	$50.63	$13,449.38
2	135	$84.06	$50.94	$13,398.43
3	135	$83.74	$51.26	$13,347.17
4	135	$83.42	$51.58	$13,295.59
5	135	$83.10	$51.90	$13,243.69
6	135	$82.77	$52.23	$13,191.46
7	135	$82.45	$52.55	$13,138.91
8	135	$82.12	$52.88	$13,086.03
9	135	$81.79	$53.21	$13,032.82
10	135	$81.46	$53.54	$12,979.27
11	135	$81.12	$53.88	$12,925.39
12	135	$80.78	$54.22	$12,871.18
13	135	$80.44	$54.56	$12,816.62
14	135	$80.78	$54.22	$12,762.40

Record: 1 of 14

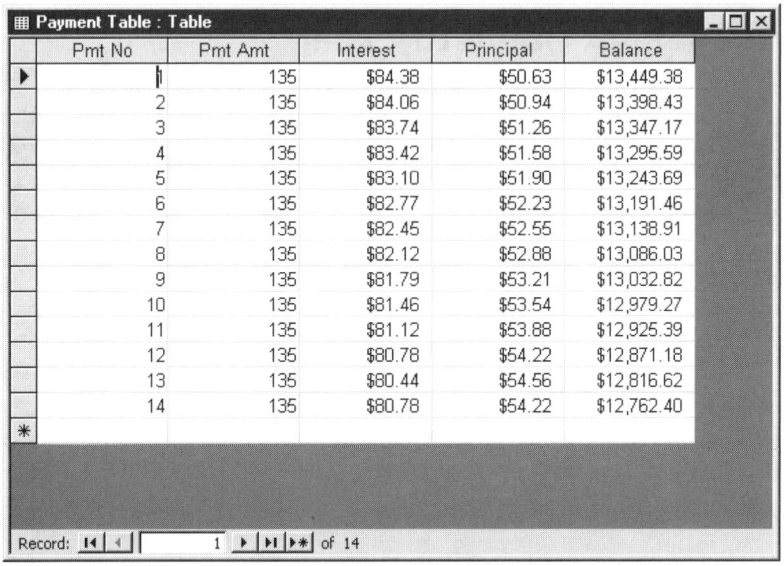

Figure 23-10. *The Payment Table imported from Excel*

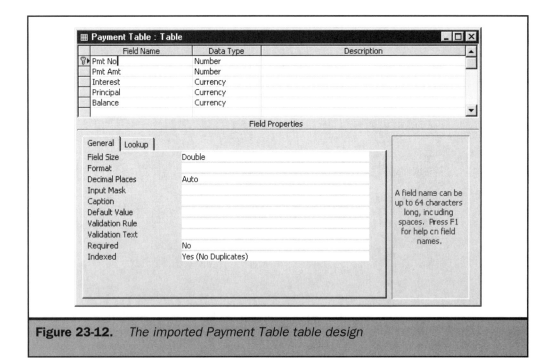

Figure 23-12. The imported Payment Table table design

Exporting a Table or Query to Excel

Exporting all or part of a datasheet to an Excel spreadsheet is similar to exporting to other file types. In the Export…As dialog box, select the desired Microsoft Excel version or other spreadsheet file type from the Save as Type list. Then locate the folder where you want to store the exported data. If you're adding the data to an existing spreadsheet, select the name; otherwise, enter a new filename in the File name box.

Exporting Access data to an existing spreadsheet can result in overwriting the data in that spreadsheet. In Excel, however, this can be avoided by saving the Access data to either the Microsoft Excel 5-7 or Microsoft Excel 97–2002 formats. These formats have workbook data structures, which have a number of worksheets. Exported Access data is added to the next available empty worksheet in these formats.

Check the Save Formatted option in the Export…To dialog box if you want to keep the same fonts and field width, as well as preserve the data that displays in the Lookup fields. The export process takes a little longer with this option, but you won't have to restore the formatting in the spreadsheet. The spreadsheet file created by Access contains the field names in the first row and data in the subsequent rows.

When you choose the Save Formatted option, the AutoStart option becomes available, which automatically launches Excel with the data on the screen when you click Export.

Using Analyze It with Microsoft Excel

The Analyze It with Microsoft Excel Office Link is useful for sending data to Excel for data analysis and charting. Although Access has some charting capabilities, you have more resources when you let Excel do it for you. Once you construct charts in Excel, you can link them to your Access form or report.

Loading database information into Microsoft Excel is done using the Analyze It with Microsoft Excel command in the Office Links menu. All the formatting done in Access, such as font styles, field size, and colors, can be transferred to the Excel spreadsheet. Report groups are saved in the worksheet as outline levels and forms are saved as simple data tables.

To load Access data into an Excel worksheet, do the following:

1. In the Database window, select the name of the datasheet, form, or report you want to load into Excel. If you want to send only part of a table, open the datasheet first and select the records you want to load.

2. Choose Tools | Office Links or click the Office Links toolbar button and click Analyze It with MS Excel.

After a moment, Excel opens, showing a new worksheet with the data from the Access object (see Figure 23-13). The selected records are saved as an Excel file (.xls) in the same folder as the Access database.

Note   *Because some of the number formatting may be different in Excel, when you choose Save Formatted, you may see a warning that some of the formatting may be lost.*

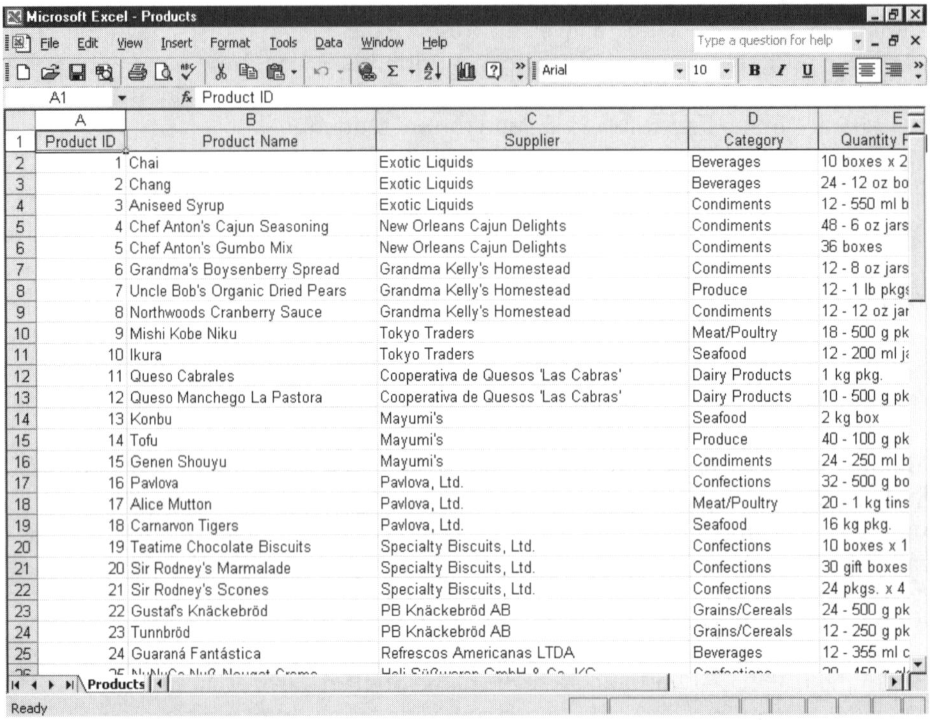

Figure 23-13. *Access data in an Excel worksheet*

Working with HTML and XML Documents

The *Hypertext Markup Language* (*HTML*) is a standard markup language you can use to create documents on the Web. HTML uses tags that the Web browser interprets to display page elements, such as text and graphics, and how to respond to user actions.

While HTML dictates how the document should look, it falls short of defining the data and the data structure. The *Extensible Markup Language* (*XML*) is the standard language for defining the content data and how it's structured on the Web. The capability to import and export XML documents is new with Access 2002.

More about both of these markup languages in Chapter 24.

Importing Data from HTML Documents

You use the same Get External Data routine to import HTML lists and tables:

1. Choose HTML Documents in the Files of Type box.

2. Locate and select the file you want to import and click Import.

The Import HTML Wizard dialog boxes are the same as the Import Spreadsheet wizard's, except for the first box where you choose between a worksheet or a named range in Excel.

A few exceptions to watch for when importing or linking to an HTML document are the following:

- Access doesn't import any .gif or .jpg image files embedded in the HTML document.

- If a table is embedded within a table cell in the HTML file, Access creates a separate table for it.

- If data spans rows or columns in an HTML table, Access duplicates the data in each cell.

Exporting Data to HTML Documents

To begin exporting an Access datasheet of form to a static HTML document, select the table, query, or form in the Database window, and then choose File | Export as usual. In the Save as Type box, choose HTML Documents.

The Save Formatted and AutoStart options work as before. If you checked Save Formatted, the HTML Output Options dialog box appears when you click Export. In this dialog box, you can enter the location of an HTML template or click Browse and look for the one you want.

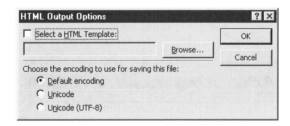

When you want to export a report to a static HTML document, Access exports the report as multiple HTML files—one for each printed page. The first file is named with the report name and subsequent files use the report name followed by Page1, Page2, and so on.

All the controls and features of the report, including any subreports, are exported correctly except for lines, rectangles, and OLE objects. You can still use an HTML template file to include images in the report header or footer. See Chapter 24 for more information about HTML templates and how they present report features.

Note *If you don't choose an HTML template for the exported Access object, you can specify the method of encoding (code page or character set) to be used by the Web browser when you view the file. You have a choice of Windows (default), Unicode, or Unicode (UTF-8). This is a new feature with Access 2002.*

Importing Data and Schema from XML Documents

You can import XML data files into Access and even select the schema you want the data to appear with. The data must be in a format that Access recognizes, either native or as seen through the use of a schema. Access supports the *XML Schema standard* (*XSD*).

To import an XML document into an Access database, do the following:

1. Open the destination database.

2. Choose File | Get External Data | Import.

3. In the Import dialog box, choose XML Documents in the Files of Type box.

4. Locate the XML file you want to import and enter the filename in the File Name box.

5. Click Import.

6. Click Options. The Import XML dialog box (see Figure 23-14) offers options with respect to the import format and tables:

   ■ The default import format is Microsoft Access Data XML, but you can choose another from the Import Format list.

   ■ The Create Table Structure option overwrites any existing Access tables that have the same name as found in the schema.

   ■ When you import the data, you have a choice of overwriting the existing Access data or appending the XML data to it.

7. When you finish with your selections, click OK, and then click Import.

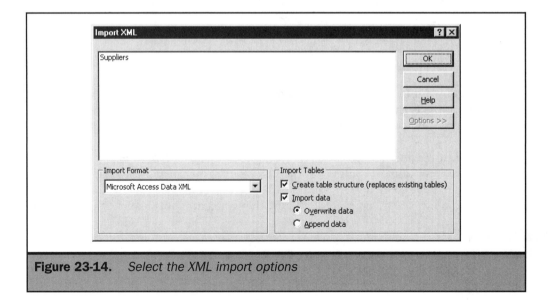

Figure 23-14. *Select the XML import options*

The imported XML document is added to the table page of the database window; it looks and behaves just like a native Access table.

 If errors occur during the import process, Access creates an Import Errors table and adds a row for each record that causes an error. The import may have resulted in duplicate primary key values, validation rule violations, or other data errors.

Exporting Data to XML Documents

You can export Access tables, queries, forms, and reports to XML documents. To export an Access object to an XML document:

1. Select the Access object you want to export in the Database window and choose File | Export.

2. In the Export dialog box, choose XML Documents in the Save as Type box, and then click Export.

3. In the Export XML dialog box, you have several options:

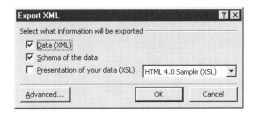

- The *Data (XML)* option is selected by default and exports the data from all four types of objects.

- The *Schema of the data* option exports an XML schema document. If both the Data and Schema options are selected, separate files are output. It's the default for tables and queries, and is available for forms and reports.

- Select the *Presentation of your data (XSL)* option if you want to apply an XML Schema standard (XSL) document to the XML document before the final write. When selected, the drop-down list shows all the available Access XML conversion options. This option is available for tables and queries, and is checked but dimmed for forms and reports.

4. If you need to refine the export further, click Advanced to open another Export XML dialog box with three tabs: Data, Schema, and Presentation (see Figure 23-15).

5. After setting all the desired options, click OK. If you checked the AutoStart option in the Export dialog box, Internet Explorer automatically launches and displays the new XML document.

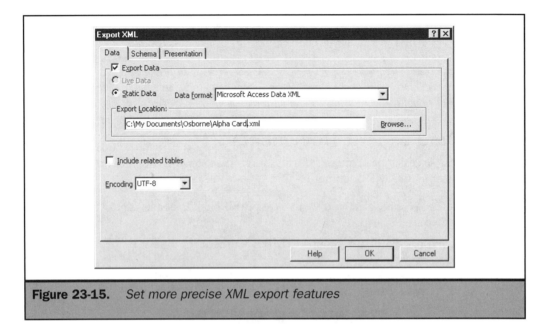

Figure 23-15. *Set more precise XML export features*

Mailing Access Objects

You can send Access tables, queries, forms, reports, report snapshots, and even modules attached to an e-mail message. You can also e-mail a data access page as the body of the message and attach other objects to it. When you attach objects or data to an e-mail message, the attachments can be converted to Excel, Rich Text Format, MS-DOS text, HTML, IDC/HTX, or ASP file formats as part of the Send To operation.

When you point to Send To in the File menu, you have two options:

- *Mail Recipient*, which can be used to e-mail a data access page as the body of the message. The data contained in the page is either bound to the database where the recipient can update the data from the page or the data is embedded in the data access page, in which case it's static and can't be updated from the page. See Chapter 24 for more information about how to create and use data access pages.

- *Mail Recipient (as Attachment)*, which attaches the selected database object to an e-mail message.

To e-mail an Access database object, you must install an electronic mail application that supports Messaging Application Programming Interface (MAPI), such as Microsoft Outlook, Microsoft Exchange, or Microsoft Mail.

To attach an Access object to an e-mail message, do the following:

1. Select the object you want to send in the Database window. If you want to send only some of the records from a table or query, open the table or query in Datasheet view and select the records you want to send.

2. Choose File | Send To or right-click the object and point to Send To in the shortcut menu, and then click Mail Recipient (as Attachment).

3. The Send dialog box opens. Choose the file format you want to use for your e-mail attachment, and then click OK. If you selected only part of the datasheet in step 1, two options become available in the Output group: All, which attaches the entire datasheet to the e-mail message, and Selection, which attaches only the selected data.

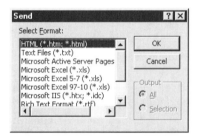

4. If you choose HTML, the next dialog box gives you the opportunity to attach an HTML template. You can accept the filename displayed in the HTML Output Options dialog box, enter a different name, and then choose Browse to locate another file, or you can clear the template box and not use a template. Click OK.

Access opens an e-mail message form where you can address your message, add text to the message, and send it out. The object you selected to send is automatically attached to the message.

Summary

In this chapter, we expanded the concepts of exchanging data with outside sources by looking at the use of Office Links to exchange data with Word, Excel, HTML, and XML documents. In addition, you looked at the challenges in importing text and e-mailing database objects. As you saw in this chapter and in Chapter 22, a large number of options and techniques are available for exporting data from Access and importing data into Access from outside sources. These techniques have many variations and, in some cases, require analysis and preparation of the data being exchanged.

This chapter and Chapter 22 both emphasized that the use of these techniques is a challenge in terms of selecting the most efficient and effective method for accomplishing the data exchange. With outside sources, this is an even greater challenge, as the effort to identify the data structure and accomplish a useful and accurate transfer can be significant.

The next chapter discusses exporting of Access data and objects to Web applications, including the development of dynamic exchanges in Web applications. The chapter also discusses the design and creation of data access pages used to post Access data dynamically on the Web.

MOUS Exam Activities Explored in This Chapter

Level	Activity	Section Title
Core	Import data to an Access table	Copying or Moving Records Importing or Linking to Excel Spreadsheets
Core	Export data from Access	Copying or Moving Records from Access to Another Application Publishing with Word Using Merge It with Word Exporting a Table or Query to Excel
Expert	Import XML Documents into Access	Importing Data and Schema from XML Documents
Expert	Export Access data to XML Documents	Exporting Data to XML Documents

Chapter 24

Access 2002
on the Internet

One of the most powerful features in Access 2002 is the data access page, which helps you share and update data across the Web. Data access pages were new to Access 2000 and have been significantly improved with Access 2002. Office XP has streamlined sharing information and collaborating activities with other people. Many of the new Office tools use Web technology to broaden the Office user's horizon and improve productivity. The data access page can be used for interactive reporting, data entry, and data analysis.

This chapter introduces data access pages and describes the basic method of creating and modifying one. Much more is involved in working on the Web than can be presented here, so this chapter simply introduces the Access object and gives you a glimpse of what you can do with it on the Web.

Understanding Data Access Pages

A *data access page* is a Web page that's connected to a Microsoft Access database. With a data access page, you can interact with others and present dynamic data at your Web site. For example, by creating a data access page, you can build a Web page that enables you and other Office XP users to search, edit, and add to a database from within your Internet Explorer browser.

You can also create a *banded data access page,* which groups and displays records similar to an Access report. For example, you can create an interactive report that groups information stored in a database to show a general summary of the data. The viewer can expand the groups to show details for a specific grouping of data. With data access pages, you can also analyze data in a variety of ways. The page can contain an Excel spreadsheet, a chart, or an Office PivotTable or PivotChart. When you edit or filter the data in the underlying table, the data access page is automatically updated.

Who Can View and Edit a Data Access Page?

To display a data access page, the user must be using Internet Explorer 5.5 or later and have a Microsoft Office XP license. When the page is loaded in Internet Explorer, the page is cached in memory, so the user is actually viewing a local version of the page. Any sorting or filtering is applied locally. The Web page doesn't change. However, if the user has access permissions to the database to which the page is connected, he or she can edit the database directly from Internet Explorer.

Creating a Data Access Page

With Access you can create a new data access page in several ways:

- Create a data access page quickly with all the fields from a table or query in a form-like style.

- Use the Data Access Page Wizard to guide you through the process.
- Create a data access page from an existing HTML document.
- Create your own data access page in Design view.

The following sections explain each of these methods for creating a data access page. When you save a new data access page, the underlying design file is contained in a Hypertext Markup Language (HTML) file with the .htm file extension, which is stored in a folder outside the database. The icon that appears on the Pages page of the Database window is only a shortcut to the file. When you select the shortcut, you can view the data on the page or modify the page design.

Note   *To view the data access pages included with the database on the CD that accompanies this book, create a new blank database and import all the objects from the database on the CD. This way, the HTML files containing the page designs are placed in the same folder on your hard drive with the database. The page shortcuts in the Database window then have the correct path to the HTML files.*

Creating a Data Access Page Using AutoPage

The fastest way to create a data access page is to use the AutoPage feature. The data access page includes all the fields and records for the table or query you choose. To create a data access page using AutoPage, do the following:

1. Click Pages in the Objects group in the Database window.
2. Click New to open the New Data Access Page dialog box.
3. Select AutoPage: Columnar.
4. Choose the table or query that contains the data you want to include from the drop-down list.
5. Click OK. The data access page appears along with the Record Navigation Bar (see Figure 24-1).
6. Choose File | Save to open the Save As Data Access Page dialog box.

Note   *You may see a warning that the connection string for this page is an absolute path. If you want to connect to the page through a network, you need to edit the string to include a UNC path. Click OK to continue.*

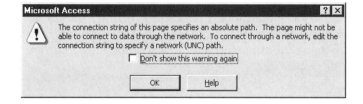

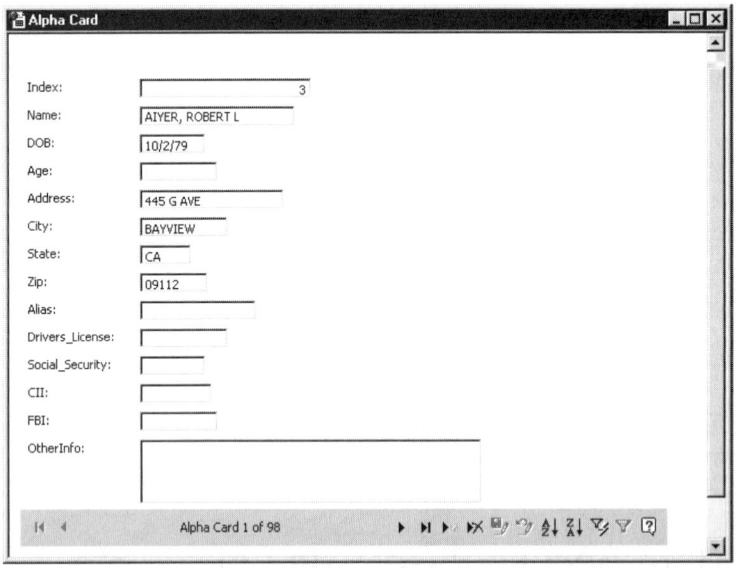

Figure 24-1. An AutoPage: Columnar option data access page

7. Accept the table or query name, or enter another name for the new page, locate the folder you want to save the page in, and then click Save.

8. Switch to Page view to see the finished AutoPage.

To see how the page will appear in your browser window, choose File | Web Page Preview, instead of switching to Page view in Access. The data access page appears in the browser window.

Note *You can also select the table or query in the Database window that you want to use as the basis for the page, and then choose Insert | Page. The New Data Access Page dialog box opens with the table or query already chosen where you can choose AutoPage: Columnar as before.*

Using the Page Wizard

The Page Wizard gives you additional options for creating a data access page. For example, you can choose fields from more than one table or query, group by values in certain fields, or select multiple fields for determining the sort order.

To start the Page Wizard, open the Pages page of the Database window, and then do one of the following:

■ Double-click the Create Data Access Page By Using Wizard item.

■ Click the New button on the Database window toolbar to open the New Data Access Page dialog box. Choose Page Wizard and choose a table or query from the drop-down list, and then click OK.

The first Page Wizard dialog box appears (see Figure 24-2).

1. Select the fields you want to display on your data access page. To add all the fields, click the double right arrow button. You may choose fields from more than one table or query.

2. Click Next after selecting all the fields you want to display on the page. The next Page Wizard dialog box enables you to group the display by certain fields. After you add a grouping level, the Grouping Options button becomes available (Figure 24-3).

3. If you want to choose the grouping interval, click the Grouping Options button. The Grouping Intervals dialog box lets you choose the grouping intervals for

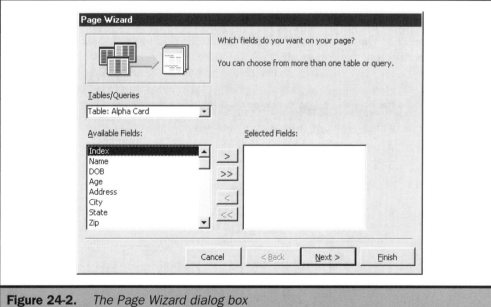

Figure 24-2.   *The Page Wizard dialog box*

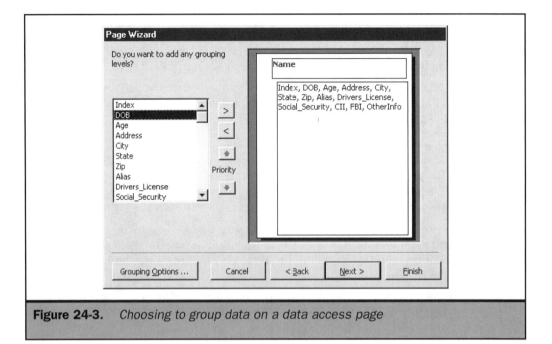

Figure 24-3. *Choosing to group data on a data access page*

each of the fields you specify as grouping levels. For example, you can group a text field by the first letter, the first two letters, and so on. Other data types present different grouping intervals. Choose the options you want to use, if any, and click OK. You then return to the previous wizard dialog box.

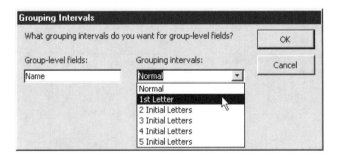

4. Click Next to open the next Page Wizard dialog box where you can set sort orders. You can select up to four fields to determine the sort order of record data in your data access page (see Figure 24-4). The field you're grouping on isn't included in the list. After selecting a field from the drop-down list, click the button next to the field to toggle the sort order to between ascending and descending order.

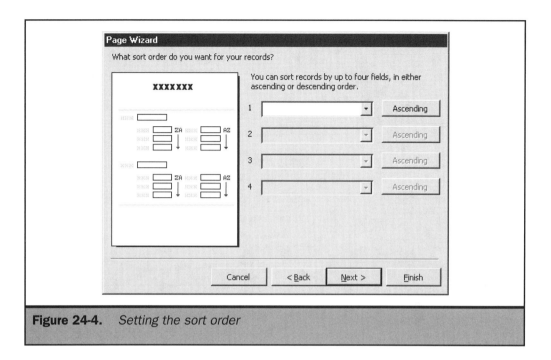

Figure 24-4.   *Setting the sort order*

5. Click Next. The final Page Wizard dialog box (see Figure 24-5) displays a text box for adding a title to your page and options for modifying the page.

6. The title you enter appears in the title bar of the browser window when the user displays the data access page. The other options are

   ■ **Open the page**   Select this option to go directly to Page view, where you can view the page with default formatting.

   ■ **Modify the page's design**   By default, this option is selected. It takes you directly to the page Design view.

   ■ **Do you want to apply a theme to your page?**   If you want to apply a set of predefined styles for your data access page, click this check box, which takes you to Design view. More about themes in the section titled "Choosing a Theme."

   ■ **Display Help on working with the page?**   If you want Help while working on the page design, click this check box.

7. Click Finish. The page appears in Design view (see Figure 24-6). Working in Design view is covered later in this chapter. The Toolbox and property sheet are also shown in the figure.

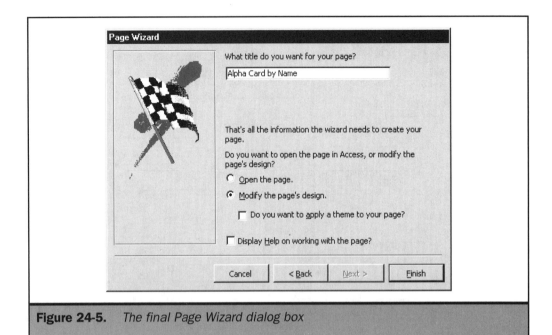

Figure 24-5. *The final Page Wizard dialog box*

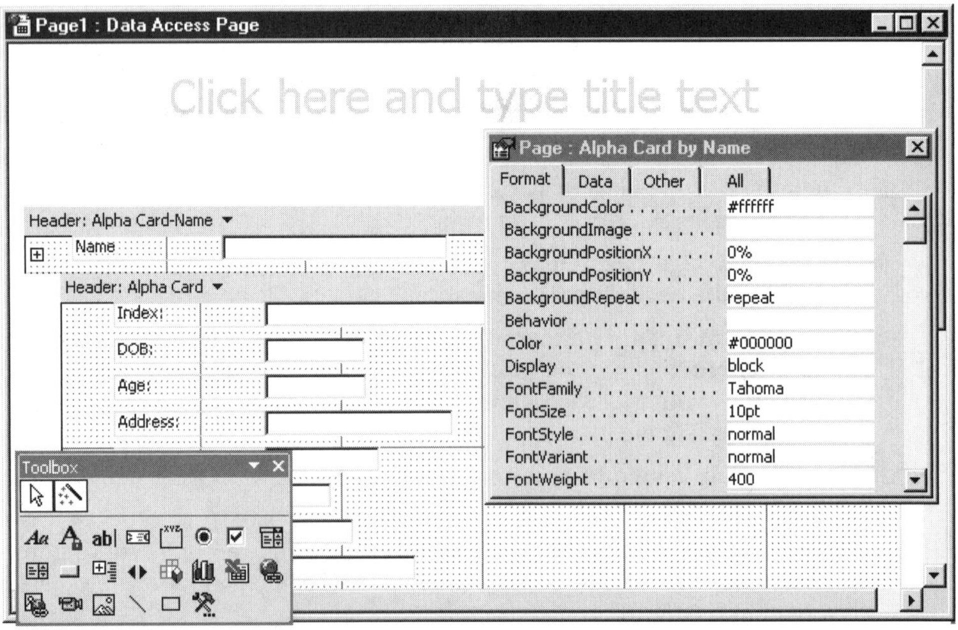

Figure 24-6. *The finished data access page*

Creating a Data Access Page from an Existing Page

In many cases, you may already have an HTML document that contains the graphics and basic text you want to use to present your access data. To create a data access page from the existing page, so you don't have to manually add all the page elements, do the following:

1. In the Pages page of the Database window, double-click the Edit Web Page That Already Exists item or click the New button on the Database window toolbar, and choose Existing Web page in the New Data Access Page dialog box. The Locate Web Page dialog box appears, showing a list of Web pages in the current folder.

2. Locate the HTML file you want to use and click Open. The page appears in Design view for you to include your Access data and modify the page elements.

If you created the page in Access 2000, you'll see a message that you must save it using Office XP Web Components before you can edit it. When you click Convert to convert the page to Access 2002, you see a message that says a backup copy has been saved just in case and displays the name for the copy. Jot it down in case you need to resort to the backup.

Creating a New Data Access Page in Design View

To create a new data access page from scratch, double-click the Create Data Access Page In Design View item in the Database window. You can also click New and choose Design View from the New Data Access Page dialog box.

A blank data access page appears in Design view with a grid for the placement of elements on your newly created page. Access may also display the Field List window for adding data fields and the Toolbox for adding controls to the data access page (see Figure 24-7). The Field List shows the collapsed lists of all the tables and queries in the underlying database. You might see the same warning as before about the absolute path to the page, which you may want to change to a UNC.

If you don't see the Toolbox, click the Toolbox button on the Page Design toolbar or right-click the toolbar and check Toolbox in the list of available toolbars. If the Field List window doesn't appear, choose View | Field List, or click the Field List button in the Page Design toolbar.

When you create a page from scratch, you can expand the Tables and Queries folders in the Field List window to display the list of all tables and queries. Expand the table or query that contains the fields you want to place in the page design. Then, drag the fields you want to add from the Field List to the page design grid. When you add the first field, the grid section is renamed to Header with the name of the table that includes the field. When you drag a text or numeric field to add it to the page, it creates a bound text box control with an attached label. If you add a Yes/No type field, the field is added as a check box.

EXCHANGING DATA
WITH OTHERS

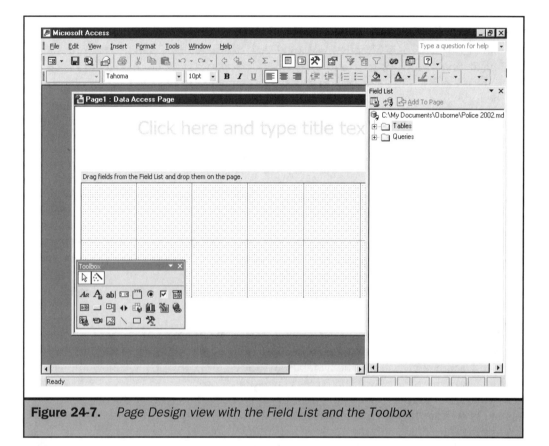

Figure 24-7.   *Page Design view with the Field List and the Toolbox*

When you create a new data access page, the page object properties are the same as for most other Access objects and are set the same way. To see the page properties, choose File | Page Properties while in Design view and click one of the four tabs on the Properties dialog box. Pages have no event properties.

Creating a Grouped Data Access Page

With a grouped data access page, you can display data that's related in a hierarchical fashion and display the information from multiple tables. A grouped data access page, also called a *banded* page, is similar to a form with subforms or a report with subreports. By grouping data on a page, you can choose to display only the topmost level of data, such as a person's name and address, and click an Expand icon to display additional data about the person.

When you group data access pages, you're adding some new sections to the page:

■ The group header, which usually displays data and calculates totals.

■ The group footer, which can also be used to calculate totals. The group footer appears just above the record navigation section for the group. The lowest level group doesn't include a group footer.

■ The group caption, which displays column headers and appears just above the group header. The data in the caption shows only when the next higher group is expanded.

■ An additional record navigation section, which displays the record navigation control for the records within the group. It appears after the group footer, if the group has a footer; otherwise, it appears after the group header section.

Usually, only the Header and Navigation sections are included. You can add or remove any of these four group sections by right-clicking the section bar and using the shortcut menu. The record source for each group is displayed on the group section bars.

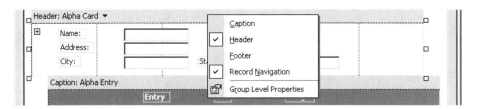

The following steps use the Police database to show how to create a grouped data access page:

1. Double-click the Create Data Access Page In Design View item on the Pages page of the Database window. If the Field List doesn't appear, choose View | Field list, or click the Field List button.

2. Click the + to the left of the Tables folder icon to display the list of tables available in the Police database.

3. Click the + to the left of the Alpha Card to display the fields available in the Alpha Card table (see Figure 24-8). Notice that Index, the primary key field, is marked with a key icon in the list.

4. Drag the Name field from the field list to the grid. When the field is in the position you want, release the mouse button. The section name becomes Header: Alpha Card and a navigation section is added.

5. Drag the Address, City, State, and ZIP fields to the grid.

Tip   *If you're satisfied with the fields arranged in the default column style, hold down* CTRL *and select all the fields you want on the page. Then, drag the group to the grid. You can also select each field name in the Field List and click Add to Page or simply double-click the field name. You can move them around later, as necessary.*

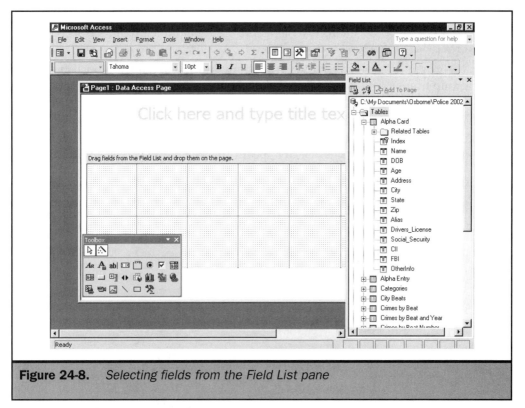

Figure 24-8.   *Selecting fields from the Field List pane*

6. To add the data from the Alpha Entry table, click the + to the left of the Related Tables folder to expand the list of related tables, and then click the + to the left of the Alpha Entry folder to see the individual Alpha Entry field names.

7. Drag the Entry field to the bottom of the page grid. A blue box displaying Create A New Section Below Alpha Card appears just above the Navigation bar.

8. Drop the Entry field in this box. The Layout Wizard offers you a choice between Columnar and Tabular layouts.

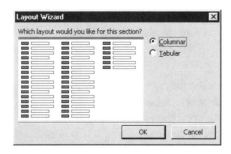

9. Choose Tabular and click OK.

10. Drag-and-drop the DR and the Purge fields to the new Alpha Entry section.

11. Click the Alpha Card section header and drag the bottom resize handle up to remove the extra space appearing after the fields. If you have extra space in the Alpha Entry section, select that section header and use the resize handle to resize it, as well.

12. Click the placeholder for the title text and add the title text you want. If you want additional text in the page header before the grouped fields, click the space below the title and enter the text you want. If you need more space, press Enter as you type to expand the section.

13. Choose File | Save to name and save your new data access page.

To browse the grouped data access page during design or after you save it, click the View button or choose View | Page View. An Expand control, a + icon, appears for each upper-level record (Alpha Card, in this example). The Expand control works as a toggle, so clicking the icon displays or collapses the additional grouped fields for the record. Figure 24-9 shows the first Alpha Card record expanded to display the related Alpha Entry records on the new grouped data access page.

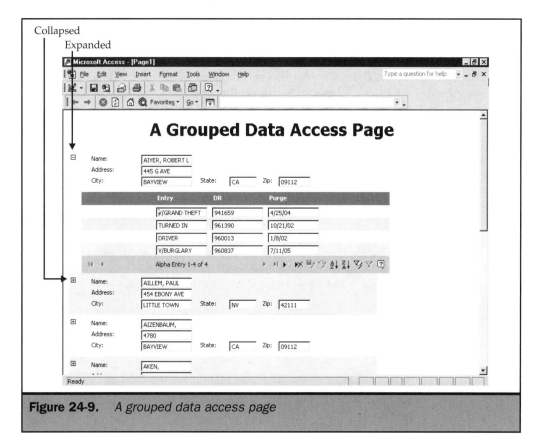

Figure 24-9.   *A grouped data access page*

Looking Behind a Data Access Page

Most Web pages are created using only standard HTML, a markup language that embeds commands, called *tags* in the code. These are used to structure and format Web pages in a browser, such as Microsoft Internet Explorer and Netscape Navigator.

Access 2002 goes beyond HTML to create data access pages. For example, data access pages are created using cascading style sheets (CSS), Extensible Markup Language (XML), and the Vector Markup Language (VML). To help you understand what's going on behind the scenes, the following sections briefly describe each of these standards and languages and how Access 2002 uses them to create data access pages.

> **Note** *If you don't want to explore the mechanics behind data access pages right now, skim through this section and return to it later for the details.*

Hypertext Markup Language

HTML is a structured markup language, not a programming language. You won't spend your time writing intricate algorithms or data structures to develop Web pages with HTML. HTML consists of markups or tags the browser uses to display a Web page. Extensive books and tutorials have been written about HTML and a complete discussion of the subject would take several chapters, if not two or more books. The following gives a basic explanation of how HTML works. Figure 24-10 shows the HTML file created for the Entries by Alpha Card data access page. To view the HTML file, choose Tools | Macros | Microsoft Script Editor, or click the Microsoft Script Editor toolbar button.

> **Note** *As you can see from the vertical scroll bar, this is quite a large file. You're viewing only a small part of it.*

When you save a file in Access as an HTML file, the file is saved as an ASCII text file with an extension of .htm or .html. Because the file is ASCII text, you can view the contents of any Web page in a text editor, such as Notepad. In HTML, the structure and formatting tags are enclosed between the angle brackets (< and >). The instructions between these symbols indicate what action the browser is to take. For example, the <P> tag indicates the following text should be formatted as a paragraph, with space appearing above and below the block of paragraph text. HTML is case-insensitive, so either <p> or <P> works.

Many tags also include *attributes*, which are used to further define the tag. For example, to center a paragraph, you would add the center attribute as follows:

```
<P ALIGN="center">
```

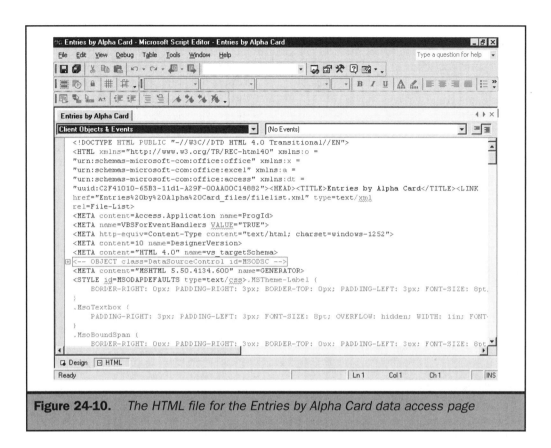

Figure 24-10. *The HTML file for the Entries by Alpha Card data access page*

Some tags support numerous attributes. For example, to insert an image, you use the IMG tag and add attributes to specify the image's height and width, what alternate text will appear as the image downloads, and how large a border to display around the image:

```
<IMG SRC="logo.gif" HEIGHT="75" WIDTH="150" ALT="Logo" BORDER="0">
```

HTML files often use tags in pairs—one opening tag and a corresponding closing tag that includes a forward slash before the instruction. The closing tag is used to specify the end of a markup operation. For example, to inform the browser that it's displaying an HTML file, you would add the opening <HTML> tag, which is the first tag in an HTML file. You end the file with the closing tag, which has the same tag name, but is preceded with a forward slash (/), </HTML>. Not all tags include both an opening and closing tag. For example, to add a line or horizontal rule to a page, you use the <HR> tag by itself.

All Web pages consist of two sections: a head and a body. The <HEAD> and </HEAD> tags appear directly after the opening <HTML> tag. The opening <TITLE> and closing </TITLE> tags appear within the head section. The text that appears inside the <TITLE>Entries by Alpha Card</TITLE> tags (see line 6 in Figure 24-10) specifies the title text that displays in the title bar of the browser. The section of the Web page that appears in the browser window appears in between the <BODY> and </BODY> tags directly after the closing </HEAD> tag. A Web page always includes the following tags:

```
<HTML>
<HEAD>
<TITLE>Page Title</TITLE>
</HEAD>
<BODY>
Page contents are inserted here...
</BODY>
</HTML>
```

For more information, *How to Do Everything with HTML,* by James A. Pence, and *HTML: A Beginner's Guide,* by Wendy Willard (both by Osborne/McGraw-Hill) are helpful references that cover HTML programming.

Cascading Style Sheets

Cascading style sheets are included in the HTML 4.0 standard to let you specify borders, fonts, and layout, such as margins and indents. If you look at the source of a data access page saved using Access, you see a <STYLE> tag followed by styles that specify the margins, font and font size, headers and footers, and so on. A style is made up of a selector and the styles you want to apply. The *selector* can be any tag for which you want to specify formatting instructions or a class, which is explained later. For example, a style might appear as follows:

```
BODY {
    FONT-FAMILY: Tahoma; FONT-SIZE: 10pt
}
```

BODY is a selector that refers to the HTML BODY tag, <BODY>. The style also consists of a *property* and a *value* together, surrounded by curly braces. You can specify multiple properties and values by separating each with a semicolon still within the curly braces. In this example, the properties are the FONT-FAMILY and the FONT-SIZE. The value of the FONT-FAMILY is Tahoma and the value of the FONT-SIZE is set to 10pt, ten points. Notice a colon separates the property and the value.

A powerful feature of styles is the capability to apply different styles to an HTML tag by creating different classes. Creating a class is similar to creating a style. A class is specified by a dot (a period), followed by a name you want to use for the class. For example, Access includes the MSTheme-Label class for labels in a data access page.

```
.mstheme-label {
    FONT-FAMILY: Tahoma; FONT-SIZE: 8pt
}
```

When you add a tag, you can add the class attribute to apply all the styles set for a class. The properties and values set in the class control the formatting of your paragraph text. Different sections of text are formatted using <SPAN> </SPAN> and <DIV> </DIV> tags. The <SPAN> </SPAN> tags are used extensively to specify where to begin and end adding the styles. The <DIV> </DIV> tags are used to specify formatting for an entire section of a document. For example, to apply the MSTheme-Label class, the CLASS attribute is added to the <SPAN> tag <SPAN CLASS="MSTheme-Label">.

Extensible Markup Language

While HTML is the standard language for creating and displaying Web pages, Extensible Markup Language (XML) is the standard language for describing and delivering data on the Web. XML protocol is a set of rules, guidelines, and conventions for designing data formats and structures. HTML determines how a Web page should look, and XML defines the data and how it should be structured. Like HTML, XML uses tags and attributes to define the data and the data structure. It leaves the interpretation of the data up to HTML.

As you saw in the last chapter, you can import XML data using File | Get External Data and export Access data to XML using File | Export. When you want to display XML data, use the XSL style sheets instead of cascading style sheets because they more closely resemble the XML syntax and style of tags. You don't have to use either one, however, to display the XML data with Internet Explorer 5 and later because the Internet Explorer has a built-in style sheet that displays the XML document as a collapsible/expandable tree. See the MSDN Web site for more information about XML and the XSL style sheets.

Modifying a Data Access Page

To make creating data access pages as simple as possible, Access ships with a variety of preformatted, grouped styles, called *themes*. While displaying your page in Design view, you can modify any of the styles or elements in the data access page. In Design view, you can use familiar tools like a property sheet, a field list, a toolbox, and control wizards to modify the page design. The controls you place on data access pages are similar to the controls you use to create Access forms and reports. Like HTML pages, data access pages also support VBScript and JavaScript. The following

sections explain how to apply a theme to format a page quickly, as well as how to add
and modify styles and elements in a data access page.

Choosing a Theme

As mentioned previously, a theme enables you to apply a special formatting scheme to
your page. For example, you can choose from a variety of preformatted templates that
include complimentary backgrounds, fonts, horizontal lines, and bullets. A default theme
is automatically applied to a new data access page. You can apply a different theme by
doing the following:

1. Open the data access page in Design view and choose Format | Theme. The
   Theme dialog box appears (see Figure 24-11).

2. Select a theme from the Choose a Theme list box. Examples of the components
   of the selected theme style are displayed in the right pane. Not all the themes
   are available by default. If the theme isn't available, an Install button appears
   instead of an example. Click the button to install the selected theme style from
   the Office XP CD.

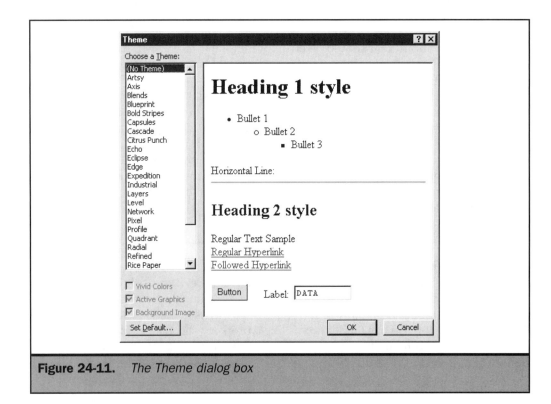

Figure 24-11.   *The Theme dialog box*

3. Once you select a theme, choose any of the following options you want to apply to your data access page:

   ■ **Vivid Colors** displays the text link and button colors using a brighter color scheme.

   ■ **Active Graphics** refers to animated graphical image files (GIFs). The animations display as static images in Access, but they display as animations in a Web browser.

   ■ **Background Image** turns on or off the background image. Clear this option if you want to see a solid background color.

   ■ **Set Default** changes the default theme to the one you're displaying. All new data access pages use the selected theme.

4. Choose OK to apply the selected theme and options.

 The final Page Wizard dialog box also offers the option of choosing a theme when you finish creating the page.

Working in Design View

 Choosing Design view from the View menu or clicking the View button in the Page Design toolbar displays the data access page in Design view, which shows the physical layout of the page. In Design view, you can add elements, and you can align and resize controls in a number of ways, for example, you can choose to align labels and controls to the left or right, and to align text at the top or bottom of a field. You can increase or reduce the height or width of controls.

When a blank data access page first appears in Design view, it includes a heading displaying "Click here and type title text." When you click this placeholder, the text disappears and the text you enter is formatted as a centered heading in the style determined by the chosen theme. Click the space below the title to enter additional text. You can enter as much text as you want. If you need more room, press ENTER and the grid section moves down on the page to make room for the multiple-line heading. The following sections explain how to add and format additional text, labels, and controls in a data access page.

 To display the page in Internet Explorer as you work on the design, save the file and choose File | Web Page Preview. If you're viewing the page in Internet Explorer, you can still return to Design view in Access by choosing File | Edit in Microsoft Access.

Adding Text, Labels, and Controls

You can enter any text you want to appear on the page in the areas above or below the grid section header. The grid section is typically the area where you add data-related text and controls. As in form design, the grid helps you place fields more uniformly.

You can add data bound fields to the area outside the grid, but this area lacks the absolute positioning features offered by the grid.

The Toolbox contains a variety of controls you can add to the page design, many of which are the same as those available for form and report design. In addition to the ones you're familiar with, the Toolbox includes other special purpose controls, such as bound span elements, scrolling text, hyperlinks, movies, lines, expand controls, and a bevy of ActiveX controls. Table 24-1 lists and describes each of the additional items in the Page Toolbox and lists their HTML or Microsoft proprietary HTML extension equivalents.

 If you want to add several controls of the same type to your data access page in one operation, lock the control in by double-clicking the Toolbox button. When you finish adding the controls, press ESC to release it or click another button.

All objects added to a page design can be selected, moved, and resized, and their properties can be customized, much the same as controls added to forms and reports.

Button	Control	Description
Aa	Label	Same as in forms and reports. Labels can contain hyperlinks, but the links work only when viewed in the browser or in an application that supports browsing, such as Word and Excel.
A	Bound Span	Displays data from a field in the database or displays the result of an expression. A bound span control is tied to a field in an underlying table or query. For example, after you add the Bound Span tool, set its Control Source property to the name of a field.
abl	Text Box	Same as in forms and reports. The HTML equivalent is the <INPUT TYPE="text"> tag.
	Scrolling Text	Adds a marquee for displaying scrolling text. This displays as scrolling, sliding, or bouncing text in Page view in Access or Microsoft Internet Explorer. You can specify the direction, speed, and type of motion. The equivalent tag is a Microsoft proprietary HTML extension <MARQUEE></MARQUEE>.

Table 24-1. *The Toolbox Control Options*

Button	Control	Description
	Option Group	Same as in forms. The option group uses XML and CSS to create the surrounding border and the name at the top of the group.
	Option Button	Same as in forms. The HTML equivalent is the <INPUT TYPE="radio"> tag.
	Check Box	Same as in forms. The HTML equivalent is the <INPUT TYPE="checkbox"> tag.
	Drop-down List	Equivalent to combo box in forms and reports. The HTML equivalent tags for creating a drop-down list are <SELECT> <OPTION>*List option*</SELECT>.
	List Box	Same as in forms and reports. The list box, like the drop-down list, is created using the HTML <SELECT> and <OPTION>*List option*</SELECT> tags.
	Command Button	Same as in forms.
	Expand	Adds a button for expanding and collapsing grouped records. Can be set to expand or collapse by default.
	Record Navigation	Adds a Record Navigation Bar that contains buttons used to display, edit, delete, sort, and filter records.
	Office PivotTable	Adds a PivotTable, which can be connected to a database. A PivotTable is a spreadsheet-like table you can use to analyze data dynamically in different ways. For example, you can rearrange row headings, column headings, and fields.
	Office Chart	Adds an Office chart to your data access page for analyzing data.

Table 24-1. *The Toolbox Control Options* (continued)

EXCHANGING DATA
WITH OTHERS

Button	Control	Description
	Office Spreadsheet	Adds an Excel spreadsheet to your data access page for adding data or importing a spreadsheet from Excel.
	Hyperlink	Inserts a link to a file or a Web page. The HTML equivalent is the anchor tag <A HREF="*http://www.somesite.com*">*Link text*</A>.
	Hyperlink Image	Inserts an image that's linked to a file or a Web page. This isn't an image map that contains multiple links. It's an image with a single link. The equivalent is the image tag surrounded by the anchor opening and closing tags, <A HREF="*http://www.somesite.com*"><IMG SRC="*filename.gif*"></A>. Formerly called "Hotspot Image."
	Movie	Inserts a movie in the data access page. The Movie control adds the Microsoft proprietary DYNSRC attribute to the IMG tag to play the movie.
	Image	Same as in forms and reports. The HTML equivalent is the <IMG SRC="*filename.gif*"> tag.
	Line	Similar to line in forms and reports, except draws the line horizontally only. The HTML equivalent is the <HR> (Horizontal Rule) tag.
	Rectangle	Same as in forms and reports.

Table 24-1. *The Toolbox Control Options* (continued)

Formatting Text and Labels for Controls

You can format text in a data access page by using the formatting toolbar; for example, you can use the Numbering or Bullets button in the Formatting toolbar to add a numbered or bulleted list to the area outside the grid on the page. To display the Formatting (Page) toolbar, right-click a visible toolbar and check it in the list of available toolbars. Table 24-2 describes the options available from the Formatting toolbar when creating a data access page. This table also includes the HTML equivalent tags for applying the formatting.

Formatting Option	Description
Style	Lists available styles you can apply to header or body text or labels. For example, you can format text with heading styles to help organize your data access page.
Font	Formats text and labels with the selected font. For another person to display the same font, the font must be installed on his or her system. The HTML equivalent is <FONT FACE="*fontname*">*Text*</Font>.
Size	Specifies the size of the font relative to point size. The HTML equivalent is the SIZE attribute, which is added to the FONT tag, <FONT FACE="Arial" SIZE="5">. The font sizes are adjusted to a number 1 through 7 for data access pages, which range from 8 points to 32 points. The default font size setting is 3.
Bold	Formats the selected text as boldface text. The HTML equivalent is the STRONG tag, <STRONG>*Bold text*</STRONG>.
Italic	Formats the selected text as italic text. The HTML equivalent is the EM tag, <EM>*Italic text*</EM>. *EM* stands for *emphasis.*
Underline	Formats the selected text with a single underline. The HTML equivalent for underline is the U tag, <U>*Underlined text*</U>. Be aware, adding underlined text can be confusing to some users because most links, by default, appear as underlined text. Use italics instead of underlining.
Align Left	Aligns text to the left margin of the page. This is the default setting, so you shouldn't have to apply it unless the previous text uses a different alignment. The HTML equivalent is the ALIGN="left" attribute, which can be added to paragraph and heading text, <P ALIGN="left">*Paragraph text*</P>.
Center	Centers text on the page. The HTML equivalent is the ALIGN= "center" attribute, which can be added to paragraph and heading text, <H1 ALIGN="center">*Heading text*</H1>. H1 refers to the Header1 style.

Table 24-2.   *The Formatting (Page) Toolbar Buttons*

EXCHANGING DATA
WITH OTHERS

Formatting Option	Description
Align Right	Aligns text to the right margin of the page. The HTML equivalent is the ALIGN="right" attribute, which can be added to paragraph and heading text, <P ALIGN="right">*Paragraph text*</P>.
Decrease Indent	Removes an indent from the text on the page. An equivalent doesn't exist for indenting text using HTML. Microsoft uses the BLOCKQUOTE tag to force an indent, so Decrease Indent removes a set of BLOCKQUOTE tags.
Increase Indent	Indents the text on the page. An equivalent doesn't exist for indenting text using HTML. Microsoft uses the BLOCKQUOTE tag to force an indent. Each time you press the Increase Indent button, BLOCKQUOTE tags are added around your text, <BLOCKQUOTE>Text</BLOCKQUOTE>.
Numbering	Formats text as a numbered list. The HTML equivalent is the <OL> and <LI> tags. *OL* stands for *ordered list* and *LI* stands for *list item*. For example, an HTML ordered list might appear as <OL><LI>*List item one*<LI>*List item two*</OL>.
Bullets	Formats text as a bulleted list. The HTML equivalent is the <UL> and <LI> tags. *UL* stands for *unordered list* and *LI* stands for *list item*. For example, an HTML unordered list might appear as <UL><LI>*List item one*<LI>*List item two*</UL>.
Fill/Back Color	Applies a color to the background of selected text or a control. If you select the grid and choose this button, the color is applied to the whole section.
Font/Fore Color	Applies color to the text in a control.
Line/Border Color	Applies the color to a line or border. You can also choose the Transparent setting to hide a line or border.
Line/Border Width	Applies a line width to the selected line or border. The options include 1-point lines for hairline borders up to 6 points for bold borders.
Special Effect	Applies a special effect such as raised, sunken, or various border styles to the selected text.

Table 24-2. *The Formatting (Page) Toolbar Buttons* (continued)

Aligning and Sizing Controls

When you select an element in the page design, moving and sizing handles appear around the element border. You can use these handles to drag the control to the location and size you want, just as you would with controls in form and report designs. By default, Access positions the controls to the coordinates in the grid. If you want to place a control without having it align to the grid, choose Format | Snap to Grid to toggle the option off.

If you're using Internet Explorer 5.5, you can select multiple controls and use the commands on the Format menu to manipulate the controls as a group. The Align, Size, Horizontal Spacing, and Vertical Spacing submenus contain the same commands you see when working with form and report designs.

If you're using an earlier version of Internet Explorer, you can't select multiple controls to format as a group. You can display the Alignment and Sizing toolbar, which contains buttons that do the same formatting as the Format menu. To display the Alignment and Sizing toolbar, choose View | Toolbars | Customize, and then check the Alignment and Sizing toolbar in the list of toolbars.

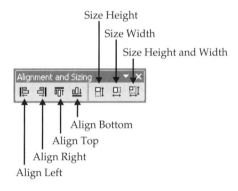

To use the Alignment and Sizing toolbar, select the control you want to use as the basis for your alignment or size pattern, and then click the button in the Alignment and Sizing toolbar that reflects the pattern you want to copy. Now click the control to which you want to apply that adjustment. The second control changes to match the position or size of the first control according to the command you select in Alignment and Sizing toolbar.

Note *If you want to apply the formatting to multiple controls, double-click the toolbar button to lock it down. When you finish, click another button or press ESC to release it.*

Table 24-3 lists the options available using the Alignment and Sizing toolbar.

Alignment and Sizing Option	Description
Align Left	Aligns the left edge of the second control with the left edge of the first control.
Align Right	Aligns the right edge of the second control with the right edge of the first control.
Align Top	Aligns the top edge of the second control with the top edge of the first control.
Align Bottom	Aligns the bottom edge of the second control with the bottom edge of the first control.
Size Height	Adjusts only the height of the second control to match the first.
Size Width	Adjusts only the width of the second control to match the first.
Size Height and Width	Adjusts both the height and width of the second control to match the first.

Table 24-3. *Alignment and Sizing Toolbar Buttons*

Note *In data access pages, you can't vertically resize a list box or a drop-down list box. The vertical size of the list box and drop-down list box is based on the font setting of the data in the control.*

Adding Images and Backgrounds

As you saw in earlier chapters, you can add a picture or other image file as data in an OLE Object control in a table. One of the limitations of a data access page is you cannot display OLE Object data from a database. So, although you can't display images from a table in a data access page, you can add a picture to the data access page design by using the Image control and adding the path to the image. The path can be relative to where the data access page is stored, a path to a local hard disk, or a full URL that includes the path to the image.

To add an image to a data access page, click the Image control, and then click the data access page where you want the upper-left corner of the image to appear. If you want to specify an area for the image to appear in, instead of clicking the page, drag the mouse until the box matches the size you want for the image. The image control is inserted in the page and the Insert Picture dialog box appears. Locate the desired image and click Insert.

You can then open the property sheet, and set the Height and Width properties to fit the image.

An image can also be tiled to create a background for a data access page or you can choose a flat color for the background. To add a background color, choose Format | Background | Color and choose a color from the palette. To add a tiled background, choose Format | Background | Picture and choose the image you want to use in the background.

 Keep contrast in mind. If you use a dark color or background image, text may be difficult to read. You can use the property settings to change the color of the text, so you can use a dark background and a light colored text.

Figure 24-12 shows a data access page with a background image. After adding the background image, you can use the page properties to change its location on the page. You can also tile the image if you want it repeated over the entire page.

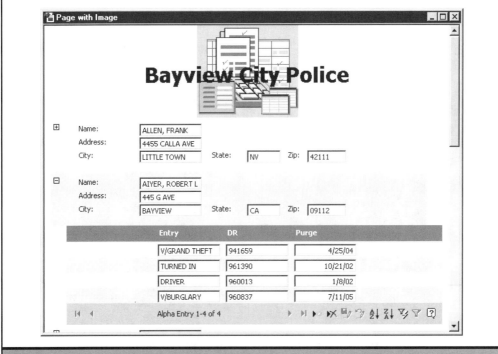

Figure 24-12. *A data access page with a background image*

EXCHANGING DATA WITH OTHERS

To make sure your page displays as fast as possible, avoid using the clip and stretch to adjust your image. Instead, use an image editor to size or crop the image to the exact size you want to display on your data access page before inserting it in the page design.

Setting Group Level Properties

When you group data access pages, you can set several properties to customize the appearance and behavior of the page. To set these properties, right-click the section bar and choose Group Level Properties from the shortcut menu (see Figure 24-13).

In the Group Level Properties sheet, set the group properties for the group, as described in Table 24-4. The default settings for the highest level group appear in bold in the table.

Setting Default Page Properties

You can change the default settings for a few page design properties. To make changes, choose Tools | Options and click the Pages tab (see Figure 24-14).

■ The Section Indent property specifies the width of the indent for each subsequently lower level section.

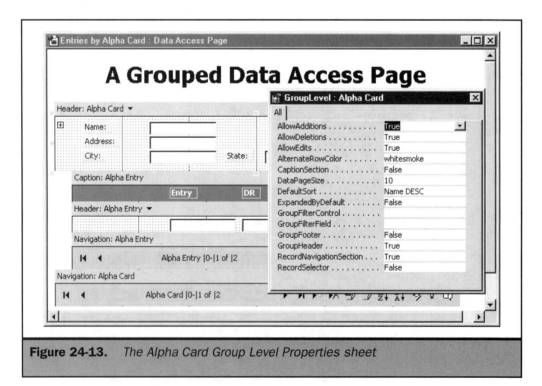

Figure 24-13. *The Alpha Card Group Level Properties sheet*

Property	Description
Allow Additions	Permits adding new records to the section. **True**/False.
Allow Deletions	Permits records to be deleted from the section. **True**/False.
Allow Edits	Permits editing of existing records in the section. **True**/False.
Alternate Row Color	Sets the background color for alternate rows of data in the group header and footer sections. **Whitesmoke**.
Caption Section	Displays or hides the caption section. True/**False**
Data Page Size	Specifies how many records to display for each group level. If no Record Navigation control is included, must be set to All. To use the page for data entry, set to 1. The lower the number, the faster the records are displayed. Default depends on the level of the section.
Default Sort	Type the name of the fields to sort on at this group level. If more than one field, separate the names with a comma. Follow each name with a space and the keyword ASC for ascending or DESC for descending order. **Ascending** is the default order.
Expanded By Default	Automatically displays the next lower group level records expanded. True/**False**
Group Filter Control	Enter the name of the combo box or list box that filters records in this group level.
Group Filter Field	Enter the name of the field containing values for which you want to filter.
Group Footer	Displays or hides the group footer section. True/**False**
Group Header	Displays or hides the group header section. **True**/False
Record Navigation Section	Displays or hides the Record Navigation Section. **True**/False
Record Selector	Displays or hides the record selector. True/**False**

Table 24-4. *Data Access Page Group Properties*

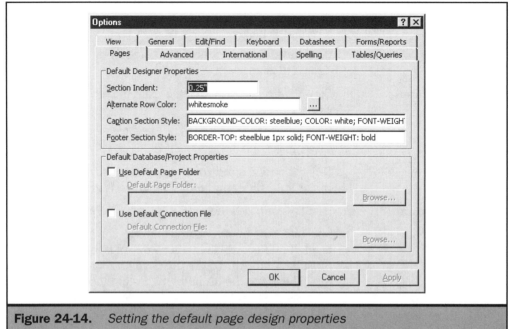

Figure 24-14. *Setting the default page design properties*

- Use the Alternate Row Color to set the color of every other row in the group header and footer sections. Click the Build button to display the color palette.

- The Caption Section Style and Footer Section Style settings specify the background and text colors, as well as the font weights for the sections.

If you change the default settings, they are applied to new pages.

Using the Data Outline

The data outline displays a tree view of the data model used by the data access page. The list includes the record sources, fields, and any calculated controls you added to the page. Click the Data Outline toolbar button to display the Data Outline pane.

You can select an item in the list and set its properties, delete fields, and redefine relationships between record sources. Right-click an item and choose from the shortcut menu. The following illustration shows the Data Outline for the Entries by Alpha Card data access page.

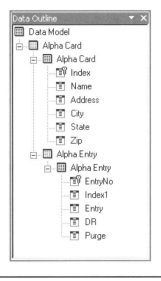

Organizing Data in a Data Access Page

When you create a data access page, you are, in essence, creating a user interface to your database. The controls you display and how you organize data can mean the difference between users getting the data they want or getting lost in your user interface. Access presents controls you can easily include to help users sort and filter records. You can also customize the groups to achieve the desired appearance. For example, you can set the number of records to display on the page and specify which group sections to include.

Once you arrange the records, you can add totals, averages, and other aggregate summaries of selected field data.

Sorting and Filtering Records

One of the most common database-oriented tasks is to sort and filter records quickly to find the information you need arranged in a helpful order. The Record Navigation Bar contains buttons you can use to sort and filter records. You can also require your server to filter the records before delivering them to you, which can save time when downloading data. If you want to establish a default sort order for records on the page in one or more groups, you can set this property in the Default Sort property in the Group Level Properties sheet.

Using the Record Navigation Bar

In addition to the standard record navigation buttons used in other windows, the Record Navigation Bar in a data access page includes commands for sorting data in either ascending or descending order and for filtering data. The Record Navigation Bar also has buttons to add a new record, save the current record without moving to another record, or undo the previous edit, and a Help button that opens the Help window.

To sort records in the page, place the insertion point in the field you want to sort by and click one of the Sort buttons on the Navigation Bar: Sort Ascending or Sort Descending. When you sort records that are grouped, the sorting operation applies only to the group. The records return to their original order when you close the data access page.

To display only those records with a specific value in a field, select the value in the field, and then click the Filter By Selection button on the Record Navigation Bar. To remove the filter, click the Toggle Filter button. You can reapply the filter by clicking the Toggle Filter button again, as long as you don't browse a different data access page. The filter isn't saved with the page, so once you load another page, the filter is lost.

Setting the Default Sort Order

The default sort order is one of the group properties you can set in the Group Level Properties dialog box. To set the default sort order of records on a data access page, do the following:

1. Open the data access page in Design view.

2. Right-click the group section bar and choose Group Level Properties from the shortcut menu (refer to Figure 24-13).

3. Enter the name of the field you want the records sorted by in the Default Sort property box. If the field name includes a space, be sure to enclose the name in square brackets. Ascending order is the default, but if you want a field sorted in descending order, follow the field name with a space, and then the keyword DESC.

4. To set the default sort order on more than one field, separate the field names with a comma.

If the control you want to sort on is bound to an expression or a grouped control, you must type the name of the control as displayed in its Control Source property, the *alias*. For example, if the Control Source property of the control you want to sort on is set to ExtendedPrice: Sum([Quantity] * [Price]), type **ExtendedPrice** in the Default Sort property. When you group on a control, Access adds the prefix "GroupOf" to the control name, creating an alias. You must use this alias if you want to specify it as the Default Sort order.

You can use another of the group properties to view more than one record on the screen at once in the data access page. The Data Page Size property specifies the number of records to display. The default is 1, but you can set it to another number or All. Try different settings until you're satisfied with the page on your display.

Calculating and Displaying Totals

The goal of a data access page isn't only to display data, but also to help analyze the data by calculating summaries. To be effective, you want to add expressions to perform calculations and include the results on your page. You can add an unbound text box control to a data access page that displays the results of a calculation using the values in other fields in the record. This is the same as adding a calculated field to a form or report.

A data access page also lets you display aggregate totals and other calculations based on grouped records. To do so, the page must have at least two group levels. You use a bound span control that's bound to the field you want to summarize. We revert to the Home Tech Repair database to show examples of calculating totals because it has more interesting currency fields. This example creates a new data access page for the Home Tech Repair database based on the Current Workorders by Supervisor query developed in Chapter 8. The query contains two calculated fields:

■ Total Cost, which sums the Material Cost and Labor Cost for each work order.

■ Extended Cost, which increases the Total Cost by 15 percent to cover overhead expenses.

The finished data access page, shown in Figure 24-15, groups work orders by supervisor and computes the total costs by supervisor, as well as a grand total of all work orders in progress. It also counts and displays the number of jobs managed by each supervisor.

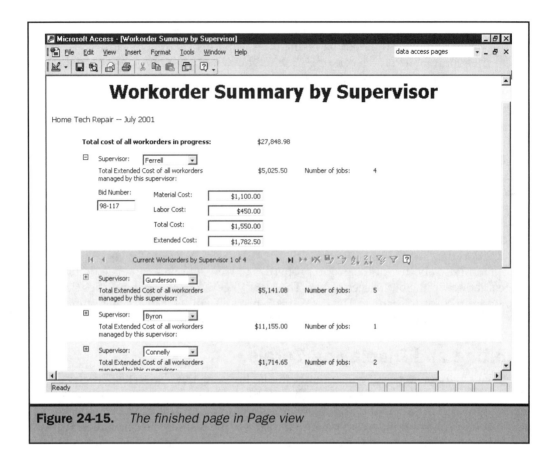

Figure 24-15.   *The finished page in Page view*

To create the page, do the following:

1. Click New in the Pages page of the Database window and choose Design View in the New Page dialog box.

2. Click the down arrow and choose the Current Workorders by Supervisor query from the drop-down list, and then click OK. The empty data access page opens in Design view and the Field List box displays the fields in the expanded query.

3. Drag the Supervisor field to the top of the page design.

4. Drag the Bid Number field to the grid below the Supervisor field.

5. Select the Supervisor field and click Promote. This creates a new group level based on the Supervisor field.

6. Select the label attached to the Supervisor control property sheet and click Properties.

7. Edit the InnerText property to remove the GroupOf prefix.

Note When you're arranging controls in a page design, you can move the attached label separately, but when you drag the control, the label moves with it. You can't drag it alone. So position the text box control first, and then move the label.

8. Reduce the height of the header section of the higher-level group, but leave room for calculated fields.

9. Drag the four cost fields to the design in a column next to the Bid Number field. You may have to drag the lower section boundary down to make room.

10. Add a title in the Title Text area, and then click in the header area below the title and add text as a subtitle (see Figure 24-16).

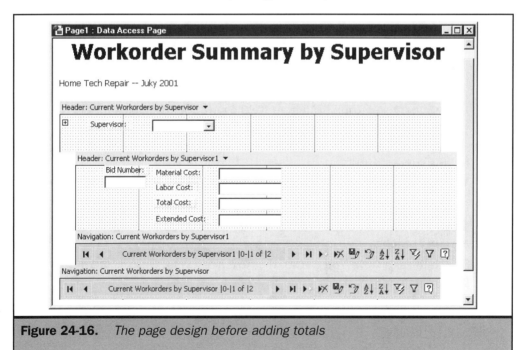

Figure 24-16. *The page design before adding totals*

EXCHANGING DATA
WITH OTHERS

The AutoSum feature in the data access page Design view offers a quick way to add calculated summaries to a page. Simply select the bound control you want to summarize and choose from the AutoSum list. Where the new summarized control appears depends on the type of page you're working with and the location of the selected control:

- If you haven't grouped records on the page or if the selected bound control is in the highest group level, Access creates a new group level and places the bound span control in the new footer section. You can move it later, if necessary.

- If the bound control is in an inner group, Access adds the new summary span control to the footer section of the next higher group level. If no footer section is showing, the span control is placed in the group header section.

To add the aggregate values to the Home Tech Repair that sum up the total workorder values for each supervisor and count the number of jobs each is responsible for, do the following:

1. In page Design view, select the Extended Cost bound control.

2. Click the arrow next to AutoSum and choose Sum from the list.

3. In the Supervisor group header, move the new bound span control to the right to make room for the label explanation.

4. Edit the control's label to read **Total Extended Cost of all workorders managed by this supervisor:**.

5. To count the number of jobs, select the Bid Number bound control.

6. Click the AutoSum arrow again and choose Count from the list.

7. Move the new bound span control to the right and edit the label to read **Number of jobs:**.

8. Switch to Page view. You can see the currency format wasn't inherited by the bound span control.

9. Switch back to Design view and double-click the Total Extended Cost control to open the property sheet.

10. Change the Format property (on the Data tab) to Currency.

If you change your mind about the type of summarizing you want in the bound span control, you can change its Total Type property. The choices are the same as in the AutoSum list.

The next task is to create a grand total of the cost of all current workorders in the top of the page. Select the bound span control you placed in the Current Workorders by Supervisor header and select Sum from the AutoSum list. A new group is added to the page and the aggregate is placed in the group footer. If you want the grand total in the group header instead, do the following:

1. Right-click the new group footer bar and select Group Level Properties from the shortcut menu.

2. Change the Group Header to True.

3. Copy-and-paste the grand total span control from the footer to the header section.

4. Right-click the group header bar and choose Group Level Properties from the shortcut menu.

5. Change the Group Footer property to False to remove it from the page.

6. Then change the grand total control's Format property to Currency.

7. Because the new level group won't contain any records, you can remove the expand control. Select the expand control in the header section that contains the grand total and press DEL.

8. If you want to change the number of Supervisor records to display on the screen at once when you switch to Page view, right-click the group header section bar and choose Group Level Properties from the shortcut menu.

9. Set the Data Page Size for the group to 5 or another number. Figure 24-17 shows the completed data access page design.

Many more options are available for grouping records and summarizing data with calculated fields. You can virtually design a data access page for any purpose and only your imagination limits the way your page looks and behaves.

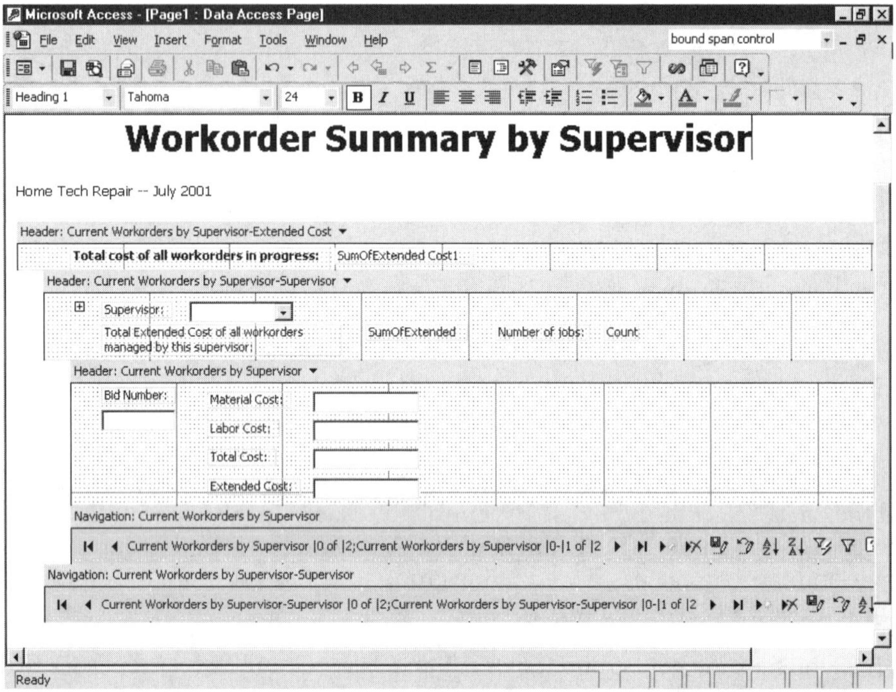

Figure 24-17. *The completed data access page design*

Editing and Protecting Data in Data Access Pages

In Access 2000, data in grouped data access pages wasn't editable but, in Access 2002, you can choose to allow or prevent editing, entering, or deleting data by setting the group level properties for each group. As long as the group section doesn't contain an aggregate or other calculated field, you can allow editing of the data in the group. The lowest level group is editable by default and you can set the Allow Editing, Allow Deletions, and Allow Additions to True for the higher level groups.

The Record Navigation Bar, described earlier, appears in all your data access pages unless you chose to hide it. It includes buttons for adding and deleting records or undoing your last editing operation. Adding and editing records in a data access page is much the same as doing so in a form.

In some cases, you may want to protect specific fields from being edited. The following sections explain how to use the Record Navigation Bar to edit, add, and delete records, as well as to undo edits. It also explains how to protect a specific field from being edited.

Adding a New Record

When you click the New Record button in the Record Navigation Bar, a blank record displays in the data access page. You can add records to the page in either Access Page view or in Internet Explorer. The following steps explain adding a new record to a data access page using Internet Explorer.

1. To view the page with Internet Explorer, choose File | Web Page Preview (see Figure 24-18). You can also start Internet Explorer and choose File | Open to load the data access page you want to work with in Internet Explorer.

2. Click the New Record button on the Record Navigation Bar.

3. Type the data you want in the first field. Press TAB to move to the next field.

4. Click the Save Record button on the Record Navigation Bar to save the record. If you add or edit another record, the changes made to the previously edited record are automatically saved.

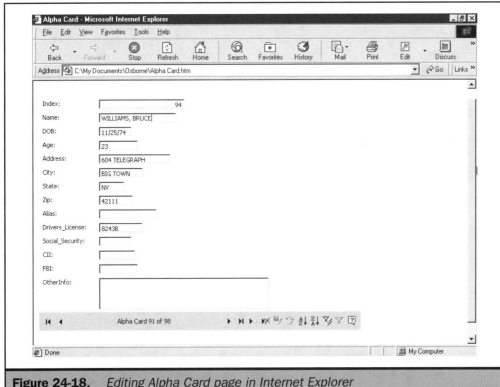

Figure 24-18.   *Editing Alpha Card page in Internet Explorer*

Editing or Deleting a Record

Use the Record Navigation Bar to move to the record you want to edit or delete. Make the changes you want to the record data and move to the next record or click the Save Record button. To delete a record, move to it and click the Delete Record button. If the data access page doesn't automatically display your changes, click the Refresh button on the Web toolbar or press F5.

Be sure to save your changes before you click the Refresh button, otherwise Internet Explorer displays a message warning that your changes may be discarded.

Protecting Fields in Data-Entry Pages

If you create a page for entering data, you may want to protect certain fields from being changed. To protect a field, you need to change the field's ReadOnly property to True.

Customizing a Record Navigation Bar

In addition to modifying data-related controls by changing the control's properties, you can also customize the Record Navigation Bar on a data access page. For example, you can change the labels that appear when a person browses the records in a data access page or remove one or more buttons from the toolbar. To customize the appearance or behavior of the Record Navigation Bar, open the data access page in Design view, select the Record Navigation Control toolbar, and do one of the following:

1. To remove a button from the Record Navigation Bar, right-click the Navigation Bar (not the section bar), point to Navigation Buttons (see Figure 24-19), and clear the check mark next to the button you want to remove. To put it back on the bar, check it again.

2. The Recordset label in the Navigation Bar tells you which record in which group is currently displaying on the page. For example, *Alpha Card 1-10 of 98* indicates you're viewing records 1 through 10 out of a total of 98 records. To change this description, select the Recordset label box, open the property sheet, and change the Inner Text property.

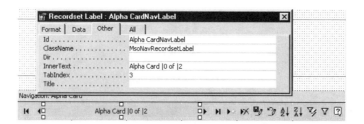

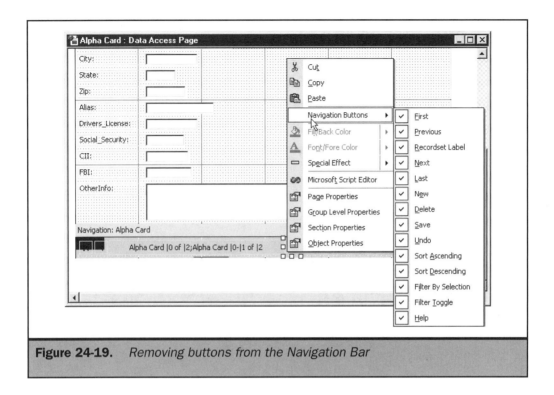

Figure 24-19.   *Removing buttons from the Navigation Bar*

3. To change the image that appears on a button, select the button, open the property sheet, and change the Scr property (on the Other tab) to a different .gif file.

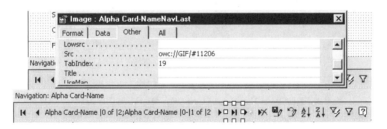

 If you have Record Navigation Bars in more than one group, you can set their properties differently.

EXCHANGING DATA
WITH OTHERS

Adding a Spreadsheet, Chart, PivotTable, or PivotChart

In data access pages you can include controls that display data in a variety of ways, such as a spreadsheet, a chart, a PivotTable, or PivotChart. Each of these options give a different visual representation of your data. For example, the spreadsheet provides some of the same capabilities you have in a Microsoft Excel worksheet to a data access page, adding a chart makes it easy for users to compare data and spot trends in data, and adding a PivotTable or PivotChart enables you to dynamically change the layout to perform calculations and analyze the data in different ways, while viewing the data access page.

Adding a Spreadsheet

When you add a spreadsheet control to a data access page, you can enter values, add formulas, apply filters, and perform many types of data analysis. You can also import data from another source, such as Excel. After you add a spreadsheet control, a toolbar appears at the top of the spreadsheet, providing a set of commands similar to those on the Record Navigation Bar. You can also use the toolbar to work with the data in the spreadsheet while you're designing it. When you view the data access page in a browser, you can also use the toolbar to work with the spreadsheet. The following section explains how to add a spreadsheet to your data access page.

1. Open the data access page in Design view.
2. Click the Office Spreadsheet tool in the Toolbox.
3. Draw a box the size you want for the spreadsheet in the data access page.
4. Enter data and formulas directly in the spreadsheet or choose File | Get External Data | Import to import data to use in the spreadsheet.
5. To make changes in the spreadsheet, activate it by clicking once to select the control, and then click a second time to activate the spreadsheet. You can tell when it's activated by the hash-mark frame.
6. Right-click the spreadsheet and choose Commands and Options from the shortcut menu (see Figure 24-20). You can also click the Commands and Options button on the spreadsheet toolbar.

Getting Visual by Adding a Chart

The Toolbox includes the Chart control to add charts to a data access page. The data for a chart can come from a table or a query, or from a spreadsheet or PivotTable list. For example, you can add a chart that uses data in a table consisting of sales figures for different regions. When you update the sales figures, the chart is updated, so the data access page displays the most current information. The Chart control lets you choose

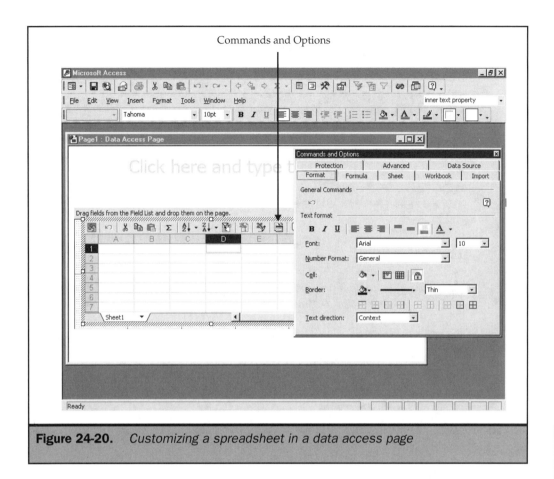

Figure 24-20. *Customizing a spreadsheet in a data access page*

from many different types of 2-D and 3-D charts. You can add text, change colors, and apply different chart formats.

To add a chart to the page, do the following:

1. Start a new page in Design view.

2. Click the Office Chart tool in the toolbox and draw a frame for the chart in the page grid (see Figure 24-21).

3. In the Commands and Options dialog box, choose Data from a Database Table or Query. Two additional tables appear in the dialog box.

4. Click the Data Details tab or click the Connection button.

5. Click Edit to locate the database that contains the data you want to see in the chart, for example, the Police database.

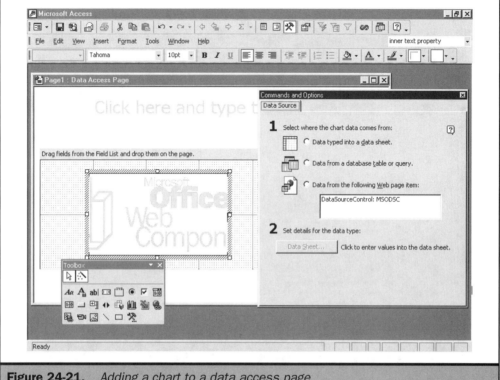

Figure 24-21. *Adding a chart to a data access page*

6. Then, select the Crimes by Beat Number query from the *Data member, table, view, or cube name* list (see Figure 24-22).

7. Click the Type tab and select from the many chart types.

8. Close the Commands and Options dialog box.

Now it's time to place the fields on the chart. Resize the chart as necessary, and then click the Field List button on the Chart toolbar. Drag-and-drop the fields to the following areas on the chart:

- Place Year in the Filter area.
- Place the BeatNo field in the Category area.
- Place the Crime Type in the Category area.
- Place the Number of Crimes in the Data area.

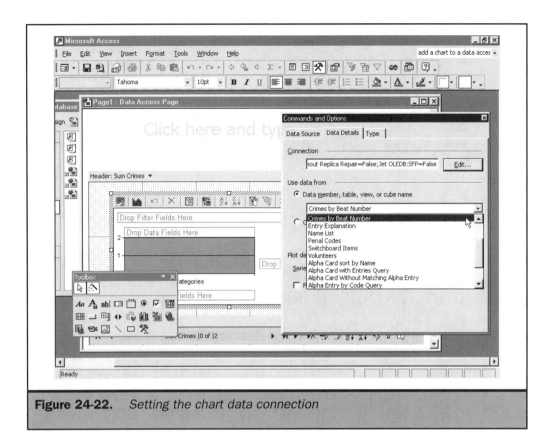

Figure 24-22.   *Setting the chart data connection*

Note   *You can also select the field name in the Chart Field List box. Select the chart area from the drop-down list at the lower left and click Add To.*

Figure 24-23 shows the chart with the Crimes by Beat Number fields placed in the chart areas.

Once you arrange the data the way you want it, you can click the Commands and Options button and customize the chart (see Figure 24-24). See Chapter 15 for details of chart features and formatting.

Creating Interactive PivotTables

As mentioned in Chapter 15, a PivotTable is a spreadsheet-like table you can use to analyze data dynamically in different ways. For example, you can rearrange row headings, column headings, and fields. When you change the layout, the PivotTable recalculates the data based on the new arrangement. If the source data changes, you can update the PivotTable to display the change.

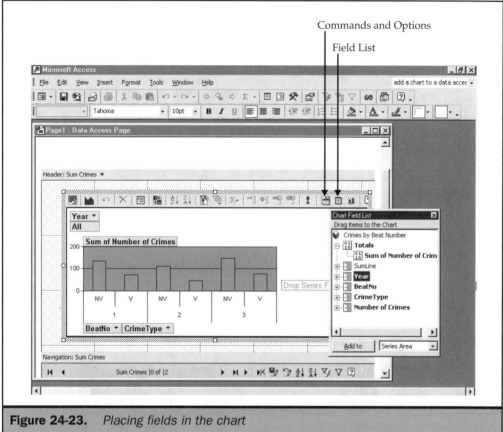

Figure 24-23. *Placing fields in the chart*

You have two ways to show a PivotTable on a data access page:

■ Create the design directly in the data access page.
■ Save a PivotTable form as a data access page.

To create a new PivotTable in the page, do the following:

1. Start a new data access page from the Database window.
2. In the page Design view, click the Office PivotTable tool and draw the frame in the page grid.
3. Expand the list of tables (see Figure 24-25) and expand the table containing the data you want to place in the PivotTable.
4. Follow the basic instructions for creating the PivotTable, as described in Chapter 15.

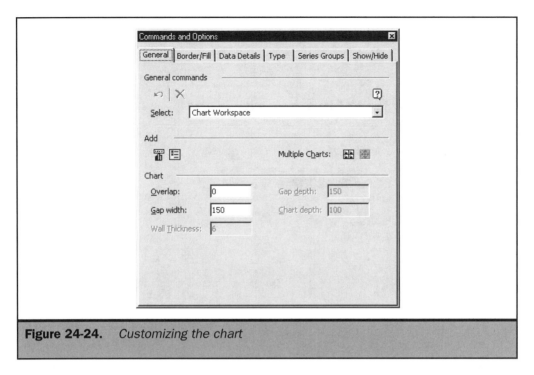

Figure 24-24. *Customizing the chart*

If you've already created the PivotTable you want and saved it as a form, you can save it again as a data access page, by doing the following:

1. Select the form name in the Database window, and then choose File | Save As. You can also right-click the form name and choose Save As from the shortcut menu.

2. In the Save As dialog box, choose Data Access Page from the As drop-down list.

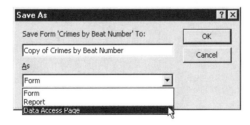

3. Click OK.

4. In the New Data Access Page dialog box, choose the location for the HTML file and enter a name for the new page. Then click OK. Figure 24-26 shows the Sum Crimes PivotTable saved as a data access page.

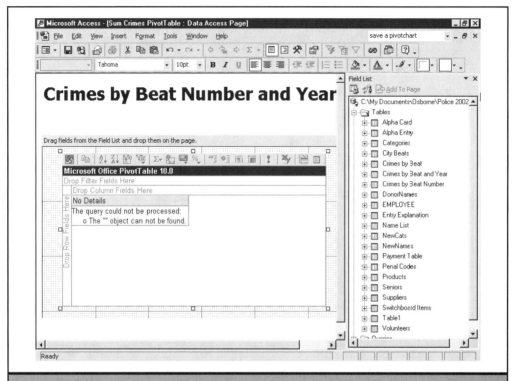

Figure 24-25. *Showing the list of tables in the Police database*

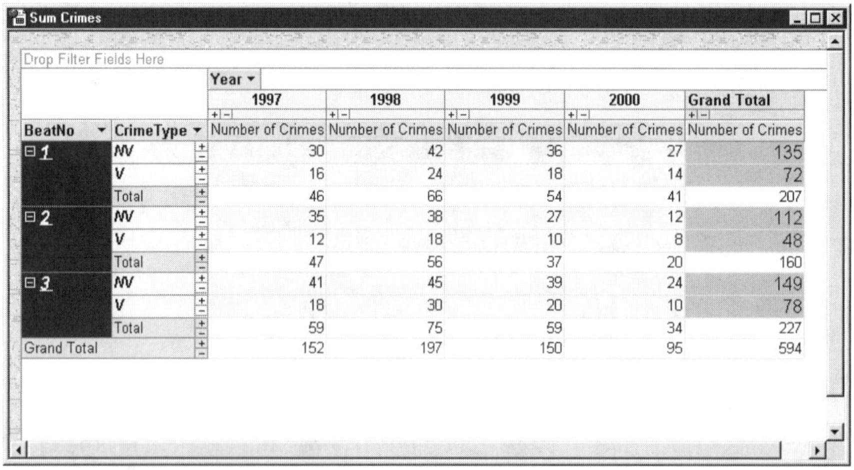

BeatNo	CrimeType	1997 Number of Crimes	1998 Number of Crimes	1999 Number of Crimes	2000 Number of Crimes	Grand Total Number of Crimes
1	NV	30	42	36	27	135
	V	16	24	18	14	72
	Total	46	66	54	41	207
2	NV	35	38	27	12	112
	V	12	18	10	8	48
	Total	47	56	37	20	160
3	NV	41	45	39	24	149
	V	18	30	20	10	78
	Total	59	75	59	34	227
Grand Total		152	197	150	95	594

Figure 24-26. *The PivotTable form saved as a data access page*

If you switch to Design view, the page design is empty. You must make changes in the design in the form and save it again as a data access page.

Creating an Interactive PivotChart

While PivotTables are controls you can build in a data access page, to create a PivotChart in a data access page, you need to change the PivotTable form to the PivotChart view, and then save it as a data access page. To add a PivotChart to a data access page, do the following:

1. Open the PivotTable form in Form view.
2. Choose View | PivotChart View to change the table to a chart.
3. Click Save, but don't close the form.
4. Choose File | Save As and select Data Access Page from the As drop-down list.
5. Click OK.
6. In the New Data Access Page, select the locations for the HTML file and enter a name for the page. Then click OK. The data access page opens in Page view (see Figure 24-27).

Note *When you close the page, the PivotChart reverts to a PivotTable.*

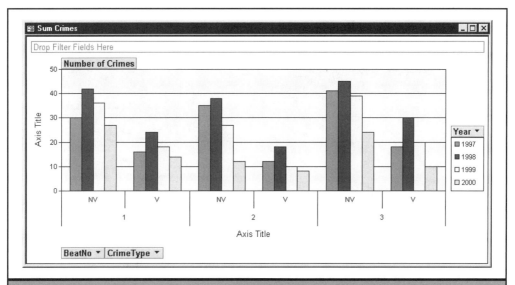

Figure 24-27. *The PivotChart in a new data access page*

EXCHANGING DATA
WITH OTHERS

The PivotChart on the data access page is truly interactive. You can filter the data in place by clicking an arrow next to one of the categories or series buttons. Then clear the check marks from the values you want to remove from the chart. Figure 24-28 shows the PivotChart filtered to show only the number of crimes from Beat 1.

You can also pivot the categories and series fields to create a different visual representation of the data. For example, drag the BeatNo field button to the Series area and the Year field button to the Categories area. You see the beat numbers in the legend and the number of crimes grouped by type within the year.

Publishing Data Access Pages

Once you create your data access page, you want to find a service provider that enables you to make your data access pages available to the world. You could easily download a Web server program and publish your Web pages from your site, but using a service provider is much less expensive than paying for a dedicated connection to the Internet. If you want to use your own company name as a part of your URL, make sure to ask if the service provider supports virtual domain names. If you publish your pages with an ISP that doesn't support virtual domains, you and others will likely have to use the service provider's address, followed by a tilde and your name, to view your Web pages.

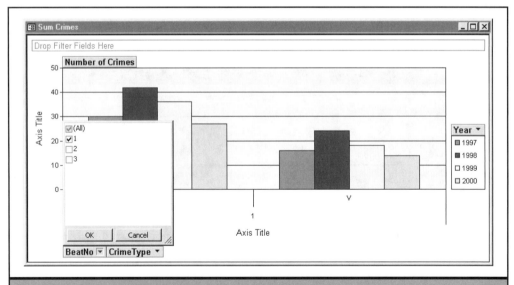

Figure 24-28. *Filtering the data in a PivotChart*

Printing Data Access Pages

When you print a data access page, you print only one page. The page contains the number of records you specified in the Page Size property. For example, if you set the property to show ten records on a page, the printed page includes all ten records. If some of the records are expanded to show records in a lower-level group, the result may take up more than one printed page.

Summary

This chapter introduced you to the basics of presenting and working with Access data on a worldwide stage. It described how to create data access pages to present data in a variety of ways. The subject of Internet access and publishing Access information on the Web is extremely variable and complex, one which would take much more room to explore than is available here. As Microsoft continues to improve and expand the capabilities of Office and Access, more capabilities are certain to arise. Armed with the elemental information in this chapter, we hope you can build a thorough knowledge of dynamic information sharing.

MOUS Exam Activities Explored in This Chapter

Level	Activity	Section Title
Core	Create and modify a data access page	Creating a Data Access Page Creating a Grouped Data Access Page Modifying a Data Access Page Sorting and Filtering Records Calculating and Displaying Totals
Expert	Save PivotTable and PivotChart views to data access pages	Getting Visual by Adding a Chart Creating Interactive PivotTables Creating an Interactive PivotChart

EXCHANGING DATA
WITH OTHERS

The Complete Reference

Access 2002

Part V

Application Development

Chapter 25

Introducing Microsoft Visual Basic

V isual Basic provides a common programming language across Microsoft products that enables you to integrate applications and share data among them. Visual Basic is a powerful object-oriented language with many capabilities and extreme flexibility.

Covering all aspects of Visual Basic in this book is impossible, so this chapter attempts to provide a solid foundation from which you can launch into more advanced study. All the basic elements of the language are discussed and demonstrations of their use are presented. Several examples of Visual Basic code are also presented, showing the many uses to which you can put the language.

Deciding Between Macros and Visual Basic

The subject of deciding between using macros to carry out actions in an application or using Visual Basic was discussed briefly in Chapter 19. For some purposes, such as defining alternative actions for certain key combinations and adding startup routines, you must use macros. Most other actions can be executed by either macros or Visual Basic. While macros are quite powerful and versatile, other activities require Visual Basic procedures, such as the following:

- When you want to discriminate between types of errors that may occur while the application is running and displays a relevant error message.

- When you want to define custom functions to perform calculations or to take the place of complicated expressions.

- When you want to optimize the performance of your application with compiled Visual Basic code, which runs faster than the equivalent macros.

- When you want to handle records individually and manipulate the data on a transaction basis.

Among the most compelling reasons to use Visual Basic code in an application are efficiency and ease of maintenance. Macros are kept as separate objects in a database, while event procedures are built into the associated form or report, where they're easy to find and maintain.

Converting Macros to Visual Basic Code

When you decide to use Visual Basic exclusively for an application, you can convert the existing macros to Visual Basic code. The method you use for converting the macros depends on how you want the code stored. If you want the code available to the entire database, convert the macro directly from the Macros tab of the Database window. If you want the code stored with a form or report, convert the macro from the associated form or report Design view.

Converting from Design View

As an example, convert the Lookup DR macro group created in Chapter 21 to Visual Basic code, so it's stored with the Lookup DR form design. Figure 25-1 shows the dialog box in Design view with the original macro group consisting of two macros. One macro closes the dialog box when the Cancel button is clicked, while the other runs a query to find the record for the DR number entered in the unbound text box.

To convert this macro to Visual Basic code, do the following:

1. Open the Lookup DR dialog box in Design view.

2. Choose Tools | Macro, and then click Convert Form's Macros to Visual Basic.

3. In the Convert form macros: Lookup DR dialog box, clear the Add Error Handling To Generated Functions option and check the Include Macro Comments option, and then click Convert.

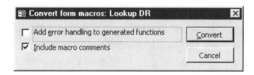

4. In a moment, the Convert Macros To Visual Basic message box shows the conversion is finished.

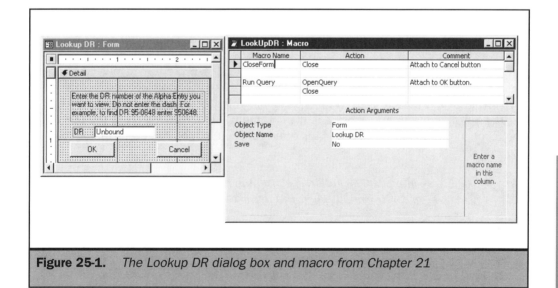

Figure 25-1. *The Lookup DR dialog box and macro from Chapter 21*

5. Click OK to close the message box.

Handling errors with Visual Basic code is discussed later in this chapter.

 When the message box closes, click the Code toolbar button to see the Visual Basic Editor window with the converted macros code. Two procedures are in the module, one for each of the command buttons. The Run Query macro that runs when you click the OK command button is converted to the OK_Click event procedure, which the following shows.

Tip *When Access adds a command button, it names the button Commandn when it's added to the form design. If you want to use a more meaningful name, rename the control in the property sheet. If you rename the control after converting the macros to Visual Basic, be sure to change the control name in the procedure as well.*

```
Private Sub OK_Click()
' Attach to OK button.
    DoCmd.OpenQuery "Lookup DR", acNormal, acReadOnly
    DoCmd.Close acForm, "Lookup DR"
End Sub
```

The first line in the procedure is the beginning of the sub procedure named OK_Click, which is attached to the OK command button's On Click event property. The Private keyword indicates the sub procedure is available only to the current document. The line beginning with an apostrophe is the comment taken directly from the macro Comment column. This is a result of the option chosen in the Convert form macros dialog box.

Note *When Access encounters an apostrophe in a line of code, it ignores the rest of the line. You can use an apostrophe anywhere in a line of code to insert comments.*

The two **DoCmd** statements run the macro actions OpenQuery and Close. The syntax of the **DoCmd.OpenQuery** statement specifies the following arguments set in the macro:

■ Lookup DR is the name of the query to open. The query gets the parameter from the text box in the Lookup DR dialog box.

■ acNormal indicates the query is to open in Datasheet view.

■ acReadOnly specifies the query results as read-only.

Having run those statements, the procedure reaches the **End Sub** statement and stops.

The second procedure that represents the converted CloseForm macro is similar, but with only one **DoCmd** statement that closes the Lookup DR form.

The procedures are saved with the form design and are always available to the form, but to no other object in the database.

Converting from the Database Window

When you convert a macro from the Database window, it's saved as a function in a global module and listed in the Modules tab of the Database window as a converted macro. Macros converted this way are available to the entire database. Instead of being converted to sub procedures, each of the macros in the group is converted to a function with a slightly different syntax. In addition, because macros may have names that aren't permitted for Visual Basic functions, Access names the new functions simply Proc with a sequence number. After the conversion, you can rename the procedure.

To convert a macro from the Database window, select the macro name in the Database window and do one of the following:

- Choose Tools | Macro and click Convert Macros to Visual Basic.
- Choose File | Save As, or right-click the macro name and choose Save As from the shortcut menu. In the Save As dialog box, enter a name for the new module in the Save Macro…To box and choose Module from the As list. Then click OK.

The same Convert macro dialog box appears with the options of including comments and error handling.

Note *You can also convert a macro from the macro Design window by choosing File | Save As, as previously shown. If the macro is part of a macro group, the entire group is converted.*

The following code shows the same Run Query macro of the LookupDR macro group converted from the Macros tab of the Database window.

```
Function LookUpDR_Run_Query()
' Attach to OK button.
    DoCmd.OpenQuery "Lookup DR", acNormal, acReadOnly
    DoCmd.Close acForm, "Lookup DR"
End Function
```

Most macro actions have equivalent Visual Basic methods that can be used with the **DoCmd** statement to carry out the macro action in a Visual Basic procedure. Some macro actions require other means to carry out the same action. Table 25-1 lists the macro actions that have no equivalent Visual Basic method and specifies alternative approaches, if any.

APPLICATION
DEVELOPMENT

Macro Action	Visual Basic for Applications Alternative
AddMenu	None
MsgBox	Use the MsgBox function
RunApp	Use the Shell function
RunCode	Use the Call statement to run the desired function directly
SendKeys	Use the SendKeys statement
SetValue	Use the Let assignment statement to set the value directly
StopAllMacros	Use the Stop or End statement
StopMacro	Use the Exit Sub or Exit Function statement

Table 25-1. *Macro Actions and the Visual Basic Alternatives*

What Is Visual Basic Made Of?

Microsoft Visual Basic is an object-oriented programming language full of special terms and expressions. The language contains all the elements useful in creating an end-user database management application. If you're already familiar with Visual Basic, skip over this part and look at the examples of procedures in the section titled, "Examples of Procedures."

Understanding Modules

A Visual Basic *module* is a group of declarations and procedures stored together as a unit. Modules come in two varieties: modules stored as separate Access objects and modules stored together with a form or report.

Module objects are listed in the Modules tab of the Database window. Procedures in a module object declared as public are available to any query, form, or report in the database. You create and edit code in module objects from the Database window.

 To make procedures in module objects easier to find, group them by purpose and give the modules meaningful names.

Form and *report modules* contain event procedures and functions associated with a single form or report. You can also add private procedures that run within the scope of the form or report module. From the form or report module, you can also run any of the public procedures saved in a module object. You create and edit code in form and report modules in Design view.

Form and report modules were called class modules in earlier versions of Access. In Access 97, saving class modules independent of the form or report design became possible, so the term has migrated from "class" to "form and report" modules.

As mentioned earlier, one of the advantages of using form and report modules is the module is stored with the form or report and is readily available. A disadvantage does exist, however, because the module must be loaded each time you open the form or report, which can be time-consuming if many procedures are in the module.

 Forms and reports have a Has Module property, which Access automatically sets to Yes. If you don't plan to attach any event procedures to the form or report, or to any of their controls, you can set the Has Module property to No and Access won't take time to look for the associated Visual Basic module.

Understanding Module Declarations

The first lines in a module are the declarations, which set requirements and defaults at the module level. Two declarations are included by default in all new modules:

- The *Option Compare* declaration specifies the default comparison method to be used when string data is compared and sorted. An argument is required if you use the declaration and must be Binary, Text, or Database. Access applies the Binary compare option if no declaration is specified. *Binary* sorts string data based on the internal binary representation of the characters. *Text* sorts in a case-insensitive text sort order. *Database* (the default when the declaration is used) can be used only within Access and results in string comparisons based on the same order as the database.

- The *Option Explicit* declaration forces the programmer to explicitly declare all the variables referred to in the module. *Declaring variables* is a process of giving each variable a unique name and specifying its data type. Declaring variables can help prevent coding errors caused by misspelling a variable in an expression.

Two other module-level Option declarations are

- *Option Private*, which is used with a multiple-project application to keep the module within a specific project.

- *Option Base*, which specifies the default lower bound for array subscripts, 0, or 1.

All the Option declarations, if used, must appear before any procedures in the module.

Understanding Procedures

A *procedure* is a block of Visual Basic code consisting of statements and methods that, together, accomplish a specific operation or calculate a value. For example, the

OK_Click event procedure discussed in the previous section used the **OpenQuery** method to run the Lookup DR query.

You can write two types of Visual Basic procedures:

■ *Sub procedures,* which perform one or more operations, but don't return a value.

■ *Function procedures,* which return a value that's the result of a calculation or a comparison.

The most common type of sub procedure is the *event procedure,* which carries out the operations in response to a specific event, such as a button click, a change in a value, or a change of focus. When the event occurs, Access runs the corresponding event procedure.

Visual Basic offers over 170 built-in functions you can use in expressions to return a value. Nearly all the built-in functions are available from the Expression Builder. You can also create your own custom functions for special purposes. An example of a custom function is the following, which creates initials from the first name, middle initial, and last name fields in a table. The underline character at the end of the first line is a line continuation character, which indicates that line and the next line are both part of the same statement. The second segment of the code line is indented, so it's immediately apparent that it is a continuation. The indent isn't required, but it helps when you read the code.

```
Function GetInitials(FirstName As String, MI As String, _
    LastName As String) As String
GetInitials = Left([FirstName], 1) & Left([MI], 1) & _
    Left([LastName], 1)

End Function
```

The **GetInitials** function uses the built-in **Left** function to extract the leftmost character from each of the three fields. The first argument in the **Left** function is the field name. The second is the number of characters to extract, beginning at the left end. The function then uses the concatenation character (&) to combine them into one string value, which is returned by the function. Figure 25-2 shows a new form with an unbound text box named Initials whose Control Source property is set to the following:

```
=GetInitials([FirstName],[MI],[LastName])
```

Once you create a custom function and save it in a module object, you can use it anywhere in the database. The custom function is also listed in the Expression Builder where you can select it and add it to another expression. The **GetInitials** function is stored in the GetInit module object in the Police database.

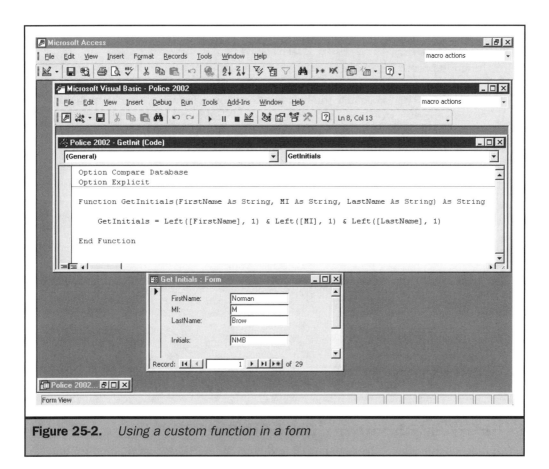

Figure 25-2. *Using a custom function in a form*

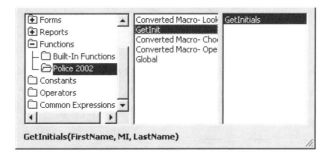

APPLICATION DEVELOPMENT

> **Tip** See the Functions Reference Help topic for a complete list of built-in functions. Open the Microsoft Visual Basic Help file from the Microsoft Visual Basic window and look in the Functions subfolder of the Visual Basic Reference folder. The functions are grouped alphabetically. Click any function name to see information about that function.

What's Wrong with This Function?

The function previously shown works fine if no blank middle initial (MI) fields are in the table. When a record has no value in the MI field, the form displays #Error in the Initials text box. This is because the **Left** function doesn't work with a blank field.

To prevent this, you need to test for a blank field and, if so, concatenate a zero-length string with the other characters instead of Left([MI], 1). You can use the **IIf** (Immediate If) function with the **IsNull** function to test for a Null value. The only complication is, for the **GetInitials** function to recognize a Null value in the MI field, you must pass the MI argument to the function as a Variant data type, instead of as a String.

The **GetInitials** function then becomes the following:

```
Function GetInitials(FirstName As String, MI As Variant, _
        LastName As String) As String
    GetInitials = Left([FirstName],1) & _
        Left(IIf(IsNull([MI]), "", [MI]), 1) & Left([LastName],
1)
End Function
```

The data types recognized by Visual Basic are discussed later in this chapter.

What Makes Up a Procedure?

Functions and sub procedures are made up of statements. A *statement* is a complete instruction to Visual Basic. It is composed of keywords, operators, variables, constants, and expressions. Three types of statements are in a procedure:

- *Declaration statements* that name variables, constants, or procedures themselves, and can also specify a data type.

- *Assignment statements* that give a value or an expression to a variable or a constant.

- *Executable statements* that trigger actions, such as executing a method or function, looping through a block of code, or branching to another location in the procedure.

All procedures begin with a statement that declares the name and type of procedure, and ends with an **End** statement.

Starting a New Procedure

Before continuing, look at the way Visual Basic describes the language. Visual Basic documentation uses typographic styles for different parts of statement syntax. Table 25-2 describes the styles and how they apply.

Style Examples	Description
Sub, Print, True, If	Language-specific keywords appear in bold with initial capitalization.
object, varname, arglist, condition	Placeholders for information you supply appear in lowercase italic.
[statements], [element]	Optional items are enclosed in brackets.
**{While	Until}**	Mandatory choices appear in braces with a vertical bar. If also enclosed in brackets, the item is optional, but must be one of the values, if used.

Table 25-2.   *Visual Basic Document Conventions*

Functions and sub procedures have similar components at the procedure level. The syntax for the Sub declaration statement is the following:

```
[Private|Public|Friend] [Static] Sub subname [(arglist)]
```

where the components in square brackets are optional. The vertical line separating two options indicates that if the component is included, it must assume one of those values. Components appearing in monospace are Visual Basic keywords and must be used as they appear in the syntax. Components in italic are originated by the user. If parentheses appear in the syntax, they must be used in the statement.

For example, in the previous syntax, the only required elements are Sub and the user-supplied sub procedure name. If you include the first component that specifies the scope of the sub procedure, it must be either Private, Public, or Friend. Static is optional. The optional argument list is supplied by the user and must be enclosed in parentheses, if used.

The syntax for the Function statement, which follows the same rules, is

```
[Public|Private|Friend] [Static] Function functionname _
[(arglist)] [As type]
```

Note   *When you convert a macro to Visual Basic from form or report Design view, Private is included in the sub procedure declaration statement by default. Converting the macro from the Database window results in a function with neither scope component.*

Component	Description
Public	The procedure is available to all other procedures in all other modules in the database.
Private	The procedure is available only to other procedures within the same module.
Friend	The procedure is available to other modules in the project outside the class module. Used only in class modules.
Static	All variables that are assigned values within this procedure retain their values between calls.
name	A unique name for a procedure or function supplied by the user.
arglist	A list of parameters passed to the procedure when it's executed. Each argument includes the name and data type. Multiple arguments are separated by commas.
type	The data type of the value returned by the function. May be Byte, Boolean, Integer, Long, Currency, Single, Double, Date, String, Object, Variant, an OLE object, or user-defined.

Table 25-3. *Procedure Components*

Table 25-3 describes the effects of each of the components of the sub and function syntax.

The list of parameters passed to the procedure from the form or report is the *arglist* component of the procedure syntax. In the **GetInitials** function example shown previously, three field names in the form are passed as arguments to the function. The *arglist* in the Function or Sub statement needn't have the same names as the fields passed to it.

The *arglist* component has its own syntax requirements in which you specify the name and data type of each parameter and how the parameter is passed. A later section in this chapter discusses passing parameters in greater detail.

Visual Basic Naming Rules

The important thing about naming Visual Basic procedures, constants, variables, and arguments is to assign a name that connects the item to its purpose, so it's easily identified and understood. After you come up with a meaningful name, you need to consider the rules for naming. Some of the rules are as follows:

- The first character must be a letter.
- The name can't contain more than 255 characters.
- Don't use a space, period (.), exclamation mark (!), or other special characters such as @, &, $, #.
- Don't use a name that's also one of the Visual Basic keywords, such as Loop or If, or the name of a Visual Basic function, statement, or method.
- Don't use the same name for two different variables in the same procedure.

Many programmers add a prefix to the name to indicate what type of item it is or, if a variable, what data type. For example, use the following prefixes:

- "rst" for a recordset
- "frm" for a form
- "int" for an integer variable
- "con" for a constant
- "dte" for a date variable
- "str" for a string variable

Visual Basic isn't case-sensitive, so it doesn't differentiate between ABC and abc. It does, however, preserve any capitalization you use when you declare and name the variable or constant.

Declaring Variables and Constants

Variables in Visual Basic are uniquely named items that contain data which can be changed during procedure execution. You can specify the data type for a variable or let Access assign it as the default Variant type. A Variant type variable can contain string, date, time, Boolean, or numeric values.

Constants in Visual Basic are also uniquely named items, but their value remains the same during execution. A constant can be a string or number value, another constant, or an expression that combines string or number values with arithmetic or logical operators. Four types of constants are supported by Access:

- *Symbolic constants* that you declare and set to a value using the **Const** statement. They retain their value throughout the procedure.
- *Intrinsic constants* or system-defined constants provided by Access or by a referenced library.
- *Conditional compiler constants* declared with the **#Const** statement.

In this chapter, we're concerned only with the symbolic constants you can declare as part of a procedure. You'll see examples of intrinsic constants, but they won't be discussed in detail. Conditional compiler constants are discussed briefly in Chapter 27 when dealing with end-user applications.

Naming variables and constants in declarations makes the code easier to read and maintain. Two types of declarations statements are used to name variables and constants:

- The **Dim** statement is usually used to declare variables.

- The **Const** statement is used to declare symbolic constants and to assign a value to them.

Declaring Variables

The position of the **Dim** statement determines the scope of the variable. Placing it at the top of a module right after the Option statements and before the first Sub or Function statement declares variables that can be used in any procedure in the module. To limit the variable to a single procedure, place the **Dim** statement after the Sub or Function statement, but before any assignment or executable statements.

You can declare more than one variable in a single statement, separating them with commas. Each variable must be accompanied by an As clause defining the data type or Access assigns the Variant data type as the default. You can declare variables as one of the following data types: Boolean (Yes/No), Byte, Integer, Long, Currency, Single, Double, Date, String, Object, Variant, New (user-defined), or one of four types of OLE objects.

Some examples of declaring variables are

```
Dim strCountry As String
Dim intAge As Integer, curRent As Currency, dteBirth As Date
```

If you declare variables with the following statement, the first variable is an integer and the other two are Variant because no other data type was specified.

```
Dim intA As Integer, intB, intC
```

Notice the use of a prefix that indicates the data type of the variable. When the variable name appears in code, the data type is evident. This is helpful during code generation and debugging. Using prefixes is good habit to form.

If you included the Option Explicit statement in the module, you must declare all the variables you intend to use in the procedure. Then, if you misspell a variable in one of the statements in the procedure, Access displays a compile-time error because the variable wasn't declared with that spelling.

The Lifetime and Scope of Variables

Understanding how long a variable retains its value and who has access to the value stored in the variable is important. The *lifetime* of a variable is the period of time in which it has a value; the value may change, but it still has a value. All variables are initialized with a default value when the procedure begins. For example, numeric variables are initialized as 0, strings are initialized as zero-length strings or fixed-length strings of the ASCII code for 0, and Variant variables are initialized as Empty.

If the procedure calls other procedures, the variables retain their values while the other procedures are running and lose value only when the procedure in which they were declared is ended.

Scope of a variable refers to the availability for use by another procedure. You specify the scope of a variable when you declare it. When a variable loses scope, it also loses its value. Understanding the scope of variables to prevent naming conflicts among procedures is important.

Three levels of scope apply to variables:

■ *Procedure level,* where the variable is declared with a **Dim** statement in the procedure.

■ *Private module level,* where the variable is declared with a Private statement in the declarations section of the module. The variable is available only to procedures in that module.

■ *Public module level,* where the variable is declared with a Public statement in the declarations section of the module. The variable is available to all procedures in the application or project.

Declaring Constants

Declaring constants involves not only naming the item and specifying the data type, but also giving the constant a value. Constants can be declared as the same data types as variables except the Object type, which doesn't apply to constants. You can declare several constants in the same statement separated by commas. Some examples of declaring symbolic constants are

```
Const conYear As Integer = 2002
Const conRent As Currency = 875, conCity As String _
= "San Francisco"
```

 When naming constants, the prefix "con" is conventionally used instead of a prefix that indicates the data type.

APPLICATION DEVELOPMENT

If you're declaring module-level variables for use by any procedure in the module, you can use Public instead of **Dim**. For constants, precede the Const keyword with Public to make the constants available to all the procedures:

```
Public intA As Integer  'Declares intA as an integer.
Public Const conRent As Currency = 875
```

Intrinsic Constants

In addition to the symbolic constants you declare with the **Const** statement, many intrinsic constants are available to the procedure. They can be used in macros and procedures with particular functions, methods, or properties. Intrinsic constants come from Access, Visual Basic, Access Data Objects (ADO), and Data Access Objects (DAO). You can also use intrinsic constants from other referenced object libraries, such as Excel.

Several categories of intrinsic constants exist, including action, ADO, event procedure, Keycode, security, Visual Basic, those that relate to the **RunCommand** method, and many miscellaneous constants.

The intrinsic constant names often include a two-letter prefix that indicates the source of the constant. For example, Access constants all start with ac, ADO constants start with ad, and Visual Basic constants start with vb. For example:

- acEdit is an Access constant used with **OpenQuery** or **OpenTable** method to specify the edit mode.

- acCheckBox specifies the Control Type property as a check box.

- adModeRead is an ADO constant that specifies the connect mode as read-only.

- adDecimal specifies the current field as a decimal data type.

- vbUpperCase is a Visual Basic constant that converts a string to uppercase characters.

- vbSunday assigns the value 1 for Sunday to a *firstdayoftheweek* argument.

Intrinsic constants also provide a measure of stability because even if the values represented by them change in later versions of Access, the names usually remain the same.

Old Access intrinsic constants that can still be used appear in all uppercase in the list of Global constants in the Object Browser window.

Methods

A *method* in Visual Basic is an action an object can perform or a procedure that acts on an object. The following are examples of methods:

- Opening or closing a form.
- Adding an item to a combo box list.
- Filtering records for a report.
- Sounding a beep when an error occurs.
- Going to a specific record in a form.
- Printing three copies of a report.
- Maximizing a window when it opens.

Access modules can use nearly 160 methods that apply to different objects. Each method has a specific syntax that further defines the object involved and the action to be taken. Table 25-4 describes a few of the more commonly used methods.

Method	Example	Description
GoToRecord	DoCmd.GoToRecord acDataForm, "Alpha Card", acGoTo, 7	Moves to record number 7 in the Alpha Card form.
SetFocus	Forms![Alpha Card]!Name.SetFocus	Moves the cursor to the Name field in the Alpha Card form.
ShowToolbar	DoCmd.ShowToolbar "CustomToolbar", acToolbarYes	Displays a toolbar named CustomToolbar in all active windows.
FindRecord	DoCmd.FindRecord "273.5"	Moves to the first record in the Alpha Entry datasheet with 273.5 in the current (Code) field.
TextWidth	Me.TextWidth("Entries by Date")	Returns the width of the text string as it would be printed in the current font of the active report.

Table 25-4. *Examples of Visual Basic Methods*

The Visual Basic language also includes over 50 methods that apply to Visual Basic and Access objects.

 *Many of the Visual Basic methods are used with the **DoCmd** object to carry out the equivalent macro actions. Figure 25-3 shows the DoCmd Help topic with the list of methods used by the **DoCmd** object.*

Arguments

When you call a function or sub procedure, you often have to supply the arguments it needs to work with. You can pass them positionally, in the same order in which they're named in the procedure statement or by name.

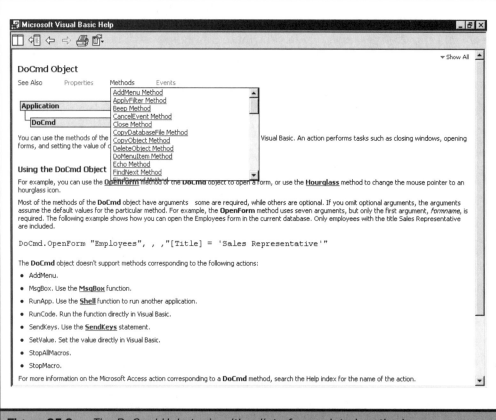

Figure 25-3. *The DoCmd Help topic with a list of associated methods*

For example, the following sub procedure statement lists four arguments:

```
Sub GetArgs(strFirstName As String, dteDOB As Date, _
      intAge As Integer, curWage As Currency)
```

When you want to run the procedure, you can use the following statement, which passes the arguments in the correct order, separated by commas and including the data type delimiters:

```
GetArgs "John", #1/15/63#, 36, 37500
```

The other way to pass the arguments to the sub procedure is by naming them in the call statement:

```
GetArgs intAge:=36, dteDOB:= #1/15/63#, curWage:=37500, _
      strFirstName:="John"
```

The named arguments are specified by the argument name followed by a colon and an equal sign, and then the argument value in the proper data type delimiter. Notice when you pass arguments by name, they needn't appear in the same order as in the argument list, but you do have to use the same names.

If an argument is optional, the Optional keyword precedes the argument name in the list. When you pass arguments by position, if you leave out one of the optional arguments, you still need to include a comma to keep the positions accurate. When you pass arguments by name, you needn't make allowances for the missing arguments.

You can also set a default value in the argument list in the procedure definition. For example, in the following procedure, the State argument has a default value of CA.

```
Sub Options(strCity As String, strState As String = "CA")
```

The Call keyword isn't required when calling a sub procedure. If you do use the Call statement to run a sub procedure, you must enclose all the arguments within parentheses:

```
Call GetArgs("John",#1/15/63#,36,37500)
```

When you pass arguments to a function, you enclose them in parentheses if you plan to use the return value. For example, to set the variable *strInitials* in a procedure to the return value of the **GetInitials** function, use the following statement:

```
strInitials = GetInitials(Name1,Name2,Name3)
```

APPLICATION
DEVELOPMENT

If you don't want to assign the return value to a variable, call it the same way as a sub procedure.

When you pass an argument to a procedure by name, the procedure may change the value during execution. To keep the procedure from changing it, pass the argument with the By Val keyword. The statement

```
Sub GetArgs(strFirstName As String, By Val dteDOB As Date)
```

specifies the dteDOB argument as a passed by value. The value passed to it cannot be changed in the GetArgs sub procedure or any procedure called by it.

Controlling Program Flow

Visual Basic offers several ways to control the flow of operations, depending on what you want to do. You can

- Skip to another location in the procedure.
- Repeat a group of statements a calculated number of times or until a certain condition is met.
- Choose from a list of next steps based on the value of a variable.
- Exit or pause the program.
- Call another sub procedure or function.

Branching Statements

You can use five types of branching statements in a procedure. Some of them transfer control unconditionally to another line of code and others branch only if a certain condition has been met.

The GoTo Statement   The **GoTo** statement branches unconditionally to a specified line in the same procedure. The syntax is as follows:

> **GoTo** *line*

where the *line* argument is required. *Line* can be any line label or line number. To keep your code simple and easy to read, use the **GoTo** statement sparingly. Structured control statements, such as **For…Next** and **If…Then…Else,** are easier to follow.

Line numbers and line labels are used to identify a single line of code. A line number can be any combination of digits that is unique within the module where it is used. A line label can be any combination of up to 40 characters that starts with a letter and ends with a colon (:). You cannot use a Visual Basic or Access reserved word in a line label. Line numbers and labels must begin in the first column of the line.

The first **GoTo** statement example in the following, branches unconditionally to line number 25 and the second example branches to the line labeled NewLine.

```
GoTo 25
25    Exit Sub
.........
GoTo NewLine
.........
NewLine:
   Exit Sub
```

The GoSub...Return Statement   The **GoSub...Return** statement combination branches to a subroutine within the same procedure and returns to the statement following **GoSub**. The syntax is as follows:

> **GoSub** *line*
> > .....
> > *line*   'First line of subroutine code
> > .....
> > **Return**   'Last line of subroutine code

The *line* argument can be a line label or a line number.

You can place **GoSub** and **Return** anywhere in the procedure, but the corresponding combination must be in the same procedure. The subroutine may contain more than one **Return** statement, so you can return to the calling procedure under varying conditions. The first **Return** statement reached sends control back to the procedure at the statement immediately following the **GoSub** statement.

The On...GoSub and On...GoTo Statements   These statements branch to one of several lines, depending on the value returned by the expression. The syntax is as follows:

> **On** *expression* **GoSub** *destinationlist*
> **On** *expression* **GoTo** *destinationlist*

The required *expression* argument is any numeric expression that evaluates to an integer between 0 and 255, inclusive. If the expression produces a number that isn't a whole number, the number is rounded off before evaluating.

The required *destinationlist* argument is a list of line labels or line numbers separated by commas.

The value of the expression determines which line is executed next. For example, if the expression evaluates to 5, control transfers to the line number or label that appears in the fifth position in the list. If the value of the expression doesn't correspond with the list, the following can occur:

- If the expression is equal to 0 or greater than the number of items in the list, the statement following the **On...GoSub** or **On...GoTo** statement is executed and none of the destinations in the list is reached.

- If the expression is negative or evaluates to a number greater than 255, an error occurs.

The destination list may contain a mixture of labels and line numbers. If you include more items than fit on one physical line in the module window, use the underscore line continuation character (_) to continue the logical line to the next physical line.

The On Error Statement   The **On Error** statement enables you to branch to an error-handling routine within the procedure when a run-time error occurs. The statement can have any one of the following forms:

- **On Error GoTo** *line*, which branches to the error-handling routine that begins at the line specified in the *line* argument. The destination must be in the same procedure as the On Error statement. Control is sent to the specified line if a run-time error occurs.

- **On Error Resume Next**, which sends control to the next statement after the one in which the run-time error has occurred.

- **On Error GoTo 0**, which disables any error handler that has been enabled in the current procedure.

Without an **On Error** statement in the procedure, any run-time error causes an error message to display and stops execution. When you create code with one of the wizards, **On Error** statements are always included. A later section in this chapter discusses error-handling in more detail and shows how you can customize the process.

Looping Statements

Looping statements are control structures that enable you to execute a block of code repeatedly. Some loops repeat the statements based on a condition, while others repeat the statement a specific number of times.

The Do...Loop Statement   The **Do...Loop** statement repeats the block of code while the condition is True or until the condition becomes True. The syntax is as follows:

Do [{**While** | **Until**} *condition*]
    [*statements*]
    [**Exit Do**]
    [*statements*]
Loop

The *condition* argument is required, but may appear with the **Do** statement or the **Loop** statement. If it's in the **Do** statement, the condition is evaluated before the statements within the loop are executed. If it's in the **Loop** statement, it's evaluated after the statements in the loop are executed and before control is transferred back to the beginning of the loop.

 One of the statements within the loop must increment or otherwise alter the value of the condition expression, or the loop will execute infinitely and your computer will appear to have crashed.

The *condition* argument is a numeric or string expression that evaluates to True or False. If the *condition* is Null, it's considered to be False.

You can insert as many **Exit Do** statements in the loop as you need. It's often used with an **If...Then** statement to exit the loop under specific conditions. When **Exit Do** executes, control transfers to the statement immediately following the **Loop** statement. If you nested **Do...Loop** statements, the **Exit Do** transfers control to the next higher level in the nested hierarchy.

The following example repeats the statements in the loop as long as the condition is True, five times in this example.

```
Dim intNum As Integer
intNum = 0
Do While intNum < 5
    .........
    intNum = intNum + 1
Loop
```

If you placed the **While** in the **Loop** statement, the loop would be repeated six times because the condition is evaluated after the statements in the loop have been executed. Using

```
Do Until intNum = 5
```

would repeat the loop the same number of times as the previous.

The For...Next Statement   The **For...Next** statement repeats a block of code a specific number of times. The loop uses a counter variable that is set to a value in the **For** statement. The syntax is as follows:

> **For** *counter* = *start* **To** *end* [**Step** *step*]
>   [*statements*]
>   [**Exit For**]

```
    [statements]
Next [counter]
```

The *counter*, *start*, and *end* arguments are required. The *counter* is a numeric variable used as the loop counter. *Start* is the initial value of the *counter* and *end* is the final value.

The optional *step* argument is the incremental amount by which the *counter* is changed with each iteration of the loop. The *step* argument can be either positive or negative. If positive, the loop executes if the value of the *counter* is less than or equal to the value of the *end* argument. If negative, the loop executes if the value of the *counter* is greater than or equal to the value of the *end* argument. If unspecified, the *step* defaults to 1.

Each time all the statements in the loop have been executed, the *step* value is added to the counter. Then, based on the test that triggered the loop in the first place, the loop is repeated or exits. After exiting the loop, execution continues with the statement following the **Next** statement.

You can have as many **Exit For** statements in the loop as you need to control the flow of operations. You can also nest **For...Next** loops.

Tip *Be sure to give each nested loop a unique counter variable or you'll get unexpected results.*

In the following example, the message box displays 55, the sum of all the numbers between 1 and 10.

```
Dim I As Integer, intTotal As Integer
intInteger = 0
For I = 1 To 10
    intTotal = intTotal + 1
Next I
MsgBox "The total is " & intTotal
```

Note *The counter variable isn't required with the **Next** statement. If you omit it, Access assumes it's there and increments it with the step value.*

The For Each...Next Statement   The **For Each...Next** statement is used to repeat a block of code for each item in an array or for each object in a collection. For example, you can use the **For Each...Next** structure to change the background colors of all the forms in a database. The syntax is as follows:

```
For Each element In group
    [statements]
    [Exit For]
    [statements]
Next [element]
```

The *element* argument is required and is used to iterate through the elements in the collection or array. When the *group* is a collection, the *element* can be a Variant variable or a generic or specific object variable, such as a form or report. If the *group* is an array, the element must be a Variant variable.

The *group* argument is also required and is the name of the object collection or the array.

> **Note**   *Collection is a Visual Basic term that refers to a group of objects usually of the same type. For example, the Forms collection is the group of all open forms and the Modules collection is the group of all open modules. Each form or report also contains a Controls collection, which includes all the controls in the form or report.*

The loop is entered if the *group* contains at least one *element* and, once entered, all the statements in the loop are executed for the first *element* in the group. The loop continues to execute as long as *elements* are left in the *group*. After the last *element* has been processed, the loop exits and control transfers to the statement following the **Next** statement.

You can insert as many **Exit For** statements as you need to control the flow of operations. You can also nest **For Each...Next** loops, but each loop must have a unique *element* argument.

The following example changes the foreground color of all the command buttons on the form to red when the form is loaded.

```
Private Sub Form_Load()
Dim btn As CommandButton
For Each btn In Me.Controls
    btn.ForeColor = "255"
Next btn
End Sub
```

The While...Wend Statement   The **While...Wend** structure is similar to the **Do While...Loop**. It executes a block of code as long as the specified condition evaluates to True. The **Do While...Loop** offers more flexibility by providing a way to exit the loop conditionally before the condition becomes False. The **While...Wend** syntax is as follows:

> **While** *condition*
>   [*statements*]
> **Wend**

The *condition* argument, a numeric or string expression that evaluates to True or False, is required. If it's Null, the *condition* is considered False.

If the *condition* is True, all the statements are executed. At the **Wend** statement, the condition is reevaluated and, if still True, the statements are executed again. If the *condition* isn't True, control transfers to the statement following the **Wend** statement.

You can nest **While...Wend** structures.

The following example iterates the statements in the loop until the CountDown reaches 0.

```
Dim intCountDown As Integer
intCountDown = 10
While intCountDown > 0
    statements
    intCountDown = intCountDown - 1
Wend
```

The With Statement   The **With** statement executes a block of code on a single object or on a user-defined type.

Note   *A user-defined type is a special data type you can create with the* **Type** *statement. It may include one or more elements of any data type.*

The **With** syntax is as follows:

With *object*
    [*statements*]
End With

The *object* argument, which is required, is the name of an object or a user-defined data type.

The **With** statement is useful for performing a series of statements on an object without having to repeat the name of the object—for example, assigning values to several properties of a control on a form. **With** works on only one object at a time. If you want to use the **With** structure with several objects, you must repeat the structure.

The following example can be part of an event procedure attached to a form's On Load event property. The structure sets the appearance properties of a label control named FormTitle.

```
With FormTitle
    .Height = 2000
    .Width = 20000
    .FontBold = True
    .FontItalic = True
    .FontSize = 16
    .Caption = "This is the Form Title"
End With
```

Decision-Making Statements

Two controlling structures can be used to execute a block of code if certain conditions are met. One of them executes one set of statements if the condition is True and can execute a different set if the condition is False. The other structure executes one of several groups of statements, depending on the value of the expression. Both structures are extremely flexible and used extensively in applications. Even the Access Wizards use these structures.

The If...Then...Else Statement The **If...Then...Else** statement executes a block of code conditionally, depending on the value returned by an expression. You can specify a group of statements to execute if the condition is True and skip to the next statement in the procedure following the **End If** statement if the condition is False. Or, you can specify a different set of statements to execute if the condition is False. The syntax is as follows:

> **If** condition **Then**
>   [*statements*]
> [**ElseIf** *condition-n* **Then**
>   [*elseifstatements*]
> [**Else**
>   [*elsestatements*]
> **End If**

The *condition* argument is required and may be a numeric or string expression that evaluates to True or False. If the *condition* is Null, it's considered to be False. The remaining arguments are optional except when the **If...Then...Else** statement is entered as a single physical line of code. Then one or more *statements* are required.

> **If** *condition* **Then** *statements* [**Else** *elsestatements*]

The single-line form of the statement is useful for short, simple tests. The block form is more flexible and is easier to read and maintain.

You can nest **If** statements by using the **ElseIf** structure. The **ElseIf** statement is reached if the previous **If** (or **ElseIf**) condition evaluates to False. The **ElseIf** imposes another condition in turn. You can include as many **ElseIf** statements as you need, but they must all appear before the first **Else** statement.

If you have many possible actions, it may be more efficient to use the **Select Case** statement.

In the following example, one message is displayed if the Balance is greater than 0 and a different message is displayed if the Balance is equal to or less than 0.

```
If Balance > 0 Then
   MsgBox "Your balance is " & Balance
```

```
Else
   MsgBox "Congratulations! Your account is paid in full."
End If
```

The Select Case...End Select Statement The **Select Case...End Select** structure executes one of several blocks of code, depending on the value of an expression. You can also include a group of statements to execute if the condition doesn't evaluate to any of the list of values specified by the **Case** statements. The syntax is as follows:

> **Select Case** *testexpression*
> > [**Case** *expressionlist-n*]
> > > [*statements-n*]
> > [**Case Else**
> > > [*elsestatements*]]
> **End Select**

The *testexpression* and *expressionlist-n* arguments are required. The *testexpression* can be any numeric or string expression that evaluates to one of a list of values. The *expressionlist-n* argument contains a delimited list of values that can result from the *testexpression*. A **Case** statement is included in the structure for each of the expected values.

The *statements-n* and *elsestatements* arguments are optional. One or more statements are executed if the *testexpression* matches any one of the items in the *expressionlist-n*.

If the *testexpression* doesn't match any of the items in the *expressionlist-n*, the *elsestatements* following the **Case Else** statement are executed.

The option group, Choose Report, in the Choose Report form, offers an excellent example of using the **Select Case** structure to open the report selected from the option group. The option group returns an integer value based on the option selected in the group. This value is used as the *testexpression* and the values from 1 through 6 are used as the *expressionlist-n* arguments with the **Case** statements. The **Select Case** structure is included in the On Click event procedure attached to the Preview command button on the form. The following code shows an example of using the Select Case structure to decide which report to preview.

```
Select Case ChooseReport     'Uses value returned by the option group.
    Case 1
        DoCmd.OpenReport "Alpha Card with Entries", _
            acViewPreview, "", ""
    Case 2
        DoCmd.OpenReport "Alpha Entry", acViewPreview, "", ""
    Case 3
        DoCmd.OpenReport "Entries by Code", acViewPreview, "", ""
    Case 4
```

```
        DoCmd.OpenReport "Entries by Qtr", acViewPreview, "", ""
   Case 5
        DoCmd.OpenReport "Entries by Year", acViewPreview, "", ""
   Case 6
        DoCmd.OpenReport "Labels Name List", acViewPreview, "", ""
End Select
```

You can use multiple expressions or ranges in any of the **Case** statements, such as the following:

```
Case 1 To 10    'Executes the statements that follow if the
                'testexpression evaluates to any number between 1 and 10.
Case A, B, C    'Executes the statements if the testexpression
                'evaluates to A, B or C.
```

Pausing or Exiting Statements

The **Exit** statement leaves a block of code, such as a loop or a called procedure, and transfers control to the statement after the end of the loop structure or after the statement that called the procedure. The **Exit** statement syntax occurs in five different forms:

- **Exit Do**, which is used inside a **Do...Loop**, transfers control to the statement that follows the **Loop** statement.
- **Exit For**, which is used in a **For...Next** or **For Each...Next** loop, transfers control to the statement that follows the **Next** statement.
- **Exit Function** exits the function procedure immediately and execution continues with the statement that follows the statement that called the function.
- **Exit Property** exits the property procedure and execution continues with the statement that follows the statement that called the property procedure.
- **Exit Sub** exits the sub procedure and execution continues with the statement that follows the statement that called the sub procedure.

The **End** statement establishes the end of a procedure or a block of code. It stops execution immediately, closes files that were opened with the **Open** statement, and resets all module-level variables and all static local variables in all modules. Like the **Exit** statement, the **End** syntax also has several forms, as follows:

- **End Function** ends a function procedure.
- **End If** ends an **If...Then...Else** structure.
- **End Property** ends a property procedure.
- **End Select** ends a **Select Case** statement.

- **End Sub** ends a sub procedure.
- **End Type** ends a user-defined type definition.
- **End With** ends the **With** structure.

The **Stop** statement suspends execution, but doesn't close any files or clear any variables. It can be used anywhere in a procedure and it works like a breakpoint in the code.

Calling Statements

Calling statements are those that declare or invoke a procedure. They include the following:

- The **Sub** statement, which declares the name, any arguments, and the statements that form the sub procedure.

- The **Function** statement, which declares the name, any arguments, and the statements that form the function procedure.

- The **Call** statement, which can be used to transfer control to a sub procedure or a function. It can also be used to call a *dynamic-link library (DLL)* procedure.

- The **Property** statements, which enable the programmer to create and manipulate custom properties. The procedure contains Visual Basic statements just like a sub or function procedure, except the statements focus on properties. Visual Basic includes three types of property procedures called by the following statements:

  - **Property Let**, which sets the value of a property.
  - **Property Get**, which returns the value of a property.
  - **Property Set**, which sets a reference to an object.

The three types of property procedures have similar syntax. See the corresponding Help topic to find out the specific arguments and use.

Writing Visual Basic Code

All the writing of Visual Basic code is done in the Visual Basic Editor window. How you reach the window depends on what type of module you want to create.

- To start a new module object, click the Modules tab of the Database window, and then click New. You can also choose Insert | Module or Insert | Class Module to open the Editor window to start a new module object.

- To edit an existing module object, select the name in the Database window and click Design or choose Tools | Macro | Visual Basic Editor.

- To start or edit the code behind a form or report, open the form or report in Design view, or simply select the form or report in the Database window, and choose Tools | Macro | Visual Basic Editor.

- You can also click the Code toolbar button from the form or report Design view. This method displays the existing procedures in the class module and also starts a new default sub procedure for the form or report.

- To write an event procedure for a control on a form or report, open the form or report in Design view and double-click the control to open the property sheet. Then click Build next to the appropriate event property and choose Code Builder from the Choose Builder dialog box.

Touring the Visual Basic Editor Window

Writing and debugging Visual Basic code actually uses several windows: the Editor window and three debug windows. This chapter discusses the Editor window and refers only slightly to using the debug windows during code generation. Refer to books that concentrate on writing Visual Basic procedures for information about the many debug features.

When you open the Editor window from a report or form that has code in the class module, you can see the procedures in the text area of the window. Figure 25-4 shows the module window with the class module for the Lookup DR form that was created by converting the macros.

> **Note**
> *If no class module exists for the form or report you selected, the module window opens with only the two default Option statements, and the first and last statement of the default event procedure. For a form, the default event is the Load event and, for a report, it's the Open event.*

The first section in the module contains the declarations and the remainder shows the sub procedures and functions that comprise the module. In Figure 25-4, the only declarations are the default Option Compare Database and Option Explicit declarations. If you want to declare any module-level constants or variables, the **Dim** and **Const** statements would also appear in this section.

Any line beginning with an apostrophe is a comment line and is ignored by Access. When Access converted the Lookup DR form macros to event procedures, it added a framed title area at the beginning of each procedure and a comment line displaying the text from the macro Comment cell. This is a good practice when you're writing your own procedures because you can readily recognize the procedure and what it's supposed to accomplish.

By default, the procedure text appears black and the comment text is green. The keywords in the procedure statements are shown in blue. The horizontal lines separate procedures and sections. The vertical bar down the left side is the indicator bar, which shows statements set as breakpoints during debugging.

APPLICATION DEVELOPMENT

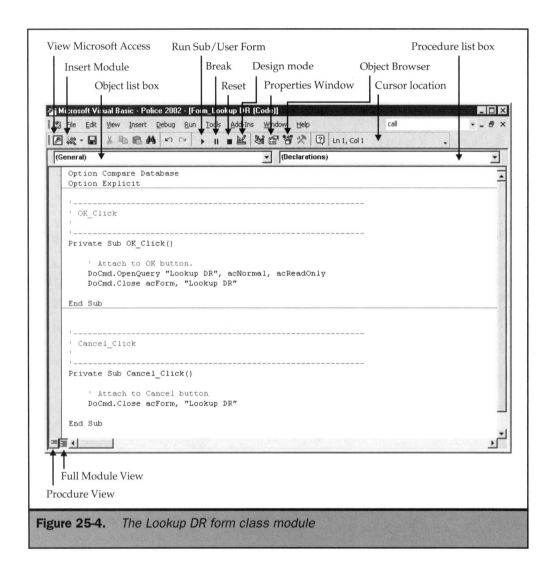

Figure 25-4.   *The Lookup DR form class module*

> **Note**   *You can change the text colors and other settings for the Editor window by choosing Tools | Options, as described in a later section.*

Two buttons at the bottom-left of the window change from Full Module view, as shown in Figure 25-4, to Procedure view, which shows one procedure at a time. When in Procedure view, you can move among procedures by pressing PGUP or PGDN.

The Object list box shows a list of all the controls in the form or report, as well as the form or report itself and all its sections and groups. Choose the item you want to write a procedure for or whose procedure you want to view if in Procedure view. The following shows the list of controls in the Lookup DR form.

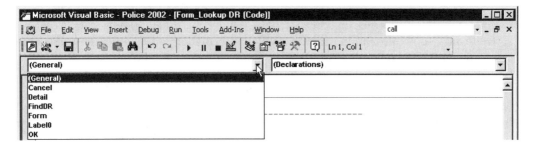

The Procedure list box displays a list of all the procedures in the module object or, if working in the form or report module, all available event procedures for the object selected in the Object list box. Event procedures already containing code appear in bold in the list. The name of the procedure that contains the insertion point appears in the box. In Figure 25-4, the following Procedure list box shows all the event procedures available for the OK command button. The Click procedure is the only one that has been written and appears in bold in the list.

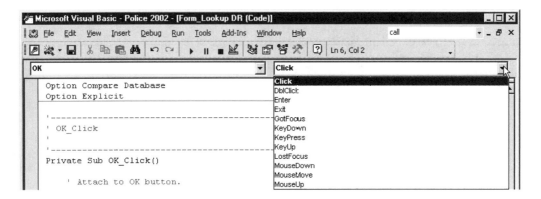

Many of the buttons on the Microsoft Visual Basic Standard toolbar are used only during program debugging, which isn't covered in detail in this chapter. Others are used during code generation. Table 25-5 lists the Standard toolbar buttons you'll use while you're writing Visual Basic procedures.

The module window also provides several tools to help you write correct and complete procedures. The Auto List Members tool displays a list of relevant objects, properties, and methods while you're entering code statements. When you type the name of an object, such as **DoCmd**, Microsoft Access automatically tries to assist you with completing the statement by displaying a list of objects, properties, or methods that might follow the name of the object. You can either select an item from the list or continue typing the statement.

The Auto Quick Info option provides syntax information while you're entering code statements. When you type a procedure or method name followed by a space or an opening parenthesis, a tip automatically appears underneath the line of code you're writing. The tip gives syntax information about the procedure, including which arguments are required and their sequence in the argument list. As you proceed to enter arguments, the next element of the syntax is highlighted.

You see how to use these and other module window tools in a later section.

Setting Visual Basic Editor Options

Many of the module window features described in the previous sections are options that can be changed. To change the module window and coding options, choose Tools | Options while in the Editor window. The Options dialog box opens showing four tabs (see Figure 25-5).

Table 25-6 describes the options available in the Editor tab of the Options dialog box.

The Editor Format tab (see Figure 25-6) enables you to specify the appearance of the different types of text in the window. You can change the colors, font, and size of any of

Button	Description
Break	Stops execution and clears all private variables.
Run Sub/User Form	Runs the procedure or, if in Step mode, executes the next step.
Insert Module	Displays a drop-down list with Module, Class Module, and Procedure choices.
Object Browser	Opens the Object Browser window.
Reset	Stops execution and clears all public and private variables.

Table 25-5. *The Visual Basic Toolbar Buttons Used During Code Generation*

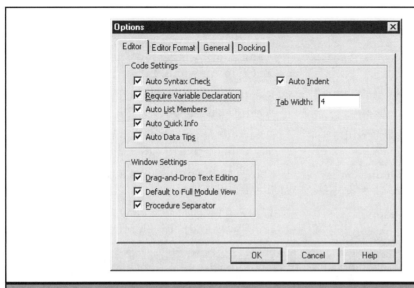

Figure 25-5.   *The Visual Basic Editor Options dialog box*

Module Option	Description
Auto Syntax Check	Checks for syntax errors as you type.
Require Variable Declaration	Includes the Option Explicit declaration in every new module.
Auto List Members	Displays a list of valid choices of keywords as you type.
Auto Quick Info	Displays syntax when you type a method or procedure name. The current statement component appears in bold in the display.
Auto Data Tips	Displays the current value of a variable when you rest the mouse pointer on the name during break mode.

Table 25-6.   *Module Options*

Module Option	Description
Auto Indent	Automatically indents a line of code to match the previous line.
Tab Width	Sets the number of characters to move when TAB is pressed.
Drag-and-Drop Text Editing	Allows drag-and-drop editing in a module as an alternative to cut-and-paste.
Default to Full Module View	Shows all the procedures in the module as the default view.
Procedure Separator	When in Full Module view, displays a horizontal line between procedures.

Table 25-6. *Module Options* (continued)

the ten different types of text. The text type list in the Code Colors group gives you the opportunity to change the colors of the characters or the background of ten different

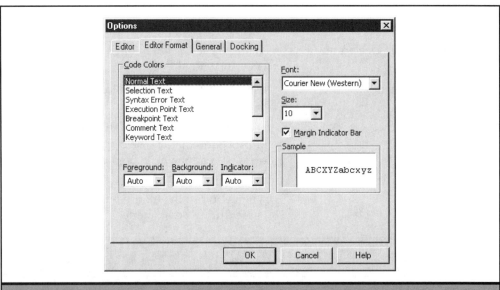

Figure 25-6. *The Editor Format tab of the Options dialog box*

areas of the module window including the Normal Text, Selection Text, Syntax Error Text, and Comment Text. When you select a text type from the list, the Sample panel at the bottom left of the dialog box shows the current setting. Click one of the drop-down arrows to display a palette of colors from which to choose, as well as the Auto option, which returns to the default colors.

The General tab of the Options dialog box contains options for specifying the form grid settings, as well as some error-trapping and compilation options.

The Docking tab enables you to select which windows are dockable. The windows include the three debug windows: the Object Browser window, the Project Explorer, and the Properties window. When a window is set to dockable, it shares the screen with the Editor window. For example, Figure 25-7 shows the Properties window docked at the left of the Editor window. The Properties window shows all the form's properties in two lists: in alphabetical order and grouped by property category. You can use the Properties window to change any of the properties of the form or report from the Editor window. Click the Close button (X) to remove the Properties window from the screen.

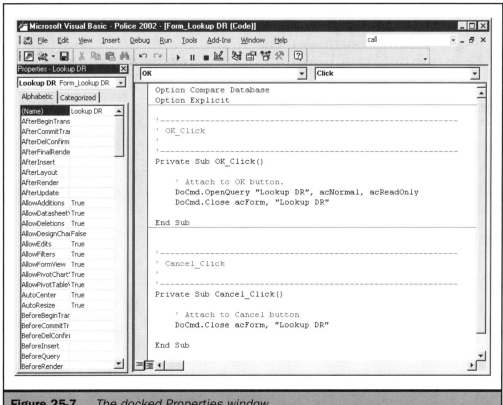

Figure 25-7.   *The docked Properties window*

Entering Procedure Statements

To start a new procedure in the current module, move to a line below all existing procedures and do either of the following:

■ Choose Procedure from the Insert Module toolbar button list.

■ Choose Insert | Procedure

The Add Procedure dialog box opens (see Figure 25-8) in which you enter the procedure name, and then select the type and scope of the procedure. You can also specify all variables in this procedure retain their values after the procedure exits. This option inserts the Static keyword in the procedure declaration. After choosing the procedure specifications, choose OK.

Access starts a new procedure with the choices you made in the dialog box and places the insertion point between the beginning and ending statements.

    *You can also begin the new procedure right in the module window by typing **Function** or **Sub**, followed by the procedure name and pressing ENTER. Access adds the **End Function** or **End Sub** statement, depending on what you typed in the first line.*

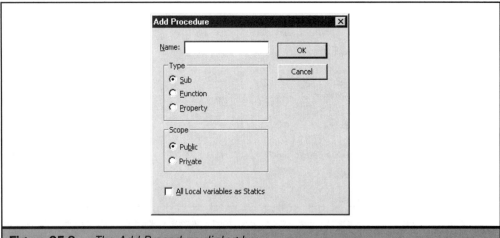

Figure 25-8.   *The Add Procedure dialog box*

If you want to write an event procedure for a control in a form or report design, click Build next to the event property to which you want to attach the procedure. Then choose Code Builder in the Choose Builder dialog box and click OK. The Editor window opens showing the **Sub** and **End Sub** statements.

If a statement is long and exceeds the width of your screen, you can continue the statement to additional lines with the line-continuation character. At the point where you want to break the line, enter a space and type an underscore character (_). Then press ENTER to move to the next physical line. It improves readability of the code if you indent the continuation line segments. You can continue the statement to as many lines as necessary.

Although you can save space by placing more than one statement on a physical line separated with colons (:), this isn't a good idea. If an error occurs in one of the statements on the line, you can't tell which statement caused the error. With each statement, however short, on a separate line, you can easily track down errors.

Adding Comments

Good programming practice is to insert comments generously throughout the procedure. You'd be surprised how quickly you can forget the details of the procedure. To add a comment line, type an apostrophe (') at the beginning of the line followed by the comment text. If the comment requires more than one line, type an apostrophe at the beginning of each line.

You can also add a comment on the same line with a statement by typing an apostrophe first, and then the comment. Visual Basic ignores everything after the apostrophe.

A Coding Example

As an example of writing Visual Basic statements, the following exercise creates a new trial form with one command button added without the help of the Command Button Wizard. We then add an event procedure that executes when the button is clicked. The procedure opens the Alpha Card form in Form view, and then sounds a beep.

1. Click New in the Forms tab of the Database window and start a new form in Design view with no underlying table or query.

2. Make sure the Controls Wizard button isn't pressed, add a command button to the form design, and then enter **Open Alpha Card** in the Name and Caption properties.

3. Click Build next to the On Click event property and choose Code Builder from the Choose Builder dialog box, and then click OK. The Microsoft Visual Basic window opens with the two default Option statements: the **Private Sub** with the procedure name and **End Sub** statements.

4. Enter an apostrophe, and then enter a comment explaining the purpose of the procedure, if desired. Next, type **DoCmd** followed by a period (.). The Auto

List Members box appears, showing a list of methods you can use with the **DoCmd** object (see Figure 25-9).

5. To choose **OpenForm** from the list, type the first few characters to scroll down the list automatically until you see **OpenForm**. Then select the item and do one of the following:

- Press TAB to enter the item to the statement and leave the insertion point immediately following it.
- Press the SPACEBAR to enter the item followed by a space.
- Press ENTER to enter the item and move the insertion point to the next line.
- Double-click the item to enter it without a following space.

6. Add a space and the Auto Quick Info box appears, showing the **OpenForm** method syntax with *FormName*, the next argument, in bold.

```
DoCmd.OpenForm |
        OpenForm(FormName, [View As AcFormView = acNormal], [FilterName],
End Su [WhereCondition], [DataMode As AcFormOpenDataMode = acFormPropertySettings],
        [WindowMode As AcWindowMode = acWindowNormal], [OpenArgs])
```

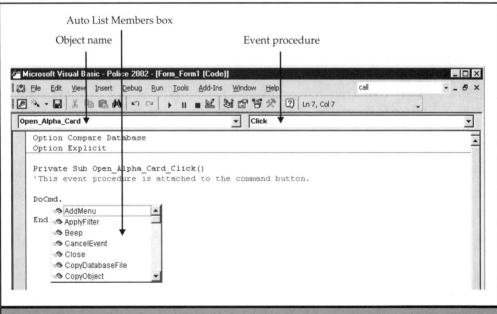

Figure 25-9. *The Auto List Members box for DoCmd*

7. Type **"Alpha Card"** (be sure to include the quotation marks), followed by a comma. The Auto List Members box reappears, now showing a list of valid views for the form display. Choose acNormal, which opens the form in Form view, and then enter a comma.

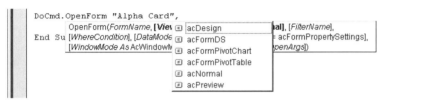

Tip *If the list is hidden behind the Auto Quick Info box, enter a space or click in the box to bring it to the front.*

8. Next, enter two sets of double quotation marks with nothing enclosed, each followed by a comma to indicate there's no filter or **Where** condition arguments included in the statement. The Auto List Members box opens again, this time with a choice of data modes.

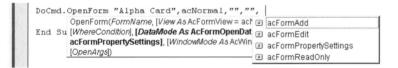

9. Choose acFormEdit to open the form for viewing and editing records. The other data mode options open the form for data entry, open the form as read-only, or open the form property sheet.

10. Press ENTER to move to the next line and enter **DoCmd** followed by a period (.).

11. Choose Beep from the Auto List Members box.

12. Click View Microsoft Access to return to the form design where you can see and name the new form.

13. Switch to Form view and click the Open Alpha Card command button.

To return to the Editor window, click the Microsoft Visual Basic button in the Windows taskbar or choose Tools | Macro | Visual Basic Editor. To close the Editor window, choose File | Close and Return to Microsoft Access.

Referring to Controls and Properties

When you refer to the value of a control or a property in an expression, you call it by name. For example, to refer to the Name text box control on the Alpha Card form, you type

```
Forms![Alpha Card]!Name
```

 If the name contains a space, you must enclose it in brackets.

If the Alpha Card form is the currently active form, however, you can use the Me property to refer to it, instead of the identifier:

```
Me!Name
```

To refer to the DR text box control on the Alpha Entry subform on the Alpha Card form, use the following:

```
Forms![Alpha Card]![Alpha Entry subform]!DR
```

The exclamation point (!) operator indicates that what follows is an item defined by the user. If what follows is defined by Access, you use the dot (.) operator. For example, use the dot operator to refer to a property of a form, report, or control. The following expression refers to the Visible property of the DOB text box control on the Alpha Card form:

```
Forms![Alpha Card]!DOB.Visible
```

Dealing with Programming Errors

Three kinds of errors can occur when programming in Visual Basic: compile-time errors, which include syntax errors; run-time errors; and logical errors. Compile-time errors are the result of incorrect code, such as the following:

- Misspelled keywords
- An **If** statement without the corresponding **End If** statement or **Select Case** without the **End Select** statement.
- Missing separators, such as commas, in an argument list.
- Syntax errors, such as unbalanced parentheses or quotation marks.

In the following example, the comma separator is missing between the acNormal argument and the pair of quotation marks that indicate no filter is applied. When you try to move to the next line, the message box appears and the whole line changes to red. After you click OK in the message box, the quotation marks are selected to show you which part of the statement caused the syntax error.

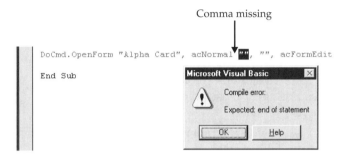

Comma missing

```
DoCmd.OpenForm "Alpha Card", acNormal "", "", acFormEdit

End Sub
```

 Access tries to correct some of your errors and doesn't always fix the problem. For example, if you left off the closing quotation mark after the form name, Access may add it at the end of the line. This wouldn't produce the correct result.

 Compile-time errors are caught when you try to run the procedure. For example, if you leave off the **End With** statement and click the Run Sub/User Form toolbar button or choose Run | Run Sub/User Form, Access displays a compile error message.

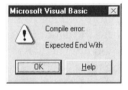

Run-time errors are errors that are detectable only when the procedure executes. The error stops the application completely and doesn't display an error message unless you included error-handling statements in the procedure. A later section in this chapter discusses more details of error handling in Visual Basic code.

Logical errors don't interfere with the execution of the procedure; they just give you the wrong result. You must go back through the logic of the application and examine intermediate results to determine the cause of the wrong answer.

Some Debugging Tools

Debugging is the process of locating and removing errors from an application. Access and Visual Basic provide many tools to help with the process. They include the following:

APPLICATION
DEVELOPMENT

■ Setting breakpoints to pause execution of the code. The code is still running, but halts between statements. While the code is suspended, you can look at the values of variables and execute each statement one at a time.

■ Stepping through code one statement at a time. This can help isolate the statement where the error occurs by looking at the results of each line of code.

■ Displaying the value of a variable or expression when you have suspended execution. With the Auto Data Tips option selected in the Editor tab of the Options dialog box, you can rest the mouse pointer over a variable or expression and see the current value.

■ Using the debug windows where you can follow the process of the code by viewing the value of controls, fields, and properties. You can also see the result of an expression or assign a new value to a control, field, or property.

■ Setting a watch over an expression, so you can see how the expression evaluates during code execution.

To find out more about the debugging tools, look in the Visual Basic Programming Help Topics.

Running Visual Basic Procedures

When you create a new procedure, you need to run the procedure to make sure it executes properly. The way you run the procedure depends on what kind of procedure it is.

If it's an event procedure, perform the action that causes the event to occur. For example, open the form for which you attached an event procedure to an On Load event. The procedure runs when the form opens.

A sub procedure that isn't an event procedure and that doesn't take arguments can be run directly from the module window. Place the insertion point anywhere in the procedure and click Run Sub/User Form or choose Run | Run Sub/User Form.

If the procedure requires arguments, such as the name of a control on a form, open the form first in Design view, and then run the procedure from the module window. Another way to run a sub procedure is by calling it from another procedure.

Procedures can also be run by adding the RunCode action to a macro, and then running the macro.

Functions cannot be run from the module window. To test a function, use it in an expression in another procedure and examine the returned value.

Getting Help with Programming

If you ran the Typical version of the Office XP Setup routine, you haven't installed the Programming Help topics. To add the Visual Basic Help topics to your system, do the following:

1. Click Start and point to Settings, and then click Control Panel.

2. In the Control Panel window, double-click Add/Remove Programs.

3. Scroll down the list of programs in the Add/Remove Programs Properties dialog box and select Microsoft Office XP, and then click Add/Remove. You're then prompted to insert the Office CD if it isn't already in the drive.

4. Click Add or Remove Features.

5. Expand the Office Shared Features list and scroll down the list to Visual Basic for Applications.

6. Expand the Visual Basic for Applications list and select Visual Basic Help.

7. Choose Run from My Computer.

8. Click Update Now to complete the setup and click OK in the message box, indicating a successful setup completion.

 If your computer uses AutoPlay for the CD drive, simply insert the Office XP Program Files disk in the drive.

With the Visual Basic Help topics installed, you can reach help using all the normal methods:

- Pressing F1 while in the Editor window.

- Type a question in the Ask a Question box. Make the question as specific as possible to get a short list of topics.

- Choose Help | Microsoft Visual Basic Help.

While you're typing statements in the Editor window, you can get some help with the syntax from the shortcut menu or the Edit menu. Five options offer the same sort of assistance as some of the coding options you can set in the Options dialog box.

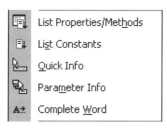

With the cursor in one of the items in the statement, choose one of the menu commands. The results depend on where the cursor is in the statement and on how much of the item you already typed. The commands display information as follows:

- The List Properties/Methods command lists all the properties and methods available for that part of the statement if you haven't typed anything. If you've begun the item, the list has scrolled down to the properties and methods that begin with the characters you've typed. This command is the same as setting the Auto List Members option.

■ The List Constants command displays a list of all the intrinsic constants that are valid for the specific item in the argument list. For example, with the **OpenForm** method, the second argument specifies the opening view, and the List Constants command displays a list including acDesign, acFormDS, acNormal, and acPreview.

■ The Quick Info command displays the complete syntax of the method if you haven't already typed an intrinsic constant. If you have, the constant is displayed together with its numeric value. For example, right-click acNormal, choose Quick Info, and then you see acNormal = 0. This command is the same as setting the Auto Quick Info option.

■ The Parameter Info command displays the complete syntax information with the current parameter showing in bold.

■ The Complete Word command finishes the word you started typing. If the first characters lead to an unambiguous entry, the whole word is filled in. If you haven't typed enough characters, the list appears showing items beginning with the characters you typed.

If you find an example of Visual Basic code in one of the Help topics that resembles what you need for your procedure, you can copy it to the clipboard and paste it into your module in the module window. Then edit the code to fit your requirements.

Examples of Procedures

This section contains a few common types of procedures that can be used for command button click events, setting control properties, navigating through records, filtering records, and handling run-time errors.

An On Click Event Procedure

When you add a control, such as a command button, to a form or report with the help of a Control Wizard, the wizard creates a procedure that carries out the actions you specified in the series of wizard dialog boxes. For example, the following code shows the On Click event procedure written by the Command Button Wizard when the Print button that prints the current record was added to the form. In the Command Button Wizard, choose the Record Operations category and the Print Record action. The wizard named the button Command2.

```
1 Private Sub Command2_Click()
2 On Error GoTo Err_Command2_Click    'Branches on run-time error.
```

```
3    DoCmd.DoMenuItem acFormBar, acEditMenu, 8, , acMenuVer70
4    DoCmd.PrintOut acSelection
5 Exit_Command2_Click:
6    Exit Sub
7 Err_Command2_Click:              'Begins error-handling routine.
8    MsgBox Err.Description        'Displays error message.
9    Resume Exit_Command2_Click    'Sends control back to
10 End Sub                         'statement that caused error.
```

Line 3 requires a little explanation. The **DoMenuItem** method carries out a menu action in Visual Basic. acFormBar is an intrinsic constant with a value of 0, which identifies the menu bar as the one displayed in Form view. acEditMenu (value 1) identifies the Edit menu from which to choose a command. The number 8, which is the value of the intrinsic constant—a SelectRecord—identifies the command to carry out.

Then the statement in line 4 carries out the **PrintOut** method with the selected record. The comments were added to the code after the wizard was finished.

Setting Control Properties

The following short procedure prompts the user to type a number between 1 and 3, and then changes the foreground color and font of the New Style label control based on the number entered. If the user enters a number outside the acceptable range, a message is displayed. When the user responds to the message, control returns to the dialog box requesting a number.

```
Private Sub Change_Style_Click()
'This procedure displays a input box asking the user
'to enter a number between 1 and 3. The number entered
'determines the change in label style.
Dim intGetNum As Integer     'Declares an integer variable
intGetNum = InputBox("Please enter a number between 1 and 3.")
Select Case intGetNum
    Case 1      'Sets the text color to red and font to 24 pts
        [New Style].ForeColor = 255
        [New Style].FontSize = 24
    Case 2      'Sets the text color to green and font to 36 pts
        [New Style].ForeColor = 845388
        [New Style].FontSize = 36
    Case 3      'Sets the text color to blue and font to 40 pts
        [New Style].ForeColor = 16711680
        [New Style].FontSize = 40
```

```
      Case Else   'Displays a message if not 1, 2, or 3.
          MsgBox "You did not enter a number between 1 and 3."
End Select
End Sub
```

Figure 25-10 shows the form with a single label control and a command button that changes the label style. The message box resulted from entering 4 into the input box.

Navigating Through Records

When you want to navigate through records in a procedure, you use the **GoToRecord** method with the **DoCmd** object. The **GoToRecord** method does the same thing as using the navigation buttons at the bottom of a form or datasheet. In the statement, you specify the type of object that contains the records: the active data object (the default), a form, query, or table. If you specify an object other than the active data object, you then type the valid name of the object you're navigating through.

The *record* argument is an intrinsic constant that identifies the destination record:

- acFirst makes the first record in the recordset the active record.

- acGoTo enables you to specify the active record by entering the record number.

- acLast makes the last record in the recordset the active record.

- acNewRec moves to a blank record at the end of the recordset ready for entering a new record.

- acNext, the default, enables you to specify how many records to move forward in the recordset to activate a record.

- acPrevious enables you to specify how many records to move backward in the recordset to activate a record.

Figure 25-10.   *Setting control properties*

If you chose acGoTo, the next argument is an integer or an expression that evaluates to an integer that specifies the target record number. If you chose acNext or acPrevious, you can specify how many records to move forward or backward. The following statement moves to the record 25 in the Alpha Card form:

```
DoCmd.GoToRecord, acDataForm, "Alpha Card", acGoTo, 25
```

This statement moves back ten records in the Alpha Entry datasheet:

```
DoCmd.GoToRecord, acDataTable, "Alpha Entry", acPrevious, 10
```

*If focus is on a particular control in a record and you use the **GoToRecord** to display a different record, focus remains on that control in the new record.*

Getting User Input and Filtering Records

This example shows how to ask the user for a value to use as a filter for limiting the records in a report before opening for print preview or printing. The built-in **InputBox** function can be used to prompt the user for the value necessary to create the **Where** condition. Figure 25-11 shows a sample form with a single button that opens the input box shown at the lower right.

The following shows the listing:

```
Private Sub ChooseState_Click()
Dim strState As String, strFilter As String
strState = InputBox("Enter the 2-character state abbreviation", _
        "Enter State")
If strState = "" Then          'User has clicked Cancel.
    GoTo Exit_This_Sub
End If
strFilter = "[State] = """ & strState & """ "
DoCmd.OpenReport "Labels Name List", acViewPreview, , strFilter
Exit_This_Sub:
    Exit Sub
End Sub
```

The *strState* variable is the value returned by the **InputBox** function and is used in the string that makes up the **Where** condition used by the **OpenReport** method. The **If...Then** statement following the **InputBox** function statement tests to see if the user clicked the Cancel button, which would return a zero-length string. If so, control transfers to the Exit_This_Sub line and the procedure exits.

APPLICATION DEVELOPMENT

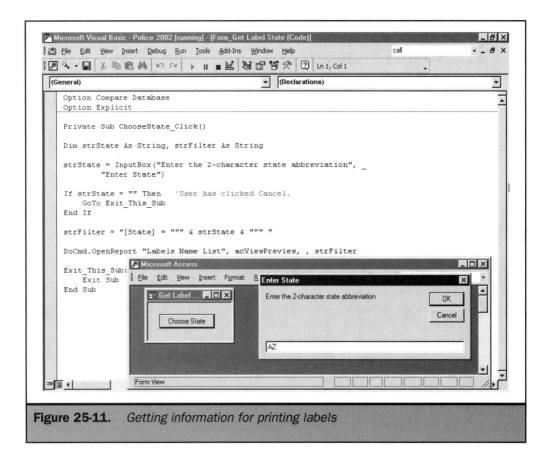

Figure 25-11. *Getting information for printing labels*

> **Note** *What hasn't been considered in this simple procedure is when the user enters a value that isn't a valid state abbreviation or a value that results in an empty report. These conditions can be accounted for with additional **If...Then** structures, possibly nested as **ElseIf** statements. Another way to handle an empty report is by attaching an event procedure or a macro to the report's On No Data event property.*

The *strFilter* variable is assigned a value comprised of the field name, state, and the value entered in the input box, *strState*. This actually creates a **Where** condition that's added to the SQL statement created by the **OpenReport** method. For the **Where** condition to show the *strState* value in quotation marks, for example, Where State = "CA", you must include the quotation marks in the filter string. The following statement encloses each of the quotation marks within another pair:

```
strFilter = "[State] = """ & strState & """ "
```

In some cases, you can use single quotation marks to embed double-quotation marks in a string but, unfortunately, Visual Basic recognizes a single quotation mark as an apostrophe and treats the rest of the statement as a comment.

The **DoCmd.OpenReport** statement includes the following arguments:

- The name of the report "Labels Name List."
- The intrinsic constant, acViewPreview, that specifies Print Preview.
- An extra comma is added to indicate no filter is applied to the records.
- The *strFilter* intrinsic constant contains a string expression used with the **Where** clause in a Select statement to limit the records.

The Exit_This_Sub line label offers a way to get out of the procedure from another line in the procedure.

 While you're debugging a procedure, such as the previous one, you might find the Run Sub/User Form and the Run | Run Sub/User Form commands dimmed and be unable to run the procedure. This can be caused by the form you're using to test the procedure being in Form view. The procedure won't run from the module window unless the form is in Design view. Click in the form and switch to Design view.

Handling Run-Time Errors

The **On Error** statement was invented specifically to trap and handle run-time errors. The statement can branch to an error-handling routine, skip over the error, or quit trapping errors. An earlier section discussed the **On Error** statement syntax.

When an error occurs, Access creates a new **Err** object. The error-handling routine tests the value of the number property of the **Err** object to determine what caused the error. The **Err** object also has a Description property that contains the error message displayed by default when the error occurs. When an error occurs, the **On Error** statement can transfer control to a block of code where **If...Then** or **Select Case** statements can isolate specific errors by number. If one of these errors has occurred, you can display a custom error message. If the error isn't one you specifically tested for, Access displays the Description of the **Err** object.

Table 25-7 lists some of the trappable errors in Visual Basic by number.

As appropriate to the application, you can create custom error messages that may also include specific instructions for correcting the error or how to avoid it in the future.

 *You can use the **Raise** method of the **Err** object to cause the numbered error to occur and test the error handler.*

Error Number	Error Description
11	Division by zero
13	Type mismatch
35	Sub, function, or property not defined
53	File not found
55	File already open
71	Disk not ready
92	For loop not initialized
380	Invalid property value
448	Named argument not found
482	Printer error

Table 25-7.   *Examples of Trappable Errors*

The following listing is an example of testing and handling run-time errors.

```
Sub HandleAnError()
On Error GoTo ErrRoutine
Err.Raise 13    'Causes the type mismatch error.
Err.Raise 92    'Causes the uninitialized For loop error.
   statements
........
Exit_This_Sub:
    Exit Sub
ErrRoutine:
   If Err.Number = 13 Then
       MsgBox "Error Number " & Err.Number & " has occurred." _
           & " You have caused a type mismatch error."
       Resume Next              'Transfers control to statement
   End If                       'after the one where the error occurred.
   If Err.Number = 92 Then
       MsgBox "Error Number " & Err.Number & " has occurred." _
           & " You may have branched into a For loop."
```

```
        Resume Exit_This_Sub  'Transfers control to exit routine.
    Else If                   'Displays error number/description.
      MsgBox "Error Number " & Err.Number & " has occurred. " _
            & Err.Description
      Resume 0                "Transfers control to error statement.
    End If
End Sub
```

 *Be sure to include the **Exit Sub** or **Exit Function** statement before the error-handling routine in the procedure or the routine will execute every time you run the procedure.*

The **Resume** statement in the error-handling routine sends execution back to the procedure. The **Resume** statement use three forms:

- **Resume** or **Resume 0**, which transfers control back to the statement where the error occurred.

- **Resume Next**, which transfers control to the statement immediately following the one where the error occurred.

- **Resume** *line label*, which transfers control to a specific line. This statement is often used to display an error message, and then to branch to a block of code that exits the procedure.

Error-trapping and handling is a complex issue, especially when you have nested procedures, each with error-handling provisions.

Summary

Presenting you with a complete guide to programming Visual Basic for Access database applications would be impossible in this book. This chapter has shown you some of the power and flexibility available with Visual Basic procedures. Several examples of simple procedures were presented and much of the code syntax has been explained. The Programming Help topics can be of great help to you when you understand the fundamentals of the programming language.

In the final section of this book, you see how to create an application to be shared among users in a workgroup. Multiple users can add complications, as well as advantages, to the job. Security becomes an issue, as does data integrity and validity. In an industrial environment, accurate real-time systems are essential.

In addition, end-user documentation must be created and delivered with the application to ensure its proper and efficient use.

APPLICATION DEVELOPMENT

MOUS Exam Activities Explored in This Chapter

Level	Activity	Section Title
Expert	Create Access modules	Writing Visual Basic CodeExample of Procedures

The Complete Reference

Access 2002

Chapter 26

Sharing with Multiple Users

Maintaining a database in a multiple-user environment isn't a simple task. When many copies of the database are on different computers accessed by different users, conflicts can occur when changes are made to the same data. Access includes several tools that can help ensure the integrity and security of the database. Access also provides useful features for conflict resolution.

This chapter discusses the process of replication, which creates copies of a database and allows synchronization of the data in all the copies in the replication set. It also discusses the concepts involved in data administration among shared databases, including ownership, permissions, and security.

Replicating a Database

Replication is the process of making copies of a database for use in different locations, but that can be totally synchronized. Each user can have a separate copy of the database with the master file centrally located where it can be updated with the changes in the remote replicas. Another use for a replica is to dedicate it as the report printer in an application that requires lengthy, time-consuming report production. This frees up the other workstations or computers for other work. You can replicate the database to your laptop and take it home with you or on a trip, and still be able to work with it productively.

Replication isn't a good idea if you expect a lot of data entry and editing in the replicas. Conflicts can arise when the same data is updated by two users and conflicts take time to resolve. Replication is also not recommended if your data must be real-time and completely current at all times. Even if the master database is updated at frequent intervals, it isn't 100 percent current between updates.

The master database where all the changes are implemented is called the *Design Master* and the copies are called *replicas*. The Design Master and the replicas may contain both replicated objects and unique objects. Each replica can be tailored to a location or a specific type of data, while the common data can be synchronized and shared with the other users.

You have three ways to create Access database replicas:

■ Use Access menu commands.

■ Drag the database to the Briefcase icon on the Windows desktop.

■ Write a Visual Basic function.

The first two methods are discussed in the subsequent sections of this chapter.

Note *If you want to upgrade a replica set you created in Access 97 to Access 2000 or 2002, you can convert each replica individually. Be sure to synchronize all members of the set before converting. See Chapter 29 for more information about converting replicas.*

Backing up the Database

Once a database is replicated, Access makes so many changes to it, there's no turning back. So, before you even think about creating a replica or performing any other act on an entire database, make a backup copy of the database. If the database is small enough, you can simply copy it to a floppy disk. If it's too large to fit on a single disk, even after compacting, you might need to copy it to a tape drive or to a removable hard disk.

You may have one of the compression programs, such as WinZip, on your computer. By compacting, and then compressing, the database, it may be small enough to fit on a floppy disk. The new WinZip program automatically spans over several disks if necessary, so you can save the backup copy to more than one disk.

Before you make a backup copy, be sure everyone who was using the database has closed it, so you save the latest and most consistent information. Use the Windows Explorer or another program to copy the database to the disk or other medium.

If you're sharing the database with a workgroup, be sure to save the system.mdw or other workgroup file, as well. This file contains the information about each user's toolbar and option settings, and if it's lost or damaged, you won't be able to start Access without reinstalling it and resetting the toolbars, options, and security settings. More about workgroups in Chapter 27.

When you replicate a database, Access offers to make a backup copy. If you respond Yes, the copy is added to the same folder as the original. You can copy it from there to another medium later.

Consequences of Replication

Before you decide to replicate your database, understanding the changes that are going to occur is important. These changes will significantly increase the size of the database while decreasing the flexibility.

Under certain conditions, several new system tables may be added to the database. The system tables are visible only if the System Objects option in the View tab of the Options dialog box is checked. They include tables created if conflicts occur between replicas or if errors occur while updating the design of a replica. The system tables also include the MSysReplicas table, which stores details of all known replicas in the set. Other tables maintain information about deleted records that's dispersed to all replicas during synchronization or details of all synchronizations that have taken place.

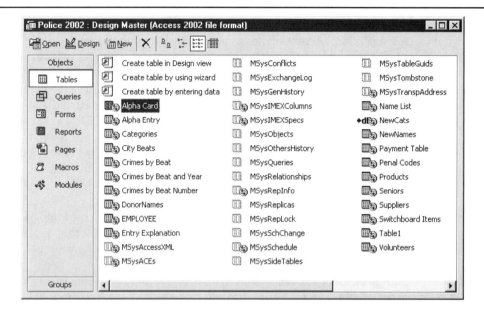

New fields are also added to the tables in the database when you replicate it:

■ The s_GUID system field is a global identifier for each record.

■ The s_Lineage system field is a binary field that stores information about the history of changes to each record.

■ The s_Generation system field stores information about groups of changes.

■ A Gen_*fieldname* field is added for every Memo and OLE Object data type.

■ The ColLineage system field is a long integer field that stores information about the history of changes to each column.

The system fields are also hidden unless you checked System Objects in the View option.

Several new properties are added to the database and its objects when you replicate it. For example, the ReplicaID property provides each member of the replica set with a unique identifier. Other properties enable you to keep tables and queries local or allow them to be replicated. To learn about these new database properties, open the Visual Basic Editor and consult the Help topics.

AutoNumber fields behave differently when you replicate a database. The AutoNumber fields set to incremental numbering change to random numbering. Existing records retain their values, but new records are assigned AutoNumbers randomly. If any applications depend on autonumbering, you can add a Date/Time field to provide sequential ordering of new records.

Certain size limitations are also the result of the addition of the three system fields. Each record may contain a maximum of 2,048 bytes. The system fields use a minimum of 54 bytes to store the identifiers, indexes, and information about changes in the record. This reduces the amount of space left for record data. In addition, a table may contain up to 255 fields, 4 of which are taken up by the replication system fields. Each Memo and OLE Object field adds a system field.

The size of the database increases because of the addition of the system tables, which can grow significantly, depending on the frequency of synchronization. Some of the tables are emptied after synchronization.

Understanding Replica Visibility

When you replicate a database, each replica is defined with a specific degree of "visibility":

- Global
- Local
- Anonymous

A *global* replica can synchronize with almost all other members of the replica set, as well as with any replica it created. When you replicate a database, its visibility is set to global. The Design Master is a global replica.

A *local* replica can synchronize only with the global replica that created it. This creates a star topology, in which synchronization always passes through the global hub to each member in the set.

An *anonymous* replica can also synchronize only with its parent global replica. Anonymous replicas are treated as single replica members, which reduces the amount of information to be stored and also reduces overhead. A global replica cannot initiate synchronization with an anonymous replica. The anonymous replica must be the one to initiate synchronization with its parent replica.

Some limitations apply to replica sets:

- If the parent replica is moved, it's updated with a new ReplicaID, and the local and anonymous replicas won't be able to find it.

- Local and anonymous replicas cannot be converted to the Design Master replica. Only global replicas can become the Design Master.

- When you create a replica from a local or anonymous replica, the new replica inherits all the parent properties, except for the ReplicaID, which must be unique. A local replica creates a local replica and an anonymous replica creates an anonymous replica.

APPLICATION
DEVELOPMENT

Creating a Replica with Access

When you make the first replica of a database, Access converts the original database to the Design Master from which you can create additional replicas. To make the first replica of a database using the Access menu commands, do the following:

1. After making certain all other users have closed it, open the database.

2. If you protected the database with a password, you must remove it. You can't synchronize replicas if they have passwords assigned. To remove the password, click Open Exclusive in the Open dialog box when you open the database. Then choose Tools | Security | Unset Database Password, and then enter the password and click OK.

3. Choose Tools | Replication | Create Replica.

4. The first dialog box asks if you want to close this database and convert it to the Design Master. (If you already created a replica, you already have a Design Master, so this dialog box doesn't appear.) Do one of the following:

   ■ Click Yes to convert the database to the Design Master.

   ■ Click No to return to the database without creating a replica.

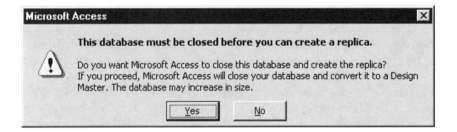

Tip   *The message box also warns that the database may be larger than the original. This is because several new system tables are added that keep track of synchronization history, conflicts, and other data management tasks. New system fields are also added to each table in the database. To see the hidden tables and fields, choose Tools | Options, and then click the View tab. Then check the Hidden Objects and System Objects options in the Show group.*

5. If you choose Yes in the dialog box, the dialog box closes and a message box appears, advising that you should have a backup of the database and offering to create one now if you haven't already done so. Do one of the following:

   ■ Choose Yes to create a backup of the database in the same folder as the original.

   ■ Choose No if you already have a backup.

   ■ Choose Cancel to quit the replication.

■ Choose Help to see what kind of changes Access is going to make to the database and the consequences of those changes.

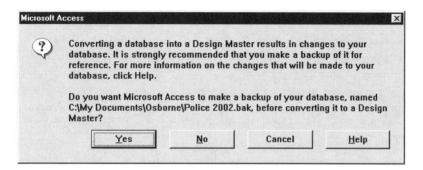

6. If you choose Yes, Access creates the backup file, and then converts the database to the Design Master. The Location of New Replica dialog box opens (see Figure 26-1), in which you select the folder where you want to store the new replica. Click OK. You can also enter a different name for the replica or accept the default "Replica of ..." name. Subsequent replicas are assigned the same name, followed by a number indicating the order of replica creation.

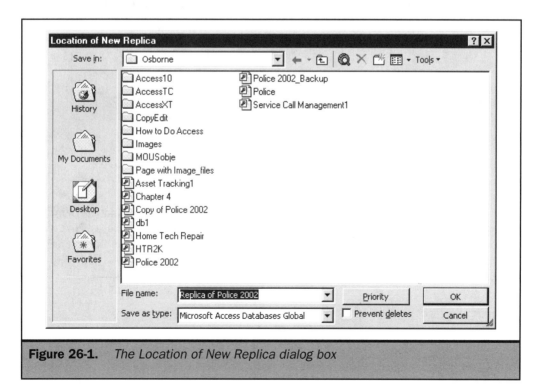

Figure 26-1.   *The Location of New Replica dialog box*

7. In the Location of New Replica dialog box, you have two other options:

- Check the Prevent deletes check box to prevent other users from deleting any records in the replica. This option is especially important in cases where scattered users may consider some of the information of no interest to them and they're tempted to delete data that's important to other users.

- Click the Priority button to open the Priority dialog box where you can set the replica priority as a percentage between 0 and 100. The default is 100 percent for the Design Master and 90 percent of the parent for the other replicas. The priority of a replica determines who wins in the case of a synchronization conflict. More about priorities later in the section "Resolving Synchronization Conflicts."

- Select the replica visibility from the Save as type list. The default is Microsoft Access Databases Global.

8. After the conversion is complete, a message box appears with information about the operation. The replica is stored in the folder you selected in the previous box, and the original database has been converted to the Design Master and stored in its original location. Click OK to end the process.

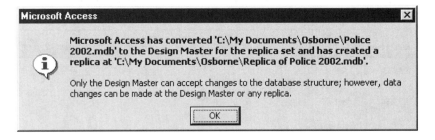

If you already created one or more replicas for the database, the Location of New Replica dialog box opens immediately after you choose Create Replica from the Tools | Replication menu.

When you open the Design Master database, the object lists in the Database window all show the Replicable icon, in addition to the object icon, as shown in Figure 26-2. These symbols also appear in the replica Database window. The Replicable icon doesn't appear with local object names. The Database window title bar also indicates whether the database is a replica or the Design Master.

Replicable icon

Figure 26-2.   *The Design Master Database window*

You can create additional replicas from either the Design Master or any of the existing replicas by opening it and choosing Tools | Replication | Create Replica, and then selecting the location, priority, and visibility for the new replica.

Setting Replica Priorities

In Access 2002, each replica in a replica set is assigned a priority when you create it. The replica with the highest priority wins in case a synchronization conflict occurs. If the priorities are the same, the replica with the lowest ReplicaID property wins.

A replica priority is a number between 0 and 100, with 100 being the highest. When you create the first replica, it's assigned a priority of 90 as the default. The Design Master has a priority of 100. Each additional replica has a default priority equal to 90 percent of the hub priority.

Local and anonymous replicas have 0 priority, so they automatically lose in case of a conflict with the global hub replica. If one of them sends a nonconflicting change to the hub, it becomes part of the global replica and assumes that replica's priority.

See the section "Resolving Synchronization Conflicts," later in this chapter, for more
information about how priorities determine conflict resolution.

Keeping Objects Local

Normally, all database objects are replicated along with the data. If you want to keep
your forms, reports, macros, and modules local, change a database property before
creating the first replica. To change the ReplicateProject property, do the following:

1. With the unreplicated database open, choose File | Database Properties.

2. Click the Custom tab and select ReplicateProject in the Properties box
   (see Figure 26-3).

3. Click the No option button next to Value, and then click Modify. The Value of
   the ReplicateProject property changes to No in the Properties list. Then click OK.

Figure 26-3.   *Change the ReplicateProject property*

Setting the Replicable Property for Individual Objects

Each object in the Design Master or in a replica can be either local or replicable. A *local* object is a table, query, form, report, macro, or module that remains in the database where it was created. The object isn't shared with other members in the replica set. A *replicable* object and any changes to it are dispersed to other members in the set.

In Access 2002, the forms, report, macros, and modules in a database are either all local or all replicable. The Replicable property applies only to the tables and queries in the database because they're the only objects that contain data. To view the General properties, which includes the Replicable property, select the table or query in the Database window, and then click the Properties toolbar button or choose View | Properties. Figure 26-4 shows the Alpha Card Properties for the Alpha Card table in the Design Master of the Police database.

If you look at the properties of a table or query in the newly created Design Master, you can see the Replicable property is checked. This indicates the object can be included in replicas. Clearing the option makes the object local to the Design Master and removes the selected object from all the existing replicas in the Replica set the next time the set is synchronized. The replicable icon is also removed from the object name in the Design Master Database window.

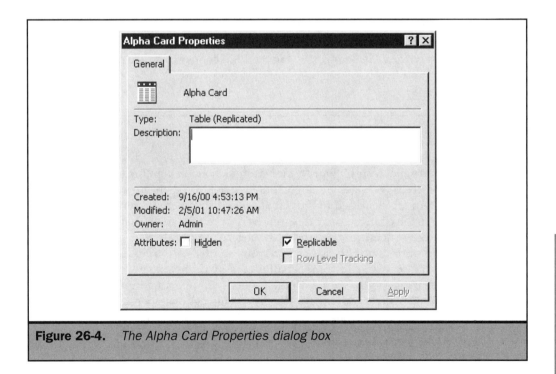

Figure 26-4. *The Alpha Card Properties dialog box*

In other circumstances, the property appears differently in the dialog box:

- When the option appears cleared and grayed out, the object is local to the active database and you cannot change the Replicable property. This is the case in a regular or nonreplicated database.

- When the option is checked, but grayed out, the object is already replicated and you cannot change the property. It appears this way in a replica database.

Creating a Partial Replica

By replicating a database, several workers in different locations can work on their own copies of the database. If they need only parts of the database or if some of the database should be kept relatively secure, you can create partial replicas for distribution. For example, a manufacturing company may have several factories in different states. The main headquarters would maintain the master database, while each local factory would have a partial replica containing only the information relating to its location and activities.

Partial replicas offer many benefits, including reduced network traffic and costs, greater security, and smaller local databases.

To create a partial replica, do the following:

1. Open the Design Master or one of the existing replicas in the set and choose Tools | Replication | Partial Replica Wizard.

2. In the first wizard dialog box (see Figure 26-5) choose to create a new partial replica or modify an existing one, and then click Next.

Reducing Storage Overhead

The storage required for the Design Master and the replicas depends on the changes to the data and to the design. Every time you make changes in the structure in the Design Master, the changes are documented in the MSysSchChg system table, one of the system tables added to the database when you create replicas. After synchronization, the changed record is removed from the table. Changing more than once between synchronizations adds to the size of the database.

The trick to minimizing the storage requirements is to compact the database on a daily basis. Also compact after making design changes, but just before synchronizing the changes with the replicas. Compacting removes the deleted records and carries out other memory-saving actions, thereby reducing the amount of information transmitted to the replicas during synchronization.

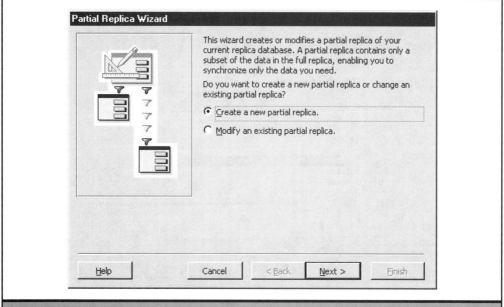

Figure 26-5.   *Create a new partial replica or modify an existing one*

3. Enter the path and name for the new partial replica in the next wizard dialog box. You have the choice between a Global, Local, or Anonymous replica. You can also specify the replica as Read-Only or Prevent Deletes. Click Next.

4. The third wizard dialog box enables you to build a filter that limits the records to be copied to the partial replica. Create the filter expression by combining the field names, the comparison operators, and the AND and OR operators. The example in Figure 26-6 limits the Alpha Entry records to those with no blank Code fields. You can build filters for any of the tables in the database using this dialog box. When you finish, click Next.

5. The next wizard dialog box (see Figure 26-7) shows a list of tables you haven't created a filter for or that aren't related (with referential integrity enforced) to tables for which you did create a filter. If you want to replicate all the records in a table, leave the table checked. To leave out all the records, clear the check mark next to the table name. When you finish, click Next.

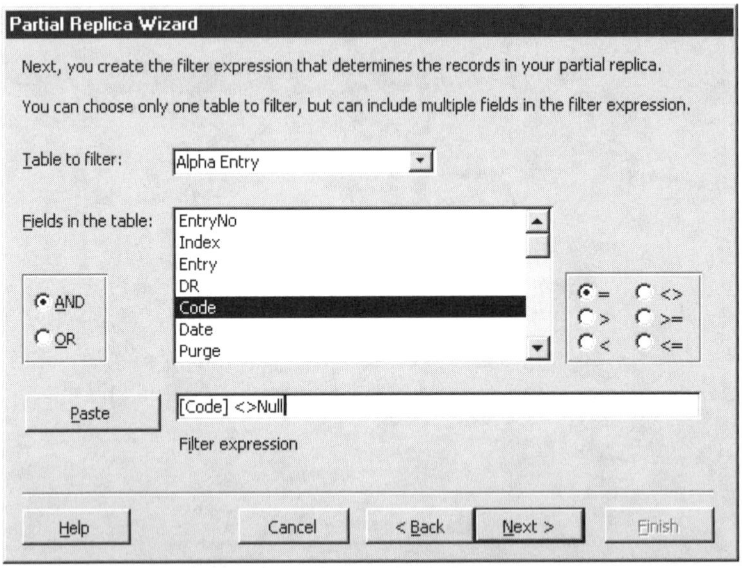

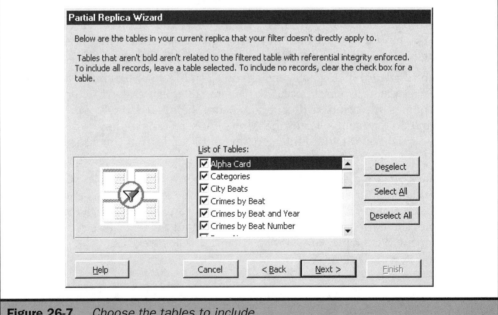

Figure 26-6. *Filtering records for the partial replica*

Figure 26-7. *Choose the tables to include*

6. In the final wizard dialog box, you have a choice to create a temporary report of changes made to the original replica when creating the partial replica or to create the partial replica without previewing the report.

Figure 26-8 shows the Partial Replica Wizard Report on Changes Made when creating the partial replica from the original Police database. Notice the Alpha Entry table is filtered in accordance with the expression entered in an earlier dialog box.

Creating a Replica with the Briefcase

The Briefcase method of creating a database replica was invented for the user who wants to take work home to continue on a laptop. Once the Briefcase replica is created, it can be synchronized with the Design Master like any other replica.

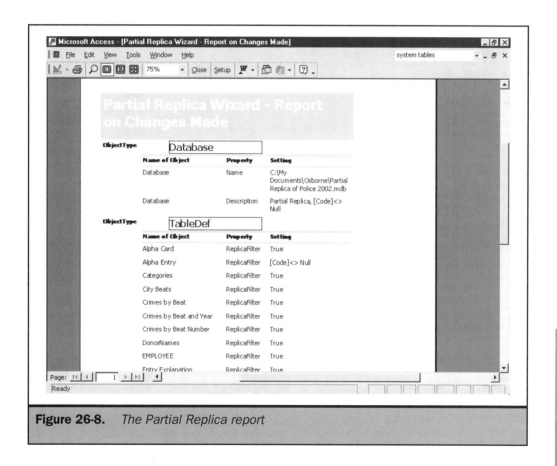

Figure 26-8.   *The Partial Replica report*

If you don't see the My Briefcase icon on your Windows desktop, refer to Windows Help topics for information about installing the Briefcase accessory.

Briefcase Replication isn't among the tools included with a typical Access installation. You may need to run Access Setup again to install it. It's included in the Database Replication feature located in the expanded Microsoft Access for Windows list in the Microsoft Office feature tree.

To make a Briefcase replica, do the following:

1. If the database you want to replicate has a database password, remove it as described earlier, and then close the database.

2. Open Windows Explorer and select the folder that contains the database.

3. Drag the database file to the My Briefcase icon on the desktop. A series of message boxes appear that ask for confirmation of the replication, offer to make a backup copy of the database before replicating, and ask which copy to designate as the Design Master.

Caution *If you select the Briefcase Copy replica as the Design Master, no one can change the design in the original copy.*

After the replication is complete, double-click the My Briefcase icon to open the My Briefcase window. To open the Briefcase replica, double-click the filename or select the file and choose File | Open.

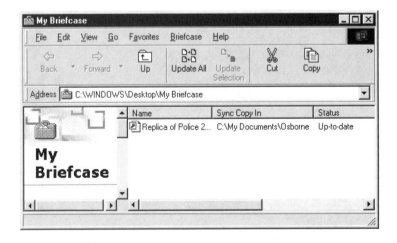

Synchronizing Replica Set Members

As objects and data change independently in each of the members of a replica set, they become quite different. To maintain database integrity, all members of the set must contain the same structure and data. The process of *synchronization* is one in which all updated records and objects are exchanged between two members.

Access provides three types of synchronization: direct, indirect, and Internet.

- Direct synchronization is the best method when all the members of the replica set are connected directly to the local area network and available via shared folders. This isn't the best solution to updating members when some are remote. If you try to directly synchronize a member who isn't found, the member is removed from the replica set.

- Indirect synchronization is used when the database must be available to remotely located, or traveling, users. Indirect synchronization must be managed by the Replication Manager, which is part of the Microsoft Office XP Developer (MOD).

- Internet synchronization is a convenient way to synchronize remote replicas in an environment configured with an Internet Server. Again, you must use the Replication Manager to accomplish Internet synchronization.

In this chapter, we discuss only direct synchronization. To synchronize two replica set members, do the following:

1. Open the replica set member you want to synchronize.

2. Choose Tools | Replication | Synchronize Now. The Synchronize Database *filename* dialog box opens.

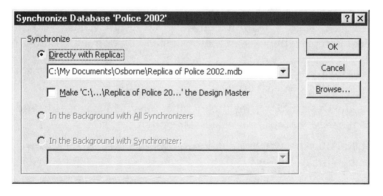

3. The Directly with Replica box shows the path and filename of the first replica created. If that isn't the one you want to use now, click the down arrow and choose from the list of other members who have been synchronized with the current database. If you still don't see the one you want, enter the path and

filename in the box or click Browse to locate it. You also have other choices in this dialog box:

- You can specify the current replica member be assigned as the Design Master in place of the existing one, as described in the next section. This option isn't available if either member to be synchronized is a partial replica.

- Choose "In the Background with All Synchronizers" to add the member to the list of replicated databases managed by any synchronizer. Synchronization takes place in the background as resources permit.

- Choose "In the Background with Synchronizer" if you want to choose a specific synchronizer from the drop-down list. Synchronization also takes place in the background.

4. Click OK. A message box appears announcing the synchronization was completed successfully and asks if you want to close and reopen the current database.

5. Choose Yes to close the database and integrate the changes. If you choose No, you return to the database, but some of the changes may not show in the database.

Tip   *If the database has a main switchboard, you can bypass it by holding down* SHIFT *while the database reopens.*

If your replica set contains more than two members, you must make two rounds of synchronization to disseminate all the changes completely. The first round copies the changes from each replica to the Design Master. The second round distributes the changes to the replicas. You needn't include that last replica from the first round in the second round because it already has been exposed to the accumulated changes in the first round.

Specifying a New Design Master

When you open a replica to synchronize it with the Design Master, you can switch roles and make the replica the Design Master instead by doing the following:

1. Choose Tools | Replication | Synchronize Now to open the Synchronize Database dialog box as before.

2. Choose the Design Master as the member to synchronize with, and then check the "Make *filename* the Design Master" option.

3. Click OK. After the synchronization, a message box asks if you want to close and reopen the database.

4. Choose Yes. The database closes and reopens with the title bar, indicating the replica is now the Design Master. The former Design Master has become a replica.

Synchronizing a Briefcase Replica

To synchronize the Briefcase replica with the Design Master on the desktop, do the following:

1. Double-click the My Briefcase icon to open the My Briefcase window. If the database isn't current, the Status shows as Needs Updating.

2. Select the database file you want to synchronize, and then choose Briefcase | Update Selection or click the Update Selection toolbar button. If you want to update all the database files in the Briefcase, choose Update All instead. The Update My Briefcase dialog box opens (see Figure 26-9).

3. Click Update.

The left column shows the status of the Briefcase replica and the right column shows the status of the copy outside the Briefcase—either the Design Master or another replica. The update action is, by default, Replace in the direction from the new version to the older version. If this isn't what you want to do, right-click one of the files and choose Replace in the other direction or Skip from the shortcut menu.

When Synchronization Conflicts Occur

In Access 95 and 97, a conflict was determined when the same record was changed in two separate replicas, even though the change affected different fields in the record. In Access 2000 and later, the conflicts are determined only if the change affects the same column in the same record. This column-level resolution is the default when the database is replicated.

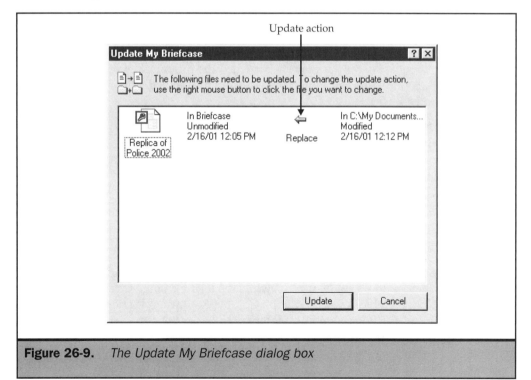

Figure 26-9. *The Update My Briefcase dialog box*

Note *If you want to retain the row-level resolution, change the RowLevelTracking property of one or more tables before replicating it. The RowLevelTracking property is a check box on the General tab of the Table Properties dialog box.*

In Access 95 and 97, two types of conflicts were defined: *synchronization conflicts,* which occurred when two users updated the same record in two members of the replica set, and *synchronization errors,* which resulted from trying to apply data changes that resulted in a referential integrity violation or some other type of data violation. In Access 2000 and later, both types of conflicts are considered synchronization conflicts and are treated the same.

Several types of conflicts can occur when you synchronize two members of the replica set.

- *Simultaneous update conflicts* occur when two replicas attempt to update the same record.

- *Unique key violation conflicts* occur when two replicas try to add a new record with the same value in the field that's defined as the primary key or a unique index. Such a conflict can also occur when the Design Master creates a unique index and the replica adds two or more records with the same value.

- *Table-level validation conflicts* occur when the data violates a rule that restricts values or types of data permitted in the table.

- *Update referential integrity conflicts* occur when the primary key value is updated in one replica and new child records using the old primary key value are added to another replica.

- *Delete referential integrity conflicts* occur when the primary key record is deleted from one replica and new child records using the deleted primary key are added to another replica.

- *Foreign key violation conflicts* occur when an invalid primary key record exists.

- *Locking conflicts* occur when a record in a replica cannot be applied during synchronization because another user has locked the table. After several tries to update the record, synchronization is abandoned and an error is returned. The conflict isn't logged.

- *Case-sensitive and sort order conflicts* may occur in replica sets that span multiple database types if the language sort orders are different or if the sort order is case-sensitive.

When a conflict occurs, the winning change is determined by the priorities assigned to the members and automatically applied while the losing change is recorded as a conflict in the Conflict table. You can use the Conflict Resolution Wizard to examine and resolve any conflicts logged in your database.

Resolving Synchronization Conflicts

After synchronizing two replicas, when you open your database, you might see a message indicating the existence of conflicts in this member of the replica set. This message means changes you tried to apply to one or more tables in the database have failed. Choose Yes to launch the Replication Conflict Viewer.

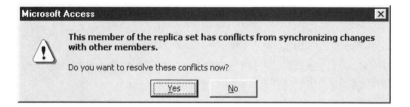

If the database is already open, you can start the Replication Conflict Viewer by choosing Tools | Replication | Resolve Conflicts. The Microsoft Replication Conflict Viewer dialog box opens (see Figure 26-10), listing the tables that contain conflicts and the number of conflicts in each table.

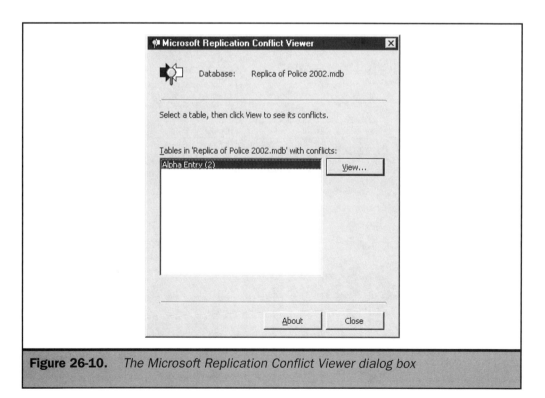

Figure 26-10.   *The Microsoft Replication Conflict Viewer dialog box*

1. Select the table you want to work with and click View. The next Conflict Viewer dialog box shows you the details of the conflict and offers four choices for resolving the conflict (see Figure 26-11).

2. The Reason For Conflict box describes the nature of the conflict. Only the system fields relating to the conflict and the fields in conflict are displayed. Click the Show All Fields option button if you want to see all the field data in the two conflicting records.

3. To resolve a conflict, do one of the following:

   ■ Click Keep Existing Data to accept the current resolution of the conflict.

   ■ Edit the data in the current resolution and click Keep Revised Data to keep current resolution with the revisions.

   ■ Click Overwrite With Conflicting Data to overturn the current resolution and keep the conflicting data.

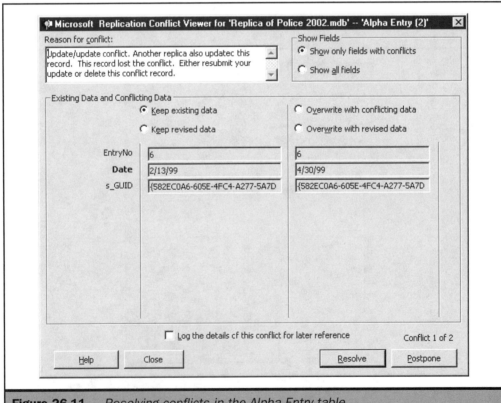

Figure 26-11. *Resolving conflicts in the Alpha Entry table*

■ Edit the conflicting data and click Overwrite With Revised Data to overturn the resolution and keep the revised conflicting data.

4. Then click Resolve. Each resolution action causes a confirmation message to display. Choose Yes to confirm the deletion or No to return to the dialog box. You can also click Postpone to leave the conflict unresolved until later and go on to another conflict.

5. You return to the earlier Replication Conflict Viewer dialog box where you can choose another conflict to examine and resolve. After all the conflicts have been dealt with, click Close to return to the Database window.

Once you decide which values are the ones you want in the database, synchronize the two replica set members again to equalize their values.

If you want to make a copy of the conflict and store it in a separate log file for later consideration, choose Log The Details Of This Conflict For Later Reference. The file is stored in the UnresolvedConflicts.log file in the DatabaseReplication folder. When you close the Replication Conflict Viewer dialog box, a message appears, offering to send the log file to the system administrator.

Note   *Other options are available in the Replication Conflict Viewer dialog box, depending on the type of conflict that occurred.*

Data errors can also occur that cannot be automatically resolved by choosing one version of a record over another—for example, if a record in the replica set has a key field or unique index field value that's a duplicate of one in another replica set member. Violating a data validation rule that's enforced in the Design Master can also cause a data error. You must locate the record causing the error and correct it manually or delete it. The Replication Manager includes a Conflict Resolver that explains data errors and helps to locate the records causing them. See the Access Help topic for more information about using the Conflict Resolver.

Launching the Replication Conflict Viewer from Windows

If you have trouble launching the Replication Conflict Viewer from within Access, you can start it independently from Windows because it's one of the shared programs in Office XP. To start the Conflict Viewer, do the following:

1. Locate the WZCNFLCT.EXE file in the Program Files\Common Files\Microsoft Shared\Database Replication folder. Then double-click the filename.

APPLICATION DEVELOPMENT

2. In the first dialog box, choose Microsoft Access Database, and then enter the path and filename in the Database Path text box.

3. Click Connect to open the first Replication Conflict Viewer dialog box where you can choose the conflict to examine and resolve as before.

Modifying a Replica Set

In a dynamic work environment, changes certainly will be required in the replicated database—for example, adding and removing individual members of the set, recovering the Design Master, or returning the replicated database to its former normal status. You may also want to make changes in some object designs and distribute them to the replicas.

Removing a Member from the Replica Set

To remove a member from the replica set, close Access and use Windows Explorer to locate the file you want to delete, and then do the following:

1. Select the filename and press DEL or right-click the filename and choose Delete from the shortcut menu.

2. Choose Yes when asked to confirm the deletion, and then close Explorer.

3. The deleted member remains in the drop-down list of members in the Synchronize Database dialog box until you try unsuccessfully to synchronize it with another. Restart Access and open another replica set member, and then choose Tools | Replication | Synchronize Now.

4. In the Synchronize Database dialog box, choose the name of the deleted member in the list and click OK. Access closes the database and displays a message stating the file wasn't found.

5. Click OK. Another message shows the replica was deleted from the set and prompts you to close and reopen the database.

6. Click OK, and then close and reopen the database.

The next time you run the synchronization, the deleted filename is gone from the list.

Recovering the Design Master

If the Design Master has been moved, renamed, deleted, or corrupted in some way, you can replace it with one of the replicas. Before converting it to the Design Master, be sure you have incorporated in it all the changes made to the other members of the replica set by synchronizing the replica with all other members of the set. Also make sure no Design Master is still in the set.

 If the Design Master hasn't been moved or corrupted, you run the risk of creating a second Design Master with this procedure. Then, you can only solve the problem by closing Access and using Windows Explorer to delete one of them.

To replace the Design Master with one of the replicas, do the following:

1. Open the replica you want to convert to Design Master.

2. Choose Tools | Replication | Recover Design Master. A dialog box opens with a lengthy explanation of the problem. The Recover Design Master command is available only when the open member is a replica.

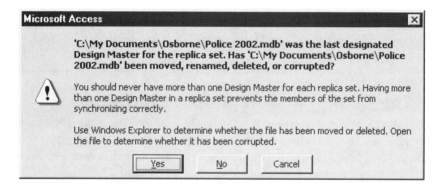

3. Click Yes to proceed. A message box says you must synchronize this member with all the others before making it the Design Master. If you already did so, click Yes. If not, click No and carry out the synchronization before trying again.

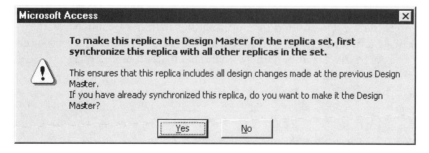

4. If you chose Yes in the previous dialog box, the replica is made the Design Master and Access closes and reopens the database to implement the change.

Troubleshooting: Two Design Masters

If you accidentally designate two Design Masters, you can no longer synchronize the replica set correctly. If you find you have two Design Masters, you can correct the problem by doing the following:

1. Identify which is the original Design Master and decide if you want to retain it as the Design Master.
2. Close Access and, using Windows Explorer, delete the faux Design Master.
3. Delete all the replicas whose most recent synchronization was with the deleted Design Master, as well as all replicas synchronized with those replicas.
4. Create as many new replicas as you need from the surviving Design Master to replace the ones you deleted.

TIP: You can tell which replica was used in the most recent synchronization because the filename appears in the Synchronize With box when you first open the Synchronize Database dialog box.

Changing the Design in a Replicated Database

Design changes can be made only in the Design Master. Before making the changes, make sure no other replica is using the name you chose for the new field or object as the name of a local object. Also synchronize with all other members before making the changes. Be aware of the size limitations that affect replicated databases.

If your database has an opening screen that displays for a short time, and then gives in to the main switchboard, you may have added a check box that gives the user the option of skipping the opening screen. The Northwind database has such a screen with that option and you see how to add one to the Police database in Chapter 28. This check box has a Visual Basic event procedure or function that changes the Display Form/Page startup property from the opening screen to the main switchboard. This constitutes a design change that isn't permitted in a replica other than the Design Master.

To replicate a database with such a feature, delete the opening screen or change the startup property to display the main switchboard instead on opening. You could also remove the check box that changes the startup option.

If you're using linked tables in the replica set, they aren't automatically replicated. A linked table is created as a local object in the Design Master and remains local until you make it replicable. Then the link and the table are sent to all replicas in the set. After the table is sent to all the members, you can change the Design Master's or another member's link without affecting the other members.

Restoring a Regular Database

No simple process exists for reversing the replication to restore the Design Master to the status of a regular Access database. If the need for replication no longer exists, you can create a new database with the same objects and data as the replicated database, but without all the extra tables, fields, and properties the replication process added. You import all the database objects to a blank database except the tables, which contain the extra system fields.

To restore the database, do the following:

1. In an empty Access window, choose File | New.

2. Choose Database from the General tab of the New dialog box and click OK.

3. Choose the location and enter a name for the new database, and then click Create. The new blank Database window opens.

4. Choose File | Get External Data | Import.

5. In the Import dialog box, choose the member of the replica set that contains the data and objects you want and click Import. The Import Objects dialog box opens where you can select the objects you want to include in the new database.

6. Choose all the objects on every tab except the tables and click OK. As the objects are imported, some conflict messages may appear. Click OK to proceed. You can resolve the conflicts later.

Once you have all the objects, other than the tables, imported, you need to reconstruct the tables with Make Table queries. In the replica database, create a make-table query for each table in the replica, leaving out the system fields added during replication. Save the new tables in the new database. The query extracts all the relevant data from the table and places it in the new table. When all the data is added to the new database, you must reconstruct all the indexes for the new tables and set all the relationships between the tables. See Chapter 9 for information about creating make-table queries.

Sharing a Database on a Network

In a multiple-user environment, you have several ways to share a single database with others, in addition to creating replicas, which was discussed earlier. Some of the options for sharing an Access database are the following:

- Placing the database in a central location where all users have access to all objects in it.

- Splitting the database, so the users share only the table data.

- Placing the entire database or part of the database on the Internet. See Chapter 24 for information about sharing data on the Web.

■ Creating an application based on the client/server model. For more information, refer to a resource such as *Microsoft Office Visual Basic Programmer's Guide*.

Sharing an Entire Database

The easiest way to share data is to put the entire database—tables and all—on the network server or in a folder that can be shared. All users then have access to all the data and use the same database objects. If everyone uses the database for the same activities and you don't want the users to customize their own objects, this is the best strategy. Figure 26-12 shows the model for sharing the entire database among multiple users.

To share an entire database on a network server, copy the database to the shared folder, and then set the Default Open Mode on the Advanced tab of the Options dialog box to Shared. Access must be installed on each computer on the network to share Access databases.

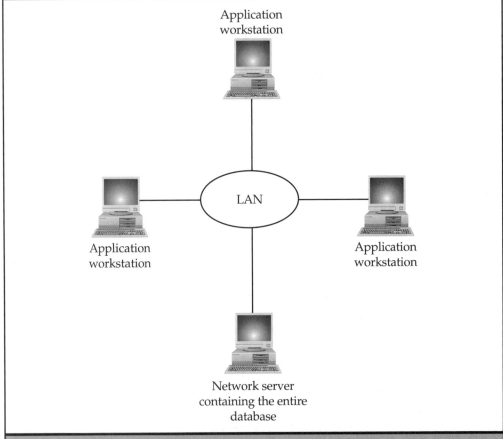

Figure 26-12.   *Sharing a database among multiple users: the entire database is stored on the network server and the workstations access all the objects via the LAN*

Splitting the Database

A faster method of sharing a database is to put all the tables on the network server and let the users keep the other objects on their own workstations. Only the data is transmitted over the network, thus reducing network traffic. This strategy is useful when the users' jobs and activities are different. The users maintain only those objects that directly pertain to their own activities.

The database containing the tables is called the *back-end* database and the one containing the other objects is the *front-end* database. The front-end database contains links to the tables in the back-end database. Access provides the Database Splitter Wizard to separate the tables from the rest of the database. Figure 26-13 illustrates the front-end/back-end model for sharing an Access database.

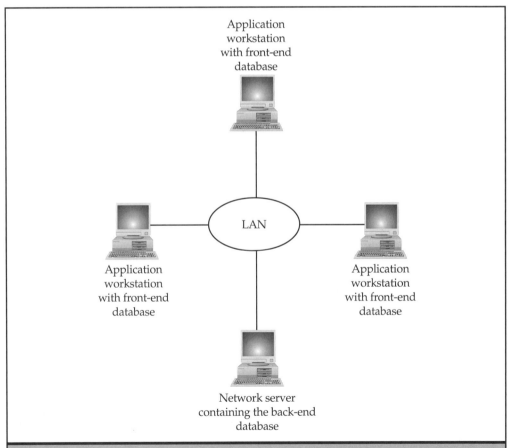

Figure 26-13.   *Splitting the database into a front end and back end: all tables are stored on the network server. The application workstations store all the other objects—queries, forms, reports, macros, and modules*

Undoing what the Database Splitter Wizard does isn't easy, so be sure to make a backup copy of the database before you attempt to split it.

To split a database into the front- and back-end elements, do the following:

1. Open the database and make sure no objects in the database are open, and then choose Tools | Database Utilities | Database Splitter. The Database Splitter Wizard opens with a message describing the process (see Figure 26-14).

2. After reading the message, click Split Database. The next dialog box lets you specify where to place the back-end database.

3. Use the Save in box (see Figure 26-15) to locate the network server on your system. The Network Neighborhood entry in the drop-down list lets you find a computer on the LAN to use as the back-end server.

4. Enter a name for the back-end database or accept the default name: the name of the current database with "_be" added.

5. Click Split. When the process is completed, a message appears announcing the successful split. Click OK to close the message box.

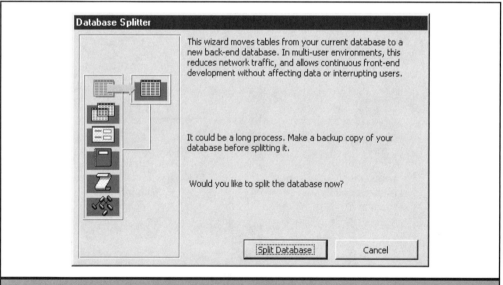

Figure 26-14. *The Database Splitter Wizard dialog box*

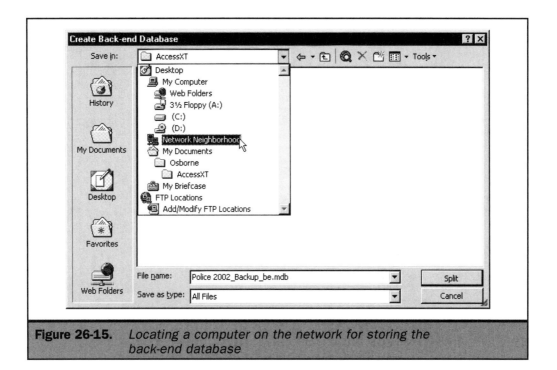

Figure 26-15. *Locating a computer on the network for storing the back-end database*

It may take a while to split a large database. The wizard is actually deleting the tables from the current database, creating a new database with the tables, and then linking the current database to the new back-end tables.

When you open the Tables tab of the current database after splitting, you can see by the link icons next to the names in the list that the tables listed are all links to another database (see Figure 26-16). If you open the new back-end database, you can see all the tables listed on the Tables tab, but the other tabs are all empty.

To customize the distributed database environment further, you can reduce network traffic even more by moving relatively static tables, such as lookup tables containing data that doesn't change often, to the front-end databases. If the data in the lookup table changes, you can make the changes in the back-end version and alert the users to copy the data to their own lookup tables. Temporary tables should also be stored locally to prevent conflicts, as well as to reduce network traffic.

If you need to change the link to any of the back-end tables, choose Tools | Database Utilities | Linked Table Manager. In the Linked Table Manager dialog box, choose the affected tables and check the Always Prompt For New Location check box (see Figure 26-17). Then when you refresh the link to the table, you have the opportunity of changing the location of the linked table in the standard file location dialog box.

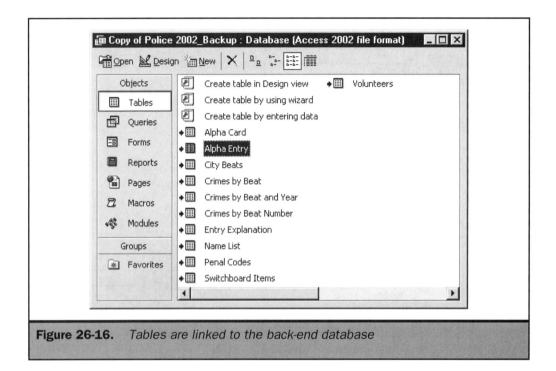

Figure 26-16. *Tables are linked to the back-end database*

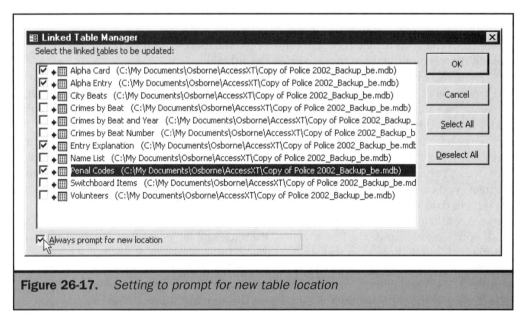

Figure 26-17. *Setting to prompt for new table location*

Preventing Exclusive Access

If one user opens the database with exclusive access, no other user can work with it. To prevent, or at least discourage, this from happening, set the Default Open Mode to Shared in the Advanced tab of the Options dialog box. Then instruct all the users not to open the database in an exclusive mode. See Chapter 27 for information about including security in a multiple-user environment.

You can also set up a security system that prevents exclusive mode opening by certain users and permitting it for others. The database administrator must be able to open the database in exclusive mode to perform duties, such as compacting and backing up the database.

Database Administration in a Multiuser Environment

As soon as more than one user has access to a database, someone should be assigned as the database administrator (DBA), who is responsible for ensuring the integrity and security of the database. Among the issues that need to be addressed by the DBA are the following:

- Controlling read/write access to the data.
- Setting up the user groups with the appropriate levels of access.
- Adding new users to a group and removing users from a group.
- Ensuring accurate, current record data and minimizing data-locking conflicts.
- Editing database objects as necessary and ensuring all users have current versions.
- Backing up and compacting the database.

Controlling Data Access

If two users attempt to edit a record at the same time, the results can be unpredictable. Some form of data locking is necessary to ensure the integrity of the database. Allowing one user exclusive access to a record is called *record locking*. When a data page, recordset object, or a database object is locked, it's read-only to all users except the one who's currently entering or editing the data in it.

Access provides three levels of record locking, ranging from no locks at all to locking all the records in the recordset. You can set the default record-locking scheme in the Advanced tab of the Options dialog box (see Figure 26-18). The choices are

- No locks (optimistic record locking)
- Edited record (pessimistic record locking)
- All records

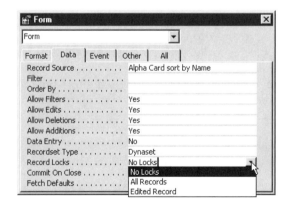

Figure 26-18. *Setting record locking on the Advanced tab of the Options dialog box*

The Default record-locking setting in the Options dialog box applies only to datasheet views of tables and queries and to dynasets. If you want to set the record locking for forms or reports, set the Record Locks property on the Data tab of the object's property sheet. The choices are the same as in the Options dialog box. Setting record locks for a report prevents changes in records in the underlying table or query while the report is previewed or printed. You can also set the Record Locks property for a query and override the default setting.

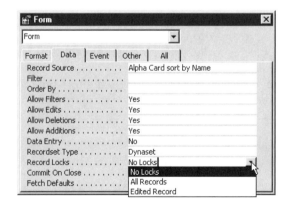

A new record-locking option that became available with Access 2000 is *record-level locking*. In support of the new Unicode format used for storing characters, the size of a page of data has doubled, from 2K bytes to 4K bytes. This can decrease performance by locking too many records if the records contain only a few bytes. For example, the Penal Codes table in the Police database contains only 54 bytes, so locking a page of Penal Codes records would actually lock over 70 records.

With the default record-level locking in effect, Access locks only a single record. This applies to accessing data only through a form. If you want to disable this option, clear the check box in the Advanced tab of the Options dialog box. The setting takes effect the next time you open the database with File | Open. It doesn't take effect if you open the database by selecting the filename from the list of recently used files at the end of the File menu. The record-locking scheme set in the Default Record Locking option group is unaffected by the record-level locking setting.

> **Note** *Whenever you have an Access database open, you can see a file in the Windows Explorer with the same name as the open database, but with the .ldb file extension. This file contains information Access uses to manage the locks in the open database. The file is automatically removed when you close the database.*

The No Locks Strategy

No Locks, the default setting when you start a new database, is called *optimistic record locking* because it's used where few record write conflicts are expected. Access doesn't lock the record during editing. The edited record is locked only at the exact moment it's being saved. The assumption here is that one user probably will have completed saving the record before another user tries to edit it. Using No Locks ensures all records can be edited at any time, but it also can cause editing conflicts among the users.

When you try to save changes to a record another user has changed since you began editing it, a Write Conflict dialog box appears with the following options:

- Save Record, which saves the record with your changes, overwriting the other user's changes.

- Copy to Clipboard, which copies your version of the record to the clipboard for further analysis.

- Drop Changes, which discards your changes in favor of the previous changes.

Edited Record Strategy

The Edited Record record-locking strategy is called *pessimistic locking* because it's assumed much competition will occur for access to records for editing. If it's important for all editing of a record to be completed before another user has access to it, the Edited Record strategy is required. As soon as one user begins to edit a record, no other user may make any changes to it until the first user saves the changes. Other users may view the record, but they cannot change it.

The only difference in the display of the record is the universal symbol for No—the circle with a diagonal line through it—appears in the record selector instead of a pencil, which appears with the No Locks method.

All Records Strategy

This restrictive record-locking strategy locks all records in the form or datasheet, as well as the underlying tables, for the entire time it's open. No one else can edit the records. One case in which this strategy would be useful is when you're running an update query that applies to several different records and you want to make sure all the affected records are locked until the query is completed.

Choosing a Locking Strategy

The strategy you choose depends on your data, how many users share the application, and how they use the data. For most multiuser environments, the No Locks strategy can be the most effective, even though some brief write conflict errors can occur. The overall performance of the system is more efficient than with the other record-locking strategies.

If more imperative reasons exist for locking records during editing, use one of the other locking strategies.

If the data in a form, report, or query is acquired from an Open Database Connectivity (ODBC) database, Access treats it as though the No Locks setting were selected and disregards the Record Locks property setting.

Minimizing Conflicts

One way to reduce the number of locking conflicts is to arrange the workload, so each user attends to different parts of the database. For example, one user updates records for sales in the western states, another for the southern area, and so on.

When two users try to update the same record and cause a conflict, Access tries several times to save the record, hoping it'll be freed from the lock, before displaying the Write Conflict message. The period of time that elapses between tries is specified in the Update Retry Interval setting. The Number of Update Retries setting determines how many times Access should try to save the record before giving up.

You can try different combinations of these two settings. For example, set the Number of Update Retries to 0 to have Access display the Write Conflict message at once. Set both to higher values to reduce the number of write conflicts by letting Access try to save the record more times, with a longer interval between attempts. However, with this arrangement, users may complain the system appears slow. Experiment with these settings to settle on the right combination for your application.

Table 26-1 describes these and other settings that help avoid data-locking conflicts. The settings are found on the Advanced tab of the Options dialog box.

Option	Settings	Description
Refresh interval	0 through 32,766 seconds. Default is 60 seconds.	Sets the number of seconds between automatic updating of records in Datasheet or Form view. Setting to 0 results in no automatic updating.
Number of update retries	0 through 10. Default is 2 tries.	Sets the number of times Access tries to save a record locked by another user before displaying a Write Conflict message.
ODBC refresh interval	0 through 32,766 seconds. Default is 1,500 seconds.	Sets the number of seconds between automatic refreshing of records accessed using ODBC. Setting to 0 results in no automatic updating.
Update Retry Interval	0 through 1,000 milliseconds. Default is 250 milliseconds.	Sets the number of milliseconds between automatic attempts to save a record locked by another user.

Table 26-1. *Advanced Options for the Multiuser Environment*

 Note *You can also set the record-locking strategy with Visual Basic code with the LockEdits property. If you set the property to False, this is equivalent to optimistic locking. Setting to True is equivalent to pessimistic locking.*

Updating Records with Refresh and Requery

If the data in your shared database changes frequently and it's important for the user to have up-to-date data, you can use two methods to keep the data current:

- *Refresh* offers a periodic quick update of the data currently on the screen.
- *Requery* completely rebuilds the underlying recordset by running the query or applying the filter again.

APPLICATION
DEVELOPMENT

Refresh updates only those records already appearing in Datasheet or Form view. When you refresh the datasheet or form, records aren't reordered or deleted, and those that no longer meet the filter criteria are also not removed. To update the recordset to reflect these actions, you must requery the records.

The default interval for refreshing records is 60 seconds, which may be too long in critical situations. You can reset the interval to 10 or 15 seconds. If you set the interval too low, Access creates a lot of network traffic.

To give the user the opportunity to refresh the data, add a command button to the form and attach code containing the statement "me.Refresh" to the On Click event property. To do so, open the property sheet for the command button and click the Build button next to the On Click event property. Next, choose Code Builder from the Choose Builder dialog box, and then enter the statement between the Private Sub and the End Sub statements.

Requerying completely rebuilds the underlying recordset. The easiest way to requery is to press SHIFT-F9. You can also use the Requery method: me.Requery.

Requerying is somewhat of a nuisance to the user because the form or datasheet returns to the first record in the recordset. If you were working with a record deep in the recordset, you must manually return to it after requerying. Remembering the record number doesn't help much because the record order may have changed with the requery.

Editing Shared Database Objects

Even though you do your best to have all the database object designs completed before setting the database up for shared access, changes are bound to be necessary later. Any local objects can be modified at any time, but the shared objects require special consideration.

Before you begin to make significant design changes to a shared database, be sure you open it in exclusive mode by selecting Open Exclusive from the Open button in the Open Database dialog box. Pick a time to do this when other users don't require access to the database, such as the middle of the night.

If the required design changes are less invasive, you can safely modify the objects while the database is open in shared mode. To make changes to a table design, the table must not be in use by another user. If the table or any query, form, or report based on the table is open, the table design cannot be changed. In this case, you can still view the table design, but Access informs you the table is read-only.

The converse is also true—if you're modifying a table design, the table and any query, form, or report based on it is unavailable to another user. A good idea is to have the changes well-thought-out and specific before opening the table design. Then keep the table design open as briefly as possible.

 The Name AutoCorrect feature keeps track of object and field name changes, and tracks down locations where they're referenced. The changes are effected in all the references. This feature isn't available for replicated databases.

Other helpful tips when you need to edit shared database objects are

- When you edit a query, form, or report design already in use by another user, that user won't see the new version until the object is closed and reopened.

- If the objects you want to change are dependent on each other, be sure to edit them all at the same time, so they'll be consistent.

- Make sure no one is using the macro you want to edit by opening the database in exclusive mode. If you change a macro someone's using, you can cause problems.

- After you make changes in a Visual Basic module, remind the other users they must close and reopen the database before they can run the updated procedures.

Data access pages are managed a little differently from the other objects. You must open the database in exclusive mode to create, rename, move, or delete a page because these changes require changes in the information in the Access database. If you only want to edit the page, you don't need exclusive rights to the database because you're only changing the HTML file that exists in the file system outside the database.

Summary

When multiple users need access to the same database, it's essential to ensure all users have the same data. One of the ways to accomplish this is to create multiple copies of the database, one of which is designated as the Design Master. The Design Master is usually the original copy of the database from which replicas are created. As users work with the database, the changes are synchronized among all copies.

As the multiple users make changes to the data, provisions must be made to prevent conflicts from occurring. Various record-locking schemes are available in Access, some of which are quite lenient, while others are more strict.

APPLICATION
DEVELOPMENT

MOUS Exam Activities Explored in This Chapter

Level	Activity	Section Title
Expert	Use the Database Splitter	Splitting the Database
Expert	Replicate a database	Creating a Replica with Access
		Creating a Replica with Briefcase
		Backing up the Database
		Recovering the Design Master
		Restoring a Regular Database

The
Complete
Reference

Chapter 27

Securing a Database

So far, we've discussed limiting user access to a database to maintain data accuracy and integrity. Record-locking helps prevent inadvertent data corruption. Now, we look at avoiding intentional interference with a database. The main purpose of database security is to prevent unauthorized access to the information, either for viewing or editing. A second, no less important, goal of database security is to prevent design modifications by unqualified individuals. Even the slightest change in a form design or a data validation rule can cause problems, which can be difficult to locate and correct.

Access provides two levels of security for databases:

■ Global protection through the use of database passwords

■ User-level security based on the Access security model

You can protect an entire database or single objects in the database, as well as distinguish between users and offer different levels of access to each.

 The subject of database security is complex and this chapter only begins to open the discussion. Consult other resources, including the Access Help topics for more complete information about security procedures and techniques.

Securing a Database with a Password

Protecting a database with a database password is more appropriate for the single-user database than for a networked, multiple-user database, however, it's the simplest way to keep the information from prying eyes. You must have exclusive use of the database to assign a password. Anyone who knows the password can open the database. You can also assign passwords to a security account, as well as for Visual Basic code protection. See the section titled "Protecting Visual Basic Code" for more information about how code security was changed with Access version 2000.

While this method is secure, it applies only to opening the database. Once open, the data and all the database objects are available to the user for viewing or editing unless other types of security have already been defined, as described later. In addition, Access stores the password in an unencrypted form, which may compromise your database security. To be safe, always make a back-up copy of the database before adding the password and store the copy in a secure location.

 Don't use a password for a database you plan to replicate. You can't synchronize replicated databases if they have assigned passwords.

To add password protection to a database, make sure all other users have closed the database, and then do the following:

1. Open the database in Exclusive mode by checking the Exclusive option in the Open dialog box.

2. Choose Tools | Security | Set Database Password. The Set Database Password dialog box appears. This menu command isn't available if the current database is a member of a replica set.

3. Enter the password you want to use in the Password box, repeat it in the Verify box, and then click OK. If the two entries aren't the same, Access asks you to reenter the password in the Verify box.

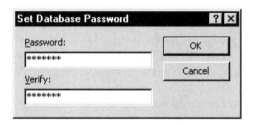

Caution *Don't forget your password! You won't be able to open the database and there's no means by which to bypass the requirement for a password. Always select a word you can remember easily, such as the name of your favorite cat. As a backup, write it down in a safe place, just in case.*

The next time you try to open the database, Access requires you to enter the password.

To remove the password, open the database again in Exclusive mode and choose Tools | Security | Unset Database Password. Then enter the password in the Unset Database Password dialog box and click OK.

Note *Some security problems may occur if one of the tables in a password-protected database is linked to a second database that doesn't require a password. The password for the first database is stored with the linking information in the second database. Then any user who can open the second database can also open the linked table in the protected database. The password is also stored in an unencrypted form in the unprotected database, making it readable to any user.*

APPLICATION
DEVELOPMENT

Securing a Multiple-User Database

When multiple users of a database exist, security becomes more complicated. Not all users require access to all parts of the database, yet someone must be responsible for every object in the database. Organizing users in groups helps simplify the security problem. You can allow each group to carry out specific actions on specific objects in the database. All the information about the workgroup is stored in a separate file called the *workgroup information file* (WIF).

Understanding the User-Level Security Model

The user-level security scheme has two advantages: no user can inadvertently break the application by making design changes and sensitive data is protected. The Access user-level security model is based on the concept of workgroups consisting of a group of users who share data in a multiuser environment. The members of the workgroups are listed in user and group accounts. A *group account* is a collection of *user accounts.*

Each member of the workgroup is allowed a specific amount of freedom with respect to the database and its objects. For example, members of one group account may be permitted to enter and edit data, but not to modify a form design. Another group may be allowed to view only specific data and be denied access to sensitive information.

The four elements of the Access security model are users, groups, permissions, and objects.

- A *user* is a person who uses the database. In a secured database, the user must sign on with his or her name and password to use the database.

- A *group* is a set of users who have the same security level and need access to the same areas of the database.

- A *permission* grants a user or group the right to perform a specific act on a database object. For example, the Open/Run permission gives the user the right to open a database, form, or report or to run a macro.

- An *object* refers to any of the Access tables, queries, forms, reports, macros, or modules in addition to the database itself.

Users and groups are granted permissions to carry out specific actions on database objects. Two types of permissions exist:

- Explicit permissions granted directly to an individual user.

- Implicit permissions granted to a user who's a member of the group that enjoys that permission. If the user is removed from the group, the permissions are revoked.

The user's set of permissions is the intersection of the two types of permissions.

Table 27-1 describes the permissions that can be granted to any user or group for specific types of objects. Permissions can be further limited to individual objects.

Permission	Allowed Actions
Open/Run	Open a database, form, or report, or run a macro.
Open Exclusive	Open a database for exclusive use.
Read Design	Open any object in Design view, but not make changes.
Modify Design	Open any object in Design view and make modifications or deletions.
Administer	Full access to all objects and the security system, including the right to assign permissions to other users.
Read Data	Open tables and queries for viewing, but not for editing or entering data.
Update Data	Open tables and queries for viewing and editing existing data, but not inserting or deleting data.
Insert Data	Open tables and queries for viewing and adding new data, but not for modifying or deleting existing data.
Delete Data	Open tables and queries for viewing and deleting data, but not for modifying or adding data.

Table 27-1.   *User-Level Security Permissions*

You can assign these permissions to users and groups in the WIF as described later in this chapter.

Another concept in the security model is that of *ownership*. All database objects must be "owned" by some user. The owner is responsible for the object and has the ultimate authority over its design, use, and availability to other users. The user who creates a new object or imports one from another database is by default the owner of the object and always has Administer permission on the object. The owner can transfer ownership to another user or group.

Built-in Groups and Users

An Access database comes equipped with a built-in group and a built-in user. The built-in Access groups are

■ The *Admins* group in which all members are administrators of the database. Administrators have full permissions on all objects in the database.

■ The *Users* group, which includes all the individual user accounts in the database. All members of the Users group by default have permissions on all newly created objects in the database.

The two groups are identical for all databases and cannot be deleted or renamed. Furthermore, neither group can be made secure.

The built-in Access user is *Admin*, who is a member of both built-in groups. The Admin user is in every copy of System.mdw, the system file created when you installed Access. Each Admin user has permission to open, view, and modify all the data and every object in every Access database, including those on other computers. As a result, the first step in securing a new database is to use the Workgroup Administrator to define new administrator and user accounts. After the new accounts are established, remove the Admin user account from the Admins group.

Creating a Workgroup

The default workgroup is defined in a workgroup file created by the Access Setup program and stored in the folder where you installed Access. When you want to define user-level security, you create a new WIF to contain the user and group accounts for all the members of the workgroup. The new WIF also contains the passwords used by the users. The security accounts in the WIF can be assigned permissions for databases and objects. The permissions are stored in the secure database, rather than in the WIF.

New with Access 2002, you no longer have to run the Wrkgadm.exe program to create a workgroup. The Workgroup Administrator is available from the Security submenu on the Tools menu.

Before creating a new workgroup, decide where you want to store the WIF. You can modify the default WIF, use an existing file, or create a new one. For a secure WIF that can't be duplicated, don't use the default file. If you want to use an existing file, be sure it was created with a unique *workgroup ID* (*WID*). The location of the WIF is stored in the Windows Registry.

To create a new WIF, use the Workgroup Administrator, as follows:

1. Close any open database and choose Tools | Security | Workgroup Administrator.

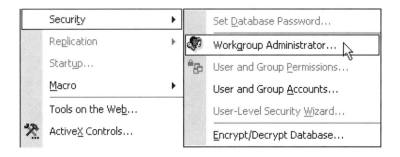

2. The Workgroup Administrator dialog box explains the purpose of a WIF and offers three buttons: Create, Join, and OK. Click Create to start a new WIF.

3. The Workgroup Owner Information dialog box (see Figure 27-1) displays the registered owner name and organization. Accept the entries or change them as necessary. The Name and Organization entries may contain up to 39 alphanumeric characters.

4. Enter a unique string of between four and twenty characters in the Workgroup ID box, and then click OK. The WID is a form of workgroup password, which is case-sensitive.

5. In the next dialog box, type a new name for the WIF. You can also change the folder where it will be stored by typing a new path or by clicking Browse to specify the new path. Then click OK.

6. The final dialog box (see Figure 27-2) asks you to confirm the workgroup information you entered. Before clicking OK, copy down all the information in the dialog box exactly as it appears. You can click Change to return to the Workgroup Owner Information dialog box and change any of the entries. Click OK when you finish. If the file already exists, you're asked to confirm the overwrite.

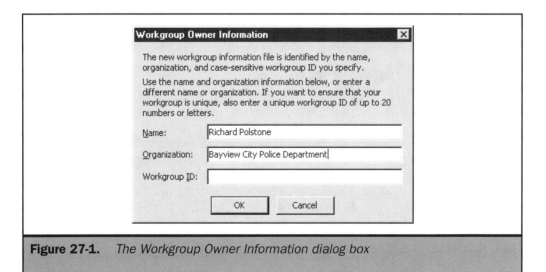

Figure 27-1. *The Workgroup Owner Information dialog box*

APPLICATION DEVELOPMENT

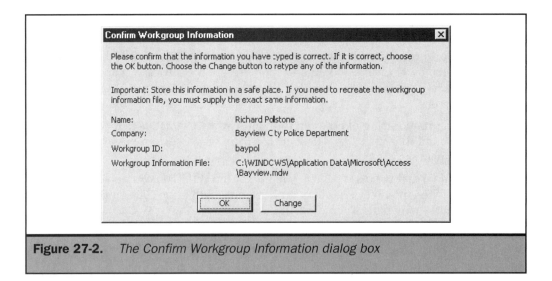

Figure 27-2. *The Confirm Workgroup Information dialog box*

 Be sure to write down the exact entries you made in the Name, Organization, and Workgroup ID boxes in the Workgroup Owner Information dialog box and keep the copy in a safe location away from unauthorized users. If the WIF is damaged and you need to restore it, you must have the exact information or you won't be able to access the database.

After you click OK, the Workgroup Administrator builds the information file and changes the system Registry, so the new WIF is used the next time you start Access. Any new accounts you add are saved in this file. If you want others to join the workgroup, save it to a shared folder in the previous step 5, and then each user can run the Workgroup Administrator to join the file.

After informing you that the file was created successfully, the Administrator returns to the first dialog box. Click OK to leave the program.

Switching to a Different Workgroup

Although only one WIF can be used at a time on the computer, you can switch between workgroups on the same computer, which is called *joining a workgroup*. You can use the Workgroup Administrator to switch from one workgroup to another if you secured databases from two different sources or if you want to return to the default system WIF. To do this, start the Workgroup Administrator as previously mentioned and click Join in the first dialog box. In the Workgroup Information File dialog box, enter the name of the WIF you want to use or click Browse to locate it. After clicking OK, the Administrator displays a confirmation message. Click OK again, and then click Exit to leave the Workgroup Administrator.

> **Microsoft Access** ✕
>
> ⚠ You have successfully joined the workgroup defined by the workgroup information file 'C:\WINDOWS\Application Data\Microsoft\Access\Bayview.mdw'
>
> OK

Note *You can also use command-line options to specify which workgroup information file to use when you open a specific database. Create the WIF and store it in an accessible location. Then create a shortcut that opens the database and add the /wrkgrp option to the command line, followed by the location of the workgroup file you want to use.*

Organizing Security Accounts

Security accounts are usually organized by groups, each with a specific set of permissions. The administrator users are members of the Admins group and have full permissions for the secure database and its objects. The Admins group may contain as many users as you want, but only one user account can own the database. Other users in the Admins group may own objects in the database and have full permissions with the objects they own.

Group accounts are made up of users and can also own database objects. Group accounts are used to assign a common set of permissions to multiple users. A user can belong to more than one group, in which case the user has the sum of all the group permissions. User accounts consist of a single user who may own objects and have permissions for those and other objects in the database. User accounts are stored in the WIF the users will join when they access the database.

Maintaining database security is much easier if the users are organized by department or function, and they're assigned to group accounts. The group is assigned permissions on the basis of its activities and needs. When users log on to a secured database, they log on with their user account, not the group account. After logging on, the users inherit all the permissions of the group, plus any permissions assigned specifically to the individual user accounts.

To create any type of security account, you must log on as a member of the Admins group. Then you can use the User and Group Accounts dialog box (see Figure 27-3) to do the following:

- Create and delete user and group accounts
- Add a user to a group
- Remove a user from a group
- Change or clear a user password

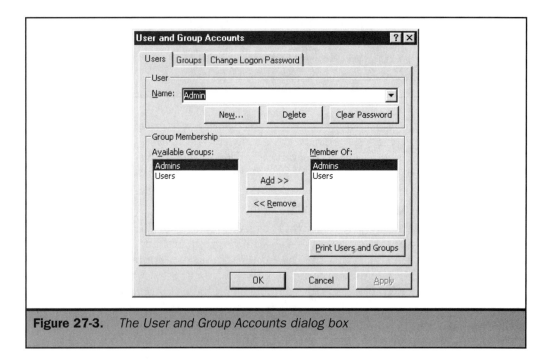

Figure 27-3.   *The User and Group Accounts dialog box*

Every account must have a *personal ID (PID)* that's saved with the account name. This is not the same as a password, which each user creates later.

Creating and Deleting User Accounts

To create a new user account, do the following:

1. Start Access with the workgroup in which you want to include the new user account, and then open a database.

2. Choose Tools | Security | User and Group Accounts.

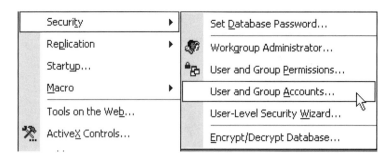

3. In the User and Group Accounts dialog box, click the Users tab, and then click New. The New User/Group dialog box opens.

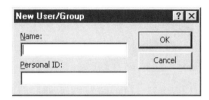

4. Type a unique name for the new user account and a PID. The user name can contain up to 20 characters and, in addition to letters, can include numbers, spaces, accented characters, and symbols, except for the following:

- Characters that have special meaning: " \ [ ] : | < > + = ; , .? *

- Leading spaces

- ASCII control characters (ASCII 10 through 31)

 For security reasons, the PID should be a unique combination of alphanumeric characters that have no actual meaning and don't form a word.

5. Click OK when you finish.

 Be sure to keep a copy of the exact name and PID you enter for the new account. You will need them if you have to re-create the account. The PIDs are case-sensitive, but the names aren't.

To delete a security user account, open the Users tab of the User and Group Accounts dialog box and select the name of the account you want to delete from the Name drop-down list. Then click Delete and respond Yes when asked for confirmation or respond No to cancel the deletion. After you make all the necessary deletions, click OK to close the dialog box.

 You can't delete any of the built-in users from the Users group and you must leave at least one user in the Admins group. You also can't delete the Admin user account.

Creating and Deleting Group Accounts

Creating a new group account is much the same as creating a new user account, except you do it in the Groups tab (see Figure 27-4) in the User and Group Accounts dialog box, instead of the Users tab.

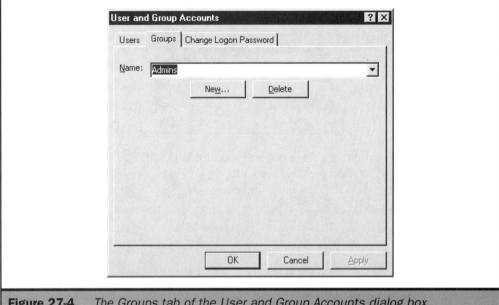

Figure 27-4. *The Groups tab of the User and Group Accounts dialog box*

When you click New, the same New User/Group dialog box opens where you enter the name and PID for the new group. The group name follows the same rules as the user name.

To delete a group, on the Groups tab, select the group name from the Name drop-down list, and then click Delete. Respond Yes to the confirmation request to delete the group or respond No to cancel the deletion, and then click OK.

 The built-in Admins and Users group accounts can't be deleted.

Adding and Removing Users from Groups

As with all activities involving database security, you must log on as a member of the Admins group to add a user to a group or to remove one from a group. To add a user to an existing group, do the following:

1. Start Access in the workgroup containing the security accounts. If you don't know whether you're starting in the right workgroup, use the Workgroup Administrator to see which workgroup is current and, if necessary, change the WIF.

2. Open a database and choose Tools | Security | User and Group Accounts, and then click the Users tab.

3. Select the name of the user you want to add to the group from the Name drop-down list.

4. In the Available Groups box, select the group you want the user added to, and then click Add. The group name is added to the Member Of list.

5. If you want to add this user to other groups, repeat step 4. If you want to add other users to groups, repeat steps 3 and 4.

6. Click OK when you finish adding users to the groups.

To create a security administrator account, create a new user account and add it to the Admins group.

To delete a user from a security group, open the Users tab of the User and Group Accounts dialog box as before and select the name of the user you want to remove in the Name box. Then select the group name in the Member Of box and click Remove. Repeat these steps for all the users you want to remove and click OK when you're finished.

The default Users group is an exception. Because Access automatically adds all users to the group, the only way you can remove a user account from the Users group is to delete the account altogether.

To document the arrangement of users and the groups they belong to, click the Print Users and Groups button on the Users tab of the User and Group Accounts dialog box. You have the option of printing only the users, only the groups, or both. The list of users includes the user names and the groups each user belongs to. The list of groups includes the group names and the users who belong to that group.

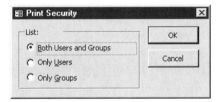

Creating or Changing Account Passwords

By default, when you add a new user account to a workgroup, Access assigns a blank password to it. The Admin account also is assigned a blank password. To make sure no one can log on using an existing user name, you should have all users enter a unique password for their accounts.

To create or change a security account password, do the following:

1. Start Access using the workgroup the account is in and log on with the user account name.

2. Open a database and choose Tools | Security | User and Group Accounts.

3. Click the Change Logon Password tab (see Figure 27-5) and enter the current password in the Old Password box. If no password has been defined for the account, leave the box blank.

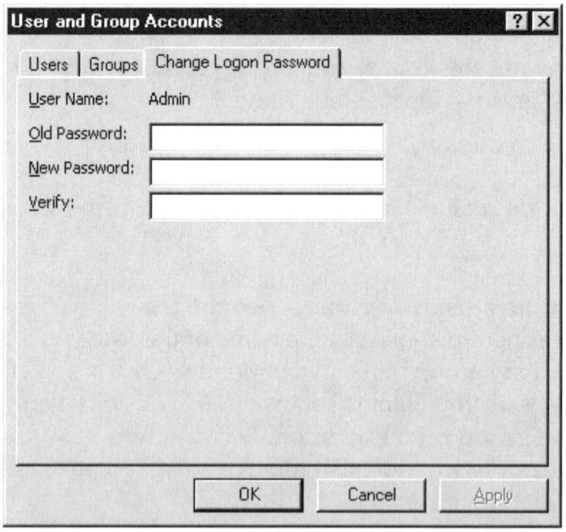

Figure 27-5. *The Change Logon Password tab*

4. Enter the new password in the New Password box. The password is case-sensitive and can contain up to 20 characters, including any except the ASCII 0 (Null) character.

5. Enter the same characters in the Verify box and click OK.

Caution *Be sure to copy the password you entered and save it in a secure place. If you forget it, an Admins user must clear the password before you can log on to the database and create a new password.*

To clear a password, you must log on as a member of the Admins group, and then do the following:

1. Open the User and Group Accounts dialog box, and then click the Users tab.

2. Select the user account name from the Name drop-down list and click Clear Password.

3. Repeat step 2 to clear other user account passwords, and then click OK when finished.

Requiring Logon

All users of a database are automatically logged on as Admin users until you add a password to the Admin user account. Then, when users try to start Access, they must enter their user account names and passwords. To activate the logon procedure, do the following:

1. Start Access using the workgroup to which you want to add the logon password.

2. Choose Tools | Security | User and Group Accounts, and then click the Users tab.

3. With the Admin user account selected in the Name box, click the Change Logon Password tab. (Refer to Figure 27-5.)

4. Leave the Old Password box blank because no password exists yet, and then type the new password in the New Password box, up to 20 characters. Passwords are case-sensitive.

5. Type the password in the Verify box, and then click OK.

The next time you or another member of the workgroup starts Access, the Logon dialog box appears. Enter the user account name in the Name box and the account password in the Password box. Then click OK.

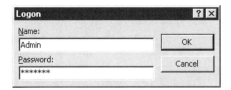

To turn off the Logon dialog box, start Access using the workgroup whose logon you want to deactivate, and then return to the Users tab of the User and Group Accounts dialog box. Select Admin in the Name box and click Clear Password. Deactivating the Logon procedure doesn't remove any user-level security you defined for the database; it only lets you start Access without logging on.

Assigning or Changing Permissions and Ownerships

Permissions are granted to a user, either explicitly to the individual user account or implicitly to the group account of which the user is a member. The owner of an object is the user who created it. To assign default permissions or to change permissions or ownerships for a database object, you must be one of the following:

■ A member of the Admins group of the WIF in use when the database was created.

■ The owner of the database object.

■ A user who has Administer permission on the object.

To view or change the permissions and ownerships, choose Tools | Security | User and Group Permissions. Figure 27-6 shows the User and Group Permissions dialog box with one tab for working with permissions and another for changing object ownership.

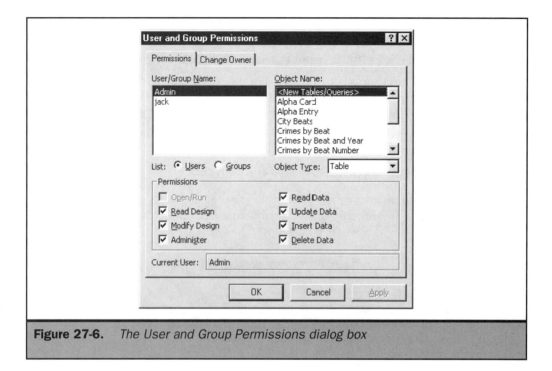

Figure 27-6.   *The User and Group Permissions dialog box*

| Note | *In addition to the list of all existing objects in the database, you can select <New Tables/Queries> to include any future tables or queries in the permissions. If you selected a different Object Type from the list, the <New...> option in the Object Name list shows that object type.* |

Assigning and Removing Permissions

To work with permissions, open the database that contains the objects using the WIF that contains the user or group accounts to which you want to assign permissions. Then open the Permissions tab of the User and Group Permissions dialog box. In the Permissions tab, you can do any of the following:

■ To see what permissions a user already enjoys with respect to a specific object, click the Users option button, and then select the user account name in the User/Group Name box. Select the type of object from the Object Type drop-down list, and then select the specific object from the Object Name box. The check boxes in the Permission area show which permissions have been explicitly granted to the user. Implicitly granted permissions show in the group permissions list.

- To see what permissions a group has on an object, click the Groups option button and select the group account name from the User/Group Name box. Then select the object type and name the same as for user account permissions. The Permission area shows the permissions currently granted to the group account.

- To change permissions, select the user or group account first, and then select the object type. Select one or more objects from the Object Name list and check or clear the permissions.

Tip *To select multiple contiguous objects in the list, drag the mouse pointer over the names. To select multiple scattered objects, hold down CTRL and click the objects you want.*

After finishing with each object or set of objects, click Apply to keep the dialog box open for more changes. When finished, click OK.

Some tips to remember when changing permissions are the following:

- Some permissions are related and, when granted, automatically grant other permissions. For example, if you click the Update Data permission for a table, the Read Data and Read Design permissions are automatically checked because they are needed to modify data. Similarly, if you clear the Update Data or Read Data permission for a table, the Modify Design permission is also automatically cleared.

- If you modify an object and save it with the same name, the permissions are unchanged. If you save it with a different name, you must reassign the permissions.

- When you change permissions on objects containing Visual Basic code, such as forms, reports, or modules, the permissions don't take effect until you close and reopen the database.

Transferring Object Ownership

To transfer ownership of an object to a different user or group, click the Change Owner tab of the User and Group Permissions dialog box (see Figure 27-7). The list in the upper box displays the objects of the type selected in the Object Type box together with their current owners.

To change ownership of an object, do the following:

1. Select the object type in the Object Type box.

2. Select one or more objects in the list. You can select them by dragging over the names or holding CTRL as you click the names.

3. Click Groups to see a list of group accounts in the New Owner drop-down list or click Users to see the user accounts.

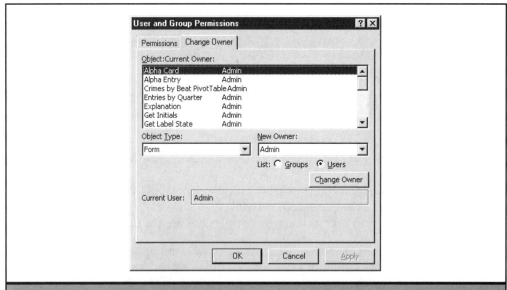

Figure 27-7.   *The Change Owner tab of the User and Group Permissions dialog box*

4. Select the group or user name from the New Owner list and click Change Owner. Ownership is transferred to the group or user selected in the New Owner list.

5. Make any other changes in ownership and click OK when finished.

Tip   *When you transfer ownership of an object to a group account, all members of the group are automatically granted ownership permissions on the object.*

You can also transfer ownership of a complete database to another administrator. Start Access using the new administrator's workgroup ID and create a new blank database. Then import all the objects from the original database to the new one.

Note   *Query objects have default permission options that control viewing data returned from the query or after running an action query. The Run Permissions option on the Tables/Queries tab of the Options dialog box can be set to Owner's or User's. If you choose Owner's, all users have the owner's permission to view or run the query. However, only the owner can change the query design or transfer ownership of the query to another user. If you choose User's, the permissions for that class of users apply and any user can change the query or transfer its ownership to another user. The change in setting applies only to new queries. Existing queries are unaffected.*

Securing a Replicated Database

Because you cannot secure a replicated database with a password, the best way is to set user permissions on each of the replicated database objects. The permissions you set don't get in the way of synchronization.

If you prefer, you can place a replica in a directory not shared by other users. Then you can use the Microsoft Replication Manager to accomplish indirect synchronization.

Removing User-Level Security

Removing the user-level security created for a database involves returning ownership to the database and all the objects in it to the default Admin user. To do this, you need to log on as the workgroup administrator who's a member of the Admins group. After logging on to the database, give the default Users group full permissions on all objects. Then exit Access and log on again as Admin, and then create a blank database in which to import all the objects from the original database.

| **Caution** | *The result of this process is a completely unsecured database. Be aware that any workgroup or user can open the new database. The workgroup information file in effect when you import the objects from the original database is the one used for the Admin group with the new database.* |

To remove the established user-level security, do the following:

1. Launch Access, log on as the workgroup administrator and open the secured database.

2. Choose Tools | Security | User and Group Permissions and click the Permissions tab.

3. Click Groups and select Users in the User/Group Name box.

4. Select Table from the Object Type drop-down list and select all the tables in the database by dragging the mouse pointer down through the whole list.

5. Select all the available permissions for that type of object and click Apply.

6. Repeat steps 4 and 5 for each of the other types of objects, and then click OK.

7. Exit Access and restart, logging on as Admin.

8. Create a new blank database and import all the objects from the original database into it.

| **Note** | *If the users are still using the current workgroup information file, clear the password for Admin to avoid the Logon dialog box. If you reverted to the default workgroup information file, this step isn't necessary.* |

Repairing a Damaged Workgroup Information File

Everyone hopes it won't happen but, sometimes, the workgroup information file becomes damaged and you won't be able to open the database that relies on that WIF. The way you can solve this problem depends on whether you used the Workgroup Administrator to create the WIF in the first place and whether you saved a backup copy of the file.

- No matter how you created the WIF, if you saved a backup copy, use Windows Explorer or other program to copy the most recent copy of the file to the folder where Access is installed or to the original path.

- If you used the default WIF and didn't make a backup copy, you must reinstall Access to re-create the default WIF.

- If you used the Workgroup Administrator to create the file and didn't save a backup copy, you must use the Administrator to re-create the file. Start the Administrator by typing in the same case-sensitive name, organization, and workgroup ID you used before.

- If you used the Workgroup Administrator to join a file on a path other than the folder where Access is installed and didn't save a backup copy, create a new copy using the same method you used to create the original file and type the same case-sensitive name, organization, and workgroup ID entries as before.

The security account information is stored in the WIF so, if you have to create a new file, you need to re-create the security accounts with the same names and personal ID entries. The permissions and object ownership are stored in the secure database and needn't be re-defined, but they must be connected with the same accounts as in the original database.

Securing a Database with the User-Level Security Wizard

The User-Level Security Wizard creates a backup copy of the current database with the same name and the .bak file extension. Then it secures the selected objects in the current database. All relationships and linked tables are retained. The secure database is owned by the user who runs the wizard.

The wizard also secures the object types you specify by revoking all permissions on them from the Users group. During the sequence of nine dialog boxes, you can specify which users belong to which groups, add and delete users, and edit passwords and PIDs. The last step in the process is to encrypt the new database. The original database remains unchanged.

When the Security Wizard is finished, it displays a report of the new workgroup information file. If you secure your Visual Basic code with a password, it's included in the Security Wizard report. Be sure to print and store the report in a safe place. If necessary, you can use the report to re-create the workgroup information file.

To secure a database with the User-Level Security Wizard, do the following:

1. Open the database you want to secure and choose Tools | Security | User-Level Security Wizard.

2. The first Security Wizard dialog box opens (see Figure 27-8) with the choice of creating a new WIF for the database or, if one already exists, modifying the current WIF. Choose Create A New Workgroup Information File, and then click Next.

3. Enter a unique WID in the second dialog box. The WID is a 4 to 20 character string that is case-sensitive. One is already provided for you, but you can replace it with your own. You can also include your name and company name if desired. In the lower pane of the dialog box, choose whether you want this to be the default WIF for this database or if you'd rather create a shortcut to open the new secured database. Click Next.

4. The third Security Wizard dialog box (see Figure 27-9) contains seven tabs showing all the objects in the current database. By default, the wizard secures all the objects, but if you want to leave some of them as they are now, clear the check marks by the object names. Click Next after setting individual object security.

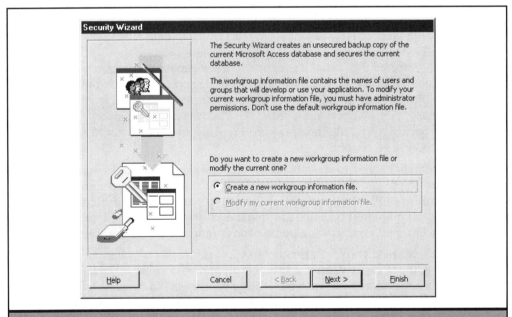

Figure 27-8. *Starting the Security Wizard*

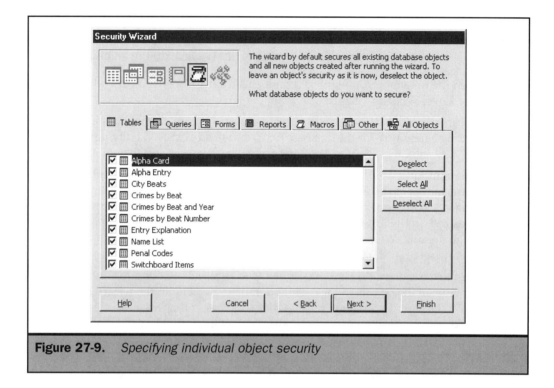

Figure 27-9. *Specifying individual object security*

5. If you protected the Visual Basic code in the database with a password, you must enter it in the next Security Wizard dialog box. The wizard won't create the WIF without it. If you haven't protected the code and you want to secure it, exit the Security Wizard and use the VB Editor to add a password. Then return to the Security Wizard. The password then appears in the wizard report after the database is secured.

6. The next dialog box (see Figure 27-10) enables you to set up the security group accounts you want included in the WIF. To see the specific permissions allowed for each predefined group, select the group name and read the text in the Group permissions box. Each group has a unique Group ID. Table 27-2 lists the groups and describes the permissions granted to each.

7. In the next dialog box, you can assign some permissions to the Users group. By default, the Security Wizard withholds all permissions from the Users group. This is because anyone who has a copy of Access is a member of the Users group and would be awarded the same permissions. If you choose Yes in this dialog box, the wizard displays a stern warning (see Figure 27-11). Choose No and click Next.

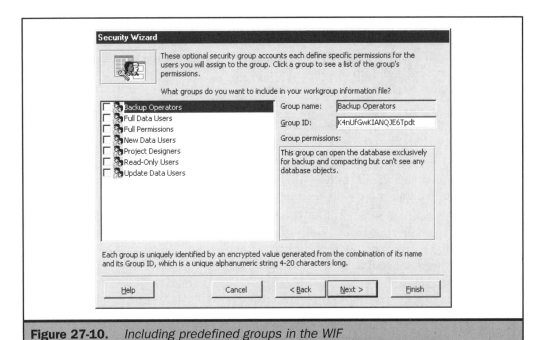

Figure 27-10. *Including predefined groups in the WIF*

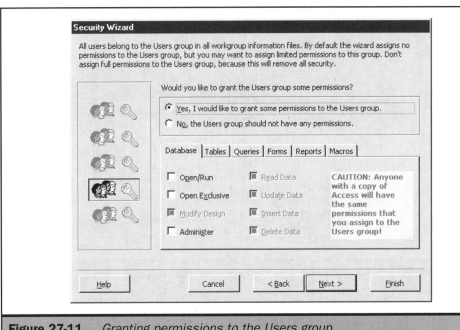

Figure 27-11. *Granting permissions to the Users group*

8. To add new users to the WIF, enter the user name, password, and PID in the next dialog box (see Figure 27-12). You can also delete a user or edit an existing password or PID by selecting the name from the list on the left. Any passwords you have created with the wizard are printed in the report the wizard creates. Click Next to move to the next dialog box.

9. In the next to last Security Wizard dialog box (see Figure 27-13), you assign the users added in the previous dialog box to a group. Actually, you can work either way in this dialog box:

■ If you choose Select a User and Assign the User to Groups, the drop-down list contains the list of users and the group names appear below. Check the group name and choose user names to add from the drop-down list.

■ If you choose Select a Group and Assign Users to the Group, the drop-down list contains the group names and the user names appear in the box below. Select a group name from the drop-down list, and then check all the user names you want assigned to the group.

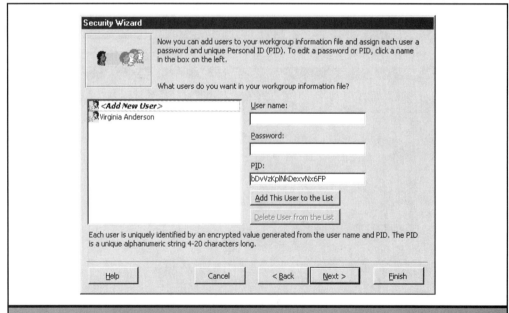

Figure 27-12.   *Adding users to the workgroup information file*

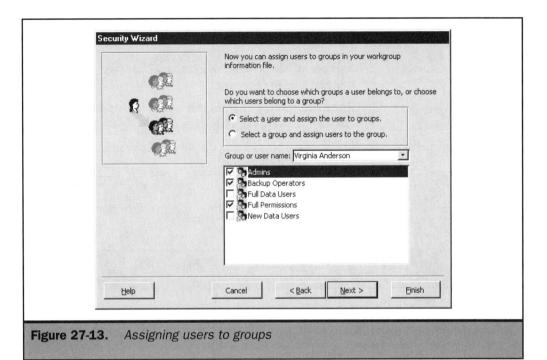

Figure 27-13. *Assigning users to groups*

10. Click Next to move to the final dialog box, where you're prompted for a name for the unsecured backup copy of the database. Click Finish to complete creating the new WIF. The backup copy has a .bak file extension.

After creating the new WIF, the Security Wizard displays a report of the setting used in the file. You can save the report as a file, or you can print and store it in a safe place. If you ever need to rebuild the WIF, you'll need all this information.

Group	Permissions Granted
Backup Operators	Open exclusively for backup and compacting, but can't see any database objects.
Full Data Users	Full permissions to edit data but can't modify any designs.

Table 27-2. *Permissions for Predefined Groups*

Group	Permissions Granted
Full Permissions	Full permissions on all objects, but can't assign permissions to other users.
New Data Users	Read and insert data, but can't delete or update data. Also can't modify any designs.
Project Designers	Full permissions to edit data and all objects, but can't alter tables or relationships.
Read-Only Users	Read all data, but can't change data or designs.
Update Data Users	Read and update data, but can't insert or delete data. Can't alter any designs.

Table 27-2.   *Permissions for Predefined Groups* (continued)

Only members of the Admins group and the Admin user have access to objects in the new database. No permissions have been granted to the Users group, so you need to add them to control the security of the database and its objects.

Other Security Measures

While creating secure workgroups can ensure complete security of a database, other, less rigorous methods exist for maintaining database safety. Encrypting a database renders it unreadable. Hiding specific objects from user view can prevent sensitive data from leaking to unauthorized users. When you deliver an end-user application, you want to make sure no user can modify any of the Visual Basic code behind forms or reports or in the database modules. If you compile the code in it, the code cannot be read or changed.

Encrypting and Decrypting a Database

When you encrypt a database, it's compacted and rendered completely unreadable by a word processor or any utility program. Encrypting a database doesn't restrict access to database objects. Decrypting the database reverses the process and restores its original form.

The database must be closed before you can encrypt it. In addition, you must have enough storage space for both the original and the encrypted versions of the database file. To encrypt a database, do the following:

1. In an empty Access window, choose Tools | Security | Encrypt/Decrypt Database.

2. In the Encrypt/Decrypt Database dialog box, select the database you want to encrypt and click OK.

3. In the Encrypt Database As dialog box, specify the drive and folder where you want to store the encrypted database, and then click OK. You can even save the encrypted database in a Web folder by choosing Web Folders from the Save In drop-down list.

If you choose to store the encrypted database with the same name and in the same folder as the original database, Access asks for confirmation before replacing the original file. If you confirm this, Access automatically replaces the original file with the successfully encrypted version. If the encryption fails, the original database isn't deleted.

 If the database is protected by user-level security, you must be a member of the Admins group with Open Exclusive permission for all the tables to encrypt or decrypt the database.

To decrypt an encrypted database, repeat the same steps as for encrypting and specify the drive and folder for storing the decrypted file from the Decrypt Database As dialog box.

 If you're trying to encrypt a version 1.x database and one of the object names includes a backquote character (`), the encryption will fail. Use the original Access version to rename the object and change all references to it accordingly. Then try the encryption again.

Hiding Database Objects

If you have objects in your database that you want to keep from view, you can prevent them from appearing in the Database window. Hiding the objects doesn't provide more security than simply removing them from view. To hide an object, do the following:

1. Select the object in the Database window and click the Properties toolbar button, or right-click the object name and choose Properties from the shortcut menu.

2. Click the Hidden option at the bottom of the General tab of the Properties dialog box (see Figure 27-14) and click OK.

When you return to the Database window, the object no longer appears. To see the names of objects that have been hidden, choose Tools | Options and click the View tab.

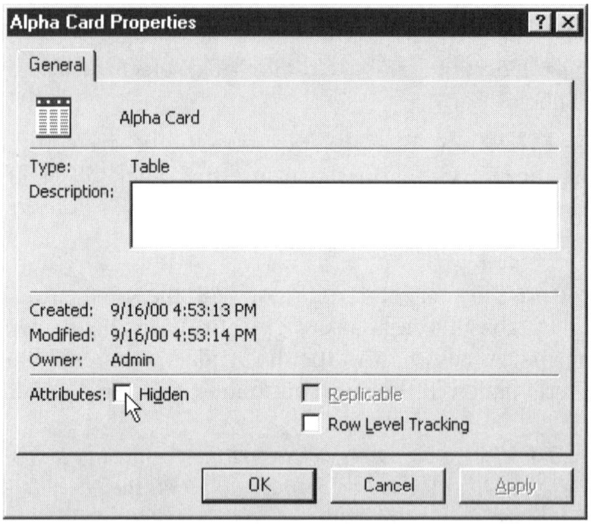

Alpha Card Properties

General

Alpha Card

Type: Table
Description:

Created: 9/16/00 4:53:13 PM
Modified: 9/16/00 4:53:14 PM
Owner: Admin

Attributes: ☐ Hidden   ☐ Replicable
             ☐ Row Level Tracking

OK   Cancel   Apply

Figure 27-14. *The General tab of the Properties dialog box*

Click the Hidden Objects option in the Show group, and then click OK. The hidden objects appear dimmed in the Database window, but they can still be opened.

To remove the Hidden property, open the General tab of the Properties dialog box and clear the Hidden option.

Another way to hide an object from view is to use a system file prefix with the object name. For example, name a new form or rename an existing form with the USys prefix and it won't appear in the Forms tab of the Database window, unless you selected the System Objects option in the Show group of the View Options dialog box. You can also use the MSys prefix to hide objects.

Protecting Data Access Pages

Securing data access pages presents a different problem because a page consists of two parts: the shortcut stored in the database and the corresponding HTML file stored separately. To protect the data access page, make the database read-only. To protect the HTML file, use the Windows security system to make the file and folder where it is stored read-only. If you already published the page, make the HTML file on the Web server read-only.

Data access pages present a two-way street through which viewers can reach the database. You must also consider protecting the Access database from unauthorized users. If the database is protected by user-level security, you can enable the security measures through the page. Make sure you specify the correct workgroup information file in the connection information for the page and that the file is in a public network accessible to all users. Use the Data Link Properties dialog box if you need to modify the connection to the page.

If you need a password to open a database connected to a page, you must enter the password the first time you view the page.

Never save the user name and password with a data access page. This would allow any user to log in to the database from the page. If you want the viewer to be prompted to log in, change the connection to the page. In the Data Link Properties dialog box, clear the Allow Saving of Password check box in the Connection tab.

Other security issues that arise when data is viewed on a data access page are the following:

- How to protect a spreadsheet in a page, so viewers cannot change data in the cells, sort or filter data, or change any of the spreadsheet properties.

- Instead of requiring a user to log on with a user name and password, you can create a page that automatically detects who the user is and displays only selected records.

For more information about these and other aspects of protecting data access pages, see the Microsoft Office and Windows Help topics.

Protecting Visual Basic Code

Modules and the Visual Basic code behind forms and reports can be protected by a password, which you set in the Visual Basic Editor. Modules are no longer protected by user-level security with the User-Level Security Wizard, but the forms and reports that refer to the code are secured by the User-Level Security Wizard.

Another way to protect the Visual Basic procedures is by saving the database as an MDE file, which compiles all the modules, removes all editable code, and compacts the database. The Visual Basic code still runs, but it cannot be read or edited. See Chapter 28 for more information about delivering a database to an end-user as an MDE file.

Always make a backup copy of your database before trying to save it as an MDE file.

Summary

This chapter has introduced you briefly to the highly complex problem of securing an Access database against both inadvertent and intentional intrusion. The techniques you can use to protect data and the database design from unauthorized users range from requiring a password to log on to the database to the multidimensional user-level security strategy.

In the next chapter, you learn how to complete an end-user application by adding user interactive tools, such as a switchboard, custom toolbars, and menus, as well as how to prepare the application for delivery.

MOUS Exam Activities Explored in This Chapter

Level	Activity	Section Title
Expert	Assign database security	Securing a Database with a Password Creating a Workgroup—Creating or Changing Account Passwords Securing a Database with the User-Level Security Wizard
Expert	Encrypt and decrypt databases	Encrypting and Decrypting a Database

Chapter 28

Developing an End-User Application

It's one thing to build a database management system for your own use and a completely different challenge to develop one for someone who isn't well acquainted with Access. Access and Office provide a number of tools that can help you create a user-friendly, graphical, and customized system for users who haven't the need or the time to study how Access works.

The end-user system can be developed to match the user's workplace in style, tone, and type of business. For example:

- You can display the company name and logo in the Access title bar and add images that depict the type of business, such as construction, medical, or financial.

- You can create a main switchboard featuring the most common work activities with subordinate switchboards containing other operations.

- For users who aren't completely computer literate, you can provide comprehensive help in the form of screen tips and What's This? Help topics.

- You can make provisions to deal with user errors in the form of understandable error explanations, a means of possible correction, or at least some user-friendly consolation.

Other features can protect the database from accidental or intentional changes and from damage. The system must also be easy to install and maintain, requiring complete documentation both for the user and for the technical staff.

The Theory Behind End-User Applications

The basic principles behind an end-user application are the ease-of-use and a specific focus on the activities the user plans to undertake. The terminology used in the displays must relate to the user's environment and be appropriate to the tasks. An Access application developer must spend time with the ultimate user (end user) in the target workplace to get a feel for the application design.

The importance of error-trapping cannot be overstated. When an application stops unexpectedly with no explanation, the user is helpless to find and correct the problem. This can be both frustrating and disenchanting. While you're developing the application, you can, of course, make it as error-immune as possible. In addition, try to forecast all errors that could occur because of user input or other data errors and add error-trapping statements with corrective actions to the event procedures. If the error cannot be corrected within the procedure, display appropriately worded messages to the user and preserve the data as well as possible. See Chapter 25 for a discussion of error-trapping with Visual Basic event procedures.

The distribution of controls on a form is important to the user. The order in which the user moves through the controls by pressing TAB is also important. Place the most commonly accessed controls early in the tab order. Others may be skipped in the tab order entirely. For example, bound text box controls that display data, but aren't to be edited by the user can be removed from the tab order by setting the control's Tab Stop property to No. They can still be viewed on the screen. Another convenience is to set, as the default on a form, the control or button most often used by the user.

When you expect a process to take quite some time to complete, a good idea is to keep the user aware that something is happening. Users often begin pressing keys at random when they think the system has stopped working. One tool is the Hourglass macro action that converts the mouse pointer to an animated hourglass turning over and over as the action progresses. You can use the Hourglass method to run the macro action in a Visual Basic procedure.

If the application is going to be used by multiple users on a network, you can split the database into a shared back-end containing all the data with linked local front-ends containing the forms, reports, and other objects relevant to each user's specific mission.

Building the Application

Designing and building an application for another user is an iterative process. You must expect to return to the design repeatedly as the user discovers how versatile and helpful an Access application can be. For example, the end-user may not be aware that you can display a form with one or more subforms to display the information from several sources at once. You can also invoke a secondary form and synchronize data between the two forms on the screen.

You can go about designing a database application for another user in two ways: top-down or bottom-up. With the *top-down* approach, you start with the user and design the user-interactive components, such as the forms and reports, and then work your way down to the distribution of data in the related tables. When you use the *bottom-up* approach, you begin with the database and work with the database architect to design the queries, forms, and reports necessary to make use of the information.

In this chapter, we concentrate on the top-down approach to designing an Access application. The first step is to find out exactly what the user wants out of the system and how the user wants the output presented. With that in mind, go about digging up the sources of the data needed to provide that output. After assembling all the data sources and identifying each item of data, you can begin to distribute the data to related tables, and then create the necessary Access objects.

The intended user should be kept in the loop while you're designing the forms and reports. The user interfaces are extremely important and the user must feel comfortable with them. Often the printed output has already been determined, for example, as preformatted standard reports, but some leeway may occur for innovation.

After completing the development, document the application with two levels of documentation:

- Technical design and program information for the application maintenance team.
- Operational manuals for the intended user that describe, with numbered steps, how to make use of the application.

APPLICATION DEVELOPMENT

Creating Startup Screens

When the application first opens, the main switchboard gives the user a choice of activities to embark on. The list contains the most frequently undertaken activities with one or more choices leading to other switchboards that list the less-popular activities. Figure 28-1 shows the Police database main switchboard discussed in Chapter 21.

The first two options open the two data entry forms most often used: Alpha Card and Alpha Entry. The third option displays another switchboard with a list of the other forms in which the user can enter and edit other types of data.

The most commonly printed report is the Alpha Card with Entries report, so that option follows in the switchboard. The Preview Other Reports option opens a report switchboard with a list of other reports that are printed less often, including mailing labels.

The final option in the main switchboard is to exit this database without exiting Access. It's important to allow the user to close the database and return to the empty Access desktop to open another database or perform other work.

Many applications also present a welcoming screen, called a *splash screen*, which appears for only a short period of time before giving way to the switchboard. Figure 28-2 shows an example of a splash screen that welcomes the user to the Bayview City Police database. The screen remains in view for five seconds.

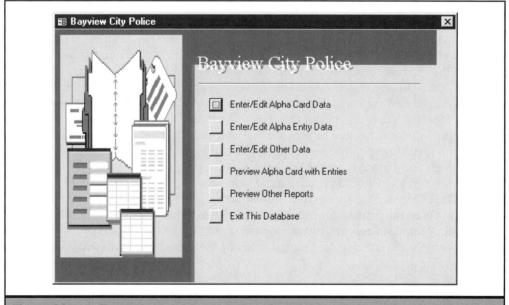

Figure 28-1. *The main switchboard for the Bayview City Police database*

Figure 28-2.   *A sample splash screen*

Tip   *Always give the user the option of preventing the splash screen from appearing when the database opens. Some users become annoyed when they have to view the welcoming screen when all they want to do is get to work. The check box at the bottom of the Welcome screen accomplishes this. You learn how to set this option next.*

To create such a splash screen, build the design and change the following form Format properties:

- Type **Welcome** in the Caption property.
- Set Default View to Single Form.
- Set Scroll Bars to Neither, and set Record Selector, Navigation Buttons, and Dividing Lines to No.
- Set Auto Center to Yes.
- Set Auto Resize to No.
- Set Border Style to Dialog.
- Set Min Max Buttons to None.

- Set the Picture property to the path of the desired background image.
- Set the Picture Size Mode to Stretch and the Picture Alignment to Center.

To limit the amount of time the form displays, you can set two event properties that relate to timing: the On Timer and Timer Interval properties found on the Event tab of the form's property sheet. The Timer event occurs when the interval set in the Timer Interval property elapses. Set the Timer Interval to 5,000 cycles, which is equivalent to five seconds. You want the splash screen to close when the time is up and the main switchboard to open in its place, so attach the following CloseSplash macro to the On Timer event property:

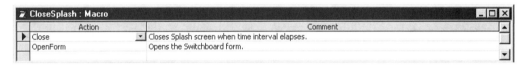

To let the user disable the splash screen, add a check box or option button control to an unobtrusive area of the screen, as shown in the previous Figure 28-2, and then do the following:

1. Enter **HideStartupForm** in the Name property box for the new control.

2. Add a label control next to the new check box and enter **Don't show this screen again** in the Caption property box.

3. Change the Fore Color property of the label to white, so you can see the text against the dark background.

Finally, attach a function to the On Close property of the form that tests the state of the HideStartupForm check box and sets the Display Form/Page startup option accordingly. The Display Form/Page is actually a property of the database that must be set in the Startup dialog box or with Visual Basic code or a macro. If the check box is checked when the form closes, the property is set to Switchboard when the splash screen closes. If not, it remains or changes to Splash. The setting takes effect the next time you open the database.

The following HideStartupForm procedure is attached to the On Close event property of the form:

```
Function HideStartupForm()
'Uses value of HideStartupForm check box to determine the setting
'for StartupForm property of Police database. (The setting is
'displayed in Display Form box in the Startup dialog box.)

If Forms!Splash!HideStartupForm Then

'HideStartupForm check box is checked so change the
'startup form to Switchboard.
```

```
   CurrentDb().Properties("StartupForm") = "Switchboard"
Else
   CurrentDb().Properties("StartupForm") = "Splash"
End If
End Function
```

After you set the On Timer and Timer Interval properties, and switch to Form view to see how the form is progressing, it closes itself when the interval is up. Luckily, Access asks if you want to save any change before closing the forms but, to be safe, save the form design before switching to Form view.

The HideStartupForm function is one of the functions stored in the Global module of the Police database. The IsLoaded and IsOpen functions are also included in the module.

Creating Custom Command Bars

When you create an end-user application, you usually replace the built-in menu bars and toolbars with customized command bars. This way, you can prevent the user from making any design changes or modifying any macros or Visual Basic procedures.

For example, when the Alpha Card form in the Police database is displayed, the user actions available in the menu bar and the toolbar should be limited to the following:

- View and edit existing data in both the Alpha Card and Alpha Entry tables.
- Add new records and delete existing records.
- Sort and filter records.
- Run Page Setup and preview or print data in the form.

The user shouldn't be permitted to switch to form Design view, to start a new database, or to open a different database from Form view.

Similarly, the report Print Preview menu bar and toolbar should limit the user's actions to:

- Zooming to a different magnification.
- Running Page Setup, and exporting or printing the report.
- Viewing multiple pages of the report.

Once the custom menu bars and toolbars are created, they're attached to the Menu Bar and Toolbar form and report properties. See Chapter 20 for the details of creating custom command bars.

Creating the Custom Police Form Menu Bar

To give the user the opportunity to use either menu commands or toolbar buttons to carry out an activity, create a custom menu bar and a custom toolbar containing

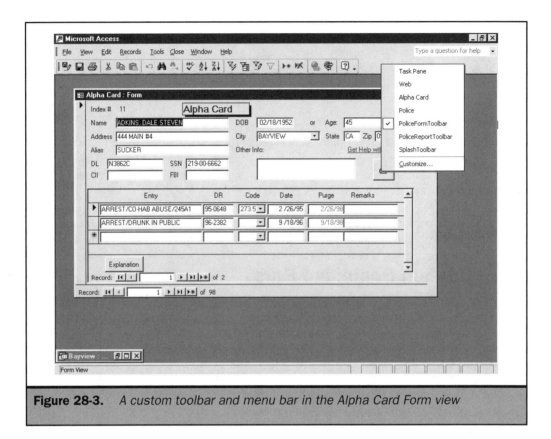

Figure 28-3.   *A custom toolbar and menu bar in the Alpha Card Form view*

relatively equivalent actions. Figure 28-3 shows the Alpha Card data entry form with customized command bars. As you can see from the shortcut menu, the visible toolbar is the custom PoliceFormToolbar.

The File menu contains only a few of the commands normally found in the built-in File menu.

To create this menu, don't try to customize the built-in File menu. Any changes you make to a copy of the built-in menu, such as removing a command, are repeated in the built-in menu. Instead, do the following:

1. Right-click one of the showing toolbars and choose Customize from the shortcut menu.

2. Click New in the Toolbars tab, enter **PoliceFormMenu** as the name for the new toolbar, and click OK.

3. Click the Properties button, change the Type property to Menu Bar, and click Close.

4. Switch to the Commands tab, and then scroll down the Categories list and select New Menu, the last item in the list.

5. Drag New Menu from the Commands box to the new menu bar.

6. Right-click the New Menu and rename it **&File** (remember, the & symbol creates an access key for the command).

7. Click slowly at the bottom edge of the File menu to create an empty command box below the edge.

8. Select the File category and drag Save from the Commands list to the empty container under File.

9. Repeat step 8 to add the other commands to the File menu.

Most of the commands on the custom File menu are found in the File category. Close is a command in the View category. Sometimes, you need to explore to find the command you want.

> **Tip** *If you can't find the command you want in one of the categories in the Customize dialog box, show a toolbar that includes the button that carries out the desired action and copy it to the custom menu. Hold CTRL while you drag it from the built-in toolbar to the custom menu. To make this look more like a command than a button on the menu bar, right-click the command and select Text Only (in Menus) from the shortcut menu.*

The View menu has only a single command, which opens the Alpha Entry datasheet in front of the Alpha Card form. To add the custom View menu to the PoliceFormMenu, show the PoliceFormMenu and do the following:

1. Add a New Menu to the menu bar as before and rename it **&View**.

2. Click slowly at the bottom edge of the View menu to create an empty menu box.

3. Choose All Forms in the Categories box and drag Alpha Entry from the Commands box to the empty container under View.

The Edit menu is also created from a New Menu command and renamed **&Edit**. All the commands placed in the Edit menu are found in the Edit category except Go To Field, which is in the Records category.

As you add menus and commands to the menu bar, you can place lines between menus by right-clicking a menu and choosing Start a Group from the shortcut menu. The dividing line appears at the left or above the selected menu item.

The Records menu includes Filter and Sort submenus in addition to several commands. The submenus are created once again by dragging the New Menu commands to the Records menu, and then renaming them **F&ilter** and **&Sort**. The specific filter and sort commands are then dragged from the Commands box to the container to the right of the submenus. All the individual commands can be found in the Records category.

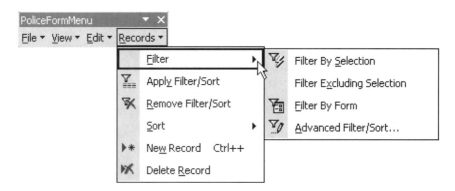

The Tools menu, also created from a New Menu command, contains only two commands:

- Spelling, which runs the Spelling Checker.
- AutoCorrect, which opens the AutoCorrect dialog box.

The Spelling command is dragged from the Records or Tools category, but the AutoCorrect command doesn't appear in any of the Commands lists. The AutoCorrect command must be copied from the Tools menu on the built-in menu bar or created by attaching a macro that carries out the desired action to the menu command.

To copy AutoCorrect Options from the Tools menu, show both the built-in menu bar and the PoliceFormMenu by checking them in the Toolbars tab of the Customize dialog box. With the Customize dialog box open, place the pointer on the Tools menu, and then press and release the left mouse button to open the list of commands. (If you click quickly, the list of commands doesn't open.) Then press and hold CTRL while you drag the AutoCorrect Options command to the Tools menu on the PoliceFormMenu. Drop it beneath the Spelling command.

 You may have to move the PoliceFormMenu menu bar out of the way to see both Tools menus at once.

As an alternative, you can write your own response to a menu command. The first step is to create a macro that opens the AutoCorrect dialog box. Then attach it to the On Action property of the Auto Correct menu command. The AutoCorr macro contains a single action: RunCommand with the AutoCorrect argument.

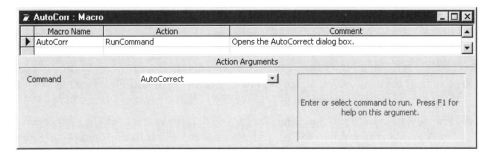

The AutoCorrect command is created as a Popup command by doing the following:

1. Show the PoliceFormMenu and open the Customize dialog box.

2. On the Commands tab, select File in the Categories box.

3. Drag the Custom command to the Tools menu and drop it under the Spelling command.

4. Right-click Custom, enter the name **&AutoCorrect**, and select Properties.

5. Click the On Action drop-down arrow, choose AutoCorr from the list of available macros, and then click Close. Figure 28-4 shows the Properties dialog box for the new AutoCorrect command.

An advantage exists to copying commands from built-in command bars. If you copied the AutoCorrect command from the Tools menu of the built-in menu bar, the control properties would automatically include the built-in Help topic. The HelpContextID property shows 3257 in the Microsoft Help file.

The remaining menus on the PoliceFormMenu are the following:

■ Close, which is a single command, the same as the command added to the File menu.

■ The Window and Help menus, which are copies of the built-in menus.

Creating the Police Form Custom Toolbar

Toolbars usually contain buttons that carry out the same actions as the more commonly used menu commands. The Police database custom form toolbar is designed to follow that pattern.

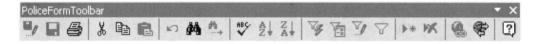

The source of the commands on the Police form toolbar, named PoliceFormToolbar, is as follows:

■ The first three buttons—Save Record, Save, and Print—are found in the File category of commands.

■ The next six buttons—Cut, Copy, Paste, Undo, Find, and Find Next—are in the Edit category of commands.

■ The next nine buttons—Spelling, the two Sort buttons, the four Filter buttons, and the New Record and Delete Record buttons—are found in the Records category.

■ The next two buttons—Hyperlink and Web Toolbar—are from the Web category.

■ The last button—Microsoft Access Help—is from the Window and Help category.

All the buttons on the PoliceFormToolbar are set to display in the Default Style, which is showing only the button image when placed on a toolbar.

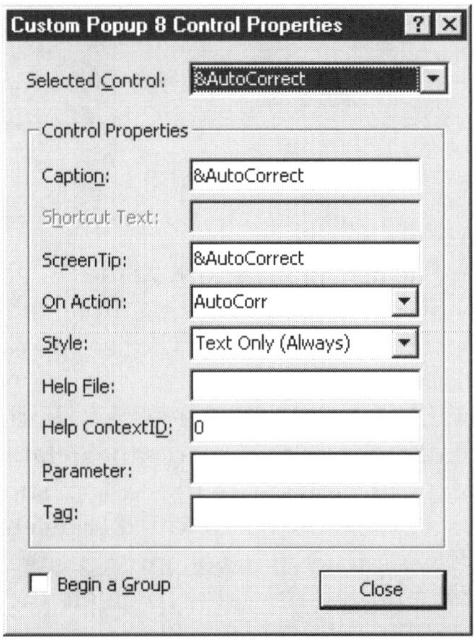

Custom Popup 8 Control Properties   ? ✕

Selected Control: &AutoCorrect   ▼

Control Properties

Caption: &AutoCorrect

Shortcut Text:

ScreenTip: &AutoCorrect

On Action: AutoCorr   ▼

Style: Text Only (Always)   ▼

Help File:

Help ContextID: 0

Parameter:

Tag:

☐ Begin a Group   Close

Figure 28-4.   *The AutoCorrect menu command properties*

Creating a Custom Shortcut Menu

Shortcut menus are a little more complicated to create. You must work with the
Custom menu on the Shortcut Menu bar. To create a shortcut menu for forms in the
Police database, open the Customize dialog box and do the following:

1. Select Shortcut Menus in the Toolbars list on the Toolbars tab and click New.

2. Enter the name **PoliceFormShortcut** for the new shortcut menu in the New
   Toolbar dialog box and click OK.

3. Select the new menu name in the Toolbars list and click Properties.

4. Change the Type property to Popup and click Close.

5. Click the Custom menu in the Shortcut Menu bar to display the new empty
   shortcut menu, and then click to the right of the empty shortcut menu to create
   the container for the menu commands.

6. Drag the commands you want to see in the shortcut menu from the Commands
   list to the container.

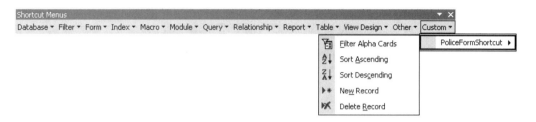

Once the commands are added to the shortcut menu, you can change their properties, just as with any other command. For example, the first command text is changed from &Filter by Form to &Filter Alpha Cards. You can also change the style to eliminate the images or change the images.

After completing the shortcut menu, set the form's Shortcut Menu property to the name of the new shortcut menu. This replaces the default form shortcut menu. Figure 28-5 shows the Alpha Card form with the custom shortcut menu displayed.

Shortcut menus are also a little more complicated to delete. If you create a shortcut menu and decide you don't want to keep it, you must change its type from Popup to Toolbar or Menu Bar before you can delete it. To delete the shortcut menu, do the following:

1. Open the Customize dialog box and click the Toolbars tab.

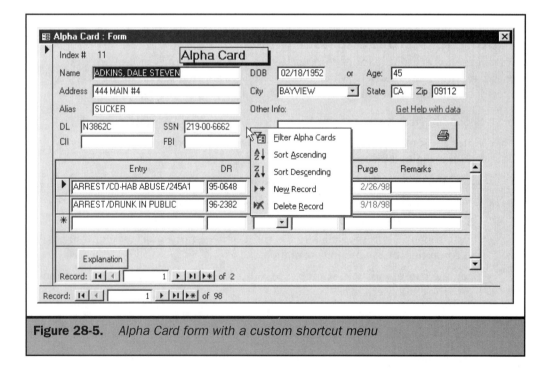

Figure 28-5. *Alpha Card form with a custom shortcut menu*

2. Then click Properties and select the name of the shortcut menu you want to delete in the Selected Toolbar box.

3. Change the type to Toolbar in the Type list. The shortcut menu name now appears in the Toolbars box on the Toolbars tab like a regular command bar.

4. Select the name of the shortcut menu and click Delete.

Creating Custom Command Bars for a Report

Reports require much simpler command bars than forms because less user interaction occurs with data in a report. Most of the actions deal with previewing the report in some magnification and printing the report. You can also add the capabilities to run Page Setup and export the report to another database or another report within the current database. Figure 28-6 shows the Alpha Card Report from the Police database in Print Preview with the custom toolbar and menu bar.

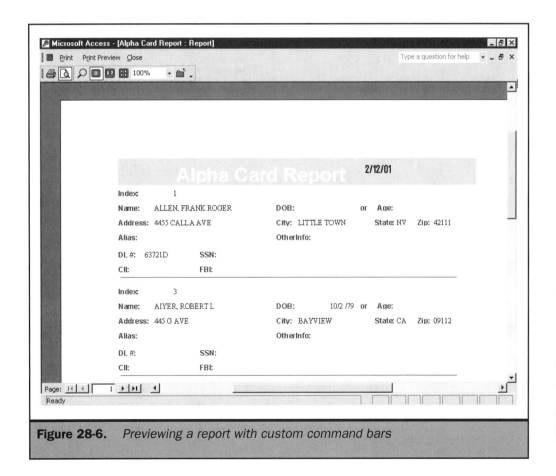

Figure 28-6. *Previewing a report with custom command bars*

Looking at the toolbar first, the Print, Print Preview, and Close buttons are dragged from the File category and the Zoom button is from the View category. The Zoom box, in which you can enter a percentage magnification, is also found in the View category. The three buttons that display the report in one or more full pages don't appear in any of the command categories, but can be copied from the built-in Print Preview toolbar.

To copy these buttons, do the following:

1. Show the built-in Print Preview toolbar by selecting it in the Toolbars tab of the Customize dialog box.

2. Hold down CTRL while you drag the buttons one by one from the built-in toolbar to the position you want in the custom toolbar. If you don't hold down CTRL, you'll remove the button from the built-in toolbar.

3. The second and last buttons are found in the File category of commands.

Once you start the new menu named PoliceReportMenu, click Properties and change the Type property to Menu Bar. In this custom menu bar, the Print menu should contain different commands than what the built-in menu contains, so create a New Menu and change its name to **&Print**. Then drag the following commands from the File Commands list in the Customize dialog box to the Print menu:

- Page Setup
- Save As
- Export
- Print

Use the New Menu tool to create a new menu named **P&rint Preview**. The Print Preview menu contains the commands that display multiple pages of the report, which can be copied from the custom toolbar or the built-in toolbar. Copy them to the Print Preview menu the same way as to the toolbar, and then change the style of the One Page and Two Pages commands to Text Only (in Menus).

Multiple Pages is actually a submenu, so you can't change its style. The command opens a grid where you can drag the mouse button over the cells to indicate the type of multiple-page preview you want.

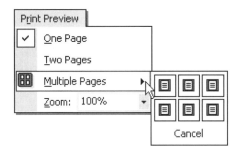

Refer to Chapter 20 for more information about customizing menus and toolbars.

Attaching Custom Command Bars

When you create a custom menu bar or toolbar for a form or report, you can display it with the form or report, instead of the built-in command bar. To do so, open the form or report in Design view, and then open the property sheet. On the Other tab, click the down arrow in the Menu Bar property and select the name of the custom menu from the list. Similarly, select the custom toolbar from the drop-down list in the Toolbar property and the shortcut menu from the list in the Shortcut Menu Bar property.

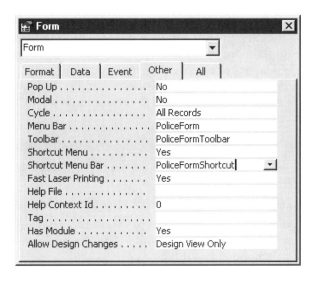

 If you forgot to change the command bar's Type property to Menu Bar, it won't appear in the list of custom menus in the Menu Bar property box.

Adding Special Touches

Any special features you can add to the forms and reports to make the user's job easier are worth the effort. ScreenTips, status bar text, customized toolbars and menu bars, visual aids, and explanations are all helpful touches to add to an end-user application. You can also add hyperlinks that jump to specific sections in the User's Manual to display help with using the data entry form. The next section discusses documenting the application and adding hyperlinks.

Adding ScreenTips and Status Bar Text

Among the special touches you can add to an application are ScreenTips and messages that display in the status bar. ScreenTips display short text relating to the control on which the mouse pointer is resting. For example, the Choose Report form that offers a choice of reports to preview has ScreenTips attached to the command buttons, as shown in Figure 28-7. The tips explain what occurs when the user clicks the button.

Status bar text appears when the corresponding control has focus. To add a ScreenTip or a status bar message to a control, type the text of the tip in the control's ControlTip Text or Status Bar Text property. You can add such tips to any type of control.

The default status bar text for a text box control is the field description you entered in the table design.

Displaying an Hourglass

Another helpful special touch is the Hourglass action, which you can use to occupy the user visually during the execution of a macro that takes a long time to run. The only argument for the Hourglass action is Hourglass On, which is set to Yes (display the hourglass icon) or No (leave the normal mouse pointer icon).

The Hourglass action usually changes the mouse pointer to an animated image of an hourglass that turns over repeatedly until the macro finishes. In Windows, you can change the icon by doing the following:

1. Click the Start button, point to Settings, and click Control Panel.

2. Double-click the Mouse shortcut to open the Mouse Properties dialog box, and then click the Pointers tab.

3. Select Animated Hourglasses in the Scheme list.

4. Select the Busy pointer and click Browse to see the icons available in the Cursors folder. Select a different icon and click Open. Figure 28-8 shows the Busy pointer changed to a rolling globe icon.

To restore an individual pointer icon to its original setting, select the pointer and click Use Default. Click OK when you finish setting the mouse properties.

Your mouse property choices may be different, depending on the brand of mouse.

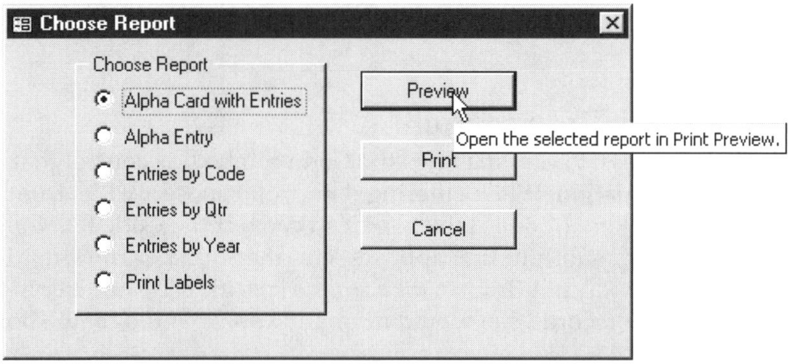

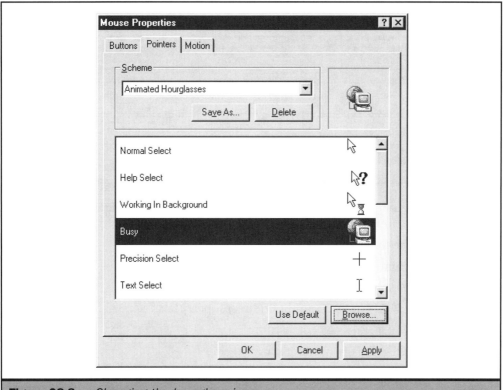

Figure 28-7. *ScreenTips describe the buttons' functions*

Figure 28-8. *Changing the hourglass icon*

In Windows NT, you set the hourglass icon in the Wait property in the Cursors dialog box of the Windows Control Panel. The default is the same hourglass icon as in Windows 95 and 98.

Displaying Lookup Information

The Alpha Entry data entry form includes the Code combo box control that displays the code with an explanation. When entering data, you choose a value from the list, which comes from the Penal Codes table. You can convert the Code text for control field on the Alpha Entry subform that appears with the Alpha Card form to a combo box. The combo box displays the information for the specific code number in the record without the other seven records that would normally appear in the combo box in the data entry form.

To convert the Code field in the Alpha Entry subform, open the subform in Design view and do the following:

1. Select the Code field and choose Format | Change To | Combo Box. The combo box down arrow is added to the control.

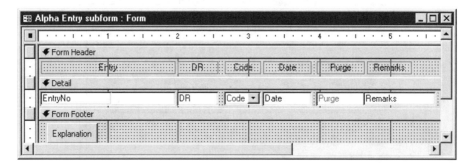

2. Open the property sheet and choose Penal Codes from the Row Source property drop-down list (Data tab).

3. Change the following Format properties:

   ■ Set Column Count to 2.

   ■ Set Column Heads to No.

   ■ Enter .5";1.5" in the Column Widths property box.

   ■ Change List Rows to 1.

   ■ Enter 2" in the List Width property box.

4. Save the form.

When you open the Alpha Card form, you can click the arrow in the Code field in the subform and see the description of the code value in the current field (see Figure 28-9).

Tip   *If the Penal Codes table doesn't have an entry for a blank (0) code value, the combo box displays the first record in the Penal Codes table when you click the arrow next to a blank field. To cure this, add a record to the table with 0 as the Code and No code entered as the Description.*

Setting Startup and Other Options

When you complete the application development and are ready to install it on the user's computer, choose Tools | Startup and set the following startup options.

- Enter the name of the application in the Application Title box—for example, **Bayview City Police**.
- Enter the name of the icon file you want to use in the application title bar in the Application Icon box. If you don't know the complete path and name, click the Build button to open the Icon Browser dialog box and search for the folder that contains the icon you want to use.

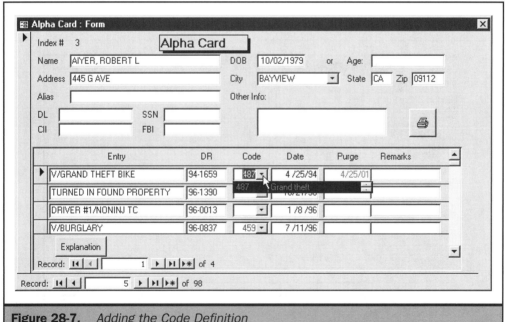

Figure 28-7.   *Adding the Code Definition*

APPLICATION DEVELOPMENT

- Choose the name of the custom global menu you want to use from the drop-down list in the Menu Bar box—for example, SplashMenu, which contains only one menu, Help.

- Choose Splash from the drop-down list of forms in the Display Form/Page box. The Splash screen was designed to display for five seconds, and then yield to the main switchboard for the database.

- Clear all the check boxes to prevent the user from having access to the built-in menus, toolbars, and shortcut menus.

- Clear the Use Access Special Keys check box. The user won't be able to display the Database window or the status bar, and won't be able to use the special keys to bypass the startup options.

Be sure to make a backup of the database before clearing the Use Access Special Keys option. If bugs are still in the application (usually some elusive ones do exist), you must be able to bypass the startup options while opening the database.

Figure 28-10 shows the completed Startup Options settings for the Bayview City Police application.

Refer to Chapter 16 for complete information about the options you can set in the Startup dialog box.

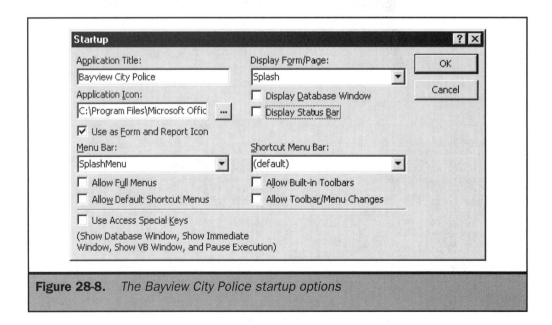

Figure 28-8. *The Bayview City Police startup options*

Setting User Workplace Options

Depending on the user environment and how the application is to be used, you can set the default workplace options to match the user's style and primary activities. Some of the default options that can be tailored to the application are the following:

- Default Datasheet options, such as the colors, column width, gridlines, and cell effects.

- Default Tables/Queries options, such as Default Field Size for Text data types, which can help conserve disk space when set to a smaller number than the default 50 characters and Long Integer setting. Set the Default Field Type to Number or Currency for an application that deals more with those types of data rather than text.

- Default View options, such as showing the status bar or the Startup dialog box when Access first starts. If you already cleared the Show Status bar in the Startup Options dialog box. you needn't clear it here, too. If you created a switchboard to display on startup, clear the Show Startup dialog box.

- Default General options, such as setting the print margins, the default database folder, and the Name AutoCorrect options. This Options tab also specifies the number of names of recently used files to display in the File menu and offers sound feedback to accompany certain tasks.

- Default Web options, such as the colors of the hyperlink before and after it's clicked, and whether to display the hyperlink underlined and with the address in the status bar. Click the Web Options button in the General tab to set these options.

- Default Edit/Find options, such as the behavior of the Find/Replace operation and whether to confirm record deletions and other irreversible actions. You can also set the Filter By Form default settings to speed the filter process.

- Default Keyboard options, such as the behavior of the ENTER, TAB, and ARROW keys.

See Chapter 16 for complete information on these default options and their settings.

Providing Maintenance with Command Line Options

As discussed in Chapter 17, it's important to optimize database performance using several techniques, one of which is to repair and compact the database regularly to check for damage, to defragment the disk space, and to consolidate the data. Repairing a database checks all the pages in the database to make sure they link properly, and validates the system tables and all the indexes. Compacting reclaims space left over from deleting objects and records, resets the incrementing AutoNumber fields, regenerates table statistics, and flags all queries so they'll be recompiled the next time you run the query.

Note *In earlier versions of Access, repair and compact were separate operations. In Access 2000 and 2002, they're combined into one database utility: Compact and Repair Database.*

When you create an end-user application, you should provide a way for the user to execute this maintenance activity without having to choose from the Tools | Database Utilities menu. You can add the /**compact** switch to the command line that starts Access and opens the database, either from the Start menu or from a shortcut on the Windows desktop.

Refer to Chapter 16 for detailed instructions for adding command-line options to the Start Menu Programs tab of the Taskbar Properties dialog box. The options control how Access starts and opens the database when you use the Start menu. To provide a different way to start Access and open a database that can repair and compact it, create a shortcut on the Windows desktop, and then add the command-line options to the command that executes when you double-click the shortcut.

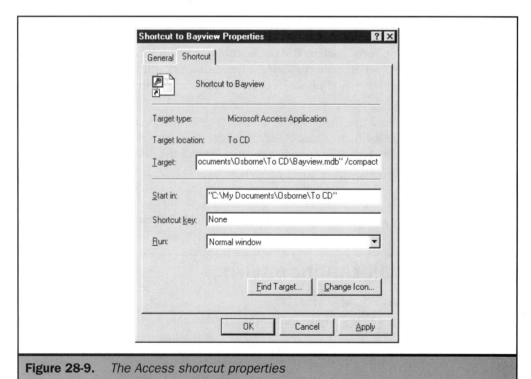

Figure 28-9. *The Access shortcut properties*

If you provide such a shortcut, the user can periodically start Access using the shortcut and automatically compact and repair the database. To create a shortcut and add the command-line option to the shortcut command, do the following:

1. On the Windows desktop, double-click the My Computer icon and locate the folder where database is stored.

2. Right-click the database icon and choose Create Shortcut on the shortcut menu.

3. Drag the new shortcut icon from the My Computer window to the desktop.

4. Right-click the shortcut and choose Properties on the shortcut menu (see Figure 28-11).

5. Click at the right end of the path after the closing quotation mark in the Target box and enter **/compact**.

6. If you want a different picture on the new shortcut, click Change Icon.

7. Select a new icon and click OK twice. The new shortcut appears on the desktop.

8. Right-click the new shortcut and choose Rename from the shortcut menu. Enter **Repair and Compact Bayview Database** as the new name.

9. Click outside the shortcut.

APPLICATION
DEVELOPMENT

When you compact a database, you must have enough disk space for two copies of the database: the original and the compacted. This is true even if you compact the database using the same name because Access first compacts to a temporary database with a different name, and then, if the operation is successful, it renames the compacted database with the original name.

In the User's Manual that you provide for the end user, include instructions about periodically using the shortcut to open the database, so it's maintained on a regular basis.

Preparing for Delivery

Even after you create, debug, and populate the database application, you're not quite through. You must generate two types of documentation for the database:

- A manual of operations for the user who needs to know how to carry out the purpose of the application.

- Detailed technical information for the database administrator and the technicians who are going to be responsible for maintaining and upgrading the application during its lifetime.

If the application is intended for a network environment, you may also need to split the database into a front-end to install on the server and back-ends to install on the local workstations. You may also need to implement a security administration system and set up work groups and permissions. See Chapter 26 for information about sharing a database with multiple users and providing security.

Creating User Documentation

The User's Manual is an important adjunct to the delivered application, especially if the intended users have little or no experience with Access. Each activity, such as entering or editing data in a form, should be described thoroughly with comments dealing with any type of mistake the user could make. Illustrations are also helpful. Figure 28-12 shows the first page of the User's Manual for the Police database system.

Once the manual is complete, you can add hyperlinks to the data entry forms that jump to the relevant text in the User's Manual. Add bookmarks to the document at the beginning of each section and at other locations the user might want to access while working in a form to get important information. Store the document in the same folder as the database, and then add a hyperlink to the form design.

Bayview City Police   User's Manual

Bayview City Police
Database Management System
User's Manual

Starting the Police Database

The Police database management system opens when you start Access 2002. The first screen is a Welcome screen that remains on the screen for five seconds followed by the Main Switchboard which offers the following choices of activity:

- Enter/Edit Alpha Card Data
- Enter/Edit Alpha Entry Data
- Enter/Edit Other Data
- Preview Alpha Card with Entries
- Preview other Reports
- Exit this Database

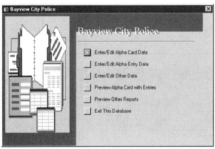

Note: If you do not want to see the Welcome screen when you start Access and open the database, check the box at the lower left of the Welcome screen, **Don't show this screen again**.

To make your selection, click on the box or in the text.

Figure 28-10.   *The Bayview City Police Database User's Manual*

The following steps show how to add a hyperlink to the Alpha Card form in the Police database that jump to the ACard bookmark at the beginning of the Enter/Edit Alpha Card Data section of the User Manual Word file that contains the manual:

1. Open the Alpha Card form in Design view, and then click the Insert Hyperlink toolbar button or choose Insert | Hyperlink.

2. In the Insert Hyperlink dialog box (see Figure 28-13), select the document file in the Current Folder that contains the User's Manual.

3. Enter **Get Help with Data** in the Text To Display box, and then click OK.

4. Drag the new hyperlink from the default upper-left corner to another position, if necessary.

5. Open the property sheet for the new hyperlink and enter **ACard** in the Hyperlink SubAddress property box.

6. Switch to Form view and try the new hyperlink.

 You can also add the subaddress directly to the hyperlink address in the Insert Hyperlink dialog box.

Figure 28-14 shows the results of clicking the hyperlink. The Access and Word windows were resized and positioned for viewing both the hyperlink in the form and the document text.

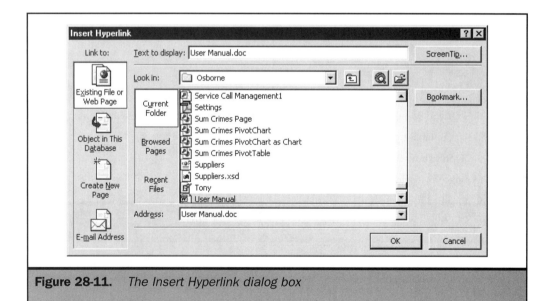

Figure 28-11. *The Insert Hyperlink dialog box*

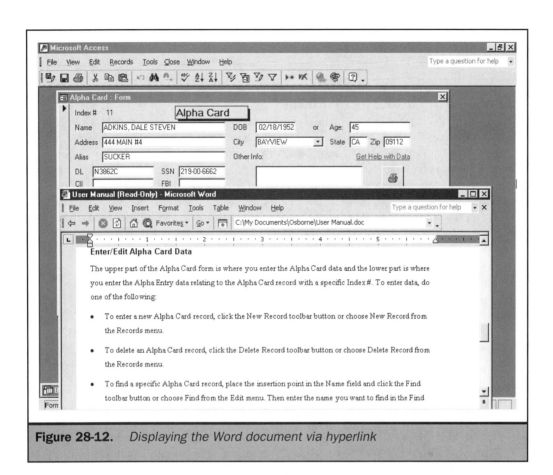

Figure 28-12. *Displaying the Word document via hyperlink*

Note *If the Access window minimizes when the Word file opens, right-click the Windows taskbar and choose Tile Horizontally to see both windows at once. You can also click Access on the taskbar and resize the windows to see the information in both windows at once.*

Depending on the ultimate anticipated file size, include explicit instructions in the User's Manual about when and how to back up the database. You may even want to add a procedure that automatically initiates the backup process at regular intervals, for example, at the end of each work day. Be sure to include instructions for restoring the database from the backup copy.

Another good idea is to keep a backup copy of the database on the local hard drive where it can easily restore the original database if it becomes damaged. Sufficient disk space must exist for this option.

If you simply want to back up individual objects, such as transaction tables that involve a lot of data changes, you can create a new empty database and import those objects to it. When it's time to back up those objects, simply import them again and confirm the overwrite.

Creating a Backup Database

Reminding the user to back up the database regularly may be the most valuable bit of advice in the User's Manual. While this isn't an insurance policy against disasters, a backup database can provide a place to start reconstruction without having to start from zero.

Unfortunately, every object you've created for the application is stored in one single file, which can become quite large—often too large to fit on a floppy disk. You can try compacting the file and see if the compressed version fits on a disk. If it's still too large, you need to back up to a tape drive or a hard drive with removable disks.

When you back up a database, you must copy two essential files to the backup medium:

■ The database file itself that contains all the objects and data in the database. The file usually has the .mdb file extension.

■ The workgroup database file that contains the workgroup security information and the users' toolbar and option settings. The system.mdw file is created automatically in the Access folder when you run Setup to install Access. You might have created a new workgroup file for the application. Be sure to copy it with the backup database.

If the workgroup file is damaged or lost, you must reinstall Access and set up the security and other options all over again. You might have created a new workgroup file for your application. Be sure to copy it with the backup database file.

To create a backup database, close the database and make sure all other users have also closed the database. If the application operates in a high-traffic, multiple-user environment, you may want to schedule backups during the night or other slow periods.

After the database is completely closed, start the backup program and copy both the .mdb and .mdw files to the destination medium. If you have additional workgroup information files, copy them as well.

If the file is small enough to fit on a floppy, open the Windows Explorer and open the folder that contains the database. Drag the filename from the Contents panel and drop it on the A: (or other floppy drive designation) icon in the All Folders panel.

You can use the Windows Backup program, which is one of the Windows Accessories, to back up the files to a floppy disk, tape drive, or other medium. Choose Start | Programs | Accessories | System Tools | Backup to start the process. Windows compresses the backup file and copies it to multiple floppy disks, if necessary. As each disk is filled, you're prompted to insert another.

NOTE: *If you don't see Backup in the System Tools menu, it might not be installed. Run Windows Setup again and add it.*

Other backup utilities, WinZip v6.3 or later, for example, can also compress and copy large files to multiple floppy disks.

Creating Technical Documentation

For the database administrator and the technical personnel, the documentation requirements are quite different from those for the end user. The administrator and technical personnel need a complete and detailed description of the database, the relationships, and every one of the objects in the database. One of the database analysis tools in Access is the Documenter mentioned in Chapter 5. With the Documenter, you can print a report of the properties, code, and permissions of all the controls on a form or report. You can document a single object or all the objects in the database. You can also print the details of the relationships between tables and the database properties.

Choose Tools | Analyze | Documenter to open the Documenter dialog box shown in Figure 28-15. The dialog box has eight tabs: one for each of the object types; one for the current database, which includes the database properties and relationships; and one listing all the objects of all types.

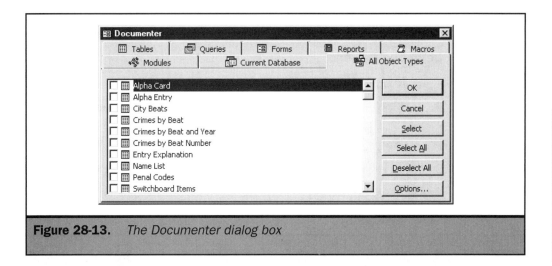

Figure 28-13.   *The Documenter dialog box*

The Documenter is one of the Additional Wizards and isn't usually installed when you run the Typical Installation. If you don't see the Documenter command on the Tools | Analyze menu, run Setup again and add the Additional Wizards component.

To create complete documentation for an application, do the following:

1. Click the All Object Types tab and click Select All.

2. If you want to specify the items to include in the description, select one of the object types and click Options. Figure 28-16 shows the options available for the table objects. To set options for other types, select one of them in the All Objects list and click Options again. Table 28-1 describes the Definition options for the other database object types.

3. Click the Current Database and click Select All. This checks Relationships and Properties.

4. Click OK.

5. After Access has created the document, you can print the object definition or export it to another file:

   ■ Click Print to print the definitions. Be forewarned, the report can be quite long.

   ■ Choose File | Export to output the definitions to an Access file as a table, an HTML file, an Excel worksheet, an RTF file, a report snapshot, or an XML document by choosing File | Export and choosing the desired output format from the Save as Type box.

Note *Creating the database definition can take quite a long time, especially if you have selected many objects.*

Object	Definition Options
Query	Same as Table, plus Parameters and SQL
Form	Include for Form: Properties, Code, Permissions by User and Group
	Include for Sections and Controls: Nothing, Names, Names and Properties (default)
Report	Same as Form
Macro	Properties, Actions and Arguments, Permissions by User and Group
Module	Properties, Code, Permissions by User and Group

Table 28-1.   *Object Definition Options for Other Database Object Types*

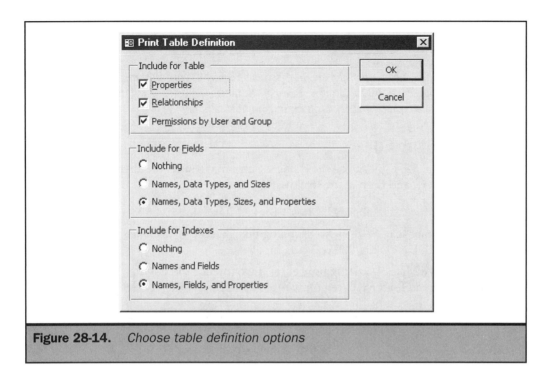

Figure 28-14.   *Choose table definition options*

Note   *The Properties button on the Forms and Report Definition dialog boxes enables you to select specific object properties to include in the documentation.*

Saving the Database as an MDE File

Creating an MDE file is a method of securing a database to be distributed to end-users. When you save a database as an MDE file, all Visual Basic code is compiled, all editable source code is removed, and the database is compacted for efficiency. The program code runs as usual, it just can't be viewed or changed. In addition, none of the forms, reports, or modules are accessible in Design view, so the design can't be viewed or modified and new objects can't be created.

No forms, reports, or modules can be imported from or exported to an MDE file. Tables, queries, and macros can, however, be exchanged with non-MDE databases because they aren't associated with any code.

Saving the database as an MDE file not only prevents changes in the code, which adds some security, but also optimizes memory use, which improves performance.

An MDE file is appropriate for the front-end database of a front-end/back-end application. In such an application, the front-end database contains the forms, reports, compiled code, and other user-interface elements of the database. The back-end

APPLICATION
DEVELOPMENT

database contains the table data. See Chapter 26 for more information about distributed processing and split databases.

 Be sure to save a backup of the original database before saving it as an MDE file. You won't be able to modify the design of any of the forms, reports, or modules in the MDE file. You must be able to work with an uncompiled version.

Creating an MDE File

Before making the MDE file, close the database and make sure all other users have also closed the database, and then do the following:

1. Choose Tools | Database Utilities | Make MDE File.

2. In the Database to Save as MDE dialog box, select the database you want to save as MDE and click Make MDE.

3. In the Save MDE As dialog box, enter the name for the database, as well as the drive and folder where you want to store it, and then click Save.

The icon for the new MDE database now shows a small padlock and a cube of blocks.

When you open the MDE database, you see the Design and New buttons on the Forms, Reports, and Modules pages of the Database window are grayed out, showing they aren't available. The Open and Design buttons are available in the Pages page. All three buttons are available on the Tables and Queries pages, but only the New button is available on the Macros page. In addition, the two or three built-in items on each page that enable you to create new objects are missing from all database pages except Tables and Queries.

Restrictions on Saving as an MDE File

In some cases, restrictions might exist on saving your database as an MDE file or you might be unable to save it as MDE at all. For example, if your database is secured with user-level security, you must meet the following requirements before saving as MDE:

- You must join the workgroup information file in use when the database was created or the one that defines the user accounts.
- Your user account must have the following permissions:
  - Open/Run and Open Exclusive permissions for the database.
  - Modify Design or Administer permissions for the tables, or you must be the owner of the tables.
  - Your user account must have Read Design permissions for all objects.

If the database is replicated, before you can save it as an MDE file, you must remove the replication system tables and properties. See Chapter 26 for information about restoring a regular database from a replica. After you save the database as an MDE file, you can replicate it again if you don't anticipate making any more changes.

If your database references another database or add-in, you must also save all the databases in the chain of references as MDE files. Start with the first database and, after saving it as an MDE file, update the reference in the next database to point to the new MDE file; then save it as an MDE file, and so on.

Summary

This chapter covered the essentials of creating an end-user application, such as startup screens and switchboards, customized toolbars and menu bars, and ScreenTips and status bar messages. It's important to set the startup and workplace options to create a productive atmosphere and, at the same time, protect the application from change or damage.

When you're ready to deliver the application, it should be accompanied by complete documentation, both for the user and for the technical staff to be responsible for maintaining the database during its lifetime.

Much more could be said about the finer points in preparing an application for delivery to an end user. The amount of help and hand-holding depends on the intended user and can be extended to visual coaching tools, such as online video instruction, pop-up help topics, and other multimedia features.

MOUS Exam Activities Explored in This Chapter

Level	Activity	Section Title
Expert	Create a Switchboard and set startup options	Creating Startup Screens Setting Startup and Other Options
Expert	Create Access Modules	Building the Application
Expert	Create an MDE file	Saving the Database as an MDE File

Chapter 29

Converting to
Access 2002

When Access 2002 arrives, you'll probably want to convert your databases to the new version immediately. You can convert from any earlier version of Access with the information presented in this chapter. You might, instead, want to keep the database in the earlier version and run it with Access 2002. This is important if your database is used by more than one user and all the users haven't upgraded to Access 2002 yet. You can convert an Access database created in Access 2.0 or later to either Access 2000 or 2002.

Secured databases present a special problem during conversion because they're associated with a user-level security workgroup information file.

This chapter discusses converting from earlier versions of Access, as well as enabling a database for use in Access 2002 without conversion. The final section in the chapter covers some of the more common problems you might encounter while attempting to convert a database.

Deciding on a Conversion Strategy

Before setting out to convert the database, you need to examine the way the database is used currently. Most likely, you'll want to convert it to take advantage of the new design features of Access 2002. You can enable the database to run in Access 2002 without conversion. *Enabling* a database lets you view and edit data, but you won't be able to save changes in the design of any of the objects. If you want to modify an object, you must open the database in the original version or convert it to Access 2002.

If your database is shared among several users, not all of whom can convert to Access 2000 or 2002, you can split the database and convert part of it and keep other parts unchanged. This way, the database can be shared by users on different versions of Access.

Once the database is converted to 2000 or 2002, you're no longer able to open it with the original version of Access. If you convert an Access 2000 database to 2002, you can't open it in 2000, but you can convert it back. You can also convert an Access 2000 or 2002 database back to Access 97, but not to version 2.0 or 95.

If you're using an Access 2000 database, you needn't convert it to 2002 unless you want to save it as an MDE file which must be in the 2002 file format. If you're converting from Access 97 or earlier, its advised you convert it first to Access 2000, and then to 2002.

Converting a Database

Before you start to convert the database, be sure to make a backup copy. Keep this copy until you're satisfied the database has converted correctly and you've mastered Access 2002. You can convert the database to a different name in the same folder or use the same name in a different folder.

To convert the database to Access 2002 file format, do the following:

1. Close the database you want to convert. If you're operating in a multiple-user environment, make sure all other users have also closed the database.

2. In an empty Access 2002 window, choose Tools | Database Utilities | Convert Database | To Access 2002 File Format.

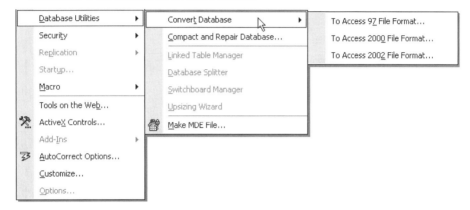

3. The Database To Convert From dialog box opens (see Figure 29-1) where you select the database you want to convert, and then click Convert.

4. In the Convert Database Into dialog box (see Figure 29-2), enter a new name for the converted database, or choose a different location and either use the same name or enter a new one. Then click Save.

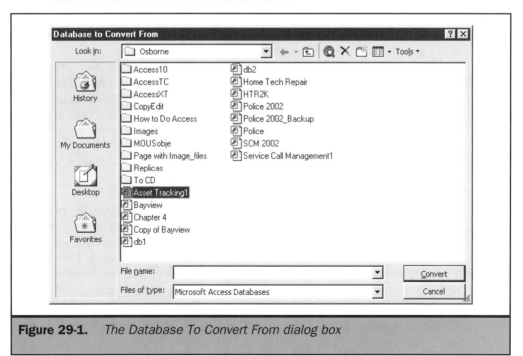

Figure 29-1. *The Database To Convert From dialog box*

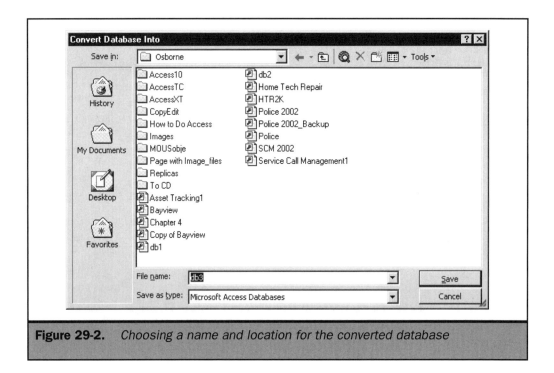

Figure 29-2.   *Choosing a name and location for the converted database*

Access converts the database to the file format you chose. You may see messages about compile errors during the conversion because some of the Visual Basic commands may no longer be valid. You can correct the code after conversion.

If the database you're converting has linked tables, make sure the tables remain in the original folder, so the converted database can find them. If Access can't find them, the converted database won't work properly. After you convert the database, you can move the linked tables to another location and use the Linked Table Manager to restore the links. The linked tables aren't converted. You must convert them separately.

Note   *Enabling or converting a secured database requires some extra steps and considerations. Converting a secured database is covered later in this chapter.*

When you convert a version 2.0 or 95 database to Access 2000 or 2002, the built-in toolbars and custom toolbars are automatically converted to the new toolbar style. Custom menu bars created in Access 95 with the Menu Builder or with macros are interpreted as the new style menu bars, but not automatically converted. Therefore, they can't be modified with the Customize dialog box until you convert them. You can use the Tools | Macro command to create new style menus, toolbars, and shortcut menus from the macros created in the earlier version. Then you can modify them with the Customize dialog box.

Converting a Workgroup Information File

If you want to take advantage of the new security and performance improvements with Access 2000 or 2002, re-create the *workgroup information file* (*WIF*) after the database has been converted. Create the new WIF by entering the exact, case-sensitive name, company, and workgroup ID you used in the previous version. If you don't get them exactly right, the Admins group will be invalid.

If you're upgrading from version 2.0 you need to convert the WIF, which is stored as an .mda file to the new .mdw file type. If you're upgrading from Access 95 or 97, you needn't convert the WIF, but you should compact it after converting the database. Then tell the users to join the compacted WIF before opening the database.

Next, re-create the group and user accounts in the new WIF, again making sure to enter the exact group or user name and personal ID for each group. When the new WIF is complete, instruct the users to use the Workgroup Administrator to join the new WIF. See Chapters 26 and 27 for more information about multiple-user environment and workgroups.

Converting Database Objects

If you don't want all the objects in the previous-version database converted to Access 2002, you can convert only the ones you want by importing them into the new 2002 database.

Converting Tables, Forms, and Reports

Database objects converted from Access 97 or 2000 should function correctly when converted to Access 2002, but objects from versions 2.0 or 7.0 (95) may experience some behavior problems. Some examples are

- If a combo box created in version 2.0 has the Limit To List property set to True, it won't accept a Null value unless Null appears in the list. In version 2002, combo boxes accept Null when the Limit To List property is set to True, whether or not it's on the list. If you want to prevent users from entering a Null value in a combo box, set the Required property of the field to Yes, which won't accept a Null value.

- In Access 2002, you can't use an expression to refer to the value of a control on a read-only form that's bound to an empty record source. In that case, the expression returns a Null value. Be sure the record source contains records before you reference the control.

- If you added a command button in version 2.0 or 7.0 that calls another application, the code will cause an error in version 2002. Delete the button and re-create it using the Access 2002 Command Button Wizard to generate the correct code.

- In Access 2000 and 2002, forms and reports have a new property, Has Module, which you can set to No if no code is behind the object. This can speed loading and save disk space because Access no longer has to look for or save room for a class module.

APPLICATION DEVELOPMENT

■ In earlier versions, you could use a control's Format Property to display different values for Null values and zero-length strings (""). In version 2000 and 2002, you must set the control's Control Source property to an expression that tests for the Null value. The IIf (immediate if) function can be used in the expression to return one string if the value is Null and another if it isn't. See Chapter 14 for an example of using the IIf function.

Converting Macros

Access 2002 uses the DoCmd object and its methods to carry out macro actions from Visual Basic code, instead of the DoCmd statement used by macros in version 2.0. When you convert your database, the DoCmd statements and accompanying actions are automatically converted to methods of the DoCmd object.

Some other macros work differently in 2002 than in earlier versions. For example:

■ The DoMenuItem macro used in Access 95 is no longer used, but is accepted for backward compatibility if you enable the database in 2002. If you convert the database, the new RunCommand macro action replaces DoMenuItem the first time the macro is saved after conversion. DoMenuItem methods used in Visual Basic code aren't affected.

■ Access 2000 and later can no longer import Excel version 2.0 or Lotus 1-2-3 version 1.0 spreadsheets. If you have a macro that uses the TransferSpreadsheet action in version 2.0, converting it to 2000 or later will change the Spreadsheet argument to Excel 3.0 (from Excel 2.0) or cause an error if the type was originally Lotus 1-2-3 version 1.0.

■ You can no longer use a SQL statement to specify the data to be used in a TransferText or TransferSpreadsheet action. For version 2002, you must first create a query that results in the data you want, and then enter the query name as the Table Name argument in the macro.

■ When you used a comparison operator to compare two expressions in a macro condition in version 2.0 and one of the expressions evaluated to Null, Access Basic returned True or False, depending on which operator you used. In Access 2000 and 2002, Visual Basic also returns Null if either of the expressions is Null. To find out whether the comparison or just one of the expressions caused the Null value, use the IsNull function with the result of the comparison.

Converting a Secured Database

To convert or even enable a secured database, you must meet specific requirements and log on with certain permissions. Access 2002 creates a new workgroup information file and makes it the current file when first installed. You must join this new workgroup information file that defines the users of the database before you can convert it. If a different file was in use when the database was secured, join that workgroup information file instead of the default Access workgroup information file.

When you log on to convert the database, you must have the following permissions:

- Open/Run and Open Exclusive permissions for the database.
- Administer permissions for the MSysACEs and MSysObjects system tables.
- Modify Design permissions for all the tables in the database or you must be the owner of them.
- Read Design permissions for all objects in the database.

The conversion process is the same as for unsecured databases once you log on with sufficient permissions.

If all the users of the database are converting to Access 2000 or later, you can convert the entire database to 2000 file format. If all the users have upgraded to 2002, convert the database to the 2002 file format. You can still use the workgroup information file without converting, but the recommendation is it should also be converted to 2002.

If they aren't all upgrading, however, you can share the database and the workgroup information file across the different versions, using methods described later in this chapter.

 Be sure to protect Visual Basic code after converting. It's no longer protected with user-level security. You must create a password for the project using the Visual Basic Editor.

Converting a Replicated Database

When all users of the replicated database have upgraded to Access 2002, you can convert the replica set. The process involves making a complete test set including a Design Master and several replicas for use in Access 2002. The test set must be kept completely isolated from the original set to be entirely safe, preferably on a separate computer.

After creating several replicas from the new test Design Master, choose Tools | Database Utilities | Convert Database to convert the test Design Master and the test replicas to Access 2002. Synchronize the converted Design Master with the newly converted replicas and operate the database as it's intended. After you're satisfied the test set works as planned with Access 2002, delete all the members of the test set and convert the original replica set.

Once the replica set is converted to Access 2002, you can no longer open it with Access 97 or 2000.

Protecting Visual Basic Code

Special attention should be paid to Visual Basic code in a database converted from Access 97 and earlier because it's no longer protected by user-level security. Both code in modules and code behind forms and reports needs to be protected with protection passwords after you convert the database. To add the code protection password, open the database whose code you want to protect and do the following:

1. Choose Tools | Macro | Visual Basic Editor to open the code window.

2. Choose Tools | *<database or project name>* Properties, and then click the Protection tab.

3. In the Protection tab, check the Lock Project For Viewing check box, as shown in Figure 29-3.

4. Enter a password in the Password box and confirm the password by entering it again in the Confirm password box.

The next time you open the database, you'll be required to enter the password if you want to view and edit any code it contains. When you choose Tools | Macro | Visual Basic Editor, you're prompted to enter the password. To remove the password, open the Protection dialog box again and clear all the information from it.

Note   *If you specify a password, but don't check the Lock Project For Viewing check box, anyone who knows the password can view and edit the code in the Visual Basic Editor window. You need to use the password, however, to open the Project Properties dialog box to change or delete the password.*

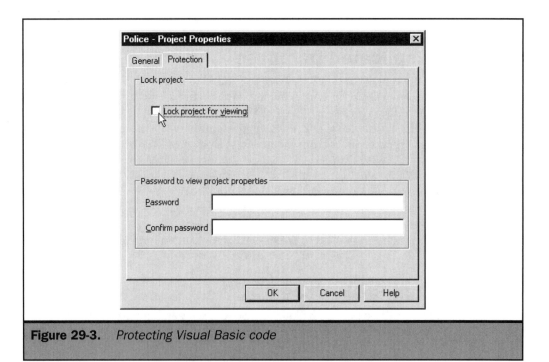

Figure 29-3.   *Protecting Visual Basic code*

Enabling a Database

As mentioned earlier, if you aren't converting the database because all users haven't yet upgraded to Access 2002, you can still use the database created in an earlier version with your version 2002. By enabling a database, you can view database objects and add, delete, or modify records, but you cannot modify any existing object design or add new objects to an enabled database from Access 2002. You must open the database using the version it was created with to modify object designs or add new objects.

To enable a previous-version database for use in Access 2002, click the Open toolbar button or choose File | Open. Choose the previous-version database you want to enable and click Open. A message appears explaining the database was created by an earlier version and you won't be able to make any changes to the database objects. It also gives you instructions for converting the database to Access 2002 if you want.

You can't link or import an Access 2002 table into an enabled database, but you can go the other way and open the version 2002 database and export tables to the previous-version database. You can also cut, copy, and paste data from version 2002 tables to previous-version tables.

When you enable a previous-version database in Access 2002, any custom toolbars are converted to the new style for consistency of viewing, but the conversion isn't saved when you close the database. Custom menu bars are also interpreted as the new version 2002 style. Menu bar macros aren't converted but are still supported.

If you're enabling a secured database, re-create the workgroup information file in Access 2002 to make sure it retains its security. If this isn't possible, use the Workgroup Administrator to join the previous-version secure WIF. Using the previous-version WIF keeps all the security except the protection for the Visual Basic code.

 Enabling a database may significantly increase the file size. If you enable it in several versions, the Visual Basic project must store all the information in each version's format.

If you're enabling a database that includes code with older versions of DAO objects, methods, and properties that rely on the DAO 2.5/3.*x* compatibility library, you may receive compilation error messages. Access 2002 doesn't support the older versions of the DAO library. Before attempting to enable the database, update the code.

Sharing a Database Across Several Access Versions

To use a one-file database with several versions of Access, you can create a front-end/back-end database out of it. Leave the data in the oldest version as the back-end and convert the other objects to the Access 2002 or another later version front-end. To build the single-file Access database, do the following:

1. Convert the entire database to Access 2002.

2. Open the converted database and choose Tools | Database Utilities | Database Splitter.

3. Split the database into a front-end and back-end, and then delete the back-end database created by the Database Splitter Wizard.

4. Then choose Tools | Database Utilities | Linked Table Manager to link the new Access 2002 front-end to the tables in the previous-version database.

Now you have both worlds: users of previous versions of Access can continue to use the previous version, while users who've upgraded to Access 2002 can add new features to their front-end databases. If the original database was created in Access 2.0, users of four different versions of Access can work with the database:

- Access 2.0 users with the original database.

- Access 95 and 97 users with either the enabled original database or a converted front end.

- Access 2000 and 2002 users with a converted front-end database linked to the previous-version back-end database.

 If the database is already a front-end/back-end application, you only need to convert the front end and leave the back end alone. Then run the Linked Table Manager to link the converted front end to the original back-end database.

Converting from Access 2002 to Access 97

If you need to use an Access 2002 database on an Access 97 system, you can convert it if it isn't a member of a replica set. You'll lose any features and functionality unique to Access 2002 in the conversion, including the following changes:

- Any of the table data that relied on the new Unicode compression may not convert correctly. Some of the characters used in the version 2002 database may not have equivalent characters in the Access 97 256-character set.

■ Any links to data access pages are lost because Access 97 doesn't include page objects. The HTML files are unaffected.

■ If the database includes a field with the new Number FieldSize property Decimal setting, the database can't be converted. You must change the FieldSize property to another setting before converting the database.

Some special conditions need to be considered when converting an Access 2002 database to Access 97:

■ If the database is protected by user-level security, remove it before trying to convert. After it is converted, you can secure the database in Access 97.

■ If the database is protected with a password, you needn't remove the password before converting the database.

■ If you secured the Visual Basic code with a password, you must enter the password in the Visual Basic Editor window before the code can be converted.

■ You must log on with Open/Run and Open Exclusive permissions for the database and Read Design permissions for all the objects in the database.

To convert an Access 2002 database to Access 97, open the database and make sure no other user has it open, and then do the following:

1. If you protected the code with a password, open the Visual Basic Editor window and choose Tools | Properties, and then enter the password in the Password box on the Protection tab of the Project Properties dialog box.

2. Return to the Access window and choose Tools | Database Utilities | Convert Databases | To Access 97 File Format.

3. In the Convert Database Into dialog box, enter a name for the previous-version database you want to create from the Access 2002 version, and then click Save.

Tip *If the 2002 version contains Visual Basic code, you may see some compile error messages caused by missing references. If you included any add-ins or library databases that you created in Access 2002, you need to convert them back to Access 97 to use them in the converted database.*

Converting from Access 2002 to Access 2000

An Access 2002 file can be easily converted to Access 2000 file format. Some features only available in 2002 aren't available in the converted database. For example, Visual Basic procedures that use objects, functions, or other elements new to Access 2002 can cause compile errors when you open the file in Access 2000.

APPLICATION DEVELOPMENT

Troubleshooting Conversion

Whenever you try to convert from one version of a program to another, some differences can cause trouble. If your conversion fails or doesn't go as expected, or if the converted database doesn't perform the way it did before, one of the following problems may have occurred.

■ One of the tables may have too many indexes. Each table can have up to 32 indexes. Complex tables involved in many relationships may result in an excess of indexes because the Microsoft Jet database engine version 3.5 automatically builds indexes on both sides on the relationships between tables. This can result in more than 32 indexes for a table. To correct this problem, delete some of the relationships before converting.

■ If an identifier causes an error, it may be reserved as one of the new Visual Basic keywords in Access 97 or later. The new keywords are: AddressOf, Decimal, DefDec, Enum, Event, Friend, Implements, RaiseEvent, and WithEvents. If you used any of these as an identifier, you get a compile error. Change the identifier to a name other than a keyword.

■ If your Visual Basic code won't compile, you may get an error message after you convert to Access 2002. To correct the code that contains the error, open a module in Design view and choose Debug | Compile All Modules. The Visual Basic Editor stops at each line of code that contains an error. You can change the syntax to correct the error.

■ If your query contains criteria based on specific date/time values, the results returned by the query may not be correct. Queries specifying dates between 1900 and 1929 may return unexpected results because of the Y2K compliance. For example, in versions 2.0 and 95, the date value #01/15/25# would be interpreted as January 15, 1925, but in versions 97 and later, the same value is interpreted as January 15, 2025. To avoid this problem, always use the four-digit year value that specifies the century.

Some problems may occur when converting Access 2.0 databases to Access 2002, including the following:

■ If a report created in version 2.0 has any margins set to 0, you may experience problems trying to print the report. Access 2002 automatically sets margins to the minimum allowed by the default printer to prevent printing data in an unprintable region. Run Page Setup to reduce the column width, column spacing, or the number of columns, so the total space required is no more than the width of the paper.

■ You may see an error message saying the connection to an ODBC driver has failed. This occurs when a table in the converted version 1.*x* or 2.0 database is linked to an ODBC data source that uses a 16-bit driver manager and driver. Access 2000 can link only to ODBC data sources using the 32-bit version of the ODBC driver manager and the appropriate ODBC driver, such as the Microsoft SQL Server ODBC driver (Sqlsrv32.dll). To solve this problem, create new 32-bit data sources for each ODBC data source and name them exactly the same as the 16-bit versions.

■ Other problems can occur because of the 16-bit versus 32-bit versions of controls and API calls. If the ActiveX (OLE custom) controls still refer to the 16-bit version, Access can automatically update the references to the 32-bit version if they're registered in your system. You can also change the API Declare statements to the 32-bit equivalent of the 16-bit call.

■ If a procedure causes an error, you may have named the procedure the same as a module. In version 2.0, you were allowed to give them the same name but, in Access 95 and later, they must have different names. Rename either the procedure or the module to continue with the conversion.

■ If you receive a message stating that you're out of memory, you might need to reduce the number of modules in the database. Access 2000 and 2002 limit the number of modules to 1,000, including all the modules behind forms and reports whose Has Module property is set to Yes. Access 97 placed a limit of 1,024 modules. To solve this problem, reduce the number of modules by setting the Has Module property to No for all forms and reports with no code behind them, reducing the number of objects in the database or even dividing the application into multiple databases as a last resort.

When you convert an Access 2002 database back to Access 97, you may see a message that one of the Access 97 object libraries is missing. Access 2002 works with the ActiveX Data Objects (ADO) and Access 97 still uses the DAO 3.51 library. If you see this message, click OK and open the converted database in Access 97, and then do the following:

1. Open one of the modules in the database and choose Tools | References in the Visual Basic Editor window.

2. In the Available References list, clear the check boxes next to the missing references, and then set a reference to the Microsoft DAO 3.51 Object Library.

APPLICATION DEVELOPMENT

Summary

This chapter guided you through the conversion process, so you can make the best use of Access 2002 and its new functionality and many new features. Because every database is different, you may have no trouble at all converting to version 2002 or you may encounter some bizarre snags not covered in this chapter. Consult the Access Help topics for additional information about converting among Access versions.

MOUS Exam Activities Explored in This Chapter

This chapter contains no information directly related to the MOUS Certification Exam activities, although the information is important to understanding how to use Access for effective database management.

Appendix A

MOUS Exam Objectives

1155

The tables in this appendix are for Access users who are preparing for the *Microsoft Office User Specialist* (*MOUS*) exams in Microsoft Access 2002. In the tables, you can find cross-references to chapters and section headings in the book where the exam activities are explained. To prepare for a MOUS exam, read the list of activities and, if you don't know an activity well, turn to the part of the book where it's explained.

Note   *At the end of most chapters in this book are tables that show where MOUS activities are explained, so you can learn more about a particular MOUS activity.*

Access 2002 Core Exam Activities

Microsoft Access 2002—Core
Total Activities: 25

Number	Activity	Chapter	Section Title(s)
AC10-1	**Creating and Using Databases**		
AC10-1-1	Create Access databases	3	Designing the Database
			Determining the Goals of the Database
			Distributing the Data
			Stepping Through the Wizard
			Starting with a Blank Database
			Starting a New Database from Windows
AC10-1-2	Open database objects in multiple views	1	Opening a Table
			Touring the Datasheet View
			Looking at Data in a Form
			Looking at a Subdatasheet
		4	Switching Table Views
AC10-1-3	Navigate among records	1	Touring the Datasheet View
			Navigating Among Records and Fields
			Navigating in Form View
		11	Navigating in the Form
AC10-1-4	Format datasheets	6	Changing the Datasheet Appearance

Microsoft Access 2002—Core
Total Activities: 25

Number	Activity	Chapter	Section Title(s)
AC10-1	**Creating and Using Databases**		
AC10-1-5	Use Access tools to maintain and repair databases	17	Backing Up and Restoring a Database Compacting and Repairing a Database Repairing with the Help Menu
AC10-2	**Creating and Modifying Tables**		
AC10-2-1	Create and modify tables	4	Creating a New Table Structure with the Table Wizard Creating a New Table from Scratch Creating a New Table in Datasheet View
AC10-2-2	Add a predefined input mask to a field	6	Customizing Data Entry
AC10-2-3	Create Lookup fields	6	Creating Lookup Fields
AC10-2-4	Modify field properties	4	Changing the Field Order Changing a Field Name or Type Changing a Field Size Modifying or Deleting the Primary Key Assigning a Default Value
		6	Adding Custom Input Masks Changing Field Names
AC10-3	**Creating and Modifying Queries**		
AC10-3-1	Create and modify select queries	8	Creating Select Queries Adding Selection Criteria Setting Query Properties Modifying a Query
AC10-3-2	Add calculated fields to Select queries	8	Adding a Calculated Field Summarizing with the Wizard

Microsoft Access 2002—Core
Total Activities: 25

Number	Activity	Chapter	Section Title(s)
AC10-4	**Creating and Modifying Forms**		
AC10-4-1	Create and display forms	10	Working in the Design Window Using AutoForm and AutoReport
AC10-4-2	Modify form properties	10	Modifying Controls Deleting Controls Changing Form and Report Properties
		11	Modifying the Form Design
AC10-5	**Viewing and Organizing Information**		
AC10-5-1	Enter, edit, and delete records	6	Entering New Data Locating Records Finding and Replacing Data Deleting Data Using the Spelling Tool Using AutoCorrect
		11	Using the Form
AC10-5-2	Create queries	8	Using the Simple Query Wizard Summarizing with the Wizard Creating Special Queries with the Query Wizard—Find Duplicates, Find Unmatched, Crosstab Queries
AC10-5-3	Sort records	7	Sorting Records Filtering with Advanced Filter/Sort
AC10-5-4	Filter records	7	Filtering By Selection Filtering By Form Filtering For Input
AC10-6	**Defining Relationships**		
AC10-6-1	Create one-to-many relationships	2 5	Types of Relationships Creating a Relationship with the Lookup Wizard Using the Relationships Window

Microsoft Access 2002—Core
Total Activities: 25

Number	Activity	Chapter	Section Title(s)
AC10-6	**Defining Relationships**		
AC10-6-2	Enforce referential integrity	2 5	Referential Integrity Modifying or Deleting a Relationship Using the Relationships Window—Enforcing Referential Integrity
AC10-7	**Producing Reports**		
AC10-7-1	Create and format reports	13	Starting a Report Choosing an AutoReport Using the Report Wizard Setting Report and Section Properties Changing the Report Style
AC10-7-2	Add calculated controls to reports	13	Selecting, Sorting and Grouping Data—Specifying Summary and Calculated Fields Placing and Adjusting Controls
AC10-7-3	Preview and print reports	13 14	Working in the Print Preview Window Using the Layout Preview Printing the Report Printing Mailing Labels and Envelopes Publishing a Report
AC10-8	**Integrating with Other Applications**		
AC10-8-1	Import data to Access	22 23	Importing or Linking Access Data Importing or Linking Other Databases Importing or Linking Text Data Using Linked or Imported Tables Copying or Moving Records Importing from and Linking to Excel Spreadsheets

Microsoft Access 2002—Core
Total Activities: 25

Number	Activity	Chapter	Section Title(s)
AC10-8	**Integrating with Other Applications**		
AC10-8-2	Export data from Access	22	Export to an Existing Access Database
			Export to Another Database Format
			Export to Text Files
			Copying or Moving Records from Access to Another Application
		23	Publishing with Word
			Using Merge It with Word
			Exporting a Table or Query to Excel
AC10-8-3	Create a simple Data Access Page	24	Creating a Data Access Page

Microsoft Access 2002—Expert
Total Activities: 31

Number	Activity	Chapter	Section Title(s)
AC10E-1	**Creating And Modifying Tables**		
AC10E-1-1	Use data validation	4	Defining Field Validation Rules Defining Record Validation Rules Ensuring Data Validity Requiring an Entry and Preventing Duplicates
		12	Validating with Properties Validating with Events
AC10E-1-2	Link tables	22	Linking Access Tables Updating Links with the Linked Table Manager
AC10E-1-3	Create lookup fields and modify lookup field properties	6 12	Creating Lookup Fields Placing and Customizing Data-Related Controls
AC10E-1-4	Create and modify input masks	6	Adding Custom Input Masks Creating a Custom Input Mask
AC10E-2	**Creating And Modifying Forms**		
AC10E-2-1	Create a form in Design view	12	Starting a New Custom Form
AC10E-2-2	Create a Switchboard and set startup options	16	Setting Startup Options Adding Startup Command-Line Options
		21	Using the Switchboard Manager Creating a Switchboard from Scratch
		28	Creating Startup Screens Setting Startup and Other Options
AC10E-2-3	Add Subform controls to Access forms	11	Creating a Hierarchical Form from Related Tables
		12	Adding a Subform

Microsoft Access 2002—Expert
Total Activities: 31

Number	Activity	Chapter	Section Title(s)
AC10E-3	**Refining Queries**		
AC10E-3-1	Specify multiple query criteria	8	Using Multiple Criteria
AC10E-3-2	Create and apply advanced filters	7	Filtering with Advanced Filter/Sort
AC10E-3-3	Create and run parameter queries	9	Creating Special Purpose Queries—Parameter Queries
AC10E-3-4	Create and run action queries	9	Designing Action Queries—Update, Append, Delete, Make-Table
		14	Creating the Parameter Query
AC10E-3-5	Use aggregate functions in queries	8	Summarizing with Aggregate Functions
AC10E-4	**Producing Reports**		
AC10E-4-1	Create and modify reports	13	Placing and Adjusting Controls Adding Page Numbers and Date/Time Adding Page Breaks
		14	Creating a New Report Design Sorting and Grouping Records in a Report
AC10E-4-2	Add Subreport controls to Access reports	14	Creating a Subreport Inserting an Existing Subreport Linking the Report and Subreport
AC10E-4-3	Sort and group data in reports	13	Selecting, Sorting and Grouping the Data—Sorting Records Selection, Sorting and Grouping the Data—Grouping Records Using the Report Wizard—Creating a Summary Report with the Report Wizard

Microsoft Access 2002—Expert
Total Activities: 31

Number	Activity	Chapter	Section Title(s)
AC10E-5	**Defining Relationships**		
AC10E-5-1	Establish one-to-many relationships	2 5	Types of Relationships Using the Relationships Window—Drawing the Relationship Line Using the Relationships Window—Specifying the Join Type
AC10E-5-2	Establish many-to-many relationships	5	How to Create a Many-to-Many Relationship
AC10E-6	**Operating Access on the Web**		
AC10E-6-1	Create and modify a Data Access Page	24	Creating a Data Access Page Creating a Grouped Data Access Page Modifying a Data Access Page Sorting and Filtering Records Calculating and Displaying Totals
AC10E-6-2	Save PivotTables and PivotCharts views to Data Access Pages	24	Getting Visual by Adding a Chart Creating Interactive PivotTables Creating an Interactive PivotChart
AC10E-6-3	Add Web browser control to Access forms	12	ActiveX Controls—Adding a Web Browser Control
AC10E-7	**Using Access tools**		
AC10E-7-1	Import XML documents into Access	23	Importing Data and Schema from XML Documents
AC10E-7-2	Export Access data to XML documents	23	Exporting Data to XML Documents
AC10E-7-3	Encrypt and decrypt databases	27	Encrypting and Decrypting a Database

Microsoft Access 2002—Expert
Total Activities: 31

Number	Activity	Chapter	Section Title(s)
AC10E-7	**Using Access tools**		
AC10E-7-4	Compact and repair databases	17	Compacting and Repairing a Database Repairing with the Help Menu
AC10E-7-5	Assign database security	27	Securing a Database with a Password Creating a Workgroup—Creating or Changing Account Passwords Securing a Database with the User-Level Security Wizard
AC10E-7-6	Replicate a database	26	Creating a Replica with Access Creating a Replica with the Briefcase Backing Up the Database Recovering the Design Master Restoring a Regular Database
AC10E-7-7	Link tables to a Structured Query Language (SQL) server database	22	Importing and Linking SQL Data
AC10E-7-8	Use SQL server 2000 functions	22	Using SQL Server Database Utilities
AC10E-8	**Creating Database Applications**		
AC10E-8-1	Create Access Modules	25	Writing Visual Basic Code Examples of Procedures
		28	Building the Application
AC10E-8-2	Use the Database Splitter	26	Splitting the Database
AC10E-8-3	Create an MDE file	28	Saving the Database as an MDE File

Appendix B

What's on the CD

Instructions for Using the Access Quick Reference on the CD-ROM

On the CD that accompanies this book is a reference resource you can use to look up specific details of properties, specifications, formats, and other items that apply to designing and creating Access databases. To use the Quick Reference, you must have Adobe Acrobat 4.0 or higher installed on your computer. If you don't already have Adobe Acrobat, there is a copy included on this book's CD. To view the Quick Reference material, double click on the PDF file. When it opens, you'll see a listing of contents in the left pane and the space where the pages will be displayed on the right side. If you select any topic on the left side, the pages associated with the topic will automatically display on the right hand side. You can use the magnification tools under the View menu to make the text more readable, and to enlarge any detail on a given page.

The following shows an outline of the information in the Quick Reference that you can readily reach on the CD.

Storing Information
Database Specifications
Database Templates
Database Objects
Database Properties
Relationships and Joins
Table Specifications
Table and Index Properties
Table Fields
    Data Types
    Field Properties
Display Formats
    Custom Formatting Symbols
    Custom Format Strings
Input Masks

User Interaction and Object Design
Built-in Toolbars
Form and Report Design
    Form and Report Specifications
    Form and Report Format Properties
    Form and Report Data Properties
    Form and Report Event Properties
    Form and Report Other Properties
    Form and Report Section Properties
    Dialog Box and Pop-Up Form Property Settings
    Controls and Control Properties

Instructions for Using the Access Database Files on the CD-ROM

The CD-ROM accompanying this book contains all the material you need to reproduce the Access database objects described in the text. You have a choice of developing the database designs from scratch using the table data or viewing and working with the completed databases. All the files are contained in the Access Database Files folder on the CD. To reach the database files, do the following:

1. Insert the CD-ROM in your CD drive. If you set AutoPlay, the CD will open and you can skip to step 4.

2. Otherwise, click Start in the Windows desktop and select Run from the list.

3. Type your CD drive letter followed by a colon (:) in the Run dialog box and click OK.

4. Double-click the Access Database Files folder icon to display a dialog box containing icons for all the files in the folder. You can tell the type of file by the accompanying icon.

You can now copy or import any of the files to your hard drive.

To use a complete sample database, you must import, rather than copy, the files to your system. If you simply copy these files rather than import them, the data access pages will refer to HTML files in the original path, rather than the path you create on your hard drive. To import the files, do the following:

1. Create a new empty database in a folder on your hard drive.

2. Choose File | Get External Data | Import.

3. Click Options in the Import dialog box, and then check Menus and Toolbars in the Import group of options. If you don't include the custom menus and toolbars, you'll get errors when you try to open the Police forms and reports that reference custom command bars.

4. Click each object tab and choose Select All to import all the objects from the database.

5. Copy all the HTML files from the CD to the same folder on your hard drive. The image files are embedded in the Home Tech Repair database, so you needn't copy them unless you want to work with them separately.

The Police welcoming splash screen includes a title in a custom font. If your system doesn't have this font installed, it substitutes a different font, which may be too large for the label box that contains the title. In this case, the first and last letters may not appear. To correct this, open the form in Design view and enlarge the label or change it to a smaller font.

To use only the tables, you can copy the HTR Tables and Police Tables databases directly to your hard disk.

The Access Database Files folder on the CD-ROM contains the following files:

Filename	File Type	Contents
Home Tech Repair.mdb	Access database	Complete Home Tech Repair database

Filename	File Type	Contents
HTR Tables.mdb	Access database	Home Tech Repair tables only
Police.mdb	Access database	Compete Bayview City Police database
Police Tables.mdb	Access database	Police tables only
Alpha Card.htm	HTML document	Alpha Card data access page design
Alpha Card by Name.htm	HTML document	Alpha Card by Name data access page design
Workorder Summary by Supervisor.htm	HTML document	Home Tech Repair data access page design
Barb.gif	GIF image	Home Tech Repair Employee picture
Charlie.gif	GIF image	Home Tech Repair Employee picture
CopdRick.gif	GIF image	Home Tech Repair Employee picture
DickS.gif	GIF image	Home Tech Repair Employee picture
Doug.gif	GIF image	Home Tech Repair Employee picture
John.gif	GIF image	Home Tech Repair Employee picture
Rick.gif	GIF image	Home Tech Repair Employee picture
Tony.gif	GIF image	Home Tech Repair Employee picture
Bay2.gif	GIF image	Scanned drawing for Home Tech Repair Workorders table
Bay window.gif	GIF image	Scanned drawing for Home Tech Repair Workorders table
Fireplace.gif	GIF image	Scanned drawing for Home Tech Repair Workorders table

The HTR Tables and Police Tables databases contain only the data from the tables in the complete databases. Each table has a primary key field identified, but no relationships have been established between tables. The Switchboard table that appears in the complete Police database isn't included among the tables in the Police Tables database.

The Home Tech Repair sample database forms include hyperlinks to other locations. You need to edit the hyperlink addresses to match their location in your system. See Chapter 6 for information about editing hyperlinks.

The Badge Picture images are embedded in the Employees table in the Home Tech Repair database. If they aren't, you can insert the images individually, using the technique discussed in Chapter 6.

If you try to run the Police database from the CD, it is read-only and you will see a run-time error message. This is caused by the check box on the splash screen that has a procedure attached to it that changes the startup display. Changes are not permitted in a read-only database. Click End and proceed with the database.

Index

Note: Bold text denotes statements in Visual Basic. Italic text denotes various code components.

Symbols

C

D

G

H

J

Q

W

Z

INTERNATIONAL CONTACT INFORMATION

AUSTRALIA
McGraw-Hill Book Company Australia Pty. Ltd.
TEL +61-2-9417-9899
FAX +61-2-9417-5687
http://www.mcgraw-hill.com.au
books-it_sydney@mcgraw-hill.com

CANADA
McGraw-Hill Ryerson Ltd.
TEL +905-430-5000
FAX +905-430-5020
http://www.mcgrawhill.ca

GREECE, MIDDLE EAST,
NORTHERN AFRICA
McGraw-Hill Hellas
TEL +30-1-656-0990-3-4
FAX +30-1-654-5525

MEXICO (Also serving Latin America)
McGraw-Hill Interamericana Editores S.A. de C.V.
TEL +525-117-1583
FAX +525-117-1589
http://www.mcgraw-hill.com.mx
fernando_castellanos@mcgraw-hill.com

SINGAPORE (Serving Asia)
McGraw-Hill Book Company
TEL +65-863-1580
FAX +65-862-3354
http://www.mcgraw-hill.com.sg
mghasia@mcgraw-hill.com

SOUTH AFRICA
McGraw-Hill South Africa
TEL +27-11-622-7512
FAX +27-11-622-9045
robyn_swanepoel@mcgraw-hill.com

UNITED KINGDOM & EUROPE
(Excluding Southern Europe)
McGraw-Hill Education Europe
TEL +44-1-628-502500
FAX +44-1-628-770224
http://www.mcgraw-hill.co.uk
computing_neurope@mcgraw-hill.com

ALL OTHER INQUIRIES Contact:
Osborne/McGraw-Hill
TEL +1-510-549-6600
FAX +1-510-883-7600
http://www.osborne.com
omg_international@mcgraw-hill.com